AMERICAN REFERENCE BOOKS

1989 VOLUME 20

AMERICAN
REFERENCE
BOOKS

ANNUAL

1989 VOLUME 20

Bohdan S. Wynar EDITOR

ASSOCIATE EDITOR
Anna Grace Patterson

ASSISTANT EDITOR
Patricia M. Leach

Comprehensive annual reviewing service for
reference books published in the United States and Canada

1989

LIBRARIES UNLIMITED
ENGLEWOOD, COLORADO

LIBRARIES UNLIMITED, INC.
P.O. Box 3988
Englewood, Colorado 80155-3988

ISBN 0-87287-758-2
ISSN 0065-9959

This book is bound with Type II nonwoven material that meets and exceeds National Association of State Textbook Administrators' Type II nonwoven material specifications Class A through E.

Contents

Journals Cited......................xii
Introduction xiii
Contributors......................xv

Part I
GENERAL REFERENCE WORKS

1—General Reference Works

Acronyms and Abbreviations..............3
Almanacs...............................4
Atlases................................4
Bibliographies.........................5
  Bibliographic Guides...................5
  National and Trade Bibliographies.......7
    International......................7
    United States......................8
    Great Britain......................9
Biographies............................9
  International..........................9
  United States........................10
  Great Britain........................11
  Mexico..............................12
  Middle East.........................12
Catalogs and Collections................12
Dictionaries and Encyclopedias..........13
  Reviewing 13
  General Encyclopedias..............15
Directories............................22
Government Publications................24
Handbooks and Yearbooks..............26
Indexes...............................28
Periodicals and Serials..................30
Quotation Books......................32

Part II
SOCIAL SCIENCES

2—Social Sciences in General

Bibliographies.........................37
Directories...........................38
Indexes...............................39

3—Area Studies

United States..........................41
  California 41
  Florida.............................41
  Louisiana...........................42
  New York...........................42
Africa.................................42
  General Works......................42
  Benin 43
  Cape Verde.........................44
  Chad 44
  Gambia 44
  Ghana 45
  Guinea.............................45
  Guinea-Bissau......................46
  Libya 46
  Mozambique........................46
  Togo...............................46
Asia 47
  General Works......................47
  India...............................49
  Japan 49
Canada 50
Commonwealth of Nations..............52
Europe................................53
  Denmark 53
  Gibraltar 53
  Great Britain........................53
  Netherlands.........................54
  Poland 54
  Sweden 55
  Ukraine 55
Indian Ocean..........................55
Latin America and the Caribbean..........56
  General Works......................56
  Argentina 57
  Bolivia 58
  Chile...............................58
  Cuba 59
  Dominica...........................60
  Mexico.............................60
  Paraguay...........................60
  Puerto Rico.........................61
  Venezuela 61

3—Area Studies (*continued*)

Middle East..........................62
  General Works.....................62
  Iran 63
  Israel 63
  Saudi Arabia.......................64

4—Economics and Business

General Works.........................65
  Acronyms 65
  Atlases............................65
  Bibliographies.....................66
  Biographies 67
  Dictionaries.......................67
  Directories........................67
  Handbooks and Yearbooks...........71
  Indexes...........................74
  Periodicals and Serials.............75
  Quotation Books...................75
Accounting 76
Business Services and Investment Guides....77
Consumer Guides......................82
Finance and Banking...................85
Industry and Manufacturing.............88
Insurance.............................93
Labor................................93
Management 96
Marketing and Trade...................98
Office Management...................103
Real Estate..........................104
Taxation 105

5—Education

General Works........................109
  Bibliographies.....................109
  Dictionaries and Encyclopedias........110
  Handbooks and Yearbooks...........111
  Periodicals and Serials.................113
Elementary and Secondary Education......114
  Bibliographies.....................114
  Directories........................116
  Handbooks........................117
Higher Education......................118
  Bibliographies.....................118
  Directories........................118
  Handbooks and Yearbooks...........125
Computer Resources...................129
**International Exchange Programs
  and Opportunities**..................131
Learning Disabilities and Disabled........132
Nonprint Materials and Resources........132
Vocational and Continuing Education.....133

6—Ethnic Studies and Anthropology

Anthropology.........................137
Ethnic Studies........................139
  General Works.....................139
  Blacks 140

Chinese-Americans 142
Eastern Europeans....................142
Germans 142
Hispanic-Americans 143
Irish-Americans 143
Jews...............................144
Native Peoples of North America.......144

7—Genealogy and Heraldry

Genealogy............................151
  Bibliographies.....................151
  Directories........................151
  Handbooks........................151
  Indexes...........................154
Heraldry 154
Personal Names.......................155

8—Geography and Travel Guides

Geography............................157
  General Works.....................157
  Atlases............................159
Place Names..........................162
Travel Guides.........................163
  General Works.....................163
  United States.......................165
  Great Britain.......................168
  Italy 169
  Oceania 169
  Tibet..............................169

9—History

Archaeology 171
American History......................172
  Archives...........................172
  Atlases............................175
  Bibliographies.....................176
  Biographies 179
  Catalogs and Collections..............181
  Dictionaries.......................182
  Directories........................182
  Handbooks........................182
  Indexes...........................184
Asian History.........................185
Australian History.....................186
British History........................186
  Bibliographies.....................186
  Biographies 188
  Catalogs and Collections..............188
  Handbooks........................189
Canadian History......................190
European History......................190
German History.......................192
Latin American History.................192
New Zealand History...................192
Russian History.......................193
Third World History....................193

World History..........................193
  Atlases...............................193
  Bibliographies........................194
  Biographies...........................195
  Catalogs and Collections..............195
  Dictionaries..........................195
  Directories...........................196
  Handbooks.............................197

10 – Law

General Works.........................199
  Bibliographies........................199
  Biographies...........................202
  Dictionaries..........................203
  Directories...........................206
  Handbooks and Yearbooks...........209
  Indexes...............................210
  Periodicals and Serials...............210
  Quotation Books.....................211
Criminology 211
Human Rights.........................213

11 – Library and Information Science
and
Publishing and Bookselling

Library and Information Science.........217
  General Works.......................217
    Acronyms and Abbreviations........217
    Dictionaries and Encyclopedias......217
    Directories.........................218
    Handbooks and Yearbooks.........219
    Indexes 222
  Careers.............................222
  Cataloging and Classification..........222
  Comparative and International
    Librarianship 225
  Conservation and Preservation........226
  Information Technologies..............226
  Interlibrary Loans...................226
  Library Automation..................227
  Library History......................227
  Library Instruction..................228
  Public Libraries.....................228
  School Libraries.....................228
  Special Libraries....................230
Publishing and Bookselling.............232
  Bibliographies........................232
  Directories..........................233

12 – Military Studies

General Works.........................237
  Bibliographies........................237
  Chronologies 237
  Dictionaries..........................238
  Handbooks............................239
Air Force.............................241

Army 243
Navy..................................244
Weapons..............................245

13 – Political Science

General Works.........................249
  Bibliographies........................249
  Biographies...........................250
  Chronologies 250
  Dictionaries and Encyclopedias........251
  Directories...........................252
  Handbooks.............................253
  Indexes...............................254
U.S. Politics and Government...........254
  Bibliographies........................254
  Biographies...........................257
  Dictionaries and Encyclopedias........258
  Directories...........................259
  Handbooks.............................261
  Indexes and Abstracts................266
  Quotation Books....................267
Ideologies 267
International Organizations..............270
International Relations..................271
Peace Movement......................273
Public Policy and Administration........276

14 – Psychology

General Works.........................277
  Bibliographies........................277
  Dictionaries..........................279
  Directories...........................280
  Handbooks and Yearbooks...........280
  Thesauri.............................281
Parapsychology 281

15 – Recreation and Sports

General Works.........................285
  Bibliographies........................285
  Chronologies 285
  Directories...........................286
  Handbooks............................286
Automobile Racing....................287
Baseball..............................288
Basketball 291
Cricket...............................291
Football..............................292
Games 294
Hockey 295
Hunting 295
Martial Arts..........................296
Skiing................................296
Treasure Hunting.....................297
Winter Sports........................297

16—Sociology

General Works........................299
  Bibliographies........................299
  Dictionaries and Encyclopedias........300
  Indexes............................300
Aging................................301
  Bibliographies........................301
  Dictionaries........................301
  Directories........................302
Death...............................303
Disabled.............................303
Family and Marriage...................305
Philanthropy.........................306
Sex Studies..........................308
Social Welfare and Social Work.........310
Substance Abuse......................311
Youth and Child Development...........312

17—Statistics, Demography, and Urban Studies

Demography..........................315
Statistics............................316
Urban Studies........................319

18—Women's Studies

Almanacs............................323
Bibliographies........................323
Biographies..........................325
Dictionaries..........................326
Directories..........................326

Part III
HUMANITIES

19—Humanities in General

General Works........................329

20—Communication and Mass Media

General Works........................333
Authorship..........................335
  Biographies........................335
  Directories........................335
  Handbooks........................336
Newspapers and Magazines.............337
  Bibliographies........................337
  Biographies........................338
  Directories........................339
  Handbooks........................339
  Indexes............................340
Radio...............................341
Telecommunication...................341

Television, Audio, and Video............342
  Bibliographies........................342
  Biographies........................343
  Dictionaries and Encyclopedias........343
  Directories........................343
  Discographies........................344
  Handbooks........................344

21—Decorative Arts

General Works........................347
Collecting...........................348
  Antiques..........................348
  Baseball Cards......................349
  Books............................350
  Coins............................350
  Glass............................351
  Toys.............................352
  Other Collectibles...................352
Crafts...............................353
Fashion and Costume.................357
Photography.........................357

22—Fine Arts

General Works........................359
  Bibliographies........................359
  Biographies........................361
  Dictionaries and Encyclopedias........361
  Directories........................363
  Indexes............................365
Architecture.........................366
  Bibliographies........................366
  Chronologies.......................367
  Dictionaries and Encyclopedias........367
  Handbooks........................367
Graphic Arts.........................368
Painting and Drawing..................369
Sculpture............................371

23—Language and Linguistics

General Works........................373
  Bibliographies........................373
  Dictionaries and Encyclopedias........375
  Handbooks........................376
English-Language Dictionaries..........376
  General Works......................376
  Abridged..........................377
  Eponyms..........................379
  Etymology.........................379
  Foreign Terms.....................381
  Idioms, Colloquialisms, and
    Special Usage...................382
  Juvenile..........................387
  Other English-Speaking Countries......387
  Spelling Guides....................389
  Thesauri..........................390

Non-English-Language Dictionaries.......390
  Arabic 390
  Chinese 390
  French 391
  Greek Romany......................392
  Russian 393
  Spanish 393
  Yiddish 394
Language Books for Travelers...........394

24—Literature

General Works........................397
  Bibliographies.......................397
  Biographies.........................398
  Dictionaries and Encyclopedias........399
  Handbooks.........................399
  Indexes............................402
Children's Literature...................402
  Bibliographies.......................402
  Biographies.........................409
  Handbooks.........................409
  Indexes............................412
Classical Literature...................413
Drama...............................414
Fiction..............................414
  General Works......................414
  Crime and Mystery..................416
  Gothic 417
  Science Fiction, Fantasy, and Horror....418
  Short Stories.......................420
Poetry..............................420
National Literature....................421
  American Literature..................421
    General Works....................421
    Bibliographies, 421; Biographies,
    422; Chronologies, 422; Hand-
    books, 423
    Drama..........................427
    Fiction..........................428
    Humor..........................428
    Individual Authors.................429
    Edward Albee, 429; Edward Bel-
    lamy, 430; James Fenimore Cooper,
    430; Emily Dickinson, 430; E. L.
    Doctorow, 431; F. Scott Fitzgerald,
    431; Robert Gover, 431; Henry
    James, 432; Anne Morrow Lind-
    bergh, 432; William March, 432;
    Herman Melville, 433; H. L.
    Mencken, 433; Toni Morrison, 434;
    Frank Norris, 434; Eugene O'Neill,
    435; Sylvia Plath, 435; Edwin Ar-
    lington Robinson, 435; Carl Sand-
    burg, 436; Gertrude Stein, 436;
    Nathaniel Tarn, 437; Diane
    Wakoski, 437; Alice Malsenior
    Walker, 437; Richard Wright, 438
    Poetry 438

British Literature.....................439
  General Works.....................439
  Fiction............................440
  Individual Authors..................441
  Algernon Blackwood, 441; Wil-
  liam Blake, 442; George Gordon
  Byron, 442; Lewis Carroll, 443;
  Geoffrey Chaucer, 443; John Cle-
  land, 444; Charles Dickens, 445;
  Margaret Drabble, 445; George
  Eliot, 446; George Herbert, 446;
  C. S. (Clive Staples) Lewis, 447;
  E. V. (Edward Verrall) Lucas, 447;
  George Moore, 447; Iris Murdoch,
  447; Walter H. Pater, 448; Alexan-
  der Pope, 448; William Shakespeare,
  449; George Bernard Shaw, 451;
  Percy Bysshe Shelley, 451; Alan
  Sillitoe, 451; John Skelton, 452;
  Montague Summers, 452; Anthony
  Trollope, 452; John Wain, 453;
  Arthur Waley, 453; H. G. Wells,
  454; William Wordsworth, 454
  Poetry 454
Australian Literature..................455
Brazilian Literature...................455
Canadian Literature..................456
Chilean Literature....................459
Chinese Literature....................459
Czechoslovakian Literature............459
Filipino Literature....................460
French Literature.....................460
German Literature....................461
Indic Literature......................462
Irish Literature......................463
Latin American Literature.............464
Nigerian Literature...................465
Russian Literature....................465
Spanish and Portuguese Literatures.....466

25—Music

General Works........................467
  Bibliographies.......................467
  Biographies.........................470
  Catalogs and Collections..............470
  Dictionaries and Encyclopedias........471
  Directories.........................471
  Discographies 473
  Handbooks.........................474
  Indexes............................475
Composers 476
Instruments..........................483
  Percussion.........................483
  Piano 484
Musical Forms........................484
  Band..............................484
  Choral 485
  Church............................486

25 — Music (continued)

Musical Forms (continued)
Classical..............................487
Opera..............................488
Popular..............................488
General Works......................488
Folk..............................490
Jazz..............................490
Rock..............................492

26 — Mythology, Folklore, and Popular Customs

Folklore..............................495
Mythology..............................497
Popular Customs......................498

27 — Performing Arts

General Works......................501
Dance..............................502
Film..............................503
Bibliographies......................503
Biographies......................504
Dictionaries and Encyclopedias........506
Directories......................508
Filmographies......................509
Handbooks......................511
Theater..............................512
Bibliographies......................512
Chronologies......................513
Dictionaries and Encyclopedias........514
Directories......................514
Handbooks......................515

28 — Philosophy

Bibliographies......................517
Biographies......................518

29 — Religion

General Works......................521
Bibliographies......................521
Dictionaries and Encyclopedias........522
Handbooks......................523
Periodicals and Serials................524
Bible Studies......................524
Buddhism..............................529
Christianity..............................529
Almanacs......................529
Archives......................529
Bibliographies......................530
Biographies......................532
Dictionaries and Encyclopedias........533
Handbooks......................534
Judaism..............................534

Part IV
SCIENCE AND TECHNOLOGY

30 — Science and Technology in General

Bibliographies......................539
Chronologies......................540
Dictionaries and Encyclopedias..........541
Directories......................543
Handbooks and Yearbooks..............543
Indexes..............................544
Periodicals and Serials................545
Thesauri..............................546

31 — Agricultural and Resource Sciences

Agricultural Sciences..................547
General Works......................547
Acronyms and Abbreviations........547
Bibliographies......................547
Directories......................547
Handbooks......................548
Food Science and Technology........548
Bibliographies......................548
Dictionaries and Encyclopedias.......549
Directories......................552
Handbooks......................552
Forestry......................554
Horticulture......................555
Resource Sciences......................557
Energy Resources..................557
General Works..................557
Oil and Gas..................558
Environmental Science................559
Natural Resources..................562

32 — Biological Sciences

Biology..............................563
Botany..............................566
General Works......................566
Aquatic Plants......................567
Flowering Plants......................567
Fungi......................569
Grasses and Weeds......................570
Medicinal and Edible Plants..........571
Trees and Shrubs......................571
Natural History......................572
Zoology..............................573
Birds......................573
Butterflies......................578
Domestic Animals......................578
Fishes......................579
Insects......................580
Mammals......................581
Marine Animals......................583
Reptiles and Amphibians..............583

33 – Engineering

General Works..........................585
Acoustical Engineering..................585
Astronautical Engineering..............586
Chemical Engineering...................587
Civil Engineering......................590
Electrical Engineering and Electronics.....591
Genetic Engineering....................592
Materials Science......................594
Mechanical Engineering.................596
Mining Engineering.....................596
Nuclear Engineering....................597
Petroleum Engineering..................598
Safety Engineering.....................598
Sanitary Engineering...................599
Steam Engineering......................599

34 – Health Sciences

General Works..........................601
  Bibliographies.......................601
  Dictionaries and Encyclopedias.........603
  Directories..........................603
  Handbooks............................605
  Indexes..............................607
Medicine...............................607
  General Works........................607
    Acronyms and Abbreviations.........607
    Biographies........................608
    Dictionaries and Encyclopedias.......608
    Directories........................611
    Handbooks..........................611
  Psychiatry...........................613
  Specific Conditions and Diseases.......614
    General Works......................614
    AIDS...............................615
    Allergies..........................617
    Birth Related Conditions...........617
    Cancer.............................619
    Heart Diseases.....................619
    Medical Genetics...................619
    Rheumatic and Skin Diseases........620
    Sports Injuries....................620
Nursing................................621
Pharmacy and Pharmaceutical Sciences....622
  Bibliographies.......................622
  Dictionaries and Encyclopedias.........622
  Directories..........................624
  Handbooks............................624
  Indexes..............................628

35 – High Technology

CD-ROM.................................629
Computing..............................629
  General Works........................629
    Bibliographies.....................629
    Biographies........................631
    Dictionaries and Encyclopedias.......631
    Directories........................633
    Handbooks and Yearbooks............634
    Indexes............................635
  Microcomputing.......................636
  Software.............................637
Robotics...............................637
Security...............................638
Video Discs............................639

36 – Physical Sciences and Mathematics

Astronomy..............................641
Chemistry..............................643
  Bibliographies.......................643
  Dictionaries and Encyclopedias.........643
  Handbooks............................647
  Indexes..............................650
Earth and Planetary Science............650
  General Works........................650
  Geology..............................651
  Mineralogy...........................655
  Paleontology.........................655
Marine Science.........................656
Mathematics............................656
Meteorology............................658
Physics................................658

37 – Transportation

General Works..........................661
Air....................................661
Ground.................................662
Water..................................663

Author/Title Index.................665
Subject Index......................701

Journals Cited

FORM OF CITATION	JOURNAL TITLE
BL	Booklist
BR	Book Report
Choice	Choice
C&RL	College & Research Libraries
CLJ	Canadian Library Journal
EL	Emergency Librarian
JAL	Journal of Academic Librarianship
JOYS	Journal of Youth Services in Libraries
LAR	Library Association Record
LJ	Library Journal
Online	Online
RBB	Reference Books Bulletin
RLR	Riverina Library Review
RQ	RQ
SBF	Science Books & Films
SLJ	School Library Journal
SLMQ	School Library Media Quarterly
VOYA	Voice of Youth Advocates
WLB	Wilson Library Bulletin

Introduction

PURPOSE AND SCOPE

American Reference Books Annual, a far-reaching reviewing service for reference books, is now in its twentieth volume. This twentieth volume covers 1988 imprints as well as some 1987 imprints that reached our editorial offices too late to be reviewed in the previous volume. The total number of books reviewed in *ARBA* 89 is 1,693. In the twenty volumes of *ARBA* published since 1970, a total of 33,120 titles have been reviewed.

ARBA differs significantly from other reviewing media in its basic purpose, which is to provide reviews of the complete spectrum of English-language reference books published in the United States and Canada during a single year. Thus, *ARBA* provides comprehensive coverage. The categories of reference books reviewed in *ARBA* and our policy regarding them can be summarized as follows: (1) Dictionaries, encyclopedias, indexes, directories, bibliographies, guides, concordances, atlases, gazetteers, and other types of ready-reference tools are reviewed in each volume of *ARBA*; coverage of this category of reference materials is nearly complete. (2) General encyclopedias that are updated annually plus yearbooks, almanacs, indexing and abstracting services, and other annuals or serials are usually reviewed at intervals of three, four, or even five years. The first review of such works usually provides an appropriate historical background. Subsequent reviews of such serial publications attempt to point out changes in scope, editorial policy, and similar matters as they occur. (3) New editions of reference books are reviewed with, if necessary, appropriate comparisons to the older editions. (4) *ARBA* has traditionally reviewed foreign reference titles only if they have an exclusive distributor in the United States. In 1987 we expanded our coverage to include Canadian publications that do not have U.S.

distributors. Prices for Canadian titles not supplied by U.S. distributors are in Canadian dollars unless otherwise indicated. We have achieved substantial coverage of Canadian reference publications and expect to increase this coverage until it is as complete for Canada as for the United States. Foreign title coverage other than Canada is still generally restricted to English-language publications from Great Britain, Australia, and India. (5) Government publications are reviewed on a highly selective basis, since other Libraries Unlimited works, *Government Reference Books* and *Government Reference Serials*, biennially provide the library profession with comprehensive coverage of government reference publications. In *ARBA* 89 only Library of Congress publications and international publications, such as those of the United Nations, are covered. (6) Reprints also are reviewed in *ARBA* on a selective basis. Reprints often are produced in limited quantities, and for this reason reprint houses are sometimes reluctant to send review copies to *ARBA* or, indeed, to any reviewing medium. (7) Titles generally produced for the mass market in areas of collectibles, travel guides, and genealogy receive selective coverage.

Certain categories of reference books are usually not reviewed in *ARBA*: reference books of less than 48 pages, reference books produced by vanity presses, reference books produced by the author as publisher, and certain types of reference materials produced by library staffs for internal use. Highly specialized reference works printed in a limited number of copies which do not appeal to the general library audience *ARBA* serves are also omitted.

Nonreference library science material is no longer reviewed in *ARBA*. *Library and Information Science Annual* (*LISCA*) 1989, edited by Bohdan S. Wynar, Ann E. Prentice, and Anna Grace Patterson, includes reviews of 1988 monographs and reference books in the fields of library and information sciences and offers reviews and overviews that are beyond the scope of *ARBA*. *LISCA* reviews library and information science periodicals, presents in-depth essays by prominent members of the library and library publishing fields, and includes a selected annotated list of recent library science dissertations.

ARBA always contains an index, and now, the author/title index is separate from the subject index. In order to facilitate the use of *ARBA*, three cumulative indexes have been produced covering the years 1970-1974, 1975-1979, and 1980-1984. The fourth cumulative index, edited by Anna Grace Patterson and covering the years 1985-1989, will be released this year.

REVIEWING POLICY

To ensure well-written and erudite reviews, the *ARBA* staff keeps an up-to-date list of scholars, practitioners, and library educators in all subject specialties; this enables us to assign books for review appropriately. This year *ARBA* has used the services of over 300 subject specialists at libraries and universities throughout the United States and Canada. Reviews in *ARBA* are signed as a matter of editorial policy.

Since *ARBA* is not a selective reviewing source such as *Choice* or *Library Journal*, our reviews tend to be somewhat longer, have a tendency to be critical and evaluative, and quite frequently discuss in some detail the strengths and weaknesses of important reference works. The editorial staff of *ARBA* has prepared standard instructions for our reviewers which are briefly summarized here: We recommend that reviewers should discuss the work and then provide well-documented critical comments, positive or negative. Usually they discuss the usefulness of a given work; organization, execution, and pertinence of contents; prose style; format; availability of supplementary materials (e.g., the index or appendices); and similarity to other works and previous editions. Reviewers are encouraged to talk about the intended audience, but it is not necessary to conclude with specific recommendations for purchase. An adequate description and evaluation of the reference book will suffice.

As in previous volumes, the list of contributors will be found following this introduction.

ARRANGEMENT

ARBA 89 consists of four parts: "General Reference Works," "Social Sciences," "Humanities," and "Science and Technology." "General Reference Works," arranged alphabetically, is subdivided by form: bibliographies, biographies, catalogs and collections, dictionaries and encyclopedias, handbooks and yearbooks, indexes, and so on. Within the remaining three parts, chapters, arranged alphabetically, are organized by topic. Thus, under "Social Sciences," the reader will find, for example, among others, chapters entitled "Economics and Business," "Education," "History," "Law," and "Psychology."

Each chapter is subdivided in a way that reflects the arrangement strategy of the entire volume: First there is a section on general works, then there is a topical breakdown. In the chapter entitled "Literature," for example, "General Works" is followed by "Children's Literature," "Drama," "Fiction," "Poetry," and "National Literature." And the latter is subdivided further, into sections entitled "American Literature" and "British Literature" — each fairly long and each subdivided — followed by sections on other national literatures including, among others, Australian, Nigerian, and Russian. Subdivisions are based on the amount of material available on a given topic and will vary from year to year. The present volume of *ARBA* contains a total of thirty-seven chapters.

ACKNOWLEDGMENTS

In closing, we wish to express our gratitude to the many contributors without whose support this twentieth volume of *ARBA* could not have been compiled. Those contributors are listed on the pages following this introduction. We would also like to thank the members of our staff who were instrumental in the preparation of *ARBA* 89: Anna Grace Patterson (who also prepared the subject index), and Patricia M. Leach (who also prepared the author/title index) of the *ARBA* office; Sharon Kincaide, who copyedited much of the material; Carmel Huestis, Louis Ruybal, and Doug Robert, who also copyedited; Gaile Martin, who proofread; Judy Gay Matthews and Kay Minnis, who provided the excellent composition work, and David V. Loertscher for his advice.   Bohdan S. Wynar

Editorial Staff

Bohdan S. Wynar, Editor-in-Chief
Anna Grace Patterson, Associate Editor

Contributors

Stephen H. Aby, Education Bibliographer, Bierce Library, Univ. of Akron, Ohio.

Robert D. Adamshick, Librarian, U.S. Army Corps of Engineers, Chicago.

Donald C. Adcock, Director of Library Services, Glen Ellyn School District 41, Glen Ellyn, Ill.

Robert Aken, Coordinator of Automated References Services, Margaret I. King Library, Univ. of Kentucky, Lexington.

Chris Albertson, City Librarian, Tyler Public Library, Tex.

Walter C. Allen, Assoc. Professor Emeritus, Graduate School of Library and Information Science, Univ. of Illinois, Urbana.

Mary Jo Aman, Business Reference Librarian, Univ. of Wisconsin Library, Milwaukee.

Mohammed M. Aman, Dean, School of Library Science, Univ. of Wisconsin, Milwaukee.

Byron P. Anderson, Asst. Professor, Northern Illinois Univ., De Kalb.

Frank J. Anderson, Librarian Emeritus, Sandor Teszler Library, Wofford College, Spartanburg, S.C.

James D. Anderson, Assoc. Dean and Professor, School of Communication, Information, and Library Studies, Rutgers Univ., New Brunswick, N.J.

Margaret Anderson, Assoc. Professor, Faculty of Library and Information Science, Univ. of Toronto, Ont.

Charles R. Andrews, Dean of Library Services, Hofstra Univ., Hempstead, N.Y.

Theodora Andrews, Pharmacy, Nursing, and Health Sciences Librarian, Purdue Univ., West Lafayette, Ind.

Susan B. Ardis, Head Librarian, Engineering Library, Univ. of Texas, Austin.

Henry T. Armistead, Head, Collection Development, Scott Memorial Library, Thomas Jefferson Univ., Philadelphia, Pa.

Bill Bailey, Reference Librarian, Newton Gresham Library, Sam Houston State Univ., Huntsville, Tex.

Jack Bales, Reference Librarian, Mary Washington College Library, Fredericksburg, Va.

Robert M. Ballard, Professor, School of Library and Information Science, North Carolina Central Univ., Durham.

Gary D. Barber, Coordinator, Reference Services, Daniel A. Reed Library, State Univ. of New York, Fredonia.

Sallie H. Barringer, Science Librarian, Trinity Univ. Library, San Antonio, Tex.

Pam M. Baxter, Psychological and Social Sciences Librarian, Psychological Sciences Library, Purdue Univ., West Lafayette, Ind.

Craig W. Beard, Reference Librarian, Harding Univ., Searcy, Ark.

Carol Willsey Bell, Genealogist, Youngstown, Ohio.

Helen Carol Bennett, Reference Collection Coordinator, California State Univ., Northridge.

Bernice Bergup, Humanities Reference Librarian, Davis Library, Univ. of North Carolina, Chapel Hill.

Ron Blazek, Professor, School of Library Science, Florida State Univ., Tallahassee.

Daniel K. Blewett, General Reference Librarian, Milton S. Eisenhower Library, Johns Hopkins Univ., Baltimore, Md.

Marjorie E. Bloss, Manager, Resource Sharing, OCLC, Dublin, Ohio.

James K. Bracken, Head, Second Floor Main Library Information Services, and Librarian for English, Communication, and Speech, Ohio State Univ., Columbus.

Carol June Bradley, Music Librarian, State Univ. of New York, Buffalo.

Robert N. Broadus, Professor, School of Library Science, Univ. of North Carolina, Chapel Hill.

William S. Brockman, Reference Librarian, Drew Univ. Library, Madison, N.J.

Ellen Broidy, History Bibliographer, and Coordinator of Library Education Services, Univ. of California, Irvine.

Simon J. Bronner, Professor of Folklore and American Studies, Capitol College, Pennsylvania State Univ., Middletown.

Judith M. Brugger, Serials Cataloger, City College, City Univ. of New York.

Betty Jo Buckingham, Consultant, Iowa Dept. of Education, Des Moines.

Robert H. Burger, Assoc. Professor of Library Administration, Univ. of Illinois, Urbana.

Debbie Burnham-Kidwell, Owner/Indexer, Burnham-Kidwell, Indexer, Kingman, Ariz.

G. Joan Burns, Principal Art Librarian, Art and Music Dept., Newark Public Library, N.J.

Helen M. Burns, formerly Chief Law Librarian, Federal Reserve Bank, New York.

Lois Buttlar, Asst. Professor, School of Library Science, Kent State Univ., Ohio.

Hans E. Bynagle, Director, Cowles Memorial Library, Whitworth College, Spokane, Wash.

Diane M. Calabrese, Noyes Research Fellow, Bunting Institute, Cambridge, Mass.

Daniel Callison, Asst. Professor, School of Library and Information Science, Indiana Univ., Bloomington.

Adam E. Cappello, formerly Instructor in English, School of Economics, Univ. of Malaga, Spain.

Esther Jane Carrier, Reference Librarian, Lock Haven Univ. of Pennsylvania, Lock Haven.

Jack Carter, Reference Librarian, Los Alamos National Laboratory, N.Mex.

James A. Casada, Assoc. Professor of History, Winthrop College, Rock Hill, S.C.

Jefferson D. Caskey, Professor of Library Science and Instructional Media, Western Kentucky Univ., Bowling Green.

Joseph Cataio, Manager, Booklegger's Bookstore, Chicago.

Dianne Brinkley Catlett, Graduate Assistant/Teaching Fellow, Dept. of Library and Information Studies, East Carolina Univ., Greenville, N.C.

G. A. Cevasco, Assoc. Professor of English, St. John's Univ., Jamaica, N.Y.

John Y. Cheung, Assoc. Professor, Univ. of Oklahoma, Norman.

Boyd Childress, Social Sciences Reference Librarian, Ralph B. Draughon Library, Auburn Univ., Ala.

Larry G. Chrisman, Technical Services Librarian, Univ. of South Florida Medical Center Library, Tampa.

Eric H. Christianson, Assoc. Professor of History, Univ. of Kentucky, Lexington.

Thomas C. Clarie, Head Reference Librarian, Buley Library, Southern Connecticut State Univ., New Haven.

Harriette M. Cluxton, formerly Director of Medical Library Services, Illinois Masonic Medical Center, Chicago.

Gary R. Cocozzoli, Director of the Library, Lawrence Institute of Technology, Southfield, Mich.

Barbara Conroy, Educational Consultant, Santa Fe, N.Mex.

Paul B. Cors, Collection Development Librarian, Univ. of Wyoming, Laramie.

Camille Côté, Assoc. Professor, Graduate School of Library Science, McGill Univ., Montreal, Que.

Nancy Courtney, Reference Librarian, Roesch Library, Univ. of Dayton, Ohio.

Brian E. Coutts, Coordinator of Collection Development, Helm-Cravens Library, Western Kentucky Univ., Bowling Green.

Richard J. Cox, Lecturer, Univ. of Pittsburgh, Pa.

Kathleen W. Craver, Head Librarian, National Cathedral School, Washington, D.C.

Karen S. Croneis, Head Librarian, Physics-Mathematics-Astronomy Library, Univ. of Texas, Austin.

Milton H. Crouch, Asst. Director for Reader Services, Bailey/Howe Library, Univ. of Vermont, Burlington.

Lisa K. Dalton, Documents Librarian, North Carolina Unit, East Carolina Univ., Greenville, N.C.

William J. Dane, Supervising Librarian and Keeper of Prints, Art and Music Dept., Newark Public Library, N.J.

Elisabeth B. Davis, Biology Librarian, Univ. of Illinois, Urbana.

Dominique-René de Lerma, Professor of Music and Graduate Music Coordinator, Morgan State Univ., Baltimore, Md.

Elie M. Dick, Marketing Operations Manager, Millipore Corp., Bedford, Mass.

Donald C. Dickinson, Professor, Graduate Library School, Univ. of Arizona, Tucson.

Dennis Dillon, Assistant for Reference Services Operations, General Libraries, Univ. of Texas, Austin.

G. Kim Dority, Editorial Director, Jones 21st Century, Englewood, Colo.

John E. Druesedow, Jr., Director of the Music Library, Duke Univ., Durham, N.C.

Susan Ebershoff-Coles, Supervisor, Technical Services, Indianapolis-Marion County Public Library, Ind.

David Eggenberger, Director, Publications, National Archives and Records Service, Washington, D.C.

Garabed Eknoyan, Professor of Medicine, Baylor College of Medicine, Houston, Tex.

Marie Ellis, English and American Literature Bibliographer, Univ. of Georgia Libraries, Athens.

Ray English, Assoc. Director, Head of Reference, Oberlin College Library, Ohio.

Jonathon Erlen, Curator, History of Medicine, Univ. of Pittsburgh, Pa.

Judith Ann Erlen, School of Nursing, Univ. of Pittsburgh, Pa.

G. Edward Evans, Univ. Librarian, Charles Von der Ahe Library, Loyola Marymount Univ., Los Angeles, Calif.

Joyce Duncan Falk, Independent Scholar, Santa Barbara, Calif.

Kathleen Farago, Reference Librarian, Lakewood Public Library, Ohio.

Evan Ira Farber, Librarian, Lilly Library, Earlham College, Richmond, Ind.

Adele M. Fasick, Professor, Faculty of Library and Information Science, Univ. of Toronto, Ont.

Eleanor Ferrall, Reference Librarian and Subject Specialist, Criminal Justice/Public Affairs, Arizona State Univ., Tempe.

Joan B. Fiscella, Head of Business Relations, Auraria Library, Denver, Colo.

Jerry D. Flack, Assoc. Professor of Gifted Education, Univ. of Colorado, Colorado Springs.

Patricia Fleming, Assoc. Professor, Faculty of Library Science, Univ. of Toronto, Ont.

Suzanne G. Frayser, Social Science Research Consultant and Faculty, Univ. College. Univ. of Denver, Colo.

Susan J. Freiband, Asst. Professor, Graduate School of Librarianship, Univ. of Puerto Rico, San Juan.

David O. Friedrichs, Assoc. Professor, Univ. of Scranton, Pa.

Ronald H. Fritze, Asst. Professor, Dept. of History, Lamar Univ., Beaumont, Tex.

David R. Fuller, Consulting Geologist, Bainbridge Island, Wash.

Sherrilynne Fuller, Director, Health Sciences Library, Univ. of Washington, Seattle.

Elizabeth Futas, Professor/Director, Graduate School of Library and Information Studies, Univ. of Rhode Island, Kingston.

Edward J. Gallagher, Professor of English, Lehigh Univ., Bethlehem, Pa.

Jack I. Gardner, Administrator, Clark County Library District, Las Vegas, Nev.

Edwin S. Gleaves, Librarian, Tennessee State Library and Archives, Nashville.

Helen M. Gothberg, Assoc. Professor, Graduate Library School, Univ. of Arizona, Tucson.

Allie Wise Goudy, Music Librarian, Western Illinois Univ., Macomb.

Frank Wm. Goudy, Assoc. Professor, Western Illinois Univ., Macomb.

Bonnie Gratch, Head of Reference, Bowling Green State Univ. Libraries, Ohio.

Leonard J. Greenspoon, Professor of Religion, Clemson Univ., S.C.

Richard W. Grefrath, Reference Bibliographer, Univ. of Nevada, Reno.

Laurel Grotzinger, Dean and Chief Research Officer, Graduate College, Western Michigan Univ., Kalamazoo.

Leonard Grundt, Professor, A. Holly Patterson Library, Nassau Community College, Garden City, N.Y.

David E. Hamilton, Dept. of History, Univ. of Kentucky, Lexington.

Deborah Hammer, Head, History, Travel and Biography Div., Queens Borough Public Library, Jamaica, N.Y.

Joseph Hannibal, Assoc. Curator of Invertebrate Paleontology, Cleveland Museum of Natural History, Ohio.

Beverley Hanson, Cincinnati, Ohio.

Roberto P. Haro, Asst. Vice Chancellor, Univ. of California, Berkeley.

Chauncy D. Harris, Samuel N. Harper Distinguished Service Professor of Geography, Univ. of Chicago.

Marvin K. Harris, Professor of Entomology, Texas A & M Univ., College Station.

Thomas L. Hart, Professor, School of Library and Information Studies, Florida State Univ., Tallahassee.

Ann Hartness, Asst. Head Librarian, Benson Latin American Collection, Univ. of Texas, Austin.

Robert J. Havlik, Univ. Engineering/Architecture Librarian, Univ. of Notre Dame, Ind.

James S. Heller, Director of the Law Library and Assoc. Professor of Law, Marshall-Wythe Law Library, College of William and Mary, Williamsburg, Va.

Jean Herold, Business Librarian, General Libraries, Univ. of Texas, Austin.

Mark Y. Herring, formerly Library Director, E. W. King Memorial Library, King College, Bristol, Tenn.

Susan Davis Herring, Reference Librarian, Univ. of Alabama Library, Huntsville.

Janet Swan Hill, Asst. Director for Technical Services, Norlin Library, Univ. of Colorado, Boulder.

Paul E. Hoffman, Assoc. Professor of History, Louisiana State Univ., Baton Rouge.

Shirley L. Hopkinson, Professor, Dept. of Librarianship, San Jose State Univ., Calif.

Renee B. Horowitz, Assoc. Professor, Dept. of Technology, College of Engineering, Arizona State Univ., Tempe.

Carmel A. Huestis, Editor, Fulcrum, Inc., Golden, Colo.

Robert P. Huestis, Property Supervisor, City of Lakewood Police Dept., Colo.

William E. Hug, Professor, Dept. of Instructional Technology, Univ. of Georgia, Athens.

C. D. Hurt, Director, Graduate Library School, Univ. of Arizona, Tucson.

David Isaacson, Asst. Head of Reference and Humanities Librarian, Waldo Library, Western Michigan Univ., Kalamazoo.

Janet R. Ivey, Automation Services Librarian, Boynton Beach City Library, Fla.

John A. Jackman, Entomologist, Texas Agricultural Extension Service, Texas A & M Univ., College Station.

E. B. Jackson, Professor Emeritus, Graduate School of Library and Information Science, Univ. of Texas, Austin.

John C. Jahoda, Assoc. Professor of Biology, Bridgewater State College, Mass.

Richard D. Johnson, Director of Libraries, James M. Milne Library, State Univ. College, Oneonta, N.Y.

Dorothy E. Jones, Reference Librarian, Northern Illinois Univ. Libraries, De Kalb.

Peter B. Kaatrude, Collection Development Librarian, Univ. of California Graduate School of Management Library, Los Angeles.

Elia Kacapyr, Asst. Professor of Economics, Ithaca College, N.Y.

Thomas A. Karel, Asst. Director for Public Services, Shadek-Fackenthal Library, Franklin and Marshall College, Lancaster, Pa.

Edmund D. Keiser, Jr., Professor of Biology, Univ. of Mississippi, University.

John Laurence Kelland, Reference/Bibliographer for Life Sciences, Univ. of Rhode Island Library, Kingston.

Dean H. Keller, Curator of Special Collections, Kent State Univ. Libraries, Ohio.

Barbara E. Kemp, Head, Humanities/Social Sciences Public Services, Washington State Univ., Pullman.

Michael Keresztesi, Professor of Library Science, Wayne State Univ., Detroit, Mich.

Cheryl Kern-Simirenko, Collection Development Librarian, Univ. of Oregon Library, Eugene.

Jackson Kesler, Professor of Theatre, Western Kentucky Univ., Bowling Green.

Norman L. Kincaide, Citation Editor, Shepard's/McGraw-Hill, Inc., Colorado Springs, Colo.

Sharon Kincaide, Production Editor, Shepard's/McGraw-Hill, Inc., Colorado Springs, Colo.

Christine E. King, Senior Asst. Librarian, State Univ. of New York, Stonybrook.

Thomas G. Kirk, Library Director, Hutchins Library, Berea College, Ky.

Kerry L. Kresse, Head, Physics Library, Univ. of Wisconsin, Madison.

Colby H. Kullman, Dept. of English, Univ. of Mississippi, University.

R. Errol Lam, Reference Librarian, Bowling Green State Univ., Ohio.

Maureen B. Lambert, Reference Librarian, Milton S. Eisenhower Library, Johns Hopkins Univ., Baltimore, Md.

Shirley Lambert, Staff, Libraries Unlimited, Inc.

Mary Larsgaard, Map Librarian, Map and Imagery Laboratory Library, Univ. of California, Santa Barbara.

Patricia M. Leach, Staff, Libraries Unlimited, Inc.

Hwa-Wei Lee, Director of Libraries, Ohio Univ., Athens.

Richard A. Leiter, Librarian, Littler, Mendelson, Fastiff and Tichy, San Francisco, Calif.

Elizabeth D. Liddy, Asst. Professor, School of Information Studies, Syracuse Univ., N.Y.

Catherine R. Loeb, Asst. to the Women's Studies Librarian-at-Large, Univ. of Wisconsin System, Madison.

David V. Loertscher, Staff, Libraries Unlimited, Inc.

Elisabeth Logan, Asst. Professor, School of Library and Information Studies, Florida State Univ., Tallahassee.

Sara R. Mack, Professor Emerita, Dept. of Library Science, Kutztown State College, Pa.

Cheryl Knott Malone, History, Government, American Studies Bibliographer and Reference Librarian, General Libraries, Univ. of Texas, Austin.

Donald J. Marion, Reference/Bibliographer, Science and Technology Library, Univ. of Minnesota, Minneapolis.

Judy Gay Matthews, Staff, Libraries Unlimited, Inc.

James F. Mattil, President, Climatran Corp., Aurora, Colo.

George Louis Mayer, formerly Senior Principal Librarian, General Library of the Performing Arts at Lincoln Center, New York Public Library.

Constance McCarthy, Asst. Head, Reference, Northwestern Univ. Library, Evanston, Ill.

James R. McDonald, Professor of Geography, Eastern Michigan Univ., Ypsilanti.

Laura H. McGuire, Documents Librarian, Eastern New Mexico Univ. Library, Portales.

Anthony A. McIntire, Teaching Assistant, Univ. of Kentucky, Lexington.

Susan V. McKimm, Business Reference Specialist, Cuyahoga County Library System, Maple Heights, Ohio.

Margaret McKinley, Head, Serials Dept., Univ. Library, Univ. of California, Los Angeles.

Philip A. Metzger, Curator of Special Collections, Lehigh Univ., Bethlehem, Pa.

Bogdan Mieczkowski, Professor of Economics, Ithaca College, N.Y.

Zbigniew Mieczkowski, Assoc. Professor, Dept. of Geography, Univ. of Manitoba, Winnipeg.

Connie Miller, Coordinator, Computer Assisted Information Services, Main Library, Indiana Univ., Bloomington.

Edward P. Miller, Consultant, Library Planning and Management Consulting, Denver, Colo.

Richard A. Miller, Professor of Economics, Wesleyan Univ., Middletown, Conn.

Diane Montag, Coordinator, Library and Media Center, Front Range Community College, Westminster, Colo.

Michael Ann Moskowitz, Library Director, Emerson College, Boston.

Andreas E. Mueller, Mathematician, Univ. of Illinois, Chicago.

Julie M. Mueller, Research Assoc., American Medical Association, Chicago.

John R. Muether, Library Director, Westminster Theological Seminary, Philadelphia, Pa.

K. Mulliner, Asst. to the Director of Libraries, Ohio Univ. Library, Athens.

James M. Murray, Director, Law Library/Asst. Professor, Gonzaga Univ. School of Law Library, Spokane, Wash.

Necia A. Musser, Head, Acquisitions and Collection Development, Western Michigan Univ., Kalamazoo.

Linda A. Naru, Head, Circulation Dept., Center for Research Libraries, Chicago.

Marie Alexis Navarro, Professor and Director, Graduate Programs in Religious Studies, Mount St. Mary's College, Los Angeles, Calif.

Charles Neuringer, Professor of Psychology, Univ. of Kansas, Lawrence.

Eric R. Nitschke, Reference Librarian, Robert W. Woodruff Library, Emory Univ., Atlanta, Ga.

Christopher W. Nolan, Reference Services Librarian, Maddux Library, Trinity Univ., San Antonio, Tex.

Carol L. Noll, Tinton Falls, N.J.

Margaret K. Norden, Head of Public Services, Marymount Univ. Library, Arlington, Va.

O. Gene Norman, Head, Reference Dept., Indiana State Univ. Library, Terre Haute.

Marilyn Strong Noronha, Reference Dept., Harleigh B. Trecker Library, Univ. of Connecticut, West Hartford.

Marshall E. Nunn, Professor and Reference Librarian, Glendale Community College, Calif.

Patrice O'Donovan, Oregon Health Sciences Univ. Library, Portland.

Herbert W. Ockerman, Professor, Ohio State Univ., Columbus.

Judith E. H. Odiorne, Librarian and Secretary/Treasurer, Barnabas Ministries, Thomaston, Conn.

Berniece M. Owen, Coordinator, Library Technical Services, Portland Community College, Oreg.

John Howard Oxley, Research Officer, Office of Institutional Analysis, Dalhousie Univ., Halifax, N.S.

Joseph W. Palmer, Asst. Professor, School of Information and Library Studies, State Univ. of New York, Buffalo.

Robert Palmieri, Professor/Coordinator, Div. of Keyboard Instruments, School of Music, Kent State Univ., Ohio.

Jean M. Parker, Interim Asst. Director, Rolvaag Memorial Library, St. Olaf College, Northfield, Minn.

Beth M. Paskoff, Faculty, School of Library & Information Science, Louisiana State Univ., Baton Rouge.

Maureen Pastine, Director of Libraries, Washington State Univ., Pullman.

Anna Grace Patterson, Staff, Libraries Unlimited, Inc.

Elizabeth Patterson, Head, Reference Dept., Robert W. Woodruff Library, Emory Univ., Atlanta, Ga.

Gari-Anne Patzwald, Information Research Specialist, OVAR/Geriatric Education Center, Univ. of Kentucky, Lexington.

James T. Peach, Assoc. Professor, Dept. of Economics, New Mexico State Univ., Las Cruces.

Susan R. Penney, Staff, Libraries Unlimited, Inc.

Martha S. Perry, Reader Services/Interlibrary Loan Librarian, Xavier Univ. Library, Cincinnati, Ohio.

Dennis J. Phillips, Head Librarian, Library Learning Resource Center, Pennsylvania State Univ., Fogelsville.

Edwin D. Posey, Engineering Librarian, Purdue Univ. Libraries, West Lafayette, Ind.

George T. Potter, Distinguished Professor of Economics and Human Development, Ramapo College of New Jersey, Mahwah.

Phillip P. Powell, Asst. Reference Librarian, Robert Scott Small Library, College of Charleston, S.C.

Marilyn R. Pukkila, Reference Librarian, Colby College, Waterville, Maine.

Richard H. Quay, Social Science Librarian, Miami Univ. Libraries, Oxford, Ohio.

Randall Rafferty, Asst. Professor and Humanities Reference Librarian, Mississippi State Univ. Library, Mississippi State.

Kristin Ramsdell, Reference/Bibliographic Instruction Librarian, California State Univ., Hayward.

Octavia Porter Randolph, Architectural Scribe, Nahant, Mass.

William G. Ratliff, Asst. Professor, Georgia Southern College, Statesboro.

Jack Ray, Asst. Director, Loyola/Notre Dame Library, Baltimore, Md.

Deborah Pearson Reeber, Librarian, Seyfarth, Shaw, Fairweather & Geraldson, Chicago.

Lorna K. Rees-Potter, Asst. Professor, Graduate School of Library and Information Studies, McGill Univ., Montreal, Que.

Richard Reid, Information Specialist, Ernst & Whinney, New York.

James Rettig, Asst. Univ. Librarian for Reference and Information Services, Swem Library, College of William and Mary, Williamsburg, Va.

James Rice, Assoc. Professor, School of Library and Information Science, Univ. of Iowa, Iowa City.

Gloria H. Richard, Attorney, Equal Employment Opportunity Commission, Falls Church, Va.

Diane Richards, Reference Librarian/Business Bibliographer, North Dakota State Univ. Library, Fargo.

Sara J. Richardson, Librarian, Methodist Hospital, Philadelphia.

Philip R. Rider, Instructor of English, Northern Illinois Univ., De Kalb.

Sandra A. Rietz, Professor of Education, Eastern Montana College, Billings.

William B. Robison, Asst. Professor, History, Southeastern Louisiana Univ., Hammond.

Ilene F. Rockman, Librarian, California Polytechnic State Univ., San Luis Obispo.

Anne C. Roess, Librarian, Peoples Gas, Light & Coke Co., Chicago.

David Rosenbaum, Reference Librarian, Education Library, Wayne State Univ. Libraries, Detroit, Mich.

Samuel Rothstein, Professor Emeritus, School of Librarianship, Univ. of British Columbia, Vancouver.

Rhea Joyce Rubin, Library Consultant, Oakland, Calif.

Emanuel D. Rudolph. Professor of Botany, Ohio State Univ., Columbus.

Siegfried Ruschin, Librarian for Collection Development, Linda Hall Library, Kansas City, Mo.

Edmund F. SantaVicca, Head, Collection Management Services, Cleveland State Univ. Libraries, Ohio.

Robert W. Schaaf, Senior Specialist in U.N. and International Documents, Serial and Government Publications Div., Library of Congress, Washington, D.C.

Jay Schafer, Librarian, Design and Planning, Auraria Library, Denver, Colo.

R. G. Schipf, Science Librarian, Univ. of Montana Library, Missoula.

Frederick A. Schlipf, Executive Director, Urbana Free Library, and Adjunct Professor, Graduate School of Library and Information Science, Univ. of Illinois.

Steven J. Schmidt, Circulation/Interlibrary Loan Librarian, Indiana Univ.-Purdue Univ. at Indianapolis Libraries.

Willa Schmidt, Reference Librarian, Univ. of Wisconsin, Madison.

John P. Schmitt, Head, Social Sciences & Humanities Dept., Morgan Library, Colorado State Univ., Ft. Collins.

Syd Schoenwetter, (deceased) Bird Cinematographer and Recordist, Miami, Fla.

Isabel Schon, Professor, College of Education, Arizona State Univ., Tempe.

Mark E. Schott, formerly Serials/Reference Librarian, Eastern New Mexico Univ., Portales.

L. L. Schroyer, Professor, Univ. Libraries, Northern Illinois Univ., De Kalb.

LeRoy C. Schwarzkopf, formerly Government Documents Librarian, Univ. of Maryland, College Park.

Ralph Lee Scott, Assoc. Professor and Head, Documents/NC Unit, East Carolina Univ. Library, Greenville, N.C.

Robert A. Seal, Director of Libraries, Univ. of Texas, El Paso.

Cathy Seitz, Social Science Librarian, Miami Univ., Oxford, Ohio.

Ravindra Nath Sharma, Asst. Director for Public Services, Univ. of Wisconsin Libraries, Oshkosh.

Avery T. Sharp, Music Librarian, Baylor Univ., Waco, Tex.

Patricia Tipton Sharp, Assoc. Professor of Curriculum and Instruction, Baylor Univ., Waco, Tex.

Gerald R. Shields, Assoc. Professor and Asst. Dean, School of Information and Library Studies, State Univ. of New York, Buffalo.

Bruce A. Shuman, Assoc. Professor, Library Science Program, Wayne State Univ., Detroit, Mich.

Stephanie C. Sigala, Head Librarian, Richardson Memorial Library, St. Louis Art Museum, Mo.

Susan M. Sigman, Staff, Libraries Unlimited, Inc.

Linda Keir Simons, Reference Librarian, Univ. of Dayton, Ohio.

George M. Sinkankas, Assoc. Professor, Graduate School of Library and Information Science, Univ. of Tennessee, Knoxville.

Robert Skinner, Music and Fine Arts Librarian, Southern Methodist Univ., Dallas, Tex.

Tom Smith, Head, Circulation Section, Loan Division, Library of Congress, Washington, D.C.

Lev I. Soudek, Professor of English Linguistics and Coordinator, Programs in Linguistics and TESOL, Northern Illinois Univ., De Kalb.

Geraldo U. de Sousa, Asst. Professor, Dept. of English, Univ. of Kansas, Lawrence.

Paul H. Stacy, Professor, Dept. of English, Univ. of Hartford, West Hartford, Conn.

Mary J. Stanley, Reference Librarian/Liaison to School of Social Work, Indiana Univ.-Purdue Univ. at Indianapolis Libraries.

Marilyn Stark, Asst. Director for Information Services, Arthur Lakes Library, Colorado School of Mines, Golden.

Patricia A. Steele, Head, School of Library and Information Science Library and Education Library, Indiana Univ., Bloomington.

Cynthia A. Steinke, Director, Institute of Technology Libraries, Univ. of Minnesota, Minneapolis.

James Edgar Stephenson, School of Library and Information Science, Catholic Univ. of America, Washington, D.C.

Norman D. Stevens, Univ. Librarian, Univ. of Connecticut Library, Storrs.

Bruce Stuart, Assoc. Professor of Health Administration, Pennsylvania State Univ., University Park.

James H. Sweetland, Asst. Professor, School of Library and Information Science, Univ. of Wisconsin, Milwaukee.

Steven L. Tanimoto, Assoc. Professor, Dept. of Computer Science, Univ. of Washington, Seattle.

Assad A. Tavakoli, Assoc. Professor, School of Business and Economics, Fayetteville State Univ., N.C.

Warren G. Taylor, Manager, Office of Facilities Use, Auraria Higher Education Center, Denver, Colo.

Wade L. Thomas, Asst. Professor of Economics, Ithaca College, N.Y.

Angela Marie Thor, Marine Studies Librarian, Univ. of Delaware, Lewes.

Elizabeth Thweatt, Technical Services Librarian/Asst. Professor, Gonzaga Univ. School of Law Library, Spokane, Wash.

Bruce H. Tiffney, Assoc. Professor of Geology, Univ. of California, Santa Barbara.

Andrew G. Torok, Asst. Professor, Northern Illinois Univ., De Kalb.

Carol Truett, formerly Assoc. Professor, School of Library and Information Science, Univ. of Hawaii, Honolulu.

Betty L. Tsai, Senior Assoc. Professor/Technical Services Librarian, Bucks County Community College, Newtown, Pa.

John Mark Tucker, Senior Reference Librarian, Humanities, Social Science and Education Library, Purdue Univ., West Lafayette, Ind.

Dean Tudor, Professor, School of Journalism, Ryerson Polytechnical Institute, Toronto, Ont.

Robert L. Turner, Jr., Asst. Library Director for Public Services, Radford Univ., Va.

Daniel Uchitelle, Manager, Online and Special Services, Modern Language Association, New York.

Felix Eme Unaeze, Asst. Professor and Business Reference Librarian, New Mexico State Univ., Las Cruces.

Robert F. Van Benthuysen, Library Director, Monmouth College, West Long Branch, N.J.

Carol J. Veitch, Director, Onslow County Public Library, Jacksonville, N.C.

Carole Franklin Vidali, Adjunct Asst. Professor, Dept. of Fine Arts, Syracuse Univ., N.Y.

Kathleen J. Voigt, Head, Reference Dept., Carlson Library, Univ. of Toledo, Ohio.

Louis Vyhnanek, Reference Librarian, Holland Library, Washington State Univ., Pullman.

Mary Jo Walker, Special Collections Librarian and Univ. Archivist, Eastern New Mexico Univ., Portales.

Lydia W. Wasylenko, Technical Services Librarian and Supervisor, Syracuse Univ. Libraries, N.Y.

Jean Weihs, Principal Consultant, Technical Services Group, Seneca College of Applied Arts and Technology, North York, Ont.

Lynda Welborn, Asst. Professor, Educational Technology, Univ. of Northern Colorado, Greeley.

Emily L. Werrell, Reference/Instructional Services Librarian, Northern Kentucky Univ., Highland Heights.

Lucille Whalen, Dean of Graduate Programs, Immaculate Heart College Center, Los Angeles, Calif.

Mary Frances White, Humanities Reference Librarian, Mary and John Gray Library, Lamar Univ., Beaumont, Tex.

Wayne A. Wiegand, Assoc. Professor, School of Library and Information Studies, Univ. of Wisconsin, Madison.

Mitsuko Williams, Head, Veterinary Medicine Library, Univ. of Illinois, Urbana.

Robert V. Williams, Assoc. Professor, College of Library and Information Science, Univ. of South Carolina, Columbia.

T. P. Williams, Head, Social Sciences Dept., Mississippi State Univ. Library, Mississippi State.

Wiley J. Williams, Professor Emeritus, School of Library Science, Kent State Univ., Ohio.

Jacqueline Wilson, Collection Development Officer, The Library, Univ. of California, San Francisco.

Glenn R. Wittig, Asst. Professor, School of Library Service, Univ. of Southern Mississippi, Hattiesburg.

Raymund F. Wood, Editor, *The Westerners*, Encino, Calif.

Hensley C. Woodbridge, Professor of Spanish, Dept. of Foreign Languages, Southern Illinois Univ., Carbondale.

Marda Woodbury, Library Director, Life Chiropractic College—West, San Lorenzo, Calif.

Dorothy C. Woodson, Social Sciences Bibliographer, State Univ. of New York, Buffalo.

Bohdan S. Wynar, Staff, Libraries Unlimited, Inc.

Lubomyr R. Wynar, Professor, School of Library Science, and Director, Program for the Study of Ethnic Publications in the United States, Kent State Univ., Ohio.

Virginia E. Yagello, Head, Chemistry, Perkins Observatory and Physics Libraries, Ohio State Univ., Columbus.

Mark R. Yerburgh, Library Director, Trinity College, Burlington, Vt.

Gary W. Yohe, Professor of Economics, Wesleyan Univ., Middletown, Conn.

Henry E. York, Documents Librarian, Cleveland State Univ., Ohio.

L. Zgusta, Professor of Linguistics and the Classics, and Member of the Center for Advanced Study, Univ. of Illinois, Urbana.

Oleg Zinam, Professor of Economics, Univ. of Cincinnati, Ohio.

Anita Zutis, Government Documents Special Collections Librarian, State Univ. of New York Maritime College, Fort Schuyler.

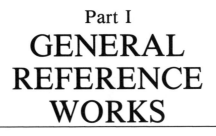

Part I
GENERAL
REFERENCE
WORKS

1 General Reference Works

ACRONYMS AND ABBREVIATIONS

1. Buttress, F. A. **World Guide to Abbreviations of Organizations.** 8th ed. Revised by H. J. Heaney. Glasgow, Scotland, Blackie; distr., Detroit, Grand River Books/Gale, 1988. 777p. $125.00. LC 87-072491. ISBN 0-8103-2048-7.

This new edition of a standard work claims twelve thousand new entries and about 40 percent of the text revised since the last edition. The scope encompasses all kinds of companies, institutions, and government and international agencies across "the whole range of human activity" in all parts of the world.

After a brief introduction and a twenty-five-item bibliography, entries are arranged in one alphabet, by the abbreviation (or by initialism or acronym) followed by the full name of the organization, in its "native" language. A new feature in this edition is the inclusion with the entry of abbreviations in other languages (e.g., NATO = OTAN). Some entries also include country of origin or parent body.

The book is well bound, and clearly printed in two columns on moderately opaque paper (that is, "ghosts" of the other side of the sheet show through, even though the paper is fairly heavy).

Since many libraries are likely to have Gale's *Acronyms, Initialisms & Abbreviations Dictionary* (see *ARBA* 88, entry 1), this source is the obvious competitor. A comparison of the present volume with the twelfth edition of *AIAD* shows the latter consistently has much better coverage for the United States, but also that it often includes other groups that the *World Guide* misses. For example, it is understandable why the *World Guide* lacks the Maine Lobstermen's Association, but why does it miss the Medical Library Association, yet include the Music Library Association? Or, why does it miss both the American Kennel Club and the Australian Kangaroo Club? Libraries with an ongoing need for this sort of tool should strongly consider Gale's *International Acronyms, Initialisms & Abbreviations Dictionary* (see *ARBA* 86, entry 1), whose second edition, at $160.00 includes more entries, and has a wider scope than the *World Guide.* James H. Sweetland

2. Miller, Stuart W. **Concise Dictionary of Acronyms and Initialisms.** New York, Facts on File, 1988. 175p. $22.95. LC 87-30468. ISBN 0-8160-1577-5.

By the compiler's own admission concise here means "a barebones dictionary, intended for ready-reference situations." Barebones it is in comparison with the exhaustive, standard work, Gale's *Acronyms, Initialisms & Abbreviations Dictionary* (see *ARBA* 88, entry 1), and even with its like competitor, *Pugh's Dictionary of Acronyms & Abbreviations,* compiled by Eric Pugh (see *ARBA* 88, entry 3). As a ready-reference source this concise dictionary is limited in two ways. First, many of its inclusions are well known to the average person, for example, U.S. postal codes, abbreviations for the months of the year, and other simple abbreviations like *VP* for Vice-President and *hr.* for hour. Second, people wanting to spell out acronyms or initialisms usually have very uncommon, not common, ones to decipher. They already know that *ed.* stands for editor, *OJ* for orange juice, and *QB* for quarterback (in football). A few corporation initials have been included for the very largest business enterprises, but since stock exchange information is frequently sought after, many more corporation initials should have been added. Some more superfluous inclusions are *EEEE* for shoe width (man's, widest size), roman numerals, *M-F* for Monday through Friday, *S* for sadism/sadist, and *T* for True,

F for False. The number of actual acronyms versus initialisms is small, and there is no reverse listing such as Gale offers. It is difficult to recommend this slender work for reference use in any size of library. There is a problem with downsizing a reference to the point that it is reduced to inutility. [R: LJ, July 88, p. 72; RBB, 1 Oct 88, p. 237]   Bill Bailey

ALMANACS

3.   International Congress Calendar. Vol. 3. 27th ed. Edited by the Union of International Associations. Munich, New York, K. G. Saur, 1987. 388p. index. $150.00pa. (4 issues). ISSN 0538-6349.

This guide to international meetings and conferences has the reliability of the Union of International Associations and the legacy of twenty-six previous editions of experience. For each meeting listed, the *Calendar* supplies information on date, place, name of organizer, type of meeting, theme, number of participants expected, number of countries represented, any concurrent exhibitions, as well as the reference to the international organization entry in the *Yearbook of International Organizations* (see *ARBA* 87, entries 70-71).

The entries are arranged geographically, chronologically, and by international organization. A title and keyword index are provided. It appears to be very comprehensive and up-to-date.

The *Calendar* now comes out in four editions per year, each of which supersedes the last. With the continuing growth of diversity in academic and research environments, this guide will be of increasing importance. It is worth its high price for those libraries where it will have frequent use.   James Rice

4.   Whitaker's Almanack 1988: The Year Book ... [and] The Reference Book.... 120th ed. London, J. Whitaker; distr., Detroit, Gale, 1987. 1236p. illus. maps. index. $57.00. ISBN 0-85021-178-6.

This British compendium of statistics and facts continues to be an important source for reference collections which require information on Great Britain. This almanac covers events and obituaries for the past year; prime ministers since 1782; vital statistics and statistics on finance, agriculture, shipping, employment, housing, and population; principal British and Irish associations; and information on Great Britain, the Commonwealth countries, and dependent territories. The main changes in this volume are related to the general election of June 1987. The section on the stock exchange

has been revised, and "included for the first time are the independent Ombudsmen for the Banking, Building Societies, and Insurance sectors."

Whitaker's is similar to the *World Almanac* (see *ARBA* 87, entry 5) in that both were established in 1868, and each contains statistics, calendars, and brief facts with emphasis on Great Britain and the United States respectively. They both also have a detailed index in the front of the book, but *Whitaker's* appears to be more extensive. *Whitaker's* is approximately one-fourth larger in size but sells for almost ten times more than the *World Almanac*. Ironically, page 1201 of *Whitaker's* indicates that the *Almanack* is available in London at 12 Dyott St., W. C. 1 for £15.25, or about $26.00. Academic and public libraries should consider purchasing this useful annual from the most affordable source.

O. Gene Norman

ATLASES

5.   The Original Cleartype United States Zip Code Atlas. Maspeth, N.Y., American Map, 1988. 146p. maps. index. price not reported. spiralbound. ISBN 0-8416-9588-1.

This specialized atlas has been developed as a tool for marketers, advertisers, and others concerned with offering goods and services. It includes separate county/town zip code maps for all the states, along with accompanying indexes which alphabetically list counties, cities, and towns (having populations of one thousand or more and five-digit zip codes). The indexes include population of the counties, as well as map location. The five-digit zip code is included for each of the cities and towns listed, along with their map location. This is an especially handy feature of the atlas. Census-designated places (CDPs) are also indicated in the indexes. The maps have a population key which uses a twelve-point scale from "under 250" to "1,000,000." They also show state capitals and county seats. The maps, in black, white, and gray, use green to mark out zip code areas and 3 digit zip code numbers. County lines are shown in light gray. The zip code information stands out clearly and is easy to read. There are also enlarged insets for areas with a great number of places in close proximity. In addition to these state maps and insets, the atlas includes special two-page, five-digit zip code maps of New York City's five boroughs, a U.S. map showing national area zip codes, and one showing time zones and area codes. There is also a world standard time zone map. These special features further enhance the usefulness of the atlas. The final section contains twenty-two pages of statistical tables. These include eleven pages of "households/household income/population statistical data for 3 digit zip code areas," then "retail sales reports/black and Hispanic markets statistical data for 3 digit zip code areas." This information is particularly valuable for marketing purposes "to measure actual performance versus potential on a zip-coded market-by-market basis" (p. 3).

The size of the atlas (8½ by 11 inches) makes it convenient to use. Although it is spiral-bound, its cover (bright yellow and green) is of heavy cardboard stock. The typeface used in the indexes and maps is particularly clear, which enhances readability.

Although there is a one-page guide, including notes on places shown on the maps and an explanation of symbols used in the indexes, there is no explanatory information on how to use the atlas. The presentation is oriented to businesspersons, professionals, and others familiar with the zip code system, rather than to students or to the uninitiated general public. However, this atlas is a valuable addition to business collections in public and academic libraries, especially because of its zip code marketing charts.   Susan J. Freiband

BIBLIOGRAPHIES
Bibliographic Guides

6. **Books for College Libraries: A Core Collection of 50,000 Titles.** 3d ed. Virginia Clark, ed. Chicago, Association of College and Research Libraries, American Library Association, 1988. 6v. index. $500.00/set. LC 88-16714. ISBN 0-8389-3353-X.

The first edition of this title was published in 1967 to replace Charles B. Shaw's *List of Books for College Libraries* which was published in 1931. The first edition of *Books for College Libraries* (*BCL1*) had a cut-off date which coincided with the beginning of *Choice*, with the hope that the journal could be used as a complementary, on-going revision and supplement. This did not materialize however. Periodic reassessments that included categories not covered by *Choice* were necessary, and *BCL2* appeared in 1975 (see *ARBA* 76, entry 141). In 1985 work began on *BCL3*. The current edition recommends approximately fifty thousand books based on college library standards revised in 1985 (one hundred faculty members per one thousand students in ten fields of study would require 104,000 volumes). With half that number recommended by *BCL3*, a small college library would have flexibility to fill needs not included in the basic subject areas. The volume

distribution related to subject areas is basically the same as with the earlier editions although there is a small increase in the number of titles in the areas of psychology, science, technology, and biography (up 17 percent from 14 percent).

Still arranged in six basic volumes with the sixth volume serving as an index to the remaining five, *BCL3* has broad subject arrangement by humanities (volume 1); language and literature (volume 2); history (volume 3); social sciences (volume 4); and psychology, science, technology, and bibliography (volume 5). Within each volume, entries are arranged in Library of Congress call number order. The title selection mirrors the qualifications of the more than five hundred college faculty and collection development librarians of the United States and Canada. Those involved in the compilation of *BCL3* included teachers in the field, reference librarians, and the referees who were chosen for their knowledge in collection development and in the various subject areas.

Entries that were listed in *BCL2* are noted with an asterisk. Although they are not annotated, entries include fairly complete bibliographic information except for price and the title's availability. Although it is understandable that an out-of-print book would be an excellent choice in a particular collection, it is also necessary that the user of this text be aware of whether it is in-print.

Effort to maintain currency is apparent; most titles in the computer area have publication dates in the 1980s, with a few earlier publications. More titles have been added to QH (natural history, biology) and Z678-686 has a totally new bibliography, the lack of which was mentioned in the review of *BLC2*. As with any undertaking of this size, one may differ with the choices of titles included, but for a basic guide this continues as a standard.

                        Anna Grace Patterson

7. **The Reader's Adviser: A Layman's Guide to Literature. Volume 4: The Best in the Literature of Philosophy and World Religions.** 13th ed. William L. Reese, ed. New York, R. R. Bowker, 1988. 801p. index. $75.00. LC 57-13277. ISBN 0-8352-2148-2; ISSN 0094-5943.

8. **The Reader's Adviser: A Layman's Guide to Literature. Volume 5: The Best in the Literature of Science, Technology, and Medicine.** 13th ed. Paul T. Durbin, ed. New York, R. R. Bowker, 1988. 725p. index. $75.00. LC 57-13277. ISBN 0-8352-2149-0; ISSN 0094-5943.

9. **The Reader's Adviser: A Layman's Guide to Literature. Volume 6: Indexes.** 13th ed. New

York, R. R. Bowker, 1988. 511p. $75.00. LC 57-13277. ISBN 0-8352-2315-9; ISSN 0094-5943.

The purpose of the *Reader's Adviser* was set forth in 1921 as a tool to help the person interested in self-education, that non-specialist interested in reading about a particular subject. The 13th edition expands that function from one traditional volume through a three-volume set for the 12th edition, to its current six-volume size.

The organization of each chapter in the volumes reviewed here move the reader from the general to the specific; from reference books, critical works, and anthologies to specific authors. Each chapter, written by a subject specialist, begins with an introductory essay, followed by general reading lists and then topical ones. Important authors receive a "main entry" which contains a brief essay about that person followed by a bibliography of works by and about that person. Each item listed has a brief evaluative description. Works cited contain complete bibliographic information and indicate whether the work was currently in print at the time of publication. There are subject, author and title indexes at the end of each volume.

The volume on religion contains a much more balanced coverage than previous editions by including more emphasis on Eastern religions. Religions and religious movements are covered from ancient to modern times with good coverage of 19th- and 20th-century groups with the exception of the "New Age" movement. Probing specific religions, Latter-day Saints for example, works both favorable and unfavorable to the movement are listed, however, coverage of the Mormon's sacred scriptures is inadequate. Philosophy is covered both by movement and by individual philosopher including Pre-Socratic to the Logical Positivists.

The volume on science, technology, and medicine is divided into usual subdivisions but has extremely useful issue subdivisions such as "Reproductive Technology: Ethical Issues," "Stress and Disease," and "Environmental Ethics." Controversial issues are not only recognized, but works both pro and con are enumerated. The biggest problem with this volume is the currency of sources, but this is not a problem that could have been solved by Bowker. Since the book literature is woefully behind the periodical literature in all three fields, sources for the beginner will have to be supplemented through the periodical literature. The author of each chapter has included books published through 1987.

Volume 6, *Indexes*, brings together all of the indexes of the previous five volumes. The first section includes a complete publisher's directory

followed by a comprehensive name index which includes not only the authors of every title cited but also the authors who have received main entry listings. The title index includes all but very generic titles such as "complete works," and the subject index integrates the topical approach of all the volumes.

The *Reader's Adviser* used to serve as a daily used tool in a time when many were interested in self-education. Are patrons of libraries still interested in "what's best to read if I don't know much about the topic?" As the amount of information and publishing continues to engulf the world, the astute librarian will become more aware of the function of information screening. Using the *Reader's Adviser* as a bible for advisory work is essential. As a basic selection tool for the general library, the librarian would be hard-pressed to find a better tool. [R: LJ, 1 Oct 88, pp. 81-82; RLR, Aug 88, pp. 233-34; WLB, Oct 88, p. 111]   David V. Loertscher

10. **Recommended Reference Books for Small and Medium-sized Libraries and Media Centers 1988.** Bohdan S. Wynar, ed. Englewood, Colo., Libraries Unlimited, 1988. 261p. index. $32.50. LC 81-12394. ISBN 0-87287-682-9; ISSN 0277-5948.

Bohdan S. Wynar, editor and publisher of *American Reference Books Annual* (*ARBA*), has selected 517 "original and unabridged" reviews from the 1988 volume of *ARBA* for this eighth annual volume. Two criteria apply: the reference work must be recommended, and it must be appropriate for small and medium-sized libraries. While many would concur with most of the choices, inevitably, some appear to be rather esoteric for such libraries, for example, *Administrative and Financial Terms* issued by the Food and Agriculture Organization of the United Nations.

Reviews, including standard citations; codes for college, public, and school libraries; and references to other reviews in standard library review media; are arranged by author, editor, or title (not AACR2 main entry) within classes based on broad subject and form (not Dewey). Among the four broadest categories, 39 reviews fall under "General Reference," 217 under "Social Sciences," 185 under "Humanities," and only 76 under "Science and Technology." Reviews are signed, and reviewers, with affiliations, are listed at the front of the volume.

Additional access is provided by an author/ title index and a rather skimpy subject index. Since the main arrangement provides broad subject access, the index ought to provide more specific access. It frequently fails. Reference works on the Bible, the saints, Christianity, the Catholic Church, liturgy, and worship may be found only under "Religion," even though there is at least one reference book on each of these topics. *Women in Science* is not listed under "Women's Studies." The entry for "mushrooms" refers to "fungi," but there is still no entry for *Wild and Exotic Mushroom Cultivation in North America.* The next edition of this standard work needs a new indexer!

James D. Anderson

11.   Reference Books Bulletin 1986-1987: A Compilation of Evaluations Appearing in *Reference Books Bulletin*, September 1, 1986-August 1987. Sandy Whiteley, ed.; Penny Spokes, comp. Chicago, American Library Association, 1987. 175p. index. $22.50pa. LC 73-159565. ISBN 0-8389-3345-9; ISSN 8755-0962.

This is the nineteenth compilation of reviews originally published in the *Reference Books Bulletin* section of *Booklist,* covering the period from 1 September 1986 to August 1987. The reviews discuss English-language reference materials for medium-sized public and academic libraries, as well as school libraries. Written by current and former members of the *Reference Books Bulletin*'s Editorial Board, individual reviews are subject to criticism and suggestions from other board members before being published.

There has been a major change in the format of the latest compilation. The reviews, which make up the great bulk of each issue, are now arranged within broad subject categories such as psychology and philosophy, religion, business and economics, and the arts. In the previous compilation the reviews were arranged alphabetically regardless of subject. There were also separate chapters on databases and software in the previous edition; these have not been included in the current volume.

As in previous editions, there are separate articles evaluating particular types and categories of reference works, for example, reference sources on the U.S. Constitution. The reviews vary in length from a paragraph or two to one page. The book is indexed by subject, type of material, and title. As the title indicates, the emphasis is on hard cover works, with almost no coverage of databases, software, or CD-ROM materials.

The virtue of this publication is that it pulls together a year's worth of reviews in one convenient place. Its coverage is geared more toward medium-sized public and college libraries, although many of the reference sources reviewed will also be found in large university libraries. *Reference Books Bulletin* is a source, on

a smaller scale than *ARBA,* for librarians to check reviews of reference items that have been published during the previous year. The individual issues of the *Bulletin* and other journals will still have to be checked for more current material. [R: LAR, 14 Oct 88, p. 605; RLR, Aug 88, pp. 182-83]

Louis Vyhnanek

12.   Swidan, Eleanor A. Reference Sources: A Brief Guide. 9th ed. Baltimore, Md., Enoch Pratt Free Library, 1988. 175p. index. $7.95pa. ISBN 0-910556-26-1.

In 1938, the Enoch Pratt Free Library of Baltimore, Maryland, issued *Guide to Reference Books.* Over the past fifty years, the publication has grown steadily in size and value. This latest update, as before, covers general reference books, the humanities, sciences, and social sciences. Now in its ninth edition, it includes, for the first time, computer-readable databases and resources in microform, necessitating a change in title from *Reference Books* to *Reference Sources.* Its stated purpose, however, remains the same: "to help the reader or library user who is bewildered by the staggering array of reference works that confront him on the shelves of the library."

As its title indicates, this guide is meant to be suggestive rather than complete. Part 1, "Reference Sources General in Scope," lists encyclopedias, almanacs, indexes, dictionaries, maps, bibliographies, and government publications. Part 2, "Reference Sources in Special Subjects," is devoted to interdisciplinary groupings in the humanities, sciences, and social sciences, which are appropriately subsumed and subdivided. Part 3 provides a succinct introduction to database research and relates to both parts 1 and 2. As in the past, inclusion is a commendation, and reference materials in medicine, law, and genealogy have been excluded.

To all libraries, public, university, or specialized, that have gotten good use out of previous editions of this valuable reference tool, this latest update can be warmly recommended. [R: JAL, Nov 88, pp. 331-32; RBB, 15 Nov 88, p. 548; WLB, Nov 88, pp. 126-27]

G. A. Cevasco

National and Trade Bibliographies

INTERNATIONAL

13.   Cumulative Book Index 1986: A World List of Books in the English Language. Nancy C. Wong and Donald M. Cannon, eds. Bronx, N.Y., H. W. Wilson, 1987. 3262p. sold on service basis. LC 28-26655. ISSN 0011-300X.

An important part of the national bibliographic apparatus since 1898, Wilson family member *CBI* is an old friend—steady, reliable, changing very gradually as needed, and increasing in size as publishing expands. Published monthly except in August and presently cumulated annually, since 1982 it has been computer-produced. *CBI* is an international bibliography of books published in the English language, and is arranged according to Library of Congress filing rules by author, title, and subject, as in a dictionary catalog. Its broad scope makes necessary exclusions: government publications, most pamphlets, "inexpensive" (no price limit given) paperbacks, maps, music scores, editions of fewer than five hundred copies, privately published genealogies, tests, tracts, local directories, etc.

The author entry usually is most complete and generally contains full name, complete title, series, edition, collation, list price, publisher, ISBN, and LC card numbers when available. Title and subject entries are usually somewhat abbreviated, but cross references abound. Subject searches produced some interesting lists: 2 pages of titles under "Fantastic Fiction," 6½ pages under "Detective and Mystery Stories," 4½ pages under "Children's Stories," and 6 pages under "Large Type Books." A directory of publishers and distributors supplies the usual information needed for ordering; it also includes lists of imprints, branch offices, agents, and representatives.

This old standard retains its usefulness for librarians and other book people, and, in varying format, should be around for a while longer to celebrate its one-hundredth year.

Laura H. McGuire

UNITED STATES

14. Bowker's Forthcoming Children's Books. Volume 1, Number 4: September 1987-January 1988. New York, R. R. Bowker, 1987. 273p. $49.95pa. ISSN 0000-0965.

This bimonthly serial companion to *Children's Books in Print* and *Subject Guide to Children's Books in Print* (see *ARBA* 88, entries 21 and 22), begun in 1987, gives bibliographic information on over eighteen hundred juvenile titles. Access is by separate subject, author, and title listings, with a final section on publisher information. The subject headings are based on *Sears List of Subject Headings* (see *ARBA* 87, entry 595), with additional terms taken as needed from the *Library of Congress Subject Headings*. The copy reviewed also contained a special section with an article on Jean Fritz's *Shh! We're*

Writing the Constitution, and other short articles relevant to the children's book industry.

Included in this issue are titles from the previous twelve months as well as expected titles for the following five months. All the information is supplied by publishers, which means that some authors are listed in several places due to variant forms of the names. Yet another addition to the growing collection of Bowker bibliographic tools, this issue is attractively produced on a better quality paper than one is accustomed to in the Books in Print series, with slightly larger type and better contrast, making it easier to read. While there is some overlap between this and *Forthcoming Books in Print*, it is minor. Those who work with children's books will be pleased to have this publication to alert them to what is on the way in the world of children's literature. Marilyn R. Pukkila

15. The Complete Directory of Large Print Books & Serials 1988. New York, R. R. Bowker, 1988. 228p. $69.95pa. LC 74-102773. ISBN 0-8352-2322-1.

Since 1970, Bowker has provided librarians with the useful *Large Type Books in Print*. Now Bowker has enhanced that title with additional indexes and issued it under the title *Complete Directory of Large Print Books & Serials*. It includes all in-print books issued by American publishers in a fourteen-point typeface or larger. The 6,191 titles can be approached through title or author indexes, or in the main body of the work under the headings general reading, textbooks, or children's books. Each of these large sections is subdivided into more specific groupings, such as cooking, gardening, poetry, and travel. In each case, the user is provided with the ordering information, publisher, price, ISBN, and edition date.

In earlier versions, this catalog was printed in eighteen-point typeface and could be used for browsing by those with limited vision. In this new directory, however, all details are given in a small typeface. Otherwise, this is a useful source for libraries that wish to select large print books and serials for their patrons. Recommended. [R: RLR, Nov 88, pp. 340-41] Donald C. Dickinson

16. Current Christian Books, 1988-89. Colorado Springs, Colo., CBA Service Corporation, 1988. 824p. $54.95pa. ISSN 0270-2347.

The goal of *Current Christian Books* (*CCB*) is to provide a comprehensive catalog of "all the Christian books in print" (preface). This edition (the first edition was published in 1975) indexes more than 34,000 titles and 21,500 authors from more than five hundred publishers—primarily

U.S. firms. Included in the front matter are a key to series abbreviations and a listing of publishers with addresses. The body of the work is divided into two indexes: a title index which gives full publishing information (title, series, publisher, year, author, binding, price, and ISBN) and recommended subject categories for each book; and an author index subdivided by publisher, with titles listed under each one.

Although there is a market for *CCB*—religious bookstores and libraries with *comprehensive* religion collections—certain factors make it a questionable acquisition for most academic and public libraries. More than 150 publishers not indexed in *Books in Print* (*BIP*) and its religion subsets are included, but these are generally more obscure firms. Omitted from *CCB*'s list are American Bible Society, Cambridge University Press, and University Press of America, all substantial sources of Christian books.

Extensive spot checking revealed several types of errors throughout the volume: in-print books not included, incorrect titles, incorrect author names, editors (and one translator) listed as authors, absence of some publishing information, and books listed in the title index but not in the author index. In addition, it often appears that the computer-stored data were not cleaned up before this volume was put into print. These flaws plus the lack of a subject index lessen *CCB*'s value as an acquisitions or research tool, especially for libraries which have *BIP*.

Craig W. Beard

17.   Rinderknecht, Carol, comp. **A Checklist of American Imprints for 1838: Items 48673-53805.** Metuchen, N.J., Scarecrow, 1988. 257p. $39.50. LC 64-11784. ISBN 0-8108-2123-0.

18.   Rinderknecht, Carol, comp. **A Checklist of American Imprints for 1839: Items 53806-59415.** Metuchen, N.J., Scarecrow, 1988. 289p. $42.50. LC 64-11784. ISBN 0-8108-2124-9.

These volumes for 1838 and 1839 in the Checklist of American Imprints series are landmarks in a sense, for they have been typeset by computer. While the text is compressed, it is very clear and readable, and the number of entries is comparable to previous volumes. Another notable change, beginning with the volume for 1838, is that U.S. documents have been omitted, due, according to the compiler, to improved bibliographic control of documents. Otherwise, the arrangement of these volumes will be familiar to those who have used previous volumes in the series (for reviews of *1835, 1836,* and *1837,* see *ARBA* 87, entries 22-24). Entries are arranged alphabetically by author; title,

place, publisher, date, and number of pages are given. Symbols for libraries holding copies are also provided. It is expected that an index of authors and titles for the decade of the 1830s will follow.

Dean H. Keller

GREAT BRITAIN

19.   **British Books in Print 1987: The Reference Catalogue of Current Literature....** London, J. Whitaker; distr., New York, R. R. Bowker, 1987. 4v. $275.00/set. ISBN 0-85021-177-8; ISSN 0068-1350.

Containing over 400,000 titles from more than twelve thousand publishers, this computer-generated set continues as the only current British list of books in print. Last reviewed in *ARBA* 86 (see entry 18), there have been few if any changes in the basic information provided. The format remains the same: alphabetically arranged, with author entries first and titles and subjects following when the entry word is the same. Keyword subject entries may be interspersed within the list. Main entries and joint authors, editors, etc., are distinguished by bold printing.

Updating is provided constantly through *The Bookseller* (J. Whitaker, 1928-), a weekly newspaper which includes a listing of all books published during the week as well as price changes and out-of-print titles. According to the preface, over 600,000 changes have been made in *British Books in Print* since the last edition.

Although the print on the verso page shows through and the typeface is very small, the entries are very readable. *BBIP* 1987 will continue to meet the needs of individuals seeking information on books published in Great Britain.

Anna Grace Patterson

BIOGRAPHIES

International

20.   **Current Biography Yearbook 1987.** 48th ed. Charles Moritz and others, eds. Bronx, N.Y., H. W. Wilson, 1988. 666p. illus. index. $46.00. LC 40-27432. ISSN 0084-9499.

Current Biography Yearbook 1987 continues in the long line of an admirable and valuable basic reference tool, providing comprehensive and accurate biographies about a variety of living leaders in the news. Each biography is approximately three thousand words in length and includes a photograph, a current address, and a list of the sources used in compiling it. Also included are an appendix obituary listing, a checklist of sources used (ranging from magazines and newspapers to basic reference works and news releases), and a classified professions listing of persons included in the yearbook. A cumulative index for 1981-1987 also is provided.

With such helpful international coverage of figures in government, business, literature, religion, education, and entertainment, *Current Biography* remains a durable resource for all libraries.   Elizabeth Patterson

21. Encyclopedia of World Biography. 20th Century Supplement. Volume 14: G-M. David Eggenberger, ed.-in-chief. Palatine, Ill., Jack Heraty, 1987. 544p. illus. maps. $249.50/set (3 vols.). LC 86-63173. ISBN 0-910081-02-6.

22. Encyclopedia of World Biography. 20th Century Supplement. Volume 15: N-Z. David Eggenberger, ed.-in-chief. Palatine, Ill., Jack Heraty, 1988. 598p. illus. maps. $249.50/set (3 vols.). LC 86-63173. ISBN 0-910081-02-6.

A review of the first supplement to the *EWB* (volume 13, A-F) published in *ARBA* (see *ARBA* 88, entry 30), noted that although the volume was hardly essential for large university collections, where much of its biographical material is readily available in other standard reference works, it probably would be put to good use in secondary schools and public libraries. The same observation can be made about these two supplements.

As would be expected, the format, style, and design of these two supplements, like the first, accord with the appearance of the basic encyclopedia. Like all *EWB* entries, each biography is the work of an academic expert or other specialist. Each entry is illustrated by a photograph or drawing of the subject. Accompanying the entries of individuals from the Third World countries are helpful locator maps that show the approximate position and relative size of the subject's country.

Each of the some three hundred biographies making up each volume, as before, runs about one thousand words and is followed by a "Final Reading" paragraph keyed to one or more study guides and to related biographies within the volumes.   G. A. Cevasco

23. Fradin, Dennis Brindell. **Remarkable Children: Twenty Who Made History.** Boston, Little, Brown, 1987. 207p. $14.95. LC 87-3820. ISBN 0-316-29126-9.

Twenty child achievers, each of whom made a rare accomplishment or discovery at a young age and left their mark on history, are featured here. The author has written an impressive personal look into the remarkable

lives of these children, some who are very well known and some who are relatively obscure. Among the famous included are Mozart, Picasso, Helen Keller, Louis Braille, and Anne Frank. The relatively unknown include Hilda Conkling, a young poetess; Maria de Sautuola, who discovered rare cave paintings in northern Spain; and Zerah Colburn, son of a Vermont farmer, who was not quite six when he first showed an ability to do complex mathematical equations in his head.

The author was able to talk to several of the persons featured and to individuals who knew them, including Shirley Tample, Pelé, Bobby Fischer, Nadia Comaneci, and Tracy Austin.

Public and school libraries will want this as a biographical and inspirational reference.

Beverley Hanson

United States

24. Culbertson, Judi, and Tom Randall. **Permanent New Yorkers: A Biographical Guide to the Cemeteries of New York.** Chelsea, Vt., Chelsea Green, 1987. 405p. illus. maps. bibliog. index. $16.95pa. LC 87-17663. ISBN 0-930031-11-3.

This is an intriguing guide to a selective number of cemeteries located in four of New York City's boroughs (Staten Island is not included), on Long Island, and in Westchester and Rockland counties. Some may consider visiting burial grounds a morbid pastime; after reading this volume the visitor will have a greater appreciation of the history, art, architecture, and cultural features such places contain.

Emphasis is on the burial places of the rich and famous, with 350 featured in brief biographies. The biographical sketches, running two to three pages, have a whimsical, witty tone. Each section of the work is introduced by directions on how to reach the particular cemetery, followed by instructions for walking tours; twelve maps, 112 photographs, a bibliography, and an index supplement the text. The biographical subjects range from the seventeenth century to modern times, with many twentieth-century figures featured.

This work is the second in a series of guides to "the most interesting cemeteries of the world's great cities." The first, *Permanent Parisians*, appeared in 1986. Both are of interest to armchair as well as actual visitors.

Robert Van Benthuysen

25. Dictionary of American Biography. Supplement Eight: 1966-1970. John A. Garraty and Mark C. Carnes, eds. New York, Scribner's,

1988. 759p. index. $80.00. LC 77-2942. ISBN 0-684-18618-7.

This is a standard, indispensable reference tool. Its purpose, as stated in the first volume (published in December 1928), is to provide scholarly biographical essays on persons "who have made some significant contribution to American life in its manifold aspects." Supplement 7 was reviewed in *ARBA* 82 (see entry 126); the review of supplement 6 appeared in *ARBA* 81 (see entry 113); and supplement 5 was reviewed in *ARBA* 78 (see entry 115). Supplement 8 contains biographies of 454 persons and extends the period of coverage through 1970, raising the total number of biographical sketches to 18,110.

Only about 15 percent of those profiled in supplement 8 are women, and this scholarly neglect of women's history in the *DAB* brought about the publication of *Notable American Women, 1607-1950* (see *ARBA* 72, entry 221). Women covered in supplement 8 include Alice B. Toklas, Sonja Henie, Dorothy Gish, Judy Garland, Janis Joplin, and Hedda Hopper. Men profiled include Jack Kerouac, Dwight D. Eisenhower, Herbert Hoover, Basil Rathbone, Martin Luther King, Jr., Joseph P. Kennedy, Robert F. Kennedy, Jack L. Ruby, and Woody Guthrie.

Readers expecting persons' "significant contributions to American life" to be positive ones may be surprised to read the biographical sketch of "reputed Cosa Nostra boss" Vito Genovese. Also a bit surprising is the inclusion of "wealthy eccentric and playboy" Thomas Franklyn Manville, Jr., whose numerous marriages and divorces were "his only claim to public attention."

The book concludes with an index guide to the supplements that covers all eight volumes.

Jack Bales

26. Smith, Carter, ed. **The Faces of America.** New York, Facts on File, 1988. 1v. (various paging). illus. index. (American Historical Images on File). $125.00 looseleaf with binder. LC 87-6707. ISBN 0-8160-1608-9.

This is the third in the Facts on File American Historical Images on File series, a looseleaf service containing a wide range of pictorial Americana, and *The Faces of America* seems the best suited to the format. The volume has three hundred portraits, including paintings, sculpture, and photographs of a diverse group of Americans from earliest times to the present. Among those included are presidents (Washington, Kennedy, Reagan), artists (Longfellow, Cassett, O'Keefe), and reformers (Debs, DuBois, Dix). The large (6 by 8 inches) por-

traits are on heavy paper, copyright-free, and easy to reproduce. At the bottom of each is an annotation that places the person in historical perspective. Each portrait is identified with artist, medium, date, and source.

The format should come in handy for reference librarians and students in academic, school, and public libraries. The price may preclude smaller libraries from purchase, but the volume will be valuable for those who can afford it. The problem will be retaining the contents, which, because of the binding, may be filched most easily. Many volumes contain portraits or photographs of famous people but they do not have as large or as easily copyable a selection as this one. *The Dictionary of American Portraits* (Dover, 1967) contains 4,045 pictures of important Americans but all are small (2 by 3 inches). The *Catalogue of American Portraits* (see *ARBA* 76, entry 918) contains many paintings (oil, watercolor, etc.), but is also small and not for copying purposes. This is a very useful volume, with an index by artist and subject, including events as subjects, but would benefit from an occupations index. [R: BR, Sept/Oct 88, p. 52; RBB, 1 Oct 88, p. 238; WLB, June 88, p. 137]   Elizabeth Futas

Great Britain

27. Sakol, Jeannie, and Caroline Latham. **The Royals.** New York, Congdon & Weed; distr., Chicago, Contemporary Books, 1987. 377p. illus. bibliog. $19.95. ISBN 0-86553-194-3.

Less a serious reference work than a hodgepodge of trivia about the British royal family, this book seems to contain as much gossip as documented fact. Among the brief biographies and tidbits about royal affairs and family ghosts can be found such information as the names of Queen Elizabeth's Corgis, the shoe size Princess Margaret wears, and the Queen Mother's favorite drink.

The arrangement is alphabetical, but not particularly useful. For example, Prince Philip is entered under "His Royal Highness the Prince Philip, Duke of Edinburgh" and filed in the "P" section under "Prince." Most people probably remember Princess Margaret's former husband as Lord Snowdon, but there is no entry under his title. They would have to look under "Her Royal Highness Princess Margaret" in the "P" section, then see Antony Armstrong-Jones in the "A" section to find biographical information about him. There are no cross-references in the book. Many of the entries have intriguing but not very enlightening headings such as "Omen of the Orchid," "One Hip Chick," and "Over the Moon." There is a bibliography of books and magazines, including special and commemorative issues, at the end. Throughout the book are attractive black-and-white photographs. Sprinkled throughout the text are the British addresses of suppliers of clothing and other items to the royal family, and also sources for souvenirs such as postcards and books in both the United States and the United Kingdom.

Probably more appropriate for the coffee table than the reference collection, nevertheless this work might prove useful in public libraries. There seems to be an insatiable interest in the royal family and this book would answer many possible questions about the British monarchy. [R: RBB, 15 Nov 88, p. 556]

Christine E. King

Mexico

28. Woods, Richard Donovon, comp. **Mexican Autobiography/La Autobiografía Mexicana: An Annotated Bibliography/Una Bibliografía Razonada.** Westport, Conn., Greenwood Press, 1988. 228p. index. (Bibliographies and Indexes in World History, No. 13). $39.95. LC 88-3129. ISBN 0-313-25945-3.

This annotated bibliography of 332 Mexican autobiographies breaks new ground in the field of Latin American bibliography, for up to now, no study has existed of autobiography in this part of the world. For each item Woods provides the basic bibliographical data, genre (e.g., autobiography proper, memoirs, diary, etc.), author's dates, narrative dates, translation or primary edition in English, and an annotation in English along with its Spanish translation (occasionally the two do not match exactly). The volume has indexes for author, title, titles in English, subject, profession or outstanding characteristic, genre, birth-decade of author and chronology by events narrated.

The introduction, though brief, is of interest for its discussion of the relative lack of autobiographies in Hispanic culture, its definition of autobiography, and its description of the composition of each bibliographical entry. The introduction, like the annotations, is in both English and Spanish.

This volume could serve as a model for future bibliographies of autobiographies in other Hispanic countries such as Spain itself, Argentina, Chile, etc. Once scholars know what exists in this field, more scholarly studies can be made in this neglected literary field.

Typographical errors are few; the indexes are very useful. The research that has gone into

locating these items has been immense; the annotations strive for fairness and usefulness and reach their goal. This volume belongs in any library interested in Mexico and its culture. Woods and his translator Josefina Cruz-Meléndez should be congratulated for a job well done. [R: Choice, Nov 88, p. 470]

Hensley C. Woodbridge

Middle East

29. **Who's Who in the Arab World 1988-1989.** 9th ed. Charles G. Bustros, ed. Beirut, Lebanon, Publitec; distr., Detroit, Gale, 1988. 992p. bibliog. index. $180.00. ISBN 2-903188-05-X; ISSN 0083-9752.

This edition of *Who's Who in the Arab World* is larger than the previous edition. It contains three sections: a biographical directory, a geographical directory, and a regional and historical survey. Part 2 of the volume provides a historical outline of the development of the Arab world, covering diverse groups, their languages, ancient cultures, and religions. Part 3 contains details and analyses on the twenty Arab countries. Lebanon is excluded from all three sections and is treated in a separate publication entitled *Who's Who in Lebanon*, also published by Publitec.

In the biographical section, entries vary in length. The information given does not follow a standard form. Perhaps this is due to the different approaches used in gathering the information. (These approaches are described in the introduction.) This reference book attempts to do much. Its uniqueness is the section on biographies, which could be expanded to include more entries. The other sections provide information that can be obtained in other regularly published sources.

Mohammed M. Aman

CATALOGS AND COLLECTIONS

30. **The Center for Research Libraries Handbook 1987.** Chicago, Center for Research Libraries, 1987. 161p. index. $10.00pa.

This is the irregularly published (since 1969) guide to the contents of the Center for Research Libraries. It represents a convenient overview of the collections if the center's *Catalog* is not available or as the only access to certain classes of material not included in the center's *Catalog*. Now thirty-eight years old, the center is a cooperative venture of 150 research libraries across the United States. From a collection of 3.5 million volumes, it lends to its members, which are of three types: "Voting," "Associate," and "User." (The *Handbook* states "any institution supporting research or having a research library is eligible to join." Users of the *Handbook* should write to the center at 6050 South Kenwood Avenue, Chicago, IL 60637 for membership information.)

The *Handbook* is a descriptive listing which characterizes the nature and size of the major components of the collection. The listings are arranged under major subject and form categories (e.g., "Africa," "Art and Architecture," "Microfilm and Reprint Collections," "Underground Press") with a slightly more detailed subject index. The volume concludes with a statement of the collecting, deposit, and loan policies of the center.

The collections (according to the *Handbook*) are strong and continue to be built in the areas of publications from the Academy of Sciences of the USSR, foreign doctoral dissertations, foreign newspapers, U.S. newspapers, state government documents of the United States, and materials from Africa and East, South, and Southeast Asia. This is an important guide for libraries that do heavy interlibrary loan in support of faculty research, but those who use the center frequently should also have its *Manual of Interlibrary Loan Policies and Procedures.*   Thomas G. Kirk

31. Nelson, Carolyn, and Matthew Seccombe, comps. **British Newspapers and Periodicals 1641-1700: A Short-Title Catalogue of Serials Printed in England, Scotland, Ireland, and British America.** New York, Modern Language Association of America, 1987. 724p. index. (Index Society Fund Publications). $250.00. LC 86-33171. ISBN 0-87352-174-9.

The latter half of the seventeenth century saw the first flourishing of periodicals in England. Civil unrest, colonization, and increasing literacy brought a demand for news. Nelson and Seccombe state that "approximately one-quarter of the publications in Britain between 1641 and 1700 were issues of serials." Until now, however, there has not been a thorough and reliable catalog of these works.

The present catalog is compatible in format with the short-title catalogs of Pollard and Redgrave (which includes serials) and of Wing (which does not). Included are all publications issued or intended to be issued at more or less regular intervals of less than a year. Arrangement is alphabetical by title, then chronological by issue. Each entry is numbered and begins with a headnote setting forth particular information about the serial: title, dates and frequency of publication, format, author/editor,

price, notes, and references to other scholarship. Variants in individual issues are given with the issue entry, along with library locations. The very informative preface details the methodology and rationale of the catalog.

An appendix lists serials published between 1701 and March 1702, thus filling the gap between the present work and the later catalog compiled by W. R. McLeod and V. B. McLeod. A second appendix differentiates variant typesettings. Six indexes complete the work: chronological, geographical, foreign language, subject, editor/author, and publisher/printer.

This carefully detailed book is rich with information for the political, cultural, social, or literary historian. Scholars of this period will find this work invaluable. [R: JAL, Sept 88, p. 262]   Philip R. Rider

DICTIONARIES AND ENCYCLOPEDIAS

Reviewing

32. **General Reference Books for Adults: Authoritative Evaluations of Encyclopedias, Atlases, and Dictionaries.** Marion Sader, ed. New York, R. R. Bowker, 1988. 614p. illus. maps. bibliog. index. (Bowker Buying Guide Series). $69.95. LC 88-10054. ISBN 0-8352-2393-0.

Designed as a buying guide for both librarians and lay people, this work contains lengthy comparative evaluations of general reference sources appropriate for adults. (Similar sources for children and young adults are covered in the first volume in Bowker's Buying Guide Series, *Reference Books for Young Readers* [see entry 35].) The more than 215 titles reviewed include online and CD-ROM products as well as print materials that were readily available in the United States as of April 1988.

According to the editor, *General Reference Books for Adults* is intended to provide "authoritative, comprehensive and objective" reviews of general encyclopedias, atlases, and dictionaries and to "apply consistent standards and criteria in evaluating each work" (p. xiii). To achieve this goal, the evaluations were prepared by a team of librarians and subject specialists, screened by consultants, and verified and revised by editorial staff. Since the final reviews are truly a collaborative effort, they are unsigned.

A lengthy introductory section includes a history of general reference books and outlines factors to consider in choosing reference materials. In addition, it contains a report of a survey in which librarians rated the usefulness of specific reference sources and also provides comparative charts containing statistical data (such as number of pages, number of entries, number of illustrations, and price) on all titles reviewed.

Reviews are organized into four sections: encyclopedias, world atlases, dictionaries and word books, and large-print reference sources. The categories for encyclopedias and atlases are then arranged alphabetically by the titles being reviewed, while the section on dictionaries is subdivided by specific type (e.g., general, etymological, synonym, and antonym). Accompanying each of the first three sections is an introductory essay that provides tips on what to look for in that particular type of reference source and a glossary of specialized terms frequently used in describing such works. In addition, each essay gives an overview of the format followed by all reviews in that section and explains the criteria considered in evaluating each feature. For example, evaluations of atlases are divided into ten categories, including "geographical balance," "scale and projections," and "currency." This consistent structure among reviews of the same type of source facilitates the comparison of specific features.

Reviews vary in length, depending on the type of source being evaluated. For example, reviews of major encyclopedias are generally at least eight pages long, while those of atlases average one and one-half to two pages. A number of reviews include facsimile pages and sample entries, and encyclopedia evaluations provide excerpts from other reviews. Although the reviews generally reflect the editor's concern for consistency and objectivity, in some instances they do not provide the currency necessary in a work of this type. For example, the evaluation of the *Oxford English Dictionary* fails to mention that a totally revised edition incorporating the supplements will be available early in 1989. Moreover, the review of *World Book* indicates that it is based on the 1987 edition, but the statistics cited, the facsimile page, and the format section all refer to the 1988 edition. Since the compilers obviously had access to information regarding the 1988 edition, it is somewhat surprising that the review does not note that the 1988 edition is the most extensive revision of *World Book* in over twenty-five years.

A bibliography near the end of the volume cites additional sources that review general reference materials. In several instances this list does not include the most recent edition of a work. For example, Kenneth Kister's 1981

Encyclopedia Buying Guide (see *ARBA* 82, entry 46) is cited rather than his *Best Encyclopedias* (see *ARBA* 87, entry 54). The well-conceived, comprehensive index includes not only the titles of works reviewed (which are distinguished by small capital letters) but also titles of other works referred to within the reviews as well as references to compilers, editors, publishers, and topics.

Librarians who have found Kenneth Kister's buying guides to encyclopedias, atlases, and dictionaries useful will welcome this new source for detailed, comparative reviews of basic reference sources. It should be a valuable selection aid in libraries that serve high school students or adults, particularly where budgetary constraints require stringent acquisition policies. It is also an excellent source for individuals trying to make wise decisions about purchasing reference titles for their home libraries. *General Reference Books for Adults* has the potential to become a standard selection tool if Bowker establishes a schedule of regular and frequent revisions. [R: LJ, Dec 88, p. 94; WLB, Nov 88, pp. 126-27]   Marie Ellis

33.   Kister, Kenneth F. **Kister's Concise Guide to Best Encyclopedias.** Phoenix, Ariz., Oryx Press, 1988. 108p. index. $15.00pa. LC 88-24044. ISBN 0-89774-484-5.

For some reason Kister is in competition with himself. Oryx Press has already published his *Best Encyclopedias* in full panoply (see *ARBA* 87, entry 54). So why a concise edition? Kister says "the guide is designed especially for busy people in search of a quick but authoritative opinion about the many titles available." Then he reduces the number of titles covered in full to thirty-three. For those titles he presents the "facts" followed by an "evaluation." Many of the facts spliced together in complete sentences appear earlier in a two-page comparison chart. Other needless repetition occurs. The *Kussmaul Encyclopedia* entry is a good example; in the space of one and one-half pages the reader is told three times that the encyclopedia is an electronic database, part of the Delphi Information System produced by General Videotex Corporation, and another three times that it is based on the print *Cadillac Modern Encyclopedia*. When comparing encyclopedias Kister repeats the same numerical facts he gives in the aforementioned comparison chart. This makes for tedious reading. Kister also commits one of the cardinal sins of evaluation; he admonishes the reader that the *Barron's Student's Concise Encyclopedia* "contains some glaring omissions" in the index without naming any of them. After the thirty-three main entries there is an annotated list of some 187 recommended specialized encyclopedias; the guide ends with a short section on recently discontinued or out-of-print works. Purchase the complete 1986 edition and continue to wonder why this one was published. [R: RBB, 15 Dec 88, p. 687]

Bill Bailey

34. **Purchasing an En-cy-clo-pe-dia: 12 Points to Consider.** 2d ed. By the Editorial Board of *Reference Books Bulletin*. Chicago, American Library Association, 1988. 40p. $4.95 pa. LC 88-2187. ISBN 0-8389-3351-3.

Except for the twelve points, this work is an almost exact copy of the reviews of the ten major multivolume encyclopedias from the 1 November 1987 "Reference Books Bulletin" section of *Booklist*. The introduction appears to be addressed to parents who wish to buy an encyclopedia for their children, indicating the age level as the first factor to consider. The other points are authority, arrangement, subject coverage, objectivity, recency, quality, style, bibliographies, illustrations, physical format, and special attributes. Each receives a one- or two-paragraph discussion. Yearbooks, alternative formats such as CD-ROM, and reviews are also discussed briefly.

The guide provides clear, brief reviews, touching on the history of the encyclopedia, the type, number and length of entries, the amount of revision, the illustrations, the index, currency, and the formats available. Kenneth Kister's guide to *Best Encyclopedias* (see *ARBA* 87, entry 54) reviews all of the encyclopedias in the ALA guide plus 42 more general encyclopedias and around 450 specialized encyclopedias. The general encyclopedia reviews it contains are longer – over seven pages for *World Book* compared to two pages in this guide, and ten pages for *The New Encyclopaedia Britannica* compared to three in ALA's guide. *Best Encyclopedias* spends more time on the history of an encyclopedia, provides purchasing information, and gives more examples in the evaluation portion of the review.

Libraries subscribing to *Booklist* or owning Kister's guide will not need the ALA guide for their own selection purposes. Libraries wishing a publication easy to check out to or sell to parents, or small libraries without access to other sources will find the low cost of this authoritative guide most appealing. [R: VOYA, Dec 88, p. 257]

Betty Jo Buckingham

35. **Reference Books for Young Readers: Authoritative Evaluations of Encyclopedias, Atlases, and Dictionaries.** Marion Sader, ed. New York, R. R. Bowker, 1988. 615p. illus.

index. (Bowker Buying Guide Series). $49.95. LC 87-38234. ISBN 0-8352-2366-3.

This first entry in Bowker's Buying Guide Series meets the need for critical information necessary to evaluate and select encyclopedias, atlases, and dictionaries for children and young adults. An additional section on large print reference materials is included. To help readers make sound choices of reference works, *Reference Books for Young Readers* discusses the effective use of reviews and gives detailed criteria for evaluating reference works.

In preparing this guide, a national survey was conducted in which public and school librarians were asked to evaluate and rate encyclopedias, dictionaries, and atlases. The questionnaire used a list of general reference works in the three major review categories and the frequency of their use by elementary, middle school, and high school students. The results of this survey provide accessible, detailed information for any school or public librarian working with children or young adults.

Comparative charts provide basic factual information about every reference book or set evaluated. Sources are current. The charts are followed by chapters containing detailed evaluations of approximately two hundred encyclopedias, atlases, dictionaries and word books, and large print reference books. Reference is made to online formats as well as CD-ROM. Specific titles are discussed, and there is generous use of facsimiles. Appendices include a selected bibliography and a list of publishers. The index is the weakest feature of this book; for example, it includes no references to online systems or CD-ROM.

This is a long needed reference source for librarians, library school students, and the general public. It provides accurate information in a clear format. [R: LJ, 15 Oct 88, p. 84; RBB, 1 Sept 88, p. 56; RLR, Aug 88, pp. 183-84; VOYA, Dec 88, pp. 257-58; WLB, June 88, pp. 143-44]

Lynda Welborn

General Encyclopedias

36. **Barron's Student's Concise Encyclopedia.** Compiled by the Editors of Barron's Educational Series, Inc. Hauppauge, N.Y., Barron's Educational Series, 1988. 1v. (various paging). illus. (part col.). maps. index. $19.95. LC 87-22976. ISBN 0-8120-5937-9.

This one-volume reference work contains thousands of entries covering twenty-three major topics, including art, biology, chemistry, computers, history, literature, living independently (first aid, drugs, checking accounts, etc.), mathematics, philosophy, and study and learning aids. The book is arranged alphabetically by topics, and within many topics alphabetically by entries which vary in length from one line to several paragraphs. Other topics are arranged in different ways; for example, "Technology" is chronological. There are cross-references within each section. Biographical information is limited to deceased people and to those living persons who did something notable many years ago (for example, Neil Armstrong). The last chapter, "Useful Tables," contains such information as proofreading marks, toll-free numbers, and constellations. Sections dealing with mathematics and the sciences include many useful drawings and graphs. The book also includes many black-and-white photographs; forty-eight black-and-white maps, eighteen color, historical maps; four color illustrations of human anatomy; and three pages of color graphs. The front and end pages show a color map of the world and a map of the time zones. The book has a thorough, detailed index, which contains the terms listed in each section as well as other words. However, the list of toll-free numbers and some other items could not be found in the index. Unfortunately, there is no place index for the detailed maps. This is a good reference source especially for high school and college students, but can also be useful to anyone in need of brief information. [R: WLB, Sept 88, p. 90]   Kathleen Farago

37. Bullock, Alan, and Stephen Trombley, with Bruce Eadie, eds. **The Harper Dictionary of Modern Thought.** rev. ed. New York, Harper & Row, 1988. 917p. $29.95. LC 87-45604. ISBN 0-06-015869-7.

This dictionary provides brief explanations of key terms "from across the whole range of modern thought" which have been contributed by experts with the lay reader in mind. The current editors have substantially revised and expanded the original 1977 edition (see *ARBA* 78, entry 83) to reflect current developments in modern thought while still restricting the survey to a single, affordable volume.

Of the original four thousand entries, roughly 80 percent have been retained, and nearly half of these have been revised or completely rewritten. Areas that have been extensively revised include contemporary history, politics, economics, anthropology, and psychology. One thousand new entries have been added, particularly in the areas of politics, medicine, the physical sciences, and the arts (e.g., *Reaganism, glasnost, genetic engineering, deconstruction*). The reading lists which supplement most entries have also been updated. References to key figures in modern thought have

been deleted, since they will now be included in a companion volume.

The selectivity demanded by a single-volume work of this type will necessarily limit its scope and content. Nevertheless, the book serves a unique reference need. The revised edition is a necessary supplement to the original volume, but would also stand alone as a useful reference tool in most collections. [R: RBB, 1 Sept 88, p. 48]

Martha S. Perry

38. **Children's Britannica.** 4th ed. Margaret Sutton, James Somerville, and others, eds. Chicago, Encyclopaedia Britannica, 1988. 20v. illus. (part col.). maps. index. $299.00/set. LC 87-81078. ISBN 0-85229-206-6.

Children's Britannica supersedes *Britannica Junior Encyclopaedia for Boys and Girls*, edited by Marvin Martin and published in fifteen volumes from 1934 to 1984. *Britannica Junior Encyclopaedia* was reviewed in *ARBA* 82 (see entry 47) and *ARBA* 78 (see entry 64).

Similar to *Britannica Junior*, the text of *Children's Britannica* is written in a simple, straightforward manner that is easy for children to understand. Like its predecessor, this twenty-volume set is curriculum-oriented and designed for use by elementary school students. Although the *Children's Britannica* is prepared under the supervision of the *Encyclopaedia Britannica*, it is a separate entity and should not be considered on the merits of the parent encyclopedia.

Under the editorial direction of Margaret Sutton with senior editor James Somerville and five associate editors, *Children's Britannica* employs a good system of cross-referencing that guides the student to related articles. The illustrations are quite adequate, with many black-and-white and several four-color illustrations. The text is often accompanied by line drawings and maps.

Volume 20 contains an analytic index to the encyclopedia that serves as the key to all information contained in the set. Also listed in volume 20 are advisors and authors contributing to this edition, plus some helpful instructions for its use. Readers are advised to consult volume 20 first, which is a very valid recommendation. For example, if the reader wishes to obtain information on the goldfinch, he or she will not find a separate article on this bird under "G" in volume 8. This is because the goldfinch has been classified as a member of the finch family, and hence, is treated under the single article of that title. The index serves to direct the reader from "Goldfinch" to "Finch Family." The same is true of cross-references listed at the end of longer articles. Many children will use them, but for most readers it is simpler to use the index, which connects interrelated topics.

The structure, content, and style of the articles reflect the encyclopedia's focus on elementary level students. For example, a two-page article on the letters of an alphabet explains that letters are actually signs which stand for sounds. The definition is followed by a brief paragraph covering early writings, and another on writing with an alphabet. To assist students in further research, the article concludes with a leading statement on the phonetic alphabet and directs the reader to an article on "Phonetics." Accompanying the article are illustrations showing some of the stages in the development of the English alphabet. One illustration shows Arabic characters, Russian letters, Chinese characters, etc., unfortunately with explanations that are at times inadequate. A string of characters is provided as an example of the various forms of the alphabet, but no translation is provided.

A much longer article has been written on American literature in volume 1, with cross-references to drama, poetry, and prose. It is well written and covers such topics as the Revolutionary period, the early nineteenth century, the New England poets, the poetry revival, the interwar period, the Southern literature renaissance, and the period since World War II. The article ends with comments about playwrights such as Tennessee Williams, Arthur Miller, and William Inge, and indicates that many of the writers mentioned in the article are covered in separate biographical sketches.

All in all, *Children's Britannica* is essentially a well-edited encyclopedia for elementary students. The format is attractive, and the cross-references and index are quite adequate. The 1988 edition was substantially revised and contains not only many longer articles but also six thousand short "capsule" entries. These brief entries give the reader instant facts which in many cases will be very helpful in the school curriculum. *Children's Britannica* is an accurate and reliable school encyclopedia and can be safely recommended for its intended audience. [R: WLB, Nov 88, pp. 121-22]

Bohdan S. Wynar

39. **The Children's Encyclopedia and Atlas.** London, Treasure Press; distr., Toronto, Doubleday Canada, c1981, 1987. 1v. (various paging). illus. (col.). maps. index. $24.95. ISBN 1-85051-213-2.

This encyclopedia and atlas is an attempt to organize information that would appeal to youngsters, although there is no introduction or suggestion of purpose or use of the work. The fifteen topics of the encyclopedia include the

universe, the Earth, plant world, history of man, etc. An index is provided to the encyclopedia and maps. The atlas index is complicated to use and, in the copy reviewed, was missing pages 54 and 55. The work is in full color and makes liberal use of diagrams, illustrations, and photographs.

Children would find the work interesting as a picture book but would have difficulty reading the fine print used in the maps. The text is clear and easy to read, albeit uninteresting. The encyclopedia would have value to parents as a source for reading to and talking with young children about the pictures and topics. Because of the organization and the limited index to the encyclopedia, the work has only marginal value as a reference tool. William E. Hug

40. **Collier's Encyclopedia: With Bibliography and Index.** Bernard Johnston, ed.-in-chief. New York, Macmillan, 1988. 24v. illus. (part col.). maps. bibliog. index. $1,399.50/set; $899.00/set (schools and libraries). LC 87-61118.

In its thirty-eighth year, *Collier's Encyclopedia* serves an adult and young adult audience with 11,500 articles in twenty-four volumes written by 5,000 scholars and contributors. For the 1988 edition, 29 articles have been totally rewritten and 919 updated. There are 53 new contributors, 176 new illustrations, and 43 revised maps. This compares favorably with the revision schedule of every other major encyclopedia. Notable additions and revisions include articles on artificial intelligence, the theory of communication, museums, steroids, the Persian Gulf war, and drama.

Comparison of *Collier's* to its competitors, *The Encyclopedia Americana* (see *ARBA 84*, entry 26), and *The New Encyclopaedia Britannica* (see entry 44) is a reviewer's favorite sport. A fair analysis shows that all three have strengths and that *Collier's* is very competitive in most areas and certainly the most reasonably priced of the three. While *Collier's* has its share of color illustrations, most are clearly printed in black-and-white and are well placed in relation to the appropriate text. The layout and type size are better than *Americana*. Detailed comparison of single articles across encyclopedias yields mixed results. For example, the article on Spain is shorter in *Collier's* than in *Americana* but longer and more detailed than in *World Book* (see *ARBA 87*, entry 52). Each of the three articles has strengths that the others do not possess, such as clearer topical maps, or details on economy and history. Some discrepancies were noted between *World Book* and *Collier's* treatment of the time line of the empire. The list of rulers was much more complete in *Collier's* than in *World Book* and was missing in *Americana*. Bibliographies in *Collier's* tend to be gathered together in volume 24 rather than appended to each article, a feature common to other encyclopedias.

An in-depth comparison leads the reviewer to the conclusion that libraries serving young adults and adults are wise to purchase a number of general encyclopedias and that *Collier's* continues to be a first choice. For the family of older children, *Collier's* would certainly serve a family's needs admirably. [R: RBB, 15 Oct 88, pp. 372-73]   David V. Loertscher

41. **The Hutchinson Encyclopedia.** 8th ed. Michael Upshall, ed. London, Hutchinson; distr., North Pomfret, Vt., David & Charles, 1988. 1273p. illus. (part col.). maps. $39.95. ISBN 0-09-172290-X.

First published as *Hutchinson's Twentieth Century Encyclopedia* in 1948, this British work offers over twenty-five thousand entries and some 2,350 illustrations, including many black-and-white photographs, diagrams, and drawings. Descriptions vary in length from one sentence to several full-page columns. Entries for persons and places offer International Phonetic Alphabet (IPA) pronunciation. The encyclopedia is very strong in science and technology and presents wide coverage of world events, history, current affairs, art, and entertainment. Illustrations are not always included on the same page as their respective article, which may confuse and inconvenience some readers. On the other hand, the page layout is attractive, the text is easy to read, and cross-references lead to additional information relevant to a particular subject. Entries for individual countries are accompanied by a location map and a table of facts and figures; in addition, there is a thirty-two page atlas section in the middle of the volume.

How does *The Hutchinson Encyclopedia* compare to one-volume encyclopedias published in the United States? Coverage in *The Hutchinson Encyclopedia* is worldwide, but its focus is more British, or Western European, than American. *The Hutchinson* is considerably more up-to-date and inexpensive than the *New Columbia Encyclopedia* (see *ARBA* 76, entry 60), which includes few illustrations and no portraits. However, the *New Columbia Encyclopedia* contains twice as many entries, often covered in greater depth and with helpful bibliographies. *The Hutchinson* is also more current and considerably less expensive than the *Random House Encyclopedia* (Random House, 1983). Although both works address a more popular audience than the *New Columbia*, *The Hutchinson* is considerably easier to use and more accurate than the Random House work. *The Hutchinson Encyclopedia* will be useful as a home reference tool and for library collections that can afford a variety of approaches to information.

Michael Ann Moskowitz

42. **Hutchinson Pocket Encyclopedia.** London, Hutchinson; distr., North Pomfret, Vt., David & Charles, 1987. 612p. illus. maps. index. $14.95. ISBN 0-09-172300-0.

"Pocket" encyclopedias share with almanacs and other tidy compilations of unrelated facts the admirable goal of putting the world literally at our fingertips. No matter what the subject, these sources operate under the illusion that art, literature, science, and technology can be reduced to a few noteworthy facts, a few notable names. This encyclopedia is a prime example of the reduction of complex social, cultural, and scientific issues and concerns to appropriate twenty-second sound bites.

The volume is divided into four major "thematic" sections: society, the arts, science and technology, and a gazetteer. Each section is then further subdivided into specific areas such as history, psychology, architecture, etc. The entries within each section are listed either alphabetically, as is the case with people, places, and things, or chronologically, by battle or event. A fairly lengthy index includes every entry and, were it not for the fact that the print is tiny to the point of illegibility, provides the best way to locate information in the encyclopedia.

The problems with this work can be summed up in two words: bias and emphasis. Women are completely ghettoized and marginalized. Though recognized in a small portion of the society section, they are systematically eliminated from inclusion in the rest of the encyclopedia (with the notable exception of Thatcher, Meir, and Gandhi). Jane Austen, the Brontës, and George Sand make up the sum total of women listed under literary greats, and no women at all appear in the psychology or philosophy sections.

In addition to the exclusion of women of note from most categories, the biographical notes provided for some of the "greats" that are listed show a tendency to either overstate the obvious or completely miss the most salient features of an individual's life and work. Two noteworthy examples of these shortcomings occur in the abbreviated, even for a pocket encyclopedia, biography of Golda Meir and the failure to note that among Michel Foucault's major contributions to intellectual discourse was his work on human sexuality. This is a serious and misleading omission.

In terms of emphasis, it should be noted that this is a British publication and as such reflects British interests and experience. The section on education, for example, focuses totally on the British system. While explanations of A levels and brief discussions of recent changes in the education system are interesting, they are neither complete enough to stand on their own, nor relevant enough to U.S. experience to make them of much practical use to Americans. The same problem holds true for the sports section where cricket reigns supreme and baseball is simply defined.

Most of what is covered here is available in any good dictionary or standard encyclopedia. Although a case might be made for a one-volume, concise source, this particular volume is fraught with too many intellectual and access problems to recommend it solely on the basis of size. [R: LJ, 15 June 88, p. 52]

Ellen Broidy

43. **Merit Students Encyclopedia.** Bernard Johnston, ed.-in-chief. New York, Macmillan, 1988. 20v. illus. (part col.). maps. index. $1,399.50/set; $579.00/set (schools and libraries). LC 87-61604.

Intended for general audiences in addition to students (it is generally considered suitable for fifth graders as well as twelfth graders), *Merit Students Encyclopedia*, first published in 1967, has had revisions each year. The editors have retained the twenty-volume status for twenty-one years and have arranged the encyclopedia alphabetically letter by letter ("foxhound" precedes "fox hunting") rather than word by word. Most major entries begin with simple information (for the younger user) and develop into more complex information (for the older user). A student's guide briefly describes the contents and organization and provides a list of related articles not covered in the entry. Cross-references in the index volume afford the user access to additional information.

Containing around nine million words, it has more than twelve thousand pages with about twenty-one thousand articles and some 200,000 illustrations and 1,570 maps, both color and black-and-white. The color plates and overlays are of excellent quality.

The reliability and usefulness of an encyclopedia depend on the accuracy and authority of its contents and of its contributors. Most articles in *Merit* are authored by special editors or by contributors listed in the index volume, but those marked with an asterisk are written by staff and only reviewed by the individuals

named. There have been some changes in the editorial staff; however, both the library advisory board and international board as well as the special editors board seem to have remained the same as for the 1985 edition (see *ARBA* 86, entry 55). Unfortunately, the editorial staff has not chosen to update the information on its contributors. As pointed out in the review of the 1981 edition (see *ARBA* 82, entry 53), John Hall Archer's credentials still have not been corrected. There are a number of persons relating to college and university articles that are no longer connected with those institutions (e.g., Abner McCall, Baylor University). Although forty-six new contributors have been added, there are some listed who have been deceased for some time.

According to promotional material there are 40 new entries; 14 articles have been completely rewritten; 412 articles have been revised slightly (e.g., "Acquired immune deficiency syndrome [AIDS]" shows a change in statistics); and new contributors, new illustrations, and revised maps have been added.

New entries of interest to young people are "Greenpeace," "Antonin Scalia," "Stevie Smith," and "Syzygy." But not included are microcomputers (there are some cross-references to "computers" in the index), terrorism, Jeane Kirkpatrick, Edward Koch, or desktop publishing. Rock stars such as Michael Jackson and Bruce Springsteen are mentioned in the entry on rock music, but lack separate entries. It would appear that the impact of these stars on today's culture certainly warrants at least a brief entry.

Although it is omitted as an entry, there is a cross-reference from sexually transmitted diseases to "venereal diseases" providing an overview of the various diseases within this category. *See also* references to more specific transmitted diseases such as herpes are given. Chlamydia, one of the fastest spreading sexually transmitted diseases, is mentioned but not accorded an entry of its own. The two titles mentioned in "Books for Further Study" are dated 1981.

Another topic of current interest is "Steroid," which is a new entry. Only a suggestion of the possible harmful side effects that may be generated by its abuse or the useful effects of some steroids, such as cortisone is given. No "Books for Further Study" is appended to this or "acquired immune deficiency syndrome (AIDS)," "syzygy," "Greenpeace," or "system analysis," among others. The entry for "Sweden" has no titles later than 1973; "Mississippi," 1982; and "Colorado," 1976. The use of biographical information on outstanding individuals, which

Merit has in many of its entries for states, is a way of maintaining currency. However, many contemporary persons such as authors popular today (e.g., Beth Henley, *Crimes of the Heart*) are not accorded their own entries or mentioned as famous individuals from their home states.

Within the last ten years, the explosion of knowledge in the information science field has dated articles such as "Library science, careers in" written under the supervision of Louis Shores who died in 1981. Obviously the expanded opportunities for those in the library and information science area are much greater than indicated here.

Although the reproduction of *Christina's World* has been added to the Andrew Wyeth article, no comment is made on his "Helga" pictures. His father, N. C. Wyeth, the noted illustrator, is referred to, but not his son, Jamie.

To maintain the good reputation *Merit* has attained, it is suggested that more attention be given to maintaining currency through the use of up-to-date bibliographies, providing more topics of contemporary interest for its intended audience, and a more diligent revision program. In spite of the caveats mentioned, *Merit* continues as an excellent choice for a young adult encyclopedia second only to *World Book* (see *ARBA* 88, entry 52). [R: RBB, 15 Oct 88, pp. 378, 380]   Anna Grace Patterson

44. **The New Encyclopaedia Britannica.** 15th ed. Philip W. Goetz, ed.-in-chief. Chicago, Encyclopaedia Britannica, 1988. 32v. illus. (part col.). maps. index. $1,399.00/set; $1,069.00/set (schools and libraries). LC 86-82929. ISBN 0-85229-473-5.

45. **Britannica Book of the Year, 1988.** Daphne Daume and Louise Watson, eds. Chicago, Encyclopaedia Britannica, 1988. 910p. illus. (part col.). maps. index. $29.95. LC 38-12082. ISBN 0-85229-486-7; ISSN 0068-1156.

Encyclopaedia Britannica has been reviewed in *ARBA* on several occasions. The most extensive review (of the 1970 edition) was published in *ARBA* 71 (see entry 171). It provided historical background for this encyclopedia plus brief comments on all significant editions, starting with the very first edition published in Edinburgh in 1768-1771. Subsequently, the 1974 (fifteenth) edition, called *Britannica 3* and divided into the *Propaedia, Micropaedia,* and *Macropaedia,* was reviewed in *ARBA* 75 (see entry 77). The review of the 1978 edition of *Britannica* (see *ARBA* 79, entry 77) emphasized the set's datedness and the inaccessibility of information in the main volumes.

Because of certain controversies, probably no other encyclopedia has been reviewed as many times as *Britannica*, particularly since the inception of its tripartite arrangement. Dorothy Cole's *Wilson Library Bulletin* review (June 1974, pp. 821-25) concludes that *Britannica 3* "contains much excellent material, but is difficult to use." *Booklist* reviewed the set several times, and one of the more in-depth reviews appeared in the 1 June 1975 issue (pp. 1021-28). *Slavic Review* (June 1975, pp. 411-12) published an interesting review of *Britannica*, indicating that articles on certain communist countries represent the official Soviet point of view and thus are of little value to Western readers. A comprehensive list of important critical reviews of *Britannica* is provided in Kenneth Kister's *Encyclopedia Buying Guide* (see *ARBA* 82, entry 46), with brief annotations discussing major criticisms and a few editorial comments. *Britannica* is also reviewed in the more recent *Best Encyclopedias: A Guide to General and Specialized Encyclopedias* (see *ARBA* 87, entry 54) and *Kister's Concise Guide to Best Encyclopedias* (see entry 33).

The 1988 edition of *Britannica* has again been published in a three-part format. This arrangement was reviewed in *ARBA* 82 (see entries 55-56), and without repeating our previous comments, let us say that the treatment is now somewhat more balanced than in earlier editions, and some of the more glaring misinterpretations have been corrected.

According to the editorial report received from *Britannica*, 5,982 pages of the new edition have been revised, including 1,972 *Macropaedia* pages, 1,338 *Micropaedia* pages, 1,926 *Index* pages, 394 *Propaedia* pages, and the 352 pages of the Britannica World Data. A total of 260 illustrations were revised, added, or replaced, and 271 new photographs were added. Index pages increased by 47, new entries increased by 4,714, and cross-references now number 43,100. In addition, the encyclopedia is updated on an annual basis by the *Britannica Book of the Year*.

Among the new articles in the *Macropaedia*, one should mention several more extensive ones on atmosphere, computer science, crime and punishment, dance, drafting, evolution, mental disorders, occupational diseases and disorders, and Yiddish literature. Several texts were revised, including those on African arts, business law, climate and weather, conservation of natural resources, Czechoslovakia, international trade, medicine, painting, public administration, the solar system, and writing. Thirty-three articles were updated, primarily those pertaining to specific countries such as Albania, Bulgaria, Burma, Denmark, Eastern Africa, Ecuador, Finland, Germany, Israel, Pakistan, the Philippines, and Uruguay. New articles have been added on the American Legion, the Communist Party of Spain, Korean art, and many other topics, including several biographies of such personalities as Arnold Toynbee, Joan Mitchell, and Walter Reynolds. There is also a new article on the Chernobyl accident, and many articles have been substantially revised, such as those on air conditioning, Argentina, the Berlin Wall, Breton literature, cocaine, Earth satellites, Earth sciences, the Italian Communist Party, medicine, Southern Africa, Margaret Thatcher, and the x-ray tube.

In conclusion, it should be mentioned that *Britannica* is, overall, an authoritative, truly international encyclopedia, providing more depth of coverage on almost all subject areas than any other general encyclopedia in the English language. A review in the 15 October 1988 issue of *Reference Books Bulletin* states that "*The New Encyclopaedia Britannica* is a unique work that continues to improve through a balanced revision program. The concise, colorful articles in the *Micropaedia*, the substantial coverage of major subjects from all areas of knowledge in the *Macropaedia*, and the supporting *Propaedia, Index,* and *Britannica World Data* combine to offer an attractive alternative to other major encyclopedias arranged in a more conventional fashion." We can only agree with these comments. [R: RBB, 15 Oct 88, pp. 382-84]

Bohdan S. Wynar

46.   Paton, John, ed. **Picture Encyclopedia for Children.** New York, Grosset & Dunlap/ Putnam, 1987. 380p. illus. (part col.). maps. index. $19.95. LC 86-81788. ISBN 0-448-18999-2.

The *Picture Encyclopedia* covers some 750 subjects in brief, attractively illustrated articles on animals, places, people, history, and science and technology. It is arranged in alphabetical order, in a two-column format. Many articles include references to other entries, in capital letters in a different type style. In addition, an index covers over twenty-seven hundred topics including the main entries. The reading and interest level would probably range from grades 3 to 6.

This encyclopedia has many more illustrations per page than multivolume encyclopedias, nearly all in color. However, larger encyclopedias cover thousands more articles. For example, the letter "H" takes 12 pages and 27 entries in *Picture Encyclopedia*, but 428 pages with over 1,000 entries in the 1988 *World Book* (see *ARBA* 88, entry 52).

In a spot check of entries, some problems were found. The article on presidents of the United States lists all presidents, but only six have separate entries and only those six appear to be in the index. The only Protestant group that rates an entry is the Quakers, although five other groups mentioned in the article on Protestants are indexed. There is a brief entry for each state, including the capital, the state flower, etc., and a drawing of the United States with the state highlighted. Canadian provinces are covered in separate articles but there is only one map, under Canada. Some cities such as London, New York, and San Francisco are included separately, while others, such as Los Angeles, Miami Beach, and Minneapolis, are not. In a similar fashion, some countries, such as Argentina, Belgium, and China, are included, but others, such as Algeria, Colombia, and Ethiopia, are not. The article on flags includes national flags for seventy-eight countries, with no explanation why others are missing.

While a person wishing to find a comprehensive encyclopedia would need to look further, this is an attractive book which should appeal to younger children and give them opportunities to look things up in alphabetical order and to use indexes and cross-references. It also is much more affordable for family purchase than multivolume encyclopedias. [R: SLJ, May 88, p. 32]   Betty Jo Buckingham

47.   **Raintree Children's Encyclopedia.** Milwaukee, Wis., Raintree, 1988. 11v. illus. (part col.). maps. index. $240.00/set; $180.00/set (schools and libraries); $145.93pa./set; $109.45 pa./set (schools and libraries). LC 87-16543. ISBN 0-8172-3050-5; 0-8172-3051-3pa.

The first edition of this set was published by Macmillan of London in 1974, with the second in 1980 and the third in 1986. All three previous editions were published under the title *Macmillan Children's Encyclopedia.* Unfortunately, this British encyclopedia was never reviewed in *ARBA*, nor was it reviewed in Kister's *Best Encyclopedias: A Guide to General and Specialized Encyclopedias* (see *ARBA* 87, entry 54).

Each of the ten volumes of the encyclopedia covers a different topic, with volume 11 serving as an index volume and brief reference section. The topics covered include people, animals, plants, Earth and beyond, famous men and women, travel and communications, modern world, countries and customs, arts and entertainment, and sports and recreation.

Perhaps the strongest point of *Raintree Children's Encyclopedia* is its illustrations, which are well executed, colorful, and blend with the text. The text, however, is less than satisfactory. For example, a very brief entry on Roman Catholics reads:

> Early Christians belonged to the one "catholic" (world-wide) Church. In time, they divided into the Roman Catholic Church and the Eastern Orthodox Churches. The head of the Roman Catholics is the Pope, the Bishop of Rome. Roman Catholics must keep the Church's rules, confessing their sins and going to the service called mass each Sunday. They believe that Christ's mother, the Virgin Mary, and the saints can help them when they pray to God.

Treatment of Protestants, Quakers, Presbyterians, and Mormons is just as brief and inadequate, and is indicative of the type of coverage provided for other subjects. An article on Roman Catholics in *Children's Britannica* (see entry 38) is much more extensive and includes information on Roman Catholic beliefs, worship, origins, and history.

Considering the price of *Raintree Children's Encyclopedia*, it seems to us that *Children's Britannica* or even *Young Students Encyclopedia* (Weekly Reader, 1982) would be a wiser investment. [R: RBB, 1 Sept 88, p. 55]

Bohdan S. Wynar

DIRECTORIES

48. Association Meeting Directory. 2d ed. Gail T. Belford, ed. Washington, D.C., Association Meeting Directory, 1988. 671p. index. $225.00pa. LC 87-654319. ISBN 0-941663-01-9.

This annual publication that provides information about association meetings and conventions is intended for companies that specialize in servicing the meeting and convention industry. It gives the following information about the meetings of some six thousand national and regional (trade, professional, and hobby) associations: meeting dates (up to five years in the future), contact person(s), meeting locations, expected number of attendees, and square feet of exhibit space. Associations are listed alphabetically in the main body of the book and are also identified by field in the "TOPS" (Trade, Occupation, Profession) index located at the end, a useful new feature.

The second edition has several other new features. The associations with political action committees and those that book professional speakers are identified. In addition, there is a geographic index of association headquarters by

state and city. Regular features of the publication include a "Planners" index and an index of "Chief Executive Officers." [R: RBB, 1 Apr 88, p. 1320]   Dianne Brinkley Catlett

49. The Community of the Book: A Directory of Selected Organizations and Programs. Carren O. Kaston, comp.; John Y. Cole, ed. New Brunswick, N.J., Transaction Books, 1987. 123p. index. $24.95. LC 86-600010. ISBN 0-88738-145-6.

Kaston's directory is a selective list of eighty-nine organizations and programs (most based in the United States) that promote books and reading, administer literacy projects, and encourage the study of books. Alphabetically arranged, the entries provide addresses, telephone numbers, and contact persons; general descriptions of the purposes of the organizations and programs; examples of their activities; names of their publications; and how the organizations and programs are funded. The directory builds upon the 1984 Library of Congress publication, *Books in Our Future*, which listed thirty-one organizations. The preface notes that international book programs are described in greater detail in *U.S. International Book Programs 1981* and *U.S. Books Abroad: Neglected Ambassadors*, both available from LC's Center for the Book.

The directory proper is preceded by an opening essay by John Y. Cole, executive director of the Center for the Book: "Is There a Community of the Book?" Following the directory is a brief list of additional organizations (e.g., Television Information Office, The Corporation for Public Broadcasting, book collecting clubs, book promotion agencies such as Great Britain's National Book League, Australia's National Book Council, and UNESCO's regional book promotion centers) and publications (*Publishers Weekly, Scholarly Publishing, American Book Trade Directory, Library Journal, American Libraries, Wilson Library Bulletin, Bowker Annual*, etc.).

The index includes information from the essay and both directories—initialisms/acronyms, names of individuals, organizations, publications, and subjects, with numerous *see* and *see also* references. Libraries with books-and-reading collections will find this a useful directory. [R: Choice, Sept 87, p. 88]

Wiley J. Williams

50. Directory of Associations in Canada. Repertoire des Associations du Canada. 9th ed. Brian Land and Liba Berry, eds. Toronto, Micromedia, 1988. 775p. index. $150.00pa. ISSN 0316-0734.

This directory, first issued in 1973 by the University of Toronto Press, now appears annually (and it seems to get more expensive every year). The *DAC* lists about 16,500 associations (there were 12,000 in the sixth edition of 1985), each indexed under one or more of twelve hundred subject classifications. The topics of some of the new associations show concerns of social welfare as they deal with abortion, multiculturalism, missing children, the peace movement, status of women, and food banks. With each edition this work looks more and more like Gale's *Encyclopedia of Associations*; that is, it has more and more descriptive data about each group. The early editions contained simply names, addresses, and subject codes. Entries now include full corporate name, mailing address, the chief executive officer's name, the number of paid staff, the number of members, title of its publications and frequencies, the date and place of annual meetings for the next three years (if known), electronic mail addresses if available (e.g., TELEX, FAX, etc.), and notes on former names or colloquial names.

Dean Tudor

51. Directory of New Brunswick Museums and Related Institutions. Répertoire des Musées du Nouveau-Brunswick et Institutions Connexes. Fredericton, N.B., Association Museums New Brunswick, 1987. 72p. maps. index. $12.00 pa.

A directory which will be of use to libraries within New Brunswick, the Atlantic provinces and, perhaps, those located in New England, especially Maine. Information given for genealogical societies will be of interest to people throughout Canada and the United States. The most useful feature for most users will be the largest section, "Museums and Historic Parks." Entries within this and the other six sections are in alphabetical order within a geographical area (Acadian Coast, Fundy Tidal Coast, Miramichi Basin, Restigauche Uplands, Southeast Shores, St. John River Valley). Individual entries include name and address of organization, contact person, special features, and visitor information (admission cost, dates open to the public, hours). There is an index to help users locate entries by name of organization. The index is also easier to use than the table of contents, which is made somewhat confusing by including an extra section devoted to museums and historic parks (perhaps a mistake in pagination).

The paperback directory is a photocopied typescript. The people of New Brunswick are obviously proud of their cultural heritage and eager to share it with others.

Milton H. Crouch

52. Encyclopedia of Associations 1988: A Guide to over 25,000 National and International Organizations…. Volume 4: International Organizations. 22d ed. Karin E. Koek, ed. Detroit, Gale, 1988. 998p. index. $195.00. LC 76-46129. ISBN 0-8103-2694-9; ISSN 0071-0202.

Describing over four thousand international membership organizations headquartered outside the United States, this latest edition represents an increase of more than two thousand entries over the nineteenth edition (see *ARBA 85*, entry 28). Those familiar with the encyclopedia's volume 1, *National Organizations of the U.S.* (see *ARBA* 88, entry 53), will notice that *International Organizations* employs the same basic format. Information provided includes association name, address, telephone number, purpose, membership, founding date, publications, telecommunications services, and regional groups. In addition, budget information is included for approximately 20 percent of the entries – an increase of about 10 percent over the last edition. Convention/meeting information has been enhanced to indicate the presence of commercial exhibits at the associations' conventions or meetings.

Because the encyclopedia is dependent upon the cooperation of the organizations in obtaining information, the treatment at times is uneven. In some cases, information on staff and standing committees has been omitted, and an affiliation category is provided but seldom completed.

Although nonprofit membership associations represent the majority of entries, nonmembership organizations such as international institutes, committees, clearinghouses, and projects are listed if they disseminate information to the general public as well as to the specialist. Informal organizations are listed as "information entries."

Though the price may be prohibitive for smaller libraries, this extremely useful source is recommended to all libraries and information centers.

Susan R. Penney

53. International Research Centers Directory 1988-89: A World Guide…. 4th ed. Darren L. Smith and Summer A. O'Hara, eds. Detroit, Gale, 1988. 2v. index. $360.00/set. LC 82-641202. ISBN 0-8103-4362-2; ISSN 0278-2731.

This two-volume guide to government, university, independent nonprofit, and commercial research and development centers, institutes, laboratories, bureaus, test facilities, experiment stations, and data collection and analysis centers, also includes foundations, councils, and other organizations that support research.

There are approximately six thousand listings from 145 countries, with volume 1 containing international and country listings from Afghanistan to Japan and volume 2 containing listings from Jordan to Zimbabwe, name and keyword index, country index, and subject index. Each listing has up to sixteen categories, which include the English name, native name, acronym, address, telephone number, organizational head, date established, parent organization, staff size, principal research activities and fields, special facilities, publications and information services, recurring programs, library description and contact person, affiliates and subsidiaries, and other miscellaneous information. This edition is a 43 percent expansion over the 1986 edition.

Printed on good quality paper, the book is well bound, with adequate type size. It is particularly important to reference libraries and personnel interested in international research.

Herbert W. Ockerman

54.   Wiggins, James M., ed. **V.I.P. Address Book, 1988-1989.** Marina del Rey, Calif., Associated Media, 1988. 800p. bibliog. $84.95. LC 87-33322. ISBN 0-938731-07-6.

The *V.I.P. Address Book* contains more than twenty thousand addresses of noteworthy leaders and celebrities in nine major areas: public service; adventure; business, religion, and education; life and leisure; communications; fine arts; sciences; entertainment; and athletics. Coverage is worldwide. The candidates for the directory, or their designated representatives, were contacted to obtain their best mailing addresses, not necessarily a home address. To meet the problem of keeping current on addresses, the publishers plan to issue *V.I.P. Address Book Updates* at regular intervals.

The directory is an alphabetical listing giving only the current mailing address of the individual and that person's occupation or title. The format is excellent for easy consultation, with running captions in large type along the side of each page. There is a brief bibliography of reference sources and various who's who publications, with the mailing address for each source-book.

While the directory has obvious interest for journalists, publicists, fund raisers, fans, and others wanting to contact various celebrities, the usefulness to libraries is more limited, since no biographical information on the personages is included. The directory has to be viewed more as a companion volume to the standard who's who, and in that capacity many libraries may find it a useful addition to their collections. [R: RBB, 15 Sept 88, p. 141]   Necia A. Musser

GOVERNMENT PUBLICATIONS

55.   **MICROLOG 1987: Canadian Research Index. Index de Recherche du Canada.** Rosemary McClelland and Janis Wheatley, eds. Toronto, Micromedia, 1987. 830p. $350.00. ISSN 0707-3135.

After some difficulties in its early years this monthly guide to Canadian technical literature appears to be on a firm footing. *MICROLOG* includes a monthly index cumulated annually (the latter is reviewed here) combined with a microfiche (or xerographic) document supply system. This system includes "research papers and studies" from all levels of Canadian government, plus those from major research institutes, professional associations, and the like. In addition, it contains annual reports, statistical reviews, and financial statements, but no other serials.

The printed index is arranged in four parts. The first is by personal and/or corporate authors (one of which is the main entry) and publisher. There are two indexes, one by title and series title, the other by subject. The fourth section (not in the copy reviewed) is a classified (?) list of partial subject collections of the fiche. The main entry gives author, title, series, and full publishing information, as well as the fiche number (and number of fiches), but lacks any author, series, or subject tracings. Additional access points provide only the main entry and the fiche information.

Certainly, given the difficulty of obtaining "grey literature," especially that produced by nonnational agencies, this is a worthy effort. However, it does exhibit some flaws. The most critical is that its indexes are *not* "bilingual" in the sense claimed, that "searching can be done in English or French." In fact, documents are indexed only in their text language. Thus, a search for any subject must use terms in both languages, a fact not helped by lack of cross-references across languages. While this approach is not wholly unreasonable, there is no point in misleading the user as do the current instructions.

Other difficulties include occasional errors in indexing (e.g., a report on press coverage of disarmament under "job hunting"), lack of any information on how to order a document, and lack of tracings with the main entry.

Even with its flaws, *MICROLOG* is by far the easiest way to get technical reports from Canadian national and provincial government, and nearly the only way for a nonspecialist to get much of the other material listed. If you do not need the full service, the subject collections might be of interest. It is unfortunate that the publisher did not include that index in this review copy.   James H. Sweetland

56.   Schorr, Alan Edward. **Federal Documents Librarianship, 1879-1987.** Juneau, Alaska, Denali Press, 1988. 215p. index. $25.00pa. LC 87-73054. ISBN 0-938737-14-7.

Given the current level of concern in the library community about diminishing access to government information, Schorr's work should be gratefully received. Arranged alphabetically by first author within ten broad subject divisions, twenty-five hundred citations provide access to more than a hundred years of writings on government information policy and practice. Access is provided to journal articles, proceedings, theses, books, news articles, and chapters within monographs. The citations appear complete and cover the topics of administration; bibliographies, guides, indexes, and abstracts; collection development; depository library programs; government information policy; microform; public services; teaching and technical services; and general publications. Although these subdivisions may provide sufficiently precise subject access for those already familiar with government documents, a detailed subject index would increase this guide's usefulness. [R: JAL, July 88, p. 198; LJ, 15 June 88, p. 44]
                    Elizabeth D. Liddy

57.   Schwarzkopf, LeRoy C., comp. **Government Reference Books 86/87: A Biennial Guide to U.S. Government Publications.** Tenth biennial volume. Englewood, Colo., Libraries Unlimited, 1988. 436p. index. $47.50. LC 76-146307. ISBN 0-87287-666-7.

This is the tenth biennial volume in this extremely useful series on government publications. The same general format used in previous editions is followed in this volume. Within four broad subject categories, such as general library reference and social sciences, nearly fifteen hundred items are listed in topical subgroupings. Each entry contains a full bibliographic citation, OCLC and *Monthly Catalog* numbers, LC card number, and, new with this edition, depository shipping list and item numbers and LC classification numbers. A descriptive, noncritical annotation is provided for each entry.

In addition to listing LC classification, depository list, and item numbers, this edition introduces several other changes. Most serial titles have been withdrawn and are now included in a new companion publication, *Government Reference Serials* (see entry 58), although some irregular or monographic series are still included. Microform titles are listed, reflecting the shift to dual formatting as part of the substantial economies and reductions in depository publication and distribution resulting from the Gramm-Rudman-Hollings deficit reduction bill of 1986. In addition, only items distributed to depository libraries by GPO itself are now listed, eliminating numerous publications now issued by privately contracted agencies in response to the deficit legislation and other Office of Management and Budget economy directives. Finally, the biennial period covered by this volume now represents the actual date of item distribution to the depository libraries, not the imprint date of the item. A more detailed author/title/subject index is included in this edition, an improvement on the limited subject access of earlier volumes.

Along with its companion volume on government serial publications, this work should continue to prove extremely helpful both to depository libraries and other libraries with large government publication collections. [R: Choice, Oct 88, p. 296]
                    Elizabeth Patterson

58.   Schwarzkopf, LeRoy C., comp. **Government Reference Serials.** Englewood, Colo., Libraries Unlimited, 1988. 344p. index. $45.00. LC 87-37846. ISBN 0-87287-451-6.

This is a companion to *Government Reference Books*, the biennial guide to U.S. government publications published since 1968/69 by Libraries Unlimited (see entry 57).

Included are government publications of reference value issued annually or biennially as well as quarterly, monthly, or even daily. Only items available for distribution through the Government Printing Office's depository library program are cited, as is the case for *Government Reference Books*. The same topical headings as found in *GRB* are used, with publications grouped under four main parts: "General Library Reference," "Social Sciences," "Science and Technology," and "Humanities."

The guide contains 583 numbered entries arranged alphabetically by title under each topic or subtopic. Entries consist of the citation, the history of the serial, and the annotation. To standard bibliographic elements used in *GRB*, the compiler has added the Library of Congress classification number, the Dewey Decimal number, the depository item number, and the GPO price list (no. 36) ID number. Separate indexes for titles, corporate authors, and subjects as well as a Superintendent of Documents (SuDocs) class number index complete the publication. The most valuable enhancement is the inclusion of the publishing history of the serial. Details include the predecessor title(s), changes in SuDocs numbers and other variations, with information on the specific issue when the change occurred.

The amount of detail provided on the many U.S. government serials of reference use is truly remarkable. Including this information has only been possible with the issuance of a separate volume for serials. Some libraries may not need this much detail, especially for older titles not in their collections, but researchers in major libraries who often need to track down elusive older material should find the publication invaluable. All libraries with sizable government collections should have *Government Reference Serials* as well as *Government Reference Books*. [R: BR, Sept/Oct 88, p. 52; JAL, July 88, p. 198; LJ, 15 June 88, p. 44; RBB, 15 Oct 88, p. 388]

Robert W. Schaaf

59.   Zink, Steven D. **United States Government Publications Catalogs.** 2d ed. Washington, D.C., Special Libraries Association, 1988. 292p. index. $20.00pa. LC 87-32353. ISBN 0-87111-335-X.

The second edition of this unique and valuable reference book contains over 370 titles of U.S. government agency publications catalogs, an increase of over 140 titles from the 1982 edition (see *ARBA* 83, entry 73). It adds a title index, expands the subject index, and provides lengthier annotations. The term "publications" is used in the broadest sense to include catalogs (as well as some bibliographies) that list printed publications, audiovisual titles, and machine-readable as well as other nonprint materials. Most of the entries are catalogs listing agency-printed publications. Most of the titles are regular serials, but a number of irregular serials have been included. The work emphasizes catalogs listing current or in-print publications; catalogs of retrospective materials have been excluded. Also excluded are publications such as annual reports, which have listings of current agency publications but which are not by themselves catalogs.

Entries are arranged in Superintendent of Documents (SuDocs) class number order and include the following information: issuing agency, title, frequency, SuDocs class number, depository item number, acquisition source, and complete address of issuing agency (including street address, and building, room, and mail stop numbers). In the case of irregular serials, complete bibliographic information is not provided for the latest edition. It includes a number of catalogs that were not printed or procured by the Government Printing Office (GPO) and thus not distributed to depository libraries.

United States government agency publications catalogs are useful research and reference tools since they frequently include non-depository and/or non-GPO publications that are not included in the GPO's *Monthly Catalog* or other standard references. Agency catalogs often provide more current information and make searching faster and easier than comprehensive catalogs. [R: WLB, Nov 88, p. 127]

LeRoy C. Schwarzkopf

HANDBOOKS AND YEARBOOKS

60.   **Book of Days 1988: An Encyclopedia of Information Sources on Historical Figures and Events....** Ann Arbor, Mich., Pierian Press, 1988. 754p. index. $98.00. ISBN 0-87650-248-6; ISSN 0891-0146.

I suspect that most library shelves are replete with single-volume handbooks which list the most important events of a given day in history. Many, if not most, of these books have in their titles "book of days" or something very close to that. Perhaps the best example of this genre is Jean Hatch's *American Book of Days* (H. W. Wilson, 1978). I would hazard a guess that at least one new "book of days" is published each year or so. This year, in addition to *Book of Days 1988* (*BOD*), we have *A Dictionary of Days*, edited by Leslie Dunkling (see entry 1251). If one also considers related works such as *An Encyclopedia of World History* (see *ARBA* 73, entry 309), the question arises, why purchase another in this genre? Well, those who have not had a chance to see the *BOD* are going to be pleasantly surprised by its unique content, which is skillfully executed and a bit eccentric, but in the most entertaining vein.

I immediately turned to my birthday (April 27) and found the entry to be a biography (three hundred to five hundred words) of Joseph Gottlieb Kölreuter, of whom I knew nothing. It turns out that Kölreuter (1733-1806) was the German botanist who provided the "irrefutable proof of sexuality in plants." I wonder how I might use that fact in some future introduction to a speech? If I can't use the latter, I surely can drop the fact that Captain James T. Kirk of the Starship *Enterprise* was born on 23 March 2228! On a more serious note, I find that the John Birch Society, an ultra-conservative group, was founded in 1958 on December 9th. I think by now you can see how the editors of *BOD* have surely created an original niche for themselves in this genre.

BOD is the second volume in a projected ten-volume set. *BOD 1988* covers "events in dates ending in '3' or '8,'" thus producing anniversary dates ending in "5" or "0." By 1992, when the set is completed, it will have come around to the point where it began in 1987. The criteria for inclusion of an event in *BOD* are sufficiently flexible to include topics from the "narrowly specific to broadly generalized" categories. Each entry, in addition to the major essay, includes reference works, works by the individual (if a biography), adult and youth works, nonprint media, suggestions for discussion, sources of additional information, and cross-reference dates (relating to the main essay). *BOD* also includes a chronology index, a subject index, and a list of contributors (including several librarians).

This is a very enjoyable work which I recommend highly.   Richard H. Quay

61. Charts on File. By the Diagram Group. New York, Facts on File, 1988. 1v. (various paging). illus. index. $145.00 looseleaf with binder. LC 87-36423. ISBN 0-8160-1721-1.

From the arts and history to paleontology and geography, *Charts on File* is a looseleaf collection of more than three hundred of what its compilers claim to be the most commonly requested charts. Of use from middle schools to college, this set of ready-to-reproduce charts will be of help to many teachers. The charts are ready to copy as handouts or as overhead transparencies (although many really contain too much information for an effective and clear visual in most classrooms).

Samples of some of the more useful charts are the Richter Scale, reproduction time spans, sound waves, evolution of organisms, and how a bill becomes law. Examples of some of the most unusual charts are food storage times in refrigerators, fundamental vase forms, the parts of a glacier, and the Beaufort scale of wind speeds.

The Facts on File publications are often expensive, and this publication is no exception. The cost is equal to about $2.00 for each chart. On the other hand, there are many transparency kits on the market which run as high as $25.00 to $40.00 per visual without any promise that the teacher will use the transparency more than once.

This reference tool is a useful guide to visuals which students can use to locate items to show in class in support of a report, and may provide some visuals for the humanities area.

Those who can afford it should invest in this set. [R: BR, Nov/Dec 88, pp. 47-48; RBB, Aug 88, p. 1899; WLB, Sept 88, p. 92]

                                      Daniel Callison

62. Henderson, Bill, ed. Rotten Reviews: A Literary Companion. New York, Viking Penguin, c1986, 1987. 93p. illus. $4.95pa. LC 87-2482. ISBN 0-14-010195-0.

It would be hard to argue that this book belongs, unquestionably, in the reference section. It has all the marks against it: it is paperback, overly small, oddly sized, and of ephemeral subject matter at best. But if these were the only criteria for books, we would have few of them in libraries.

Rotten Reviews is a godsend to every writer who has ever written a book, poured his life blood out in it, risked his family, his sanity, and his health over it, only to have reviewers destroy it in, oh, say fifteen or twenty minutes' worth of writing. Of course there are reviewers who read every word of every book they are asked to review. But their number, in this fast-paced, quick-minded world of cheddar-melts and chicken nuggets, grows smaller with each passing day.

Rotten Reviews serves as a reminder to reviewers that their opinions are as fleeting as the wind, and as insubstantial as snow in the bright sunshine. What must uplift writers of every simile is the knowledge that nearly every important writer is found here, in the hands of some mean-spirited critic. Perhaps those who can, do, and those who can't, review. But let's hope the profession of criticizing rises above blather on most occasions.

The authors are listed alphabetically. The title of the author's work, however, often precedes his or her name, lending confusion to the arrangement of thumbing through the As only to find Winesburg, Ohio listed first, before Sherwood Anderson's name. This is, however, a collection of literary greats: Anderson, Arnold, Brontë, Huxley, Ibsen, Johnson, Joyce, Wilde, and Woolf. The fun, however, is to read the unbridled anger of the reviewer over, say as "insignificant" a work as *Babbitt*, or *As I Lay Dying*, or *Madame Bovary*. Ah, well, that is the life of the mind of reviewers. We take our potshots, but we also take our chances. Besides, we can't *always* be right.

                                      Mark Y. Herring

63. Slavens, Thomas P. Number One in the U.S.A.: Records and Wins in Sports, Entertainment, Business, and Science. Metuchen, N.J., Scarecrow, 1988. 196p. index. $20.00. LC 88-14823. ISBN 0-8108-2140-0.

Users of this compilation by Slavens (School of Information and Library Studies, University of Michigan) and his research assistants should be aware that for the most part only 1987 U.S. records (and those of U.S. citizens abroad) are included. There are in addition some entries for earlier years (especially 1986); a few entries cite early 1988 honors. More than 70 percent of the text is devoted to sports and entertainment records (44 and 28 percent, respectively). Business and science records (the third and fourth categories) are covered in 11 and 17 percent of the text. In each category entries are arranged under subject headings (listed A-Z in each category) "suggested by the Library of Congress."

The source note for entries appears to be unusually complete for newspaper references (e.g., *Ann Arbor News, Billboard, New York Times, Sporting News, USA Today, Variety, Wall Street Journal,* and *Washington Post*), including author/title, date and page number. In passing it should be noted that many of the entries concluding with references to, say, the *Ann Arbor News*, indicate that the source of the information is in fact the Associated Press. This means, of course, that one's local newspaper may have picked up the item. It is likewise evident that the source note provides a clue as to when to expect the next award; for example, the richest person in the United States in 1988 (cf. p. 148, wealth). It is also true that librarians and their patrons will increasingly use online sources for currency. Periodical sources indicate title, date, and page but not volume.

Random sampling will quickly suggest the selective nature of topics included. The first topic under sports records, automobile racing, lists forty entries (plus eight other winners listed, without cross-referencing, in winners). (*Facts on File*, 1987, indexes sixty-seven winners.) The only entry for political science (in science records, for there is no separate social science section) identifies the first woman executive director of the American Political Science Association. None of the fourteen ASPA awards listed (without winners) in the seventh edition (1988) of *Awards, Honors & Prizes* (Vol. 1, Gale) are listed.

Patrons often want lists of winners going back to the earliest award, in which case such sources as almanacs, encyclopedia yearbooks, and Bowker's *Literary and Library Prizes* are valuable.

Number One includes entries as diverse as the most popular types of Christmas trees (p. 133) and the city where the most prunes per capita are consumed (p. 173). It is unclear why the fullest entry for the longest married U.S.

couple in 1986 and 1987 are in different subjects (pp. 91, 103). Nor, in light of the attention to sports winners, is it clear why *Sports Illustrated* is not among the sources.

In summary, it may well be that libraries having the types of sources mentioned in this review will not need *Number One in the U.S.A.*

Wiley J. Williams

64. **The Statesman's Year-Book: Statistical and Historical Annual of the States of the World for the Year 1988-1989.** 125th ed. John Paxton, ed. New York, St. Martin's Press, 1988. 1701p. index. $59.95. LC 4-3776. ISBN 0-312-02094-5.

This volume is a compact but extensive treatment of vital world information for those needing a quick reference for social, political, economic, and historical data. Weights and measures conversion tables are included. A chronology of key events from April 1987 to March 1988, tables of comparative economic data, and descriptions of the make-up and charge of many international organizations precede an alphabetical presentation of each country.

For each country the following are described: history; area and population; climate; constitution and government; defense; international relations; economy; energy and natural resources; industry and trade; communications; justice, religion, education, and welfare; and diplomatic relations. Detailed data for these areas are often available for states, provinces, territories, and other political subdivisions or affiliates of individual countries. The quantity and quality of population, economic, energy and natural resources, and industry and trade data are typically superior for the more industrialized countries.

The volume is well indexed by place and international organization, product, and names. An *Historical Companion* is available for those desiring greater historical treatment than the abridged information in this volume. The *Year-Book* is a worthy acquisition for every library.

Wade L. Thomas

INDEXES

65. **Abridged Biography and Genealogy Master Index: A Consolidated Index to More Than 1,600,000 Biographical Sketches....** Barbara McNeil and Amy L. Unterburger, eds. Detroit, Gale, 1988. 3v. (Gale Biographical Index Series, No. 11). $375.00/set. LC 87-25397. ISBN 0-8103-2149-1.

This index of more than 1,600,000 biographical sketches in 115 biographical dictionaries is a spinoff of the larger *Biography and Genealogy Master Index* from the same publisher. The index is designed for the smaller library which would contain more popular biographical works such as the *Dictionary of National Biography* (for a review of the 1961-1970 editions, see *ARBA* 83, entry 96), *Fifth Book of Junior Authors* (see *ARBA* 85, entry 1030), and *The McGraw-Hill Encyclopedia of World Biography* (see *ARBA* 74, entry 106). Coverage is wide and includes political figures; women; and persons in the arts, music, mass media, literature, and the sciences. Many entries are duplicates of the same person with differing forms of the name. Some entries with birthdates help clarify which person is being sought.

The decision to buy this tool should be based on the number of works owned by the library which are indexed, the call for biographical information, and the time saved by such an index. Its coverage through 1987 makes it a current and valuable source if the above stipulations have been met. [R: Choice, July/Aug 88, p. 1671; LJ, 1 June 88, p. 102; RBB, 1 June 88, p. 1652; WLB, May 88, p. 103]

David V. Loertscher

66. Breen, Karen. **Index to Collective Biographies for Young Readers.** 4th ed. New York, R. R. Bowker, 1988. 494p. $34.95. LC 88-19410. ISBN 0-8352-2348-5.

This greatly expanded edition of this valuable work for children's and school libraries indexes the contents of 1,129 collective biographies listing 9,773 people. The index aims more at inclusion than exclusion so that its judgment of quality biographical material is not consistent with previous editions.

The main alphabetical section is a listing of persons including their birth and death year, nationality at birth and current country of residence, occupation, and the book code indicating the volume indexed. A second section lists names alphabetically by subject and country of origin and residence. Thus it is easy to find a Spanish violinist by looking under "Musicians" and the subdivision "Violinists." Full listings by nationality such as "Jamaicans" are included. The final section of the book lists each title with master lists of all persons indexed from that source. Also included are the lists of books by their code and finally a key to the publishers. The print and layout make reading easy.

Clearly, this is an essential book in all school and public libraries where access to biographical information is a regular part of reference services.   David V. Loertscher

67. **Canadian Magazine Index 1987. Volume 3.** Luci Lemieux and Carol Wiltshire, eds. Toronto, Micromedia, 1988. 1586p. $350.00. ISSN 0829-8777.

This index, first published in 1985, is a guide to over three hundred popular, special interest, and academic magazines from Canada, which have been selected for their wide availability in Canadian libraries. Included are a number of regional Canadian magazines, such as *Edmonton Magazine*, Canadian editions of U.S. magazines such as *Time* and *Reader's Digest*, serious journals such as *Canadian Historical Review*, and a group of thirty major Canadian business journals. The index also covers eighteen key U.S. magazines, such as *Psychology Today, Scientific American,* and *Hot Rod.*

The work is divided into two sections, the subject index and the personal name index. Corporate authors and governmental units are included, but these entries are located in the subject index. For each entry the magazine title, volume, date, and page number are given. Entries under subject are listed chronologically. There is extensive coverage of reviews of books, art, movies, plays, and other performances. These reviews, listed under author in the personal name index, serve to swell the number of entries. The subject indexing is also quite detailed, down to the level of news briefs. In fact, little selectivity is evidenced in this all-inclusive system of indexing. While the work is not in the typical Wilson index format, it is professionally done. Publication is monthly, with annual cumulations. Micromedia Limited, the publisher, also sells microforms for 158 of the titles indexed.

A similar publication, the *Canadian Periodical Index*, has been published since 1947 by the Canadian Library Association, and since 1987 by Info Globe. That index, reviewed in *ARBA* 88 (see entry 77), covers four hundred titles, including French-Canadian titles, and is similar in format to the *Readers' Guide to Periodical Literature*. Although it was not available to this reviewer for inspection, there is probably quite a bit of overlap between the two indexes, although the *Canadian Magazine Index* may cover more special interest titles. In fact, most U.S. academic libraries will hold only the more scholarly Canadian titles. But for those libraries interested in coverage of a wide range of popular Canadian magazines, this index meets their requirements.

Necia A. Musser

68. **Canadian Periodical Index 1920-1937: An Author and Subject Index.** By Grace Heggie

and others. Ottawa, Canadian Library Association, 1988. 567p. $200.00. ISBN 0-88802-187-9.

An index to twenty Canadian periodicals covering the years 1920 to 1937. The index will greatly improve access to the early years of these basic Canadian periodicals and improve the *Canadian Periodical Index*'s coverage of this earlier period. The format follows that of the *CPI*, listing articles in one alphabetical sequence by author and subject. The subject headings follow those of the later issues, with appropriate additions to reflect the contemporary subject matter. Full citation is given for each entry. Book reviews are entered in one section under that heading. This index is a necessary addition to any retrospective collection of Canadian material.   Lorna K. Rees-Potter

PERIODICALS AND SERIALS

69. **MLA Directory of Periodicals: A Guide to Journals and Series in Languages and Literature.** 1988-89 ed. Eileen M. Mackesy and Dee Ella Spears, comps. A Companion to the *MLA International Bibliography*. New York, Modern Language Association of America, 1988. 732p. index. $100.00. ISBN 0-87352-471-3.

70. **MLA Directory of Periodicals: A Guide to Journals and Series in Languages and Literature: Periodicals Published in the United States and Canada.** 1988-89 ed. Eileen M. Mackesy and Dee Ella Spears, comps. A Companion to the *MLA International Bibliography*. New York, Modern Language Association of America, 1988. 300p. index. $30.00pa. ISBN 0-87352-472-1.

The 1988-89 *MLA Directory of Periodicals* is available in two versions. The complete, hardbound edition, which has been published biennially since 1979, includes all 3,146 journals and series that are screened regularly for items suitable for inclusion in the *MLA International Bibliography*. The paperback version, issued since 1984, is limited to the 1,170 titles in the MLA master list that are published in the United States and Canada. The scope and the binding are the two essential differences between the volumes; otherwise, the format and arrangement are identical. Appearing near the front of each volume is a list of all the publications covered, arranged by MLA acronym.

The directory portion of each edition is arranged alphabetically by the title of the periodical or series. The consecutively numbered entries generally contain six parts: (1) editorial address; (2) publication information, such as

beginning date, sponsoring organization, and ISSN; (3) subscription information, including frequency, subscription price, address (if different from the editorial address), and availability in microform; (4) advertising information, which notes if advertising is accepted, and in some instances provides rates; (5) editorial description, which includes a brief annotation outlining the scope of the publication, indicating whether book reviews and notes are published, which languages are accepted, and whether manuscripts are reviewed anonymously; and (6) submission requirements, noting the average length of articles, number of copies required, style manual followed, disposition of rejected manuscripts, number of reviewers, average time before a decision is reached and between acceptance and publication, and number of manuscripts submitted and published each year. Not all of the listings include information in all of these categories, however.

Concluding each version of the directory are four indexes that provide access to the listings by names of editorial personnel, sponsoring organizations, subjects, and languages published (excluding English, French, German, Italian, and Spanish). Entries in the subject index are based on the scope notes provided by the editors of the publications and on the titles of the publications.

The complete version of the *MLA Directory of Periodicals* continues to be the most comprehensive and detailed listing available of current journals and series pertaining to language, literature, and folklore. It is an invaluable source for librarians seeking subscription information as well as for those involved in selection decisions and collection evaluation projects. In addition, it is particularly useful for humanities scholars seeking to identify potential publishers of their manuscripts. Although medium-size and large academic and research libraries will undoubtedly need the international coverage provided by the clothbound edition, smaller libraries and individuals may find the more limited, and considerably less expensive, paperbound version more appropriate for their needs. [R: RBB, 15 Dec 88, p. 692]

    Marie Ellis

71. Nagar, Murari Lal, and Sarla Devi Nagar. **TULIP: The Universal List of Indian Periodicals. Bouquets One-Four.** Columbia, Mo., International Library Center, 1986-1988. 4v. $45.00pa./vol. LC 87-26291. ISBN 0-943913-03-9.

TULIP is truly a remarkable bibliographic effort and an indispensable tool for serious scholars of India. The authors have undertaken an immense project. With little or no funding in the initial stages of the project, the Nagars, who are outstanding bibliographers at the University of Missouri-Columbia, set out to produce a comprehensive reference to Indian periodicals held in major research libraries around the world. In order to understand what has been accomplished, some qualifications to this description are necessary. First, the publications under review here are the first four volumes of an ongoing project and contain only the A through F entries. Second, India is defined broadly and includes both Pakistan and Bangladesh. Third, "research libraries around the world" refers to major libraries in the United States, India, and the United Kingdom. Finally, the authors refer to *TULIP* as a "union catalog." In other words, *TULIP* is a guide that points users to one of several catalogs that, in turn, indicate which particular library contains the periodical of interest. Each periodical listed is described in great detail. The descriptive entries have been organized into a standard format which is surprisingly easy to learn and, more important, easy to use. *TULIP* was designed with the computer in mind and is also available in machine-readable form. In a short review, a comprehensive evaluation of this effort is not possible. It should be enough to indicate that even researchers with considerable expertise on India will be suitably humbled by the number of entries and the immensity of the effort.   James T. Peach

72.   **The Serials Directory: An International Reference Book.** 3d ed. Birmingham, Ala., EBSCO Publishing, 1988. 3v. $289.00/set. ISBN 0-913956-33-3; ISSN 0886-4179.

According to the publisher, there are now more than 118,000 entries following the same arrangement as in the premier edition (see *ARBA* 87, entry 82). The information is still derived from the CONSER file, EBSCO's own internal database, and questionnaires sent to over 100,000 publishers.

The titles are still arranged under 147 major subject headings with 135 subheadings, plus eighteen thousand or more cross-references. Information in most entries includes, among other data, key title, varying form of a title, publisher name and address, telephone number, editor, index/abstracts, LC classification, Dewey Decimal classification, CODEN designation, cumulative index availability, book reviews, circulation, and former titles. The third volume contains an alphabetical title index, ceased title index, and ISSN index. Currency is maintained with a quarterly issue of *The Serials Directory Update* with the latest issue being cumulative.

It was noted in the review of the first edition that information had been omitted in entries on *Information Economics and Policy* and *Vertica.* This has now been corrected. *Booklist*, which did not appear as a current journal in the two earlier editions, is now shown as a current title. Some newsletters in library and information science (e.g., *Library Personnel News*) are listed in *Ulrich's International Periodicals Directory 1988-89* but do not appear in *The Serials Directory.*

On the plus side, the third edition is more easily read because of its larger print, better quality paper, and greater use of boldface type. Since reference tools such as this are heavily used, it is important the information be reliable. With greater attention paid to accuracy, *The Serials Directory* not only complements *Ulrich's* and *Irregular Serials and Annuals*, now published under one title (see entry 73), but may challenge its competitor.

Anna Grace Patterson

73.   **Ulrich's International Periodicals Directory 1988-89.** 27th ed. New York, R. R. Bowker, 1988. 3v. index. $279.95/set. LC 32-16320. ISBN 0-8352-2563-1; ISSN 0000-0175.

The twenty-seventh edition of *Ulrich's* has now been expanded to include *Irregular Serials and Annuals.* As a result, *Ulrich's* contains current periodicals which are issued on a regular basis more frequently than once a year, titles issued annually or less frequently than once a year, and those issued irregularly. The current edition provides information for over 108,590 titles from 61,000 publishers in 197 countries; over 6,700 titles have been added and 65,000 have been updated. Quarterly supplements will be published in *Ulrich's Update* (formerly *The Bowker International Serials Database Update*), issued free of charge to purchasers of the directory.

As the editor states, this edition continues Bowker's dedication to providing accurate and complete acquisition and research information on serials. It also incorporates a number of enhancements and changes which are the result of surveys, studies, and feedback from users on how to make the directory more efficient and useful. Combining *Ulrich's* with *Irregular Serials and Annuals* is just one such improvement.

The first two volumes of the three-volume set contain the classified subject listing. Entries provide title, Dewey Decimal Classification number, ISSN, country of publication, frequency, publisher's name and address, price, abstracting and indexing information, circulation, online and CD-ROM availability, and special features. Included for the first time in this edition are brief descriptions for 10,770 publications, 16,000 Library of Congress Classification numbers, and 7,840 CODEN. Serials which began publication in the last three years are now highlighted with an inverted triangle.

The third volume includes a listing of serials available online, vendors of online serials, cessations, ISSN and title indexes, and an index to publications of international organizations. Cessations have been expanded to include titles which have ceased during the past three years, rather than just the past year.

To make the directory easier to read and use, the main entry type size has been enlarged, main entry numbers in the title index appear in boldface type, and section tab guides have been added to help locate alphabetical sections and indexes. Four new subject headings ("Animal Welfare," "Men's Health," "Women's Health," and "New Age Publications") have been added to the subject heading classification scheme, which currently includes 554 headings.

In addition to the print product, three new services will be offered to *Ulrich's* users. *Ulrich's News* is a free, bimonthly newsletter devoted to news of changes and information on serials development. *Ulrich's User's Guide*, a separately published booklet, and *Ulrich's Hotline*, a toll-free number for assistance, are both available for standing order customers.

As previous reviews have noted (see *ARBA 88*, entry 93, *ARBA 86*, entry 83, and *ARBA 83*, entry 23), the directory displays bias towards American and European publications and, of course, can never be completely comprehensive, but it is an indispensable resource for all libraries.   Martha S. Perry

QUOTATION BOOKS

74. Burke, John Gordon, Ned Kehde, and Dawson Moorer, eds. **Dictionary of Contemporary Quotations.** rev. ed. Evanston, Ill., John Gordon Burke, 1987. 302p. $45.00. ISBN 0-934272-13-1; ISSN 0360-215X.

This revised edition continues "to record contemporary quotations which are historically, sociologically, and politically significant," but some quotations have been deleted in this volume. The editors have gleaned the new quotations, which amount to a 20 percent increase, from over 180 periodicals and newspapers covering 1981 to 1987. The first 132 pages arrange quotations alphabetically by author, and the last part of the book primarily lists quotations by broad subject. Each quotation in the author section contains a complete citation to a source,

usually the original one. The bibliographical history of this book indicates that "this is volume 6," which supplements "volume 5, published in 1981." Plans call for monthly updates on an electronic database that will be made available to standing order subscribers.

The *DCQ* was compared with *What They Said in 1986* (Monitor, 1987), which covers spoken quotations of prominent people for one specific year. Even though limited to one year, *What They Said* is a more comprehensive source of quotations, with a detailed subject index and longer quotations. *What They Said* has 549 pages compared with 302 pages in *DCQ*, and *What They Said* contains more than twice the three quotations that *DCQ* lists for George Bush. *What They Said* also lists twenty-nine quotations by Mikhail Gorbachev and four by C. Everett Koop, both omitted from *DCQ*. *DCQ* does contain quotations not found in *What They Said* or other standard sources. Therefore, it may be considered a supplement to basic and more comprehensive quotation books. [R: RBB, 1 Jan 88, p. 762]

O. Gene Norman

75. Marsden, C. R. S., comp. **The Dictionary of Outrageous Quotations.** Topsfield, Mass., Salem House, 1988. 128p. index. $9.95. LC 87-35586. ISBN 0-88162-367-9.

This slim volume contains quotations arranged alphabetically by seventy-five broad topics with an index by person quoted, but most quotations are unlikely to be found in standard quotation books. The author, a British governmental psychologist, admits to including a variety of types of outrage, including paradoxes, blasphemies, insults, obscenities, and lies. He identifies the person, or source, quoted but omits the specific citation of each quotation. Persons quoted include such diverse personalities as Al Capone and John Wayne on America, Nancy Reagan and John Wilkes Booth on crime and punishment, Billy Graham and Adolph Hitler on God, Voltaire and Zsa Zsa Gabor on marriage, and Pope Pius XI and Xaviera Hollander on sex.

Only two overlapping entries were found during a check of fifty-five entries in *The Dictionary of Outrageous Quotations* against the *Dictionary of Contemporary Quotations* (see entry 74). Several of the contemporary persons probably will not be found in other similar sources. For libraries which have a need for provocative and unusual quotations, *The Dictionary of Outrageous Quotations* supplements other standard quotation books.

O. Gene Norman

76. Simpson, James B., comp. **Simpson's Contemporary Quotations.** Boston, Houghton Mifflin, 1988. 495p. index. $19.95. LC 87-37867. ISBN 0-395-43085-2.

The quotations of this volume, while not as impressive as the brilliance of the mind of Plato, or the coruscating genius of the eloquence of Augustine, still impress. That so much quotable material could be found since 1950 staggers the mind, in a mysterious way. "The fireworks begin today," writes Mayor Koch. "Each diploma is a lighted match. Each one of you is a fuse." Or consider the inimitable Dorothy Parker: "[Robert Benchley] and I had an office so tiny that an inch smaller and it would have been adultery." And we even have Vice President Bush's perfect image of the press corp covering the 1984 elections: "A bullpen seething with mischief." It's all here: William F. Buckley, Jr., C. S. Lewis, Albert Schweitzer—in short, all of those people who have tried their best to make the world a more interesting, and, in some cases, even a better place to live.

The book grows out of Simpson's *Best Quotes of '54, '55, '56,* but adds enormously to that outstanding collection. Now eclipsing that first book, the present one contains about ten thousand quotes from nearly four thousand namecunds. The book is arranged under twenty-four subheads, grouped together under three major headings: the world, humankind, and communications and the arts. Subheadings include topics such as law, business, love, religion, sports, theater, art, and science. Author and subject/key lines indexes should make even the hottest crossed bun smile.

Libraries wanting to complete the phrase should add this book to *The Wit and Wisdom of the 20th Century* (see *ARBA* 88, entry 95). With both Simpson and Pepper seasoning the quotation shelves, finding the right author, or the right way of saying it, will be but a fingertip away. [R: Choice, Oct 88, pp. 297-98; LJ, 15 June 88, p. 53; RBB, Aug 88, pp. 1906-7]

Mark V. Herring

77. Van Ekeren, Glenn. **The Speaker's Sourcebook: Quotes, Stories and Anecdotes for Every Occasion.** Englewood Cliffs, N.J., Prentice-Hall, 1988. 393p. $29.95; $12.95pa. LC 87-29192. ISBN 0-13-824608-4; 0-13-824590-8pa.

Drawn from a variety of sources, including the author's own experience, this collection offers quotes and anecdotes to help a speaker liven up a speech or make a point. Entries are arranged alphabetically by topic from "Ability" to "Worry." Some topics have several pages of material devoted to them but others have only a single page. Another disparity in coverage can be seen in the topics chosen. Some, such as "Self-image" and "Self-talk" seem to overlap, while such often requested topics as "Education" and "Knowledge" have no entries at all. Although some speakers might find useful material here, it is hardly a source that would enable one to "put together an effective speech on any topic in minutes," as is stated on the cover. The Prochnows's *A Treasure Chest of Quotations for All Occasions* (see *ARBA* 85, entry 69) and other similar titles provide much the same type of material and generally broader coverage but, of course, there is not complete duplication of material among any of the books. Librarians often must find elusive quotes and an additional source, however flawed, is welcome. [R: WLB, June 88, p. 144]   Barbara E. Kemp

Part II
SOCIAL SCIENCES

2 Social Sciences in General

BIBLIOGRAPHIES

78. Encyclopedia of Public Affairs Information Sources: A Bibliographic Guide.... Paul Wasserman, James R. Kelly, and Desider L. Vikor, eds. Detroit, Gale, 1988. 303p. $125.00. LC 87-25902. ISBN 0-8103-2191-2.

This new encyclopedia is a "holistic" directory of information sources on approximately three hundred topics of wide public interest such as business, education, government, politics, law, sociology, and urban affairs. By "holistic" I refer to both the format and contents of this directory. The format is alphabetical by topic with each topic containing the following types of resources: (1) abstract services, indexes, information systems; (2) annuals and reviews; (3) associations and professional societies; (4) bibliographies; (5) biographical sources; (6) directories; (7) encyclopedias and dictionaries; (8) handbooks and manuals; (9) online databases; (10) periodicals; (11) research centers, institutes, clearinghouses; and (12) statistical sources. Therefore, the user is presented with a variety of logical sources and formats. Under most categories, the editors provide anywhere from two or three sources to a dozen. The citations include addresses, but they are not annotated, nor do they give editions or starting dates in some cases; they do generally note the source as being issued, say, monthly or annually.

My biggest single criticism of this directory is the varying degree of quality of selection of entries under many categories; no firm criteria for selection are given in the preface. For example, under the topic "education," the editors list five journals (heading: "periodicals"), only one of which seems all that relevant, namely, the weekly newspaper of record for public education *Education Week*. Another example is found under "crime and criminals" where the statistical sources include the FBI's *Uniform Crime Report*, but not the Justice Department's *Sourcebook of Criminal Justice Statistics*. Some additional care is also needed in the selection of cross-references; for example, there is no cross-reference from "education" to "higher education," or in this case, "colleges and universities." Accordingly, I give the editors high marks for the concept, but only passing grades on the contents. [R: Choice, July/Aug 88, p. 1674; JAL, May 88, p. 129; LJ, July 88, p. 72; RBB, 1 June 88, pp. 1656-57]   Richard H. Quay

79. McLaughlin, Judith A., comp. **Bibliography of the Works of Jean Piaget in the Social Sciences.** Lanham, Md., University Press of America, 1988. 148p. index. $24.00. LC 87-26136. ISBN 0-8191-6730-4.

McLaughlin has compiled a bibliography of over five hundred published works by Piaget appearing as books, journal papers, chapters in edited works, interviews, and published speeches. Unpublished speeches, most introductory essays written by Piaget for works compiled by others, and works published exclusively in languages other than French or English are excluded. Citations are listed chronologically by the year of first publication. Original publications, re-editions, and published translations are listed together so that citations are not duplicated. For citations in French, English translations of titles are provided. There are indexes by collaborating authors, titles (both French and English), and keyword subject.

The title is not completely accurate, as the compiler includes citations to literature in the disciplines of philosophy and religion. She also notes the difficulty of being comprehensive, given the dispersed nature of Piaget's publications and the breadth of his intellectual contributions.

The most comprehensive bibliography of Piaget's works remains *Catalog of the Jean Piaget Archives, University of Geneva*, published in 1975 (see *ARBA* 76, entry 1492). Nonetheless, McLaughlin's contribution is easy to use, cites the most accessible publications by Piaget, and includes material published after the *Catalog* cut-off date. It should find an audience among faculty, graduate students, and under-graduates in sociology, education, and psychology. [R: Choice, Nov 88, p. 464]

Pam M. Baxter

80. Nordquist, Joan, comp. **Herbert Marcuse.** Santa Cruz, Calif., Reference and Research Services, 1988. 60p. index. (Social Theory: A Bibliographic Series, No. 9). $15.00 pa. ISBN 0-937855-16-2.

Herbert Marcuse is best known both as a member of the Frankfurt School and as an intellectual influence on the student movement of the 1960s and early 1970s. His work has been cited across many disciplines, making bibliographic control an important and challenging task. This bibliography is intended to provide a guide to the English-language books, articles, and essays written by and about Marcuse. Though a cut-off date is not specified, it appears that works written as recently as 1987 are included.

The bibliography is arranged into four sections. The first is an alphabetical list of twelve books, not including edited works, written by Marcuse. Accompanying each title is a list of all of the reviews and articles written on that particular book; the articles are arranged alphabetically by author. Section 2 lists seventy-nine essays written by Marcuse; these are arranged alphabetically by title. Reprints of these essays are cited in chronological order. Articles about a particular essay are cited as well. To facilitate access to the one hundred plus entries in this section, there is a title keyword index. Section 3 is a list of over fifty books about Marcuse, though not necessarily exclusively on him; these are arranged alphabetically by author. The fourth section includes 268 articles on Marcuse, arranged alphabetically by author. This section, too, is accompanied by a title keyword index. Five other bibliographies on Marcuse are also cited.

Because Herbert Marcuse is an important social theorist, his work and the reactions to it warrant the accessibility provided by this up-to-date bibliography. Three small reservations can be noted, however. First, the criteria for including works in the bibliography are not fully explained, raising questions concerning its coverage. Second, an author index to all four sections would have been useful in tracing a particular writer's analysis of Marcuse. Third, for those concerned about durability, the cover and binding are not sturdy. These reservations aside, this is a valuable bibliography both for its coverage of Marcuse and for its contribution to improved access to scholarship on the Left.

Stephen H. Aby

DIRECTORIES

81. **Directory of Social Science Information Courses, 1988.** By the Social and Human Sciences Documentation Centre and the Social Science Information and Documentation Committee of the International Federation for Documentation. New York, Berg and Paris, UNESCO; distr., New York, St. Martin's Press, 1988. 167p. index. $50.00. ISBN 0-85496-240-9.

This directory was compiled by the Social and Human Sciences Documentation Centre and the Social Science Information and Documentation Committee of the International Federation for Documentation. UNESCO helps support the research for this directory, especially through the use of its DARE Data Bank. The DARE facility is part of UNESCO's Social and Human Sciences Documentation Centre.

DSSIC identifies 257 "major academic and practical courses in social science information." The courses vary according to the emphasis placed on the background of the potential student. Some courses emphasize the basics of social science information development/transfer, while others are directed toward advanced students. Most of the courses are part of a formal program leading to an academic degree. An example of the latter is the course in social science information offered as part of the master's in library science at the School of Information Studies, Syracuse University.

Each entry within the directory contains the name of the course, address of institution, name of contact person, type of course, target group, course level, admissions requirement, teaching methods, course duration, language course is taught in, fees, and principal instructor(s). The *DSSIC* coverage is worldwide, although about 30 to 40 percent of the entries are from either the United States or the United Kingdom. The directory includes an author/acronym index, an index of contact persons, and an index by discipline/subject, which is subdivided by host country of the institution offering the course.

The principal value of this directory is that it compiles, in a handy format, information generally available in several other sources, but requiring considerable effort by the user to duplicate. The price for this effort however is a bit high. [R: Choice, Sept 88, p. 78]

Richard H. Quay

INDEXES

82.   ASSIA: Applied Social Sciences Index & Abstracts. Volume 1, No. 3, 1987. P. F. Broxis, ed. London, Library Association; distr., Birmingham, Ala., EBSCO Publishing, 1987. 283p. $756.00 (6 issues). ISSN 0950-2238.

Many publishers of printed indexes/ abstracts are rushing to convert to machine-readable formats, especially CD-ROM. Many information providers have already elected to produce their products in automated format only. Although few publishers are abandoning the printed versions of their indexes, it seems clear that with advances in computer technology (e.g., multiple access to a single CD-ROM station) and the pressure of diminishing resource budgets, many librarians could be forced to opt for one format only. Within this context, it is somewhat unusual to see the appearance of a new printed index on the scale of *ASSIA*.

The purpose of *ASSIA*, although not clearly defined in the promotional materials, seems to be an interdisciplinary approach to the literature of the social and behavioral sciences, linking subjects that are not adequately covered in a single traditional indexing service alone. Accordingly, in 1987 *ASSIA* covered 538 titles, of which 146 were also indexed in the *Social Sciences Index*, 206 in *Psychological Abstracts*, and 186 in *Sociological Abstracts*. Several titles in *ASSIA* (e.g., *American Journal of Psychology*) were covered in all three of the indexes/ abstracts cited above; however, the majority were indexed in just one of the three. Using *ASSIA* does, in fact, greatly diminish, but not fully eliminate, the need to consult multiple indexes, depending upon the subject and depth of one's research.

In any event, the Library Association is to be praised for *ASSIA* both as a concept and in its design, which incorporates excellent subject access through numerous cross-references linking "leading subject heading terms and qualifying terms." The abstracts are somewhat brief (50 to 150 words), but adequate to convey the key elements of the article. *ASSIA* includes an author index providing the author's name, title of article, and subject heading under which the full bibliographic entry will be found.

Approximately 46 percent of the titles are United States imprints, 40 percent are from Great Britain, and the remainder are from Europe and the Commonwealth countries. *ASSIA* is published bimonthly, with an annual cumulation.   Richard H. Quay

83.   Gilbert, Dennis A. Compendium of American Public Opinion. New York, Facts on File, 1988. 438p. maps. $60.00. LC 88-16531. ISBN 0-8160-1619-4.

This collection, intended to make public opinion data readily accessible to readers at all levels from the novice to the expert, will be most appreciated by the nonexpert. The preface delineates the purpose and scope of the book and the meaning of percentages. The introduction discusses the development of polling, how polls work (including factors that affect their accuracy), and cautions in evaluating the data.

The polls used are publicly reported, scientifically selected random samples, conducted mostly between 1984 and 1986. They cover a wide variety of topics from expected ones such as crime, drugs, education, and minorities to less obvious ones such as confidence, gambling, sports, and values. The table of contents provides the only access to the information, but the need for a separate index is not strong. Each of the twenty topic chapters has an introductory essay, essays on each subtopic, and graphic representations (charts, maps, graphs), which are all redrawn in a standard style for this publication. In only the simplest cases are lists or tables used instead of graphics. Thus this work differs from the *American Public Opinion Index* (see *ARBA* 85, entry 131), which is a paper index with responses on microfiche. This *Compendium* lists the sources of the data it prints but makes no reference to other sources of information such as the indexes just noted, the magazine *Public Opinion*, the resources of the Inter-University Consortium for Political and Social Research, or pertinent bibliographic tools.

With that limitation in mind, the *Compendium* serves its purpose well: it provides a convenient selection of U.S. public opinion in the mid-1980s and a useful introduction to public opinion polling. [R: WLB, Dec 88, pp. 116-17]
          Joyce Duncan Falk

3 Area Studies

UNITED STATES

California

84. Hart, James D. **A Companion to California.** rev. ed. Berkeley, Calif., University of California Press, 1987. 591p. illus. maps. $38.00; $15.95pa. LC 86-30903. ISBN 0-520-05543-8; 0-520-05544-6pa.

This is a revised edition of a work published nine years ago. Approximately two hundred new entries on topics of contemporary interest have been added. Many of the entries carried over from the earlier edition have been updated, and 191 have been significantly expanded or emended. Concise information is given on persons from all walks of life and all periods of time, cities and towns, geographic features, organizations and institutions, historic events, crops and resources, indigenous plants, animals and birds, universities and colleges, works of literature, newspapers, television series, motion pictures, and performing groups, all of which are important to a knowledge of California from earliest times to the present.

Entries are arranged in one alphabetical sequence from ABAG, the acronym for the Association of Bay Area Governments, to film producer Adolph Zukor. Ample cross-references are provided when there is significant information to be found in additional entries. Special features include entries on national and ethnic groups in California, lists of governors and of counties with statistical data and county seats, and a thirteen-page chronology of events from 1510 to 1986. The compilation is illustrated by four maps and forty-one black-and-white photographs of persons, places, and facsimiles of historic documents or their title pages. Entries in a one-volume work are of necessity brief, but they will serve as ready-reference aids to identification or to placing a topic in a particular framework, as well as starting points for further research. Recommended for all types of libraries and for all grade levels. [R: RBB, Aug 88, p. 1899]

Shirley L. Hopkinson

Florida

85. **Florida Almanac 1988-89.** 7th ed. Del Marth and Martha J. Marth, eds. Gretna, La., Pelican Publishing, 1988. 468p. illus. maps. index. $11.95pa. ISBN 0-88289-670-9; ISSN 0361-9796.

Begun in 1972 as a detailed and authoritative almanac furnishing comprehensive coverage of facts and statistics relative to economic, social, demographic, cultural, and other conditions of the state of Florida, the publication has grown and expanded through the years, increasing its utility as a reference tool. For a review of the fifth edition, see *ARBA* 84, entry 324. The new edition, of course, is essentially an update of those sections for which new data are available and relevant as well as a reprint of those sections (historical, geographical, etc.) which retain their basic characters.

Beginning with state symbols, the table of contents identifies thirty-three different sections of coverage, including, among others, history; chronology; rivers, lakes, springs, forts, and battlefields; boating; crime; constitution; and elections. Obviously there is something for every information seeker depending on his or her needs and interests. Sections on parks, forests, historic landmarks, hunting/fishing, and attractions are well develolped and informative. The publication is as up-to-date as possible, as affirmed in a prefatory note by the authors stating that they were aware of the critical need for current data and even juggled printing deadlines to incorporate last-minute changes. The new edition retains the work's identity as a first-rate publication and an excellent source of information on Florida — comprehensive in coverage yet sufficiently detailed in each of its parts.   Ron Blazek

Louisiana

86. **Louisiana Almanac 1988-89.** 12th ed. Milburn Calhoun and Susan Cole Doré, eds. Gretna, La., Pelican Publishing, 1988. 526p. illus. maps. index. $15.95; $11.95pa. ISBN 0-88289-695-4; 0-88289-688-1pa.; ISSN 0896-6206.

People engaged in the search for information on a topic frequently wish that all relevant facts, names, dates, and places were available in one spot. The *Louisiana Almanac* seeks to provide just that sort of one-stop shopping. Unfortunately, what it makes up for in convenience, it loses in substance, style, and just plain readability. A confusing mix of Louisiana-specific information and general facts, without the benefit of a table of contents (although there is an index), the almanac also suffers from a very unprofessional-looking typesetting job. The printing on some of the lengthy charts is so small as to be practically useless. Attempts at illustrative matter are of equally poor quality.

On the plus side, the almanac is a storehouse of information on Louisiana ranging from matters of more universal interest, like temperature and climate, government, and finances, to issues that would be of limited concern to people outside the state, like reservoir data (close to illegible) and results of district elections. Regrettably, the organization, or lack thereof, the bad printing, and the absence of any explanatory notes that might clear up why, suddenly, the middle paragraph of three describing a university should appear in noticeably darker type than the rest of the text. If the publishers intend a thirteenth edition they might consider, along with making needed improvements in the physical look of the volume, updating some of their language as well, particularly in the descriptions of "historically black colleges."   Ellen Broidy

New York

87. Lopez, Manuel D. **New York: A Guide to Information and Reference Sources, 1979-1986.** Metuchen, N.J., Scarecrow, 1987. 372p. index. $35.00. LC 87-16531. ISBN 0-8108-2018-8.

This book is an update of Lopez's 1980 volume of the same name (see *ARBA* 81, entry 379). Format and subject headings are the same but the materials included cover the years 1979 to 1986. Books, serials, and government publications predominate; periodical entries are few.

However, all sources listed are fully annotated and were selected, in large part, for their availability to the general public and for the reader information they provide (e.g., bibliographies and indexes). Equally divided between New York City and New York State, the diversity of subjects represented is admirable. In one place the reader can locate current books on black Americans in New York City, geology, the New York State Fair, the Jewish Museum, and the Mets along with a socioeconomic atlas of the state. As a result, Lopez makes no claim for comprehensiveness and his choices are representative of what is available. Not a book for the advanced scholar, but the general reader or student can easily use this bibliography to begin to research a wide variety of topics about New York. [R: Choice, May 88, p. 1384]

Deborah Hammer

AFRICA

General Works

88. Blackhurst, Hector, comp. **Africa Bibliography 1986.** Manchester, England, Manchester University Press; distr., New York, St. Martin's Press, 1987. 269p. index. $39.95pa. ISBN 0-7190-2630-X; ISSN 0266-6731.

Africa Bibliography began in 1984 as an annual listing of books, articles, pamphlets, and theses covering all of the continent and associated islands. In this particular edition, 137 collective works have been indexed as well. Though published under the auspices of the International African Institute (IAI), *Africa Bibliography* is not to be confused with the *International African Bibliography* (*IAB*) (Carfax Publishing, 1971-), formerly sponsored by the IAI, but now produced by an independent publisher. The two bibliographies are very similar in scope. Because it only appears annually rather than quarterly like the *IAB*, *Africa Bibliography* is easier to browse through, though one must wait longer to do so. Neither one, however, approaches the *African Book Publishaing Record* (Hans Zell, 1975-) for thoroughness in terms of newly published monographs.

In addition to a detailed subject index, subject subdivisions within the main body of the work provide direct access. Most of the items included are either in English or French. For South Africa though, only one item appeared in Afrikaans — so there is considerable selectivity here. The *IAB*, on the other hand, includes a vast number of foreign-language items but does not have the useful subject subdivisions. An introductory article by Roger Stringer on publishing in Zimbabwe is quite informative. Overall,

Africa Bibliography is an extremely useful reference to sources on African topics.

Dorothy C. Woodson

89.   Fenton, Thomas P., and Mary J. Heffron, comps. and eds. **Africa: A Directory of Resources.** Maryknoll, N.Y., Orbis Books, 1987. 144p. illus. index. $9.95pa. ISBN 0-88-344-532-8.

This is an updated and greatly expanded version of the authors' chapter in their *Third World Resource Directory* (see *ARBA* 86, entry 93). While occasionally useful (certain chapters such as "Organizations" are especially good), it is a most peculiar volume to be labeled "resource directory." Instead of references to books and indexes to periodicals dealing with *how* to find information on sub-Saharan Africa, we are given citations to books that discuss various (and highly diffuse) topics on Africa, such as *The Crisis in Zaire, King Solomon's Mines Revisited*, or *Women Farmers in Africa*. With the dazzling array of books on Africa currently in print and with no rationale given for inclusion or exclusion, it would seem that much of this book does not really serve the purpose for which it was intended.

The chapter on periodicals is also curious. Rather than indicating where one can find references to articles (such as in indexes, abstracts, databases, etc.), we are told, for example, to be "placed on (publishers) mailing lists"—a sloppy and serendipitous way in which to conduct research or keep abreast. Despite these peculiarities, the volume has extremely useful information, such as the chapter on organizations and an informative chapter on audiovisuals. [R: Choice, July/Aug 88, p. 1674]

Dorothy C. Woodson

90.   Kirchherr, Eugene C. **Place Names of Africa, 1935-1986: A Political Gazetteer.** Metuchen, N.J., Scarecrow, 1987. 136p. maps. bibliog. $17.50. LC 87-20765. ISBN 0-8108-2061-7.

This thin volume is a completely revised edition of the author's earlier work *Abyssinia to Zimbabwe: A Guide to the Units of Africa in the Period 1947-1978* (see *ARBA* 82, entry 528). In view of the frequent political changes occurring on the African continent, the periodic updating of African gazetteers and other reference works has become mandatory. The base year for this book was arbitrarily set at 1935.

The chief appeal of this reference work is its simplicity. In its center we find an eighty-page dictionary, "Place Names of the Principal African States and Adjacent Islands." The dictionary gives geographical definitions of political entities of Africa, with some comments. Variant names are cross-referenced to the current usage. In all, 330 former and current names are included. Twenty-three map inserts help locate places cartographically.

Historical depth is provided in a forty-page section under the title "Supplementary Notes." Here, the author addresses such topics as African territories with special status, former colonial possessions of European powers, African islands and their status, secessionist states (e.g., Katanga, Biafra), and "independent homelands" of South Africa. A selected bibliography lists about one hundred relevant source books, maps, and documents. The basic nature of this reference book and its reasonable price make it suitable for both public and academic libraries. It updates nomenclature on Africa found in encyclopedias and standard geographical dictionaries, which are updated less frequently. [R: Choice, Sept 88, p. 82; RBB, 1 Sept 88, pp. 52, 54]

Michael Keresztesi

Benin

91.   Decalo, Samuel. **Historical Dictionary of Benin.** 2d ed. Metuchen, N.J., Scarecrow, 1987. 349p. maps. bibliog. (African Historical Dictionaries, No. 7). $35.00. LC 86-27989. ISBN 0-8108-1924-4.

The first edition of this work appeared under the title *Historical Dictionary of Dahomey* (see *ARBA* 77, entry 313). This country is located on the West African coast between Togo and Nigeria. Following a coup d'état in 1975 which proclaimed a Marxist-Leninist state, Dahomey's name was changed to the People's Republic of Benin.

This dictionary remains one of the few authoritative sources of information on the recent history of this country in the English language. It purports to provide in capsule form authentic information on some of the dominant features of the history, politics, economics, and social aspects of Dahomey/Benin. The biographical articles of the key players in the tumultuous arena of public life of the country are especially valuable contributions.

The second half of the book brings together a bibliography of about two thousand items, mostly in French, that cover key aspects of the country's history, life, and culture. Relatively few citations are of recent vintage. Although the book has no indexes, access to the literature is made easy by means of a detailed subject structure. The work's reference value is enhanced by a list of acronyms; a chronology beginning with 1958; a fairly detailed background essay on Dahomey's history; and maps and tables dealing with ethnic, linguistic, demographic, and economic matters.

In all, this is a competently produced reference work on a little known country in Africa with a fascinating past and a turbulent present. This dictionary must continue to remain a mainstay in American libraries for students and specialists. [R: Choice, Sept 88, p. 78]

Michael Keresztesi

Cape Verde

92. Lobban, Richard, and Marilyn Halter. **Historical Dictionary of the Republic of Cape Verde.** 2d ed. Metuchen, N.J., Scarecrow, 1988. 171p. maps. bibliog. (African Historical Dictionaries, No. 42). $22.50. LC 87-34559. ISBN 0-8108-2087-0.

Richard Lobban and Marilyn Halter have through this second edition made substantive new additions and revisions to the previous work, *Historical Dictionary of the Republics of Guinea-Bissau and Cape Verde* (see *ARBA 81*, entry 337), published almost seven years ago. Cape Verde has emerged from one of Africa's smallest and poorest countries to one of historical and political importance because of Amilcar Cabral's Nationalist party, the PAIGC, that championed the long-armed struggle against the Portuguese colonialists. Therefore, the need for a separate dictionary on Cape Verde is obvious.

This dictionary, the forty-second in the African Historical Dictionaries series, is well researched, organized, comprehensive, and annotated. It treats various aspects of the islands including its people, both at home and abroad, politics, and social and economic issues. Also included at the beginning is a detailed historical narrative of Cape Verde, the main entries, and a comprehensive bibliography.

This work is impressive and should be regarded as a "researcher's companion." It is highly recommended to all libraries, scholars, and students of African history, ethnic studies, and geography.   Felix Eme Unaeze

Chad

93. Decalo, Samuel. **Historical Dictionary of Chad.** 2d ed. Metuchen, N.J., Scarecrow, 1987. 532p. maps. bibliog. (African Historical Dictionaries, No. 13). $47.50. LC 86-15611. ISBN 0-8108-1937-6.

Formerly part of French Equatorial Africa, Chad is one of the largest and least known parts of the world. Samuel Decalo has added immeasurably to our store of facts on Chad with the publication in 1977 of the first edition of the *Historical Dictionary of Chad*, and now with

the second edition, he brings the work up-to-date by covering the extremely turbulent years since 1977.

Among the most useful features of the work are the list of acronyms and abbreviations (given the frequent political shifts and the use of French, this is indispensable), the "selected" chronology, and the two introductions, a reprint of the introduction to the first edition and an updated introduction prepared for this edition. The chronology and introductions identify the names, places, and events that Decalo describes in some detail in the actual dictionary section.

The dictionary itself is arranged in one running alphabet without chronological, geographical, or subject subdivision. Each entry includes a brief description, the length of which clearly has been determined by its importance. Since Decalo strives to be inclusive here, some entries are extremely brief, particularly those of minor officials or political parties wielding little power or influence. On the other hand, major events and forces in the country are described more fully and often include *see* references to related subjects.

One of the most important parts of the book, for both scholars and interested general readers, is the two-hundred-page bibliography with which the book concludes. Decalo introduces this section with an informative essay that provides an overview of the literature on Chad. The bibliography itself is arranged by broad subjects and much of the material cited is in French. Although unannotated, it furnishes a comprehensive list of monographic and periodical literature on Chad. The final section of the bibliography lists additional sources and bibliographies for further study. [R: Choice, July/Aug 88, p. 1672]   Ellen Broidy

Gambia

94. Gailey, Harry A. **Historical Dictionary of the Gambia.** 2d ed. Metuchen, N.J., Scarecrow, 1987. 176p. maps. bibliog. (African Historical Dictionaries, No. 4). $22.50. LC 87-9897. ISBN 0-8108-2001-3.

With the publication of the second edition of this reference tool, the compiler has remedied the major defects noted in the first edition (see *ARBA 76*, entry 251). More attention has been paid to the historical period prior to 1900 and bibliographic coverage of the materials relating to the Mandino tribe has been increased. The chronology and the bibliography have also been updated to make the tool more useful for those engaged in current research. This volume differs slightly from others in the African Historical

Dictionaries series in that it devotes the greater part of the space (120 pages) to the dictionary of historical, demographic, geographical terms, but it shares one flaw which is noticeable throughout the publications. The map that is included is virtually useless. Perhaps the series editors could publish a single volume of legible and comprehensible maps of all the countries in the series.   Margaret Anderson

95.   Gamble, David P., comp. **The Gambia.** Santa Barbara, Calif., ABC-Clio, 1988. 135p. maps. index. (World Bibliographical Series, Vol. 91). $32.50. ISBN 1-85109-068-1.

Comparable in scope to the other bibliographies in this series, this work brings together materials to permit "an understanding of the Gambia and its people, the effect of the river on economic conditions, the country's present economic and political states, the complications that exist even within a very small territory (due primarily to historical factors) and the problems to be faced in the future" (preface). As is the norm for the series, the emphasis is on English-language sources, but some French listings have been provided as well, and the compiler, long familiar with the territory, says he has made an effort to maintain a balance among American, British, and Gambian writers. The historical overview, provided by the introduction, is adequate, though brief; the descriptive annotations are for the most part informative. One serious flaw in production is to be found in the map, which, rather than demonstrating the geopolitical relationship between Gambia and Senegal, sometimes described as that of "a long, swollen-knuckle finger pointing deep into the heart of Senegal," leaves one thoroughly confused. It is difficult to tell which lines indicate what boundaries, and the use of a numbered key to indicate the location of *all* towns and cities, even where there is space to print their names on the map, simply adds to one's frustration.   Margaret Anderson

Ghana

96.   Sarfoh, Joseph A., comp. **Population, Urbanization, and Rural Settlement in Ghana: A Bibliographic Survey.** Westport, Conn., Greenwood Press, 1987. 124p. index. (African Special Bibliographic Series, No. 8). $35.00. LC 87-19627. ISBN 0-313-26073-7.

Ghana, the first independent black African nation, has been a focus of extensive study in many areas of academic endeavor since 1957 when it attained independence from Britain.

Since independence, researchers have done an elaborate study on Ghana's population, urbanization, and rural settlement. Much of this study has been given considerable coverage in professional literature in both volume and context, but some remains relatively inaccessible to researchers and others due in part to the lack of a bibliographic guide or a single source to materials that already exist. This work comes at the most opportune time to fill this gap.

The bibliography is not annotated, but it is a comprehensive compilation of most works covering population, urbanization, and rural settlement in Ghana.

This work is arranged in sections as follows: preface, introduction, sources of papers, abbreviations, bibliographies, books, articles in periodicals and chapters in books, Ph.D. dissertations, official documents, and author index. The author index is keyed to item numbers rather than to page numbers, which makes cross-reference easier.

This bibliography will be very useful to economists, planners, and researchers interested in the formulation of a comprehensive policy on population, migration, and rural settlement in Ghana and Third World countries. It is highly recommended to libraries, students, and scholars of African and Third World studies and to researchers in demography, social sciences, and urban and regional geography. [R: Choice, Apr 88, pp. 1224, 1226]   Felix Eme Unaeze

Guinea

97.   O'Toole, Thomas E. **Historical Dictionary of Guinea (Republic of Guinea/Conakry).** 2d ed. Metuchen, N.J., Scarecrow, 1987. 204p. maps. bibliog. (African Historical Dictionaries, No. 16). $22.50. LC 87-9830. ISBN 0-8108-2000-5.

Another title in the quality series African Historical Dictionaries providing reference information for African states which may not be widely known to North Americans, this work provides an updated chronology of events to nearly the end of 1986 (for a review of the first edition, see *ARBA* 79, entry 354). The reviewer of the first edition made no suggestions for major changes, and so this edition differs from the previous one only by virtue of its updates. It is particularly gratifying to see that the compiler has not hesitated to include many French-language materials in the bibliography, since the country has a long historical relationship with France and such material is essential to the study of the region. The tool does have one flaw, however, which seems to be common to the series: the detailed map of the country is rendered, by virtue of exceedingly small print, very difficult to read.   Margaret Anderson

Guinea-Bissau

98. Lobban, Richard, and Joshua Forrest. **Historical Dictionary of the Republic of Guinea-Bissau.** 2d ed. Metuchen, N.J., Scarecrow, 1988. 210p. maps. bibliog. (African Historical Dictionaries, No. 22). $25.00. LC 87-32298. ISBN 0-8108-2086-2.

This dictionary will serve as a good source of historical information about the African country of Guinea-Bissau. It is an expansion of the first edition, which combined Guinea-Bissau and the Cape Verde Islands. The production of this work was made possible because of the personal interests and knowledge of Lobban and Forrest of Guinea-Bissau and Cape Verde. Forrest visited Guinea-Bissau, Senegal, and Portugal from 1982 to 1984.

The dictionary is arranged in various sections which contain explanations of abbreviations and acronyms, historical chronology for Guinea-Bissau, introduction, the dictionary, and a comprehensive bibliography. An appendix is also included.

This dictionary will be of interest to all libraries and research centers in African studies, and is highly recommended.

Felix Eme Unaeze

Libya

99. Lawless, Richard I., comp. **Libya.** Santa Barbara, Calif., ABC-Clio, 1987. 243p. maps. index. (World Bibliographical Series, No. 79). $47.75. ISBN 1-85109-033-9.

Like other volumes in Clio's World Bibliographical Series, this bibliography provides annotated entries covering various aspects about a given country. Richard Lawless has competently compiled information covering the history, economy, geography, politics, and culture of Libya, one of the most controversial countries in North Africa. He can be credited for avoiding the pitfalls from which some of the other bibliographies in this series have suffered. Lawless is selective and meticulous. Coverage is balanced and the informative annotations are of approximately equal length. Most entries represent materials published over a span of twenty years, with a heavy concentration on information in print covering the 1980s. This makes the bibliography quite useful to the average researcher since there is a high probability that most of the cited publications are available in American universities.

A scholar of Libyan studies may find the bibliography useful only as a complement to other more detailed and scholarly bibliographies, such as Hans Schluter's *Index Libycus*

(see *ARBA* 82, entry 359). The introduction is well written and provides an objectively balanced point of view. The author, title, and subject index is comprehensive and easy to use. This bibliography should be followed as a model by future contributors to the series. [R: Choice, Oct 88, p. 292]

Mohammed M. Aman

Mozambique

100. Darch, Colin, with Calisto Pacheleke, comps. **Mozambique.** Santa Barbara, Calif., ABC-Clio, 1987. 360p. maps. index. (World Bibliographical Series, No. 78). $55.00. ISBN 1-85109-025-8.

This is another volume in a series, all the volumes of which are formatted in the same way: a brief overview of the country's history in this century with additional information concerning both the social situation and the geography and climate. The classified bibliography is well, although chiefly descriptively, annotated, and contains materials in both Portuguese and English, with occasional items in French and German. The section devoted to languages provides access to grammars, dictionaries, and linguistic notes about some of the major languages of the country.

The authors state in their preface that the work is "the first comprehensive and critically annotated general bibliography on Mozambique to be published, and the first general bibliography since the 1940s." Their focus was "first of all on specialized bibliographies and reference works, and only then on the important or representative books and articles in a given area." They further note that by including "representative works" they have therefore listed some works, such as those defending the Mozambican National Resistance, which put forward ideas they cannot themselves support. A bibliography providing materials to outline various positions is more useful to researchers than one following a single direction or bias. [R: Choice, Nov 88, p. 456]

Margaret Anderson

Togo

101. Decalo, Samuel. **Historical Dictionary of Togo.** 2d ed. Metuchen, N.J., Scarecrow, 1987. 331p. maps. bibliog. (African Historical Dictionaries, No. 9). $32.50. LC 86-29813. ISBN 0-8108-1954-6.

Similar to the first edition published in 1976, this edition has expanded its coverage of Togo, one of West Africa's least-studied countries. There is much valuable information in this work that would not be retrieved easily elsewhere since very little study has been done previously on this fascinating country.

Arranged like the original edition in the same organizational format as the majority of others in this series, this dictionary includes a historical foreword prepared by the series editor, a note on spelling, abbreviation and acronyms, statistical tables, an important recent political chronology, and an extensive introduction, followed by the dictionary and bibliography.

The dictionary and bibliography form the two major parts of this volume. Included in the dictionary are entries on biographies of important personalities who have played a role in the sociopolitical and economic development of Togo. Others include entries of general interest and on military and religious topics. Some of the entries are more than one page in length while others are only one or two lines; the latter is suggestive of the dearth of available information on this country.

The multilingual bibliography is comprehensive, arranged in sections but not annotated. Entries are in German and French with a few in English; the bibliography should prove useful to those seeking further sources of information on Togo.

Considering the quality of work that Decalo has put into this volume, the price is fair and this work is highly recommended to libraries, scholars, and students of African history, ethnic studies, and minority relations.

Felix Eme Unaeze

ASIA

General Works

102. Basu, Asok. The Himalayas: A Classified Social Scientific Bibliography. Calcutta, K. P. Bagchi; distr., Columbia, Mo., South Asia Books, 1987. 318p. index. $48.50. ISBN 81-7074-013-4.

This is a classified bibliography of selected social sciences literature in English, published up to the first quarter of 1983, that would be helpful in area studies of the Himalayas, including Bhutan, Nepal, Tibet, and Himalayan areas of India and China.

The book has two parts. Part 1 contains the introduction, classification scheme, and author and subject indexes. Part 2 is the classified bibliography.

In part 1, the author states his understanding of area studies in relation to the Himalayas, and provides a rationale for the classification scheme used in part 2. This scheme begins with geographic areas, proceeds through a thematic

schedule based upon the eighteenth edition of the *Dewey Decimal Classification*, and finishes with some common aspects that may be used to extend the thematic notation. The scheme, printed in full, is not indexed, but it is short enough to grasp in a few minutes. There is an overly brief and unclear discussion of the sources of the entries in part 2. The author implies that some items were not examined, but does not specify which ones.

Part 2 consists of 4,417 bibliographic entries arranged according to the classification scheme designed by the author. This arrangement creates many small groups, each consisting of materials that discuss a subject as it occurs in a particular area of the Himalayas. To uncover entries on a subject as it occurs throughout the Himalayas, or all items by a particular author, one must use the indexes. Every entry in part 2 has a unique number, which is used as the reference in the author and subject indexes. Most entries give enough information to be distinctive, but are not annotated, and give no location data.

An examination of the imprint dates of the first 20 percent of the entries (884 of 4,417) revealed citation dates from 1716 to 1983.

Many errors were encountered when checking dates. Eighteen entries lacked a date. Robert S. Elegant's surname was misspelled, and could not be found in the author index under any spelling. One person's name was treated three different ways within four entries on the same page: Dattaray, Datta Ray, and Dutta Ray. Numerous typographical errors were also encountered. All this indicates that many of the entries may be unreliable. The book is in dire need of a thorough proofreading and cross-check between bibliography and indexes. The reviewer's copy is beginning to fall apart. The binding allows the book to lie open properly, but gives the impression that it is not robust enough to withstand even ordinary handling.

The whole approach *is* thoughtful of the reader's convenience. All, however, is explained in a style that refuses to make any direct commitment. One must assume, where one should simply have been told.

Recommended with caution for university libraries that support Asian area studies.

George M. Sinkankas

103. Bibliography of Asian Studies 1983. Wayne Surdam and others, eds. Ann Arbor, Mich., Association for Asian Studies, 1988. 391p. index. $30.00pa.; $60.00pa. (institutions). ISSN 0067-7159.

This valuable but late annual bibliography of Western-language publications on Asia remains as useful as earlier volumes (see *ARBA* 76, entry 257; *ARBA* 83, entry 310; and *ARBA* 86, entry 118). The most notable change from previous issues is a new typeface that, despite (on close examination) being quite legible, makes the pages look busy and seems to demand a magnifying glass. As with past issues, a foreword, explanation of entries, list of journal abbreviations and analyzed works, and a seventy-page author index accompany the 321 pages of bibliographical entries arranged by geographical region followed by countries within a region, with each subdivided by subject. Rather than the detailed table of contents of previous volumes, only page numbers of regions and countries are given, followed by a page describing the general subject headings arrangement. For libraries with a run of previous volumes, this 1983 volume is a necessary continuation. Libraries lacking such runs gain little by adding an isolated annual volume. What this serial needs is less concern about fonts and software by the editors and greater emphasis on producing computer-accessible bibliographies which cumulate several years, preferably on CD-ROM. Past printed cumulations have covered 1941-1965 and 1966-1970; therefore, anyone looking for more recent information needs to consult thirteen individual volumes.   K. Mulliner

104.   **The Far East and Australasia 1988.** 19th ed. London, Europa Publications; distr., Detroit, Gale, 1987. 1015p. $170.00. LC 74-417170. ISBN 0-946653-36-4; ISSN 0071-3791.

Simply put, this is a remarkable reference work on Asia and a short review cannot convey adequately its usefulness. The volume is divided into three main parts. Part 1 contains general survey articles about selected Asian topics. Part 2, which contains addresses and short descriptions of regional organizations (from the Asian Development Bank to UN organizations with Asian operations), is particularly useful. Part 3 contains country-specific surveys and is the heart of the book. Each of the country surveys includes sections on geography, history, and economics as well as detailed statistical tables, a directory of organizations and useful addresses, and a selected bibliography. The authors of the country surveys are, in general, widely respected scholars of Asian affairs.

The country survey of Bangladesh is typical. It is twenty-two pages in length, while others range from only a few pages for Brunei to over sixty pages for China. Appropriately for a nation with a small land area, the Bangladesh geography section is only one page. The sections on the history and economy of Bangladesh,

however, are sufficiently detailed and, more important, accurate enough to provide a solid introduction to that troubled nation. The Bangladesh statistical survey contains thirty tables of basic social and economic data. Most of the tables for Bangladesh end with 1985 or 1986 data, as do the statistical tables for many other countries. The Bangladesh "Directory" contains a brief description of the constitution and government, a listing of government officials, and names and addresses of government agencies, diplomatic missions, and trade/industry organizations. The selected bibliography, though brief, provides a good start toward further research on a variety of topics.

In short, this is a reference work which libraries, "old Asia hands," and those simply seeking an introduction to an Asian nation will find to be detailed, accurate, up-to-date, and most useful.   James T. Peach

105.   Jenkins, Esther C., and Mary C. Austin. **Literature for Children about Asians and Asian Americans: Analysis and Annotated Bibliography, with Additional Readings for Adults.** Westport, Conn., Greenwood Press, 1987. 303p. index. (Bibliographies and Indexes in World Literature, No. 12). $39.95. LC 87-23627. ISBN 0-313-25970-4.

This work on children's literature about Asians and Asian-Americans is an exemplary bibliography for teachers, librarians, and others responsible for selecting and recommending suitable reading materials for children and young adults to increase their knowledge and understanding of Asian peoples and cultures. The presence of children of all ethnic groups in American schools has made reading about other cultures an essential part of the curriculum. Public libraries serving a multiethnic community also find this bibliography a helpful readers' guide.

Of the 592 books included, 167 are concerned with Chinese and Chinese-Americans, 211 with Japanese and Japanese-Americans, 50 with Koreans and Korean-Americans, and 164 with Southeast Asians and Southeast Asian-Americans. Within each of the four major groupings there are three sections. The first is an overview of the literature for children, subdivided by folk literature, contemporary literature, and books about the ethnic group in America. Fiction and nonfiction are separately analyzed. The second is an annotated bibliography of the children's literature in different categories ranging from single tales to collections, and from fiction to nonfiction. Suitable grade levels for each book are indicated. The third is an annotated bibliography of titles for adults which suggests further background readings.

In addition to the main chapters, the book begins with a general introduction and ends with two appendices (one on criteria for selection and the other containing glossaries of Asian language terms) and separate indexes for author, title, and subject. The author index also includes the names of translators and illustrators. This bibliography is highly recommended for its quality and timeliness. [R: RBB, 15 May 88, p. 1584]   Hwa-Wei Lee

106. Shulman, Frank Joseph, comp. and ed. **Doctoral Dissertations on Asia: An Annotated Bibliographical Journal of Current International Research, Winter/Summer 1987. Volume 10, No. 1 & 2.** Ann Arbor, Mich., Association for Asian Studies, University of Michigan, 1988. 154p. index. $20.00pa. ISSN 0098-4485.

This tenth volume (see *ARBA* 86, entry 120 for a review of volume 7) continues a valuable guide to doctoral research on Asia. The availability of *Dissertation Abstracts* on CD-ROM (*Dissertation Abstracts Ondisk*) seems likely to eliminate many traditional paper bibliographies of dissertations, but this volume demonstrates why specific print guides are likely to remain as unparalleled research tools. Most important, Shulman carries his coverage well beyond the dissertations included in *Dissertation Abstracts International*. The compiler combed the world to identify doctoral dissertations relevant to Asia. His definition of Asia ranges from Afghanistan to Japan and the Philippines but is broadened to include works on Western perceptions of Asia and on Asians abroad. Beyond the nearly two thousand dissertations identified and briefly noted (or translated), introductory pages provide background on this serial, on Shulman's and others' bibliographies of dissertations on more specialized geographical areas within Asia, and a guide to obtaining dissertations. The alphabetical arrangement within divisions and the author index are particularly notable, as Shulman attempts to reconcile the form of individual Asian names consistent with the practice in each nation. With the previous volumes, no collection supporting doctoral research or Asian studies can be without this title.

K. Mulliner

India

107. **A Social and Economic Atlas of India.** New York, Oxford University Press, 1987. 254p. maps. (col.). $65.00. ISBN 0-19-562041-0.

Understanding most of the world's economically less advantaged countries and formulating workable plans for their development are activities frequently handicapped by the absence of a comprehensive, timely database. Information is collected almost randomly by a variety of marginally related agencies, resulting in a sort of statistical jungle in which it is impossible to gain much overall insight. The problem has been resolved for India by publication of this immensely detailed and surprisingly up-to-date atlas, which permits nearly all facets of the complex national picture to be seen at a glance.

An enormous labor of research and cartography, the atlas offers 246 maps (all in color) and 370 charts, combining with a rather dense text to detail nearly all aspects of India's social and economic fabric. Fittingly, particular attention is given to the ethnic and cultural components of the nation, as well as to the crucial agricultural and resource sectors, but the physical base and such nontraditional atlas subjects as tourism and foreign aid are also addressed. The data presented are satisfactorily current. Although restricted by the fact that the last general census of India – the most basic source – was taken in 1981, the compilers have been able to collect and utilize much information from as recently as 1986.

Cartographic quality is good, but little imagination has been used in the presentations, which are all basic tables, national maps at various scales, bar graphs, and pie diagrams. Detailed maps of major urban areas and some innovative ways of showing interregional relationships would have made for a more interesting volume. An overall index of sources is an unfortunate omission, and the use of modest quality paper (an endemic problem in Indian publishing) gives a slightly fuzzy image to the printing. Nonetheless, the price is attractive and the atlas should be widely used as a basic reference on one of the world's most important and complicated nations. [R: WLB, Nov 88, p. 127]

James R. McDonald

Japan

108. Collcutt, Martin, Marius Jansen, and Isao Kumakura. **Cultural Atlas of Japan.** New York, Facts on File, 1988. 240p. illus. (part col.). maps. bibliog. index. $40.00. LC 88-2967. ISBN 0-8160-1927-4.

Attractively published and well edited, this book is an excellent reference source at a low price. It provides a historical panorama with easy to absorb reference tables; a fairly detailed text that covers geography (including climate, vegetation, and geology); archaeology and anthropology; and the various aspects of culture, including court and economic life, politics, institutions, religion, art, architecture, gardens, theater, and relations with foreign countries. Cultural life is organized by historical periods. Coverage is from the prehistoric period up to the present, including 1987. There are captivating and well-chosen color photographs, and a number of informative and clear maps. The volume includes a basic bibliography; a list of Japanese rulers, including Meiji leaders and all prime ministers; a glossary; a list of illustrations; gazetteer; and an index. The book contains a wealth of information, easily retrieved with the use of the gazetteer and the index. Highly recommended for public and college libraries.

Bogdan Mieczkowski

109.   Keresztesi, Michael, and Gary R. Cocozzoli. **Japan's Economic Challenge: A Bibliographic Sourcebook.** New York, Garland, 1988. 440p. index. (Garland Reference Library of Social Science, Vol. 425). $57.00. LC 88-322. ISBN 0-8240-6608-1.

This bibliography lists 2,619 English-language books and articles on the historical, social, and cultural backgrounds of Japan's spectacular emergence as an industrial giant since World War II. Most of the items were published from the late 1970s to the mid-1980s, although a few earlier, even some pre-1940, items are included. The cut-off date is June 1987. Entries are arranged under eleven broad categories: reference books; general works on history, society, culture, and foreign relations; background to the economy; industrial policy; trade and trade relations; labor, social policy, employment, and women; the Japanese corporate world; Japanese management; productivity, quality, and quality control; dimensions of the Japanese economy; and response to the economic challenge. These categories are divided into appropriate subtopics, which are further subdivided by the nature of the publication (monograph or article). Each category is assigned a letter of the alphabet and subdivisions are assigned a second letter. Entries are numbered in sequence within each subdivision. A fifty-nine page topical locator provides detailed subject access to the entries by referring to the publication's alphanumeric code. A list of periodicals in which cited articles were published gives city and country of publication. There is also an author index. The entries give standard bibliographical information. The bibliography is strictly enumerative; there are no annotations. It is well organized and the topical locator provides rapid reference consultation. This will be a

valuable addition to the literature of the field and to subject reference collections.

Shirley L. Hopkinson

CANADA

110.   **Canada Year Book 1988: A Review of Economic, Social and Political Developments in Canada.** 120th ed. Ottawa, Statistics Canada, 1987. 1v. (various paging). illus. (part col.). maps. index. $49.95. ISBN 0-660-11801-7.

In a single volume to which over three hundred persons have contributed, we are provided with a review of the economic, social, and political development in Canada through the early and mid-1980s. Its compilers state, justifiably, that it provides "a composite portrait of Canada in all its diversity and richness" (preface). They also point out, equally justifiably, that this work is "the standard statistical reference source on Canada."

A few new features have been added to mark the 120th anniversary of the publication. At the beginning of each chapter interesting details and facts drawn from yearbooks published since Confederation (1867) have been supplied. There is also an informative table showing metric conversion, since most quantitative measures in Canada are now in metric terms. Some Canadian Imperial and U.S. units of measure have been supplied for comparison purposes. All tables, graphs, and maps supplied are clear, legible, and informative.

Margaret Anderson

111.   **Canadian Almanac & Directory 1988.** 141st ed. Toronto, Copp Clark Pitman; distr., Detroit, Gale, 1988. 1v. (various paging). index. $80.00. ISBN 0-7730-4742-5.

First published in 1848, this directory has become a standard authoritative reference about Canada (for a review of the 137th edition, see *ARBA* 85, entry 102). Now divided into seven sections, it provides names and addresses of financial institutions, libraries, museums, radio and television stations, boards of education, and universities and colleges among many others. Included also is information on municipalities, forms of address, flags and badges (with black-and-white illustrations), and a section on lawyers in private practice.

There is a slim table of contents for the seven sections followed by "Frequently Used Information," "Alphabetical Factfinder," and "Topical Table of Contents." The index listings are arranged according to the main word of the entry with some duplication of information when it is difficult to determine the main word.

Herein lies the frustration of use. Individuals outside Canada and/or unfamiliar with some of the organizations may have trouble in locating the information they seek. Better access would enhance the use of the volume.

Another Canadian reference is *Corpus Almanac and Canadian Sourcebook* (see *ARBA* 87, entry 129), which contains much of the same information. Although the index is sometimes difficult to use, *Canadian Almanac & Directory* is less expensive than *Corpus Almanac* and continues as one of the major sources of current Canadian information.

Anna Grace Patterson

112. **The Canadian Encyclopedia.** 2d ed. James H. Marsh, ed.-in-chief. Edmonton, Alta., Hurtig, 1988. 4v. illus. (part col.). maps. index. $225.00/set. ISBN 0-88830-326-2.

The first edition of this encyclopedia was published in 1985, with the help of a grant from the provincial government of Alberta. It was five years in the making, and the editors continued to refine and expand their efforts in the interim in order to produce this greatly enlarged edition. The intent of this work is to provide a national encyclopedia that will contribute to the understanding of the Canadian identity as a nation, a work which would be priced within the means of most Canadian families. The encyclopedia, therefore, does not attempt to duplicate the information found in a true general encyclopedia, although many of the subject headings are the same. There is a much greater representation of biography, with over thirty-seven hundred entries providing information on people from all periods, regions, and subject areas, while emphasizing those, including contemporary Canadians, who have made lasting contributions to Canadian society.

In addition to the biographical material, articles include the wide variety of subjects one would expect to find in an encyclopedia, with an emphasis on Canada and things Canadian. Thus, the history, geography, and economy of the country are extensively covered; flora and fauna, political themes, the arts, and ethnic groups receive similar in-depth coverage. General subjects, such as plate tectonics and heart disease, are given a general description, then related to Canada (the article on heart disease mentions work by several Canadian physicians). More extensive information on subjects of this nature will be found in a general encyclopedia.

In comparing this work to existing works like *The New Encyclopaedia Britannica* (see entry 44) and *The Encyclopedia Americana* (see *ARBA* 84, entry 26), one is struck by the quantity, variety, and excellent quality of the artwork. Neither *Britannica* nor *Americana* offers as many illustrations, nor is there the liberal use of color that there is here. In addition, many of the photographs in the above-mentioned works appear dated. The *Canadian Encyclopedia* contains over two thousand illustrations, many in full color, which include photographs, reproductions of works by well-known artists, original art especially commissioned for this edition, maps, charts, graphs, and diagrams. The color and clarity of the illustrations are outstanding; the paper used in the encyclopedia is of exceptionally high quality, very white, with a finish that lends itself well to color reproduction.

In addition to the superb artwork and comprehensive coverage of its intended subject, the encyclopedia has succeeded in its effort to be extremely current. Statistics utilize census data from 1986, and there is even a photograph taken at the 1988 Winter Olympic Games in Calgary (although the textual material was set prior to the Games and therefore does not include this year's results).

This edition has not only been updated, but revised and expanded. Over 90 percent of the entries have been changed, some to a much greater degree than others. Subjects such as politics and the arts have had the most revision; biographies and entries for populated places or religious groups needed only minor adjustment. Expansion of the work has resulted in the addition of 1,700 new articles, for a total of nearly 10,000 entries, as well as over 350 new photographs and 150 other illustrations, for a total of 695 additional pages. The index is four times larger than in the previous edition and contains numerous cross-references for ease of use.

The reviewer compared entries for the Haida Indians in the *Canadian Encyclopedia* and the *Encyclopedia Americana*. *Americana* had the longer article under the specific entry. The article described the geographic location, dialects, way of life (both now and before the arrival of the white man), economy, dwellings, social customs, art, and religion of the tribe. The bibliography was dated (latest article: 1955). The *Canadian Encyclopedia* article provided some of the same information, but contained several *see* and *see also* references (potlatch, Northwest Coast Indian art, and native people). These entries contained extensive material on the Haida people and illustrated the similarities and differences among the various tribes in political and social structures, customs, and art. Bibliographic references under the *see* and *see also* references were both extensive and current.

Publication of this encyclopedia was an enormous undertaking; the editors are to be congratulated for their thoroughness and dedication to comprehensiveness. On the whole, the selection of articles reflects a truly Canadian identity, as it was meant to do, and the information presented is both accurate and current.

Shirley Lambert

113. **Canadian Statistics Index 1988.** Rosemary McClelland, ed. Toronto, Micromedia, 1988. 359p. $225.00 (with suppl.). ISSN 0832-655X.

114. **Canadian Statistics Index 1988 (Supplement).** Rosemary McClelland, ed. Toronto, Micromedia, 1988. 267p. $225.00 (with annual). ISSN 0832-655X.

With volume 4, *Canadian Statistics Index* (*CSI*) becomes an annual publication providing bibliographical access to publications of Statistics Canada and of other public as well as private sources of Canadian statistics. Sources include both monographs and periodicals which feature statistics of significant general interest in both English and French. Volume 4 covers new and updated publications issued between June and December 1987 with a paperback supplement covering annual titles received January through May 1988. *CSI* is divided into five sections. The abstracts section provides bibliographic information on publications and descriptive abstracts which include information on time periods and geographical areas covered. The subject section lists documents under selected Library of Congress subject headings. The categories section is designed to provide broad subject access to documents (e.g., by city, social welfare). The title section lists descriptive titles, excluding such general designations as "annual report." The publishers section provides addresses of publishers.

In addition to bibliographic information, *CSI* provides ordering information for the publications listed, most of which are available in either microfiche or paper from *CSI*'s publisher, Micromedia, Ltd.

CSI's broad coverage makes it an essential resource for those who use Canadian statistics and should be acquired by libraries and agencies needing this data.   Gari-Anne Patzwald

115. **Quick Canadian Facts: The Canadian Pocket Encyclopedia.** 39th ed. Surrey, B.C., Canex, 1988. 486p. illus. maps. index. $6.50pa. LC 66-9362. ISBN 0-9692048-5-X; ISSN 0316-1943.

The first edition of this annual was in 1946; in 1981 it was sold to Canex Enterprises. The

format has remained almost the same year after year, but each edition does seem to get slightly larger as, of course, there is one more year's information to deal with. This handbook is a cross between the *Canada Year Book* (see entry 110) and the *Canadian World Almanac* (International Press, 1988). It is also cheaper than either of them.

Quick Canadian Facts begins with tables indicating the holidays celebrated in Canada; weights and measures; kilometers between cities; time zones; maps, currency; and data on banking, taxes, governments (federal and provincial), health and welfare, sports, trade, manufacturing, tourism, history, etc. The sources for the tables indicate Statistics Canada or Canada Commerce; other sources are the information centers of the various provincial governments. (The back issues, should you need them, are available from Micromedia, a well-known Canadian vendor of microfiche reprints.) New to this issue is material about the 1988 Winter Olympics held in Calgary, Alberta.

Since I last looked at *Quick Canadian Facts*, it has cleaned up its many typographical errors, and it has reduced its leading for a clearer, all-round cleaner look. Still, it confuses library numbers: while it does give the LC card number, it claims that the National Library of Canada's card number is 317.105, when in fact it is this book's Dewey Decimal number. And for some reason the material in the book is copyrighted 1985, even though there is material in it dealing with 1988.   Dean Tudor

COMMONWEALTH OF NATIONS

116. **The Commonwealth Yearbook 1988.** 2d ed. By Foreign and Commonwealth Office. London, Her Majesty's Stationary Office; distr., Lanham, Md., UNIPUB, 1988. 551p. illus. (col.). maps. index. $43.00pa. ISBN 0-11-580237-1.

Formerly the *Yearbook of the Commonwealth*, this is the second edition of the annual published under the current title. It traces the evolution of the Commonwealth and describes its organization. The major part of the work deals with the individual member countries and their dependent territories. The geographical, political, economic, and educational structures of each country are described. A short history of each one together with a summary of its constitution is given. A list of major government office holders is also included. At the end of the book is a chapter of tables covering such subjects as geographic areas, population, economic, social, and educational statistics. It also includes time differences between Commonwealth countries, their national days, and a bibliography of publications (including British parliamentary papers) relating to the Commonwealth. Most of the statistics are drawn from sources available elsewhere, such as the publications of the United Nations and the World Bank. The *Europa Year Book* (see *ARBA* 86, entry 91) and the other Europa publications such as *Africa South of the Sahara* (see *ARBA* 88, entry 113) contain as detailed information on individual countries. The *Statesman's Year Book* (see *ARBA* 86, entry 92) also contains comparable descriptions. The major advantage of the *Commonwealth Yearbook* is that it draws together this information in a single work and has more detail about the organization's administration.   Christine E. King

EUROPE

Denmark

117. Miller, Kenneth E., comp. **Denmark.** Santa Barbara, Calif., ABC-Clio, 1987. 216p. maps. index. (World Bibliographical Series, Vol. 83). $45.00. ISBN 1-85109-042-8.

Perhaps this bibliography of popular reading materials will help break down the view that Denmark equals Copenhagen and Copenhagen equals Denmark. True, over one-quarter of the Danes live in Copenhagen and 84 percent live in cities. However, there is a great deal more to this interesting country, as a reader will quickly learn if he or she follows up with just a few of the suggested items. Overall, Miller followed the series pattern in compiling this bibliography. His selections appear to favor a higher percentage of older titles (pre-1980) than is typical of the series. "Political Parties and Elections" appears to have the greatest number of post-1980 titles: sixteen out of twenty-nine. In most sections, seldom are more than 40 percent of the items recent titles. In my opinion this is a reflection of Miller's good judgment and knowledge of the literature. Certainly in a selective bibliography (in this case 730 items), some of the reviewer's favorite titles will not be on the list. Only two omissions are worth noting. One is the lack of any reference to the controversy that took place when Mogens Glistrup attempted to establish a new type of university in the mid-1970s. The other is the omission of the two-volume *Norse Discovery of America* by Anne Ingstad (Oslo University Press, 1985). The latter omission is surprising in view of the number of books on the Vikings that are on the list (twenty-two). None of the listed items is more comprehensive. There are sections on the Faroe Islands and Greenland; most people are not aware that both are part of Denmark. In all, this volume is worth adding to reference collections with an interest in Denmark or the Nordic countries. [R: Choice, Oct 88, p. 294]

G. Edward Evans

Gibraltar

118. Shields, Graham J., comp. **Gibraltar.** Santa Barbara, Calif., ABC-Clio, 1987. 100p. maps. index. (World Bibliographical Series, Vol. 87). $27.50. ISBN 1-85109-045-2.

This book, like the tiny British dependent territory it chronicles, is small and compact. It is a selective, annotated bibliography on all aspects of Gibraltar's history and culture intended mainly for the informed general reader but also useful for researchers and tourists of a serious mind.

The 260 entries for articles, books, government documents, maps, and dissertations are arranged in twenty-eight sections, such as guidebooks, flora and fauna, politics, economy and finance, engineering, and environment and planning. The largest sections, history and the Anglo-Spanish dispute, are also more selective than other sections. Dissertations are illogically put in a separate section rather than in appropriate subject sections and are exclusively British. Some Canadian and U.S. dissertations, although few in number, are as relevant as the ones listed.

Entries have ample, clear, and frequently critical annotations and sometimes include references to additional works. Items on the Anglo-Spanish dispute are identified as representing British, Spanish, Soviet, objective, or a variety of viewpoints. Approximately 30 percent of the items were published in the 1980s and about 50 percent in the 1950s-1970s. The remainder are classic or unusual works from the eighteenth century through the 1940s.

A twenty-page introduction traces the history of the sieges, sovereignties, modern development, and recent diplomatic troubles of the Rock. It gives a succinct and informed sketch of the essential features and issues of Gibraltar today, although the question of the joint use or internationalizing of the airport (p. xxiii) could have had more explanation. Also included are a chronology, a map, and an author/title/subject index. [R: Choice, Oct 88, p. 297]

Joyce Duncan Falk

Great Britain

119. Jackson, Paul. **British Sources of Information: A Subject Guide and Bibliography.**

New York, Routledge, Chapman & Hall, 1987. 526p. $79.50. LC 86-26125. ISBN 0-7102-0696-8.

For people interested in any aspect of Great Britain, *British Sources of Information* is an excellent introductory guide. It is divided into four parts. The first part, "Select Bibliography," comprises about half the volume. There is a further subdivision into forty subject areas (e.g., "Cities," "History," "Religion," and "Women"). Each section of the bibliography attempts to list works that are standard reference works or introductions to the subject, readily accessible, or recent outstanding publications. No attempt is made to be comprehensive, but generally the selection of works is quite good for introductory purposes. Part 2, "Periodicals, Journals, and Magazines," lists the names and addresses of various publications under twenty-four subjects (e.g., "Economics," "Film and Video," and "Law"). Particularly useful is the "Press" section which supplies the addresses of the national newspapers along with a selection of the locals. In part 3, "Sources of Information," the addresses for various organizations and institutions are arranged by subject along with addresses for museums, galleries, and institutions of higher learning. Finally, part 4, "Teaching Resources," lists the addresses and subject interests of various publishers, film distributors, video workshops, and audiovisual suppliers. As a convenient and unique ready-reference source for introductory bibliography and addresses concerning Great Britain, this book is quite useful. Its one serious drawback is the rather high price of the volume given its size.

Ronald H. Fritze

Netherlands

120. King, Peter, and Michael Wintle, comps. **The Netherlands.** Santa Barbara, Calif., ABC-Clio, 1988. 308p. maps. index. (World Bibliographical Series, Vol. 88). $52.50. ISBN 1-85109-041-X.

Following the format of the series, this highly selective (1,025 entries), critical, annotated bibliography covers all aspects of the country's history, culture, and current conditions. It serves the general reader and is a good beginning for the specialist. Rather than summarizing the long, complex history of the Netherlands, the authors, both specialists in Dutch studies at the University of Hull, use the introduction to explain the problems of selectivity and their emphases on the economy, sociopolitical divisions, hydraulic engineering, and demography. It is a serious mistake not to index the introduction in the author/title/subject

index; there is no reference in the index to the important explanations in the introduction (e.g., why the Frisians are not included in the section on minorities [p. xviii]).

One wishes for a more logical order of the thirty-five sections; for example, philosophy and the history of ideas would be better placed near history and religion rather than far away between the arts and sports. One-third of the sections are helpfully subdivided, which should also have been done with the one on social conditions, to separate historical studies from those of the current scene. The history section covers topics from early modern primary sources, to classics by Huizinga, Geyl, and Boxer, to a 1987 article on historiography, and the legal system section ranges from a fourteenth-century jurist to an American translation of the business corporation code. And, yes, there are serious works on tulips, windmills, and wooden shoes. The annotations are descriptive and often critical, describing works as standard, classic, impressive, authoritative, brilliant, inaccurate, lightweight, lurid, amusing, etc. There are also a map and a short glossary.

This excellent bibliography entices the tourist, new resident, technician, businessperson, or scholar to learn more about its subject. [R: Choice, Nov 88, p. 462]

Joyce Duncan Falk

Poland

121. Kanka, August Gerald. **Poland: An Annotated Bibliography of Books in English.** New York, Garland, 1988. 395p. index. (Garland Reference Library of the Humanities, Vol. 743). $47.00. LC 88-4064. ISBN 0-8240-8492-6.

Kanka is a librarian at Macomb Community College. His bibliography on Poland is more comprehensive than R. Lewanski's *Poland* (see *ARBA 85*, entry 108) but it does not include bibliographies published in journals, such as J. Hapak's bibliographical essay "Solidarity and Its Antecedents" (*Choice* [February 1983]) or those found in *The Polish Review* (Polish Institute of Arts and Sciences of America, 1956-). Books covered were published from the eighteenth century to 1986. Works not devoted exclusively to Poland (e.g., in economics by P. T. Wiles, G. Grossman, and the present reviewer) are not included, indicating existence of a much larger font of information about Poland than ever covered in a bibliography. The present volume has a good coverage, and is arranged alphabetically by topic, from aeronautics to *wycinanki* (ornamental paper cut-outs). It includes also general works, plus author and title indexes. History and Poles abroad receive special attention. The annotations are clear and informative. Recommended for all college libraries, larger public libraries, and all libraries with ethnic and international coverage.

Bogdan Mieczkowski

Sweden

122. Sather, Leland B., and Alan Swanson, comps. **Sweden.** Santa Barbara, Calif., ABC-Clio, 1987. 370p. maps. index. (World Bibliographical Series, Vol. 80). $55.00. ISBN 1-85109-035-5.

The eightieth (there are eighty-four in print) of a series which will eventually include all the world's countries, this annotated bibliography offers a comprehensive view of one of Europe's most successful and admired nations. Designed to interest both the serious student and the more casual observer, these works aim to present a broad range of information, from historical and geographic background to economic aspects, literature and the arts, and such "lifestyle" subjects as folklore and cuisine. References are principally to English-language materials and include both books and important journal articles; there are also a list of newspapers and a particularly useful section "Professional Periodicals." A twenty-four-page introduction provides a helpful overview of the country and the influences that have shaped its character. As in other numbers of this series, there is a good map, and the book's utility is enhanced by an extensive cross-referencing system and a detailed (eighty pages) index.

The diversity of the material is suggested by the fact that there are forty-four major subject headings (for a total of 1,015 entries). Many of these are necessarily limited to a few citations; but in all cases, key works seem to have been included. There is a certain bias toward historical materials (145 entries, plus the historical aspects of other areas); but this does not seem excessive. It seems clear that the compilers have gone to considerable length to provide comprehensive coverage across the academic spectrum and to unearth materials that appear as sections of larger works.

Attractively presented and well-edited, this volume is an excellent starting point for anyone interested in learning more about Sweden at any level. It should form part of many basic reference collections. [R: Choice, Sept 88, p. 88]

James R. McDonald

Ukraine

123. Kubijovyč, Volodymyr, ed. **Encyclopedia of Ukraine. Volume II: G-K.** Toronto, published for the Canadian Institute of Ukrainian Studies, Shevchenko Scientific Society (Sarcelles, France), and the Canadian Foundation for Ukrainian Studies by University of Toronto Press; distr., Englewood, Colo., Libraries Unlimited, 1988. 737p. illus. (part col.). maps. $125.00. ISBN 0-8020-3444-6.

The first of the five projected volumes, *Encyclopedia of Ukraine. Volume 1: A-F*, was published in 1984. Edited by one of the most prominent Ukrainian scholars, Volodymyr Kubijovyč, with the assistance of the editorial board and subject editors, the *Encyclopedia of Ukraine* serves as a complementary volume (for English-speaking people) to *Entsyklopediia ukrainoznavstva*, a multivolume Ukrainian encyclopedia initiated some forty years ago by the Shevchenko Scientific Society. The first volume contains approximately 2,800 entries with over 450 black-and-white illustrations, 5 color prints, 83 maps, and numerous diagrams, charts, and other illustrative material. Volume 2 contains approximately 3,000 entries, 450 black-and-white illustrations, 3 color photographs, and 40 maps. Some one hundred scholars from around the world contributed articles. Longer articles are signed and frequently contain bibliographies of relevant works published in several languages. The somewhat modified system of Library of Congress transliteration has been used in most of the text, with the exception of linguistics. A map of Ukraine and gazetteer are bound separately.

This encyclopedia is a first-rate source book to the history and culture of Ukrainians, both in Ukraine and abroad. However, the younger generation of Ukrainian scholars is not well represented among the contributors. Also absent are non-Ukrainian scholars, some of them outstanding specialists in certain areas of Ukrainian history and culture. It is hoped this lack will be remedied in the forthcoming third volume.

Taking into consideration the scope of this work and its overall excellent execution, these few critical comments may be of a minor nature. This remarkable encyclopedia is highly recommended to all scholars as one of the most important works on Ukrainian matters published in the last decade.

Bohdan S. Wynar

INDIAN OCEAN

124. Gotthold, Julia J., with Donald W. Gotthold, comps. **Indian Ocean.** Santa Barbara, Calif., ABC-Clio, 1988. 329p. maps. index. (World Bibliographical Series, Vol. 85). $55.00. ISBN 1-85109-034-7.

This annotated bibliography contains 804 citations for books, articles, atlases, maps, and bibliographies on the Indian Ocean, including the Red Sea and the Persian Gulf. The compiler's stated purpose was to provide a selected list of items on the history of the discovery of the ocean, its scientific revelations and resources, and its strategic military and political importance, in sufficient number to enable a student or researcher to gain a reasonably comprehensive knowledge of the area. Entries are arranged alphabetically by title under 109 subtopics, which are grouped in eleven broad subject or form categories from history to Indian Ocean island groups. The annotations summarize the content of each item, point out special features and special approaches to the subject matter, and comment on the special value of the publication in reference to the study of the ocean itself. An introduction defines the parameters of the ocean; describes its physical characteristics, climate, natural resources, vegetation, and animal life; and gives a short history of its exploration and an assessment of its importance as a military area. There are a chronology of important events in or related to the area, an eighty-nine page index of authors' names, place names and subjects in one alphabet, and one black-and-white map. It is evident that the research has been thorough, that the compiler's goal has been accomplished, and that this work meets the usual high standards of the Clio World Bibliographical series. It is highly recommended for subject collections. [R: Choice, Dec 88, p. 628]   Shirley L. Hopkinson

LATIN AMERICA AND THE CARIBBEAN

General Works

125.   Grieb, Kenneth J. **Central America in the Nineteenth and Twentieth Centuries: An Annotated Bibliography.** Boston, G. K. Hall, 1988. 573p. index. (Reference Publications in Latin American Studies). $95.00. LC 87-28240. ISBN 0-8161-8130-6.

This is an annotated interdisciplinary bibliography of monographic works from about 1810 through 1980 with an emphasis on the social sciences. The author states in his preface that "this volume is intended to facilitate research about and knowledge of Central America and its nations by providing a broad but selective guide to books dealing with Central America since independence."

The quality of the entries is predicated on subject knowledge and experience and Kenneth Grieb has both. Among his earlier works were

five monographs about Latin America and *The Research Guide to Central America and the Caribbean* (see *ARBA* 86, entry 139). Grieb's annotations are generally balanced and as complete as necessary. Since many of the titles listed were written in Spanish, the English-language abstracts give the volume utility for laypersons and scholars of many disciplines.

The scope of this bibliography includes the five core countries—Guatemala, Honduras, El Salvador, Nicaragua, and Costa Rica. Belize is included although its recent cultural heritage is essentially British. The Hispanic nation of Panama is omitted, which is unfortunate because in this century Panama symbolizes the political volatility that is Central America and has geographical proximity. The author does have sound historical reasons for omitting Panama. In colonial times that country was ruled from Bogota in what is now Colombia. The nations covered by this bibliography were governed from Guatemala City or Antigua as an *audiencia*, subordinate to the viceroyalty at Mexico City.

Kenneth Grieb's regional bibliography is nevertheless an excellent one, recommended for all collections interested in an unstable but important part of our hemisphere. [R: Choice, June 88, p. 1534]   T. P. Williams

126.   **Handbook of Latin American Studies: No. 48: Humanities.** Prepared by a number of scholars for the Hispanic Division of the Library of Congress. Dolores Moyano Martin, ed. Austin, Tex., University of Texas Press, 1988. 764p. index. $65.00. LC 36-32633. ISBN 0-292-73041-1.

This is the standard bibliographic reference serial for Latin American bibliography. First established in 1935, it has continued to provide comprehensive coverage of Latin American scholarship in the fields of the humanities and social sciences. Rapid growth in the literature by the 1960s prompted the editors in 1965 to begin issuing separate volumes for the humanities and social sciences in alternating years. The present volume focuses on the literature of the humanities in the fields of art, film, history, literature, music and philosophy.

The handbook has never remained static, and it continues to make changes and improvements. Noticeable in this volume are an expanded table of contents and the elimination of certain standard subject headings in the subject index. Recent themes noted by the editors include: an explosion of literature on Latin American film and Spanish American theater, expanded writings on Caribbean history, and new attention to topics such as disease and epidemics, the changing role of the Catholic Church, and Ecuadorean history.

One problem the editors have yet to deal with is the increasingly dated nature of most of the entries. A survey of the sections on music and Brazilian history revealed the following: 22 percent of the citations were to literature published in 1982, 26 percent to literature published in 1983, 25 percent to literature published in 1984, and 15 percent to literature published in 1985. Less than 2 percent referred to literature published since 1985. While this was excusable in the days when Latin American acquisitions were in a disordered state, it is less excusable today in an era of Latin American approval plans and reputable American suppliers. If the handbook is to maintain its important role in Latin American scholarship, a dramatic improvement in the currency of citations is certainly needed.   Brian E. Coutts

127. Macdonald, Roger, and Carole Travis. **Libraries and Special Collections on Latin America and the Caribbean: A Directory of European Resources.** 2d ed. Atlantic Highlands, N.J., published for Institute of Latin American Studies, University of London by Athlone Press; distr., Atlantic Highlands, N.J., Humanities Press, 1988. 339p. index. (University of London, Institute of Latin American Studies Monographs, 14). $75.00. LC 87-24114. ISBN 0-485-17714-5.

This directory, which is described in the introduction as the second edition of the *Directory of Libraries and Special Collections on Latin America and the West Indies*, by Bernard Naylor, Laurence Hallewell, and Colin Steele (London, Athlone Press, 1975), provides information on 468 British and European libraries and special collections with significant holdings on Latin America and the Caribbean. It is a complete revision of the earlier work, and its coverage has been expanded to include Europe as well as the United Kingdom. Emphasis is still on the United Kingdom, with 195 entries devoted to its libraries, and 273 entries covering nineteen other countries. Information was gathered by questionnaire, and in the case of the United Kingdom, by personal visits if no response to the questionnaire was received. In the case of Europe, brief entries for known Latin American collections were made from published sources, or the existence of a collection was merely noted, if the questionnaire was unanswered. As a result, information for libraries of the United Kingdom is more complete than that for many European libraries.

The geographical area covered is defined as "the whole of the mainland south of the Río

Grande together with the reasonably adjacent islands" (p. 2). Data provided include name of library, address, telephone and telex numbers, head librarian, access, services offered, and a brief description of the library's history and holdings. Emphasis is on printed matter, although materials in many formats are included. No effort was made to collect information about manuscript collections, but it is included when libraries provided it. A thorough index lists libraries, subjects, and special named collections. This publication will be a useful addition to any library supporting research in Latin American studies.   Ann Hartness

128. **Statistical Yearbook for Latin America and the Caribbean. Anuario Estadistico de America Latina y el Caribe.** 1986 ed. By Economic Commission for Latin America and the Caribbean. New York, United Nations, 1987. 782p. $65.00pa. ISBN 92-1-021024-7; ISSN 0251-9445. S/N E.S.87.II.G.1.

Statistical materials of any quality or extent have long been difficult to obtain for Latin America. This volume's ninety-four indexes of social and economic development and 269 tables of measurements and absolute values for various economic and social series present the most recent refinements of data for the twenty-four nations in the region. Some tables have information from 1960, 1970, and 1975, as well as the more normal 1979 or 1980 to 1985. An appendix gives estimated values for fourteen series for 1986.

The book is organized into five parts. The introduction and technical notes are essential for understanding the quality and limitations of the numbers in each table. The list of sources is organized by topics, then by country. The third and fourth sections are the indexes and tables noted above. The final section is the appendix for 1986. All text and table headings are in both Spanish and English.

This is a major reference resource for persons interested in the area during recent times. Its value cannot be too highly stated. Even so, it illustrates how difficult it still is to obtain comparable, reliable figures on many aspects of Latin America's economic and social development. Recommended for libraries with strong Latin American and business interests.
                                        Paul E. Hoffman

Argentina

129. Horvath, Laszlo, comp. **Peronism and the Three Persons: A Checklist of Material on Peronism and on Juan Domingo, Eva, and Isabel Peron and Their Writings in the Hoover**

Institution Library and Archives and in the Stanford University Libraries. Stanford, Calif., Hoover Institution Press, 1988. 170p. (Hoover Press Bibliographical Series, 71). $16.95pa. LC 88-14851. ISBN 0-8179-2712-3.

This checklist of books, pamphlets, serials, and archival material on the Peróns and of "Peroniana" produced by them or by Argentine government agencies representing them, reflects the collections of a library with strong holdings on this subject. Its significance lies in the major role played by Juan Domingo Perón (and, by extension, his two wives) in twentieth-century Argentine history and in the continuing influence of his political and ideological legacy on contemporary politics.

The unannotated list provides full bibliographic information, including pagination, for each item cited and indicates its location within the Stanford University libraries. The six sections (works on Juan Perón and *Peronismo*, and on Eva and Isabel Perón, and works by each one of them) cite a variety of primary and secondary sources in various languages. The former include writings and speeches of the Peróns, government plans and statements of policy, statistical compilations, texts of laws, and similar publications, while the latter include a potpourri of bibliographies, scholarly monographs, and polemical writings by a variety of observers of and participants in Argentine politics of the period and since.

The lack of numbered entries makes use of this checklist more cumbersome than it need be, complicating the task of referring back to items located once. The work also lacks indexes of any sort. Since this work covers the holdings of a single library system, it should be used in conjunction with related bibliographies if complete coverage is desired, such as Gabriela Sonntag's *Eva Perón Books, Articles, and Other Sources of Study: An Annotated Bibliography* (Seminar on the Acquisition of Latin American Library Materials, 1983). Since much of the material cited is primary source material, this work would be most useful to a specialist doing in-depth research in this field, although interpretative monographs are certainly to be found by others willing to scan the bibliography in order to identify them.   Ann Hartness

Bolivia

130. Yeager, Gertrude M., comp. **Bolivia.** Santa Barbara, Calif., ABC-Clio, 1988. 228p. maps. index. (World Bibliographical Series, Vol. 89). $41.00. ISBN 1-85109-066-5.

Each volume in the World Bibliographical Series seeks to present an expression and flavor of the country and an appreciation of its national aspirations. This volume on Bolivia provides information on the country and its people, geography, tourism, travelers' accounts, flora and fauna, prehistory and archaeology, history, politics, foreign relations, constitution and local government, population, employment, economy, banking, agriculture, social conditions, health, languages, religion, education, literature, art, music, and other brief sections on different aspects of this nation. There are also sections dealing with culture, bibliographies, reference works and encyclopedias, dictionaries, and indexes of authors, titles, and subjects.

The entries are numbered to facilitate access via different means. Within the different sections, each citation identifies the topic and provides a bibliographic citation to the pertinent publication where the information can be located. Each entry is annotated, some with just a line, while others of some interest have a well-developed, short paragraph. While most of the citations are to relatively current works, there are a few important ones that date back to the early twentieth century. The introduction provides a brief narrative (approximately five pages) concerning Bolivia. After the indexes, there is a one-page map that is of little utility.

This particular volume on Bolivia is a useful introductory work that provides the layperson with a broad array of information concerning this South American country. It can serve as a useful access device to more important and reliable information on Bolivia. It is recommended for most libraries, especially larger public libraries and four-year academic libraries. Others would do well to rely upon a strong encyclopedia, or other travel guides that provide sources of further information.

Roberto P. Haro

Chile

131. Bizzarro, Salvatore. **Historical Dictionary of Chile.** 2d ed. Metuchen, N.J., Scarecrow, 1987. 583p. maps. bibliog. (Latin American Historical Dictionaries, No. 7). $55.00. LC 87-4681. ISBN 0-8108-1964-3.

Much has transpired in Chile since the first edition of this historical dictionary appeared in 1972. Most significant was the coup d'état of 11 September 1973, which led to the overthrow and murder of the socialist president, Salvador Allende Gossens. Since 1974, Chile has existed under the military dictatorship of Augusto Pinochet Ugarte.

The author of this revised edition, Salvatore Bizzarro, a professor of romance languages at Colorado College, has traveled extensively in Latin America, including several research trips to Chile, and is the author of a book on Pablo Neruda.

This edition is almost twice as long as the first and adds hundreds of new entries including an extended sketch of President Pinochet, a revised and expanded entry on Salvador Allende, an entry for the Constitution of 1980, and many other new and revised entries. A sampling of the "A" section revealed the following added entries: agrarian reform, air force, air transport, alcabala, Fernando Alessandri, entries for members of the Allende family (including one for Isabel Allende Lloren, Salvador's cousin and a noted novelist), the army, automobile industry, and avion rojo.

Like the first edition, there are biographical sketches of all of Chile's many presidents, sketches of Chile's ten constitutions, and useful entries on Chilean newspapers and periodical press. The volume is complemented by a fifty-page bibliography. It would make a useful addition for all Latin American collections. [R: Choice, May 88, p. 1378]

Brian E. Coutts

Cuba

132. Pérez, Louis A., Jr., comp. **Cuba: An Annotated Bibliography.** Westport, Conn., Greenwood Press, 1988. 301p. index. (Bibliographies and Indexes in World History, No. 10). $45.00. LC 87-28017. ISBN 0-313-26162-8.

Prepared by one of the better historians of modern Cuba, this bibliography of 1,120 annotated entries is intended for the general reader and for the scholar working outside his or her area of specialization. In selecting items, the compiler gave preference to what he considered to be major works that are comprehensive, up-to-date, and likely to provide bibliographical leads for more detailed study. Where possible, English items are used, but Spanish-language books, articles, and journals are nonetheless heavily represented because much of the best literature on Cuba is in that language.

Similar in organization to the ABC-Clio national bibliography series, this work has forty-five major headings that cover topics such as geography, history, women, forestry, the arts, mass media, and bibliographies. Entries under each heading are arranged alphabetically by title, except for travelers' accounts, which are arranged by date of original publication. An analytical index of authors, topics, and titles of books concludes the work.

The large number of Spanish-language items cited will probably present a difficulty for the general library user both for understanding the titles and for access (via interlibrary loan in many places) and use. Still, this is an important reference work that belongs in libraries whose users have an interest in Cuba, whatever their language capabilities. [R: Choice, Sept 88, pp. 76, 78]

Paul E. Hoffman

133. Suchlicki, Jaime. **Historical Dictionary of Cuba.** Metuchen, N.J., Scarecrow, 1988. 368p. bibliog. (Latin American Historical Dictionaries, No. 22). $39.50. LC 87-28406. ISBN 0-8108-2071-4.

Jaime Suchlicki has prepared a valuable and useful new reference book that brings together in a single volume essential historical facts and events, as well as information on prominent leaders in Cuban history, culture, and economic development, from pre-Columbian times to the present. This work has added value because special emphasis has been placed on the Cuban Revolution and the changes that have taken place in Cuba since Fidel Castro assumed power in 1959.

The work is easy to use, given its format. It includes a list of abbreviations, a section on chronology that provides a year-by-year outline of important events, the dictionary of alphabetical entries, a good bibliography, and appendices in four parts: (1) a brief description of the country, (2) diplomatic relations with other nations, (3) Cuban membership in international organizations, and (4) a list of Cuban presidents. The entries in the dictionary range in length from a few lines to several pages, such as the entry for Fidel Castro Ruz. For personal entries, years of birth and, where appropriate, death, are given. Artists, writers, and musicians are included and major works are identified.

This new reference work will be an important addition to the collections of reference departments in academic and public libraries. It is easy to use and authoritative, and provides quick access to pertinent information. There are some cross-references, *see also* guides, and other referral notes. There are a few items that are either omitted, or not well identified; for example, there is no separate entry for the Caribs, a neolithic warlike people who controlled about one-third of the island when Columbus arrived in Cuba. Aside from such minor exceptions, this remains an important new book that should be purchased by all academic and large public libraries. [R: Choice, Nov 88, p. 470; RBB, 1 Oct 88, pp. 240-41]

Roberto P. Haro

Dominica

134. Myers, Robert A., comp. **Dominica.** Santa Barbara, Calif., ABC-Clio, 1987. 190p. maps. index. (World Bibliographical Series, Vol. 82). $40.50. ISBN 1-85109-031-2.

One of the smallest (155th out of 178) and least populus (166th) nations in the world, Dominica has long been of special interest to scholars, visitors, and its own residents for its rich human and natural histories. From a literature said to be in a dozen languages (p. xiii), the author has selected 493 items in three languages (481 in English, 10 in French, 2 in Carib) for annotation. Many items are articles or portions of regional studies, since Dominica has seldom been the object of monographic study.

As is customary in volumes in this series, an effort was made to include both classic and more recent studies that might be readily available in larger U.S. libraries and that would adequately introduce the researcher to the unique features of a country's history, geography, and modern culture and life. In this case, entries are especially numerous for the island's human and natural histories, the sources of its distinctiveness. Of the categories usually found in volumes in this series, three (banking, sciences and technology, recreation) are omitted because nothing could be found on them, and one (public administration and local government) has few entries because of a lack of literature. Most topics also include cross-references to items annotated under other headings.

An introduction to the history and present condition of Dominica, a map, and an analytical index complete the apparatus of this useful bibliography. Recommended for larger libraries with special interest in the Caribbean. [R: Choice, Oct 88, p. 294]

Paul E. Hoffman

Mexico

135. Camp, Roderic Ai. **Who's Who in Mexico Today.** Boulder, Colo., Westview Press, 1988. 183p. (Westview Special Studies in Latin America and the Caribbean). $45.00. LC 87-29823. ISBN 0-8133-7397-2.

This new biographical work on prominent Mexicans is a most welcome addition to the information books in this area. The author has expended considerable effort to gather pertinent information about nearly four hundred prominent living Mexican leaders from different sectors of society—entrepreneurial, cultural, military, political, religious, and social. Groups that have been traditionally excluded from previous biographical works on Mexico have been given special attention in this book, especially women, prominent clergy, and opposition political leaders from the left and right. The focus on Mexican women is particularly significant and of added value to the user.

The arrangement of the book is quite straightforward. There is an opening preface that provides the user with the author's intention and rationale for the inclusion of the biographees. This is followed by a brief section on how to use the book, abbreviation of sources for information, and a list of acronyms. The biographees are listed in alphabetical order. Under the biographee, information is provided on date and place of birth, schooling or educational background, elective political offices, if any, political party offices or candidacies for elective office, appointive governmental posts, leadership of any national interest group, private sector positions in Mexico or elsewhere, familial ties and important professional and personal friendships, military activities, if appropriate, selected national awards and prizes, and additional sources of information.

The author has done an excellent job of researching his subjects and providing useful information for the user. A few minor additions such as cross-references or a quick-check index would be desirable but are not essential. Overall, this is an important new biographical reference book that belongs in any library with an interest in Mexico. Strongly recommended for all four-year college and university libraries and major public and special libraries dealing with Mexico. [R: Choice, Oct 88, pp. 284, 286]

Roberto P. Haro

Paraguay

136. Nickson, R. Andrew, comp. **Paraguay.** Santa Barbara, Calif., ABC-Clio, 1987. 212p. maps. index. (World Bibliographical Series, Vol. 84). $45.00. ISBN 1-85109-028-2.

Of the eighty-four volumes published in the World Bibliogrpahical Series, this is the thirteenth to focus on a Latin American country. The compiler, a lecturer in Economics at the University of Birmingham, has previously written *Paraguay, Power Game* published by the Latin American Bureau in 1980. Since Paraguay is one of the least written-about republics in Latin America, this is one of the shorter volumes in the series. It includes some six hundred annotated entries organized into thirty-three chapters. The longest of these focuses on history (125 entries), immigrants, emigrants, and minorities (48 entries), and the economy (42 entries). In the chapter on history, forty-two books and articles are in Spanish, two are in

German, and one is in Russian. Since Paraguayan history and culture have been dominated by three lengthy dictatorships (Dr. José Rodriguez de Francia, 1814-1840; Carlos Antonio Lopez, 1844-1862; and General Alfredo Stroessner, 1954-present) and two devastating wars (War of the Triple Alliance, 1865-1870; and the Chaco War, 1932-1935) much of the English-language literature has focused on these people and events. Little has been written on most other topics.

In his excellent introduction, Nickson laments the recent difficulties of doing research in Paraguay and suggests topics in need of research. Hopefully, this bibliography, and the popularity of the recent film *The Mission*, will stimulate renewed interest in one of our least-known neighbors. [R: Choice, Nov 88, p. 466]

Brian E. Coutts

Puerto Rico

137. Fowlie-Flores, Fay, comp. **Index to Puerto Rican Collective Biography.** Westport, Conn., Greenwood Press, 1987. 214p. bibliog. (Bibliographies and Indexes in American History, No. 5). $39.95. LC 87-8374. ISBN 0-313-25193-2.

This index to collective biography covers Puerto Ricans and others closely associated with Puerto Rican history and development from colonial times to the present. It indexes 146 titles, including twenty-two English-language sources, thereby providing access to Puerto Rican biography to those who do not read Spanish. Since coverage of Puerto Ricans in standard U.S. biographical reference tools is generally very limited, the inclusion of these sources is welcome.

The publications indexed include books published before 1986 containing a minimum of three biographies, with no limit on the maximum number. Books of collective biography, collections of essays, histories, and anthologies were indexed. Information provided for each biographee includes significant dates, profession and/or reason for importance, and sources of biographical data. Unlike the other two indexes to Puerto Rican collective biography discussed below, this work cites the exact location (volume, when applicable, and page numbers) of biographies, and indicates the existence of illustrative material. Its format is readable and easy to use.

Although there were no indexes of Puerto Rican collective biography until recently, this is the third one published since 1984. The other two are Sara de Mundo Lo's excellent *Index to Spanish American Collective Biography,*

Volume 3: The Central American and Caribbean Countries (see *ARBA* 85, entry 116) and *Indice biográfico: apuntes para un diccionario de puertorriqueños distinguidos* (San Juan: Colección HIPATIA, 1985). The former, which indexes 186 titles, covers about one hundred in the title under review. It is arranged by subject with an index of biographees, in contrast to the *IPRCB*, which is arranged by biographee. *Index to Spanish American Collective Biography* and *Index to Puerto Rican Collective Biography* complement each other in biographical coverage, while the *Indice biográfico* is more limited. *Index to Puerto Rican Collective Biography* is a significant contribution to this field. College and university libraries as well as those serving Hispanic communities will want to add it to their reference collections.

Ann Hartness

Venezuela

138. Sullivan, William M., comp. **Dissertations and Theses on Venezuelan Topics, 1900-1985.** Metuchen, N.J., Scarecrow, 1988. 274p. index. $30.00. LC 87-13111. ISBN 0-8108-2017-X.

This bibliography lists 1,504 dissertations from French, German, British, Irish, Dutch, and, predominantly, North American universities. Dissertations presented at universities in Venezuela itself or in other Latin American countries, except Mexico, are not included.

Divided into sixteen sections, the bibliography covers a wide variety of subjects related to Venezuelan geography, history, literature, etc. There are many sociological and scientific studies, with those related to geology particularly numerous. Given the importance of the petroleum industry in Venezuela, on the other hand, it is surprising that "Petrology and Mineralogy" is one of the shortest sections in the book. The list of sources for this bibliography comprises some two hundred items. Some of the entries are annotated, mostly by quoting from the abstracts or the introductions of the dissertations.

There is a good, comprehensive author index. The subject index is less satisfactory. For example, the names of seven former presidents appear in entry 1027. But one would search the subject index in vain for two of them, Isaias Medina Angarita and Carlos Delgado Chalbaud. Moreover, in the annotation itself the latter is called "Chalbaud Delgado," a curious mistake in a work of this kind.

There are a few other mistakes. German words are erratically capitalized or sometimes misspelled (e.g., *diagnostiche* in entries 116 and

117). More careful copyediting should have eliminated these distracting minor mistakes, which blemish an otherwise excellent work.

Though this is a purely descriptive guide to dissertations and theses that undoubtedly are of varying significance and quality, the compiler's diligence has made it a comprehensive tool that should prove useful and even indispensable to students and researchers in this special field.

Siegfried Ruschin

MIDDLE EAST

General Works

139. Adams, Michael, ed. **The Middle East.** New York, Facts on File, 1988. 865p. illus. maps. index. (Handbooks to the Modern World). $45.00. LC 86-29274. ISBN 0-8160-1268-7.

This handbook on the Middle East contains valuable information on the countries of the region, bringing together factual and analytical articles on each country. The factual information is similar to that published in *The Middle East and North Africa* (see *ARBA* 86, entry 145) and *The Worldmark Encyclopedia of Nations* (Wiley, 1988). In addition to fifteen Arab countries treated in the handbook, Iran, Israel, and Turkey are also included. North African countries, except Libya, are not included in the "Basic Information" section, and none of the North African countries is included in the "Comparative Statistics" section. The statistics are taken from secondary sources such as United Nations publications, Lloyds Bank economic reports for individual countries, *Middle East Economic Digest*, and IMF *International Financial Statistics*.

In part 2, each of the nineteen countries and the Maghreb (Algeria, Morocco, and Tunisia) is treated in detailed analytical articles written by prominent authorities and scholars. Each article concludes with a select, brief list of readings that should be helpful for further research. Separate articles, about fifteen pages each, concentrate on political affairs (e.g., Arab nationalism, Zionism, East-West rivalries); economic issues (e.g., industrialization, labor organization, technological change, foreign aid, the importance of petroleum); and social issues (e.g., Westernization, communications, the position of women in the Middle East). Of particular interest is the treatment of the Palestine problem from Arab and Zionist points of view.

This handbook should be a valuable reference tool for any type of library, especially for one whose daily job responsibilities include Middle Eastern affairs. The information is current, the treatment is concise, the maps and index are helpful, and the price is right. [R: BR, May/June 88, p. 47; C&RL, July 88, pp. 351-52; LAR, 15 July 88, p. 408]

Mohammed M. Aman

140. Blake, Gerald, John Dewdney, and Jonathan Mitchell. **The Cambridge Atlas of the Middle East & North Africa.** New York, Cambridge University Press, 1987. 124p. maps. bibliog. $75.00. LC 87-6548. ISBN 0-521-24243-6.

This Cambridge atlas is an excellent introduction to and overview of this complex and often misunderstood part of the world. It is particularly extensive, covering such staples as physical environment, demographics, culture, and economics. In addition, an entire section is devoted to "special topics," providing unique information on such focal points as the Straits of Hormutz, the Turkish Straits, Gilbralter, the Suez Canal, military strength, and political conflicts. The explanatory comments accompanying the data for each topic are clearly written and include key references to more detailed information, beyond the sources in the bibliography. Although there are none of the expected full-color maps, businesspersons, politicians, soldiers, and scholars will find this authoritative atlas useful, informative, and valuable. [R: RBB, Aug 88, p. 1898]

James F. Mattil

141. **The Cambridge Encyclopedia of the Middle East and North Africa.** Trevor Mostyn and Albert Hourani, eds. New York, Cambridge University Press, 1988. 504p. illus. (part col.). maps. index. $39.50. LC 88-10866. ISBN 0-521-32190-5.

This volume, containing articles by eighty-two academics and journalists considered to be international experts in their individual fields, is intended to provide a general, comprehensive introduction to the history, society, and culture of a region spreading west to east from Morocco to Afghanistan, and north to south, from Turkey to Djibouti and Somalia. The volume is divided into six parts: "Lands and Peoples," "History," "Societies and Economies," "Culture," "The Countries," and "Inter-State Relations." The historical section spans the period from the ancient Near East to the beginning of the World War II; in "Societies and Economies" the emphasis is on changes in the areas of agriculture, banking, industry, energy production, and society, including those wrought by increasing urbanization, migration, legal systems, and trade unions, as well as on the changing role of women, and new developments in education and communications. Under "Culture" we find discussions of the three major religions which saw their beginnings in this area, classical and modern Arabic, Hebrew, Persian and Turkish literatures, the arts, music and dance, and Islamic science and medicine. In the section devoted to the individual countries the emphasis is on current and recent developments. Also included in this section are articles on three "Peoples without a Country": Armenians, Kurds and Palestinians. The final section focuses on such topics as the role and activities of the "Great Powers" in the Middle East, International Islamic movements and Institutions, inter-Arab relations, and the Iran-Iraq War.

The volume is reasonably well provided with illustrations and maps, but the maps, although clear and easy to read, could benefit from being larger, at least one-half page in size. It is unfortunate the general maps of the entire region are presented only as endpapers, where the pale color wash used in the printing makes them harder to read than one might wish. Most of the articles include brief English-language bibliographies, and though some of the items listed date from the 1960s, they do, for the most part, represent good, standard, still useful titles. Comparable in quality to *The Cambridge Encyclopedia of Latin America and the Caribbean* (see *ARBA* 87, entry 135), this book is a good general introduction to the history, culture, and politics of an important international region of the world; an introduction useful both for the general public and for use by students in the senior levels of secondary schools and undergraduate programs.   Margaret Anderson

Iran

142. Navabpour, Reza, comp. **Iran.** Santa Barbara, Calif., ABC-Clio, 1988. 308p. maps. bibliog. index. (World Bibliographical Series, Vol. 81). $52.00. ISBN 1-85109-036-3.

The author has prepared an excellent bibliography of approximately eight hundred selected and annotated items about Iran. He has followed the general guidelines of the World Bibliographical Series, aimed at an audience ranging from the informed general reader to the scholar who wishes to obtain background information for more specialized research. Priority has been given to publications that are still in print and widely available. This survey is extremely thorough, covering special features and topical issues of contemporary Iran. It includes geography and geology, democracy, religion, social structure, politics, military, economy, education, science and technology, literature, arts, etc. Current issues such as the Gulf War, foreign relations, the revolution, and Ayatollah

Khomeni are given particular emphasis. [R: Choice, Nov 88, pp. 464, 466]

            Assad A. Tavakoli

Israel

143. Purvis, James D. **Jerusalem, the Holy City: A Bibliography.** Metuchen, N.J., American Theological Library Association and Scarecrow, 1988. 499p. index. (ATLA Bibliography Series, No. 20). $42.50. LC 87-4758. ISBN 0-8108-1999-6.

A holy city for three major religions, the site of friction and tension since its earliest days, Jerusalem symbolizes both peace and conflict and has been used as an example of humanity's noblest aspirations and basest actions. The writings on this special city are voluminous, covering a myriad of topics and a plethora of opinions. James D. Purvis's *Jerusalem* attempts to gather and organize much of this literary treasure trove.

The bibliography is divided into eight major sections, each covering a historical or religious epoch. These eight are further subdivided, occasionally by historical event, most frequently by important religious site. For example, part 6, "Christian Jerusalem," is divided into numerous subsections such as "Jerusalem in the New Testament," "The Church of the Holy Sepulchre," "The Church of St. Stephen," and others. Most of the entries are in English; French, German, and Italian make up the bulk of non-English-language materials cited. There are a few items in Hebrew (with titles translated into English), but Purvis elected not to include Arabic-language materials because of accessibility problems.

In spite of the preponderance of entries in English and other Western European languages, accessibility remains a major problem. The bibliography lists over five thousand items and although the bibliographic information is sound and the division into chapters and parts somewhat helpful, basically this is a very long, not always selective, list. The fact that there are no annotations severely diminishes the bibliography's usefulness. The wide range of topics addressed and the tremendous variety among the sources cited also mediate against truly effective or efficient utilization. The addition of author and subject indexes offsets some of the access difficulties; however problems in the indexes point up another difficulty with the work. Muslim history is not given the attention it deserves, either in the chapter subdivisions or in sheer number of pages devoted to the Islamic experience of and in Jerusalem. Part 7, "Jerusalem as a Muslim City," has but one subdivision;

it takes a careful reading of the subject index to extract the rich and varied historical moments (not to mention architectural masterpieces) that make up Muslim Jerusalem. Both Christianity and Judaism, but especially Christianity, stand out in much greater relief in the pages of this bibliography. [R: Choice, Sept 88, p. 88; LJ, 15 June 88, pp. 52-53]   Ellen Broidy

Saudi Arabia

144. Clements, Frank A., comp. **Saudi Arabia.** rev. ed. Santa Barbara, Calif., ABC-Clio, 1988. 354p. maps. index. (World Bibliographical Series, Vol. 5). $55.00. ISBN 1-85109-067-3.

The first edition of this work appeared in 1979 and listed 789 entries (see *ARBA* 81, entry 372). The expanded edition lists nearly twice as many and provides an update of publications through 1986, with one or two early 1987 entries being included. Particularly useful in this new edition are the sections on the economy and finance and banking, listing items published in the 1980s and providing fairly current information for Western businesspersons considering investment and other commercial ventures in the country. With Saudi Arabia's steadily rising political and economic preeminence in Arab affairs and in the Middle East in general, this updated bibliography is a timely publication.

Margaret Anderson

4 Economics and Business

GENERAL WORKS

Acronyms

145. **Business Acronyms: A Selection of Approximately 25,000 Acronyms, Initialisms, Abbreviations, Contractions, Alphabetic Symbols, and Similar Condensed Appellations....** Julie E. Towell, ed. Detroit, Gale, 1988. 414p. $60.00. ISBN 0-8103-2549-7; ISSN 0899-3726.

For the second time Gale has raided its comprehensive work, *Acronyms, Initialisms, and Abbreviations Dictionary* (*AIAD*), to produce a subject-specific collection (*Computer and Telecommunications Acronyms* [see *ARBA* 87, entry 1645] was the first). Not a complete raid; some newly collected terms appear in this volume. The scope is international, with translations provided. Not all entries are in common use: "many are listed for their historical interest." Terms can be searched either by acronym or by meaning; many entries have a mnemonic code indicating the source of the information. All of the new entries will be included in the next edition of *AIAD* and so on into the future, with *Business Acronyms* staying one step ahead. To guarantee accuracy, standard reference works were consulted, but more often than not the terms surfaced from a variety of outside sources; having a line on them makes this work uniquely authoritative. The editors repeat several times that "considerable effort was made to ensure complete coverage in a broad range of business-related fields." And so they have. It remains to be seen how this first edition will be received; most libraries already own *AIAD*. The decision to purchase rests on whether certain business acronyms not in *AIAD* are missed; if nearly all of them can be found in *AIAD* except for a few obscure ones, then the decision is clear-cut. Recommended for business-related special libraries. [R: RBB, 1 Dec 88, p. 620]

Bill Bailey

Atlases

146. **The Original Cleartype Business Control Atlas 1988.** Maspeth, N.Y., American Map, 1988. 172p. maps. index. $16.95 spiralbound. ISBN 0-8416-9700-0.

This fine little book can best be described as a "poor man's commercial atlas and marketing guide." It contains excellent 8½-by-11-inch state and province maps for the United States and Canada, maps showing such valuable detail as county lines, all towns with population over one thousand, and boundaries for standard metropolitan statistical areas (SMSAs). Additional maps show world time zones, U.S. area codes and world direct dial codes, and U.S. zip codes. It is worthwhile for these maps alone, which are a convenient size, easily reproducible, and hard to find elsewhere. However, far more than maps is available here. There is a good deal of statistical information for each SMSA. Population totals are given, with a breakdown by age and major ethnic group. Number of households and household income figures are here, as well as retail sales figures, divided by major retail grouping.

For libraries owning the much larger *Commercial Atlas and Marketing Guide* (see *ARBA* 87, entry 150), this will not be a necessary or desirable purchase. However, for the small library, or the small business, this should be considered a standard reference tool.

Diane Richards

Bibliographies

147. Bick, Patricia Ann. **Business Ethics and Responsibility: An Information Sourcebook.** Phoenix, Ariz., Oryx Press, 1988. 204p. index. (Oryx Series in Business and Management, No. 11). $32.50. LC 87-23191. ISBN 0-89774-296-6.

Bick's *Sourcebook* is an annotated bibliography of business ethics arranged by broad subject areas that are divided into more specific topics. It also includes a listing of other sources of information such as research centers, lists of major journals, and organizations concerned with business ethics. The "Core Library Collection," which concentrates on reference materials such as indexes, abstracts, directories, and bibliographies, will be particularly helpful to a library with limited resources. An appendix includes the text of the important "Sullivan Principles"; the work concludes with author, title, and subject indexes.

Bick introduces each subject area with a brief definition or description and, where appropriate, Library of Congress subject headings and classification numbers. She includes materials on business ethics, corporate social responsibility, self-regulation, international business, South Africa, employee rights, discrimination, the consumer, and the role of organized religion in business.

Bick omits or superficially covers some major contemporary ethical issues in business such as Acquired Immune Deficiency Syndrome, women's health in the workplace, computerization, and substance abuse. The few references to these which are included are not well indexed. On the other hand, international business and multinational corporations are given very strong coverage, thus filling a gap left by Jones and Bennett in their *Bibliography of Business Ethics 1981-1985* (E. Mellen, 1986).

This *Sourcebook* could be strengthened by a more detailed preface explaining the author's method of identifying sources and her criteria for choosing subject areas and works. A more developed subject index would improve the work.

On the whole this work is a useful addition to the growing body of literature on business ethics, particularly for the inclusion of material on the international dimensions of business. [R: Choice, Oct 88, p. 284]

Joan B. Fiscella

148. Strauss, Diane Wheeler. **Handbook of Business Information: A Guide for Librarians, Students, and Researchers.** Englewood, Colo., Libraries Unlimited, 1988. 537p. illus. index. $37.50. LC 88-23093. ISBN 0-87287-607-1.

The *Handbook of Business Information* is an impressive entry into the burgeoning field of business reference "how-to" type manuals. What distinguishes this work from the more casual sources is its clear, well-articulated focus. As the title indicates, this study is geared towards "librarians, students, and researchers." Commendably, the author successfully meets this formidable challenge.

The handbook is arranged into two parts, "Formats of Business Information" and "Fields of Business Information." Part 1 provides coverage of eight major categories, including basic business reference sources, government information and services, looseleaf services, and vertical file collections. Part 2 covers nine categories, including money, credit and banking, real estate, and stocks. All categories are further outlined in an expansive table of contents. The book employs twelve appendices ranging from "Free Vertical File Materials for Business Collections" to "Ten Key Monthly Federal Periodicals and the Statistics They Contain." Additionally, there are over 150 illustrations (including many unique and original diagrams) and an extensive index providing author, title, and major/minor subject coverage.

The author has correctly identified a niche which this title expertly fills. As stated in the preface, this work is not inclusive. Its purpose is to "give librarians, students, and other researchers a grounding in business basics and to identify, describe, and in many instances illustrate the use of key information sources." By creating a methodological context, adeptly suggesting research strategies, and skillfully providing business reference examples, this well-polished guide belongs on all business reference shelves with its respective complements, Lorna M. Daniells's *Business Information Sources*, revised edition (see *ARBA* 86, entry 158) and Michael R. Lavin's *Business Information: How to Find It, How to Use It* (see *ARBA* 87, entry 190).

Peter B. Kaatrude

149. **UNCTC Bibliography 1974-1987.** New York, United Nations, 1988. 83p. illus. $12.00 pa. ISBN 92-1-104218-6. S/N E.87.II.A.23.

This bibliography presents an overview of the work along with the complete bibliographic references of the United Nations Centre on Transnational Corporations (UNCTC). The Centre serves as the secretariat to the Commission on Transnational Corporations, which was established in 1974 as an intergovernmental subsidiary body of the UN Economic and Social Council (ECOSOC). The Commission's main functions are to discuss and keep under review all issues related to transnational corporations

(TNCs), to draft the UN Code of Conduct on TNCs, and to advise ECOSOC on all matters relating to TNCs.

The references are listed in seventeen chapters covering the different aspects of UNCTC's activities, such as code of conduct; international arrangements and agreements; international standard of accounting and reporting; national policies, laws, and regulations; contracts and agreements between TNCs and host countries; manufacturing and extractive sectors; service sectors and transborder data flows; technology transfer; political, social, cultural, and environmental impact; TNCs in South Africa and Namibia; East/West industrial cooperation; individual countries; activities of the Centre and its joint units; reports of the sessions of the commission; and the *CTC Reporter* and other journals.

The references are divided into sales documents and documents and articles. Brief content notes are given for the sales documents along with a few reviews. Titles of the references are in boldface type for easy browsing. The number of pages, the sales number, and the price are provided along with pictures of the covers of some of the publications. Since there is no subject index, the user must depend on browsing. Ordering information for the publications is provided in the back of the book.

Another chapter presents an introduction to UNCTC and its work. This bibliography is a useful reference tool for learning about the activities of UNCTC.   Anne C. Roess

Biographies

150. Sobel, Robert, and Bernard S. Katz, eds. **Biographical Directory of the Council of Economic Advisers.** Westport, Conn., Greenwood Press, 1988. 301p. index. $49.95. LC 86-14984. ISBN 0-313-22554-0.

The President's Council of Economic Advisers (CEA) was created by the Employment Act of 1946. Since that time forty-five distinguished economists have served on the council. This volume contains a short (two to nine pages) biographical essay on each member. The standard personal details regarding birth, education, employment, and dates of service on the council are presented, as is a distillation of key professional accomplishments and ideological bent. The authors, primarily academic economists, do an admirable job of placing each of the forty-four men and one woman council members in historical context. This is a tightly edited, concisely written, accessible work. The essays are largely free of technical jargon, demonstrating that at least some economists are literate in the

English language. If there is a weakness, it is that the introductory essay describes only the events leading up to the creation of the CEA. A reader interested in the organizational and political factors that have shaped the council over the years must construct it through the lives of its individual members.   Bruce Stuart

Dictionaries

151. Pennant-Rea, Rupert, and Bill Emmott. **The Pocket Economist.** 2d ed. New York, *The Economist* and Basil Blackwell, 1987. 252p. illus. bibliog. $24.95; $9.95pa. ISBN 0-631-145-869; 0-631-15591-0pa.

There is probably no other reference book on the "dismal science" of economics that is simultaneously so well written, humorous, and informative. Many readers will want to read this delightful reference from cover to cover. From the first entry (*above par*) to the last (*zero-sum game*) the authors have combined accuracy, good humor, and social commentary into concise but informative definitions of the jargon of economics. Written with an unmistakably British flair, the definitions of distinctly American terms are frequently among the most insightful. My own very unscientific estimate is that there are less than a thousand entries, but the entries have been carefully selected and include many of the most commonly used and most commonly misunderstood economic concepts. The revisions and new entries in the second edition clearly indicate that the authors are aware that economics is a dynamic and evolutionary discipline. Thus, while this reference work is not intended to be comprehensive, it has much to offer. In short, the dismal science will seem much less dismal to users of this highly informative reference.   James T. Peach

Directories

152. Bard, Ray, and Susan K. Elliott. **The National Directory of Corporate Training Programs.** 2d ed. New York, Doubleday, 1988. 373p. bibliog. index. $27.50; $14.95pa. LC 88-298. ISBN 0-385-24202-6; 0-385-24203-4pa.

The National Directory of Corporate Training Programs is intended primarily for new college graduates, new graduates of MBA programs, and "career changers." For individuals from any of these groups, or anyone else anxious to embark on a managerial career, *The National Directory* is a source of information on training programs for professionals at more than 300 major organizations (the Library of Congress among them).

The entry for each organization in *The National Directory* includes a company profile, lists of qualifications and functional specialties (e.g., accounting, engineering, marketing) sought in job candidates, and descriptions of training programs. Information on recruitment and placement practices, salaries and benefits, and company contacts is provided as well as information on special opportunities such as assignments abroad. Interspersed throughout the company listings are interviews with successful training program graduates, recruiters, training managers, university career-placement advisers, and corporate executives—individuals capable of providing sound advice to job-seekers.

Company listings in *The National Directory* are based on information supplied by the organizations themselves in questionnaires, follow-up telephone calls, personal interviews, and recruitment literature. Some information came from outside sources, including *Fortune* rankings and College Placement Council salary reports.

The National Directory is well organized and easy to use. An introduction provides a helpful overview of company-sponsored training explaining how it differs from traditional school situations. In the main section of the work, training programs are listed by company, in alphabetical order from Abbott Laboratories to Zenith. A useful bibliography on resume preparation, interviewing, career strategies, etc., follows. Training program, industry, and geographic indexes appear at the end. A highly affordable reference tool, *The National Directory* can supplement other sources of information on employment opportunities such as Dun's *Career Guide*. [R: LJ, 15 Nov 88, p. 67; RBB, 15 Dec 88, pp. 694-95]

Lydia W. Wasylenko

153. **Directory of American Research and Technology 1988: Organizations Active in Product Development for Business.** 22d ed. New York, R. R. Bowker, 1987. 763p. index. $199.95. LC 21-26022. ISBN 0-8352-2417-1; ISSN 0886-0076.

The number of research and technical organizations in the United States is very fluid, covering a vast array of functions and technologies. For this reason, and also because of continuing corporate changes, Bowker now publishes this large directory annually. Its revised title and purpose were described earlier in *ARBA* 87 (see entry 167). This edition lists 11,642 organizations, 977 of which have never been listed before. Since the 1986 issue listed 10,991 organizations, the turnover is quite

apparent. The directory is available on Pergamon Orbit Infoline, but it is updated only once per year when the new edition of the directory is published. The anticipated amount of usage will then be a factor in the purchase of this volume versus searching online, since the continuous update capabilities of online services is not taken advantage of and the information in both versions is identical.

Robert J. Havlik

154. Korsmeyer, Pamela, ed. **The Development Directory: A Guide to the US International Development Community.** Madison, Conn., Editorial Pkg., 1988. 333p. $60.00pa. LC 88-16250. ISBN 0-945939-01-9.

The aim of the directory is to help coordinate development efforts by providing information about the individual members of the international development community. It is based on questionnaire data and followup contacts. The main alphabetical list of organizations—limited to those in the United States—contains address, categorization by type, names of principal officers, purpose, sectors of activity, geographic area(s) of involvement, and publications. Part 1 also includes separate lists of organizations by type, by sector, and by the geographic area of interest, as well as publications by sector and by geographic area. Finally, there is a list of organization personnel. Part 2 provides three lists of individuals active in international development: the main list gives position, address, affiliation, publications, experience, sectors, geographic areas, and comments; additional lists are by sector of the individuals' proficiency and activity, and by geographic area. An appendix shows the new listing and correction forms used in the questionnaire. The directory is useful to those interested in specific publications or in publishing, for cross-information and contacts, and for coordination of development efforts. [R: LJ, 1 Sept 88, p. 162]

Bogdan Mieczkowski

155. Levine, Michael. **The Corporate Address Book: How to Reach the 1,000 Most Important Companies in the U.S.** New York, Putnam, 1987. 268p. index. $8.95pa. LC 87-11162. ISBN 0-399-51384-1.

The Corporate Address Book is a reasonably priced desktop directory, aimed at those who correspond with corporate America. The introduction offers three scenarios for applying the company listings: "Consumer Complaints," "Idea Suggestions," and "Employment."

Approximately one thousand U.S. corporations are profiled. Each corporate entry includes name and address, business line, list of key officers, revenues, net worth, number of employees, and names of U.S. subsidiaries. Companies are arranged alphabetically within thirty general categories. An index is provided that lists parent company names, but omits names of subsidiaries. Inclusion in this directory is admittedly aided by *Barron's, Business Week, Forbes, Fortune,* and *The Wall Street Journal.* Nowhere is this more apparent than in the appendices, where several *Fortune* magazine ranking lists are featured.

All in all, this reference source should be of use to those who need a "quick look up," without entailing the expense of a *Million Dollar Directory Series* (see *ARBA* 87, entry 176), *Standard & Poor's Register of Corporations, Directors and Executives* (see *ARBA* 87, entry 182), or *Directory of Corporate Affiliations* (see *ARBA* 85, entry 177). Of course, coverage in *The Corporate Address Book* does not attempt to rival the well-established directories. Recommended for the occasional corporate address chaser, who will not go wrong at this price.

Peter B. Kaatrude

156. National Directory of Corporate Public Affairs 1988: An Annual Guide.... Arthur C. Close and Gregory L. Bologna, eds. Washington, D.C., Columbia Books, 1988. 579p. index. $65.00pa. ISBN 0-910416-68-0.

The *National Directory* is a unique reference book that provides an excellent profile of the public affairs programs at the most significant corporations in the United States. It consists of four main sections. The first and most important section is an alphabetical listing of some fifteen hundred companies involved in public affairs programs. Each entry includes the name of the company, its main business, the address of its headquarters, its Washington, D.C., office address, its political action committee, its corporate foundation and contributions, the names and titles of its public affairs personnel and their activities, and other relevant facts such as publications. The second section is an alphabetical listing of the personnel mentioned in the first. In the third section the companies are arranged by the type of business they are engaged in, while in the fourth they are arranged geographically.

This directory is a useful tool for any group interested in tracking the public affairs and political activities of the major corporations in this country.

Elie M. Dick

157. Rosenbaum, Virginia K. **Takeover Defenses: Profiles of the Fortune 500.** Washington, D.C., Investor Responsibility Research Center, 1987. 227p. $175.00pa. ISBN 0-931035-13-9.

The antitakeover defenses of 424 Fortune 500 firms are presented. The ones omitted include cooperatives, privately held firms, and foreign subsidiaries. The act of taking a company private is in itself a major antitakeover device, but firms that have done so are not covered here.

Each firm included is profiled as to ownership (percent owned by institutions, percent by officers and directors, and major individual shareholders), antitakeover provisions, and severance provisions for major executives forced out by a merger. A glossary defines the various types of defense, such as *greenmail* or *poison pill.* Information is taken from SEC documentation and other public sources, and companies were permitted to comment on their own entries. The appendices consist of several tables; the first table shows whether or not each company uses each of seven possible antitakeover ploys. The next seven tables redundantly list each ploy in turn and the companies that use them. There are five more tables listing additional possible merger provisions and the companies that use them. Large corporations and major investment firms may want to buy this book, but most libraries will find this small volume too pricey for their needs.

Susan V. McKimm

158. Seminars Directory, 1989: A Guide to Approximately 10,000 Seminars and Workshops Held in the United States and Canada.... Detroit, Gale, 1988. 973p. index. $125.00. ISBN 0-8103-2842-9.

This directory lists approximately ten thousand seminars given by two thousand vendors. The information is obtained from Seminar Clearinghouse International, and compiled from "publicly held seminars, external training consultants, self-study courses and training films."

Each entry includes the title of the seminar; the vendor's name, address, and telephone number; description of topics; length, cost, and location; and an evaluation of the seminar (if there are ten or more evaluations submitted by seminar participants). There are thirty-one general subject areas, including administration, computers, engineering, environment, finance, government, health care and medicine, industry, management, science, and small business. The larger subjects are divided into subsections.

There is also an alphabetical listing of each subject, subsection, topic, and *see* reference. The directory, additionally, indexes the seminars by title and by vendor.

This will be a useful tool for those libraries with professional development or continuing education collections. Its currency and comprehensiveness will supplant those titles that are limited to seminars dealing with one or two subjects.   Mary Jo Aman

159.   Silverstein, Lorne, comp. and ed. **Alberta Business Who's Who & Directory.** 3d ed. Edmonton, Alta., Alberta Business Research, 1987. 896p. illus. $59.50. ISBN 0-9692200-0-6.

A directory of business information on Alberta, two-thirds of the text of this work is biographical information on over one thousand business leaders, including information on position, education and career background, association memberships, and personal life (sometimes including home address). Photographs accompany many entries. Also found is information on financial institutions; banks; computer consulting firms; securities and stock exchange; accountants; engineers and architects; exporting; government at the federal, provincial, and municipal levels; and native business organizations. Advertising is included and there is an advertisers' index towards the back of the text. There is a cross-index to companies with their executives names. The text would be more useful if there were a subject and possibly a name index at the back of the book leading to a page reference.

Generally this directory contains business information that is not found in other directories on Alberta or on Canada. The directory would be of use to Canadian business collections, especially any that concentrate on western Canada.   Lorna K. Rees-Potter

160.   **Ward's Business Directory of U.S. Private Companies.** Belmont, Calif., Information Access, 1988. 3v. maps. $800.00pa./set.

This directory set, now in its twenty-seventh edition, presents noticeable changes from previously reviewed editions (see *ARBA 86*, entry 188 and *ARBA 88*, entries 180-81). Immediately apparent are the chronic title alterations. Whereas before, *Largest U.S. Companies*, *Major U.S. Companies*, and *Major International Companies* were in vogue, now *U.S. Private Companies* is found on each of the three volumes comprising the twenty-seventh edition.

Missing is the category for international company listings. In fact, unless a U.S. parent company has a foreign office, international company coverage is nonexistent. Even for those U.S. companies with foreign affiliates, information is sparse and found only in the "Ranked by S.I.C." category. Oddly enough, *Ward's* maintains in the introduction that inclusion "includes domestic and foreign public and private companies [with] at least $.5 million in annual sales." Additional cuts include the "Special Features" where three sections have been deleted, including the "30 Financial Indices for Public Companies."

Overall arrangement is now much more logical. Volume 1 lists private and public companies with annual sales of $11.5-plus million and volume 2 lists those with annual sales of $.5 to $11.5 million. Volume 3 is now devoted exclusively to ranked companies by sales size within industry. Private company coverage has also increased from 75,749 in the last edition to 85,357 in the recent edition.

Given these changes, it appears as though *Ward's* is now more focused on what it does best, providing brief listings for a large number of U.S. private companies. That strength is now all the more obvious due to the aforementioned changes. *Ward's* is therefore recommended as a unique and comprehensive corporate directory set. [R: WLB, June 88, pp. 144-45]
                    Peter B. Kaatrude

161.   Weiner, Richard. **Professional's Guide to Public Relations Services.** 6th ed. New York, American Management Association, 1988. 483p. illus. index. $95.00. LC 87-47829. ISBN 0-8144-5932-3.

This edition greatly expands the coverage of the fifth edition (see *ARBA 86*, entry 878), especially in the areas of research and electronic communications. Weiner feels it is increasingly important for the modern public relations professional to purchase services beyond what can be performed in-house. This unique directory not only tells the publicist where to find such services, but gives extensive advice on how to purchase and use them. Weiner includes useful comments and opinions regarding each service, and includes only these he feels are of good quality, though he acknowledges that he may have occasionally overlooked others that are equally good. The increased coverage of research sources will make this edition more useful to libraries than the previous one, particularly in its coverage of books, periodicals, and online information services. Pricing information has been updated, and useful information on negotiating contracts is inserted throughout the book, when relevant. Beyond being merely a directory, this book contains a wealth of nitty-gritty information for the practitioner that is unavailable in any other handy reference book.
                    Susan V. McKimm

Handbooks and Yearbooks

162. The Consultant's U.S. Statistical Guide and SourceFinder. rev. ed. Glenelg, Md., Consultant's Library, 1987. 75p. bibliog. $39.00pa. ISBN 0-930686-31-4.

A publisher's brochure claims that this work is "the only comprehensive fact book and source finder for the consulting profession" and "the consultant's ultimate power tool." The slim volume does not live up to this extravagant billing, but it does have some useful features.

The chapter "Books on Consulting" is a bibliography containing seventy citations. Names and addresses of publishers whose works appear in the bibliography are given in "Book Publishers on Consulting." "Computer Software for Consultants" identifies twenty-nine computer programs for functions such as accounting, client-tracking, and forecasting.

Names and addresses of fifty-one remarkably diverse organizations are provided in "National Consultant Organizations." Given the range of the list, which covers everything from financial and management consultants to bridal and food service consultants, it is difficult to view consulting as a unified profession about which one can generalize. Business conditions for consultants (e.g., demand for services, competition, fee structures) undoubtedly vary considerably across specializations.

Several chapters of *The Consultant's Guide* seem less than substantive. These include "Cassettes" (twelve citations), "Professional Periodicals" (five citations), and "Certification and Accreditation" (list of seven certification/accreditation programs).

"Consulting Economics, Statistics, and Analyses" presents findings from a semiannual study of the economics of consulting. Reprinted from "The Professional Consultant and Seminar Business Report" (May 1987), this chapter is interesting and informative, but doomed to be superseded by the next semiannual study. A brief and highly superficial concluding chapter, "Overview and Forecast," is also likely to become dated soon.

The Consultant's U.S. Statistical Guide and SourceFinder contains little information that is not available in standard reference tools and other sources. It may be convenient to use, but it is not indispensable. [R: RBB, 1 Apr 88, pp. 1320-21]   Lydia W. Wasylenko

163. Davis, James E., and Regina McCormick. **Economics: A Resource Book for Secondary Schools.** Santa Barbara, Calif., ABC-Clio, 1988. 354p. index. (Social Studies Resources for Secondary School Librarians, Teachers, and Students). $28.50. LC 87-18670. ISBN 0-87436-479-5.

Often the teaching of economics takes on the form of following the stock market. Although this exercise can be educational and interesting, it is not economics. This resource guide should be very useful to teachers of economics in secondary schools; it does a good job of defining economics and delineating the resources available to teach economics.

The definition of economics and the fundamental economic problems are explained in the first chapter of this resource book. The second and weakest chapter gives a chronology of American historical events and their economic impact. The chronology runs from 1500 to 1986 and can be useful, although many significant events are missing such as the abandonment of the gold standard in 1971 and the Bretton Woods Economic Summit of 1944.

Chapter 3 provides sixteen short biographies of famous economists. These biographies are a pleasure to read and should provide valuable information to secondary school teachers. Chapter 4 merely presents twenty-four tables and much used economic data and the sources of these data.

Chapters 5, 6, and 7 are perhaps the most valuable part of this work, for it is in these chapters that the resources are listed. Chapter 5 is a directory of economic organizations, providing addresses, telephone numbers, statements of purpose, and publications. Chapter 6 lists all sorts of economic reference books. A notable omission is *The New Palgrave: A Dictionary of Economics* (see *ARBA* 88, entry 165). The final chapter is over 150 pages of classroom materials for teaching economics. The listed materials cover everything from books, films, and videos to computer software. The descriptions of these materials along with their sources and prices makes this a truly valuable resource book. [R: BR, Sept/Oct 88, p. 51]

Elia Kacapyr

164. Factor, Regis A. **Guide to the *Archiv für Sozialwissenschaft und Sozialpolitik* Group, 1904-1933: A History and Comprehensive Bibliography.** Westport, Conn., Greenwood Press, 1988. 214p. index. (Bibliographies and Indexes in Law and Political Science, No. 9). $65.00. LC 88-17770. ISBN 0-313-22837-X.

The purpose of this guide is to present the history of *Archiv für Sozialwissenschaft und Sozialpolitik* which was first published in Germany in 1904 and appeared regularly until its suspension in 1933. Most of the contributors were outstanding political economists of this period who wrote about the growing complexity of political and socioeconomic problems facing society. The articles in *Archiv* were addressing the crucial theoretical and practical issues of their era. The guide consists of four parts: (1) introduction, (2) biographical information, (3) author bibliography index, and (4) subject bibliography index.

In his introduction, Factor outlines the *Archiv*'s history, its foundation by Max Weber, Werner Sombart, and Edgar Jaffe and its success in attracting contributions of numerous eminent scholars. The journal consisted primarily of essays and reviews of pertinent literature. After 1910 it included "Chronicles of Social Policy." In addition, it has published series of monographs which could not be included in the journal due to their inordinate length or too specialized character. Biographical information contains a brief description of persons performing editorial functions and writing essays and reviews. The rest of the volume consists of the bibliography index divided into author bibliography index, which lists alphabetically the authors with their contributions chronologically arranged, and subject bibliography index, listing all contributions by subjects arranged in alphabetical order.

Well organized and clearly written, this guide is recommended for scholars doing research in economics, history of economics, European history, and social philosophy.

Oleg Zinam

165. Input-Output Tables of China, 1981. Compiled by the Centre of Economic Forecasting, State Planning Commission of China and Department of Statistics on Balances of National Economy, State Statistical Bureau, People's Republic of China. Beijing, China Statistical Information and Consultancy Service Centre and Honolulu, East-West Population Institute; distr., Honolulu, University of Hawaii Press, 1987. 107p. $14.95pa. LC 87-24457. ISBN 0-86638-104-X.

Input-output analysis is a quantitative method of describing technological and economic relationships among different sectors of a national economy. It is considered to be an important tool for analyzing economic data for a particular reporting period and for forecasting economic development for future planning. The twenty data tables are organized in two parts. The first group contains summary data for six broad economic classifications: agriculture; heavy industry; light industry; construction; transport, mail, and telecommunications; and commerce. In the second, figures are given for twenty-four specific production sectors such as farming, animal husbandry, metallurgy, food,

textiles, heavy chemicals, etc. The tables are set up according to Marx's theory of political economy. The vertical columns show input, the materials, and labor used by each industry in the process of production. The horizontal rows show the output, that is, products distributed to each industry. Gross output includes intermediate products, which are consumed during production, and final products, those not consumed but used for other purposes. The tables show the balance between input and output. The statistics are seven years old, but since this is the only compilation of production statistics to be translated and published in English in this format, it will be of interest in subject collections in area studies and economics.

Shirley L. Hopkinson

166. Key Indicators of County Growth 1970-2010. Washington, D.C., NPA Data Services, 1987. 529p. maps. $195.00 spiralbound. ISBN 0-936555-01-7.

Based in Washington, D.C., with ready access to federal government statistics, NPA Data Services, Inc., can collect and organize an enormous body of data for the determination of county growth. Eight years are covered: 1970, 1980, 1985, 1986, 1987, 1990, 2000, 2010. Ten key indicators are given for each year: total population, population under twenty, population sixty-five and older, total households, persons per household, personal income of resident population, personal income per capita, personal income per household, total employment, and earnings per job. Completing the extensive tabulation are growth rates for the periods 1970-1987, 1987-2000, and 2000-2010. In all there are 346,280 data items, which also can be purchased on diskettes (thirteen PC-readable disks arranged in the ASCII read files and formatted for ready application in LOTUS 1-2-3 and similar spreadsheet analyses).

NPA Data Services derived the data from its own 1986 Economic Projections Series with the inclusion of available historical data and a number of new data sets based on the estimates of Dr. George S. Masnick of Harvard and M.I.T. The first forty-three pages, "Analyzing County Economies," explain how the data were obtained and prepared; in addition in this section there are twelve maps and two tables to illustrate the text. Three appendices are equally helpful: "Metropolitan Statistical Areas with County FIPS Codes," "States with County FIPS Codes," and "State Maps with Counties." The wealth of data here surpasses any other such compendium and, for those libraries electronically minded, having so much valuable data in PC storage will be of prime importance. Highly recommended to all libraries for its convenient and comprehensive inventory of essential data.

                Bill Bailey

167. McHugh, Francis P. **Keyguide to Information Sources in Business Ethics.** New York, Nichols/GP Publishing, 1988. 173p. bibliog. index. $34.50. LC 88-19693. ISBN 0-89397-327-0.

First published in England (1988), this guide to information resources for business ethics includes an historical context for understanding the place of ethics in business. McHugh provides useful perspectives on the subject by articulating the distinction between academic discussions and practical business approaches, by noting the differences between the United States and other countries, and by using codes of ethics as a vantage point.

Other introductory chapters include information on the origins and use of information on business ethics, suggestions for identifying academics and practitioners in the field, an overview of business literature, and special sources of information, including codes and nonbook materials. A separate section lists selected organizations worldwide including academic centers, business organizations, libraries, and organizations that use codes of ethics. A single index lists authors, titles, subjects, and organizations.

The bibliography of almost seven hundred entries is limited to a "representative selection" of citations to books and articles, including a few popular magazines, with an emphasis on contemporary literature. Almost one hundred entries refer to codes and discussions of codes of ethics. According to McHugh only the most important articles and books are abstracted and annotated.

Unfortunately, the guide leaves a lot to be desired. The abstracts and annotations do not consistently indicate the importance of a particular work. The most current works cited date from the mid-1970s to early 1980s; of the few entries dating from 1986, most are codes of ethics. That Elliston and Davis's *Ethics and the Legal Profession* (Prometheus Books) 1986 is noted as forthcoming indicates that there may have been a long time lag between the completion of this work and its publication. Finally, the index is not adequate: while a number of titles are omitted, others are entered simply as subjects.

In spite of its limitations, the guide is worthwhile for identifying worldwide resources and highlighting extremely useful materials, such as case studies, for curriculum development and classrooms. With the reservations noted above, this guide is recommended for academic libraries, particularly with curricula concerning business ethics.

                Joan B. Fiscella

168. Paradis, Adrian A. **The Small Business Information Source Book.** White Hall, Va., Betterway Publications, 1987. 136p. index. $7.95pa. LC 87-15925. ISBN 0-932620-81-7.

This book tells where and how to find information on "almost 150 principal subjects" (p. 7) of interest to small business. Part 2 lists organizations by subject, giving addresses only, with no telephone numbers, key personnel, or descriptions. Appendices include a glossary of business terms and a directory of publishers, again sans telephone numbers, names, or annotations.

Although ostensibly chosen for small business, the topics do not seem well selected. For instance, topics include "First Facts and World Records," "Passports," "Biographical Information," and "Antitrust," but do not include such sought-after topics as business plans, home-based businesses, venture capital, or Subchapter S corporations. The information in most entries is cursory, but whole books have been written on many of the topics, such as exporting. Some entries seem strange, such as "Small Business Services," which is entirely devoted to describing the services of Dun & Bradstreet.

The chief advantage of this title is its price. For organizations, Gale's *Encyclopedia of Associations* (see *ARBA* 88, entry 79) and *National Trade and Professional Associations of the United States* (see *ARBA* 88, entry 58) are far more complete, but also costlier. Innumerable bibliographies do a more detailed job on business publishers. Gale's *Small Business Sourcebook* (see *ARBA* 88, entry 220) is the most comprehensive and best-edited directory of small business resources of which I am aware, though it costs far more than the Paradis title. [R: LJ, Jan 88, p. 80]   Susan V. McKimm

169. Walter, Ingo, and Tracy Murray, eds. **Handbook of International Business.** 2d ed. New York, John Wiley, 1988. 1v. (various paging). index. $75.00. LC 87-35545. ISBN 0-471-84234-6.

This handbook is a series of twenty-three scholarly signed articles on general topics relating to international business, such as balance of payments or the OECD (Organization for Economic Cooperation and Development). Most chapters have bibliographies, and extensive use is made of charts and tables. This work has a United States orientation, as reflected in topics such as "The U.S. Merchant

Marine," "Import Letters of Credit," and "Assistance Provided by the U.S. Department of Commerce." The scholarly level of writing may inhibit its use by small business owners without a formal business education, even though it contains much concrete practical and legal information. For instance, sample import letters of credit and bank forms having to do with import are reproduced here. All major areas of international business seem to be covered, except that there is little on foreign securities, or direct foreign investments such as joint ventures. International treaty groups appear herein, but the specific characteristics of individual countries are generally outside this handbook's scope.

Much of this book is worth reading for background information, and understanding of economic concepts, but the price alone will dictate that it be reference in many libraries. This is a solid text that should be of long-term value in a business collection.

Susan V. McKimm

Indexes

170. **Business Periodicals Index: August 1986-July 1987.** Walter Webb and Hiyol Yang, eds. Bronx, N.Y., H. W. Wilson, 1987. 2388p. sold on service basis. LC 58-12645. ISSN 0007-6961.

Since last reviewed (see *ARBA 85*, entry 178) this work has had a change of editors, but seemingly not of editorial policy, which can alter a standard work for better or worse. The previous editor, Bettie Jane Third, has been succeeded by Walter Webb. The subject fields indexed are still the same, as are the main policies followed. The Committee on Wilson Indexes of ALA's Reference and Adult Services Division still advises the publisher in accordance with in-depth content studies, and subscriber vote still determines selection of periodicals for indexing. What has changed, though, is that the volume has grown stouter, from 1,612 pages for the year August 1982-July 1983 to 2,388 pages for this year. An increase of 776 pages is sizable, leading one to guess that now more business periodicals are indexed. However, this is not the case: the total count of titles indexed for both years is 310. This means that the stalwart *BPI* indexers (six in all) are indexing more closely and using more subject headings and *see also* references to ensure a better product. Also accounting for the thicker volume, business publications are adding more articles, thereby increasing their page counts, which gives *BPI* more to do. *BPI* is still the best index for business research, in spite of its computerized competitors. The new editor and his staff deserve a heartfelt thanks from the library world for

keeping a staple of research going strong and more responsive to user needs.   Bill Bailey

171. **Business Rankings and Salaries Index: An Annotated Bibliographic Guide to More Than 8,000 Listings....** Compiled by Brooklyn Public Library, Business Library. Detroit, Gale, 1988. 587p. index. $140.00. LC 87-32668. ISBN 0-8103-1827-X.

Information on salaries and rankings of businesses and industries is found through special issues resources, indexes, and browsing of industry-related literature. The librarians of the Brooklyn Public Library who have identified and collected references to such lists in the eighteen hundred periodicals, eighteen newspapers, and various statistical annuals and directories received at the library have made their work available through this new Gale index.

Each ranking entry provides the ranking title, the criteria used, the number ranked, the name of the highest ranked, and a bibliographic citation. "Also noted" includes names of others ranked or additional useful information. Ranking lists include such varied topics as the Fortune 500 lists, top art patrons by donations, ten top electronics contractors for the Pentagon to the ten most admired petroleum refining companies.

Each salary entry gives a subject heading, generally the occupation or industry, a bibliographic citation, and a short note on the contents. The approximately 125 salary categories include accountants, athletes, book reviewers, economists, and systems analysts.

Each of the major sections is organized alphabetically. Indexes to sources provide additional points of access. Entries date from the mid-1980s.

While other indexes, such as *Statistical Reference Index Annual* (see *ARBA 86*, entry 835), provide access to a broader scope of statistical information more useful to researchers, Gale's work provides immediate information and thus would be quite valuable for telephone or desk reference personnel. However, the information will become quickly dated unless regular updates are made available. [R: Choice, July/Aug 88, p. 1672; LJ, 15 May 88, p. 77; RBB, 1 June 88, p. 1654; WLB, May 88, p. 106]

Joan B. Fiscella

172. Lea, Richard S. **Job Title Index to SIC (Standard Industrial Classification) Codes.** Jefferson, N.C., McFarland, 1988. 93p. bibliog. $19.95. LC 87-43167. ISBN 0-89950-311-X.

This small volume is offered solely as a partial reference guide, correlating generic job titles to the appropriate Standard Industrial Classification Code (S.I.C. number). It is partial because it is not comprehensive. It is, however, reasonably complete. It should be useful for individuals trying to determine where their job aspirations fit into the contemporary American economy. It would, however, be a cumbersome tool for a researcher who wants to survey from one code classification to comparable employment opportunities in unrelated industries. [R: WLB, June 88, p. 141]

Gary W. Yohe

Periodicals and Serials

173. Geahigan, Priscilla C., and Robert F. Rose, eds. **Business Serials of the U.S. Government.** 2d ed. Chicago, Business Reference and Services Section, American Library Association, 1988. 86p. index. $11.95pa. LC 88-3428. ISBN 0-8389-3349-1.

This revised, selective bibliography lists and annotates 183 U.S. government serials judged useful for business information by the Business Reference Services Committee of ALA. Each citation lists title, issuing agency, initial date of publication, frequency, previous title(s), indexing sources, and SuDocs number.

The bibliography is organized into sixteen areas, including general sources, economic conditions, demographics, international business, agriculture, environment, labor, small business, patents, government contracts, public finance, taxation, consumers, and fifteen specific industries. Title and subject indexes are included. A preface carefully explains the criteria for inclusion and other decisions made in compiling the bibliography.

The serials include handbooks, journals, pamphlets, and looseleaf services. The signed annotations give fairly extensive descriptions of the scope of each serial and refer to other titles when appropriate. The amount of evaluative comment varies greatly. Annotations, notes on the interrelations of, differences among, and history of titles will help nonspecialists find their way through the government's business serials.

Box indexes are helpful, although there are gaps in each. For example, some superseded titles are listed; others are not. The subject indexing appears to be selective, but it isn't clear on what basis (for instance, the mining entry refers to two titles, neither of which is in the mining industry section).

In spite of the lapses in indexes, this is a highly recommended resource for the business information needs of small and medium-sized public and academic libraries, particularly those

without *American Statistics Index.* [R: LJ, 1 Sept 88, p. 148; RBB, 15 Oct 88, p. 388]

Joan B. Fiscella

Quotation Books

174. Hay, Peter. **The Book of Business Anecdotes.** New York, Facts on File, 1988. 296p. bibliog. index. $22.95. LC 87-20211. ISBN 0-8160-1522-8.

The Book of Business Anecdotes is an entertaining, well-rounded collection of business stories. Hundreds of biographies, histories, and similar works, including *The Percy Anecdotes*, supply material for the scintillating tributes contained herein. Quotes are aptly placed into a concise narrative context by the author. The resultant pieces are labeled with catchy titles, such as "Chairman of the Bored," a recounting of John De Lorean's tribulations at General Motors Corporation.

Over five hundred of these oftentimes poignant and consistently inspiring tales are arranged into twelve categories, encompassing "Business and the Muses," "Corporate Culture," and "The Spirit of Enterprises," among others. The work is complemented by an extensive index, listing personages, places, and publications cited.

This expertly crafted work should be the cornerstone of collections of this genre that no business library should be without. [R: BR, Sept/Oct 88, p. 46; LJ, 15 Apr 88, p. 74; WLB, June 88, pp. 137-38]   Peter B. Kaatrude

175. Manser, Martin H., comp. **The Chambers Book of Business Quotations.** New York, Cambridge University Press, 1987. 211p. illus. index. $19.95. ISBN 0-550-20488-1.

Numerous quotation books appear every year in *ARBA*, and many of these have dealt with business. This particular title is designed to provide quotes that could be used in a report or speech. Entries seem primarily to have been selected for their entertainment value, and this aspect is enhanced by the book's attractive graphics. Several quotes have been illustrated with cartoons.

Only two thousand quotes are included, compared to five thousand in the *Macmillan Book of Business and Economic Quotations* (see *ARBA* 86, entry 209) or three thousand in *The Great Business Quotations* (see *ARBA* 88, entry 203). As in these other books, quotes are taken from a wide variety of sources besides business-related ones, ranging from Woody Allen to the Bible. The book is divided into nine major topics, such as "Time" or "Human

Resources." A major weakness is that there is no keyword indexing, so to find a particular quote one would do better to consult a general quote book such as *Bartlett's Familiar Quotations* (see *ARBA* 82, entry 109) that does provide such indexing. There is an index that combines authors and very general subjects such as "Management," which lists the pages that the quotes concerning management begin on (there are only fifteen of these).

This book would be useful in a public library, but is more for use as a resource for speeches or papers than as a reference tool for looking up specific quotations. In fact, libraries might consider this for their circulating collections, as this kind of resource is frequently asked for by patrons. [R: WLB, June 88, pp. 137-38]   Susan V. McKimm

ACCOUNTING

176.   Siegel, Joel G., and Jae K. Shim. **Dictionary of Accounting Terms.** Woodbury, N.Y., Barron's Educational Series, 1987. 472p. $8.95 pa. LC 87-29056. ISBN 0-8120-3766-9.

This pocket-sized, soft cover dictionary has more than twenty-five hundred terms covering financial, managerial, and cost accounting; auditing; financial analysis; and tax terms. In addition, some related business terms from finance, operations research, computers, and economics are defined. Charts, examples, graphs, and tables clarify the definitions. *See* references are provided along with cross-references, which are indicated by small capital letters either in the body or at the end of the definition. Closely related or special meaning terms in the definitions are in italics to indicate that these are defined. Organization and associations for this field are also listed, along with a brief statement of purpose. A list of acronyms and abbreviations, and tables of various values of the dollar are at the end of the volume.

The dictionary is designed for business people and students who are unfamiliar with these accounting related business practices and for accountants who need quick reference information. The price makes it affordable for the individual. With its coverage of new terms such as *alternative minimum tax* (*AMT*), this dictionary is also useful for libraries.

Jean Herold

177.   Spiceland, J. David, and Surendra P. Agrawal. **International Guide to Accounting Journals.** New York, Markus Wiener Publishing, 1988. 291p. $18.00. LC 87-21035. ISBN 0-910129-63-0.

The purpose of this reference guide is to assist accounting researchers in identifying resources for research. It includes information about journals publishing unsolicited articles on accounting in approximately thirty-three countries. Journals were included in this book based upon an assessment of the leading professional and academic works found in business libraries in Europe and the United States.

The text is divided into two parts: information listed alphabetically by journal, and journals listed by country. While the latter is merely a list of the journals under the name of each country, the former is very informative, including facts on such things as primary readership, percentage of articles on accounting topics, language of the publication, circulation, sponsoring organization, length, style, and publisher. In all, approximately thirty or so pieces of helpful information allow the reader to determine the usefulness of the journals described in the first part.

The work will also be useful to authors searching for a journal most likely to publish their manuscripts. As such, academic libraries will find this reference book most useful. [R: Choice, Sept 88, p. 90]   James M. Murray

178.   Woelfel, Charles J. **Budgeting, Pricing & Cost Controls: A Desktop Encyclopedia.** Chicago, Probus Publishing, 1987. 319p. $35.00. ISBN 0-917253-91-4.

This specialized source is aptly subtitled a desktop encyclopedia since entries range in length between full-blown encyclopedia articles and dictionary definitions. Written by a CPA and professor of accounting who has authored college textbooks and professional monographs, the entries are succinct and clear. Formulas, sample charts illustrative of the topic, and examples are scattered throughout the text.

Entries are alphabetical, with a table of contents to aid the user. There are slightly over one hundred definitions, which demonstrates that this source does not attempt to be comprehensive. At least one reference is provided for further reading on each topic. The preface states that it is aimed at the practicing executive as well as the academician.   Maureen B. Lambert

179.   Woelfel, Charles J. **The Desktop Encyclopedia of Corporate Finance & Accounting.** Chicago, Probus Publishing, 1987. 518p. $27.50. ISBN 0-917253-65-5.

Designed for day-to-day use by managers, executives, bankers, and accountants, this encyclopedia is more explanatory than a dictionary but less detailed than a handbook. It covers more than 270 major accounting and financial concepts with alphabetically arranged short articles providing detailed explanations with formulas, graphs, charts, and balance sheet examples. In addition, more than twenty-five hundred concepts have shorter explanations. The references to other terms at the end of an entry provide access to related topics. Many entries also have citations to primary and secondary sources of information in books and accounting documents. Special situations such as personal financial statements, nonprofit enterprises, partnerships, estates and trusts are also included. The introduction has a list of underlying principles, major concepts, terms associated with cost and managerial accounting, and auditing that provides a systematic approach to accounting and finance and is useful for anyone trying to understand the basic structure of accounting and finance. The preface mentioned a detailed, general index that was not included in the review copy.

The primary audience for this book is anyone unfamiliar with accounting practices. Accountants would generally prefer *Kohler's Dictionary for Accountants* (see *ARBA 85*, entry 182) since it includes twice as many terms with briefer explanations. Large business collections may want this encyclopedia, but smaller collections would find *Kohler's* adequate for most needs. Accounting textbooks supply basic information on accounting practices and could be checked out for an individual to use.

Jean Herold

BUSINESS SERVICES AND INVESTMENT GUIDES

180. Blum, Laurie. **Free Money for Small Businesses and Entrepreneurs.** New York, John Wiley, 1988. 229p. $12.95pa. LC 87-20978. ISBN 0-471-85802-1.

Readers seeking a pot of gold at the rainbow's end will be disappointed by this limited directory to sources of "free money." This directory is divided into two sections identifying sources of either "program-related investments" (PRIs) or of flow-through funding and federal money. The former provide money directly to private businesses, while the latter interpose some intermediary, such as a nonprofit institution.

The book explains that PRIs are made to further the charitable objectives of the various groups; however, listings fail to identify the objectives of most of the institutions. This makes it difficult, if not impossible, to properly use the directory to target appropriate contacts. The

section on flow-through funding and federal money mentions certain money sources but gives no listing of likely intermediaries needed to apply for and/or receive funding. Little guidance is offered explaining how a businessperson would actually proceed to solicit funding, or the steps involved in the process.

This directory is neither comprehensive, extensive, well-researched, nor particularly useful.

James F. Mattil

181. Bond, Robert E. **The Source Book of Franchise Opportunities.** 1988 ed. Homewood, Ill., Dow Jones-Irwin, 1988. 513p. index. $24.95pa. LC 88-50647. ISBN 1-55623-090-7.

While most fair-minded people agree that one ought not to judge a book by its cover, these same members of the multitude would accept the book's table of contents as a valid bellwether on which to form a judgment. A book that has nineteen pages of text and hundreds of pages of listings reminiscent of a government (no-copyright-infringement-problems) document, *Franchise Opportunities Handbook* (Government Printing Office, 1980-) has the noxious odor of a rip-off. A closer glance, glad to report, reveals just the opposite: Bond's book is a true "value-added" effort, the work of a knowledgeable, highly regarded consultant who has distilled years of experience in the brief text, the six-page annotated bibliography, and the design of his forty-one-item questionnaire.

Intended as "a sourcebook for the sophisticated potential franchisee," *Opportunities* offers detailed profiles on roughly one thousand franchises, far more data than one ever finds in the above-cited government publication or Info Press's *Franchise Annual* (see *ARBA 88*, entry 213), among others. The franchises are grouped into forty-five categories such as lawn and garden, rental services, travel, etc. Each profile addresses three areas: history, financial, and franchisor training/support. Among the specific data elements are membership in the International Franchise Association, states where franchises are registered, if passive ownership is possible, contract period, and if co-op advertising is available. About twenty-two hundred additional franchises have less detail.

In his introduction, Bond presents the rationale for each question, stressing that his opus is merely "the first step in the long and tedious process of selecting a franchise." His comments seem prudent and to the point. The brief bibliography contains forty-seven items. While some of the annotations are verbatim reprints of comments from *Franchise Opportunities Handbook*, many are not, and he has several newer titles noted which did not appear in the most recent edition of that government document. Although time will rapidly date the book's utility, and there is no indication of it being an annual, purchasers need not fear another rip-off with this one. For all business collections, especially in public libraries.   Richard Reid

182.   Chapman, Karen J. **Investment Statistics Locator.** Phoenix, Ariz., Oryx Press, 1988. 182p. $45.00. LC 87-24746. ISBN 0-89774-367-9.

A busy reference librarian, especially the non-expert-in-business librarian, needs a quick source to get to the location of business/investment statistics for today's investment-oriented populace. Chapman's work fills this important need well. Trying to remember the location of recurring statistics in this rapidly changing field can be daunting; now it will become easier.

Arranged by subject, the *Locator* leads the researcher to a wide variety of investment-related data found in twenty-two standard business serials such as *Barron's, Commercial & Financial Chronicle, Moody's* various handbooks and manuals, and so on. Printed with boldface subject headings on good quality non-glare paper, the book has an easy to use format with excellent *see* references and certain data under multiple headings. A reader can find statistic sources on operating incomes, quick ratios, old master painting prices, inventories, and many more investment choices. Much less ponderous than the *American Statistics Index* (see *ARBA* 76, entry 818), the volume still provides a good base for key investment data sources, both government-generated and otherwise. Use this book as an adjunct to Daniells's *Business Information Sources* (see *ARBA* 86, entry 158) to round out a business reference shelf. It can be of good use in a variety of libraries from small public ones to the technical/business libraries. [R: Choice, June 88, p. 1530; RBB, 1 May 88, p. 1487; WLB, May 88, p. 111]
                Robert D. Adamshick

183.   Colby, Robert W., and Thomas A. Meyers. **The Encyclopedia of Technical Market Indicators.** Homewood, Ill., Dow Jones-Irwin, 1988. 581p. index. $45.00. LC 87-73023. ISBN 1-55623-049-4.

Investing in the stock market, while always risky, has become increasingly complex if one indulges in following the indicators of the market; a hunch may be worth millions or bankruptcy, so indicator-followers have come to rely more on the established indicators and on new ones derived by the gurus of Wall Street. This encyclopedia attempts to explain over one hundred of the "top" indicators of stock market

performance to the investing public. In one volume, it compiles a vast amount of detailed research in this area, written by acknowledged experts in the field. Part 1 puts forth the rationale behind and the methods used to research the indicators chosen. The computer software utilized to test the indicators is thoroughly discussed. Part 2 gives detailed information on each of the selected indicators with definitions, examples, charts, and tables. The authors sometimes include the name and address of the indicator's "creator" or printed sources for further consultation.

The authors tested their indicators using a variety of software packages, and the results of the tests are provided in either textual or graphic format (or both). Dow Jones-Irwin has produced a valuable work for the *serious* investor, not for the novice. The $45.00 price buys a solid investment into hundreds of hours of research presented in a technical but lucid style, replete with excellent examples, and printed in an attractive typeface. Cross-referencing in the index could use improvement (e.g., "Hughes Breadth Index" is found in the "Indicators" section, under "Advance/Decline Noncumulative," but "Hughes" is not in the index).

The book deserves a place on the shelves of serious stock market investors and libraries serving this type of clientele.
                Robert D. Adamshick

184.   **Consumer Guide Best-Rated Investments for 1988.** New York, New American Library, 1987. 160p. index. $6.95pa. ISBN 0-451-82173-4.

The information in *Best-Rated Investments* is intended to provide investors with a comprehensive guide to all the popular vehicles of investment. It covers the stock market, mutual funds, real estate, the bond market, government securities, and other forms of investment from the perspective of where the "smart money" will be going in this year and next. The editors of *Consumer Guide*, a Chicago-based publisher of books, cannot be faulted for the ease with which they have explained and analyzed strategies for investing. It is all quite understandable to the veteran investor, and the novice can use the glossary to find terms he or she is not familiar with. The discussions here are complete and well rounded, though not as extensive as those in Currier's *The Investor's Encyclopedia* (see *ARBA* 86, entry 225) or Blume's *Encyclopedia of Investments* (see *ARBA* 83, entry 767). In fact, considering the turmoil that has bedeviled the securities markets recently, many of the statements made seem remarkably prescient. Consider: "Make no mistake that a bull, or up, market entails risk ... from a Dow Jones average of 2700-plus is a long way to fall." Or: "[Portfolio insurance] adds to the volatility of the market and virtually guarantees that we will eventually see a day when the Dow Jones Industrial average declines by more than 10 percent."

No individual companies are recommended or mentioned here other than the names of the top five mutual funds in several categories. This is more of a primer than an advisor. Its price represents real reference value, but it comes with the caveat that its paperback binding and cheap paper stock will not stand up to the hammering given to a popular book by library patrons.

Randall Rafferty

185. Consumer Guide 100 Best-Rated Stocks. Compiled by the editors of *Consumer Guide* and Zacks Investment Research. New York, New American Library, 1987. 128p. $3.50pa. ISBN 0-451-15174-7.

This small, even slight, handbook will appeal to the individual speculator. It will act as a supplement to a library's larger investment advisory services, such as the weekly Standard & Poor's *Outlook*, *Valueline*, or United Business Service. The words "best-rated" in the title mean that the compilers surveyed the major brokerage firms as to which stocks the firms were recommending most highly. While the book is concise, usually an advantage, it is at the same time too brief, giving as it does just a bare minimum of facts about each company. It labors under two other faults. First, it lacks any sort of index; it is alphabetical. Librarians seem to prefer having too many access points to any given book than too few. Seen in that light, an index by line of business would have been helpful, as would a ranking of companies by their relative attractiveness. Had this book been more substantial, it could have avoided the second fault, which has to do with format. Its small size and newsprint pages make it tantamount to a piece of ephemera that could get lost on the reference shelf. Unfortunately for the publishers, this handbook made its appearance just ahead of the worldwide stock market crash of 19 October 1987, an event that rendered all opinions suspect. Considering the frequency and rapidity with which economic and political conditions change and the increasing volatility as reflected on the trading floor, one marvels at the presumptuousness of those who make it their business to predict, and one wonders as a librarian at the staying power or "shelf life" of this book in light of all that has happened.

Randall Rafferty

186. Directory of Franchising Organizations, 1988. 29th ed. Babylon, N.Y., Pilot Books, 1988. 78p. $5.00pa. LC 62-39831.

Issued for twenty-nine years, the directory lists new franchises and offers potential franchisees unimbellished data on the nature and cost of each franchise, how to avoid unsubstantiated claims, plus other ways to help an individual avoid mistakes in franchise selection. It provides a method to shop for, compare, and select franchises.

Franchises are arranged alphabetically by broad subject headings under which the company name and address and a brief description of the franchise and investment costs are presented. Since it is published annually, many of the items are duplicates of previous editions and some redundancy occurs. There is no alphabetical index approach to franchise names, suggesting less reference value. The *Franchise Opportunities Handbook*, published by the U.S. Department of Commerce on an irregular basis, and the recently published *Source Book of Franchise Opportunities* (see *ARBA 86*, entry 222) provide a plethora of franchise information, but neither is priced at $5.00 nor is as current as this slight title. Designed for a year's use only, it is recommended for obtaining new franchise materials.

Jack I. Gardner

187. Emerging Stock Markets Factbook 1988. Washington, D.C., International Finance Corporation and World Bank, 1988. 91p. maps. $100.00pa. ISBN 0-8213-1105-0.

This is a very expensive and small book developed by the International Finance Corporation for a very small and specialized audience of international stock market investors. It pulls together a wide variety of data from many sources on the stock markets of nineteen developing/emerging nations of the Third World, principally in Latin America and south Asia. The data are not readily found in any *one* other source. The book is an offshoot of the International Finance Corporation's database on emerging markets, as is the *Quarterly Review of Emerging Stock Markets*. The database itself is available on a subscription basis on diskettes for that audience beyond the scope of the *Factbook*.

The book is in four parts: introduction, stock market indexes, overview of emerging markets, and market profiles. The introduction is very brief and gives the address for the database subscription. Part 2 provides stock market indexes such as cumulative total returns, performance indexes, and price indexes. The overview contains charts and graphs with comparisons by country. Some charts also compare with "developed" nations such as the United States or United Kingdom. Country-specific information is found in the profiles of part 4. Here you will find market capitalizations, trading values, exchange rates, etc. The serious investors who might use this work may also wish to work with the *Yearbook of National Account Statistics* (see *ARBA* 77, entry 762) for other financial data on the nineteen nations covered. This book may find a home only in the largest business reference collections or libraries of international investment houses, not in the general library. Nations covered include Argentina, India, Taiwan, Zimbabwe, Greece, Portugal, and the Philippines, to name a few.

Robert D. Adamshick

188. Foster, Dennis L. **The Rating Guide to Franchises.** New York, Facts on File, 1988. 298p. index. $29.95. LC 88-3740. ISBN 0-8160-1891-X.

This work differs from other reference materials on franchising in that it analyzes the "financial and legal status and relative position in the marketplace" of each company. The companies are then rated using a system of one to four stars according to individual and industry experience, financial strength, training and services, fees and royalties, and satisfied franchisees. To accomplish this, the author conducted "an exhaustive, independent research effort" (introduction). Each company profile is about one page in length (approximately thirty-five lines). Information provided includes description of business, franchisee profile (whether experience in the area is needed, characteristics of preferred applicants); projected earnings, franchisor's services (training provided, discount purchase opportunities, etc.), initial initial investment, advertising requirements and benefits, contract highlights (length of contract, renewal specifications, etc.); fees and royalties; and, in summary, franchise highlights (a short list of the numbers presented above, including date founded, number of outlets currently operating, fees, training length, etc., designed for quick scanning).

The book is arranged by broad category (apparel and soft goods, automotive, business services, etc.). It is indexed by specific type of service or good provided and by franchise name. The introduction presents the caveat that the information provided here should be used only as a guideline, and that a franchise's requirements may change rapidly. The author recommends sending for a franchise information kit, among other steps, before applying for a contract. This work provides facts difficult to obtain elsewhere, and will be useful, not only to prospective franchisees, but to students seeking information on these companies for class projects. [R: WLB, Sept 88, pp. 96-97]

Maureen B. Lambert

189. Hildreth, Sandra S. **The A to Z of Wall Street.** Chicago, Longman Trade, 1988. 299p. $13.95pa. LC 87-22615. ISBN 0-88462-711-X.

Another in the recent spate of financial/investment dictionaries, this one offers its users ("both the individual and professional") clear, brief (most are three lines or less) meanings of over twenty-five hundred investment words and phrases. After the basic alphabetical arrangement, the author—who boasts experience as a stock/commodity broker, radio commentator, and financial columnist—offers one welcome and two necessary appendices. The latter are "Common Abbreviations" (not all are listed in the main body) and "Cross References" (something the main body is weak on). The former, "How to Interpret *The Wall Street Journal* Reports" is a nifty twenty-two page explanation of financial columns and charts' abbreviations found in that venerable newspaper. Those collections already possessing Lehmann's *Dow Jones-Irwin Guide to Using The Wall Street Journal* (2d ed. Dow Jones, 1987) or Downes and Goodman's *Barron's Finance & Investment Handbook* (see *ARBA* 87, entry 204) with its thirty-eight-page section, "How to Read the Financial Pages," may find Hildreth's appendix a less than compelling reason to buy the book.

The *Barron's* book also features a 384-page, 2,500 word "Dictionary of Finance & Investment." Comparison of ten randomly selected terms from Hildreth with *Barron's* showed eight of them included, in contrast to six in Rosenberg's *Dictionary of Banking & Financial Services* (see *ARBA* 87, entry 224) and four in Thomsett's *Investment & Securities Dictionary* (see *ARBA* 88, entry 222). Thomsett's book comes closest, of those cited here, to Hildreth's in scope and recency. While only offering about two thousand terms, Thomsett's definitions are better than twice as long on the average. Of ten randomly selected entries in the dictionary, Hildreth matched nine of them and at less than half the price.

A to Z incorporates thirty-three figures and charts from *Trendline* and *Chartcraft*, which help to further clarify various trading concepts. With its large, pleasing layout and typography, Hildreth's work best can be recommended as an inexpensive way to stay current with the latest financial terminology. For all business collections. [R: RBB, 1 Mar 88, pp. 1101-2]

Richard Reid

190. Lesko, Matthew. **The Investor's Information Sourcebook.** New York, Perennial Library/Harper & Row, 1988. 433p. index. $19.95; $9.95pa. LC 87-45636. ISBN 0-06-055110-0; 0-06-096237-2pa.

Lesko has become the unofficial ombudsman of consumer and government-related information sources. His highly popular and widely used *Information USA* (see *ARBA* 84, entry 451) is a hard act to follow, and his latest work may also be hard to beat. Lesko sets the tone of the *Investor's Information Sourcebook* with this preface: "The key to successful investing is information ... [and] knowing where to find it." This sourcebook is just such a place. The snappy prose style and good tips on investment sources make this work both a "good read" and a handy reference source for librarian and investor.

The book is divided into four sections: "Starting Points," guides for the beginner, with book sources, hotline numbers, and hard to find company information; "Economic Resources," covering economic indicators and their role in investing; "Investment Vehicles," explaining the myriad types of investments available, with caveats and sources; and "Investing for Lifelong Security," which fills the reader in on plans for retirement and heirs. Appendices round out the work with teaching aids, programs, comics for the kids to learn investing, and information on where to turn if you feel you have been cheated by securities dealers.

The section on free government advice and key telephone numbers is especially helpful, following Lesko's successful *Getting Yours— The Complete Guide to Government Money* (see *ARBA* 83, entry 781). The chapter on "freebies" is a must for the novice investor and for librarians wanting to build up vertical files on investing. The readable typeface and index enhance the use of the book.

For the price, this book is very much a bargain. Keep it on the ready-reference shelf with Lorna Daniells's *Business Information Sources* (see *ARBA* 86, entry 158) and other basic business sources, and get several copies for circulating collections. [R: Choice, Dec 88, p. 683; RBB, 1 Apr 88, pp. 1322, 1324]

Robert D. Adamshick

191. Miller, Herbert A., Jr. **Retirement Benefit Plans: An Information Sourcebook.** Phoenix, Ariz., Oryx Press, 1988. 207p. index. (Oryx Sourcebook Series in Business and Management, No. 8). $39.50. LC 87-22500. ISBN 0-89774-282-6.

This sourcebook's compiler is both an employee benefits specialist in a major employee benefits consulting firm *and* a librarian. From these two differing perspectives, he provides a near-comprehensive guide to the bibliographically difficult literature of retirement benefits. Miller divides the work into types based on format, including monographs, periodicals, theses (dissertations), company promotional literature, surveys, and databases. Many of the eighteen hundred plus entries have a brief annotation to help the user grasp the nature of the publication. Chapter introductions explain the rationale behind Miller's listings and include caveats as to the availability and/or reliability of some of the bibliographic entries. These warnings show the reader the intensity of Miller's research in a subject area notorious for hard-to-find publications, especially for back-dated issues. His chapter "Core Library Collection" can serve as an excellent guide to important works in employee benefits literature for those active in the field or for librarians charged with building a collection in industry or government. Typeface and organization are straightforward and clear, while indexing by author, title, and subject is good; the subject entries are sub-arranged by date, a nice touch for getting to recent materials. Librarians and businesses in the subject area may wish to add Miller's *Retirement Benefits Plans* to their shelves, along with *A Bibliography of Research: Retirement Income & Capital Accumulation Programs* (see *ARBA* 83, entry 787). [R: Choice, Sept 88, p. 84]

Robert D. Adamshick

192. Monk, J. Thomas, Kenneth M. Landis, and Susan S. Monk. **The Dow Jones-Irwin Investor's Guide to Online Databases.** Homewood, Ill., Dow Jones-Irwin, 1988. 715p. index. $55.00. LC 87-73534. ISBN 0-87094-751-6.

Like other Dow Jones-Irwin guidebooks, this one is an excellent compendium of information on the online database industry. It can be used as both a textbook and a reference source for the field. The volume consists of a narrative introduction to electronic database searching (when and how), database vendor company profiles, and file information descriptions. Useful appendices include database providers (e.g., Dialog), information gateways (e.g., OCLC), a quick list of communications software (e.g., Crosstalk XVI), and an index to the volume.

Three excellent matrices are included. The first covers the target audience of the database producer. The second is a useful analysis of database producers by subject covered. The final matrix covers individual databases by subject. These three matrices alone are worth the price of the volume. The profiles and file descriptions are well written and contain a wealth of information, including telephone numbers for additional assistance.

Most business collections will find this book an excellent, handy, one-volume source that they will want to keep near the online searching desk. Patrons interested in the value of computerized information files will find that the introductory sections will help them better utilize the information they retrieve. Despite its rather high cost, few libraries can afford to be without this reference book. The only drawback is that this volume, like others by Dow Jones-Irwin, sometimes drifts into too general a discussion of the topic. In most cases, however, this general discussion is of benefit to the novice.   Ralph Lee Scott

193.   Scott, David L. **Wall Street Words.** Boston, Houghton Mifflin, 1988. 404p. bibliog. $18.95. LC 87-21444. ISBN 0-395-43747-4.

This excellent and timely compilation of over 3,600 finance terms accomplishes its aim admirably: it puts "financial literacy for a changing market," as the subtitle proclaims, within the reach of its readers. A comparison with Barron's *Dictionary of Finance and Investment Terms* (see *ARBA* 87, entry 205) serves to highlight the strengths of each source. While some necessary overlap does occur, each contains terms that the other lacks.

Among the terms in *Wall Street Words* which did not appear in Barron's dictionary are *electronic funds transfer*, *fallen angel*, *flipper*, *greater fool theory*, and *Reagonomics*. Definitions in Barron's dictionary are on the whole more detailed. For example, the explanation for *fiscal year* in *Wall Street Words* is: "The twelve month accounting period for an organization. Since many firms end their accounting year on a date other than December 31, the fiscal year often differs from the calendar year." Compare with Barron's definition, which states the previous facts (in slightly different style), then adds: "a seasonal business will frequently select a fiscal rather than a calendar year, so that its year-end figures will show in its most liquid condition, a choice which also has the advantage of having less inventory to verify physically. The fiscal year of the U.S. government runs from October 1 to Sept. 30." This information, while not strictly necessary, is often quite helpful to the student (and to reference staff looking for just such a tidbit).

Wall Street Words has more acronyms than Barron's as well, and includes them in the main body of the book, while the latter source has a separate listing in the back. Among the acronyms in *Wall Street Words* which are absent from Barron's are ECU (European Currency Unit), ICAA (Investment Counsel Association of America), and JTWROS (Joint Tenancy with Rights of Survivorship). The last term in this group does appear in spelled out form in Barron's, however.

Two other very nice and unique features of *Wall Street Words* are its inclusion of eighty-seven investment tips, contributed by a group of experts, and case studies which illustrate the meanings of some of the terms. Finally, a four-and-a-half page section of technical analysis chart patterns in the back of the book enhances its utility to the student. [R: LJ, 15 Feb 88, p. 161; RBB, 1 Mar 88, pp. 1101-2]

Maureen B. Lambert

CONSUMER GUIDES

194.   **The Complete Car Cost Guide.** 1988 ed. Steve Gross, ed. San Jose, Calif., IntelliChoice, 1988. 1v. (various paging). illus. index. $30.00 pa. ISBN 0-941443-04-3.

For many of us, a new car comes down to a choice between the unaffordable and the unacceptable. Research and homework have increasingly become the answer for a beleaguered buyer trying to find the middle ground. For many years, *Consumer Reports* and other magazines have published the results of their tests. But until this "guide to the economics of buying and owning over 500 new automobiles" was published, it has not been possible to compare easily the cost per year of owning the various makes and models of cars. Before, a prospective buyer would have had to consult many sources, and even then would not have had a clear picture. The editors of this guidebook have eased that task. The coverage of the differing makes of cars, import and domestic, is indeed impressive. Light trucks, wagons, and vans are also included. For this 1988 edition, arrangement is alphabetical instead of by car size, as in previous editions. Another change is the elimination of past model years' analyses in favor of current (1988) models only.

In order to use the book, it is necessary to understand how concepts of depreciation, insurance, financing costs, fuel, repairs, and maintenance combine to produce a profile of future costs of ownership. It is all based on computer modeling, using a sophisticated program devised by the editors. Data were gathered from the publisher's own research and other sources, including *Auto Age* (1966-), *Chilton's Labor Guide and Parts Manual*, *Consumer Reports* (1936-), *Motor Age Professional Mechanics* (1927-), and some others. This is an important new reference book, and is strongly recommended to any library which serves the car buying public. It should be placed alongside the April issue of *Consumer Reports*, the annual car issue. [R: LJ, Aug 88, p. 150]

Randall Rafferty

195. *Consumer Guide* **Consumer Buying Guide.** 1988 ed. Skokie, Ill., Consumer Guide Books, 1987. 384p. index. $4.50pa. ISBN 0-451-15201-8.

This annual guide covers new and used automobiles, major appliances, and consumer electronics. Unlike the *Consumer Reports Buying Guide Issue* (the December issue of *Consumer Reports* magazine), it covers the same products every year, adding new consumer electronics as they arrive on the market. Each section has an introduction giving terminology, special features, and other purchasing information for that particular type of product. This is followed by a section discussing "best buys" and "recommended" brands. Nonrecommended brands are not included. Efforts are made to recommend brands in a variety of price ranges and with a variety of features. Unlike Consumers Union (the publisher of *Consumer Reports*), Consumer Guide Books has no testing laboratories, but calls in experts to comparison shop and recommend the brands to include. Many library patrons will prefer the *Consumer Guide* approach because it includes many of the most-asked-about products, such as compact disks, every year, while it may be two years between *Consumer Reports* evaluations. However, *Consumer Reports* ultimately includes a wider variety of products and has a five-year index, so that the two-year-old report can be found. Both *Consumer Guide* and *Consumer Reports* are cheap titles, and many public libraries will want more than one copy of each due to the high demand for product evaluations.

Susan V. McKimm

196. **Consumer Sourcebook: A Subject Guide....** 5th ed. Kay Gill and Robert Wilson, eds. Detroit, Gale, 1988. 473p. index. $175.00. ISBN 0-8103-2523-3; ISSN 0738-0518.

Consumerism is a growing movement, but much of the problem that prevents consumers from fighting back lies in not knowing whom to fight and how to go about it. With the fifth edition of this work, Gale continues to do an excellent job of telling us where to find an ally—generally a free or inexpensive one—in our battle for justice.

A striking new organization to this edition is apparent on first opening the volume: twenty-six chapters arranged by broad subject category. This eminently sensible arrangement enables one to easily identify the appropriate category

and flip to it. Further divisions of the chapters by federal, state (including county and municipal governments), and private associations and organizations aid speedy location. Almost all chapters have an additional "special topics" section, where the most common feature is a listing of corporate consumer contacts. Each chapter, section, and subsection is arranged alphabetically. A master name and keyword index (from words in the organization's name) provides specific name entry as well as moderately good additional subject access points. A sampling of topical chapters includes aging, education, employment, energy, funerals, health care, insurance, politics, and veterans.

The approximately sixty-two hundred unique entries are compiled by Gale based on direct contact with the organizations and agencies. The completeness, or amount of information provided, of an entry varies considerably and appears to be based on editorial views of how much needs to be explained about an organization. Always included will be name, address, and telephone number. Governmental agencies and nationwide organizations are usually explained in great detail the first time the entry appears with only minimal details for state and local offices or chapters. In the detailed listing the editors usually provide founding date, membership, staff, and descriptions of purposes, functions, and activities. The existence of local groups will also be noted but only occasionally detailed.

Another significant departure from previous editions is the dropping of coverage of company and trade names. This information now appears in Gale's *Trade Names Dictionary* (see *ARBA* 87, entry 183). The use of cross-references within the topical chapters to specific related organizations is another new and useful feature. Attempts by the editors to expand on their "how to" special topics sections in each chapter are welcome but greatly inadequate to the task. There are approximately ten of these brief explanations (usually less than five hundred words each) on various consumer topics, but almost all of them are only beginning hints to complex issues.

Overall, this volume continues the usual fine reference work publishing that we have come to expect from Gale. The price is a bit steep but not out of line with today's market and the value of the work. The volume has a sturdy binding and hard board covers that will surely be needed to protect it in a busy ready-reference section of an academic or public library. For librarians, this edition will be as essential as earlier ones. [R: RBB, July 88, p. 1792]

Robert V. Williams

197.　Hoy, Michael, comp. **Directory of U.S. Mail Drops: With an Appendix for Foreign Countries.** Port Townsend, Wash., Loompanics; distr., Boulder, Colo., Paladin Press, 1987. 52p. bibliog. $9.95pa. ISBN 0-915179-59-8.

A mail drop, also known as a remail service or mail forwarding service, is a private operation that allows a person to use the mail drop as his or her mailing address for a specified period of time. The user of the mail drop can then have mail held or forwarded by the mail drop. Use of the mail drop, after paying specified monthly fees, may be under real or assumed identities and may be for legal, quasi-legal, or illegal purposes. An individual mail drop may also perform a variety of other services, such as lockbox, copying, secretarial, and telephone answering services.

This is a directory of approximately twelve hundred mail drop services in the United States, with about one hundred additional ones in other countries. Organization of individual entries is alphabetical by state, city, and name of service. Each entry contains name, address, telephone number, and letter codes that refer to the specific services offered by the mail drop.

Exactly how the information in the directory was compiled is not clear, but it appears to be based on direct contact with the mail drop operator. It is also difficult to determine completeness because of a lack of comparative sources. (A brief bibliography of items on this and related topics at the end of the volume lists an earlier U.S. based as well as an international directory with fewer entries.) An interview with a former operator of a mail drop service appears at the front of the volume and contains good information on their operation and uses and U.S. laws affecting their operation and use. The U.S. Postal Service does regulate these operations, but the compiler leaves the distinct impression that these regulations are generally ignored by operators and users.

Reference librarians will find this an interesting and useful source that has its place in a strong reference collection. For those collections with specialties in alternative (or underground) literature, this has a definite place because it is closely allied to the survivalist, libertarian, anarchist literature. Loompanics is a key publisher and distributor in this area and an ideal source for continuing identification and acquisition of this literature.

Robert V. Williams

198.　Oppenheim, Joanne F. **Buy Me! Buy Me! The Bank Street Guide to Choosing Toys for Children.** New York, Pantheon Books/Random House, 1987. 311p. illus. index. $11.95pa. LC 87-43044. ISBN 0-394-75546-4.

The sad fact is that most parents let the $12-billion-a-year toy industry choose their children's toys, through television advertising and marketing schemes. As a result, many of the toys they buy are overpriced, easily broken, have little play value, and limit rather than enrich their children's play.

The aim of this book is to help parents deal with the "buy me" syndrome that has resulted from changes in the way toys are conceived and manufactured. Individual toys are rarely introduced anymore; rather the emphasis is on lines of toys or "play systems." An incredible 50 percent of the toys sold today are based on licensed characters. And as any five-year-old can tell you, one He-Man figure (or Care Bear or Transformer) is useless, you need *lots.* The first section of the book gives an overview of the toy industry and describes how parents have lost control of their toy-buying decisions. It catalogs the harmful effects many of these toys are having on their children, both directly and by replacing toys with real play value. Then suggestions are given on dealing with television and other pressures to buy inappropriate toys.

Section 2 lists and discusses toys appropriate for different ages and developmental stages, from infant through age eleven. It gives general guidelines for choosing toys as well as specific brand-name suggestions. It also points out instances when a simple homemade toy will perform as well and cost nothing. Throughout, the emphasis is on selecting the best, most appropriate, and longest lasting toys, and not showering the child with a glut of flashy throwaway items. To help in this aim, section 3 is a directory of catalog companies, toy manufacturers, and parent action groups. This is a fascinating and much-needed resource for beleaguered parents lost in toyland. [R: RBB, July 88, p. 1796]

Carol L. Noll

199.　Star, Nancy. **The International Guide to Tipping.** New York, Berkley, 1988. 240p. $5.95 pa. ISBN 0-425-11058-3.

TIP (To Insure Promptness) is certainly much older than modern tourism. However, questions about whom to tip, when, and how much still cause much confusion. This book attempts to provide "enough information to attain tipping confidence." The book consists of two distinct parts. The first part contains six chapters dealing with various aspects of tipping. Chapter 1 deals with "ground rules" such as The Thank You Tip, given on departure, and The Power Tip, given upon arrival. Chapter 2 contains advice on tipping on cruises, and chapter 3 discusses the dilemma: cash or gift. Chapter 4 handles special holiday situations (like Christmas), chapter 5 (the longest in this part) is devoted to tipping in the United States and chapter 6 discusses the customs of tipping in thirty-five countries (grouped alphabetically). The second part of the book (almost 75 percent of the entire book) presents the "Encyclopedia of International Tipping," in which the reader finds the various tipping categories discussed in alphabetical order. Within each category the national peculiarities are presented, also alphabetically according to countries.

The book will interest not only tourists but also the nontraveling U.S. public. It provides useful and reliable information. Some overlaps (repetitions) are unavoidable considering the arrangement of the material described above. [R: LJ, 1 Oct 88, p. 87]

Zbigniew Mieczkowski

200. The Wholesale-by-Mail Catalog 1988. By The Print Project. Prudence McCullough, ed. New York, St. Martin's Press, 1988. 464p. index. $10.95pa. LC 87-28673. ISBN 0-312-01532-1.

Mail-order shopping is big business these days and supposedly continuing to grow faster than any other sector of the merchandising industry. Discount mail-order shopping is a large component of this market, and an increasingly popular one since we all want to be able to brag about "getting it wholesale." The new edition of this work is a nice addition to the several other directories that attempt to cover this area.

The volume is arranged alphabetically by major subject categories of related products (e.g., appliances, audio, television, and video). Entries within each of the twenty-five subject categories detail the specifics about a particular wholesale company or store. Each entry contains the name of the store, mailing address (and shopping addresses if the store has one or more shopping locations), catalog availability/price, the compiler's estimation of approximate percentage of discount available, payment methods, brief listing of major products sold, symbols indicating acceptance of mail orders, telephone orders, whether shipments will be made to Canada, compiler's rating of dollar savings from the store, and a one hundred- to five hundred-word summary of the products and name-brands offered by the store. The summary is particularly effective because it enables the reader to get a "feel" for the store by emphasizing its specialties, tradition, and, particularly, an extensive listing of name brands available from it.

A wide variety of products is covered here, and almost any type of discount shopper will find his or her needs well covered. Each product category section contains cross-references to stores in other categories that carry the same or related goods but happen to be listed in another section more appropriate to their specialization. Two indexes, by product and by store, complement this cross-reference approach and make it unlikely that one would miss any of the stores relevant to a particular product. The compilers also provide, in both the entries themselves and in a separate, forty-page section, good advice to the shopper about mail-order problems such as warranties, delayed orders, complaint procedures, returns, shipping costs, and ordering from foreign countries. Each category section also has a brief discussion of particular problems that could arise when ordering the kinds of goods listed in it.

Overall, the volume is easy to use and read and contains most of the information a user could want when trying to make a decision to order from a particular company. I found the individual store entries more informative than those in its nearest competitor, Sue Goldstein's *The 3rd Underground Shopper* (see *ARBA* 88, entry 235), but there were fewer of them than in Goldstein, who has 750 entries compared to about 500 in this volume. One could profitably own both volumes since there is overlap as well as unique listing in both volumes. Similarly, both volumes are good on consumer advice but emphasize different kinds of problems and solutions. For the library attempting to provide exceptional coverage in the area of mail-order discount shopping, this volume will be a good addition to the collection.

Robert V. Williams

FINANCE AND BANKING

201. Alarid, William M. Free Help from Uncle Sam to Start Your Own Business (or Expand the One You Have). Santa Maria, Calif., Puma Publishing; distr., Lake Bluff, Ill., Quality Books, 1988. 158p. illus. index. $9.95pa. LC 88-2411. ISBN 0-940673-37-1.

This small paperback covers federal loan programs, loan guarantee programs, direct payment programs, grant programs, and information and counseling services that are designed to help business. Some of these programs are for a very specific type of industry, such as a direct compensation fund for damages to fishing vessels and gear. Unlike some larger directories of business resources, such as the *Government Assistance Almanac* (see *ARBA* 87, entry 222),

Free Help does not list any local government offices, only national headquarters. The programs are arranged by Federal Domestic Assistance Program number, so this title can serve as an index to the *Catalog of Federal Domestic Assistance* (see *ARBA* 84, entry 651), a comprehensive and inexpensive annual giving in-depth information on all federal assistance programs. The trouble with the *Catalog* is that it is complicated to use, and therefore a smaller index such as *Free Help* that gives very succinct information would be useful in narrowing a search before going to the larger title. *Free Help* also includes some examples of how businesses have used federal aid, drawn from Matthew Lesko's book, *Getting Yours* (Penguin Books, 1984), a popular guide to many government programs. In all, this is not nearly as comprehensive as some other reasonably priced titles that are available, but it might prove to be handy, especially in helping unsophisticated patrons. [R: RBB, 1 Sept 88, pp. 46, 48]

Susan V. McKimm

202. *American Banker* **1988 Year Book.** William E. Zimmerman, ed. New York, American Banker; distr., Detroit, Gale, 1988. 482p. illus. index. $95.00. ISBN 0-9618162-1-X.

A fascinating collection of articles, statistics, surveys, and other information about the domestic and international financial services industry. This yearbook is invaluable not only for the amount of data presented but also for its concise and logical arrangement.

The *American Banker 1988 Year Book* has broad applications for the individual as well as the academic, public, or special library. For example, the chronology, extensive ranking tables, and the professional directory listings would appeal to all user segments. This work is separated into five distinct areas: "Key Trends and Developments," "Dates and Events," "Statistics: Historical and Current," "Surveys and Special Reports," and "Directories." The equal attention given to commercial banks, international banks, nonbanks, and thrifts throughout each section works well in unifying the excellent reporting and analyses.

The book is a definite purchase recommendation. The comprehensiveness of coverage, the level of detail, and the excellent arrangement make this source worthwhile.

Peter B. Kaatrude

203. Avneyon, Eitan A. **Dictionary of Finance.** New York, Macmillan, 1988. 486p. illus. $50.00. LC 87-28326. ISBN 0-02-916420-6.

Avneyon's dictionary is a solid, no-frills reference book: good attention to shades of

meaning and substantial detail where required, but no extras of any consequence. (There are a few ink sketches of economists, often used to illustrate a theory, such as Thorstein Veblen and the "leisure class" or Jevons and the "sunspot theory," but these constitute the sole extra.) Otherwise, there are some sixty-two hundred entries in a letter-by-letter alphabetical order covering, as the preface states, "every aspect of finance and investment: economics, accounting, trading procedure in the securities & commodities market, banking, private and public financing, consumer and tax legislation, as well as management, marketing, statistics, and other related fields."

The definitions vary in length from a few lines up to about one-third of a column. When a word has several senses, such as *abatement*, the general description and the specialized meanings in the law, taxation, and accounting fields follow. The author includes newer terms, slang, and industry jargon according to "the extent that it has lasting relevance and it is not mere ephemeral jargon." Obviously such a yardstick leaves a wide margin for personal taste. Case in point: two words that have evolved from mergers and acquisition jargon to the business pages of every magazine and newspaper: *white knight* is included by Avneyon, but not *greenmail*.

There are plentiful cross-references, both as separate entries and as italics in the text. Besides the words, major international organizations are included as text entries. In spite of the many cross-references, there are not enough in some cases. *Market maker*, a fairly common industry term, is not listed either as a main or as a secondary entry. The concept is treated, though, under *make a market*. These minor weaknesses should not obscure this book's principal advantage: its broad coverage. By treating many topics superficially, it becomes the ideal purchase for those libraries that can only afford a single business dictionary. Even specialized collections may find the good sense of its definitions warrant its purchase. [R: WLB, Dec 88, p. 117]

Richard Reid

204. Balachandran, M. **A Guide to Statistical Sources in Money, Banking, and Finance.** Phoenix, Ariz., Oryx Press, 1988. 119p. index. $45.00. LC 87-21941. ISBN 0-89774-265-6.

The main emphasis of this annotated bibliography is on serial sources of banking and monetary statistics, covering "capital and credit markets, interest rates, consumer finance and credit cards, money supply and currency, treasury operations, bank deposits, bank loans, assets, liabilities and profitability of financial institutions, and foreign exchange markets" (introduction).

The groupings of entries suggest the coverage and the variety of sources: (1) states (48 entries, with all states except Massachusetts, Nevada, Ohio, South Carolina, West Virginia, and Wyoming represented); (2) regional (29 entries, primarily regional Federal Home Loan Bank boards and Federal Reserve Banks); (3) national (150 entries, such as American Bankers Association, Bank Administration Institute, Federal Deposit Insurance Corp., Federal Home Loan Bank Board, Mortgage Bankers Association of America, Federal Reserve Board, Comptroller of the Currency, Treasury Department – all with multiple entries – and a host of additional public and private organizations); (4) foreign countries (110 entries from ninety-eight countries; no entries from People's Republic of China, USSR, or East European countries, except Hungary with one entry); (5) international (79 entries, involving data or comparisons of several countries); and (6) databases (64 entries, with the vendor indicated; presumably these are all in machine readable form).

Each entry is annotated with fifteen to sixty words of content description. A directory of publishers (about 275), a title index, and a subject index complete the volume. An extremely useful source of information on where to look and whom to contact for banking and monetary data worldwide. [R: Choice, June 88, p. 1529; RBB, 15 June 88, p. 1720; RQ, Spring 88, p. 429]   Richard A. Miller

205. IBI International Business Intelligence Development Aid: A Guide to National and International Agencies. Compiled by Eurofi (UK) Limited. Stoneham, Mass., Butterworths, 1988. 587p. $160.00. LC 87-35543. ISBN 0-408-00991-8.

There are now several hundred governmental organizations that provide development aid to Third World nations. The form, structure, objectives, and purposes of such agencies differ greatly. Some operate on a bilateral basis, others are multilateral. Some provide only financial assistance, others provide technical assistance and a variety of other forms of aid. Some have a short-term focus, others fund primarily long-term, capital-intensive projects. Indeed, the development aid process has become so large and complex that even seasoned development specialists have difficulty finding their way through the maze of development agencies. This reference work will provide specialists and nonspecialists alike with a highly useful tour through most of the important development agencies. For each development

agency there is a brief summary of its organization, its members, its purposes, and recent activities. When appropriate, there is also an organizational diagram. Many users will find the guide to abbreviations and the mailing address of each organization to be the most useful parts of this reference. Since some developing nations also engage in providing development aid to other developing nations, the short section describing that activity is an informative and possibly unique feature. The one obviously irritating feature of this relatively expensive reference is that the publishers apparently saved a great deal of money by publishing typescript. Nevertheless, this is a very useful and highly recommended reference work.   James T. Peach

206. Jud, G. Donald, and Charles J. Woelfel. The Desktop Encyclopedia of Banking. Chicago, Probus Publishing, 1988. 397p. $37.50. ISBN 0-917253-29-9.

This work is a lightweight entry into the bulging arena of business "encyclopedias." This source, while touted as a "complete guide to lending, credit analysis, asset-liability management and much more," falls short of the mark. Missing are discussions of many expected banking terms, such as *call loan, fiat money, insufficient funds, mint, private banking,* and *withdrawal.* Further omission of more specialized terms, such as *cumulative voting, revolving check credit, visitorial powers,* and *without recourse,* compounds the work's slightness.

Added to this dearth of banking terminology is an odd, potentially confusing arrangement. Basically the book is proportioned into two broad categories: the "encyclopedia" and "glossaries." While limitations of the "encyclopedia" portion are suggested above, redemption is not forthcoming from the complementary sections. The "glossaries" number five. Four of the glossaries are imbedded within "encyclopedia" entries and one of the glossaries is placed as the final section of the book. The work lacks cross-references for location purposes and an index.

Those needing a reference source that will provide what this title fails to do should consult Glenn G. Munn's *The Encyclopedia of Banking and Finance* (see *ARBA 84,* entry 753). This latter work remains a seminal source, and even though slightly dated, is vastly superior to the title in question.

Peter B. Kaatrude

207. Presley, John R., ed. Directory of Islamic Financial Institutions. New York, Croom Helm/Routledge, Chapman & Hall, 1988. 353p. bibliog. $120.00. LC 87-30403. ISBN 0-7099-1347-8.

The editor states that the primary object of this directory is "to give detailed information on the principles, theory, and institutions of Islamic banking and to explore the progress which has already taken place in many Muslim states towards the introduction and operation of Islamic financial institutions" (preface). Islamic banking practices differ in several respects from those of Western commercial banks, not least of all because the Qur'an forbids the giving or charging of interest, considerable adjustment with respect to money markets and monetary policies are needed on both sides if the two types of institutions are to function alongside each other as they are having to do in various parts of the Muslim world. The past quarter century has seen the establishment of more than fifty Islamic financial institutions, and the development of strong support for the concept of Islamic banking, thus making this directory a very welcome publication indeed.

The book is divided into three parts. "Islamic Banking: The Background" covers an overview of the Islamic economic system, Islamic banking operations, the International Association of Islamic Banks, and the Role of the Islamic Development Bank, as well as providing a selected bibliography on Islamic economics and banking. Part 2, a "Directory of Islamic Financial Institutions," supplies the address of the head office, telephone/telex/cable information, the date of formation, the background and areas of operation, the names of the founder members, the present directors and, if available, the senior management staff, the objectives of the institution and the value of its assets in U.S. dollars. The addresses of individual branches are listed as well. Part 3, "Islamic Banking: Case Studies and Banking Laws," includes studies of banking in the Islamic Republic of Iran and in Pakistan. A third section discusses the major issues of transition in Islamic banking, and appended to it are the Islamic banking laws in Malaysia and Turkey.

This is a well-researched, well-prepared tool, useful for those engaged in banking and commerce on the one hand, and, on the other, those interested in the theory of Islamic banking.   Margaret Anderson

208. Weiner, Andrew. *The Financial Post Moneywise Magazine* **Dictionary of Personal Finance.** Mississauga, Ont., Random House of Canada, 1987. 205p. index. $12.95pa. ISBN 0-394-22007-2.

This dictionary includes about one thousand entries, arranged into nine topic chapters: personal budgeting, real estate, financial services, life and health insurance, property and casualty insurance, investing in the (stock) market, personal taxation, retirement, and family finances and estate planning. The defined terms range from very common (e.g., *stock, proxy, net worth, taxation, earnings per share*) to less common (e.g., *random walk theory, rule of 72, annuity certain, beta factor, codicil, GTC, SWIFT*). Each definition (from 5 words to about 150 words, usually about 25-30) is clearly and lightly written for the nonprofessional reader, who is the sponsor's (Canada's *The Financial Post Moneywise Magazine*) audience. The definitions are authoritative but not sufficiently detailed to serve in all cases as the sole source of information. The line between included and excluded items seems about right; thus *puts* and *calls* are included, *straddles* are not.

A major attribute is the Canadian orientation, with almost no mention of differences with U.S. (or English or any other) laws, agencies, or institutions. Thus there is no mention of the IRS, the FDIC, or the FSLIC, but included are Revenue Canada and Canada Deposit Insurance Corporation. Similarly there is no mention of 1040, 1040A (or EZ), or W-2, but defined are the T1 General, T1 Special, and T4. References to U.S. terms include items with some currency north of the border: Wall Street, Dow Jones Averages, AMEX and NYSE (and Big Board), Manhattan duplex. For non-Canadians this orientation can be a benefit (if one wants Canadian institutions and laws), a minor drawback (if a term is missing), or a major problem (if one gets led astray, as with the incomplete definition of zero-coupon bond—under stripped bond—or with the Canadian laws on personal taxes, which differ from U.S. and other tax laws). Humor makes for interesting reading; for example, "Revenue Canada: What the folks at the Department of National Revenue prefer to call themselves. We can't print what you'd prefer to call them."   Richard A. Miller

INDUSTRY AND MANUFACTURING

209. **The Blue Book of Canadian Business 1987.** Edited by Canadian Newspaper Services International. Toronto, Canadian Newspaper Services International, 1987. 1300p. illus. $150.00. ISBN 0-9692531-1-7; ISSN 0381-7245.

Now in its eleventh edition, this reference source has become a standard for Canadian business information. Arrangement is within three broad sections: "Profiles of Leading Canadian Companies" (134 companies), "Rankings of Major Canadian Companies" (reproduced from other sources), and the "Canadian Business Index" (approximately 2,200 companies).

Parameters for company inclusion are defined as those Canadian firms having "(1) annual revenues of $10 million or more, (2) assets of $5 million or more, or (3) 500 employees or more."

The strengths of *The Blue Book* are with its "Profiles," the first section. These comprehensive reports are unsurpassed in the quality of information that they provide. Standard in these profiles are lengthy sections on individual company history, activities, management philosophy, and social responsibility. Added to this detailed reporting are board of director and functional officer listings. Completing each report is an executive biography (oftentimes including photograph) profiling at least one of the chief officers from each of the 134 leading companies.

There are two indexes—a "Profile Index" and an "Executive Biography Index"—both of which apply to the first section only. Neither of the other two sections offers indexing.

The latter two sections, especially the "Business Index," with its brief directory listings for approximately twenty-two hundred companies, are not unique by any means. Both the *Canadian Key Business Directory* (Dun's Marketing Services, 1975-), providing coverage of 20,000 Canadian companies, and the *Canadian Trade Index* (Canadian Manufacturers' Association, 1900-), covering 14,500 Canadian manufacturers, are far more comprehensive given the sheer number of directory listings available. The hallmark and the strong selling point of *The Blue Book* is definitely the "Profiles." The other sections appear to be more of an afterthought, and without indexing a halfhearted one at that.

Peter B. Kaatrude

210. Boger, Karl. **Postwar Industrial Policy in Japan: An Annotated Bibliography.** Metuchen, N.J., Scarecrow, 1988. 208p. index. $22.50. LC 87-26535. ISBN 0-8108-2080-3.

The rise of Japan from the ashes of total defeat to a position as a world economic power that rivals its former occupier is one of the great economic and political events of modern history. Although not comprehensive, this handy little volume provides a list of sources that can be used to study this situation. The author is an economics bibliographer who has also studied the American industrial system (see his *U.S. Industrial Policy: An Annotated Bibliography of Books and Government Documents, 1980-1985* [The Council of Planning Librarians, 1986]).

Why this topic is so important to the United States is explained by the author in a

three-page introduction. The eight chapters of this book cover broad subject areas, such as "Japan's Economic Development," "Finance and Financial Organization," and "International Economic Relations." The 520 entries are all individually numbered and described. Three indexes ("Authors and Editors," "Title," and "Subject") at the end of the book include the entry numbers for easy access to the citations. Books, journal articles, and U.S. and Japanese government documents can be found here, while articles from newspapers and news magazines are excluded. Only English-language items are included, and for the most part, these materials reflect an American point of view. A related bibliography with a Japanese perspective is the *Bibliography of Japanese Publications on Economics, 1946-1975* by the Union of the National Economic Associations of Japan, edited by Sakae Tsunoyama (University of Tokyo Press, 1977).

Most of the citations within this volume have post-1970 dates. This is because Americans did not really become interested in the Japanese economy until the 1970s and 1980s, when the Japanese began to surge ahead of America in many fields. The basis of their success was laid, however, during the 1950s and 1960s, and more citations from those time periods would have been useful.

Librarians will want to compare this book with a similar publication: *Japan's Economic Challenge: A Bibliographic Sourcebook* by Michael Keresztesi and Gary Cocozzoli (Garland, 1988). Boger's less expensive work is appropriate for economists, businessmen, and historians and is recommended for academic and specialized libraries. [R: Choice, Sept 88, p. 74]

Daniel K. Blewett

211. **Corporate Technology Directory.** 1988 U.S. ed. Wellesley Hills, Mass., CorpTech, 1988. 4v. maps. index. $795.00/set. ISBN 0-936507-13-6; ISSN 0887-1930.

The dynamic growth of high-tech industries increases the difficulty of locating information on small, privately owned companies. This annual directory with quarterly updates provides company and product information and can be used for potential job opportunities.

In volume 1, two index sections are the keys to companies and products. The three-part business index section is an alphabetical list of company names, and also has a geographic index and a foreign parent company listing. One of the three-part product indexes is an alphabetical list of sixteen thousand products and technologies, which includes the CorpTech Code, Standard Industrial Classification (S.I.C.) numbers, and citations to the company associated with the product/technology. The index to the three thousand-item CorpTech Code, developed by the publisher, has seventeen industry segments such as automation and biotechnology, with sub-segments, further subdivided into more specific products. An S.I.C. code listing to the comparable CorpTech Code entry is also provided. More than twenty-five thousand companies are alphabetically arranged in volumes 2-5. The company profile has the address, sales, number of employees, executives' names, products by four-digit S.I.C. codes, and the date of the information.

Since this directory covers all areas of high-tech industries, it does not include as many companies for a segment of the industry. *Cahners/ Bowker MMP 1987: Microcomputer Market Place* (see *ARBA* 88, entry 1718) lists nine thousand companies, some of which are in the CorpTech directory.

Directories for high-tech industries are costly and require annual purchase to keep the information relatively current. Even with a discount for libraries, this is an expensive publication, but buying directories for each high-tech area is also expensive. Although there are limitations, large business, computer science, engineering, public, and some corporate libraries will find this directory a useful addition to their collections.   Jean Herold

212.   Dibner, Mark D. **Biotechnology Guide U.S.A.: Companies, Data and Analysis.** New York, Stockton Press/Grove's Dictionaries of Music, 1988. 378p. bibliog. index. $175.00. LC 88-4952. ISBN 0-935859-40-3.

This exhaustively indexed directory of U.S. biotechnology companies lists some 360 firms involved in this burgeoning high-tech area. In addition to the firms directly involved, this guide also details the involvement of major organizations in the field, such as large corporations. For the key companies comprising the core group, details of personnel, products, financing, revenues, and date of founding are provided.

The companies are first listed in a straight alphabetical listing by name, followed by another alphabetical listing which includes addresses, telephone numbers, major product lines, the names of the chief executive officers and the R&D manager, type of financing, date started, and S.I.C.s for the industry type.

Another useful index is by major product. Numerous other indexes provide information on patents, partnerships with foreign companies, R&D budget by company type, state biotechnology centers, etc.

In view of the high cost of this item, as well as the volatility of the field, it can only be recommended for special libraries serving companies active in biotechnology, either as producers or as providers of goods and services, and possibly to academic libraries serving clienteles with strong research interests in the area.   Edwin D. Posey

213.   **Encyclopedia of American Business History and Biography: Railroads in the Age of Regulation, 1900-1980.** Keith L. Bryant, Jr., ed. New York, Facts on File, 1988. 518p. illus. maps. index. $75.00. LC 87-36493. ISBN 0-8160-1371-3.

214.   **Encyclopedia of American Business History and Biography: Railroads in the Nineteenth Century.** Robert L. Frey, ed. New York, Facts on File, 1988. 491p. illus. maps. index. $75.00. ISBN 0-8160-2012-4.

These volumes are part of what is intended to be a fifty-volume set covering all aspects of U.S. business; if the rest of the set meets the standards set by these titles, it will become a major reference for all libraries concerned with business history.

Written by sixty-one transportation historians (eighteen contributed to both volumes), the signed, alphabetically arranged articles include histories of individual railroad companies, biographies of railroad leaders, accounts of major federal legislation and court cases affecting railroads, and a few discussions of general topics (e.g., brakes, operating ratio). Coverage is limited to major steam railroads and the emphasis is strongly on railroad management and finance; technological developments are treated from the economic viewpoint. *Age of Regulation* biographies are exclusively of company executives; *Nineteenth Century* coverage is somewhat broader, including some financiers, inventors, politicians, etc., who were important in railroad history even though they never served as C.E.O. of a railroad company. Eugene Debs is the only labor leader included, and there are no articles on labor unions. Most of the railroad histories include maps; the biographies include portraits. Most articles include a bibliography of published sources, a list of archival collections, or both. The treatment is analytical and objective, neither an exposé nor an apology. There are comprehensive indexes of names and topics.

The information on railroad companies is available elsewhere, but the biographical information is not; there is no comparably comprehensive and authoritative source. These volumes make an important contribution to scholarship in the field. [R: BR, Nov/Dec 88, p. 48; Choice, Oct 88, p. 288; LJ, 15 June 88, p. 53; RBB, Aug 88, p. 1901; WLB, May 88, p. 112]

Paul B. Cors

215. Financial Times Industrial Companies. Harlow, England, Longman; distr., Chicago, St. James Press, 1987. 2v. index. $105.00/vol. ISBN 0-912289-92-9 (v.1); 0-912289-91-0 (v.2).

This title is not a British emphasis directory, but a reference guide to notable and major international electric and electronic companies (volume 1) and chemicals, petrochemical, and pharmaceutical companies (volume 2). It is the new addition to the annual volumes prepared by *Financial Times:* (*World Insurance, Mining,* and *Oil and Gas*).

Each entry contains name, address, telex and telephone numbers, and FAX information, principal officers, business, subsidiaries, description of operations, capital structure, ownership, where traded, three-year financial results (table format), in addition to other pertinent information for each corporation. An introductory chapter for each volume analyzes trends in its particular industry with its world trade, its markets, its national competition, and each nation's production figures and statistics. There is an extensive alphabetical index to corporations and subsidiaries that provides access to the smaller companies as a part of the whole.

The entries are set in a double-column format, thorough, and provide comparative information (e.g., found in *Moody's, Standard and Poor's,* etc.) on the firm's recent activity, including financial and common stock trading activity. It is bound well and should last indefinitely, but the print is also comparable to *Moody's* (i.e., difficult to read). It is certainly consistent in price with ongoing services in the United States.   Jack I. Gardner

216. Knowledge Industry Publications 200. 1987 ed. Ira Mayer, ed. White Plains, N.Y., Knowledge Industry; distr., Detroit, Gale, 1987. 421p. $250.00. ISBN 0-8103-4254-5; ISSN 0736-6795.

Knowledge Industry Publications 200 (KIP 200) covers public and private companies producing intellectual property for broadcast, cable, print, and electronic consumption. Companies which distribute but do not produce intellectual property are not included. The two hundred companies profiled in this directory account for $106.8 billion in media revenues (the cut-off for inclusion is $35 million in media revenues per organization). For each company, financial data, a listing of corporate officers and directors, information on subsidiaries, and a description of the company are provided. Where appropriate, the descriptions include details on corporate structures and divisions, specific publications, magazines, radio and television stations, daily newspapers, databases, etc. For publicly held companies, balance sheet financials are given. Because *KIP 200* provides a strong overview of the trends among those companies active in the media property sweepstakes, it is a valuable reference guide for corporate management, investors (domestic and foreign), bankers, etc., who need to know who is doing what, who owns who, and how much money they are making (or losing).

Assad A. Tavakoli

217. Moskowitz, Milton. The Global Marketplace: 102 of the Most Influential Companies outside America. New York, Macmillan, 1987. 708p. illus. bibliog. index. $24.95. LC 87-15897. ISBN 0-02-587590-6.

The author of this title is the coauthor of *Everybody's Business* (see *ARBA* 81, entry 872) and *The 100 Best Companies to Work for in America* (see *ARBA* 86, entry 257). The biographies of 102 companies from twenty countries include information on sales, profits, rank, number of employees, when founded, headquarters, address(es) and telephone number(s), plus a history of how, when and by whom the company was started, as well as its present status. The appendix provides tables of the world's largest (1) industrial corporations outside the United States, (2) coal producers, (3) banks outside the United States, (4) steel making countries, (5) industrial corporations, and (6) U.S. multinationals. There are also tables listing the numbers of telephones, robots, and telecommunications equipment throughout the world.

A table of contents lists the companies alphabetically, while another table lists them by countries. There is an extensive index, as well as a comprehensive bibliography. Although many of the facts and figures can be located elsewhere, this title brings all of that information, plus the companies' "inside stories," together in one book. This is fascinating as well as informative reading. [R: BL, 15 Jan 88, p. 814; LJ, Jan 88, pp. 77, 80]   Mary Jo Aman

218. Mulligan, William H., Jr., ed. A Historical Dictionary of American Industrial Language. Westport, Conn., Greenwood Press, 1988. 332p. bibliog. index. $55.00. LC 87-37544. ISBN 0-313-24171-6.

This dictionary will serve as a guide for researchers exploring the "culture of work" in America, particularly during the preindustrial and industrializing periods on the North American continent. Designed to create an understanding of the "vocabulary of work" in earlier time periods, it is a reference guide providing brief definitions and descriptions which invite lengthy discussions on industrial language.

It is alphabetical in arrangement, and the main body of work is followed by an appendix which lists industrial classifications subdivided by alphabetically arranged, significant words pertinent to that classification. Following the appendix are a five-page bibliography indicating the sources searched and an index of institutions and people mentioned in the main body of the work. Greenwood Press provides wide margins, enhanced headings, and clearly printed pages in this necessary and probably definitive reference title for those interested in an historical approach to industry and labor in America.

Jack I. Gardner

219. Pardoe, Geoffrey K. C., ed. **Space Industry International: Markets, Companies, Statistics and Personnel.** Harlow, England, Longman; distr., Detroit, Gale, 1987. 353p. index. (Companion for Industry). $155.00. ISBN 0-582-00314-8.

This modestly sized directory provides descriptive company information within the context of industry analyses. Focused toward the practitioner in need of international marketing data for highly specialized manufacturers, this source is invaluable.

The book is conveniently arranged into twelve chapters, each highlighting an industry-important area of the world. For example, the "Middle East" is presented as one unified area, as is "Canada." Tabulations preface each of the twelve sections, providing regional chronological overviews of satellite launch activity. Each country within the specified region is then profiled to include background information on space administration, space policies, programs, industry, and market. Following these country overviews are the company listings. Each entry includes standard directory information, plus unique marketing information on customers, operational sites, product areas, and senior staff. Indexing includes company name, organizational name, product area, and personal name. Also provided are a "Glossary" and a "Reference Sources and Further Reading List."

This third title in Longman's Companion for Industry series is almost guilty of taking on more than can be covered adequately between two covers. The statistics and the capsulized overviews of the space industry are convenient, but not absolutely necessary. *Jane's Spaceflight Directory 1986* (see *ARBA* 87, entry 1730) is much more comprehensive in scope for the industry overviews as is *Jane's Aerospace Dictionary* (see *ARBA* 87, entry 1727) for its coverage of space terminology. However, for those not having ready access to these two latter sources, the new addition can be of limited use. Therefore, as a purchase primarily for the industry content, it is recommended to use the more comprehensive tools. Otherwise, the real forte of this work lies in its presentation of company marketing information. This unique data should justify acquisition of this source for business libraries supporting research in the area of space marketing.

Peter B. Kaatrude

220. Spiewak, Scott A. **Cogeneration and Small Power Production Manual.** 2d ed. Lilburn, Ga., Fairmont Press, 1988. 577p. illus. $85.00pa. LC 87-46191. ISBN 0-88173-059-9.

The second edition of this manual contains essentially the same material as the first edition (see *ARBA* 88, entry 267). Very few sections have been revised and the revisions are not extensive. Four pages describing the rescinding of the fuel act natural gas prohibitions replace pages 48-51 in Section A, "Regulation of Cogeneration and Small Power Production." Section F, "Tax and Cogeneration," in the first edition is eliminated as a separate section. It is replaced with Appendix E-4, "Tax and Cogeneration," in Section E, "Finance and Cogeneration." This Section F of ninety-one pages is replaced with twenty-two pages on major tax changes for cogeneration and small power production facilities and the same article on the impact of the deficit reduction act of 1984 and the "Wallop Amendment" on energy sales contracts which was in the first edition.

Again, nowhere is there an indication of what material has been updated or the currency of the material in the manual. The editorial board and the preface are the same. No changes were made in the list of officials of state utility commissioners concerned with cogeneration or in the appendix on description and prices of cogeneration equipment. It also would have been helpful if a subject index was included in this second edition. This manual is useful for the person who has to initiate a cogeneration facility feasibility study. However, with the very few revisions made, this reviewer wonders why a new edition was issued so quickly.

Anne C. Roess

221. **U.S. Manufacturers Directory.** 1988-89 ed. Omaha, Nebr., American Business Directories, 1988. 2v. $495.00pa./set. ISBN 0-945041-00-4.

This two-volume directory set purportedly lists "every manufacturing firm in the U.S. with 10 or more employees." The listings provide company name, address, telephone number, executive name and title, S.I.C. codes (up to three per entry), and broad category codes for employee size (seven) and sales volume (nine). The arrangement of the entries is (1) alphabetical, (2) alphabetical by state and city, and (3) alphabetical within S.I.C. number. A special feature offers a census of companies contained herein by S.I.C. and by county. Company information was drawn from "Yellow Pages" and "enhanced using Department of Commerce statistics ... and telephone verification."

The appearance of the entries in this directory set is similar to *Ward's Business Directory of Major U.S. Private Companies* (see *ARBA* 88, entry 181). The companies are listed in a straightforward tabular sequence and the type is very small. The content of the information is similar to *Electronic Yellow Pages Manufacturers Directory* (Market Data Retrieval, 1987) which contains over 435,000 company records, and to *Thomas Register of American Manufacturers and Thomas Register Catalog File, 1982.* 72nd ed. (see *ARBA* 83, entry 785). The 78th edition of the *Thomas Register* provides coverage of over 145,000 manufacturers. Other content comparisons can be made with *MacRae's Blue Book* (MacRae's Blue Book, 1987) and with the *U.S. Industrial Directory, 1984* (see *ARBA* 85, entry 229).

Overall, the *U.S. Manufacturers Directory* is interesting but not sufficiently unique to distinguish itself in the already overcrowded manufacturers' directory field. Its drawbacks include the reliance on the S.I.C. classification (the *Thomas Register*'s expansive topical index is much more specific) and its broad company coverage. The *Electronic Yellow Pages Manufacturers Directory* is far more comprehensive. For $5.00 less than the cost of the *U.S. Manufacturers Directory*, one could purchase *MacRae's Blue Book*, *Thomas Register*, "and" the *U.S. Industrial Directory*.

Peter B. Kaatrude

annotated insurance references are organized into six broad classifications: general insurance and risk management reference sources, lines of insurance (including social insurance), insurance operations, the legal environment of insurance, consumer guides, and miscellaneous sources. The entries are up to date and include books, periodicals, directories, policy and rate manuals, statistical compilations, audiovisual programs, and computerized databases. Particular emphasis is placed on looseleaf services. Coverage is limited to works in the English language and, other than Canadian, there are few foreign references. Older material is restricted to a few classics. Separate author, title, and subject indexes are keyed to the numbered references.

Although perhaps most useful to insurance students and practitioners, this work is clearly designed to meet the needs of a broadly defined audience. For libraries interested in building or expanding their insurance collections, 212 of the listed works are included in a separate "core library collection" section. A chapter on insurance education describes professional education and training programs available in the United States, and it lists, by state, all colleges and universities with undergraduate and graduate degree programs in insurance and actuarial science. An alphabetical listing of insurance and insurance-related organizations and trade associations contains brief descriptions of the purpose, activities, and services offered by each group. A short chapter describes and gives representative examples of the research activities of several insurer organizations such as the Health Insurance Association of America and the American Council of Life Insurance. Rounding out the volume are chapters listing the names and addresses of insurance libraries, computerized insurance databases, and regulatory authorities in the United States and Canada. Much of what is in this volume can be found elsewhere, but no other single source contains the breadth of coverage or packages it better. [R: Choice, Dec 88, p. 633]

Bruce Stuart

INSURANCE

222. Weiner, Alan R. **The Insurance Industry: An Information Sourcebook.** Phoenix, Ariz., Oryx Press, 1988. 278p. index. (Oryx Sourcebook Series in Business and Management, No. 16). $45.00. LC 88-1433. ISBN 0-89774-307-5.

This indispensable guide contains the most useful collection of references, annotations, and other source material on the insurance industry to appear in print. More than twelve hundred

LABOR

223. Arden, Lynie. **The Work-at-Home Sourcebook: How to Find "at Home" Work That's Right for You.** 2d ed. Boulder, Colo., Live Oak, 1988. 219p. illus. bibliog. index. $12.95pa. LC 87-35699. ISBN 0-911781-07-2.

Somewhat changed from the 1987 edition (see *ARBA* 88, entry 274), this new edition is divided into nine chapters covering over one thousand work-at-home opportunities in art, crafts, telecommuting, computer-based home work, office support positions, work with people, industrial home work, and sales. The first chapter provides tips on getting the job, optimizing the work-at-home opportunity, labor laws, and independent contractor status and tax savings.

Provided with each entry are the name of the company offering at-home work, the address, type of work available, requirements, and provisions. Entries are listed alphabetically by company, and a geographic index at the end of the book aids the user in locating companies by state. Several companies in each section are highlighted by a brief essay. These essays give the reader a better understanding of the company's views and expectations concerning at-home workers; however, they often tend to be a bit too "promotional" in nature. A "Resource Guide" provides additional periodicals, books, and organizations pertinent to the subject, and an index to opportunities for the disabled concludes the work.

Because interest in at-home work is increasing, both for companies as well as employees, public libraries might want to consider having a book such as this in their collection.

Susan R. Penney

224. **Bibliography of Published Research of the World Employment Programme.** 7th ed. Washington, D.C., International Labor Office, 1988. 126p. index. (International Labour Bibliography, No. 4). $12.25pa. ISBN 92-2-106390-9.

First published in 1978, this work is one of the results of World Employment Programme (WEP) efforts. The WEP was created in 1969 by the International Labour Organization (ILO) in support of an international development strategy for the Second United Nations Development Decade. The publication is current to December 1987.

The brief but useful work is divided by topic into twelve chapters: general publications on the World Employment Programme; comprehensive employment planning; manpower planning and labor market information systems; basic needs and income distribution; labor market analysis and the informal sector; rural poverty, rural industrialization, and employment; migration and urbanization; population and employment; technology and employment; special employment programs and vulnerable groups; structural adjustment and the international division of labor; and women.

Each chapter is divided into ILO publications, ILO works published by commercial and nonprofit publishers, and related books and articles. Each of the entries is noted in geographical and chronological order in its respective category. Entries include all relevant information such as publisher, price, pagination, date, and ISBN. This bibliography also indicates if an item is available in more than one language, or if the document is either confidential or unavailable.

The text's introduction provides an example on how to read the entries, and indicates how to order or obtain listed items found in the bibliography. The text is followed by helpful author, country, and area indexes.

James M. Murray

225. **Directory of U.S. Labor Organizations.** 1988-89 ed. Courtney D. Gifford, ed. Washington, D.C., Bureau of National Affairs, 1988. 104p. index. $18.50pa. ISBN 0-87179-582-5; ISSN 0734-6786.

This is the fourth private edition of a directory published by BNA since 1982, when the previous, long-running government work, *Directory of National Unions and Employee Associations*, was discontinued for budgetary reasons. This edition includes relevant information on nearly three hundred American labor organizations representing nearly seventeen million workers. It is recommended for all public, academic, and business libraries.

The directory is divided into three main parts. Part 1 is an introductory outline of the structure of the ninety-union American Federation of Labor-Congress of Industrial Organizations (AFL-CIO) and the role of the AFL-CIO executive council. Excellent charts on pages 2 and 3 outline how these bodies are structured. Part 2 lists all AFL-CIO headquarters and central body offices. Part 3 includes information on all major AFL-CIO and independent American unions. In addition to listing officers and the address and telephone numbers of relevant organizations, part 3 also includes such information as convention dates, when the union was founded, the number of locals, membership, and publications.

The text is supplemented by helpful appendices and indexes. The two appendices give AFL-CIO membership data and the latest U.S. Bureau of Labor statistics data on American union membership. Three indexes list labor organizations by abbreviations and by common name, and list the names of union officers.

James M. Murray

226. Dryden, Laurel, comp. **Employment Creation Policies and Strategies: An Annotated Bibliography, 1980-86.** Washington, D.C., International Labor Office, 1987. 400p. index.

(International Labour Bibliography, No. 3). $15.75pa. ISBN 92-2-106173-6.

The aim of this bibliography is to bring together theoretical and applied works on remedies for unemployment in both developing and industrialized countries. The preface states that the works included fall into the categories of research papers, government reports, books, and conference proceedings published from 1980 to 1986. Materials were taken from the ILO's Labordoc and Laborinfo databases.

The book is divided into seven sections covering different solutions, with a final section devoted to bibliographies. Personal and corporate author, country or geographic area, and subject indexes facilitate use of the work. Some entries contain short abstracts or merely lists of descriptors that provide clues to each item's scope. Due to the computerized source of the book, unedited slashes appear throughout some of the abstracts. Information on the items includes language of text, ISSN where appropriate, and some price information.

Maureen B. Lambert

227. Greenfield, Gerald Michael, and Sheldon L. Maram, eds. **Latin American Labor Organizations.** Westport, Conn., Greenwood Press, 1987. 929p. index. $125.00. LC 86-33613. ISBN 0-313-22834-5.

This work provides information in English about the history and development of the labor movement in twenty-six Latin American and Caribbean countries as reflected in labor organizations. Each chapter covers a specific country, beginning with an essay placing the labor movement within the context of the country's historical, social, and political development, followed by a bibliography. A section in dictionary format entitled "Labor Organizations" concludes each chapter; it covers the origins, development, and activities of important past and present organizations.

Depth of coverage in the latter sections varies from chapter to chapter, reflecting the uneven development of labor movements in different countries, the availability of information about different organizations, and the preparation of chapters by different authors. The editorial decision to list names of organizations under awkward English translations instead of under the names by which they are known in their original national languages is unfortunate, hampering access to the information in these sections (which are otherwise the most useful features of this work). Cross-references from names in the vernacular and acronyms help, but they require an extra step in locating information about the desired organization.

Appendices supply data on international labor organizations associated with Latin America, chronologies of major historical/labor movement events for each country, and a "Glossary of Terms, People, and Events." A thorough index completes the work. Overall, this publication provides much useful information in one place about a subject which has heretofore been difficult to pursue because of the multiple sources one had to consult in order to address it. [R: Choice, July/Aug 88, p. 1675]

Ann Hartness

228. Kelly, Matthew A. **Labor and Industrial Relations: Terms, Laws, Court Decisions, and Arbitration Standards.** Baltimore, Md., Johns Hopkins University Press, 1987. 200p. index. $26.50; $10.95pa. LC 86-21353. ISBN 0-8018-3310-8; 0-8018-3311-6pa.

According to the introduction, one of the objectives for writing this book was to provide "a source book for labor-management practitioners as well as scholars." Equally important, states the author, was creating an instructional aid for courses in this subject. Though not voluminous, it succeeds on both counts.

Part 1 is a glossary of over three hundred definitions of terms. Definition length ranges from a single sentence to a full page. In the lengthier definitions, other related terms may be in boldface type; the reader who has looked up these terms separately is given a *see* reference to the main topic. Definitions are clearly written and sometimes refer to landmark cases.

Part 2, "Compendium of Labor Legislation," presents summaries of legislation arranged by topic and subarranged chronologically. Examples of topics covered under "Labor Relations Laws" are Conspiracy Doctrine, antitrust laws, the private sector, and federal employees. Under "Protective Labor Legislation," Kelly includes maximum hours, minimum wages, child and women's labor, workmen's compensation, and social insurance. Part 3 discusses arbitration and outlines major court decisions and arbitration standards.

A well-chosen and up-to-date bibliography appears at the end of the book. Two indexes—one for the terms (including organization names) and one for court decisions—facilitate use of this handbook. In summary, this work is a good first place to look for information on this specialized topic. [R: Choice, Oct 87, p. 286]

Maureen B. Lambert

229. **National Directory of Safety Consultants.** 13th ed. Des Plaines, Ill., American Society of Safety Engineers, 1987. 94p. $25.00 pa. ISBN 0-939874-37-7.

This directory consists of the names, addresses, telephone numbers, professional credentials, and areas of expertise of five hundred members of the American Society of Safety Engineers (ASSE) Consultants Division. Its intent is to facilitate the society's work in the areas of accident, injury, and illness prevention and control. While there are over twenty thousand safety professionals, most of the people listed in this directory are independent consultants who specialize in product liability, occupational safety, industrial hygiene, and construction. One point the directory makes is that every forty minutes someone in the American workplace dies in an accident, and every ten minutes, someone is injured seriously enough to lose time from the job. These facts are the driving force behind the creation of this directory and its parent society.

The largest segment contains an alphabetical arrangement of the biographical information, but the directory also has two other sections of interest. The first consists of the members arranged by state, and the second is a listing by specialty or expertise. This directory should be of interest to anyone involved in safety or product liability work.

Susan B. Ardis

230. **Training and Development Organizations Directory: A Descriptive Guide....** 4th ed. Janice McLean, ed. Detroit, Gale, 1988. 684p. index. $270.00. LC 81-643973. ISBN 0-8103-4348-7; ISSN 0278-5749.

The new edition of *Training and Development Organizations Directory* (*TDOD*) lists twenty-three hundred organizations and individuals that offer training programs for business, industry, and government. The directory also points out companies that develop and market training programs on videotapes and computer-based formats. *TDOD* contains three indexes that provide a variety of access points. First, entries, previously arranged geographically, are now listed alphabetically by training organization name. Second, users seeking geographic access may find training organizations by consulting the new geographic index, which lists training organizations by state and then by city. Third, *TDOD* contains a subject index which lists hundreds of terms that lead the user to the appropriate training program sought. Also given are addresses, telephone numbers, principal executives, and a brief description of training courses of each organization. Because *TDOD* contains information on a wide range of training programs and services, it will be of use to corporate training managers and human resources development directors,

department heads locating training for their personnel, small businesses looking for affordable packaged training programs, and individuals seeking personal growth.

Assad A. Tavakoli

231. Way, Harold E., and Carla M. Weiss, comps. **Plant Closings: A Selected Bibliography of Materials Published through 1985.** Ithaca, N.Y., ILR Press, 1988. 206p. index. $15.00pa. LC 87-31762.

This bibliography of more than eight hundred items—books, parts of books, government reports, research papers, and articles from scholarly and professional journals, general interest magazines, and labor union periodicals/newspapers—is "intended to provide a comprehensive listing of publications" located in the Martin P. Catherwood and other Cornell University libraries collections. While there are a few entries from the 1930s-1960s, the emphasis is on the 1970s-1985. The full bibliographic, numbered entries, arranged alphabetically by personal or corporate author (or by title if anonymous), are accompanied by a wide variety of subject headings relevant to plant closings, including those for geographic areas (e.g., "Geographic Location Study—Canada—Ontario," "Geographic Location Study—United States—Illinois," "Legislation—United States—California") and types of industries ("Industry—Glass," "Industry—Textile—Case Studies"). Alphabetical indexes by subject headings and authors (including coauthors) refer the user to entry numbers.

According to the preface, supplements are to be published as needed. The compilers are, respectively, head of the Central Library, Johnson County Library, Shawnee Mission, Kansas (and formerly a reference librarian at the Catherwood Library at Cornell), and a reference librarian at Catherwood. Their compilation is a substantial bibliography.

Wiley J. Williams

MANAGEMENT

232. Patten, Thomas H., Jr. **A Bibliography of Compensation Planning and Administration Publications 1975-1985.** 3d ed. Phoenix, Ariz., American Compensation Association, 1987. 105p. $30.00pa.

Compensation costs, which include direct pay and employee benefits, continue to rise due to influences such as public policy, union negotiations, productivity, pensions, and retirement. These costs must be based on the needs and goals of the business as well as the employee's needs. To help the compensation professional balance these needs, this list covers books and articles from 1975 through 1985 on topics related to compensation planning.

This bibliography, used in conjunction with the American Compensation Association development courses, primarily includes journal articles arranged by nineteen primary topics such as job evaluation, wage administration, hours of work, executive compensation, incentive plans, benefits, and the impact of unions on pay levels. The 123 secondary categories provide access to specific subjects for the broad areas. A detailed table of contents lists the specific subjects, since there is no index. The cross-references are given at the beginning of the bibliography, not in the bibliography itself.

Although aimed at the compensation professional, the small business person can benefit from the suggested titles. Large public library business collections and colleges and universities with business schools will find this a useful, specialized publication. To keep the material up-to-date, serial publications such as *Personnel Literature* (U.S. Office of Personnel Management), *Personnel Management Abstracts* (Personnel Management Abstracts), or *Work Related Abstracts* (Information Coordinators, Inc.) index articles and books covering the topics in this bibliography.   Jean Herold

233. **Personnel Management Abstracts: Accumulating Index, 1987. Vol. 33, No. 4.** Gloria J. Reo, ed. Chelsea, Mich., Personnel Management Abstracts, 1987. 271p. $55.00 (4 issues). ISSN 0031-577X.

Personnel Management Abstracts is a quarterly publication edited by Gloria J. Reo. It is an index that lists all the current articles from a large number of academic and trade journals dealing with management of people and organizational behavior. The index is arranged in two separate sections, by subject matter and by author. Each index notation includes a brief description of the article and information about the journal in which it appeared. To further facilitate research, many articles appear under several headings in the subject index. In addition, for requests of reprints, a list of addresses of many publishers of the journals is provided. Finally, the last section of this publication features book abstracts on related management topics. This index is an excellent reference tool on scholarly research for the most recent management techniques, issues, and problems.
                                        Assad A. Tavakoli

234. Walter, Ingo, and Tracy Murray, eds. **Handbook of International Management.** New York, John Wiley, 1988. 1v. (various paging). index. $75.00. ISBN 0-471-60674-X.

Walter and Murray's handbook aims to be "a comprehensive overview of managerial issues confronting firms doing business internationally." In twenty-four chapters, the twenty-five, largely academic, experts cover such topics as "country-risk assessment," "forecasting exchange rates," "technology transfer," and "international financial accounting." They also confront "international labor relations," "organization design," "marketing research in the international environment," and "offshore sourcing, subcontracting, and manufacturing." As the chapter titles suggest, the work is wide-ranging, with a nice mixture of the practical and the theoretical. It amply earns its claim to the status of a handbook.

The book's genesis hearkens back to 1982 when the first edition of the *Handbook of International Business* was first published. So diverse has the international field become that when it came time for a second edition, it gave birth to this companion with all the concerns of managers housed between its covers. All? Well, hardly, but it does offer fine starting places for further investigations, especially with each chapter's "Sources & Suggested Readings" as a guide. Students should find much of use here, so it is regrettable that $75.00 seems to be the average price for state-of-the-art handbooks. Still, most large public and academic libraries will want to have it on the shelves.

Aside from the companion already noted, there have been few management-oriented handbooks which have given more than cursory treatment to the international scene. There are a detailed subject index and many useful charts and illustrations.   Richard Reid

235. Zembicki, Christine. **Production and Factory Management: An Information Sourcebook.** Phoenix, Ariz., Oryx Press, 1988. 176p. index. (Oryx Sourcebook in Business and Management, No. 18). $38.50. LC 88-15415. ISBN 0-89774-340-7.

Production and factory management is a field which cuts across several disciplines. Management skills are required, as well as thorough technological grounding in such areas as industrial engineering, computerization, and robotics. Appropriately enough in such a field, this is a wide-ranging bibliography, offering a guide to book and periodical literature and other sources of information for "managers at all levels of factory operations and students of industrial engineering" (p. vii).

Individual chapters deal with such topics as site selection, plant layout, quality control, and budget and cost analysis. Within the chapters, entries are divided by type of source (e.g., dictionaries, handbooks, online databases, major periodicals, etc.). One useful and interesting feature is the inclusion of nonprint sources of information. Professional organizations and major research centers are listed, with full information on how these may be contacted. A valuable appendix lists Library of Congress subject headings covering information in this field, an important inclusion because of the interdisciplinary nature of the knowledge.

This bibliography is representative rather than exhaustive. A huge field is being covered; some of the chapters deserve (and probably have) book-length bibliographies in their own right. Most of the literature cited is reasonably current, though for some areas, older material is included. This is a good introduction to the information sources in production and factory management.   Diane Richards

MARKETING AND TRADE

236. DiPrima-LeConche, Patricia, comp. **The National Directory of Product Publicity Sources.** 1987/88 ed. Westbury, N.Y., Asher-Gallant Press, 1987. 167p. index. $95.00pa. LC 87-17542. ISBN 0-87280-157-8.

An innovative comprehensive directory focusing on the advertising and marketing fields. This unique work should prove to be well worth its cost to both the research specialist and the library providing support for this industry. Inclusion in this directory is limited to those journals which provide space for free product publicity, be it photographs, press releases, or even descriptive detailed articles.

Over eight hundred trade and industry publications are reviewed for key directory information, contact person, circulation, editorial coverage, release format, readership profile, and specific submission criteria. The mixture of periodicals surveyed includes popular mainstream publications, as well as more narrowly focused ones. Circulation distribution figures for the periodicals range from 150 issues or less to upward of one million.

Sections that comprise this reference source include an alphabetical journal entry listing, a target market index, a circulation index, a new product section index, a literature section index, and an article index. The five indexes categorize relevant titles only, and cross-referencing back to the body of the work is required. This is not a major drawback, but unique code numbers located within the main entry could very easily supplant most of the indexes.

This directory is such a tremendous convenience and so germane to what it purports to accomplish that it is a wonder it was not produced years ago. The potential cost benefits for the user of the directory are enormous and should very quickly offset the price of acquiring this excellent source. Recommended for advertising and marketing specialists as well as libraries serving this clientele.   Peter B. Kaatrude

237. **Findex 1988: The Directory of Market Research Reports, Studies and Surveys.** 10th ed. Sharon J. Marcus, ed. Bethesda, Md., Cambridge Information Group, 1988. 779p. index. $285.00pa. LC 80-645160. ISBN 0-942189-00-0; ISSN 0273-4125.

Now in its tenth edition, this comprehensive guide to market research reports, studies, and surveys offers its users over eleven thousand reports from 520 American and international publishers. Industry reports are grouped into twelve major and about 175 subcategories. Company reports are alphabetical and account for only about three hundred studies. Indexes list report titles by publisher, geographically, and by subject. There is also a directory of publishers/distributors with address, contact, and telephone and telex numbers for ease of ordering. The subscription price entitles the user to a midyear supplement, and to a telephone inquiry service to see whether the database contains reports more current than those in print.

The book also has a serious, although not fatal, flaw: the subject index is terrible. Several titles checked at random revealed partial or no subject indexing under the keywords in the report title, despite the subject index using those words or similar ones for indexing terms. Examples: "Competitive Strategies for the Speciality Camera Store" was not indexed under "cameras" or "retail." The study "Office Furniture" did not list under "office" or "furniture." "Biotechnology Patentwatch," a bimonthly newsletter, did not appear with "patents" in the index. Only three reports are noted under the heading "service industries," and the survey "Review of Professional Services Marketplace" was not among them. If the percentage holds, half or more of the titles could be partially or totally unindexed. Of course a user could get around this by scanning each listing in the subcategories in the main text, or even calling the telephone service, but that is not the point. The subject index could also be vastly improved by including methodologies employed by the surveys as subject terms, listing those reports which give rankings of top companies within industries, and by restoring an S.I.C. code approach (dropped from earlier editions). A master report title index would also facilitate matters.

Competitors are few: *Directory of Industry Data Sources* (see *ARBA* 84, entries 756-757) incorporates market reports, but also many other types of documents. *Research Alert* (Alert Publishing, 1981-), a biweekly newsletter, only covers about six hundred studies a year. Unless one anticipates heavy use, those libraries with access to Findex online are better off signing on when needed. All others are cautioned.

Richard Reid

238. Herold, Jean. **Marketing and Sales Management: An Information Sourcebook.** Phoenix, Ariz., Oryx Press, 1988. 167p. index. (Oryx Sourcebook Series in Business and Management, No. 12). $39.50. LC 87-32444. ISBN 0-89774-406-3.

This annotated bibliography is limited to English-language materials published primarily from 1980 to the present and commercially available. "Exceptions are made if there are no later publications to cover the subject" (introduction). Few textbooks are included. Other types of materials not cited are trade journals and newsletters for specific types of businesses, journal articles, and marketing reports on products and industries produced by marketing research firms.

The databases included in this bibliography are limited to BRS, DIALOG, NEXIS, and VU/TEXT, as well as the CD-ROM systems of INFOTRAC and ABI/INFORM. There are separate indexes for author, title, and subject.

The bibliography is arranged by marketing topics and by the format of the cited book within each section. A separate section lists titles for a core collection in the basic areas represented in the bibliography.

This is a carefully produced bibliography which will be useful to business libraries and schools.

Mary Jo Aman

239. **International Marketing Handbook: Detailed Marketing Profiles for 141 Nations....** 3d ed. Frank E. Bair, ed. Detroit, Gale, 1988. 3v. maps. $235.00/set. ISBN 0-8103-2580-2; ISSN 0734-712X.

The third edition of this directory set is similar in format and content to the second edition (see *ARBA* 86, entry 272) and the intervening supplement (see *ARBA* 87, entry 288). The bulk of the text continues to be drawn from the U.S. International Trade Administration's *Overseas Business Reports* (1962-). The directory includes sixteen new or revised reports published since 1986 out of a total of eighty-six dating back through the 1970s. None of the shorter fifty-three country profiles provides data more recent than 1983. The last one thousand pages of the set, as in the second edition, are devoted to a marketing briefs section. This

material, also culled almost exclusively from U.S. government sources, includes information on international holidays, trade fairs, business guides, and trade regulations.

While the convenience of having the *Overseas Business Reports* readily available in one bound set continues to be an attraction, it is this reviewer's opinion that there are not enough new or revised reports to have warranted a possible supplement, let alone a complete third edition. By contacting a U.S. Government Printing Office bookstore one can purchase the sixteen latest *Overseas Business Reports* published since 1986 at a fraction of the cost of this third edition. However, with the advent of more timely updating of these important reports by the ITA (e.g., the USSR survey was last revised in July 1977) it is expected that the heavily dependent *International Marketing Handbook* will once again become indispensable.

Peter B. Kaatrude

239a. **International Trade Names Dictionary 1988-89: A Guide to About 40,000 Consumer-Oriented Trade Names, Brand Names, Product Names, Coined Names, Model Names, and Design Names....** Donna Wood, ed. Detroit, Gale, 1988. 366p. $240.00. ISBN 0-8103-0690-5; ISSN 0899-7586.

239b. **International Trade Names Dictionary 1988-89: Company Index.** Donna Wood, ed. A Companion Volume to *International Trade Names Dictionary....* Detroit, Gale, 1988. 350p. $210.00. ISBN 0-8103-0691-3; ISSN 0899-7594.

These directories are much needed additions to the limited information available on international trade names. The arrangement of this reference source is similar to the *Trade Names Dictionary 1986-87* and the *Trade Names Dictionary 1986-87: Company Index* (see *ARBA* 87, entries 183 and 184).

Emphasis in this first edition is on "every type of consumer-related product, from apparel to food and beverages to pharmaceuticals to recreational items." Coverage focuses extensively on eleven countries and partially on others. Source information is drawn from twenty-one different publications compared to ninety-nine sources in the *Trade Names Dictionary*. According to the preface, the *Trade Names Dictionary* has also been used as a source of information. Those international entries that once appeared in the *Trade Names Dictionary* now appear in this new publication.

These directories are necessary references providing valuable coverage of a company's international operations. For example, listed under the trade name "Jack Daniels" are names of twenty-one distributors and importers located in other countries. Therefore, this new reference tool acts as an indispensable complement to its domestic counterpart as well as a unique source of foreign trade name identification. What remains to be seen is whether the publishers increase the number of companies and trade names covered and include entries printed in the vernacular.   Peter B. Kaatrude

240. Jagoe, John R. **Export Sales and Marketing Manual.** Minneapolis, Minn., Export USA, 1987. 1v. (various paging). index. $295.00 looseleaf with binder. LC 87-19952. ISBN 0-943677-00-9.

Working with numerous government agencies, corporations, and trade associations, the author, an international marketing consultant with twenty years of exporting experience, has assembled a looseleaf manual offering knowledgeable, step-by-step guidance for anyone wishing to export goods or services from the United States. The verbs of action in the chapter titles (securing, writing, selecting, pricing, etc.) neatly encapsulate Jagoe's enthusiastic approach, walking the reader through the process in twelve succinct chapters (plus three reference ones: information sources, export glossary, and subject index).

At $295.00 a year (plus an additional $200.00 for four quarterly updates, reputed to be each twenty to fifty pages long), the advice does not come cheap. Comparison with Dun & Bradstreet's comparably priced *Exporters Encyclopedia* (1982-), which is an annual bound volume of the biweekly *World Marketing Fact File* service, finds many similar areas of coverage but with a few key differences. A telling example: the treatment of a SED (Shippers Export Declaration). Jagoe covers the basic points in a page and refers the reader to the Commerce Department brochure on how to fill out a SED. *EE* spends nine pages, with big chunks from that brochure. Jagoe also shows a blank SED form, while *EE* offers a filled-in one marked "Sample Copy."

One suspects that businesspersons will prefer the clipped, essence-only style of Jagoe, with its well-organized form, to the large lumps of *EE*, which are not without their own rewards. Last, although Jagoe is well-illustrated, with more than eighty illustrations, flow charts, graphs, and checklists, *EE* manages to come up with several overlooked basics, such as international symbols and cautionary marks. Both of these books have a third competitor: the Small Business Foundation of America's *Exportise* (1983). While it cannot compare with Jagoe (only two paragraphs on a SED and no form),

its price and general good sense make it worth commending for budget-conscious libraries. If your collection needs exporting information and lacks *EE*, Jagoe should provide it handsomely. [R: WLB, Feb 88, pp. 99-100]

Richard Reid

241. **Japan Marketing Handbook.** London, Euromonitor; distr., Detroit, Gale, 1988. 160p. maps. index. $160.00. ISBN 0-86338-213-4.

In spite of its title, this book is much more an overview and analysis of the current state of the Japanese economy than a practical guide to doing business in Japan. There is an abundance of information on different aspects of the economy and much statistical data — a section at the end contains forty tables. Also included is a directory of useful names and addresses. Published by Euromonitor (London), this book has a European bias.

A major problem with this book, as with all those of its type, is dated information. Overall trends may stay the same, at least for a while, but the statistics and other details become very quickly of historical interest only. At approximately a dollar per page, the book seems overpriced. Similar information is available other places for less. The Japan External Trade Organization (JETRO) publishes some excellent material, as does the U.S. Department of Commerce. The absence of specific detail on operating a business in Japan seems unfortunate. It is in this area that the JETRO publications and the U.S. Department of Commerce *Overseas Business Reports* are at their best.

Overall, this is not a bad book. It contains much excellent statistical and general economic information. However, it will not serve as a guide to the specifics of marketing in Japan. Recommended for those libraries desiring an overview of the Japanese economy.

Diane Richards

242. **Japan Trade Directory 1988-89.** Tokyo, Japan External Trade Organization; distr., Detroit, Gale, 1988. 1v. (various paging). illus. (part col.). maps. index. $265.00. ISBN 4-8224-0410-2.

This directory of Japanese businesses and associations engaged in overseas trade gives information on twenty-nine hundred companies that export or import eighteen thousand products or services. The format of this seventh edition has been revised, with directory information on companies separated from the descriptive and pictorial material on the prefectures. In the 539-page main section, entries are arranged alphabetically by the English translation of the company name, which is followed by the romanized Japanese name, address, telephone and telex numbers, cable and facsimile codes, name of the president, type of business, year of establishment, capital, annual sales, number of employees, bank references, office hours, major overseas offices, trade names, catalog availability, contact preference, company interests, departments and personnel to contact, and languages spoken. Each entry is accompanied by lists of products exported and imported and preferred countries or regions for trading. Indexes provide access by exports, imports, company names, trade and industrial associations, and trade names. A prefecture guide of two hundred pages provides information on each prefecture, including maps showing cities, airports, and rivers; general tourist information; lists of sister cities throughout the world; a text profile of the prefecture; and color photographs depicting places of interest, industries, and crafts. Pie charts show categories of regional products. With its primary emphasis on trade and industry, this directory will find its greatest use in subject collections. The material in the prefecture guide, however, can answer a number of general reference questions.

Shirley L. Hopkinson

243.   **Marketsearch International Directory of Published Market Research.** 12th ed. Compiled by Arlington Management Publications Limited with The British Overseas Trade Board. Evanston, Ill., Marketsearch, 1988. 648p. index. $215.00pa. ISBN 0-906616-09-3.

The publisher states in the news release that this directory lists approximately eighteen thousand market research studies in 150 countries, with the United States and the United Kingdom appearing to be most heavily covered. There are four sections. First is an alphabetical listing of products and services, from Alzheimer's disease to tour operator. These products/services are assigned codes using the British Standard Industrial Classification scheme. There are approximately sixty-four hundred products and services listed; for approximately one quarter of these there are no studies. Second, the title and a very brief description of each study are given. Each product/service is categorized according to the general BSIC, and then further subdivided alphabetically by the country(ies) covered in the study. The user must browse the category in order to locate the study. This is not a problem when the category is devoted to one or two products/services, but when there are several, the search can take longer. Also included are the language(s), date, frequency, publisher, and price of each study. The third section lists the studies by publisher and reiterates the BSIC,

title, and countries covered. In the fourth section publishers are listed alphabetically by name, with their addresses and telephone and telex numbers.

Except for having to search for the actual study and publisher, anyone wishing to find recent market research studies here and abroad should find this directory valuable. Although this volume is not all encompassing, it should satisfy most needs. The $215.00 cost of this paperback may be prohibitive to all but the larger business libraries, schools, or companies. This item is superior to *Findex: The Directory of Market Research Reports, Studies and Surveys 1979* (see *ARBA* 80, entry 789). [R: RBB, 1 Oct 88, p. 242]   Mary Jo Aman

244.   Neri, Rita E. **U.S./Japan Foreign Trade: An Annotated Bibliography of Socioeconomic Perspectives.** New York, Garland, 1988. 306p. index. (Garland Reference Library of Social Science, Vol. 403). $40.00. LC 87-34805. ISBN 0-8240-8471-3.

The balance of trade between the United States and Japan is a source of much concern to the citizens of both nations. One reason for the tension is that neither country fully understands the other, despite the close and unique history they have shared since 1945. The author has compiled and annotated a selective list of 965 English-language items which, if studied, should enable one to better understand the background of this complicated international situation.

The items listed here emphasize the Japanese perspective on the problem. The five-page introduction provides an overview of how Japan's economy reached its present position and the interaction between the United States and Japan. Sections of the bibliography cover Japanese culture, society, law and politics, as well as science, business and economic matters, and U.S.-Japanese relations. The preface states that works on Japanese companies or investments in the United States or Japanese and American reactions to the trade situation are not included. There are also few U.S. government documents. Most of the materials were published between 1970 and early 1987.

Citations are arranged within the various sections by the author's name. For convenience, the Western style of putting the surname last is used here for Japanese names. The entry numbers in the author, title, and subject indexes refer back to the individual citation numbers. The book is printed on acid-free paper with a 250-year life expectancy.

The work under review is similar in purpose to another new publication from Garland, *Japan's Economic Challenge* (see entry 109).

There is also the chapter "International Economic Relations" in Karl Boger's *Postwar Industrial Policy* (see entry 210). Most libraries will not need all three books. Neri's volume is suitable for public and academic libraries. [R: RQ, Summer 88, p. 579]   Daniel K. Blewett

245. Ostrow, Rona, and Sweetman R. Smith. **The Dictionary of Marketing.** New York, Fairchild Publications, 1988. 258p. illus. $25.00. LC 87-82654. ISBN 0-87005-573-9.

Ostrow and Smith, whose previous effort, *The Dictionary of Retailing* (see *ARBA* 86, entry 275) filled such a long-neglected niche, are back with another well-done dictionary. It should not make anyone want to toss the industry standard, Shapiro's *Dictionary of Marketing Terms* (see *ARBA* 82, entry 895), for their approximately nineteen hundred terms cannot compare with his five thousand plus, but their work nicely updates and supplements his opus.

The Dictionary of Marketing offers its users good-sized definitions, not only of words and phrases, but also profiles of principal marketing trade associations that sound like a narrative summary of an entry in the *Encyclopedia of Associations*. Other than a handful of graphs and charts and numerous cross-references, there are no extras. Call it a no-frills dictionary—lean but well-focused.

A comparison of fifteen randomly selected entries from Shapiro's book shows only four are found in Ostrow and Smith's book. Conversely, Shapiro had eight words and phrases found here. Shapiro fell short with the more recent terms. (It *is* eight years old.) Thus, recent concepts such as "telemarketing" and "metropolitan statistical area" as well as colorful jargon ("pig in a python" and "low-ball price") and technical concepts ("backward market segmentation" and "Screening stage") not in Shapiro's most recent edition are found here.

Although there are other marketing dictionaries such as Jefkin's *Dictionary of Marketing, Advertising and Public Relations* (Transatlantic, 1983) and Baker's *Dictionary of Marketing and Advertising* (Nichols, 1985), they are not as current nor as precisely focused as Ostrow and Smith's. Their well-crafted dictionary is worth commending to all business collections. [R: Choice, June 88, p. 1539; LJ, 15 May 88, p. 77; RBB, Aug 88, pp. 1900-1901]

Richard Reid

246. **Trade Contacts in China: A Directory of Import and Export Corporations.** London, published with China Prospect Publishing House by Kogan Page; distr., Detroit, Gale, 1987. 357p. maps. $110.00. ISBN 1-85091-340-4.

This latest directory of import and export corporations in China is one of many publications of this kind available. Like most of them, this one is grossly overpriced (see *ARBA* 88, entry 208 for an example).

First published in Great Britain in 1987, this directory contains three parts. Part 1 briefly describes trading institutions, practices, business laws, and regulations. Part 2 lists over six hundred national and local branch offices of Chinese trading corporations, with addresses and business activities. Part 3 provides two indexes of corporations, one by industry and one by province. There are also three appendices. The first contains four maps showing the major industrial areas of China, including special economic zones, the fourteen coastal cities, the coal mines, and the railway systems. The second is a list of government ministries and commissions, while the third lists names and addresses of Chinese commercial offices in the United Kingdom and United States, Chinese embassies and representatives abroad, and additional readings.

While browsing through the directory, one mistake (p. 350) was found: Education was listed as a ministry instead of as a commission. In China, the national educational administration is called State Education Commission, which is a higher status than ministry.

Despite this one mistake and the obvious high price, the directory is a useful guide for anyone interested in doing business with China and may be good to have in larger business reference collections. [R: Choice, July/Aug 88, p. 1678]   Hwa-Wei Lee

247. **Trade Shows and Professional Exhibits Directory: An International Guide to Scheduled Events Providing Commercial Display Facilities....** 3d ed. Martin Connors, Charity Anne Dorgan, and Valerie J. Webster, eds. Detroit, Gale, 1988. 1138p. index. $159.95. ISBN 0-8103-2748-1; ISSN 0886-1439.

This third edition provides information on over forty-five hundred shows in sixty countries. So far, main editions of this publication are coming out biennially, with a supplement issued in the off year. Information is obtained by questionnaires and telephone interviews. The listings include show name, sponsor, manager, anticipated attendance, intended audience, number of exhibits, price, frequency, and relevant special features. Dates and locations are listed into the 1990s, if that information is available. Organization is by broad subject heading, with five additional indexes providing access by location, chronology, sponsoring organization, exhibit topic, and show name keyword.

Laid out in the usual attractive style of Gale publications, this directory is an excellent choice for libraries needing trade show information. It is intended for a more general audience than the comparable *Tradeshow Week Data Book* (see entry 248), which, with its multiple layers of indexing and annual publication, is targeted more at marketing professionals.

Diane Richards

248. **Tradeshow Week Data Book, 1988: The Annual Statistical Directory of U.S. and Canadian Tradeshows and Public Shows.** 4th ed. Darlene Zonca, ed. Los Angeles, Calif., with Trade Show Bureau by Tradeshow Week; distr., New York, R. R. Bowker, 1988. 1v. (various paging). index. $195.00pa. ISBN 0-8352-2460-0; ISSN 0000-1023.

Published in cooperation with the Trade Show Bureau and its fourteen sponsoring associations, the 1988 *Tradeshow Week Data Book* provides show information on 2,638 U.S. and 237 Canadian trade shows and conferences being held in 1988 and 1989. The intended audience is corporate exhibit managers, trade show managers, and trade show service executives. Information was obtained through questionnaires sent to show management companies. Organization of the main section is by broad subject category, or industrial classification. Seven other indexes provide additional access points to the main section. These include listings by show title, location, size, date, management, and rotation pattern. In addition, there is an index which provides second- and third-level subject access. The main entries themselves contain all the information a potential exhibitor might need to know, including show sponsor and management, entry fees, cost for space, estimates of numbers of both exhibitors and attendees, and profiles of both exhibitors and attendees.

This directory is full of invaluable information for those individuals or companies who market by exhibiting at trade shows. The information is complete, well organized, and attractively presented. For any library with a large business collection, or a significant business clientele.

Diane Richards

249. Williams, Emelda L., and Donald W. Hendon. **American Advertising: A Reference Guide.** New York, Garland, 1988. 208p. index. (Garland Reference Library of Social Science, Vol. 398). $28.00. LC 87-32148. ISBN 0-8240-8490-X.

Written by two marketing professors, this selective, annotated bibliography lists 648 references to books and journal articles on advertising. The emphasis is on American publications from 1970 to date, but a number of older classics are included. The volume has sections on the history of advertising; ethical, economic, and social issues; motivation and psychological concerns; planning and selection of media; creativity; local advertising; reference books; and professional journals. The author index assists the reader in locating references by author, but the lack of a subject index hampers access to specific topics, such as color in advertising (cited in number 333 on page 95).

American Advertising appears to be one of the few recent bibliographies available on the topic. Neither the *Subject Guide to Books in Print 1987-88* (Bowker, 1987) nor the July 1988 issue of *Forthcoming Books* (Bowker, 1988) lists "Advertising—Bibliography" as a heading. Surprisingly, *American Advertising* contains only ten of the twenty titles on the topic in Lorna M. Daniells's *Business Information Sources* (see *ARBA* 86, entry 158), and Daniells also lists later editions of at least three titles in *American Advertising* (see numbers 160, 203, and 214). Despite the minor flaws noted above, the book should be a worthwhile addition to most business collections. [R: Choice, Sept 88, p. 92]

O. Gene Norman

OFFICE MANAGEMENT

250. McCauley, Rosemarie. **Professional Reference for the Office.** Mission Hills, Calif., Glencoe, 1987. 536p. illus. maps. index. $13.68 spiralbound. LC 86-9771. ISBN 0-02-683010-8.

As do other office handbooks, *Professional Reference* covers all the basics for secretaries and office workers, such as English skills and document formatting. Many other areas of office operation are covered as well, including up-to-date information on financial and banking matters, math operations, time management, the electronic office, information processing, telecommunications, records management, reprographics, personnel policies, and résumé preparation.

Divided into eighteen units, it is arranged in a concise, alphabetical presentation with cross-references, main headings, subheadings, and an index facilitating easy access to the information desired.

Comparable to *Secretary's Almanac and Fact Book* (see *ARBA* 86, entry 281) in content, *Professional Reference* is a spiralbound, softcover edition, while *Secretary's Almanac* is in hardcover.

Beverley Hanson

251. **Webster's Guide to Business Correspondence.** Springfield, Mass., Merriam-Webster, 1988. 400p. illus. index. $12.95. LC 87-31333. ISBN 0-87779-031-0.

Designed for anyone writing business-related correspondence, this new guide by a well-known dictionary publisher covers a variety of topics, including style, forms of address, mechanics of writing, composition and grammar, tone in writing, samples and guidelines, correspondence with U.S. government agencies, and using the mail. Each chapter is introduced by its own table of contents and discusses in detail one of these topics. The text is often enhanced by many line drawings, tables, and facsimiles, including tables for stationery and envelope sizes, complimentary closes, and stylings for envelope addresses. Over forty sample letters are provided for virtually every type of business correspondence, such as credit letters, letters about discounts, job letters, sales letters, introduction letters, invitations, price quotations, reminders of overdue payment, and thank-you letters. A well-done index and an index of sample letters conclude the work.

In essence, this is a combination of information from *Webster's Secretarial Handbook* (2d ed. Merriam-Webster, 1984), and *Webster's Standard American Style Manual* (see *ARBA 86*, entry 889)—information carefully selected and expanded on to create a comprehensive reference source pertaining specifically to business correspondence. [R: LJ, July 88, p. 73]

Susan R. Penney

REAL ESTATE

252. Harris, Jack C., and Jack P. Friedman. **Barron's Real Estate Handbook.** 2d ed. Hauppauge, N.Y., Barron's Educational Series, 1988. 700p. illus. bibliog. index. $19.95. LC 88-3345. ISBN 0-8120-5758-9.

Little has changed between this second edition and the first one (see *ARBA 86*, entry 280). Half of the book is devoted to definitions of real estate terms. The other half repeats the information of the first edition: tables of monthly mortgage payments, loan progress, mortgage value, maximum premiums, discount points, depreciation percentages, proration percentages, and graduated payment mortgages. Unlike the first edition, the depreciation tables are based on the Tax Reform Act of 1986. The metric conversion and mathematical tables are still here, as are the diagram and definitions of the parts of a house. There are samples of real estate forms and worksheets, such as Qualifying Income, Debt Obligation, Form 3903 Moving Expenses, Residential Loan Application, etc.

There is an extensive bibliography with materials from as early as 1969 and as late as 1987, as well as an index and a list of publishers and their addresses.

One important item—the price—has changed, increasing $7.00 over the first edition. There is no need to replace the first edition with this one. [R: LJ, 15 Oct 88, pp. 83-84; RBB, 15 Dec 88, p. 688]   Mary Jo Aman

253. **Real Estate Index: January 1975-June 1985.** Chicago, National Association of Realtors, 1987. 2v. $225.00/set. LC 86-23878. ISBN 0-938785-00-1.

In this day of online and CD-ROM databases, an extensive, two-volume, ten-year printed index is unusual. Done as a service for members of the National Association of Realtors, the volumes cover real estate and related topics in 127,000 citations. From five hundred English-language journals, they are selectively indexed to include only general interest articles on real estate. More than twenty thousand monographs, including corporate and university studies, looseleaf services, directories, census publications, and income/expense analysis statistics, are cited. A list of the indexed periodicals is provided at the beginning of each volume.

In volume 1, the "Author Index" only lists titles, with the complete citations given in the "Title Index." Volume 2, the "Subject Index," includes real estate terms, specific businesses (e.g., beauty shops, liquor stores, and motels), names of cities, states, real estate associations, and federal government housing agencies. Broad subjects are subdivided. "Mortgages" covers seven pages and when subdivided covers a total of eighty-six pages. Real estate acronyms such as REIT (Real Estate Investment Trust), ARM (Adjustable Rate Morgage), and TIMS (Trusts for Investment in Mortgages) are not listed. These abbreviations are indexed by "Investment Trusts, Real Estate" for REIT, "Morgages—Variable Interest Rates" for ARM, and "Mortgages as Investments" for TIMS. The acronyms are also located in the broad subject headings and in the "Title Index," if they are the first word of the title.

The library with a comprehensive real estate collection will need this compilation, even if the researcher has to be creative in locating specific information and uses online searches for updated material. Other libraries will have to consider the price, the lack of many of the indexed titles, and the needs of their users before purchasing this retrospective index. [R: Choice, July/Aug 88, p. 1676; WLB, Jan 88, pp. 102-3]   Jean Herold

254. Thomsett, Michael C., comp. **Real Estate Dictionary.** Jefferson, N.C., McFarland, 1988. 220p. illus. $29.95. LC 87-43196. ISBN 0-89950-321-7.

Over eleven hundred terms pertaining to residential and commercial real estate are defined in this volume. The emphasis is on the legal and financial aspects of the real estate transaction (sales, listings, investments, mortgages, etc.) and not on slang or jargon. Most explanations run several sentences to a short paragraph in length, and there is a chart or graph to illustrate concepts on nearly every page. Definitions are sophisticated but are quite readable and will be understood by most adult readers. There are also between two and eleven *see also* terms for each entry, with most definitions having about five referrals. Users will find these helpful, but it does get complicated because each of the definitions that are referred to has numerous *see also* references that need to be followed up for a complete explanation of a concept.

Some useful addenda for the home buyer include checklists for evaluating neighborhoods, for home inspection and layout, and for assessing terms of a mortgage. The loan amortization charts printed here cover loans from 5 percent to 16.5 percent in 0.5 percent increments from one to thirty years and have detailed instructions on how to use them. There is also a chart for calculating the remaining balance on a loan. The list of abbreviations at the end is actually a list of acronyms common in the real estate field. Relatively inexpensive, this dictionary would be a worthwhile acquisition for most reference collections. [R: Choice, Sept 88, p. 90; RBB, 1 Oct 88, pp. 244-45; RQ, Summer 88, pp. 576, 578; WLB, June 88, p. 143]

Gary R. Cocozzoli

255. Webster's New World Illustrated Encyclopedic Dictionary of Real Estate. 3d ed. By Jerome S. Gross. New York, Prentice Hall Press, 1987. 418p. illus. $12.95pa. LC 87-2360. ISBN 0-13-947318-1.

The numerous short definitions in this dictionary cover a broad universe of terms: land, geography, housing, construction, and law pertaining to real estate. Jargon, real estate slang, and colloquial terms are also included; most of these definitions are unlikely to be satisfactorily defined in either a regular or legal dictionary. Illustrations are limited, but those given are very helpful. For example, there is a visual comparison of fifteen different styles of roofs, and a land plat showing a cul-de-sac in a modern subdivision. The definitions are readable, but vary in quality: the majority are acceptable, some are inadequate (such as the one for *Cape Cod house*), some are confusing (*tri-level*), while others are seemingly incorrect (*bi-level*). There are no entries for such terms as *lanai, quad-*

level, or *biweekly mortgage*, which might be expected to be included.

An unusual feature is the collection of eighty-two sample forms that might be encountered in real estate rental or property purchase. These are not designed to be reproduced but will be enlightening nonetheless for the user. A table of contents simplifies finding the proper form.

Other extras include a cross-section diagram of a house with ninety-four terms identifying the parts and a method of figuring loads for house framing. There is a short list of real estate associations with addresses and a loan amortization table for calculating monthly payments for mortgages lasting five, ten, fifteen, twenty, twenty-five, or thirty years from 5.5 percent to 21 percent in 0.5 percent increments. The reprint of the National Association of Realtors Code of Ethics and Standards of Practices is another convenient addition.

The reasonable cost of this item makes it attractive and worthwhile for most libraries, but it is not an essential purchase for the reference collection of libraries already owning other similar or more sophisticated titles. [R: RBB, 15 Apr 88, p. 1412]

Gary R. Cocozzoli

TAXATION

256. Bernard, Yolande. Lexique de la Fiscalité. Taxation Glossary. Ottawa, Canadian Government Publishing Centre, 1988. 304p. bibliog. (Terminology Bulletin, 177). $12.95pa.; $15.50pa. (U.S.). ISBN 0-660-53874-1.

This publication contains terms relevant to Canadian income tax legislation. Both English-French and French-English glossaries are given. This editor expands on a previous one published in 1983. In addition to entries extracted from the Income Tax Act and Regulations, the work now includes terms drawn from technical notes relating to the income tax, bills amending the Income Tax Act since 1983, *The Glossary of T1 Forms* issued by the Revenue Canada Taxation Translation center, and The White Paper on Tax Reform tabled in 1987. Most entries in the glossary refer users to the pertinent documentary source. A user's guide and a bibliography are included. The terminology given in this work is to be used in all federal government communications, and the desire is expressed that, for the purpose of uniformity, it also will be used by organizations outside the government. It is a useful and valuable publication, essential to those who are concerned with Canadian taxation.

Helen M. Burns

257. **Facts & Figures on Government Finance.** 1988-1989 ed. By Tax Foundation. Baltimore, Md., Johns Hopkins University Press, 1988. 359p. index. $30.00; $24.95pa. LC 44-7109. ISBN 0-8018-3612-2; 0-8018-3619-0pa.; ISSN 0071-3678.

Founded in 1937, the Tax Foundation's primary purpose is to conduct nonpartisan research on the fiscal and managerial aspects of the U.S. government with a view to publishing its findings. In addition to this title, the foundation publishes two monthlies, one quarterly, an annual proceedings, and a series of special studies and reports. As a research center it has proved time and again that it is preeminent in the compilation of statistics that reveal "the taxing and spending practices of government at all levels."

This work contains 283 tables of statistics with over 60,000 entries. Each table is self-explanatory, and all but a few are retrospective, making them ideal for comparative purposes. The sections look at federal, state, and local governments together, covering such data as revenue, expenditures, and debt, then at each type of government separately in more depth. Each section begins with summary data, then advances to the more specific: death and gift-tax collections, tobacco tax, pari-mutuel tax rates, etc. At the end the glossary of terms will aid the novice and the index will provide ready access to an already neatly organized work.

Last year's twenty-third edition took the shape of an experimental looseleaf version, which has been discontinued in favor of a return to hard- and softbound copies. For a book of just numbers the format and distinctive type are excellent; there are no crowded figures, there is ample spacing throughout, and the tables do not tire the eye. *All* reference departments should have this statistical compilation at the desk and refer to it often for such questions as, When was the last year the United States showed a surplus and not a deficit? (1969, Nixon's first year as president—the country was $8.4 billion in the black). Highly recommended (both the surplus and the book).   Bill Bailey

257a. **Guide to Income Tax Preparation.** 1989 ed. By Warren H. Esanu, and others. Mt. Vernon, N.Y., Consumer Reports Books, 1988. 554p. index. $10.95pa. LC 87-71005. ISBN 0-89043-252-X.

For those who are apprehensive about the changes in tax law and not looking forward to dealing with the federal government's arcane instructions, here is an answer from a publisher that inspires trust: Consumer Reports has produced a guide which strives "to provide informa-

tion and strategies to help you avoid problems and pitfalls" (introduction). To that end, the authors have written a guide in clear prose which contains tips, notes for clarification, and cautions down the left margin of the book for maximum visability. The detailed table of contents allows the user to locate relevant information quickly, and an even more specific index isolates specific facts.

A section at the beginning outlines changes resulting from the Tax Reform Act of 1986 and the Revenue Act of 1987. This section discusses changes affecting individuals, pensions and IRAs, taxation of trusts, estates, minor children, and some changes affecting corporations.

Special chapters on choosing a tax preparer and what to do if you are audited enhance the book's usefulness. One tip on choosing a preparer: avoid those whose fee is based on the amount of tax saved or the size of your refund. The manual also details differing credentials of preparers and advises on whether to choose a seasonal commercial preparer, an enrolled agent, an accountant, or tax attorney. The audit chapter discusses how to guard against being audited as well as how to handle yourself once the process is initiated.

Sample forms illustrating different financial situations are very helpful as is the glossary of terms and the IRS toll free numbers. The authors' credentials are reassuring: one of the four worked as an IRS agent and all are attorneys. The price is very reasonable and makes it nearly impossible for librarians to avoid rushing this book through cataloging for anxious patrons with tax questions.

     Maureen B. Lambert

257b. **U.S. Master Tax Guide, 1989.** 72d ed. By CCH Tax Law Editors. Chicago, Commerce Clearing House, 1988. 648p. index. $19.50pa.

This edition seems not to have incorporated any of the changes suggested by the last review (see *ARBA* 87, entry 308). A broad survey of the tax laws, nonetheless, it contains references to the publisher's more detailed publication, *Standard Federal Tax Reports*. An overview at the beginning covers tax law changes applying to individuals, corporations, trusts, etc. It tells the user where to file returns and lists due dates.

The valuable "Checklists" section enumerates items which are taxable and nontaxable, lists possible medical expenses, and details items relating to special groups such as armed forces, farmers, and senior citizens. Examples scattered throughout illustrate various financial problems. Editors continue the dual numbering scheme with page numbers at the top and paragraph numbers at the bottom. The index is detailed and refers one to the specific paragraph.

Libraries that receive many tax questions will want this source, even if they cannot afford the companion, *Standard Federal Tax Reports*, since the guide provides enough detail to answer basic questions. Legal collections and government documents libraries will want both this source and *Standard Federal Tax Reports*.

Maureen B. Lambert

5 Education

GENERAL WORKS

Bibliographies

258. Lester, Paula E. **Teacher Job Satisfaction: An Annotated Bibliography and Guide to Research.** New York, Garland, 1988. 324p. index. (Garland Bibliographies in Contemporary Education, Vol. 7: Garland Reference Library of Social Science, Vol. 448). $47.00. LC 88-9768. ISBN 0-8240-8922-7.

The emphasis of this bibliography is on research reports related to teacher job satisfaction. Some of these cover methodologies, findings, and conclusions of particular studies; others review the literature related to several studies. Variables investigated in these studies are related to educational level, subject taught, personal and demographic characteristics (age, sex, length of service, school size), preservice versus in-service, and factors that contribute to job satisfaction and dissatisfaction. A large percentage of the studies described include those in which a questionnaire was constructed to measure teachers' attitudes toward various aspects of their jobs.

Items for inclusion in the bibliography were identified in *Education Index, Dissertation Abstracts, Psychological Abstracts, RIE (Resources in Education)* and *CIJE (Current Index to Journals in Education)*, from 1975 to 1987. Entries are arranged in nine categories: beginning teachers, elementary school teachers, college teachers, subject area teachers, teacher motivation, teacher-administrator relationships, teacher stress, teacher burnout, and teaching. Information in each entry includes a complete bibliographic description and a brief (one sentence) annotation describing the major purpose of the research study, report, or article.

The introduction carefully outlines the structure of the bibliography, the rationale, and criteria for selection of entries. It includes "History of Research on Teacher Job Satisfaction,"

a review of the literature on the topic. In addition, it provides an overview of each of the nine major topics included in the bibliography, and a list of reference sources.

Access to the bibliography is possible through author, title, and subject indexes. The educational researcher who is interested in any aspect of teacher job satisfaction or dissatisfaction would find this coverage of the research in the field for a period of over ten years both comprehensive and current. [R: Choice, Dec 88, p. 630]   Lois Buttlar

259. O'Brien, Nancy Patricia, comp. **Test Construction: A Bibliography of Selected Resources.** Westport, Conn., Greenwood Press, 1988. 299p. index. $39.95. LC 87-25119. ISBN 0-313-23435-3.

This comprehensive bibliography is intended for scholars, researchers, educators, and practitioners. The 2,759 unannotated entries deal with the subject in general and, as well, with the construction and design of specific tests, whether published or "unpublished" (the latter being tests available only from private sources, not from commercial publishers). Surveys and questionnaires are excluded. Matters such as test reliability, test bias, and test validity are included only as they relate to construction and design.

The citations were gathered from published materials and from online database searches of Psychological Abstracts, ERIC (*RIE* and *CIJE*), and Dissertation Abstracts. Other sources searched were the *Education Index* and online, Social Sciences Citation Index, Science Citation Index, and Sociological Abstracts. Citations are to books, reports, journal articles, dissertations, and ERIC documents. There is an addendum for materials published 1983-1986.

Criteria for inclusion are "lack of inclusion elsewhere, historical research value, and need for additional information on the subject" (p. xii). The compiler states that "there are few bibliographies that deal specifically with the subject and those that are available are outdated. This bibliography duplicates only a few significant entries contained in those works" (p. xi). It is odd that those bibliographies, outmoded though they be, are not identified in the introduction nor cited in the bibliography proper.

There is an author index and a detailed subject index which enters tests by title, thereby providing one more useful source for locating information on specific tests. [R: Choice, June 88, p. 1539]   David Rosenbaum

260. Woodward, Arthur, David L. Elliott, and Kathleen Carter Nagel. **Textbooks in School and Society: An Annotated Bibliography and Guide to Research.** New York, Garland, 1988. 176p. index. (Garland Bibliographies in Contemporary Education, Vol. 6; Garland Reference Library of the Social Sciences, Vol. 405). $25.00. LC 87-35302. ISBN 0-8240-8390-3.

An excellent and thorough classified bibliography on a topic of increasing importance, the title encompasses research and critical commentary of school textbooks and their relation to teaching and learning and to educational policy. As the authors point out, serious study of the textbook is relatively recent with most of the published work occurring in the past decade.

Within the two sections "Textbook Producers and Consumers" and "Evaluation and Criticism of Textbooks," there are five broad categories—"Textbooks and School Programs," "Production and Marketing of Textbooks," "General Discussion and Special Topics," "Subject Matter Content Coverage," and "Ideology and Controversy." Narrower topics are arranged with the broad ones covering such subjects as textbook industry; treatment of ethnic minorities and women; specific content areas (e.g., science, reading, language arts, etc.); censorship and evolution and creationism. Browsing within these sections is useful and the three-to-four-sentence annotations are very informative. The subject index provides good access to topics not reflected in the outline, such as the treatment of the elderly and handicapped. There are a few cross-references, but more would have been preferable. For example, there are no main entries for "blacks," "aged," or "women"; rather, they are embedded under other headings. Standard indexes and other reference sources in education were used to identify the pertinent litera-

ture in books and journal articles published since 1975. Most helpful are the authors' section overviews and suggestions about topics and issues needing further research.

The stated purpose, "to provide a comprehensive, up-to-date reference work for researchers and educators" has been successfully achieved. Highly recommended for all academic libraries, larger public libraries, and any library or research center affiliated with teacher education programs. [R: Choice, Sept 88, p. 92]

Bonnie Gratch

Dictionaries and Encyclopedias

261. **World Education Encyclopedia.** George Thomas Kurian, ed. New York, Facts on File, 1988. 3v. bibliog. index. $175.00/set. LC 82-18188. ISBN 0-87196-748-0.

This is a well conceived and carefully edited handbook that provides a concise yet comprehensive overview of the history and structure of formal educational systems in 179 countries. Accordingly, perhaps a more precise title would have been World Encyclopedia of Educational Systems, since the present title suggests more than it delivers. In any event, this is a relevant addition to the research literature of pedagogy.

WEE was compiled with the assistance of sixty-seven contributors worldwide. The arrangement is alphabetical by country within three broad categories: "Major Countries," "Middle Countries," and "Minor Countries." These categories were based primarily on a scale of availability of information. I suspect that the cultural attaché of Liechtenstein (a "minor country") might object to this categorization, in spite of his country's size. For the countries listed as "major," *WEE* includes the following information: (1) "Basic Data" (statistical); (2) "History and Background"; (3) "Overview of the System" (grading system, textbooks, etc.); (4) "Primary and Secondary Education"; (5) "Secondary Education"; (6) "Higher Education"; (7) "Administration, Finance, and Educational Research"; (8) "Nonformal Education"; (9) "Teaching Profession"; (10) "Summary" (a general assessment of the system and projections for the future); (11) "Glossary of Terms"; and (12) "Bibliography" (often containing both primary and secondary materials). The work also includes an essay on the history of education worldwide and a variety of statistical tables drawn primarily from the 1984 edition of the *UNESCO Statistical Yearbook*. Some but not all of the information cited above is included for the "middle" and "minor" countries. Most of the "major" countries, furthermore, contain tables depicting the structure of the national system in graph format.

WEE compares favorably by virtue of content, scope, and quality of data to the *International Handbook of Education Systems* (Wiley, 1983-1984). However, I still prefer over both of these the 160 educational system profiles that appear in *The International Encyclopedia of Education* (see *ARBA* 86, entry 292), especially in comparison to the shorter reviews in *WEE* for primarily Third World nations. [R: Choice, Nov 88, p. 472; WLB, Oct 88, p. 112]

Richard H. Quay

Handbooks and Yearbooks

262. Ambert, Alba N. Bilingual Education and English as a Second Language: A Research Handbook, 1986-1987. New York, Garland, 1988. 457p. index. (Garland Reference Library of Social Science, Vol. 464). $63.00. LC 88-16446. ISBN 0-8240-6625-1.

This new handbook represents a welcome update and a substantial widening of the scope of research issues and applications covered in Alba Ambert's *Bilingual Education* (see *ARBA* 86, entry 335) published three years ago. The editor wrote four separate essays; she also invited seven contributing authors to discuss areas of their research or expertise. Each essay covers an important field or application in the wide interdisciplinary domains of bilingualism, bilingual education, and English as a second language learning and teaching. Most essays focus on research done in the past two years. An essay will typically contain a general, but quite thorough, characterization of research in a particular area, an analysis of current research results, suggestions for further work, and a very useful annotated bibliography that usually covers the most representative sources.

Some of the topics discussed in greater detail are first language acquisition, second language learning, early bilingualism, bilingual education programs, English as a second language (for minorities and immigrants in the United States), assessment of children with limited proficiency in English, and vocational education of non-native users of English.

With a few exceptions, most essays implicitly concentrate on situations and conditions prevailing in the United States and Canada. In this respect, the *Research Handbook* can complement C. B. Paulston's *International Handbook of Bilingualism and Bilingual Education* (see entry 262) which surveys the bilingual and multilingual settings and problems in many countries of the world.

Several appendices and detailed author and subject indexes enhance the quality of this good reference work.   Lev I. Soudek

263. Educational Media and Technology Yearbook 1988. Volume 14. Donald P. Ely, Brenda Broadbent, and R. Kent Wood, eds. Englewood, Colo., with Association for Educational Communications and Technology by Libraries Unlimited, 1988. 293p. index. $50.00. ISBN 0-87287-609-8; ISSN 8755-2094.

The *Educational Media and Technology Yearbook* is a useful guide to associations, publishers, and educational programs in the field of instructional systems technology. This fourteenth volume will be added to most collections in universities that have this special degree at either the master's or Ph.D. level. The review by Clark and Sugrue, "Research on Instructional Media 1978-88," is well done and has great merit as a concise piece that covers a decade of educational technology, but most of the other articles are flat and do not add much to the field. One can find much of the same material in current journals of the field and will find much more detail and depth. For the $50.00 price tag on each volume of this yearbook series, I would be willing to think in terms of purchasing every other or every third year for the address updates, and letting the "research" or "state-of-the-articles" slip on by. The biographical sketches on James D. Finn and James W. Brown, two real pioneers in this field, are nicely done and add a bit of something special to this volume.

An extensive mediagraphy is given in the back, and covers such areas as video, photography, and computers. There is also a section on online databases, which I think is a bit out of the instructional technology territory. Why not leave that one to the information science people?   Daniel Callison

264. Franck, Irene M., and David M. Brownstone. Scholars and Priests. New York, Facts on File, 1988. 196p. illus. bibliog. index. (Work throughout History). $16.95. LC 87-36011. ISBN 0-8160-1449-3.

This volume examines curators, librarians, monks and nuns, priests, scholars, school administrators, and teachers. Teachers and priests receive the lion's share of attention, while curators, school administrators, and librarians receive the least attention.

The article on the priests starts with prehistoric times in the Near East, then addresses Greece and Rome, India, the Jews, early Christianity, changes in the East, the Druids, Islam, medieval Christianity, the Protestant

Reformation, modern cults, and priestly occupations. Neither this chapter nor the others look at these vocations in Africa, except basically for Egypt, and in the Western Hemisphere except for that part of it now known as the United States, after the arrival of the European settlers.

Each article includes *see* references to other chapters of this volume and to chapters of other volumes in the series. The index appears to be complete. The bibliography, however, includes only one title from the 1980s. Over 78 percent of the titles are dated in the 1960s or earlier. A number of terms are italicized, apparently just for emphasis. Many of these terms are in the *see* references or the index. A number are not. Nothing in the introductory material explains use of italics.

Since the book seems to be addressed to middle school and older students and adults, entries were checked against *World Book Encyclopedia* (1987). The coverage in *World Book* was more attractive, with lots of full color illustrations, and more complete in most cases, but the information was much more scattered. *Scholars and Priests* provides more information about history in some instances, and has fewer illustrations, all black-and-white.

While care needs to be taken to be sure users are aware of the limitations of this set, libraries whose users need historical information on occupations will find it very helpful to have this kind of information presented in such a compact fashion.   Betty Jo Buckingham

265.   Harris, Sherwood, and Lorna B. Harris, eds. **The Teacher's Almanac 1988-89.** New York, Facts on File, 1988. 320p. index. $35.00. LC 87-647888. ISBN 0-8160-1986-X; ISSN 0889-079X.

This compilation of statistical data, directory information, and other material on a broad range of topics relating to education is arranged into eleven chapters: "The Teacher's Year"; "State Rankings"; "Teacher Salaries and Jobs"; "The Teaching Profession"; "Student Performance"; "Awards and Achievements"; "Issues and Challenges"; "Books, Periodicals, Computers, and Tests"; "Enrollment, School Districts, and Attendance"; "Finances"; and "Higher Education." Each of these chapters contains information on as many as a dozen subtopics. Some of these include the teacher job market, state textbook adoption schedules, student standardized test performance, desegregation, the year's major educational events in review, illiteracy, book censorship, current student enrollments and projections, school expenditures per pupil, teacher burnout, computers in schools, state teacher certification requirements, student

dropouts, and college salaries and enrollment trends.

Much of the data presented here is drawn from either professional associations, such as the National Education Association, or U.S. government departments and agencies, such as the Department of Education. In a number of cases (e.g., student SAT performance; levels of federal aid to education), the almanac also presents retrospective data. Subject access to the almanac is provided by the detailed table of contents and the subject index; the latter excludes most proper names found within the almanac's lists, tables, and directories. There is also a prefatory "Quick Reference Index to State Information," which aids in locating comparative state data.

Though some of the government data included here is readily available in large government documents collections, that does not diminish the value and convenience of the almanac. Keeping in mind their audience, the editors have carefully selected the government information and have skillfully blended it with more obscure material from professional associations. The result is a desk reference volume that should be of great interest and utility to educators.   Stephen H. Aby

266.   Schmidt, William D. **Learning Resources Programs That Make a Difference: A Source of Ideas and Models from Exemplary Programs in the Field.** Washington, D.C., Association for Educational Communications and Technology, 1987. 111p. illus. index. $19.95pa. ISBN 0-89240-046-3.

The author visited some thirty learning resources programs throughout the United States to identify and describe exemplary programs that could be used as models for structure and practice. Programs chosen for study provide institutionwide (or systemwide) service rather than department- or building-level service and are at five levels: doctorate-granting universities, comprehensive universities and colleges, two-year colleges and institutions, public school districts, and regional education agencies. The terms *learning resources program* and *instructional media support programs* are used synonymously, and defined as programs "which provided a full range of learning resources (both print and audiovisual or audiovisual only) for use in instructional programs" (p. xii).

Schmidt's methodology incorporated a national survey of leaders requesting nominations of outstanding programs. Of 356 programs located in forty-two states, 101 received more than one nomination and were sent a questionnaire to solicit information about the program.

Thirty-two programs were selected for visitation. Of those visited, twenty-seven individual case studies provide several (two to five) pages of information, including illustrations and photographs, about each institution's learning resources program. Each case study includes the institution name, location, type, enrollment (FTE), number of campuses served, number of faculty that can access the center, operating budget, name of the learning resources program, program type, year established, staff (FTE), square footage, operating budget (including charge back and fees, but excluding grants), narrative descriptions which include information related to program strengths, current projects and practices, contact person, floor plans, budgeting and funding information. An additional fourteen programs were selected because of some unusual or interesting aspect and are described briefly.

Another section includes information not discussed in the case studies, such as opinions about the use of film or video format, use of charge backs, use of computers, staffing patterns, sources of program strengths, and strategies for promoting program image and viability. While an index to institutions described would be useful, the only index to this publication is one entitled, "Index of Learning Resources, Applications, Projects, and Services." A table summarizing the characteristics of the twenty-seven programs reported in the case studies would have provided a useful overview, as would one summarizing data reported by the 86 institutions that returned the questionnaire, particularly information related to the context of the learning resources program within the institutionwide organizational structure.

In spite of the lack of this summary information, Schmidt has compiled a worthwhile collection of model-generating, exemplary learning resource programs.   Lois Buttlar

267. **World Yearbook of Education 1988: Education for the New Technologies.** Duncan Harris, ed. New York, Nichols/GP Publishing, 1988. 330p. bibliog. index. $42.50. LC 32-18413. ISBN 0-89397-299-1; ISSN 0084-2508.

This is a wide-ranging collection of articles addressing the theoretical and practical aspects of educating students and staff for the new information technologies (NIT). The sixteen articles, written by scholars from all over the world, are organized into four broad subject areas: "Basis and Needs for Education for the New Technologies," "National Perspectives," "Specific Initiatives," and "Some Questions."

Throughout the collection, the articles are varied in their level of analysis, topical focus, and interpretation of the concept "new information technologies." Some articles are broadly theoretical, political, or philosophical in their discussion of the issues related to NIT. For example, Ian Jamieson and Mary Tasker's "Schooling and the New Technology: Rhetoric and Reality" provides an excellent examination of some assumptions and societal implications of the advent of NIT in schools. Similarly, in "The Myth of Vocationalism," George Chryssides presents a philosophical critique of vocationalism and, by implication, some of the potential uses of NIT in schools. Articles in the "National Perspectives" section not only discuss national programs and policies, but also allow a comparative analysis of the connection between a country's political and social goals and its educational policy. Many of the other articles review local programs designed to initiate students, adult students, faculty, and staff into the use of NIT.

Because the editor did not want to dictate how the contributors framed the issues, this collection has inherent pluses and minuses. On the positive side, the reader is rewarded with a variety of insights, concerns, program models, and practical ideas. On the negative side, as an exploratory collection, these articles are not well integrated: it is sometimes difficult to find and synthesize the common elements of the essays. Overall, however, the focus on students and educators, on specific initiatives and national policies, and on practical applications and theoretical concerns makes this a valuable collection.

Stephen H. Aby

Periodicals and Serials

268. Collins, Mary Ellen, comp. **Education Journals and Serials: An Analytical Guide.** Westport, Conn., Greenwood Press, 1988. 355p. index. (Annotated Bibliographies of Serials: A Subject Approach, No. 12). $49.95. LC 87-31442. ISBN 0-313-24514-2.

This is an annotated bibliography of over eight hundred journals and serial publications in education and education-related fields. It is international in coverage, including titles from the United States, Canada, the United Kingdom, Ireland, Australia, New Zealand, South Africa, Nigeria, India, Pakistan, and Israel. Its purpose is "to provide an overview of English language publications in the field of education; to assist scholars and other professionals in education with the choice of journals for reading or for the submission of manuscripts; and to assist librarians in collection development" (p. x).

The entries are arranged alphabetically by title under four broad subject headings: education—general; levels of education; teaching methods, curriculum, and professional issues—general; and topical areas in education. In addition, there are approximately forty subheadings, making for easy location of journals by subject category. Access to entries is supplemented by publisher, title, geographical, and subject indexes. Bibliographic citations for each title are thorough, including such information as the date founded, title changes, mergers, frequency, price, publisher, editor, circulation, advertisements, means of manuscript selection, sources for microforms and reprints, inclusion of book reviews, availability through indexes/abstracts and databases, and target audience. Annotations, ranging from one to two paragraphs, are descriptive, evaluative, and/or comparative. There is also a list of index, abstract, and database abbreviations with full titles, as well as a directory of microform and reprint publishers.

As a collection development tool and as an overview of education journals and serials, this is a comprehensive and well-executed bibliography. As a guide to publishing opportunities, it does not provide as detailed annotations as *Cabell's Directory of Publishing Opportunities in Education* (see *ARBA* 86, entry 294). However, it is more current and covers far more journals (804) than either *Cabell's Directory* (234) or Joel Levin's *Getting Published: The Educator's Resource Book* (274) (Arco, 1983). The breadth of coverage, clear organization, and thorough indexing make *Education Journals and Serials* an important addition to education collections. [R: Choice, Sept 88, p. 76]

Stephen H. Aby

ELEMENTARY AND SECONDARY EDUCATION

Bibliographies

269. **Annual Summary of Investigations Relating to Reading July 1, 1986 to June 30, 1987.** Sam Weintraub, ed. Newark, Del., International Reading Association, 1988. 293p. index. $23.00pa. ISSN 0197-5129.

This notable series of annual summaries has a long history. In 1925 William S. Gray published his retrospective (1884-1924) *Summary of Investigations Relating to Reading* (University of Chicago Press, 1925), a landmark survey of four hundred studies. This was followed by annual summaries appearing in one or another prominent education journal. In 1961

the series, commonly known as "the Gray summary," was taken over by the International Reading Association, and began appearing annually in the *Reading Teacher*. In 1965 the *Summary* was moved to the new-born *Reading Research Quarterly*, occupying thenceforth one entire issue yearly. And finally the *Summary* achieved separate publication, under the IRA imprint, beginning with the 1 July 1978-30 June 1979 edition (swollen to a whopping eleven hundred entries, just about double the previous year). This 1978-1979 *Summary* was reviewed in *ARBA* (see *ARBA* 81, entry 731), as was the 1984-1985 *Summary* (see *ARBA* 87, entry 313).

In its life as a separate publication the series has kept to a standard format: the entries have held steady in the eight hundred to eleven hundred range; the same six categories, five of them subdivided, still hold good; and the classified arrangement plus table of contents is still in place, substituting for a subject index (there is an author index). Yet there has been one important, and underpublicized, development. We learn from an inconspicuous note on p. vii (the note made its first appearance in the 1982-1983 *Summary*) that a microfiche edition of the annual *Summary* is available, that is to say (1) the full text of all the cited publications, on microfiche; (2) the annotated citations on eye-readable cards; and (3) printed author and subject indexes. Indeed, *all* publications cited in *every* previous annual *Summary*, and in the 1884-1924 retrospective *Summary*, are also available. Furthermore "a demonstration workshop is available to train staff and students in the use of the collection"—all this to be had from the Alvina Treut Burrows Institute (P.O. Box 49, Manhasset, NY 11030, 516/869-8457). In point of fact the Institute is the publisher of the *William S. Gray Research Collection in Reading*, a formidable microfiche collection which encompasses the entire contents of the series here under review (1884-to date) *plus* a substantial number of additional documents, mainly books, monographs, and research reports, as well as journal articles drawn from a somewhat wider, more international list of monitored periodicals.

To clarify: Subscribers to the *William S. Gray Research Collection in Reading* received at its inception in 1977 the entire "Gray summary" output, 1884-1976, and, thereafter, annual supplements (all full-text microfiche) beginning with 1977-1978. The annual *Supplement*, while composed largely of the IRA's annual *Summary*, regularly fleshed it out with additional publications (everything, of course, in full-text, except for the occasional copyright item), on average about one hundred additional documents in each annual *Supplement*. The upshot is that persons obtaining the microfiche edition of the *Summary* get even more than they bargained for.   David Rosenbaum

270.   Clay, Katherine, ed. **The School Administrator's Resource Guide**. Phoenix, Ariz., Oryx Press, 1988. 104p. index. $22.00pa. LC 87-23190. ISBN 0-89774-446-2.

Many additional annotated bibliographies will probably be compiled by searching several related major electronic databases. This bibliography from Oryx Press is an example of such publications, which are a gathering of sources from several general searches. Annotations are exactly as they are given by the original database with little or no additional insight concerning the quality of the source from the editor, Katherine Clay. Although the introduction tells us that four major databases (ERIC, PsycINFO, Sociological Abstracts, and Social SciSearch) were used, over 80 percent of the citations come from ERIC. Given the $22.00 price tag, any school administrator, researcher, or librarian who has access to ERIC on CD-ROM will want to bypass this guide to educational resources. [R: RBB, 1 May 88, p. 1488]   Daniel Callison

271.   Henderson, Anne T., ed. **The Evidence Continues to Grow: Parent Involvement Improves Student Achievement**. Columbia, Md., National Committee for Citizens in Education, 1987. 76p. index. $10.00pa. LC 87-60762. ISBN 0-934460-28-0.

The key point of this book is that parent involvement is an indispensable component in any educational equation geared toward student success and achievement. Edited by Anne T. Henderson for the National Committee for Citizens in Education, and funded by the Steward Mott Foundation, this annotated bibliography is a follow-up to a work published in 1981. The editor makes clear the concern supported by the studies described in the document: "It is central to our democracy that parents and citizens participate in the governing of public institutions. Parent involvement is not a quick-fix; it is absolutely fundamental to a healthy system of public education." She cites a wide array of studies from which a clear picture arises. When parents are actively involved in the education process, students achieve higher grades and test scores, exhibit more positive attitudes and behavior, and have greater long-term achievement.

The purpose of this book is surely hard to fault. There are, however, critical questions which may be asked about both the selections and the annotations. While many of the works described are recent, a large number of the documents are ten- to twenty-years old. The scholarship would carry more weight if the editor had relied less upon ERIC documents and emphasized more research found in juried journals. While it is understandable for the author to eschew the citing of complicated statistics in a work addressed to a broad and general audience, the nearly total lack of data makes it difficult for readers to gauge the true import of many works cited. Even popular press coverage of education typically utilizes percentile figures and states levels of significance.

A further concern is the overall conclusion the editor arrives at after surveying the related literature. No one would seriously dispute the need for parent involvement in education. However, it seems to be stating the obvious to argue that when parents are actively involved in their children's education, the children are likely to succeed. Such children have a substantial support system. Another very different set of circumstances exists for millions of children who live in less ideal situations. For example, where do single parents who must hold down three jobs in order to provide food and shelter for their family find time and energy to become actively and substantially involved in the formal education of their children?

These criticisms aside, the contribution of *The Evidence Continues to Grow* and its predecessor is important. The business community, professional educators, and the general public are rapidly coming to realize that the key to successful educational programs today is vital partnerships. This annotated bibliography provides a valuable roadmap to concerned people who wish to access resources critical to the success of such connections. [R: VOYA, Aug 88, p. 153]
                    Jerry D. Flack

272.   Hladczuk, John, and William Eller, comps. **Comparative Reading: An International Bibliography**. Westport, Conn., Greenwood Press, 1987. 174p. index. (Bibliographies and Indexes in Education, No. 4). $35.00. LC 87-25407. ISBN 0-313-26004-4.

Hladczuk and Eller's *Comparative Reading* compiles close to two thousand studies, articles, periodicals, and books related to reading in a design which expands and lends flexibility to the more strict definition of comparative reading. Selected comparative and noncomparative works are both grouped according to their relationships to cross-cultural, world regional, and national concerns in the field. Ten additional categories of works whose topics are correlated to the act of reading itself are also provided: comparison, learning to read, basic skills, language, culture, the organization of reading, the improvement of reading, evaluation in reading, research in reading, and the psychology of comparative reading. These last ten categories are further divided under appropriate social, psychological, theoretical, methodological, and other subheadings. The overall effect of the collection, aside from providing lists of references, is to offer a system of classification that, by itself, raises intriguing suggestions regarding the possible dimensions of comparative reading. Its presentation of interdisciplinary "sets," alone, hints at opportunities for the student of reading and the researcher to design investigations which might redefine relationships and connections among the many and various aspects of reading. It proposes a different way to think about comparative reading by providing a structure within which unforeseen patterns might be discovered. At the same time, the construction into which the selected works are fitted is not so prejudicial as to preclude the imposition of many varied and inventive systems upon it.

Comparative Reading is offered as a tool for contemplation and for invention. It should have many utilities for the reading professional, not the least of which is the proposal, by virtue of its design, of an heuristic from which new and relevant questions having to do with the nature and scope of comparative reading can be generated.

Sandra A. Rietz

Directories

273. **Desktop Reference to the International Reading Association 1988-1989.** Newark, Del., International Reading Association, 1988. 224p. illus. index. $15.00pa.

When last reviewed as *International Reading Association Directory* (see *ARBA* 82, entry 674) this annual directory ran 117 pages and was priced at $1.50. With the organization continuing to expand and prosper, the 1988-1989 directory weighs in at 224 pages priced at $15.00 (cause? effect? of the prosperity?). The IRA now has "80,000 members in 90 nations ... over 1,200 local councils ... over 78 committees." Information is supplied on a wide range of activities: conferences, finance and administration, membership and council relations, publications, research and professional development, awards, special funds and services, professional relations and projects, committees and other groups, councils and affiliates, and for good measure, a calendar of dates and deadlines, a list of IRA periodicals, the bylaws, an index of personal

names, and, for unsatisfied information junkies, a list of IRA information sources.

David Rosenbaum

274. Mintz, Jerry, ed. **National Directory of Alternative Schools.** Glenmoore, Pa., National Coalition of Alternative Community Schools, 1987. 98p. illus. bibliog. $12.50pa. ISBN 0-939996-00-6.

The work contains an eclectic blend of information. It begins with a brief introductory essay on the purpose and activities of the National Coalition of Alternative Community Schools (democratic, nondiscriminatory schools). This is followed by section 1, a listing of 460 NCACS members in forty-seven states and sixteen foreign countries (Africa, Asia, Europe, Middle East, and South America). The members are alphabetically arranged by geographic area and subdivided by title of school. Each entry contains only the school's name and address; sometimes the name of a contact person is provided. There is no information regarding telephone number, grade levels, number of students or teachers, curriculum, or cost. The section concludes with another list of sixteen alternative boarding schools and thirteen alternative colleges.

Section 2 includes photographs and additional school details (cost, school description, etc.) based upon questionnaire responses and promotional brochures supplied by the schools. Section 3 unevenly describes thirty-five home-based schools and programs, again from questionnaire responses. Section 4 is another blend of disparate information – a listing of schools with innovative programs, an editorial from *Home Education Magazine*, and ideas for brochure contents and fund raising.

The last section is a bibliography of over one hundred titles primarily from the 1960s and 1970s (some with superseded editions), over fifty journal articles (none written since 1972), and six government documents published between 1971 and 1977.

Although a noble attempt to fill a publication gap, this modestly priced source is uneven in its scope and coverage, contains typographical errors, and is poorly bound. Updates are planned, but the quality must improve for this source to be considered a staple of reference collections. [R: RBB, 1 Mar 88, pp. 1120-21]

Ilene F. Rockman

275. Osborn, Susan. **Free Things for Teachers.** rev. ed. New York, Perigee Books/Putnam, 1987. 127p. illus. $6.95pa. LC 87-2409. ISBN 0-399-51334-5.

This softcover booklet is addressed to elementary school teachers and purports to fill a need for supplementary classroom materials at little or no cost other than postage and handling. A random reading of the items shows them consisting predominantly of pamphlets, coloring books, and other printed materials. The booklet is pleasantly illustrated with line drawings, and the approximately 250 items are listed in a table of contents under sixteen categories, such as arts and crafts, health and safety, mathematics, sports, games and hobbies, etc. The publication would appear to be of some interest to teachers in the primary grades.

Adam E. Cappello

Handbooks

276. Encyclopedia of School Administration and Supervision. Richard A. Gorton, Gail T. Schneider, and James C. Fisher, eds. Phoenix, Ariz., Oryx Press, 1988. 321p. index. $74.50. LC 87-34959. ISBN 0-89774-232-X.

ESAS is a comprehensive guide to the topics and issues which confront and engage school administrators. The list of over 200 contributors reads like a who's who of American education, including names such as Mary Hatwood Futrell, Rita Dunn, Ralph W. Tyler, and Herbert Kohl. The nearly 300 articles are short, direct, and succinct, yet simultaneously highly informative and free of educational jargon. Important terms are defined and relevant issues are clarified in each article. Each entry further includes a list of suggested resources for more indepth reading and research. One of the excellent features of the text is the inclusion of "A Guide to Related Topics" which appears early in the text and provides readers with an overview of all topics subsumed under broad category headings such as "Curriculum Areas and Issues" and "Administrative Processes." The article topics represent a wide array of issues and concerns of interest to today's school administrator. Matter-of-fact topics such as administrative salaries and graduation requirements are explicated, as are contemporary and controversial issues and developments such as split brain research and gifted education.

It is hard to imagine a more difficult position to hold in today's society than that of school administrator. The school administrator must be a business manager, a personnel specialist, an instructional leader, a community relations expert, and sometimes disciplinarian and counselor. To function intelligently, this super administrator must have at his or her disposal an amazing amount of information about a seemingly endless number of theories, research,

issues, and concerns. Editors Gorton, Schneider, and Fisher have assembled a great deal of information in a format that is accessible and easily read. Their work is an achievement to be appreciated by today's school administrators. [R: Choice, Nov 88, p. 460; RBB, 15 Dec 88, p. 690; WLB, Sept 88, p. 95]   Jerry D. Flack

277. Harrison, Charles. Public Schools USA: A Comparative Guide to School Districts. Charlotte, Vt., Williamson Publishing, 1988. 366p. index. $17.95pa. LC 87-34313. ISBN 0-913589-36-5.

This is an excellent guide for anyone concerned with the comparative merits of public schools located in proximity to major metropolitan areas. Approximately five hundred school districts with enrollments of twenty-five hundred or more students are profiled; all are located within twenty-five miles of a large city. Comparisons of twenty-two statistics include enrollment, current expenses per student, average combined score on the SAT or ACT, percentage of 1986 graduates who enrolled in two-year or four-year colleges, subjects in which advanced placement courses are offered, teacher-student ratios in elementary and secondary grades, teacher salaries, and number of students per music and art specialist in elementary grades.

In addition, an "Effective Schools Index" has been computed for each district that returned its statistical profile. This index rates the school district in each category against the national average. This information is very helpful in comparing district to district. A "Fair Appraisal" is compiled from interviews with "knowledgeable" lay people, who were asked to assess the quality of the educational leadership, instruction, and school environment.

Because the statistics are objective, the reader gains a fairly complete and accurate picture of the schools in any given district. For example, 93 percent of the high school students in Lexington, Massachusetts, take the SAT with an average score of 1,017. Not surprisingly, 87 percent of the graduates continue on to college. The average ESI for Lexington is 88. A family seeking an excellent college preparatory program might choose to reside in that district, rather than in Waltham or Watertown, also suburbs of Boston, which have ESI indexes of 60, fewer advanced placement courses, and a college preparatory program rated only "good" or "getting better."

This is a fascinating book to read, but will be of particular use for families relocating to another area of the country, to real estate agents, and to teachers and administrators. Most public libraries will want to have a copy. [R: Choice, Nov 88, p. 460; LJ, 15 June 88, p. 56]

Shirley Lambert

HIGHER EDUCATION
Bibliographies

278. Herring, Mark Youngblood. **Ethics and the Professor: An Annotated Bibliography, 1970-1985.** New York, Garland, 1988. 605p. index. (Garland Reference Library of the Humanities, Vol. 742). $77.00. LC 87-17800. ISBN 0-8240-8491-8.

This selective, descriptively annotated bibliography covers 1,905 English-language sources published in the United States from 1970 to 1985. Included are journal articles, books, essays in books, newspaper editorials, conference proceedings, and some dissertations and pamphlets. Excluded are reference materials and government publications. Coverage is eclectic, ranging from academic freedom and collective bargaining to moral and ethical behavior practices inside the classroom and on the athletic field. The title implies a higher educational setting (as does the Library of Congress Subject Headings "College teachers—Professional ethics—Bibliography"), but a careful reading of the citations indicates many journals devoted to a K-12 setting. The terms *teacher* and *professor* seem to be used interchangeably, which confuses the purpose of the work.

Entries are arranged by subject within ten broad chapter headings (e.g., ethics and government, personal values) and are preceded by a three-to-five-page introductory essay. An author, title, and subject/keyword index concludes the source.

As with other books in this publication series, the body of the work is reproduced from typed (not typeset) camera-ready copy. This fact, plus the relatively high price, may preclude purchase by all but the most comprehensive library collections. [R: Choice, June 88, p. 1534]

Ilene F. Rockman

279. Young, Arthur P., comp. **Higher Education in American Life, 1636-1986: A Bibliography of Dissertations and Theses.** Westport, Conn., Greenwood Press, 1988. 431p. index. (Bibliographies and Indexes in Education, No. 5). $49.95. LC 88-10996. ISBN 0-313-25352-8.

The primary goal of this book is to enhance bibliographic access to research conducted at the graduate level in the form of doctoral dissertations and master's theses. The expansive title underscores the breadth and variety of influences which characterize the history of academic institutions, including curricula, athletics, disciplines, and personalities. Part 1 is arranged alphabetically by state and territory and is subdivided by institution; part 2 contains topical studies arrayed under sixty-nine headings. There are 4,570 entries—3,290 dissertations and 1,280 theses—covering some one thousand colleges and universities. Each entry has author, title, degree, degree-granting institution, year, and the University Microfilms International order number, if available. There are author and subject indexes. A researcher or librarian could gather much of this information from the *Dissertation Abstracts International* and *Comprehensive Dissertation Index* sets (University Microfilms International, 1861-) and *Master's Theses in Education* (Research Publications, 1951/1952-). However, *Higher Education* gathers information from several hundred sources, and in doing so, has brought comprehensive coverage to the subject. The information in the volume is a valuable source to history in general, and, in particular, the history of higher education. The book would aid historians and educators, and is recommended for academic libraries with graduate-level coursework in these fields.

Byron P. Anderson

Directories

280. **American Universities and Colleges.** 13th ed. New York, with American Council on Education by Walter de Gruyter, 1987. 2024p. index. $119.50. LC 28-5598. ISBN 0-89925-179-X; ISSN 0066-0922.

This work has long been one of the standard directories for U.S. colleges and universities, listing information for about nineteen hundred institutions that offer the baccalaureate or higher degree. There has been little change since the last *ARBA* review (see *ARBA* 84, entry 558). The directory consists of three main parts. Part 1 includes six essays on the history, structure, and characteristics of higher education in this country; many interesting statistical tables are interspersed here. Part 2 is principally a listing of accrediting agencies, both general and those specific to professional associations, and those colleges that are accredited by these agencies. Part 3, comprising the bulk of the work, includes the list of institutions of higher education and various data about each (e.g., enrollment, history, institutional governance, freshman characteristics, admission requirements). Most of the data are stated to be current for the 1986-1987 academic year, except for tuition and financial aid figures, which are usually from 1985.

This source provides significantly more information than one finds in most other college directories, for example, data on faculty and administrators, publications from the institution and its departments, library collections, and buildings and grounds. Not all information is available for every college, but the detail generally is very good. The quality of editing and verification appears to be excellent; virtually no errors could be located. The major drawbacks to this work, compared to other directories, are lack of currency for important data, such as tuition (the four years between editions assures data up to six years old before the next edition); the decision to exclude two-year colleges; and the hefty price. [R: WLB, May 88, p. 104]   Christopher W. Nolan

281. Blum, Laurie. **Free Money for Humanities and Social Sciences.** 2d ed. New York, Paragon House, 1987. 194p. bibliog. (Blum's Guides to College Money). $8.95pa. LC 87-8918. ISBN 0-913729-81-7.

Free Money is a 1987 revised second edition of *Free Money for Humanities Students* (1985). In paperback this directory provides low-cost information on sources of grants and scholarships for humanities students.

An introductory section offers valuable information concerning how to apply for scholarships and grants, although the review copy had duplicative sentences. Basic concepts as well as specific information on applying for federal and athletic grants and scholarships are outlined in the introduction rather than in the body of the work. Basic federal aid sources are described and requirements given. The introductory section closes with a final note on the likelihood that, given the nature of the data included in the directory, some information may be dated. Dated material may be updated by contacting the organization offering specific programs.

The directory portion of the work is divided into three sections: geographic, miscellaneous, and subject. Approximately eleven hundred entries provide information about programs, including address, amounts given, deadlines, contacts, and restrictions. Along with traditional humanities and social science disciplines, subject entries are given for architecture, education, library science, and public administration.

Free Money fills a useful niche in the world of collegiate financial aid directories. It is a low-cost option for students seeking financial aid and is certainly useful for general library reference collections.   Warren G. Taylor

282. Cass, James, and Max Birnbaum. **Comparative Guide to American Colleges: For Students, Parents, and Counselors.** 13th ed. New York, Harper & Row, 1987. 777p. index. $35.00; $15.95pa. ISBN 0-06-055090-2; 0-06-463725-5pa.; ISSN 0893-1216.

This guide provides both descriptive and comparative information on well over one thousand colleges. The college profiles, which are arranged alphabetically by the name of the institution, cover such information as admission requirements, academic environment, faculty, graduates' career data, student body, religious orientation, campus life, varsity sports, and annual costs. Most of these sections include detailed statistical data, which can be used for comparative purposes. For example, admissions information often includes the percentage of students accepted, the SAT scores of incoming students, and the percentage of students graduating in the top one-fifth and two-fifths of their high school class. This and other information is used in assigning a selectivity rating for the college, indicating the level of competition for admission and academic success. Academic environment provides a percentage breakdown of degrees conferred by major. The section on graduates' career data includes, whenever the data are available, percentages of students pursuing various graduate and professional degrees, percentages of students entering business, and a list of graduate programs and corporations taking many of these students.

Supplementary indexes allow one to find schools by state, religious affiliation (if any), and selectivity rating. There is also a comparative listing of majors which alphabetically lists majors, the colleges offering those majors, and the number of each college's students graduating with that major in a designated year.

The *Comparative Guide to American Colleges* is comparable in many ways to Peterson's *Guide to Four-Year Colleges* (see *ARBA 87*, entry 351). Like Peterson's, it is more descriptive than the *Narrative Descriptions* volume of *The College Blue Book* (see *ARBA 88*, entry 372). It also surpasses Jack Gourman's *The Gourman Report: A Rating of Undergraduate Programs in American and International Universities* (National Education Standards, 1987) in providing comparative facts on a large number of colleges, prestigious and otherwise. These features, plus its selectivity ratings and graduates' career data, clearly make the *Comparative Guide to American Colleges* one of the very best one-volume guides to colleges.

Stephen H. Aby

283. Cassidy, Daniel J. **The Graduate Scholarship Book: The Complete Guide to Scholarships, Fellowships, Grants, and Loans for Graduate and Professional Study.** Englewood Cliffs, N.J., Prentice-Hall, 1988. 366p. index. $19.95 pa. ISBN 0-13-362229-0.

Cassidy's latest effort is a continuation of his well-received editions of *The Scholarship Book* (see *ARBA* 88, entry 370 and *ARBA* 85, entry 293). The format has remained the same, but there have been textual changes specifically aimed toward the prospective graduate student.

The preface contains sections that discuss money for graduate school, awards available in the private sector, and suggestions for organizing one's scholarship search. These sections, though brief, provide practical information and guidance to the student who is seeking financial aid for graduate school.

The 1,657 scholarships and awards are arranged alphabetically within broad areas of study, including a large section headed "General," which lists those scholarships and awards that are not designated for a particular field of study. Each entry includes the name, address, and telephone number of the organization offering financial aid, the amount of the award, application deadlines, field(s) of study, and the briefest of descriptions. Because of the necessary brevity and the changing nature of qualification information, the author stresses the book be used only as a guide.

The "Quick Find Index" and the "Field of Study Index" provide straightforward access. There is also a page that gives assistance in using the book.

This clearly written, well-organized book is appropriate for academic libraries because of the emphasis on graduate studies. Considering the reasonable price, a potential reader may be apt to purchase his or her own copy. [R: Choice, Oct 88, p. 286]   Phillip P. Powell

284. **The College Handbook Foreign Student Supplement 1988-89.** New York, College Board, 1988. 247p. maps. $12.95pa. LC 88-070964. ISBN 0-87447-320-9.

The College Board, a nonprofit association of U.S. colleges, educational institutions, and agencies has been publishing its *College Handbook* since the early 1940s. Now it has also published a separate *Foreign Student Supplement* to its useful handbook. The supplement addresses many special information needs of foreign students who want to pursue their undergraduate, graduate (M.A. and/or Ph.D.), or postgraduate studies in the United States.

Part 1 surveys general aspects of U.S. higher education, types of colleges, foreign student admission policies, requirements, costs, etc. It also includes a useful glossary of frequently occurring college terminology.

Part 2 consists of tables providing detailed information on 1,955 institutions, with separate sections for undergraduate and graduate studies. The tables include columns listing degrees offered, numbers of American and foreign students enrolled at a given college, tests and other requirements, application deadlines, costs, financial aid available for students from abroad, etc.

A predeparture calendar, several worksheets, and checklists are designed to help foreign students in their difficult and confusing tasks of selecting appropriate institutions and starting the application process.

Lev I. Soudek

285. **Consider a Christian College: 75 Colleges Combining Academic Excellence and Enduring Spiritual Values.** By Christian College Coalition. Princeton, N.J., Peterson's Guides, 1988. 127p. illus. maps. index. $12.95pa. LC 88-9915. ISBN 0-87866-688-5.

There is a great amount of entry overlap in this guide and the eighteenth edition of *Peterson's Annual Guide to Undergraduate Study Four-Year Colleges* (Peterson's Guides, 1987). In a comparison of the seventy-five institutions included in *Consider a Christian College* to *Peterson's Annual Guide*, seventy-three colleges were listed in the latter publication. Both guides follow an identical format of providing statistical data on enrollment patterns, admission requirements, expenses, financial aid, athletics, and majors. *Peterson's Annual Guide*, however, offers an additional two-page profile of each college which fully describes the religious aspects, facilities, faculty, and geographic area of each institution. *Consider a Christian College* provides information only on the seventy-five member colleges of the Christian College Coalition. Many Christian colleges such as Dallas Baptist University, Liberty University (Virginia), and Nazareth College (Michigan), which are included in *Peterson's Annual Guide*, are not listed in this guide. Although *Consider a Christian College* provides an introduction concerning the rationale for selecting a Christian institution that no other college guide gives, almost all of the information contained in this guide can be found by a patient and thorough perusal of *Peterson's Annual Guide*. This guide should only be a supplemental purchase for high school libraries. [R: Choice, Dec 88, pp. 622, 624]

Kathleen W. Craver

286. Exploring Common Ground: A Report on Business/Academic Partnerships. Washington, D.C., American Association of State Colleges and Universities Press; distr., Lanham, Md., University Publishing Associates, 1987. 206p. $24.00; $9.75pa. LC 87-27068. ISBN 0-88044-090-2; 0-88044-089-9pa.

Not a reference book per se, this report relates the history of thirty-six exemplary business/academic partnerships. The histories average six pages each, canvas the United States, and concern a diversity of joint ventures. The introduction is in two parts: the corporate perspective on partnership and the university perspective. The studies also follow a prescribed pattern: the president or chancellor of the university, in tandem with the corporate liaison, describes the institutional setting and the collaborative program. Examples are Southeast Missouri State University's partnership with Atlas Plastics Corporation, or the University of Wisconsin-Green Bay's research on waste recovery at FEECO International.

These are all success stories; in fact, they glow too easily with accomplishment. If there were any stumbling blocks along the way there is no evidence of them here. Each study is a fait accompli and reads like a news item in an alumni publication. There is no reason to doubt these successes, but this report would have been much better if the case study approach had been used. A critical examination of each partnership would have been more to the point. Otherwise it sounds as if cementing such partnerships, receiving large sums of money from private and government sources, and managing fairly complex joint ventures are simple matters any university can master.

There is no index or bibliography. Recommended for reference collections that include program descriptions, notices of research, and business sketches.   Bill Bailey

287. The GIS Guide to Four-Year Colleges, 1989. By the Editors of the Guidance Information System. Boston, Houghton Mifflin, 1988. 630p. $14.95pa. ISBN 0-395-47348-9; ISSN 0897-8956.

This guide is a basic college directory to over fifteen hundred U.S. schools offering baccalaureate degrees. Like similar guides, it comprises an introduction proposing how to search for a suitable college, an index of majors, and the listings themselves. Distinctive to this publication is a set of tables which represent by symbols each school's key features, such as selectivity and cost. Users can list the symbols on a card and run it down the columns to find "matches" with their desired criteria. Also

included are about twenty lists of the "best" schools in different categories (e.g., best dormitories, friendliest students), as rated by an undescribed group of three hundred high school counselors.

Entries for most colleges include the basic information on addresses, costs, financial aid, admissions requirements, majors offered, and extracurricular activities. A selected group of colleges (apparently less than 20 percent) that the editors consider especially interesting receive somewhat longer descriptions, including "student comment" on locale and "campus character."

Although the information here is helpful, the descriptions are much briefer than those found in several other guides. There are no data on libraries or computer facilities. The short "student comment" appears to be the comment of exactly one student per institution; thus one finds the expected range of pithy to useless statements which yield little help to the prospective student. The initial search guidance chapter is much less useful than those in other guides. The editors have also filed several entries, such as The George Washington University, under the article "The," where they may be totally missed. Libraries will be much better off purchasing Peterson's annual *Guide to Four-Year Colleges* (see *ARBA* 87, entry 351) or *Barron's Profiles of American Colleges* (see *ARBA* 87, entry 344).   Christopher W. Nolan

288. Graduate Schools and Financial Aid: A Guide to Reference Sources in the Robarts Library. Patricia Bellamy, comp. 3d ed. Toronto, University of Toronto Library, 1987. 52p. index. $5.00pa.

Bellamy's guide covers graduate schools, specific areas of graduate study, financial aid for graduate study, proposal writing, and other materials related to graduate study. The main sections of the book are the geographic areas of Canada and the Commonwealth, United States, and international. There are 161 titles listed, and all are from the reference department collection of the Robarts Library at the University of Toronto.

Each listing contains title, basic publication information, LC classification number, and an annotation. Beyond this information, each title has an abbreviation for its location in the Robarts Library. Though the guide appears oriented toward Canada, it is in effect a bibliography of core literature to materials that identify graduate schools and financial aids for institutions of higher learning throughout the world. The book is an excellent collection development tool for libraries that want strong collections in guides to graduate schools and financial aid. Also, the book is a good source for prospective graduate students to begin searching for information on graduate schools and/or financial aid.

The guide lists most main reference sources for the topic, but some titles are missing, such as *Lovejoy's College Guide, Peterson's Grants for Graduate Students*, and the Writers Digest Books' *Internships*. The information in *Graduate Schools and Financial Aid* is easily accessed through an extended table of contents and three indexes (personal name, corporate name, and title). The information is up-to-date.
                                        Byron P. Anderson

289.   **The Grants Register 1989-1991.** 11th ed. Craig Alan Lerner, ed. New York, St. Martin's Press, 1988. 779p. index. $75.00. LC 77-12055. ISBN 0-312-02118-6.

The Grants Register has long been a standard resource for information on financial awards given to students and professionals pursuing graduate or postgraduate education. This directory includes not only traditional scholarships and grants, but also competitive prizes, honoraria, and travel funds for conference attendance. It is especially noteworthy for including many sources of aid for non-U.S. nationals, particularly from nations of the Commonwealth and the Third World.

Entries describe each award's name, sponsoring organization, eligibility rules, value of grants, and application guidelines. The detailed subject index indicates which awards are restricted to persons of a particular national citizenship. Since this work was last reviewed (see *ARBA* 86, entry 321), the editor has expanded the index by including more cross-references, and has updated all other descriptive data. The editor has also seen fit to omit the bibliography of other financial aid sources included in the ninth edition. Otherwise, this continues to be an essential purchase for libraries supporting postbaccalaureate students, in spite of its partial overlap with sources such as *Grants for Graduate Students* (see *ARBA* 88, entry 355) and *DRG: Directory of Research Grants* (see *ARBA* 88, entry 328).   Christopher W. Nolan

290.   **Guide to Federal Funding for Education, 1988.** Abby D. Rich and Charles J. Edwards, eds. Arlington, Va., Education Funding Research Council, 1987. 2v. index. $134.95 looseleaf with binders/set. LC 81-643087. ISBN 0-933538-24-3; ISSN 0275-8393.

This directory lists 168 federally funded programs supporting educational efforts by state and local education agencies, postsecond-

ary institutions, and other educational organizations. Sixteen new programs have been added since the publication of the 1987 guide, and there are many updates to the other programs. The first volume lists, describes, and indexes the programs, while the second volume holds the monthly updates that arrive as part of the subscription.

The programs are arranged into broad subject areas, such as "School Improvement Programs." Each major subject area begins with a several-page summary of recent governmental actions having an impact on funding for those programs. The program descriptions themselves give information on who is eligible, the types of activities that can be funded, what legislation and regulations authorize the programs, and how one should apply. Appendices provide indexing by subject, application deadline, and *Catalog of Federal Domestic Assistance* number.

The descriptions of programs and procedures for applying are very clearly written and easily perused, and the updating service is useful during times when changes in federal appropriations are common. However, all of these programs can be found in the Office of Management and Budget's *Catalog of Federal Domestic Assistance* (see *ARBA* 84, entry 651), a publication costing about $100.00 less than this item. The text of the *CFDA*, while not quite as clear, contains additional information not found in this guide. Also compare *The Complete Grants Sourcebook for Higher Education* (see *ARBA* 87, entry 346) and *DRG: Directory of Research Grants* (see *ARBA* 88, entry 328) for many other funding sources for education not included in the aforementioned publications.
                                        Christopher W. Nolan

291.   **The Insider's Guide to Colleges, 1987-1988.** 13th ed. Compiled and edited by the staff of the *Yale Daily News*. New York, St. Martin's Press, 1987. 804p. bibliog. index. $25.00; $10.95 pa. ISBN 0-312-00234-3; 0-312-00136-3pa.

Now in its thirteenth edition, this guide provides a brief "snapshot" of life at over 290 colleges and universities in the United States and Canada. Although the descriptions of the individual institutions are valuable, accurate, and quick to read, the more valuable information is given in the first sections of this publication. Understandable, clear language describes the considerations the student must make in order to "get in" or be admitted to the college of his or her choice. Topics in this first section include "tests," "interviews," "the application form," and "transfers." Important terms are also defined.

By limiting coverage to fewer than three hundred colleges, this source leaves more institutions out than it covers. Significantly in short supply are institutions of higher education that have a substantial minority population. Most of the colleges given here have under a 15 percent enrollment reflecting American minorities.

Information for each school was compiled and written by a local "expert." The information, however, is very heavy on social life and whether or not beer is available. Little attention is given to financial aid possibilities.

Daniel Callison

292. Jones, Constance. **Beat the MBAs to the Top! A Guide to over 500 Courses Most Valuable to Business People on Their Way Up.** Reading, Mass., Addison-Wesley Publishing, 1987. 360p. index. $14.95pa. LC 87-11363. ISBN 0-201-11310-4.

Business education continues to be a popular educational path. However, with much talk of a glut of MBAs, guides to alternative methods of education for business are especially welcome. This directory lists a selected number of nondegree educational opportunities in the United States, including university executive and correspondence programs, as well as seminars and workshops by independent and professional organizations. Educational programs range from general business topics, such as marketing and management, to industry-specific training, such as preparation for work in travel agencies, real estate, and bookselling.

In addition to basic directory information, the guide lists some of the topics or courses offered, the possibility of continuing education credit, costs, and prerequisites. The reader can get a feel for the content of very specific programs, but the many university entries are fairly general and less helpful. A good introduction advocates supplementing any directory data with advice from businesspersons who can comment on the quality of particular programs.

This directory gives a good sampling of the types of business education available to those who are not considering more traditional degree programs. However, little is presented here which could not also be obtained through the use of several other, more comprehensive guides to continuing education, such as *Continuing Education: A Guide to Career Development Programs* (see *ARBA* 82, entry 714) or *The Encyclopedia of Associations* (Gale, 1988). For those people considering the pursuit of certificates, rather than baccalaureate or master's degrees, *The College Blue Book* volume *Occupational Education* (see *ARBA* 88, entry 372) is

also a good choice. [R: RBB, 15 Feb 88, p. 980]

Christopher W. Nolan

293. **Peterson's College Money Handbook 1989: The Only Complete Guide to Scholarships, Costs, and Financial Aid at U.S. Colleges.** 6th ed. Andrea E. Lehman, ed. Princeton, N.J., Peterson's Guides, 1988. 587p. (Peterson's Annual Guides). $17.95pa. ISBN 0-87866-702-4.

This handbook has changed little from the edition reviewed in *ARBA* 84 (see entry 572). The main body of the work lists accredited colleges and universities which offer four- or five-year baccalaureate programs. For each school, data are given on typical expenses, types of financial aid offered *by the school*, a profile of which students receive aid and how much they receive, and a contact name in the school's financial aid office. Also present are a short but useful introduction to the financial aid process in higher education and an index of institutions listed according to the types of aid they provide (such as athletic and merit scholarships).

The data will be of major interest to high school students and transferring undergraduates considering college costs. About half of the expense figures given are for 1987-1988, the rest for 1988-1989; thus readers should be able to compare prospective costs accurately. *The College Cost Book 1987-1988* (see *ARBA* 88, entry 373) covers much the same ground as this guide for a somewhat lower price. In spite of Peterson's subtitle, neither it nor *The College Cost Book* is a complete guide to college financial aid information. Libraries will also need to provide directories of aid from noncampus sources, such as the *Scholarships, Fellowships, Grants and Loans* volume of *The College Blue Book* (see *ARBA* 88, entry 372) or Feingolds's *Scholarships, Fellowships and Loans* (see *ARBA* 88, entry 367). Christopher W. Nolan

294. **Peterson's Guide to Certificate Programs at American Colleges and Universities.** George J. Lopos and others, eds. Princeton, N.J., Peterson's Guides, 1988. 343p. index. $35.95pa. LC 88-43018. ISBN 0-87866-741-5.

This new work by Peterson's Guides is a first attempt to collect and organize pertinent information about certificate programs at *four*-year American colleges and universities. A certificate program is defined as a program that focuses on an area of specialized knowledge or information that is developed, administered, and evaluated by the institution's faculty or by faculty-approved professionals. The popularity of many certificate programs is well known across the country, as enrollments in such specialized programs seem to increase annually.

This reference book provides some basic information about the development of certificate programs, a definition of such, and what the attainment of a certificate may mean. The section on how to use the book is brief, and not as useful as it could be.

The book is organized in an alphabetical series by states, with institutions listed in alphabetical order. Those that are members of the National University Continuing Education Association are identified. Under the entry for each college or university is another alphabetical listing of certificate programs offered. Each entry provides a brief paragraph of general information, program format, evaluation, enrollment requirements, program costs, housing and student services, and the name of a contact person with full address and telephone number(s). The appendices list NUCEA member institutions, as well as a taxonomy/classification of instructional programs. The indexes are composed of an alphabetical list by program classification and a list of institutions.

With this first attempt to gather information on certificate programs, the compilers have been fairly successful. In time the work will be expanded and refined. It is limited and hardly inclusive, perhaps because of the definition of the subject matter, and the first attempt to capture the data. Recommended for public libraries, community colleges, and institutions with an interest in continuing education.

Roberto P. Haro

295. **Peterson's Higher Education Directory 1988.** Kim R. Kaye, Robert E. Henne, and Richard E. Bohlander, eds. Princeton, N.J., Peterson's Guides, 1988. 1057p. index. $34.95pa. ISBN 0-87866-644-3; ISSN 0896-2944.

This core directory of Peterson's series profiles over thirty-five hundred U.S. institutions and seventy-five thousand key administrative personnel. The data for each institution are collected through surveys and other print material. Institutions must be formally accredited to be included in the directory.

Information about each institution is detailed and extensive, including such items as address, county, congressional district, codes, campus description, enrollment headcount, costs, etc. Information concerning support facilities is also provided. Appendices provide listings of government offices of higher education and higher education asociations, consortia, and accrediting organizations. Extensive indexes identify academic unit heads and administrative officers, institutions with specialized accreditation, and institutions by geographical location.

As with any directory some information may be out of date at the time of publication or at the time the directory is used. For example, one institution that changed its name at least two years prior to publication of this directory is listed under its former name. Personnel changes are another area where the directory may be out of date.

Peterson's Higher Education Directory, however, continues to be the standard. It is convenient to use and provides access to extensive relevant data. This directory should be a basic addition to any reference collection serving people working directly with or anyone wishing to apply to U.S. higher education institutions. [R: Choice, Nov 88, p. 466; RBB, 15 Oct 88, p. 391]   Warren G. Taylor

296. Rugg, Frederick E. **Rugg's Recommendations on the Colleges 1988-1989.** 5th ed. Haydenville, Mass., Rugg's Recommendations, 1988. 105p. $14.95pa. LC 87-061711. ISBN 0-9608934-3-1.

The fifth edition of this guide makes its recommendations from a pool of 500 colleges, up from 336 in the third edition, and 400 in the fourth edition, but this still excludes from consideration a great number of institutions. Expanded also is the category of specialized majors (cinematography, black studies, etc.), a useful addition to the standard thirty-nine majors (economics, geology, etc.). There are on average sixty recommendations per standard major, up from forty-four in the third edition; for specialized majors, there are far fewer, varying from a single recommendation to a dozen or so. Another feature, new to this edition, is the designation of a "top choice" for each of the thirty-nine standard majors.

Among the numerous college guides, Rugg stands out as unique in listing "recommended departments by academic major"—always excepting the unfathomable *Gourman Report: A Rating of Undergraduate Programs in American and International Universities* (6th ed., National Education Standards, 1987), which, in its parading of ultraprecise rankings, is even more unique. Rugg's recommendations provide a degree of reassurance to bewildered novices, their families, and to the counselors they depend on. But how reliable are these recommendations and the (implied) nonrecommendations? The editor continues to rely largely on student opinion. Although the numerical strength of his student informants has jumped from a risible one or two per institution (in the third edition) to ten or more, there is little here to inspire confidence. To his credit, he does not attempt a numerical ranking à la Gourman. Rugg's trilevel classification by "selectivity" under each standard major merely indicates "difficulty in gaining admission," not quality of the departments. Even the "top choice" for each of the thirty-nine majors is simply asterisked and left in its alphabetical place. The injustice lies rather in the preliminary selection, by fiat ("totally my opinion," p. 1), of five hundred colleges and the automatic disbarment of more than one thousand baccalaureate institutions with their many thousands of academic departments. Fairness requires a precise, factual explanation of the selection procedures, but none is given. [R: RBB, 1 June 88, p. 1660]   David Rosenbaum

297. Schlachter, Gail Ann, and R. David Weber. **Financial Aid for Veterans, Military Personnel and Their Dependents 1988-1989: A List of: Scholarships, Fellowships, Loans, Grants, Awards, and Internships....** Redwood City, Calif., Reference Service Press, 1988. 238p. bibliog. index. $32.50. ISBN 0-918276-07-1.

This directory is one of several well-crafted, special interest, financial aid directories compiled by Schlachter and others. Previous titles in this series include the *Directory of Financial Aid for Minorities* (see *ARBA* 85, entry 323), and the *Directory of Financial Aids for Women* (see *ARBA* 87, entry 858), both published biannually by Reference Service Press.

Financial Aid for Veterans is divided into nine sections. The first six, representing the main body of the directory, include the following: scholarships (433 references); fellowships (69 references); loans (67 references); grants (64 references); awards (16 references); and internships (15 references). The remaining chapters include a list of state-level financial aid programs, a useful bibliography of financial aid resources, followed by indexes which identify aid sources by sponsoring organizations, geographically, by subject, by title, and by date the application is due.

In the main sections, each entry is well documented to include availability, purpose of aid, eligibility, duration of aid, limitations, number awarded each year (this part is weak, since most entries say "varies each year"), and title. Some of the entries in this directory are to sources generally well known, others document obscure sources. From my rough sampling, I would estimate that about one-third of the entries could be found in such standard sources as Norman and Finegold's *Scholarships, Fellowships and Loans* (Bellman Publishing, 1982). The number of eligible persons (both veterans and their

dependents), plus the content and format of this directory, make its purchase very attractive, especially for school and public libraries. [R: RBB, 1 June 88, p. 1657; WLB, Apr 88, pp. 101-2]   Richard H. Quay

298. **World List of Universities. Liste Mondaile des Universites.** 17th ed. New York, Stockton Press/Grove's Dictionaries of Music, 1988. 666p. index. $90.00. LC 79-645502. ISBN 0-935859-18-7; ISSN 0084-1889.

As in previous editions (see *ARBA* 77, entry 594 and *ARBA* 86, entry 328), the main purpose of this English-French directory is to facilitate educational exchanges. The latest edition includes updated addresses on those universities previously listed and adds some five hundred new educational institutions.

The format has remained the same, with the first part consisting of a listing of universities and other institutions by country with the address and founding year. Because names of university officials are seldom included with entries in the directory, other sources such as the *International Handbook of Universities* (see *ARBA* 88, entry 359) or *World of Learning* (see *ARBA* 88, entry 331) must be used. For most countries, various departments of each institution are included; however, information for China and the USSR is limited.

The second section of each chapter lists international and regional organizations concerned with higher education and includes descriptive notes. More detailed descriptions can be found in part 2 of the directory where the history, aims, structure, and activities of each major group are outlined. The information in part 2 is provided by the organizations themselves; hence, the entries tend to vary in the type of information provided. Academic associations and scholarly bodies concerned with only specific disciplines are excluded.

Though other sources must be consulted for more detailed information, this directory proves to be a useful quick reference to names, addresses, and departments of worldwide universities and educational institutions.
                              Susan R. Penney

Handbooks and Yearbooks

299. **The A's & B's of Academic Scholarship.** 11th ed. By Priscilla S. Goeller. Alexandria, Va., Octameron, 1988. 105p. illus. $5.00pa. ISBN 0-945981-04-X.

Goeller lists academically based scholarships for undergraduate studies from approximately twelve hundred American colleges and universities, as well as a very few federal and state sources. Unlike most other scholarship guides, which concentrate on governmental or private funding sources, this tool gives prospective students information on which schools offer scholarships mainly on academic merit. Very clear charts indicate the names of the colleges, names of the scholarship programs, the number and value of the awards, award criteria (including grade point average and SAT or ACT scores), restrictions, and application dates.

Only those schools which elected to respond to the compiler's questionnaires were included; thus several hundred accredited American colleges and universities are not included. However, many of these, such as Harvard and Amherst, have no publicly promoted scholarships that are not related to financial need, says Goeller. Consequently, though this guide has incomplete coverage and no other special features, it fills a niche ignored by most other aid publications and is a bargain for the price.

Christopher W. Nolan

300. Chandler, Lana J., and Michael D. Boggs. **The Student Loan Handbook.** White Hall, Va., Betterway Publications, 1987. 159p. illus. bibliog. index. $7.95pa. LC 87-15918. ISBN 0-932620-82-5.

Libraries wishing to furnish current information about the most popular forms of financial aid will find this handbook a valuable resource. Written by two West Virginia bank-loan officers in a concise, comprehensible style, this review of federally supported loans and grants available to postsecondary students who are seeking financial aid for college, trade school, or technical training is easy to access. Part 1, entitled "The Guaranteed Student Loan Program," gives information regarding loan qualifications, application procedures, loan amounts, and repayment requirements. Part 2, "Campus-Based Programs," provides facts concerning the Pell Grant, Supplemental Educational Opportunity Grant (SEOG), the Perkins Loan (formerly the National Direct Student Loan Program), and the College Work Study Program. Part 3 lists and discusses other "Money Sources Worth Exploring" such as the Cooperative Education Program, Junior Fellowships, military supported programs, and ethnic/minority student aid programs. Part 4 furnishes guidelines concerning the development of a personal financial plan. Appendices include a description of the Student Aid Report (SAR), a state-by-state list of guaranteed student loan program sources, and a student loan department table with instructions and work-

sheet. [R: LJ, 15 Feb 88, p. 159; SLJ, Mar 88, p. 219]   Kathleen W. Craver

301. **Chronicle Student Aid Annual: For 1988-89 School Year.** Moravia, N.Y., Chronicle Guidance, 1988. 431p. index. $19.95pa. LC 79-640360. ISBN 1-55631-067-6; ISSN 0190-339X.

This annual lists over thirteen hundred financial aid programs offered by private and governmental organizations for baccalaureate, graduate, and postdoctoral studies. There has been little change since it was last reviewed by *ARBA* in 1986 (see entry 330) and 1982 (see entry 693). The aid includes scholarships, grants, loans, and work/study programs, as well as contest awards. A unique feature is the information on the National Apprenticeship System, which has been reprinted from a Department of Labor publication, offering a much different tactic for students in some career paths. Entries give application addresses and institutions, eligibility requirements, amounts of awards, and criteria for selection. A separate section is included on aid from states for their own residents. All other programs are indexed by subject, names of sponsoring organizations, and names of specific programs. The editors have usefully added a bibliography of other financial aid guides currently available.

There is a high level of quality and accuracy of information in this guide. When its coverage was compared with another standard source, *The College Blue Book* (see *ARBA* 88, entry 372), over half of the Chronicle entries were not included in *The College Blue Book*. However, the latter also has many entries exclusive of the Chronicle guide. Thus the *Chronicle Student Aid Annual* would be a good addition to a collection of the many overlapping guides in this area.

Christopher W. Nolan

302. **A Classification of Institutions of Higher Education.** 1987 ed. Princeton, N.J., Carnegie Foundation for the Advancement of Teaching; distr., Princeton, N.J., Princeton University Press, 1987. 148p. (Carnegie Foundation Technical Report). $6.50pa. LC 85-28030. ISBN 0-931050-26-X.

Originally developed in 1973, this classification groups U.S. colleges and universities on the basis of the comprehensiveness of their educational programs, their size, and level of degree offered. There are ten categories: "Research Universities" in two categories; "Doctorate-Granting Universities" in two categories; "Comprehensive Universities and Colleges" in two categories; "Liberal Arts Colleges" in two categories; "Two-Year Community, Junior and Technical Colleges"; and "Professional Schools and Other Specialized Institutions."

The primary arrangement is in these categories with public and private institutions listed within states alphabetically. Each institution is listed with its enrollment. There is an index of all of the institutions by name with its category as an access point (page numbers would have been more helpful).

As a classification scheme only, this tool will be of limited use to many patrons. There are some tables, however, in the beginning that provide a bit of additional data such as the number of institutions in each category and the shifts within categories between 1976 and 1987.

All in all, the classification is well prepared and straightforward. Selectors will have to decide if a tool of such limited but unique scope is of value in their environments.

James Rice

303. **The College Handbook 1988-89.** 26th ed. New York, College Board, 1988. 1978p. index. $16.95pa. LC 41-12971. ISBN 0-87447-313-6.

304. **Index of Majors 1988-89.** 11th ed. New York, College Board, 1988. 784p. index. $13.95 pa. LC 80-648202. ISBN 0-87447-314-4.

The College Board *College Handbook* and *Index of Majors* for 1988-1989 constitutes a valuable reference set. These editions are based on information gathered and verified in the winter and spring of 1988. They provide information for over three thousand institutions. Each volume has a convenient section with explanations for efficient and effective use of the information.

The College Handbook has been updated, highlighted, and made much easier to use. A review of the entries revealed that information is current and accurate. The pertinent categories of information covered in the handbook include a description, majors/academic programs, academic regulations, admissions, student activities, annual expenses, financial aid, and address/telephone number. Also, many indexes are included to provide multiple access points to the information.

The *Index of Majors* lists over five hundred major fields of study offered by the institutions presented in *The College Handbook*. The basic taxonomy used in the list is the CIP (Center of Instructional Programs) taxonomy. The index allows prospective students to identify institutions geographically by majors offered by level. The index is a valuable companion to *The College Handbook*.

The College Handbook and *Index of Majors* provide a firm foundation of information for students to utilize in selecting an institution of higher education to attend. The College Board has a long history of offering concise, accurate information regarding colleges and universities. These works are an excellent investment for reference collections as well as for prospective students.

Warren G. Taylor

305. Fiske, Edward B., with others. **Selective Guide to Colleges.** 4th ed. New York, Times Books/Random House, 1987. 646p. $10.95pa. LC 86-30102. ISBN 0-8129-1702-2.

Written by the education editor of the *New York Times*, this is a selection aid for prospective college students and their parents. It is a selective sampling of nearly three hundred colleges and universities located in forty-five states, eight of which are represented by only one school. Moreover, better than 25 percent of the institutions are clustered in three Eastern states: New York, Massachusetts, and Pennsylvania. Schools appearing in the guide are categorized by cost (inexpensive, moderate, expensive, very expensive), and each is rated academically on a one- to five-star rating scale. Entries are arranged alphabetically by name and begin with statistical data including median SAT/ACT scores, enrollment figures, ratio of male and female students, percentage of students on financial aid, number of students who apply, and percentage of students accepted.

Each school is profiled in an essay ranging in length from two to three or more pages. Many of the essays are dotted with comments from students. Topics range from curriculum and faculty to student housing and social life. Data were gathered primarily from questionnaires distributed to students and administrators. College catalogs and other materials contributed by the institutions provided additional information. Interestingly, college administrators were invited to comment on write-ups appearing in previous editions of the guide, presumably to prevent misrepresentation, since some controversy had arisen over previous profiling of some schools.

Students who use the guide to help with college selection should find it lively and entertaining reading, but also should be encouraged to consult more traditional (comprehensive and objective) college directories such as the *College Blue Book* (see *ARBA* 88, entry 372), *American Universities and Colleges* (see entry 280), and others. [R: VOYA, June 88, p. 107]

Dianne Brinkley Catlett

306. Fry, Ronald W., ed. **Internships. Volume 1: Advertising, Marketing, Public Relations & Sales.** Hawthorne, N.J., Career Press, 1988. 253p. index. (Internship Series). $11.95pa. ISBN 0-934829-27-6.

307. Fry, Ronald W., ed. **Internships. Volume 2: Newspapers, Magazine and Book Publishing.** Hawthorne, N.J., Career Press, 1988. 284p. index. (Internship Series). $11.95pa. ISBN 0-934829-28-4.

These two volumes make up the Internship Series, and represent a very clear, concise explanation of internships available in the areas listed in each volume. The introduction claims that the series "offers more information on internships in these specialized areas than any book ever published," which is valid. Information on internships in general, including those fields found in the Internship Series, can be found in titles such as the annual *Internships* volume from Writer's Digest (see *ARBA* 88, entry 360). In comparison, the Internship Series has more information for the specialized areas. The Internship Series complements the Career Press's six-volume Career Directory Series (*Newspapers Career Directory*, etc.). Each section of the Internship Series begins with introductory articles adapted from the Career Directory Series. Each internship listing is nicely formatted with company or agency name, address, telephone number, total employees, internship contact, internships offered (salaried or non-salaried), average yearly number, applications received, period of availability, duties/responsibilities, qualifications, application procedure, and application deadline. There are appendices which list industry and allied trade organizations and publications, and volume 2 has an additional appendix on summer institutes and publishing courses. Both volumes have an index to text and publisher listings. Recommended for libraries with collection development in financial aids, and academic libraries with campus curriculum areas in business or journalism. [R: LJ, 1 Oct 88, p. 85]   Byron P. Anderson

308. Goldstein, Amy J., ed. **Accounting to Zoology: Graduate Fields Defined.** Princeton, N.J., Peterson's Guides, 1987. 378p. index. $16.95pa. LC 86-22612. ISBN 0-87866-537-4.

This presents "a comprehensive look at 300 graduate fields of study." The signed entries are written by graduate educators currently involved in education in their field. The book is divided into four major sections: humanities and social sciences; biological, agricultural, and health sciences, which include biological sciences, agricultural and natural resource sciences, and health-care professions; physical sciences and mathematics; and engineering and applied sciences.

Entries are not elaborate, being more like abstracts than full descriptions. Nevertheless, the book provides a succinct reference that will be helpful to counselors wishing to give students advice on careers and academic preparation for those careers. For the most part each entry strives to define the field, describe graduate programs and degrees, identify trends in the field, give an idea of job prospects, and point out some recent significant research. An alphabetical index of fields covered in the book gives easy access and the table of contents is detailed.

The book will be most useful to high school counselors; but higher education counselors will also find it a brief, quick reference. Of course, to find academic institutions offering programs in the various fields one will have to refer to other Peterson guides, unless satisfied with the institution represented by the author of the individual entry in this volume. Public, school, and college libraries should give this book serious consideration for purchase.

Edward P. Miller

309. Sparks, Linda, and Bruce Emerton, comps. **American College Regalia: A Handbook.** Westport, Conn., Greenwood Press, 1988. 380p. index. $45.00. LC 88-188. ISBN 0-313-26266-7.

If you have spent hours trying to locate the alma mater for the University of Michigan, or the name of the school paper for Cornell, your task has been made less time-consuming with this new reference source that brings together in one volume previously hard-to-find data on American college and university regalia. Regalia consists of school nicknames, mascots, newspapers, colors, yearbooks, alma maters, and fight songs. This handbook provides this information for 469 colleges and universities with enrollments of at least twenty-five hundred. Information was compiled from letters sent out to each institution. The inclusion and completeness of institutional information is dependent on the extent of the material received and is therefore not uniform for each school.

Arrangement is alphabetical by state and then by name of college or university. Information is quickly located by a table of contents arranged by school name, and separate indexes arranged by school name, school color, and school mascot. This well-organized volume fills a basic reference need in a simple, easy-to-use format. [R: WLB, Oct 88, p. 106]

Marilyn Strong Noronha

310. Vacation Study Abroad. 38th ed. Edrice Marguerite Howard, ed. New York, Institute of International Education, 1987. 449p. index. $19.95pa. ISBN 0-87206-154-X; ISSN 0271-1702.

The 1988 *Vacation Study Abroad* is the thirty-eighth edition reviewing summer and short-term study abroad. This guide provides information on non-American worldwide programs in a format similar to other guides issued by the publisher, such as *Study in the United Kingdom and Ireland, 1988-89*, edited by Edrice Howard. There is a section on how to use the guide, which includes a description of the elements of each entry and a planning guide to study abroad. The planning guide presents useful concepts related to researching options, making educational choices, and making financial, travel, and living arrangements. Such information increases the usefulness of the guide.

Over one thousand programs are listed. Each entry provides information concerning location, dates, cost, subjects, credits, eligibility requirements, instruction, housing, and deadline. Also helpful is the inclusion of the language of instruction. The entries are presented in an alphabetical and hierarchical arrangement. The listing moves from geographic area, to country, city, and institution. The most useful item in each entry is the name, address, and telephone number for each program. *Vacation Study Abroad* is further enhanced by two appendices—a listing of consortia abroad and "U.S. Study Abroad Census"—as well as two indexes—a listing of sponsoring institutions and a listing arranged by fields of study.

As with other Institute of International Education guides, *Vacation Study Abroad* will be most useful to students seeking to study abroad and to libraries, particularly academic libraries, where the reference collection serves a large student-oriented population.

Warren G. Taylor

311. Yearbook of American Universities and Colleges, Academic Year, 1986-1987. George Thomas Kurian, ed. New York, Garland, 1988. 653p. bibliog. index. $60.00. ISBN 0-8240-7942-6; ISSN 0896-1034.

This volume is a selective collection of "reports, essays, statistics, speeches, lists and legal cases" (p. 5) relating to the 1986-1987 academic year in higher education. The contents, most of which are reprinted from other sources, are arranged into fifteen chapters: "Introduction," "Principal Sectors of Higher Education," "Issues," "Statistics," "People," "Speeches and Documents," "Lists and Rankings," "Collective Bargaining," "Corporate Aid to Education,"

"Selected State Reports on Higher Education," "Major Court Decisions Affecting Colleges and Universities 1986," "Campus and Community," "Centenaries and Anniversaries," "Institution Changes," and "Bibliography." It is intended not only as a source of information for administrators and other interested scholars, but also as a "permanent historical record for higher-education watchers" (p. 1).

While the yearbook is interesting throughout, a number of its sections are particularly noteworthy. The "Issues" chapter contains fifteen original essays on such topics as faculty development, Christian colleges, black colleges, public relations, instructional improvement, education's high-tech future, and faculty careers. The "Speeches and Documents" section includes speeches by William J. Bennett and Derek Bok, as well as reports on higher education by such bodies as the Carnegie Foundation for the Advancement of Teaching. The section on court decisions summarizes the facts, decisions, and reasoning of the courts in cases relating to higher education. The "Collective Bargaining" chapter provides both statistical data and a summary of the developments in faculty unionization for the year. For all of the sections in the yearbook, a representative selection of issues and information has been provided. In addition to the topical arrangement of sections, subjects can be found using the subject index, which includes not only subjects but also names, titles, and court cases.

This is an excellent yearbook, and it seems well designed to meet the needs of its intended audience. Hopefully, future editions will be as thoughtful in their organization and content and as faithful to the year's developments in higher education.   Stephen H. Aby

COMPUTER RESOURCES

312. Diem, Richard A. **Computers in Education: A Research Bibliography.** New York, Garland, 1988. 167p. index. (Garland Bibliographies in Contemporary Education, Vol. 8; Garland Reference Library of Social Science, Vol. 369). $27.00. LC 88-23642. ISBN 0-8240-8541-8.

Diem has assembled 1,064 citations with one-sentence annotations covering the research literature of educational computing in four main topical areas: preschool, elementary school, secondary school, and general computing. The bibliography is a combination of items located in *Education Index, Dissertation Abstracts, Books in Print, Current Index to Journals in Education,* and *ERIC.* There is a name and subject index appended. The items included cover 1975-1986.

While the bibliography purports to cover only research, there are many scholarly papers included which are obviously opinion pieces. A few classical works such as *Mindstorms*, while based on research, are more expository in nature. In the early 1980s, a flurry of research summaries on computer education appeared. That flood has diminished to a trickle so that it is difficult to find a good up-to-date summary of what we know about computer education from the research. The current bibliography will save scholars time in locating sources, but the one-sentence annotations are little help in describing or summarizing the research. Thus, the bibliography is merely a checklist at best. Recommended for those searching for educational computing research who would spend at least the $27.00 price tag doing online searches and culling out all the duplicate and nonrelevant documents.   David V. Loertscher

313. Directory of Software in Higher Education. Compiled from *The Chronicle of Higher Education* October 1987 by Sandy Albanese. Dublin, Ohio, OCLC Online Computer Library Center, 1987. 85p. $5.00pa. ISBN 1-55653-033-1.

Compiled from data recently appearing in *The Chronicle of Higher Education*, this useful guide directs one to many computer programs with academic implications, covering the expected areas of administration, the sciences, language, and engineering, but also other fields such as criminology, fashion, nutrition, and ecology. The entries are fully annotated, but the description of the program itself is necessarily brief (addresses and telephone numbers can elicit the details). Prices vary down from $89,000.00. Most programs are unexpectedly inexpensive, and some are even free. Because the entries appear in one alphabet, the indexes become useful. One lists the program name under the disciplines, while the applications index (CAI, data analysis, and programming among them) also indicates which processor is required, with the IBM PC appearing most frequently. Because this is compiled from a previous publication, one can only lament that the word processing program Nota Bene (which cares for many of the utility tasks individually listed) was not included. Destined to be dated soon if not revised, this directory is most valuable as it stands for immediate interests.
                     Dominique-René de Lerma

314. Directory of Software Sources for Higher Education: A Resource Guide for Instructional Applications. Compiled by the Educational Software Library of Carnegie Mellon University. Peggy Seiden, ed. Princeton, N.J., Peterson's Guides, 1988. 169p. index. $29.95pa. LC 87-29123. ISBN 0-87866-679-6.

When faculty look for information on the use of software in instructional settings, they need information to identify appropriate software and evaluate its quality. Existing directories of educational software list only a small percentage of sources available and generally focus on commercial sources. Information on instructional software is scattered throughout numerous directories that are hardware specific, such as *Educational Software for the IBM Personal Computer* (Electronic Communications, 1985), include all grade levels from preschool through graduate, such as *T.E.S.S.: The Educational Software Selector* (see *ARBA 88*, entry 392); or are discipline specific, such as *Educational Resources for Microcomputers: The 1985 Science and Math Software Directory* (Information, 1986). The uniqueness of the *Directory of Software Sources* is in its pulling together existing sources of information about software appropriate for use in higher education, particularly noncommercial software developed at colleges and universities. Besides listing commercial and noncommercial software, the directory lists other directories of educational software, software evaluation sources, journals, and organizations. All entries are abstracted and list title, address, telephone number, and contact, if available. The directory itself is not evaluative. The information is well indexed through title, subject, and organization indexes. Unfortunately, information on the hardware or operating software required to run the program is sometimes missing. The directory would be useful for librarians, faculty, and academic computing staff. Recommended for academic environments that use instructional software.
                     Byron P. Anderson

315. Software for Schools 1987-88: A Comprehensive Directory of Educational Software Grades Pre-K through 12. New York, R. R. Bowker, 1987. 1085p. $49.95. ISBN 0-8352-2369-8; ISSN 0000-099X.

An indispensable tool for educators, *Software for Schools* provides access to computer software for educational as opposed to recreational needs. The bulk of the tool is divided into two major sections. The first is an extensive listing by machine, then by subject and grade level. The second is an alphabetical listing of software by title with extensive bibliographic information, including a brief description of the package.

The subject index (by machine) provides educators with an excellent tool when searching for a specific application. This listing is worth the price of the tool, since it takes much of the guesswork out of software identification. By cross-referencing the title found in the subject index with the alphabetical indexing, enough information is provided to order the product on preview.

Other useful but briefer sections include an educational computer periodicals directory, a publishers' index, an index to professional software of use to educators in managing educational operations, and a few introductory articles about computer education in the schools.

Compared to *T.E.S.S.* (see *ARBA* 88, entry 392) guide to computer software, this directory is not as comprehensive, but provides much more detailed information and indexing access. Every school/school district with heavy investments in computers and computer education should own this tool. It is well worth the price. [R: JOYS, Spring 88, p. 366; RBB, 15 May 88, p. 1588]   David V. Loertscher

INTERNATIONAL EXCHANGE PROGRAMS AND OPPORTUNITIES

316. Cassidy, Daniel J. **The International Scholarship Book: The Complete Guide to Financial Aid for Study Abroad.** Englewood Cliffs, N.J., Prentice-Hall, 1988. 333p. index. $19.95pa. ISBN 0-13-473539-0.

A one-volume guide to private-sector financial aid for university students, this work is based upon the data collected by the National Scholarship Research Service. The purpose of the volume is to provide information on some seven billion dollars in private sector scholarships available to students interested in education abroad.

The guide includes a "Quick Find Index" for awards specifically intended for students with physical handicaps, certain racial or family ancestry, or for students interested in studying in a specific country (the index covers nations from Albania to Zimbabwe). A "Field of Study Index" lists awards based on a student's intended field of study, for example, architecture, engineering, literature, humanities, and is broken down into undergraduate and graduate classifications. Each listing contains a brief description of the award, its eligibility requirements, deadline dates, and sources for additional information. *The International Scholarship Book* also provides an extensive selection of

low-cost books and pamphlets providing information on a variety of college financial aid topics. An alphabetical index is included.

The guide provides in one convenient source a wealth of information for students interested in financial assistance for foreign study.
William G. Ratliff

317. **Directory of Overseas Educational Advising Centers.** New York, College Board, 1988. 149p. $9.95pa.

This directory (*DOE*) was compiled and edited by the Office of International Education, College Board, with the assistance of the National Liaison Committee on Foreign Student Admissions, American Association of Collegiate registrars and Admissions Officers. *DOE* is a directory, arranged alphabetically by country, of advisors who can provide information on overseas study for American students. The directory includes only those centers which are operated by or work closely with the United States Information Service. With some countries, in addition to a national center, additional regional centers are also identified. In the case of France, that included regional centers in Bordeaux, Lyons, Marseille, and Strasbourg. The national center is located in Paris.

Entries include the center's name, address, and, in some cases, the telex and/or cable codes. Appendices include a partial list of national advising center directors' names and a small, but useful, bibliography of resource materials.

Readers wanting information on courses of study overseas may wish to consult *Academic Year Abroad 1988-89* (see *ARBA* 87, entry 368) or *Study Abroad* (UNESCO, 1949-) before writing to the agencies listed in the *DOE*. Finally, for information on overseas study by country, or regions within a country, the *Directory of Resources for International Cultural and Educational Exchanges* (United States Information Agency, 1987) may be useful in that it gives addresses, within the United States, where one can gain additional help.   Richard H. Quay

318. **Directory of National Institutions of Educational Planning and Administration in Asia and the Pacific.** By UNESCO Regional Office for Education in Asia and the Pacific. Bangkok, Thailand, UNESCO Regional Office for Education in Asia and the Pacific; distr., Lanham, Md., UNIPUB, 1987. 69p. $10.00pa.

UNESCO surveyed twenty-seven national institutions of educational planning and administration to obtain the information for this directory. By country, those included are Australia (five), Bangladesh (three), China (one), India (three), Malaysia (one), Nepal (one), New Zealand (two), Pakistan (two), Philippines (one), Republic of Korea (four), Socialist Republic of Vietnam (one), Sri Lanka (one), and Thailand (two). In addition to the usual directory data, it also gives the size of staff, facilities, working languages used, and historical background for the institutions; and it states the objectives/purposes, activities, training programs, and research/studies undertaken in support of each institution.

With so much information supplied, one would think this directory an indispensable item. But some of the entries are verbose and poorly written. For example, the objective of the Beijing Municipal Institution of Educational Administration is "to train high school leading figures" who "well know education laws" and "call a spade a spade." Instead of research on children's emotions, it is on "kid's" emotions. Typographical errors appear throughout as do glaring grammatical errors. Too many of the listings are fillers and repetitious. Editing would have improved the contents dramatically. For libraries that specialize in international education.   Bill Bailey

319. International Directory of Research Institutions on Higher Education. 2d ed. By the European Centre for Higher Education. Paris, UNESCO; distr., Lanham, Md., UNIPUB, 1987. 134p. $10.00pa. ISBN 92-3-002516-X.

This updated edition has been expanded beyond the European regions in the first edition to include other world regions. Each entry contains relevant information in fifteen categories, such as official name, telephone number, address, director, and publications, including series, periodicals, reports, etc. Countries and institutions are listed alphabetically and publications are listed chronologically and by author. Titles are in the language of issue; however, English translations are provided for non-English titles.

Of interest is an introduction by Robert Cowen presenting the directions and trends in higher education research. Topics addressed are minorities, finances, governance, quality, social awareness, and networking. The introduction provides a concise overview.

Access to the information in this directory is by country and institution. There is no subject access or index. Location of a publication requires reading the entire work. The information in the directory is very useful for specialized research in higher education. This directory will be most useful to higher education libraries and research centers on higher education.
                         Warren G. Taylor

LEARNING DISABILITIES AND DISABLED

320. Directory of Facilities and Services for the Learning Disabled, 1987-88. 12th ed. Betty Lou Knotsville and Carol A. McCabe, eds. Novato, Calif., Academic Therapy, 1987. 154p. maps. free pa. ($2.00 handling fee). ISSN 0092-3257.

This slim volume tries to accomplish many things. The brief introduction is apparently aimed at parents attempting to place a learning disabled child. The bulk of the directory consists of nearly five hundred entries for schools, services, and professionals. Included are address and telephone number, population served, type of fee scale, services offered, and types of therapeutic environments and approaches. Entries are listed by state, with facility and service type indexes. For professionals, there is a list of publishers, largely those publishing testing or diagnostic tools for use with LD children. Additional lists contain professional associations and advocacy groups, educational and professional journals and newsletters aimed at parents, and college guides for the LD student.

Since the tenth edition of this title was reviewed (see *ARBA* 85, entry 314), there have been several very good directories for locating educational opportunities and services for exceptional children, and for LD children in particular. *Directory for Exceptional Children* (see *ARBA* 88, entry 381) and the *FCLD Learning Disabilities Resource Guide* (see *ARBA* 87, entry 375) are better choices for inclusiveness. That said, this title is a bargain for the circulating collection or for the personal reference shelf of the professional.
                         Pam M. Baxter

NONPRINT MATERIALS AND RESOURCES

321. Professional Resources Catalogue 87. Edmonton, Alta., Alberta Education, 1987. 133p. $14.80 looseleaf. ISBN 0-920794-47-5.

The catalog is a list of professional educational materials available through three different agencies serving educators in the province of Alberta, Canada: Instructional Technology Center, Learning Technology Unit, and Professional Resources Collection. Materials can be located by looking under Library of Congress subject headings or by using an alphabetical list of titles. Summaries and suggested use (e.g., moral education) of each resource are provided under the alphabetical directory.

Professional Resources Catalogue 87 has limited use outside the province of Alberta, Canada, since the materials listed are only available to province educational personnel. The catalog is not recommended as a comprehensive list of available professional resources in education.

William E. Hug

VOCATIONAL AND CONTINUING EDUCATION

322. **Chronicle Career Index: For 1988-89 School Year.** Moravia, N.Y., Chronicle Guidance, 1988. 169p. $14.25pa. LC 79-640396. ISBN 1-55631-068-4; ISSN 0276-0355.

Occupational information is essential to guide initial and midcareer decision making. This guide to over eight hundred publications and audiovisual resources is valuable for career and guidance personnel and students and adults considering their work and educational options. The guide indexes catalogs, directories, pamphlets, periodicals, and surveys. Often these are from trade and professional associations, so they are unlikely to appear in other reference sources.

Listing is alphabetically by publisher or source, so access by career field is through a cross-reference index using occupational titles from the *Dictionary of Occupational Titles* (Government Printing Office, 1984). This index uses categories such as graphic arts, executive secretarial studies, and radio broadcasting. Cross-references are given from unused terms. Newly emerging fields, such as mediation and negotiation, however, are not reflected even though a growing abundance of information is becoming available.

Primary users of this volume will be career and guidance personnel. A helpful section entitled "Educational and Professional Information" indexes listings by functions such as educational information (financial aid, study abroad, military training), counseling (concepts and theories, counseling with parents), or curriculum.

This is a relevant and useful volume to tap materials that are otherwise elusive or obscure since they are not in the usual publishing mainstream. However, career counselors still are an essential link between this volume and current occupational trends and local resources.

Barbara Conroy

323. **Chronicle Vocational School Manual: For 1988-89 School Year.** Moravia, N.Y.,

Chronicle Guidance, 1988. 409p. index. $16.50 pa. LC 82-643014. ISBN 1-55631-064-1; ISSN 0276-0371.

The first section of this manual lists programs of study by subject specialty, giving the state and name of school. Coverage includes 771 programs of study at forty-three hundred plus postsecondary occupational education institutions. These range from special institutes to academies to vocational-technical schools. Prefacing this first section is an index to the various programs of study, abundant with cross-references, which helps with newly emerging fields or those known by multiple names.

The charts in the second section indicate admissions requirements, tuition and fee costs, current enrollment, financial assistance (including government aid), and student services. Additional specialized information about many programs is given in an appendix, and another gives a surprisingly short list of accrediting associations.

The value of this volume is in the detail of the charts. Often, trade schools are difficult to locate when career counselors are guiding clients to specialized training opportunities. Consequently, the extent of available training is overlooked. This volume is as current as possible in the field and offers a valuable resource.

Barbara Conroy

324. Costa, Marie. **Adult Literacy/Illiteracy in the United States: A Handbook for Reference and Research.** Santa Barbara, Calif., ABC-Clio, 1988. 167p. bibliog. index. (Contemporary World Issues Series). $34.95. LC 87-31696. ISBN 0-87436-492-2.

This handbook is intended to provide "teachers, students, writers, researchers, volunteers" (p. x) and others with basic information about the problem of adult illiteracy in the United States. This information is divided into six chapters: "Chronology"; "Biographical Sketches"; "Facts and Data"; "Directory of Organizations, Associations, and Government Agencies"; "Reference Materials"; and "Computer Network, Databases, and Nonprint Media." There are also a glossary of literacy-related terms, a list of references, and a combined author/subject/title index.

The "Chronology" section lists important events, laws, etc., from 1647 to the present, and is intended to provide an historical context for understanding U.S. literacy efforts. "Biographical Sketches" provides background information on twenty-three prominent individuals in the adult literacy movement. The "Facts and Data" section includes information on the various definitions of illiteracy, different techniques for measuring it, results of surveys of adult reading habits, measures of the readability of material, adult education legislation, and proclamations from the 1987 Adult Literacy Congress. The "Directory" section provides a selective, annotated list of the more important organizations, along with a list of some of their publications. "Reference Materials" selectively includes bibliographies, handbooks, yearbooks, monographs, and periodicals dealing with literacy/illiteracy. The last section includes descriptions of online databases and computer-readable tapes, films and videocassettes, audiocassettes, and television series.

While this handbook generally succeeds in providing a foundation for those researching adult literacy/illiteracy, one criticism can be noted. The events in the "Chronology" section are listed, but are not related to one another in a coherent fashion. As a result, this section does not really illuminate the historical context of literacy efforts. An historical essay, involving some analysis, would have done this better. On the whole, however, this is a useful handbook with a good selection of material. Those individuals beginning research on the topic should find this work quite helpful.

Stephen H. Aby

325. ETS Test Collection Catalog. Volume 2: Vocational Tests and Measurement Devices. Compiled by Test Collection, Educational Testing Service. Phoenix, Ariz., Oryx Press, 1988. 160p. index. $39.50pa. LC 86-678. ISBN 0-89774-439-X.

Vocational tests and measurement devices help educators, researchers, and testing personnel to guide individuals looking at their careers and worklife. This volume lists over fourteen hundred such tools: work sample tests, attitude measures, vocational interests, planning aids, aptitude instruments, and self-assessment measures. Some are commercially available, standardized tests; others are hard-to-locate research instruments. These are applicable to all ages from elementary school to adult.

Of particular value are instruments that assess organizational climate, managerial style, and interpersonal competence within organizational settings. With increasing focus on effective organizations and in-house career development programs, this scope is unique and valuable. Some evaluation measures can be used to assess professionals in specific fields such as administrators, teachers, or nurses.

Each entry gives full citation, descriptors, availability, and a brief abstract. Three indexes

—title, author, and subject—adequately lead the user to entries. The subject index uses ERIC descriptors and gives several subject access points for each entry. As with any such catalog, however, tests developed or discontinued since its publication are not included.

This volume adds to the growing bank of resources for career planning, counseling, and employee assistance programs. [R: RBB, 15 May 88, p. 1582; WLB, Mar 88, p. 98]

Barbara Conroy

326. Malone, Cheryl Knott. Gender, Unpaid Labor, and the Promotion of Literacy: A Selected, Annotated Bibliography. New York, Garland, 1987. 148p. index. (Garland Reference Library of Social Science, Vol. 401). $27.00. LC 87-25753. ISBN 0-8240-8469-1.

The role of unpaid female workers in education and American society is emphasized in this annotated bibliography of books, articles, government publications, and dissertations published since World War II. There are 494 entries covering volunteers in schools, libraries, after-school programs, higher education, and literacy campaigns. Materials published prior to 1960 (from 1946 to 1959) are lumped together in one category. From 1960 on, materials are listed by year, through 1986.

In the preface Malone indicates the bibliographic sources she searched, either manually or online, and the subject headings she consulted to identify items for inclusion. An eight-page introduction traces the history of volunteer workers as teacher's assistants and librarians; in inner-city after-school programs in education; in various hospital roles in health care; and as tutors to illiterate adults and students in national and international literacy programs.

Annotations are limited to one or two sentences in most cases. Three indexes—author, title, and subject—provide access to specific titles in this attempt to control the literature on a unique aspect of women's studies in America. [R: Choice, June 88, p. 1538]

Lois Buttlar

327. Sudak, Diane, and Phyllis Kozokoff. Senior Citizen Education Programs: Opportunities on College Campuses in the Southeast. Metuchen, N.J., Scarecrow, 1988. 284p. illus. index. $32.00. LC 87-20789. ISBN 0-8108-2063-3.

The first of its kind, this guide was developed in response to the growing numbers of older learners attending college. It identifies and describes programs specifically designed for people of retirement age, as well as traditional course offerings available to senior citizens in

Alabama, Florida, Georgia, Louisiana, Mississippi, North Carolina, South Carolina, and Virginia.

According to the introduction, the guide "is intended as a first step in the process of selecting from many alternatives available in the Southeast.... Our summary of a given school is as comprehensive and up-to-date as available information permits."

The directory is divided into sections by state. Each state section begins with an alphabetical list of cities with their institutions. Each institution is then listed alphabetically, with the following information provided: type of college, enrollment, degrees granted, GED preparation available, campus environment, and tuition arrangements. Any special or favorable tuition advantages for older learners are indicated. A helpful note gives the availability of public transportation. Each institution listing has a "Senior Adult Information" section of particular interest. It presents the following information, if applicable: number of seniors enrolled in traditional courses, specific programs (academic and otherwise) for seniors, contact, description, senior enrollment, cost, aids for the handicapped, and availability of Elderhostel programs. The index lists each college. Several black-and-white photographs enhance the text. This work is very good in what it covers; if it does not cover something, the authors state their reasons for exclusion and provide further sources of information. [R: LJ, 1 Sept 88, p. 163; RBB, Aug 88, p. 1906; WLB, June 88, pp. 141-42]   Carmel A. Huestis

328. **Technical, Trade, & Business School Data Handbook 1988-90: Northeast/Southeast Regions.** Deborah Otaguro, ed. Concord, Mass., Orchard House, 1988. 736p. index. $45.00pa. ISBN 0-933510-70-8.

This is the third edition of the handbook. It is a two-volume work; the other volume covers the Midwest and Western regions of the United States. Schools in Puerto Rico are included, as are several foreign schools. The handbook is updated biannually and is intended as a first-step guide for high school students, guidance counselors, librarians, and parents to locate information on vocational programs. All schools listed are accredited by at least one national or regional accreditation group.

A "How to Use This Handbook," glossary of terms, and list of accreditation group abbreviations precede the main body of the work. Part 1 is a state-by-state alphabetical listing of approximately thirty-six hundred trade schools located in northeastern and southeastern states. Some eighteen hundred entries

include detailed information about the admissions process, academic programs, expenses, environment, and living conditions. These entries also include the school's address, telephone number, and accrediting agency. A brief entry containing the school's name, address, telephone number, and accrediting agency is provided for an additional eighteen hundred schools. Data were obtained from school catalogs and admissions offices. No attempt was made to evaluate or recommend any school. Part 2 provides a state-by-state list of community and junior colleges and state-operated vocational-technical schools. These entries provide only the school's address and telephone number. Part 3 lists the programs which have been indexed, then provides an alphabetical listing for all schools which offer this program. Part 4 is an alphabetical list of the schools and colleges listed in the handbook.

High school librarians, guidance offices, and public libraries will find this a useful addition to their collections. Recommended.
                                      Carol J. Veitch

329. **VGM's Careers Encyclopedia.** 2d ed. Craig T. Norback, ed. Lincolnwood, Ill., VGM Career Horizons/National Textbook, 1988. 484p. index. $29.95. LC 87-62404. ISBN 0-8442-6132-7.

VGM Career Horizons continues to build on their many occupational titles with this eight-year update of the first edition. This volume claims to cover the most common 180 careers, though one questions the inclusion of areas such as jockey and cartoonist. Of greater benefit would be listings covering areas of gerontology or health care, two of the fastest growing employment areas. Each career area is listed with a description, qualifications, and education and training required. Moreover, this revised edition gives more details on the places of employment, working conditions, potential for advancement, salary, and additional sources of information. The career listings are accessible through one alphabetical index which contains the careers, cross-references, national associations, and acronyms. The volume is similar to other titles such as *Career Choices Encyclopedia* (Walker, 1986) or the more comprehensive, three-volume *Encyclopedia of Careers and Vocational Guidance*, seventh edition (see *ARBA 88*, entry 394). Also similar are the brief career outlines available in pamphlet format, such as "Career Summary" cards by Careers, Inc. of Largo, Florida, or the "Chronicle Occupational Briefs" by Chronicle Guidance Publications of Moravia, New York. Though not unique, *Careers Encyclopedia* would be useful for students, parents, and career counselors, and would be of value to schools and libraries involved with vocational guidance or career information. [R: BR, May/June 88, p. 37; RBB, 15 Apr 88, pp. 1406-7]   Byron P. Anderson

330.   Where to Start Career Planning: Essential Resource Guide for Career Planning and Job Hunting. 6th ed. Carolyn Lloyd Lindquist, ed. Ithaca, N.Y., Cornell University Career Center; distr., Princeton, N.J., Peterson's Guides, 1987. 288p. $14.95pa. ISBN 0-87866-384-3.

This annotated bibliography offers a current and rich resource for individuals making career moves and career counselors who offer guidance—always needing ready access to new information sources. Concise annotations and full citations are given for publications grouped under twenty-one broad career fields: business, psychology, public interest, travel, etc. Most materials are current, issued in the 1980s. This is a valuable contribution, for it becomes increasingly necessary to cull older titles that sound relevant but, on inspection, turn out to be obsolete in their information.

In addition to the career field groupings, fifteen special topical areas offer an especially rich resource. Materials are listed for those with disabilities, those needing financial aid, and those looking at study and travel opportunities. A particularly welcome section is that on alternative patterns of study and work options. Audiovisual resources are listed separately, as are career information series and periodicals related to careers and giving job listings.

Increasing interest in career transitions makes this volume invaluable in public and college libraries. Sections on career planning and development and on job search directories and techniques offer ready and reliable access to the rapidly proliferating self-help materials for individuals engaging in personal career planning as well as those active in the job search. Many materials include strong components in specialized educational strategies for leaving a profession or those attempting to shift to a new field. Materials range from those aimed at the new graduate to those for people seeking second careers. [R: RBB, 15 Feb 88, p. 988]

Barbara Conroy

6 Ethnic Studies and Anthropology

ANTHROPOLOGY

331. Bibliographic Guide to Anthropology and Archaeology 1987. Boston, G. K. Hall, 1988. 382p. $165.00. ISBN 0-8161-7069-X; ISSN 0896-8101.

This book lists materials cataloged between June 1986 and August 1987 by Harvard University's Tozzer Library (formerly the Library of the Peabody Museum of Archaeology and Ethnology). It is the first annual supplement to the *Author and Subject Catalogues of the Tozzer Library*, second enlarged edition, on microfiche (G. K. Hall, 1988), which is the successor to the *Catalogue of the Library of the Peabody Museum of Archaeology and Ethnology*. This book contains full cataloging information, compiled from OCLC records, for books and other materials on topics related to cultural anthropology, physical anthropology, archaeology, and linguistics, most published from 1982 through 1986. There are entries for authors, titles, subjects, etc., in a dictionary arrangement. Both LC and Dewey Decimal Classification numbers are given. Periodical analytics are not included as they are in the *Catalogue*, but articles in periodicals are now indexed in the Tozzer Library's *Anthropological Literature: An Index to Periodical Articles and Essays* (see *ARBA* 81, entry 834).

This is an attractive, well-done work, with a format much improved over the familiar retrospective catalogs consisting of photographs of catalog cards. Although the basic cataloging information in this book can be retrieved using OCLC, this will still be a useful work, especially for subject access, not available on OCLC.

Joseph Hannibal

332. Biographical Directory of Anthropologists Born before 1920. Compiled by Library-Anthropology Resource Group. Thomas L. Mann, ed. New York, Garland, 1988. 245p. illus. index. (Garland Reference Library of the Humanities, Vol. 439). $45.00. LC 87-29219. ISBN 0-8240-5833-X.

This directory, compiled by the Library-Anthropology Resource Group (LARG), contains biographical information of people from various professions and geographic areas born before 1920 who have contributed to the field of anthropology. Each of the 3,488 entries contains such data as time of birth and death, birthplace, major publications as well as published sources of bibliographical information. For the purpose of this compendium, anthropology is broadly defined as the study of humankind. Anthropology as a discipline is an outgrowth of numerous contributions of a large number of scholars from various professions and countries.

Despite extensive efforts to make this directory as complete as possible, some eligible persons might have been inadvertently omitted. Therefore, a revised edition is planned to add the missing biographies. The compilation of the directory started in 1971 by means of a systematic search through anthropological journals, histories of anthropology, bibliographical reference works, directories, and subject catalogs. Before completing this volume, LARG produced three closely related publications: two editions of *Serial Publications in Anthropology* (1973 and 1982) and *Anthropological Bibliographies: A Selected Guide* (1981).

This volume is a significant contribution to anthropological research, as it will greatly facilitate the search for existing contributions and bibliographical data in the field. Among the entries are 889 archaeologists, 555 anthropologists, 464 ethnologists, 202 folklorists, 188 historians, 157 orientalists, 140 linguists, 138 priests, 105 missionaries, and several hundreds from other fields and professions. A subject index enhances the value of this excellent reference volume, which is highly recommended for college and public libraries. [R: Choice, June 88, pp. 1529-30; WLB, Apr 88, p. 98]

Oleg Zinam

333.   Gacs, Ute, and others, eds. **Women Anthropologists: A Biographical Dictionary.** Westport, Conn., Greenwood Press, 1988. 428p. bibliog. index. $55.00. LC 87-11983. ISBN 0-313-24414-6.

This is a collection of biographies of fifty-eight female anthropologists, mostly American, but a few of British or other nationalities, born between 1835 and 1935. Most are cultural or social anthropologists; some are archaeologists or physical anthropologists. Individual biographies are three to seven pages in length, and are accompanied by a selected list of works by the anthropologist and, usually, also by a list of references and works about the anthropologist.

The biographies are often based on interviews with the subjects or with people who knew them, as well as on written sources. In addition to the usual items covered in biographies (information on birthplace, parents, career highlights, etc.), the biographies are "intended to reveal something of the special nature of being female in the domains of fieldwork, research, formal higher education or training, and public life" (p. xv). Both advantages and disadvantages of being a female in the field of anthropology are noted. Most of the biographies are sympathetic (some writers even acknowledge the support and/or help of their subjects).

Although the experiences of selected female anthropologists have been chronicled previously, this book is unique in its breadth of coverage, making it a very useful contribution. [R: Choice, July/Aug 88, p. 1679]

Joseph Hannibal

334.   Gravel, Pierre Bettez, and Robert B. Marks Ridinger. **Anthropological Fieldwork: An Annotated Bibliography.** New York, Garland, 1988. 241p. index. (Garland Reference Library of Social Science, Vol. 419). $33.00. LC 87-32876. ISBN 0-8240-6642-1.

Social sciences tend to become more specialized, and in this process of specialization, each develops its own peculiar method of gathering, classifying, and evaluating data. As a consequence of this trend, research in anthro-

pology has become almost identified with its technique. This valuable reference book is devoted to fieldwork in anthropology, its methods and techniques, its personal dimensions, and its ethics. It contains seven hundred bibliographical items, covering books, chapters in books, and articles published in professional journals, most written from 1925 to 1986, though a few selected entries go back as far as 1800. These selected contributions cover about one hundred countries and geographic areas and are written in English, French, and German. Individual entries are arranged in alphabetical order by authors. At the end of the volume are indexes by subject matter and by the geographic areas covered.

Since the writings on the techniques of gathering data, such as observations, photography, and inspection of records and archives, are extremely numerous and not of equal historical significance, this annotated bibliography was forced to be selective. To keep the collection at a manageable level of complexity, many otherwise valuable items, such as introductory chapters on methodology in many textbooks and volumes on ethnography, were not included. The authors attempted to present the most important aspects of anthropological fieldwork and make the sources of its otherwise fragmented and heterogeneous heritage accessible to scholars, students, and the general public. Since individual annotations are concise and clearly written, they can be easily understood by the educated layperson. Overall, this volume can be used as a valuable complement to anthropological bibliographies compiled by Library-Anthropology Resource Group (LARG). [R: Choice, Sept 88, p. 80]   Oleg Zinam

335.   Rogers, Susan Carol, David D. Gilmore, and Melissa Clegg, comps. **Directory of Europeanist Anthropologists in North America.** Washington, D.C., American Anthropological Association, 1987. 106p. maps. bibliog. index. $6.00pa. ISBN 0-913167-20-7.

This is the premier project of the Society for the Anthropology of Europe (SAE) of the American Anthropological Association. The SAE identified a need for networking and communication among Europeanist anthropologists. The directory is an excellent vehicle for meeting these needs. This listing for the directory was developed from a survey, which is presented in the appendices. The directory list of 340 entries is arranged alphabetically by last name. Each entry includes basic demographic information, including address, title, and institution. Academic information is also provided for each individual and includes degree awarded, awarding institution, and date of award. Background information in the list also provides geographic specialty, field research sites, and topical specialties. The entries are concise and provide useful information for networking. There are twenty-four topical entries for several areas of interest (aging, class, ecology, etc.), as well as listings by geographic area.

In addition, the directory contains many access points to the main list. The several indexes are arranged by country, European region, non-European area specialty, and topical specialty. Another useful tool is the section of maps illustrating the location of each field research site. One of the most productive networking and communications items in the work is the bibliography of publications written by the individuals listed in the directory. The directory is well formatted to assist in the utilization of the access points.

Although the *Directory of Europeanist Anthropologists in North America* is designed for a select audience, college and university libraries will find it a useful reference tool. The work is a basic item for professionals in European anthropology.

Warren G. Taylor

336. Tattersall, Ian, Eric Delson, and John Van Couvering, eds. **Encyclopedia of Human Evolution and Prehistory.** New York, Garland, 1988. 603p. illus. maps. (Garland Reference Library of the Humanities, Vol. 768). $87.50. LC 87-23761. ISBN 0-8240-9375-5.

This encyclopedia covers two major, interrelated areas of anthropological inquiry, human evolution and prehistoric archaeology. It includes entries on a wide range of topics, including various fossil and extant primates, methodologies used to study evolution, classic sites, paleolithic artifacts, and major workers in the field.

The entries, which range from a few sentences to several pages in length, are arranged alphabetically. Longer entries are followed by a few current references. There is no index, but the book contains abundant cross-references and a list of major subjects. All articles end with the initials of their authors, specialists who are listed at the beginning of the book.

Although the quality of writing varies, and there is some overuse of jargon, the book is basically well written and accurate, and is suitable for use by college students, professionals, and the informed layperson. The book contains numerous photographs, line drawings, maps, charts, and diagrams, most of which are well executed and reproduced. The omission of an index, however, is a deficiency.

Although other books, such as C. Loring Brace and others' *Atlas of Human Evolution* (see *ARBA* 81, entry 822), have covered some of the same material, this is the most up-to-date and wide-ranging encyclopedic work on human evolution available. [R: Choice, Dec 88, p. 626; WLB, Nov 88, p. 124]   Joseph Hannibal

ETHNIC STUDIES

General Works

337. Allen, James Paul, and Eugene James Turner. **We the People: An Atlas of America's Ethnic Diversity.** New York, Macmillan, 1988. 315p. maps. (part col.). index. $85.00. LC 87-28194. ISBN 0-02-901420-4.

It took the compilers seven years to produce this informative atlas and it is worth every one of those years. While the basic data used to compile the maps can be found on the 1980 U.S. census tapes, the presentation of the data and the accompanying text make this book special. Using 115 maps (111 in color), the compilers show the U.S. distribution of sixty-seven ethnic and racial groups, as well as population shifts between 1920 and 1980. In addition to the sixty-seven major groups, subgroups are covered in the text; for example, Catholic and Protestant Irish, Flemish-speaking Belgians, French Canadians, ethnic Chinese from Vietnam and Hmong from Laos, and Sephardic Jews.

The first three chapters of the book discuss the preparation and interpretation of the maps and cartograms and why the compilers selected the county as the basic mapping unit and single ancestry as the source data. The remaining ten chapters present the data by broad areas of geographic ancestry origin and then by country. The chapters are "Early North American" (Indian and Eskimo); "Western," "Northern," "Eastern," and "Southern European"; "Middle Eastern"; "African"; "Middle and South American"; "Asian and Pacific Island"; and "General Patterns of Ethnic Identity." Each country or racial group has at least one large colored map showing the 1980 geographic distribution and text outlining the group's historical background in the United States and present-day situation. A "Summary" table for each group presents data on the number of persons claiming single ancestry, multiple ancestry, the total number of persons claiming membership in the group, and lists the five U.S. counties with the largest population, as well as the five U.S. counties with the largest percentage of that group. The final third of the atlas is made of appendices of county by county ethnic census data. The only weaknesses are the two brief indexes ("Ethnic Populations" and "Place"), but this is a very minor concern as the data are easy enough to locate. A good addition for any general medium-sized or larger reference collection. [R: Choice, May 88, p. 1377; RBB, 15 Apr 88, p. 1399; WLB, Apr 88, pp. 103-4]   G. Edward Evans

338. Sigler, Jay A., ed. **International Handbook on Race and Race Relations.** Westport, Conn., Greenwood Press, 1987. 483p. index. $95.00. LC 86-33651. ISBN 0-313-24770-6.

This volume contains essays on race relations written by experts on the current racial/ethnic situations in the twenty countries represented. Primarily, the essays are intended to be honestly descriptive, without lengthy analysis of the reasons for racial attitudes or prescriptions for remedy. All the essays are constructed similarly, with an introductory section that sets the context of the following descriptive narrative; all include substantial notes and bibliographies.

The editor introduces the work with comments on the scholarly debate about race and its meaning as an anthropological, physical, or social factor. The editor's motivation for compiling these essays is to demonstrate the prevalence of racial categories in many societies and the relevance of "race" in even apparently homogeneous nations such as Switzerland and Japan. To date, most of the race relations literature has focused on conditions in the United States, but Sigler contends that the importance of race relations is global and would benefit from a comparative approach.

The volume includes an adequate index and an appendix with data on population and percentages of population in the major racial/ethnic groups for each of the twenty countries. Commendably, the book is published on permanent paper. [R: Choice, May 88, p. 1482]
        Linda A. Naru

Blacks

339. Litwack, Leon, and August Meier, eds. **Black Leaders of the Nineteenth Century.** Champaign, Ill., University of Illinois Press, 1988. 344p. illus. bibliog. index. (Blacks in the New World). $24.95. LC 87-19439. ISBN 0-252-01506-1.

This book could be described as one of the leading volumes in the series dealing with Afro-American leaders that have been published recently. Litwack and Meier have done a fantastic job in editing those scholarly essays written by sixteen contributors who have in the past written

various valuable works in the advancement of Afro-American history.

This book contains sixteen chapters of scholarly essays on selected Afro-American leaders of the nineteenth century. It serves as a supplement to two earlier volumes on a similar subject published by the University of Illinois Press. The choice of individuals selected for treatment in this book was based on their importance and significance, including the availability of adequate primary and secondary materials concerning them. This volume has attempted to include important black leaders of the nineteenth century but has left out some significant leaders and personalities such as Prince Hall, founder of the black Masons, and Richard Allen, prominent bishop of the African Methodist Episcopal church. The reason for this obvious omission is space limitations. It is important also to mention that the individuals covered were exhaustively treated with their pictures at the beginning of each chapter.

I recommend this book without reservations to all libraries including scholars and students of Afro-American history, black politics, and sociology. [R: LJ, 15 May 88, p. 80]
        Felix Eme Unaeze

340. Michael, Colette V. **Negritude: An Annotated Bibliography.** West Cornwall, Conn., Locust Hill Press, 1988. 315p. index. $35.00. LC 88-8848. ISBN 0-933951-15-9.

Michael has indicated in the preface that this work is the first bibliography of books and essays relating solely to "Negritude" on a broader spectrum, that is, as a political, sociological, philosophical, or literal concept. This bibliography is comprehensive and annotated. It is arranged in various "user-friendly" sections. The bibliography section is organized in three subdivisions: (1) selective listings, (2) anthologies and bibliography, (3) secondary sources. The index section contains a list of books, dissertations, names of individuals, and subjects referred to in the entire work.

This bibliography is impressively done and has definitely filled the gap in the availability of a single source of materials on this subject. It is recommended to scholars and students and others who are interested in further readings and research in Negritude. [R: Choice, Nov 88, p. 464]

        Felix Eme Unaeze

341. Smith, Jessie Carney, ed. **Images of Blacks in American Culture: A Reference Guide to Information Sources.** Westport, Conn., Greenwood Press, 1988. 390p. illus. index. $49.95. LC 87-24964. ISBN 0-313-24844-3.

The editor, Fisk University Librarian, has been provoking scholarly talents nationally in many areas for two decades and has now gathered ten specialists to address imagery as found in literature, theater, music, film and television, the graphic arts, children's literature, and cultural artifacts previously thought ephemeral (toys, games, and dolls), looking also at male and female portraits. Names of the contributors (e.g., David C. Driskell, Thomas Riis, T. J. Anderson, Lois Anderson, and Janet Sims-Wood) will be known already by their previous work on these subjects. Each presents an essay on the subject, followed by excellent bibliographies and other appropriate reference materials. The foreword, by Nikki Giovanni, is as direct and honest as one might expect from such a figure. This will prove to be an important contribution, not only for the subject of images which the title promises, but with regard to the subjects through which those themes emerge. [R: Choice, Dec 88, pp. 628, 630; RBB, 1 Dec 88, pp. 630-31]

Dominique-René de Lerma

342. Stevenson, Rosemary M., comp. **Index to Afro-American Reference Resources.** Westport, Conn., Greenwood Press, 1988. 315p. index. (Bibliographies and Indexes in Afro-American and African Studies, No. 20). $39.95. LC 87-28028. ISBN 0-313-24580-0.

This index is a valuable single document containing listings of a great wealth of reference sources dealing with diverse aspects of the Afro-American experience. It is an important compendium of reference resources in dictionaries, encyclopedias, catalogs, indexes, bibliographies, social commentaries, and history texts on the Afro-American experience.

Stevenson did an excellent job in compiling this index, considering the scope and context of topics covered. Approximately 181 sources are cited in this work, which is suggestive of its comprehensive nature. This index covers mainly works done on the United States, but citations on Canada, the Caribbean, and South America comprise a significant portion of the volume. Selectively included in this index are sources on the black experience in Africa, Asia, and Europe, especially those that are of relevance to such issues as African cultural survival in the Americas (e.g., African art, music, and religion).

This index is arranged in sections beginning with acknowledgments, introduction, cited works, index to Afro-American reference resources, author and title indexes. The author and title indexes make the entries easily accessible.

The "Index to Afro-American Reference Resources" is highly recommended to scholars and students of ethnic studies, especially those researchers needing additional sources of research in the Afro-American experience. [R: Choice, June 88, p. 1540; RBB, 1 Sept 88, p. 50; WLB, June 88, p. 141]

Felix Eme Unaeze

343. Tyler, Elizabeth Ann, comp. **Research in Black History: A Guide to Resources in the Birmingham Public Library.** rev. ed. Revised by Don M. Veasey. Birmingham, Ala., Birmingham Public Library Press, 1987. 61p. $10.00pa. LC 87-29958. ISBN 0-942301-06-4.

Tyler's compilation is a job well done. This work contains a wealth of material that will enhance the activities of researchers of black history. Although most of the resources listed are available at Birmingham Public Library, this work reveals other availability and locations. It includes important works relating to the black experience in America, ranging from the introduction of slavery in America to the Civil Rights movement. Included are guides to research procedures, studies of individual families, general reference sources, and historical and sociological articles and books. Pictures of historic places and people cover thirteen pages.

This work is limited in scope, but is valuable and recommended to some researchers of black history.

Felix Eme Unaeze

344. **Who's Who among Black Americans 1988.** 5th ed. William C. Matney, ed. Detroit, Gale, 1988. 870p. index. $99.50. LC 76-643293. ISBN 0-9-30315-26-X.

This fifth edition expands upon and increases entries for black Americans who have emerged as leaders and policy makers in their chosen fields. Those individuals listed in this work were living at the time this publication was compiled. This work represents a comprehensive compendium of biographies of high-achieving black Americans in their various professional lives. It covers approximately fifteen hundred entries on black American men and women whose achievements have contributed, in some way, to the advancement and enhancement of the quality of life in our society.

I highly recommend this "treasure" to all types of libraries, educational institutions, black fraternal organizations, government agencies, and all individuals engaged in research about blacks in America and black history in general. [R: VOYA, Apr 88, pp. 52-53]

Felix Eme Unaeze

Chinese-Americans

345. Brownstone, David M. **The Chinese-American Heritage.** New York, Facts on File, 1988. 132p. illus. maps. bibliog. index. (America's Ethnic Heritage Series). $16.95. LC 88-10970. ISBN 0-8160-1627-5.

Intended for young adults, this book is a very fine treatment of Chinese-American history. It is well written and documented and is full of interesting and historically valuable illustrations.

After an opening chapter on the historical and cultural background of the early Cantonese immigrants, the author follows the standard treatment of the subject. He examines the push and pull factors of Chinese-American immigration in the middle of the nineteenth century, the immigrants' arduous journey to the Golden Mountain, their lives inside the urban Chinatowns, their contributions to the building of the American West, the long years of hardship following the passage of the exclusion act of 1882, and the life of the new immigrants arriving since 1965. There is a special chapter on Chinese-Americans in Hawaii. The author does include some discussion of the major social problems Chinese-Americans have faced, past and present. Regrettably, there is no mention of Chinese from Vietnam under the section "Recent Chinese Immigrants"; this is a large and important group of recent Chinese arrivals in the United States.

A brief bibliography identifies the most important sources in this field.

Marshall E. Nunn

Eastern Europeans

346. Jacobs, Sonia L., and Eugene E. Petriwsky, comps. and eds. **Rare Books Slavica in the University of Colorado Libraries, Boulder, Colorado: An Annotated Bibliography.** Boulder, Colo., Roberts Rinehart, 1987. 91p. illus. (part col.). index. $40.00. LC 87-62074. ISBN 0-911797-39-4.

Assuming that the University of Colorado maintains a valuable collection of Slavic rare books, Eugene Petriwsky, assistant director of the University of Colorado Libraries in charge of collection development, and Sonia L. Jacobs, acting head of Special Collection Development, prepared a valuable bibliographic of rare Slavic publications. In her introduction, Jacobs correctly states that the development of a collection of rare Slavic books at the Colorado University library is associated with the late Professors Eugene M. Kayden and S. Harrison Thomson and presently with Eugene Petriwsky; all of them contributed to the growth of this, in many respects, unique collection. One has to acknowledge the role as well of Dr. Ralph E. Ellsworth, who understood the value of special collections at the University of Colorado, and for many years supported the development of Slavic and rare book collections at the University of Colorado. Presently Dr. E. Petriwsky and his associates constitute the major force in furthering the scope of "rare book Slavica" in this noted university library.

Lubomyr R. Wynar

Germans

347. Miller, Michael M., comp. **Researching the Germans from Russia: Annotated Bibliography of the Germans from Russia Heritage Collection....** Fargo, N.D., North Dakota Institute for Regional Studies, 1987. 224p. illus. maps. index. $20.00pa. LC 86-61716. ISBN 0-911042-34-2.

The present annotated bibliography of the Germans from Russia Heritage Collection, located at the Institute of the North Dakota State University Library, lists print and nonprint materials. In addition to the bibliographic information, it contains "A Brief History of the Germans from Russia Heritage Society," "A Brief History of the Germans from Russia," and "Calendar of Events in the Life of the Colonists."

The bibliography is arranged into three parts covering various topics, ranging from Volga Germans to German colonies in Bessarabia. It is rather unfortunate that neither in the preface by Dr. Timothy J. Kloberdanz nor in the introduction are there clear definitions of Germans from Russia, southern Russia, Bessarabian Germans, and other important concepts. Surely, Miller, the compiler of this bibliography, knows that German colonies in Bessarabia were not located in ethnic Russia, and German colonists residing in the Black Sea region were located in Ukraine. It is important to use objective historical terminology in reference publications. Volhynian Germans also resided in Ukraine, and the enclosed section on the Amish is not related to the topic of this bibliography.

It is hoped that the Institute and the Germans from Russia Heritage Society will clarify this terminological confusion and introduce an appropriate terminology (e.g., Germans from Russia, Germans from Ukraine, Germans from Rumania, etc.). This reviewer finds the present bibliography valuable and hopes that the next edition will incorporate our recommendations.

Lubomyr R. Wynar

Hispanic-Americans

348. Schorr, Alan Edward. **Hispanic Resource Directory.** Juneau, Alaska, Denali Press, 1988. 347p. index. $37.50 (unbound). LC 88-70503. ISBN 0-938737-15-5.

This is a welcome addition to a growing number of new reference books dealing with Hispanic groups in the United States. This work attempts to provide information on almost one thousand local, regional and national Hispanic associations, academic programs, foundations, research centers, museums, and other groups in the United States. To be included, the groups must be active in one or more of the following services: educational, advocacy, cultural, economic, legal, library and information, health, political, religious, research, scholarships, and social services.

Information in this new directory is arranged alphabetically by state resulting in 951 entries which include name, address and telephone number for the group; contact person and title; services offered; year established; number of members; staff; chapters; budget; narrative statement; and publications, if any. Nine appendices include data and information on postsecondary educational institutions with more than 20 percent Hispanic enrollment, Hispanic-oriented publishers, human and equal opportunity rights groups, minority and small businesses, migrant education, migrant health, bilingual education, Hispanic statistical data, and federal Hispanic employment program managers in Washington, D.C. There are three indexes: organizational names, contact persons, and services.

In any compilation of this magnitude, some groups are overlooked. Several important organizations omitted were the Texas Association of Chicanos in Higher Education (TACHE); the National Hispanic University; the Latino Issues Forum in San Francisco; and Raza Advocates for California Higher Education (RACHE) to list but a few. It is important, therefore, to use this new work in conjunction with others such as *Hispanic American Voluntary Organizations* (see *ARBA* 86, entry 368), *Chicano Organizations Directory* (see *ARBA* 86, entry 367), and *Latinos in the United States* (see *ARBA* 88, entry 413). The statistical data included should consist of more than a reprint of dated information. Nevertheless, this directory is recommended for all libraries and as a convenient reference tool for the interested researcher or layperson.

Roberto P. Haro

Irish-Americans

349. Eleuterio-Comer, Susan K., comp. **Irish American Material Culture: A Directory of Collections, Sites, and Festivals in the United States and Canada.** Westport, Conn., Greenwood Press, 1988. 107p. bibliog. index. (Material Culture Directories, No. 1). $35.00. LC 88-11038. ISBN 0-313-24731-5.

This first number in the Material Culture Directories series includes description of Irish-American holdings of ninety museums, libraries, historical societies, and archives as well as a list of forty-four historical sites in the United States, including monuments, churches, houses, and other architectural structures. A separate section is also devoted to the description of Irish festivals in the United States. A brief historical introduction, "Irish-American History from 1600" and a selective bibliography of materials pertaining to reference and general works concludes this interesting volume. This volume was patterned on Greenwood's *Museums, Sites, and Collections of Germanic Culture in North America* compiled by M. Hobbie, the editor of the present series (see *ARBA* 81, entry 471). The study of material ethnic culture, institutions, and collections expands the scope and content of Irish-American studies. The compiler of this compendium states in her preface that "Irish-American objects are difficult to identify in part because of the lack of a 'foreign language' to signify their ethnicity" (p. x). This is a rather questionable assumption since ethnic publications appear in three linguistic patterns—non-English, bilingual, and English—and in the case of Irish-Americans, they maintain strong ethnic identity in the United States in the context of their cultural institutions, publications, historical heritage, and political activities.

The methodology used in collecting necessary data for this reference tool raises another question. According to the compiler: "The collections included in this directory were chosen through a variety of methods. About two hundred questionnaires were sent to potential repositories during 1984-1987" (p. xi). At the same time, in the chapter "National Register Sites" one finds an important statement that "the entries were abstracted from the 1976 edition of the National Register of Historic Places," which is complete through the end of 1974" (p. 51). We do not know how many questionnaires were returned (out of 200) and how many were rejected. It is important to provide an explanation of the variety of methods mentioned by the compiler in order to understand the informational base of this publication.

Despite some dated information, this reviewer feels that *Irish American Material Culture* will fill an important gap in ethnic reference sources. However, the relatively high price for this small guide will make it inaccessible to many libraries due to limited library budgets.

Lubomyr R. Wynar

Jews

350. Bubis, Gerald B. **Saving the Jewish Family: Myths and Realities in the Diaspora Strategies for the Future: An Analysis and Cumulative Bibliography 1970-1982.** Lanham, Md., Jerusalem Center for Public Affairs/Center for Jewish Community Studies and University Press of America, 1987. 201p. $27.75; $14.50pa. ISBN 0-8191-6574-3; 0-8191-6575-1pa.

This work analyzes the trends and developments that have buffeted the contemporary Jewish family in the United States, in Israel, and in the rest of the world. Among the sociological variables examined and documented are the nuclear nature of the Jewish family, divorce and fertility rates, the movement towards zero population growth, late marriages, the aging of the population, the evolution of personal values, and the feminist movement. The author maintains that, despite these findings, the Jewish family is fundamentally vital and adaptable. He urges the American Jewish community to revitalize this bulwark of society and makes some specific suggestions towards this end. A classified bibliography of over twelve hundred articles appearing in American periodicals between 1970 and 1982 follows.

The Jewish family has been discussed for millenia and the number of writings on the subject has grown dramatically in recent decades. References to reading material are scattered in general indexes (such as *Index to Jewish Periodicals* [Index to Jewish Periodicals, 1963-]) and in a few books. Bubis makes no pretense that his bibliography is comprehensive. However, he has compiled a handy start to bibliographic research that is also thought-provoking and interesting reading. It is recommended for collections in sociology, public libraries that support a large Jewish community, and synagogues.

Margaret K. Norden

351. Edelheit, Abraham J., and Hershel Edelheit. **The Jewish World in Modern Times: A Selected, Annotated Bibliography.** Boulder, Colo., Westview Press, 1988. 569p. index. $65.00. LC 87-35200. ISBN 0-7201-1988-X.

This reference work is ambitious! It is a selective, annotated bibliography of English-language books, pamphlets, and journal articles on Jewish life over the last 350 years. A brief introduction outlines modern European Jewish history. There follow two major parts: part 1, "The Jewish World," and part 2, "Important Jewish Communities." The first section covers sociology, religious and cultural trends, antisemitism, public affairs, the Holocaust, and Zionism. The second describes Jewish communities in chapters on Central Europe and Scandinavia; Eastern Europe and the Balkans; Western Europe; the USSR; the United States and Canada; Central-South America; the Middle East; Israel; and Africa, Asia, and the Pacific. For each subject, general surveys precede specific subjects. The book concludes with a list of bibliographies and guides (unannotated), a glossary, and author/title indexes.

The compilers have actually seen and reviewed all of the material included in this guide; the references are, therefore, available to researchers. This adds to the tool's importance. Other positive attributes are the informative annotations, the abundance of cross-references, and the direct, concise style. However, users should be aware that the coverage is uneven. For example, the sections on Jewish art and on the Holocaust are inadequate. Researchers and teachers will find more complete listings in a collection or reference tools (including *Index to Jewish Periodicals* [Index to Jewish Periodicals, 1963-]). This work serves only as an introduction and general guide to a broad subject.

Margaret K. Norden

Native Peoples of North America

352. Blumer, Thomas J., comp. **Bibliography of the Catawba.** Metuchen, N.J., Scarecrow, 1987. 547p. index. (Native American Bibliography Series, No. 10). $55.00. LC 87-4389. ISBN 0-8108-1986-4.

The Catawba nation was a fully recognized southeastern power in the sixteenth and seventeenth centuries, but its population was decimated by smallpox, wars, and the American Revolution. Despite these setbacks, this native American tribe remains one of the best-documented societies because of a series of land treaties and the Catawba nation's efforts to obtain justice in the American court system. This fine work presents a comprehensive bibliography of the Catawba nation of South Carolina covering the period from the seventeenth century to 1985. Over forty-two hundred briefly annotated entries, drawn from newspapers, journals, government reports, legal documents, and private papers, are arranged in chronological order. A comprehensive index of subjects and place and personal names is included. An excellent choice for academic collections, especially those with native American studies. [R: Choice, June 88, p. 1530]   Julie M. Mueller

353. Edmunds, R. David. **Kinsmen through Time: An Annotated Bibliography of Potawatomi History.** Metuchen, N.J., Scarecrow, 1987. 217p. index. (Native American Bibliography Series, No. 12). $25.00. LC 87-16679. ISBN 0-8108-2020-X.

Almost eleven hundred sources relating to Potawatomi life and history for the period between 1600 and 1980 are presented here.

The major strength of this work is Edmunds's familiarity with and scholarship in this area. That mastery shines through in the thoughtful annotations given each entry. The annotations in this work inform the reader, summarize the work annotated, and often contain evaluative "hints" regarding point-of-view or possible value. An example is entry 588: "The Indians of Iowa in 1842," *Iowa Journal of History and Politics* 13 (April 1915), 250-64. The article contains a primary account of the visit of two Quakers to the Osage River Sub-Agency in Kansas in 1843. They mention a mixed-blood interpreter education at Hamilton School in New York (J. N. Bourassa), and generally describe the Potawatomis in favorable terms, although they indicate that they were "addicted to all the vices and immoralities common to Indians." The members of the Wabash band (Catholic Potawatomis) were described more favorably than other members of the tribe. [R: Choice, June 88, p. 1532]
          M. David Guttman

354. Heard, J. Norman. **Handbook of the American Frontier: Four Centuries of Indian-White Relationships. Volume I: The Southeastern Woodlands.** Metuchen, N.J., Scarecrow, 1987. 407p. (Native American Resources Series, No. 1). $39.50. LC 86-20326. ISBN 0-8108-1931-7.

Drawing information from many sources, this handbook pulls together a variety of information about Indian-white relations in the frontier days of the southeastern United States. Plans call for four additional volumes: three to cover the rest of the United States and a final "comprehensive index, chronology and bibliography" volume for the set. All the entries, in alphabetical order, are for individuals or tribes with a text ranging from under one hundred to more than one thousand words. At the end of each entry is a list of sources used to develop the text. Cross-references are provided in the text

and occasionally at places where one might expect to find an entry, for example, "Mendez de Canzo, Gonzalo de, see Canzo, Gonzalo Mendez de" (p. 244). However, there are not always such entries, for example, there is no reference for the Miccosukees either in the "Ms" or in the text on the Seminole. Lacking any index or bibliography in this volume, it is time-consuming to check the overall comprehensiveness of the work. In checking twenty names, I found sixteen, but the time needed to do this was excessive. Variations in the spelling of names may account for some of the missing names; however, with no index, no definite answer can be given. Final judgment about the value of the volume must await the completion of the set. At this time, only institutions with a strong interest in Indian-white relations need buy this book. [R: C&RL, July 88, p. 353; Choice, Sept 88, p. 80; LJ, 1 Apr 88, p. 80; RBB, 15 May 88, pp. 1583-84]
          G. Edward Evans

355. **Indians of North America: The Nanticoke.** By Frank W. Porter, III. New York, Chelsea House, 1987. 96p. illus. (part col.). maps. bibliog. index. $16.95. LC 86-31775. ISBN 1-55546-686-9.

356. **Indians of North America: The Osage.** By Terry P. Wilson. New York, Chelsea House, 1988. 111p. illus. (part col.). maps. bibliog. index. $16.95. LC 87-34105. ISBN 1-55546-722-9.

357. **Indians of North America: The Potawatomi.** By James A. Clifton. New York, Chelsea House, 1987. 98p. illus. (part col.). maps. bibliog. index. $16.95. LC 87-5170. ISBN 1-55546-725-3.

358. **Indians of North America: The Yankton Sioux.** By Herbert T. Hoover with Leonard R. Bruguier. New York, Chelsea House, 1988. 111p. illus. (part col.). maps. bibliog. index. $16.95. LC 87-18221. ISBN 1-55546-736-9.

The Chelsea House series on Indians of North America is to be a fifty-two-volume set. The four volumes reviewed here are tribal volumes, as are forty-seven other volumes, and are probably representative of the series. The individual volume authors are subject experts writing for a young adult audience. Tribal coverage includes both well-known groups, such as the Yankton Sioux, Apache, Navajo, and Iroquois, and less-known groups such as the Nanticoke, Lumbee, Quapaw, and Tunica-Biloxi. There are even volumes on the Aztec, Maya, Tarahumara, and the Eskimo. Topical volumes do or will cover native American literature, archaeology, federal Indian policy, urban native Americans, and women in native American society. Porter's general introduction starts off every volume and there is a very general pattern to all the tribal books. The relationship between the tribe and the national government is always covered in some manner. Historical material is included but the focus is on contemporary problems and cultural issues. Photographs, both black-and-white and color, illustrate the books along with line drawings and maps. A short bibliography, which includes whenever possible one bibliographic work, directs the reader to additional material. A glossary of special terms helps the reader understand the text, which is at times complex. This is probably due both to the nature of the issues covered and to having specialists write the material. One example will illustrate this point. In the discussion of pipestone the author wrote: "All the Sioux considered this quarry a holy place and came to it often to mine the special stone they used to make Sacred Pipes. In their traditional religion, they contacted the Supreme Being Wakantanka Tunkasina by means of the Pipe, just as Christian believers prayed to God through the person of Jesus as the intercessor" (p. 25). While most of the words are reasonably simple, the concept is not, and the young adult audience of these books may find it hard going at times. Overall the books are factually sound and a refreshing change from the usual fare offered to children and young adults about native Americans. It would be worthwhile reviewing some of the topical and Meso-American volumes to determine if they maintain the same high level of the four reviewed here.   G. Edward Evans

359. Johnson, Bryan R. **The Blackfeet: An Annotated Bibliography.** New York, Garland, 1988. 231p. index. (Garland Reference Library of Social Science, Vol. 441). $35.00. LC 87-32693. ISBN 0-8240-0941-X.

It will be some time before there is a more comprehensive bibliography on the Blackfeet. Johnson's coverage is almost exhaustive. Some of the less frequently covered items include popular novels, "coffee table" books, motion pictures, audio recordings, government documents, and manuscripts. Certainly there are bibliographies covering these formats, but seldom is there such a wide range in one bibliography. The compiler says he "under represented" Canadian government publications, especially on the provincial level. He also claims he underrepresented daily newspaper articles, small press books, and transcripts of radio and television broadcasts. Despite these self-proclaimed short-

comings, there are references to works in Blackfeet, German, French, Dutch, Spanish, and even a few in Japanese. In truth the work is very thorough. The depth of the bibliography is evident. Most of the annotations are short descriptive sentences. Occasionally there are lengthy notes, and these are usually evaluative. In all the compiler lists 1,186 items and arranges them in alphabetical order by main entry. He also identifies twenty-one major manuscript collections about the Blackfeet in Canada and the United States. The detailed index is as thorough as the bibliography itself. Given the scope of Johnson's effort, the bibliography contains useful citations on other native Americans and on the fur trade in addition to the Blackfeet. [R: Choice, Sept 88, p. 82]

G. Edward Evans

360. Justice, Noel D. **Stone Age Spear and Arrow Points of the Midcontinental and Eastern United States: A Modern Survey and Reference.** Bloomington, Ind., Indiana University Press, 1987. 288p. illus. (part col.). maps. bibliog. index. $37.50. LC 86-45399. ISBN 0-253-35406-4.

Fifty projectile point "clusters" (a group of related point types) are described in this book. All of the clusters have a geographic distribution that includes some portion of the Mississippi River basin. This is not a serious limitation as many clusters stretch from the Atlantic Ocean to the Great Basin. The descriptions are arranged in chronological order starting with Clovis (12 to 11,000 B.C.) and ending with Morris (A.D. 900-1200). Each cluster description contains some general text identifying sites and published references, then provides information about age and cultural affiliation, geographic distribution (with a map), and finally, morphological correlates. There are line drawings and cross-sections with a scale for each cluster. Eight good-quality color plates at the front of the book catch the reader's attention. A bibliography provides full bibliographic citation for works mentioned in the text. A comprehensive index completes the volume. The audience for this book is wide ranging. Most of the text will be fully comprehensible only to the specialist; however, almost anyone could use the illustrations to begin to identify and roughly date "my arrowhead." Thus, this could be a very high-demand book in a public library used by collectors or people making surface finds. A short basic introduction on projectile point manufacturing further enhances the book's value for the layperson. In any case, it should go into a noncirculating collection.

G. Edward Evans

361. Salzmann, Zdeněk, comp. **The Arapaho Indians: A Research Guide and Bibliography.** Westport, Conn., Greenwood Press, 1988. 113p. index. (Bibliographies and Indexes in Anthropology, No. 4). $35.00. LC 87-32274. ISBN 0-313-25354-4.

In terms of books and articles listed, this bibliography is close to comprehensive (702 items). However, for access to those items, it is not nearly as satisfactory. Coverage is for the Northern and Southern Arapaho, but there is no coverage for the Gros Ventre who are very closely related.

The background essay covering the history of the Arapaho is short, concise, accurate, and informative for the lay reader. In checking the coverage, I found twenty of the twenty-one titles I thought might be omitted. The missing item was a missionary history that does contain substantial Southern Arapaho material, but this is certainly not a major omission. There is an extensive listing of U.S. government publications, but it is convenience packaging. All the government documents listed are from S. L. Johnson's *Guide to American Indian Documents in the Congressional Serial Set: 1817-1899* (see *ARBA* 78, entry 382), *CIS U.S. Serial Set Index* (Congressional Information Service, 1975-1977), *CIS U.S. Congressional Hearings Index* (Congressional Information Service, 1981-1985), the *Monthly Catalog*, and other GPO publications. Unfortunately, each source is a separate listing, thus there is a high degree of duplication. There is a good listing of archival sources with brief descriptions of the collections. The lack of in-depth indexing limits access to the bibliographic citations, which are in alphabetical order by author. Only a thirty-six-term "topical" index provides subject access to the material, and there is no title index. One other problem exists in terms of listings for unpublished materials—the compiler does not provide location information.

This is a book for the comprehensive native American collection. [R: Choice, Sept 88, p. 88]
G. Edward Evans

362. Stuart, Paul. **Nations within a Nation: Historical Statistics of American Indians.** Westport, Conn., Greenwood Press, 1987. 251p. bibliog. index. $45.00. LC 86-33618. ISBN 0-313-23813-8.

Reference books labeled convenience packages are often considered suspect. That should not be the case here. It is true that all data in this book have appeared in other publications over the past one hundred years, but in hundreds of different books, articles, and reports. Stuart has pulled together statistical data from various sources to create an excellent compendium of facts and figures on the native American. The majority of tables and charts were prepared from twentieth-century sources; there is little pre-1870 data as the early statistical information is unreliable. After the introductory chapter (which explains how the data were acquired and presented), Stuart organizes his material into eight general sections: "Land Base and Climate"; "Population"; "Removal, Relocation and Urbanization"; "Vital Statistics and Health"; "Government Activities"; "Health Care and Education"; "Employment, Earnings and Income"; and "Indian Resources and Economic Development." With the exception of the sections on "Population" and "Removal" there are very few tables with tribal level data. Each table and chart lists the sources used in its preparation. This is a good source for general statistical information on native Americans, but will be of little assistance for those seeking detailed information on tribes. [R: WLB, Mar 88, p. 100]
G. Edward Evans

363. Verrall, Catherine, comp. **Resource/ Reading List 1987: Annotated Bibliography of Resources by and about Native People.** Toronto, Canadian Alliance in Solidarity with the Native Peoples, 1987. 111p. illus. index. $7.00 spiralbound. ISBN 0-921425-01-5.

The purpose of this publication is "to indicate the most useful books and other resources for the general public" that will convey "the wealth of Native heritage" (p. iv). Two priorities guided the selection process. First, resources which involved native people in the decision-making process (publishers/producers, authors/ filmmakers, or consultants) received top priority. Second, current or at least in-print items received preference over out-of-print titles. If appropriate, works by non-natives appear in the bibliography.

While most of the items listed are books, there is a good selection of other formats such as film, video, sound recordings, posters, slides, and a variety of curriculum items. Although intended for Canadian institutions, U.S. libraries and schools will find some excellent suggestions for additions to their collections. The compilers provide some indication of the most appropriate age level that could use the item. There are sixteen pages of books for children and elementary schools, twenty pages of teaching resources (nonbook), and a fifty-six-page section of youth and adult books. Topical categories (the arts, critiques, and women, for example) provide the subdivision in the adult section. Some topics are surprisingly broad; for example, "general" covers history, society today, and other general subjects. Annotations are brief but evaluative, if at times condescending, as in the comments about *Black Elk Speaks* (Dover, 1979): "The reader must guard against stereotyping the spiritual and ceremonial practices of all Aboriginal people on the basis of one nation." There is a title index which will aid the known item search, but there is no tribal, band, nation, or group index. In a library that is building a popular collection of native American materials, this will be a useful tool. [R: CLJ, Aug 88, p. 250]

G. Edward Evans

364.   Waldman, Carl. **Encyclopedia of Native American Tribes.** New York, Facts on File, 1988. 293p. illus. (part col.). maps. bibliog. index. $35.00. LC 86-29066. ISBN 0-8160-1421-3.

If you purchased Carl Waldman's *Atlas of the North American Indian* (see *ARBA* 86, entry 380) you know what to expect in this book: a first-class, accurate, well-illustrated reference work that can be used in school media centers (middle and high school) and in public libraries. It is not really appropriate for an academic library, not because of the text, but rather the illustrations are lacking in detail, which may make academic users think the text is too elementary.

In addition to the 140 individual tribes discussed, there are general entries for regional groupings, such as Southeast Indians and Subarctic Indians. The main entries are in alphabetical order by tribe or region. Major tribes, either in terms of present-day numbers or historical significance, receive longer treatments; for example, three pages for the Navajo and four pages for the Iroquois. Band/clan divisions are noted and indexed. Entries provide an overview of tribal culture and history up to the present time. Over three hundred color illustrations will encourage browsing use. If a reader is interested in individuals, material culture, or subjects such as religion, the index provides references to the pages where the topic is covered; for example, shellwork is mentioned in seventeen different entries, while quillwork appears in twelve, and beadwork in fourteen. As seen from the example, the level of indexing is detailed and distinctions carefully drawn. The suggestions for further reading are at the end of the book, not with the main text, and almost all are general/popular titles rather than scholarly works. Highly recommended for schools and public libraries. The only concern is that the binding of the review copy already showed signs of wear and this will be a high-use item in most libraries. [R: BR, Sept/Oct 88, p. 52; Choice, Sept 88, p. 90; LAR, 14 Oct 88, p. 608; SLJ, May 88, p. 36; VOYA, Aug 88, p. 154]   G. Edward Evans

365.   Wolf, Carolyn E., and Nancy S. Chiang. **Indians of North and South America: A Bibliography Based on the Collection at the Willard E. Yager Library-Museum, Hartwick College, Oneonta, N.Y. Supplement.** Metuchen, N.J., Scarecrow, 1988. 654p. index. $59.50. LC 88-6055. ISBN 0-8108-2127-3.

Eleven years and 3,542 entries later, a supplement to *Indians of North and South America* (see *ARBA* 78, entry 682) is available. All items listed are in the library's collection. The cut-off date for the supplement is May 1987. (That is, every item listed in the bibliography was on the library's shelves ready for use on that date.) While providing no call numbers, the item's OCLC number is part of the entry, so interlibrary loan staff can locate needed call numbers. Presumably the original offer to loan any circulating item still stands, although there is no explicit statement to that effect in the supplement. As in the original volume, the formats covered are extensive: (1) books about native Americans, (2) periodical articles or issues of periodicals added to the Yager Collection (primarily relating to the Oneida land claims case), (3) essays or chapters about native Americans in collected works, (4) anthropological and archaeological books that are primarily about native Americans, (5) doctoral dissertations on native Americans that the library purchased through University Microfilms, Inc., and (6) major collections of native American documents on microfilm. Without conducting a true random sampling, my impression is that about 70 percent of the entries are for items published since 1977, so one will need to consult both volumes for pre-1977 materials. The two volumes list more than eight thousand items, with an expected emphasis on North America. Spot checking both volumes failed to turn up any entry for an item in any language other than English. The format for entries remains the same: item number, author, title, publication information or a reference to an item number if the citation is for an essay, and the OCLC number. Extensive title and subject indexing assists in locating items of interest. If you have the first volume, you will probably wish to purchase the supplement. The compilers do not claim that the book is more than a list of their library's holdings; however, because they index collected works there is some general reference value for almost any library with a large collection of native American material. [R: Choice, Dec 88, pp. 633-34]

G. Edward Evans

366.   Wolfson, Evelyn. **From Abenaki to Zuni: A Dictionary of Native American Tribes.** New

York, Walker, 1988. 215p. illus. maps. bibliog. index. $17.95. LC 87-27875. ISBN 0-8027-6789-3.

Intended for children (probably fifth to eighth graders) this book provides short descriptions of sixty-eight native North American tribes in the United States. There are no entries for Alaskan or Canadian tribes. The author has written several other children's books about native Americans and is well qualified to compile this book. The content of the entries is accurate and easy to follow. Most entries are two and one-half to three pages long, with an occasional four-page entry having a full page of illustrations. There are 250 black-and-white illustrations and maps, and each entry has a small U.S. map indicating where the tribe lived.

Historical/ethnographic information makes up the majority of each entry, with a concluding paragraph about present day conditions. All the entries start with a guide to the pronunciation of the tribal name, its meaning, culture area, geographic location, dwelling type, clothing material, modes of transportation, and staple foods. A glossary, a selected bibliography, a list of recommended readings, and an index complete the book.

Carl Waldman's *Encyclopedia of Native American Tribes* (see entry 364) is similar, but for the higher grades. The opening entries in both books provide some insight into their differences. Wolfson gives the entry *Abenaki*, while Waldman has *Abnaki*, and provides the alternative spelling used by Wolfson. Wolfson discusses the Abenaki long houses and dome-shaped wigwams, while Waldman describes conical wigwams. Who is right? Both are correct, as Wolfson is describing western Abenaki and Waldman bases his material on the eastern Abnaki. Unfortunately, neither author mentions the tribal division and its resulting cultural differences. Because of the overlap and differences, both books need to be in the school collection. If a choice is necessary, Waldman's book covers more than double the number of tribes. [R: BR, Nov/Dec 88, pp. 49-50; VOYA, June 88, pp. 107-8]

G. Edward Evans

7 Genealogy and Heraldry

GENEALOGY

Bibliographies

367. Filby, P. William, ed. **Passenger and Immigration Lists Bibliography 1538-1900: Being a Guide to Published Lists of Arrivals in the United States and Canada.** 2d ed. Detroit, Gale, 1988. 324p. index. $100.00. LC 84-13702. ISBN 0-8103-2740-6.

The second edition of the bibliography lists more than 2,550 published sources containing names of persons arriving in the United States and Canada from 1538 through 1900. This edition includes all the information from the first edition (see *ARBA* 83, entry 413) and its supplement (see *ARBA* 85, entry 380) and adds more than 750 new lists.

Arranged alphabetically by author, full publication information is given in the numbered entries, followed by a descriptive annotation. The annotations give all the important particulars concerning the value of each title. All numbered entries correspond with the source numbers used in the multivolume *Passenger and Immigration Lists Index* (for latest supplement review, see *ARBA* 88, entry 426), also published by Gale. An extremely detailed index triples the value of this work, by assisting the researcher to locate specific topics, such as "Alabama—arrivals, French to, Germans to, Irish to, naturalization." "Remonstrance [ship], New Netherland, 1650" and "Oberhochstadt, Germans from."

This bibliography meets all the criteria we have come to expect from its editor, and the work is highly recommended to all libraries, particularly to those holding the companion volumes. [R: RBB, 1 Nov 88, p. 464]

Carol Willsey Bell

Directories

368. Johnson, Keith A., and Malcolm R. Sainty. **Genealogical Research Directory 1988: National & International.** Carmel, Calif., Genealogical Research Directory, 1988. 959p. maps. $23.50pa. ISBN 0-908120-70-2.

The 1988 edition is greatly expanded from previous editions. More than 100,000 entries were submitted by over six thousand contributors from thirty countries. Each edition contains new genealogical queries, not repeating previously published items.

The work is arranged in alphabetical order by surname, including the time period, locality, and contributor's number. The contributors' list is arranged numerically, giving names and addresses. A large number of contributors are from Australia, New Zealand, and the British Isles. The value to Americans is making contact with a foreigner working on the same family lines. An appendix, "Guide to Genealogical Societies," presents addresses of worldwide societies, although the United States section is woefully incomplete.

This series has generated much interest in the genealogical community, and the volumes are heavily used in libraries. The cloth edition is recommended for library use.

Carol Willsey Bell

Handbooks

369. Bell, Carol Willsey. **Ohio Guide to Genealogical Sources.** Baltimore, Md., Genealogical Publishing, 1988. 372p. maps. $30.00. LC 88-82274. ISBN 0-8063-1228-9.

The *Ohio Guide* lists the eighty-eight Ohio counties alphabetically, presenting a complete and detailed roster of all of the pertinent genealogical information for each. Given in each county sketch are the names and addresses of the county courthouses, libraries in the county seats, and historical and genealogical societies;

relevant land surveys; lists of court records on microfilm; itemizations of available census records; and comprehensive lists of bibliographical references to published sources. Locations for the bibliographical references are given in eight libraries, among them the Ohio Genealogical Society Library, Ohio Historical Society Library, State Library of Ohio, Family History Library of the LDS Church in Salt Lake City, and the Library of Congress.

This guide is a model of its kind, identifying in depth the record repositories and giving detailed inventories of existent records. For instance, under court records there are listings for the auditor, clerk of courts, county home, probate court, etc. Census records include agricultural, industrial, and veterans' records. The bibliographies include many privately printed items, all with library locations. The scope is truly impressive. As an added bonus the work is nicely formatted and easy to consult. Genealogical and historical libraries will find the guide a superb source for beginning a hunt in Ohio genealogical records.   Necia A. Musser

370. Cerny, Johni, and Wendy Elliot, eds. **The Library: A Guide to the LDS Family History Library.** Salt Lake City, Utah, Ancestry Publishing, 1988. 763p. index. $32.95. LC 87-70109. ISBN 0-916489-21-3.

The collections and services of the Family History Library of the LDS Church in Salt Lake City and its network of branch libraries provide the most comprehensive genealogical resource in the world. The current volume is an indispensable guide to that collection for any patron intending to do serious family research.

Thirteen specialists have prepared brief guides to the library's collection in their own area of expertise. The United States is divided into ten regions and for each state within those regions, the following is covered: historical background, settling and migration information, maps, cemetery records, census records, church records, court records, directories, genealogies, immigration/emigration records, land and property records, military records, native races, naturalization records, newspapers, probate records, vital records, and voting records. Many charts show county-by-county coverage of records held by the library.

Records for the rest of the world are covered in fourteen different essays. Europe is well covered; chapters on South America and Africa are presented. Each essay is arranged in a slightly different manner but represents the types of records available for that country. For example, each parish of England is listed showing whether the library contains the parish registers, Bishops' Transcripts, Boyd's Marriage Index, or whether the library has indexed those records by computer (known as the Parish Register Printouts). So vast a project is the latter that it is now possible to compile a list of persons (for example, Richard Knowles born somewhere in England between 1780-1790) born in every county in England for any period of time.

For persons who use or anticipate using the LDS Family History Library or for those who want to know what records are in existence for a particular state or country, the guide provides an invaluable listing. Recommended for individuals, and every library with a genealogical or family history section, but will need to be supplemented by more comprehensive research tools for in-depth research.

David V. Loertscher

371. Gilmer, Lois C. **Genealogical Research and Resources: A Guide for Library Use.** Chicago, American Library Association, 1988. 70p. index. $9.95pa. LC 87-32534. ISBN 0-8389-0482-3.

This work was prepared by a librarian for use by librarians who are unfamiliar with the research methodology needs of genealogists. It was designed to serve as a concise guide to direct researchers to sources of possible answers, to assist the librarian in posing better questions, to advise patrons of available sources, and to refer patrons to other repositories.

It is arranged in chapters covering these topics: genealogical reference service, genealogical research and organization of data, primary and secondary sources, and concluding the search. A selected bibliography accompanies each topic. An appendix contains a directory of major organizations and societies.

In addition to being a handy desk reference for busy librarians, this useful guide will be very helpful to the amateur genealogist. It is well written, simply arranged, and indexed to useful subject headings. [R: Choice, Nov 88, p. 460; LJ, 1 Oct 88, p. 81]   Carol Willsey Bell

372. Kemp, Thomas J. **Vital Records Handbook.** Baltimore, Md., Genealogical Publishing, 1988. 229p. illus. $19.95pa. LC 88-80164. ISBN 0-8063-1220-3.

Vital records are, as the name suggests, concerned with central life events: birth, marriage, and death. Frequently people need documentation certifying the occurrence of these events for driver's licenses, passports, jobs, or social security. Vital records are also critically important in genealogical research. This book has been designed to facilitate obtaining copies of these vital records. It is divided into three parts: (1) the United States; (2) United States Trust territories; (3) selected foreign countries. Application forms issued by the various record offices and the current procedures for obtaining a birth, marriage, or death certificate are given for each state, province, territory, or country. Interested persons may photocopy the needed form and send the required fee and the completed form to the appropriate record officer. Regulations, fees, and application forms often change which means this work may be quickly outdated. Libraries serving genealogists and other patrons who require copies of vital records will find this work useful. [R: RBB, 1 Nov 88, p. 465; WLB, Oct 88, p. 111]

Robert F. Van Benthuysen

373. Lester, DeeGee, comp. **Irish Research: A Guide to Collections in North America, Ireland, and Great Britain.** Westport, Conn., Greenwood Press, 1987. 348p. index. (Bibliographies and Indexes in World History, No. 9). $49.95. LC 87-25150. ISBN 0-313-24664-5.

This work is a resource guide to Irish research collections in the United States, Canada, Great Britain, and Ireland, and covers the topics of literature, history, current events, biography, Celtic studies, and the arts. Libraries, archives, organizations, the media, and government information services are among the collections described. Questionnaires were sent to nearly thirteen hundred facilities, and many were personally surveyed by the compiler.

Arranged first by country, the entries are then alphabetical by the name of the repository. Complete addresses are provided, as well as hours and special notes relating to the collections. Individual collections are described in detail. A very comprehensive index leads the user to the entry number relating to the topic. Appendix A lists special bookstores and bookdealers, while appendix B describes Irish local newspapers.

This guide is invaluable to the scholar, historian, writer, and genealogist seeking the location of important Irish collections. The compiler has achieved the goal of identification and has saved the user untold hours of footwork. [R: Choice, May 88, p. 1382]

Carol Willsey Bell

374. McGinnis, Carol. **West Virginia Genealogy: Sources & Resources.** Baltimore, Md., Genealogical Publishing, 1988. 129p. maps. bibliog. index. $18.50. LC 88-82275. ISBN 0-8063-1230-0.

This work focuses on genealogical resources in West Virginia. It contains six chapters and three appendices. The first chapter is a brief history of the state; the second deals with vital and county records and lists the records in the individual counties. The third chapter discusses alternate sources for vital records, while the fourth deals with census, land, and related records. The fifth chapter lists genealogical collections on the state, regional, and county levels. The sixth chapter discusses historical and genealogical societies and lists societies in individual counties. The information for chapters 2, 5, and 6 came from written surveys that were mailed to county clerks, libraries, and historical societies in late 1987 and early 1988.

The appendices include an excellent bibliography on West Virginia genealogical resources, an inventory to the historical records survey archives done by the Works Project Administration, and "West Virginians Filing Civil War Damages Claims with the Southern Claims Commission (1871-1880)."

This book will give those doing genealogical research in West Virginia enough current information to speedily start them on their search for information on their ancestors.

Robert L. Turner, Jr.

375. Noyes, Sybil, Charles Thornton Libby, and Walter Goodwin Davis. **Genealogical Dictionary of Maine and New Hampshire.** Baltimore, Md., Genealogical Publishing, 1988. 795p. $35.00. LC 79-88099. ISBN 0-8063-0502-9.

This reprint edition was previously reviewed in *ARBA* 73 (see entry 370). The work was originally published in five parts from 1928 to 1939, and reprinted in 1972, 1976, 1979, 1983, and 1988. The popularity of this work is obvious from the demand for reprints.

Arranged in alphabetical order, each primary immigrant is discussed in a paragraph under his or her given name. Content varies from brief entries to in-depth treatment of each family. Included are earliest dates found, offices held, names of spouse and children, and frequent references to sources.

It is good to see this important work made available once more. Libraries will certainly want to add it to their collections.

Carol Willsey Bell

376. Ryan, James G. **Irish Records: Sources for Family & Local History.** Salt Lake City, Utah, Ancestry Publishing, 1988. 562p. illus. maps. index. $34.95. LC 87-70107. ISBN 0-916489-22-1.

This attractive guide to Irish genealogical research leads the user through the maze of various record types by presenting them in a country-by-country arrangement. An abbreviated introduction contains an overview of Irish history and sources, with a brief discussion of record types.

The work is arranged by Irish counties, covering topics such as history, census, church records, commercial and social directories, family history, gravestone inscriptions, newspapers, wills and administrations, research sources and services, and miscellaneous sources. For each civil parish, details are given including dates covered, location on the county maps, and addresses. Examples of various records are scattered throughout the text.

The guide is recommended for the more advanced student of family and local history, after the exact locality has been determined. It is certainly a nice addition to the ever-growing number of "how-to" works for foreign research.

Carol Willsey Bell

377.   Sinko, Peggy Tuck. **Guide to Local and Family History at the Newberry Library.** Salt Lake City, Utah, Ancestry Publishing, 1987. 202p. index. $16.95. LC 87-70110. ISBN 0-916489-24-8.

This guide to genealogical materials in the Newberry Library is written for the serious genealogist, but will also have value for any researcher planning to use the Newberry collections. The author served on the staff of the Newberry Library's Local and Family History Section for nearly ten years. She has succinctly described its genealogical holdings and supplied plentiful lists of bibliographies, guides, periodicals, and serial publications in each chapter. An introductory chapter gives the reader some practical hints on locating material in the catalogs of this closed-stack collection. The next nine chapters cover types of materials: published sources, census records, church records, ethnic sources, military records, heraldic societies, passenger lists, special Newberry sources, and various miscellaneous collections.

The remaining chapters describe the specific source works for the various states, arranged by geographic region. There is a general description of the chief sources for each state and an assessment of the overall quality of Newberry coverage for the state, with bibliographies of books and serials pertaining to the history and genealogy of the state. A somewhat sketchy index concludes the book.

Since the Newberry Library is one of the premier historical libraries containing a collection of fifteen thousand genealogies, this new reference guide will be useful to academic and public libraries of all sizes who have patrons actively engaged in genealogical research.

Necia A. Musser

Indexes

378.   **Genealogical Periodical Annual Index: Key to the Genealogical Literature. Vol. 26: 1987.** Karen T. Ackermann, comp. Laird C. Towle, ed. Bowie, Md., Heritage Books, 1988. 266p. $17.50. ISBN 1-55613-126-7.

This periodical index was first reviewed in *ARBA* 85 (see entry 373). This twenty-sixth volume in the series bears out the statements in the earlier review that this is an important tool for accessing genealogical periodicals, and a wish fulfillment for the family researcher. The current volume covers 272 periodicals with over eleven thousand citations. The indexing is chiefly to surnames and to localities. Counties are listed under the appropriate state. The periodicals are mostly the publications of various local genealogical societies in the United States. Societies wishing to have their publications indexed are invited to send current and back issues to the editor for inclusion in the next volume. By covering these genealogical quarterlies and newsletters not otherwise indexed, this reference work performs a unique service. It should be highly valuable to all genealogical collections. [R: RBB, 1 Sept 88, p. 48]

Necia A. Musser

HERALDRY

379.   Shearer, Benjamin F., and Barbara S. Shearer. **State Names, Seals, Flags, and Symbols: A Historical Guide.** Westport, Conn., Greenwood Press, 1987. 239p. illus. (part col.). $39.95. LC 86-27135. ISBN 0-313-24559-2.

Here is a current handbook of state flags, seals, names, and assorted symbols—the first such guide to appear in fifty years. It supersedes George Shankle's *State Names, Flags, Seals, Songs, Birds, and Flowers, and Other Symbols* (rev. ed. Scholarly Press, 1971, c1938).

This work is comprehensive. The table of contents lists the state mottoes, seals, flags, birds, and so on, with a chapter for each. Using the historical perspective, the ten chapters describe and document the various state symbols. The most frequently cited sources in chapter 1, "State Names and Nicknames," are Shankle's work and John P. Harrington's "Our State Names" from the *Smithsonian Institution Annual Report* (1954). In subsequent chapters the documentation stems mainly from the statutes of the various states.

The volume has ten pages of color illustrations depicting state seals, flags, flowers, trees, and birds. A compact book that lives up to its title, it is an excellent and moderately priced volume that belongs in virtually every U.S. library. The only complaint from this reviewer, and a petty one at that, is in so systematic and thorough an effort, why did the authors choose to exclude the emblems of America's commonwealths and dependencies? [R: Choice, May 88, p. 1386; WLB, Apr 88, p. 103]

T. P. Williams

PERSONAL NAMES

380. Ellefson, Connie Lockhart. **The Melting Pot Book of Baby Names.** White Hall, Va., Betterway Publications, 1987. 204p. $7.95pa. LC 87-15916. ISBN 0-932620-84-1.

The number of people who have emigrated to this country in the past one hundred years has made our society richer and more diverse. Most new Americans want to adopt their new country's ways, but still retain some elements of the old country. Many parents still search through their family history for appropriate names for their children. This interesting work compiles more than eighty-five hundred names from over thirty countries. Included are Arabic, Chinese, Hawaiian, North American Indian, Ugandan, and Vietnamese names as well as the standard European names, and British, French, Norwegian, Russian, and Polish names. Arranged alphabetically, the entries describe the culture of the country, the emigration history to the United States, and a selection of contemporary and traditional male and female names and their meanings. The names were selected by contacting resources such as ethnic organizations, language professors, foreign students, and older immigrants. This work would be appropriate for public libraries, ethnic studies collections, or even fiction writers.

Julie M. Mueller

381. Fraser, P. M., and E. Matthews, eds. **A Lexicon of Greek Personal Names. Volume I: The Aegean Islands, Cyprus, Cyrenaica.** New York, Clarendon Press/Oxford University Press, 1987. 489p. $125.00. LC 87-12344. ISBN 0-19-864222-9.

The last comprehensive dictionary of Greek proper names was prepared in 1862: G. Benseler's revision of W. Pape's *Wörterbuch der griech. Eigennamen* (Braunschweig: Vieweg, frequently reprinted). Concerning the epigraphic sources, there is no doubt that while the inscriptions supplied only a fraction of the material to Benseler, they by now represent the source of names, particularly of personal names, *kat' exokhén*. Fortunately, Fraser and Matthews started the project of a new dictionary of personal names, and this is the first volume. Volumes on Attica, Greece and Western Greece, the area north of Greece to Southern Russia, the west coast of Asia Minor, and a volume on unassignable names will follow. (Egypt, Syria, Asia Minor, etc., are part of a parallel project.) The volume is organized alphabetically by name, and within each entry by individual regions. This second alphabetic sequence is somewhat awkward; for example, in the entry *Zo:ílo*, one finds Chios, Crete, Cyprus, Cyrenaica, Delos, Euboia, etc. (listing the islands by the alphabet). A more geographically based organization of the regions might have been more useful to the reader, although perhaps not easy to establish. Within this sequence, the occurrences of names are organized prosopographically and numbered by the *numerus currens* from, for example, Amorgos to Thera. Only references (in the nominative) to the crucial edition are given, with no encyclopedic information—this can be defended by the multiplication of years and pages another policy would entail. Nor can fully fledged textual criticism be offered, but as stated, the best editions are chosen.

There is no doubt that this work, and its subsequent volumes, will be indispensable for any serious study touching on Greek names. [R: C&RL, July 88, pp. 342-43]   L. Zgusta

8 Geography and Travel Guides

GEOGRAPHY

General Works

382. Chambers World Gazetteer: An A-Z of Geographical Information. 5th ed. David Munro, ed. New York, Cambridge University Press, 1988. 1v. (various paging). maps. (part col.). $34.50. ISBN 1-85296-200-3.

A pronouncing geographical dictionary with over twenty thousand entries, this work is international in scope with the emphasis on Great Britain. The *Chambers World Gazetteer* (*CWG*) has appeared in several editions, including one titled the *Macmillan World Gazetteer and Geographical Dictionary*, issued in the United States in 1955.

The *CWG* updates and supplements more definitive, comprehensive gazetteers such as *Columbia Lippincott Gazetteer of the World* (Columbia University Press, 1962) and the London Times *Index-Gazetteer of the World* (Houghton, 1966). All but the smallest and most specialized libraries need at least one of the large gazetteers. Unfortunately, they are ponderous and entirely too unwieldy for frequent desktop use. This reviewer has long kept a copy of *Webster's Geographical Dictionary* close to his desk. A copy of *CWG* will join it. There is nothing so handy as a small format gazetteer.

Two features of this work are especially useful. Near the entry for each country is a map depicting that nation's political or administrative subdivisions. (Even large atlases often fail to provide maps of states, provinces, and departments.) Also, a world atlas of some 112 pages is appended.

One will not find an entry for Starkville, Mississippi, in *Chambers World Gazetteer*; it has about half as many entries as *Webster's*

Geographical Dictionary. The political maps, the atlas, and the handy, attractive format are the compensations. T. P. Williams

383. Huber, Thomas P., Robert P. Larkin, and Gary L. Peters. Dictionary of Concepts in Physical Geography. New York, Greenwood Press, 1988. 291p. index. (Reference Sources for the Social Sciences and Humanities, No. 5). $49.95. LC 87-29582. ISBN 0-313-25369-2.

Students of geography, and librarians who help them, will be pleased with this third *Dictionary of Concepts in ...* title issued by Greenwood Press. Although the scope appears limited, with only eighty-eight entries, each concept is defined in great detail, with definitions approaching the character of bibliographic essays.

Each entry has four parts. Concise definitions precede the major descriptions, which average three pages in length, and contain an overview of the subjects' development over time, significant researchers and theories, and an assessment of the terms' impact within the field of physical geography. Bibliographical data for references mentioned in the text follow the narratives, and the entries conclude with a list of sources (frequently annotated) for additional research on the concept. This work will be at least as much a guide to research in physical geography as it will be a book of definitions.

Additional features include an "Outline of Concepts," which lists 185 terms (not all are defined in the work) in hierarchical categories, and an index. Both the main text and the index are liberally supplied with cross-references.

Because of the limited number of entries, the *Dictionary of Concepts in Physical Geography* should not be the only geographical dictionary in a research collection. However, it serves as a useful complement to Andrew Goudie's *Encyclopaedic Dictionary of Physical Geography* (see *ARBA* 86, entry 404) or to Monkhouse and Small's *Dictionary of the Natural Environment* (see *ARBA* 80, entry 569). [R: Choice, Oct 88, p. 370; RBB, 1 Nov 88, pp. 460, 462]   Lisa K. Dalton

384. Parry, R. B., and C. R. Perkins. **World Mapping Today.** Stoneham, Mass., Butterworths, 1987. 583p. illus. maps. index. $195.00. LC 87-25604. ISBN 0-408-02850-5.

The object of this work is to provide information about current, available maps and atlases, including thematic and series maps, that is, to provide something approaching a *Books in Print* for maps, but not on as ambitious a scale as *Geokatalog* (GeoCenter, 1985). After the list of graphic indexes comes a section of essays (fifty-five pages) on the state of world mapping, map acquisition, map evaluation, remote sensing, digital mapping, and future trends in digital mapping. Following this is the body of the volume, the indexes to mapping, arranged alphabetically by continent and within continent alphabetically by country. For each map area, there is an introductory text (e.g., what agencies map, when established, etc.), further sources of information, addresses, and then the list of maps, with atlases first, followed by general maps, topographic, and various thematic maps. Then comes a glossary, a geographic index (not an index of all geographical names in the book, but rather an alphabetical list of nation-states and other mapping units), and an index to publishers. All of this is presented in an oversized (31 cm) volume, with easily readable type and clear graphic indexes (it might perhaps have been a good idea to present what is basically an index in looseleaf). This is an excellent reference work, appropriate for academic and public libraries alike.   Mary Larsgaard

385. Portinaro, Pierluigi, and Franco Knirsch. **The Cartography of North America 1500-1800.** New York, Facts on File, 1987. 319p. illus. (part col.). maps. index. $60.00. LC 87-20028. ISBN 0-8160-1586-4.

Two Italian map-collecting, cartographic scholars selected the maps and edited the text of this large-format (9½ inches by 12¾ inches) volume. Displayed within the book are maps produced by Juan de la Cosa, the Blaeus, Ortelius, Mercator, John Smith, Champlain, and others. The period covered is post-Columbus to the American Revolution, with emphasis on maps as historical documents. Most of the maps, 129 out of 180, are in color. Fifty-one are from Italian cartographers or map publishers.

Front matter includes an introduction, a survey of the history of cartography, "The Production of Old Maps," and an illustrated essay, "The Exploration of North America." The main body of the work is divided into three chapters covering the years 1500-1600, 1600-1700, and 1700-1800. Each chapter begins with an explanation of the extent of geographical knowledge and the state of the cartographic arts during the century. The maps are presented as individually numbered plates with captions identifying the maker, indicating the significance, and for the rarer maps, indicating an institutional location. The size of the map is given in millimeters. Portraits and pictures are included. Back matter includes biographical notes on cartographers and explorers who have contributed to the geographical knowledge of North America. There is an index.

The book was printed in Hong Kong on heavyweight, coated paper, and the color printing is in precise register. The maps have been reduced in size for reproduction purposes, resulting in displays of maps that are one-quarter to one-half their original size. This presents problems in trying to read lettered or printed textual matter; even a magnifying glass will not help. Most of the maps shown are on two-page spreads and the tight gutter margins of the book prevent examining the map at the gutter. A popular book designed to tantalize and pique interest, this is a supplemental rather than a primary reference work. [R: BR, May/June 88, p. 41]   Frank J. Anderson

386. **Sheppard's International Directory of Print and Map Sellers.** London, Europa Publications; distr., Cincinnati, Ohio, Seven Hills Books, 1987. 268p. illus. bibliog. index. $42.00. ISBN 0-946653-25-9.

Two overview essays open this directory—one on the international map trade, the other on the international print trade. Both are informative especially for the novice. They report on the public's increased interest in collecting these items for investment purposes and on the accompanying rise in price. Maps and prints have been doing brisk business in the world's auction houses and the trade has burgeoned in response to the demand. All of which has led to this first effort listing of seven hundred plus print and map sellers worldwide. *Sheppard's* does not tell how it compiled its list; for instance, the U.S. entries are hit-and-miss. Presumably, membership directories were used and advertisements read. Even with omissions, this directory offers a good beginning. Pertinent periodicals and reference books are also listed for the trade along with an afterthought glossary of only fifteen words. There are three categories of listings for most of the countries: organizations, auctioneers, and print and map sellers. Of the two indexes—alphabetical and specialty—the latter one is indispensable. Thus, botanical prints are found under "Botanical" and star charts under "Celestial." For too long this information could only be located in directories for the antiquarian and secondhand book trade. Now it is available in a single volume of selected listings. Recommended. [R: RBB, 15 Apr 88, pp. 1410, 1412]   Bill Bailey

Atlases

387. Sivin, Nathan, ed. **The Contemporary Atlas of China.** Boston, Houghton Mifflin, 1988. 200p. illus. (part col.). maps. index. $39.95. LC 88-9452. ISBN 0-395-47329-2.

In recent years, several introductory reference works on China have appeared, including, among the more notable, the *Cultural Atlas of China* (see *ARBA* 85, entry 92). This atlas is similar in content and format to the *Cultural Atlas.* Both contain extensive maps, photographs, charts, diagrams, and drawings, with equally attractive layout and design. In this *Contemporary Atlas,* however, regional maps are more detailed and the contents in general are more up-to-date. In addition to the maps section, the volume has sections on the history, society, and culture of China. The last section, "China Today," provides brief information on China's natural resources, agriculture, industry, trade, economy, transportation, communication, defense, science, and technology up to 1987 or 1988. Serious shortcomings include the failure to credit sources for statistics and lack of a bibliography for further reading. Even so, the volume is a welcome addition to general library collections and will satisfy the needs of most readers.   Hwa-Wei Lee

388. **The Illustrated World Atlas.** New York, Crescent Books/Crown, 1987. 1v. (various paging). illus. (part col.). maps. index. $9.98. LC 86-675542. ISBN 0-517-63607-7.

The British-produced *Illustrated World Atlas,* with data given in metric measures, contains sixty-five pages of good, solid regional maps displaying physical and political information. However, in atlases (and especially in desk atlases, which this is) the importance of scale cannot be overestimated. The largest scale used in this volume is 1:5,000,000 (except for the UK maps and the Benelux map, which are at 1:2,000,000 and 1:2,500,000, respectively). The seventeenth edition of *Goode's World Atlas* (see *ARBA* 87, entry 435), on the other hand, as a

general rule uses maps at a scale of 1:4,000,000, with the result that far more detail is shown. Though admittedly subjective, esthetically as well, *Goode's* is far superior. The introductory chapters in this volume, however, are excellent— clear, informative, and well illustrated. The essays examine issues of concern to the world, and bear such titles as, "A Crowded Planet," "Environment in Danger," and "Energy Alternatives." The manner in which photographs appear, juxtaposing scenes of scarcity with scenes of plenty, is very effective. However, the maps an atlas make, and the maps in this volume, while containing only a few errors (Montreal is shown as being larger than Toronto on page 41; the "City" was left off Kansas City on page 41), and while showing considerably fewer features than *Goode's,* still are quite sophisticated cartographically, and they render this a very respectable work. The administrative map of the United Kingdom and Ireland on page 10 is useful, and is an item generally excluded from American-produced atlases. [R: RBB, Aug 88, pp. 1903-4]
        Dorothy C. Woodson

389. **Philip's Atlas of Canada & the World.** London, George Philip; distr., North Vancouver, B.C., Whitecap Books, 1988. 1v. (various paging). maps. (part col.). index. $59.95. ISBN 0-88665-488-2.

The appearance of a major new atlas is always a significant event, reflecting as it does enormous investments of both cartographic skill and editorial expertise. Given the inevitable production costs involved, new atlases need access to large potential markets if they are to compete successfully. In this case, the British firm Philip was commissioned to produce an atlas for the giant W. H. Smith bookstore chain, to be featured in their many Canadian outlets. The unique feature of the work is thus its initial forty-seven pages of detail on Canada, featuring thirteen regional maps (covering the country), ten urban blow-ups, and an index of six thousand names. The remainder of the book is a generally conventional world atlas, in which 144 pages of maps are followed by a 55,000-item index.

A handsomely bound volume at a reasonable price, the atlas is unfortunately flawed at a number of points. Elevation shading is inconsistent between plates; and while cities are symbolized according to a seven-part division by size, there is no hint as to what the size ranges are, nor is there any recognition of national capitals. In many countries (France as a classic case), names of modern and ancient political units and regions are confusingly jumbled, with no key to the distinction. Many other examples of dubious symbolism catch the eye. Finally, the quality of printing (done in Italy) also falls short of expectations. Color registry is slightly off on some of the plates, the use of less than top-quality paper gives a somewhat fuzzy image, and print tone (especially in the index) is very uneven. This atlas should have a reasonable appeal to a Canadian audience, but its overall quality falls well short of comparable volumes.

James R. McDonald

390. **Rand McNally Cosmopolitan World Atlas.** Skokie, Ill., Rand McNally, 1987. 288p. illus. (part col.). maps. index. $55.00. LC 87-42818. ISBN 0-528-83284-0.

Intended for adult readers, this large-format comprehensive world atlas contains 170 pages of color maps, an index of seventy-five thousand place names, and a sixty-page almanac of population, zip codes, and world political information.

For the first time it contains a fourteen-page section of thematic maps and charts illustrating population patterns, languages, climates, etc. There is also a new thirty-two-page section of satellite imagery and illustrative color maps showing the dramatic effects of natural and human forces on the face of the Earth.

The basic map section is almost indistinguishable from previous editions. Name changes, roads, and impounds have been updated, but the maps suffer from the same muddy colors and indistinct use of shading and symbols as in previous editions. The color differentiation is so poor that it is almost impossible to pick out the South African homelands, while the complete lack of altitude tinting makes it difficult for the inexperienced map user to tell where the mountains begin and end in Colorado. The atlas would benefit from a few physical maps, at least of the continents, and better use of color, shading, symbols, and tints.

The use of scale is the same as in previous editions, which is to say, more inconsistent than in most world atlases. California is shown at almost 1:4,000,000 while Rhode Island is at 1:300,000. Despite its problems, the *Cosmopolitan* can be relied upon to be factually accurate, relatively easy to use, and reasonably priced. [R: Choice, June 88, pp. 1539-40; RBB, 1 June 88, pp. 1659-60]   Dennis Dillon

391. **Rand McNally Desk Reference World Atlas.** Skokie, Ill., Rand McNally, 1987. 528p. illus. (part col.). maps. index. $17.95. LC 87-42819. ISBN 0-528-83287-5.

The idea behind this book is quite good: to have a combined world atlas, gazetteer, and

general reference volume at a convenient size, about 7 by 10 inches, to stand along with the dictionary on an ordinary bookshelf. The cartographic and other resources of Rand McNally have been utilized to produce this work. The problem with it lies in the reference maps with political boundaries and in the metropolitan area maps, both drawn for reproduction at a larger size. When reduced to the small format they are hard to read without a magnifying glass. The thematic maps and the historical maps, however, have been simplified and redrawn for the smaller format and are clear and effective. The "Gazetteer of the World," with brief information on countries, the guides to major world cities and major U.S. cities, "United States City and County Population and ZIP Codes," and "Colleges and Universities of the United States" are useful and handy compendia. An index to the reference maps completes the volume. The book is a reasonably priced, convenient, quick-reference tool for the items included, but for most maps a larger format atlas is still to be preferred. [R: RBB, 15 Sept 88, p. 132]   Chauncy D. Harris

392. **Rand McNally Student's World Atlas.** Skokie, Ill., Rand McNally, 1988. 96p. illus. (part col.). maps. index. $5.95pa. LC 87-62450. ISBN 0-528-83286-7.

One wonders how many times a publisher will repackage the same information. This little atlas has appeared in 1985, 1983, and in 1982 (as the *Young Student's Atlas*). Many of the illustrations in it, however, have appeared in a variety of Rand McNally titles over the past several years.

Maps are presented in a continental arrangement, each continent allotted approximately twelve pages. Each section contains maps of terrain, environment, animals, and countries and cities. Also, each continent is shown on one or more physical-political maps, which are the only pages indexed. Generally, individual maps of countries are not provided.

While each section shows the relative position of its continent on a tiny world map (approximately one by two inches), there is no full-page world map in the volume, a curious omission in a world atlas.

The index (544 entries) is keyed to the alphanumeric grids along the edges of the physical-political maps, which are presented in an array of projections, including conic, sinusoidal, and Lambert's Azimuthal. The elementary school students for whom this book is designed must realize that they cannot expect to come straight across and up to find their target at the intersection of two lines. Rather, they must track within the lines of longitude and latitude. Even adults have trouble with this method.

There is a need for inexpensive atlases. However, schools and libraries should be willing to invest a little more for any of several higher quality children's atlases which are available. *The Facts on File Children's Atlas*, for example, by David Wright and Jill Wright (see *ARBA* 88, entry 455), is excellent. [R: RBB, 1 Sept 88, pp. 56-57]   Lisa K. Dalton

393. Rand McNally World Atlas. Skokie, Ill., Rand McNally, 1988. 224p. illus. (part col.). maps. index. $16.95. LC 88-060753. ISBN 0-528-83327-8.

Judging by its appearance, one might wish initially to make comparisons with *Goode's World Atlas* (see *ARBA* 87, entry 435), but the *Rand McNally World Atlas* has been written on an entirely different level. Rand McNally has compiled an atlas which should satisfy the needs of the novice user.

The atlas begins with a new section titled "The Planet Earth." The thirty-two pages include a well-written user's guide and brief two-page discussions describing various aspects of the solar system, the Earth's evolution and anatomy, the oceans, and the atmosphere. The color drawings and photographs make it an attractive addition to this new edition.

The maps are entirely political. There are no physical maps or maps describing world social and economic conditions. Europe and North America, specifically the United States and Canada, receive the most attention. Maps of Africa, Asia, and South America are less detailed. The maps themselves are of the usual high quality associated with Rand McNally, with name changes current through 1987. Following the maps is a place index of twenty-seven thousand names and their map locations, a section giving information about U.S. states and cities, and a list of world populations.

The atlas does a good job providing the type of information a high school student or undergraduate who has little experience with atlases might require.   Phillip P. Powell

394. Rand McNally World Atlas of Nations. Skokie, Ill., Rand McNally, 1988. 208p. illus. (col.). maps. index. $34.95. LC 88-060112. ISBN 0-528-83315-4.

This encyclopedia-style atlas is arranged alphabetically by country. Each entry consists of factual information in tabular form, a small map, a short accompanying place name index, color photographs, and brief textual information

on three subjects: people, economy and land, and history and politics.

Most countries are covered in one page, though some European countries take two or more pages, and some small Third World countries are covered in half a page. The atlas also includes a sixteen-page section of physical maps and a general place name index with nine thousand entries.

This is an atlas in name only. Any general encyclopedia has better maps of individual countries, and textual information of greater depth. Roughly one-fourth of the atlas is devoted to high-quality color photographs. The principal value of this atlas is as a quick reference. Its alphabetical arrangement and high-quality graphics convey brief information on 168 world countries.

Suitable for the home, classroom, or school libraries, but it is not an adequate substitute for an atlas such as *The Times Atlas of the World* (7th ed., Times Books, 1985) or for an inexpensive atlas such as the *New York Times Atlas of the World* (2d ed., Times Books, 1987).

                                    Dennis Dillon

395. The Times Family Atlas of the World. Topsfield, Mass., Salem House, 1988. 1v. (various paging). illus. (part col.). maps. index. $24.95. LC 88-675200. ISBN 0-88162-346-6.

This atlas is made up of two separately paged segments. The sixty-eight-page introductory section includes gazetteer-type, brief descriptions of the states and territories of the world in alphabetical order (in forty pages) with flags and with inset location maps for the countries described on each double-page spread, a short section on geographical comparisons, the physical earth by seven striking semi-hemispherical views, and nine worldwide thematic maps. The second section of 156 pages includes general reference physical maps of regions, political maps of the world and of the continents, city plans for fifty major world cities, a geographical dictionary, and an index to the maps (thirty thousand place names). Endpapers show coverage of individual atlas maps and distances between major cities of the world in miles and in kilometers. The maps reveal an intelligent selection of level of detail that can be depicted with clarity on the scales selected. The volume is well produced and easy to utilize and understand.

This atlas is not a substitute in a reference collection for a large general atlas such as the *Times Atlas of the World* (7th ed., Times Books, 1985). Compared with other recent small atlases, such as *Goode's World Atlas* (see *ARBA* 87, entry 435), *Rand McNally Concise*

World Atlas (see *ARBA* 88, entry 451), or *Rand McNally Desk Reference World Atlas* (see entry 391), this atlas generally contains less detailed information but surpasses them in legibility and attractiveness. Designed, as the name suggests, for family use, this new small atlas admirably succeeds in its goal of providing a simple, beautiful, and reliable volume easily usable by non-specialized individuals regardless of age or purpose. It would be an appealing addition to the library of any family.   Chauncy D. Harris

396. **Webster's New World Atlas.** New York, Prentice Hall Press, 1988. 325p. illus. (col.). maps. index. $39.95. ISBN 0-13-948134-6.

This affordable atlas contains very readable and attractive maps by France's Institut Geographique National.

A thirty-five-page general information section contains graphics and text on physical, social, and cultural topics. The presentations on subjects such as vegetation zones and climate are effective, but the essays are too brief for more than superficial treatment of topics such as religion, communication, or agri-politics. These are the only thematic maps in the atlas.

The main section is divided into six geographical sections: Europe, Africa, Asia, the Americas, Australia-Oceania, and the North and South Poles. The sections are easy to find thumbing through the volume: the separating pages have a black background and contain summary information for all the countries in the region and a table of contents for maps in the section. The introductory spread is followed by small-scale (1:33,000,000) physical and political maps of the whole region, then by larger-scale (1:5,000,000) maps of areas.

The indexing is good, with variant names indexed, not cross-referenced. A glossary lists non-English terms for physical features, with their languages and translations. A handy locating device is printed on the endpapers: a world map with sections outlined and references to the corresponding page numbers in the volume. The physical book is not unwieldy in size and has good quality color, paper, and typography.

This atlas is appropriate for anyone needing a moderately priced, up-to-date world atlas and requiring only general, small-scale political maps.   Linda A. Naru

PLACE NAMES

397. Barnes, Will C. **Arizona Place Names.** Tucson, Ariz., University of Arizona Press, 1988. 503p. maps. bibliog. $15.95pa. LC 87-35835. ISBN 0-8165-1074-1.

This is an unrevised reprint of the 1935 edition, with an introduction by historian Bernard L. Fontana, who adds a few recently published titles to the bibliography. Barnes, a soldier, cattleman, and rural politician, first came to Arizona in 1880 as an army private assigned to Fort Apache, where he won the Medal of Honor. He had a long career with various federal agencies such as the U.S. Forest Service, the Board of Geographic Names, and the Geological Survey. His compilation of names was the result of more than thirty years of criss-crossing the state gathering information from a wide range of sources. Each entry is precisely located geographically within the state, then the origin of the name and its meaning are given and documented, followed with the date of establishment of the first post office and the name of the first postmaster. Within the body of the text there is a section headed "First Things in Arizona," with seventy entries. Barnes includes conflicting stories as to the origin of some names, where the historical record is cloudy. Many things have happened since the 1935 publication date, including an influx of people into Arizona and the establishment of new towns and cities (Bapchule, Bullhead City, Carefree, Sun City, etc.), which, of course, are not listed in this book. Libraries will now be able to replace their deteriorating copies of the original edition inexpensively, new residents of Arizona can get acquainted with the history of their new home, and Western history buffs can add another title to their libraries.

Frank J. Anderson

398. Boone, Lalia. **Idaho Place Names: A Geographical Dictionary.** Moscow, Idaho, University of Idaho Press, 1988. 413p. illus. bibliog. $15.95pa. LC 87-30211. ISBN 0-89301-119-3.

Several years ago, a woman appeared at the reference desk in the University of Montana Library to ask the origin of the name of the small community of, as she pronounced it, "POTTO-mack." We had not heard of this hamburger-sounding locale, so we asked her to write it down. Well, it seems that she had a variant way to say "Potomac" (as in the river which flows through our nation's capital city). As it turns out, this sort of query is not uncommon in libraries, so place-name books are always welcomed by library staff. In the book at hand, each "place" (towns, creeks, etc.) is given a location, name of county, other information as appropriate, and the origin. Pronunciations are not offered here, so one has to guess at things such as "Leadore" and "Kamiah." This is a reasonably complete listing, but *all* place names, in any state, cannot generally be included—

additions are always appropriate. Boone has given Idaho a better start than we have in Montana.   R. G. Schipf

399. Gazetteer of Inuit Place Names in Nunavik (Quebec, Canada). Repertoire Toponymique Inuit du Nunavik. By Ludger Müller-Wille with the Inuit Elders of Nunavik and Avatag Cultural Institute. Inukjuak, Que., Avatag Cultural Institute, 1987. 368p. illus. maps. $39.95; $29.95 pa. ISBN 1-55036-000-0.

Inuit is the name that the Eskimo of the Arctic regions of Alaska, Canada, Greenland, and Siberia call themselves. *Nunavik* is the Inuit name for the northern portion of the province of Quebec. The Inuit have a strong tradition of geographical names which represent the relationship between these people and their environment. Because these names are generally passed along only orally, and because governmental mapping tends to reflect the Euro-Canadian place names applied by white explorers and settlers, a project to collect the indigenous place names of the area was undertaken.

In this gazetteer are published for the first time all place names of the Nunavik region of Quebec, some 7,797 entries. With this publication, the Inuit people and the Canadian government hope to ensure the preservation of this part of the native culture.

Place names are presented by region, with each list arranged by the geographical coordinates of the location. Each place name is listed in both the Roman alphabet and in Inuktitut syllabics, with an identification of the geographical feature (in English and French). Also listed are the Canadian National Topographic System quadrangle on which a site is mapped, and a survey code. An alphabetical index of place names repeats all this information, and supplies a region identifier. A separate section lists non-Inuit names used in the area and gives the preferred Inuit name. Introductory text and the "How to Use the Gazetteer" section are presented in English, Inuktitut, and French.

There is a wisdom in preparing a work like this. Though it will appeal primarily to those in a limited geographical area, or to those with strong interests in native cultures, this gazetteer is an important and significant publication.

Lisa K. Dalton

400. Room, Adrian. Place-Names of the World: A Dictionary of Their Origins and Backgrounds. rev. ed. London, Angus & Robertson; distr., Topsfield, Mass., Salem House, 1987. 259p. bibliog. $12.95pa. ISBN 0-207-15539-9.

A popular, selective guide to the origins of one thousand plus world place names, the new

edition includes countries, capital cities, major natural geographical features, and political subdivisions, along with some places chosen for historical, economic, or tourist interest. Each brief entry consists of a general location guide to avoid confusion and a sentence or two giving the names' derivation and/or alternate theories when applicable. There are no pronunciation guides. The introduction discusses patterns of place naming and how they have changed over the centuries. Room has written several standard guides to place names as well as other studies on language. This book is aimed at the general reader looking for a fast fact and not the historian doing substantial research. For the more inquisitive person, Room has provided an excellent bibliography. [R: RBB, 1 Sept 88, p. 54]

Deborah Hammer

401. Urdang, Laurence, ed. Names & Nicknames of Places & Things. Boston, G. K. Hall, 1987. 327p. index. $39.95. LC 86-25675. ISBN 0-8161-8780-0.

A book for browsing as well as for reference; it is more than a compilation of trivia and would be useful in a reference collection. The "places" and "things" are primarily in the United States, the United Kingdom, and Western Europe. The alphabetical arrangement, and geographical and subject index, make the book easy to use. Entries are printed in boldface type, with the explanatory information indented and printed in an adequately sized, legible roman typeface. Running heads assist in locating information quickly; and there are numerous cross-references. The definitions range in length from one line to more than half a page. The time frame is from around the mid-nineteenth century into our own times. The editor's foreword explains the rationale and scope of the book, and credits various persons and organizations who were helpful in supplying information. Nicely printed on quality paper and sturdily bound. Urdang is the editor of *Verbatim: The Language Quarterly*, and a prolific editor of dictionaries, encyclopedias, and other reference books. [R: C&RL, Jan 88, pp. 57-58; SLJ, May 88, p. 30]   Frank J. Anderson

TRAVEL GUIDES

General Works

402. Hamilton, Malcolm. Travel Index: A Guide to Books and Articles, 1985-86. Phoenix, Ariz., Oryx Press, 1988. 237p. $47.00pa. LC 87-34890. ISBN 0-89774-403-9.

The compiler, "an inveterate traveler" and therefore engaged in a labor of love, has produced an outstanding work. It provides comprehensive coverage of articles, books, and other printed sources of travel information for the years 1985 and 1986. Orderly and expedient, this index is a pleasure to thumb through. Part 1 indexes articles from various magazines and the Sunday *New York Times*; part 2 is a selective index to books cited or reviewed in travel magazines and newspapers; and part 3 indexes specialized travel newsletters and magazines. All three parts are arranged by subject and geographical area. In addition to LC subject headings, terminology found in the literature itself is used; perhaps a departure from standard employment of subject headings but welcome at times when LC fails to recognize common usage.

This index is so attractive that it is difficult to voice criticism, but why are only two years considered? For *Travel Index* to be of value it should be ongoing and retrospective, to constitute a set. Any reference book that considers so short a span of years is destined to oblivion, and this one should not be. From the viewpoint of popular culture the sizable number of pages here on travel attests to an abiding interest in the subject. Recommended as a first-rate index which marks a slight period of time. [R: Choice, Sept 88, p. 80]   Bill Bailey

403. Hecker, Helen. **Directory of Travel Agencies for the Disabled.** Vancouver, Wash., Twin Peaks Press, 1988. 1v. (unpaged). $9.95 pa. LC 86-24951. ISBN 0-933261-04-7.

This directory lists over two hundred travel agencies that specialize in travel arrangements for persons with special needs or that have a person on staff who provides such services. Agencies are listed by country. Approximately 70 percent are located in the United States and are listed thereunder by state. Basic information on each agency includes address, telephone number (including TTY/TTD and toll-free numbers, if available), and the name of a contact person who specializes in travel for those with special medical needs or physical limitations. Many entries also include a brief description of the specialized services available: the types of handicapping conditions they can accommodate, staff fluent in sign language or who are trained to handle medical emergencies, newsletters aimed toward handicapped travelers, wheelchair accessible vans and buses, and the like.

An amazing number of agencies specialize in travel to medically or physically restricted individuals, including dialysis patients, diabetics, those with respiratory disorders, the vision or hearing impaired, and the developmentally disabled. Some even specialize in certain types of excursions, such as safaris, cruises, and wilderness trips.

A more "compleat" guide is Louise Weiss's *Access to the World* (Henry Holt, 1986). Depending on demand, libraries owning *Access to the World* and Hecker's own *Travel for the Disabled: A Handbook of Travel Resources and 500 Worldwide Access Guides* (see *ARBA* 87, entry 456) might consider this directory a supplemental purchase.

        Pam M. Baxter

404. Jordon, Dorothy Ann, and Marjorie Adoff Cohen. **Great Vacations with Your Kids: The Complete Guide to Family Vacations in the U.S.** New York, E. P. Dutton, 1987. 311p. index. $9.95pa. LC 87-13595. ISBN 0-525-48338-1.

The authors know whereof they speak. Jordon founded and directs Travel With Your Children (TWYCH), an information center for parents planning vacations with their children. Cohen, a contributing editor to *Family Travel Times*, the TWYCH newsletter, and author of travel books, like Jordon, has two children. In the early chapters of this how-to book-cum-travel-opportunities-catalog they pass on useful and time-proven advice collected from experiences of traveling with children. Through their personable first-person approach, they suggest strategies for the best way to deal with travel agents, how to prepare for and handle various modes of transportation, what sort of toys and games to take along, how to find sitters on the road, what sort of lodgings to choose, and what books to consult for additional information. The "Where to Stay" chapter suggests a variety of hotel/motel chains whose properties meet varying needs and suit varying budgets.

Most of the book describes specific vacation packages available in eight categories — adventure, city vacations, resorts, tennis and golf, skiing, farms and dude ranches, camping and cabins, and cruises. Descriptions of each place's offerings detail its services and activities available to families and their children as well as typical costs and dates of operation (if less than year-round). The chapter on city vacations (Boston, Chicago, Los Angeles, New York, San Francisco, and Washington) offers a lot of good advice on attractions that ought to appeal to children. In this chapter and in the chapters on resorts, etc., the recommended lodging places tend toward the expensive, a point sometimes acknowledged by the authors. Most families will do better when planning a stay in one of these cities to shop for something more affordable by consulting the lists of chains and calling their toll-free reservations numbers.

Jordon and Cohen have neglected two categories of vacations popular with some families—autumn color tours and visits to historical sites and restorations. Rather than a criticism, this should be taken as a suggestion for expanding this very useful guide, sure to be a hit in the travel reference section of public libraries.

James S. Rettig

405. **World Business Travel Guide.** By Uniglobe Travel. Toronto, SP Travel Books/Summerhill Press; distr., New York, Sterling Publishing, 1987. 495p. maps. $9.95pa. ISBN 0-920197-39-6.

The growing integration of the world's economy has resulted in increased international business travel. In order to succeed, one requires pertinent information about various aspects of the foreign area visited. The answer is this compact guide to world business travel, which is composed of two parts. The first part contains general information on air travel (including jet lag), health tips, currency and exchange (some advice is totally superfluous), doing business abroad, and safety warnings. It is supplemented by a number of tables—international flying time between twenty-one major business centers (some significant omissions), data on various aircraft types (all nonmetric), currency exchange rates, worldwide weather (temperatures in degrees Fahrenheit), hotel and meal costs in various countries, telephone codes, clothing sizes, metric conversion, and vocabulary in English, French, German, and Spanish. The second regional part provides the essential facts about fifty-six economically important countries in the world grouped into four regions. Countries of less economic importance (e.g., all Central America, sub-Saharan Africa except Nigeria and Kenya) or suffering from political instability (e.g., Lebanon, Lybia, Iran, Iraq) have been omitted. The arrangement of material for each country is standardized for quick reference. The presentation is concise and clear; the standardized form is very helpful. There are only a few misprints. Intended for U.S. business people, especially novices in international travel, this guide is sure to be valuable.

Zbigniew Mieczkowski

United States

406. **Access America: An Atlas and Guide to the National Parks for Visitors with Disabilities.** Burlington, Vt., Northern Cartographic, 1988. 444p. illus. (part col.). maps. bibliog. $89.95 spiralbound. LC 87-072038. ISBN 0-944187-00-5.

This guidebook to National Parks represents an attempt at making the parks accessible to and usable by all persons who are physically handicapped. The format of the guide is oversized with large print to enable use by the visually disabled as well.

The access information included in the guide was obtained through questionnaires submitted to *selected* parks and also through surveys taken within the parks during 1986-1987. The collected information was reviewed by the parks before publication. The introduction fully explains terms and features presented in the guide and a color-coded legend is included. The tools can be easily understood and should provide adequate information for those considering National Park excursions. It will be useful for nonhandicapped persons too.

Included periodically throughout the guide are brief entries by various individuals who relate their experiences as a disabled visitor to the parks. The editors note in their introduction that these entries reflect access at the time of the individuals' visits and encourage readers to refer to the current information elsewhere in the guide for the park cited. These entries are interesting and add an additional flavor to the guide.

This unique tool will be a valuable resource for any library. The appendices include climate charts, various centers and hospitals within the regions, and additional resources and programs. Extensive research has gone into this volume and the end result is a thorough, exhaustive reference on over thirty-five of our National Parks. It is highly recommended for all libraries, especially public. [R: Choice, Dec 88, p. 621; RBB, 1 Dec 88, pp. 626, 628; WLB, Sept 88, p. 89]

Mary J. Stanley

407. Bloomfield, Brynna C., and Jane M. Moskowitz, comps. **Traveling Jewish in America: The Complete Guide for Business & Pleasure.** rev. ed. Lodi, N.J., Wandering You Press, 1987. 472p. $9.95pa. LC 86-51617. ISBN 0-9617104-1-1.

This guide lists over twenty-four hundred synagogues alphabetically by state then city, including denomination, address, telephone number, name of rabbi, and service schedule. Under each state and city it also provides information on where to buy kosher food, groceries, supermarkets, co-ops, etc., with name, address, and telephone number. There is a section on accommodations, including kosher hotels, motels with kitchen facilities, and motels within walking distance of synagogues. Finally, information on *mikve* is included (address, telephone number, and contact person). A short section on how to use the guide and a key to abbreviations are included. Area codes for cities are given, which makes telephoning easier. Another helpful feature is the cross-references, which facilitate use.

The book was designed to serve the needs of the Jewish traveler or tourist in the United States. However, it is far from a "complete guide," since it does not include sites of Jewish interest, historical or cultural information that the Jewish traveler might well be interested in when visiting different states and cities. Rather it is limited to brief facts on synagogues, eating places, buying food, accommodations, and *mikve*.

Although the information is presented clearly (using boldface and different sizes of type), and is relatively easy to read, the physical format of the book could be improved. Specifically, the margins, especially the most important inner margin, are very narrow, which makes handling more difficult. The paper quality is only fair, since print can be seen from both sides. It appears doubtful that the book would hold up well under hard use. In spite of these defects, the guide would be useful as part of temple, synagogue, or Jewish community center library collections, as well as collections in public libraries located in cities with significant Jewish populations.

Susan J. Freiband

408. Fitzgerald, Daniel. **Ghost Towns of Kansas: A Traveler's Guide.** Lawrence, Kans., University Press of Kansas, 1988. 348p. illus. maps. bibliog. index. $25.00; $12.95pa. LC 88-26. ISBN 0-7006-0367-0; 0-7006-0368-9pa.

This is a fascinating volume for the casual reader and traveler, as well as for historians of the establishment and growth of Kansas. The author describes the settlement, politics, colorful figures, legends, and decline of ninety-nine Kansas towns. The entries are organized by region and each vignette is illustrated with old photographs and etchings. Information on how to reach the site is also given. The author's definition of what comprises a ghost town is somewhat elastic since the book includes not only abandoned or now nonexistent communities, but also those which are currently inhabited but only a shadow of their former selves. The author provides a preface describing, in general, the forces that led to Kansas towns coming into existence, as well as the circumstances that led to their dissolution. A selected bibliography for further reading and an index are provided.

Charles Neuringer

409. **North Carolina: The WPA Guide to the Old North State.** By the Federal Writers' Project of the Work Projects Administration. Columbia, S.C., University of South Carolina Press, 1988. 601p. illus. bibliog. index. $29.95; $14.95 pa. LC 88-17763. ISBN 0-87249-604-X; 0-87249-605-8pa.

Originally published as part of the Federal Writers' Project, this volume, which provided employment to out of work writers during the Great Depression, is a fascinating flashback to America in the late 1930s. Written primarily as automobile touring guides, the WPA guide series became a benchmark standard for writing in America. The best local writers were hired to put down on paper the folklore of rural and urban America. The guides are useful not only as historic "looking glasses to the past," but also as reflections of the ideas, ideals, and future aspirations of the United States. Few readers have failed to find the unique charm of the WPA guide series. This North Carolina volume provides a valuable insight into a diverse southern state, with roots going back to 1585.

Libraries will want to own this volume for the valuable introduction by William S. Powell, the "dean" of North Carolina historians. His insights place the guide in its historical context and give important information on the actual writing project as it progressed in North Carolina. The volume is well bound, and the type is actually easier to read than the original. The illustrations, alas, are copies of copies, that fail to do justice to the fine quality of FWP originals. Too bad the editor was unable to locate the originals in the National Archives, and thereby give the current generation the benefit of the fine photography done during this period. Highly recommended reference book for most libraries.   Ralph Lee Scott

410. Perry, John, and Jane Greverus Perry. **The Sierra Club Guide to the Natural Areas of Idaho, Montana, and Wyoming.** San Francisco, Calif., Sierra Club Books; distr., New York, Random House, 1988. 435p. maps. index. $12.95pa. LC 87-26312. ISBN 0-87156-781-4.

With these guides to the natural areas of the United States, the Sierra Club provides alternatives to America's overcrowded national parks and recreation areas where 95 percent of all travelers go each year. The fifth addition to this series (see *ARBA* 87, entry 464 for a review of the fourth volume) covers over two hundred natural areas, including public domain and Bureau of Land Management (BLM) lands. A guide for the sightseer, camper, hiker, fisherman, and skier, or any lover of outdoor activities, this volume identifies the "quiet places" where a visitor can simply enjoy nature. According to the introduction, "many are roadless areas, some truly pristine."

The three states covered here are subdivided into several zones. Each state chapter begins with a zone map and at the beginning of each zone section, a map listing sites is provided. Arranged alphabetically within zones, the entries present information about the agency administering the area, acreage, how to get there, and visiting hours. Interesting background information on terrain, vegetation, wildlife, and history gives a broader perspective. Easy reference symbols indicate the activities available at each site, a truly helpful feature. Another very useful feature is the listing of publications (maps, trail guides, etc.) available at each site; additional references are given for many sites. An index listing each site concludes the book.

This reviewer was impressed with the quantity and the quality of the information provided here. Indeed, it is one of the best guidebooks to these places available.

Robert P. Huestis

411. *Reader's Digest* **America's Historic Places: An Illustrated Guide to Our Country's Past.** Pleasantville, N.Y., Reader's Digest Association, 1988. 352p. illus. (part col.). maps. index. $26.95. LC 87-4757. ISBN 0-89577-265-5.

This profusely illustrated guide to five hundred historic sites in the United States includes famous American homes, museum villages, forts, battlefields, government buildings, historic districts, churches, ghost towns, and such engineering wonders as bridges, mines, and monuments. Purely natural wonders, such as the Grand Canyon and Niagara Falls, are not included. The fifty states are divided into five regions: northeastern, southeastern, north central, south central, and western (including Alaska and Hawaii). Individual states appear alphabetically within each regional chapter. There are detailed maps for each region, with numbered dots used to pinpoint the locations of sites described in the text. The numbers correspond to a convenient state-by-state listing of the sites located on the facing page. Colored photographs are included for almost all of the sites.

Useful tourist information includes each site's address, dates when open, and if admission is charged. Specific visiting times and entry fees are not given because of their susceptibility to change. The concisely written text provides just enough information to entice the inveterate sightseer. [R: BL, 15 May 88, p. 1568]

Gary D. Barber

412. Tegeler, Dorothy. **Moving to Arizona: The Complete Arizona Answer Book.** Phoenix, Ariz., Fiesta Books, 1988. 179p. illus. maps. bibliog. index. $9.95pa. LC 88-11291. ISBN 0-943169-75-5.

Librarians may take umbrage over the subtitle on the title page: "The Complete Arizona Answer Book." There is no information about libraries in the state! For most users this may not be a serious oversight; but the author could have included some reference to the field of library science at least in the section on professional and trade organizations (appendix C), particularly since some rather obscure associations are included. Nevertheless, other than this, the book is quite complete. As the title suggests it is published for those who are considering or have decided on a move to Arizona. And the facts provided are accurate, up-to-date, and comprehensive. Individual entries are written in chatty, conversational tone, succinct and clear in their description of even complex systems of government. The print is easy to read and the paperback format makes the book easy to carry around: in a glove box in the car for quick reference or even in a purse. As a reference item it would be of value in a public library or a special library associated with an organization having direct dealings in Arizona. For the student of geography, other more scholarly works provide information about the state; but this book will find much practical use. It is well indexed and includes names and addresses of sources in the state giving more information on the topics and items covered. Recommended for general reference collections.

Edward P. Miller

413. Wayburn, Peggy. **Adventuring in Alaska.** rev. ed. San Francisco, Calif., Sierra Club Books; distr., New York, Random House, 1988. 375p. illus. maps. bibliog. index. $10.95 pa. LC 87-23578. ISBN 0-87156-787-3.

The guide encompasses four parts. Part 1, constituting about 30 percent of the book, begins with general information about geography, geology, climate, and wildlife migrations. The historical outline follows, notable for the author's attention to (and respect for) native history before European exploration and penetration. Subsequent chapters (essays) provide information and know-how about external transportation links of Alaska, wilderness travel (hiking, boating, and flying) and equipment (the last as long as fourteen pages). Interesting is the detailed advice about behavior with respect to bears. Part 1 closes with discussion of land tenure, with special emphasis on national parks and other nature reserves. Advice is also given on visiting native villages.

The next three parts of the book present detailed information about the three regions of Alaska: the southeast, the south central and southwest, and the interior and the Arctic. This is the author's division, based on physiography and practical tourist needs. Not all places in Alaska are described in this guide: the author focuses on the most accessible and attractive areas.

The objective of the book to provide a high-quality, useful, and reliable guide for outdoor adventurers has been attained. The physical format is modest to keep the cost low: black-and-white photographs; drawings of animals, birds, and plants; black-and-white maps. However, the supporting materials are adequate and the figures useful (e.g., the diagram on sunlight, p. 25). Appendices provide valuable information for naturalists: a list of birds (about four hundred), habitats of colonial seabirds, and a list of mammals. Also very good is the bibliography (about seventy positions). The reviewer regrets that the international system (metric) was not used, even in brackets.

Zbigniew Mieczkowski

Great Britain

414. **AA Touring England.** Basingstoke, England, Automobile Association; distr., Topsfield, Mass., Salem House, 1987. 608p. illus. (part col.). maps. index. $69.95. ISBN 0-86145-619-X.

It is impossible to say whether anglophiles or bibliophiles would be more impressed by *Touring England*. Published by the Automobile Association, this beautiful book is a road atlas, town atlas, and tour guide all rolled into one. Directions are provided for over 130 automobile trips, while information and photographs are supplied for thousands of England's many tourist attractions. The book is divided into four geographical sections: the West Country, South and South-East England, Central England and East Anglia, and the North Country. Wales and Scotland are not included. Each of the four sections is further divided into three subsections on automobile trips, town maps, and road maps. Each town map has a street index, while the road maps have a master index at the end of their subsection. The maps are full color and very detailed (one inch equals three miles on the road maps). Numerous photographs, almost all in color, fill those pages not covered by the maps. Furthermore, the cover and dust jacket are attractively designed, the book lies flat

when opened, and it includes two ribbon bookmarks.

After perusing this volume, readers come away closing their eyes and wishing they were in England. I do, however, have two small complaints. First, there is no town map of Winchester, which is strange since it is a lovely tourist center and a very important town, historically. Second, the Cambridge town map does not show the railroad station. That is a bit difficult given the town's layout, but it might cause some poor tourist confusion. Otherwise, *Touring England* is a wondrous book to hold and to browse. Any library providing tourist information will want to acquire it. Furthermore, its detailed maps might also be of some use to genealogists. [R: RBB, 15 June 88, p. 1724]

Ronald H. Fritze

415. **The National Trust Atlas.** 3d ed. By The National Trust and The National Trust for Scotland. London, National Trust/George Philip; distr., Dobbs Ferry, N.Y., Sheridan House, 1987. 224p. illus. (part col.). maps. index. $29.95. ISBN 0-540-05526-3.

Once again the National Trust authorities have published a treasure trove of information about the properties that they own throughout the United Kingdom, from the remote uninhabited islands of Northern Scotland down to the Land's End peninsula and Isles of Scilly in the south. For the casual reader or tourist, the atlas offers fascinating glimpses of historic buildings and inviting landscapes, while the more professional reader can use it to plan tours of facilities designed by particular architects or built during specific periods. The expert too will find the atlas useful, since it includes information about recent acquisitions, such as Kedleston Hall in Derbyshire, the ancestral home of George Nathanial Curzon, 1st Marquess Curzon of Kedleston, which was designed by Robert Adam in 1761.

The properties are indexed alphabetically by architects, builders, geographic locations, and previous ownership, and there is a separate index by county, plus a series of road maps covering all areas. A key to the road maps appears on page 8, which also includes a reference guide to the symbols used in the maps to designate places of special interest. Unfortunately, these references are not repeated on the maps themselves, so newcomers may need to refer back to the key to decode these symbols as they travel toward their destinations. Finally, as they complete their tour of the selected property, travelers may gain additional appreciation of its features through reference to the glossary of architectural terms and to the brief biographical information on architects and craftsmen, also included in this very attractive publication. [R: RBB, 1 Feb 88, pp. 916, 918]

George T. Potter

Italy

416. Hofmann, Paul. **Cento Città: A Guide to the "Hundred Cities & Towns" of Italy.** New York, Henry Holt, 1988. 388p. illus. maps. $19.95. LC 87-28512. ISBN 0-8050-0728-8.

The author has lived in Italy for thirty years and has picked his favorite one hundred small cities to describe. The descriptions will usually focus on a central church or piazza and then explore the town from there. None of the larger, tourist cities such as Rome, Naples, or Florence is described. Others do that. The cities described here are off the beaten tourist paths and are more of the "real" Italy.

The book is divided into six sections, each covering a region of Italy. Each section has a map showing the location of each of the cities discussed as well as an introductory essay describing the region. This is a delight for those who have lived in Italy or those who would like to travel there. There is an appendix listing practical travel information, including travel time to the city by train from major cities, restaurant information, museums, and collection information. The only problem with this book is the black-and-white photographs. It would have enhanced the book greatly to have color photographs, for most of the areas pictured are breathtakingly lovely. This is for all collections interested in Italy.   Robert L. Turner, Jr.

Oceania

417. Margolis, Susanna. **Adventuring in the Pacific: The Sierra Club Travel Guide to the Islands of Polynesia, Melanesia, and Micronesia.** San Francisco, Calif., Sierra Club Books; distr., New York, Random House, 1988. 406p. illus. maps. bibliog. index. $12.95pa. LC 87-23558. ISBN 0-87156-780-6.

Travel guides published by the Sierra Club have a tradition of being down to earth. *Adventuring in the Pacific* is no exception. Margolis provides an excellent guide to the three major island cultural areas in the Pacific: Polynesia, Melanesia, and Micronesia. Each of the island groups within these cultural areas is concisely described. An overview of an island group and description of the geography, topography, and climate provide the traveler with a good background of what to expect in addition to the usual "getting there" information. Sections on

politics and history also provide insight. For instance, it is important to know that the government in the Cook Islands limits the number of flights into the country. The government also limits the number of tourist facilities by requiring licenses. This ensures that tourism will not overwhelm the island.

Following the introduction to each island group is a guide to each of the major islands, with maps, and some of the more interesting remote smaller islands. A local code of behavior alerts the traveler to customs that if not observed might bring offense. In Western Samoa shorts are frowned upon. Also ones does not eat while walking through a village. Tips such as these make stays much more enjoyable. Information on unusual sights or unique opportunities such as hikes or reef snorkling focus the traveler's attention, saving considerable time in planning and effort in discovering these unusual places.

The guide has an excellent introductory section on the exploration of the Pacific, with chapters covering the creation of islands, prehistory of the Pacific islanders, Western contact, basic travel information, and a vital chapter on the literature about Oceania. Helpful appendices giving time charts, airlines serving the Pacific, field research trips, alerts to birders, notes on yachting, and recommended itineraries for time-limited travelers round out the guide. The work ends with a basic but good bibliography and index. *Adventuring in the Pacific* is an excellent guide for the traveler who wants good solid information about the beautiful and romantic Pacific.

Jack Carter

Tibet

418. Batchelor, Stephen. **The Tibet Guide.** Newburyport, Mass., Wisdom, 1987. 466p. illus. (part col.). maps. bibliog. index. $26.95 pa. ISBN 0-86171-046-0.

For twenty-five years (1959-1984) travel to Tibet by westerners was severely restricted by the Chinese. Though tourists are now welcome in this fascinating land, a well-written and informative travel guide is a necessity for even the most experienced and adventurous traveler. And, while Batchelor has succeeded in providing the prospective visitor to Tibet with an excellent guide, this book is much more than a simple travel guide. In addition to the essential tourist information concerning hotels, restaurants, customs, and places to visit, the chapters on the history of Tibet and Tibetan Bhuddism are remarkably informative. There are numerous photographs (mostly color) and the photography is in the best tradition of the *National Geographic*. Perhaps the most refreshing feature of this guide, however, is the author's honesty and candidness concerning the potential difficulties of travel in Tibet and how quickly official travel policies, prices, and other conditions may change. Thus, the author warns the potential visitor not to expect a trip to Tibet to conform to "your preconceived notions" or "what you might read in travel books." This warning is also good advice for the reader of this delightful guide that should be good reading even for those who have no immediate travel plans.

James T. Peach

9 History

ARCHAEOLOGY

419. Jelks, Edward B., and Juliet C. Jelks, eds. **Historical Dictionary of North American Archaeology.** Westport, Conn., Greenwood Press, 1988. 760p. bibliog. index. $95.00. LC 87-17581. ISBN 0-313-24307-7.

Dictionary is too limiting a term for this book; however, had the editors used *encyclopedia*, reviewers might expect too much. Nevertheless, it is closer to the latter than the former. The editors and 151 American archaeologists prepared over eighteen hundred entries for prehistoric cultures, archaeological sites, and major artifact types. They make no claim of comprehensive coverage; however, there is great depth to the book. The editors and thirteen regional consultants selected topics that in their opinion "contributed uniquely to the essential body of information upon which current major classifications and interpretations of North American prehistory are based" (p. xvi). The compilers appear to have chosen more rather than less coverage of lesser-known sites and topics; they include the reviewer's unpublished master's thesis and some of his other obscure archaeological publications in the bibliography and text. The alphabetically arranged entries, prepared by an archaeologist, provide basic information about the topic and its contribution to archaeological knowledge. Entries for each site indicate who excavated it and when, what artifacts and features are notable, and its cultural affiliation. The signed entries provide a brief list of sources of further information. The book's bibliography is 135 pages long and the index is 53 pages. To check coverage for artifact types, the reviewer used the forty-six projectile point "clusters" described by N. D. Justice in *Stone Age Spear and Arrow Points* (see entry 360). All of the clusters appeared in some form in this book, although not always using precisely the same term. For example Justice's Hi-Lo Cluster has no entry (type site Hi-Lo) but two other related

sites have coverage, Bull Brook and the Itasca Bison Kill site. If one has a limited budget for North American archaeology and ethnology reference titles, one could not go wrong with just this book for archaeology and the Smithsonian Institute's *Handbook of North American Indians* (1978-) set for ethnology. [R: LJ, July 88, p. 72; RBB, 15 Sept 88, pp. 136, 138]

G. Edward Evans

420. Marx, Robert F. **Shipwrecks in the Americas.** rev. ed. Mineola, N.Y., Dover Publications, 1987. 482p. illus. bibliog. index. $10.95 pa. LC 87-23756. ISBN 0-486-25514-X.

It would have been nice to have had an updated edition of this book reflecting wreck finds and technological advances in diving since 1971. An updated bibliography would have been good. However, the only changes from the original 1971 edition are a revised selection, a change in layout of the pictures and index to the pictures, and substitution of the original preface with the preface from the 1975 reissue. Previous issues of this book have sold out rapidly. This newly available, inexpensive paperback issue will probably be snapped up by a new generation of those interested in shipwrecks, diving, underwater archaeology, and treasure hunting.

Frank J. Anderson

421. Spriggs, Matthew J. T., and Patricia Lehua Tanaka, comps. **Nā Mea 'Imi I Ka Wā Kahiko: An Annotated Bibliography of Hawaiian Archaeology.** Hololulu, Social Science Research Institute; distr., Honolulu, University of Hawaii Press, 1988. 303p. maps. index. (Asian and Pacific Archaeology Series, No. 11). $17.00 pa. LC 87-9895. ISBN 0-8248-1135-6.

Unlike David Kittelson's *The Hawaiians* (see *ARBA* 86, entry 103), this is a highly focused bibliography dealing with Hawaiian archaeological literature. It is intended to replace the *Hawaii Register of Historic Places: Bibliography of Hawaiiana* (Division of State

Parks, 1970). It is difficult to determine just how many unique entries the work contains. There are 2,003 numbered entries, but duplication occurs when a publication covers more than one island or *ahupua'a* (traditional land unit) as the full entry is repeated and given a new number. What is unusual about this bibliography is that it includes unpublished reports, primarily work done to comply with environmental impact statements that are required before an area is developed. The compiler (a trained archaeologist) estimates that 95 percent "of the substantive archaeological reports for the period in question have been included" (p. vii). It is current for unpublished material through 1984 and to about March of 1986 for published items. Not included are newspaper reports and popular publications such as the Bishop Museum Association publication *Ka Ele'ele*. Although the title indicates the entries are annotated, the annotations are minimal but informative, providing site location by island, district, and/or ahupua'a, and the type of research (e.g., excavation, intensive survey, or reconnaissance survey). Entries are arranged in author order within general references: *Hawai'i Island, Kaho'olawe, Kaua'i and Ni'ihau, Lana'i, Leeward Islands (Nihoa and Necker), Maui, Moloka'i,* and *O'ahu*. Author, island, district and ahupua'a indexes complete the volume. Any library with a strong Hawaiian collection will want to order this book if no standing order exists for the series.   G. Edward Evans

422.   Whitehouse, Ruth D., ed. **The Facts on File Dictionary of Archaeology.** rev. ed. New York, Facts on File, c1983, 1988. 597p. illus. bibliog. index. $29.95; $16.95pa. ISBN 0-87196-048-6; 0-8160-1893-6pa.

No identifiable changes exist in the softcover edition in comparison to the 1983 hardcover version. It remains a good single volume for finding a variety of terms used in archaeological literature. The worldwide coverage means that all the entries are brief; most are less than two hundred words long. One of the longer entries is for radio carbon dating, one page of text and a one-page chart. The longest text-only entry (two and one-half pages) is for megalithic monuments. Its length is due to the wide distribution of megaliths across Europe, Asia, Africa, and Oceania.

The layperson may have trouble using this work because of its technical nature and concise definitions. Suggestions for further information are provided in a five-page listing at the end of the book, not in the entry where it would be most helpful for the nonspecialist. Line drawings should help the general user, but this is not always the case. The entry for *flake* has a drawing labeled *primary flake*. Unfortunately, the definition does not use that phrase, leaving the general user in doubt if primary flakes are the same as a *blank*, the word employed by the editors in the definition (p. 174). One other example will illustrate the fact that this is a dictionary for the well-informed rather than general user. In the entry for *neolithic states* one of the differences is the use of ground and polished stone tools. There is no entry for either ground or polished stone tools that would explain how such tools differ in technology and utility from flake tools.

A topical subject index does provide an interesting secondary method of access to the entries. That is, if you want to find all the entries relating to *site technology*, the index lists all the entries from *aerial photography* to *triangulation*. Thirty topical divisions make it clear this volume has a strong European orientation. There are five pages of topical listings for China, Japan, Southeast Asia, Australasia and Oceania, North America, Meso-America, and South America, while there are nine pages of European and African listings.

Overall this is a fine dictionary for students of archaeology and it will be useful for the general reader, if a less technical work such as *Penguin Dictionary of Archaeology* (Penguin, 1982) or the *Concise Encyclopedia of Archaeology* (Hutchison, 1974) is available.

G. Edward Evans

AMERICAN HISTORY

Archives

423.   **Archival and Manuscript Repositories in North Carolina: A Directory.** Raleigh, N.C., Society of North Carolina Archivists, 1987. 109p. illus. maps. index. $12.00pa.

This directory lists the archival/manuscript collections of 125 institutions in North Carolina. Entries are arranged alphabetically by city, and then by institution. Each entry provides the name, address, and telephone number of the institution; hours of operation; any prior arrangements needed to use the facilities; description of holdings; restrictions on the use of the collection; types of material solicited; reference services provided; copying facilities provided; equipment allowed in the repository (e.g., electric typewriters, portable microcomputers, cameras, recorders); published and unpublished guides to the collections; whether the institution reports holdings to the National Union of Manuscript Collections; and staff size.

The directory includes four indexes — by institutional name, county, type of repository (i.e., college/university, community/technical college, historical society, museum, public library, religious, special, governmental), and subject (with a few *see* references). There is no mention of supplements or future editions.

Wiley J. Williams

424. Directory of Archives and Manuscript Repositories in the United States. 2d ed. By National Historical Publications and Records Commission. Phoenix, Ariz., Oryx Press, 1988. 853p. index. $55.00. LC 87-30157. ISBN 0-89774-475-6.

This volume, here published by Oryx Press, marks the second edition of this directory, updating that published by the National Archives and Records Service in 1978. The new edition contains information on historical documents collections in 4,560 corporate, academic, city, and state archives in all fifty states, the District of Columbia, Puerto Rico, and the U.S. Virgin Islands. Based largely on information drawn from questionnaires, the second edition contains material on fourteen hundred repositories not included in the earlier edition, as well as updated information on previously listed locations.

Entries in the second edition, as in the first volume, are arranged alphabetically by state and, within each state, by city and institution. Following a brief description of each state's program for local government records, individual entries list the following information, if available: institution name, street address, mailing address, telephone number, days and hours of operation, user fees, access restrictions, copy facilities, acquisitions policies, volume of total holdings, a brief description and inclusive date of the holdings, and references to other guides and finding lists.

There is one change in the indexing of the second edition from the first volume. Both volumes contain a subject index, but the new edition also contains an alphabetical listing, while the first volume indexed entries by type of repository, such as state, university, etc., and then alphabetically by institution code. It should be noted that, while entry information has been updated and verified, errors sometimes crop up. For example, this reviewer turned up a mistake in checking the hours of operation for the Manuscripts, Archives, and Special Collections Division at Washington State University.

The new edition of this standard work will be very useful for historians and other researchers seeking current information on special collection materials. It is reasonably priced and should be an essential addition to any college,

university, and archival reference collection. [R: Choice, Oct 88, p. 286; RBB, 1 Oct 88, pp. 237-38]

Louis Vyhnanek

425. Guide to the National Archives of the United States. Washington, D.C., National Archives and Records Administration, 1974, 1987. 896p. index. $25.00. LC 87-28205. ISBN 0-911333-23-1.

The National Archives's decision to reissue this mammoth finding aid may be a welcome one for researchers and libraries assisting researchers needing access to federal records. This volume provides descriptions to over a million cubic feet of records of numerous federal agencies as well as concise administrative histories of these agencies. This new version also includes descriptions of some significant record groups added to the National Archives between 1970 and 1977 and a new introduction by Frank B. Evans about how the guide fits into the National Archives's finding aid program.

Although Evans's introductory essay may be of more interest to the archivist than the researcher, it is important to mention this introduction because it reinforces the fact that the guide has some fundamental flaws as a reference to the archival records of our national government. Evans's essay covers recent developments in the ways that archivists are arranging and describing records and new interests by researchers in using the records. Evans notes that the 1974 finding aid might be "regarded as marking the end of one era and the transition to another" in seeing that archives are effectively used to increase human knowledge and aid scholarship. The truth is, the guide is a dinosaur. Its descriptions of records are extremely concise, and the guide's index is to these descriptions, *not* the records. Guides such as this are dying out as both archivists and researchers become more accustomed to automated catalogs and networks. The computer has also begun to transform access to voluminous quantities of records. And the record group used as the basis of organization and description in this guide may give way to other, more efficient methods of arrangement and description. The best news in this guide is the statement that it is being reissued only because it is out-of-date, and new automated systems of access will be available in the next several years. Libraries should acquire the guide only if their 1974 copy is worn out, missing, or if they neglected to acquire it the first time around.

Richard J. Cox

426. Larsen, John C., ed. Researcher's Guide to Archives and Regional History Sources.

Hamden, Conn., Library Professional Publications/Shoe String Press, 1988. 167p. index. $27.50. LC 88-15081. ISBN 0-208-02144-2.

The premise for the preparation of this book was that increasingly archival materials, historical records, and traditional library resources are used in combination by those involved in historical research. It is intended primarily as a guide for beginning researchers who need to go beyond printed library holdings by consulting archival records, public records, local historical collections, oral history collections, and similar specialized resources.

This guide presents fourteen essays, each written by an experienced archivist in the fields considered. The first essay is a general introduction to archival research which reviews the types and range of material available and appropriate research techniques. Other chapters provide information and advice on using archives and archival reference tools. Specific types of material, including business, religious, public, and genealogical records; nonmanuscript and cartographic sources; and oral histories are covered. The notes and bibliography section provides extensive leads for pursuing in greater depth these topics.

This title could serve as a text in an introductory course on historical research or as a guide for persons embarking on their own into searching archival resources. It fortunately offers both practical, specific, "how-to-do-it" information with a scholarly overview and orientation to archival research. [R: WLB, Dec 88, p. 104]   Henry E. York

428. Smith, Allen. **Directory of Oral History Collections.** Phoenix, Ariz., Oryx Press, 1988. 141p. index. $49.50. LC 87-22868. ISBN 0-89774-322-9.

A number of guides and catalogs pertaining to subject, institutional, and regional oral history collections have appeared in the last decade. This directory covers the collections of 476 libraries, museums, societies, and associations across the United States. For each entry it lists the address, names of contact persons, size of the collection, hours and conditions of access, catalogs or finding aids available, the purpose of the collection, and notable holdings. The information gathered is based on responses to questionnaires filled out by the individual institutions. In this regard, descriptions of the collections vary according to the size of the collection and the thoroughness of the individual who answered the questionnaire. The largest collections are necessarily described in less detail than smaller ones, yet the detail of most entries is quite full.

The directory is arranged geographically and its contents are made accessible through a subject index which also includes entries for the institutions and the cities in which they are located. Happily, the index is very good, although it proved difficult to identify easily those institutions described as having interviews of naval officers. On the whole, however, this is a fine work that will be useful to historians and librarians. [R: Choice, July/Aug 88, p. 1678; RBB, 15 June 88, p. 1719]

Eric R. Nitschke

428. Szucs, Loretto Dennis, and Sandra Hargreaves Luebking. **The Archives: A Guide to the National Archives Field Branches.** Salt Lake City, Utah, Ancestry Publishing, 1988. 340p. illus. index. $35.95. LC 87-70108. ISBN 0-916489-23-X.

When most researchers think of the National Archives they imagine the monumental structure in Washington, D.C. This guide to the National Archives's eleven field branches located throughout the country shows that the research resources of that institution are a rich treasury of historical materials beyond those located in the nation's capital.

These field branches hold over 300,000 cubic feet of archival records, 60 percent of which are district court records. The records are important sources for local, regional, and national historical studies on genealogy and family history, politics, culture, the military, and economics. Records from the General Accounting Office to the Bureau of Indian Affairs to the Office of the Army Surgeon General are held. These records span the two centuries of the federal government.

This reference is a well-organized and presented volume with brief descriptions of how to conduct research in the branches, summaries of the branches' holdings, explanations of textual and microfilm holdings held in common by all the branches, and more detailed descriptions of specific records holdings (arranged alphabetically by title of the record groups). A topical and name index to the guide is also included.

The Archives is a useful reference to this component of the National Archives. Even when the National Archives succeeds in creating a national computerized database to all of its holdings, this publication will be of assistance for introducing prospective researchers to the riches of the field branches. [R: LJ, 1 Oct 88, p. 80]

Richard J. Cox

Atlases

429.   Ferrell, Robert H., and Richard Natkiel. **Atlas of American History.** New York, Facts on File, 1987. 192p. illus. (part col.). maps. index. $24.95. LC 87-675628. ISBN 0-8160-1028-5.

A nice combination of high school atlas and history text, this volume does well. Farrell's facile pen and Natkiel's cartographic skills carry the work. About 200 two- and four-color maps are supplemented by sound narrative history and nearly 150 color and black-and-white illustrations. Most of this is packaged neatly into six chronologically arranged chapters covering 160 pages. Final sections include selected statistical information, territorial expansion and population maps, and maps for each presidential election since 1800. A three-page alphabetically arranged index completes the work. Index entries refer back to page number for both narrative and map information; however, the authors provide no coordinates to facilitate access to the latter.

In part, this last point illustrates both the strengths and weaknesses of this book. The format is clean, the narrative history is sound, but the cost of combining the two into 190 pages comes at the expense of enough information to make the work sufficiently useful to library audiences. Few maps cover an entire page; in fact, illustrations and narrative combined consume more space than maps. Why does George Washington get two full-page portraits? And the angle of vision here is heavily weighted toward U.S. diplomatic and political history; social history gets light treatment. For example, one looks in vain for maps on population densities of ethnic minorities or religion. [R: BR, May/June 88, p. 47; LAR, 14 Oct 88, p. 601; LJ, Jan 88, p. 76; RBB, 1 Mar 88, p. 1102; RQ, Spring 88, p. 421; WLB, Jan 88, pp. 97-98]
                                          Wayne A. Wiegand

430.   McEvedy, Colin. **The Penguin Atlas of North American History.** New York, Viking Penguin, 1988. 112p. maps. index. $6.95pa. ISBN 0-14-051128-8.

This book, by the author of *The Penguin Atlas of Ancient History* (see *ARBA* 77, entry 357) and *The Penguin Atlas of Recent History: Europe since 1815* (Penguin, 1982), presents North American history from 20,000 B.C. to 1870 in maps and text. The book concentrates on the continental United States, but some events in the Caribbean and Middle America (Mexico and Central America) are also included. The atlas contains forty-eight full-page, blue, black, white, and gray maps and nine small insert maps. The layout is attractive, with text on the lefthand pages and maps on the right. The maps, usually depicting broad events, are clear and uncluttered, showing a particular area in a given year. The text is primarily a narrative history of boundary changes, which can be followed on the accompanying maps. Events which did not cause boundary changes (e.g., the War of 1812) are dealt with only briefly. The text is highly readable, although it contains some unsupported opinions. The book lacks an index to the maps; however, it does contain an index to the text, through which one usually can find the information on the maps. For events beginning with 1492 this work does not take the place of more detailed atlases such as *Atlas of American History* (see *ARBA* 86, entry 458) and Ferrell and Natkiel's *Atlas of American History* (see entry 429), but it is a handy atlas which will be useful for high school and undergraduate students.   Kathleen Farago

431.   Scott, James W., and Roland L. De Lorme. **Historical Atlas of Washington.** Norman, Okla., University of Oklahoma Press, 1988. 1v. (various paging). illus. maps. bibliog. index. $27.95. LC 87-40557. ISBN 0-8061-2108-4.

This atlas is the latest volume in a series of historical atlases published by the University of Oklahoma Press. Written by James W. Scott, Professor of Geography, and Roland L. De Lorme, Professor of History at Western Washington University, the atlas is the first comprehensive reference guide to the historical geography of the state of Washington. It contains seventy-seven maps, each accompanied by a page of textual explanation, covering Washington's physical geography as well as its history from the prehistoric period to the present.

The atlas is divided into fourteen chapters, including ones on the physical environment, Indian history, early exploration and settlement, fur trade, missionaries, early territorial history, population growth and characteristics, political divisions, place names, transportation, production, urbanization, and cultural and park resources. Within each chapter there are maps and text covering that particular aspect of Washington's history or geography. The excellent black-and-white maps are clearly drawn and the text does a superb job of providing a one-page summary of each topic. There is also an alphabetical name and subject index as well as a bibliography of reference sources for each individual map.

This atlas meets a definite need for a current reference source on Washington's history and geography; it will be a useful addition to the reference collections of Washington libraries and the main collections of large academic libraries. The work is also an excellent one-volume source that will be used in college and university courses on Washington history and the history of the Pacific Northwest. [R: Choice, Dec 88, p. 704]   Louis Vyhnanek

Bibliographies

432. **American History: A Bibliographic Review. Volume III: 1987.** Carol Bondhus Fitzgerald and others, eds. Westport, Conn., Meckler, 1988. 211p. illus. $59.50. ISBN 0-88736-224-9; ISSN 0748-6731.

This third volume of *American History* represents a substantial shift in focus for its publishers. Unlike previous issues (see *ARBA 86*, entry 481), this latest annual issue has dropped the thematic bibliographic essay in favor of a general "bibliographic review," surveying recently published bibliographies, guides, indexes, catalogs, and databases of interest to historians. As in previous volumes, this issue contains a preliminary checklist of the work of a noted historian, provides a directory of publishing awards in American history and their 1986 recipients, and provides selected book reviews for eight recently published bibliographical guides in history. Most interesting is the "national registry" for the bibliography of history, providing a record both of recently completed research and of works in progress in American history.

This publication provides much interesting information, and its aim of forming a centralized source for indexing published bibliographic essays is a commendable one. But so much of what is provided is already so widely available both in print and nonprint sources – and often easier to access – that it is hard to justify either this publication or its price tag. It is an interesting idea which has yet to be developed, an idea still in search of realization. Given the explosion in journal publication, and the fact that much of what is provided in this title is readily covered by many other publications, it is hard to justify this publication.

                              Elizabeth Patterson

433. Burnham, Alan. **New York City, the Development of the Metropolis: An Annotated Bibliography.** New York, Garland, 1988. 366p. illus. index. (Garland Bibliographies in Architecture and Planning, Vol. 5; Garland Reference Library of the Humanities, Vol. 408). $52.00. LC 88-10220. ISBN 0-8240-9133-7.

This bibliography is based on the New York City portion of the American Architec-

tural Archive, once the personal collection of the editor. Alan Burnham was a New York-based architect with an intense interest in historical architecture and preservation. His *New York Landmarks* (Wesleyan University Press, 1963) is a standard reference source. This new work's focus is on Manhattan; only forty pages cover the other boroughs. The bibliography is arranged in chapters both by type of work (e.g., guidebooks, picture books), and by type of structure (e.g., park, church, bank, government building). The entries are alphabetical and annotated. There are author, title, personal name, and subject indexes. Architectural and urban historians and historic preservationists as well as those with an interest in New York City local history will appreciate this book, which is appropriate for libraries in the New York area and larger architecture collections elsewhere.

                              Deborah Hammer

434. Buxbaum, Melvin H. **Benjamin Franklin: A Reference Guide 1907-1983.** Boston, G. K. Hall, 1988. 796p. index. (Reference Guide to Literature). $55.00. LC 82-12144. ISBN 0-8161-8673-1.

This annotated bibliography is a companion to the first volume published in 1983, covering the period 1721-1906 (see *ARBA 84*, entry 348). Following the same methodology as that employed in volume 1, all entries are grouped by year of publication, and they are arranged alphabetically by author within the year that they were originally published. The entries provide succinct summaries of the original authors' views on Franklin and his works.

The author seems to have supposed that those who purchase this second volume are already acquainted with his earlier publication. Hence he does not repeat the nine-page introduction that was included in volume 1, and which outlined the objectives of this project as follows: To preserve comments in early publications that have deteriorated with age; to make available references to works that are in reserved collections; to include both familiar and unfamiliar entries to give a balanced view of Franklin; to illustrate how some comments reveal more about their authors than Franklin; to study Franklin's status as the archetypical American character.

In the main this volume successfully achieves these objectives, although some criticisms of Franklin are regarded as "shallow and unfair," and we are reassured that he "did have in mind moving on to higher and finer realms of life." It was not his fault that "he was claimed by the American Society of Heating and

Ventilating Engineers as their Patron Saint."

George T. Potter

435.   Cole, Garold L. **Civil War Eyewitnesses: An Annotated Bibliography of Books and Articles, 1955-1986.** Columbia, S.C., University of South Carolina Press, 1988. 351p. index. $29.95. LC 87-34273. ISBN 0-87249-545-0.

Travel literature has long been both a popular literary genre and a valuable resource for historians. The documentation of Southern primary accounts began with Thomas D. Clark's *Travels in the Old South* (Books on Demand, 1956-1960) and *Travels in the New South* (University of Oklahoma Press, 1962), as well as E. Merton Coulter's *Travels in the Confederate States* (University of Oklahoma Press, 1948). These excellent bibliographies have served historians well over the years, and Cole's *Travels in America from the Voyages of Discovery to the Present* (see *ARBA* 86, entry 416) continues that bibliographic tradition, as does *Civil War Eyewitnesses.* This book includes almost fourteen hundred entries representing books and periodicals published from 1955 to 1986. Each entry includes a full bibliographic citation and annotations ranging in length from one brief sentence to a full paragraph. An extensive seventy-page index provides broad subject, author, and title access to the entries.

The volume is divided into three subject areas: the North, the South, and anthologies. In turn, each of these is subdivided. Sources selected for the bibliography include books, collected essays, memoirs, autobiographies, and both popular and scholarly periodicals. With an ever-growing body of literature, the Civil War continues to attract scholars and writers. Books such as *Civil War Eyewitnesses* ensure that historians will have bibliographic control of their needed source material. [R: Choice, Oct 88, p. 286]

Boyd Childress

436.   Cummins, Light Townsend, and Alvin R. Bailey, Jr., eds. **A Guide to the History of Texas.** Westport, Conn., Greenwood Press, 1988. 307p. index. (Reference Guides to State History and Research). $59.95. LC 87-15021. ISBN 0-313-24563-0.

Texans justly take pride in the rich history of their state and now they have this handy guide to help them explore it further. This book is the second volume to be published in the series, whose guides are intended to serve as introductions to the available secondary literature and research collections. The first part of the Texas volume consists of eleven historiographical essays written by specialists on various chronological periods and topics, for example,

"Antebellum Texas" and "Women in Texas History." In the second part of the volume, sixteen chapters describe selected research collections located in Texas. Fifteen of the chapters deal with individual major collections as they relate to Texas history. The final chapter surveys twenty-four lesser collections. These collections were included in the guide as general historical collections and to provide an even geographical distribution. Each chapter is written by a person intimately acquainted with the collections as an archivist, a librarian, or an officer. Finally, there are two brief appendices which supply a chronology of Texas history and a list of the addresses of various Texas historical societies. A detailed index of authors and selected subjects completes the volume. This guide is well done and should be a must purchase for institutions specializing in Southern, Southwestern, or Texas history or those supervising graduate work in Texas history. It is unfortunate that the high price of the volume will deter many individual scholars and graduate students from buying a personal copy.

Ronald H. Fritze

437.   Doenecke, Justus D. **Anti-Intervention: A Bibliographical Introduction to Isolationism and Pacifism from World War I to the Early Cold War.** New York, Garland, 1987. 421p. index. (Garland Reference Library of Social Science, Vol. 396). $60.00. LC 87-8635. ISBN 0-8240-8482-9.

Justus Doenecke's annotated bibliography on anti-intervention begins with opposition to American intervention in World War I and ends in the late 1950s with the defeat of isolationist elements in the U.S. Congress and the general bankruptcy of anti-interventionist ideas and policies. Doenecke identifies two anti-intervention groups, pacifists and isolationists. Although these two groups may have supported one another on certain issues, their motivations were quite different. Pacifists refuse to support any conflict, while isolationists oppose U.S. intervention outside of its own hemisphere, binding alliances, and participation in world organizations that would impinge upon U.S. sovereignty.

The book is divided into five chapters: general works; World War I and its aftermath; the twenties, thirties, World War II, and the Cold War era; opinion-making elements; and interest and ideological groups and leaders. Chapter 1 deals with general works on the nature of pacifism and isolationism. Chapter 2 on World War I deals with opponents of Woodrow Wilson's policies and with works on William Jemmings Bryan, Robert La Follette, and Jane Addams. There are also sections on the radical Left and its advocates of nonintervention: Eugene Debs, Emma Goldman, John Reed, Crystal and Max Eastman, and William ("Big Bill") Haywood. This chapter also deals with the ratification of the League of Nations Covenant and the revisionist view of U.S. intervention in World War I represented by Charles A. Beard and Harry Elmer Barnes. Chapter 3 covers Congress in the interwar years, pacifist and isolationist tendencies in the United States prior to its entry into World War II (including the German-American Bund and the America First Committee). Congressional leaders covered include Everett Dirksen, John W. Bricker, Arthur Vandenberg, and other leaders such as John Foster Dulles, Herbert Hoover, and Hamilton Fish. Chapter 4 deals with publicists and journalists who have had an impact upon U.S. foreign intervention: William Randolph Hearst, H. L. Mencken, Ezra Pound, and the McCormick-Patterson Press chain. Chapter 5 discusses special interest and ideological groups and leaders, including ethnic and religious groups, extreme right- and left-wing political movements, Roman Catholic and Protestant pacifism, and anti-interventionism.

Doenecke's work is an excellent guide to primary and secondary source material on anti-interventionist thought, tendencies, and movements in U.S. politics since the beginning of this century for students of U.S. foreign policy, ideology, and domestic U.S. politics, and is highly recommended for college and university reference collections. [R: Choice, Oct 88, pp. 286, 288]   Norman L. Kincaide

438.   Jenkins, John H. **Basic Texas Books: An Annotated Bibliography of Selected Works for a Research Library.** rev. ed. Austin, Tex., Texas State Historical Association; distr., College Station, Tex., Texas A & M University Press, 1988. 648p. illus. index. $29.95. LC 87-22899. ISBN 0-87611-086-3.

Fire destroyed most of the first edition (1983) of this essential guide. Since at the time it was well received and thought destined to become a classic, reprinting was called for. Now in a new revised edition it is again available. Jenkins, the compiler, self-published the first edition; the Texas State Historical Association is the current publisher. Since the work received justifiable plaudits the first time around, at question here is the amount of revision undertaken. Added to the preface are three sentences acknowledging the fire, the new publisher, and the fact of revision, but not the extent of it. The number of entries, the number of pages, the size of the appendix, the length of the index, and the layout are exactly the same. Jenkins states that

he incorporated additional printings of the main entries published since the first edition, and surely they are there. But to advertise his guide as a revised edition is misleading; an amended reissue is more truthful. Nevertheless, because of its scholarship and insightfulness it is a must buy for libraries interested in Texas history (excluding belles lettres, histories of religious denominations, counties, towns, schools, and institutions along with other omissions), and a superfluous buy for libraries already owning the first edition.   Bill Bailey

439.   Kaufman, Martin, John W. Ifkovic, and Joseph Carvalho III, eds. **A Guide to the History of Massachusetts.** Westport, Conn., Greenwood Press, 1988. 313p. index. (Reference Guides to State History and Research). $59.95. LC 87-12026. ISBN 0-313-24564-9.

This two-part guide to state and local Massachusetts history is intended as a noncomprehensive survey of the bibliographical and archival sources with the particular aim of serving as a starting point for the beginning researcher in the field. Part 1 contains six chronological and three topical (urban life, women, and oral history) essays on Massachusetts historiography. Each describes the sources available, analyzes the changing approaches to the history, and suggests areas for future research. The essays are unusually well written and extremely accessible to the general reader. Part 2 lists, alphabetically, major historical repositories throughout the state. The entries give an overview of what is held and highlight special collections. This guide is the third volume in Greenwood's Reference Guides to State History and Research series (Louisiana and Texas are already in print). It is a fine example of a scholarly yet readable research tool that will interest students throughout Massachusetts and New England.   Deborah Hammer

440.   Kyvig, David E., and Mary-Ann Blasio, with others, comps. **New Day/New Deal: A Bibliography of the Great American Depression, 1929-1941.** Westport, Conn., Greenwood Press, 1988. 306p. index. (Bibliographies and Indexes in American History, No. 9). $45.00. LC 87-37568. ISBN 0-313-26027-3.

Historians working in the period from 1929 to 1941 will welcome this bibliographic tool. Its forty-six hundred book, article, and dissertation entries are organized into subject headings, including "Overviews & General Histories," "Participant Accounts," "The Hoover Administration," "The Roosevelt Administration," "The Economy," "Foreign Relations," and seven others. There is also an author index.

The compilers disclaim complete coverage, but their compilation is quite thorough, particularly for materials appearing in the last twenty-five or thirty years. At $45.00 the volume may be overpriced for all but Depression Era specialists, but it is a must for any research library. [R: Choice, Nov 88, p. 462; RBB, 15 Dec 88, p. 692]

David E. Hamilton

Biographies

441. Duffy, Bernard K., and Halford R. Ryan, eds. **American Orators before 1900: Critical Studies and Sources.** Westport, Conn., Greenwood Press, 1987. 481p. index. $75.00. LC 86-33610. ISBN 0-313-25129-0.

The spoken word has always held an important place in American social and political discourse. The eighteenth and nineteenth centuries were particularly blessed with practitioners of oratory, that most democratic form of mass communication. Listeners need only be at the right place at the right time to hear the likes of Frederick Douglass, William Lloyd Garrison, Elizabeth Cady Stanton, or Sojourner Truth. *American Orators before 1900* brings together in one volume biographical and bibliographical information about fifty-five of the best, and most persuasive, public speakers of that tumultuous period.

The arrangement, alphabetically by orator, is mildly problematic as it mitigates against following the development of American oration either thematically or chronologically. In part this problem is addressed by the inclusion of a subject index that allows the reader to locate all mention of women's suffrage by individual speakers as well as topics addressed by a particular speaker in a given speech. A second index lists orators and names of speeches referenced in the text.

The main body of the work consists of signed essays on each of the fifty-five orators. The introductory paragraphs contain brief biographical information, but is most useful for setting the individual in his or her historical context. The remainder of the entry discusses the content and style of some of the individual's major speeches.

A brief, highly selective list of "information sources" following each entry is divided into three parts: research collections and collected speeches, selected critical studies, and selected biographies. The last item included with each entry is a chronology of major speeches, keyed to the research collections. For those unfamiliar with the art (and science) of oratory, the editors have kindly provided a glossary of rhetorical terms to help lay readers decipher some of the more technical language that occasionally appears in the text.

Ellen Broidy

442. Dunlap, Leslie W. **Our Vice-Presidents and Second Ladies.** Metuchen, N.J., Scarecrow, 1988. 397p. index. $35.00. LC 88-4123. ISBN 0-8108-2114-1.

John Nance Garner, one Texan vice-president, once remarked to Lyndon Johnson, another Texan vice-president, that "the vice presidency isn't worth a pitcher of warm spit." But, in spite of that judgment, Leslie W. Dunlap has produced an entertaining reference book on a seemingly unpromising subject. The book deals with vice-presidents from John Adams to George Bush. Each of the forty-three office holders is given a biographical headnote followed by an anecdotal essay on the relationship between the vice-president and his wife. The many fascinating personal facts and stories included in this volume make it a treasure trove to browse. It turns out that the Coolidges were cruelly mistreated and snubbed by first lady Mrs. Harding. In contrast, Mrs. Coolidge was a very fine woman. The quote "What this country needs is a really good five cent cigar" was made by Thomas R. Marshall, vice-president under Woodrow Wilson, while he was presiding over the Senate during a particularly dreary speech. (Marshall, by the way, was the fourth, and so far last, Hoosier to serve as vice-president.) Unfortunately, the rambling organization of the individual essays and the book's perfunctory index preclude this work from being used as a ready-reference tool. In addition, some of the historical judgments are a bit idiosyncratic. The essay on John Tyler glosses over his very serious disagreements with the Whig Party leadership after he succeeded the deceased William Henry Harrison. Millard Fillmore also receives a surprisingly favorable assessment, although no mention is made of his widow's burning of his papers. Still, the book's focus on the marital relations of the vice-presidents makes it a unique addition for the well-stocked reference collection with an interest in American political history.

Ronald H. Fritze

443. Healy, Diana Dixon. **America's First Ladies: Private Lives of the Presidential Wives.** New York, Atheneum, 1988. 254p. illus. $18.95. LC 88-3365. ISBN 0-689-11873-2.

This book, by the author of *America's Vice-Presidents: Our First Forty-three Vice Presidents and How They Got to Be Number Two* (see *ARBA* 85, entry 648), contains brief (three to nine pages) biographies of the forty-one

"First Ladies," mostly wives of the presidents, but in some cases other women who served as official hostesses. Arranged chronologically by administrations, the biographies give brief background information (date and place of birth, early life, etc.), but concentrate on each woman's role, attitude, and behavior during the presidency. A black-and-white picture of almost all of the first ladies is included. The biographies are well written, witty, interesting, and compassionate. They capture each personality and the social atmosphere during each administration. There are many tidbits of information in this work which would be useful in answering trivia questions, but due to the lack of an index they are not readily accessible. Although it cannot be recommended as a reference work, it can serve as a lively addition to general collections. Paul F. Boller, Jr.'s *Presidential Wives* (Oxford University Press, 1988) covers much of the same material in more detail, but only deals with wives; and while it does contain a name index, its use is also limited by the lack of a subject index.   Kathleen Farago

444. Notable Americans: What They Did, from 1620 to the Present: Chronological and Organizational Listings of Leaders.... 4th ed. Linda S. Hubbard, ed. Detroit, Gale, 1988. 733p. index. $150.00. LC 87-32671. ISBN 0-8103-2534-9.

The *Conspectus of American Biography*, first issued in 1906, has undergone numerous revisions and title changes over the years. This new fourth edition bears both a new name and a new look, updating the 1973 edition, *Notable Names in American History*. Coverage now extends from 1620 through 1986. As with previous editions, this register is divided into nineteen broad subject sections providing chronological listings of over forty-two thousand notable persons and organizations in such areas as government, education, religion, business, and labor. A personal name index is provided for easy access. New with this edition is an organizational index allowing for access to personal names by institutional or other type of affiliation.

Some sections simply have been updated, while others such as the "Corporate Executive" section have undergone substantial redesign in criteria for inclusion and scope of coverage. So many name changes have occurred in the organization listings that notes indicating previous institution/group names often are included.

As with previous editions, this register is best used in conjunction with biographical directories such as the *National Cyclopaedia*

of American Biography (White, 1892-) and comparable historical biographical listings. Topical access continues to be the greatest value of this research tool, but without access to the detailed biographical information available in the *Cyclopaedia* and related works, this register on its own can provide only brief data on Americans of note. [R: BR, May/June 88, pp. 47-48; RBB, 15 May 88, pp. 1585-86]
                                Elizabeth Patterson

445. Sifakis, Stewart. Who Was Who in the Civil War. New York, Facts on File, 1988. 766p. illus. bibliog. index. $45.00. LC 84-1596. ISBN 0-8160-1055-2.

This comprehensive, illustrated biographical dictionary contains nearly twenty-five hundred entries of principal Union and Confederate military participants in the Civil War. All officers—583 Union and 425 Confederate—of the rank of general are included plus lower rank officers who led forces larger than a regiment for a lengthy period in a major action or in distinguished service. Also treated are federal and state officials, congressional members, political activists, journalists, artists-correspondents, medical personnel, diplomats, religious commissioners, relevant foreign leaders and observers, and engineers. The data in each entry concentrate on the respective subject's actions during the period of the war and generally omit pre-and postwar activities unless pertinent to the conflict. The entries are concise, supplying such information as birth/death dates, ranks and positions, major contributions, and historical perspective. One valuable feature is the inclusion for each entry of further sources of information when available. Approximately 250 primary source illustrations and photographs are furnished. There are two appendices: a monthly chronology of the major events of the war and a listing of officers who received the thanks of the U.S. Congress. A selected bibliography includes annotations of valuable books and periodicals. There is an index of people and places as well as headings of interest relative to the war for the respective entries (e.g., abolitionists and artillerists). This is an interesting source containing much accessible, comprehensive data. It provides adequate condensed information with suggestions for more in-depth research if desired. [R: LJ, July 88, pp. 72-73; RBB, 1 Oct 88, p. 245; WLB, Dec 88, pp. 115-16]   Jackson Kesler

446. Thrapp, Dan L. Encyclopedia of Frontier Biography. Glendale, Calif., Arthur H. Clark, 1988. 3v. index. $175.00/set. LC 88-71686. ISBN 0-87062-191-2.

This three-volume set, containing approximately forty-five hundred names of western pioneers, includes seventeenth- and eighteenth-century frontier settlers in both New France and New England as well as the trans-Appalachia country. But the vast majority are nineteenth-century men and women who discovered, settled, fought for, governed, or merely lived in the unsettled lands west of the Mississippi River.

Each alphabetical entry begins with a one-word identification—frontiersman, desperado, Indian chief, cowboy, or sometimes just "character." The average length of each biography is about one-half of a double-columned page, shorter or longer for westerners like Custer or Kearny. It offers no illustrations or pronunciations, but accents are sometimes given. A bibliography follows each entry. For famous persons, "literature abundant" appears in place of bibliography.

Coverage for the plains and mountain states is very good: Cochise, Sacajawea, Escalante, Kino, Laframboise, Jedediah Smith, Carrie Nation, "Calamity Jane," and so forth are discussed. Coverage of California is less complete, omitting many Hispanic names. Most of the Franciscan missionaries as well as Consul Thomas O. Larkin, pioneer enthusiast John Marsh, and alcalde Edwin Bryant are left out. Also omitted is the name of New Mexico's Archbishop Lamy. Coverage of Alaska is even less complete—Baranoff, Bering, Rezanov, and Wrangel do not appear though Baranoff is referred to in passing as "a Russian official."

The index, over seventy double-columned pages, is valuable. It covers many topics—gunmen, Mormons, vigilantes, Indian tribes, many names, including those listed, and others having any relationship to persons appearing in the book. Thus, "Wild Bill" Hickok has twenty-seven citations to other persons; Custer and Geronimo each have about one hundred citations. This feature adds to the reference value of the book.

The work is highly recommended and will be invaluable to all western history buffs as well as to reference librarians with a similar clientele.
Raymund F. Wood

Catalogs and Collections

447. **The Collections and Programs of the American Antiquarian Society: A 175th-Anniversary Guide.** By the Staff of American Antiquarian Society. Worcester, Mass., American Antiquarian Society; distr., Charlottesville, Va., University Press of Virginia, 1987. 183p. illus. index. $12.95pa. LC 87-14480. ISBN 0-912296-93-3.

The purpose of *Collections and Programs* is "to illuminate the rich variety and depth" (p. 14) of the American Antiquarian Society's collections, to provide guidance in accessing them, and to commemorate the society's 175th anniversary. It contains a brief history of the society; articles on its collecting, cataloging, and conserving activities; and descriptions of the society's research programs and physical plant. There are also many well-composed photographs, which are pertinent to the text.

The society's general collections consist of broadsides, almanacs, miniature books, and other publication categories. The topical collections include children's literature and school books and the Hawaiian Collection, as well as the usual historical, literary, and genealogical categories one expects in this type of library. The articles generally describe the materials in each collection, recount the historical and continuing development of the collection, provide guides for accessing materials, and note any unusual or important features.

The book is well arranged and the articles are well written. The index, however, is merely an alphabetization of the table of contents. A reference librarian might have appreciated the inclusion of titles mentioned in the text, but this is a minor criticism since the authors did not intend *Collections and Programs* as a tool for locating specific titles. The authors successfully accomplish their purpose of showing what one can expect to find in the society's library and how to find it. This is a fitting tribute to the society's 175th anniversary and is a worthy acquisition for any library interested in America's heritage. [R: C&RL, July 88, pp. 365-68]
Mark E. Schott

448. Kramer, Ilse E., comp. **Die Wunderbare Neue Welt: German Books about the Americas in the John Carter Brown Library, 1493 to 1840.** Providence, R.I., John Carter Brown Library, 1988. 229p. illus. index. $20.00pa.

The first task of a scholar in history or literature is to determine what sources exist for research on a topic and where they can be located. This task can be particularly frustrating if guides are lacking to collections in libraries and archives. For German and German-speaking scholars of the new world, the pilot edition to the collection of German books and related materials on the American continent from 1493 to 1840 will provide an introduction to the materials lodged in the John Carter Brown Library, Brown University. This edition covers the material from 1493 to 1619, which includes roughly one-quarter of the fifteen hundred items on this subject in the library. The entries are arranged by year of publication, then alphabetically by author. Each entry includes author, title, publication data, and condition and contents of the work.

A little over one-third of the works cited are in German, while others are in Latin. The catalog lists works by German authors in any language and non-German authors whose works were translated into German. Two indexes list authors and geographical location. This work arose out of the card index of the materials compiled by Professor Duncan Smith of the German Department at Brown University. It is the result of the need to advertise the collection to a wider field of scholars. This volume is essential to scholars researching the German view of the New World as it became known to Europeans through the age of discovery and exploration. It is highly recommended for college and university library reference collections and particularly for graduate and postgraduate students and scholars of this period.

Norman L. Kincaide

Dictionaries

449. Olson, James S. **Historical Dictionary of the 1920s: From World War I to the New Deal, 1919-1933.** Westport, Conn., Greenwood Press, 1988. 420p. bibliog. index. $55.00. LC 87-29987. ISBN 0-313-25683-7.

This historical dictionary is another in the excellent series compiled by James Olson of Sam Houston State University. The dictionary is a collection of essays, from 350 to 1,200 words in length, on the most prominent individuals, social movements, organizations, legislation, treaties, political events, and ideas of the period between 1919 and 1933: from the Versailles Treaty to the inauguration of Franklin D. Roosevelt. The entries are arranged in alphabetical order and include brief bibliographical citations. Relevant cross-references are included. The dictionary also includes a chronology of events between 1919 and 1933. The author provides a selected bibliography, arranged according to topic, covering the decade. A comprehensive index rounds out this useful, informative volume. The *Historical Dictionary of the 1920s* is certain to be an essential reference for the advanced high school student in the humanities, university undergraduates, and beginning graduate students in U.S. history. [R: Choice, Dec 88, p. 631; RBB, 15 Nov 88, p. 554; WLB, Oct 88, p. 109]

William G. Ratliff

Directories

450. **Directory of Federal Historical Programs and Activities.** By Society for History in the Federal Government and American Historical Association. Washington, D.C., American Historical Association, 1987. 84p. $6.00pa.

This small guide is more a directory of historians than it is a guide to historical programs on the federal level. The seventeen-page name directory is an alphabetical listing of historians employed by the federal government and includes approximately seventeen hundred names. In addition to a complete telephone number, each entry gives a page reference to the second section, which lists historical programs operated by federal government agencies. Examples include the Government Printing Office, the extensive programs of the Department of the Interior, and the Equal Opportunity Office. These departmental or agency listings are divided by the three major branches of the government – cabinet-level departments, independent agencies, and the Department of Defense. Five pages of related programs conclude the volume.

The program description of each entry is brief. For example, the entry for the Postal Service mentions the function of the historian in two sentences, a typical entry. Most descriptions list major responsibilities with only a brief mention of organized programs. Addresses for these offices are included and codes are used to indicate status as archivist, historian, contractor, preservationist, program manager, or visiting scholar.

Earlier editions of the directory were published in 1981 and 1984, and the 1987 volume appears more complete and should provide broad access to federal history until replaced by a newer edition. [R: Choice, Sept 88, p. 78]

Boyd Childress

Handbooks

451. Prucha, Francis Paul. **Handbook for Research in American History: A Guide to Bibliographies and Other Reference Works.** Lincoln, Nebr., University of Nebraska Press, 1987. 289p. index. $21.95; $9.95pa. LC 86-30871. ISBN 0-8032-3682-4; 0-8032-8719-4pa.

Francis Prucha, professor of history at Marquette University, in his introduction states that "the purpose of this Handbook is to introduce beginning historians to the helps that await them in the reference sections of the library. Established historians, too, may find it of value as they seek the newer reference guides, and non-historians can use it to locate historical materials" (p. 1). As a single-volume reference guide listing over fifteen hundred titles in American history, this work should serve well the informational/reference need of a student of American history and a reference librarian.

This modestly priced volume is divided into two major parts. Part 1 consists of seventeen sections covering traditional library reference sources (bibliographies, library catalogs, periodical indexes, archival guides, dissertations, etc.), and separate chapters on oral history materials, governmental sources (federal, state, and local), guides to legal sources, geographical sources, and databases. Part 2 is devoted to individual historical disciplines, and covers in fifteen sections such topics as political, military, social, economic, and technological histories. Separate sections are devoted to ethnic groups, women, regional materials, and travel accounts. Each chapter is subdivided into separate sections arranged according to reference typology of listed materials (e.g., general bibliographies, general bibliographies of U.S. history, bibliography of bibliographies, other bibliographies). Prucha uses an alphanumeric system to arrange the listed entries, and includes necessary cross-references. Some entries are annotated, and according to the compiler the "more important works are discussed in the text; more specialized items are generally simply listed, with only brief annotations or none at all" (p. 3). The comprehensive author/title/subject index concludes this interesting volume.

Although Prucha's reference compendium is an important addition to the historical reference literature, several critical comments pertaining to its scope, bibliographic features, and methodology are in order. First of all, the author's designation of this bibliographic reference guide as a "handbook" is rather questionable. A *handbook*, in general, provides concise information including various statistical tables and charts on a special subject as well as a balanced bibliographic coverage of American history. Thus, from a reference typological point of view, the author's *handbook* in reality constitutes a standard bibliographic guide.

It is unfortunate that Prucha does not discuss the subject structure of American history, nor does he explain the role of auxiliary historical disciplines in historical research. For instance, there are no separate sections on historical research methodology (a must for any historical handbook), or American historiography (however, there is a section on American historical bibliography). Also, there are no separate sections on cultural and intellectual history. In this respect the subject coverage in this guide, in my view, should be expanded.

The author correctly states that immigration "has been an important element in the historiography of the United States," and in recent years "the study of ethnic groups has grown rapidly" (p. 166). He covers immigration and ethnic topics in three separate chapters: "Ethnic Groups," "Blacks," and "American Indians." American Jewish reference sources are included in the chapter on religion. Unfortunately, many entries listed in the chapter "Ethnic Groups" are not annotated, and the author's brief discussion of some major reference works (e.g., *Harvard Encyclopedia of American Ethnic Groups* [see *ARBA* 82, entry 438]) is not critical or evaluative, but descriptive. This also constitutes a "weak spot" in this bibliography.

The author clearly states in his introduction that this publication "is not intended to be a definitive listing." This reviewer fully agrees with the compiler's assessment of his work. Finally, I wish to recommend that in a future revised edition of this bibliography, all entries should have a complete bibliographic description, including pagination. From a reference and bibliographic point of view, it is an important matter. Despite the uneven coverage of some historical topics, this publication, as a general introductory guide to American history, is an important addition to our reference literature. [R: Choice, Mar 88, p. 1070; C&RL, July 88, p. 353]   Lubomyr R. Wynar

452. Roberts, Robert B. **Encyclopedia of Historic Forts: The Military, Pioneer, and Trading Posts of the United States.** New York, Macmillan, 1988. 894p. illus. maps. bibliog. index. $95.00. LC 86-28494. ISBN 0-02-926880-X.

Interest in American military history continues unabated, and the author (who died in November 1986 at the end of forty years of research) has compiled a unique encyclopedia. Covering the time period from 1562 to 1985, it is composed of clear, concise, and easy to read articles along with interesting drawings and photographs of the sites. The fifty states are covered, but not other American territories or possessions. Spanish, French, Russian, and English camps are included. United States Navy, Marine Corps, and Air Force bases, along with various other minor posts, are generally not considered here. (The histories of Navy and Marine Corps bases are well treated with lengthy essays in *United States Navy and Marine Corps Bases, Domestic* and *Overseas* [see *ARBA* 86, entries 637 and 638].) With over three thousand forts included (many of which are still in operation), this book will be of assistance in answering reference questions; it is also fun to browse through.

The entries, with headings in boldface type, are arranged by state and then by the name of the fort. Each article usually includes the general location of the fort, who established it and when, and sometimes the date when it ceased operations. Cross-references are inserted where needed. A four-page glossary and a diagram of a bastioned fortification appear after the preface. A directory of state archives and libraries (lacking telephone numbers) is at the end of the book. There is also a bibliography (whose citations lack publishers) and an "Index to Forts," but not a general index, which would have been more helpful.

Since some of the sites are still active or have been transformed into parks or museums, a short paragraph at the end of each entry stating how to get to the site, and its address and telephone number would have been helpful. Perhaps some maps showing the location of the fort in relation to the surrounding area could have been added to this volume. More illustrations would have been nice, too.

Still, the book's strengths outweigh its weaknesses. It is well constructed, with wide margins on the pages, and the typography is uniformly good. One would have to check a wide variety of sources to find the same amount of information as is contained within these pages. This reference tool is recommended for large public and academic libraries and those institutions interested in state and military history. [R: Choice, Mar 88, p. 1070; RBB, 1 May 88, p. 1484; WLB, Feb 88, pp. 98-99]

Daniel K. Blewett

Indexes

453. **Index to Historic Preservation Periodicals.** By National Trust for Historic Preservation Library of the University of Maryland.... Boston, G. K. Hall, 1988. 354p. $95.00. ISBN 0-8161-0474-3.

Based on the idea that historic preservation is of growing importance in modern America, this index offers a compilation of the monthly listing of articles issued by the Library of the National Trust for Historic Preservation. The over six hundred serials examined include those issued by international, national, regional, state, and local historic preservation organizations, plus popular and scholarly periodicals that include material relevant to the historic preservation movement. The National Trust for Historic Preservation Library currently is housed as a special collection in the Architecture

Library of the University of Maryland, College Park.

The over 350 pages of separate periodical entries are entered in the index as complete bibliographic citations, many of them annotated. The six thousand entries represent such topics valuable to historic preservation as architecture, law, historical research, design review, interior treatments for historic buildings, restoration, real estate, fund raising, tax incentives, and federal policy matters.

The only drawback to the volume is the lack of a subject index. Since a single heading is assigned to each citation, it is necessary to scan for more than one subject to complete a thorough search. Otherwise, the index provides a valuable reference source for preservationists and historians. [R: Choice, Dec 88, p. 630; WLB, Oct 88, pp. 109-10]

William G. Ratliff

454. Kinnell, Susan K., ed. **People in History: An Index to U.S. and Canadian Biographies in History Journals and Dissertations.** Santa Barbara, Calif., ABC-Clio, 1988. 2v. $125.00/set. ISBN 0-87436-493-0; ISSN 0894-0916.

When an organization labors as diligently as ABC-Clio does to produce its widely used and respected bibliographic volumes, *America: History and Life*, its editors are perpetually faced with the temptation to skim off a small portion of the database, repackage it, and market it as a brand-new, "how-did-you-get-along-without-it" product. ABC-Clio has succumbed to this temptation with the publication of its latest reference work, *People in History*.

This work is being marketed as a "unique new reference tool ... a landmark two-volume publication ... a rich, new vein of exploration for historians, genealogists, and scholars concerned with the history of specific ethnic or religious groups, schools of thought, or occupations in the United States and Canada." In fact, *People in History* is simply a selection of citations and abstracts for biographical materials, journal articles, and dissertations, culled from the America: History and Life database. The biographee's name is the main entry, and each article is assigned one or more subject terms which then appear in the index at the end of the second volume. This will all be quite familiar to users of the print version of *America: History and Life*, as it employs the same indexing system.

Since America: History and Life is available online through DIALOG, it would be difficult to justify the purchase of this work in a library that provided adept database searching for its patrons; it would be still harder to justify it if the library already possessed the print version of *America: History and Life.* [R: Choice, Oct 88, pp. 294-95; LJ, Aug 88, p. 151; WLB, June 88, p. 143]   Daniel Uchitelle

ASIAN HISTORY

455. **Encyclopedia of Asian History.** Ainslie T. Embree, ed.-in-chief. New York, Scribner's, 1988. 4v. illus. maps. index. $275.00/set. LC 87-9891. ISBN 0-684-18619-5.

A distinguished editorial committee recruited leading scholars of Asia from throughout the world to contribute entries to this landmark encyclopedia. From Iran and Central Asia on the west through Japan and the Philippines on the east, these four volumes offer an unparalleled view of most of the world's populace over thousands of years. Even more important than the breadth, the alphabetical entries—each signed by a recognized authority on the subject—provide detail on significant events, countries, locales, and more than twelve hundred influential men and women. Most of the entries are accompanied by cross-references to related articles and brief bibliographies of important works (with a preference for books) in English on the topic. Cross-references from blind headings are also included in alphabetical arrangement.

The entries comprise most of the more than 2,050 pages in four volumes, enhanced by 63 original maps and 160 photographs, drawings, and other illustrations. A brief, informative preface leads into the articles, and more than 150 pages of additional material follow the entries in volume 4. Included are a list of entries, a directory of contributors, a list of maps, a Wade-Giles/Pinyin conversion table for romanized Chinese, and acknowledgments for illustrations. A twenty-five-page synoptic outline presents the intellectual organization and provides an alternative to the alphabetical arrangement to identify entries of interest. This is followed by a sixty-five-page index with cross-references and subdivisions, that largely repeats the alphabetical organization of the entries.

Most contemporary encyclopedias prefer mediocrity to controversy, a tendency evident in these volumes in the emphasis on facts over analyses. This modest complaint pales, however, when viewed against the range of authoritative entries on almost any subject relevant to the variegated, heterogeneous Asian cultural and political tapestry over the past 5,000 years and more. The scholarly integrity of the individual entries and overall plan are presented in large, sturdy, attractive, and easy to use volumes. The encyclopedia is an essential and

incomparable reference work for academic, public, and most other libraries. [R: Choice, June 88, p. 1532; C&RL, July 88, pp. 350-51; LJ, 15 June 88, p. 52; RBB, 1 Sept 88, p. 45; RQ, Summer 88, p. 573]   K. Mulliner

456. Mehra, Parshotam. **A Dictionary of Modern Indian History 1707-1947.** New York, Oxford University Press, c1985, 1987. 823p. maps. index. $36.00. ISBN 0-19-561552-2.

Indian civilization is one of the oldest in the world, yet no comprehensive dictionary for modern Indian history has ever been prepared. The author of this first dictionary on the topic certainly has filled a major gap by producing this much-needed book. It covers the period from the death of Muslim ruler Aurangzeb in 1707 to Indian independence in 1947, with the exception of a few entries such as the death of Indian Prime Minister Nehru in 1964. Four hundred entries are arranged in alphabetical order. Entries range from a short paragraph to a few pages in length depending on the importance of the event. Many entries have short bibliographies.

Persons, places, battles, movements, societies, treaties, political parties, and many other important events are covered in this well-prepared dictionary. Well-known Indian leaders such as Nehru, Gandhi, Abdul Kalam Azad, M. A. Jinnah (creator of Pakistan), and many British governors are included. The book has a select chronology of events and covers many important events such as the Khilafat movement, the Jallianwala Bagh tragedy, the government of India acts, the Indian Universities Act, the Gandhi-Irwin Pact, various committee reports, and the rebellion of 1857. A detailed index is helpful. Other attractions of the book are many historical maps, a list of abbreviations, glossary of terms, and a complete list of British governors, governor generals, and viceroys of India from 1774 to 1947. In fact it is a total picture of modern Indian history in a compact form.

This up-to-date version of events put together in dictionary form is highly recommended for all types of libraries interested in developing their collections on Indian history.

Ravindra Nath Sharma

457. Olson, James S., ed. **Dictionary of the Vietnam War.** Westport, Conn., Greenwood Press, 1988. 585p. maps. bibliog. index. $65.00. LC 87-12023. ISBN 0-313-24943-1.

Olson designed this dictionary to be "a ready reference tool for students and scholars." It is precisely that, containing some nine hundred entries on people, events, institutions, jargon, and other subjects. Entries range from brief descriptive paragraphs to two-page essays, and the editor has cross-referenced each item that is the subject of another entry.

The dictionary also includes appendices tabulating South Vietnam's population by province as of 1971 and listing its minority groups in 1970. A separate list defines many of the sometimes arcane acronyms and slang expressions of the war, while yet another appendix contains maps of Vietnam by military region and province. Also useful is a chronology of major events in Vietnam from 1945 to 1975. A reasonably up-to-date categorized bibliography (which unfortunately lists only published books), seventeen pages of index, and a list of contributors complete the volume. Olson himself wrote most of the entries, based on various secondary sources, while others (many from Olson's home state of Texas) contributed many of the longer entries, each of which is signed.

Olson's book, which supplements Harry Summers's *Vietnam War Almanac* (see *ARBA* 86, entry 519), is longer, broader, and more comprehensive. The entries are accurate and clearly written. This is certainly a valuable guide for students bogged down in the Vietnam quagmire, as well as for researchers needing a quick refresher on an obscure item. But at a cost of $65.00, and with the publisher planning no paperback edition, it would appear to be a reference tool unfortunately confined to libraries. [R: Choice, July/Aug 88, p. 1674; LJ, 1 Mar 88, p. 61; RBB, 1 May 88, pp. 1483-84; WLB, June 88, pp. 138, 140]   Anthony A. McIntire

AUSTRALIAN HISTORY

458. **Australians: A Historical Library.** Alan D. Gilbert and others, eds. New South Wales, Australia, Fairfax, Syme & Weldon, and New York, Cambridge University Press, 1987. 10v. illus. (part col.). maps. index. $665.00/set. ISBN 0-521-34073-X.

This comprehensive multivolume guide to the history of Australia is outstanding. Although there is no shortage of good reference works on Australia, this is by far the best single source for general historical information, for a wide range of factual and statistical information, and for other sources of information. The set comprises ten volumes containing more than two million words and over three thousand illustrations. Five of the volumes take a historical look at the country at critical points: to 1788, in 1838, in 1888, in 1938, and since 1939. There are also five reference volumes that include a historical atlas, a historical dictionary, a chronological listing of events since 1788 and a guide

to historical places, a set of historical statistics, and a guide to bibliographic and library resources. A short guide and index volume ties the references in the various volumes together and also provides listings of political personages (e.g., prime ministers) and art and literary awards. The volume on sources, which is truly excellent, starts with a general chapter on resources that takes a comprehensive look at archives, galleries, libraries, and museums. It is followed by a careful consideration of general reference works and major statistical sources. Finally there are forty-five compact essays under eight headings: environment, aborigines, general history, European discovery and colonization, politics, the economy, society, and culture. Each of these essays is written by an outstanding scholar and summarizes the theme in narrative form, touching on the important writings on the topic. As a complete and comprehensive look at all aspects of Australian life and culture over the course of its bicentenary, this set is an invaluable reference source. [R: Choice, Sept 88, p. 73; LJ, July 88, p. 72; RBB, 15 Sept 88, pp. 128, 130]

Norman D. Stevens

BRITISH HISTORY

Bibliographies

459. Armitage, Christopher M., comp. **Sir Walter Ralegh: An Annotated Bibliography.** Chapel Hill, N.C., for America's Four Hundredth Anniversary Committee by University of North Carolina Press, 1987. 236p. index. $14.95. LC 87-40134. ISBN 0-8078-1757-0.

Sir Walter Ralegh (*Ralegh* rather than *Raleigh*) was a multitalented person, gifted as a poet, writer, and historian. The present bibliography joins an impressive body of materials chronicling the life, works, and influence of this Renaissance man from 1576 through 1986. Earlier bibliographers, Wilberforce Eames and Thomas Brushfield, cataloged some Ralegh materials; Humphrey Tonkin and Jerry Leath Mills have a narrower time frame and a different focus. By comparison, this bibliography is much more extensive. Sponsored by America's Four Hundredth Anniversary Committee, the project was begun by the late Herbert R. Paschal, who had been a member of the committee, and was completed by Armitage.

Armitage has organized the more than nineteen hundred entries into broad sections for biography, geography, literary and artistic works, with an overall emphasis on the historical and colonizing aspects of Ralegh's career. Most entries are annotated, the terse comments pointing out a singular characteristic or particular relevance of a work. The two geographical sections contain many interesting items. For example, entry 512 recounts legends concerning Ralegh and tobacco; entry 1149 describes Ralegh's notions of the North American Indians.

Ralegh's place in literary history and criticism and his influence in literature, music, the visual arts, and books for children are documented in the appropriate sections. An index of authors and selected topics is appended. The sectional arrangement obviates the need for a more detailed subject index.

Meticulous attention to detail is evident throughout. Scholars will use the work in conjunction with Peter Beal's *Index of English Literary Manuscripts* (see *ARBA* 82, entry 1352), which catalogs Ralegh's manuscripts. [R: Choice, June 88, p. 1529]

Bernice Bergup

460. O'Brien, Philip M. **T. E. Lawrence: A Bibliography.** Boston, G. K. Hall, 1988. 724p. illus. index. $60.00. LC 87-11993. ISBN 0-8161-8945-5.

With this bibliography, the author has presented scholars with an astounding record of works by and about one of the most fascinating, complicated, and mysterious figures of this century. Known to most people as Lawrence of Arabia, T. E. Lawrence came from an obscure background as the illegitimate son of an Oxford scholar to become the military hero of the Middle Eastern campaign during World War I. Through his efforts, and his often overlooked warnings, the face of the postwar Middle Eastern scene was changed forever. But Lawrence was much more than a colorful and romantic figure as portrayed by Lowell Thomas and other reporters, he was a respected authority on the Crusades, military history, and archaeology, and a noted writer and translator of numerous historical and literary works. He remains the subject of considerable study more than fifty years after his death.

This bibliography is divided into two sections, the first focusing on Lawrence's own writings. It contains a chronological listing of books, pamphlets, essays, contributions to other works (introductions, prefaces, etc.), periodical and newspaper articles, and materials published posthumously after his sudden death in 1935. English and American editions are listed first, followed by all other language editions. A brief description of the origins of the work prefaces each grouping of editions. The second section chronologically lists works about Lawrence, including books which contain considerable references to him, as well as one of the most thorough listings of periodical and newspaper articles and foreign-language publications about Lawrence yet compiled. Only print materials are included in this bibliography; films, slides, and recordings have been omitted.

Within each section all entries contain a detailed descriptive cataloging statement, including descriptions of paper and binding, signature patterns, and notes on locations of extant copies. A detailed index is included.

Much effort has gone into this bibliography, and although the omission of nonprint works is regrettable, the compiler is the first to acknowledge that more still needs to be done. In its present form, however, scholars will find this bibliography one of the most thorough and accessible tools available for the study of a fascinating figure. [R: LAR, 14 Oct 88, p. 614]

Elizabeth Patterson

461. Palmegiano, E. M. **The British Empire in the Victorian Press, 1832-1867: A Bibliography.** New York, Garland, 1987. 234p. index. (Themes in European Expansion, Vol. 8: Garland Reference Library of Social Science, Vol. 389). $42.00. LC 86-29624. ISBN 0-8240-9802-1.

With some three thousand entries, this bibliography provides access to sources for the study of British imperial and colonial history drawn from fifty popular London-based magazines printed in the mid-Victorian years. These magazines constituted an important element of the contemporary press, which both strongly influenced and reflected the British public's interest and the conception of the "colorful fabric which was the British Empire at the height of its grandeur" (introduction). Since most of these journals are now relatively obscure, this reference work facilitates research into largely untapped sources. This bibliography consists of a listing of relevant articles for each magazine included with no annotations, except a few words when needed to clarify the subject matter of vague titles. Completing the book are two indexes: an author index and a subject index that has a few topical entries but consists mostly of names of colonies. These headings are not subdivided: the list of entries for India runs over three pages.

In addition to this core section which identifies articles on the British Empire found in periodicals with a wider coverage of topics, there is also a checklist, with full bibliographic information, of thirty-seven magazines, which published exclusively or extensively on imperial matters. An introduction provides an overview of the themes and ideas published in this literature. This title will be welcomed by researchers in the scholarly specialization covered who previously had only more general tools such as *Poole's Index* (P. Smith, 1963) and the *Wellesley Index to Victorian Periodicals* (University of Toronto, 1966-1979). [R: Choice, Sept 87, pp. 90, 92]   Henry E. York

462. **Royal Historical Society Annual Bibliography of British and Irish History: Publications of 1986.** D. M. Palliser, ed. Brighton, England, for the Royal Historical Society and with the Institute of Historical Research by Harvester Press; distr., New York, St. Martin's Press, 1987. 165p. index. $29.95. ISBN 0-312-01587-9.

The aim of this annual is to collect, as quickly as possible, books and journal articles on British history published during the preceding year. The editors admit that this "has meant subordinating absolutely total coverage and refinements of arrangement to speed of production" (p. ix). Although the majority of the items cited in this twelfth edition were published in 1986, some from as far back as 1984 are included. The work also contains citations from non-British sources. There are no annotations. Access is provided by an author index and by a detailed subject index, which covers all major subjects of the books and articles listed, whether or not they are named in the titles. There is also more general access through the thirteen broad, primarily chronological, divisions of the book, which are further divided by more specific subdivisions such as politics, external affairs, and religion. There has been no change in format since this work was last reviewed in *ARBA 84* (see entry 366). (See also *ARBA 77*, entry 404; *ARBA 79*, entry 431; and *ARBA 80*, entry 398). This continues to be an important reference source in any research library serving scholars of British history.   Christine E. King

Biographies

463. **Great Lives from History: British and Commonwealth Series.** Frank N. Magill, ed. Englewood Cliffs, N.J., Salem Press, 1987. 5v. index. $325.00/set. LC 87-26511. ISBN 0-89356-535-0.

Biographical reference works are heavily used and frequently browsed since questions about other people's lives perennially fascinate us. The British series of *Great Lives from History* should do its part to answer those questions in a satisfying way. It is the second part of a five-part set; the U.S. set has already appeared. The remaining sets will cover the rest of the world in (1) ancient and medieval times, (2) ca.1450-1900, and (3) the twentieth century. In the five British and Commonwealth volumes there are 483 biographical essays written by about 250 contributors. The time period cov-

ered by the essays is from A.D. 800 to the present and some of the subjects are still alive. Most are English but a significant number come from Scotland, Wales, Ireland, Canada, Australia, New Zealand, and South Africa. Although people involved in politics predominate, writers, artists, musicians, scientists, and athletes frequently appear in these volumes. Each essay consists of two thousand to three thousand words, organized in a set format. At the beginning of an essay there are notes providing the dates and places of birth and death, the area of achievement, and a brief statement of the individual's place in history. The main body of the text is divided into three parts: early life, life's work, and summary. An up-to-date annotated bibliography to guide further study concludes each essay.

Although the set claims to include every English monarch, William II Rufus was inexplicably left out. It is wonderful to find essays on popular writers like Agatha Christie and Sir Arthur Conan Doyle, but what about H. Rider Haggard and H. G. Wells? Most contributors have done a fine job on their essays; however, in a work employing over two hundred contributors, quality will vary. Volume 1 starts out on a high note with an excellent essay on Lord Acton. But just a bit down the alphabet, Lancelot Andrewes is quite ill-served in an essay that neglects any mention of his connections with English Arminianism. The annotated bibliography on Oliver Cromwell is up-to-date only if it is compared with the *Dictionary of National Biography*'s entry, written in the nineteenth century. Still, these are the exceptions. For quick, reliable, and readable information on Margaret Thatcher, Harold Laski, Sir Francis Drake, Geoffrey Chaucer, the Beatles, and many others, this set is a good place to go.

Should a library that already owns the *DNB* buy this set? Yes, the two sets are quite different. As a ready-reference work, *Great Lives from History* is less comprehensive, less detailed, and usually less scholarly. But it is more up-to-date in its sources, typographically easier on the eyes, has an easy to use standardized format, and includes a few people not found in the *DNB* or its supplements. The series is aimed at the general public and undergraduate readers and it will serve their needs in a workmanlike fashion. [R: RBB, 1 June 88, pp. 1657, 1658]   Ronald H. Fritze

Catalogs and Collections

464. **Subject Catalogue of the House of Commons Parliamentary Papers 1801-1900.** By Peter Cockton. Alexandria, Va., Chadwyck-Healey,

1988. 5v. index. $1,500.00/set. LC 87-5128. ISBN 0-85964-133-3.

Clearly, it is a monumental task to prepare this subject catalog for an entire century of the House of Commons parliamentary papers—a formidable undertaking. However, despite the complexity and scale of the project, the author has produced a series of volumes that should prove to be useful to scholars exploring the ways in which the House of Commons functioned in the nineteenth century. As indicated in the instructions that explain the use of the catalog, the contents are divided into nineteen well-defined chapters, and when subjects overlap between one chapter and another all the relevant paper titles are given in each chapter to avoid cross-referencing. Although this is reassuring, and generally well carried out, U.S. readers may be puzzled to note that the section "Wars" in the chapter "Defence and the Armed Services" makes no specific reference to the declaration of war with the United States in January 1813, nor to the Treaty of Peace and Amity that was reached at Ghent in December 1814. Some papers relative to these hostilities are appended to a section on the Napoleonic Wars, but we see no reference to these key documents until we explore the section regarding the United States of America in the chapters on foreign affairs and diplomacy. Perhaps this reflects the parliamentary view of what we think of as the War of 1812, but it also indicates that the author occasionally falls short of the high standards that he has set for this useful publication. [R: Choice, Nov 88, p. 456]   George T. Potter

Handbooks

465.   Havighurst, Alfred F. **Modern England 1901-1984.** 2d ed. New York, for North American Conference on British Studies by Cambridge University Press, 1987. 109p. index. (Conference on British Studies Bibliographical Handbooks). $39.50. LC 87-20927. ISBN 0-521-30974-3.

The Conference on British Studies Bibliographical Handbooks series has supplied scholars, teachers, students, and nonspecialists with useful guides that are introductory but reasonably comprehensive for many years now. Havighurst is the first author of one of the existing volumes to provide a second edition. This new volume extends coverage through 1984 (the first edition's coverage was through 1970). Much useful information on the Margaret Thatcher period has been included. The second edition contains 2,670 entries to reference books, monographs, and journal articles as compared to 2,502 entries in the first edition. Although most of the earlier entries have been retained, a large number have been replaced by listings of more recent works. A new category entitled "Labour History" has been added. Otherwise, the format and indexing are the same as the other volumes in this familiar series. Those owning the first edition will need to acquire this excellently updated bibliography along with those who do not own the first edition, but who are interested in twentieth-century British history.
                    Ronald H. Fritze

466.   Mitchell, B. R. **British Historical Statistics.** New York, Cambridge University Press, 1988. 886p. index. $135.00. LC 86-24513. ISBN 0-521-33008-4.

This volume replaces *Abstract of British Historical Statistics* (1962) and *Second Abstract of British Historical Statistics* (1971), compiled by Mitchell in collaboration with Phyllis Deane and Hywel Jones, respectively. Its principal aim continues to be the presentation of economic statistics (like those used by Deane and W. A. Cole in their classic study of economic growth), though more "social statistics" are now included. The data are mostly "raw," though some are unavailable except in "processed" form. The book is divided into sixteen chapters on population and vital statistics, labor, agriculture, fuel and energy, metals, textiles, building, miscellaneous industrial statistics, external trade, transport and communication, public finance, financial institutions, consumption, prices, miscellaneous statistics, and national accounts. Mitchell begins each chapter with a complete list of the tables included and an introduction discussing the sources of the statistics, their strengths and weaknesses, methods applied in interpreting them, the historiography associated with their subject matter, and the (by no means infrequent) controversies over their usefulness (e.g., E. A. Wrigley and R. S. Schofield and their critics on population history). This is particularly helpful since the increased size of the new volume and the tremendous growth of relevant literature have prevented the inclusion of bibliographies for each chapter. Not only does the present volume contain a great deal more material, the statistical series are in some cases much more accurate—for example, the numbers concerning national accounts are almost entirely different from those in the original volume. Mitchell is also careful to point out the limitations of his sources, whether the early compilations of Gregory King and Arthur Young or more recent information like that in the censuses. The tables are well laid out, documented, and indexed. This is an invaluable research tool.
                    William B. Robison

467. Outlines of English History: Dates, Facts, Events, People. rev. ed. George Carter, comp. London, Ward Lock; distr., North Pomfret, Vt., David & Charles, 1987. $9.95pa. ISBN 0-7063-6582-8pa.

This convenient handbook covers, in chronological order, key events in English history from the Roman invasion in 55 B.C. through 1986. A brief description of each event is included. The work also features genealogical tables for all of England's ruling dynasties, and some fifty pages of short biographical sketches. This is a revised, updated, and expanded version of a work which has been around since 1962, and the fact that it has gone through several previous revisions is suggestive in regard to its value. Students of English history, those who want a convenient, inexpensive reference work covering a broad range of events, and certainly public and academic libraries will find this book quite useful.   James A. Casada

CANADIAN HISTORY

468. Bercuson, David J., and J. L. Granatstein. **The Collins Dictionary of Canadian History: 1867 to the Present.** Don Mills, Ont., Collins, 1988. 270p. illus. maps. $24.95. ISBN 0-00-217758-7.

This new reference work on Canadian history since Confederation is an important addition to recent reference works on Canada including the *Canadian Encyclopedia*, 2d ed. (see entry 112), and the *Historical Atlas of Canada* (see *ARBA* 88, entry 529). It represents the combined talents of two of Canada's most prominent historians, David Bercuson, of the University of Calgary, and J. L. Granatstein, of York University. Bercuson has written extensively on labor history while Granatstein has published on topics ranging from conscription to foreign policy. The present volume includes some 1,600 alphabetized entries on topics ranging from politics to agriculture. There are numerous cross references, some black-and-white illustrations, a helpful timeline, and numerous appendices listing governors general, prime ministers, provincial premiers, election results, immigration statistics, etc. The entries are short and in some cases critical. Pierre Trudeau warrants one and one-fourth pages and no picture, while René Lévesque gets one-half page and likewise no picture. There are entries for such widely diverse topics as the Group of Seven (artists), *Saturday Night* (literary magazine) and the Munsinger Affair (political scandal). Politics and labor are extensively covered while coverage of the arts and sports is a bit eclectic. For example, there is an entry for Jean Beliveau, former Montreal Canadien, but none for Wayne Gretzky. Singers Paul Anka, Neil Young, and Anne Murray are included, but Gordon Lightfoot and Joni Mitchell are not. Despite these shortcomings, this new volume should prove helpful for students of Canadian history and culture.   Brian E. Coutts

EUROPEAN HISTORY

469. Cook, Chris, and John Stevenson. **The Longman Handbook of Modern European History 1763-1985.** White Plains, N.Y., Longman, 1987. 435p. maps. bibliog. index. (Longman Handbooks to History). $36.95; $19.95pa. LC 86-18618. ISBN 0-582-48585-1; 0-582-48584-3pa.

This work covers political, diplomatic, social, and economic history, mainly for France, Germany, Austria-Hungary, Italy, and Spain. (Great Britain is covered in the authors' *The Longman Handbook of Modern British History, 1714-1980*, 1983). The book is divided into eight sections, which are mostly arranged chronologically. The sections contain a list of principal rulers and ministers; a rundown of twenty-seven major events relating to one country (e.g., Spain 1909-1939) or to several countires (e.g., Europe and the French Revolution); a brief description of principal wars, campaigns, and treaties; statistical information (e.g., population figures, output of coal); 180 brief biographies, arranged alphabetically; an alphabetical glossary of terms; a "topic bibliography" (brief description of thirty-five topics, with a brief bibliography and a few suggested essay topics for each); and eleven gray-and-white historical maps. There is also a detailed index.

Some of the facts and dates disagree with those in other sources. Also there are some inconsistencies, such as in the first section, where for some of the countries there are no presidents or prime ministers listed, and for some, no explanation of the country's status before 1910. Some people (e.g., Dubcek, William I of Prussia), and some terms (e.g., anarchist, Paris Commune) should have been included in the biography and the glossary. Because of its wide coverage, the book may be used as an introduction or as a quick reference to a subject; however, other, more detailed works should prove more useful. [R: RBB, 1 Feb 88, p. 916]   Kathleen Farago

470. Magocsi, Paul Robert. **Carpatho-Rusyn Studies: An Annotated Bibliography. Volume 1: 1975-1984.** New York, Garland, 1988. 143p. maps. index. (Garland Reference Library of the

Humanities, Vol. 824). $28.00. LC 87-29288. ISBN 0-8240-1214-3.

In his introduction, Magocsi indicates that the marked growth in Carpatho-Rusyn studies during the 1970s is a result of two unrelated phenomena: (1) the consistent and longtime support of scholarly research by the Soviet regime, and (2) a new initiative on the part of individual scholars in the United States to study the Carpatho-Rusyn problem. The author has collected 649 publications (articles and books published in several languages) and arranged them by year of publication. Entries show full bibliographic citations and are accompanied by brief descriptive annotations. Magocsi is the author of several publications dealing with the so-called Carpatho-Rusyn question in the United States, but we still do not quite comprehend the scope and purpose of this technically well-prepared bibliography. Thus, for example, while speaking of the "homeland" (e.g., Carpathian Region in the Ukrainian RSR), no longer does anyone refer to the "Carpatho-Rusyns"; rather, scholarly literature is written in Ukrainian (or Russian) and considers this region a part of Ukraine. Thus, entry 171, *The Wooden Architecture of Ukrainian Carpathians*, written by Ivan Hvozda, has very little to do with the Carpatho-Rusyn problem, as is the case with several other entries (172-176, etc.). It is apparent that the book is mistitled, especially when one thinks about the Carpathian oblast of the Ukrainian Republic.   Bohdan S. Wynar

471. Paxton, John. **Companion to the French Revolution.** New York, Facts on File, 1988. 231p. maps. bibliog. $24.95. LC 84-21489. ISBN 0-8160-1116-8.

This dictionary covers persons, events, and terms associated with the French Revolution. Its emphasis is on the period 1769-1804 but some topics go back further in time. Entries are generally two or three sentences long, but some (e.g., *American Revolutionary War, Revolutionary Calendar, Danton, Battles, Wars*) are a page or more in length. Political terms, newspapers, songs, slogans, doctrines, customs, and a great many battles are discussed. Entries may either be in French or in English translations of the French. (One subject is treated twice, once as *Bed of Justice* and once as *Lit de Justice*). There are few cross-references from one language to the other, but French terms are translated in the text. The *Companion* concludes with a chronology, a select bibliography, and maps of revolutionary France and Paris.

Libraries owning Boursin's *Dictionnaire de la Révolution française* (Paris, 1893; still available from Kraus Reprint) and whose readers are not dismayed by French will not need Paxton's *Companion*. Boursin covers more topics more extensively. For English-language users, the *Historical Dictionary of the French Revolution, 1789-1799* (see *ARBA* 86, entry 494) is at the same time more comprehensive and detailed than Paxton. But for libraries who have neither Boursin, the *Historical Dictionary*, or the budget for either, Paxton (at one-quarter the price of the other titles) is a good choice. Its information is adequate for identification and quick reference and its range of topics appropriate. [R: BR, Sept/Oct 88, p. 52; LJ, Jan 88, p. 80; RBB, 15 Apr 88, p. 1404]

Eric R. Nitschke

472. Sable, Martin H. **Holocaust Studies: A Directory and Bibliography of Bibliographies.** Greenwood, Fla., Penkevill, 1987. 115p. index. $20.00. ISBN 0-913283-20-7.

Much more than just a bibliography, this slim volume is an important resource for tracing information about the Holocaust. It is divided into two distinct sections. The first is a listing of all published bibliographies on the Holocaust up to 1986. Unfortunately a substantial work published in 1986, *Bibliography on Holocaust Literature* (see *ARBA* 87, entry 522), by Abraham Edelheit and Hershel Edelheit is not included.

The second half of the work is the "Holocaust Studies Directory," which is a unique source. It is arranged into three sections. The first covers associations, community councils and federations, foundations, charitable and social service agencies, government agencies, and survivor organizations. The second section includes archives, libraries, publishers, information and research centers, and school and university teaching programs. Section 3 covers events, historical and Holocaust museums and memorial buildings, memorial parks, streets, gardens and sites, monuments, statues, sculptures, obelisks, gravestones, tombs, tablets, markers, and plaques.

The scope of the directory is worldwide, but the author does not claim it is complete. The primary arrangement within each section is by country then alphabetically by entity, except for the United States where the arrangement is by state. Within the countries where the Holocaust occurred only museums and monuments in major cities and the biggest concentration camps are identified, with the exception of Romania, where the coverage is almost complete. No explanation is given for this inconsistency in coverage. There is a useful geographic subject index.

This book would be of use to professional researchers, families of Holocaust victims, and anyone else interested in tracing primary sources and information about this ignominious episode in world history. It is also useful as a guide for those wishing to visit memorials and museums. The author intends to update this work periodically. [R: Choice, May 88, p. 1386]

Christine E. King

GERMAN HISTORY

473. Freeman, Michael. **Atlas of Nazi Germany.** New York, Macmillan, 1987. 205p. illus. maps. bibliog. index. $55.00. LC 87-12261. ISBN 0-02-910681-8.

This atlas provides a useful graphic presentation of the development, structure, and dynamics of the Third Reich. The work is divided into six sections: "The Rise of the Nazi Party," "Administrative and Political Structure," "Society," "Population and Economy," "The Search for Living Space" (which includes territorial annexation, conquests, and the movements of armies during World War II), and "The War Machine" (which discusses wartime administration of the Army and SS, military logistics, and the concentration camps and Holocaust). Over 130 pages of maps, charts, graphs, and photographs are included in the volume. The graphic representations of the Hitler era are accompanied by a narrative, explanatory text. The atlas also includes a list of abbreviations, a glossary, a bibliographic guide of general works on the Third Reich, and an index. The list of references consulted in the compilation of the work includes both general surveys of the period and published and unpublished primary sources.

This volume is an excellent reference source for the general reader, high school student, or university undergraduate. It successfully helps to clarify this confusing and often contradictory era in German history. [R: Choice, Apr 88, p. 1222; WLB, Feb 88, pp. 96-97]

William G. Ratliff

LATIN AMERICAN HISTORY

474. Weeks, John M. **Maya Ethnohistory: A Guide to Spanish Colonial Documents at Tozzer Library, Harvard University.** Nashville, Tenn., Vanderbilt University Publications in Anthropology, 1987. 121p. index. (Vanderbilt University Publications in Anthropology, No. 34). $8.75pa. ISBN 0-935462-25-2.

This typescript guide to Spanish documents relating to the Maya (1520-1800) contains 526 entries representing some twenty-four thousand frames of microfilm and leaves of typed transcripts and photocopies. The first eighty-four entries are of materials from the Archive of the Indies in Seville, Spain, and cover the bulk of the material, some 21,216 frames and leaves. The following 439 entries are for 2,488 leaves and frames from the Archivo General de la Nación in Mexico City. These are followed by one entry from the Archivo Notarial in Merida, Mexico (52 leaves), and two from the Biblioteca Nacional in Madrid, Spain (218 leaves). Each entry indicates the archival section, a title, certain descriptive and critical information, and the Tozzer Library identification number for the items in the entry. Proper names have been modernized and place names standardized using Peter Gerhard's *A Guide to the Historical Geography of New Spain* (Cambridge University Press, 1972). Indexes of entries are by decades, by personal names, by place names, and by subjects. A brief bibliography concludes the work.

Collected mostly during the 1930s as part of the Carnegie Institution's History of Yucatan Project, the materials described in this catalog are strongest for the periods 1570-1579 and 1640-1720. Various sorts of judicial inquiries are especially well represented, a plus since those records often contain the detail from which ethnohistorians can reconstruct a variety of life ways.

Recommended for libraries with specialized Latin American or Mexican history collections.

Paul E. Hoffman

NEW ZEALAND HISTORY

475. **Bateman New Zealand Encyclopedia.** 2d ed. Gordon McLauchlan, ed. Auckland, New Zealand, David Bateman; distr., Boston, G. K. Hall, 1987. 640p. illus. (part col.). maps. index. $49.00. ISBN 0-908610-21-1.

As a reference volume, this encyclopedia is intended for a wide range of readers in age and background. The topics range across a standard array: geography, explorers, arts (writers, musicians, artists), agriculture, sports, natural history, with particular strength in individuals (of all sorts—explorers, artists, politicians, sports figures, particularly in rugby, religious leaders), Maori culture (individuals, names, places, history), flora, fauna, and whaling, but with less extensive coverage of business and commerce, history (as connected with Europe), demographics, and politics. General or popular knowledge for an interested general reader, from fifth grade up, is stressed, so this encyclopedia, while accurate and authoritative, does not provide the detail or world coverage one expects in *Encyclopaedia Britannica* or *The Encyclopedia Americana.*

The coverage in this second edition goes through mid-1987, including Prime Minister Lange's reelection, which is mentioned in the eighteen-page historical chronology (from A.D. 925) but not in his personal entry. A subject index (twelve pages) covers only the headings of the approximately nineteen hundred entries but not topics or people who merit mention but no individual entry. Colored maps cover climate, vegetation, forest, minerals, land use, soils, and New Zealand's Antarctic claim. A foldout map shows topography, cities, and major roads. Forty-eight pages of colored plates depict stamps, flags, coats of arms, war ribbons, Maori artifacts, geothermal, geologic, glacial, and river features, sheep, industries, art, insects, birds, flowers, fruits, and butterflies.

This volume is a delight to browse through. The text is extremely readable, a popular as distinguished from a technical approach to New Zealand. With a wealth of information, this extremely useful single-volume work for libraries and individuals serves as a quick reference on New Zealand. [R: RBB, 1 Dec 88, pp. 628, 630]

Richard A. Miller

RUSSIAN HISTORY

476. **The Blackwell Encyclopedia of the Russian Revolution.** Harold Shukman, ed. New York, Basil Blackwell, 1988. 418p. illus. index. $65.00. LC 88-10360. ISBN 0-631-15238-5.

The purpose of this encyclopedic work is to describe and analyze the revolutionary events in the Russian empire in order to show how they affected the political, social, economic, and ethnic history of the old empire. Over fifty contributors, primarily from England, contributed a variety of unsigned articles. Most longer articles, such as "The Ukrainian Revolution and the Civil War," contain brief bibliographies, but unfortunately the authors are occasionally unfamiliar with a specific language (see nine citations under "Further Reading," p. 225; one in Ukrainian, with a number of errors). Beginning on page 297, brief biographies of prominent personalities are provided, including one paragraph on Petliura, a prominent Ukrainian leader, and two pages on Plekhanov, a well-known leader of Russian communism.

We are not familiar with Harold Shukman, the editor of this volume, and a brief introduction written by him unfortunately tells us very little about the scope of this work, the authority, or the sources used. For example, there are many encyclopedic works covering the Civil War and the October Revolution written in several languages in the Soviet Union, plus encyclopedias and dictionaries published in other Eastern European countries, such as Poland and Czechoslovakia. None of these works is mentioned here, nor is there any mention of the rather impressive American output on all aspects of the Civil War and the Revolution.

All in all, this is a handy volume for the uninitiated, but will be of marginal assistance to scholars and advanced students of Soviet affairs.[R: RBB, 1 Nov 88, p. 460]

Bohdan S. Wynar

THIRD WORLD HISTORY

477. Gorman, G. E., and J. J. Mills. **Guide to Current National Bibliographies in the Third World.** 2d ed. Munich, New York, Hans Zell/ K. G. Saur, 1987. 372p. index. $75.00. ISBN 0-905450-34-5.

This is a second considerably revised edition of a work which first appeared five years ago. The updating indicates both the work's original popularity and the rapidly changing nature of bibliographical information in Third World countries. Unlike many works in the area, this is not a numerical listing of existing Third World bibliographies perhaps accompanied by brief annotations. Instead, the authors have chosen, and wisely in this reviewer's opinion, to offer what is essentially a narrative coverage arranged by geographical region. For each geographical region the basic national bibliography is cited with accompanying information on where it is published, frequency of appearance, subscription costs, and the like. While this information will prove vital to acquisitions librarians, the guide's value grows with its offering of history, scope and contents, and analysis of each national bibliography. While much remains to be done in this burgeoning field, this is a work that libraries supporting studies of Third World subjects cannot overlook.

James A. Casada

WORLD HISTORY

Atlases

478. Boyd, Andrew. **An Atlas of World Affairs.** 8th ed. New York, Methuen, 1987. 216p. maps. index. $39.95; $12.95pa. LC 87-675084. ISBN 0-416-01172-1; 0-416-01182-9pa.

This concise handbook focuses on national and international events and organizations appearing in current news reports since 1945. The individual chapters, rarely more than two pages in length, focus on such diversified topics as *nuclear geography, three worlds?*, *minorities and micro-states*, and the *long arm of war*, as well as on specific geographic regions and countries. The maps are small, often filling less than one page, and done only in black-and-white, but they are very clear, and the author has avoided overcrowding them with extra information. The purpose of the volume is to supply basic, current, factual information about the various regions of the world, as well as locating places in the news for the nonspecialist inquirer.

As a basic current affairs tool, the atlas does the job it attempts, although the user might welcome the addition of some suggested readings for further background information.

Margaret Anderson

479. **The Harper Atlas of World History.** Pierre Vidal-Naquet, ed. New York, Harper & Row, 1987. 340p. illus. (part col.). maps. index. $29.95. LC 87-675015. ISBN 0-06-181884-4.

Historical atlases have changed dramatically over the years. They have grown sleeker, more inclusive, glossier, and, in the case of world history atlases, clearly less ethnocentric. All of these trends are apparent in the atlas under review. It represents a good, medium-sized alternative in a publishing area which stretches from the student atlas to *The Times Atlas of World History* (see *ARBA* 85, entry 477).

Like its competitors, *The Harper Atlas* has basic qualities and features which separate it from the pack. Certainly it is the most colorful of the lot; almost every page is ablaze with maps, photographs, and charts which when combined with explanatory prose, chronologies, etc., create an overly busy, hyperactive effect. This "all but the kitchen sink" approach requires that the maps be somewhat smaller and more confined than one would normally expect.

Undeniably, *The Harper Atlas* serves up a lot of information for the money. One glaring weakness, however, is the lack of a table of contents. The index, though comprehensive, does not highlight references to maps. The user has no idea, for example, which of the seventy-five references to China will produce an actual map.

The introductory "History of Cartography" is most informative, yet will do little to soften the disappointment of those seeking large, easily accessible maps. On the other hand, individuals in search of striking graphics and a volume that frequently approximates a lavishly illustrated world history text will be very pleased, indeed. [R: Choice, Mar 88, p. 1066; LJ, 1 Feb 88, p. 60; RBB, 15 Feb 88, p. 984]

Mark R. Yerburgh

480. **Rand McNally Atlas of World History.** rev. ed. Skokie, Ill., Rand McNally, 1987. 191p. maps. (col.). index. $17.95pa. LC 81-51409. ISBN 0-528-83288-3.

The editor states in his introduction that "the first aim of an historical atlas is to show, through the combined use of maps and text, the development of human society in its physical setting" (p. 10). The combination provided here covers the record of this development from the earliest Ice Age to 1986.

The maps are clear; each deals with a specific historical period or happening (e.g., the Reformation and counter-Reformation in Europe; the rise of Muscovy; the Golden Age of Islam), and each has sufficient pertinent detail to make it very informative. They are also sufficiently large. The smallest maps are allotted one-half of a page, the largest are printed as a double-page spread.

The accompanying texts, although unsigned, are equally informative and written with no perceivable historical bias. The reader wanting more information is directed to additional English-language sources listed as further reading.

A valuable, useful addition to both personal and library reference collections. [R: RBB, 15 June 88, pp. 1722, 1724]

Margaret Anderson

Bibliographies

481. Richardson, R. C., comp. **The Study of History: A Bibliographical Guide.** Manchester, England, Manchester University Press; distr., New York, St. Martin's Press, 1988. 98p. index. $55.00. ISBN 0-7190-1881-1.

This slim volume, compiled by R. C. Richardson, Head of History and Archaeology at King Alfred's College, Winchester, England, is a select bibliography of twentieth-century historiography sources, including books as well as journal articles. The work is the first of a new series published by Manchester University Press, History and Related Disciplines, Select Bibliographies, of which Richardson is also the general editor. This volume covers mainly English-language material and does not include material from historians writing prior to the twentieth century.

Like all future volumes in the series, Richardson's work is arranged with an initial chapter of general works on historiography and the historiography of particular regions and countries followed by the historiography of periods from ancient to twentieth-century history. Within these chronological chapters the briefly annotated entries are divided geographically, covering primarily Great Britain, the United States, and Europe. The only exception is the final chapter, "Twentieth Century," where the entries are arranged by the historiography of particular schools and types of history, for example, the "Annales School" and "Women's History."

The broad title of this work is a bit misleading because it is very selective in its coverage. A much more comprehensive recent source is the two-volume work, *Historiography: An Annotated Bibliography of Journal Articles, Books, and Dissertations* (see *ARBA* 88, entry 545), which contains over eight thousand entries and a great deal of foreign language material. Richardson's work would be a good place for an undergraduate student or a person with an interest in recent historiography to start, but the two-volume *Historiography* would be a much better place for history graduate students and researchers to begin. The Richardson volume would be more useful in small colleges or public libraries, not needing or unable to afford the *Historiography* volumes. Eight additional volumes are projected in this series, but this reviewer does not feel they will provide the depth of coverage of the *Historiography* volumes for their projected cost. [R: Choice, Oct 88, pp. 295-96]

Louis Vyhnanek

Biographies

482.   **Great Lives from History: Ancient and Medieval Series.** Frank N. Magill, ed. Englewood Cliffs, N.J., Salem Press, 1988. 5v. index. $325.00/set. LC 88-18514. ISBN 0-89356-545-8.

The latest addition to the Magill stable of summaries, this is the third of a projected five-set series. Sets already published are the *American Series* (see *ARBA* 88, entry 513) and the *British and Commonwealth Series* (see entry 482). This *Ancient and Medieval Series* covers non-British persons from antiquity through the Middle Ages (midfifteenth century). There are 455 articles of two thousand to three thousand words in length, in the characteristic Magill format. A brief factual summary is at the beginning, including dates of birth and death, the subject's areas of achievement, and major contributions to history. The main portion of each entry is divided into three parts: early life, life's work, and a summary, which is "an overview of the individual's place in history" (p. v). Finally, an annotated list of references for further study is included. Each entry is signed and written "by an academician who specializes in the area of discussion" (p. v). The biographies are clear and

readable, suitable for undergraduates or general readers.   Nancy Courtney

Catalogs and Collections

483.   Shailor, Barbara A. **Catalogue of Medieval and Renaissance Manuscripts in the Beinecke Rare Book and Manuscript Library Yale University. Volume II: MSS 251-500.** Binghamton, N.Y., Medieval & Renaissance Texts & Studies, State University of New York, 1987. 578p. illus. index. (Medieval & Renaissance Texts & Studies, Vol. 48). $36.00. LC 84-667. ISBN 0-86698-030-X.

This is the second volume of a projected three-volume work. The first volume was published in 1984 and described MSS 1-250. Interested purchasers should refer to the review of volume 1 (see *ARBA* 86, entry 503) for details on the catalog's coverage. There is little to be added to the earlier review, except to emphasize that this work is expertly researched and written, beautifully produced, and priced so that even an individual could conceivably afford to own it.

The manuscripts in volume 2 range in date from a thirteenth-century Greek *Euchologium* to a midnineteenth-century collection of miniatures removed from another manuscript (also in the Beinecke) and rebound in red velvet. Sixty-two plates illustrating calligraphy, illuminations, and bindings complete the work. Descriptions of individual manuscripts are very detailed and knowledgeable.

This series is unquestionably one of the finest manuscript catalogs ever produced. Scholars will look forward eagerly to the final volume.   Philip R. Rider

Dictionaries

484.   **Dictionary of the Middle Ages. Volume 10: Polemics-Scandinavia.** Joseph R. Strayer, ed. New York, Scribner's, 1988. 708p. illus. maps. $75.00. LC 82-5904. ISBN 0-684-18276-9.

485.   **Dictionary of the Middle Ages. Volume 11: Scandinavian Languages-Textiles, Islamic.** Joseph R. Strayer, ed. New York, Scribner's, 1988. 719p. illus. maps. $75.00. LC 82-5904. ISBN 0-684-18277-7.

486.   **Dictionary of the Middle Ages. Volume 12: Thaddeus Legend-Zwart^{c}noc^c.** Joseph R. Strayer, ed. New York, Scribner's, 1989. 750p. illus. maps. $80.00. LC 82-5904. ISBN 0-684-18278-5.

With the appearance of these three volumes, the *Dictionary of the Middle Ages* is now complete. All that remains is the comprehensive index, slated for publication in 1989.

The dictionary represents an enormous collaborative effort bringing together some of the ablest scholars, whose work encompasses a broad geographic area within the medieval timeframe. Like their predecessors these volumes contain brief definitions as well as lengthy articles on art, architecture, language and literature, music, economics, geography, history, politics, religion, and philosophy. Updated bibliographies, especially for the lengthier articles, are critical and evaluative.

Because the consonant "q" is considerably more common in Arabic than in English, volume 10 is particularly rich with references to Islam. The entry *qirmiz* for "crimson dye" is traced to its Armenian origins. In volume 11, the entry on *shoes and shoemakers* suggests that "the pointed shapes for both architecture and footwear appear to have originated with the Seljuks, and the styles spread to Europe via travelers and crusaders." The discussion of *wine and winemaking* in the Middle Ages traces its Greek and Roman origins, and much later its connection with medicinal experimentation in the Islamic world. Of such is the dictionary's expansive historical range.

The volumes contain numerous instances of broad geographic coverage as well. The entries on *Viking navigation* and *Vikings* in volume 12 detail the sweep of these "adventurers" from Scandinavia to the British Isles, Ireland, Greenland, the North American continent, present-day France, the Iberian Peninsula, Italy, North Africa, and Russia. Or, to take another example, consider the three topical articles (totaling sixteen pages) on roads: *roads and bridges, European; roads and communications, Byzantine;* and *roads in the Islamic World.* The variations in phraseology accommodate the historical development of the respective areas. Among the Europeans bridge building combined both practical matters and the spiritual aspect of the bridge as a "pious work." In the Islamic world, however, roads were significantly influenced by the use of camels rather than oxen for transport. These articles illustrate well the diverse character of collective scholarship. The Europeanist discusses not only the geographic and historical aspects, as does the Byzantinist, but also, at greater length, the social and religious ramifications. Likewise, the articles on *ships and shipbuilding* in volume 11 are divided regionally into Mediterranean, Northern European, and the

Red Sea and Persian Gulf, with corresponding shifts of emphasis.

Perhaps the dictionary's chief merit lies not only in its comprehensiveness but in its ready accessibility to the student seeking a summary treatment of the *War of the Roses*, as well as to the scholar pursuing more specialized research. Even brief entries like *rose window* and *vizier* usually cite additional sources as well as related articles. Indeed, the system of cross-references reinforces the interdisciplinary character of the dictionary, and weaves together the many strands of medieval scholarship.

In such an undertaking the whole does become larger than the sum of its parts. Uneven coverage is perhaps one hazard of such a collaboration. The article on Western European weights and measures is more than ten times the length of the Byzantine entry. Similarly, twelve pages are allotted to *vehicles, European* but only slightly more than one page to *vehicles, Islamic*. The more significant feature is that the dictionary's geographic range extends well beyond Western Europe and the Near East, to the Scandinavian and Eastern European countries, and to Russia.

The format of the twelve-volume work is attractive, using several typefaces to distinguish the article from its bibliography and cross-references. Each volume is illustrated with a judicious selection of black-and-white photographs, maps, and line drawings. And a single handsomely colored plate appears opposite the title page of each volume. The paper used conforms to standards for permanence and durability.

The dictionary is a major work, indispensable to research libraries and other academic institutions. Most public libraries except for the smallest should consider it for purchase. [R: SLJ, May 88, pp. 35-36]

Bernice Bergup

Directories

487. International Directory of Medievalists. Répertoire International des Médiévistes. 6th ed. Compiled by Institut de Recherche et d'Histoire des Textes. Munich, New York, K. G. Saur, 1987. 2v. index. $150.00/set. ISBN 3-598-10683-1.

The medieval period is so grossly misunderstood by our own time that one wonders that any layperson can know anything more than the usual banality of "The Dark Ages." Any work that sheds light on an age that brought us Gower, Chaucer, and Dante deserves recognition.

Now in its sixth edition, the directory brings together all these birds of a feather who call themselves *medievalists*. The text includes nearly five thousand entries in over twenty-five languages and contains citations to the research of medievalists covering the period from late antiquity through the Renaissance. The new subject index is a most helpful addition, allowing users of the directory to group together, even further, those of similar precious faith.

Each name in the text is followed by title and function, professional address, home address, telephone numbers, research area, and bibliography. The bibliographical citations include works published in print and in preparation. The subject index is arranged under broad headings such as "National Histories," "Philosophy," "Sigillography" (the study of seals or signets), "Iconography," and "Prosopography" (character studies).

Medievalists range the world over, as this volume shows, with entries from Argentina, Denmark, Luxembourg, the USSR, the United States, and many more. The material gleaned from the text came from ten thousand questionnaires mailed to known medievalists.

Such a work is a welcome addition to the area of medieval studies. One hopes that the future will witness continued updated editions of this significant work.

Mark Y. Herring

Handbooks

488. Grant, Michael, and Rachel Kitzinger, eds. **Civilization of the Ancient Mediterranean: Greece and Rome.** New York, Scribner's, 1988. 3v. illus. maps. index. $225.00/set. LC 87-23465. ISBN 0-684-17594-0.

This work fits into what is becoming almost an identifiable genre: the two- to four-volume encyclopedic work, covering a subject area of intermediate scope, featuring long articles or essays (no definitions or brief entries), aimed at a wide range of users, and perhaps, as in this case, arranged not alphabetically but in some systematic topical fashion. Previous examples of the type include the *Encyclopedia of American Economic History* (see *ARBA* 81, entry 857) and the *Encyclopedia of the American Religious Experience* (see *ARBA* 88, entry 1394). One difference here is that the word *encyclopedia* does not appear in the title. Will that perhaps occasion some reflection on whether a work such as this must necessarily go in the reference collection? What distinguishes a "reference work" from any other collection of essays that attempts to provide a comprehensive survey of its subject?

Comprehensiveness, in any case, is one important aim of this set: a comprehensiveness that is considerably broader than traditional emphases in the study of "classics." The full scope of its treatment of "the public and private lives and achievements" of the Greeks and Romans is difficult to convey, short of reproducing the entire table of contents, but this sampling of topics is suggestive: farming and animal husbandry; transportation; alphabets and writing; slavery; insurance and banking; piracy; ruler worship; Roman associations, dinner parties, and clubs; Greek/Roman attitudes toward sex; birth control, childbirth, and early childhood; women in Greece/Rome; and urban planning. All this in addition to the traditional material of classical studies: philosophy, religion and mythology, the major literary forms, political theory and practice, the visual arts, and of course, wars and military exploits. There are ninety-seven essays arranged under fourteen broad headings such as "Population," "Technology," "Government and Society," "Religion," "Private and Social Life," etc. The opening section, "History," with two historical summaries, one for Greece and one for Rome, establishes a chronological framework for the more thematic approaches of the other essays. A "Chronological Table" in the front of volume 1 is also helpful to that end.

Eighty-eight contributors are listed in volume 3. All appear eminently qualified. About one-third (including editor Grant) are British — testimony, perhaps, to the rich heritage of classical studies in British education and scholarship. No attempt has been made to eliminate differences of opinion among the contributors, or even to standardize their use of varient forms or spellings of ancient names. Potential problems created by the latter are handled fairly well by cross-references in the index (e.g., *Corcyra/Kerkyra*).

The index, in volume 3, is thorough, though not exhaustive (not all mentions of place names are indexed). Commendably, each index page has a note indicating the page breaks among the three continuously paged volumes.

One regret to be registered about this fine work is that it has rather few illustrations and none in color. Illustrations (some 175, according to the introduction) are confined almost entirely to articles on crafts, technique, and the visual arts. Among the best are the line drawings and diagrams in volume 1 illustrating ancient engineering achievements. Eleven maps are provided near the end of volume 3. [R: LJ, 1 May 88, p. 71; WLB, May 88, p. 108]

Hans E. Bynagle

10 Law

GENERAL WORKS

Bibliographies

489. **Bowker's Law Books & Serials in Print 1988: A Multimedia Sourcebook.** New York, R. R. Bowker, 1988. 3v. $425.00/set. ISBN 0-8352-2413-9; ISSN 0000-0752.

Bowker's Law Books is an attempt to do what sounds and possibly is impossible: publish a comprehensive list of all titles of law books available in the United States. Others have tried. The virtue of such attempts at compiling a comprehensive list of law books in print is in the numbers of titles that do make it into the list. In this case, with nearly twelve thousand titles listed, the result is a very useful resource.

The challenge of producing the book and making it a useful resource for working librarians is in the nature of legal literature in general. Because of the rapidly changing nature of law, legal writers have been hard pressed to publish a book that did not need substantial revision or updating by the time it made it onto library shelves. For the most part, too, the more useful the book is when published, the more quickly it will go out-of-date. Any comprehensive list of law books will decidely face similar problems. By the time it is published, editions and supplements will have been further revised. This is indeed the case with the present volumes.

But putting aside such limitations, *Bowker Law Books & Serials in Print* is a success. The format is very easy to use and it is well indexed. Subject headings are very logical and the *see* and *see also* references are complete.

A very welcome feature in this set is the annotations. These are provided in a remarkable proportion of entries. They include content notes and remarks about how an item is published. The information provided for each item is complete and well placed. Editing of the work as a whole appears to be of a very high calibur; no glaring errors were discovered.

Overall, *Bowker's Law Books & Serials in Print 1988* is an excellent resource that should be found in any active law library. [R: LJ, 15 Oct 88, pp. 82-83]

Richard A. Leiter

490. **Encyclopedia of Legal Information Sources: A Bibliographic Guide to Approximately 19,000 Citations for Publications, Organizations, and Other Sources of Information on 460 Law-Related Subjects....** Paul Wasserman, Gary McCann, and Patricia Tobin, eds. Detroit, Gale, 1988. 634p. $140.00. LC 87-25901. ISBN 0-8103-0245-4.

The intended audience for this book includes law professionals as well as laypersons needing legal information, so the result is a curious mixture of highly specialized law books (restatements, citators) and simple texts and dictionaries.

In traditional encyclopedic style, editors have arranged this source book alphabetically by its 460 topics; however, the introduction suggests that researchers use the "Outline of Contents" to locate topics quickly. Headings were selected for "timeliness" and "importance" in the field of law. They range from the very specific (railroads) to the very general (foreign law).

Under each heading the citations may be grouped by as many as nineteen different kinds of sources—statutes, restatements, handbooks, annuals, associations, audiovisuals, etc. Except for a few classic titles, the editors excluded material published before 1980. Future editions and "interedition" supplements are planned.

The format is the clear, two-column style found in other Gale reference books. Listings include full addresses for publishers. There are no annotations except for very brief ones in the legal research section. There is no index.

This encyclopedia provides no definitions or discussion of terms and topics. It directs users to other resources. As such it occupies a niche not filled by any other legal reference tool. [R: Choice, Oct 88, pp. 288-90; LJ, 1 Sept 88, p. 162; RBB, 1 Nov 88, p. 462]

Berniece M. Owen

491. Kapp, Marshall B., comp. **Legal Aspects of Health Care for the Elderly: An Annotated Bibliography.** Westport, Conn., Greenwood Press, 1988. 166p. index. (Bibliographies and Indexes in Gerontology, No. 7). $39.95. LC 88-15428. ISBN 0-313-26159-8.

This volume contains a selective listing and annotation of sources at the intersection of two rather disparate fields, health law and geriatric medicine. The bibliography is organized into thirteen sections: general sources, informed consent and mental competency issues, financing and the law, disability determinations, abuse and neglect, involuntary commitment and protective services, provider regulations and standards of care, decisions regarding the critically ill and the suicidal, resuscitation, disability planning, death and organ donations, research on older human subjects, and legal and advocacy services. Author and subject indexes are provided. Coverage is extensive rather than exhaustive. The annotations are clear, concise, and informative. Unfortunately, entries are listed only once even when they cut across the somewhat arbitrary divisions established by the author. The subject index is rudimentary at best. A valuable resource despite its shortcomings.   Bruce Stuart

492. Kavass, Igor I. **Soviet Law in English: Research Guide and Bibliography 1970-1987.** Buffalo, N.Y., William S. Hein, 1988. 653p. $48.50. LC 87-83674. ISBN 0-89941-631-4.

This book attests to the fact that there is much written in English on the subject of Soviet law. The bibliography lists more than sixteen hundred titles. However, even given the amount of material, there is a dearth of material on the subject of *doing research on* Soviet law. This lack of research materials has come to an abrupt end. *Soviet Law in English* provides the researcher with a useful tool for identifying the English sources on any topic in Soviet law.

The book is broken down into five different sections. Part 1 is a forty-page essay on researching Soviet law. In this section one is introduced to the hazards of doing research on Soviet law and, at the same time, is given a tremendously helpful description of just what it means to be doing research, in English, on Soviet law.

The second part of the book, "Soviet Law: Subject Checklist," is useful because it not only introduces the reader to the subject headings used in the book, but also provides a topical overview of Soviet law. For example, it is interesting to note that there is a subject entry, "Parasites," with a *see* reference to "Criminal Law and Procedure." The third part of the book is a well laid-out subject bibliography complete with page length and full bibliographic information.

Part 4 is an author checklist. The importance of the checklist is that each Soviet author is identified with an asterisk at the left of his or her name. And this is perhaps the only flaw that could be detected in the book: It is altogether unclear why the asterisks could not be placed in the annotated author bibliography. Under the present arrangement of the book, one must refer to the checklist in order to determine if the author is a Russian national or not.

The final portion of the book is a 380-page annotated bibliography by author. As with the rest of the book, this section is handled beautifully with but one small flaw: Not all entries in this section are annotated. Perhaps 90 percent of the entries *are* annotated; however, an entry listing an encyclopedia of Soviet law, for example, is not. While an annotation may not be necessary to describe the encyclopedia's coverage, one would be useful to describe the reliability of the encyclopedia itself.

All in all, this book is a must for any library that may have patrons doing research in Soviet law. In this day and age, I cannot imagine any public institution that would not.

Richard A. Leiter

493. Kirsh, Harvey J., comp. **Kirsh: Selected Bibliography of Construction Law Writings in Canada.** Agincourt, Ont., Carswell, 1988. 43p. index. $19.25. ISBN 0-459-31371-1.

A selected bibliography of approximately 210 English-language journal and law report articles, monographs, papers, and reports on construction law in Canada, this bibliography is organized into two parts: an author index and a subject matter index. Individual items are in standard legal citation form with no annotations. The selective coverage is oriented to the practitioner in Canadian common law jurisdictions although there are a few English-language citations to articles on the Quebec Civil Code. Coverage of the smaller jurisdictions in Canada (e.g., Saskatchewan, Nova Scotia) is poor or nonexistent. The bibliography covers the core literature of interest to the practitioner; consequently the emphasis is on current material although some older treatises still in use are cited. The author's preface is dated September 1987. A quick check of citations reveals coverage to the end of August 1987. The author noted that the bibliography was primarily created as "a research tool for my own use, and incidentally to assist others." The subject matter index terms are at an appropriate level of specificity for a specialized subject bibliography.

This bibliography may be appropriate for the larger Canadian law library collection, considering the lack of comprehensive legal bibliographies in Canada. However, it is unfortunate that a less expensive format could not be used to disseminate such bibliographic tools.

Lorna K. Rees-Potter

494. **Law Books in Print: Books in English Published throughout the World and in Print through 1986.** 5th ed. Nicholas Triffin with Alice Pidgeon, comps. and eds. Dobbs Ferry, N.Y., Glanville, 1987. 6v. $700.00/set. ISBN 0-87802-025-X.

Law Books in Print is one of those impossible attempts to provide the law library world with a comprehensive catalog of available legal materials and aid in the very important business of legal research by facilitating the work of law libraries. The preface of the six-volume set very wisely uses phrases such as: "Our goal has been to include *virtually* all major types of law books ..." and "the major impediment in our attempt to be comprehensive...."

A book which strives to be a comprehensive list of legal materials must, by its nature, be mammoth. The task of editing such a work is herculean. It is with this in mind that *Law Books in Print* must be evaluated. It cannot be comprehensive and the editing cannot be faulted, really, for frequent omissions and odd duplications. What there is of the work is sufficiently useful to make it a required part of any reference or acquisitions collection.

More than once *Law Books in Print* lists the same title twice, with but minute, subtle, albeit insignificant, differences. For example, Frank Houdek's classic bibliography, *Freedom of Information Act*, published by the Tarlton Law Library, is listed twice; once listing Houdek as editor, and once not. Surprisingly, the subject headings assigned to each entry are different. One entry's subject headings are listed as "Freedom Of Information; Legislative Histories; Bibliography," while the other entry's subject headings are "Legal Bibliography; Freedom Of Information." The ISBNs are listed as 0-9356-3013-9 and 0-935630-13-9, respectively. While it would be easy to say that this is sloppy editing and beride the editor for carelessness, the enormity of the task and the harmlessness of such errors must sympathetically be taken into account.

Such editing *faux pas* can be forgiven. But there are other errors that are harder to forgive. For instance, on at least one occasion, a title is listed twice, each listing different publishers without indicating which is a reprint. This can confuse and frustrate a user. Additionally, there are some other puzzling editorial decisions featured in the publishers' listings in volume 6. Commerce Clearing House is only listed as "CCH" with no cross-references. Clark Boardman Company Ltd. is listed as "Boardman," again with no cross-references. This is especially confusing when another two-name company such as Bancroft-Whitney is listed as "Bancroft Whitney" (sans hyphen), not as "Whitney." What's more, Bancroft-Whitney has only *two* titles listed, as has the notable law-related publisher, Ronald Press Company. Each could have, indeed, should have had, numerous titles listed as in print. While some of these criticisms may appear trivial at first glance, their number and their scope do affect the overall usefulness of the work.

A final criticism of the format of the book is in the publishers' directory. While the list is as complete as anyone would want, it lacks one feature that many users demand of such a directory: telephone numbers. In order to find out the publication date of City Lights Book Store's title *Unamerican Activities* by Geoffrey Rips, you either have to write or call San Francisco information.

Richard A. Leiter

495. Miller, Oscar J., and Mortimer D. Schwartz, comps. **Recommended Publications for Legal Research 1978.** Littleton, Colo., Fred B. Rothman, 1988. 141p. index. $37.50pa. ISBN 0-8377-1153-3.

This publication is a valuable collection development tool which fills the void left by the discontinuance of *Law Books Recommended for Libraries*, after which it is modeled. It is the seventh volume of a monographic series which when completed is expected to cover the period 1970 to date. Publications included in each volume are selected from announcements made during the year covered.

Under each of fifty subject categories, titles are arranged alphabetically by main entry. The following information is included for each listing: main entry, title, place of publication, publisher, date, pagination, price, series, LC card number, LC classification number, and when available, the ISBN. Each title carries a collection development rating for recommendation as follows: (A) basic collection, (B) intermediate collection, and (C) in-depth research collection. The majority of items included are recommended for research collections and less than 5 percent carry a recommendation for basic collections. There are two indexes. The subject index indicates the page on which a subject category begins; the main entry index is an alphabetical list with reference to item listings.

The selections include very few foreign-language publications, although several foreign presses, especially Canadian, British, and European, are represented. Reprint editions, of which there are many, include bibliographic information on the original edition. Legal periodicals are not included. The most valuable feature of the publication for collection development is the rating given to each item.

Elizabeth Thweatt

496. Schultz, Jon S. **Comparative Statutory Sources: U.S., Canadian, Multinational.** 3d ed. Buffalo, N.Y., William S. Hein, 1987. 177p. $30.00. LC 87-082494. ISBN 0-89941-585-7.

This third edition was prepared, in the author's words, "to sort out the growing number of publications that provide continuing comparisons of the statutes of multiple jurisdictions" (preface). Researchers wishing to compare the statutory laws of several states will find this annotated directory helpful in expediting their research.

The third edition is a significant expansion over the second edition, published in 1978. The number of sources indexed, over one hundred, has more than doubled. Similarly, the four hundred subject headings and seven hundred entries are approximately double those of the second edition. Furthermore, this edition indexes selected materials that compare Canadian provincial legislation, and a number of sources comparing the laws of different nations.

The work is not comprehensive. Only publications revised or supplemented at least annually are indexed. Materials updated less frequently, monographs, and periodical articles comparing the laws of different jurisdictions, by design, have not been indexed.

The author's helpful "Introduction: How to Use This Book" provides insight and guidance into multijurisdictional statutory research. Schultz generously refers to other helpful materials that may assist the researcher. (He surprisingly fails to mention Eis's *Legal Looseleafs in Print* [see *ARBA* 84, entry 484].) He also has included in this new edition a brief introduction using the Lexis and Westlaw legal databases to conduct comparative statutory research.

Notwithstanding occasional editing errors, the third edition of *Comparative Statutory Sources* should prove to be even more valuable

than its predecessors. This book is recommended for most law libraries.

James S. Heller

497. Teitelbaum, Gene. **Justice Louis D. Brandeis: A Bibliography of Writings and Other Materials on the Justice.** Littleton, Colo., Fred B. Rothman, 1988. 128p. illus. $30.00. LC 87-25962. ISBN 0-8377-1215-7.

From the introduction through the well-organized and well-researched sections of this bibliography, the author displays an obvious reverence for the subject and his work. Teitelbaum builds this bibliography on Mersky's *Louis Dembitz Brandeis...* (Yale Law School, 1958), by referring readers to Mersky for pre-1957 sources rather than duplicating this effort. He does, however, pick up references missed or omitted.

Following a brief chronology, the book is divided into ten chapters, with most entries annotated. The chapters cover (1) books and pamphlets, (2) law review articles, (3) parts of books, (4) essays, (5) nonlegal periodicals, (6) correspondence, (7) speeches by Brandeis, (8) speeches about Brandeis, (9) miscellany, and (10) sources used and guide for further research.

The approach, citations, and annotations all display a high degree of scholarship. The work is accurate and thorough. Chapter 10 will be particularly helpful to Brandeis scholars. All libraries and sources used are well documented, including periodical indexes consulted, methods of searching, and the closing dates of the search.

The book concludes with lists of people who were in contact with Brandeis (presidents, Supreme Court justices, law clerks) and concepts (such as the Balfour Declaration) with which Justice Brandeis was involved. [R: Choice, Oct 88, p. 298]

Helen Carol Bennett

Biographies

498. Kingston, Charles. **Famous Judges and Famous Trials.** New York, Frederick A. Stokes, 1923; repr., Littleton, Colo., Fred B. Rothman, 1988. 257p. index. $32.50. LC 87-36177. ISBN 0-8377-2336-1.

This is a reproduction of a work published in 1923 except that it lacks the nine portraits of the original edition. Twelve randomly selected, yet famous judges of British, Irish, and Scottish extraction are included along with a variety of cases over which they presided.

Each chapter is devoted to a single judge. Generally limited biographical material, which may include personal qualities, family background, political connections, education, physical description, and professional and public images, introduces these gentlemen who are regarded as outstanding judges. Another prevailing feature of each chapter is the description of selected cases over which these judges presided. Facts of the crimes are often detailed and involved and the personalities of the criminals are revealed. The predominant crime is murder, but fraud, gambling, bigamy, and theft are included. The cases follow one upon another without connection or transition. Each chapter concludes with a description of the retirement years of the judge. A very brief index completes the book.

The book is considered to be of general interest.   Elizabeth Thweatt

Dictionaries

499. Brown, Archibald. **A New Law Dictionary and Institute of the Whole Law: For the Use of Students, the Legal Profession, and the Public.** London, Stevens & Haynes, 1874; repr., Littleton, Colo., Fred B. Rothman, 1988. 391p. $45.00. LC 87-32130. ISBN 0-8377-1949-6.

This reference tool provides succinct explanations of the rules and principles of English common law, chancery law, real property or conveyancing law, mercantile law, constitutional law, and international law. The author was a barrister-at-law of the Middle Temple, and presented a one-volume "institute" of the whole law of England. Arranged alphabetically, the entries are in boldface, uppercase letters. *See* and *see also* cross-references provide access to related entries. The main body of the dictionary is preceded by a detailed table of contents which is intended to serve as a synopsis to the institute of the whole law and classifies the law under distinct headings.

The contents have been limited to material that is currently useful, eliminating that which was old and totally disused. Recommended for large public libraries, academic libraries, and law libraries.   Gloria H. Richard

500. Burrill, Alexander M. **A Law Dictionary and Glossary: Containing Full Definitions of the Principal Terms of the Common and Civil Law....** 2d ed. New York, Baker, Voorhis, 1867; repr., Littleton, Colo., Fred B. Rothman, 1987. 2v. $135.00/set. LC 87-13018. ISBN 0-8377-1946-1.

It is always interesting to examine an old law dictionary. The law on the whole is constantly changing, evolving. The words of law must therefore change and evolve as well,

sometimes considerably. But in evaluating the usefulness of an old dictionary for libraries one has to think about the ways that such material can be used.

Perhaps the only value of an old dictionary to the modern researcher is in making it possible to learn the definitions of words in their own time frame. It is one thing to read a modern dictionary that treats obsolete uses and meanings of words, but it is quite another to read a one-hundred-year-old dictionary's definition of the word. The dictionary under consideration, *A Law Dictionary and Glossary*, was first published in 1867. If one were reading a legal writing from that era and wanted to learn the definition of a word that is used in the document that either is not found in a modern legal dictionary or that has a definition in a modern dictionary that does not quite fit the context, referring to this dictionary might help.

But Burrill's work is more than a dictionary of old law terms. It contains numerous references to law treatises of the day as sources of various definitions and uses, and it also contains a substantial number of definitions of Latin words and phrases, as well as other languages and legal systems, such as French and Spanish and the civil law. It was also intended, *in its day*, to provide the contemporary researcher with definitions of obsolete words. Legal terms that were obsolete in 1867 may be all but unknown in the present day.

Another interesting feature of the book to the modern researcher is the preface, in which the author explains something of the process of compiling the dictionary, and in so doing describes, in an indirect way, contemporary legal bibliography. Much can be learned, albeit much of it trivia, from Burrill's essay, in which he refers to the standard works of the day as if they were eternal statements of the law. Forgotten works by forgotten authors which may prove to be gold mines of nineteenth-century legal thought.   Richard A. Leiter

501. English, Arthur. **A Dictionary of Words and Phrases Used in Ancient and Modern Law.** Washington, D.C., Washington Law Book, 1899; repr., Littleton, Colo., Fred B. Rothman, 1987. 979p. $85.00. LC 87-12973. ISBN 0-8377-2104-0.

A great number of old and relatively modern nineteenth-century legal terms have been defined in this comprehensive work. In keeping with the intent of the author, definitions have been kept brief and as short as possible. Many Latin terms are, of course, included.

Unlike other dictionaries published at the turn of the century, the origins (i.e., Latin,

French, Anglo-Saxon) of the defined words and phrases are not included. The text of the definitions are simple, clear, concise, and unusually brief for dictionaries of the period. However, this in no way detracts from this dictionary as both a quick and simple reference guide for locating legal words for historical and retrospective legal research purposes. It is clear that the author drafted this dictionary in order to assist readers in quickly understanding and locating legal terminology.

The appendix includes a number of useful reference sources. Included are the American Constitution and Amendments to 1899, the Magna Carta, and the regnal years of British monarchs. The appendix ends with an extensive and excellent abbreviations section.

James M. Murray

502. Fox, Elyse H., comp. **The Legal Research Dictionary: From Advance Sheets to Pocket Parts.** Newton Highlands, Mass., Legal Information Services, 1987. 83p. $9.50 spiralbound. ISBN 0-941991-00-8.

The main aim of this pocket-sized dictionary (4 by 6 inches) is to assist first-year law students who are unfamiliar with legal research. The compiler, a law librarian and law library consultant, believes her book "fills a gap in the traditional legal research teaching approach," and that law clerks, practicing attorneys, paralegals, and law librarians will all benefit from using it. She explains that her book is not comprehensive and cannot be, and that there are other books of every description available that are more useful, without naming one of them. This work appears to be taken from lecture notes for the first month of an introduction to law course, but does not even satisfy classroom needs. For example, the definition given for *Key Number* is "a subdivision of a digest topic that corresponds to a particular point of law." Her definition is overly truncated to the point of obfuscation; a first-year law student is not assisted by it; and it does not explain that key numbers are ingenious timesavers that allow the user to locate relevant law cases on a topic throughout the extensive National Reporter System. Many of the other definitions are better defined in *Black's Law Dictionary*, the abridged fifth edition (West, 1983), if the idea is to purchase a carry-along. The compiler certainly began with a good idea: to produce a brief work (under one hundred pages) to provide law students with a ready-reference for legal research. Perhaps this dictionary might suffice for some law students and for that reason should be sold in the campus bookstore. It is hard to imagine, though, that any legal community professionals

would find it of lasting value, and because of its size it would get lost on a library shelf.

Bill Bailey

503. Kinney, J. Kendrick. **A Law Dictionary and Glossary: Primarily for the Use of Students but Adapted Also to the Use of the Profession at Large.** Chicago, Callaghan, 1893; repr., Littleton, Colo., Fred B. Rothman, 1987. 706p. $65.00. LC 87-4498. ISBN 0-8377-2334-5.

This dictionary is a reprint of a book published in 1893 by Callaghan and Company. The book was intended for use primarily by students. However, its use today is limited since it mostly serves as a reference work for individuals conducting historical research on legal terms and their use in the legal field.

Unlike current law dictionaries such as *Black's Law Dictionary*, fifth edition (West, 1979) and *Ballentine's Law Dictionary, with Pronunciations*, third edition (Lawyers Co-op., 1969), the linguistic origin of legal terms is included, indicating whether the words are Latin, French, or Anglo-Saxon. Some of the definitions are quite long; and as is the case with most dictionaries, words are arranged and defined in alphabetical order. Because this work was intended for students, it includes a larger number of entries than a number of other legal dictionaries or glossaries published during the turn of the century, such as Stimson's *A Concise Law Dictionary of Words, Phrases and Maxims with an Explanatory List of Abbreviations Used in Law Books* (see entry 507).

James M. Murray

504. Leonard, Robin D., and Stephen R. Elias. **Family Law Dictionary: Marriage, Divorce, Children & Living Together.** Berkeley, Calif., Nolo Press; distr., Emeryville, Calif., Publishers Group West, 1988. 193p. illus. $13.95pa. LC 88-60701. ISBN 0-87337-061-9.

At a time when one out of two marriages ends in divorce, fourteen states permit "no fault" divorce, and books on how to do your own divorce are on sale in every bookstore, it is highly appropriate that the Nolo authors produce an easy to understand dictionary covering the field of family law. *Family Law Dictionary* includes terms relating to marriage, divorce, adoption, support, custody, guardianship, living together, paternity, and abortion. It includes legal and nonlegal terms, in alphabetical order without sections or parts. Unlike any other dictionary in the field, all definitions are in clear, concise English, often translations of "legalese." Difficult entries contain case examples and all entries contain the context in which terms are used. The charts and examples, a novel approach, are an invaluable aid to the novice or expert attempting to comprehend legal language. For example, a one-page chart "Who is your kin?" clearly sets forth the degree of kinship, a complicated definition which is hidden in multiple entries and various sections of the state probate codes. Effective cross-references (both *see* and *see also*) and state by state charts, ranging from incest and marital prohibitions to parental liability laws, enhance its usefulness. Delightful illustrations lighten a serious and often depressing subject. The large print, boldface type, and index tabs make it an attractive as well as a readable volume.

Laypersons, students, teachers, and even lawyers will find it useful for current simple, clear definitions of family law terms and their usage. [R: RBB, 1 Oct 88, p. 240]

Helen Carol Bennett

505. Olver, Graham. **A French-English Dictionary of Legal and Commercial Terms.** London, Stevens, 1925; repr., Littleton, Colo., Fred B. Rothman, 1988. 170p. $26.00. LC 88-11415. ISBN 0-8377-2515-1.

A 1988 reprint of the 1925 edition, this book is rated "B" by the Association of American Law School's (AALS) six-volume work *Law Books Recommended for Libraries* (1970). That is, Olver's dictionary is recommended for any academic library in "the intermediate phase of development" which is "progressing toward support of a research program and an enriched curriculum which includes seminar offerings."

While apparently somewhat brief and selective, the text is still valuable for retrospective research. However, the dated nature of the book when combined with the vast economic developments during the last sixty-three years render it essentially useless in current international legal and commercial practice. Consequently, only academic law libraries with large research collections would find this work useful for their collections.

Terms are briefly defined in nontechnical language. Most of the terms and expressions may be found in the French Codes of 1925. In many cases, the equivalent English term is given first, and some commercial terms have been introduced in order to make meanings clear and because they have been used in legal proceedings.   James M. Murray

506. Shumaker, Walter A., and George Foster Longsdorf. **The Cyclopedic Dictionary of Law: Comprising the Terms and Phrases of American Jurisprudence....** St. Paul, Minn., Keefe-Davidson Law Book, 1901; repr., Littleton, Colo., Fred B. Rothman, 1987. 976p. $85.00. LC 87-12974. ISBN 0-8377-2614-X.

For those academics with an interest in legal history or for those whose scholarly pursuits will lead them into studying American case law at the turn of the century or earlier, *The Cyclopedic Dictionary of Law* is an important, and perhaps, necessary book.

If any legal dictionary can claim to be comprehensive, this one comes as close as is possible, given its historical context. In nearly one thousand pages, definitions of almost twenty thousand classic legal terms are clearly and concisely set forth. The only criticism that can be made of this monumental work is that, in 1987, the definitions are generally out of date by nature of the fact that it was published in 1901. While it is true that many of the legal terms described in the work are not obsolete, many are, and there is no question but that the case references included in the definitions are necessarily dated.

But case annotation is one of the book's strong points. Each definition is carefully annotated with case authority that substantiates the author's definition. He has also noted relevant scholars and commentators when appropriate. In its day, the annotations undoubtedly made this book an invaluable resource for the legal researcher because each definition contained enough information to make a good starting point for any research project.

Additionally, despite the book's title, it often goes beyond American legal definitions. Definitions of legal terms from ancient French, Roman, and commonwealth legal systems are covered. When appropriate, the evolution of the definition is treated thoroughly and accurately. Alternate definitions are also given when the definitions of a term vary substantially in different legal systems.   Richard A. Leiter

507. Stimson, Frederic Jesup. **A Concise Law Dictionary of Words, Phrases, and Maxims with an Explanatory List of Abbreviations Used in Law Books.** Revised by Harvey Cortlandt Voorhees. Boston, Little, Brown, 1911; repr., Littleton, Colo., Fred B. Rothman, 1987. 346p. $35.00. LC 87-4497. ISBN 0-8377-2611-5.

This law dictionary is most valuable as a reference tool for those scholars and other individuals conducting retrospective or historical legal research. It is a reprint of the 1911 edition originally published by Little, Brown and Company.

In comparison with legal dictionaries in use today, such as *Black's Law Dictionary*, fifth edition (West, 1979) or *Ballentine's Law Dictionary, with Pronunciations*, third edition

(Lawyers Co-op., 1969), there is a somewhat larger number of Latin terms. This is not unusual, since Latin terms were used to a greater degree in law at the turn of the century.

As is the case with modern law dictionaries, many of the alphabetically arranged definitions have references or citations to prior legal authority in order to lead the reader to further resource or study material. An unusual feature of this dictionary is the list of abbreviations found alphabetically arranged under "A." This list covers over fifty pages—a substantial portion of this work.

Another helpful feature of this dictionary is the practice of including the derivation of defined words. For example, symbols such as *l*, *fr.*, and *sax.* following each word indicate whether the word is Latin, French, or Anglo-Saxon in origin. This practice has not been continued in most current law dictionaries. The appendix following the text is a table of British regnal years listing the names and commencement of reigns of the various monarchs.

James M. Murray

508. Wharton, J. J. S. **The Law Lexicon, or Dictionary of Jurisprudence: Explaining All the Technical Words and Phrases Employed in the Several Departments of English Law....** Harrisburg, Pa., I. G. M'Kinley and J. M. G. Lescure's, 1848; repr., Littleton, Colo., Fred B. Rothman, 1987. 1073p. $85.00. LC 87-12975. ISBN 0-8377-2740-5.

Wharton's legal lexicon or dictionary of jurisprudence is a lengthy but classic work. It is a complete dictionary of technical words and phrases or legal terminology used by the English legal profession during the early half of the nineteenth century. Each word, phrase, or technical term is listed alphabetically with as clear and concise a description as possible. There are also references to the historical origin of the terms defined (such as Latin, Hebrew, French, etc.) as well as occasional passages from early Jewish, Greek, and Roman works that illustrate a doctrine.

A list of principal authorities relied upon is found in the front of the book. The authorities are referred to within the descriptions of each word or phrase for those scholars interested in further in-depth research into the historical and legal aspects of a particular legal term.

Legal and other scholars will benefit the most from using this work. Academic law libraries would be well advised to have this dictionary in their collections, but it is doubtful this dictionary would have use in any other library.

James M. Murray

509. Williamson, A. **A French-English Dictionary of Legal Words and Phrases Including Legal Commercial Terms Most Commonly in Use.** London, Stevens, 1911; repr., Littleton, Colo., Fred B. Rothman, 1988. 135p. $24.00. LC 88-11417. ISBN 0-8377-2743-X.

A French-English dictionary of approximately 950 terms which have a technical legal meaning and are found in the French civil codes or in French legal texts, this dictionary is a reprint of the full text, including title page and preface, of the 1911 publication. The orientation is to legal terms that are important in the field of business. The dictionary is organized in alphabetical order of the major French-language term with fairly brief definitions in English following. Entries for legal phrases follow the entry for the major term, for example, *affrête-ment*, followed by *affrêtement à forfait, affrêtement acueillette*, etc. If these phrases are compounds of two major terms they will appear in alphabetical order under each major term, for example, *contrat d'affrêtement* appears under *affrêtement* and under *contrat*.

The text reproduction quality is not as good as a reader would wish; however, the publisher noted a problem with the condition of the original text. This is a minor problem compared to the improved availability of this long out-of-print dictionary. Law libraries in Canada or elsewhere with French civil code collections will find this reprint a very useful addition.

Lorna K. Rees-Potter

Directories

510. **Almanac of the Federal Judiciary.** Barnabas D. Johnson and others, eds. Chicago, LawLetters, 1988. 2v. index. $250.00 looseleaf with binder/set. LC 84-080461. ISBN 0-914239-09-0.

Directories of members of the federal judiciary are readily available. *United States Court Directory, 1987* (Administrative Office of the United States Courts) and *Judges of the United States, Second Edition* (Bicentennial Committee of The Judicial Conference of the United States, 1984) are both available from the U.S. Government Printing Office, as is the annual *United States Government Manual*, which also names judges. *Almanac of the Federal Judiciary*, however, offers a unique contribution as an annotated directory, one that adds both profiles and evaluations to standard data on individual judges and enlightening comments on the separate circuit courts. First issued in 1984, volume 1 includes all sitting judges of the district courts, which cover the District of

Columbia and the eleven circuit courts, plus those of special courts, namely, tax, claims, international trade, and military appeals. Information on individual judges notes appointor; education; positions held; professional associations; pro bono, political, and other activities; bar association evaluations; honors and awards; publications; noteworthy rulings; media coverage; lawyers' evaluations; and miscellany. Of interest to lawyers will be the performance guidelines espoused by specific judges. Volume 2, initially appearing in 1985, covers the judges of the courts of appeals and, with the 1988 edition, those of the Supreme Court. This is the volume that presents lawyers' comments on each circuit court and the federal court. Information noted for individual judges corresponds to that listed for volume 1 entries. Looseleaf in format, the 8½-by-11-inch pages are double-columned with boldface headings providing contrast and easy legibility. Volume 1 offers an alphabetical index by judges' names. Volume 2, with no index, lists within the introduction each judge by court and seniority. Libraries serving any active legal program or involved citizenry will find this set expensive but invaluable for pertinent details.　　　　　　　Eleanor Ferrall

511. BNA's Directory of State Courts Judges and Clerks: A State-by-State Listing. 2d ed. Compiled by Kamla J. King and Judith Springberg with the BNA Library Staff. Washington, D.C., Bureau of National Affairs, 1988. 446p. index. $50.00pa. LC 88-22264. ISBN 0-87179-598-1.

This directory provides a state-by-state listing for each of the fifty states, the District of Columbia, and U.S. territories of almost thirteen thousand judges, clerks, and administrators in over two thousand courts. The information was verified in May 1988. Information for each court listing includes the official name of the court; name, address, and telephone number for each clerk; and name, title, city, and telephone number of each judge. In cases where there is a chief judge, that name is listed before other judges.

A new feature of the second edition is the chart of court structure showing the line of appeal or petition for the fifty states, District of Columbia, and Puerto Rico. Chart information is derived from the Court Statistics and Information Management Project (CSIM) and includes common elements, but configurations vary, reflecting the complexity and variety of the state court systems. Arrows indicate the line of appeal or petition. An "A" on a chart indicates that the appeal comes directly from decisions of an administrative agency.

An appendix arranged alphabetically by state followed by U.S. territories gives the name, official title, address, and telephone number for the court administrators. The publication concludes with a personal name index which is an alphabetical compilation of all judges, clerks, and administrators. Each name is followed by the appropriate abbreviation: (J) for judge, (C) for clerk, or (A) for court administrator. The state abbreviation is then given, followed by the page reference to the state section in the work.　　　　　　　Elizabeth Thweatt

512. Directory of Intellectual Property Lawyers and Patent Agents. 1988-89 ed. Lynn M. LoPucki and Ann T. Reilly, eds. New York, Clark Boardman, 1988. 1721p. index. $145.00. ISBN 0-87632-611-4.

Information from records of the U.S. Patent and Trademark Office was merged with data gathered from survey forms completed by intellectual property lawyers and patent agents to compile this directory. A copy of the information gathering form is included in the volume and experts who were omitted are invited to submit the completed form for inclusion in the next edition of the directory.

The directory is divided into six sections as follows: (1) lawyer and patent agent profiles, (2) firm profiles, (3) type of work index, (4) language index, (5) lawyer and patent agent index, and (6) firm index. Section 1 constitutes the major portion of the directory and is arranged by state, subarranged by city with an alphabetical listing of experts. The extent of information provided for each entry varies. At a minimum, it includes the name, telephone number, registered patent agent or attorney number, and address. More extensive entries include birth date, educational background, bar admittance, practical experience, and specializations. Following the state listing is a single page with experts for Venezuela, Hong Kong, and the Philippines.

Section 2 is arranged by state, subdivided by city, followed by firm. Information includes address and number of attorneys or patent agents. The general description is followed by a single name or list of experts with telephone numbers for the firm listed. Section 3 lists profiled individuals by their type of work. Cross-references are made to related terms. Section 4 identifies experts who are able to conduct business in foreign languages. It is a listing by language, arranged by state, city, and expert. Section 5 is an alphabetical listing of individuals, giving the city and state of practice. Section 6 is an alphabetical list for firms that appear in the firm profiles and gives cross-references for the cities in which the firms are located. This is an extensive index for intellectual property lawyers and patent agents.

Elizabeth Thweatt

513. Joyner, Al. **Directory for Successful Publishing in Legal Periodicals.** Charleston, Ill., Qucoda, 1987. 694p. $44.99pa. LC 86-62889. ISBN 0-940579-00-6.

This work is highly recommended for academic law libraries, since law faculty and legal scholars will usually have the greatest need for the extremely useful information found in this publication. Over 450 journals are included, as well as those from more than fifty countries. If a journal has not been included, it is because that journal's editors failed to supply requested information.

In summary, the material found in this guide gives general information about each legal periodical and detailed information about the periodical's manuscript review process. More specifically, three classes of information are included about each periodical. First is such information as the mailing address, telephone number, name of the editing organization, average length of each issue, number of subscribers, and average number and type of manuscripts a journal publishes in each issue. Not every published feature of a periodical is included here (e.g., columns, news items, or editorials); the focus is upon manuscripts. However, features such as notes and comments are also included.

The second class of information includes the particulars, or preferred manuscript characteristics, of each periodical. Such things as the preferred topics and the total number of pages are mentioned. Finally, the particular nature of the review process of each periodical is provided. For example, whether a periodical is "refereed" is included; that is, if the periodical is reviewed by persons not on the periodical's staff and who are generally recognized experts on the subject of the manuscript.

Four major classes of legal periodicals are included: law school journals, journals by professional associations, journals by state and local bar associations, and periodicals published by private companies. This work also has a series of twelve excellent appendices providing the following information: journals exclusively refereed, journals accepting all legal subjects, journals accepting specific subjects, journals periodically publishing special issues, journals with preferred page length of manuscripts, journals published by or through law schools, journals published by private companies or individuals, journals by professional associations, journals by bar associations, journals by

the U.S. government, journals paying fees for manuscripts, and journals disapproving of simultaneous mailing of manuscripts.

James M. Murray

514. **Law Librarian's New Product Directory.** New York, Garland, 1988. 524p. illus. index. $125.00 looseleaf with binder.

This is one of those ideas that is destined to remain just that: a good idea and nothing more. Basically, the *New Product Directory* is supposed to be a convenient way of obtaining information about new law books and services. It is actually nothing more than an index of selected publishers' new book announcements along with reproductions of publishers' flyers and brochures. The concept of a new product directory is interesting. Since a law librarian is typically deluged with mailings announcing new publications, the idea for an organized arrangement of these mailings is thought to make the work of an acquisitions librarian easier. The reason that the execution of the concept fails is that in the end it does not actually serve its purpose effectively or efficiently.

First of all, the *New Product Directory* is not comprehensive. If it is not comprehensive it cannot serve as an efficient substitute for regularly reading the mailings from publishers. A diligent acquisitions librarian regularly reads all of the incoming mail for ideas of new books to add to his or her library. If the *New Product Directory* is meant to relieve the librarian of the burden of wading through the mail, then by using it the librarian should be able to ignore the mail and rely totally on the directory. Since it is obviously *not* comprehensive, the librarian cannot ignore the mail for fear of overlooking an announcement about a useful new title. Therefore, the librarian is stuck with reading the mail just as thoroughly as before, looking for materials that are not in the directory. Thus the *New Product Directory* becomes not a convenience but an additional burden. It is merely another thing to read on a regular basis when looking for announcements about new materials to purchase.

Second, even if it were comprehensive, the directory would fail to alleviate the burden of scanning the mail looking for announcements about new products and services. Undoubtedly librarians will receive more announcements about new materials in direct mail from publishers than they will through the directory.

Perhaps the only useful purpose that the *New Product Directory* serves is that it obviates the necessity for collecting the new product announcements in pamphlet boxes. Since all of the flyers are reproduced on three-hole-punched

8½-by-11-inch paper, they all fit neatly into a binder that one receives with a subscription. A dubious advantage over collecting the real thing.

Richard A. Leiter

Handbooks and Yearbooks

515. **The Canadian Yearbook of International Law. Volume XXV: 1987. Annuaire Canadien de Droit International.** C. B. Bourne, ed. Vancouver, B.C., University of British Columbia Press, 1988. 568p. index. $60.00. ISBN 0-7748-0303-7; ISSN 0069-0058.

The twenty-fifth edition of a yearbook in the field of international law published under the auspices of the Canadian Branch of the International Law Association, this annual has come to be a basic authoritative work of Canadian scholarly contributions to this growing field. The text is divided into a number of sections, including articles, notes and commentaries, practice, cases, and book reviews. This edition starts with a review article by Maxwell Cohen on developments in Canada in the field of international law over the last twenty-five years. This is followed by equally authoritative articles by Ivan Head on international law and development and by Jacques-Yvan Morin on the relationship between sovereignty and international law. These articles are followed by equally notable experts writing on diverse themes in international law such as fundamental norms, world citizenship, contemporary Soviet theories, aviation terrorism and the International Civil Aviation Organization, the cultural dimension of the Canada/U.S. Free Trade Agreement, the Charter of Rights and Freedoms and extradition, and the Labour Conventions Reference decision. The notes and comments section has a number of brief commentaries on selected issues such as sovereignty and the Arctic, the International Law Commission, and the International Court of Justice. The practice section surveys current Canadian practice and activity in the Canadian Parliament and at the Canadian Department of External Affairs in international law. There is as well a list of treaty actions taken by Canada in 1986. One chapter gives a summary of 1986-1987 cases in international law organized by topic and when appropriate by jurisdiction. The main text is completed by a number of book reviews of recently published major works in the field.

The articles appear in either the French or the English language. Most of the articles and the commentaries have a brief summary of the contents in the other language. The text is followed by a detailed analytical index by name, title, case, topic, and statute. This is a basic,

scholarly work that should be included in any collection in the field of international law and purchased by any individual seriously working in this field.

Lorna K. Rees-Potter

516. Gibson, Ellen M. **New York Legal Research Guide.** Buffalo, N.Y., William S. Hein, 1988. 404p. maps. index. $32.50. LC 88-80721. ISBN 0-89941-622-5.

Navigating through legal reference materials constitutes this guide, not methods of research. Knowledge of basic legal bibliography and research techniques is assumed. The first of its kind for New York law, it should be "a useful resource for anyone interested in the development and use of New York legal publications." From it the reader learns about not only the standard print, microform, and online database sources, but also media sources that provide significant legal and law-related information. The fifteen chapters and eight appendices are incisive and logically arranged. Since New York has a long history, explanations of its legal evolution are welcome, especially concerning New York constitutions, the state legislative process, and judicial procedure. Within a chapter each section covers the topic employing easy to follow subdivisions, illustrative lists, and footnotes. An annotation follows each reference title mentioned in the text. The 102-page appendices section leads the reader to major New York law reviews and bar association periodicals, legal newspapers, publishers, law libraries, and other informative miscellany. The name index contains authors of the law publications, while the subject index concentrates on listing broad topic areas and law titles. Not a wasted word in this guide, its 404 pages attest to the intricate history and functioning of New York law as reflected in its myriad legal reference publications. Recommended nationwide since New York and California law are pervasive influences.

Bill Bailey

517. Reams, Bernard D., Jr., and Stuart D. Yoak. **The Constitutions of the States: A State by State Guide and Bibliography to Current Scholarly Research.** Dobbs Ferry, N.Y., Oceana, 1988. 554p. index. $60.00. LC 88-19621. ISBN 0-379-20970-5.

The authors designed this book to be a companion volume to their previously published work *The Constitution of the United States* (see *ARBA 88*, entry 578). *The Constitutions of the States* is organized in an alphabetical arrangement with a single chapter for each state. Entries are subarranged by section or article for each state constitution and presented in reverse chronological order. Under each article or section, entries are arranged in alphabetical order by author. Emphasis is placed on current periodical literature and articles published between 1975 and 1987 are included. In the introduction, the authors list major reference sources which used in combination with the current work will give a broad historical perspective. The current *Guide and Bibliography* includes many "Comments" from periodical literature. Since state constitutions have undergone many revisions, those currently in force are used as the source in this volume. The header for each state gives the date the constitution was ratified.

Three separate indexes (author, title, and case name) complete the volume. The author index lists the author's last name only with page references to the work.

This publication will be a welcome addition to the legal and general reference collection of any library.   Elizabeth Thweatt

518. Soled, Alex J. **The Essential Guide to Wills, Estates, Trusts, and Death Taxes.** updated and expanded ed. Washington, D.C., American Association of Retired Persons and Glenview, Ill., Scott, Foresman; distr., Boston, Little, Brown, 1988. 261p. illus. index. $21.95; $12.95pa. LC 87-18858. ISBN 0-673-24891-7; 0-673-24890-9pa.

Many people procrastinate in preparing a will until it is too late. When no will is available, there is no guarantee that property will pass to the desired heirs, death taxes may be higher, and provisions for survivor benefits will probably take somewhat longer. Through this book, the American Association of Retired Persons and author Soled encourage individuals to protect their wishes for estate disbursement by making wills.

The Essential Guide provides information for estate planning and is not intended as a "do it yourself" guide. Written in question and answer format, it enables the user to question the professional properly and work with him or her to reduce the heirs' tax liability. Because it is organized for selective use, one is easily able to use the table of contents and index to find specific information. The guide is divided into sections on wills, terminology, estates, trusts, and death taxes, concluding with an appendix covering various federal and state laws relating to these areas. In addition to the question and answer format, case studies are used to enlighten the reader.

Most of the terminology is clearly defined in simple terms. However, occasionally one has to use the index to find a more complete meaning of a term (e.g., "living trust" is used as a definition, but one must refer to the index for a reference to a broader interpretation).

In spite of this, every public library should have a copy of this in the reference section, with one or more in circulation. Individuals would be wise to have a personal copy as well. [R: BL, 1 May 88, p. 1465]   Anna Grace Patterson

Indexes

519. **Code of Federal Regulations Index 1988: Covering 1986 Regulations.** Lucille Boorstein, ed. New York, R. R. Bowker, 1988. 3v. $399.00/set. ISBN 0-8352-2439-2; ISSN 0000-1058.

This is a monumental work and will be a welcome addition to the reference or documents collection. It was developed with the legal researcher in mind. Each title of the index was assigned to one or more experts with law-related or indexing backgrounds. The index is easy to use and much more extensive than any other index currently available for the *Code of Federal Regulations.*

Volume 1 of the three-volume set provides separate index information for each of the fifty code titles, title by title, except for Title 1 (General Provisions), Title 3 (The President), and Titles 2 and 6 (Reserved). Titles 1 and 3 were purposefully omitted due to the nature of the material they contain. Volumes 2 and 3 provide subject access through a merged topical index for the same titles that are in volume 1. Each index section in the work is preceded by a list of major headings for easy reference. *See* and *see also* references are used throughout the work.

The initial index covers the 1986 *Code of Federal Regulations.* There are plans to supplement the index three times a year. During the first year of publicaiton the changes for 1987 and 1988 will be incorporated into the supplements of the first edition. When the 1989 edition is published, it is expected that the index will be only three months out-of-date. [R: LJ, 15 Oct 88, pp. 82-83]   Elizabeth Thweatt

Periodicals and Serials

520. DeLashmitt, Eleanor, comp. **Annuals and Surveys Appearing in Legal Periodicals: An Annotated Listing.** Littleton, Colo., Fred B. Rothman, 1987. 140p. $37.50 looseleaf with binder. LC 87-28393. ISBN 0-8377-2033-8.

This work is designed to help law librarians locate regularly published law journal articles that survey particular developments in the law. The author has divided her work, which is published in looseleaf format for annual updating, into three sections: "State," "Federal Courts," and "Subject." The "State" section, which is arranged by state name, identifies articles providing an overview of legislative, judicial, or administrative developments in the laws of particular states. The researcher can use the "Federal" section to locate articles surveying judicial decisions rendered by the United States Supreme Court and the federal circuit courts of appeals. The "Subject" section can be used to locate survey articles on a wide range of procedural and substantive law topics.

Each listing contains the title of the survey article, the name of the publication in which the article appears, the author, descriptive notes, and citations to where each article is published. As the author states, "[t]he notes are of particular importance because they indicate the scope of coverage, the strengths and weaknesses of the survey and the frequency of publication" (introduction). DeLashmitt is correct in stating that researchers "often overlook or are unaware of the valuable articles found in the surveys that appear in law reviews, bar journals and annuals" (introduction). Her work certainly makes locating such articles easier and should substantially benefit legal researchers. Recommended for most law libraries.   James S. Heller

Quotation Books

521.   James, Simon, and Chantal Stebbings, comps. and eds. **A Dictionary of Legal Quotations.** New York, Macmillan, 1987. 209p. index. $14.95. LC 87-12255. ISBN 0-02-916002-2.

Most of the quotations come from Britons, as befits the compilers' nationality. The remaining chestnuts are American, with a few international and classical ones mixed in. The over two thousand quotations are arranged under 160 topics. Some of the topics contain little; for example, there are only six quotations under "Perjury," all culled from Shakespeare. Taken out of context, Shakespeare usually supplies an emphatic statement not meant to stand alone, as good quotations should be able to do. An asterisk identifies the authors or source quoted from more than twenty-five times: the *Bible*, Ambrose Bierce, Edmund Burke, Lord Denning, Thomas Fuller, Frank McKinney Hubbard, James Kelly, and Shakespeare. Of these it is reassuring to see that Ambrose Bierce (*The Devil's Dictionary*) is still sardonically appropriate. The quotations range from Aristotle to Mick Jagger – "Marriage is like signing a 356-page contract without knowing what's in it." Stevenson's *Home Book of Quotations* (Dodd, 1984) and *The International Thesaurus of Quotations* (see *ARBA* 88, entry 96) include more legal quotations but with a difference. Many of

the entries here derive from actual court cases and legal literature and are not just literary witticisms. Given that the majority of these quotations are serious in nature, not as humorous or barbed as in other sources, this collection is recommended.   Bill Bailey

CRIMINOLOGY

522.   Cohen, Daniel. **The Encyclopedia of Unsolved Crimes.** New York, Dodd, Mead, 1988. 323p. illus. bibliog. $17.95. LC 88-239. ISBN 0-396-08944-5.

This selection of sixty-nine unsolved crimes is divided into six categories and subarranged chronologically, with one case dating back two thousand years and the latest cases occurring in 1980. The predominant crime is murder, often multiple, sensational, and well known. There are a dozen cases included in which the author questions if a crime actually occurred at all. No index exists, but the contents at the front of the volume makes finding a case easy.

The case reports range in length from one and a half to eight pages. Some details are included about each crime, but there is definitely an air of mystery about the events and persons involved in each case. The author sometimes questions reported evidence and the multiplicity of information provided. There is often the conjecture that perhaps new evidence will still surface. Some cases are related to others reported in the volume and in these instances cross-references are made.

A selected bibliography can be found at the end of the book. Many of the listings include brief explanations or annotations. Although throughout the work references are made to sources of information, no footnotes are used and it would be very difficult to trace references. Some historical facts are included, especially for older cases, which aid the reader in understanding circumstances surrounding certain historical events such as human sacrificial offerings. In the introduction the author states: "What I am primarily interested in is the mystery. Whodunit? Why? Was anything done at all?" This statement indicates accurately the tone and quality of the book.   Elizabeth Thweatt

523.   De Sola, Ralph. **Crime Dictionary.** rev. ed. New York, Facts on File, 1988. 222p. bibliog. $24.95. LC 87-20133. ISBN 0-8160-1872-3.

The present volume is an expanded and updated version of a work first published in 1982 (see *ARBA* 83, entry 517). There is, of course, an extensive language of crime and criminal justice, both official and unofficial. The entries in this dictionary fall principally into several categories. There are an especially large number of acronyms and abbreviations, such as FBI (Federal Bureau of Investigation, as most people would know) and ACJS (Academy of Criminal Justice Sciences). Under this latter entry the *Journal of Criminal Justice* is identified as the academy's official journal, when in fact *Justice Quarterly* has been the official journal since 1985. It is a bit odd, to say the least, that in a 1988 volume the only definition of AIDS is: "Automated Identification Division System." In view of the considerable impact of the disease AIDS on the correctional system, and the attendant legal issues, it might well be properly identified here. On the other hand, some peculiar irrelevancies are included, such as Molly Pitcher, the Revolutionary heroine.

The acronyms and the correctional institutions which are identified might have been more efficiently organized as appendices, rather than being scattered through the volume. Braunschweig is quite mistakenly, to the best of my knowledge, identified as one of the Nazi concentration camps. We also learn what some abbreviated terminology (e.g., *Ex Med*) stands for (*Excerpta Medica*), but we do not learn in this case exactly what *Excerpta Medica* is. As one would expect, there are many clinical terms for different types of criminal offenders (e.g., *kleptomaniac*) and basic legal terms or types of offenses (e.g., *expunge*; *vehicular homicide*). These definitions are generally very brief. An impressively large number of slang or argot terms are included. In general, the very rudimentary, uncritical, and sometimes simplistic definitions, and the lack of information regarding origins, is a basic limitation of this work. It may indeed have some value as a starting point for someone attempting to identify names, terms, and acronyms. It is limited beyond this level. There are other dictionaries in this area, including Erki Beckman's *The Criminal Justice Dictionary* (see *ARBA* 80, entry 524 and *ARBA* 84, entry 485), George Rush's *Dictionary of Criminal Justice* (Allyn & Bacon, 1977), and Dermot Walsh and Adrian Poole's *A Dictionary of Criminology* (see *ARBA* 85, entry 516). The first two works tend to stress criminal justice terms, rather than criminological terms (a difference of emphasis), but otherwise have some of the same limitations as the present volume; the last-named work is more substantial, but much more selective. [R: BR, Nov/Dec 88, p. 48; Choice, Nov 88, p. 458; RBB, Aug 88, pp. 1899-1900]   David O. Friedrichs

524. Newton, Michael. **Mass Murder: An Annotated Bibliography.** New York, Garland,

1988. 378p. index. (Garland Reference Library of Social Science, Vol. 427). $45.00. LC 87-24588. ISBN 0-8240-6619-7.

The topic of mass murder has been one of enduring fascination. In recent years, however, there has been an apparent increase in mass murders, and related serial murders, with an attendant interest in understanding these patterns of behavior more fully. The present volume provides us with a very useful guide to the formidable literature on this topic. It is divided into three sections: general and encyclopedic works; specialized/psychological works; and, by far the longest section, case histories. Of course a great deal of this literature is directed toward a general public, and is "sensationalistic," or geared more toward entertainment than toward enlightenment. But the compiler of this bibliography, to his credit, notes the limitations of many of the items he lists and describes (e.g., the various books produced by Jay Robert Nash). While the emphasis on the case history listing may not be ideal for most scholarly research purposes, the index allows for identification of sources on some basic topics (e.g., women and killers, arson). Although the local press and pulp press are deliberately (and sensibly) excluded, this bibliography is quite thorough on other sources. It is also very up-to-date, with sources through at least 1986 included. The paucity of serious social science research on mass murders, relative to the popular literature, is made quite evident (the compiler notes an important recent exception to this tendency: Jack Levin and James Alan Fox's *Mass Murder*, 1985). But students and scholars interested in mass murder and serial murder, and especially in specific celebrated cases, will certainly find this volume a helpful point of departure. [R: Choice, June 88, pp. 1538-39; WLB, May 88, p. 111]

David O. Friedrichs

525. Radelet, Michael L., and Margaret Vandiver. **Capital Punishment in America: An Annotated Bibliography.** New York, Garland, 1988. 243p. index. (Garland Reference Library of Social Science, Vol. 466). $34.00. LC 88-23249. ISBN 0-8240-1623-8.

Despite the fact that capital punishment is imposed in only a very small number of cases, it continues to be an issue of formidable and emotionally charged interest, and it continues to inspire a large literature of research and commentary. The present bibliography contains one thousand items, briefly annotated, which focus on this issue. It stresses works published since 1972 (the year of the landmark *Furman* case), produced in the United States, which are reasonably accessible. Some exceptions to these criteria include earlier "classic" contributions to the literature. The listing is divided into books and articles, congressional publications, and U.S. Supreme Court decisions. The books and articles are listed alphabetically by author. An index facilitates locating items on particular aspects of capital punishment (e.g., Catholic views, juries, competency, racial discrimination, etc.). Since many of the items listed have appeared in the mid- and later 1980s, this volume clearly supersedes existing works such as Charles Triche's *The Capital Punishment Dilemma, 1950-1977: A Subject Bibliography* (Whitston, 1979). As the book happened to arrive while the reviewer was working on an invited essay on capital punishment, he was able to put it immediately to use, and can personally testify to its helpfulness. Computerized search systems have not rendered this type of portable bibliography entirely obsolete!

David O. Friedrichs

526. Smandych, Russell C., and others. **Canadian Criminal Justice History: An Annotated Bibliography.** Toronto and Cheektowaga, N.Y., University of Toronto Press, 1987. 332p. index. $65.00. ISBN 0-8020-5720-9.

This annotated bibliography covers both published and unpublished materials written between 1867 and 1984 on the history of Canadian criminal justice to approximately 1970. Over eleven hundred English- or French-language citations with English-language abstracts are included. The bibliography is divided into four major chapters: police; crime deviance and dependency; courts and administration of justice; and prisons and social welfare institutions. The text is completed with an appendix of sources searched and an author index and a subject index. Within each chapter citations are arranged by author or editor and chronologically if there is more than one citation per author. Each citation is in standard citation format, with a fairly detailed descriptive annotation. The materials cited include monographs, journal and monograph articles, papers and report literature, government documents, and theses. The author index is detailed, covering primary and secondary authors and editors. The subject index gives headings and subdivisions at appropriate levels of detail and numerous cross-references.

This volume is a must for those interested in scholarly research and collections on Canadian criminal justice as well as any Canadian social history collection. [R: Choice, July/Aug 88, p. 1678]

Lorna K. Rees-Potter

527. Torres, Donald A. **Handbook of State Police, Highway Patrols, and Investigative Agencies.** Westport, Conn., Greenwood Press, 1987. 375p. illus. bibliog. index. $49.95. LC 86-27142. ISBN 0-313-24933-4.

This handbook covers an area of information that has remained dormant for many years. Researchers familiar with the author's *Handbook of Federal Police and Investigative Agencies* (see *ARBA 86*, entry 556) will welcome this new reference, which covers similar information at the state level.

This reference is divided into three basic parts. Part 1 gives a historical overview, examines the relationship between federal, state, county, and municipal agencies in law enforcement, and provides background on the establishment of the state enforcement agencies. Part 2 is comprised of photographs of badges and patches from the different states. Part 3 gives historical and organizational data, headquarters and training locations, and hiring and training qualifications for sworn members of each state police, highway patrol, or state investigative agency in the United States. Lines of authority are clearly indicated in organizational charts for each state. Textual information is followed by appendices of sample application forms and outlines of sample training course schedules.

Statistics are current through 1986. Photographs are clear and charts are easy to read. Parts 2 and 3 are arranged alphabetically by state and are uniform in coverage. A bibliography and short but adequate index complete the book. All information has been verified and reviewed with the appropriate state agency before publication, according to the preface. [R: Choice, Mar 88, p. 1072]

Elizabeth Thweatt

HUMAN RIGHTS

528. Charny, Israel W., ed. **Genocide: A Critical Bibliographic Review.** New York, Facts on File, 1988. 273p. index. $40.00. LC 87-33215. ISBN 0-8160-1903-7.

This interdisciplinary collection of essays, each including a critical annotated bibliography, brings together a wide variety of materials on genocide. Its intention is to present "an authoritative, encyclopedia-like statement of the knowledge base in a given field or area of study of genocide" (p. vii). Each chapter, written by an expert in the field, brings the reader up-to-date on the state-of-the-art concerning a particular aspect of genocide. The editor is Executive Director of the Institute of the International Conference on the Holocaust and

Genocide in Jerusalem. The book is a publication of this Institute. Included are chapters on the study of genocide, its intervention and prevention, history and sociology, psychology, philosophy, literature, art, and film. In addition, the book includes sections on the Holocaust, the Armenian genocide, genocide in the USSR, the Cambodian genocide, and other types of genocide. Although the scope of the book is broad, it does not cover legal conventions and tools for the punishment of genocide. A variety of definitions and approaches to genocide is presented in the various chapters. The introduction serves as a good overview and summary of the book. There is also an index (author, title, and subject), including citations to specific bibliographic entries, and cross-references.

The collection represents an important contribution to genocide scholarship. It is a useful guide and resource tool for students and scholars from a variety of subject disciplines interested in this field. It is also important for academic, public, and special librarians in collection development. Because of the annotated, selective bibliographies, it serves as a valuable selection tool in this field. [R: Choice, Dec 88, pp. 626, 628]   Susan J. Freiband

529. Gastil, Raymond D. **Freedom in the World: Political Rights and Civil Liberties 1987-1988.** Lanham, Md., Freedom House; distr., Lanham, Md., University Press of America, 1988. 450p. index. $29.50; $12.95pa. LC 82-642048. ISBN 0-932088-23-6; 0-932088-22-8pa.; ISSN 0732-6610.

The tenth edition of this country-by-country evaluation of "freedom in the world" is similar to previous editions (see *ARBA* 84, entry 503). An opening essay describes why the book focuses on civil and political rights and how these rights are defined. Following this are tables showing each country's rating relative to other countries, ratings for previous years, elections and referendums held in 1987, and social and economic data. More essays follow, on censorship, development, and the science (or art, depending on one's view) of developing schemes for rating such things as democracy and human rights. The core of the book is a concise write-up on each country, describing its political structure and current state of civil liberties. The summaries are arranged alphabetically by country; an index at the end covers countries and concepts addressed in the essays.

This book may be compared to two other annual country-by-country reviews: Amnesty International's annual report, and the Department of State's *Country Reports on Human*

Rights Practices (see *ARBA* 81, entry 596). As the introduction to *Freedom in the World* makes clear, however, its scope is much narrower than these other two works, focusing only on "freedom" as expressed in political and civil rights, not on economic or human rights. Each of these three books has its own political motivations and biases, and therefore complement, rather than duplicate, each other.

Cathy Seitz

530. Stormorken, Bjørn, and Leo Zwaak. **Human Rights Terminology in International Law: A Thesaurus.** Dordrecht, The Netherlands, Martinus Nijhoff; distr., Norwell, Mass., Kluwer Academic, 1987. 234p. $52.00. LC 87-31352. ISBN 90-247-3643-9.

The terminology of human rights presents problems not only in translation from and to many languages but in the various interpretations of the concepts themselves. The need for a controlled vocabulary has been known for a long time, but it was at the Human Rights Centre of the Council of Europe in Strasbourg that an attempt to fulfill this need was brought to fruition with the present volume. It is intended for use in human rights case law of national and international bodies, but refers only to case law as it is found in the *Digest of Strasbourg Case Law Relating to European Convention on Human Rights* (Heymanns, 1984-). The terms selected are taken directly from human rights documents, such as the Universal Declaration of Human Rights and the European Convention on Human Rights, and are placed in a simple hierarchical structure using the following abbreviations: TT (top term), BT (broader term), NT (narrower term), and RT (related term). The body of the work is composed of four lists: (1) a master list in alphabetical order where the term is followed by hierarchical information on interrelationships with other terms, (2) a simple alphabetical list for quick reference, (3) a KWOC (key word out of context) list, and (4) a list by article number for each of the human rights documents using the terminology found in the thesaurus (e.g., in article 1 of the American Convention on Human Rights the reader would find the terms *discrimination* and *obligations of states*). The volume is useful not only to those working in case law on human rights but also to those who are concerned with proper terminology in writing and research in the field of human rights.   Lucille Whalen

531. **World Directory of Human Rights Teaching and Research Institutions, 1988.** By the Social and Human Sciences Documentation Centre and the Division of Human Rights and

Peace. New York, Berg and Paris, UNESCO; distr., New York, St. Martin's Press, 1988. 216p. index. $49.95. LC 87-23188. ISBN 0-85496-229-8.

As part of UNESCO's World Social Science Information Directories, the *World Directory of Human Rights Teaching and Research Institutions* presents basic information on institutions around the world, governmental and nongovernmental, that promote human rights research and teaching. Although the preface and introductory material are in English, Spanish, and French, the directory section and indexes are in English. For the publication, *human rights* refers to those rights found in the Universal Declaration of Human Rights, the 1966 International Covenants on human rights, and the other instruments adopted by the specialized agencies. The editors have attempted to identify those institutions which offer programs of instruction and research in human rights and document the nature of these programs, giving also admission requirements and any scholarship aid that is offered. As in other works of this type, the information was obtained by means of a questionnaire. Developed by the Canadian Human Rights Foundation and sent to some ten thousand institutions throughout the world, the questionnaire understandably elicited less than a total response. The work makes it possible, however, to access information by country, subject of research or teaching areas, and scholarship aid. The full description is found under the title of the institution. Titles are arranged alphabetically under international and regional groups and then by country. Although there is incomplete information for some entries, this is an excellent beginning for information on human rights programs that is not easily found elsewhere. [R: Choice, Sept 88, p. 92]

Lucille Whalen

11 Library and Information Science and Publishing and Bookselling

LIBRARY AND INFORMATION SCIENCE

General Works

ACRONYMS AND ABBREVIATIONS

532. Sawoniak, Henryk, and Maria Witt. **New International Dictionary of Acronyms in Library and Information Science and Related Fields.** Munich, New York, K. G. Saur, 1988. 449p. $88.00. ISBN 3-598-10697-1.

In an age when acronyms are an integral part of language, any 449-page dictionary, international in scope, will be of value to members of a designated profession. This dictionary lists acronyms used in library and information science and related fields of publishing, printing, archive management, journalism, reprography, and some in computer science and management. It includes, in addition to the well-known international languages, the less popular languages of Central and Eastern Europe, Asia, Africa, and Latin America. This new edition includes 28,500 entries, compared to 12,700 in 1976.

It is difficult to understand the logic used in the selection of related fields and terms, as judged by the U.S. listings checked. Another discrepancy noted was the lack of criteria for inclusion of universities (e.g., four of the nine University of California campuses are included and five omitted, as is the University of Southern California). The California state universities are excluded, yet Colorado and Ohio state universities are included. Errors were detected (e.g., American Association of Law Libraries, AALL, is listed as ALL).

Since library acronyms are included in the three-volume twelfth edition of *Acronyms, Initialisms & Abbreviations* (see *ARBA* 88,

entry 1), which lists 420,000 entries, most general reference collections would be better served by purchasing one comprehensive, up-to-date source rather than acquiring marginal, specialized resources. [R: RLR, Nov 88, p. 333]
Helen Carol Bennett

DICTIONARIES AND ENCYCLOPEDIAS

533. **Encyclopedia of Library and Information Science. Volume 42, Supplement 7.** Allen Kent, ed. New York, Marcel Dekker, 1987. 428p. illus. $65.00. LC 68-31232. ISBN 0-8247-2042-3.

534. **Encyclopedia of Library and Information Science. Volume 43, Supplement 8.** Allen Kent, ed. New York, Marcel Dekker, 1988. 395p. illus. $65.00. LC 68-31232. ISBN 0-8247-2043-1.

The main set as well as several supplements to the *Encyclopedia of Library and Information Science* have been reviewed in *ARBA* as well as *Library and Information Science Annual.* For example, supplements 39, 40, and 41 were reviewed in *Library and Information Science Annual 1987* (see entries 11-13). In that review it is indicated that among other things, the purpose of the supplements is "to update articles in the main set; to add new articles on topics currently important in the field; to include recently deceased prominent librarians; and, finally, to include articles originally commissioned for the main set but not received in time for inclusion." The main set and first two volumes were reviewed in *Library Science Annual 1985* (see entries 6-9). That review incorporated references to previous reviews of individual volumes and also reviewed early supplements.

The two present supplements include a number of interesting articles. Volume 42 contains "Libraries in Denmark," by Preben

Kierkegaard and Hans Lemming, and "The United Nations Bibliographic Information," by Nathalie Dusoulier and S. Stein. Articles in volume 43 include "Congressional Research Services," by Robert Lee Chartrand and Sandra N. Milevski; "Copyright and the Information Professionals," by William Z. Nasri; "Information Resource Management," by Eileen M. Trauth; and "Machine-Readable Cataloging (MARC): 1986," by Henriette D. Avram. The articles are thorough and well documented, and the contributors are recognized authorities in their respective fields.

As mentioned in previous reviews, the impact of technology on the field of library science in recent years has been significant, and it is hoped that once the editor and his staff complete the supplements, a new edition of the encyclopedia will be produced.

Bohdan S. Wynar

DIRECTORIES

535. American Library Directory 1988-89. 41st ed. New York, R. R. Bowker, 1988. 2v. index. $164.95/set. LC 23-3581. ISBN 0-8352-2462-7; ISSN 0065-910X.

Pertinent factual information on over thirty-four thousand U.S. and Canadian libraries is included in this two-volume biennial edition. Almost every type of library is covered; however, the directory still lacks a listing of school libraries. Entries are comparable to previous editions and provide not only addresses and personnel information, but collection size, expenditures, and a wide variety of other information about the library. Arrangement is by state or province and then alphabetically by city. An index by library name is provided. Information is supplied by the libraries listed.

Special sections give added value to the volumes. Included are lists of networks, library schools (not just ALA accredited), libraries of the handicapped, state libraries, Army libraries, and USIA centers.

Spinoff publications include the entire database available on DIALOG and access to mailing labels from the publisher. Thus, libraries who cannot afford the $165.00 price can access the information contained through electronic means.

ALD is an indispensable and current tool for all who need information about libraries, including library professionals, publishers, and the general public who want to learn about libraries available not only in their local area, but in areas where they will be traveling.

David V. Loertscher

536. Directory of Library & Information Professionals. Woodbridge, Conn., with American Library Association by Research Publications, 1988. 2v. index. $345.00/set. ISBN 0-89235-125-X; ISSN 0894-7031.

This directory was designed by its publisher in cooperation with ALA to replace *Who's Who in Library and Information Services* (1982). The idea was to publish a work that would be not only more comprehensive than its predecessor, but also machine-readable on CD-ROM. Computerization also provided many different access points to the professionals other than by name. The arrangement of volume 1 is alphabetical by the person's name. Volume 2 provides indexes to names by specialty, employer, consulting expertise, and geographical area.

Information was gathered by massive mailings to the professionals of twenty library and information societies. Self-reports included detailed information on education and positions but restricted prolific writers to three publications of interest. A single followup mailing and some telephone solicitation was done to include as many persons as possible. Individual listings were edited by the publisher but were not returned to respondents for proofreading.

The effort to provide a wider listing of professionals is a great one. However, this publication is full of errors and lacks the comprehensive coverage originally intended by its designers. Its cost to produce both in-print and CD-ROM formats is evident from the price, which puts it out of range of most libraries and library professionals in the country. One would almost wish that the alphabetical access to persons in volume 1 had been published as a separate publication at less than half the price with access by other database fields being limited to an online search or to the CD-ROM application alone. Users of volume 2 will quickly come to the conclusion that access by computer and self-reporting of a single item such as library specialty leads to the most confusing maze of terminology for the same specialty. For example, there are at least fifty different titles which school librarians gave themselves, and the computer generates them as reported. Is computer access to a hodge-podge of information of value? This publication is a good example of what computerization is doing to publishing. Quality standards and information access needs should be evaluated before we drown the world in a morass of information from which we may never recover.

Conclusion? If the person you are looking for responded to the questionnaire, the source is valuable, but don't expect miracles. [R: Choice, Nov 88, p. 458; JAL, May 88, p. 111; LJ, 1 May

88, p. 64; RBB, 1 Apr 88, p. 1319; WLB, Mar 88, pp. 96-97; WLB, June 88, p. 124]

David V. Loertscher

537. Looney, Jim, and Colleen Smith, comps. **FOCUS: The Directory of Library Services in British Columbia.** 4th ed. Vancouver, B.C., British Columbia Library Association, 1987. 191p. index. $20.00 looseleaf with binder.

This directory is a couple of years overdue, but its quality makes it well worth the wait. To begin with, it is commendably comprehensive, giving listings not only for conventional libraries but also for such organizations as archives, associations and "reading centres." The coverage is particularly good for those notoriously hard to find out about libraries maintained by law firms, companies, and small societies; this directory's net seems to have caught all the fish around.

The editors have also included a number of very useful features not usually found in a regional directory. Detailed information is given for each branch as well as for the parent institution as a whole. The descriptions of collections give not only number of volumes but also indication of nonbook materials in twenty-seven categories. A geographical index provides access by locality (the main listing being alphabetical by official title), and an index by library type enables one to find, say, all the community college libraries in one grouping. ENVOY (the TransCanada electronic messaging system) and FAX numbers are supplied in addition to the usual telephone numbers and postal addresses. The personnel data indicate whether the staff members are professional, support persons, or technicians and show how many of each there are, down to fractions of FTE. And, most helpfully for the forgetful, an index of personal names enables you to find out where that person you met at a conference is working.

All this adds up to a remarkable amount of information in one source. Since this information is also presented accurately (no mistakes discovered) in legible and convenient format and at reasonable cost, FOCUS is by every standard a considerable achievement of its kind. Other regional library directories, please imitate!   Samuel Rothstein

538. **World Guide to Libraries. Internationales Bibliotheks-Handbuch.** 8th ed. Munich, New York, K. G. Saur, 1987. 1279p. index. (Handbook of International Documentation and Information, Vol. 8). $220.00. ISBN 3-598-20536-8; ISSN 0000-0221.

This work contains a staggering 37,784 current library entries in 167 countries, an increase

of 4,000 entries since the seventh edition (3,000 of which are in the United States). Criteria are that special libraries have holdings of five thousand volumes and general libraries thirty thousand volumes; some Third World countries are excepted.

The directory is arranged in order by continent, country, type of library, then city. A typical entry provides data on the size, specialization and accessibility of each library, including library name in the appropriate language and in English, mailing and telegraph addresses, telephone and telex numbers (no telefax), data of founding, name of director, main departments, special collections, statistics on holdings, participation in data networks and/or interlibrary loan programs, and reference number. There is an alphabetical index by library name (unfortunately, by complete name so that, for example, the John G. Shedd Aquarium Library is found under "John" instead of "Shedd"), but no subject index.

Specific personnel information may already be outdated in many cases since the editorial deadline was 5 August 1987, but the directory is valuable in identifying or verifying institutions, especially those outside of the United States. It also has great potential for library trivia, such as that the national library of Kiribati is located in Tarawa and has thirty-five thousand volumes. However, the price will cause many libraries to hesitate before purchasing it. [R: RLR, Nov 88, pp. 334-35]   Jay Schafer

HANDBOOKS AND YEARBOOKS

539. **ALA Handbook of Organization 1987/ 1988 and Membership Directory.** Chicago, American Library Association, 1987. 905p. $10.00pa. LC 80-649998. ISBN 0-8389-5706-4; ISSN 0273-4605.

The 1987/1988 handbook is identical in format to those of previous years. It serves the dual purpose of being an organizational manual and a membership directory. It is arranged in such a way that if size should ever dictate doing so, two separate volumes could easily be produced. The handbook, appendices, and indexes are in the first section of the book. Included in the handbook are the mission statements of the American Library Association and its various components, with names and business addresses of officials. The constitution and ALA policy manual are included in their entirety, as are lists of periodicals published by the association and awards given in 1988. The appendices provide a variety of useful information, including a calendar of events with location and dates of meetings of ALA and other library associations, and membership application forms with the current dues structure.

The index to the membership directory follows the general index. This places it in front of the directory, but causes no apparent difficulty in use. The 1987/1988 membership directory uses slightly larger print than did the 1986/1987 membership directory. The result is a volume which is approximately 15 percent longer in pages, but is definitely easier to read. There is an entry for each of the more than forty thousand personal members of the association. There are few questions about the American Library Association that one could ask which could not be answered by use of this handbook.

Robert M. Ballard

540. **The ALA Yearbook of Library and Information Services: A Review of Library Events 1987. Volume 13 (1988).** Roger H. Parent and Helen K. Wright, eds. Chicago, American Library Association, 1988. 419p. illus. index. $80.00. ISBN 0-8389-0489-0; ISSN 0740-042X.

Continuing the series begun in 1976, this year's volume follows very closely the format of recent years: a few feature articles, a number of special reports, a review of the year's library events, and reports from the fifty states. All of this is published in a large volume, attractively designed, with many illustrations. One of the two feature articles, "Libraries and Adult Literacy," is a competent introduction to the subject; the other, "Leadership and the Information Professions," is provocative, but too brief. The fifteen special reports, all one or two pages in length, are on a wide variety of topics: libraries and the AIDS crisis, The Center for the Book's first decade, nontax sources of revenue for public libraries, ACRL Planning Project for Historically Black College and University Libraries, etc. The 130 items that comprise the "Review of Library Events 1987" consist of reports of activities of library and library-related organizations and groups, and topical reports on a range of subjects such as information technology, library press, copyright, library education, and sound recordings—very useful summaries of recent developments. The fifty state reports provide some basic information about each state library association plus a narrative report on library news and activities in the state. There is a name and subject index, and finally a cumulative index to *ALA Yearbook* features (1976-1988). This last index is welcome, but even more welcome would have been the inclusion in that index of the special reports. This reviewer finds those almost always interesting, and often important professional reading. The same is true of many of the items in the review

of library events. All libraries should have the *ALA Yearbook*, and make it easily available to staff members, both for reference purposes and for professional reading.

Evan Ira Farber

541. **The Bowker Annual of Library and Book Trade Information 1988.** 33d ed. Filomena Simora, comp. and ed. New York, R. R. Bowker, 1988. 743p. index. $99.95. LC 55-12434. ISBN 0-8352-2468-6; ISSN 0068-0540.

The thirty-third edition of the *Bowker Annual* continues its important role of providing librarians and booksellers with essential information on both fields. Coverage and structure are the same as in previous editions, including, for example, "Reports from the Field"; "Legislation, Funding, Grants"; "Library/Information Science Education, Placement, and Salaries"; "Research and Statistics"; "Reference Information"; and "Directory of Organizations." Special topics of value in this edition are reading and literacy, the U.S.-U.S.S.R. Agreement on Library Cooperation, and a report on the progress of the sex versus salary/position issue. Important bibliographies such as "The Librarian's Bookshelf" are more up-to-date than in previous editions and statistics are current through 1987.

Because of varying features edition to edition, it is still a good idea to keep the last five volumes at one's fingertips. With such a battery of information at the reference librarian's disposal, it remains the preeminent handbook for librarians and booksellers. Indispensable. [R: LJ, 15 Oct 88, p. 62]

David V. Loertscher

542. Felknor, Bruce L. **How to Look Things Up and Find Things Out.** New York, Quill/ William Morrow, 1988. 290p. index. $22.00; $9.95pa. LC 87-22096. ISBN 0-688-07850-8; 0-688-06166-4pa.

As its title indicates, this book was written more for the inexperienced information seeker than for seasoned researchers. Yet there is information to be gleaned here by anyone who has ever experienced frustration with libraries and reference materials, whatever the reason. Writing in a friendly, conversational style, Felknor offers both encouragement and advice to would-be information seekers. He begins by identifying finding devices that are common to most reference books. He then provides clues to obtaining information about people, places, and various subject fields (e.g., geography, history, the arts, religion, science, mathematics, the social sciences, medicine, technology)—the major portion of the work. Although there are some recommended titles given in each subject category, this is not a bibliography per se.

Included in the volume is a concise yet informative chapter on computers and computer databases. And there is an index complete with cross-references.

The real "hero" of the book, however, is the reference librarian, whom the author both implicitly and explicitly advises the reader to seek anytime help is needed. This practical advice comes from Felknor's own experiences with libraries and research. [R: LJ, 1 Feb 88, p. 60; WLB, Apr 88, p. 102]

Dianne Brinkley Catlett

543. Library and Information Science Annual 1988. Volume 4. Bohdan S. Wynar, Ann E. Prentice, and Anna Grace Patterson, eds. Englewood, Colo., Libraries Unlimited, 1988. 325p. index. $37.50. ISBN 0-87287-683-7; ISSN 8755-2108.

Volume 4 of *Library and Information Science Annual*, continuing the basic format of the first three volumes, is divided into four main sections: (1) essays, (2) reviews of books, (3) reviews of periodicals, and (4) abstracts of library science dissertations. The editors have broadened their original objectives by reviewing all English-language (formerly selected) books in library science published in the United States and by extended coverage of Canadian, British, and Australian imprints. The size of the volume has increased considerably, particularly in the book review section, which has doubled from 253 reviews (volume 1) to 549 (volume 4).

By all objective standards *LISCA* is an excellent reference source. It is physically attractive, has sturdy binding, good quality paper, large boldface type, excellent format and arrangement, and separate author/title and subject indexes. A previous reviewer noted a discrepancy in style and quality among the 180 reviewers and suggested that more editing is needed. While this may be true, one could also argue that because the reviews are not "packaged" by professional reviewers but instead are written by librarians and educators with expertise in the subject, the reviews reflect the profession's diversity and therefore appeal to an equally diverse audience, and that stylistic variation makes the reviews more interesting to read. Reviewers are given guidelines and suggested format, but the style is their own. This reviewer has not detected a single bibliographical nor typographical error.

While some of the material in *LISCA* can be located in other sources, this sturdy, one-volume annual compilation of state-of-the-art essays, book and periodical reviews, and abstracts of library science dissertations is an invaluable addition to the literature of our field. [R: LJ, 15 Nov 88, p. 52]

Helen Carol Bennett

544. The Library Association Yearbook 1988. R. E. Palmer, comp. London, Library Association; distr., Chicago, American Library Association, 1988. 403p. $40.00pa. ISBN 0-85365-578-2; ISSN 0075-9066.

This sturdily bound yearbook provides current information about the Library Association of the United Kingdom. It is arranged in three parts. Part 1 contains pertinent information about the staff and officers of the association, its branches, special interest groups, publications, grants and awards, and other organizations affiliated with the association. Part 2 contains documentary sources such as the Royal Charter, the bylaws, regulations, and code of professional conduct. Part 3 is an alphabetical listing of its members as of February 1988.

This carefully wrought work is a useful reference source for all library professional collections. [R: LAR, 14 Oct 88, p. 614]

Robert H. Burger

545. Wygant, Alice Chambers, and O. W. Markley. **Information and the Future: A Handbook of Sources and Strategies.** Westport, Conn., Greenwood Press, 1988. 189p. bibliog. index. $37.95. LC 87-36063. ISBN 0-313-24813-3.

Naming and packaging are two important components of our late twentieth-century world. With *Information and the Future* we have an interesting example of the uses of both these trends. On the face of it, judging that is from the title and the introductory remarks, one might think that here was a revolutionary new (or at least markedly different) approach to information seeking. Instead, what we have for the most part is today's model clothed in tomorrow's terminology.

This book is basically a guide to using library and other information resources intelligently. This, in and of itself, is admirable. Anyone who works in a library, or indeed has ever needed to use a library, can testify to the need for well thought out, clearly articulated guides to the madness frequently encountered in the "ordered" world of libraries. Unfortunately, this book offers no more (and, to be honest, certainly no less) guidance, advice, strategic planning, etc., than countless other attempts to make the library intelligible to the user. The problem with this particular work is its pretentiousness.

Reviewed for what it is rather than what it purports to be, *Information and the Future* is a decent, if somewhat cumbersome, introduction to research strategies and sources. Designed to address a wide audience (ranging, according to the introductory chapter, from high school students to professional librarians), the book presents exactly the type of information one would (should) expect a book of this nature to present. The obvious statement sums up this work quite succinctly. Greenwood Press is charging almost $40.00 for information available elsewhere. The selections chosen as examples of guides to the literature, encyclopedias, and indexing and abstracting services are predictable. Perhaps the choices were dictated by the authors' efforts to keep to the letter, if not necessarily the spirit, of the title.

The one section that does stand out is part 3, "Applications." Here the authors present two conceptual tools designed to help researchers "learn about, forecast, and influence the process of social change on topics of importance" (p. 119). The two concepts, the "issue emergence cycle" and the "strategic intelligence cycle," are not so much discussed as drawn, presented in, to quote the text, "graphical illustrations." Some of this is fascinating, although two problems emerge. First, the brief introduction may serve to confuse rather than illuminate. And second, there is no clearly drawn connection between these highly theoretical constructs and the rather pedestrian tone of the earlier sections.

Ellen Broidy

INDEXES

546. Library Literature 1987: An Index to Library and Information Science. Cathy Rentschler and Mary M. Brereton, eds. Bronx, N.Y., H. W. Wilson, 1988. 655p. sold on service basis. LC 36-27468. ISSN 0024-2373.

Library Literature, a popular Wilson index, has been reviewed several times in *ARBA* (see *ARBA* 82, entry 155). The most recent review can be found in *Library Science Annual: Volume 1* (Libraries Unlimited, 1985). First published in 1936, this indexing service is well known to the library profession. The 1987 volume indexes 244 periodicals and includes coverage of books, pamphlets, films, filmstrips, microcards, microfilms, and library school theses dealing with library and information science. Monographic material in English is handled quite well, indexing 60 and 70 percent of books and pamphlets published in this country and Canada, respectively. Publications of Eastern Europe and other developing countries are not as well represented.

As noted in previous reviews, a time lag in indexing periodicals is evident, especially with regard to foreign titles. Nationally known periodicals published in the United States (*Library Journal, Wilson Library Bulletin*, etc.) have a time lapse of only one to two months. Regional publications and subject-oriented periodicals published in this country average around six months, and the time lapse for foreign periodicals is more significant at one to three years.

As in previous volumes, entries for book and nonbook materials are arranged in one alphabet by author and by specific subject heading.

A comprehensive, well-executed, and reliable indexing service, *Library Literature* is recommended to all institutions interested in the professional literature of library and information science.   Susan R. Penney

Careers

547. Librarian Career Resource Network Directory. Chicago, Office for Library Personnel Resources, American Library Association, 1987. 37p. index. $2.00pa. ISBN 0-8389-7205-5.

The aim of this ALA Office for Library Personnel Resources publication is to provide a "list of practicing librarians who have volunteered to answer career related questions." Volunteers are listed in alphabetical order along with particulars concerning their position, address, areas of expertise, and indications of the method of contact they prefer. Geographical and subject indexes are included. ALA/OLPR assumes responsibility for maintaining the directory.

The philosophy behind such a directory is apparently well founded. Certainly it seems reasonable to identify willing experts to guide other librarians in career choices and explorations. The problem I have encountered with other such directories is that they are often uneven, poorly maintained, and inadequately distributed. Only responses from users and volunteers and time will tell if this effort can escape those pitfalls. The start is adequate and propitious. We hope that the directory will grow and increase in usefulness.

Patricia A. Steele

Cataloging and Classification

548. Binding Terms: A Thesaurus for Use in Rare Book and Special Collections Cataloguing. By the Standards Committee of the Rare Books and Manuscripts Section (ACRL/ALA). Chicago, Association of College and Research Libraries, American Library Association, 1988. 37p. $10.00pa. ISBN 0-8389-7210-1.

549. Provenance Evidence: Thesaurus for Use in Rare Book and Special Collections Cataloguing. By the Standards Committee of the Rare Books and Manuscripts Section (ACRL/ ALA). Chicago, Association of College and Research Libraries, American Library Association, 1988. 19p. $9.00pa. ISBN 0-8389-7239-X.

For years most rare book libraries and departments have developed and maintained local files recording examples of various physical characteristics of books and manuscripts found in their collections. With the advent of machine-readable cataloging it became necessary for libraries to express the information in these local files in a uniform way so that this valuable information could be shared by others. In 1979 the Independent Research Libraries Association issued *Proposals for Establishing Standards for the Cataloguing of Rare Books and Specialized Research Materials in Machine-readable Form*, which called for a new field to be added to the MARC format for terms indicating the physical characteristics of materials cataloged. At the same time it was proposed that the Standards Committee of the Rare Books and Manuscripts Section of ACRL undertake the development of a thesaurus of such terms. This thesaurus, it was decided, should be issued in separate parts, and the first, *Printing and Publishing Evidence*, was published in 1986. The next two – *Binding Terms* and *Provenance Evidence* – are under discussion here, and other subjects, such as paper and papermaking and type evidence, are being prepared.

The thesaurus for *Binding Terms* is arranged in two parts, an alphabetical list of terms used to describe materials, techniques and styles of bindings, and a hierarchical list which displays the relationships between broader and narrower terms. Many of the terms in the alphabetical list are defined, often with quotations from Paul Needham's *Twelve Centuries of Bookbinding 400-1600* (Pierpoint Morgan with Oxford University Press, 1979), and the introduction contains a list of references useful to the understanding of the terms.

Provenance Evidence is also divided into an alphabetical list and a hierarchical list, with definitions provided in the alphabetical list. It is important to note that " 'provenance' is here interpreted in its broadest sense to refer not only to former owners in the legal sense, but also to any who may have had temporary custody of the material (such as auction houses or library

borrowers) and have left their mark in some way on it" (p. 1). A list of works useful for detailed descriptions of provenance evidence is also provided in the introduction.   Dean H. Keller

550. Canadian Thesaurus 1988: A Guide to the Subject Headings Used in the *Canadian Periodical Index* and *CPI Online*. Thésaurus Canadien 1988. Robert Lang and others, eds. Toronto, Info Globe, 1988. 465p. $85.00 spiral-bound. ISBN 0-921925-04-2; ISSN 0838-3553.

This thesaurus "is designed to facilitate retrieval of material when searching the *Canadian Periodical Index* online or in print." *CPI* indexes more than 375 periodicals, including those in the French language and the eighteen U.S. titles most commonly found in Canadian libraries. This "bilingual list of over 35,000 terms covering all major subject areas and emphasizing Canadian topics ... reflect[s] the content of magazines indexed in *CPI*. The level of specificity given to each subject corresponds to the level of detail found in the periodical literature." The fact that the publisher, Info Globe, is owned by the *Globe and Mail*, an influential Toronto-based newspaper available throughout Canada, gives this list authority.

The *Canadian Thesaurus* can also be used as an adjunct to *Canadian Subject Headings*, second edition (Ottawa, National Library of Canada, 1985) and to *Répertoire de vedettes-matière*, ninth edition (Québec, Université de Laval, 1983). Its value to catalogers lies in the provision of subject headings not found in either of the two subject heading lists used by most Canadian libraries. Catalogers in bilingual libraries will find the French-English equivalencies very helpful.

This work is a recommended purchase for large cataloging departments or those that do in-depth cataloging, and for reference departments where *CPI* is consulted frequently. Updated and revised editions are planned for the future.

Jean Weihs

551. Dickstein, Ruth, Victoria A. Mills, and Ellen J. Waite. **Women in LC's Terms: A Thesaurus of Library of Congress Subject Headings Relating to Women.** Phoenix, Ariz., Oryx Press, 1988. 221p. $28.50. LC 87-34766. ISBN 0-89774-444-6.

This thesaurus is a guide to the Library of Congress's (LC) subject headings used for and about topics dealing with women. The terms included in this work are taken from the 1983 microfiche update of the *Library of Congress Subject Headings* (*LCSH*). Also included are any new or changed headings beginning with the word *women* from the tenth edition of *LCSH*.

The thesaurus begins with an alphabetical listing of all included terms. Following this are individual chapters organized by specific topical terminology relating to women. Chapters include "Communication and Information"; "Economics and Employment"; "Education"; "History and Social Change"; "International Women"; "Languages"; "Literature"; "Religion and Philosophy"; "Law, Government, and Public Policy"; "Health and Biological Sciences"; "Natural Science and Technology"; "Social Science and Culture"; and "Visual and Performing Arts." Introductory scope notes begin each chapter.

Four appendices describe the subdivisions used with LC subject headings. The fifth appendix provides a listing of LC call numbers assigned to women and topics relating to them.

The intended users of this thesaurus are researchers and librarians using subject catalogs and indexes when researching women's studies materials as well as librarians who catalog and index such materials. Unquestionably this work will provide significant value for its audience as it is well organized, complete, and serves as a springboard to other related indexes and databases pertaining to this growing interdisciplinary field. [R: LJ, July 88, p. 58; RBB, 1 Sept 88, p. 57]   Marjorie E. Bloss

552. Olson, Nancy B. **Audiovisual Material Glossary.** Dublin, Ohio, OCLC Online Computer Library Center, 1988. 41p. illus. bibliog. (OCLC Library Information and Computer Science Series, No. 7). $8.50pa. ISBN 1-55653-026-9.

This slight volume is a valuable resource, well worth its purchase price. It is not perfect—the title is misleading, there are some structural problems, and it would be a mistake to regard all definitions as authoritative—but for many general catalogers and other librarians faced with handling a variety of nonbook materials, this glossary may be precisely what is needed.

In choosing terms to include, the compiler interpreted *audiovisual* as encompassing virtually everything that is not a printed book of text. Thus atlases, music scores, broadsheets, computer software, and anything that requires special equipment to use are all included. Definitions are taken from various sources, and attributed when quoted directly or modified within defined limits. Definitions cover only audiovisual materials, sometimes only *some* audiovisual materials (e.g., *sleeve* is defined only for sound recordings and microfiche, *border* is defined only for maps). The impetus for definition modification is not always clear (e.g., *artifact* is changed from the *ALA Glossary*'s

"made or modified by human workmanship" to "made or modified by man," while the definition for *puppet film*, which defines a film as movement itself rather than as a representation of movement, is unchanged from OCLC's *Audiovisual Media Format*). Coverage seems uneven, being more inclusive, for example, for cartographic than for graphic materials. A network of *see, see also,* and *cf.* references among terms is helpful, but occasionally incomplete (e.g., no references like *puppet film* to *animation*).

Many terms appear in the *ALA Glossary* (see *ARBA 84*, entry 86). Most special format terms can be found in separate manuals, which are themselves more comprehensive for the particular formats (e.g., H. L. Stibbe's *Cartographic Materials: A Manual of Interpretation for AACR2*, ALA, 1982). The *Audiovisual Material Glossary*'s strength is combining deeper coverage of audiovisual material than the *ALA Glossary*, gathering major terms for all sorts of audiovisual materials into a single place, and including terms which have only recently come into library usage (e.g., *optical disc*). Another asset is the presence of drawings to augment certain definitions (e.g., *isometric view, stereograph reel,* etc.).

Janet Swan Hill

553. Olson, Nancy B., comp. *Cataloging Service Bulletin* **Index: An Index to the** *Cataloging Service Bulletin* **of the Library of Congress: No. 1-40, Summer 1978-Spring 1988.** Lake Crystal, Minn., Soldier Creek Press, 1988. 127p. $20.00 (unbound). ISBN 0-936996-32-3.

Information from the *Cataloging Service Bulletin* is vitally important to catalogers, but it is difficult to keep track of, so indexes to it are greeted enthusiastically. This new index covers the full run of *CSB*, including the entire AACR2 era. It is unbound, and sized to file with the bulletins themselves. Entries file under all important terms (e.g., creating added entries for the name of a manuscript repository is indexed under added entries, repository, and manuscript, and the relevant rule). Coverage is unpredictably incomplete. For example, *CSB* 13, page 7, under AA1.48B, discusses treatment of privately published works, but the occurrence is not indexed, although the previous version in *CSB* 12, page 7 *is*. Cursory checking also found no entries for "Initialisms in title proper" (*CSB* 13, p. 19); for Korean word division (*CSB* 14, pp. 71-78); or for Macroreproductions (*CSB* 14, p. 58) (but the previous version, *CSB* 12, p. 16 *is* indexed). The ease with which these omissions were detected makes more seem likely. Vocabulary is occasionally inconsistent. For example,

CSB 13, page 27, and *CSB* 14, page 24 contain versions of the same RI, the first indexed as "Series Tracing," the second as "Series Tracing Guidelines." Other entries under "Series Tracing Guidelines" and "Series Tracings" mean that catalogers will need to follow up on multiple citations before being assured of having exhausted the possibilities of the *index*.

Because of omissions, catalogers may never be assured of having exhausted the possibilities of the bulletins themselves. LC's own index to its *Library of Congress Rule Interpretations* (1988) will eventually reduce interest in detailed indexing for much *CSB* content, but for libraries that do not acquire the separate publication, and for all non-*LCRI* items, independent indexes will still have a place. Catalogers will be glad to have this one, but they should be aware of its shortcomings.   Janet Swan Hill

554. Taylor, Arlene G., with Rosanna M. O'Neil. **Cataloging with Copy: A Decision-Maker's Handbook.** 2d ed. Englewood, Colo., Libraries Unlimited, 1988. 355p. illus. bibliog. index. $35.00. LC 88-13840. ISBN 0-87287-575-X.

This book is misnamed. It is an excellent, maybe essential, manual for all librarians seeking to turn collections into coherent information retrieval systems using current practices for description, indexing, and classification. The theme of the book is absolutely true: rules for description, indexing, and classification and their application, no matter how expert, cannot and will not make an integrated, coherent catalog or classified collection. Each catalog surrogate and each classified document must be fit into the existing catalog and collection, and it is the care or carelessness with which these fundamental processes are performed that determine the quality of the information retrieval they support. It matters little, in terms of these functions, whether the cataloging data or "copy" comes from inside or outside the library (for example, from the Library of Congress or cooperating libraries via cataloging utilities).

This book emphasizes the integrating function with its step-by-step description and analysis of every consideration, enhanced by numerous illustrations. It is indeed "A Decision-Maker's Handbook." After an opening overview of the whole situation, the handbook takes decisionmakers through each major component of the library retrieval system: document description, choice and form of name, title and subject access headings, classification, and the exceedingly complicated problem of author, title, and issue notation. Subsequent chapters address sources of cataloging information,

cataloging media and the impact of computer-based cataloging. The volume concludes with a very brief bibliography and a useful index.

No book, especially one dealing with such a complicated and technical subject, can be perfect, but this book is remarkably problem and error free. In a comparison of journal arrangement by title rather than by classification notation, the need to shift the collection as it grows unevenly across the alphabet is likewise a problem with classified collections (p. 183). In discussing Dewey Decimal Classification notation supplied by the Library of Congress, the claim is made of "the lack of a means of drawing together materials on the same subject" (p. 242). These small quibbles do not measurably affect the value of the book as a whole.

All librarians, and especially administrators and directors, should be required to read at least the first paragraph of the concluding chapter which includes: "It has been shown throughout this book that it is possible to use outside copy exactly as it appears *only* if the library and its users are willing to accept the potential consequences" (p. 3328). Professionals should want to know what these consequences are, and for that, they will have to read the rest of the book.
                                    James D. Anderson

Comparative and International Librarianship

555. Wei, Karen T., comp. **Library and Information Science in China: An Annotated Bibliography.** Westport, Conn., Greenwood Press, 1988. 273p. index. (Bibliographies and Indexes in Library and Information Science, No. 3). $39.95. LC 88-17767. ISBN 0-313-25548-2.

This comprehensive bibliography lists 991 books, chapters in books, periodical articles, conference papers, theses, dissertations, and ERIC documents on all aspects of library and information science in pre-1949 China, the People's Republic of China, and the Republic of China. The scope is broad, covering books and printing; the history of Chinese libraries; national, college and university, public, special, school and children's libraries and archives; cataloging, classification, Chinese collections, and acquisition; automation and information services; education for librarianship; publishing and trade; international exchange and activities; librarians; copyright laws; library associations; and research librarianship.

Most of the cited works are in the English language. A few important Chinese, French, German, and Japanese works have been included if they are accompanied by a translation or an abstract in the English language. Almost all of the titles are twentieth-century works, although a very small number date from the late nineteenth century. About 96 percent of the entries have descriptive annotations which are well written and effectively summarize the contents and indicate the scope of the work. Entries are arranged in ten subject categories and a section on bibliography and reference works, which contains forty-four entries. Rapid reference access is provided by author and subject indexes. This compilation, the only comprehensive bibliography on the subject to date, will be an extremely useful research aid for students of the field and for scholars generally.

Shirley L. Hopkinson

Conservation and Preservation

556. Preservation Education Directory. 5th ed. Susan G. Swartzburg, comp. Chicago, Resources and Technical Services Division, American Library Association, 1988. 30p. index. $5.00 pa.

The main body of this work, now in its fifth edition, lists preservation programs and courses offered at accredited library schools in the United States and Canada and preservation components in other library school courses. The only preservation degree program listed is at Columbia University, where students may earn either an M.S.L.S. or an advanced certificate in preservation. Both programs are described. Many library schools now offer individual courses in preservation. Schools are listed alphabetically by name, and each entry describes the course content and, usually, the number of course credits given. Schools which incorporate preservation information into other courses, such as rare books, history of books and printing, and collection management, are also listed with briefer entries. A second section of the book lists institutes and associations in North America which offer courses or workshops on preservation. Section 3 describes five conservation training programs for conservators who perform hands-on restoration work. Section 4 tells the reader how to acquire information about programs abroad from the International Centre for the Study of the Preservation and the Restoration of Cultural Property in Rome. It is followed by a geographic index for the institutions in the United States and Canada. This book will be useful to individuals who wish to study preservation management or conservation techniques. And since it lists which library schools in each state offer preservation courses, it can also help library administrators recruit preservation/conservation specialists for their

staffs. It should be available to both library staff and patrons.   Linda Keir Simons

Information Technologies

557. Jones, C. Lee, ed. **Directory of Telefacsimile Sites in Libraries in the United States and Canada.** 3d ed. Buchanan Dam, Tex. C B R Consulting Services, 1987. 128p. $18.00pa.

This edition lists close to seven hundred sites in the United States and Canada that have reported the use of telefacsimile equipment to the editor. A brief introduction describes how this information was obtained and contains a summary by manufacturer of the hardware installed in the participating libraries.

The directory is organized by state or province (separate sections) and lists libraries alphabetically within each section. Each entry contains the name of the institution or library, address, fax telephone number, contact person, voice telephone number, and equipment used. Three indexes supplement the main directory. These indexes provide access to the entries by state and city, by institution, and by fax telephone number beginning with the area code. The institution and fax telephone number indexes would be more useful if they provided geographic information so that the reader could go directly to the desired entry in the main directory.

Although its value is limited by the rapid growth and changes occurring in telefacsimile services, this type of book is needed by libraries involved in the technology.

Dennis J. Phillips

Interlibrary Loans

558. Morris, Leslie R., and Patsy Brautigam. **Interlibrary Loan Policies Directory.** 3d ed. New York, Neal-Schuman, 1988. 781p. index. $87.50pa. LC 87-35001. ISBN 1-55570-024-1.

This third edition of the standard interlibrary loan policies directory provides the most current printed information available for over fifteen hundred academic, public, and special libraries in the United States, plus a few Puerto Rican and Canadian universities. (Inevitably a few libraries are omitted.)

Arranged alphabetically by state and then by name of library or institution, the information received in response to a survey questionnaire includes ILL address and telephone number; acceptable methods of transmission; average turnaround time; policies regarding the loan of books, periodicals, newspapers, doctoral dissertations and master's theses, government documents, technical reports, microforms, audiovisual materials, and computer software; photoduplication services; billing procedures; packing requirements for mailing; time service is suspended during Christmas holidays; lending policies to foreign libraries; and groups of libraries for which fees are waived. Several of the categories are new to this edition.

Also included are three useful indexes: name of library/institution index with state identification, an index to libraries with facsimile transmission and receiving capabilities (with fax number when supplied), and an index to those libraries that charge for loaning books (fees range from $0.75 to $15.00). Unfortunately, the number of libraries charging for book loans is growing. All blank or indefinite ("varies") responses were considered as "No."

This directory should be very useful to all librarians working with interlibrary loans. Although some of this information is available in OCLC's online interlibrary loan file, the policies of many more libraries are included here, and frequently more detailed information is listed. Although all prices and policies are subject to change, for the present this is a very convenient and comprehensive directory. [R: WLB, Oct 88, p. 110]   Esther Jane Carrier

Library Automation

559. Dyer, Hilary, and Alison Gunson, comps. **A Directory of Library and Information Retrieval Software for Microcomputers.** 3d ed. Brookfield, Vt., Gower Publishing, 1988. 75p. index. $41.95pa. LC 87-23646. ISBN 0-566-05586-4.

The most dramatic change in this third edition is the new print format, which greatly improves both readability and searchability. As in past editions, the major portion of the book contains entries listed alphabetically by program name. The degree of detail varies considerably among entries depending upon how much is included in the Notes field; however, no entry contains any type of evaluation. Listings are found for both British (costs in pounds sterling) and U.S. (costs in dollars) products.

Especially useful are the hardware, supplier, and function indexes. These have no page numbers, but since the entries are arranged alphabetically, it is not a serious problem. The hardware index, while certainly helpful, can be misleading. The PC compatibles list contains only a fraction of the listings found under the IBM PC heading, presumably because the software producers did not think to include this category in their description.

A brief section gives guidelines for choosing software, but although the advice is good, the entries themselves do not contain enough information for making any choices. The book does, however, serve as a good initial reference source.

Despite these few caveats, the book is a good source of basic information on microcomputer software for libraries and information environments. [R: LAR, 15 Sept 88, p. 522]
                Elisabeth Logan

Library History

560. Young, Arthur P. **American Library History: A Bibliography of Dissertations and Theses.** 3d ed. Metuchen, N.J., Scarecrow, 1988. 469p. index. $39.50. LC 88-10072. ISBN 0-8108-2138-9.

Every new edition of *American Library History* is a significant improvement of an already useful reference book. This third edition was long overdue, since the second was published in 1974. The current work is a bibliography of 1,174 items, of which 964 are annotated listings of doctoral dissertations and master's theses and 210 are unannotated listings of unpublished reports and papers. The book begins with a brief chapter describing and listing the various reference sources for American library history. These items are not numbered. The second and main part of the book is the bibliography of dissertations and theses, which is divided into fourteen sections. Each section concerns a type of library (e.g., public, school, etc.) or a topic (biographical or education). The annotations are basically descriptive and range from 40 to 120 words in length. Enough information is provided to indicate whether the item is of interest for further study, although no critical evaluation is provided. Part 3 is a listing of unpublished papers and reports, largely organized in the same manner as part 2. Separate indexes to authors and subjects are provided. Amazingly, no one apparently had written a thesis or dissertation on the Allen County Public Library of Fort Wayne, Indiana! All library schools, education programs, history departments, and individuals studying American library history should acquire or have access to this useful publication. It provides the invaluable service of locating materials that are difficult or impossible to find. Professor Young deserves our gratitude. [R: JAL, Nov 88, p. 314]
                Ronald H. Fritze

Library Instruction

561. Penchansky, Mimi B., Evelyn Apterbach, and Adam Halicki-Conrad, comps. **International Students and the Library: An Annotated Selective Bibliography on the Theme of the LACUNY 1988 Institute.** Flushing, N.Y., Library Association of the City University of New York, 1988. 29p. $3.00pa.

This bibliography provides a brief guide to significant information on orienting foreign students to the college or university library. It covers books, journal articles, reports, and studies. Organizations that work with international students are included, as well as tips on helping these students use the library. It must be emphasized that it is a selective bibliography – coverage is somewhat limited – but each entry has a long, detailed annotation that is particularly helpful. While it would hardly be an exhaustive source for the subject, this work would help librarians who are faced with serving a large population of international students begin to familiarize themselves with the issues of this area. Also, the section of tips on helping foreign students in the academic library would be useful for those librarians looking for immediate ways of better serving this special group of library users. In short, almost everything included could be found by searching recent volumes of *Library Literature* or ERIC, but for a minimal price, the Library Association of the City University of New York has done it for you.   Sallie H. Barringer

Public Libraries

562. Gutierrez, David, and Roberto G. Trujillo, comps. **The Chicano Public Catalog: A Collection Guide for Public Libraries.** Encino, Calif., Floricanto Press, 1987. 188p. index. $39.00pa.

The compilers state that this core bibliography "represents a solid, basic collection in Mexican American Studies" (p. i). It includes 487 titles of Chicano materials almost exclusively in the English language in such fields as social science, language, literature, and history. Even though most academic areas of Mexican-American studies are well represented in this work, many important areas such as education are virtually ignored. The most glaring omission in this core bibliography, however, is in the area of fiction. One must question the inclusion of only two novels, a few short stories, and a few plays in what is supposed to be a collection guide for public libraries. [R: Choice, Feb 88, p. 882; WLB, Apr 88, pp. 98-99]   Isabel Schon

563. **University Press Books for Public Libraries.** 10th ed. New York, for Public Library Association, American Library Association by Association of American University Presses, 1988. 87p. index. free pa. ISSN 0731-2857.

The latest edition by the Public Library Association's Small and Medium-Sized Libraries Section highlight the 1987 offerings of university presses. Judged by eleven public librarians, this work continues the practice of the ninth edition in excluding university press journals and serials. Each entry, arranged in Dewey Decimal Classification order with an author and title index, is annotated with liberal quotes from the reviewing media. Still useful for the smaller library wanting guidance in selecting titles from the annual university press output.

Chris Albertson

564. **Young Adult 1987 Annual Booklist.** Los Angeles, Calif., Adult Services, Los Angeles Public Library, 1987. 71p. $5.00pa.

Published by the Los Angeles Public Library, this thin 8½-by-11-inch stapled paperback lists books published in 1985 and 1986 that the Los Angeles adult services staff judged would be of interest to young adults. The list is divided into twenty-three pages of fiction entries and eight pages of nonfiction entries with brief annotations, an unannotated list of twenty-two career titles and two songbooks; fifteen pages of unannotated listings of "Adult Books Having YA Interest and/or Assignment Value"; and twenty-one pages of unannotated listings of "Selected Uncataloged Paperbacks."

This is not an essential purchase for any selector. Most individuals selecting young adult materials would have already been aware of these items from reviews, while those inexperienced selectors may seek help directly from the annual "Best Books" lists of the American Library Association's Young Adult Service Division or the H. W. Wilson catalog series (*Junior High School Catalog* [see *ARBA* 86, entry 596] or *Senior High School Catalog* [see *ARBA* 88, entry 640]).   Chris Albertson

School Libraries

565. **The Elementary School Library Collection: A Guide to Books and Other Media. Phases 1-2-3.** 16th ed. Lois Winkel with others, eds. Williamsport, Pa., Brodart, 1988. 1028p. index. $79.95. LC 87-24974. ISBN 0-87272-092-6.

The sixteenth edition of this important selection tool for school and public libraries continues its long-standing provision of a core book and audiovisual media collection. Books and other media of high quality available and/or published between 15 April 1985 and 15 April 1987 are included. As with previous editions, standards of quality including allegiance to certain "current trends of education" must be met before a title is listed. Arrangement is by Dewey Decimal Classification (eleventh abridged ed.) with author, title, and subject indexes.

ESLC has almost twice the titles as its competitor, *Children's Catalog* (see *ARBA* 87, entry 619), and contains audiovisual media that the H. W. Wilson list does not. Annotations in *ESLC* are descriptive for the most part, while the *Catalog* annotations contain excerpts of reviews. *ESLC* includes sections for reference, professional publications, and periodicals not included in the *Catalog*. Both tools have a heavy overlapping of titles and their revision policy is quite different. *ESLC* is published in its entirety annually, while the *Catalog* is published at five-year intervals with annual supplements. Each policy of revision has its own set of advantages for collection building.

In both lists, fiction and easy books predominate, biasing the lists toward literature and away from curricular nonfiction. This bias is as much a publisher's bias as a conscious one by the editors. Realizing this and other biases of basic lists such as "the best of what is in print," users who purchase and use the list must do so carefully, as instructed by the editor. School librarians will need to use the list to build more curriculum-oriented collections in contrast to public librarians who will want broader coverage of children's interests for the community as a whole. Purchasing the entire collection in phases for new schools or public libraries is not a wise practice where a focused collection matching local needs is desired. Use of the list for topical development of collections is a wiser practice.

While one may quibble with the selection of individual titles, the list is as current as the "in-print nightmare of U.S. publishing" will allow. The professional collection needs a thorough revision to reflect needs of both librarians and teachers in the school. Otherwise, the list is highly recommended for those who are beginning and building collections. Since the list is expensive, a system of cooperative purchase within a local area is recommended. [R: BL, July 88, p. 1844]   David V. Loertscher

566. **School Library Media Annual 1988. Volume Six.** Jane Bandy Smith, ed. Englewood, Colo., Libraries Unlimited, 1988. 297p. index. $29.50. ISBN 0-87287-635-7; ISSN 0739-7712.

This volume was compiled by a team of editors who tried to follow the tradition of excellence established by the previous co-editors. The first concern of this book continues to be reading, but most recently this topic has come under new labels such as literacy, and has drawn the attention of a number of people and organizations. The school library media not being a classroom, the editors kept the practitioners in mind and geared their publication to current practice, dealing with such topics as continuing education, issues, research and studies, information, and publications.

The first part of the book reports on the "whole language approach," a student-centered, integrated language arts approach that requires an expanded role of library media personnel to assist students in their work. This also means that the library media center must have a wide assortment of quality literature to meet the needs of the students. It must develop active participation between teachers and media specialists.

Another section of the book looks at the publishing industry and its pressures and practices in the corporate political arena; its profit making business orientation is not always in line with pedagogical objectives. One California experience (the "whole language approach") and another in Georgia about the censorship issue in Gwinnett County are reported. Some attention is focused on research and the need for better bibliographical control. Concern is expressed for training, use, cost, and supervision in technology. In the field of automation, library media specialists are showing special interest in two areas: automated circulation and cataloging.

The last part of this volume is like an almanac dealing with information on a variety of topics. This book is a wealth of information and the editors must be commended for their good work.   Camille Côté

567. **University Press Books for Secondary School Libraries.** 20th ed. New York, for American Association of School Librarians, American Library Association by Association of American University Presses, 1988. 49p. index. free pa. ISSN 0887-1345.

Selected by secondary school librarians, this annotated list of over two hundred titles from university presses is intended to increase the awareness of titles which can add depth and breadth to a secondary school collection on topics less frequently published by commercial publishers. Titles are arranged in Dewey Decimal Classification order and each entry contains complete bibliographic information as well as an annotation taken from recognized reviewing sources or provided by members of the committee. Each entry is coded for level (high school or junior high school) and expected appeal (general, regional, or special, for those libraries with in-depth collections in the field). Titles were selected which enhance the curriculum, are of interest to young adults, are new editions of previously published works, or are scholarly titles that require a basic knowledge of the subject. A directory of contributing publishers with addresses is located on the inside covers. Author and title indexes are included.

The largest group of titles is in history, geography, and biography, with the next largest group in the social sciences. The literature section is the third largest group, and the pure sciences and the arts have about an equal number. The other subject areas of Dewey have a limited number of titles. While all secondary school libraries will find this a helpful selection aid, those in schools offering honors or advanced placement courses will find it particularly useful.	Donald C. Adcock

Special Libraries

568.	**Directory of Special Libraries and Information Centers 1987: Colorado, South Dakota, Utah, Wyoming.** Denver, Colo., Rocky Mountain Chapter, Special Libraries Association, 1987. 114p. index. $20.00pa.

Information on nearly three hundred special libraries and their resources has been gathered together in this very useful publication, described in its introduction as "the first attempt by the Rocky Mountain Chapter/Special Libraries Association to create a regional directory of special libraries." The book is not a comprehensive listing of all special libraries in the four-state region encompassed; some six hundred questionnaires were sent out, but many of the libraries (especially smaller ones) either did not respond or declined to be listed. However, for those who did respond, the directory provides just the right amount of concise and helpful information.

The entries are organized first by state, then within state alphabetically by parent organization. Elements of each entry include organization, library, and head librarians' names; address and telephone number; subjects; special collections; number of books, periodicals (bound volumes), and subscriptions; availability of public access, telephone reference, and interlibrary loan; computer databases, telecommunications, and systems in use; OCLC/RLIN symbol; and notes of other appropriate information supplied by the individual libraries. A

check of selected entries indicates that they are both correct and current. (Special librarians must have a fairly low job-change rate!) Two indexes—geographic (by city/town) and subject (basic but complete)—round out the directory.

This publication will be a welcome resource for anyone looking for information in the four states covered, and will be especially useful to special librarians trying to find other information professionals in specific subject areas. The chapter and association are to be congratulated on the results of their collaboration, and encouraged to update the directory on a regular (biannual?) basis.	G. Kim Dority

569.	Filby, P. William, comp. **Directory of American Libraries with Genealogy or Local History Collections.** Wilmington, Del., Scholarly Resources, 1988. 319p. index. $75.00. LC 87-37109. ISBN 0-8420-2286-4.

More Americans are searching for their ancestors than ever before; genealogy is now outranked in popularity as a hobby in the United States only by stamp and coin collecting. The purpose of this directory is to help that horde of researchers to locate collections, identify what they contain, and discover how they may be accessed. The information is based on a mailing of over 4,000 questionnaires sent to U.S. and Canadian libraries; the return rate was 37 percent. Part 1 of the questionnaire contained fifteen questions concerning basic information on the collection, and part 2 asked respondents to indicate what items they owned from a checklist of twenty-six book titles and nine periodicals. As a result of the low rate of return many important collections have been omitted. A spot check of New Jersey reveals the omission of the state university collection, at least five county historical societies with substantial genealogical collections, and many town libraries that collect local history. The compiler's name is synonymous with genealogical research, and, therefore, it is a surprise to find him associated with this enterprise. Anyone seeking a genealogical or local history collection will be as well served by the *American Library Directory* (see entry 535) or the directory prepared by the American Association for State and Local History. This title is recommended for only the most definitive of genealogical collections. [R: Choice, Oct 88, p. 290; LJ, 1 Oct 88, p. 81; RBB, 15 Nov 88, p. 552; WLB, Sept 88, p. 95]	Robert F. Van Benthuysen

570.	Poland, Ursula H., ed. **World Directory of Biological and Medical Sciences Libraries.** Munich, New York, K. G. Saur, 1988. 203p. (IFLA Publications, 42). $30.00. ISBN 3-598-21772-2.

This directory of 1,371 life sciences libraries from more than one hundred countries was compiled from responses to questionnaires. It was a project of the Biological and Medical Sciences Libraries Section of the Division of Special Libraries, International Federation of Library Associations and Institutions. Libraries with collections in biomedical sciences (including allied health), dentistry, veterinary sciences, and pharmaceutical sciences (nonprofit organizations only) are included. For developing countries all libraries with such collections are included; for developed countries, the twenty-five major resources (as selected by each country's organization of biomedical sciences librarians) are listed.

The directory is arranged alphabetically by country, and within country, alphabetically by city. Entries typically include the name of the library or parent institution; address, telephone and telex numbers; contact person at the library; subjects included in the collection; number of titles in the collection; lending status; and names of union lists to which the library/institution contributes.

The volume concludes with three appendices: a bibliography of national and regional directories of biological and medical libraries; a list of associations of biomedical librarians; and addresses of union lists and cooperative service centers. The limited coverage of libraries in developed countries (previously mentioned) makes it clear that the directories listed in the first appendix and others (such as the *American Library Directory* [see entry 535], *Directory of Special Libraries and Information Centers* [see *ARBA* 88, entry 644], and *Subject Directory of Special Libraries and Information Centers* [see *ARBA* 88, entry 64]—each covering U.S. and Canadian libraries) must be used to provide a truer picture of life sciences collections. Furthermore, users of this volume will not fail to note the attention that Ursula Poland, the editor, gives in the introduction to questions "that yielded inconsistent results." The final paragraph of the introduction states: "Nonetheless, the Working Group for this ... project is pleased to present the results of this survey and expresses hope that ... future editions will address the shortcomings of this work, as well as fill its gaps." It thus remains to be seen exactly how useful this directory will be.

Wiley J. Williams

571. **Tools of the Profession.** Hilary Kanter, ed. Washington, D.C., Special Libraries Association, 1988. 129p. $15.00 spiralbound. ISBN 0-87111-338-4.

This collection of bibliographies is the product of members of seventeen divisions of the Special Libraries Association. As such, it represents the collective expertise of information professionals working in various special library settings. Each bibliography includes complete citations; and in some cases, annotations and/or classified groups by format are included. Seventeen subject areas are covered: advertising and marketing; aerospace; business and finance; chemistry; engineering; food, agriculture, and nutrition; insurance and employee benefits; metals/materials; natural resources; nuclear science; pharmaceuticals; physics, astronomy, mathematics (including statistics and computer science); public utilities; publishing; social science; telecommunications (broadcasting); and transportation. Each bibliography provides a sound base for reference, research, and collection development within the particular subject area.

This volume will be most beneficial to those conducting research in relevant fields, and to other information professionals who may be faced with the task of creating or developing a special library collection. Recommended for special library, academic library, and appropriate public library collections.

Edmund F. SantaVicca

572. **Who's Who in Special Libraries 1988-89.** Washington, D.C., Special Libraries Association, 1988. 298p. maps. index. $25.00pa. ISBN 0-87111-339-2.

The 1988-1989 membership directory of the Special Libraries Association remains substantially unchanged from those of previous years. The first section, which totals forty-seven pages, may be correctly termed an organizational handbook. Among other items of interest, this section includes names, addresses, and telephone numbers of the current board of directors, a list of association staff members, information about the organizational structure, the complete bylaws, history, honors and awards, and past presidents. This section also includes the locations and dates of future meetings, the location of SLA student groups with names and telephone numbers of faculty advisors, and the names and addresses of all division and state chapter officers.

As much routine information is repetitive and identical to the previous year, change is accomplished by inclusion of additional information as opposed to revision. The division, chapter, and business indexes are in reality alphabetical listings of the membership by subject division, state chapter affiliation, and organizational affiliation. The alphabetical listing of the more than twelve thousand members of the association includes organizational affiliation, addresses, and telephone numbers when known, and comprises one-half of the volume. Until 1980, *Who's Who in Special Libraries* was published as the annual directory issue of *Special Libraries*, the official journal of the association. A true name index with page references as in the earlier publications may have been deemed prohibitively expensive, but making a distinction between the handbook and the directory on the title page would not be. Nor does the title of the separate section reflect the true nature of the publication. Nonetheless, this is a useful and informative work. Mailed without charge to members of the association, *Who's Who in Special Libraries* would be of interest to vendors, suppliers, and all who have an interest in activities of the Special Libraries Association.

Robert M. Ballard

PUBLISHING AND BOOKSELLING

Bibliographies

573. **Bookman's Price Index: Subject Series. Volume 1: Modern First Editions.** Daniel F. McGrath, ed. Detroit, Gale, 1987. 1154p. $125.00. ISBN 0-8103-2535-7.

This work is essentially a list of the current (mid-1980s) U.S. market values (prices) of collectible twentieth-century U.S. and British novels, plays, and books of poetry. Some thirteen thousand titles (some titles have multiple entries so that the total number of entries is about thirty thousand) are listed alphabetically by author. Each entry has been taken directly from the 1984, 1985, or 1986 catalog(s) of one (or more) of 178 U.S. and/or British bookdealers specializing in collectible twentieth-century fiction and thus consists of both basic card catalog information and a detailed description of the physical condition of the book. Coverage is strongest for collectible twentieth-century U.S. novels and weakest for science fiction and fantasy titles. Since there is no way of knowing if these titles actually sold at their listed catalog price or were eventually sold at a lower price to another dealer, collectors must also consult the yearly *Book Auction Records*, keeping in mind that auction prices are usually lower (when there is no competition for a given title) or higher (when there is a bidding war for a given title) than catalog prices.

Since the last edition of Van Allen Bradley's *The Book Collector's Handbook of Values* (see *ARBA* 83, entry 864) was published six years ago, and since Mildred Mandelbaum's *The Used Book Price Guide* is only published every five years and tends to list the less expensive fiction titles, there is no real competitor to this work save the yearly *Bookman's Price Index*, which is based on fewer dealer catalogs. It is to be hoped that future editions of this time-saving work will expand its coverage of science fiction, fantasy, and mystery titles and include auction prices (when available) of titles whose catalog value exceeds $500.00.

Joseph Cataio

574. Melanson, Holly, comp. **Literary Presses in Canada, 1975-1985: A Checklist and Bibliography.** Halifax, N.S., School of Library and Information Studies, Dalhousie University, 1988. 187p. bibliog. index. (Occasional Papers Series, 43). $16.50pa. ISBN 0-7703-9717-4.

Holly Melanson, Coordinator of Collections Development at Dalhousie, defines a literary press "as one that is created solely to encourage and provide a forum for new Canadian poets, novelists, dramatists and other creative artists" (p. i). Her directory has entries for 240 English Canadian presses active during the eleven years following publication of Grace Tratt's standard *Check List of Canadian Small Presses, English Language* (Halifax: Dalhousie University Libraries and School of Library Service, 1974). This bibliography is similar in format to the original with arrangement by name of press and entries consisting of ISBN, full postal address if available, names of founders, dates of operation, literary publications by year, and bibliography of articles about the press. There are two indexes: regional by province and nominal for the founders. Unfortunately, there is no index to the more than 4,000 literary press publications included as part of the entries. Apart from a few problems with margins, the format and production are equal to the careful work of compilation.   Patricia Fleming

575. Morton, Herbert C., and others. **Writings on Scholarly Communication: An Annotated Bibliography of Books and Articles on Publishing, Libraries, Scholarly Research, and Related Issues.** Lanham, Md., with American Council of Learned Societies by University Press of America, 1988. 151p. index. $27.50; $14.75pa. LC 87-32931. ISBN 0-8191-6825-4; 0-8191-6826-2pa.

This bibliography seeks to suggest the range of published materials on the topic of scholarly communication in the humanities and social sciences. Writings in the sciences and the professions are excluded. Works selected for inclusion are intended as illustrative of the literature, not a definitive listing; nor do the authors claim they have systematically combed the literature. The work includes lengthy abstracts of eighty-seven journal articles, books, and reports, followed by citations (at times with annotations) to 146 related publications. They are arranged in eleven chapters according to broad subjects (e.g., book publishing, libraries and computing, scholars and technology). An author index completes the volume. Morton's excellent introductory bibliographical essay provides a good overview of the following sections. The work has its principal value as a guide for the individual seeking an introduction to the literature on this amorphous subject, not the researcher seeking detailed information on specific subjects.

Richard D. Johnson

576. Wagner, Henry R., Eleanor Bancroft, and Ruth Frey Axe. **A Check-list of Publications of H. H. Bancroft and Company 1857 to 1870.** Berkeley, Calif., Friends of the UCLA Library and Friends of the Bancroft Library, 1987. 85p. index. $10.00pa.

The original compilers of this list of Bancroft publications, Henry R. Wagner and Eleanor Ashby Bancroft, died within six months of each other in the mid-1950s, leaving the work unfinished. Only recently has the work surfaced, and it is presented here with additions and revisions. Wagner was a collector, bibliographer, and historian, and Bancroft was assistant to the director of the Bancroft Library. H. H. Bancroft is best known as a historian, but he and his brother Albert were successful publishers (1857-1886) until a complete breach ended the relationship. Axe sketches the history of the two main Bancroft imprints (H. H. Bancroft and Company and A. L. Bancroft and Company); Bancroft-Whitney, founded by A. L. in 1886, and the Bancroft Company, founded by H. H. in 1887, are not considered here. In her introduction Axe also discusses the reasons for the break (a disastrous fire in their underinsured building seems to have been the last straw in a long-simmering feud). There are 212 entries, arranged chronologically. Bibliographic and copyright data are given. Locations in dozens of libraries are noted in addition. Valuable for students of Western publishing history.

Walter C. Allen

577. Woolmer, J. Howard. **The Poetry Bookshop 1912-1935: A Bibliography.** Revere, Pa., Woolmer/Brotherson, 1988. 186p. illus. (part

col.). index. $75.00. LC 87-51103. ISBN 0-913506-19-2.

Small, private, financially precarious publishing houses have generally been the outlets for twentieth-century poetry; few commercial presses will bother with it because it seldom sells well enough to justify the costs of publication. One of these small publishers was The Poetry Bookshop, established by poet Harold Monro in 1912 and remaining in business until 1935. Although the quality of both its poetry and its printing was seldom as great as that of Virginia Woolf's Hogarth Press, the Poetry Bookshop did publish Robert Graves's first work (*Over the Brazier*) as well as books by Charlotte Mew, Frances Cornford, Richard Aldington, Ford Madox Hueffer (Ford), and others.

J. Howard Woolmer has produced bibliographies of several of these private presses, basing them on his own extensive collection of their works. The present bibliography describes, in separate sections, books, "rhyme sheets" (broadsides), pamphlets, Christmas cards, periodicals (the Bookshop published two—*Poetry and Drama* and *The Chapbook*), books from other publishers distributed by the Poetry Bookshop, ephemera, and ghosts. A useful secondary bibliography is appended; the index is thorough and accurate. Full bibliographical details are provided for each item. There are many photographs (some in color) of title pages and covers. Facsimile reproductions of a rhyme sheet and a Christmas card are tipped in.

Collectors and scholars alike will welcome this attractive book. It does much to further our knowledge of a small but important corner of the publishing world.

Philip R. Rider

Directories

578. **Advertising and Publicity Resources for Scholarly Books.** New York, Association of American University Presses, 1988. 864p. index. $200.00pa. LC 87-73317. ISBN 0-945103-00-X.

Published as an aid to marketing scholarly books, this directory provides a listing of scholarly periodicals worldwide in which a publisher might advertise or send review copies of publications. Accordingly, the periodicals (and other publications of value in marketing scholarly books) are grouped by subject, such as "African Studies," "Agriculture," "History," "Oceanography," etc. Each entry provides the title, address, and telephone number of the periodical, subjects covered, types of articles, audience, language, date begun, frequency, circulation, and what percent of the circulation is in the U.S. and what percent is to individuals as opposed to institutions. Names of key contacts, such as the book review editor, are noted, as well as availability of the mailing list and whether advertising is accepted. Advertisement specifications and rates are also listed.

This work is only a starting point; it is no substitute for careful research. For example, many of the subject areas contain questionable inclusions, such as *Western Horseman* (primarily a popular periodical) under "Agriculture and Animal Science," when *Equus*, a far more scholarly periodical, is omitted. Many periodicals included in Katz, *Magazines for Libraries*, 5th ed. (see *ARBA* 87, entry 80), have been missed, but *National Librarian*, with a circulation of 400, has been included. *Emergency Librarian* is included, but not *The Book Report*.

Much of the information was supplied directly by the publishers, but unfortunately, no attempt was made to fill the gaps. The uneven coverage detracts greatly from this work's value; *The Serials Directory* (see entry 72) and *Ulrich's International Periodicals Directory* (see entry 73) are much more complete. [R: LJ, July 88, p. 71]

Shirley Lambert

579. American Book Trade Directory 1988-89. 34th ed. New York, R. R. Bowker, 1988. 1812p. index. $159.95. LC 15-23627. ISBN 0-8352-2461-9; ISSN 0065-759X.

This directory, now in its thirty-fourth edition, provides users with a convenient compilation of current information about American and Canadian booksellers. Arranged first by state, then by city, each book outlet is described as to size of stock, telephone number, specialties, name of owners and buyers, chain affiliation (if any), and SAN (Standard Address Number). In the case of antiquarian dealers, the directory indicates the number of catalogs issued annually. The newest version of the directory lists 25,395 retailers and wholesalers, an increase of 1,423 names over the previous year. Since information is gathered annually by questionnaire and telephone inquiry, accuracy is one of the volume's hallmarks. In addition to the listing of book outlets, one can use the directory to locate addresses of bookstore chain and franchise headquarters, wholesalers of books and magazines, auctioneers and appraisers of literary property, foreign-language specialists, and exporters and importers. The main section of the book is followed by a topically divided index enabling the user to locate dealers who specialize, for example, in dolls, dance, or railroadiana. The *American Book Trade Directory* gives the user the benefit of Bowker's many years of publishing experience. No public or

academic library should be without this thorough and well-organized volume.

Donald C. Dickinson

580. BookGuide 1988-89: Ontario Sellers of Used & Rare Books. Cobalt, Ont., Highway Book Shop, 1988. 146p. maps. index. $5.95pa. ISBN 0-88954-324-0.

This is a nicely executed, moderately priced guide to some 312 used bookdealers, antiquarian print and map dealers, and comic book dealers in Ontario, Canada. The first section lists 93 dealers in Toronto, the second 120 dealers in southwestern Ontario, the third 56 dealers in southeastern Ontario, the fourth 26 dealers in Ottawa, and the fifth 17 dealers in northern Ontario. These lists are either alphabetical by the name of the bookstore or alphabetical by city. Up to nine items of information are provided for each dealer, including name, address, telephone number, hours open, name of proprietor, subject specialties, size of book stock, special services (catalogs and search service), and the names of accepted credit cards. There are also a fifteen-page essay on bookselling and book collecting, a two-page calendar of events, and alphabetical and subject specialty indexes. The identification of dealers who issue catalogs along with their subject specialties makes this guide a valuable tool for the specialized collector who buys primarily from catalogs. There is no equally inexpensive, equally up-to-date, and equally detailed guide to the used book, map, and print dealers of Ontario; and any collector, dealer, or library seeking new sources of these items would be well advised to purchase it.

Joseph Cataio

581. Cassell & The Publishers Association Directory of Publishing 1988. 13th ed. London, Cassell; distr., Philadelphia, Taylor & Francis, 1987. 387p. index. $55.00pa. ISBN 0-304-31442-0.

This directory, now in its thirteenth edition, provides facts on over eleven hundred publishing firms, with the majority located in the United Kingdom and the Commonwealth. Firms in the United States are excluded. Users of this directory can obtain for each firm, the address, telephone number, description of publishing specialty, number of titles published annually, number of employees, and names of chief officers. In addition to the identification of publishing firms, the directory supplies lists of author's agents, trade and professional societies, book clubs, remainder houses, literary and trade events, and periodicals of the trade. All this is drawn together by a thorough listing of publishers by field of activity and an index of personal names. This useful volume should be purchased by any academic or public library that is involved in overseas purchasing or whose staff needs to answer reference questions on overseas publishers. The directory will serve as a supplement to *Books in Print* and has a greater variety of information than is found in *British Books in Print*.

Donald C. Dickinson

582. Directory of Book, Catalog, and Magazine Printers. 4th ed. By John Kremer with others. Fairfield, Iowa, Ad-Lib Publications, 1988. 191p. illus. bibliog. index. $15.00pa. ISBN 0-912411-13-9; ISSN 0895-139X.

This directory lists almost one thousand printers of books, catalogs, magazines, and other bound publications, including annual reports, calendars, journals, newsletters, yearbooks, etc. Along with the alphabetical listing of printers are included a how-to-use section, how to request printing quotations, tips for saving money on printing, how to read the printer listings, working with overseas printers, list of overseas printers, and appendix material that provides print-user survey results, resource guides, recommended reading, and indexes— many of them: by main focus, by printed items, by in-house binding capabilities, services offered, optimum print runs, Canadian and foreign printers, and an alphabetical index of all printers listed in the directory.

Each listing includes company name, address, telephone number, print runs preferred, binding capabilities, other services offered such as typesetting, color separations, and fulfillment, size of printing presses, typical turnaround times for printed material, and terms of payment.

The directory material is also available as a database program for IBM-PC compatible and Macintosh computers. Advertisements are sprinkled throughout, which is somewhat distracting.

A disclaimer is included in the foreword: "Most of these listings are based on the printer's self-report and some printers are not above exaggerating their capabilities, services, and turnaround times." Amen! Getting reliable quotations for printing takes time and using this book and some of its specialized sections will certainly help maximize your efforts.

Judy Gay Matthews

583. The International Directory of Little Magazines and Small Presses. 24th ed. Len Fulton, ed. Paradise, Calif., Dustbooks, 1988. 887p. index. $35.95; $22.95pa. ISBN 0-916685-05-5; 0-916685-04-7pa.

The twenty-fourth edition of this directory continues to grow in volume and stature. It is of inestimable value to writers, scholars, and librarians as it is the most up-to-date source on those difficult to find little magazines and small presses. Listings are of three kinds—magazines, presses (book publishers), and cross-references —all arranged in one alphabet. For magazines, entries include title, name of press, editor(s), address, telephone number, date founded, type of material published, information on contributors, frequency of publication, number of issues published in 1987 and anticipated issues for 1988 and 1989, subscription price, average number of pages, page size, production method, length of reporting time on manuscripts, payment rates, copyright arrangements, number and type of reviews, advertisement rates, and membership in small magazine or press organizations. Press listings include similar information. This 887-page paperback provides detailed information on over forty-six hundred markets for writers and is updated by new listings which appear in the *Small Press Review*. It is of particular value to academic and large public libraries with special collections of contemporary fiction, art, and poetry; women's studies; countercultures; ethnic or minority studies; science fiction and/or fantasy; and the avant-garde. But any library, any writer, anyone interested in the new, the unusual, trends and developments in the literary and artistic worlds, etc., will find this publication fascinating and valuable in tracing the nontraditional, out of the mainstream periodical publication. The subject index ranges from little magazine and small press publications on African literature, Americana, book reviewing, classical studies, comics, futurism, and gardening to the occult, visual arts, the West, women, and Zen. A regional index covers little magazines and small presses by state and country. This directory of little magazines and small presses continues to be a "must" for every library of any size. Maureen Pastine and
Martha S. Perry

584. LMP 1988: Literary Market Place: The Directory of American Book Publishing with Names & Numbers. New York, R. R. Bowker, 1987. 1181p. index. $85.00pa. LC 41-51571. ISBN 0-8352-2391-4; ISSN 0075-9899.

Several minor changes have occurred with the publication of the forty-eighth edition of *LMP*. Indexes, now appearing in the back of *LMP*, are "Names & Numbers," "Publisher Toll Free Directory" (new with this edition), "Index to Sections," and "Index to Advertisers." Another new section is "Magazines" (73), which lists not only periodicals that carry book reviews, but also those that excerpt and serialize books as well as those that are vehicles for book trade advertising.

For inclusion in *LMP*, entrants and nominations for new entrants are sent questionnaires. Those who do not respond and who cannot be verified by public sources or who fail to meet entry criteria are then dropped. *LMP 1988* contains "11,757 total entries, 24% of which are new," according to the preface.

LMP is divided into fifteen general areas with each subcategory assigned a section number. Among the major groups are "Book Publishing," "Book Clubs," "Literary Awards, Contests & Grants," "Radio & Television," and "Newspaper & Magazine Publishing." Entries provide, along with other information, name, address, telephone number, key personnel, brief statistics, and descriptive annotations.

As Dority pointed out in her review (see *ARBA* 86, entry 609), there is no substitute for the breadth of coverage that *LMP* provides. It remains a necessary and recommended tool in spite of its new increased price ($85.00 for the 1988 edition compared to $54.95 for the 1985 edition).   Anna Grace Patterson

585. Robinson, Ruth E., and Daryush Farudi, comps. **Buy Books Where—Sell Books Where 1988-1989: A Directory of Out of Print Booksellers and Their Author-Subject Specialties.** 6th ed. Morgantown, W. Va., Ruth E. Robinson Books, 1988. 274p. index. $29.75pa. ISBN 0-9603556-7-7.

This directory lists the subject and author specialties of over twenty-one hundred American used book dealers. Section 1 gives the names and addresses of dealers specializing in specific authors, ranging from Edward Abbey to Stefan Zweig. Section 2 supplies the names and addresses of dealers specializing in specific subjects, ranging from the Adirondacks to zoology. Section 3 lists dealers who are generalists. The geographic section lists dealers alphabetically by state (and alphabetically by city within the given state) and is particularly helpful because it also identifies those dealers who issue catalogs. The main weakness of this helpful directory is its omission of major specialty dealers. Under Chicago, for example, no mention is made of the main dealer in Chicagoana, Chicago Historical Bookworks in Evanston, Illinois. Similarly, the listings under "Literature, Modern" and "First Editions, Modern" fail to include two of the finest dealers: Joseph the Provider and Serendipity. A third example of what could be a much longer list is the omission of Articles of War Bookshop under "Military History." In addition to improving its comprehensiveness, future editions of this directory could be improved by including the size of the book stock, the telephone number, and the name of the proprietor.

Joseph Cataio

12 Military Studies

GENERAL WORKS

Bibliographies

586. Harnly, Caroline D. **Agent Orange and Vietnam: An Annotated Bibliography.** Metuchen, N.J., Scarecrow, 1988. 401p. index. $37.50. LC 88-22657. ISBN 0-8108-2174-5.

A Vietnam veteran recently recalled that the Fire Support Base at which he was stationed never had any weeds around it. "They sprayed chemicals." He paused, then said, "You know, I had an operation a while back for a tumor. With all the noise about Agent Orange, you really have to wonder." Indeed, a combat hazard little appreciated at the time, chemical contamination, has wrought catastrophe on the lives of some Vietnam veterans. But those who attempt to investigate face a bewildering labyrinth of documents: army denials, Veterans Administration confusion, press reports, antiwar polemics, and advocacy group publications. Caroline D. Harnly's *Agent Orange and Vietnam: An Annotated Bibliography* is a map for the maze.

It effectively categorizes and briefly describes and evaluates the literature on Agent Orange. The first section is on ethical and political questions involved in the spraying: was its use justified and legal? Other sections catalog literature about the effects on Vietnam's ecology, the social—especially medical—costs to the Vietnamese, and the controversy over disposal of leftover spray. But over half of the book is devoted to literature on the effects on the veteran: health issues, political issues, and litigation.

The volume references books, journals, reports from a variety of sources, television programs, and various newsletters; it does not include newspaper citations because they are too numerous and available through various newspaper indexes.

By organization and content, this bibliography is geared to research scholars. But I also recommend at least an awareness of it to those librarians who sometimes encounter a Vietnam veteran who "wonders."

Anthony A. McIntire

Chronologies

587. Hannings, Bud. **A Portrait of the Stars and Stripes.** Glenside, Pa., Seniram Publishing, 1988. 430p. illus. bibliog. index. $39.95. LC 88-092574. ISBN 0-922564-00-0.

This is a stand-straight, salute smartly, eyes-right paean of patriotism in the form of a military history of the United States 1770-1918. Except for a short essay opening each of seven chapters, the history is told chronologically. In truth, the title is somewhat misleading in that only 4 of the 415 text pages are devoted to the national flag itself, including several undistinguished tributes. There is no mention of the 1794 law that established the fifteen-striped fifteen-starred flag that became the "Star Spangled Banner."

The chronology is extensive and accurate. The writing style is somewhat "active" but reflects the author's purpose of lauding the accomplishments of American fighting men. There are many lists—historical sites and museums; colonies and states, presidents and vice presidents; twenty-eight pages of Civil War generals, naval officers, and naval actions; and thirty-nine pages of Medal of Honor winners from 1863 to 1918—and they vary in reference value.

The bibliography is disappointing. The great majority of the 106 citations are for either nineteenth-century works or material provided by the armed services. There is very little scholarly retrospective here—no Bruce Catton, H. S. Commager, R. E. Dupuy, T. N. Dupuy, D. S. Freeman, S. E. Morison, K. Williams or T. Williams. And flag references from two pioneers in the field—Admiral Preble (early) or Whitney Smith (modern)—are absent.

The reading for this review was from galley photocopies so no evaluation of the illustrations, type, paper, or binding was possible. Volume 2 (1919-1945) is projected for 1989 publication, volume 3 (post World War II) for 1990.

David Eggenberger

Dictionaries

588. Chandler, David, ed. **Dictionary of Battles: The World's Key Battles from 405 BC to Today.** New York, Henry Holt, 1987. 255p. illus. (part col.). maps. index. $24.95. LC 87-12046. ISBN 0-8050-0441-6.

Dictionary of Battles is a hardcover reading book of eight essays containing accounts of 155 key battles, well illustrated in two and four colors; it carries 150 maps ranging from locators to battle plans.

The essays open with the classical world and close with modern warfare. Each essay has its own battle accounts arranged in alphabetical order (except for the essay on the two world wars which seems to be in three alphabets). In addition to the battles, the essays discuss the evolution of weapons, armor, and formations, among other topics, plus changes in military science caused by the introduction of such "technologies" as the stirrup, gunpowder, railroads, and air power.

The dictionary authorship is impeccable. Four of the essayists, including general editor David Chandler, have connections with the British West Point at Sandhurst. One might debate why some battles are "key" and others are not or raise an eyebrow over such statements as "It is an open question, too, whether the Viet Cong would have achieved success in South Vietnam without the support provided by regular troops from the north and Soviet and Chinese arms." In general, however, the judgments are informed and sound, as expected from such authorship.

Clearly recommended over Joseph Mitchell and Edward Creasy's, *Twenty Decisive Battles of the World* (1964) and George Bruce and Thomas Harbottle, *Dictionary of Battles* (see *ARBA* 72, entry 1834). [R: RBB, 15 June 88, p. 1718]

David Eggenberger

589. **The Official Dictionary of Military Terms.** Compiled by the Joint Chiefs of Staff. New York, Science Information Resource Center/Hemisphere Publishing, 1988. 478p. $49.50. LC 87-23694. ISBN 0-89116-792-7.

This dictionary establishes definitions for military terms in order that usage be standardized among all the Department of Defense agencies and military forces. Definitions are included for Inter-American Defense Board and NATO terminology. The words and phrases in the dictionary range from the common to the fairly specialized, although those for equipment and weapons are restricted to major modern systems. In general, the definitions are concise and helpful, but not always: "PERSONAL PROPERTY--(DOD) Property of any kind or any interest therein, except real property, records of the Federal Government, and naval vessels of the following categories: aircraft carriers, battleships, cruisers, destroyers and submarines." Presumably an oiler ("a naval or merchant tanker specially equipped and rigged for replenishing other ships at sea") is considered personal property. *See* and *see also* references are provided.

There are two parts to this publication, the dictionary proper and an appendix containing a directory of the Department of Defense and the Coast Guard. Both, with minor editing, are reprints of two government publications. The dictionary is identical to the 1986 edition of *Department of Defense Dictionary of Military and Associated Terms*; the appendix is taken from the *1986/87 United States Government Manual*. The 1987 edition of the *Department of Defense Dictionary* is available for $21.00 and depository libraries may receive it under Item 315-C.

Eric R. Nitschke

590. Robertson, David. **Guide to Modern Defense and Strategy: A Complete Description of the Terms, Tactics, Organizations and Accords of Today's Defense.** Detroit, Gale, 1987. 324p. $65.00. LC 87-082651. ISBN 0-8103-5043-2.

First of all, let it be said that this is a very fine reference work. It is, however, not a guide, and it is a shame that the publisher chose to change the title under which the book was published in Great Britain (*A Dictionary of Modern Defence and Strategy*) to its present form. Whereas a guide discusses the literature of a subject, examines its organization, and cites major titles, the present work is a dictionary—a vocabulary of strategic planning and prediction, arms control, offensive and defensive philosophies, national defense policies and international military alliances, and lastly, strategic weaponry.

This is not the place to find definitions of *heads up display* or *AK-47*. This dictionary is concerned with a higher level of terminology: *zero option*, *phased array radar*, *equivalent megatonnage*, *first strike*, *Moscow option*, *MIRV*, *SS-22* and *SS-23*, etc. The four hundred or so definitions are substantial (about one page per term) and written without jargon. Despite the dictionary's origins, the emphasis is on Western and NATO, not British, terminology. Michael Stephenson and John Weal's *Nuclear Dictionary* (Longman, 1985), while covering the same subject matter, has briefer definitions but more data on weapons than Robertson. A library could well use both works, but Robertson's work is the more exhaustive and will be useful to a wide range of readers. [R: Choice, July/Aug 88, p. 1677; RBB, Aug 88, p. 1903; WLB, June 88, pp. 140-41]

Eric R. Nitschke

Handbooks

591. Complete Guide to Federal and State Benefits for Veterans, Their Families and Survivors. 10th ed. By Robert L. Berko. South Orange, N.J., Consumer Education Research Center, 1987. 174p. $8.00pa. LC 87-5229. ISBN 0-934873-05-4.

Berko's guide to current veterans benefits contains much that is useful for veterans and their families. The inclusion of state benefits contributes greatly to the volume's uniqueness and to its reference value. Another plus is the book's organization. Following an introduction by Senator Robert Dole and the preface, there are four concise instructional paragraphs. This is followed by a section of definitions that includes such important terms as *Vietnam Era*, *service-connected*, and *wife*. This last term, incidentally, refers to the spouse of a veteran, even if male.

Every possible concern of the veteran is addressed here, including disability pensions, death benefits, health care, education, loans, etc. The state benefits vary widely and sometimes amount to little more than free fishing and hunting licenses for disabled veterans or special license plates.

My chief complaint about this handbook is its format. A very diminutive paperback, printed on cheap paper, it could easily get lost on the reference shelf. The price seems exorbitant for a paperback of this size but, in all fairness, the information provided could pay back the investment many times over.

There are more substantial sources for those seeking federal veterans benefits. One is the *Catalog of Federal Domestic Assistance*, published annually by the President's Office of Management and Budget. Another is the *Ency-*clopedia of U.S. Government Benefits* (see *ARBA* 86, entry 688). These sources are fine if one disregards the real need for a guide to state benefits. The Veterans Administration publishes free or nominally priced guides, including *A Summary of Veterans Administration Benefits* (VA Pamphlet 27-82-2, revised June 1986).

Berko's guide is conditionally recommended for all libraries willing to deal with its format.

T. P. Williams

592. Franck, Irene M., and David M. Brownstone. Warriors and Adventurers. New York, Facts on File, 1988. 182p. illus. bibliog. index. (Work throughout History). $14.95. LC 87-19947. ISBN 0-8160-1452-3.

Being a pilot, sailor, or soldier is an honorable profession, but would you want your children to become gamblers, gamesters, robbers, or some other type of criminal? They now can read all about those occupations in this new work for juveniles. The publicity sheet for this multivolume series states that it is "designed to be the definitive reference on the history of work." Sections on flyers, gamblers and gamesters, robbers and other criminals, sailors, soldiers, and spies, using historical examples from all over the world, describe a broad variety of activities within each general occupation. For information on the responsibilities and training required today for legitimate jobs, the U.S. Department of Labor's *Occupational Outlook Handbook* is a good place to start.

The chapters are of a general nature, similar to encyclopedia articles. Important concepts, slang terms, and names are italicized. At the end of each chapter there is a list of related occupations in this book and in other volumes in the series. An index and "Suggestions for Further Reading" appear at the end of the book; some of the suggested titles may be too scholarly for juvenile readers. Nearly sixty illustrations are included, and the typeface is large and easy to read.

Other titles in this series include *Helpers and Aides* (see *ARBA* 88, entry 279), *Scholars and Priests* (see entry 264), and *Communicators* (see *ARBA* 87, entry 869). (Where do they place librarians?) For reviews of additional titles in this series, see *ARBA* 87, entries 187, 261, and 712. Probably more suitable for circulating than reference collections, this book is appropriate for school and public libraries. [R: BR, May/June 88, p. 42; VOYA, June 88, p. 100]

Daniel K. Blewett

593. Jordan, Gerald, ed. British Military History: A Supplement to Robin Higham's *Guide to the Sources*. New York, Garland, 1988. 586p.

(Military History Bibliographies, Vol. 10; Garland Reference Library of Humanities, Vol. 715). $75.00. ISBN 0-8240-8450-0.

British Military History is a supplement to Robin Higham's *Guide to the Sources of British Military History* (see *ARBA* 73, entry 347) published in 1971. The book is divided into twenty-five chapters, each comprising an article and bibliography that covers topics dealing with British military history in a wider context than battle and campaign narrative. Topics include economic, scientific, and technological background from the beginning of British history to 1914, military developments to 1485, the army in the nineteenth century, World War I on land, the British army 1919-1945, and other articles dealing with dominion forces in Canada, New Zealand, and Australia. The authors of these articles, all scholars of British military history, had considerable freedom to deal with their individual topics, hence some are more detailed than others.

The articles describe sources for research in British military history, covering guides to private papers, government documents, archival collections, and recently published works which indicate the trends coming into the field of military history. This work only supplements that information in the earlier guide and is not a comprehensive bibliography. It provides significant discussion of sources for British military students and historians, and criticizes British government policy on the release of government documents, but in a rather reserved manner. A clear, concise discussion of British government policy on declassifying and releasing government documents (military documents, unit war diaries, headquarters reports and orders, situation reports, and reports from frontline fighting) was needed here, but was not provided. Without a clear discussion of government policy, such as the American thirty-year rule, students and scholars may search in vain for documents that have not yet been released. These scholars also fail to discuss the location of captured enemy documents in British archival collections.

This book is a valuable source of information for students and scholars of British military history and military history in general, despite its failure to discuss British government policy concerning the declassification of military documents and where documentary collections on specific army commands and units can be found. With excellent articles on trends in military history research, it is recommended for college and university library reference collections.

Norman L. Kincaide

594. **The Military Balance 1987-1988.** London, International Institute for Strategic Studies; distr., New York, Jane's Publishing, 1987. 246p. maps. index. $27.00pa. ISBN 0-86079-126-2; ISSN 0459-7222.

When the United States and the Soviet Union are very close to confirming a treaty on eliminating a whole class of medium-range nuclear weapons, with the prospect of a reduction in long-range nuclear weapons in the near future, and with the continuing negotiations between NATO and the Warsaw Pact to reduce conventional weapons and troop strengths in Europe, a convenient guide to comparative military expenditures, nuclear and conventional weapons, and troop strengths is all the more important and valuable. This volume, divided into three sections, provides just such a source of information.

The first section groups national entries regionally: the United States, Soviet Union, Europe, the Middle East and North Africa, sub-Sahara Africa, Asia and Australasia, and Latin America. Entries for each country provide available information on gross domestic product, economic growth, national debt, inflation, defense budget, and rate of exchange, along with population, military manpower, terms of service, and strength of the individual armed services as of 1 July 1987.

The second section provides tables of comparative information on nuclear delivery systems around the world. This section sets out the geographical distribution of substrategic nuclear systems subject to current or foreseeable arms-control negotiations such as the Strategic Arms Limitations talks. Other tables provide information on major known arms procurement contracts worldwide, military manpower levels, and defense expenditures from 1955 to the present.

The third section provides essays dealing with estimating the strategic nuclear balance according to the rules established by the Strategic Arms Limitation Treaties and on the problems of attempting to assess the conventional weapon and manpower balance between NATO and the Warsaw Pact. Tables aggregate figures for both sides for the NATO guidelines area considered under the Mutual and Balanced Force Reduction negotiations, along with the area from Europe to the Atlantic to the Urals, and the world at large. This book is a valuable source of information for students and scholars of economics, history, and military science, as well as government officials and defense industry and military analysts. With its concise, well-organized format for quick and easy reference on military and economic data, it is recommended for all college and university, defense industry, and governmental reference library collections.   Norman L. Kincaide

595. Military Uniforms in America. Volume IV: The Modern Era—From 1868. By The Company of Military Historians. John R. Elting and Michael McAfee, eds. Novato, Calif., Presidio Press, 1988. 139p. illus. (part col.). index. $40.00. LC 74-21513. ISBN 0-89141-292-1.

The Company of Military Historians has provided a very interesting representation of military uniforms in America in its fourth volume on military uniforms in America in *The Modern Era—From 1868*. The book is divided into four chapters: "The Indian Wars, 1868-1892," "The Small Wars, 1893-1916," "The World Wars, 1917-1945," and "The Modern Wars, From 1946- ." Color plates depicting period uniforms are accompanied by text describing parts of the uniform and their function either in combat or dress ceremony. A brief history of the unit depicted in a dress or combat scene is included as well as descriptions of the weapons and other military equipment pictured. The material is very well researched, and this is an excellent source for understanding the sometimes halting development of military attire in America as well as the regional differences indicated. American, Canadian, Mexican, and Caribbean military attire is depicted in dress and combat situations. Most of the plates are excellent portraits, while some are not so well done. Some plates depicting more recent periods were created by veterans of the conflicts or periods they portray.

It is hoped the Company of Military Historians will include a volume on native American military dress in the near future. This work is a valuable source of information for military, American, and Canadian historians and military science students for the development of military attire and its sometimes illogical as well as practical developments in providing suitable or unsuitable clothing for the soldiers who served in America, and is recommended for secondary school, public, college, and university library reference and history collections.

Norman L. Kincaide

596. Strait, Jerry L., and Sandra S. Strait. **Vietnam War Memorials: An Illustrated Reference to Veterans Tributes throughout the United States.** Jefferson, N.C., McFarland, 1988. 226p. illus. index. $29.95. LC 87-46385. ISBN 0-89950-329-2.

In addition to the justly famous Vietnam Memorial in Washington, there are nearly four hundred monuments in cities nationwide which honor those who fought and died in Indochina. Jerry Strait, himself a Vietnam combat veteran, and his wife Sandy have compiled an excellent directory of these memorials, arranged state-by-state, with approximately 140 photograph illustrations. Each entry includes a description of the monument and often a well-researched account of its history.

Many of the monuments are traditional in design, with plaques listing the war dead, accompanied by symbols like the bald eagle and the Vietnam Service Medal. Some have sculpture portraying GIs in combat, often consoling wounded comrades. Monuments at military bases tend to emphasize the accoutrements of war; for example, the monument at Elgin Air Force Base has a full-sized mounted helicopter atop it. Others include a mounted B-52 bomber, and mounted F-111 and F-105 airplanes. The most artistically creative may be the memorial in Augusta, Maine, which features two huge steel plates, the first of which has a pattern cut out in a way which casts a shadow on the second of a larger-than-life-sized image of two soldiers helping a wounded buddy.

Not only does this catalog demonstrate a nationwide desire to honor and heal, there is also the intriguing aspect of these monuments as alternatives to the sometimes controversial memorial in Washington, with its original emphasis on the names of the war dead. The "monument ot the living survivors" in Minneapolis, for instance, is a statue of a weaponless GI in combat gear, shrugging his shoulders enigmatically. In Angel Fire, New Mexico, there is a modernistic sanctuary chapel designed for quiet reflection.

The photographs are somewhat amateurish, but the text is written from the heart, and in its own way this is a very moving compilation every bit as important as the many books already published about the Vietnam Memorial in Washington. [R: VOYA, Oct 88, p. 211]

Richard W. Grefrath

AIR FORCE

597. Angelucci, Enzo, and Paolo Matricardi. **Combat Aircraft of World War II 1940-1941. Volume IV.** New York, Orion Books/Crown, 1988. 62p. illus. (part col.). $17.95. ISBN 0-517-56843-8.

This is volume IV of a series of poster books that cover World War II aircraft (see also entries 598 through 601). Each volume in the series is devoted to an illustration of the major aircraft production of a given year during the period 1938-1945. (Volume I introduces the series by covering prewar aircraft back to 1933.) Allied and Axis aircraft typical of the time period covered are illustrated by poster-sized, full color (at times double-page) illustrations. Narrative accompanying the drawings outline aircraft specifications and production development. Volume IV contains an essay on prewar bomber development.

The series appears well thought out and will prove highly useful for reference questions on aircraft during the period. Posters in the volumes may be removed easily for mounting and the publishers have included instructions for their removal should this thought not have already struck the reader. (Librarians will lament this do-it-yourself guide to book multilation.) The series will prove valuable to aircraft modelers, restorers of antique World War II aircraft, and history buffs. Most general reference collections will find the volumes attractive and appealing to patrons. Young adults interested in aircraft modeling will find many projects in the series.   Ralph Lee Scott

598. Angelucci, Enzo, and Paolo Matricardi. **Combat Aircraft of World War II 1941-1942. Volume V.** New York, Orion Books/Crown, 1988. 62p. illus. (part col.). $17.95. ISBN 0-517-56844-6.

599. Angelucci, Enzo, and Paolo Matricardi. **Combat Aircraft of World War II 1942-1943. Volume VI.** New York, Orion Books/Crown, 1988. 62p. illus. (part col.). $17.95. ISBN 0-517-56845-4.

600. Angelucci, Enzo, and Paolo Matricardi. **Combat Aircraft of World War II 1943-1944. Volume VII.** New York, Orion Books/Crown, 1988. 62p. illus. (part col.). $17.95. ISBN 0-517-56846-2.

601. Angelucci, Enzo, and Paolo Matricardi. **Combat Aircraft of World War II 1944-1945. Volume VIII.** New York, Orion Books/Crown, 1988. 62p. illus. (part col.). $17.95. ISBN 0-517-56847-0.

Of all the equipment used during World War II, probably the type which has received the most attention from publishers continues to be aircraft. These four volumes continue the trend of oversized books filled with numerous illustrations and relatively little text. They are part of an Italian eight-volume series that covers the time period 1933-1945.

Each volume deals with a little over twenty planes. For each airplane there is usually a page of text describing its development and evaluating it combat effectiveness. Photographs are

provided, but the centerpiece of these books is the color paintings of the aircraft. These paintings present three views of the individual planes (front, top, side), and sometimes cover two pages. Since these were designed as poster books, the pages have dotted lines to show where they can be cut for framing, although doing so decreases the value of the books. Short essays on various topics (e.g., the strategic bomber) are also scattered throughout the books, as are some brief chronologies. In the review copies, the tables of contents appear at the end of the books.

These books are only marginally useful as reference tools, despite their lists of aircraft specifications (weight, speed, armament, etc.). Only the most important and famous planes are included. A better reference book by the same authors is the *Rand McNally Encyclopedia of Military Aircraft, 1914-1980* (see *ARBA 83*, entry 1590). Modelers, however, will value this set for the interesting, full-color aircraft camouflage patterns. This series is not an essential purchase. It is suitable for public libraries and those institutions interested in military/aviation history.

Daniel K. Blewett

602. Taylor, Michael J. H. **Encyclopedia of the World's Air Forces.** New York, Facts on File, 1988. 211p. illus. (part col.). maps. index. $35.00. LC 88-6970. ISBN 0-8160-2004-3.

Not all of the world's nations maintain a military air force, but some 150 of them do, ranging in size from the USSR's 15,000 planes and 824,000 personnel to Comoros's one plane and "very few" personnel. All are listed and described, to the extent that accurate information could be obtained, in this convenient handbook aimed at the nonspecialist.

The entries, arranged alphabetically by country, vary in length from one-third of a page to six pages. Each normally includes country population, number of air force personnel, official names of the air force in the local language, location (and, usually, mailing address) of the headquarters, number of major air bases, number of airplanes (in four categories: fixed-wing combat, fixed-wing noncombat, combat helicopters, noncombat helicopters), a tabular list of aircraft by model, a narrative description, and one or more (mostly color) photographs of aircraft. The information is logically organized and easy to use. The use of some British spellings (especially *aeroplane*) should not be a problem for U.S. readers.

Following the country listings are an alphabetical table of aircraft specifications, a glossary (mostly an explanation of acronyms and abbreviations), and an index of aircraft.

Paul B. Cors

ARMY

603. Beaumont, Roger. **Special Operations and Elite Units, 1939-1988: A Research Guide.** Westport, Conn., Greenwood Press, 1988. 243p. index. (Research Guides in Military Studies, No. 2). $39.95. LC 88-25083. ISBN 0-313-26001-X.

Beaumont's bibliography of those unconventional, highly trained, commonly misunderstood, often romantic and covert groups known as special forces or elite units will be of interest to both the general reader and the researcher of military history and affairs. As the author says in his preface, the guide is subjective and arbitrarily organized; much material has been excluded, and the "purpose of inclusion has often been illustrative … and a full compilation might well run to several volumes." Be that as it may, this annotated, ten-section bibliography presents a fascinating and useful gathering of sources. Sections such as "Elite Units," "Special Operations in Major Wars," "Biography/Autobiography," and "Popular Images" list entries alphabetically arranged by author. Occasionally the annotations are uneven. The entries are drawn from a wide spectrum of books, field manuals, and reports as well as periodicals ranging from the *Reader's Digest* and *Soldier of Fortune* to *U.S. Naval Institute Proceedings* and *Jane's Defense Weekly.*

Four appendices on current national elite forces, various elite forces formed since 1939, counterterrorist operations since World War II, and principal airborne combat operations precede three indexes—author, title, and subject. Almost worth the price of the volume alone is Beaumont's information-packed, highly readable forty-eight page introduction.

Charles R. Andrews

604. Chant, Christopher. **The Handbook of British Regiments.** New York, Routledge, Chapman & Hall, 1988. 313p. illus. index. $55.00. LC 87-3009. ISBN 0-415-00241-9.

The high-water mark for the British army came in 1881 and coincided with the demanding overseas commitments of Victorian England. That imperial force—31 regiments of cavalry and 113 of infantry—now stands as 16 regiments of armor and 39 of infantry (including four of Gurkhas). Chant's purpose in this book is to trace the order of battle and antecedents of the current British units back to the 1661 creation of a standing army under Charles II.

For each regiment Chant provides a small illustration of its badge, command, administrative headquarters, music, motto, nicknames, dress uniforms, allied and affiliated units, and, yes, its museum(s). In addition—and with almost audible drum rolls—are each regiment's battle honors and history. Passing in review are so many of the milestones of Western history: Blenheim, Quebec, Waterloo, Balaclava (and the charge of the six hundred 93rd Highlanders), the Somme, El Alamein, etc.

The regiments and corps are presented in order of British military precedence. Thus the leader is the Household Cavalry (the Life Guards and the Blues and Royals) with the Queen as the colonel-in-chief. And last is the Women's Royal Army Corps, "commanded" by the Queen Mother, founded in 1917 and given its present form in 1949. In between are the units with the names so romantic that they camouflage the horrors of war: Coldstream Guards, Black Watch, Royal Scot Greys.

This is a fascinating book, particularly for Anglophiles and military historians. It ranks with the author's *Encyclopedia of Codenames of World War II* (see *ARBA* 88, entry 674).

David Eggenberger

605. Fletcher, Marvin. **The Peacetime Army 1900-1941: A Research Guide.** Westport, Conn., Greenwood Press, 1988. 177p. index. (Research Guides in Military Studies, No. 1). $37.95. LC 88-21433. ISBN 0-313-25987-9.

This initial volume in Research Guides in Military Studies series provides extensive bibliographic coverage of the United States Army between the turn of the century and the beginning of the Second World War. The 971 annotated entries—consisting of books; articles from scholarly, professional, and popular journals; and dissertations—are divided into two chapters: "1900-1917" and "1919-1941." Within each of these groupings are sixteen topics ranging from the very general ("History of the United States Army") to the very specific ("George S. Patton's Student Days at the Army War College"). The topics include among others: biography, social issues, National Guard, engineers, strategy, and technology. Under the "Miscellaneous" topic, the reader will find such entries as "*Aux Armes!*: The Rise of the Hollywood War Film, 1916-1930," "A History of the United States Army Band to 1946," and "Kidnapping the Kaiser." Entries are repeated in both sections if they span the two periods.

Users will want to note that all entries are limited to English-language sources published, for the most part, since World War II. Excluded are materials dealing primarily with the development of airpower, the Spanish-American War, and World War I. A helpful chronology and introduction begin the volume. This is a well conceived, useful, and recommended bibliography, but its two-part division, however, may strike nonspecialist users as unnecessary (even though its logic is understandable).

Charles R. Andrews

606. Grover, David H. **U.S. Army Ships and Watercraft of World War II.** Annapolis, Md., Naval Institute Press, 1987. 280p. illus. bibliog. index. $44.95. LC 87-15514. ISBN 0-87021-766-6.

The result of a major research project treating the Army's World War II fleet in its entirety, this specialized volume will prove invaluable to scholars of military history. The book's fourteen chapters describe the size and nature of the Army's waterborne activities between 1941 and 1945, delineating each class of vessel operated by the commands within the Army, for example, the Corps of Engineers, the Army Airforces, the Coast Artillery Corps, and the Signal Corps. That the Army's "navy" numbered 127,793 vessels – nearly twice as many as in the U.S. Navy – may surprise even the historian.

Each chapter is devoted to a class of vessel, such as transports, hospital ships, minecraft, tankers, tugs, and communication ships. Within the chapter are details on hull, dimensions, tonnage, engines, and builder, and in the case of larger vessels, the postwar fate of each. Concluding the volume are a glossary, a bibliography, and an alphabetical ship-names index. In the case of ships named for individuals, the user must know the full name, as all alphabetizing is done by first name and/or rank. For example, to locate the mineplanter *Harrison*, one must know the ship's official name was the *Colonel George F. E. Harrison* (indexed under *Colonel!*). Indexing all such entries by last name would have been more helpful. Nevertheless, this photograph-filled study is fascinating and comprehensive. It is highly recommended for all military science collections.

Charles R. Andrews

NAVY

607. Colledge, J. J. **Ships of the Royal Navy: The Complete Record of All Fighting Ships of the Royal Navy from the Fifteenth Century to the Present.** rev. ed. Annapolis, Md., Naval Institute Press, 1987. 388p. $37.95. LC 87-72201. ISBN 0-87021-652-X.

This book completely revises volume 1 of the classic two-part set published in 1969 giving details of British ships, those from the Royal Indian Marine, nations of the British Commonwealth, and the East India Company and its successors. The volume unifies widely scattered material, and its disposal notes provide more detail than found in *Conway's All the World's Fighting Ships* (see *ARBA 85*, entry 598), *Jane's Fighting Ships* (see *ARBA 87*, entry 672), or Lenton and College's *Warships of World War II* (London, Ian Allen, 1971). The author is a leading authority on Royal Navy warships since, as editor of the World Ship Society's *Warship Supplements*, he keeps abreast of changes in warship status.

Nine pages of introductory materials preface 370 pages listing over 14,000 entries with brief descriptions of vessel type, tonnage and dimensions, armament, builder, and launch/disposal data. Names are arranged alphabetically; numerical designations are treated as spelled. If several ships have the same name, entry order is roughly chronological, although captured and impressed vessels are not in sequence.

The lack of inclusion criteria makes comprehensiveness difficult to judge. Some, but not all, requisitioned trawlers, drifters, and whalers are cited; similarly, landing craft are handled inconsistently. The occasional misprint and a few errors (e.g., on p. 247 the loss of H. M. S. *Ocean* is described misleadingly) cannot detract from the worth of the whole since a random sample of entries proved accurate.

Overall, this version is a useful, quick-reference source laid out for effective retrieval of basic data, well-printed on good quality paper in a sturdy binding.

John Howard Oxley

608. **Combat Fleets of the World 1988/89: Their Ships, Aircraft, and Armament.** Jean Labayle Couhat and Bernard Prézelin, eds. Annapolis, Md., Naval Institute Press, 1988. 876p. illus. index. $96.95. LC 78-50192. ISBN 0-87021-194-3.

With a modest $2.00 increase over the 1986/1987 edition (see *ARBA 87*, entry 671) and an additional 124 pages, this comprehensive, up-to-date resource is still a best buy. New to this seventh edition are the additions of ships of twelve nations, among them those of the Cook, Faeroe, Falkland, and Marshall Islands, the Central African Republic, and Zimbabwe. Many new ships, especially United States, Soviet, and Chinese, have been added.

Combat Fleets retains its alphabetical arrangement by country and includes as before highly detailed descriptions of and technical information about surface and undersea vessels of every conceivable kind, as well as naval aircraft and weapons/sensor systems. Some thirty-seven hundred clear, black-and-white photographs and meticulously keyed drawings add to the volume's appeal. Again, an index of ships by their full names (including class names for ships of the USSR and China) concludes the volume, along with an addendum with photographs, bringing the coverage through February 1988. Libraries with recent editions and limited budgets may wish to pass this one by unless clientele needs dictate acquiring the most current information. [R: LJ, 1 Nov 88, p. 91]

Charles R. Andrews

609.   Whitley, M. J. **Destroyers of World War Two: An International Encyclopedia.** Annapolis, Md., Naval Institute Press, 1988. 320p. illus. bibliog. index. $32.95. LC 87-63596. ISBN 0-87021-326-1.

This highly specialized study attempts to record all destroyers extant, completed, or constructed ("laid down") during the period 1939-1945 by the world's naval powers, both combatant and neutral. The arrangement is alphabetical by country and within by class of destroyer (e.g., Great Britain: J, K, & N classes; U.S.: Fletcher class; Germany: Type 36 class). Each class is described under three headings: design, modifications, and service, preceded by data of the class—displacement, length, beam, draught, machinery (i.e., boilers and turbines), performance, bunkerage (i.e., fuel tonnage), armament, and complement. Each country's destroyers are introduced by an interesting one- or two-page history. A highly informative seven-page essay on the torpedo boat/destroyer, beginning with the nineteenth century, introduces the volume.

More than 480 clear photographs and profile drawings of individual ships are included. The alphabetical index is of ship names. Most large military science collections will want this comprehensive, reasonably priced, and well-designed volume.

Charles R. Andrews

WEAPONS

610.   Chant, Christopher. **A Compendium of Armaments and Military Hardware.** New York, Routledge & Kegan Paul/Methuen, 1987. 568p. index. $99.00. LC 86-31326. ISBN 0-7102-0720-4.

Nicely organized with just the right amount of information for the nonspecialist, reasonably priced for a tool of this complexity, well bound, and presented in an attractive, easy-to-use format, the *Compendium* is a sensible purchase for those libraries that do not need—or cannot

afford—the more comprehensive, fully illustrated Jane's series of weapons and hardware.

The volume is divided into four sections: "Land Weapons," "Warships," "Aircraft," and "Missiles." Each section is arranged by type of weapon system. For example, land weapons include main battle, medium, and light tanks; armored cars, reconnaissance vehicles, and scout cars; armored personnel carriers; artillery; antiaircraft systems; multiple rocket systems; unguided antitank weapons; and machine guns and mortars. Within each weapon system, the arrangement is alphabetical, whether by country (land weapons), system (missiles, warships), or manufacturer (aircraft). Detailed information is provided within these subdivisions in the manner best suited; for example, in "Warships," the categories are type, displacement, dimensions, armament, aircraft, electronics, propulsion, performance, and complement.

Each of the four sections has its own alphabetical index, simplifying overall index use. If the volume has any shortcoming, it is the lack of illustrations. [R: Choice, July/Aug 88, p. 1672; RBB, July 88, pp. 1807, 1810]

Charles R. Andrews

611.   Colen, Donald J. **The ABCs of Armageddon: The Language of the Nuclear Age.** New York, World Almanac/Random House, 1988. 208p. illus. bibliog. index. $16.95. LC 87-50913. ISBN 0-345-35224-6.

There is demand for this type of reference work; it is at least the third published in the past year: Paul Fleisher's *Understanding the Vocabulary of the Nuclear Arms Race* (see entry 612) and Eric Semler's *The Language of Nuclear War* (see *ARBA 88*, entry 690) are the other two. With its modest, alphabetized 250-entry list of acronyms, euphemisms, and inside the defense establishment nomenclature, it ranks third in the group (300 and 500 respectively for the other two). If the reader first perused the Semler volume, the Colen book will be more generally appreciated. Unlike the other two, Colen's book is particularly concerned with the political, military, and psychological power of language. Perhaps as only a former "insider" could define them, these entries express a cogent unifying theme not found in other works of the genre. As a public relations man for Martin-Marietta Corporation during the research and development of the Titan ICBM project in the early 1960s, Colen honed his skills at packaging concepts that the Department of Defense would champion, and that taxpayers would have no choice in financing. The "ultimate package," of course, is nuclear Armageddon (p. 11). When it comes to nuclear war strategies and the nomenclature that sustains them, the author is concerned that the fate of the earth is left to those who can whip up a verbal cloud of obfuscation. As befitting a reference work, there is a reliable index, and a separate glossary of acronyms. In addition to the bibliography, most entries have source notes; most of the others have internal citations. This book would make a useful addition to collegiate and public libraries. [R: RBB, 15 Nov 88, p. 549]

Eric H. Christianson

612. Fleisher, Paul. **Understanding the Vocabulary of the Nuclear Arms Race.** Minneapolis, Minn., Dillon Press, 1988. 192p. illus. bibliog. (Peacemakers). $14.95. LC 87-15430. ISBN 0-87518-352-2.

This reference work contains over three hundred alphabetically arranged entries with brief descriptions. The overall format, illustrations, and the various display types are user-friendly and visually attractive; the entries (acronyms such as CEP, MAD, MIRV, and INF and concepts or weapons such as neutron bomb and rad) are displayed in enhanced type when employed within other entries. There is an appendix listing more than two dozen organizations seeking to end the nuclear arms race and commercial nuclear power plants. The select bibliography for future reading is intended for grades 5-12.

This admirable effort is not without shortcomings. Some important terms and pertinent events are conspicuously absent, notably the Three Mile Island reactor core-meltdown and the fission by-products 137-cesium and 131-iodine. While the Chernobyl accident is mentioned, there is neither explanation nor entry for core-meltdown and the radioactive isotopes produced by such an event. The entry for *fallout* is thus lacking important and comprehensible information; this applies to other entries as well. For example, the entry for the Nevada Test Site contains statements that are misleading, at the very least. Regarding underground tests at NTS, we are told that (p. 117) "now and then some radioactive material [what kinds?] leaks into the air from the ... explosions. The long-term effects of these leaks are hard to measure. The U.S. government says they are harmless." True, the DOD/DOE does not say that such tests are hazardous to livestock or humans, but the long-term effects of these ventings are measureable, and their devastating effects are being identified (see Howard T. Ball's *Justice Downwind* [Oxford University Press, 1986] and John G. Fuller's *The Day We Bombed Utah* [New American Library, 1984]. Without revisions it is not as useful as the five-hundred-entry paperback by

Eric Semler, *The Language of Nuclear War* (see *ARBA* 88, entry 690).

Eric H. Christianson

613. Gunston, Bill. **The Illustrated Encyclopedia of Aircraft Armament: A Major Directory of Guns, Rockets, Missiles, Bombs, Torpedoes and Mines.** New York, Orion Books/Crown, 1988. 208p. illus. (part col.). index. $24.95. ISBN 0-517-56607-9.

Bill Gunston, a former RAF pilot and flight instructor, has produced an excellent guide to aircraft ordnance and armament in *The Illustrated Encyclopedia of Aircraft Armament*. In five chapters Gunston covers developing technology from World War I to the present, unguided ordnance, guided weapons (air-to-surface missiles, anti-tank missiles, air-launched torpedoes), guided weapons (air-to-air missiles), and machine guns and cannon. Gunston provides excellent analysis of aircraft weapons systems and ordnance, beautifully reproduced color plates of aircraft depicting their armament and ordnance, and excellent cut-away drawings and descriptive diagrams illustrating how certain weapons systems function.

Each chapter begins with introductory text explaining the development trends in that field of ordnance or weaponry. Chapter 1 covers the technological development of aircraft weapons systems from World War I to the present, indicating the trends which this development will take. Covering developments country by country, chapter 2 deals with certain developments in free fall bombs, aerial rockets, dispenser systems, mines, and depth charges. Each entry describes the origin, dimensions, weight, and warhead of each weapon, plus a brief analysis of the weapon. The same format follows the discussion of systems in chapters 3, 4, and 5. At a time when it is essential to know the worth and cost of weapons systems, the quality, detail, and analysis in this book make it an excellent guide to aircraft armament for military historians, students of military science, defense analysts, and government employees, as well as defense contractors and congresspersons investigating defense contractors and Pentagon officials, and is highly recommended for college, university, public, industry, and government library reference collections.   Norman L. Kincaide

614. Nicolle, David C. **Arms and Armour of the Crusading Era 1050-1350.** White Plains, N.Y., Kraus International, 1988. 2v. illus. maps. bibliog. index. $225.00/set. LC 87-3566. ISBN 0-527-67128-2.

This extensive two-volume set belongs in any serious collection of military costume or of medieval history. The work covers the years 1050 through 1350 and crosses many cultural and geographic lines. European arms and armor are included, as are those of the Byzantine, Islamic, Central Asian, and Indian armies. The information in the work is divided into three main categories: the illustrations, the dictionary of terms, and the bibliographies.

Volume 1 contains the commentary on the illustrations in volume 2. This arrangement makes it simple to read the description while looking at the drawing. There is no tedious flipping back and forth from the front to the back of a single volume. The illustrations are all line drawings, with careful attention to detail. Some are fairly small and it can be difficult to spot all the significant details without a magnifying glass. The illustrations are grouped into the main geographical and cultural zones of medieval Christian and Muslim civilizations. Information is included on Buddhist, shamanist, and Hindu regions, as these areas influenced the two main civilizations. Within each group the material is generally grouped in chronological order. There are brief introductions to each section.

The dictionary of terms is fairly extensive, but Nicolle warns that many meanings are unclear or unknown. The author feels much work remains to be done in this area. The bibliographies are also fairly extensive, but Nicolle makes no claim to be comprehensive. The bibliography is broken into two parts: "Arms, Armour and Art Sources" and "Military, Cultural and Social Background Sources." Each is further divided into unpublished primary sources, published primary sources, and unpublished and published secondary sources. As there is necessarily overlap, the user should consult both parts. There is also a general index provided. An excellent work.

Susan Ebershoff-Coles

615. Rogers, Paul. **Guide to Nuclear Weapons.** New York, Berg; distr., New York, St. Martin's Press, 1988. 123p. index. (Bradford Peace Studies Papers. New Series, No. 2). $17.95. LC 87-21711. ISBN 0-85496-150-X.

Though brief, this is a useful and well-produced annotated guide to the global glut of nuclear weapons and to their expanding array of delivery systems. Sea, air, and land-based weapons of all known configurations are listed for each nation. In addition to the major nuclear powers (United States, USSR, United Kingdom, France, People's Republic of China, Israel, and India) are entries for those nations with capability or intent (South Africa, Pakistan, Argentina, Brazil, Iraq, Iran, Libya, and Taiwan). Proliferation is documented through entries for Warsaw Pact and NATO countries, and other nuclear alliances.

Based on the data that he compiled, the author observes that the development and production of new weapons continue, entirely unaffected by the intense arms control negotiations of the 1980s. However, it does not seem unreasonable to argue that the increases in nuclear weapons and delivery systems research and development and deployment are, indeed, related closely to negotiations; new weapons systems, or additions to those in service, seem to be tailor-made to fit within existing or probable parameters of the restrictions sought by arms control negotiations.

For a comprehensive and detailed analysis of U.S. nuclear weapons, see Thomas B. Cochran's *Nuclear Weapons Data Book*, volume 1, *U.S. Nuclear Forces and Capabilities* (National Resources Defense Council, 1984). (A revised edition is available from Ballinger.) Given its global scope, and with its nine tables, reliable index, and list of abbreviations, this volume will make a useful addition to public and college libraries. [R: WLB, Oct 88, p. 108]

Eric H. Christianson

13 Political Science

GENERAL WORKS

Bibliographies

616. **International Bibliography of Political Science. Vol. XXXIV: 1985. Bibliographie Internationale de Science Politique.** By the International Committee for Social Science Information and Documentation for UNESCO. New York, Routledge, Chapman & Hall, 1988. 596p. index. (International Bibliography of the Social Sciences). $190.00. ISBN 0-415-00087-4; ISSN 0085-2058.

This indispensable index continues to be among the most efficient and most authoritative information gathering sources in political science, as long as neither a current nor a comprehensive search is required. Coverage is international. Books and reports, as well as articles from about 550 journals, are included.

Unlike many indexes we have become accustomed to using in recent times, this bibliography gives consistent evidence of human intervention, thought, and care. First, it is selective. The editors choose only the books and articles they believe to be the most scholarly and significant, eliminating those which are merely informative or polemical. The principles which govern this selection process are presented in a table following the preface. Selectivity has its drawbacks, of course, but most of the time it is exactly what is needed by most people. Another evidence of human effort is the excellent indexing. A classified arrangement of entries with a topical subject index provides two approaches, and the geographical breakdown by country within the subject index is a boon to students of comparative politics. There is an author index as well.

As in previous years, articles abstracted in *International Political Science Abstracts* are cross-referenced here.

The only regrettable aspect of this volume is the cost, which has increased by more than 70 percent over the previous year.

Constance McCarthy

617. Reid, Darrel R. **Bibliography of Canadian and Comparative Federalism, 1980-1985.** Kingston, Ont., Institute of Intergovernmental Relations, Queen's University, 1988. 492p. index. $39.00pa. ISBN 0-88911-451-X.

Queen's University's Institute of Intergovernmental Relations has produced its latest bibliographic resource in response to the demand for access to information on Canadian federalism. The bibliography comprises 3,418 consecutively-numbered entries, in both English and French, for books, parts of books, government publications, and journal articles. The entries are arranged under six broad headings, including "Federalism and Federal Countries," "Courts and Constitutions," and "Intergovernmental Relations." The main focus is on "items that relate to the interaction of the various levels of government within [Canada]" (p. v), but selected references on federal theory, comparative federalism, and federations other than Canada are included.

Entries include the bibliographic information needed to locate the items (e.g., author, title, publisher, date, page numbers, series). There are author, title, and subject indexes. The subject index has some omissions (e.g., a brief on equality by the Canadian Advisory Council on the Status of Women is not indexed under either "Women's Rights" or "Women, Status of"). Consequently, the user cannot be assured of finding all relevant entries under a given heading. The subject index also employs a system of boldface headings with subheadings that is somewhat confusing. Nevertheless, this resource is appropriate for the student of Canadian government of history or of federalism in general. Its exhaustive nature makes it particularly helpful to those who have previously lacked access to relevant Canadian federal, provincial, and municipal government documents.   Gari-Anne Patzwald

Biographies

618.   Alexander, Robert J. **Biographical Dictionary of Latin American and Caribbean Political Leaders.** Westport, Conn., Greenwood Press, 1988. 509p. index. $75.00. LC 87-17805. ISBN 0-313-24353-0.

These 460 biographical sketches by fifteen contributors were intended to provide basic data on the family backgrounds, education, and especially the political significance of persons selected as the "most important political figures" in the nineteenth and twentieth centuries in Latin America and the Caribbean (p. ix). Living as well as dead persons are profiled. Entries are of variable length; most are less than a page but a few exceed two pages. All entries include as many as five bibliographic items for those wanting further information. A chronology of significant political events 1804-1985, a list of biographees by country, an analytical index, and short biographies of the contributors complete the presentation. Most of the contributors are political scientists.

Criteria for selection of biographees are not stated except to say that twentieth-century figures were favored. Review of the country list confirms this bias and shows that at least two biographees were selected for each nation-state or territory. Country coverage does not have any apparent correlation to size or traditional notions of historical importance. Thus Chile has thirty-eight entries, Barbados has nine, and Brazil, Costa Rica, Cuba, and Mexico have twenty-three each. Presidents and leaders of twentieth-century leftist parties and unions dominate the lists.

This work will be of value in any library whose patrons have an interest in Latin America and the Caribbean, especially in recent decades. [R: Choice, Dec 88, p. 622; RBB, 1 Nov 88, p. 460]   Paul E. Hoffman

619.   Weeks, Albert L., comp. **The Soviet Nomenklatura: A Comprehensive Roster of Soviet Civilian and Military Officials.** Washington, D.C., Washington Institute Press, 1987. 133p. maps. index. $69.95 spiralbound. LC 87-18954. ISBN 0-88702-030-5.

This excellent directory has been "compiled on the basis of day-by-day examination of Soviet publications and official yearbooks published in Moscow." It is divided into six sections; the introductory one describes the method used to compile the directory, lists abbreviations used, and provides two maps. The subsequent sections are devoted to the Communist Party of the Soviet Union; Republican, Krai, and Oblast party officials; governmental officials; officials and ambassadors within the Ministry of Foreign Affairs; and finally leaders within the Ministry of Defense including the armed forces. Entries, accurate as of June 1987, are of two kinds. The most common is the recording of a person's name, birthdate, and current position. The other type, used for the Politburo and principal leaders of the armed forces, includes the same information as the first plus additional information about appointment dates and previous positions held. A final part, consisting of a personal name index and an index of governmental bodies, provides alphabetical access to the directory's contents.

This directory will be useful for reference departments in public and academic libraries. It overlaps in part with various CIA publications, updated often, that are available through the GPO depository program. This directory is easier to use than its CIA counterpart, provides alphabetical access, and contains more information in its expanded entries. Unless updates are provided, however, the directory will soon contain obsolete information. [R: Choice, July/Aug 88, p. 1679]

Robert H. Burger

Chronologies

620.   Lentz, Harris M., III. **Assassinations and Executions: An Encyclopedia of Political Violence, 1865-1986.** Jefferson, N.C., McFarland, 1988. 275p. bibliog. index. $29.95. LC 87-46383. ISBN 0-89950-312-8.

The first entry is for the assassination of Abraham Lincoln on 14 April 1865; thereafter assassinations and executions increased in number dramatically, especially in the latter half of the twentieth century. It takes seventy-seven pages to cover the progress of death from Lincoln to the year 1940. From 1940 to 1986 the death count rises and occupies 161 pages. Murder of the powerful reached new heights in the 1940s and 1970s. This encyclopedia, which records it all, is an even more telling book because of the chronological arrangement it employs. If an alphabetical arrangement by victim's name had been used instead, the impact would be less. Listing those assassinated or executed by year marks that year as a violent one and for those highly violent years reveals near-global unrest. The reader begins to see a pattern emerging, a mosaic of murder that has affected millions of people.

The prologue lists some of the more promi-nent victims of political violence prior to 1865 and is a helpful reminder of earlier mayhem beginning with the murder of Julius Caesar. Lentz writes brief sketches, often a sentence or two, of the lesser-known victims, while he pro-vides a fuller picture of those who were well known. He also includes unsuccessful attempts at murder and distinguishes them in his text by leaving their names in roman type as opposed to the names of those victims who were murdered, which appear in boldface type. About compre-hensive coverage, he says in his introduction that Third World nations present a problem; it is vir-tually impossible to name every victim "where political violence seems to be a way of political life." Throughout the book Lentz is conscien-tious about giving the facts regarding the violent event, "including the manner, the motive, and the assailant, when known." Occasionally a name looks out of place such as that of George Armstrong Custer who was neither assassinated nor executed. Recommended as a unique refer-ence work. [R: RBB, 15 Oct 88, pp. 386, 388; WLB, Sept 88, pp. 89-90]   Bill Bailey

Dictionaries and Encyclopedias

621. Bogdanor, Vernon, ed. **The Blackwell Encyclopaedia of Political Institutions.** New York, Basil Blackwell, 1987. 667p. index. $65.00. LC 87-6571. ISBN 0-631-13841-2.

The six hundred topics in *The Blackwell Encyclopaedia of Political Institutions* (*BEPI*) are intended to provide "a succinct guide to the central concepts used in the study of political in-stitutions of advanced industrial societies, the principal political organizations and movements in these societies, and the main types of political community." It aims to complement another specialized work, *The Blackwell Encyclopaedia of Political Thought* (*BEPT*) (Basil Blackwell, 1986), whose 350 articles emphasize the major ideas and doctrines and protagonists (fully one-half of the articles are biographical) of the Western tradition of political thought.

Because of the interrelatedness of the sub-ject matter of the volumes, it is perhaps not surprising that nearly one hundred of the essays appear in both volumes—for example, essays on absolutism, anarchism, bureaucracy, democ-racy, feminism, Thomas Hobbes, John May-nard Keynes, law, James Mill and John Stuart Mill, Plato, Rousseau, state, totalitarianism, Beatrice Webb and Sidney Webb, Max Weber, and welfare state. The essays are, however, usually written by different persons so that we are provided with two different perspectives. In-deed, very few of the 130-odd contributors to

the *BEPT* are among the 247 contributors (mostly British and European academicians) to the *BEPI*. The great strength of the volumes is the perceptive signed essays—sometimes run-ning to several columns, sometimes only a few lines—followed by monographic and periodical suggestions for further reading (often into the mid-1980s) appended to all but the shortest entries. Each volume is fully cross-referenced and indexed.

As to a more precise interpretation of *polit-ical institutions* in *BEPI*, the following random sampling of unique main entries in *F*, *P*, and *S* may be helpful: *faction, field service adminis-tration, First Amendment freedoms, freedom of information, functional representation, funda-mental rights, parliamentary system* (and four other entries beginning with *parliamentary*), *party convention* (and four other *party* entries), *political action committee (United States)* (and twenty-six other *political* entries), *public admin-istration* (and five other *public* entries), *secret police, Speaker, strong mayor plan,* and *Supreme Court.*

All in all, because of its scholarly essays cum bibliographies on such a diverse range of subjects, this volume is a substantial contribu-tion for students of political analysis and thought. They will use it frequently alongside *The Blackwell Encyclopaedia of Political Thought.* Academic and public libraries with such titles as Riff's *Dictionary of Modern Political Ideologies* (see *ARBA* 88, entry 739), Scruton's *A Dictionary of Political Thought* (see *ARBA* 84, entry 421), and Robertson's *A Dic-tionary of Modern Politics* (see *ARBA* 87, entry 689) and such standard sets as *The Dictionary of the History of Ideas* (see *ARBA* 74, entry 1198), *The Encyclopedia of Philosophy* (Macmillan, 1973), and *International Encyclopedia of the Social Sciences* (Macmillan, 1979) will appre-ciate its breadth of up-to-date coverage all in a single volume. [R: C&RL, Jan 88, pp. 60-61; Choice, Sept 88, p. 74; RBB, Aug 88, p. 1898]
Wiley J. Williams

622. Shimoni, Yaacov. **Political Dictionary of the Arab World.** New York, Macmillan, 1987. 520p. $50.00. LC 87-12392. ISBN 0-02-916422-2.

The compiler states that this work is, to some extent, a revised, updated edition of the *Political Dictionary of the Middle East in the 20th Century* (see *ARBA* 73, entry 397). The review of the original dictionary criticized it for being "frequently biased" and anti-Arab. The present dictionary omits specific references to the state of Israel, but the bias is still quite plain, although the compiler does offer the statement that "a measure of subjective judgment" was used in selecting entries.

The articles show some surprising variations in length. The one dealing with the Arab-Israeli conflict gets twenty pages, followed immediately by nearly one dozen more on the "Arab-Israel Wars." In the articles referring to individual Arab countries Egypt is allotted twenty pages, followed by Lebanon with sixteen and Jordan and Syria with ten each. Iraq, Libya, and Saudi Arabia receive eight each.

The articles were prepared by several contributors, some of whom are identified with their work in the foreword and some of whom are simply listed as having contributed. No sources or suggested readings are supplied, even with the longest articles, although maps and tables are included as appropriate, and both are easily read. Since, the compiler notes, this was not intended as a who's who, the work is shorter on biographical sketches than it might be; many were removed at the last minute to conserve space. Almost eighteen pages are devoted to an article entitled "Oil in the Middle East," thus marking the importance of oil revenues to funding developments in the Arab world.

The problem of transliteration and spelling of Arabic terms and names has been met by using those normally "used in the international press" (foreword) with the omission of diacriticals, and this poses no real problem to the user, since cross-references to variant forms are supplied. One device, presumably used to save space, is somewhat annoying and frustrating to a reader moving from one article to the next, as one may do with a work of this type. Abbreviations are used for each entry once the heading has been supplied, and these abbreviations are often a single letter. When one moves from the article on "Arafat" to the ones on "Aref" and "al-Asad," as one might easily wish to do, the use of the same abbreviation, *A*, requires one to concentrate closer attention on one's reading to ensure that one does not think one article is a continuation of another. Abbreviations already existing as acronyms pose no problem, but space could have been saved in many cases by marginal shortening of the articles. [R: Choice, May 88, p. 1386; LJ, 15 Feb 88, p. 161; RBB, 1 Apr 88, pp. 1324, 1326]   Margaret Anderson

497) and *ARBA* 86, entry 666), is to provide "within a single volume concise, current and objective data on all the world's political parties, placed within the context of the prevailing constitutional, electoral, and parliamentary situation in the particular country or territory." Containing numerous 1987 and early 1988 references, the new edition includes more than twenty-one hundred political parties in more than two hundred countries and territories (with particular attention to minor parties), compared to some one thousand and thirteen hundred in the earlier works — considerably more than in any other source. Illegal, guerrilla, and terrorist groups continue to be generally excluded; they are, however, in the publisher's companion volume, *Revolutionary and Dissident Movements* (see entry 664).

Entries for parties range in length from a line or two to a few pages. The longer entries, covering major parties, include party name (in English and the native language), address, names of leaders, orientation (e.g., center-left, basically communist, conservative progressive), date founded, history, structure, membership, publications, and international affiliations (often those listed in the appendices cited below). Minor parties and other political alliances receive abbreviated entries. The five appendices identify international party organizations such as Democratic Socialists, Christian Democrats, Liberals, Conservatives, or Greens (environmental parties). The index to organizations, personal names, and publications replaces the two indexes of prior editions. This third edition is recommended for larger public and academic libraries.

The fact that *Political Parties* appears quadrennially means that researchers and librarians should be aware of certain other publications, such as the annual *Political Handbook of the World* (see *ARBA* 88, entry 704) (its section on parties includes both legal and illegal/revolutionary groups — see its objective treatment of the Palestine Liberation Organization), *Yearbook on International Communist Affairs 1988* (see entry 671), and (to a lesser degree) *Europa Year Book* (see *ARBA* 86, entry 91). The second (1987) edition of the apparently quadrennial *World Encyclopedia of Political Systems & Parties* (see *ARBA* 88, entry 698) has excellent coverage of parties as of 1985.

Wiley J. Williams

Directories

623. Day, Alan J., ed. **Political Parties of the World.** 3d ed. Chicago, St. James Press, 1988. 776p. index. (Keesing's Reference Publication). $85.00. ISBN 0-912289-94-5.

The aim of the third edition, like that of the 1980 and 1984 editions (see *ARBA* 82, entry

624. Fenton, Thomas P., and Mary J. Heffron, comps. and eds. **Middle East: A Directory of Resources.** Maryknoll, N.Y., Orbis Books, 1988. 144p. illus. index. $9.95pa. LC 88-1603. ISBN 0-88344-533-6.

This is the sixth in the series of twelve resource directories being compiled on Third World regions and issues. The volumes are intended to expand and update the *Third World Resource Directory* published in 1984 (see *ARBA* 86, entry 93). Included in this directory are the five African nations north of the Sahara (Tunisia, Algeria, Libya, Egypt, and Morocco) which are closely affiliated with the Middle East. The compilers note in their introduction that they "endeavored to identify and acquire resources on the Middle East from organizations in all parts of the world." Organizations are included if their work is mainly focused on the Middle East, since the size of the directory precludes the listing of those whose work is international or global.

This is a directory of alternative resources on each of the countries in the region and on as wide a variety of topics as possible. It is noted that "the bulk of the resource materials available to us were concerned with the countries and issues that preoccupy the attention of activists, educators, journalists, policy-makers, and concerned citizens" (p. xiii). The resources selected, the compilers tell us "reflect the thinking of dedicated and thoughtful women and men who have come to the conclusion that genuine and equitable development in the Middle East demands *fundamental* changes in the status quo" (p. xiv).

The book is divided into five chapters: organizations; books; periodicals; pamphlets and articles; and audiovisuals. Appended to them are (1) a list of university centers with Middle East outreach programs, and (2) a list of religious organizations with Middle East interests. Each of the five chapters is divided into an annotated listing followed by a supplementary, unannotated list. Each concludes with a brief section headed "Information Sources." Five separate indexes allow access by organizations, individuals, titles, geographical areas, and subjects.

This is an informative and useful tool, even though, as the compilers point out, it is clearly biased in favor of a particular political orientation. They have stated their position clearly enough and are offering alternatives to traditional patterns of Western thinking.

Margaret Anderson

Handbooks

625. Cole, Wayne, and Lise Boucher. **Lexique des Élections. Elections Glossary.** Ottawa, Canadian Government Publishing Centre, 1988. 141p. bibliog. (Terminology Bulletin, 182). price not reported. pa. ISBN 0-660-53998-5.

The *Elections Glossary* is a list of approximately six hundred terms that apply primarily to the Canadian electoral system, although some terms would be applicable to the United States as well. As can be expected with a Canadian government sponsored publication, it is divided into an English-French and French-English glossary. While this title provides many terms that one might not find in typical U.S. political dictionaries, no definitions of these terms are provided. Certainly this source would have been eminently more useful had such definitions been supplied. Because of this severe limitation this work is suggested for only the most complete political science collections.

Frank Wm. Goudy

626. Waller, Robert. **The Almanac of British Politics.** 3d ed. Beckenham, England, Croom Helm; distr., New York, Methuen, 1987. 638p. maps. index. $22.50pa. ISBN 0-7099-2798-3.

Patterned after the highly successful *Almanac of American Politics* (most recently reviewed in *ARBA* 86, entry 695), this compilation is described by its author as a "personal and impressionistic" guide to the British political landscape. Just as *The Almanac of American Politics* focuses on each congressional district, *The Almanac of British Politics* provides a series of profiles on each parliamentary seat, or constituency. Waller describes the social, economic, and political character of each seat; recent electoral data are provided, as well as the area's prospects in the next general election. Supplemental statistics analyze the electorate by type of housing, occupations, and racial groupings. Most of the profiles fill an entire page in the book; occasionally two constituencies will be profiled on the same page. Hence, the descriptions are fairly brief and lack much of the anecdotal flavor found in the American counterpart. Still, the information is concise and useful in understanding the political make-up of the district.

Waller has organized the profiles into broad geographic groupings: Greater London, metropolitan counties, nonmetropolitan counties, Scotland, Wales, and Northern Ireland. He provides an introductory "Regional Survey," which gives an overview of the current political climate in Britain. A series of maps and specialized lists and tables (e.g., "Retiring MPs and Replacement Candidates") complete the information package that Waller has assembled. Waller is also the author of a companion volume, *The Atlas of British Politics* (see *ARBA* 87, entry 678), which treats broader trends in British politics quite effectively.

Most library collections will probably not need quite so detailed a source on British politics. However, this kind of work is highly recommended for university libraries supporting graduate study in this area. Already in its third edition (the previous edition was published in 1983), this title will most likely become the standard work for detailed information on politics in Great Britain.

Thomas A. Karel

Indexes

627. Index to Federal Programs and Services 1987. 8th ed. Ottawa, Canadian Government Publishing Centre, 1987. 552p. index. $14.50 pa.; $17.40pa. (U.S.). ISBN 0-660-12222-7; ISSN 0715-7193.

This convenient book describes about fifteen hundred programs or services offered through 180 Canadian federal government departments and ABCs (agencies, boards, and commissions) as of 15 November 1986. It is not an organization manual, although there are descriptions of some of the government bodies as well as addresses and telephone numbers of the various regional and district offices serving the public in Canada (this is only useful if you actually reside in the locality, otherwise a letter or telephone call to the head office normally in Ottawa will suffice). There is a keyword subject index that appears to be adequate.

Each program/service is described with a summary and a piece about "organizational responsibility." For example, under the National Library of Canada (NLC) there are twenty-nine descriptions of services, ranging from "Cataloguing in Publication" through "ISBN and ISSN assignments," the "DOBIS search service" for union catalog book information, and the "*Canadiana*" service, which is Canada's national bibliography available in print form as a serial. Libraries serving patrons living outside of Canada should be aware that these fifteen hundred services and programs are normally open to all Canadian citations and landed immigrants (permanent residents), but that some may not be available to aliens, such as the Access to Information Act or programs dispensing grants.

Dean Tudor

U.S. POLITICS AND GOVERNMENT

Bibliographies

628. Bowman, James S., and Ronald L. Monet. **Gubernatorial and Presidential Transitions: An Annotated Bibliography and Resource Guide.** New York, Garland, 1988. 113p.

index. $37.00. LC 87-25152. ISBN 0-8240-7218-9.

This slender volume consists of a fifty-nine-page annotated bibliography and fifty-one pages of appendices. The bibliography is divided into six chapters, three relating to presidents and three to governors. The topics covered for each office are transitions between administrations; management, leadership, and executive functions; and the executive office, including staff and appointments. The compilation of material on the presidency is of questionable value. There is a large body of literature on these topics and the basis for the small selection chosen is not apparent, unless it was to achieve an approximate equality in the number of citations provided for each of the two offices. Material on gubernatorial transitions and management, however, is much harder to locate, and the 101 citations on these topics may well be a nearly comprehensive list. It is chiefly for the sake of this small bibliography that the book might be considered for purchase by libraries with an interest in this field.

The materials in the appendices are reprints, mostly from publications of the National Governors Association and the Council of State Governments. The gubernatorial materials include a model gubernatorial transition act, a suggested timetable, and some state-by-state tables of dates and procedures, while for the presidency a detailed timetable and checklist prepared by the General Services Administration in 1985 is included. The volume concludes with an author index. [R: Choice, Sept 88, pp. 74, 76]

Constance McCarthy

629. Casper, Dale E. **Richard M. Nixon: A Bibliographic Exploration.** New York, Garland, 1988. 221p. index. (Garland Reference Library of Social Science, Vol. 415). $30.00. LC 87-28064. ISBN 0-8240-8478-0.

Once again, Garland has published an exceptional reference work. The compiler is to be congratulated for such a thorough listing of works by, about, and with pertinent reference to the man who had no choice but to resign the presidency in 1974. With more than 1,744 citations, this work provides quick and reliable reference to the material with an index and a sensible organizational format that includes sections on periodical literature, biographies, Alger Hiss, Nixon's political campaigns, and the various offices he held. Both domestic and foreign policies and practices are detailed. Included are useful references to Watergate, the impeachment proceedings, and the revisionist literature about the man and his activities. This is a bibliographical tour de force of Nixon as subject in an impressive array of literary genres. Academic and political research libraries should have this volume on their shelves. [R: Choice, June 88, p. 1530]   Eric H. Christianson

630. Gould, Lewis L., and Craig H. Roell. **William McKinley: A Bibliography.** Westport, Conn., Meckler, 1988. 238p. illus. index. (Meckler's Bibliographies of the Presidents of the United States, 24). $45.00. LC 88-15531. ISBN 0-88736-138-2.

Carol Bondhus Fitzgerald edits the Meckler Corporation's Meckler's Bibliographies of the Presidents of the United States series. Her introduction states that "few of the presidents have been the subject of comprehensive monographic bibliographies," a situation that Meckler has committed itself to rectifying. The first two books in this new series appeared in 1988, the present volume, plus John F. Marszalek's bibliography on Grover Cleveland. Lewis Gould and Craig Roell corroborate Fitzgerald's view about the paucity of bibliographic sources as applied to McKinley and they evidence considerable pleasure at the opportunity to fill a major gap. Gould is especially appropriate as a coauthor, given his stature as a prominent historian of the Progressive Era.

The compilers introduce their work by commenting on the obscurity of McKinley as an individual despite the fact that many events of his turn-of-the-century administration bore directly on later developments. Gould and Roell arranged more than seventeen hundred entries into chapters that identify manuscript and archival resources and writings by and about McKinley; sections of the bibliography point to writings on major events of the McKinley period and key individuals in his cabinet. Author and subject indexes are appended.

The seriousness with which the compilers and the publisher have approached this series of publications is underscored by the choice of Arthur Schlesinger, Jr., to write the foreword. Schlesinger comments on historiography that "the tide of historical interest is ... turning again — from deep currents to events ... to the insights of classical history ... that the state, political authority, military power, elections, statutes, wars, the ideas, ambitions, delusions, and wills of individuals, make a difference to history." Schlesinger concludes that the Meckler series "fills a great lacuna in American scholarship," placing "the study of American presidents on a solid bibliographical foundation."

Gould and Roell have presented a vital and ambitious series with an admirable inauguration. One hopes that future volumes in this series will match the work of Gould and Roell for scholarship and accuracy.

John Mark Tucker

631. Lincove, David A., and Gary R. Treadway, comps. **The Anglo-American Relationship: An Annotated Bibliography of Scholarship, 1945-1985.** Westport, Conn., Greenwood Press, 1988. 415p. index. (Bibliographies and Indexes in World History, No. 14). $49.95. LC 88-7225. ISBN 0-313-25854-6.

This ambitious and comprehensive bibliography provides an interdisciplinary survey of the unique relationship that has existed between the United States and Great Britain. Although the bibliography is limited to materials published between 1945 and 1985, the scope of the bibliography extends back to 1783.

The bibliography is divided into two sections. Part 1 (110 pages) deals with the social and cultural interaction between the two countries. Among the specific topics covered are the love-hate relationship; social movements; immigration; religious, educational, cultural, and political influences (and contrasts); foreign trade; and financial cooperation. Part 2 focuses on diplomatic and military relations and is the more substantial section of the volume (245 pages). This section is organized into eight broad chronological subsections, with several specific topics highlighted within each grouping (e.g., the War of 1812, the Trent Affair, competition in the Pacific, Ireland between the two World Wars, nuclear weapons, etc.).

Only English-language material is included in this bibliography, but British (as well as American) publications are well represented. The compilers have concentrated on scholarly material, so no popular magazine articles have been selected. Within each subdivision of the bibliography, the following types of publications are listed alphabetically by author: scholarly books, essays in books, journal articles, British and American doctoral dissertations, and some Canadian dissertations. Each item is annotated, with the exception of the dissertations (which include, wherever possible, a full *Dissertation Abstracts* citation). The annotations vary in length, though most are sufficiently substantial and reflect the compilers' careful research.

Appended to the bibliography are lists of the chief American diplomats who have served in England, and the chief British diplomats who have served in the United States. There is also a selected list of reference sources consulted. An index of authors and a detailed subject index are provided.

This volume will be most useful in support of graduate research in American or British history and international relations, and is highly recommended for large university library collections. The usually high standards for paper and binding used by Greenwood Press are clearly evident in this volume.

Thomas A. Karel

632. **Lyndon B. Johnson: A Bibliography, Volume Two.** Craig H. Roell, comp. Austin, Tex., University of Texas Press, 1988. 362p. index. $30.00. LC 83-23264. ISBN 0-292-74017-4.

Lyndon Johnson's career presents a problem for many researchers: the formidable mass of material discourages all but the most stouthearted. Fortunately, through the efforts of the Johnson Library and Craig Roell, some semblance of order – if not reduction in bulk – has been imposed upon it. *Lyndon B. Johnson: A Bibliography, Volume Two*, is a result of those efforts.

The follow-up to a 1984 volume (see *ARBA 86*, entry 681), this work catalogs recent additions to the Johnson literature and works overlooked in the first volume, as well as revisions, updates, and corrections to earlier material. The compiler organizes this bibliography by subjects broadly grouped into two sections: one on Lyndon Johnson himself and one on Lady Bird Johnson and the Johnson family. Each part is further divided into chronologically based categories; naturally, the longest of these (some 250 pages) lists works relating to the Johnson presidency. The volume also sports a helpful author index.

This durable hardbound book would be an excellent addition to research and university libraries. It shows no partiality to literature either for or against Johnson. Furthermore, it indexes not only scholarly books and articles, but also dissertations, the popular press, manuscript collections, interviews, and much more. In fact, the only major weakness in the compilation seems to be a rather skimpy approach to foreign literature; perhaps a future volume will remedy that.

As a guide through the morass of Johnson literature, serious scholars should start with this series of bibliographies. They probably will save quite a lot of time by doing so.

Anthony A. McIntire

633. Marszalek, John F. **Grover Cleveland: A Bibliography.** Westport, Conn., Meckler, 1988. 268p. illus. index. (Meckler's Bibliographies of the Presidents of the United States, No. 22). $45.00. LC 88-9096. ISBN 0-88736-136-6.

This bibliography is one of the first in a planned series of forty volumes focusing on the presidents of the United States. In an effort to fill in perceived gaps in the literature, this series hopes to provide comprehensive, annotated bibliographies covering archival sources and relevant monographs, periodical articles, dissertations, government documents, and even iconographic resources for each president.

This particular edition is divided into nineteen topical sections covering manuscript and archival sources, personal writings, biographical publications, and fifteen sections (mostly containing monographs and periodical articles) covering Cleveland's childhood, early career, terms in office, and post-presidential activities. One large section is devoted to information about Cleveland's two administrations and those who served under him during his twenty-second and twenty-fourth presidential terms. Some entries come with very brief annotations. A chronology of his life and a list of periodicals cited in the bibliography are provided. An author index and a far too brief subject index also are included.

Within each section materials are arranged, according to the author, "in order of importance," variously defined as the most recent publication, the most "significant" publication, or the most inclusive. This makes browsing difficult, and the limited subject index does little to improve access. For those doing in-depth study of Cleveland, this work will prove quite handy. For those doing basic, general research into his interesting career, this bibliography may be too much to handle. Elizabeth Patterson

634. Miles, William, comp. **The People's Voice: An Annotated Bibliography of American Presidential Campaign Newspapers, 1828-1984.** Westport, Conn., Greenwood Press, 1987. 210p. index. (Bibliographies and Indexes in American History, No. 6). $37.50. LC 87-11969. ISBN 0-313-23976-2.

It is taken for granted nowadays that the visual message as seen on television is much more important than the printed word, especially when it comes to politics. Before the twentieth century, however, political campaigns were marked by the appearance of numerous newspapers devoted to one cause or another. (As an example of how radio and television have changed the distribution of political campaign messages, there are twenty-one newspapers listed for the 1828 election year, and only one each for 1980 and 1984.) These short-lived publications, very partisan in their outlook and support for a particular candidate, are useful items for historical research in American politics. Due to the ephemeral nature of these publications, along with the amount of time that has passed since they were produced, there is sometimes only limited information available for a specific title.

The problem for researchers and librarians is finding that information, and it can be difficult to track down who owns the newspapers. There are, of course, computer networks and union lists, but one can spend a lot of time searching for the correct record. This specialized bibliography should simplify the searching process, as it brings together bibliographic and holdings information in one volume. The newspapers are first arranged chronologically by campaign year, then by the candidate that they supported, and finally by title. Each numbered entry for the 733 titles includes the place of publication, frequency and dates published, name of the publisher, masthead slogans, and a note directing one to other reference books that list the newspaper.

The twenty-two-page introduction discusses the history of these interesting publications and the relationship between the candidates and the press. There is a list of related reference books, along with title, geographic, and editor/publisher/candidate indexes. Interlibrary loan librarians should be aware of this work as each entry includes the OCLC screen number, library symbol, and holdings information. The book is well constructed, and the typeface, although like that of a typewriter, is easy to read. Recommended for academic and large public libraries. [R: Choice, Mar 88, p. 1068]

Daniel K. Blewett

635. Weatherson, Michael A., and Hal Bochin. **Hiram Johnson: A Bio-Bibliography.** Westport, Conn., Greenwood Press, 1988. 151p. index. (Bio-Bibliographies in Law and Political Science, No. 3). $35.00. LC 87-28030. ISBN 0-313-25574-1.

This new bio-bibliography on Hiram Johnson is a useful addition to American history between the turn of the century and the end of World War II. U.S. senator, governor of California, and Theodore Roosevelt's running mate in the 1912 presidential election, Hiram Johnson played an important role in the progressive movement.

The compilers have gathered primary and secondary information on Hiram Johnson and packaged it in this monograph to provide a lengthy summary of his career and an annotated bibliography of selected works mentioning him, articles he wrote, and a collection of speeches taken from the *Congressional Record*.

This is the third in the Greenwood Press series Bio-Bibliographies in Law and Political Science; the earlier ones were on Wayne Morse and Will Herberg. The format for these works is similar, providing a biographical sketch that highlights the activities and accomplishments of the biographee, an annotated list of works about the person, some materials regarding the biographee's writings or speeches, and sources for additional information (primary and secondary). This particular work has an appendix that identifies the location of manuscript collections. The index is not very detailed and therefore somewhat limited in value.

There are a few typographical errors in the book that do not detract much from the text. An example is on page xiii in the "Chronology," where in the second line for the 1920 entry, "the" is repeated. Other than these minor things, the book is useful and readable.

Because of its specialized focus, this book is recommended for large public and academic libraries that have strong collections on American history from the turn of the century to 1945. It is not suitable as a reference work for use in a general library, but instead would be of value as an addition to a strong biography section. [R: Choice, July/Aug 88, p. 1679]

Roberto P. Haro

Biographies

636. Champagne, Anthony. **Sam Rayburn: A Bio-Bibliography.** Westport, Conn., Greenwood Press, 1988. 147p. index. (Bio-Bibliographies in Law and Political Science, No. 4). $35.95. LC 88-21341. ISBN 0-313-25864-3.

Besides holding the office of Speaker of the House longer than anyone else in American history, Sam Rayburn (1882-1961) served significantly in Congress under eight presidents and acted as Lyndon Johnson's political mentor. Therefore, it is not at all surprising that he appears in this Greenwood Press series. The volume is a handy introductory guide to research on Sam Rayburn. It begins with a brief chronology of Rayburn's life, followed by a sixty-page chapter of biographical narrative. Next comes a chapter which consists of an annotated bibliography of 186 items about Rayburn. Entries are numbered and listed alphabetically by author with complete bibliographic information. Each annotation is normally about fifty words in length. Besides listing relatively easy to find books and articles, the bibliography performs the valuable service of supplying information on relevant theses and dissertations and various important oral history interviews with people who knew Rayburn which are held by the Sam Rayburn Library in Bonham, Texas. The third chapter lists the writings of Sam Rayburn, particularly letters and speeches. It is a short chapter, since Rayburn conducted most of his business orally and did not keep detailed records. Finally, the last chapter lists and describes thirteen archival collections of interest to researchers on Rayburn. A subject index assists readers in finding specific information. The wide range of material found in this work make it of use for beginning students all the way up to advanced researchers.

Ronald H. Fritze

637. Day, Glenn, comp. **Minor Presidential Candidates and Parties of 1988.** Jefferson, N.C., McFarland, 1988. 228p. illus. index. $19.95. LC 88-42570. ISBN 0-89950-357-8.

This small volume introduces us to no less than sixty-seven minor candidates for president of the United States during the 1988 electoral year. Some were seeking nomination by one of the major parties, while others ran either independently or under the banner of a minor party (Libertarian, Socialist, Prohibition, etc.). Featured are the candidates' political statements (often unedited), their photographs, and reproductions of campaign literature. Also included are the platforms of eleven minor parties and the names and addresses of a dozen more. Sources used include the files of the Federal Election Commission, contacts with the candidates, and statements of the parties. Of interest among the appendices are the primary votes cast for minor parties, fund-raising data, and numbers of signatures required for ballot access in the various states, ranging from a low of zero in some to a high of 128,340 in California. Updated to March 1988, the book offers an interesting look at some of the less known byways of the American electoral process. While primarily a work of political curiosity, this book is also a reminder that our country is still one where the road to the nation's highest office is open to all.

Adam E. Cappello

Dictionaries and Encyclopedias

638. Elliot, Jeffrey M., and Sheikh R. Ali. **The State and Local Government Political Dictionary.** Santa Barbara, Calif., ABC-Clio, 1988. 325p. index. (Clio Dictionaries in Political Science). $37.50; $17.00pa. LC 87-18722. ISBN 0-87436-417-5; 0-87436-512-0pa.

With 290 entries arranged alphabetically in eleven subject-based chapters, this dictionary provides basic information about the organization and functions of state and local govern-

ment. The approach follows that used by the same authors in their earlier work, *The Presidential-Congressional Political Dictionary* (ABC-Clio, 1984). A one-paragraph definition of the term is accompanied by a one-paragraph analysis of its significance. Thus, the user can find an explanation of the city manager's role and an account of the poll tax's purpose. Definitions include helpful *see also* references to related entries, and the compilers cite their sources, making it possible for readers to locate more detail than the necessarily broad generalizations characteristic of each entry can provide. This dictionary is a sound addition to public and academic library collections. [R: LJ, 15 Feb 88, p. 160]

Cheryl Knott Malone

639. O'Toole, G. J. A. **The Encyclopedia of American Intelligence and Espionage: From the Revolutionary War to the Present.** New York, Facts on File, 1988. 539p. illus. bibliog. index. $40.00. LC 87-30361. ISBN 0-8160-1011-0.

The study of intelligence and espionage, for which the author has coined the term *espionology*, has greatly expanded over the last two decades. O'Toole, a former CIA employee, states in his introduction that scholarly research in this field has been hampered by the lack of appropriate reference tools; most publications are too popular or too broad in scope, such as *The Whole Spy Catalogue: An Espionage Lover's Guide* by Richard L. Knudson (see *ARBA* 88, entry 1144). O'Toole has tried to rectify this situation by compiling a work that is focused on just one country.

This encyclopedia was produced by combing through a variety of reference books, biographies, and histories of the American intelligence community. The result is that the well-written entries are filled with details that one would have to search several different sources to find. Biographical material makes up a large portion of this book, and includes more data about Americans than found in *Who's Who in Espionage* (see *ARBA* 86, entry 660). Numerous cross-references are included, and at the end of each entry are listed the authors and titles of the books consulted.

American history from the Revolutionary War to the present is covered, but the colonial period is left out. Several of the entries, such as those on the Civil War and the Bay of Pigs, are essays running to several pages; an entry on the funding of American intelligence agencies would have been useful. There is a three-page list of abbreviations, but the jargon of intelligence work is not covered as well as in *The Dictionary of Espionage* (see *ARBA* 88, entry 696), or *Top Secret: A Clandestine Operator's*

Glossary of Terms (see *ARBA* 88, entry 697). Not nearly enough pictures are included (there are two of the Lockheed SR-71 Blackbird), but the ten-page bibliography and index are very helpful.

This well-constructed book is worth the price, and should join Ronald Seth's *Encyclopedia of Espionage* (Doubleday, 1972) on the reference shelves. Suitable for all libraries. [R: WLB, Oct 88, p. 108]   Daniel K. Blewett

640. Shafritz, Jay M. **The Dorsey Dictionary of American Government and Politics.** Chicago, Dorsey Press, 1988. 661p. illus. $34.95; $18.95pa. LC 87-72401. ISBN 0-256-05639-0; 0-256-05589-0pa.

Jay Shafritz describes his work as "a tool for those who seek information on American national, state, or local government and politics" (preface). *The Dorsey Dictionary* defines and explains terms and concepts used for the executive, legislative, and judicial branches of American government. Also included are descriptions of major federal laws and landmark decisions of the United States Supreme Court, brief biographies of significant political figures, and chronologies of important events in American history. The book's appendices include a guide to federal government documents and guides to statistical information and online databases on American government.

Shafritz's professed goal is to "capture the language, concerns, and professional literature of American governance in one volume" (preface); he succeeds quite admirably. Following many definitions he has included references to books or journal articles where one may further research the term defined. While many of these references are current and provide valuable information to the reader, too many others are dated.

Notwithstanding some minor shortcomings, this dictionary will be a useful addition to most academic and public libraries. In paperback for $18.95, it is a real bargain. [R: Choice, Oct 88, p. 296; LJ, 15 Mar 88, p. 51; RBB, 15 June 88, pp. 1719-20]   James S. Heller

641. Shavit, David. **The United States in the Middle East: A Historical Dictionary.** Westport, Conn., Greenwood Press, 1988. 441p. bibliog. index. $65.00. LC 87-24965. ISBN 0-313-25341-2.

Principally a biographical dictionary listing those Americans involved in work or travel in the Middle East, this book also includes notes on institutions or organizations founded or supported primarily by American funding. The biographical notes are brief, but include references to the individual's education and training, length and place(s) of service, and known writings or files of papers left behind. Each entry concludes with a list of sources in which more extensive information concerning the individual can be found.

A chronology of events from the late eighteenth century (when American involvement in this area appears to have begun) begins with the Ottoman-Russian war in 1787, and ends, a bit unauspiciously, with the United States air raid on Libya. We are also provided with a listing of the chiefs of American diplomatic missions in the Middle East from 1831 to 1986.

One valuable supplement to the work is a listing of all those included, classified by profession or occupation. This allows the user to work out for him- or herself the type and intensity of U.S. involvement in various parts of the region.

Any compilation of this type will be likely to have omitted or overlooked some individuals who were also involved in Middle Eastern affairs, and no criticism of such omissions need be offered. It is to be hoped, however, that a second edition of this work will contain a longer introductory essay presenting a more detailed analysis of the overall picture of American involvement in this part of the world. [R: Choice, Oct 88, pp. 296-97]

Margaret Anderson

Directories

642. **The Almanac of the Unelected 1988: Staff of the U.S. Congress.** By Charles C. Francis and Jeffrey B. Trammell. Washington, D.C., Almanac of the Unelected, 1988. 749p. illus. index. $250.00. ISBN 0-8191-6979-X.

The unelected referred to in the title are the estimated twenty thousand individuals who work for the congressional leadership, for the legislative committees, or on the personal staffs of the members of the Senate and the House of Representatives. This volume presents information on six hundred of these, who are considered key members, the persons basically responsible for translating the policies of the members of the congressional committees into the reports of those committees and into legislative language to be embodied into statutory law.

The selection of these six hundred was, in the words of the publishers, "something of an art, something of an organizational science, and in many ways an impossibility." The six hundred highly individualized profiles are presented under their respective committees, and include photographs, addresses, and telephone numbers, together with data on their educational background, employment experience, areas of expertise, specific accomplishments, political orientation, and, in many cases, personal evaluations by their colleagues or other observers.

There are an alphabetical index of the six hundred key members and a subject matter index with some 250 alphabetized entries, including such topics as abortion, AIDS, currency, gun control, Soviet Union, space policy, weapons, and welfare.

The volume would appear to be of special value to government officials, journalists, political organizations, educational and scientific institutions, lobbyists, labor union officials, and others who have a need to deal with the law-making branch of the federal government. [R: Choice, Dec 88, p. 621; RQ, Winter 88, p. 262-64]

Adam E. Cappello

643. County Executive Directory. Washington, D.C., Carroll Publishing, 1988. 350p. $95.00 (2 issues). ISSN 0742-1702.

644. Federal Executive Directory. Washington, D.C., Carroll Publishing, 1988. 464p. index. $140.00 (6 issues).

645. Federal Regional Executive Directory. Washington, D.C., Carroll Publishing, 1988. 353p. maps. index. $95.00 (2 issues).

646. Municipal Executive Directory. Washington, D.C., Carroll Publishing, 1988. 409p. index. $95.00 (2 issues).

647. State Executive Directory. Washington, D.C., Carroll Publishing, 1988. 441p. index. $125.00 (3 issues).

Among the major frustrations of reference work is the inability to keep abreast of personnel changes in governmental organizations. Most directories of government personnel are published on an annual basis only and are out-of-date by the time they appear on library shelves. Also, many directories only list the names of key officials and a user must rely on a telephone call to retrieve more specific information. Both of these deficiencies are addressed by the series of executive directories prepared by the Carroll Publishing Company. Each of the directories under review is very comprehensive, and while the updating schedule varies by title, these directories are generally more current than anything else available.

Of the five titles, the *Federal Executive Directory* is the most impressive. A new edition is published every two months, which gives this directory extremely high marks for timeliness. A

typical volume contains over eighty-six thousand entries, providing exhaustive coverage of the federal executive branch and the U.S. Congress. This directory may lack the handy background information and descriptions found in the *U.S. Government Manual* (Government Printing Office, 1974-), but its listing of personnel is far more useful. The volume is organized into four major sections: an alphabetical listing of executives; a breakdown of cabinet departments and seventy administrative agencies; a listing of congressional offices, committees, and related offices (including the General Accounting Office, Government Printing Office, and the venerable Library of Congress); and a very detailed keyword index. Each entry in the index is keyed to a consecutive five-digit number, which makes for very quick and precise searching.

A related volume, the *Federal Regional Executive Directory*, provides access to information that is normally not found in standard governmental directories. This volume contains listings for over thirty thousand regional offices of federal agencies, cabinet departments, congressional home district offices, military bases, and federal district and appeals courts. Included in this volume are FBI field offices, U.S. marshals, and the state directors of the USDA Extension Services. This title is only published twice a year, but personnel turnover tends to be less frequent at this level of government service.

The remaining volumes in the set cover state, county, and municipal government. In each of these volumes, the scope and detail of the coverage are equally impressive. The *State Executive Directory* is similar in arrangement to the federal volume – listings for departments, agencies, and the legislature – with a handy section of "special listings." These include telephone numbers for legislative reference information, a list of historical preservation offices, and dates for state legislative sessions. The state directory is updated three times a year and contains over twenty-eight thousand names.

The *Municipal Executive Directory* (published twice a year; forty thousand names) is divided by size of municipality. There are brief entries for places under fifteen thousand in population: the only data given are the population, name of the mayor (or the top elected official), address, and telephone number. The listings for places over fifteen thousand are more comprehensive: most major officials are listed, sometimes even the librarian! The *County Executive Directory* (also published twice a year) is similarly divided by size, with divisions at the twenty-five thousand and fifty thousand population marks. Listings for counties larger than fifty thousand can be quite extensive. Lake County, Ohio, for example, has seventy-five offices listed. In many of the listings, a wide array of county offices is reported, including surveyor, sanitation supervisor, constable, friend of the court, drain commissioner, dog officer, and risk manager.

There is a uniform look and arrangement to these directories; the major sections are color-coded to enhance ease of use. Because they are published in paper binding, they might not withstand heavy reference use – though the federal volume is published frequently enough to prevent this problem. Each of these titles is recommended for large public and academic libraries; smaller libraries will need to decide on the basis of the number of questions asked in these areas.

Thomas A. Karel

648. **The New York State Directory 1988.** Louise S. Erlick, ed. Bethesda, Md., Cambridge Information Group, 1988. 423p. index. $95.00 pa. LC 84-641421. ISBN 0-942189-32-9; ISSN 0737-1314.

Sixth edition of a mammoth publication which has as its purpose to identify and enable the user to contact those "public and private officials who, because of their positions and knowledge have an impact on public policy and the political process," this work lists officials in the state executive, legislative, and judicial branches as well as state executive departments and agencies that formulate and implement policies. Federal departments and agencies and private sector individuals are included when appropriate. The directory is organized first by branches of government and then by policy areas. The twenty-five policy areas include banking, commerce and industry, education, environment, health, transportation, and tourism. Each is arranged with executive departments and agencies, followed by state and regional offices, legislative committees, federal departments and agencies, and private sector sources. The names, work addresses, and telephone numbers of *each* major member of *each* of the above agencies/departments are printed. Section 3 lists state government public information in a similar arrangement. Extensive appendices include county and municipal government officials, chambers of commerce, and news media services throughout the state. There are separate indexes for personal names, state government, and private sector sources. The usefulness of this volume is that a large number of people in government become easily accessible to the average citizen. The question is how often it will be updated. Presently accurate

through June 1988, it will be useful in libraries throughout New York State.

Deborah Hammer

649. **State Legislative Leadership, Committees & Staff 1987-88.** Lexington, Ky., Council of State Governments, 1987. 284p. $30.00pa. ISBN 0-87292-073-9.

This title acts as a supplement to the *Book of States*. The type of information provided is identical to the earlier edition published in 1981-1982 (see *ARBA* 83, entry 473). Section 1 provides an overview of the state legislatures including the chairs of the major committees and support staff offices along with the appropriate names, addresses, and telephone numbers. Section 2 is arranged by area and state and is divided into three parts. The first part is a legislative directory, the second part includes a detailed list of standing committees, and the third part names those support staff services that are involved with legislative functions. Again, the appropriate contact person is listed along with address and telephone number. Included are not only the fifty states but also the District of Columbia, American Samoa, Guam, Northern Mariana Islands, Puerto Rico, and the Virgin Islands. This title is excellent for those requiring current information on key persons to contact in the legislative area of state government.

Frank Wm. Goudy

Handbooks

650. Bosnich, Victor W. **Congressional Voting Guide: A Ten Year Compilation of the 99th Congress.** Washington, D.C., Congressional Voting Guide, 1987. 630p. index. $19.75pa. LC 87-91609. ISBN 0-9618958-0-2.

A handy reference to the voting records of the members of Congress, this single volume includes what the author has deemed "major votes" of the 1977 to 1986 period. The House measures are listed first, followed by the members' voting records, then the Senate measures and the Senators' votes. The measures are arranged in reverse chronological order by official number and a short version of the measure's name. An index of full, formal titles of measures and one for popular names would have been useful. The only index is to names of members of both houses of Congress. Nevertheless, the guide makes it convenient to find how each member of the 99th Congress voted on a particular issue, as well as to research a single member's voting record on a variety of issues. The author also provides a "Presidential Support Score" indicating the degree to which each member of Congress voted in favor of the measures promoted by the White House. The guide, and its subsequent editions, will be of service at any library attempting to assist an informed electorate. [R: Choice, Apr 88, pp. 1219-20; RBB, 15 Apr 88, p. 1404; RQ, Spring 88, pp. 424-25]   Cheryl Knott Malone

651. Congress A to Z: CQ's Ready Reference Encyclopedia. Washington, D.C., Congressional Quarterly, 1988. 612p. illus. bibliog. index. $75.00. LC 88-20336. ISBN 0-87187-447-4.

This is an excellent reference source that unequivocally measures up to its billing as a "ready reference encyclopedia." The workings of the U.S. Congress, legislative terminology, historical information, and biographical sketches are presented in 280 clearly written entries. Most of the entries (which are arranged in an alphabetical sequence, with ample cross-references included) are brief, ranging in length from one paragraph to two pages of text. Scattered throughout the book, however, are thirty substantial essays (five to eight pages long) on a variety of broad topics. Among these "core essays" are the budget process, committee system, impeachment power, legislative process (complete with a chart on how a bill becomes a law), lobbying, war powers, and the Watergate scandal. The essays on the House of Representatives and the Senate each include a page that depicts a typical day's activity in Congress. Some of the entries in the book (both long and short) include brief bibliographies, and many entries are accompanied by photographs, cartoons, charts, and an occasional map.

Congress A to Z is an extremely accessible reference work. The table of contents lists every item in the book (including the cross-references) and there is a more detailed index of names and subjects at the end of the book. A wealth of appended material is provided: fourteen specialized listings of members of Congress (e.g., party leadership, women members, censure proceedings); fifteen lists dealing with the work of Congress (e.g., vetoes and overrides, congressional salaries, organization charts); floor plans of the Capitol building; a map of Washington, D.C., and some major official attractions in the city; a U.S. government organization chart; the Constitution; and an eight-page bibliography. In addition to the general index, there is also an index of the members of Congress.

This is an ideal source for reference collections in all types and sizes of libraries. *Congressional Quarterly's Guide to Congress* (see *ARBA* 83, entry 478) is by far more comprehensive and is a true encyclopedia of congressional history and activity. This work, however, is

recommended for the kind of quick understanding and background information most library patrons (academic and public) need, and the material here is more substantial than that found in other political dictionaries, such as *The Presidential-Congressional Political Dictionary*, by Jeffrey M. Elliot and Sheikh R. Ali (see *ARBA* 86, entry 687). It is a safe bet that *Congress A to Z* will become a very heavily used reference work in most libraries. [R: WLB, Nov 88, p. 122]   Thomas A. Karel

652. The Handbook of State Legislative Leaders 1988. Centerville, Mass., State Legislative Leaders Foundation, 1988. 560p. illus. index. $60.00pa. ISSN 0743-0728.

According to the preface, this publication on state legislative leaders is the fifth edition of the title. A ten- to twelve-page section is devoted to each state, but much of this is white space. Within these sections a full page, including a 2½-by-3-inch photograph, is devoted to each major legislative leader (president of the senate, speaker of the house, pro tempore president and speaker, and majority and minority leaders of each house). This page provides addresses and telephone numbers, names of assistants, brief biographical information, a list of responsibilities of the office, and memberships and interests of the incumbent. Other information provided for each state: a list of committee chairs, party composition of the legislature, dates of convening and adjourning, and deadlines.

Except for the photographs and personal information, nothing has been added to information available in *State Legislative Leadership, Committees and Staff* (see entry 649), a biennial supplement to the *Book of the States* (see *ARBA* 88, entry 727), which includes more officers, each with individual addresses and telephone numbers, as well as separate lists of major offices and important committees by state, including incumbents and chairs.

Constance McCarthy

653. Mullaney, Marie Marmo, comp. American Governors and Gubernatorial Elections 1979-1987. Westport, Conn., Meckler, 1988. 101p. bibliog. $35.00. LC 88-13248. ISBN 0-88736-316-4.

Mullaney's compilation is an updated edition of *American Governors and Gubernatorial Elections, 1775-1978*, compiled by Roy R. Glashan and reviewed in *ARBA* 80 (see entry 502). Both works provide brief biographical information on the governors (date and place of birth, date of and age at becoming governor, party, major occupation, residence, and death date and age), and basic election statistics (election date, vote for Democratic, Republican, other significant candidates, and total scattered vote and percentage.

Public and academic libraries with files of *Almanac of American Politics* (see *ARBA* 86, entry 695) and *Politics in America* (see *ARBA* 87, entry 449) will know that while both sources give most of their attention to the members of Congress they do add the college degrees, religious affiliation, and marital status to the governors' biographical statements and that both include recent gubernatorial election results for the candidates. The biennial *America Votes* (see *ARBA* 87, entry 717), likely to be held by these libraries, provides even more data on elections for governors, presidents, senators, and congresspersons. Smaller libraries may find *American Governors and Gubernatorial Elections 1979-1987* sufficient for their needs on governors and will appreciate its bibliographic note listing sources of biographical information and election statistics for governors and other state and national political officials.

Wiley J. Williams

654. Ornstein, Norman J., Thomas E. Mann, and Michael J. Malbin. **Vital Statistics on Congress, 1987-1988.** Washington, D.C., Congressional Quarterly, 1987. 275p. $16.95. LC 87-30088. ISBN 0-87187-451-2.

This is the third update of the 1980 work prepared to contain data on the Congress, and the first to be published by Congressional Quarterly. It differs from the previous works by including new arrays of data in the areas of campaign finance and budgeting. The work focuses on Congress as an institution and provides statistics about overall congressional performance, about groups of legislators, categories of legislators, and their behavior. It includes materials about the House and Senate taken together and separately. The statistics included are aggregated, designed to present an overall iinstitutional perspective. As such, this is a tool most suited for the highly specialized researcher or layperson interested in the Congress as an institution.

The book is divided into eight major areas: (1) members of Congress, (2) elections, (3) campaign finance, (4) committees, (5) congressional staff and operating expenses, (6) workload, (7) budgeting, and (8) voting alignments. The appendix is lengthy, containing current information about the legislators.

This particular work does not replace nor compete with *Politics in America* (see *ARBA* 86, entry 694), or the *Almanac of American Politics* (for review of 1986 edition, see *ARBA* 86, entry 695). Rather, this is a companion work

to those items, one that provides an institutional scrutiny. Its approach, then, is to provide an institutional perspective on the Congress that identifies previous activities, shifts, and different directions. As it is highly specialized, smaller libraries may not want to consider this item for purchase. Those libraries that have purchased the previous editions will need to purchase this work to complete their collections. As mentioned above, the specialized focus of this book recommends it mainly to the major libraries and political science research collections.

Roberto P. Haro

655. Scammon, Richard M., and Alice V. McGillivray, comps. and eds. **America at the Polls 2: A Handbook of American Presidential Election Statistics 1968-1984.** Washington, D.C., Congressional Quarterly, 1988. 594p. maps. $60.00. LC 87-33221. ISBN 0-87187-452-0.

This title is an update to Congressional Quarterly's first *America at the Polls*, which covered presidential elections from 1920-1964. It also serves as a companion volume to the America Votes series (see *ARBA* 87, entry 717). As in the America Votes series, each chapter includes a county outline map of each state and the detailed county-by-county vote election results. Minor party votes with explanations as necessary are provided. A separate chapter details the presidential preference primary vote by state and candidate for each election from 1968 through 1984.

Basically, the information detailed here is the same as that which the America Votes series includes on these five elections. For those libraries that do not have past editions of this series, or that need a cumulative edition of this information, this work should definitely be purchased. [R: Choice, Nov 88, p. 468; RBB, 1 Nov 88, pp. 456, 458; WLB, Oct 88, p. 105]

Frank Wm. Goudy

656. Sharp, J. Michael. **Directory of Congressional Voting Scores and Interest Group Ratings.** New York, Facts on File, 1988. 2v. $125.00. LC 87-9047. ISBN 0-8160-1464-7.

The legislative voting behavior of members of Congress is a fruitful subfield of political research. Many current sources, from reference works to periodicals, provide ratings or other measures of congressional behavior. The publication of this directory provides a convenient and comprehensive source for this kind of data.

The two volumes compiled by Sharp (a former legislative aide to presidential candidate Richard Gephardt) constitute a major quantitative study of the voting behavior of each member of Congress (House and Senate) since 1947. By combining the member's voting history with a variety of interest group ratings, Sharp provides a "panoramic view" of an individual's voting record. To achieve this, he devised four basic voting scores: party unity, presidential support, conservative coalition support, and voting participation. Additionally, the ratings from eleven prominent interest groups are given for each member. The groups include Americans for Democratic Action, Chamber of Commerce of the United States, the AFL-CIO's Committee on Political Education, and the National Taxpayer's Union.

The data in these volumes range from 1947 (when the Americans for Democratic Action first began rating the performance of congressmen) to 1985. The major sources of data used by Sharp are several Congressional Quarterly publications: *The CQ Weekly Report, Congressional Quarterly Almanac,* and *Politics in America* (see *ARBA* 86, entry 694); also, he used the *Almanac of American Politics* (see *ARBA* 86, entry 695). Thus, for libraries lacking long runs of these publications, this new source will be a gold mine of data.

The arrangement of the directory is alphabetical by the names of the members of Congress. Each entry gives brief biographical information, including the member's religious affiliation, education, occupation, and political background. This section, however, is not intended to provide a complete political profile of the individual. For example, political activities after serving in Congress are generally not mentioned (Gerald Ford's presidency *is* noted, but this book does not indicate that Congressman David Stockman later became Budget Director). Beneath the background information, the voting scores and interest group ratings are listed in columns which match the length of the member's service in Congress. An appendix lists the members of each congress, from the eightieth to the ninety-ninth, arranged by state.

A most convenient source for voting behavior data, this will serve as a heavily used supplement to the abovementioned sources for most academic libraries. The publisher is planning to update the work with a new edition after the election of every second new congress. [R: BR, May/June 88, p. 48; Choice, June 88, p. 1540; RBB, July 88, p. 1811; RQ, Summer 88, p. 572; WLB, May 88, pp. 109-10]

Thomas A. Karel

657. Stanley, Harold W., and Richard G. Niemi. **Vital Statistics on American Politics.** Washington, D.C., Congressional Quarterly, 1988. 403p. bibliog. index. $16.95; $11.95pa.

LC 88-3594. ISBN 0-87187-472-5; 0-87187-471-7pa.

This unusual new reference book is a collection of statistical tables, lists, and graphs relating to political topics. The value and interest of these data lie in the fact that they have been gathered from a wide variety of books and journal articles, and from machine-readable survey data from the National Opinion Research Center and the Inter-University Consortium for Political and Social Research, as well as from the standard sources of political statistics. Some of the subject matter covered is also somewhat unexpected: for example, public opinion on abortion, gun control, and the death penalty in the chapter on the Constitution; content analysis on coverage of campaigns and elections in the chapter on the media; and teenage unemployment by race and sex in the chapter on economic policy. In every case, the source is cited at the end of the table, making the book a useful finding tool for additional data.

The volume has been arranged for use as a supplementary textbook, with questions at the end of each chapter. Each of the thirteen chapters has a brief introduction, which comments on the tables presented and on the availability of statistical information on the topic under discussion.

In the future editions one hopes will appear, several improvements would make this a better reference book. For really satisfactory use, the index should be more detailed. Page numbers and running chapter heads should be preserved where tables are presented sideways on the page; it is very disorienting to be confronted with twenty or more consecutive pages without page numbers. A single numbering sequence for tables and figures (graphs) within each chapter would also help the user. Despite these inconveniences, this grouping of a wide variety of data previously available only through rather extensive research will be gratefully used in reference departments. [R: RBB, 15 Dec 88, p. 695; WLB, Oct 88, p. 105]

Constance McCarthy

658. Trattner, John H. **The Prune Book: The 100 Toughest Management and Policy-Making Jobs in Washington.** Lanham, Md., Madison Books/University Press of America, 1988. 625p. index. $34.95. LC 88-8253. ISBN 0-8191-7000-3.

This unusually titled book turns out to be a very useful and timely reference guide to the "toughest managerial/policy jobs" in the federal government. The title derives from the so-called "Plum Book" (*Policy and Supporting Positions*), which lists approximately three thousand appointive positions throughout the executive branch (and which is in very high demand around election time). The "Plum Book" is a simple inventory of the positions and contains no description or background information. *The Prune Book*, on the other hand, isolates and carefully analyzes the most challenging of these positions.

The positions covered in *The Prune Book* are the key appointed positions that lie just below Cabinet level: the deputy secretaries, undersecretaries, directors of special programs, assistant directors, and general counsels. The editor claims that *"The Prune Book* is non-partisan and has no agenda"; its purpose is "to improve the selection of the men and women who fill the crucial – but often vaguely understood – senior positions in the critical management and policy-making area." A great deal of the information contained in this book is the result of staff research and interviews with past officeholders. The interview process is described in detail, and there is a useful chapter on the various forces which shape the appointments: transition, timing, political contexts, organizational contexts, and the whole appointment process.

The book is organized by cabinet departments, then subdivided by the key positions. There is a brief sketch of each department, which describes the work, responsibility, and major subdivisions from a perspective different than that found in the official *U.S. Government Manual* (see *ARBA* 84, entry 456). Also, an organization chart is provided for each department. For each of the positions listed, the following information is included: the major responsibilities of the position; the necessary background, experience, and personal skills; "insights," which provide an overall analysis of the position as well as some viewpoints of the interviewees; key relationships (within the department, outside the department, and outside the federal government); and the holders of the position since 1969.

The Prune Book is appended by a list of sixty-nine additional "tough" positions (which came close to being included), a list of nearly four hundred interviewees, brief biographical sketches of the "Prune Book Departmental Teams" (the research staff), and an index of names. This source will be heavily used by students of American politics and may even be required reading for some advanced courses. Academic and large public libraries should acquire it as a supplementary reference source which can accompany standard works like *The Almanac of American Politics* (see *ARBA* 86,

entry 695), *The U.S. Government Manual*, and the major Congressional Quarterly publications.

Thomas A. Karel

659. Zink, Steven D. **Guide to the Presidential Advisory Commissions 1973-84.** Alexandria, Va., Chadwyck-Healey, 1987. 643p. index. (Government Documents Bibliographies). $85.00. LC 87-13196. ISBN 0-85964-122-8.

This publication represents an interesting compilation of presidential commissions between the years 1973 and 1984. While it does not include the text of the different commission reports, it does provide some valuable and useful information.

The work is arranged by year, and then by the name of the commission, not necessarily in alphabetical order. There is a useful table of contents in the front, and three different indexes in the rear: personal name, title, and subject. The introduction contains a brief section on how information is packaged under each entry, including availability of the final report.

Each entry contains the official name of the advisory body and a popular name in parenthesis, date of establishment and termination, statement of functions, activities and recommendations, dates and places of meetings, membership, title of reports issued, and availability of such reports. The summary of recommendations is in short sentences listed in random order. As mentioned above, there is no attempt to abstract or include passages from the original documents.

The value of this compilation of information rests with its access to pertinent publication materials on significant issues dealt with by the various presidential commissions. The period covered, 1973-1984, was a particularly significant one which will be carefully researched by scholars and interested laypersons. The one-sentence account of each recommendation assists the user in determining whether a particular commission report may be important to review in its full text. Moreover, it provides a convenient way to gauge the work and the extent of effort undertaken by the commission to accomplish its purpose.

At $85.00 a copy, the work is not inexpensive. It is recommended for large public libraries and academic libraries, particularly those that do not have a government publications section or that are not U.S. government document depositories. [R: Choice, Sept 88, p. 92]

Roberto P. Haro

Indexes and Abstracts

660. Index to the Iran-Contra Hearings Summary Report: A Concordance Index to Both Versions—The U.S. Government Printing Office and the *New York Times*. By James Joseph Sanchez. Jefferson, N.C., McFarland, 1988. 82p. $19.95pa. LC 88-42555. ISBN 0-89950-356-X.

661. Index to the Tower Commission Report. By James Joseph Sanchez. Jefferson, N.C., McFarland, 1987. 57p. $10.95pa. LC 87-3116. ISBN 0-89950-299-7.

These two publications provide handy and extensive indexing to two important recent public documents dealing with the Reagan administration's efforts to supply arms to Iran and divert those funds to the Nicaraguan Contras. *The Tower Commission Report*, issued in February 1987 (under its official title, *Report of the President's Special Review Board*), was the first authorized investigation into the Iran-Contra affair. The text which Mr. Sanchez has chosen to index is that published by Bantam Books in a mass-market paperback edition (a wise decision, as it is difficult to locate the official version in most libraries). Sanchez has indexed the complete text of the *Report* and has made generous use of cross-references. Brief explanatory notes are set off in brackets (e.g., "al-Mugarieff" [Libya, opposition leader]), and a glossary of acronyms is integrated into the index. This is an extremely detailed and creative index. In addition to predictable references (e.g., over two pages on Oliver North), there are a host of unusual phrases and descriptive entries: "Kidnapping for profit," "Spare parts for HAWK missiles," "Nice crowd you run with," "Chocolate cake carried by McFarlane to Tehran meeting," and so forth.

Sanchez's indexing is even more intricate in the *Index to the Iran-Contra Hearings Summary Report*. This book indexes not only the official Government Printing Office version of the report (*Report of the Congressional Committees Investigating the Iran-Contra Affair*; H. Rept. No. 100-433; S. Rept. No. 100-216) and the popular paperback version published by the *New York Times*, but also four critical studies of the controversy (including Bob Woodward's bestselling *Veil*). The index terms are based on those used in the *Index to the Tower Commission Report*, with the page references coded to the pertinent publication. Although this index is somewhat cumbersome to use, it is an extremely valuable reference tool for these reports. Sanchez has provided an introductory section in which he compares the amount of coverage of material in both reports, and a lengthy explanation of how to use the index. Libraries with any version of these reports will benefit greatly by the addition of these indexes to their collections.

Thomas A. Karel

662. U.S. Governmental Advisory Organizations Publications on Microfiche 1987: A Microfiche Collection of Approximately 175 Complete Publications and Reports. Index and Abstract Service: Part 2. Denise M. Allard, ed. Detroit, Gale, 1988. 53p. with microfiche. index. $1,040.00pa./set (2 issues). ISBN 0-8103-0682-4; ISSN 0895-477X.

To complement its *Encyclopedia of Governmental Advisory Organizations* (see *ARBA* 87, entry 703), Gale has issued this new subscription service that provides the complete text of selected publications from numerous governmental advisory organizations. Not every organization in the encyclopedia is represented here; the editors chose only those documents felt to be most important. Draft reports and hearings can be found for earlier years while final reports are prevalent for the more recent past. Some of these items were never issued by the Superintendent of Documents, and many are no longer in print. Libraries trying to fill gaps in their historical collection or replacing hard copies with microforms should examine this service.

Each edition will be issued in two installments; the first edition has 315 microfiche. There are 173 documents, some going back to 1969, with the majority published after 1980. Manufactured to the NMA standard with diazo film from silver halide masters, each sheet holds ninety-eight frames. The eye-readable header section for each fiche contains the fiche number, the document numbers, and the titles of the documents to be found on that fiche. The fiche is produced with negative polarity and a 24x reduction rate. A printed "Index and Abstract Service" is included, of the usual Gale quality, with clear, easy-to-read printing and good organization. A "Title, Organization, and Keyword Index" at the back provides both fiche and document numbers. One can then look up the document numbers in the "Publications Abstracts" section to find the bibliographic citation and accompanying short abstract for each publication. SuDocs numbers are provided for the majority of citations.

This service does duplicate to some degree the existing government distribution program. The federal document microfiche project that began in 1975 was also selective until 1983, when it was expanded to cover virtually all GPO publications. Approximately 75 percent of the listed documents included in this service are also depository items, and many may therefore already be in the library. (Some examples are reports on the *Challanger* disaster and from the Tower Commission.) Since many, if not most, libraries will probably have a good number of the post-1980 publications, they might be more interested in this service if the selection of items focused to a greater degree on the pre-1980 documents. The editor has told this reviewer that Gale is planning to include publications from before 1969 in future editions. This would be very useful, since it is doubtful that the government will ever conduct a retrospective microfiche project.

Another drawback is that different documents frequently share the same fiche; therefore, if one fiche is lost, two documents are incomplete rather than just one. Finally, the fact that this is a subscription service means that the purchaser gets the entire collection at one price. A library cannot at this time buy the printed "Index and Abstract Service" separately and choose which documents it wishes to purchase individually. Such a procedure is under discussion at Gale, but it has not yet been implemented. Flexibility in ordering items would make this service more attractive to libraries.

Gale is to be commended for providing another way to acquire these older publications. The value of this service will become greater as Gale makes available on microfiche more pre-1983 documents and allows libraries to buy single documents. Until then, libraries will want to carefully consider whether the number and type of documents included are worth the cost and possible duplication when compared to interlibrary loan or going to the government directly for individual documents. Recommended.

Daniel K. Blewett

Quotation Books

663. Frost, Elizabeth, ed. **The Bully Pulpit: Quotations from America's Presidents.** New York, Facts on File, 1988. 282p. bibliog. index. $23.95. LC 87-24381. ISBN 0-8160-1247-4.

This collection of presidential statements includes about three thousand quotes taken from speeches, diaries, letters, books, and overheard remarks. The book focuses on the presidential years, but includes before and after statements as well. Quotations were selected "on the basis of their historic significance, intrinsic human interest, and colorful or eloquent language" (p. xiii).

About one hundred general topics are covered, along with comments by the presidents about each other. There is a good mixture of minor and major themes; it is interesting, for example, to learn what some presidents said about ambition, character, duty, and success, as well as more heavyweight topics such as civil rights, democracy, foreign affairs, and slavery. The most extensive topic covered is the presidency followed by war and peace, respectively. Topics are arranged alphabetically and then chronologically within headings. Dates and sources are cited whenever possible. An appendix lists each president's birth and death dates and terms of office. A five-page bibliography is included, along with author and subject indexes.

The only comparable work is Caroline Harnsberger's *Treasury of Presidential Quotations* (Fodlett, 1964). Frost's compilation updates that title, adding many different quotes from the same time period and adding the sayings of Presidents Johnson, Nixon, Ford, and Reagan. [R: BR, May/June 88, p. 40; RBB, Aug 88, p. 1898; RQ, Spring 88, pp. 422-23; WLB, May 88, pp. 104, 106]

Gary D. Barber

IDEOLOGIES

664. Degenhardt, Henry W., ed. **Revolutionary and Dissident Movements: An International Guide.** Harlow, England, Longman; distr., Detroit, Gale, 1988. 466p. bibliog. index. (Keesing's Reference Publication). $140.00. LC 87-29718. ISBN 0-8103-2056-8.

Like its predecessor, *Political Dissent* (see *ARBA* 85, entry 625), this revised and updated edition is based on information contained in *Keesing's Record of World Events*, formerly *Keesing's Contemporary Archives*. It does not cover legal political parties, which are treated in a complementary volume of the Keesing's Reference Publication series, *Political Parties of the World* (see *ARBA* 86, entry 666). Nor does it duplicate the directory of peace movements, *Peace Movements of the World* (see *ARBA* 88, entry 754). Similarly, pressure groups which are not an actual or potential threat to the stability of a country and revolutionary or liberation movements which have come to power are excluded. In short (as in the first edition), this book lists more than one thousand organizations, most (but not all) of which have used violence to achieve their purposes, as well as illegal political parties, parties in exile, and groups representing religious dissent and coming into conflict with the authority of the state.

In this edition, unlike the 1983 one, the countries (more than 160) are arranged alphabetically (followed by a brief list of international revolutionary movements) and subdivided by revolutionary/dissent groups. For example, under Iran a brief introduction on the prevailing political and security situation in that country is followed by descriptions of the history, leadership, and aims of fifteen organizations classified as left-wing movements, the moderate opposition, separatist movements, a monarchist group, and religious minorities.

Entries range from a sentence or two (e.g., *Unit of Martyr Kalahi* and *Arya* – in Iran) to several pages (e.g., *Moro National Liberation Front* – in the Philippines; *Solidarity* – in Poland). The brief, selected bibliography emphasizes materials from about 1970 to 1987. The index to organizations and personal names replaces the separate subject and name indexes of the earlier volume. This book is recommended for academic and medium to large public libraries. [R: Choice, Sept 88, p. 78; RBB, 1 Sept 88, pp. 54-55]   Wiley J. Williams

665. Knight, David B., and Maureen Davies. **Self-Determination: An Interdisciplinary Annotated Bibliography.** New York, Garland, 1987. 254p. index. (Canadian Review of Studies in Nationalism, Vol. 8; Garland Reference Library of Social Science, Vol. 394). $40.00. ISBN 0-8240-8495-0.

The purpose of this bibliography is to provide multidisciplinary access to the literature of self-determination. The compilers have attempted to include works that explore "the changing definitions, interpretations and applications of the concept of self-determination" (p. 2). The introduction briefly discusses the evolution of the concept of self-determination and describes the parameters of each of the four divisions of the bibliography.

The bibliography is suggestive rather than exhaustive. It consists of 535 entries for "major works" – mainly books, parts of books, and journal articles – arranged in four categories: practice and interpretations; theoretical considerations: identity, territory, and power; world regional perspectives and state case studies; and the fourth world: indigenous peoples. All but a few of the resources listed are in English. Annotations, averaging about two hundred words, are informative and well written.

Given the flexibility of modern computer databases, one may dispute the compilers' contention that researchers are likely to miss materials in their subject areas but outside their disciplines. Furthermore, the bibliography's highly selective nature and language limitations restrict its coverage. More sources and shorter annotations might have made it more helpful. Given these reservations and the indefinite nature of the topic, this bibliography is recom-

mended only to those who will take the time to read its introduction and determine its relevance to their individual research needs. [R: Choice, Mar 88, p. 1066]   Gari-Anne Patzwald

666. Lubitz, Wolfgang, ed. **Trotsky Bibliography: A Classified List of Published Items about Leon Trotsky and Trotskyism.** 2d ed. Munich, New York, K. G. Saur, 1988. 581p. index. $120.00. ISBN 3-598-10754-4.

For several decades, the subject of Trotsky and his intellectual bequest (Trotskyism) has spawned a sizable literature in numerous languages. Though some of it is mainstream, much remains fugitive and/or ephemeral. This bibliography offers a fair measure of control to all aspects of Leon Trotsky (1879-1940) as individual, ideologue, cult figure, and devil.

Trotsky Bibliography is relatively simple to use. The classification scheme divides and subdivides the subject into logical chunks. Major divisions, for example, include "Biographical Items and Related Material," "Trotsky's Political, Philosophical, Socio-Economic and Military Thought," and "The Internal Trotskyist Movement." The 5,009 entries are numbered and arranged alphabetically by author within each subsection; annotations are not offered. The author index provides ready access to the citations as do several other approaches too numerous to mention. Suffice it to say that most of the relevant material is reflected here: 33.5 percent of it is in English, 25.1 percent is in Russian, and most of the others are in French, German, or Italian.

Although large academic libraries will undoubtedly give *Trotsky Bibliography* serious consideration, it does seem somewhat premature for K. G. Saur to be offering this $120.00 second edition only six years after the appearance of its $50.00 predecessor. The issuance of a supplement would have been a less costly alternative for as the editor suggests only 13 percent of the citations are from the 1980-1987 period. Other potential drawbacks include a flimsy binding and a very stilted preface. Despite these observations, the bibliography is both scholarly and responsive.   Mark R. Yerburgh

667. Maoláin, Ciarán Ó. **The Radical Right: A World Directory.** Santa Barbara, Calif., ABC-Clio, 1987. 500p. index. (Keesing's Reference Publications). $70.00. ISBN 0-87436-514-7.

This volume is a comprehensive directory of more than twenty-five hundred far-right organizations, movements, and publications in over eighty countries – from Afghanistan to Zimbabwe – in which "there has been organized ultra-right activity in the postwar (i.e., 1945-)

era." Within each country listing, those groups thought to be active in 1985-1987 receive fullest treatment. The author regards the radical right as consisting of three strands: ultraconservatism, anticommunism, and right-wing extremism. These terms are flexible enough to include groups with orientations such as anti-gun control, anti-immigrant, anti-Semitic, anti-union, racist, neofascist, neo-Nazi, Christian fundamentalist (e.g., Moral Majority), and mainstream conservative (U.S. Republican Party).

Within each country chapter, the order of information follows a uniform format. An introduction (an overview of relevant historical developments in each country) is followed by an alphabetical listing of active organizations, which in turn is followed by lists of defunct organizations, less important and lesser-known groups, and individual right-wing activists with no known far-right group connection.

The amount of information given for an organization varies widely, from only its vernacular and English name to its address, telephone number, leadership (president, general secretary, etc.), political orientation, history, policies (ideology, aims, and objectives), membership, publications, associated organizations, and international affiliations. It should be noted that in some instances organizations are listed under a country other than that of their headquarters address; for example, Americans for Human Rights in Ukraine and Association for the Liberation of Ukraine are listed under the USSR, and Co-ordinating Committee of Hungarian Organizations in North America and Hungarian Freedom Fighters Federation of the USA are entered under Hungary.

The seven-thousand-entry index will be most helpful in identifying a given group, publication, or individual. Its lack of a subject approach, however, limits easy retrievability for such groups with anti-abortion/right to life/pro-life or tax reform interests. With the present index one finds but three entries beginning "Tax" or "Taxpayers," another tax committee under *N* as National Tax Limitation Committee, and yet another one under *A*, the American Tax Freedom Committee. For the United States and Canada, the annual *Guide to the American Right: Directory and Bibliography* (Laird Wilcox) and its update, *The Wilcox Report*, provide such access.

Maoláin, formerly an associate editor of *Keesing's Record of World Events*, is compiler and editor of *Latin American Political Movements* (Facts on File, 1986). *The Radical Right* will be a valuable source in academic and larger public libraries for researchers in this area of political science and/or political journalism. [R:

Choice, Sept. 88, p. 86; RBB, 1 Sept 88, pp. 54-55]   Wiley J. Williams

668. Nicholls, David, and Peter Marsh, eds. **Biographical Dictionary of Modern European Radicals and Socialists. Volume 1: 1780-1815.** New York, St. Martin's Press, 1988. 291p. index. $49.95. LC 87-36961. ISBN 0-312-01968-8.

Because Britons are included in a companion set, *Biographical Dictionary of Modern British Radicals* (see *ARBA* 80, entry 396), they are excluded from this volume, the first of seven projected volumes on European radicals and socialists active between 1780 and 1980. While volume 1 covers 1780 to 1815, subsequent volumes will treat the following periods: 1816-1848, 1849-1870, 1871-1890, 1891-1914, 1915-1939, and 1940-1980. A supplementary volume will contain entries for those originally omitted.

Edited by two historians at Manchester Polytechnic, volume 1 includes signed articles on 187 men and women, eighty-six of them French, forty-three German, fourteen Italian, eight Austraian, seven Dutch, six Polish, six Swiss, five Hungarian, five Russian, three Belgian, and one each Czech, Greek, Norwegian, and Spanish. Written by forty-eight scholars worldwide, the biographies are arranged alphabetically from Abbamonti to Zschokke, and vary in length from less than one page to more than five pages.

Each article describes a radical's life, highlights his or her major contributions, and concludes with a bibliography in narrative form. Although the entries are in English, most of the bibliographic works cited are in other languages. To assist the reader, cross-references are supplied in the articles. The index, unfortunately, is limited to names of biographees. Nevertheless, this useful, well-produced publication belongs in all research libraries serving students of European history and politics. [R: Choice, Nov 88, p. 455; WLB, Oct 88, p. 106]   Leonard Grundt

669. Nordquist, Joan, comp. **Georg Lukacs.** Santa Cruz, Calif., Reference and Research Services, 1988. 64p. index. (Social Theory: A Bibliographic Series, No. 11). $15.00pa. ISBN 0-937855-20-0.

This slim, no-frills item represents the tenth installment in a bibliographic series devoted to contemporary social theorists such as Foucault, Habermas, Derrida, and Lacan. The purpose is to provide a rough and ready list of English-language works both by and about these influential individuals. Georg Lukacs (1885-1971), the distinguished Hungarian neo-Marxist writer, philosopher, and activist, seems a natural for inclusion in the series.

As the Lukacs bibliography is identical in size, scope, format, and retrieval systems to those that have already appeared, it seems unnecessary to closely reexamine those features. Suffice it to recall that there are no annotations; individual sections include "Books by Georg Lukacs," "Essays by Georg Lukacs," "Books about Georg Lukacs," and "Articles about Georg Lukacs." The only external entry is via a keyword in the title index which is limited to journal articles about Lukacs.

The price seems rather high to pay for these stapled, pamphlet-like offerings. As most of the individuals presented are currently undergoing intense study and scrutiny, will the publisher soon be issuing second and third editions? Such could become confusing and expensive. If, however, *Georg Lukacs* and its clones are merely bibliographic pontoons designed to serve the scholarly community only until more permanent structures have been raised, then this series is a useful and enlightened one.

Mark R. Yerburgh

670.   Wolfe, Gregory. **Right Minds: A Sourcebook of American Conservative Thought.** Lake Bluff, Ill., Regnery Gateway; distr., New York, Kampmann, 1987. 245p. index. $16.95. LC 86-20388. ISBN 0-89526-583-4.

From the *Federalist Papers* (1787-1788) to the latest George Will column, conservative thought has been with us for a long time, according to Wolfe. This sourcebook bears witness to the proliferating literature and to what is called the movement — since conservatives like to say victory is not yet complete. What that victory involves is the subject of these polemical works. William F. Buckley, Jr., wrote the foreword, which is a paean to the cause and ends with "It is a very full life, in Conservative City." Part 1, half of the book, is a bibliography of conservative writings classified under twenty-two headings (e.g., "The Welfare State," "Urban Studies," and "Education"). Part 2 is a who's who among conservatives from the founding of the Republic to "Conservatism Redirivus, 1945-1985." Part 3 lists journals and periodicals, think tanks, publishers, and collections of private papers. A name index concludes the offerings. As a sourcebook it is thorough, perhaps too much so. Wolfe selects some authors who are either only partly conservative or forced to fit his definition. If Wolfe perceives a grain of conservative thinking in an author's work, he seizes it. Because an author dislikes growing violence in America, promiscuity, or current cinema, he or she is not necessarily a conservative, but more likely simply concerned. True conservatives are a breed apart. Recommended as a guide to who whey are and who they claim as their own. [R: Choice, Mar 88, p. 1072]   Bill Bailey

671.   **Yearbook on International Communist Affairs 1988: Parties and Revolutionary Movements.** Richard F. Staar and Margit N. Grigory, eds. Stanford, Calif., Hoover Institution Press, 1988. 598p. bibliog. index. $49.95. LC 67-31024. ISBN 0-8179-8801-7; ISSN 0084-4101.

First appearing in 1967, this distinguished annual requires only the briefest of introductions. Its presence is required in all research libraries. The yearbook provides a detailed, country-by-country analysis of communist activities in 1987. Entries range in length from forty-two pages for the USSR to a single page for Haiti. They contain a wealth of information on party officials, elections, programs, and major activities. Eighty contributors were involved in this project. Standard equipment includes an introductory essay which highlights major trends, themes, and developments during 1987. Entries are arranged alphabetically by country within each of six regional groupings (e.g., Africa, the Americas, Asia, and the Pacific). A select bibliography is appended for 1986-1987 monographs. This is followed by a name index and a subject index.

At $49.95 the *Yearbook on International Communist Affairs* is an exceptional bargain. Its systematic purchase over the years will negate the need to acquire somewhat similar monographic offerings such as ABC-Clio's *Communist and Marxist Parties of the World* (see *ARBA* 87, entry 724). For a systematic, ongoing view into communist activities, this serial has no peer. An excellent reference choice for all but the smallest public and academic libraries.   Mark R. Yerburgh

INTERNATIONAL ORGANIZATIONS

672.   Baratta, Joseph Preston, comp. **Strengthening the United Nations: A Bibliography on U.N. Reform and World Federalism.** Westport, Conn., Greenwood Press, 1987. 351p. illus. index. (Bibliographies and Indexes in World History, No. 7). $45.00. LC 87-134. ISBN 0-313-25840-6.

For both critics and proponents of world government, this work will be a valuable resource. The advocates will find it more useful and complete than the critics, but there is richness in it for both groups. For those who still see hope in the United Nations as the precursor of world federalism, the volume provides more than adequate entrée to a vast literature. The introduction by the compiler is a brief but interesting review of the issues involved in past efforts to establish some type of world government, particularly as it relates to world peace. He is unabashedly in favor of a world federation approach but has been careful to include items that argue differently or that point out the multitude of problems involved in reforming the United Nations to that end.

The volume contains twenty-four chapters, or sections, dealing with specific aspects of world federalism and UN reform. The compiler notes that the chapters are organized "according to the end sought ...: union of democracies, United Nations, international control of atomic energy, universal federation ... European federation, and world order" (p. 16). This is not the most useful arrangement for purposes of topical searching, but it generally makes sense in terms of the overall topic of world government. A beginning chapter of "essential items" is excellent for the novice and a final chapter listing other bibliographies on the topic should satisfy the expert. The list of current organizations worldwide involved in efforts at world government will be useful for the expert, or any other persons, who may wish to contact them.

A wide variety of items is listed here: books, major journals in the field, individual articles, government documents (especially UN documents), dissertations, films, plays, videos, and, very usefully, major archival and personal manuscript collections relating to the issues. Such a vast listing (over thirty-two hundred citations) would, however, be difficult to use if not well annotated. Fortunately, the authors have done a superb job with brief but informative descriptions of about 75 percent of the items listed here. This makes the work extremely useful. The author index is also quite good; the subject index is less useful because of the many citations under a particular entry.

Overall, an outstanding resource for a wide variety of uses and users: scholars, librarians, students, and the casual reader. [R: Choice, Mar 88, p. 1061]   Robert V. Williams

INTERNATIONAL RELATIONS

673. **Directory on European Training Institutions in the Fields of Bilateral and Multilateral Diplomacy, Public Administration and Management, Economic and Social Development.** By United Nations Institute for Training and Research (UNITAR). New York, United Nations,

1987. 496p. index. $30.00pa. ISBN 92-1-057006-5. S/N E/F.87.III.K.DS/7.

The stated purposes of this directory are threefold: (1) to identify institutions with which the UN Institute for Training and Research (UNITAR) European Office could work more closely, (2) to provide guidance for those interested in these fields in Europe, and (3) to facilitate the exchange of information among similar institutions in Europe. There are two main criteria for selection: that an institution's activities in these fields go beyond teaching for university degrees, and that the institution be involved in *direct* training rather than just research.

The information was obtained by means of questionnaires returned by the institutions in the twenty-four countries included. Entries are arranged in English alphabetical order under each country. Although the bilingual title page would imply that the entire directory is bilingual, this is not the case—entries are given in English *or* French, depending upon what language the institution responded in. The format of the entries, however, is standardized to facilitate making the information available on computer in the near future. This will allow more detailed indexing by specialty and subject. (The present index is by name only, in the original language, English, and French.) Information provided includes address and telephone number, financial support, objectives, main activities, training and research areas, etc. The volume concludes with a section on UNITAR's activities in Geneva.

A specialized reference, of use to those interested in training in these fields.

Sharon Kincaide

674. Echard, William E., comp. and ed. **Foreign Policy of the French Second Empire: A Bibliography.** Westport, Conn., Greenwood Press, 1988. 416p. index. (Bibliographies and Indexes in World History, No. 12). $75.00. LC 87-37566. ISBN 0-313-23799-9.

The French Second Empire lasted from 1852 to 1870; it encompassed the reign of Napoleon III; the Crimean War; colonial expansion in Algeria and Indochina; the support of Archduke Maximillian in Mexico; and wars with Italy, China, and, finally, Prussia. The present bibliography covers these topics and others as documented in source materials and secondary studies produced during the past century.

The compiler, who edited the *Historical Dictionary of the French Second Empire, 1852-1870* (see *ARBA* 87, entry 512), wished "to include every book, article, and doctoral dissertation concerned entirely or primarily with the foreign policy of the French Second Empire ... in English, French, German, Italian or Spanish" (p. xix). Realistically, as he admits, this goal could not be attained, but the forty-one hundred items cited make this the most complete, indeed only, bibliography on the subject. The work is arranged in chapters which group together materials on French policy toward a particular country, geographic region, or problem (such as colonies). Citations, in typescript, are generally not annotated and those for books contain the place and date of publication but not the publisher. There are an author index and a fine subject index. This work is certainly suitable for undergraduate research and will serve as a fine aid for those working at more advanced levels. [R: Choice, Dec 88, p. 626]

Eric R. Nitschke

675. Grenville, J. A. S. **The Major International Treaties 1914-1945: A History and Guide with Texts.** New York, Routledge, Chapman & Hall, 1987. 268p. maps. index. $140.00 (with ... *since 1945* below). LC 87-14091. ISBN 0-416-08092-8.

676. Grenville, J. A. S., and Bernard Wasserstein. **The Major International Treaties since 1945: A History and Guide with Texts.** New York, Routledge, Chapman & Hall, 1987. 528p. index. $140.00 (with ... *1914-1945* above). LC 87-11250. ISBN 0-416-38080-8.

The ever-changing pattern of foreign relations in the world provides a never ending source of international economic, military, and cultural agreements. Grenville and Wasserstein have provided an essential guide to and collection of the major international agreements from 1914 to the present. This two-volume set is an updated version of Grenville's single-volume work *The Major International Treaties, 1914-1973* (1973). This set is intended for students of international affairs, as well as the general reader interested in international relations, especially the making of treaties. These volumes will also serve as a quick reference guide to the formation of foreign policy, treaty arrangements, and a collection of the texts of treaties for scholars of world affairs and international relations.

The first volume deals with treaties from 1914 to 1945, with some overlap into the second volume. Grenville provides an introduction to the treaty section describing the role of treaties during that era, their form and structure, how they were drafted, the vocabulary used, plus a section on treaties imposed by force. Grenville and Wasserstein follow a similar pattern in the second volume, which covers treaties since 1945. They preface each geographic section with text

on diplomatic developments during that period and the reasons behind the agreements. They have edited the text of the treaties to provide the reader with the essential points of the agreements, leaving out superfluous language. This work is by no means a dull recitation of treaty texts, but is rather a very useful and analytical tool for students, scholars, and lay readers. This set is highly recommended for college, university, and government library reference and history collections, as well as for individual scholars.

Norman L. Kincaide

677. Mickolus, Edward F., and Peter A. Flemming, comps. **Terrorism, 1980-1987: A Selectively Annotated Bibliography.** Westport, Conn., Greenwood Press, 1988. 314p. index. (Bibliographies and Indexes in Law and Political Science, No. 8). $55.00. LC 87-32275. ISBN 0-313-26248-9.

When there is a statement on the verso of the title page that reads, "This book was produced from copy provided by the author and without editing or proofreading by the publisher[,]" one wonders what lies between the book's covers. Upon examining this book, however, one finds a reference tool that is a sequel to Mickolus's previous bibliography on this subject, *The Literature of Terrorism* (see *ARBA* 82, entry 547).

"Fiction," "Terrorist Infastructure," and "Philosophical Approaches" are three of the eleven chapters in a book that organizationally parallels *The Literature of Terrorism*. The approximately twenty-four hundred entries cover "a broad cross section of research and opinion on terrorism" (p. vii). Publications in languages other than English are included, and some titles have English translations. There are author and title indexes, but no subject index. The vast majority of entries are not annotated.

This reviewer does have a few criticisms. One is that every line of a citation begins at the left margin; there is no indentation. Nor is there a section for reference works, other than a chapter on bibliographies. Also, the second author of a joint effort is not listed in the author index. And in the journal citations, the volume and issue numbers appear before the journal title, which can lead to confusion. Finally, the entries are not numbered, which presents some difficulty when referring back from the title index.

For comparison, librarians should examine *International Terrorism: A Bibliography* (see *ARBA* 87, entry 682). This unannotated work includes many of the same items as the Mickolus and Flemming book, but it is restricted to English-language material. Despite some flaws,

Terrorism, 1980-1987 is useful for public and academic libraries. [R: Choice, Nov 88, p. 464]

Daniel K. Blewett

678. Newton, Michael, and Judy Ann Newton. **Terrorism in the United States and Europe, 1800-1959: An Annotated Bibliography.** New York, Garland, 1988. 508p. index. (Garland Reference Library of Social Science, Vol. 449). $72.00. LC 88-21848. ISBN 0-8240-5747-3.

According to the authors of this bibliography on terrorism, it is "designed to offer students of the modern terrorist phenomena the necessary background and foundation for a survey of the history behind the headlines" (p. ix). For the purposes of this volume, terrorism is defined "as any resort to violence or coercive action by a group in pursuit of social, economic, or political objectives" (p. x).

The book consists of three parts. Part 1 covers general works. Part 2 covers Europe, subarranged alphabetically by country. Part 3 covers the United States, subarranged by such topics as anarchism, economic violence, lynching, and racial violence. Chronologically the book covers the years from 1800 to 1959.

The subtitle of this volume is something of a misnomer. The majority of titles listed here are not annotated. The authors contend that "annotations are provided in the case of books and articles whose titles are not self-explanatory" (p. xi). An examination of the entries reveals that this guideline for supplying annotations is not strictly adhered to. For example, the article "Why We Hate the Bolsheviki" contains the annotation: "Castigates the IWW for alleges [sic] subversive activities"; while "Bolsheviks of the West" is not annotated. When annotations are provided, they rarely exeeed one or two sentences in length.

In spite of the aforementioned limitation, this bibliography should be of some interest to students of terrorism seeking a listing of books and articles on terrorism in the United States and Europe between 1800 and 1959.

Larry G. Chrisman

679. Plano, Jack C., and Roy Olton. **The International Relations Dictionary.** 4th ed. Santa Barbara, Calif., ABC-Clio, 1988. 446p. index. (Clio Dictionaries in Political Science). $42.95; $18.00pa. LC 87-26943. ISBN 0-87436-477-9; 0-87436-478-7pa.

"Language precision is the primary tool of every scientific discipline.... [However, the] political and social sciences suffer more than most disciplines from semantic confusion" (series statement). The attempt to rectify this situation has long been the mission of Plano

(the series editor) and Olton. Since the first edition of this work in 1969 (see *ARBA* 70, Vol. 1, p. 92), the authors have tried to explain the basic concepts of international relations rather than simply define individual words or phrases.

Changes since the third edition (see *ARBA* 83, entry 500) include thirty-four new entries, an eleven-page "Guide to Major Concepts," deletion of the "Guide to Countries," and numbering each of the 570 entries, which greatly facilitates finding the correct entry from the index. The "National Political Systems" chapter has been replaced by the chapter "Patterns of Political Organization," and the number of pages has been reduced to 446. Also, chapter titles are now at the top of every other page.

The entries continue to be well written and easy to read; the printing is clear and the headings are in boldface type. Each entry has a "Significance" paragraph that relates each term to its place in the field of international relations; sometimes this section is longer than the preceding definition.

The *Dictionary of International Relations Terms* (3d ed. GPO, 1987) contains fewer and shorter entries, but it is more up-to-date on contemporary terminology (e.g., "gray area weapons"), while Plano's volume tends to be historical in its treatment. The GPO publication also includes a bibliography and helpful notes at the end of the entries, which the ABC-Clio book lacks.

Plano and Olton's work continues to be useful to all classes of patrons and should be available with its companion in the series, *The International Law Dictionary* (see *ARBA* 88, entry 560). [R: RBB, 1 Oct 88, pp. 241-42]

Daniel K. Blewett

PEACE MOVEMENT

680. Abrams, Irwin. **The Nobel Peace Prize and the Laureates: An Illustrated Biographical History, 1901-1987.** Boston, G. K. Hall, 1988. 269p. illus. index. $39.95. LC 88-16313. ISBN 0-8161-8609-X.

One cannot help wondering if this book, focusing on peace as it does, is not yet one more sign of the times. Whatever the motivation, Irwin Abrams has provided readers with a good beginning for exploring the peace prize awardees.

Perhaps more important than the actual entries are the first three chapters. Here Abrams discusses Alfred Nobel, the Norwegian Nobel Committee, and the transformation of the prize over the years from a strict interpretation of Nobel's wishes, to a more liberal interpretation. Written in a lively style, the reader is taken behind the scenes as a witness to the establishment of the prize, what is done with the money, how it has helped establish the peace movement, and more.

The individual biographies of awardees is less satisfying to this reviewer. For example, the entry for the 1973 prize jointly awarded to Henry Kissinger and Le Duc Tho is written with gloves on. The award was considered controversial not only in the United States, but also in Norway. The prize winner for 1987, Oscar Arias Sanchez, might not be considered a peace giant. And the Arias plan was criticized at the time, and has subsequently been shown to be a failure. Some discussion of the merits of the plan, both pro and con, would have been more helpful.

Despite the occasional hagiographical tone of the entries, however, the volume should find its way into libraries of every description. While such information is likely to be there already, no one source will be able to offer more.

Mark Y. Herring

681. **The ACCESS Resource Guide: An International Directory of Information on War, Peace, and Security.** 1988 ed. William H. Kincade and others, eds. Cambridge, Mass., Ballinger, 1988. 238p. index. $34.95; $14.95pa. ISBN 0-88730-260-2; 0-88730-262-9pa.

Peace is currently a hot topic, what with summit meetings, arms limitation agreements, and a new federal peace institute in Washington, D.C. Certainly there have been many reference books published on this subject, and this is one of the latest to appear.

This guide has entries for 657 organizations concerned with war and peace. Each entry, arranged by country, has the address, telephone number, name of the director, and the number of information staff, along with statements regarding the purpose and type of institution, subjects covered, publications and products produced, and the intended target audience. Names of staff subject specialists are also included, although this information could become out-of-date very quickly. The eighteen-page "Guide to Publications" is composed of approximately 150 citations for many useful periodicals and reference books. There are easy to understand instructions and a clear definition of editorial objectives and criteria.

The ten-page introduction is a survey of information on war, peace, and security. Also included is a list of abbreviations and a multilingual vocabulary aid for keywords in this field. The organizations are indexed by topic, product, service, and U.S. state. There is a general institution index, along with one for individuals. The print is clear and easy to read, and the price for the paperback version makes this book affordable for all.

However, does the world need another such directory? There are other sources for librarians to turn to: Gale's *Encyclopedia of Associations* and numerous research center directories are obvious choices, as are the UNESCO *World Directory of Peace Research and Training Institutions* (see entry 685) and *Peace Movements of the World* (see *ARBA* 88, entry 754). The fourth volume of the *World Encyclopedia of Peace* (see *ARBA* 88, entry 760) has a longer bibliography and list of journals than does *ACCESS*, and the individual organization entries contain short "Brief History" and "Principal Activities" paragraphs. For libraries which can afford only one such peace directory, the *Peace Resource Book 1988-1989*, by the Institute for Defense and Disarmament Studies (see entry 683), should also be examined. Although U.S.-oriented, it includes more organizations than the *ACCESS Resource Guide*.

The directory under review is suitable for all institutions, especially if they aim for a comprehensive reference collection in political science, international relations, or security studies.

Daniel K. Blewett

682. Chmielewski, Wendy E., ed. **Guide to Sources on Women in the Swarthmore College Peace Collection.** Swarthmore, Pa., Swarthmore College Peace Collection, 1988. 118p. index. $7.00pa.

This small guide is an attempt to make more readily accessible the materials about women that are located in an important archival repository and research collection relating to the establishment of permanent peace through pacifism, disarmament, and nonviolent change. Half of the material in its 149 document groups is about or by women. Included in the collection are papers of individuals, records of organizations, diaries, journals, photographs, posters, and memorabilia, as well as nine thousand volumes of history, biography, etc.

The first part of the guide lists the pertinent document groups, including collective groups from the United States and other countries. Descriptions of the thirty-four major groups that are exclusively of an individual women or a ·women's organization, from Jane Addams to the Women's Peace Union, vary in length from a paragraph to several pages, and include dates, size of collection in linear measures, availability of checklists and other finding aids, microfilming, and any restrictions on use. There are extensive lists of correspondents. The second part presents materials under thirteen broad subject headings, with cross-references. There are also lists of diaries and journals, of memorabilia, and of articles, booklets, essays, and pamphlets. The index is invaluable in pulling out references within the documentary groups. This inexpensive little publication should be extremely useful to researchers and scholars studying almost any aspect of women's social roles or women's part in the social reform or pacifism movements.

Laura H. McGuire

683.   Conetta, Carl, ed. **Peace Resource Book 1988-1989: A Comprehensive Guide to the Issues, Organizations, and Literature.** Cambridge, Mass., Ballinger, 1988. 440p. illus. index. $14.95pa. ISSN 0740-9885.

People concerned about nuclear weapons, chemical/biological warfare, or the arms race usually have few options more salient than fretting. Concerned, highly motivated citizens might try to join a peace advocacy group, but many such potential activists would rapidly find their initiative stymied by a lack of information about organized peace efforts.

They should turn to the *Peace Resource Book*, as should anyone interested in current information about the global military situation. The first of three sections, "Guide to Peace Issues and Strategies," examines the world's military system, critiques arms control negotiations, and explains the ideology and strategy of the peace movement. The second section lists some three hundred national peace advocacy groups, annotates peace-oriented educational programs in the United States, and indexes some seven thousand national and local peace groups both alphabetically and by zip code. (For those anxious only to write to their representatives, it also lists the names and addresses of members of Congress.) The final segment, "Guide to Peace-Related Literature," arranges published resources available for peace advocates—reference works, books, pamphlets, etc.—by subject headings, and includes ordering information.

Skeptics might scoff at these ideals, label them pipe dreams, and write off the whole business. But the *Peace Resource Book* can fill what is essentially a vacuum in most library reference departments: it puts in one place information important to those who are not content merely to dream the dream of peace but who are instead determined to work for it.

Anthony A. McIntire

684.   Meyer, Robert S. **Peace Organizations Past and Present: A Survey and Directory.** Jefferson, N.C., McFarland, 1988. 266p. illus.

bibliog. index. $24.95. LC 88-42515. ISBN 0-89950-340-3.

Although the title implies equal coverage of peace organizations both past and present, the greater part of this volume consists of profiles of ninety-two currently active peace organizations, most of which are based in the United States. Entries range from one to eight pages in length and generally include a brief history of the organization, its philosophy, goals, descriptions of past and current activities, and excerpts from publications submitted in response to the author's survey.

Coverage of past organizations consists of an introductory chapter which provides a condensed review of the development of the peace movement from prehistory to the present. Following the directory the author recaps the survey findings and discusses their implications; he concludes with his recommendations for the future of the movement and a call for action. Appendices include a directory of addresses and position statements from selected peace organizations. A brief bibliography and index complete the volume.

As stated in his conclusion, the author's intention is to stimulate involvement, broaden awareness of activities and resources, and encourage financial support of the movement. The broad range of information included here should help reach that objective. More comprehensive but less detailed coverage can be found in the *Peace Resource Book* (see *ARBA* 87, entry 736), *The International Peace Directory* (see *ARBA* 86, entry 721), and *Peace Movements of the World* (see *ARBA* 88, entry 754). [R: WLB, Nov 88, p. 126]   Martha Perry

685.   **World Directory of Peace Research and Training Institutions 1988.** 6th ed. By the Social and Human Sciences Documentation Centre and the Division of Human Rights and Peace. New York, Berg; distr., New York, St. Martin's Press, 1988. 271p. index. $49.95. ISBN 0-85496-156-9.

This title is among a growing number of guides and directories dealing with the theme of peace and disarmament. Over 650 entries from international and regional organizations as well as from forty-six individual countries are provided. First published in 1966, and subsequently updated in 1973, 1978, 1981, and 1984, the earlier editions did not include training institutions. It is important to note that the focus of this work is on those institutes dealing with peace research as distinguished from those that are a listing of peace organizations such as the *International Peace Directory* (see *ARBA* 86, entry 721).

The format of the directory is basically an index followed by seven sections. Illustrative of these indexes are the following: an index of research subjects with the host country of the institution, a geographical index of the countries and regions covered by the research activities, and an index of courses and subjects taught with the indication of the responsible host country. Representative information for listings in each country include address, date organized, staffing, field of coverage, titles of journals published and other recent publications, and a brief annotation describing the scope of the organization.

This is a well-organized, well-researched volume that would be most useful to academic libraries with a strong international affairs collection.   Frank Wm. Goudy

PUBLIC POLICY AND ADMINISTRATION

686. Bergerson, Peter J. **Ethics and Public Policy: An Annotated Bibliography.** New York, Garland, 1988. 200p. index. (Public Affairs and Administration, Vol. 20; Garland Reference Library of Social Science, Vol. 414). $30.00. LC 87-32997. ISBN 0-8240-6632-4.

Peter Bergerson, an active participant on the Committee on Professional Standards and Ethics of the American Society for Public Administration, adeptly interprets the literature of ethics and public policy. From a comprehensive search of eleven online databases he has culled 330 scholarly entries published over the last twenty-five years in book, journal, and dissertation format. He labels interest in the field, strong in the 1980s, as "episodic."

Grappling with the octopus-like extensions of ethical issues into all areas of public management, Bergerson creates a typology to define and organize the literature. The nine topical divisions he chooses are "State and Local Governments," where interest is strong; "Comparative Government and Foreign Policy," with wide variations of approach; "Health Care/Medical/Bio-Scientific" issues; "Interrelationship of Government and Business," including the ethics of privatization; "Codes of Ethics for Policy Analysis," the largest section (eighty-one citations) with entries analyzing codes by both description and prescription; "Multiple Roles of Policy Analysis," noting the players among which are whistleblowers; "Criteria for Analysis of Alternatives and Principles of Decision-Making"; "Case Study Application"; and "Competing Paradigms and Theoretical Frameworks," where what is policy and what should

be policy interrelate. Annotations, descriptive in content, vary considerably in length. Summaries for each dissertation entry are lengthy, but the author does not clarify whether the short to long discussions of other entries indicate their significance. Adequate white space creates easy legibility for pages with no print highlighting.

This valuable bibliography joins others in Garland's useful Public Affairs and Administration series, the latest of which were reviewed in *ARBA* 88 (see entries 250, 693, and 761). [R: Choice, Oct 88, p. 284]

Eleanor Ferrall

687. Chandler, Ralph C., and Jack C. Plano. **The Public Administration Dictionary.** 2d ed. Santa Barbara, Calif., ABC-Clio, 1988. 430p. bibliog. index. (Clio Dictionaries in Political Science). $39.50; $17.00pa. LC 87-32045. ISBN 0-87436-498-1; 0-87436-499-Xpa.

This revision of the 1982 edition follows the same organizational structure and includes the same features which made the first edition an excellent selection. Entries are arranged alphabetically within seven subject matter chapters, which are all fundamental areas of study in public administration, financial administration, bureaucracy and administrative organization, etc. This type of organization allows for use as a supplement or complement to public administration texts and readings, making this title a valuable resource to students of political science and public policy studies. The nearly sixteen-page index provides access to all the definitions, and distinguishes by boldface type the entries containing definitions from the entries in regular type, which contain additional information.

The second edition includes twenty-five new entries and numerous revisions of other entries. Some of the new entries are *robotics, decision tree, Theory Z, coproduction*, and *Circular A-95*. Important cases affecting public administration are also included. The authors, both professors of political science at Western Michigan University, have done an excellent job of updating the entries and linking each definition to its contemporary environment or historical period by the inclusion of a "significance" paragraph. Cross-references are used extensively to connect entries and a bibliography provides access to additional sources for further information.

This source, if kept current, will become a standard reference book for the field of public administration. Highly recommended for academic and public libraries [R: WLB, Oct 88, p. 110]

Bonnie Gratch

14 Psychology

GENERAL WORKS

Bibliographies

688. Benson, Hazel B., comp. **The Dying Child: An Annotated Bibliography.** Westport, Conn., Greenwood Press, 1988. 270p. index. (Contemporary Problems of Childhood, No. 6). $39.95. LC 88-11008. ISBN 0-313-24708-0.

Benson has compiled an exhaustive bibliography on terminally ill children and their families. Over seven hundred references to English-language material in popular and professional periodicals, books and book chapters, government documents, published conference proceedings, and doctoral dissertations were culled from the voluminous publishing output between 1960 and 1987, with limited previous coverage. All citations, with the exception of dissertations, are descriptively annotated, the quality of annotations being one of the volume's strengths. Citations are arranged under six broad categories (general topics, children, adolescents, family aspects, caregivers, and somatic care) and further divided under a total of forty subject areas.

The helpful appendices include annotated references to children's books, citations to audiovisual materials, a list of support groups for terminally ill children and their families, names and addresses of wish-granting and hospice organizations, and a very basic list of print and online bibliographic tools. Finally, there are a list of the journal abbreviations used and author and keyword subject indexes.

There have been several fine bibliographies published over the past decade on death and dying, most of which Benson herself cites. However, *The Dying Child* stands out for several reasons. First, the narrower subject focus is welcome and warranted given a literature that is both abundant and dispersed. Second, the breadth of literature assembled is admirable: literature from law, pediatrics, medicine and nursing, social work and clinical psychology, child development, philosophy, and education accompanies popular material. Finally, the annotations are excellent and the references are well organized and accessible under categories reflecting the body of literature.

Pam M. Baxter

689. Bruhn, John G., and others. **Social Support and Health: An Annotated Bibliography.** New York, Garland, 1987. 504p. index. (Garland Library of Sociology, Vol. 13; Garland Reference Library of Social Science, Vol. 412). $64.00. LC 87-17796. ISBN 0-8240-8348-2.

This annotated bibliography encompasses 1,247 references from the literatures of health and social sciences through December 1986, compiled with the aid of reference librarians and computerized information systems. Most of the works are in English, with a sampling of other literatures, especially French, German, and Dutch. They embrace many concepts in the somewhat fuzzy literature of social support, including concepts related to the risks of illness, coping and adaptation, rehabilitation, life span development, social networks and social connectedness, pace of clinical progress, ethnic and cultural factors, and consumer criticism of current health systems. The authors have spent two decades studying the phenomena of social support among the sick and the well at the individual, family, and community levels.

The book is logically arranged in seven chapters that have from five to eleven subdivisions, supported by an author index and a well-thought-through subject index. Within each section, materials are arranged by format: books, articles, dissertations, chapters, and conference proceedings. The annotations are structured; each includes a brief statement of purpose, a phrase noting the type of work (e.g., research, text, literature review), a few sentences indicating the main themes or findings, and a list of suggested audiences.

This work should be useful to psychologists, sociologists, anthropologists, health workers, social workers, clergy, and to students in the social, behavioral, and medical sciences. [R: Choice, May 88, p. 1386; Choice, Sept 88, pp. 88, 90]   Marda Woodbury

690. Horowitz, Michael, Karen Walls, and Billy Smith. **An Annotated Bibliography of Timothy Leary.** Hamden, Conn., Archon Books/Shoe String Press, 1988. 305p. illus. index. $37.50. LC 87-30816. ISBN 0-208-02064-0.

This volume is an exhaustive annotated listing of everything known to be written by or about Timothy Leary. The entries range from the scholarly books written by Leary to bumper stickers, posters, and slogan buttons referring to Leary. The items also list phonograph records, tape recordings, films, and television appearances as well as unpublished materials. Whenever possible the annotators have included material describing the physical appearance of the items as well as a description of their contents. Illustrations of some items are included. A title index of Leary's works is supplied. The work will be of great value to those interested in the life and philosophy of Timothy Leary. It will also serve as a useful reference to those scholars studying the social history of the decades between 1950 and the present. [R: Choice, Dec 88, p. 628]   Charles Neuringer

691. Lubin, Bernard, and others, comps. **Family Therapy: A Bibliography, 1937-1986.** Westport, Conn., Greenwood Press, 1988. 470p. index. (Bibliographies and Indexes in Psychology, No. 4). $49.95. LC 88-18682. ISBN 0-313-26172-5.

In an effort to manage the proliferation of family therapy literature, the compilers of this comprehensive bibliography have brought together fifty years of articles, monographs, book chapters, and book reviews that are relevant to families, couples, and marital therapy. The 6,167 entries were gleaned from a "thorough search" of *Psychological Abstracts, Sociological Abstracts, Cumulated Index Medicus, Cumulative Index to Nursing and Allied Health Literature, International Nursing Index, Dissertation Abstracts, Current Contents, Books in Print*, and reference lists from books in the relevant areas.

Although the attempt to bring family therapy materials together in a single reference source is a laudable effort, the organization of the source inhibits its use. The entries are arranged alphabetically by author and followed by author and subject indexes. Since the entries are already arranged alphabetically by author, the author index seems redundant. Furthermore, the classifications for the subject index do not provide a useful entreé into the references in the text. Many are so broad (e.g., family therapy, counseling; marital therapy, counseling) that they are useless. The only recourse for the reader interested in a specific topic is to wade through sometimes hundreds of references under an indexed topic or laboriously seek information by inspecting each of the entries, one by one. Organization of the entries by meaningful topical areas within the body of the book with cross-references to other subjects would greatly improve the utility of this work. It is surprising that Greenwood Press would allow the preparation of such ineffective indexes, particularly in a series entitled Bibliographies and Indexes in Psychology.   Suzanne G. Frayser

692. Meurs, Jos van, with John Kidd. **Jungian Literary Criticism, 1920-1980: An Annotated, Critical Bibliography of Works in English (with a Selection of Titles after 1980).** Metuchen, N.J., Scarecrow, 1988. 353p. index. $32.50. LC 88-18276. ISBN 0-8108-2160-5.

The editor of this reference work has gathered together 902 English-language bibliographical items (published between 1920 and 1980) that deal with literary criticism from a Jungian point of view. There are some post-1980 entries. The entries range from dissertations to full length books. All citations, except for dissertations, are annotated. The author has exercised the prerogative of adding evaluative comments to those entries which he feels are particularly meritorious or particularly critical of Jung. It is sometimes difficult for the reader to separate the editor's critical comments from the summary of the original authors' writings.

An excellent introductory historical survey of English-language Jungian based literary criticism, as well as an author/subject index are provided.

This volume is an important resource to both literary scholars and followers of Jungian psychology.   Charles Neuringer

693. Saraswathi, T. S., and Ranjana Dutta, with Anjoo Sikka. **Developmental Psychology in India 1975-1986: An Annotated Bibliography.** Newbury Park, Calif., Sage Publications, 1987. 327p. index. $35.00. ISBN 0-8039-9528-8.

This selective bibliography of research in India is divided into six sections: (1) physical, motor, and mental development; (2) cognitive, perceptual, and language development; (3) socialization and personality development (the longest section); (4) developmental research and social policy; (5) cross-cultural studies; and (6) general. These sections are further divided into subsections. Journal articles are arranged by author within subsections. The abstracts are preceded by brief essays providing overviews of the six sections. There is an author index. The studies included represent the best in Indian research (in the compilers' opinions). The bibliography has been assembled with careful attention to detail; the annotations are extensive and clearly written. Since the subjects of studies included are Indian children and adults, this bibliography will be most useful to anthropologists or psychologists involved in cross-cultural research.   Margaret McKinley

694. Stoloff, Michael L., and James V. Couch. **Computer Use in Psychology: A Directory of Software.** Washington, D.C., American Psychological Association, 1987. 1v. (unpaged). $22.50 spiralbound. LC 87-72765. ISBN 1-55798-029-2.

This directory lists 290 software packages of interest to clinical, academic, and research psychologists. All listings are divided among three categories: teaching (92 listings); research aids for statistical analysis, manuscript formatting, and modeling (43 listings); and programs for clinical practice (155 listings). Each entry contains the title and author(s) of the package, address of the producer or supplier, a brief description, the type and level of documentation provided, hardware required and the versions available, and (usually) the price. All but a few are intended for use with personal computers. There are indexes by title, by author(s), and for each subject area (academic, clinical, and research), listing software under specific functions. The compilers state that inclusion of a product does not constitute endorsement, as much of the information was obtained from software producers, published reviews, or blurbs. Users are encouraged to provide information on additional software for future editions.

Computer Use in Psychology begs comparison with Samuel Krug's *Psychware Sourcebook* (see *ARBA* 88, entry 773). Krug aims at a narrower audience, listing three hundred psychological measurement products used for vocational, educational, and clinical assessment. Stoloff and Couch list half as many products in their clinical section and include less information about each, and there are no examples of report formats as in *Psychware Sourcebook*. However, the listings for psychology teaching tools and research-oriented packages are unique, and their numbers should grow, making

this title especially appropriate for academic libraries.   Pam M. Baxter

Dictionaries

695. Hersen, Michel, and Alan S. Bellack, eds. **Dictionary of Behavioral Assessment Techniques.** Elmsford, N.Y., Pergamon Press, 1988. 519p. index. (Pergamon General Psychology Series, Vol. 147). $95.00. LC 86-25352. ISBN 0-08-031975-0.

Nearly three hundred behavioral assessment techniques are described in one- to three-page critical essays written by academicians or therapists familiar with the techniques. Each essay observes a standard format: description, purpose, development, psychometric characteristics, clinical use, future directions, and a brief bibliography. There is an index listing sources for each of the techniques. A "User's Guide" is arranged by "Focus of Assessment" (aggression, anxiety, etc.), followed by names of relevant tests and their assessment methods (self-report, physiological test, structured interview, etc.). While authors' credentials are not provided, each of the essays is competently and succinctly written, showing evidence of careful editing. A few essays are written by the developers of the techniques being discussed, but this is obvious from consulting the index of sources. A few of the essays, such as that for the MMPI (Minnesota Multiphasic Personality Inventory), will be most useful to students, since the existing literature is voluminous. Well-organized information about the wide array of behavioral assessment techniques that have been developed is very difficult to locate. This work will, therefore, be a much-used reference tool in academic libraries whose institutions include programs in clinical psychology and in other libraries whose clientele includes behavior therapy professionals.

Margaret McKinley

696. Petrovsky, A. V., and M. G. Yaroshevsky, eds. **A Concise Psychological Dictionary.** Moscow, Progress; distr., New York, International Publishers, 1987. 358p. index. $10.95. ISBN 0-7178-0657-X.

This small dictionary of psychological terms was translated from Russian into English. Because of its small size, many terms from what the editors feel to be peripheral areas of psychology (e.g., medical psychology, psychophysics, and psychopathology) are excluded. Entries are cross-referenced and name and subject indexes are supplied. Its small size, while attractive, is also a drawback in terms of breadth and completeness. There are many other dictionaries and encyclopedias of psychology that are more useful than this reference work. However, the dictionary does give the reader a clue to the orientations and areas of psychology that are of special interest to Russian scientists. The more than occasional intrusion of political ideology in the definitions may be either of great interest, or an irritation, to the reader. One example will suffice. In the definition of *behavior therapy*, the editors write, "in equating psychopathologic phenomena and actions against the injustices of capitalistic society, B.T. is an ideologically reactionary theory" (p. 37).

Charles Neuringer

697. Popplestone, John A., and Marion White McPherson. **Dictionary of Concepts in General Psychology.** Westport, Conn., Greenwood Press, 1988. 380p. index. (Reference Sources for the Social Sciences and Humanities, No. 7). $65.00. LC 88-3120. ISBN 0-313-23190-7.

The authors of this dictionary have gathered short review essays examining selected concepts in behavioral psychology. Each entry defines the concept, traces its historical development, and presents the cogent empirical evidence. In addition, the work offers bibliographical citations and sources of information. Some of these are annotated. Entries are cross-referenced and a name and subject index is supplied.

The entries are well written and filled with information. The major drawback with this volume, as with other limited dictionaries, is the selecting of concepts to be reviewed. The authors do not present any criteria for the selection process. The authors, one assumes, selected those concepts which they thought to be important. Some readers might question the absence of certain concepts from this volume. However, for the information presented, the book is an excellent starting point for scholarly research, and a boon to reference librarians.

Charles Neuringer

698. Zusne, Leonard. **Eponyms in Psychology: A Dictionary and Biographical Sourcebook.** Westport, Conn., Greenwood Press, 1987. 339p. index. $65.00. LC 87-255. ISBN 0-313-25750-7.

An eponym is a term or process that has been named after an individual (e.g., "Zeigarnik Effect") or a place (e.g., "Hawthorne Effect"). Over eight hundred eponyms of current or historical interest from the field of psychology are to be found here, alphabetically arranged, in this engaging reference work.

Each entry consists of a definition of the eponym followed by a short biographical or historical sketch based on the eponymous item. The bulk of the entries come directly from psychology, but some eponyms from statistics, physiology, psychiatry, neurology, linguistics, and computing are included because they have become part of the language of psychology. A joint eponym definition and name and place index is provided.

This dictionary will be a valuable resource for all scholars interested in psychology and the history of psychology. It is also a delight for the casual reader. [R: Choice, July/Aug 88, pp. 1679-80; RBB, 15 Feb 88, p. 982]

Charles Neuringer

Directories

699. **American Psychological Association's Guide to Research Support.** 3d ed. Kenneth Lee Herring, ed. Washington, D.C., American Psychological Association, 1987. 276p. bibliog. index. $30.00pa. LC 87-17460. ISBN 0-912704-83-7.

This reference work is an important updating of the American Psychological Association's guide to locating and securing funding of basic and applied research in the behavioral sciences. Aside from the alphabetical listing of federal and private research support sources, there are also a glossary of funding-associated terms, a listing of publications about private and public funding, a name index of funding agencies, a subject index, and a listing of research fellowship opportunities.

The heart of the reference work is the listing of federal and private research support agencies. Each of the entries follows a detailed, clear, and consistent format that provides all the information needed by the potential seeker of research funds to determine the feasibility of approaching the agency, and how to initiate the application procedure.

This work is a "must" for researchers in the behavioral sciences. A copy of it should be part of the resource tools of academic departments, research institutes, and laboratories.

Charles Neuringer

Handbooks and Yearbooks

700. **The Supplement to the Ninth Mental Measurements Yearbook.** Jane Close Conoley, Jack J. Kramer, and James V. Mitchell, Jr., eds. Lincoln, Nebr., Buros Institute of Mental Measurements, University of Nebraska; distr., Lincoln, Nebr., University of Nebraska Press, 1988. 279p. index. $55.00pa. LC 39-3422. ISBN 0-910674-30-2.

This is a supplement to that important reference work, the *Ninth Mental Measurements Yearbook* (see *ARBA* 88, entry 777). It is composed of reviews of new and significantly revised commercial tests published from the appearance of the *Ninth Mental Measurements Yearbook* up to and including 1987.

The supplement follows the standard *Mental Measurements Yearbook* presentation format (title, group for whom the test is intended, acronym, validity and reliability data, forms, length, time of administration, publisher, literature citations, reviews, etc.). Several indexes are supplied for these new and revised tests. There are a list of contributing reviewers, test subject index, publishers' directory, test name index, acronym index, subscore index, etc. The editors plan to incorporate the materials found in this supplement into the *Tenth Mental Measurements Yearbook*.

Because of the rapid introduction of new and revised testing instruments, this supplement serves the important function of filling in the gaps between publications of the *Mental Measurements Yearbook*. With the addition of this supplement, the *Mental Measurements Yearbook* retains its position as the premier reference work in the psychometric area.

Charles Neuringer

Thesauri

701. **Thesaurus of Psychological Index Terms.** 5th ed. Washington, D.C., American Psychological Association, 1988. 291p. $65.00 spiralbound. LC 82-70075. ISBN 0-912704-67-5.

Constructing a controlled vocabulary that is current and uniform is a challenge, and especially so in such a volatile field as psychology. Since publication of the first thesaurus in 1974, the total number of terms has more than doubled to over sixty-six hundred in this edition, with approximately forty-seven hundred being postable terms. Features have been added to enhance the value of the thesaurus as a retrieval tool for use with all of PsycINFO's products.

The "Relationship Section" includes 250 new postable and 100 new nonpostable terms since the fourth edition (1983), and these are listed in appendices A and B, respectively. A third appendix contains the "Content Classification Categories," most useful for computer searching. For each postable term in the "Relationship Section," the number of postings through June 1987 and the unique subject code used for online access are provided. The date indicating in what year a term was added to the controlled vocabulary is included, as well as for

each term in the accompanying lists of broader, narrower, and related terms. The number of "Scope Notes" assigned to postable terms has increased to about seventeen hundred, and these are essential in a discipline where use of ambiguous terminology is frequent.

A new feature in this edition is that the "Rotated Alphabetical Terms Section" includes both postable and cross-reference terms. Nonpostable terms are marked with an asterisk to indicate that the user should consult the "Relationship Section." Since the third edition was reviewed (see *ARBA* 84, entry 1409), the "Postable Terms and Term Codes" list has been dropped.

In addition to being an excellent example of thesaurus construction, this work is indispensable for users of *Psychological Abstracts*, PsycLIT, and PsycINFO's online files.

Pam M. Baxter

PARAPSYCHOLOGY

702. Crabtree, Adam. **Animal Magnetism, Early Hypnotism, and Psychical Research, 1766-1925: An Annotated Bibliography.** White Plains, N.Y., Kraus International, 1988. 522p. index. (Bibliographies in the History of Psychology and Psychiatry). $150.00. LC 87-29746. ISBN 0-527-20006-9.

First postulated by Austrian physician Franz Mesmer, the theory of "animal magnetism" held that the magnetic properties of celestial bodies influenced human health and disease. Applying this belief to contemporary medical practice, Mesmer advocated use of magnets and hand movements as treatment for a variety of illnesses. Although animal magnetism as a form of treatment lost credibility by the early 1800s, it gradually became a founding force behind the theory of hypnotism and hypnotic states and the study of the subconscious mind, and stimulated serious study of psychic phenomena.

Adam Crabtree has compiled a bibliography of nearly two thousand references to the primary literature published from 1766 to 1925. Approximately one-third of the entries are annotated, and the international scope of the works cited represents the major contributors from psychology, medicine, and psychical research. Books, journal articles, proceedings, pamphlets and treatises, and other scholarly papers are listed chronologically, then alphabetically by author. Thus, the progress and influence of Mesmer's original works and their impact on others are apparent. Each citation contains a code to identify the focus of the work as hypnotism, psychical research, or both. The compiler also provides a very good historical introduction and a glossary of terms. There are name, title, and subject indexes.

The scope of this work being narrow, it will be of interest only to scholars. It will be a valuable addition to research collections in the history of psychology, history of medicine, hypnotism, and psychical research.

Pam M. Baxter

703. Cunningham, Scott. **Cunningham's Encyclopedia of Crystal, Gem & Metal Magic.** St. Paul, Minn., Llewellyn Publications, 1988. 221p. illus. (col.). bibliog. index. (Llewellyn's Sourcebook Series). $12.95pa. LC 87-46256. ISBN 0-87542-126-1.

The main part of this book, a chapter entitled "The Stones," discusses in eighty pages over one hundred stones and minerals in an A to Z arrangement of seventy-eight major stones. For each stone, Cunningham lists common name, folk names, basic energy type (projective or receptive), planet, element, any deity associated with the stone, metals or herbs associated with the stone, and the stone's basic powers/magical lore/magical uses. In a second major chapter (twenty pages long), the author discusses metals, using the same format. Twelve shorter chapters are entitled "The Powers of Stones"; "Magic"; "Stone Energies"; "The Rainbow of Power"; "Hearts, Diamonds and Stars"; "Obtaining Stones"; "Cleansing the Stones"; "The Stories within Stones"; "Stone Divinations"; "A Stone Tarot"; "The Magic of Jewelry"; and "Stone Spells."

Material at the book's end includes tables (planetary rulers, birthstones; projective/receptive stones); sources from which to obtain stones; a four-page, thirty-nine-item glossary; a seventy-item, briefly annotated bibliography; and an eleven-page index.

The author states that "crystals, gemstones and metals have their own inherent powers and abilities just waiting to be used." He has written this work to reveal those secrets. Cunningham has written over thirty nonfiction and fiction books, many of them for this volume's publisher, a major occult book publisher.

This very well done book covers a great deal of interresting ground for its low price, and is recommended for purchase by all types of libraries. Its very attractive purple and red cover, adorned with pictures of a half-dozen large, gleaming stones, will magically draw patrons to it.

A related title is George F. Kunz's *Curious Lore of Precious Stones* (Dover, 1970), which covers thirty-three stones in an A to Z arrangement in sixty pages.   Thomas C. Clarie

704. Gettings, Fred. **Dictionary of Demons: A Guide to Demons and Demonologists in Occult Lore.** North Pomfret, Vt., Trafalgar Square Publishing; distr., North Pomfret, Vt., David & Charles, 1988. 255p. illus. (part col.). $24.95. LC 88-70614. ISBN 0-943955-05-X.

In entries ranging in length from one sentence to more than a page, this dictionary lists names of demons, demonic systems, and other related terms that appear in Western occult and magical circles. Containing approximately three thousand names, this work is compiled from the grimoires of the main demonological traditions and from the great literature in which demons proliferate. Also included are short biographical entries on important demonologists. There is a lengthy introduction, which gives a history of Western demonology. Included are many fine illustrations, including some color plates. The bibliography at the end contains only those works referred to in the text; there is no recommended reading list.

This is a scholarly work on a rather narrow aspect of the occult. It is so specialized, in fact, that its use will be limited. Though the author is somewhat vague about his intended audience, one interested group would seem to be those researchers working with art and literature that contain references to demons. Lengthy entries on the demonologies of Dante, Milton, and Blake are of particular note. As long as the occult remains of high general interest, this book will also have some popular appeal, though it is not a popular treatment. For libraries with large humanities collections or a strong interest in the occult. [R: RBB, 15 Dec 88, p. 689]

Diane Richards

705. White, Rhea A. **On Being Psychic: A Reading Guide.** Dix Hills, N.Y., Parapsychology Sources of Information Center, 1987. 108p. $15.00pa. ISBN 0-944446-02-7.

White's guide is a listing of 1,357 sources, which include books, chapters, theses, and journal articles, providing extensive coverage on the psychic experience with both scholarly and popular works represented. Publications range from those published in the late 1800s to the present. Citations are listed by author under nine broad subject headings.

A large portion of the work is devoted to works about individual healers, mediums, and psychics. The researcher will undoubtedly find a wealth of information here plus many esoteric sources not easily located elsewhere. For specific sources not available, photocopies of up to sixty pages may be obtained from the publisher for a fee. Several parapsychological organizations are listed at the end of the volume from which additional information and sources may be obtained.

This is a valuable source for the psychic researcher, but the paperback format may not stand up to heavy use in libraries.

Marilyn Strong Noronha

706.　White, Rhea A. **Parapsychology: A Reading and Buying Guide to the Best Books in Print.** Dix Hills, N.Y., Parapsychology Sources of Information Center, 1987. 99p. index. $12.00 pa. ISBN 0-944446-00-0.

This is the third annual listing of books in print, as of 1 July 1987, on the topic of parapsychology. The subjects covered include precognition, reincarnation, mediumship, and out-of-the-body experiences, to name a few. This edition lists 420 books, arranged by author and subject in four major categories. The main divisions are current books (published from 1960 to date) and classics (published prior to 1960) that are still in print.

The introduction states that the books were selected for inclusion for at least one of the following reasons: quality of presentation, special topic, authority, or presence of a special feature such as a bibliography. The books are listed alphabetically by the author's last name with the usual bibliographic information plus other important details about the book that might include the price, presence of a glossary or bibliography, computer program, and if the original edition is out of print.

At the end of the volume are a title index, subject index, name, and supplemental subject index covering areas of the book not accessible through the main subject list. This bibliography contains titles not easily located elsewhere and can save researchers a great deal of time. However, the paperback format may not stand up to heavy use.

Marilyn Strong Noronha

15   Recreation and Sports

GENERAL WORKS

Bibliographies

707. Redekop, Paul. **Sociology of Sport: An Annotated Bibliography.** New York, Garland, 1988. 153p. index. (Garland Library of Sociology, Vol. 14; Garland Reference Library of Social Science, Vol. 387). $23.00. LC 87-31176. ISBN 0-8240-8464-0.

This annotated bibliography is intended to represent "the core of sport sociology, as described in refereed articles in sociological journals, articles in a range of readers and sourcebooks, and a fairly limited list of relevant monographs" (p. xiv). Arrangement is alphabetical by author listed in seven subject-oriented chapters that cover various aspects of the major topic. Examples include "Theory and Method in the Sociology of Sport," "Sport and Society," "Minority Relations," and "Deviance and Sport." Some chapters are further subdivided by more specific aspects of the topic covered. This is the only subject access that the book provides and the table of contents must suffice as a kind of subject index.

Annotations, when provided, generally range from twenty-five to fifty words and touch on the type of methodology employed if the article abstracted is a research report. Unfortunately, no explanation is provided regarding why some titles are abstracted and others are not.

There is a list of periodicals represented at the front of the book and an author index in the back. Generally, however, this work is lacking in features and some basic explanatory information usually included in scholarly reference works. Nevertheless, it should serve as a useful introduction to the literature on the author's narrowly defined subject. [R: Choice, July/Aug 88, p. 1676]   Larry G. Chrisman

708. Shoebridge, Michele. **Women in Sport: A Select Bibliography.** London, Mansell; distr., Rutherford, N.J., Publishers Distribution Center, 1987. 231p. index. $52.00. LC 87-24006. ISBN 0-7201-1858-1.

More women competed in the 1988 Olympics than ever before, reflecting their greater overall participation in sports, and their rising standards of performance. This helpful bibliography aims to bring together much of the research on women in sports, be it recreational or competitive, as participant or as facilitator.

This bibliography is divided into several categories. General sections include bibliographies and conference proceedings. Topical subjects include sports medicine, coaching, the Olympic Games, works on individual sports, biographies of women athletes, as well as selected serial publications and organizations focusing on women in sports. An author index and subject index are also included.

Only English-language publications are included, and coverage excludes most materials focusing on women in sports before 1890 and the start of the Modern Olympic period. Emphasis is heavily weighted in favor of British and Commonwealth publications. Many recent imprints such as Elizabeth Day and Ken Day's useful *Sports Fitness for Women* (David & Charles, 1986) are omitted. Even with these drawbacks, however, this bibliography should prove extremely useful and is a welcome addition to the literature. [R: Choice, Sept 88, p. 88]   Elizabeth Patterson

Chronologies

709. Carruth, Gorton, and Eugene Ehrlich. **Facts & Dates of American Sports.** New York, Perennial Library/Harper & Row, 1988. 373p. index. $27.50; $12.95pa. LC 87-46126. ISBN 0-06-055124-0; 0-06-096271-2pa.

With the contemporary American penchant for sports, as well as for books full of facts and figures, sports records books are becoming a glut on the market. There are too many poor ones, and too much duplication, but there is always room for another good one. *Facts & Dates of American Sports* is a useful and welcome addition primarily because it approaches its task in a new way. Arranged not by sport but rather chronologically on a year-by-year basis, from 1540 (the introduction of the horse into the United States) to 31 January 1988 (the Washington Redskins' Super Bowl victory), and by day within the year, this is a kind of sports almanac. That intriguing primary arrangement is supplemented by a detailed index of personal names and sports as well as some general subjects (e.g., women). There are also brief descriptions of ten memorable sports events, 38 tables of records and statistics for eleven major sports, and 222 brief biographies of major sports figures all located at appropriate chronological spots throughout the volume. This approach offers an interesting chronological view of the growth and development of sports in the United States and also serves as an excellent first source for those looking for information about what happened today in sports history. The lack of an adequate binding is particularly unfortunate for a volume like this that is apt to receive intensive use. Despite that flaw this is a significant addition for all sports information collections and libraries.   Norman D. Stevens

Directories

710. Carlson, Raymond, and Eleanor Popelka, eds. **Directory of Theme & Amusement Parks.** Babylon, N.Y., Pilot Books, 1988. 55p. $3.95pa. LC 87-29206. ISBN 0-87576-138-0.

This very short book lists by state, and within state by city/town, nearly five hundred theme and amusement parks in the United States. On the book's back cover the publishers state that "the material covered is stripped of time consuming and wasteful verbiage." Indeed, the entries are very short (two to four lines), with a typical entry giving title of park; attractions, specific ride names; special features (boardwalk, picnicking, swimming pool); telephone numbers; and sometimes, but not always, addresses. Admission prices and operating hours are not listed "since they change so frequently."

There are no indexes in the book, a shame when one considers how useful an index by type of feature (boardwalk, fun houses, haunted houses, miniature golf, railroads, skating rinks) would be. Also, we would like to see more infor-

mation under each entry, giving such important data as the maximum number of visitors allowed each day, the number of parking spaces available, the number of buildings, the number of rides, the date the park was founded, who owns/operates it, handicapped facilities, and the like. A rough idea of admission fees and hours is also a needed inclusion. Furthermore, it would be nice to see the editors comment on the nature and flavor of each park.

While the book is useful and very inexpensive, it needs a great deal of expansion (in spite of the publisher's campaign to stamp out "wasteful verbiage") and much deeper involvement and work by the editors to make it of real use. We hope the editors are ready for the challenge and hard work involved when/if they tackle another edition.

Thomas C. Clarie

Handbooks

711. Greenberg, Stan. **Olympic Games: The Records.** Enfield, England, Guinness Books; distr., New York, Sterling Publishing, 1987. 176p. illus. (part col.). index. $17.95. ISBN 0-85112-896-3.

712. Wallechinsky, David. **The Complete Book of the Olympics.** rev. ed. New York, Viking Penguin, 1988. 680p. illus. $12.95pa. ISBN 0-14-010771-1.

Interest in the Olympic games in 1988 produced a number of volumes which covered the games through 1984. These two volumes provide excellent coverage for different audiences. The Greenberg volume is of a more popular nature. Each Olympic games event from 1896 through 1984 is briefly covered, with a short newsy article accompanied by an event picture and a list of medals won by country. The second section provides a profile and photograph of seventeen of the most popular winners of events. The final section covers the major sporting events, providing lists of winners in each category.

The Wallechinsky volume, on the other hand, is a much more serious attempt to provide extensive factual information on winners. The almost seven-hundred-page listing is arranged by event and then by year of games. Names of the top finalists (usually five) in each match are listed and comments about the match are provided. Several useful reference lists are available in both volumes.

Scholars of the Olympic games will have to be extremely careful in using both volumes. Many facts are contradictory and names are spelled differently in each work. Neither can be considered authoritative without extensive tracking of the facts given. [R: BL, 15 Feb 88, p. 964]   David V. Loertscher

713. **Guinness Sports Record Book, 1988-89.** David A. Boehm, ed. New York, Sterling Publishing, 1988. 256p. illus. index. $16.95; $10.95 pa. LC 82-642136. ISBN 0-8069-6811-7; 0-8069-6810-9pa.

From the standard sports records, such as the regular season National Basketball Association records, to the more unusual records, such as the most golf rounds played in one day, the *Guinness Sports Record Book* for 1988-1989 once again has it all. Although a variety of other authoritative sources contain more complete and detailed records for specific sports, and although there are a number of other overall compilations of all kinds of sports records, this compact volume, which covers ninety-one major and minor sports, has established itself as *the* accepted and classic source of general information. This edition, like its predecessors, contains all of the usual data, arranged alphabetically by sport, for everything from aerobatics to yachting, including both well-known sports such as baseball and little-known sports such as joggling (running while juggling). Guinness's usual strict rules for acceptance of a record, now fortunately coupled with their rejection of gratuitously hazardous categories and oddities, once again makes this a reliable and valuable guide that will always be in high demand in libraries. New editions, like this one, should be added to library collections on a regular basis both because more current information is provided and because these volumes either disappear or are soon worn out from intensive use. Both as a standard reference source and as a volume that is fun to browse through, the *Guinness Sports Record Book* is a winner. [R: RBB, 15 Sept 88, p. 136]   Norman D. Stevens

714. Mallon, Bill. **The Olympic Record Book.** New York, Garland, 1988. 522p. $33.00. LC 87-22511. ISBN 0-8240-2948-8.

Each Olympic year produces scores of record books documenting the Olympic success of athletes from all nations; 1988 was no exception. Mallon's unique book, however, is an exception to the illustrated volumes that generally list the feats of U.S. athletes with only bare mention of other medal winners. Mallon also includes records of the Winter Olympic Games, and that, added to his comprehensive listings of records and medal winners, makes this a most useful reference volume.

Mallon's book begins with overall Olympic records in categories such as most medals won by an individual, most years winning a medal, and most years between medals. These categories are given for men and women. Such records are also listed for the Summer and Winter Olympic Games. Records are then listed by individual sport. A distinct feature of the book is a brief summary of the Olympic success of each participating nation. Records of each separate Olympiad conclude the volume. Although there is no index, each section of the book serves as a guide to the others. For example, the section on total medals can lead the reader to the summaries of each Olympic game. Since the volume includes records of the 1984 games, the book is almost as complete as possible. A truly invaluable guide to Olympic records. [R: Choice, July/Aug 88, p. 1676; LJ, 1 Apr 88, p. 80; RQ, Summer 88, pp. 575-76; WLB, June 88, p. 142]   Boyd Childress

AUTOMOBILE RACING

715. Morrison, Ian. **Motor Racing: The Records.** Enfield, England, Guinness Books; distr., New York, Sterling Publishing, 1987. 192p. illus. (part col.). index. $14.95pa. ISBN 0-85112-890-4.

A special Guinness record book, this compilation of motor sports statistics deals primarily with European racing. Included are facts and figures on Formula One, World Sports Car Championship, Formula Two, Formula 3000, the European Formula Three Championship, the British Formula Three Championship, the Indianapolis 500, and miscellaneous series like the Mille Miglia, Targa Florio, Can-Am, and the Tasman Cup. There is little coverage of American racing. Except for the Indianapolis 500, Indy car racing is not covered nor is stock car, sprint, midget, off-road, or drag. For European racing, however, the book contains a great deal of information.

For Formula One, the work provides the date, the first six finishers, the constructor, fastest lap, and pole sitter for each of the races in the series arranged by year. It also provides the series standings for drivers and constructors. There is also a diagram of each track used by Formula One, along with a complete list of all circuits used in the World Championship series. The emphasis of the work is on Formula One racing. Other European events are well covered but in less detail than the coverage given to Formula One. The book is well illustrated with many photographs in both color and black-and-white as well as line drawings. There are a number of informative short articles sprinkled throughout the text. Many of these cover individual drivers but some describe specific events or tracks. A minor irritant is the practice of listing drivers with only the first initial and then surname. It would be nice to have complete first names.   Susan Ebershoff-Coles

BASEBALL

716.   Deane, Bill. Award Voting: A History of the Most Valuable Player, Rookie of the Year, and Cy Young Awards. Kansas City, Mo., Society for American Baseball Research, 1988. 72p. illus. bibliog. $6.00pa. ISBN 0-910137-32-3.

In this little book Deane provides not only the histories of the awards named in the subtitle, but also a year-by-year breakdown of election results for each award. For example, it can be determined that in the 1946 National League MVP voting, Stan Musial won with 319 votes, Dixie Walker finished second with 159, Enos Slaughter third with 144, and so on down the line to Carl Furillo and Oscar Judd with one vote apiece. There is no index by player's name. The information is clearly presented and will be useful for baseball research collections.

Jack Ray

717.   Ercolano, Patrick. Fungoes, Floaters and Fork Balls: A Colorful Baseball Dictionary. Englewood Cliffs, N.J., Prentice-Hall, 1987. 219p. illus. bibliog. $6.95pa. LC 86-25306. ISBN 0-13-345075-9.

Over 1,500 words and phrases related to baseball are defined in this book. Cross-references are included, archaic phrases are explained, and fascinating and often unusual etymologies are offered. Added along the way are short histories of varied aspects of the sport, such as the beginning of night baseball and the evolution of the World Series.

Ercolano captures the rich vocabulary of the national pastime effectively. Geography is prominent: Chicago slides, Cuban fastballs, and Texas Leaguers. There are animals too: bird dogs, dead fish, rabbit balls, and goose eggs. But most often, food is involved: a near beer pitcher may put mustard on his potato in a hamburger league game. Because baseball is so deeply ingrained in American popular culture, this book will also serve as a lexicon of American slang.

Ercolano's research is thorough; this reviewer found no significant terms omitted. Baseball fans will enjoy quizzing themselves with this book, and it will probably serve to resolve a few arguments. In short, *Fungoes, Floaters, and Fork Balls* will give new meaning to Casey Stengel's famous words, "You can look

it up." [R: WLB, Mar 88, pp. 98-99]

John R. Muether

718.   Hoppel, Joe. The Series. St. Louis, Mo., The Sporting News, 1988. 336p. illus. $12.95pa. ISBN 0-89204-272-9; ISSN 0896-680X.

There probably can never be enough books on baseball, and especially on the World Series, to satisfy the avid sports fans who make heavy use of library collections. Here is another good one. Glenn Dickey's *The History of the World Series since 1903* (Stein & Day, 1984) and Donald Honig's *The World Series* (Crown, 1986) are two standard volumes that, along with the numerous general works on baseball, serve most needs, but they obviously lack coverage for the past few years. *The Series*, which is the latest in a series on the World Series published by The Sporting News, brings the picture up-to-date for now and, above all, provides a good general concise history of the fall classic. Arranged chronologically, starting with the first games in 1903, this is simply a year-by-year description of this important sporting event consisting of a brief narrative history accompanied by a game-by-game box score. In addition to the coverage of the World Series itself, the same information is provided for each of the American and National League Championship Series beginning in 1969. For both the World Series and the Championship Series, there is also a tabulation of all-time batting and pitching leaders. There are excellent black-and-white photographs, typically including the classic scenes, accompanying each year. The coverage ends with 1987. The written text is short and simple using all of the standard baseball clichés that one might expect. As a quick introduction to these major sporting events, *The Series* is a good solid contribution that is inexpensive and will wear well.

Norman D. Stevens

719.   Honig, Donald. The Greatest First Basemen of All Time. New York, Crown, 1988. 148p. illus. index. $18.95. LC 87-22208. ISBN 0-517-56842-X.

720.   Honig, Donald. The Greatest Pitchers of All Time. New York, Crown, 1988. 168p. illus. index. $18.95. LC 87-32960. ISBN 0-517-56887-X.

From famed baseball writer Honig (*Baseball When the Grass Was Real, The 100 Greatest Baseball Players of All Time*) come these two greatest-players-by-position books. They are identical in format, with sketches of the players averaging seven to eight pages in length (including photographs) and arranged chronologically. Twenty-two pitchers and nineteen first basemen are featured, and each book has a short chapter, "They Also Ran," which discusses some of the outstanding players who were not included. The complete record of each featured player is given at the end. Honig's essays are no wooden encyclopedia-style renderings, but wonderfully rich and evocative mini-biographies that bring the players to life. Observations of contemporaries, as well as numerous photographs of players and their teammates, provide an added dimension to Honig's material. Of course, one may always question the selections in books of this sort. With Honig, short-term brilliance obviously takes priority over lifetime achievement; hence, Dizzy Dean with 150 lifetime wins and Sandy Koufax with 165 are featured, while Early Wynn with 300 and Phil Niekro with 318 are not even mentioned with the also-rans. Similarly, Don Mattingly, who at age twenty-seven has played four full seasons, is a featured first baseman. Also, the rationale for a book on pitchers seems stronger than for one on first basemen, since the latter are known primarily for their hitting. Nevertheless, these are delightful books; they can be used for reference or read cover-to-cover equally as well.   Jack Ray

721. Kelly, Robert E. **Baseball's Best: Hall of Fame Pretenders Active in the Eighties.** Jefferson, N.C., McFarland, 1988. 200p. bibliog. index. $16.95pa. LC 88-42507. ISBN 0-89950-352-7.

Each year, millions of baseball fans speculate on who, among retired players, will receive baseball's highest honor, election to the Hall of Fame (HOF). The HOF, in Cooperstown, New York, is a shrine to professional baseball; and only a select few are chosen by ballot each year, which makes the honor infrequent, coveted, and controversial.

Robert E. Kelly, who has written analytical essays for several national baseball magazines, here ventures his predictions and analyses of the chances of (1986 season) active players of making the HOF, based on their prior and projected achievements. Kelly's analyses, written at the completion of the 1986 season, may be affected by subsequent events and records, but this cannot be helped short of publishing an annual edition.

Calling those with a fair shot at HOF election "pretenders," Kelly discusses specific players and their chances of election, individually and in groups by position. Analyses are provided, with performance and position/classification charts, short biographies, a history of the HOF, a discussion of how selection juries are

formed and operate, and the intriguing chapters "The Fairness Issue" and "The Neglected Ones."

Picking away at Kelly's methodology, one might say that he is strongly subjective, despite attempts to be statistical and analytical. His criteria for rankings (production per at bat, earned run average) are supposed to buttress his contentions with the appearance of objectivity, which is nowhere in evidence in his prose. One must, however, give him credit for attempting to be fair towards the players he discusses, despite perhaps unavoidable omission or dismissal of other people's favorites. Kelly has simply chosen what he calls "the best" for entry into his group of pretenders. The problem lies not in who is a good player, but rather with how Kelly decided on who is *better* (and thus more deserving) than whom.

Updated editions would help (the 1986 season seems so long ago now) but there is much readable information, accompanied by calculations and justifications in this little volume, which should please most baseball fans, while infuriating the rest. Recommended for sports collections in larger public libraries.

Bruce A. Shuman

722. Reidenbaugh, Lowell. **The Sporting News Selects Baseball's 25 Greatest Teams.** St. Louis, Mo., The Sporting News, 1988. 256p. illus. $19.95. LC 88-42860. ISBN 0-89204-280-X.

Lowell Reidenbaugh has been covering baseball for *The Sporting News* since 1947. No one can deny, therefore, that he knows whereof he speaks when he becomes so bold as to identify the twenty-five greatest teams in major league history, even though he freely admits to room for dispute. In this big, yet attractively priced, book, Reidenbaugh takes a detailed look at the greatest teams to play the game, and accompanies his contentions with large, black-and-white photographs and statistics, as documentation.

His number one, all-time team is the 1927 New York Yankees (do the names Ruth and Gehrig ring a bell?), which, he asserts pugnaciously, will never be equaled or bettered. Other teams giving the '27 Yanks a run for their money are the '61 Yankees (Maris, Mantle, Ford), the '06-'08 Cubs (Tinker to Evers to Chance) and the pitching-rich, ill-fated '54 Indians. He freely admits, furthermore, that anyone who lists "the best" and omits or forgets about the Dodgers, of whatever year, is going to have a serious fight on his hands.

Each of the twenty-five team editions is analyzed, position by position, with the year's statistics listed, and a ten-page narrative of the season in question. Reidenbaugh did not do all this alone; he merely presents the distilled consensus of the knowledgeable sports writers of *The Sporting News*. Sure, one might quarrel with the rankings presented here (baseball fans give new meaning to the word *partisan*) and many will find their favorite teams left off the list. This book will settle no bar bets or arguments; it may provide vindication for one opinion over another, but the "loser" will remain unconvinced. The reviewer, for example, has *always* hated the Damnyankees, and refuses to let objectivity taint his passions and prejudices. This book is a must for all libraries with patrons who think that the last two words of the national anthem are "play ball!" Get another one for the circulating collection and keep close tabs on it.   Bruce A. Shuman

723.   Smith, Myron J., Jr. **The Dodgers Bibliography: From Brooklyn to Los Angeles.** Westport, Conn., Meckler, 1988. 153p. index. (Sports Teams and Players Bibliography Series, 1). $29.95. LC 87-11249. ISBN 0-88736-206-0.

For this first in a new series of team bibliographies, Smith has selected baseball's most successful franchise, the Dodgers. The emphasis in this compilation is on "published (non-newspaper) items written in this century." Following a short introduction to the team, Smith arranges the sources as follows: (1) "Reference Works and General Histories" (which includes lists of libraries and archives, as well as many general indexes, such as *Readers' Guide to Periodical Literature*); (2) "Team Bibliography"; and (3) "Player Bibliography." The section on team bibliography would have been more useful had entries been arranged chronologically, rather than by author or title, particularly since there is an author index at the end of the book. Fortunately, a subsection on Dodgers in the World Series is arranged by year.

This source immediately invites comparison with Smith's *Baseball: A Comprehensive Bibliography* (see *ARBA* 87, entry 763). The latter has separate listings for Brooklyn and Los Angeles, which provides a rough chronological division that the present work lacks. While *The Dodgers Bibliography* covers some team-generated sources (e.g., *Dodger Scorecard Magazine*) and other more recent ones, it does not always include every relevant item from the larger work. For example, Don Drysdale has twenty-nine entries in the larger bibliography, twenty-two in this one, with no new sources listed. The same is true for Carl Erskine (ten and six, respectively). Overall, this book gives you about 8 percent of the number of cites for 54 percent of the price of the comprehensive bibliography.

However, in areas where patrons bleed Dodger blue, this book will be a useful resource, particularly if the larger work is not available. [R: Choice, June 88, p. 1540]   Jack Ray

724.   Tomlinson, Gerald. **The Baseball Research Handbook.** Kansas City, Mo., Society for American Baseball Research, 1987. 120p. index. $6.00pa. ISBN 0-910137-29-3.

This specialized primer introduces the user to the rudiments of research from topic selection through source acquisition to publication solicitation. Tomlinson lists twenty-four "contributors" (including David Q. Voigt and Philip Lowry), but their only appearance in the text is in passing references. A valuable checklist of eighty sources (most of which are annotated) covers many useful general sources (but omits *Biography and Genealogy Master Index, Magazine Index,* and *Comprehensive Dissertation Index*) and essential baseball reference tools (except *Sport Bibliography* [Human Kinetics]), along with examples of biographies, newspapers, magazines, and published books. Some sections (e.g., "The Self-Publishing Option") provide little guidance except for references to more detailed sources. More detail concerning the location and use of papers (a critical source for much baseball research) would strengthen the work, as would more discussion concerning oral history basics (e.g., requesting interviews). The photography section is strong but does not explain copyright bylines from photograph services and newspapers. Other sections discuss the use of libraries (librarians are touted often as invaluable resources) and Society for American Baseball Research resources, and methods for assuring accuracy.

This inexpensive, cheaply bound volume will be useful to the first-time baseball researcher, but users should be cautioned concerning its limitations. [R: Choice, June 88, pp. 1540-41]
                                       Robert Aken

725.   Westcott, Rich. **Diamond Greats: Profiles and Interviews with 65 of Baseball's History Makers.** Westport, Conn., Meckler, 1988. 389p. illus. $22.50. LC 87-24023. ISBN 0-88736-220-6.

In this collection of short biographies, each player is either interviewed or covered by a short five-page sketch written by Westcott.

This is only marginally a reference book. There is no index. Westcott had no real criteria for which players he included and which he excluded. Some of the players are in the Hall of Fame, some were Most Valuable Players, some were outstanding hitters or pitchers, and some performed memorable feats. Because the table of contents is arranged neither alphabetically, chronologically, nor by position played, it is difficult to locate who is included and who is not. Babe Ruth, Ty Cobb, and Pete Rose are not included; Lou Brock, Ted Williams, and Minnie Minoso are.

The selections are fascinating and well written, giving both a picture of the times and of the men who lived them. There is no comparable collection of short baseball biographies, but because of the small number of players included and the idiosyncratic selection criteria, this work is better suited to the general collection than for reference.   Dennis Dillon

BASKETBALL

726. CBA Plays America: 1988/89 Official Guide and Register. Denver, Colo., Continental Basketball Association, 1988. 302p. illus. $12.95 pa.

The Continental Basketball Association (CBA) was founded in 1946 as the Eastern Basketball League. Despite franchise relocations and constant player movement, the CBA has survived and continues to grow. The twelve teams play a fifty-four-game schedule plus playoffs, and have their own rule exceptions (p. 4) and complete affiliation system with the National Basketball Association (p. 5). With franchises in cities like Albany, New York, Pensacola, Florida, and Rockford, Illinois, the CBA is a fast-paced proving ground for future NBA hopefuls. Numerous players with CBA experience have gone on to stardom in the NBA – players such as Michael Adams (Denver Nuggets) and Rickey Green (Charlotte Hornets). The guide parallels somewhat the *Official NBA Guide* (see entry 728) and *NBA Register* (see entry 727) and includes background information on the league, its teams, CBA coaches, playoffs, and CBA records. Almost one hundred pages of the guide are profiles of players with CBA experience, whether they were with NBA or CBA teams in 1987-88. For example, Rod Higgins, now with the NBA's Golden State Warriors, played with Tampa Bay of the CBA in the 1985-86 season. Another section features team standings, playoff records, and statistical leaders for the past ten CBA seasons. The collection needing complete basketball coverage should have this book.   Boyd Childress

727. NBA Register. 1988-89 ed. Alex Sachare and Dave Sloan, eds. St. Louis, Mo., The Sporting News, 1988. 368p. illus. $10.95pa. ISBN 0-89204-289-4; ISSN 0739-3067.

In earlier reviews (see *ARBA* 81, entry 747 and *ARBA* 86, entry 763), reviewers have been less than enthusiastic concerning the *Register*,

and one concluded the *Official NBA Guide* (see entry 728) would suffice as the primary tool for NBA fans and statistics buffs. The *Register* includes statistical profiles of all active players from the previous year. Additional listings include collegiate records of prominent rookies, great stars in the history of the game, and career records of NBA coaches. The volume is primarily statistical in nature and is intended as a companion resource to the *Guide*. Inarguably, The Sporting News is the authoritative source for NBA statistics, and the *Register* reflects that accuracy. As one previous reviewer commented, the *Register* is player-oriented, and the exact information found in it is packaged in a team format in the *Guide*. For libraries which are forced to scrutinize their budgets, the *Guide* is the more attractive volume.

Boyd Childress

728. Official NBA Guide. 1988-89 ed. Alex Sachare and Dave Sloan, eds. St. Louis, Mo., The Sporting News, 1988. 496p. illus. index. $10.95pa. ISBN 0-89204-288-5; ISSN 0078-3862.

The Sporting News is the long-standing sports statistics leader, and the *Official NBA Guide* is an annual example of its excellence. The volume includes a statistical summary of the past season, present season rosters and schedules, NBA records and award winners, and season-by-season team records since the 1946-1947 season. These records include team and individual records, making this volume an indispensable source for NBA information. When compared to the *NBA Register* (see entry 727), the *Guide* provides the same information with a different approach. Since the *Register* includes information on players from the past season and present season, the *Guide* is the only source for information on greats of the game like Connie "The Hawk" Hawkins, who is not listed among the greats in the *Register*. When hard purchasing decisions have to be made, the *Guide* is the preferable choice.

Boyd Childress

CRICKET

729. Allen, David Rayvern. **Early Books on Cricket.** London, Europa Publications; distr., Lanham, Md., UNIPUB, 1987. 128p. illus. index. $25.00. ISBN 0-946653-26-7.

Cricket is a very popular game in England and in many Commonwealth countries. Allen has filled a major gap in the history of cricket by compiling a much-needed annotated bibliography on the subject.

The book is divided into two parts. The first part is a historical survey of the game, covering the period from the eighteenth century to 1977. It also deals with the changes in the game since its introduction in England in the early twelfth century. This well-written essay discusses many works on the subject published during the period covered in the book.

The second part, entitled "Bibliographical Notes on Early Books," is an annotated bibliography in chronological order covering the period from 1706 to 1895. Each entry has full bibliographic information—author, title, place of publication, publisher, year of publication, and total pages. Many pamphlets are included in the bibliography. The annotations are clear, varying from a few lines to a few paragraphs. An added attraction of the book is the inclusion of forty illustrations on cricket from old books. The index leads to entry numbers, and the boldface type refers to page numbers of illustrations.

It is certainly a well-prepared bibliography. Though expensive, this collector's item is recommended for cricket lovers and for all libraries interested in developing their collections on cricket. [R: LAR, Apr 88, p. 236]

Ravindra Nath Sharma

FOOTBALL

730. Baldwin, Robert. **College Football Records: Division I-A and the Ivy League, 1869-1984.** Jefferson, N.C., McFarland, 1987. 198p. index. $25.95. LC 87-42500. ISBN 0-89950-246-6.

This college football guide provides scores for all games played through 1984 since Princeton played Rutgers in 1869. It is limited to Division I-A schools and the Ivy League. The Atlantic Coast, Big Eight, Big Ten, Ivy League, Mid-America, Pacific Coast, Pacific Ten, and the Southeastern, Southwestern, and Western conferences are all included, as are all the independents in Division I-A. Each entry gives the school nickname, colors, location, stadium name and capacity, the year the school began its football program and the year it entered its conference, and the number of championships won. Each entry also includes wins-losses-ties records with each conference opponent, each Division I-A opponent, and all other opponents played. Also given are total overall record, total conference record, and overall bowl game record for each school. There are 111 schools included in the work. They are grouped together by their conferences with the independents listed last. Some historical data about each conference are also provided. These list the best overall Division I-A record, best bowl game records, most

bowl appearances, conference bowl game records, the longest Division I-A rivalries, and a list of Division I-AA football teams. No individual performances are included. The work is devoted to charting the schools and the success of the institutions in maintaining competitive football programs. [R: VOYA, Oct 88, p. 210; WLB, Feb 88, pp. 97-98]

Susan Ebershoff-Coles

731. **Football Register.** 1988 ed. Howard Balzer and Barry Siegel, eds. St. Louis, Mo., The Sporting News, 1988. 488p. $10.95pa. ISBN 0-89204-286-9; ISSN 0071-7258.

732. **Pro Football Guide.** 1988 ed. Dave Sloan, ed. St. Louis, Mo., The Sporting News, 1988. 408p. illus. $10.95pa. ISBN 0-89204-285-0; ISSN 0732-1902.

Football Register is a compendium of every NFL player and coach. Facts such as age, weight, birthplace, education, awards, honors, and records are combined with detailed, year-by-year performance statistics for each player's entire pro career. All facts are up-to-date through January 1988. Each chapter gives a simple alphabetical listing by name which helps the librarian who knows nothing about football.

Pro Football Guide is a compilation of facts about all NFL clubs, 1987 NFL statistics, all-time pro records, team year-by-year standings, draft choices, and the 1988 schedule. Team listings include player rosters, draft picks, front office facts, 1987 results, and 1988 schedules. A complete account of the 1987 NFL season, week-by-week with team and individual statistics for each game from week one through the Super Bowl, complements this volume.

In summary, both *Football Register* and *Pro Football Guide* are fact filled volumes which will be helpful to those with questions about the NFL. Both should be updated annually.

Janet R. Ivey

733. Hoppel, Joe, Mike Nahrstedt, and Steve Zesch, eds. **The Sporting News College Football's Twenty-Five Greatest Teams.** St. Louis, Mo., The Sporting News, 1988. 254p. illus. $14.95pa. LC 88-42855. ISBN 0-89204-281-8.

Any list of the twenty-five greatest anything is sure to generate much discussion and argument among aficionados of the topic. This group of twenty-five college football teams is no exception. From the 1924 Notre Dame team to the 1986-87 version of the Miami Hurricanes, this list compiled by The Sporting News represents the results of a 1983 poll of leading coaches and a 1988 survey of a TSN panel of football experts. The experts were asked to consider the events of the last five years and come up with an updated list of the twenty-five greatest teams.

Each team has a chapter of its own with both a textual and statistical analysis of its performance and the qualities which merited inclusion on such a select list. Statistics include a rundown of the season, statistical leaders, the final wire service rankings when available, and a collection of facts and figures presenting the high spots of the season.

Comparing teams of different eras is difficult in any sport. How would the legendary Four Horsemen of Notre Dame stack up against the powerful defense of the 1934-35 Minnesota Gophers or the elaborate and sophisticated defenses of the modern era? Personnel strengths and weaknesses were factors as well as coaching staffs, schedules, and a variety of intangibles. The teams are ranked one through twenty-five with the 1971 Nebraska Cornhuskers heading the list and ending with the 1933 Princeton Tigers.

Black-and-white photographs of each team provide a complete roster and other black-and-white action shots emphasize how much has changed—and how much has remained the same. While this book will be very popular with armchair quarterbacks and Monday morning coaches and generate lots of lively discussion, a standard football encyclopedia would be much more useful on a reference shelf.

Susan Ebershoff-Coles

734. Official 1988 National Football League Record & Fact Book. New York, Workman Publishing, 1988. 368p. illus. $12.95pa. ISBN 0-89480-587-8.

Every pro football nut should keep this work at an elbow from preseason to the Super Bowl. It will answer a wide range of questions. Who has the highest average gain in rushing yardage for a season, who gained the most yards returning punts in a season, who was the Most Valuable Player in Super Bowl IV? It is very handy for settling arguments.

A detailed NFL schedule leads off the book. Each week is listed in detail and nationally televised games noted. The playoff dates are given along with explanations of how playoff sites are determined. A list of dates including when clubs can sign free agents and when the roster must be down to forty-five players as well as the more routine information is provided. The tie-breaking procedures for determining postseason play are explained and rules for determining next year's schedules are given.

A four-page summary on each team lists the conference, division, corporate address and the club officials, the schedule, record holders, and last year's statistics. It also lists the current year's roster and coaching staff. Short biographical sketches accompany the list of coaches. Rookies are listed also.

The next section reviews the previous season in detail. Trades, preseason and regular season standings, game results, and week-by-week game summaries are covered. Awards; All-Pro teams; and rushing, passing, and receiving leaders are listed. Team and individual statistics and a paid attendance breakdown are also included. A statistical history of the NFL provides a wide variety of information. A register of the Pro Football Hall of Fame and a chronology of NFL history will provide answers to numerous questions. A list of number-one draft choices, Monday-night results, past NFL standings and much more information make this a very useful place to locate pro football information. Hopefully this will be an annual publication.

Susan Ebershoff-Coles

735. Porter, David L., ed. Biographical Dictionary of American Sports: Football. Westport, Conn., Greenwood Press, 1987. 763p. index. $75.00. LC 86-29386. ISBN 0-313-25771-X.

This biographical dictionary lists more than five hundred players, coaches, and executives who have had significant achievements relating to football and have had impact on the history of the sport. Arranged alphabetically and averaging about one page in length, the signed entries provide basic background information about the biographees, with primary emphasis on their sports careers. Each entry also has a brief bibliography of other sources of information. There are several appendixes: entry by main category (player, coach, or executive); entry by main position played; players by place of birth; biographees who have or are playing professional football; members of the College Football Hall of Fame; members of the Pro Football Hall of Fame; and a list of college and professional football conferences, leagues, and associations. There is a general index, which provides access to information within the essays but which, unfortunately, has some minor errors.

As evidenced by the bibliographies provided, much of the factual information found in this book can be found in other sources, but having such information and the analyses of impact in one volume will be very useful to reference librarians, researchers, and football fans. [R: Choice, Apr 88, p. 1219; LJ, 15 Apr 88, p. 31]

Barbara E. Kemp

GAMES

736. Clark, Thomas L. **The Dictionary of Gambling & Gaming.** Cold Spring, N.Y., Lexik House, 1987. 263p. bibliog. $48.00. LC 87-082866. ISBN 0-936368-06-3.

Here is a long-awaited, definitive gambling dictionary that includes not only historic terms and slang, but the ongoing rich and descriptive language used in today's casino and gambling world by gamblers and those who perpetrate the games. Gambling is pervasive and usually criminal in our society, which means this title provides all the culled slang, jargon, and underworld argot associated with illegal and legal gambling. Clark's linguistic and lexicographic scope includes modified, historical principles in searching and comparing: subculture dictionaries, other dictionaries, and illustrative quotations (including oral and fugitive quotes). Each entry provides the word, part of speech, pronunciation, source language (if needed), spelling variants, multiple definitions, status of term (obsolete, rare, etc.), synonyms, cross-references and related terms, source citations, explanative quotations, glosses with quotation, date of first occurrence from historical dictionaries and other source materials, etymological remarks, and sporatic editor's comments. Definitions are lucid and complete; several terms elicit short "articles" that further explore the word, game, or concept.

The book is double columned, well bound, and will serve as the standard gambling dictionary for a score of years. Many popular and standard lexicons include gambling terms and half or less of gambling literature may include gaming glossaries, but Clark's work combines a scholarly intuitive effort with common perseverance in rooting out gaming life's juicy jargon in a thorough and conclusive manner. [R: Choice, June 88, p. 1530; RBB, Aug 88, p. 1900; WLB, Apr 88, p. 100]

Jack I. Gardner

737. Eiss, Harry Edwin. **Dictionary of Mathematical Games, Puzzles, and Amusements.** Westport, Conn., Greenwood Press, 1988. 278p. illus. bibliog. index. $49.95. LC 87-280. ISBN 0-313-24714-5.

Intrigued by mathematics, man has created mind games and puzzles ranging from simple brain teasers such as number patterns or match tricks to sophisticated strategic games like chess. This book is a compilation of over two hundred such mathematical wonders. Included are mathematical excursions and genuine puzzles which influenced today's state of the science such as Euclid's Fifth Postulate of Parallels or the trisection of an angle. All the games are placed in their proper historical perspective.

Over fifty alphabetic entries include individual games or entire topics. For example, "logical paradoxes" includes a brief history of logical puzzles as well as quotations from poetry, literature, and mathematicians. Several "magic square" puzzles include the origins of these puzzles, solution formulas, and variations on the basic square. Each entry concludes with a list of cross-references to related topics or similar games found within the dictionary. A short but comprehensive bibliography of suggested readings at the end of each entry completes the text. Well over one hundred drawings of varying quality illustrate and exemplify the games, puzzles, and mathematical concepts.

The index is comprehensive, but functions more like a table of contents. This fascinating and unique collection of mathematical facts, puzzles, and games is a very worthy addition to any general or academic library. [R: Choice, July/Aug 88, p. 1723; RBB, 15 May 88, p. 1582]

Andreas E. Mueller

738. Waters, T. A. **The Encyclopedia of Magic and Magicians.** New York, Facts on File, 1988. 372p. illus. $35.00. LC 87-13464. ISBN 0-8160-1349-7.

In this volume of over one thousand one-paragraph entries, the author states: "My purpose in writing this book has been to provide a Technical Encyclopedia and Who's Who." This is done in one A to Z arrangement. The author tries "to provide a basic description of most known effects and routines, and, where feasible, briefly describe the technique involved." He also has tried very hard "to give credit where it is due" and tell who invented a trick.

There are no indexes, but *see* references are frequent. It would have been very helpful to include an index by "type" (cards, dice, handkerchiefs, water tanks, levitations).

Biographical entries are very brief, with little personal or evaluative information. Most biographical items have accompanying black-and-white photographs and a list of books the person wrote (due to the brevity of information on people, the author might well consider doing another volume just on people, with far lengthier, in-depth articles). Most other entries are for tricks, consisting of a ten-line paragraph each, telling what the audience sees and then how the trick is really done.

The large pages show a lot of white space which, combined with ten or so capitalized headings per page, gives the volume a "beginner's/fun book" look. There is a great deal of hard to find, fascinating material here. A richer, more sophisticated typeface, toned-down headings, and much less blank space would give the volume the more finished, powerful look it now lacks. [R: BR, Nov/Dec 88, p. 49; LJ, 15 Feb 88, p. 162; RBB, 15 June 88, p. 1720; VOYA, Oct 88, p. 211]   Thomas C. Clarie

HOCKEY

739.   **Hockey Guide.** 1988-89 ed. Larry Wigge, ed. Frank Polnaszek, comp. St. Louis, Mo., The Sporting News, 1988. 240p. illus. $10.95pa. ISBN 0-89204-290-7; ISSN 0278-4955.

740.   **Hockey Register.** 1988-89 ed. Larry Wigge, ed. Frank Polnaszek, comp. St. Louis, Mo., The Sporting News, 1988. 400p. $10.95pa. ISBN 0-89204-291-5; ISSN 0090-2292.

These companion volumes, published by The Sporting News, provide extensive coverage of the hockey scene. The *Hockey Guide* reviews the National Hockey League's (NHL) previous season and playoffs; gives the coming season's schedule; the current year entry draft; and complete NHL team directories, including management, team rosters, and records. It also gives team and player statistics for every North American hockey league and American college team. The *Hockey Register* provides information on the careers of any player who played even one NHL game during the previous season, as well as some selected players invited to the training camps. The information is quite up-to-date, covering events as late as August 1988. With names listed alphabetically in each section, one section covers forwards and defensemen and the second covers goaltenders. Each entry gives basic vital statistics, injuries suffered, shooting side, and compact career statistics. *The National Hockey League Sourcebook* (see entry 741) covers much the same information about the NHL and is probably better for in-depth team statistics and NHL history. The Sporting News volumes, however, do broaden coverage in the area of semiprofessional, amateur, and collegiate hockey and provide more information about players' careers.   Barbara E. Kemp

741.   **The National Hockey League Sourcebook 1987-88.** New York, Henry Holt, 1987. 256p. illus. $9.95pa. LC 87-82762. ISBN 0-8050-0782-2.

This first edition sourcebook will be of great interest to all hockey fans and anyone needing basic information or statistics about the National Hockey League. An official publication of the NHL, the book covers the league in depth. Part 1 covers the 1987-1988 NHL. The initial section analyzes each of the twenty-one teams in the league, giving an outlook for 1987-1988, individual players nearing milestones, the 1987 entry draft selections, up to twenty years of the overall team record, the team's playoff history, club and individual records, and a summary of the 1986-1987 scoring. This section is followed by a summary of the 1986-1987 season highlights. The third section is a scouting analysis of the 1987 first and second round draft picks. Part 2 covers the history of the NHL and a variety of individual and team awards and records. Part 3 details the history of the Stanley Cup, the NHL's championship trophy. The fourth and final part is an index to the 1986-1987 statistical records of the players who either played in the NHL or in one of the minor, collegiate, or European leagues and were drafted by the NHL or were on an NHL club reserve list.

Nowhere else can one find so much information about professional hockey presented so concisely. With hockey having a devoted and growing following in the United States, this book will be useful in most libraries and the personal collections of sports fans.

Barbara E. Kemp

HUNTING

742.   Schuh, Dwight. **Bowhunter's Encyclopedia: Practical, Easy-to-Find Answers to Your Bowhunting Questions.** Harrisburg, Pa., Stackpole Books, 1987. 574p. illus. index. $39.95. LC 87-6473. ISBN 0-8117-0258-8.

Bowhunters are a varied lot. Some are occasional dabblers who hunt only one particular game in one part of the country, while others roam from state to state hunting anything in season. And some are purists, using only a specific type of equipment. For all bowhunters of the United States, this massive compilation should be a welcome addition – and at a reasonable price – to their library shelves.

As the title indicates, the work is encyclopedic in structure since arrangement is alphabetical by major topical categories. Topical entries vary considerably in length, with some only a few sentences long, while others may take up a dozen or more pages. Longer articles are nicely subdivided for easy scanning for specific information. In general, entries are in noninverted format, so that one goes directly to the desired topic. This scatters some related material but generally works well for the overall volume. Cross-references, though not extensive, complement the encyclopedic approach, and a brief subject index provides additional access to longer entries. Photographs, most taken by the author, are used extensively throughout the text and add immensely to the usefulness of the volume.

In terms of content, the volume is remarkably complete for all aspects of bowhunting: equipment selection and repair, types of game, dressing and care of game, emergency procedures, and descriptions of hunting opportunities in all fifty states. Identification, selection, use, repair, and problems with bowhunting equipment are particularly strong features of the volume. The writing style is generally well balanced and appropriate to the topic, being terse and factual when needed and casually folksy when giving advice about hunting a particular type of game. Overall, the articles are both informative and easy reading.

The distinctive western states bias is the central weakness of the volume. The author is obviously much more knowledgeable about — and experienced in — states west of the Mississippi, and relies principally on published materials for what appears on the other states. This weakens the overall value of the volume but not to any significant extent, because most hunters are familiar with the possibilities for bowhunting in their own and neighboring states. There are similar omissions in a few other places, where attention to detail has been neglected. (For example, in the list of archery manufacturers, Jeffery Enterprises, of Columbia, South Carolina, and a major bow manufacturer, is missing.)

These are weaknesses that should be corrected in future editions. This reviewer hopes there will be future editions because it would be a shame if this work, the most encyclopedic treatment the sport is ever likely to have, is allowed to get too far out-of-date. It is much more complete on hunting aspects than the annual *Archery Digest* (Action Enterprises, Inc.) and is an improvement over the now out-of-date *Archery World's Complete Guide to Bowhunting* (Prentice Hall, 1975).

Robert V. Williams

MARTIAL ARTS

743.   Nelson, Randy F., with Katherine C. Whitaker. **The Martial Arts: An Annotated Bibliography.** New York, Garland, 1988. 436p. illus. index. (Garland Reference Library of the Social Sciences, Vol. 451). $62.00. LC 88-11243. ISBN 0-8240-4435-5.

This bibliography provides a detailed list of English-language sources for Asian martial arts. As such it omits arts associated with other countries such as French Savate, Hawaiian Kajukenbo, and numerous others.

After an introductory chapter of general reference materials, the chapters are divided according to major systems of martial arts. Entries within each chapter are classified according to the following divisions: general, history, biography, philosophy, instruction, and juvenile. The first chapter also includes handicapped, medical aspects, legal aspects, sociological aspects, and guides for beginners. The last three chapters are devoted to weapons, miscellaneous other arts, and works prior to 1920. Author and subject indexes complete the volume.

Most of the entries are journal articles. Only the book entries are annotated. Videotapes and other nonprint media are omitted. Illustrations are limited to a picture at the front of each chapter depicting practitioners from the chapter's system.

The volume is well-organized and probably the largest bibliography of the martial arts available today. Considering the popularity of the martial arts, the volume is a welcome addition to all types of libraries.

Andrew G. Torok

SKIING

744.   Pickard, Brent K. **A Skier's Guide to North America.** Miami, Fla., Wise Guide Publishing; distr., Boulder, Colo., Johnson Books, 1988. 236p. illus. $11.95pa. LC 88-50618. ISBN 0-944982-01-8.

Those planning ski vacations have many options to consider: terrain, snow conditions, costs, area facilities, and accessibility. In attempting to assist the planner, this guide profiles over seven hundred popular ski areas in the United States and Canada.

An orientation, offering tips on budgeting, equipment, apparel, etc., precedes the main section, which is divided into three geographic areas. Within these areas, ski resorts are alphabetically arranged under their respective state. Listings, ranging in length from one to six pages, include address, resort information, skiing conditions, lodging and dining reports, directions on getting there, and, once there, getting about. An appendix lists telephone numbers of transportation companies, and black-and-white photographs of resorts illustrate the guide.

Because of the extent of coverage, some localities, such as the Northeast, receive short shrift, and some excellent areas are left out. A chart, summarizing resort facilities and price ranges and including area maps, would further assist the vacation planner. *Frommer's Dollarwise Guide to Skiing U.S.A.* (Prentice-Hall,

1988), besides the abovementioned features, offers editions for the East and West, limiting scope and thus providing more detail.

Much information is involved in preparing for a ski vacation, and the more complete and current the data are, the better. Frequent updating is essential, and a combination of a comprehensive guide, periodical information, and communication with the resort(s) in question will provide the most satisfactory results.

Anita Zutis

TREASURE HUNTING

745. Reed, John H. **Directory of Treasure Hunting, Prospecting, and Related Organizations: An International Directory....** Gibson, La., Research & Discovery Publications, 1987. 191p. bibliog. index. $10.95pa. LC 86-063262. ISBN 0-940519-00-3.

It is likely that treasure hunting is coincidental with the discovery of gold. Years ago, I can remember seeing hunters, headphones at the ready, going slowly over the ground with their strange-looking metal detectors in the public parks. New discoveries in the Florida Keys show that the ancient urge is very much with us still. Some hunters often prefer to hunt in solitude; yet this book is proof of a strong desire to band together by forming clubs.

The compiler, John Reed, has apparently sent out many hundreds of queries to clubs and dealers around the world. His rate of return must have been disappointing, if the rather large proportion of clubs whose names and addresses are given but whose note reads "present status unknown" is an indication of response rate. Reed's purposes are to help hunters to locate clubs in "one's own area," and to aid travelers in finding and contacting other clubs. Defunct and inactive clubs have been retained in order to have a complete list and to ameliorate the possibility of searches for nonexistent organizations, if that term for these loosely structured clubs is not too strong.

These are essentially hobby clubs. Besides the aforementioned surveys, Reed has also scanned books and old magazines in the hunt for former and active clubs. There are several curious appendices: "Treasure Hunting Organizations Whose Locations and/or Names Could Not Be Determined" and "Acronyms Whose Meanings Are Unknown" are two. The bibliography includes twenty-one books and a complete (or nearly so) list of periodicals, some of which are no longer published. Arrangement is state by state, then country by country (nine countries included). The *Directory of Directories 1987* (see *ARBA* 87, entry 47) shows no comparable publications. [R: RBB, 1 Sept 88, p. 46]

Randall Rafferty

WINTER SPORTS

746. Gélinas-Surprenant, Hélène. **Lexique de Sports D'hiver. Winter Sports Glossary.** Ottawa, Canadian Government Publishing Centre, 1988. 340p. bibliog. index. (Terminology Bulletin, 179). $22.75pa. ISBN 0-660-53887-3.

The popularity of winter sports in Canada has prompted the publication of this glossary, which lists over five thousand terms related to competition in thirteen winter sports. General terms (i.e., those pertaining to two or more sports) and those common to various divisions of a sport, such as skating and skiing, are also included. The text is in English and French.

An explanation of graphic symbols used (e.g., the significance of semicolons or parentheses) and codes for the various categories precede the main section. Entries are alphabetically arranged by the English word(s). Each contains a two-letter code, the term, its English synonym(s), and the French equivalent and its synonym(s). Further information or definitions are supplied as deemed necessary.

An index links the French term to the page in the text where it is found. Both English and French titles comprise the bibliography of research works used as sources.

The guide is not meant to be exhaustive, but rather to serve as a practical reference. However, while entries associate terms with winter sports, there is no index providing the converse. Some descriptive information is included, but more definitions would be appreciated, especially by those not familiar with a particular sport.

Anita Zutis

16 Sociology

GENERAL WORKS

Bibliographies

747. Nordquist, Joan, comp. **Talcott Parsons.** Santa Cruz, Calif., Reference and Research Services, 1987. 60p. index. (Social Theory: A Bibliographic Series, No. 8). $15.00pa. ISBN 0-937855-14-6.

This is the eighth publication in a series: Social Theory: A Bibliographical Series, sponsored by Reference and Research Services at Santa Cruz, California. The series represents a reference source for researchers seeking to locate important books and journal articles on contemporary social theory, reprinted in English. Both primary and secondary sources are covered by each bibliography.

In a modern world—complex, interdependent, and dynamic—socioeconomic problems, to be understood, must be brought into theoretical perspective. Users of libraries have developed a great interest in publications of social theorists. There is a growing need for comprehensive bibliographies of these scholars and for quick and easy reference to their work either in translation or in reprinted form. One of the objectives of this bibliographical series is to provide references to social theorists and to the issues they are addressing.

This issue is on Talcott Parsons (1902-1979), a major theorist and a proponent of "structural-functional theory." Section 1 contains the books written by Parsons and the book reviews and essays about these books. In section 2 are listed Parsons's essays, arranged alphabetically by title and accompanied by a chronological list of the sources of the reprints. "Related Articles," critical work of other writers about Parsons's ideas in his essays, are listed alphabetically after each of the original essays. A keyword index to the essays is found at the end of the section. Books in English about Parsons's work are listed in section 3. Articles in books and journal articles containing critical literature in English about Parsons's writings are found in section 4. This issue is highly recommended for university and public libraries as a useful addition to their reference collections.

Oleg Zinam

748. Nordquist, Joan, comp. **Theodor Adorno.** Santa Cruz, Calif., Reference and Research Services, 1988. 52p. index. (Social Theory: A Bibliographic Series, No. 10). $15.00pa. ISBN 0-937855-18-9.

The series introduction makes clear that the intention is to provide a "quick and easy to use" rather than a comprehensive or research bibliography. As such this number proceeds in a straightforward manner to provide a bibliography for Theodor Adorno, the German sociologist, philosopher, and music critic perhaps best known in this country for his 1950 book *The Authoritarian Personality*. There are four sections in this listing: books by Adorno with book reviews and related essays cited, essays by Adorno, books about Adorno's works, and articles and essays about Adorno's works. There are key-word-in title indexes to the second and fourth sections. Citations in all sections are limited to English-language materials or translations into English from German. Although one could readily think of additional features to enhance this work, such as annotations for the major titles cited or an introductory essay on Adorno's social theory, these do not fall within the series scope which is to provide a convenient list of the author's works and of selected critical works. As such this is a useful finding aid for beginning research. This book, or pamphlet, has a folded and stapled binding.

Henry E. York

749. Salerno, Roger A. **Louis Wirth: A Bio-Bibliography.** Westport, Conn., Greenwood

Press, 1987. 143p. index. (Bio-Bibliographies in Sociology, No. 1). $35.00. LC 87-19631. ISBN 0-313-25473-7.

Louis Wirth (1897-1952) was one of the most important figures in American social sciences in this century. He exemplified the "scholar in action" (preface), the academic sociologist whose writings influenced public policy, especially in the areas of urban development, city planning, and civil rights. This bio-bibliography was prepared by Roger A. Salerno, assistant professor in the Social Sciences Department at Pace University in New York City, whose Ph.D. dissertation was on Wirth.

This guide provides several sections that comprehensively cover the life and scholarship of Louis Wirth. It begins with a one-page chronology. There follows a forty-five-page biography based on published and unpublished materials, which traces Wirth's personal background and professional development. The bibliography of works by Wirth is exhaustive, including public addresses, government reports, and transcripts of radio appearances as well as books, essays, and journal articles. The archival sources for Wirth's papers are noted. The final section is a bibliography of material about Wirth. All citations are annotated. Salerno's work will be a useful reference tool for scholars and a much-appreciated find for students seeking a convenient source for beginning research on Wirth. [R: Choice, May 88, p. 1386]

Henry E. York

Dictionaries and Encyclopedias

750. Mackenzie, Kenneth R. H., ed. **The Royal Masonic Cyclopaedia.** Wellingborough, England, Aquarian Press; distr., New York, Sterling Publishing, 1987. 781p. illus. (Masonic Classics Series). $19.95pa. ISBN 0-85030-521-7.

The Royal Masonic Cyclopaedia was originally published in six parts over a two-year span from 1875 to 1877. This one-volume reprint is part of the Masonic Classics Series, which includes a variety of literature on freemasonry now out-of-print. Each title in the series consists "of a facsimile of the original text ... prefaced by a critical introduction by an acknowledged authority on the subject."

The excellent introduction to Mackenzie's "idiosyncratic" *Royal Masonic Cyclopaedia* discusses its lack of critical acceptance, placing the blame for its failure largely on its "over-emphasis on the higher, or additional, degrees, on quasi- and pseudomasonic Orders, and on frankly esoteric subjects, none of which was likely to appeal to the average member of the Craft" (p. v). Its strength is attributed to

distilling "the essence of Victorian esoteric thought" and, in so doing, unwittingly providing "a primary sourcebook for the history of the 'Occult Revival' " (p. vi).

Entries are arranged alphabetically in dictionary format and range in length from one or two sentences to over twenty pages. The writing is sometimes highly stylized, by twentieth-century standards, and readers may find the longer entries slow reading at best. It is safe to say that libraries interested in the subject should treat this title as supplementary to the standard works on freemasonry. Its emphasis on the occult aspects of the topic, however, may result in its wider acceptance now than when it was first published. Nevertheless, its greatest appeal remains as a curiosity.

Larry G. Chrisman

Indexes

751. **Cumulative Index of Sociology Journals 1971-1985.** Judith C. Lantz, comp. Washington, D.C., American Sociological Association, 1987. 763p. $65.00pa.

This one-volume cumulative index of ten sociology journals is the first work of its kind to be produced by the American Sociological Association. Covering the years 1971-1985, it includes all ASA journals as well as the *American Journal of Sociology* and *Social Forces*.

The work is divided into two parts: an author index and a subject index. Articles, book reviews, and review essays are referenced in both sections; notes and comments are not included. Entries in each section contain essentially the same information: title of the journal, date, and pagination.

Overall, this work is a convenient source for searching select publications over a fifteen-year period. Unfortunately, it suffers from an inconsistent format in the subject index; both subject headings and a keyword-like approach to indexing are utilized. As a reference tool, it would also benefit from the addition of two other features: full bibliographic information for entries (author entries exclude article titles; subject entries exclude article titles and authors' names) and more cross-referencing. The latter is especially important given the absence of a thesaurus.

In spite of these deficiencies, Lantz has done an admirable job in providing accurate coverage and compiling a tool that is easy to use. The work would be of particular value to scholars interested in retrospective searching of select publications.

L. L. Schroyer

AGING

Bibliographies

752. Guttmann, David, comp. **European American Elderly: An Annotated Bibliography.** Westport, Conn., Greenwood Press, 1987. 122p. index. (Bibliographies and Indexes in Gerontology, No. 6). $35.00. LC 87-17809. ISBN 0-313-25583-0.

The fact that over one-third of all ethnic elderly in the United States are from European-origin groups would seem to indicate the need for further information on these groups. This annotated bibliography brings together books, including dissertations, articles, and documents on those sixty-five and older representing what is termed the *Euro-American elderly*. The works are arranged alphabetically by author under general subject areas, which include (1) basic knowledge about the group; (2) adjustment to life in America; (3) factors in well-being; (4) problems, needs, and services; (5) research; and (6) the education of those working with this group. The bibliographical data for each entry are generally the same, but the annotations vary in length from three to four lines to half a page. There are author and subject indexes in addition to a list of the journals cited in the bibliography and a section on other bibliographies. The 310 publications listed are limited to those in English published within the past fifteen years. They are carefully chosen to meet the specified criteria and the annotations are well written. The compiler, David Guttman, is a significant contributor to this literature, so the reader has some confidence that the works selected are indeed worthy of inclusion. Both researchers and practitioners should find this volume a welcome addition to gerontological literature. [R: Choice, Apr 88, p. 1222]   Lucille Whalen

753. Oriol, William E., comp. **Federal Public Policy on Aging since 1960: An Annotated Bibliography.** Westport, Conn., Greenwood Press, 1987. 127p. index. (Bibliographies and Indexes in Gerontology, No. 5). $35.00. LC 87-8343. ISBN 0-313-25286-6.

A recent addition to the Greenwood series Bibliographies and Indexes in Gerontology, this volume focuses on both public policy itself and the issues that lead to public policy on aging. Covering the years 1960 through early 1986, the work is divided into two main sections, one on general works on federal public policy and the other on specific issues such as health, housing, discrimination, and women. Each of the 751 annotations was written by the author, who is a former Staff Director of the U.S. Senate Special

Committee on Aging. Using the National Gerontology Resource Center in Washington, D.C., with heavy reliance on its computerized database, Ageline, the author has provided an excellent selection from the vast array of material available to him and has made every effort to select only those items relevant to public policy issues. If the user is interested in specific items, there are author and subject indexes to make searching easier. Additionally, there is an appendix providing sources of further information on congressional committees, publications, and organizations that frequently give background data or accounts of difficulties or achievements relating to public policy issues on aging. Most of the organizations are devoted to aging, but there are also some that are more general but have committees or programs specifically for problems of the aging (e.g., the American Psychiatric Association's Council on Aging). This work should be of special significance for those concerned with public policy issues. [R: Choice, Feb 88, p. 884; RBB, 15 Jan 88, p. 844; RQ, Summer 88, pp. 573-74]

      Lucille Whalen

754. Schlesinger, Benjamin, and Rachel Schlesinger, comps. and eds. **Abuse of the Elderly: Issues and Annotated Bibliography.** Toronto and Cheektowaga, N.Y., University of Toronto Press, 1988. 188p. index. $13.95pa. ISBN 0-8020-6694-1.

This sourcebook on abuse of the elderly contains ten essays on the subject and an annotated bibliography of 267 items from Canadian and American sources. The essays, written by medical and social sciences professionals, provide an overview of elderly abuse issues and summarize some of the current research on the subject. The bibliography section is arranged by subject and contains a selective listing of primary and secondary sources published between 1979 and 1987. This useful source on a timely topic is recommended for academic and public libraries.   L. L. Schroyer

Dictionaries

755. Harris, Diana K. **Dictionary of Gerontology.** Westport, Conn., Greenwood Press, 1988. 201p. index. $37.95. LC 87-25142. ISBN 0-313-25287-4.

Gerontology is a growing interdisciplinary field, with terminology drawn from both the social and physical sciences. This dictionary is intended to help develop that terminology and to clarify it for interested "students, scholars, researchers, and practitioners" (p. ix). It provides brief definitions of approximately eight hundred terms, theories, research methods, statistical techniques, organizations/associations, drugs, medical conditions, and other key concepts in the study of gerontology. Each definition is accompanied by one or more bibliographic references to books, articles, or other publications that discuss the term further. In some cases, the definition also mentions who first used the term. Words within a definition that are defined elsewhere in the dictionary are indicated with an asterisk. Many of the entries are accompanied by *see* and *see also* references to preferred and related terms, respectively. A name index, which includes some organizational names, provides additional access. The dictionary also includes a timetable of important developments from 1935 through 1986; each of these developments is defined in the volume.

The strengths of this dictionary are its clear, concise definitions and its handy references to further reading. While many of the terms defined here are also included in *The Encyclopedia of Aging* (see *ARBA* 88, entry 819), the latter source has longer entries, and therefore may be meeting a different and more comprehensive informational need. Libraries supporting research and/or instruction in gerontology would probably want both works. In any event, the *Dictionary of Gerontology* is well done and should be a useful addition to the reference literature in this increasingly important field. [R: Choice, Dec 88, p. 628; RBB, 1 Nov 88, p. 462]　　　Stephen H. Aby

Directories

756. National Directory of Educational Programs in Gerontology. 4th ed. By David A. Peterson, David Bergstone, and Joy C. Lobenstine. Washington, D.C., Association for Gerontology in Higher Education, 1987. 855p. $45.00pa. ISSN 0148-4508.

This fourth edition directory is the result of a national data collection project undertaken by the Association for Gerontology in Higher Education (AGHE) in cooperation with faculty from the Universities of Southern California, Oregon, and Utah. Funded by the U.S. Administration on Aging, the project was designed to gather information on the extent of gerontology instruction in institutions of higher education.

Users familiar with the form and content of previous editions will note some differences in the fourth edition. The first of the two sections lists all Canadian and accredited U.S. institutions initially surveyed and includes information on the number of courses offered, number of faculty, availability of noncredit courses, membership in AGHE, offerings for the elderly, and

number of academic units. Listings in the second section are arranged alphabetically by state and provide a full description of programs offered by each academic unit for institutions offering four or more credit courses in gerontology. Also in section 2 is a new index to programs by academic level (associate, bachelor's, master's, etc.).

This is a very useful and well-organized directory of particular value to students, faculty, and professionals working in the field. As a reference tool, however, it would benefit from more clearly delineated divisions by state in section 2. Recommended for academic and private libraries.　　　L. L. Schroyer

757. National Directory of Retirement Facilities. 2d ed. Phoenix, Ariz., Oryx Press, 1988. 878p. index. $175.00pa. LC 88-19628. ISBN 0-89774-450-0.

This second edition directory is intended to introduce the user to residential alternatives designed for persons of retirement age. The current edition lists more than eighteen thousand facilities, a reported increase of about six thousand listings since the first edition was published in 1986. Listings in the directory were compiled from state licensing agencies, membership directories, and a computerized search of Dialog's Electronic Yellow Pages. The majority of information was prepared from completed questionnaires and telephone contact, the remainder from secondary sources.

Entries are arranged geographically by state and city and then alphabetically by name of facility. Each entry includes name, address, and telephone number. The majority also include name and title of the contact person, type and size of facility, cost, services, ownership, affiliation, and entrance age requirement. In addition, some facilities paid for a one-hundred-word description of unique or interesting features they offer. Completing the directory is an alphabetical listing of facilities.

This is a vital directory and should be an important resource for those seeking basic information on residential alternatives. Unfortunately some entries contain only the name, address, and telephone number of the facility, while others are ambiguous regarding the facility's type. The introduction, for example, states that "multiple care" is used to identify facilities which "offer several unspecified forms of care," a vague designation. A more complete description of "multiple care" and more complete information for all of the facilities listed would have improved the usefulness of this work. Even without these improvements, this work represents the most current national listing of retirement facilities available. Unfortunately, its price makes it prohibitive except for libraries with a strong interest in collecting resources for the elderly.

L. L. Schroyer

DEATH

758. Simpson, Michael A. **Dying, Death, and Grief: A Critical Bibliography.** Pittsburgh, Pa., University of Pittsburgh Press; distr., New York, Harper & Row, 1987. 259p. index. (Contemporary Community Health Series). $27.95. LC 87-6011. ISBN 0-8229-3561-9.

This is an updated and expanded version of Simpson's 1979 publication (see *ARBA* 81, entry 1553). Unlike the previous edition, this bibliography contains only books. The main body of fourteen hundred citations acts as an updated list to the 1979 publication, as most are post-1978 titles. All are rated on a scale of one to five stars (not recommended to highly recommended), with the rating of zero reserved for the truly awful. Arranged alphabetically by title, the vast majority of citations in this section are annotated, although the length of the annotations ranges from a few words to a few paragraphs. Two "stop press" sections include another three hundred titles, some as recent as 1987. Additional sections on murder, terrorism, and nuclear holocaust and megadeath are comprehensive lists of books, unannotated and unindexed. There are an author index and a classified subject index similar to that of the previous edition.

The comprehensiveness of the bibliography is commendable. One can hardly find a topic in death and dying not covered here, and the coverage of books intended for children and young adults is particularly welcome. The aspect of this work that is most objectionable is the tone of the critical annotations. For example, books that rate a zero or one star according to Simpson can be accompanied by two-hundred-word annotations railing against the authors and/or books, usually in hyperbolic and condescending terms, whereas four- or five-star books may have annotations half that length. A book on the use of morphine with terminal cancer patients can be described in better terms than "too much of a good thing." It is unfortunate that the compiler's tone of expression detracts from an otherwise sound contribution. [R: Choice, May 88, p. 1386; RBB, 15 Apr 88, p. 1406]

Pam M. Baxter

DISABLED

759. **American Foundation for the Blind Directory of Services for Blind and Visually Impaired Persons in the United States.** 23d ed. New York, American Foundation for the Blind, 1988. 378p. index. $39.95 spiralbound. ISBN 0-89128-147-9; ISSN 0899-2533.

This directory has modified its title in this edition. In addition, it has also added a new chapter, "How to Find Services," which includes several tables of statistics concerning the visually impaired population of the United States, as well as definitions of visual terms. This chapter also has a quick reference guide to major federal programs. There are many indexes as well as state listings, providing numerous access points for users to find relevant information. The directory is organized to enable blind and visually impaired people, their families, and their friends to locate services they need quickly and efficiently. It will be a valuable resource for professionals in the field as well.

The directory is most comprehensive in that it describes programs and services for impaired people from childhood through the elderly. The format is easy to use. It is not clear how information is gleaned for agencies, but since I am employed at the IUPUI Medical Center and University Campus in Indianapolis, Indiana, I am aware of a low vision clinic in the Ophthalmology Department that is not included in the directory. However, this is only a minor flaw. It does indicate the low vision clinic through the Optometric Center here at the campus.

The directory is excellent and fulfills a serious need for the visually impaired. Recommended for all types of libraries and agencies dealing with vision impairment.

Mary J. Stanley

760. **Directory of Agencies and Organizations Serving Deaf-Blind Individuals.** rev. ed. Compiled by Helen Keller National Center for Blind-Deaf Youths and Adults. Sands Point, N.Y., Helen Keller National Center for Deaf-Blind Youths and Adults, 1987. 140p. $10.00 looseleaf with binder.

This directory is a listing of agencies and organizations reporting to have worked with deaf-blind individuals and is intended to serve as a resource and aid to securing services for that clientele. The directory is divided into two categories: federally funded programs and public and privately funded programs. Listings of public and privately funded programs appear alphabetically according to state, city, and name of agency. Information for the directory is based on a survey conducted by the Helen Keller National Center for Deaf-Blind Youths and Adults in 1986. It is the intention of the center to update the directory periodically. Although the material appears to be thorough, its loose-leaf format is cumbersome and information has to be decoded from the legend provided. Overall, the directory stands to be an excellent resource tool for the deaf-blind community.

Janet R. Ivey

761. Hedges, Donna M., Betty Wong, and R. Bruce Macdonald, comps. and eds. **Employment of the Learning Disabled: An Annotated Bibliography of Resource Materials for Education and Training.** Vancouver, B.C., Vancouver Association for Children & Adults with Learning Disabilities, 1987. 159p. index. $15.00 loose-leaf. ISBN 0-9693284-0-0.

Prepared as a result of a grant from the Canada Employment and Immigration Commission, this annotated bibliography was compiled under the auspices of the Vancouver Association for Children & Adults with Learning Disabilities (VACLD). The publication contains approximately three hundred original titles on employment and the learning disabled, most of which have been published since 1980. Included are field studies, videotapes, directories, theses, guides, games, microforms, articles, and books.

The work is divided into three main sections: (1) employers, (2) adults with learning disabilities, and (3) instructors and other professionals. Entries in each section are arranged alphabetically by author and include a brief abstract, location of the item (within Canada), and subject headings. Separate name, title, and subject indexes are included.

This is a needed bibliography which should greatly assist its intended audiences. As a reference tool, however, it would benefit from the elimination of duplicate items and more clearly defined subject headings. Location codes primarily serve the Vancouver area; however, many items may be obtained through interlibrary loan. Recommended for public and academic libraries.   L. L. Schroyer

762. Schlachter, Gail Ann, and R. David Weber. **Financial Aid for the Disabled and Their Families 1988-1989.** Redwood City, Calif., Reference Service Press, 1988. 269p. index. $32.50. LC 87-063263. ISBN 0-918276-04-7.

Millions of dollars in financial aid are set aside each year for the disabled, and yet most are unaware of this. *Financial Aid for the Disabled and Their Families* identifies hundreds of scholarships, fellowships, loans, grants, awards, and internships designed exclusively for the disabled, their spouses, parents, children, and siblings.

Over six hundred references and cross-references guide the reader to programs sponsored by professional organizations, foundations, educational associations, military and veteran organizations, and state or federal government agencies. Each entry provides detailed information on program title, sponsoring organization address and telephone number, purpose, eligibility, funding awarded, duration, special features or limitations, number of awards, and deadline dates.

The volume is enhanced by its five indexes: program title, sponsoring organization, geographic, subject, and calendar. In addition, this directory lists the addresses and telephone numbers of several state sources of benefits and describes the seventy-five key directories that any individual (disabled or not) can use to find additional sources of financial assistance.

If updated regularly, this directory will assuredly be a major reference tool in most libraries. [R: LJ, 1 Oct 88, p. 82; RBB, 15 Dec 88, pp. 690-91; WLB, Sept 88, p. 89]

Janet R. Ivey

763. Sherman, Barbara Smiley, ed. **Directory of Residential Facilities for Emotionally Handicapped Children and Youth.** 2d ed. Phoenix, Ariz., Oryx Press, 1988. 284p. index. $74.50pa. LC 87-27316. ISBN 0-89774-407-1; ISSN 8756-2170.

This is a revised edition of Sherman's *Directory of Residential Treatment Facilities for Emotionally Disturbed Children* (see *ARBA 86*, entry 823). The scope and organization differ little from the previous edition. One introductory essay details the legal and educational responsibilities of schools toward handicapped students and the process of student placement. A second outlines procedures for selecting a treatment facility. Both are detailed yet jargon-free, appropriate for parents as well as professionals.

The information contained in entries remains the same: address, telephone number, and the name of a contact person; a brief description and client profile; fees, sources of institutional funding, and the services available; referral information requirements; and the therapeutic orientation. Data were collected by a mail questionnaire, and the appearance of these facilities in the directory indicates their responsiveness to the survey, not the compiler's endorsement. This section has been supplemented considerably since the 1985 edition: the number of entries has more than doubled to include about one thousand facilities, with each entry presented in a more concise format. Indexes by funding sources and specific type of disability remain. An index providing access to specialized programs has been added but needs enhancement. Two indexes in the previous edition (type of placement and ages of clients served) have been omitted.

Those who have found the previous edition useful will probably want the additional coverage afforded here. This volume is especially appropriate for collections serving social workers, counselors, special educators, and others who make referrals of this nature. [R: RBB, July 88, pp. 1811-12]

Pam M. Baxter

FAMILY AND MARRIAGE

764. Gondolf, Edward W. **Research on Men Who Batter: An Overview, Bibliography and Resource Guide.** Bradenton, Fla., Human Services Institute, 1988. 93p. index. $4.95pa. LC 87-34229. ISBN 0-943519-05-5.

This guide is intended to introduce social workers, therapists, and researchers to the research literature on abusive men. The scope and content of the bibliography, however, expand its audience to students and those involved in a variety of criminal justice and human services areas.

The references themselves are preceded by a brief overview of the literature on abusive males. The bibliography of approximately a thousand unannotated references follows, organized under five conceptually broad areas: the dynamics of spouse abuse, the etiology of abuse, research on men who batter, intervention approaches and strategies, and resources for use in education and intervention. Entries are further subdivided under nearly sixty categories in a hierarchical arrangement. This provides effective subject access, supplemented by an author index.

For the most part, references represent the published, readily accessible literature: journal articles, books and book chapters, and federal government documents. Other types of material are papers from professional conferences and research institutes, items from microfiche document services, and a few in-press and forthcoming titles. Popular magazine literature is omitted. Lists of self-help books for both abuser and victim, program manuals for therapists, films, resource centers, periodicals, and reference books are included in the "Program Resources" section. References are duplicated in the bibliography in lieu of a detailed subject index or cross-references, which, fortunately, are few in number. Reflecting the body of research, entries date from the mid-1970s with the majority from 1980 to 1987.

Gondolf's contribution supplements Eugene Engeldinger's *Spouse Abuse* (see *ARBA* 87, entry 793). Engeldinger provides comprehensive coverage of the conjugal violence literature, whereas Gondolf affords better access to research on the abusive male. [R: RBB, Aug 88, p. 1895]

Pam M. Baxter

765. Sadler, Judith DeBoard. **Families in Transition: An Annotated Bibliography.** Hamden, Conn., Archon Books/Shoe String Press, 1988. 251p. index. $30.00. LC 87-37347. ISBN 0-208-02180-9.

As pointed out in this book's introduction, the structure of the American family is changing. In addition to the nuclear family, there are many single-parent families, commuter families, stepfamilies, and a variety of other forms of the family. This annotated bibliography is a guide to information on changing family structures and their related problems, and is intended to be a resource for individuals, groups, family professionals, and members of nontraditional families. It provides one-paragraph, descriptive annotations on almost one thousand books, articles, handbooks, media materials, research studies, popular works, and other sources. Over 90 percent of these materials were published since 1975; 65 percent were published in the 1980s, including some as recently as 1987.

The entries are arranged into sixteen chapters; within each chapter, entries are sorted into subsections for books or articles, and then arranged alphabetically by author. Chapter titles include "Single-Parent Families," "Stepfamilies," "Divorce," "Adoptive and Foster Care Families," "Divorce and Remarriage," "Custody and Child Support," "Parental Kidnapping," "Children of Divorce," "Working Parents & Latchkey Children," "Fathers," "Teen Pregnancy and Parenthood," "Homosexual Relationships," and "Works for Children & Youth." There is also a chapter listing films, videocassettes, and audiocassettes, as well as two general chapters covering such topics as surrogate parents, commuter families, househusbands, living together arrangements, communal living, and other miscellaneous works. A final chapter lists bibliographic citations for recently identified works. Additional access to the entries is provided by separate subject, author, book title, and article title indexes. The appendix lists names and addresses of family-related associations and organizations.

This is a commendable bibliography, both for its broad coverage of topics and for its inclusion of material for lay and professional audiences. However, it would have been helpful if the author had included relevant indexes, abstracts, and databases for those wanting to do further research. For example, the Family Resources database produced by the National Council on Family Relations, the *Sage Family Studies Abstracts* (Sage, 1979-), and the *Inventory of Marriage and Family Literature* (see *ARBA* 88, entry 834) are useful guides to the literature, which might be of particular interest to this book's professional or research-oriented audience. These and other titles would have complemented those sources that are included. Still, for locating many current and retrospective sources on the changing family, this bibliography will be a valuable resource. [R: Choice, Oct 88, p. 296; RBB, 1 June 88, p. 1657; WLB, Apr 88, p. 101]

Stephen H. Aby

766. Watkins, Kathleen Pullan. **Parent-Child Attachment: A Guide to Research.** New York, Garland, 1987. 190p. index. (Reference Books on Family Issues, Vol. 11; Garland Reference Library of Social Science, Vol. 388). $27.00. LC 87-23614. ISBN 0-8240-8465-9.

The phenomenon of parent-child attachment and how it begins has attracted the attention of researchers for more than seventy years. During that period several theoretical models of the attachment process have been developed and numerous empirical studies have been undertaken. In this guide to research in this area, Watkins lists a number of studies published between 1976 and 1986 as well as some classic older works. The publications are grouped in eleven chapters dealing with such topics as "Theories of Attachment Relations," "Attachment Relations in the Adoptive Family," "Attachment to the Child with Chronic Illness or Congenital Anomaly," and "Attachment in Adolescent and Other Single-Parenting Situations." Each chapter includes a six- to ten-page essay analyzing the current developments and issues in the area as well as a bibliography listing approximately twenty to fifty studies. Brief descriptive annotations are given for items listed. Only English-language material is included, and most of the items are monographs rather than journal articles. Both scholarly writing and those aimed at the general public are listed; sometimes both the scholarly and popular versions of the same work can be found. While not pretending to be a comprehensive bibliography of this important topic, this volume will be a good starting place for undergraduate

essays as well as for readers seeking basic information in the field. [R: Choice, July/Aug 88, p. 1679; RBB, Aug 88, p. 1906]

Adele M. Fasick

PHILANTHROPY

767. **Corporate Foundation Profiles.** 5th ed. New York, New Foundation Center, 1988. 688p. $75.00pa. LC 80-69622. ISBN 0-87954-237-3.

768. **The Foundation Center Source Book Profiles January-March 1988: A Quarterly Information Service....** Francine Jones, ed. New York, Foundation Center, 1988. 1v. (various paging). index. $295.00 (4 issues). LC 77-79015. ISBN 0-87954-235-7.

Concentrating on company-sponsored foundations to the exclusion of direct giving, *Corporate Foundation Profiles* notes 771 top American business donors with assets of $1,000,000 or more and annual giving of $100,000 or more. With forty-seven new listings, mainly established during the 1980s by service industries, and forty-two deletions due to mergers and terminations, this fifth edition analytically describes 240 foundations in detail in part 1. Timely two-to-six-page entries, arranged alphabetically by company, include the foundation's address, telephone number, contact, purpose, limitations, personnel, financial data, number of staff, sponsoring companies and background, grant analysis (by types, support recipient type, geographical distribution, and sample grants), foundation publications, policies and application guidelines, funding cycle, and sources. Part 2 presents in a single-line entry the foundation name, state location, total giving, grant amounts, number of grants, asset amount, and fiscal date of both part 1 entries and 531 additional corporate foundations. The subject index is preceded by a list of the subjects used. Corporate names in boldface type give regionally or nationally; others are geographically restrictive. Additional indexes are by type of support, geographical location with *see also* references, and name. For similar information on corporate foundations consult the costlier titles, *Taft Corporate Giving Directory* (see *ARBA* 86, entry 809) or *Corporate 500* (see *ARBA* 88, entry 841).

Corporate Foundation Profiles, which is paperbound, reproduces entries of business-based grantmakers drawn from *Source Book Profiles*, which also includes other charitable foundations. Issued quarterly (three in paper, one bound) on a two-year publishing cycle,

Source Book lists 125 foundations per cumulated volume, until the top one thousand are covered. Its value lies in its currency and accuracy. Its entries account for 60 percent of grant dollars awarded in a year, while the entry verification by the foundations themselves stands at 85 percent. Entry and index formats have been described above. Producers note an expanded and more precise index vocabulary, but a keyword index would prove even more valuable. A "U" following the index entry indicates new information will be found in that entry; the "Foundation Profile Updates" section lists these changes separately. Active university development offices and libraries with in-depth foundation collections may utilize both *Corporate Foundation Profiles* and *Source Book Profiles*. Budget may well determine the choice made by many libraries.   Eleanor Ferrall

769.   Dolnick, Sandy F., ed. **Fundraising for Nonprofit Institutions.** Greenwich, Conn., JAI Press, 1987. 268p. illus. index. (Foundations in Library and Information Science, Vol. 19). $28.25; $56.50 (institutions). LC 87-31200. ISBN 0-89232-387-6.

Seventeen authors, all with practical experience in trying to get funds for nonprofit agencies, have contributed their best thinking to this volume. While not focused on libraries as such, a number of examples are drawn from our turf, and most of the information presented is certainly relevant.

The book is organized in two sections: six general discussions on types of fundraising and ten very specific "how-we-do-it-good" case studies. Unlike many works aimed at the library profession, the discussion ranges far beyond government and corporate grants. The general section includes, in addition to the expected chapters on government and foundation funding, discussions of marketing, community assessment techniques, retail business operations, and the use of Friends groups. The case studies are even more instructive: among the techniques used are direct-mail campaigns, personal solicitation of individuals, use of personal contacts with the wealthy, celebrity dinners, and "fun runs." Rather than using a grant as the example of government funding, Richard Waters presents the bond issue for the Dallas Public Library. While not presented as such, Daniel Switzer's detailed discussion of the operation of a "ball" is probably the most detailed case, and certainly one of the most interesting.

In any collection covering so much ground, detail tends to get lost. In fact, perhaps the least satisfactory sections are those on the grant process, which is covered better in such sources as Emmett Corry's *Grants for Libraries* (see *ARBA* 87, entry 584). As an idea stimulator and for outlines of "ideas that work," this text is excellent, but no one should go out and do likewise based solely on this. In fact, the paucity of bibliographic or other references is a serious flaw.

This book is generally well written; its photographs, sample stationery, posters, and the like are surprisingly clear for nonphotographic reproductions; and the index is adequate. However, this reviewer objects strenuously to the price: the spread of two-tier pricing to a monograph is an abomination. Aside from the philosophical issue, there is a practical point: this book is worth $28.25; for $56.50, many will prefer other available titles.

James H. Sweetland

770.   Gilbert, Sara. **Lend a Hand: The How, Where, and Why of Volunteering.** New York, William Morrow, 1988. 160p. index. $11.95. LC 87-32077. ISBN 0-688-07247-X.

The purpose of *Lend a Hand* is to list "voluntary organizations that perform a wide variety of useful services and that welcome the assistance of young people" (p. xv). The title of this reference work is somewhat misleading since it does not indicate or imply the book's major emphasis (volunteer work for young people).

The book includes over one hundred nonprofit organizations that responded to a letter/questionnaire from the author. Over 250 nonprofit organizations were selected from the *Encyclopedia of Associations* for possible inclusion. Those who responded were included and descriptions are in the words of the organization in question.

The work is divided into three main categories: "Why Volunteer?" "Where to Volunteer," and "How to Volunteer." It is further subdivided into seven chapters which fall within the main categories. Chapter 3, "Who Needs Help; What They Do; How to Find Them," contains the list of organizations arranged under broad subject categories such as animals, the elderly, politics and government, etc. There are a generally useful alphabetical list of organizations and a subject index at the back of the book.

In addition to the information provided on service-oriented organizations, there are many helpful "guidelines" provided for those interested in volunteering. Young people and guidance counselors who work with young people should find *Lend a Hand* useful in a variety of ways. It is an obvious selection for public library and junior/senior high school library reference collections.   Larry G. Chrisman

771. **Grants for Museums.** New York, Foundation Center, 1988. 87p. index. $40.00pa. ISBN 0-87954-259-4.

One in a series of twenty-six that The Foundation Center calls its COMSEARCH: Broad Topics, this selective listing of grants sources will prove a time saver to fund seekers in museums, historical societies, or archives; arboretums; botanical gardens; planetariums; zoos; wildlife and nature preserves; aquariums; and art galleries, centers, institutes, associations, or commissions. Opening tables depict grant amounts given by each foundation, grant amounts by recipient locations, and the top fifteen recipients by single highest grant amount. Entries in the main section, culled from the *Foundation Grants Index* (see *ARBA* 83, entry 48), provided 2,001 grants of $5,000.00 or more, most awarded in 1986 and 1987. Donor names appear alphabetically under each state and the District of Columbia, followed by number-identified recipients, amount of grant, date of authorization, and description of activity funded. Users are urged in the introduction to study carefully the limitations to giving that are succinctly summarized under each donor foundation. Three indexes are provided to the grants entries: recipient name, recipient location (geographic), and subject (keyword). An alphabetical directory of the foundations follows the indexes, again, but briefly, noting limitations. Type is small but legible on the 8½-by-11-inch double-column pages. Updated since its 1982 initial appearance, this specialized directory will justify its cost to those in the specialized areas it serves.   Eleanor Ferrall

772. Layton, Daphne Niobe. **Philanthropy and Voluntarism: An Annotated Bibliography.** New York, Foundation Center, 1987. 308p. index. $18.50pa. LC 87-12032. ISBN 0-87954-198-9.

This "annotated" bibliography lists 1,614 books and articles on philanthropy and voluntarism. The author indicates that "I have highlighted through annotations, 244 works of scholarly quality or other exceptional value in illuminating aspects of giving, volunteering, and associated topics" (p. xii). The annotations appear to average approximately 150 words in length and tend to be descriptive rather than evaluative. It should be noted, however, that the selection of a title to be annotated in this work is in itself a type of evaluation. The book is organized into four parts and twenty chapters, and the organizational scheme is explained in detail in the author's preface. An author index and a subject index facilitate the reader's use of this bibliography.

In the foreword by Stanley N. Katz, president of the American Council of Learned Societies, it is noted that "until now there has been no comprehensive bibliography of philanthropy and voluntarism, with the result that students, scholars, and the general public have no systematic aid to understanding the field." This appears to be the first attempt at a comprehensive bibliography of the subject. As such, all library users interested in philanthropy and voluntarism should find it an extremely useful introduction to the literature of this field. [R: Choice, Dec 87, p. 602]
                    Larry G. Chrisman

773. **National Data Book.** 12th ed. New York, Foundation Center, 1988. 936p. $75.00pa. LC 81-71421. ISBN 0-87954-234-9.

774. **National Data Book: Index.** 12th ed. New York, Foundation Center, 1988. 191p. $65.00pa. LC 81-71421. ISBN 0-87954-234-9.

Revised and enlarged annually, *National Data Book* appears in two volumes. Entries in the main volume include 25,639 private grant making foundations and 250 community foundations awarding grants of $1.00 or more, plus eighteen community foundations with no current awards and 677 private operating foundations that support only their own research or programs. Arrangement is by state, then by grant amount in descending order within three main divisions: private grant making foundations, community foundations, and operating foundations. Entries note address, principal officer, fiscal information, annual report availability, and IRS number. The index volume provides a single alphabetical listing of all entries with their state, with their sequence entry numbers in the main volume. As always in Foundation Center publications, valuable materials are provided in the introductory material. This title includes hints for its usage, foundation characteristics, statistical analyses, and a bibliography of state and local foundation directories. Both Mary W. George (see *ARBA* 82, entry 78) and Charlotte Georgi (see *ARBA* 86, entry 807) gave thumbs-up recommendations to the fifth and ninth editions, respectively, of this reference tool. I follow suit for this twelfth edition.
                    Eleanor Ferrall

SEX STUDIES

775. Everett, Jane, and Walter D. Glanze. **The Condom Book: The Essential Guide for Men and Women.** New York, New American Library, 1987. 139p. $3.95pa. ISBN 0-451-15173-9.

Written for a popular audience by a New York City journalist (Everett) and a prolific editor of reference works and other books (Glaze), this short paperback is designed to promote the correct, consistent use of condoms. The dominant theme of the text is the inherent danger and health hazards posed by contemporary sexual relations and the necessary use of condoms as prophylactics. Almost no attention is given to the use of condoms as contraceptives. A twenty-two-page question and answer primer presents detailed, practical information on the usage of condoms that facilitates their acceptance and helps to dispel myths and stereotypes about them.

The bulk of the book is an annotated alphabetical list of over 108 specific brands of condoms. Each annotation has information on the name of the product, its manufacturer or distributor, packaging, description of the condom (e.g., material, shape, lubrication, odor, taste, color), and comments by users of the product.

The major value of the book is its importance as a consumer guide to condoms. Until now, practically no information was available for consumers to use in making their choices of prophylactics. Although the book's emphasis on the danger of not using condoms may encourage better sexual hygiene, the association of sexual relations with so much fear and danger of disease may have the unfortunate side effect of equating sexual relations in general with danger and disease. Such a view does not promote psychological well-being.

Suzanne G. Frayser

776. **Gay/Lesbian Events of 1988.** Chicago, Envoy Enterprises, 1987. 96p. $5.95pa. ISBN 0-945043-00-7.

This new annual publication aims to list events of interest to lesbians and gay men for the coming year throughout the United States. Although this is not stated, data were gathered via questionnaires from lesbian and gay organizations. The main body of the directory is a 1988 calendar, with events arranged under the day on which they are scheduled to occur. Entries include a brief description of the event plus sponsoring organization, address, and telephone number. Along with events, brief descriptions of historical events of interest to lesbians and gay men are scattered throughout. At the end of each month are events for the month for which a particular date was not known at the time of publication. A similar list follows the entire year. Events connected with annual Gay and Lesbian Pride celebrations are listed in a separate section. A subject index

provides access to events by type, with entries for alumni and students, bowling tournaments, camps and retreats, community organizations, concerts, contests, fairs and festivities, film festivals, political organizations, religious organizations, sports, square dancing and clogging, tours, women's gathering, etc.

This first edition lists a small fraction of lesbian- and gay-oriented events in the United States. If the publisher is able to increase its coverage, this should become a useful annual reference publication. [R: RBB, 1 June 88, p. 1648]

James D. Anderson

777. **An Index to *The Advocate*: The National Gay Newsmagazine 1967-1982.** Robert B. Marks Ridinger, comp. Los Angeles, Calif., Liberation, 1987. 280p. $30.00pa. ISBN 0-917076-08-7.

An index to all feature articles, news items, interviews, columns, reviews, and portfolios that appeared in *The Advocate* from September 1967 through December 1982, this specialized tool should be in every large public library and in academic libraries that support social science curricula. It will prove to be of great value for those researchers in the fields of sociology, law, political science, urban studies, anthropology, and psychology – to name but a few areas.

The work is arranged in fourteen sections, including a subject index to feature articles and news items; a geographical index to these same items; subject indexes to film, record, theater, and book reviews; a listing of all lesbian/gay periodicals cited; a chronological listing of all issues indexed; and a table of abbreviations of reviewers' names. Geographical and subject indexes list entries in chronological order under geographic subdivisions; reviews are indexed by author, title, composer, and/or group, as appropriate. Interviews are indexed by surname of interviewee, and portfolios, by artist's surname.

Thorough and well designed, this index is a welcome addition to the reference setting, by virtue of its providing avenues of access previously unavailable. Very highly recommended. [R: RBB, 1 June 88, p. 1647]

Edmund F. SantaVicca

778. Maggiore, Dolores J. **Lesbianism: An Annotated Bibliography and Guide to the Literature, 1976-1986.** Metuchen, N.J., Scarecrow, 1988. 150p. index. $18.50. LC 87-20613. ISBN 0-8108-2048-X.

This slim volume is half bibliography and half bibliographical essay and guide to the social science literature on lesbianism. Some three hundred entries in sociology, psychology, law, and feminist theory introduce the researcher to various aspects of lesbian existence such as identity, family relations, minority status, oppression, and health. The citations are from the period 1976-1986 and include descriptive and evaluative annotations. In addition, certain entries are marked with an asterisk to denote "those works which exemplify the best in each category" (p. 1). Not included are works that deal with gay men exclusively or that use data from research on gay men to generalize about lesbians. Also excepted are "works whose perspective on lesbianism is negative or contains erroneous information" (p. 1). The entries are arranged under five major topical headings, which are divided into sections. Some sections conclude with references to organizations which can be contacted for further information. Author and title indexes and a listing of other resources (bookstores, periodicals, and directories) are included.

The author/compiler is herself a social worker and the book is aimed specifically at social service practitioners whose clients may be lesbians. The lengthy "Overview of the Findings" is an excellent introduction to the special problems and needs of lesbians that must be considered by social workers in order to serve this population. It also points out areas where there is need for more research. [R: Choice, July/Aug 88, pp. 1675-76; RBB, 1 June 88, p. 1650]   Nancy Courtney

779. Richter, Alan. **The Language of Sexuality.** Jefferson, N.C., McFarland, 1987. 151p. bibliog. index. $19.95. LC 87-42520. ISBN 0-89950-245-8.

In this small book, the author attempts to demonstrate "how much of our ordinary language or terminology serves to provide metaphors for describing or understanding sexual activities, attitudes, organs, and so on" (p. 15). Chapter 1 deals with the general link between language and sex in humans and provides the theoretical context within which the remaining four chapters can be couched. Richter points out that although language does not totally reflect reality, its grammar and content reveal the importance of sexuality in English-speaking cultures. Their importance is brought out by identifying classes or types of words with sexual meanings, dividing them by levels of acceptability and spheres of usage (scientific, slang, informal expression, euphemism, taboo), and parceling out the focus of the content.

Each of the remaining chapters attempts to illustrate the general points in the first chapter by organizing sexual language into classes of terms related to different aspects of sexuality:

intercourse, female sex organs, male sex organs, and other aspects (actions, oral sex, people, states, aids, and objects). Within these classes, terms are grouped according to their association with such content categories as nature (e.g., flowers, animals) and culture (e.g., food, clothes, tools). Richter discusses the etymology of some words and briefly speculates on the reasons for the meaning of others. The glossary provides a quick overview of the extensive terminology discussed in the text and serves as an abbreviated dictionary.

Although he accomplishes much of what he set out to do, Richter stops short of substantive explanations for why the terms and meanings cluster as they do. However, his focus on the language itself highlights an important perspective from which other investigators can analyze the meaning of sexuality in our culture, where there are almost no current dictionaries or encyclopedias on the subject. [R: Choice, Mar 88, p. 1070; WLB, Feb 88, p. 101]

Suzanne G. Frayser

SOCIAL WELFARE AND SOCIAL WORK

780. **INFO LINE Taxonomy of Human Services.** By Georgia Sales. El Monte, Calif., Information and Referral Federation of Los Angeles County, 1987. 376p. bibliog. $75.00pa. ISBN 0-938371-00-2.

This INFO LINE taxonomy is an effort to establish a classification of human services that would be common to all agencies and personnel dealing with human services. The taxonomy includes major service categories and target groups: basic subsistence, consumer services, criminal justice and legal services, education, environmental quality, health care, income security, individual and family life, mental health care and counseling, organizational, community services, and target groups. The target group section enables users to access specific services for special groups such as teen family planning programs.

The work is arranged in a hierarchial system of broad terms and then broken down into more specific components. Definitions have been provided for all terms to ensure consistency throughout the hierarchy. *See also* references indicate related terms that will be useful access points for the user. The term identification numbers identify where the terms fall in the hierarchy (e.g., under health care, the broad term *health care* is designated as L, under it we find LD, *emergency medical care*, and broken down even more narrowly is LD-15, *emergency medical transportation* and LD-15.050, *air ambulance*. Each of these terms is then defined as to its specific category. The preface explains all of the descriptives used in the taxonomy. It includes an alphabetical listing and appendices for certain target groups.

INFO LINE is located in Los Angeles County, California, and provides twenty-four-hour (confidential) telephone information and referral services to human service agencies to meet the needs of the callers. Although designed primarily for this organization, this taxonomy could prove valuable for all human services agencies. Mary J. Stanley

781. NASW Register of Clinical Social Workers: Fall Addendum to the 1987 Fifth Edition. Silver Spring, Md., National Association of Social Workers, 1988. 263p. index. $60.00pa. LC 75-42777. ISBN 0-87101-162-X; ISSN 0277-0695.

The fifth edition of the *1987 NASW Register of Clinical Social Workers* and this *Fall Addendum* serve as an updating and inclusion of previous and new registrants in the field. In order to appear in the listing, applicants must give evidence of meeting the criteria and this evidence is reviewed by a peer board before acceptance. The listing is a voluntary process so there may be eligible social workers who meet the criteria but do not appear in the listing. Criteria for register listing and definition of clinical social work are included. Entries for individuals are similar to previous editions, containing addresses, telephone numbers, institutional affiliations, specializations, and experience. Entries are arranged by state and by city; there is also an alphabetical listing. This addendum is a good supplement to previous editions and is a complement to other directories of the helping professions. Mary J. Stanley

782. Public Welfare Directory, 1988/89. Amy Weinstein, ed. Washington, D.C., American Public Welfare Association, 1988. 473p. $55.00 pa. LC 41-4981. ISBN 0-910106-19-3; ISSN 0163-8297.

This annual publication provides a guide to the public human service programs throughout the United States and Canada. The information provided includes agencies; contact persons within these agencies; and a description of services offered by federal, state, territorial, county, and major municipal agencies.

The first segment lists the federal agencies by department with a short history and program development section. This is followed by agencies and divisions within the departments and key personnel, their addresses, and telephone numbers.

The state agencies section is in alphabetical order by state and specifically notes where to write for certain services (e.g., client inquiries or assistance services). Canadian agencies and provincial and territorial agencies follow the state agency section, formatted in the same manner.

Appendices include detailed information on such topics as interstate compacts, the Uniform Child Custody Jurisdiction Act, and Supplemental Security Income program. Each annual issue adds new listings in issue areas. This years' edition includes a listing for a contact person for immigration issues in each state. The 1987/1988 edition included a listing for a contact person in adolescent pregnancy programs in each state.

Agencies change in personnel frequently enough to warrant updating this annual publication. It is important in the field of public service and especially important for referral within the social work community.

Mary J. Stanley

SUBSTANCE ABUSE

783. The Directory of Addiction Professionals, 1988-89. John P. Sulima, Ann Simon, and Jeanie Charness, eds. Providence, R.I., Manisses Communications Group, 1988. 195p. index. $49.95pa.

This edition of an annual directory contains brief biographical information about two thousand individuals who deal with alcohol and drug abuse issues. A wide variety of occupations is listed, including addiction counselors, psychologists, social workers, writers, nurses, etc. The publication indicates that individuals were invited to be listed but does not indicate how these individuals were selected. The goal of this work is to identify a broad spectrum of individuals working in the alcohol and drug abuse fields. The multidisciplinary nature of these fields makes it difficult to assess the comprehensiveness of this publication. The paperback directory is divided into four sections which contain individuals grouped by name, by location (state and city), by profession, and by training programs grouped by state. The most comprehensive listing is the name index, which includes each person's job title, current employer, employer's address, and telephone number. Other information such as education, awards, professional associations, publications, etc., may also be included. The brief list of accredited training programs in alcoholism and drug abuse at colleges and universities in North America was compiled by the National Association of Substance Abuse Trainers and

Educators. Advertisements are interspersed throughout the directory.

Jacqueline Wilson

784. Miletich, John J., comp. **Work and Alcohol Abuse: An Annotated Bibliography.** Westport, Conn., Greenwood Press, 1987. 263p. index. (Bibliographies and Indexes in Sociology, No. 12). $39.95. LC 87-23619. ISBN 0-313-25689-6.

This is an English-language bibliography of more than one thousand references covering the years 1972-1986. Included are annotated references to books, articles, dissertations, theses, conference proceedings, and government publications. Although many countries are mentioned in the work, most of the materials listed were published in the United States, Canada, or Great Britain.

The references are presented in chapters headed as follows: "(1) Definitions, Identification, Diagnosis," "(2) Companies and Management," "(3) Unions, Safety, Employee Dismissal," "(4) Government," "(5) Specific Occupations," (6) Women," and "(7) Counseling and Treatment." There are author, subject, and company name indexes. The annotations for the most part are short, perhaps only a few lines, although some are a paragraph in length.

Since alcohol abuse by employees is a problem for many, including employers, employees, coworkers, families, and friends, this work should have broad appeal. It should interest company and government employees at all levels, medical professionals, and social workers as well as those interested in alcohol abuse and social problems in general. [R: Choice, Apr 88, p. 1223; RBB, 1 Apr 88, p. 1328]

Theodora Andrews

YOUTH AND CHILD DEVELOPMENT

785. Erickson, Judith B. **Directory of American Youth Organizations, 1988-89: A Guide to Over 400 Clubs, Groups, Troops, Teams, Societies, Lodges, and More for Young People.** Minneapolis, Minn., Free Spirit, 1988. 154p. bibliog. index. (Do Something! Book). $14.95 pa. LC 88-295. ISBN 0-915793-11-3.

The body of this directory is a list of four hundred national adult-sponsored, nonprofit organizations serving those through high school age. The spectrum of interests is broad: athletic, educational, service, civic and political, vocational and career, religious, honor societies, ethnic heritage, and a host of other areas. Entries are divided among sixteen interest categories and thereunder alphabetically by name.

Basic information for each organization includes name and date of formation, address and telephone number, and president or names of contact persons. For most entries, a brief description follows, generally about one hundred words long. An index provides access to organization names, acronyms, and subjects. The typefaces and layout enhance ease of use.

The nature of the supplemental material is indicative of the directory's broad audience. One introductory section advises children and adolescents on how to select an organization matching their interests, and another offers advice to parents. Material after the entries is directed toward youth leaders and counselors: a history of youth organizations in America, the potentials and problems inherent in volunteer youth groups, and future trends; a list of organizations concerned with youth advocacy, volunteerism, and leadership issues; and an annotated list of about sixty references to similar directories, general works on the role and impact of youth organizations, and histories of specific organizations.

The first edition of this directory was published in 1983 (see *ARBA 85*, entry 721). Overlap with the annual *Encyclopedia of Associations* and the spinoff *Youth-Serving Organizations Directory* (Gale, 1980) is considerable and not unexpected. As a specialized directory, however, it would be a valuable addition to school libraries at all levels and to public library reference collections. [R: RBB, 15 Dec 88, pp. 689-90; VOYA, Dec 88, p. 258]

Pam M. Baxter

786. Sheiman, Deborah Lovitky, and Maureen Slonim. **Resources for Middle Childhood: A Source Book.** New York, Garland, 1988. 138p. index. (Reference Books on Family Issues, Vol. 12; Garland Reference Library of Social Science, Vol. 433). $27.00. LC 88-18046. ISBN 0-8240-7777-6.

Middle childhood covers the years from six to twelve, the years during which most children are in elementary school. The format of this book is a series of short chapters covering physical development, psychosocial development, cognitive development, family interactions, play, peer relationships, schooling, and societal impact in relation to middle childhood. The six-to-eight pages of text in each chapter are followed by an annotated bibliography of related books. Most of the books listed were published during the 1980s although a few are from the late 1970s and there is a sprinkling of classics of the 1950s and 1960s. One of the authors, D. L. Sheiman, holds an Ed.D. degree (which is perhaps why the chapter on schooling is longer than the others), but the authors' affiliations are not listed and none of the chapter bibliographies lists publications by them. Because the chapters are so brief, they contain a number of sweeping generalizations such as: "The love of horses emerges [for girls]" as though every preteen girl went through this phase. The chapters are written in nontechnical style; indeed many of the references are to general publications such as the *New York Times Magazine*, and the bibliographies include mainly practical and popular treatments of the subject. A useful guide for parents and teachers who are dealing with elementary school age children.   Adele M. Fasick

787. Washington, Valora, and Ura Jean Oyemade. **Project Head Start: Past, Present, and Future Trends in the Context of Family Needs.** New York, Garland, 1987. 377p. bibliog. index. (Source Books on Education, Vol. 13; Garland Reference Library of Social Science, Vol. 378). $58.00. LC 87-11873. ISBN 0-8240-8521-3.

At $58.00 this is a rather expensive monograph, but in 377 pages it covers its subject well. While providing an excellent overview of the history of Project Head Start, the unique focus of the book is its concern with Head Start as a vehicle for helping poor families to achieve economic self-sufficiency. In its identification of current trends in family development the book will be of interest not only to those involved with the Head Start program, but also to all who are interested in family social policy.

For many of its years, Head Start has enjoyed wide popularity and is often cited as an example of a successful federal program. While recognizing positive aspects of the program, the authors urge caution and continued vigilance in monitoring Head Start's success. Particularly, they point to unresolved issues such as administrative changes, service delivery, and program effectiveness in light of the changing needs of today's families. A section that outlines specific responses the program can make to these challenges is a concise summary of a variety of solutions already suggested by agencies, groups, and individuals involved in the program.

Topically divided, the book succeeds in reviewing Head Start as a comprehensive child development program in the context of changing family trends. Essays, extensive reference lists, an annotated bibliography, and author/name and subject indexes provide and make accessible the information needed to promote more collaborative interaction between academic researchers, public policy makers, and program providers and users.

     Debbie Burnham-Kidwell

788. Wilson, Miriam J. Williams. **Help for Children: Hotlines, Helplines, and Other Resources.** 3d ed. Shepherdstown, W. Va., Rocky River, 1988. 114p. $5.95pa. ISBN 0-944576-00-1.

This updated third edition directory lists over two hundred hotlines, clearinghouses, associations, and other support systems that provide help with problems or emergency situations concerning children. Entries in each of the seven chapters contain the name of the organization, address, telephone number, and a brief description of the services offered. A useful index of names and telephone numbers is also included for quick reference by subject.

Intended to be representative of the major problems and issues concerning children, this book provides information on a variety of topics including child safety, drug abuse, missing and exploited children, health care, mental and physical handicaps, maternal care, and terminal illness. For both parents and child care professionals, it is a valuable reference source. An alphabetical arrangement of headings and entries, however, would have improved its readability. [R: RBB, 15 Apr 88, p. 1407]

     L. L. Schroyer

17 Statistics, Demography, and Urban Studies

DEMOGRAPHY

789. Biracree, Tom, and Nancy Biracree. **Almanac of the American People.** New York, Facts on File, 1988. 336p. index. $29.95. LC 88-3882. ISBN 0-8160-1821-9.

This almanac tries to present the main facts and statistics of American life in areas such as health, love, recreation, religion, housing, and money. Mostly presented in narrative form, statistics have been pulled from a wide range of government and private sources, including the Gallup Poll, Clairol, and the Census Bureau. The statistics as they are presented sometimes leave more questions than answers. For instance, in a very short section entitled "Who Uses the Library," we learn that 27 percent of Americans say they never go to a library. No attempt is made to differentiate this 27 percent from the other 73 percent in terms of age, education, income, or any other characteristics. Other tables are more complete, but in general a serious researcher will want the original source. Many of the statistics selected have entertainment value, such as a list of foods most people hate, or allow readers to compare themselves with others, such as a table listing what averages people actually weigh, rather than what they *should* weigh, or what people wear to bed as well as what they dream about when they get there.

This book will appeal to general readers, and especially in a public library can be used by those looking for pop sociology or demographics. The standard compendium of social, political, and economic statistics, of course, remains *The Statistical Abstract of the United States* (see *ARBA* 83, entry 725), and it is possible to subscribe to the Gallup Poll results on an annual basis, but even a library with these two sources will not have all the survey and other private data that appear herein.

Susan V. McKimm

790. Hillman, Thomas A. **Catalogue of Census Returns on Microfilm 1666-1891. Catalogue de Recensements sur Microfilm.** Ottawa, Canadian Government Publishing Centre, 1987. 289p. $18.00pa. ISBN 0-660-53711-7.

This is the official catalog published by the Public Archives of Canada listing the Canadian population census returns on microfilm available from the Public Archives for censuses from 1666 through 1891. It supersedes two previous catalogs published in 1978 and 1981, the first covering 1825-1871, the second covering 1666-1881. In addition to microfilms of the original census records in its own collection, the Public Archives has microfilmed copies of census records held in original form in the provincial archives of Ontario, New Brunswick, Nova Scotia, and Prince Edward Island.

The census listings are arranged by province and within province alphabetically by census subdistrict, with citations to the Public Archives reel numbers. The microfilm may be borrowed, three reels at a time, by any library participating in interlibrary loan. The reels are also available for sale from the Public Archives. The introduction to the catalog contains brief information on the various censuses, as well as general information for the census user. Since identifying the appropriate reel number is essential in requesting the film for purchase or for loan, this catalog is mandatory for any library with patrons using Canadian census materials.

Necia A. Musser

791. **The Population Atlas of China.** Compiled and edited by the Population Census Office of the State Council of the People's Republic of China and the Institute of Geography of the Chinese Academy of Sciences. New York, Oxford University Prress, 1987. 217p. maps. (col.). $195.00. LC 87-675262. ISBN 0-19-584092-5.

China, with 1,031,887,961 persons according to the 1982 census, is the most populous country, accounting for 22 percent of the world's total population. This monumental and authoritative atlas graphically summarizes the statistical data gathered in the 1982 census (the third), following censuses in 1953 and 1964, and is the first population atlas ever published by the Chinese government. It reflects four years of painstaking work by a large number of trained staff and specialists from the Population Census Office and the Institute of Geography of the Chinese Academy of Sciences. This immense volume (15 inches by 21 inches) contains 137 color maps, 32 pages of statistical tables, and explanatory text. For easy reference, the maps are grouped in eight sections: "Background Maps"; "Population Distribution"; "Ethnicity"; "Sex and Age"; "Population Change"; "Educational Level"; "Employment"; and "Family, Marriage and Fertility." Three appendices encompass main population indicators by county and city unit, autonomous areas of the People's Republic of China, and an index of county- and city-level administrative divisions.

The outstanding cartographic work combines technological sophistication and visual appeal. Most of the maps use a conical equal-area projection and are drawn on three common base maps: 1:8,000,000 (two pages), 1:12,000,000 (one page), or 1:16,000,000 (half page). The Gauss Kruger projection was used for six medium-scale maps in the population distribution section. To emphasize the demographic theme, the content of the base maps is highly selective and generalized. Two transparent overlays (in a pocket at the back) provide detailed identification of cities and counties omitted from the base maps to facilitate reading.

This long-awaited and comprehensive compilation of the census data should be a welcome addition to libraries and demographic collections. Researchers on contemporary China will find the wealth of information in the atlas valuable and easy to use. [R: Choice, June 88, p. 1539; LJ, 1 Apr 88, p. 80; RBB, 15 Apr 88, p. 1410]   Hwa-Wei Lee

792. Schulze, Suzanne. **Population Information in Twentieth Century Census Volumes: 1950-1980.** Phoenix, Ariz., Oryx Prress, 1988. 317p. maps. bibliog. $82.00. LC 88-17937. ISBN 0-89774-400-4.

Schulze's third census volume completes coverage of all the U.S. censuses beginning in 1790. Like the previous volumes (see *ARBA* 85, entry 740 and *ARBA* 86, entry 841), the format remains consistent. It allows the user clear and easy access to the often-confusing Census volumes. The inside covers, front and back, serve as guides detailing the subjects covered in

each volume of each Census. Once the particular volume is determined, the user goes into the guide to learn any pertinent bibliographic information about the volume and then to find in which specific table within the volume the data are located. One change from the earlier efforts is that Dubester Numbers no longer serve as base numbers for each volume.

In addition to tabular information, the author writes an introduction for each Census. Information is given regarding the "Major Population Reports" and even how these reports are bound. Also, within each introduction a section entitled "Population Inquiries" discusses the manner in which data were gathered for that particular Census. This includes the changes from house-to-house visitation to questionnaires through the mail. Also, sampling methods for various kinds of sociological and economic information are discussed. Very helpful, too, is the section entitled "Terminology Used in This Volume." It defines terms used in each Census as they pertained to each particular Census.

This volume, along with its predecessors, is invaluable to the librarian who has any contact with Census data. Schulze has presented it both thoughtfully and concisely. With it in hand, the librarian no longer needs to relearn the organization of each Census volume and report.

Phillip P. Powell

STATISTICS

793. **Encyclopedia of Statistical Sciences. Volume 8: Regressograms to St. Petersburg Paradox, The.** Samuel Kotz and Norman L. Johnson, eds.-in-chief. New York, John Wiley, 1988. 870p. illus. $115.00. LC 81-10353. ISBN 0-471-05556-5.

794. **Encyclopedia of Statistical Sciences. Volume 9: Strata Chart to Zyskind-Martin Models.** Samuel Kotz and Norman L. Johnson, eds.-in-chief. New York, John Wiley, 1988. 762p. index. $125.00. LC 81-10353. ISBN 0-471-85474-3.

Ambitious, impressive, and authoritative are the adjectives that come to mind in describing the *Encyclopedia of Statistical Sciences* (*ESS*). The nine handsome volumes that comprise the set are truly comprehensive. There are more than twenty-five hundred entries from over 750 contributors covering everything from "Abacus" to "Zyskind-Martin Models." All of the fields and subfields of statistics are included, along with more recent developments such as fractals and their applications.

ESS is designed to be comprehensible to experts and nonexperts, but novices should beware: elementary topics, such as standard error, are treated curtly. Most contributors have assumed a certain level of understanding in their entries, and this is as it should be. The more esoteric topics are written at a higher level. Experts will not be ashamed to refer to this encyclopedia.

Many of the topics, but not the elementary ones, are given extensive treatment. Computational techniques and examples are sometimes shown in detail; other entries give applications and historical backgrounds. Each entry is cross-referenced to related topics, and any references are listed in full. The entry for "U-Statistics" is eight pages long and lists sixty-nine references. In addition, many topics include a bibliography.

It can be a pleasure just to browse through these volumes. Biographies of the most eminent statisticians concentrate on their contributions and the significance of their work. All of the entries are informative and scholarly, and a few are even entertaining. Glenn Shafer's exposition of the St. Petersburg Paradox is an example of the latter.

A decade in the making, *ESS* is a must purchase for college and university libraries, government agencies, and private concerns that need an authoritative reference to the statistical sciences. The editors plan a supplementary volume and invite those interested in the development and execution of *ESS* to read their article in the *Journal of Official Statistics* (3 [1987]: 93-99).   Elia Kacapyr

795. **European Directory of Non-Official Statistical Sources 1988.** London, Euromonitor; distr., Detroit, Gale, 1988. 281p. index. $160.00 pa. ISBN 0-86338-258-4; ISSN 0953-0258.

The first detailed guide to European nonofficial statistics to be published, this directory lists in alphabetical order organizations which regularly produce, in over two thousand published titles, time-series statistics on particular markets, industries, products, and sectors. Included are trade associations (and their journals and periodicals), research organizations, financial institutions, and databases. Although the emphasis is on statistics from Pan-European sources and EEC countries, material from twelve other European countries is included.

The entries are compact, but detailed. They include name and address; title and frequency of publication; content coverage summary; code letter indicating origin of data; price; address and name of contact when available; telephone number, telex, and facsimile numbers when available; and comments with miscellaneous

information such as ISBN or ISSN, availability of publication, and language. There are two indexes: publishers by country and subject. The latter is sufficiently detailed, but user time could have been saved had the entries been numbered consecutively and the indexes referenced to an entry number rather than a page.

Since budget and cost conscious governments are publishing less and less, nonofficial sources are becoming more important. While there are some drawbacks to using nonofficial statistics, they are often more up-to-date, are sometimes more detailed, and may include types of material not included in official publications. Therefore, this carefully compiled directory should be very valuable to special libraries, very large public libraries serving the business community, some libraries of government agencies, and libraries in schools of business.

Laura H. McGuire

796. Evinger, William R., comp. **Federal Statistical Data Bases: A Comprehensive Catalog of Current Machine-Readable and Online Files.** Phoenix, Ariz., Oryx Press, 1988. 670p. index. $125.00. LC 86-42609. ISBN 0-89774-255-9.

This directory provides a complete listing of databases available from the federal government of the United States. Most of these databases are on tape, but the volume also catalogs online databases, diskettes, and microfiche files. The staggering amount of machine-readable information available from the federal government is conveniently summarized in this work, which supplants the Department of Commerce's *Directory of Federal Statistical Data Files*.

Each listing includes a concise description of the statistical information contained on the tape or other media. Geographic and time-period coverage are explicitly indicated. A short technical description provides information, such as the recording mode and character set used, that may be useful when reading the file. Other reference materials and related files are cross-referenced within each listing. Additionally, each entry gives the address and telephone number of contacts for the file along with the price.

The entries are alphabetically arranged within the various departments and agencies of the federal government. The Bureau of the Census provides most of the listings in the volume. Entries are easily located through the subject index.

I found this volume to be remarkably complete. The few obscure databases I know of are listed and the descriptions that accompany each entry are useful and informative. [R: Choice, Oct 88, p. 290; JAL, Sept 88, p. 265]

Elia Kacapyr

797. **Statistical Yearbook 1987.** Paris, UNESCO; distr., Lanham, Md., UNIPUB, 1987. 1v. (various paging). $81.00pa. ISBN 92-3-002480-5.

This standard reference work from the United Nations is a massive compilation of statistics related to education and educational expenditures, science and technology, libraries and publishing, archives and museums, film, radio and television, and the performing arts. Included are 207 countries. A detailed table of contents serves as an index. New tables introduced in the text are identified in this list by the symbol #. The work is not easy to use because of its bulk and the necessity for thin paper pages to accommodate the many data presentations and the multilingual introductions to each section. The introduction to each section includes text in English, French, and Spanish. An appendix at the end of the volume gives these introductions in Arabic. The tables are compiled from reports filed periodically by the member states with UNESCO on laws, regulations, and statistics related to "educational, scientific and cultural life and activities." Every effort is made for accuracy and completeness by using whatever sources are available to the Secretariat of UNESCO. In most instances the data are presented in tabular form. Some line graphs, pie charts, and block diagrams illustrate reports, particularly in the section on science and technology. Although it is expensive, this reference item should be available in every library except the smallest.   Edward P. Miller

798. **USA by Numbers: A Statistical Portrait of the United States.** Susan Weber, ed. Washington, D.C., Zero Publication Growth, 1988. 164p. illus. maps. $8.95pa. LC 88-58. ISBN 0-945219-00-8.

Users of statistics today can select from a number of compilations according to their needs; this new addition to the field sets out to be a "guided tour through the thicket of statistics that underlie and punctuate a host of American public policies, social problems, and environmental issues," and it succeeds admirably. It gives the broad picture, not details of small areas. In thirteen chapters, with eighty-five charts, graphs, and maps, it presents population-linked data for the United States, with time series long enough to show trends. Included are statistics on population, age, fertility, adolescent sexuality, abortion, immigration (legal and illegal), rich and poor, water use, airborne poisons, etc. Each chapter begins with a brief summary of its contents, and the easy to read tables have unusually clear explanatory notes. Statistics have been pulled out of a mass of published and unpublished data collected by agencies of the federal government (Bureau of the Census, National Center for Health Statistics, Geological Survey, etc.) as well as from materials furnished by important private sources, such as the Alan Gutmacher Institute, which supplied information on adolescent sexuality. Most of the information dates from the mid-1980s, with some as recent as 1987. In some instances figures shown are the result of calculations based on raw data, much of it difficult to find. The volume has no index, but because of a very good table of contents and excellent overall organization, one scarcely notices this lack.

This affordable little reference gem is a *must* for all kinds of libraries. A caution: although this paperback is sturdily bound, prepare for heavy use by protecting the cover and reinforcing the spine as soon as it arrives. [R: LJ, 15 June 88, p. 53]

Laura H. McGuire

799. **The World in Figures.** Compiled by *The Economist*. Boston, G. K. Hall, 1988. 296p. illus. maps. index. $65.00. ISBN 0-8161-8954-4.

This handsome and impressive volume is loaded with excellent maps, charts, graphs, and tables. It even comes with book-ribbons to mark frequently used pages.

The statistical information, covering over two hundred countries, is arranged into two sections. The first section considers a statistical category, such as gross domestic product, and ranks the countries in descending order. A few of the many statistical categories covered are inflation, trade, tourism, and finance. This section also includes some wonderful charts, such as the one on page 51, that neatly condense a myriad of information on world trade.

The second section considers each nation individually. The data for each country include a small map that demonstrates location and all the standard demographic statistics. Political and economic summaries are given along with a host of other economic and financial information. It seems that more information is provided for the countries with larger economies. Then again, these larger economies collect more statistical information.

Econometricians and other diligent data gatherers will notice that this volume is no substitute for the original sources of the data. The most recent year for most of the data is 1985 and time series data are not provided. Yet one will frequently use this comprehensive, unique volume as a quick and reliable source of international economic data. [R: RBB, 15 Apr 88, p. 1412]

Elia Kacapyr

URBAN STUDIES

800.   Chandler, Tertius. **Four Thousand Years of Urban Growth: An Historical Census.** Lewiston, N.Y., St. David's University Press/Edwin Mellen Press, 1987. 656p. maps. bibliog. index. $89.95. LC 86-31122. ISBN 0-88946-207-0.

This book is a complete revision, with new population estimates and sources and longer time coverage, of Chandler's previous work. It is the standard work on the populations of cities (that is, urban areas including suburbs but excluding rural areas) from 2250 B.C. to 1975.

Population estimating for periods in which no census data are available—by far the largest portion of this book—is achieved by considering known events or population subtotals and determining a relevant multiplier. For example, by knowing the number of public baths in a Moslem city and using the scholarly estimate of one thousand people per bath, one can calculate a reasonable estimate for total urban population. Other information used includes the number of guilds, battle casualties, plague victims, or Catholic Church communicants.

The population estimating method requires a considerable amount of research, and the author has compiled a sixty-three-page bibliography. Works cited include dissertations, scholarly monographs, and journal articles.

The main section of the volume includes data for ancient cities. This information is subdivided into pre-800 and 800-1850, then by broad geographic division: Europe, the Americas, Africa, and Asia. For each city, the author cites years, populations, notes, and sources for the population estimates. Other sections of the work are outline maps and tables of the world's largest cities, and there is an index of place names.

As the standard work in the field, this volume belongs in research libraries. [R: Choice, June 88, p. 1530]

Linda A. Naru

801.   **Cities of the United States: A Compilation of Current Information on Economic, Cultural, Geographic, and Social Conditions. Volume 1: The South.** Deborah A. Straub and Diane L. Dupuis, eds. Detroit, Gale, 1988. 403p. illus. maps. index. $69.95. ISBN 0-8103-2501-2; ISSN 0899-6075.

Cities of the United States is to provide information on more than one hundred cities in four volumes devoted to the South, West, Midwest, and Northeast, respectively. Volume 1 includes thirty cities in the South.

Information on each city follows a regular structure: the city in brief (key statistics), introduction, geography and climate, history, population profile, municipal government, economy, education and research, health care, recreation, convention facilities, transportation, and communications. The section on recreation is particularly full and useful, including subsections on sightseeing, arts and culture, festivals and holidays, sports for the spectator, sports for the participant, and shopping and dining. The section on education and research covers elementary and secondary schools, colleges and universities, and libraries and research centers. The section on the economy discusses major industries and commercial activity, labor force and employment outlook (including number of workers in major activities and largest employers), and cost of living. The information is based on federal government statistics, local authorities (including chambers of commerce, convention and visitors' bureaus, and other local sources), and diverse publications.

Each city is illustrated by two or three photographs and a simple but clear map showing the regional context, access by interstate highways, and the location of universities and colleges. A useful addition would be a simple map of the downtown area, showing the location of hotels, convention centers, restaurants, shopping streets and malls, museums and galleries, libraries, concert halls, theaters, sports facilities, parks, banks and office buildings, and other points a visitor is likely to look for, often on foot from a hotel or convention center.

The volume is designed for people vacationing, conventioneering, or relocating: businesspersons, market researchers, students, media professionals, researchers, and decision makers. The value of the work consists mainly in the convenience of having standard comparable information for larger American cities, culled from numerous sources, handily assembled, well organized, and clearly presented in a single publication.

Chauncy D. Harris

802.   **Consumer Guide Best-Rated Retirement Cities & Towns.** New York, New American Library, 1988. 160p. maps. $6.95pa. ISBN 0-451-82174-2.

Although his name does not appear on the cover or title page, Norman D. Ford, who has written several books on retirement living and travel, is the contributing author of this work. It describes ninety-two cities and towns across America judged the most attractive retirement locations. Ratings are based on twelve criteria: climate and elevation, quality of life, affordability, housing, leisure activities, cultural activities, health care, community services, safety and law enforcement, employment opportunities, volunteer opportunities, and economic outlook. Ninety of the communities are in sixteen states—Alabama, Arizona, Arkansas, California, Colorado, Florida, Georgia, Louisiana, Mississippi, Missouri, Nevada, New Mexico, North Carolina, South Carolina, Texas, and Utah—and two in Mexico. Colorado Springs, Colorado, and Chapel Hill, North Carolina, share the highest ranking, with Key West, Florida, at the bottom.

Unlike the *Rand McNally Retirement Places Rated* (see *ARBA* 88, entry 874), which covers 131 places and is divided into chapters devoted to subjects of concern to retirees, this guide is organized geographically, with brief alphabetically arranged chapters for each state included and for Mexico. Locations of specific communities are not shown on the maps provided and sources of statistical information are not cited, but addresses of local chambers of commerce are furnished. This book, although not nearly as comprehensive as the *Rand McNally* guide, can be useful in public libraries.

Leonard Grundt

803.   Ekstrom, Brenda L., and F. Larry Leistritz. **Rural Community Decline and Revitalization: An Annotated Bibliography.** New York, Garland, 1988. 203p. index. (Garland Reference Library of Social Science, Vol. 443). $28.00. LC 88-2418. ISBN 0-8240-2433-8.

This work examines the decline and revitalization of rural communities within the industrialized countries in North America, Europe, and Australia. Only materials written in English, generally between 1975 and 1987, are included. The book is divided into two broad categories, rural economic decline and revitalization. The first category is subdivided into five sections: demographic, economic, public service, social and psychological effects, and policies and issues. The second section is divided into six sections: general topics, improving the efficiency of existing resources, expanding and diversifying the economic base, financing, planning and assessment, and policies and issues. The literature cited reviews the economic, demographic, public service, fiscal, and social and psychological effects of a declining economic base. It also examines a variety of economic development strategies and analyzes major policy issues associated with economic decline and revitalization. Many of the items cited are special reports, which are often difficult to find, prepared by a number of different economic development organizations. The compilers tried to make sure that the works cited were available through interlibrary loan.

Included are two detailed indexes, one by author, the other by subject. This is a good addition to the literature. [R: Choice, Oct 88, p. 288]   Robert L. Turner, Jr.

804.   **Metro Insights.** 1989 ed. Lexington, Mass., Data Resources, 1988. 1137p. maps. $449.00. ISBN 0-07-607001-8.

Published by a nationally known forecasting and marketing demographics firm, *Metro Insights* presents economic, demographic, and marketing information for one hundred of the "top" U.S. metropolitan areas. (Although some states are represented by several cities, each state has at least one city listed.) The information is drawn from Data Resources's own private database and from public resources such as the consumer price index and business market indexes.

The purpose of the compendium is to offer in a single source concise information that can be easily compared across the urban markets covered. Consequently, all entries follow a consistent format, presenting information on critical industries, employment, consumer spending, local economy, manufacturing and nonmanufacturing fields, market potential, demographic breakdown, infrastructure, construction markets, and the area's strengths and weaknesses. Several paragraphs are devoted to each of these topics; although brief, the analyses are thoughtful and timely. The points made in the text are supplemented throughout by intelligently chosen, clearly rendered graphs and charts. Two appendices—one on metropolitan area definitions by county and the other an overview of data sources and definitions (especially helpful to the novice researcher)—conclude the book.

Metro Insights would be a useful resource for any company needing to compare economic, market, industrial, or demographic data across major urban markets. Which is the fastest growing metropolitan area in a given region? How does per capita growth compare across markets? Does New York, Los Angeles, or Chicago have the largest concentration of college-educated twenty-five to forty-five-year-olds? These are the kinds of questions that *Metro Insights* is designed to answer. It does not, of course, take the place of more in-depth local information sources such as the regional chambers of commerce, but for business libraries, it can provide a handy, one-stop source for a vast amount of easily compared metropolitan data.

G. Kim Dority

805.   **A Survey of Income and Expenditure of Urban Households in China 1985.** By State

Statistical Bureau, People's Republic of China. Beijing, China Statistical Information and Consultancy Service Centre, and Honolulu, East-West Population Institute, East-West Center; distr., Honolulu, University of Hawaii Press, 1988. 171p. maps. $29.95pa. LC 87-36588. ISBN 0-86638-105-8.

In recent years a new pattern of joint publication has emerged in China. This statistical compilation copublished by the State Statistical Bureau of the People's Republic of China and the East-West Center Population Institute is a recent example. Other joint publications by the State Statistical Bureau have included the *Statistical Yearbook of China* (see *ARBA* 86, entry 827) and *China Urban Statistics, 1985* (see *ARBA* 87, entry 841), both with different copublishers.

As is evident from the title, this compilation of urban household income and expenditure in China was based on a survey conducted in 1985. It gathered data on family composition, employment, income and expenditure, consumer structure, and quantities of major consumer goods in nonagricultural households from 106 cities and 77 county towns randomly, but systematically, selected throughout China. The 1985 samples, much expanded from previous annual surveys, also included, for the first time, non-wage-earner households (pension recipients, individual laborers, etc.) in addition to wage-earner households. Other than a one-page introduction and a two-page note, "Concepts and Definitions," the publication consists of fifteen tables of basic household statistics and forty-seven tables of economic statistics. The detailed information from the survey should be of value to researchers on recent Chinese social and economic conditions.

Hwa-Wei Lee

18   Women's Studies

ALMANACS

806. Clark, Judith Freeman. **Almanac of American Women in the 20th Century.** New York, Prentice Hall Press, 1987. 274p. illus. index. $24.95; $15.95pa. LC 86-43172. ISBN 0-13-022658-0; 0-13-022641-6pa.

Clark has produced an intriguing combination of substance and trivia in this work. Almanac-style date-and-event entries are interspersed with short essays, primarily biographical but also covering general topics such as "Early Labor Activists and Organizers," "The Baby Boom," and "The Vietnam War." The biographies focus on women active in social change, with lesser emphasis on literary and artistic figures, scientists, sports figures, and business women. Almanac entries are arranged chronologically and identified with general headings such as "Women's Issues," "Popular Culture," "Sports," "Arts and Culture," "Ideas/Beliefs," "Business," "Military," "Judicial," and "Legislative." The almanac is fun to read and educational, providing a fascinating overview of women's history during the twentieth century as well as highlighting important individuals and movements. Unfortunately, it is seriously marred as a reference work by a names-only index that makes it almost impossible to trace events or movements over time or to answer "who did what" questions when only the "what" is known. [R: LJ, Aug 87, p. 115; RBB, 15 Oct 87, p. 374]   Susan Davis Herring

BIBLIOGRAPHIES

807. Brady, Anna, comp. **Women in Ireland: An Annotated Bibliography.** Westport, Conn., Greenwood Press, 1988. 478p. index. (Bibliographies and Indexes in Women's Studies, No. 6). $45.00. LC 87-25043. ISBN 0-313-24486-3.

Brady, an assistant professor and bibliographer for Irish Studies and Women's Studies at Queens College, City University of New York, warns readers in her preface that her work is "neither exhaustive, definitive, nor fully comprehensive." In all likelihood, readers will be more astonished by what this ambitious bibliography does include than disappointed by what it omits. Nearly five hundred pages long, *Women in Ireland* lists over twenty-three hundred primarily English-language sources (books, chapters in books, articles, dissertations and theses, pamphlets, and more) arranged in fourteen subject areas. The focus is on "women of Irish ancestry whose lives were spent primarily in Ireland [and] those of whatever ancestry or place of residence whose achievement or recognition was related to Irish affairs or to intimate connection with well-known Irish figures" (p. xv) from early Celtic times to "the present" (which appears to mean 1985). Better than 50 percent of the items fall in the three largest sections: "Biography and Autobiography"; "Employment and Economic Life"; and "Literature, Folklore and Mythology." Fiction, poetry, and most literary criticism are excluded; material on Northern Ireland is "probably underrepresented" (p. xi). Brady provides descriptive annotations of varying length for most entries, scope notes at the beginning of major topical sections and subsections, and author and subject indexes to aid the user in finding and sorting through the voluminous material.

Brady offers the bibliography as "a useful beginning resource" (p. xii) to stimulate further research. Although they will surely appreciate the headstart Brady gives them, U.S. researchers will likely find the next step a challenge. "[M]ost of the relevant literature ... is only, or more readily, available in Ireland" (p. xi), Brady informs us, and indeed many of the sources are published by small Irish presses or periodicals. Still, with Brady's contribution, research on Irish women has taken a significant step forward. [R: Choice, July/Aug 88, p. 1671; C&RL, July 88, p. 349]

Catherine R. Loeb

808. Duffy, Susan, comp. **Shirley Chisholm: A Bibliography of Writings by and about Her.** Metuchen, N.J., Scarecrow, 1988. 135p. index. $17.50. LC 88-2073. ISBN 0-8108-2105-2.

The 1,140 items in this bibliography are divided into four major sections: "Primary Source Material," "General Bibliography," "Newspaper Articles," and "Miscellaneous

Material." Each section is organized by the format of the material. The first section contains references to books, essays, letters, newspaper and periodical articles, and speeches written by Shirley Chisholm, as well as to recordings, videotapes, and films of her. The introduction states "this bibliography does not include the numerous citations in *The Congressional Record*, 1971-1977." However, the subsection "Speeches" lists three references to that publication within that time period, as well as several earlier references. It is unclear what the criteria were for deciding to include references from the *Record*. "General Bibliography" refers to books and periodicals about Chisholm in addition to ERIC documents, dissertations and theses, government publications, and children's books. Also included in this section are a list of references to articles in *Congressional Quarterly Almanac* (see *ARBA* 88, entry 728). "Newspaper Articles" lists citations to eight newspapers, including the *Christian Science Monitor* and *Wall Street Journal*. There are also two sections on miscellaneous New York and national newspapers. The final section, "Miscellaneous Material," contains references to material found mainly in the Schomburg Center for Research in Black Culture at the New York Public Library. A number of references to newspaper articles are without complete bibliographic information but refer to the vertical file at the Schomburg Center. Very few of the references are annotated. There is an index to personal names and a brief subject index. [R: Choice, Oct 88, p. 288]

                        Nancy Courtney

809. Frost, Wendy, and Michele Valiquette. **Feminist Literary Criticism: A Bibliography of Journal Articles 1975-1981.** New York, Garland, 1988. 867p. index. (Garland Reference Library of the Humanities, Vol. 784). $120.00. LC 87-35325. ISBN 0-8240-7788-1.

    Frost and Valiquette define feminist literary criticism as one facet of "the broader feminist enterprise," in which the feminist critic "by taking gender as the starting point ... generates radically new visions" of literature (p. xiii). This work attempts to bring such visions together. Covering only seven years, the authors have concentrated on a period during which many of the basic theories were developed, but much of the work was not indexed.

    The bibliography includes nearly 1,950 entries from over 460 journals ranging from mainstream academic to radical feminist. Each entry includes a full citation, subject headings, and occasional notes. No annotations are given, but the subject headings, while not evaluative, provide some sense of the content. The headings

have been created by the compilers to fill a perceived gap; they are highly detailed and specific but sometimes seem exceedingly convoluted, for example, "Critical Schools, Other, Relation to Feminist Criticism — Freudian/Psychoanalytic Criticism." The entries are arranged in seven general categories: textual and contextual criticism by period (antiquity to twentieth century), interviews and self-profiles, multiple time periods, folklore and oral tradition, language and gender, pedagogy and research, and theory.

    Indexes provide good access to entries by subject heading, author/work, and critic. The lengthy, well-documented introduction gives a solid historical and theoretical background to feminist literary criticism as a radical movement and could be useful as a survey article. Other nice touches include the clear, concise users' guides to the bibliography and to the subject index.

    Overall, this is a well-done, comprehensive work. Despite its fairly high cost, it will be useful to any institution dealing with literary topics or women's studies. Any confusion caused by the unfamiliar subject headings will be more than balanced by the depth and breadth of the material. [R: Choice, Oct 88, pp. 290-92]

                        Susan Davis Herring

810. Glenn, Judith A., comp. **Select Bibliography of Women's Studies: Holdings of the Women's Center Library at Oregon State University 1987.** Corvallis, Oreg., for William Jasper Kerr Library by Oregon State University Press, 1987. 271p. (Kerr Library Bibliographic Series, No. 21). $6.95pa. ISBN 0-87071-281-0.

    This is a simple bibliographic listing of approximately one thousand monographs held by the Women's Center Library at Oregon State University. Separate author and title listings contain complete bibliographic information for each item. The citations are repeated under twenty-eight subject headings such as anthologies, computers, family, and lifestyles. There are no annotations. A two-page list of periodical holdings is included, most of which "represent incomplete runs and/or miscellaneous special issues" (268), as well as a fourteen-item list of "miscellaneous" material, some of which is available "at desk" (271).

    There is nothing particularly new or hard to locate in this bibliography which will best serve only members of the Oregon State community.

                        Nancy Courtney

811. Leavitt, Judith A. **Women in Administration and Management: An Information Sourcebook.** Phoenix, Ariz., Oryx Press, 1988.

228p. index. (Oryx Sourcebook Series in Business and Management, No. 7). $39.50. LC 87-23192. ISBN 0-89774-379-2.

This annotated bibliography is essentially a supplement to Leavitt's *Women in Management* (see *ARBA* 84, entry 668). It includes journal articles, books, dissertations, ERIC documents, journals, and government documents from 1981 to 1986. Annotations are concise and helpful, although in several cases source documents are mentioned that are not included. The journals indexed range from the popular through business, trade, and scholarly publications. The journal articles—740 of the total 913 entries—are arranged by chapters covering topics such as salaries, sex-role stereotypes, black women managers, women directors, obstacles, and advice. The other sources are entered under either "General Literature" or "Core Library Collection." A brief introduction, giving an overview of the literature and the changing status of women in management, an appendix of associations and directories, and author, titles, and subject indexes complete the volume.

This valuable resource should be part of any collection serving researchers studying women in administration and management. Used in conjunction with other sources such as *Women's Studies* (see *ARBA* 88, entry 894), it could also serve as a useful tool for collection development. [R: Choice, Oct 88, p. 292; LJ, 15 June 88, p. 44]   Susan Davis Herring

812. Ruud, Inger Marie. **Women and Judaism: A Select Annotated Bibliography.** New York, Garland, 1988. 232p. index. (Garland Reference Library of Social Science, Vol. 316). $45.00. LC 87-29109. ISBN 0-8240-8689-9.

This bibliography aims "to provide access to all sorts of works dealing with as many aspects as possible of women's life from ancient to modern times." The scope is very broad, covering materials on Jewish women in all countries with a Jewish population of any importance, focusing on women in religion, education and employment, marriage and family, and politics and society. However, women in Israel and the United States are emphasized. The majority of the items included have been published within the last twenty years. The bibliography includes books, sections of books, journal articles, and doctoral dissertations in English, German, French, and the Scandinavian languages. An important limitation is that materials in Hebrew are not included. A listing of the journals represented, including complete title and address, is a useful feature. The majority of the items included have been personally examined by the compiler and annotated.

The annotations, descriptive in nature, vary in length from a single sentence to a short paragraph. The entries, numbered serially, are arranged alphabetically by author. There are no cross-references. Separate topographic, subject, and author indexes conclude the book. However, the subject index is not specific and includes, for example, many numbered entries under such broad topics as "feminism," "legal status," "marriage and marriage ceremonies," and "religious life." The usefulness of the book could have been enhanced with better subject access. A more detailed introduction including specific selection criteria for inclusion would also have been helpful. However, the book provides a useful, convenient compilation of citations with a strong international emphasis that will serve as a valuable resource for Jewish studies collections in academic and public libraries, as well as temple, synagogue, Jewish day school, and community center libraries. [R: Choice, July/Aug 88, p. 1677; RBB, 15 Sept 88, p. 142]   Susan J. Freiband

BIOGRAPHIES

813. Garland, Anne Witte. **Women Activists: Challenging the Abuse of Power.** New York, Feminist Press at The City University of New York; distr., New York, Talman, 1988. 146p. illus. $29.95; $9.95pa. LC 88-401. ISBN 0-935312-79-X; 0-935312-80-Xpa.

The fourteen women profiled in this book are *extraordinary* "ordinary" women. Readers are unlikely to recognize any of the women's names. These are women who were catapulted into politics by personal experiences that angered them, frightened them, or assaulted their assumptions about American justice. In most cases, there is nothing in the woman's background that would have predicted her recourse to public action. Garland singled out *women* activists because of her belief that women form the backbone of present-day grassroots American activism. The women's organizing efforts encompass the key issues of our times: rural development, environmental destruction, corporate power, urban renewal, nuclear power and nuclear weapons, toxic waste hazards, and automobile safety.

Bernice Kaczynski stood up to General Motors when the company convinced the city of Detroit to raze her Polish neighborhood to make way for a new Cadillac plant. Mary Sinclair became a pariah in her Michigan community when she fought to stop the building and licensing of a nuclear power plant. Cathy Hinds was spurred to action when she discovered a toxic waste dump almost in her backyard.

Women of Greenham Common found that through collective resistance they could fight the fear and despair bred by the nuclear threat.

Combining the author's narrative with direct quotes, the profiles run from ten to twenty pages in length—long enough to give the reader a real sense of the women, their motivations, and the issues. Garland's interviews elicited not just the details of the women's political work, but also the women's reflections on why they became involved and how their experiences changed their own lives. The stories are as engaging as they are informative; they have much to say to anyone interested in contemporary activism and social change. *Women Activists* would be equally appropriate in school, public, and university libraries.

Catherine R. Loeb

DICTIONARIES

814. Walker, Barbara G. **The Woman's Dictionary of Symbols and Sacred Objects.** San Francisco, Calif., Harper & Row, 1988. 563p. illus. bibliog. index. $32.95; $19.95pa. LC 88-45158. ISBN 0-06-250992-5; 0-06-250923-3pa.

Walker's dictionary is a fascinating guide to the history and mythology of woman-related symbols. Twenty-one different sections, including "Round and Oval Motifs," "Sacred Objects," "Deities' Signs," "Zodiac," "Animals," "Body Parts," and "Minerals, Stones and Shells," give a unique history of symbols. Each section includes an introductory essay about the type of symbols discussed in that section. The 753 entries include symbols such as "Three-Rayed Sun," "Corn Dolly," "Satyr," "Tongue," and "Cosmic Egg." Over six hundred illustrations enhance the work. Most entries include footnote references to the extensive bibliography. The index is both a general subject index and an alphabetical guide to all the symbols listed. The symbols are set in boldface type.

Janet R. Ivey

DIRECTORIES

815. **Library and Information Sources on Women: A Guide to Collections in the Greater New York Area.** Compiled and edited by The Women's Resources Group of the Greater New York Metropolitan Area Chapter of the Association of College and Research Libraries and the Center for the Study of Women and Society of the Graduate School and University Center

of the City University of New York. New York, Feminist Press at The City University of New York, 1988. 254p. index. $12.95pa. LC 87-35068. ISBN 0-935312-88-9.

The women's studies researcher eager to tap the vast information resources of the New York area might be expected to plan forays into the libraries of institutions such as Sarah Lawrence College, Princeton, New York University, Columbia, Barnard, and The City University of New York. But would one think of contacting Butterick's Fashion Information Center or the Fashion Institute of Technology for a study of women and fashion? Or, were the topic comparable worth, would one be likely to know of the Ruth Milkman Collection at the Barnard Women's Center?

The Feminist Press's new guide offers profiles of 171 collections in the five boroughs of New York City, Long Island, Westchester County, and eastern New Jersey. The collections are strikingly diverse in size, institutional setting, and focus: alongside generalist giants like the New York Public Library, there are idiosyncratic personal collections, the highly focused libraries of associations and political action groups, and the parochial collections of local historical societies. Some of the collections are tiny and obscure; a few seem to offer little on women. On the whole, however, the guide presents a fascinating patchwork.

The compilers asked each collection to provide the following information as applicable: name and address, telephone number, contact person, objectives, access privileges, hours, description of women's materials, collection by format (books and monographs, serials, government documents, pamphlets, clippings, manuscripts or archives, etc.), services, and publications. Entries are arranged alphabetically, with cross-references and a brief subject index provided to aid the reader in locating collections of interest. For the larger collections, of course, the guide provides only the roughest outline; the serious researcher will need to follow up on the leads found here.

This guide will no doubt serve New York area researchers best. However, its usefulness will not end there. Women's studies researchers elsewhere will turn to the guide as they search for collections with undiscovered treasures in their research areas. Further, it is to be hoped that *Library and Information Sources on Women* might serve as a model for the creation of similar guides in other geographic locales.

Catherine R. Loeb

Part III
HUMANITIES

19 Humanities in General

GENERAL WORKS

816. Benet's Reader's Encyclopedia. 3d ed. New York, Harper & Row, 1987. 1091p. $35.00. LC 87-45022. ISBN 0-06-181088-6.

Now named for its former editor who died in 1950, *Benet's Reader's Encyclopedia* contains over nine thousand entries. The scope of these entries includes short biographical notes on writers, artists, musicians, philosophers, and historical figures; plot and character synopses of important works; explanations of myth, folklore, and legend; and descriptions of literary terms, awards, schools, and movements. Arranged in alphabetical order, the encyclopedia employs the use of cross-references to lead readers to their literary destination.

Compared to the second edition, this version claims to be "expanded, completely revised, and updated." Expanded and updated it is; completely revised it is not. Literary figures such as Harold Pinter, John Updike, Lawrence Ferlinghetti, and Erich Fromm, who have enjoyed greater notoriety since the second edition was published in 1965, have more complete entries than in previous editions, including their most current works and philosophy. New entries include Alice Walker, B. F. Skinner, Neil Simon, Richard M. Nixon, Sam Shepard, Andy Warhol, Dr. Doolittle, *The Fountainhead*, and theater of the absurd.

Entries on literary standards such as Faust and Dostoyevsky are relatively unchanged from the second edition. Furthermore, a significant number of entries from the second edition are nonexistent in the third edition, such as certain biblical and mythological references and lesser known Shakespearean characters. The second edition included over one hundred illustrations; the third has none.

This third edition is easily readable. The large boldface letters in each referent stand out from the typeface in the ensuing definitions.

The owner of both second and third editions will have the most comprehensive sources of literary allusions available. But if the library chooses not to acquire the latest edition, the older one contains all of the information to which the classics of literature refer. [R: Choice, Mar 88, p. 1061; RBB, 1 Mar 88, p. 1102; WLB, Feb 88, p. 97]   Susan M. Sigman

817. Blazek, Ron, and Elizabeth Aversa. **The Humanities: A Selective Guide to Information Sources.** 3d ed. Englewood, Colo., Libraries Unlimited, 1988. 382p. index. (Library Science Text Series). $56.00; $23.00pa. LC 87-33907. ISBN 0-87287-558-X; 0-87287-594-6pa.

The first and second editions of this text, by A. Robert Rogers, were published in 1974 (see *ARBA* 75, entry 174) and 1979 (see *ARBA* 81, entry 153). Dr. Rogers's unexpected death in 1985 led Blazek and Aversa to revise and update this bibliography. The resulting text continues to be useful to library school teachers and students, reference librarians, humanities bibliographers, as well as scholars in these fields.

Because there are so many thousands of reference sources which could be included in such a broad interdisciplinary bibliography, this book is aptly subtitled "a selective guide." It includes 973 major entries (pared down from 1,200 in the second edition), representing the authors' selection from titles in previous editions, new sources, and the recommendations of subject specialists. Although some would argue that history deserves to be included among the humanities, coverage was limited to philosophy, religion, the visual arts, the performing arts, and language and literature. An excellent introductory chapter discussing the nature of humanities scholarship is followed by a chapter listing and annotating some of the most important general humanities reference sources (e.g., the *Arts and Humanities Citation Index*). Subsequent odd-numbered chapters provide advice in accessing information in each discipline, while the even-numbered chapters consist of annotations, divided by bibliographic type, of key reference sources. Following the practice of the second edition, the chapter on accessing information in philosophy discusses major LC classification headings as an illustration of how students can use the card catalog to discover other sources on their own.

A typical annotation is 100 to 235 words, with numerous cross-references to other entries. A typical entry is objective and descriptive, but evaluative comments and frequent comparisons to other sources make this book especially useful to students. This is truly a thoroughly revised new edition: the new authors have frequently (according to this reviewer's sample) improved the annotations of the earlier editions by being more precise. While there is some competition from *Reference Books in the Social Sciences and Humanities* by Rolland E. Stevens and Donald G. Davis (see *ARBA* 78, entry 4), *The Humanities* is more comprehensive, more up-to-date, and more thoroughly annotated. [R: Choice, Sept 88, p. 74; LJ, Aug 88, p. 86; RBB, 15 Sept 88, p. 138; RQ, Winter 88, pp. 274-75]
David Isaacson

818. Burroughs, Lea. **Introducing Children to the Arts: A Practical Guide for Librarians and Educators.** Boston, G. K. Hall, 1988. 306p. illus. bibliog. $35.00. LC 88-14770. ISBN 0-8161-8818-1.

Introducing Children to the Arts, written for the educator and librarian, covers seven arts: architecture, art, dance, music, poetry, story, and theater. Burroughs presents each tradition through its history or its internal structure, explains how children experience and understand the form, and offers several workshops for children of varying ages, including directives for special children. Each chapter provides a bibliography and filmography spanning the wide range of ideas mentioned in the chapter, and often includes a discography and videography. A short bibliography for adults is at the end of the book.

Particularly helpful within the various bibliographies are the specific subject headings. These will help educators and librarians quickly move to the topic they wish to discuss as they plan a workshop. For example, in the music chapter the discography lists titles which elucidate the following elements: counterpoint,

melody, harmony, texture, instruments, rhythm program, color, and combinations thereof.

The bibliographies contain books from the turn of the century to the present, with more than a casual number from the 1960s, and relatively few from the 1980s. The author has acknowledged this in the introduction, stating that she has chosen "books that live" and that smaller libraries will already have these books in their collections. Many of the books included are the "classics" children need to be exposed to at a young age to develop their cultural literacy.

Burroughs's treatment of history throughout the book, though brief and directed toward the reader who has little background knowledge, is commendable. For a book of this length, the overview is far reaching. Although in certain chapters she exhibits an American focus (which she admits and explains), Burroughs generally presents complementary histories of European as well as non-Western countries.

This book is recommended especially for the school library.
Susan M. Sigman

819. **The Eighteenth Century: A Current Bibliography, n.s. 9—for 1983.** Jim Springer Borck, ed. New York, AMS Press, 1988. 793p. index. $76.50. ISBN 0-404-62214-3; ISSN 0161-0996.

Under general editor Jim Springer Borck, the ninth in the new series of *The Eighteenth Century* provides an indispensable research tool for the serious scholar. The 740 pages of text are composed of annotated bibliographic entries (many entire book reviews are provided) on all aspects of eighteenth-century studies. The work is arranged topically into printing and bibliographical studies; historical, social, and economic studies; philosophy, science, and religion; the fine arts; literary studies; and individual authors. The volume includes books and articles in all the major world languages which have appeared between 1980 and 1983 and covers historical and literary topics ranging in scope from the Enlightenment in Germany to British colonial policy in America. The index provides a list of authors, editors, and reviewers in the entries of the bibliography, and includes names mentioned significantly in the reviews and annotations.
William G. Ratliff

820. Grote, David. **Common Knowledge: A Reader's Guide to Literary Allusions.** Westport, Conn., Greenwood Press, 1987. 437p. $49.95. LC 87-10710. ISBN 0-313-25757-4.

Common Knowledge is a dictionary of names from sources such as mythology, religion, history, literature, and popular culture that have become a part of general literature. Some examples to illustrate are "poor as Job's turkey," "Out Herod Herod," and "melancholy as Hamlet." The purpose of the book is three-fold: (1) to identify for the general reader the origins of characters that have become a part of our literary heritage, (2) to include a wide range of the writers whose works are most likely to be encountered, and (3) to give adequate descriptions of the characters and the source or sources of their origin.

Use of the volume is facilitated by entering the allusion by name rather than the phrase or sentence of origin. It is well cross-referenced and variant names are listed.

This book along with a good biographical dictionary and *Bartlett's Familiar Quotations* will serve general readers well in understanding most of the allusions that will be encountered in their literary reading. It would be ideal in personal libraries of serious graduate and undergraduate students of literature. Certainly every university and college library will want to have it represented in its collection. [R: Choice, Apr 88, p. 1222; RBB, 1 May 88, p. 1483; WLB, May 88, pp. 108-9]   Jefferson D. Caskey

20 Communication and Mass Media

GENERAL WORKS

821. Allen, Martha Leslie, ed. **Directory of Women's Media, 1988.** Washington, D.C., Women's Institute for Freedom of the Press, 1988. 91p. index. $12.00 spiralbound.

This edition of the directory (for review of the 8th edition, see *ARBA* 83, entry 701) follows much the same format as previous issues. Published since 1975 by the Women's Institute for Freedom of the Press, a nonprofit organization interested in assisting networking among women, women's organizations, and women's media, the directory is compiled solely by volunteers. Costs are kept to a minimum to produce an inexpensive guide which is readily affordable to all interested users.

Focusing primarily on media owned and operated by and for women, the directory is arranged in two broad categories. The first, women's media groups, is subdivided into twenty sections focusing on such topics as women's periodicals, films, music, and bookstores. Within each section, listings are arranged in geographical order by zip code and country. An alphabetical cross index is provided at the end of this listing.

The second category, individual media women and media-concerned women, is arranged alphabetically, with a geographical cross index provided. Also included in the directory is a statement of philosophy of communication, the "Radical Feminist Analysis of Mass Media."

Listing in this directory is voluntary, and the information is provided solely by the organization or individual listed. As a result, listings and coverage are somewhat erratic. The organization of the women's media group section is very cumbersome, but the work still should prove of value to those interested in this field. [R: RBB, 1 June 88, p. 1648; RBB, July 88, p. 1812] Elizabeth Patterson

822. Hull, Debra L. **Business and Technical Communication: A Bibliography, 1975-1985.** Metuchen, N.J., Scarecrow, 1987. 229p. index. $22.50. LC 87-4749. ISBN 0-8108-1971-6.

Designed as a resource for business and technical communication instructors, this 1,133-item annotated bibliography provides access to articles published in the field from 1975-1985. It is arranged in three major sections. Section 1 presents articles concerning the business communication classroom. Topics deal with definitions, evaluations of teaching programs, teaching methods, and grading techniques. Section 2 includes articles that examine the communication process. Topics include audience analysis, style, written documents, oral presentation, and graphics. Section 3 emphasizes the use of computers and telecommunications.

A list of selected bibliographies and books appears at the end of the volume. Author and subject indexes provide easy access to materials. Although the bibliography is aimed at instructors in the field, there is much information here of value for those wishing to improve their skills in business communication. [R: Choice, June 88, p. 1536] Marilyn Strong Noronha

823. Kelly, Kevin, ed. **SIGNAL: Communication Tools for the Information Age: A Whole Earth Catalog.** New York, Harmony Books/ Crown, 1988. 226p. illus. index. $16.95pa. LC 88-13165. ISBN 0-517-57084-X.

Readers will no doubt recall the first *Whole Earth Catalog*, published some twenty years ago, which offered many alternatives to the traditional lifestyles of most Americans. "Making do with less" in a consumer-oriented economy was the hallmark of the earlier guide to building a self-sufficient lifestyle. This current offering explores global communications in a "more with less" framework. Topics covered range from personal computers to "how to get published on a low budget." *SIGNAL* covers virtually every aspect of human communication: television, radio, packet switching networks, robots, libraries, public speaking, oral history, cellular telephones, teleconferencing, "Big Brother," marketing, propaganda, dreams, gossip, citation indexing, government databases, word processors, hackers, computer viruses; in short, a wide variety of communications tools for the 1990s.

Like the earlier Whole Earth offerings, this volume is heavily illustrated with reproductions from other books. The editors have attempted to give the reader a kernel of information on each work cited. For the most part they are successful and give what is needed to make an intelligent purchasing decision. Most readers will find this volume, like the others, a fascinating book to read. I have always had trouble putting a Whole Earth book down. Each time I pick one up I want to spend hours filling my mind with the wealth of information presented. The editors have produced a volume that is the ultimate "communication tool." Most libraries will find that this book, which is paperback, will wear out just as quickly as the other Whole Earth volumes did. A highly recommended introduction, guide, and catalog to the information society. This is the best bargain in "computer books" around, with an exceedingly modest price for the amount of information provided. Highly recommended.

Ralph Lee Scott

824. Matlon, Ronald J., and Peter C. Facciola, eds. **Index to Journals in Communication Studies through 1985.** Annandale, Va., Speech Communication Association, 1987. 645p. $40.00pa. LC 87-061400.

This index covers the tables of contents for primary articles from fifteen major speech journals from their inception through 1985. Book reviews, editorial comments, convention remarks, and similar features are not included.

The organization of this index is not conventional and therefore tends to be difficult to use. For each issue of every volume, the date is given and the table of contents, including titles, author(s), and pagination noted. Each article title entry is numbered or lettered and numbered. Part 2 of the index contains a list of contributors in alphabetical order and the journal article designation. The reader must figure out which of the journal titles received what letter designation by thumbing through the first part of the index. No key is provided either in the preface or in the second part, and journal listings are not in alphabetical order. However, the reader may be fortunate enough to find the key in part 3.

Part 3 is the "Index of Subjects." It contains four chapters. In chapter 1, the purpose and content of the next three chapters are explained. Chapter 2 is an outline of the coded classification, based on the National Center for Educational Statistics areas in communication study. Chapter 3 is a classified index to subjects using these codes. This index then refers the reader back to the first part of the book using the appropriate number, letter/number designation for specific articles. Chapter 4 contains a keyword index of subjects; the numbers used in this chapter refer to the coded classification found in chapter 3.

Readers wanting articles on communication published since March 1978 would do much better with *Communication Abstracts*, which covers one hundred journals and fifty books, and is published quarterly. On the other hand, what this index does do is cover the earlier works, some of them going back as far as 1915. Libraries that have *Communication Abstracts* and an earlier edition of the index will not find a serious need for this latest edition. However, it is probably useful as an office reference work for faculty in the field of communication.

Helen M. Gothberg

825. Signorielli, Nancy, and George Gerbner, comps. **Violence and Terror in the Mass Media: An Annotated Bibliography.** Westport, Conn., Greenwood Press, 1988. 233p. index. (Bibliographies and Indexes in Sociology, No. 13). $39.95. LC 87-29556. ISBN 0-313-26120-2.

An important addition to the literature of media portrayals of violence, this was prepared by students and staff at The Annenberg School of Communication. The bibliography includes articles from scholarly journals and books, the popular press, government reports, conference papers, and relevant dissertations through spring 1987. The focus is primarily on the United States, although relevant research from other countries is also included. The introduction summarizes approaches to the issues and provides a useful overview to the four topical bibliographies that follow. These include sections on violence and mass media content, violence and mass media effects, terrorism and the mass media, and pornography and the mass media. Emphasis is clearly on the first two areas – mass media content and mass media effects – with annotated citations for these areas comprising close to two hundred pages compared to only thirty-two pages for terrorism and pornography in the mass media. The annotations in each section are very good, with excellent descriptions of methods and findings. However, following the predilections of Signorielli and Gerbner, the annotations tend to focus on aspects of the articles of interest to those involved in cultivation research. A separate author and subject index bring together entries in all four areas. [R: Choice, June 88, p. 1540; RBB, 1 Sept 88, p. 57]

Michael Ann Moskowitz

AUTHORSHIP

Biographies

826. **Who's Who in the Writers' Union of Canada: A Directory of Members.** 3d ed. Toronto, Writers' Union of Canada, 1988. 483p. illus. $16.95pa. ISBN 0-9690796-2-1.

With almost as many entries as the first and second editions combined, this edition offers concise information on nearly five hundred writers all of whom have at least one book in print. Entries consist of a photograph; a biographical sketch; selected publications (with ISBN); awards; critical comment; availability for readings, lectures, and workshops; and mailing address. Very few French-Canadian writers are included. The volume concludes with a name list of more than one hundred additional members and notes on the union and its activities. Even though not all Canadian writers are members, and not all members are represented in the detailed entries, TWUC's directory provides information which cannot be found in any other source.   Patricia Fleming

Directories

827. **Grants and Awards Available to American Writers.** 15th ed. New York, PEN American Center, 1988. 144p. index. $6.00pa.; $10.50 pa. (institutions). LC 73-648098. ISBN 0-934638-08-X.

Following a statement about the inherent limitations of this type of directory, the editor notes supplementary sources of information for writers seeking grants. Nevertheless, this work lists hundreds of grants and awards for American and Canadian writers. Symbols indicate the writing specialties, and an index by category also helps to pinpoint the type of work considered.

In addition to category, information about each award includes its sponsor, focus, type of recipient sought, deadline, and application details. An appendix provides addresses of state arts councils in the United States and Canada, so that they may be contacted for information about their literature programs. With an index of awards and an index of organizations, writers can easily find information about a particular grant. However, the directory probably will best serve writers who browse through it without a specific award in mind.

Renee B. Horowitz

828. **The Guide to Writers Conferences, 1989.** 2d ed. Coral Gables, Fla., Shaw Associates, 1988. 345p. index. $14.95pa. LC 88-90514. ISBN 0-945834-02-0; ISSN 0897-4195.

Not only does this guide present valuable information about conferences and workshops for writers, it also organizes the material in several useful ways. For example, main entries include such items as purpose of the conference, schedule, instructors, facilities, and tuition. The appendix provides a twelve-month conference calendar. Conferences are also indexed geographically and by such specialties as juveniles, screenwriting, mysteries, romances, inspirational works, and technical writing.

Unfortunately, the editors have omitted at least one important technical and professional writing conference: the Professional Communications Society Conference (of the Institute of Electrical and Electronics Engineers). Inasmuch as the editors request information from readers about unlisted conferences, future editions of the guide should correct such oversights.

Renee B. Horowitz

829. **Literary Agents of North America: The Complete Guide to U.S. and Canadian Literary Agencies.** 3d ed. Compiled and edited by Author Aid/Research Associates International, New York, Author Aid/Research Associates International, 1988. 203p. index. $19.95pa. LC 83-208290. ISBN 0-911085-04-1.

In addition to an alphabetical directory of literary agents, this book offers various indexes to help writers find the most appropriate agents. Perhaps the subject index is most useful, for it lists agents according to the types of material they handle. Another valuable section of this directory is the policy index. Agents are grouped into such categories as those who charge reading or evaluation fees, do not charge reading fees, encourage new writers, do not encourage new writers, read unsolicited manuscripts, or do not read unsolicited manuscripts. Other sections list agencies by size and geographical location. An index of personnel helps writers to locate specific agents.

The introduction to this work, "Do You Have a Mega-Book?," presents practical information for writers about the state of the publishing industry. In particular, the editors examine whether the new writer's chances for publication have improved. They point out that an established writer who produces a "mega-book" will have no difficulty locating an agent. But, "if you're new and writing an essentially noncommercial book, not so good." The editors recommend smaller agencies and smaller presses and also provide useful hints for dealing with agents. [R: Choice, May 88, p. 1384]

Renee B. Horowitz

830. O'Gara, Elaine. **Travel Writer's Markets.** 1987-88 ed. Berkeley, Calif., Winterbourne Press, 1988. 181p. index. $12.95pa. LC 87-50510. ISBN 0-9609172-6-8.

Although *TWM* includes over ten times the number of travel magazine entries as does *Writer's Market*, these entries are briefer. In addition to title, editor, address, pay rates, and article length, the book includes guidelines for submission of articles and, whenever possible, a sampling of the titles of their previously published travel articles. A particularly useful feature is the "Washout" section which gives information on magazines that have either gone out of business, do not take freelance articles, or do not pay well. Travel writers can easily go to other sources for lists of appropriate book publishers (e.g., *Literary Market Place*); however, *TWM* is the only guide available to newspaper travel markets. This section includes national newspapers and syndicates as well as newspapers throughout the United States and Canada.

The chapters on manuscript submission, tax tips for writers, and helpful organizations and publications can also be found in other reference sources. Yet, any library frequently serving freelance travel writers will certainly consider this a useful addition. [R: RBB, 1 May 88, p. 1491]   Michael Ann Moskowitz

831. **The Writers Directory 1988-90.** 8th ed. Chicago, St. James Press, 1988. 1045p. $95.00. ISBN 0-912289-87-2.

With its latest revision and expansion, this biennial reference work includes entries for more than sixteen thousand living authors who write in English. A very useful listing of the writers by category of writing under the headings "Creative Writing," "Nonfiction," and "Other," precedes the entries. Further subdivisions range from administration/management to

zoology. These listings, the "yellow pages," are helpful in finding all entrants writing about a particular subject.

Entries furnish pseudonyms in addition to real names, birthdates, areas of specialization, and mailing addresses of authors. Most useful for students and researchers are a summary of the type of writing and a bibliography for each writer.

This book proves not only an invaluable source of reference material for serious students and researchers, but also a delightful browsing arena for recreational readers who would like to know more about their favorite contemporary authors. In fact, any page in the directory provides enough interesting information to sidetrack readers from their intended research.

Renee B. Horowitz

Handbooks

832. Gibaldi, Joseph, and Walter S. Achtert. **MLA Handbook for Writers of Research Papers.** 3d ed. New York, Modern Language Association of America, 1988. 248p. illus. index. $8.95pa. LC 88-5195. ISBN 0-87352-379-2.

The second edition of the *MLA Handbook for Writers of Research Papers* (see *ARBA* 85, entry 46) heralded the multitude of revisions the Modern Language Association of America made in research paper style. Now the third edition continues to clarify and amplify the MLA format for writers.

Over two-thirds of the handbook still covers the rules in detail, with a slew of examples for documenting and citing sources. Lists of abbreviations for geographical names, publisher names, and titles are included in this section, as well as sample pages of a research paper and a comprehensive subject index. The remainder of the text discusses basics such as library research, plagiarism, spelling, language usage, and other elements important to producing a quality paper.

This edition covers more thoroughly the help word processors can offer students in their writing. Suggestions for drafting and revising papers are specified. Safety measures such as the proverbial backup disk are also touched upon. Fully covered, too, is the process of documenting nonprint sources (e.g., computer software, online searches, etc.), an addition necessary to keep pace with technology.

Although some academic disciplines use other style guides, such as *A Manual for Writers of Term Papers, Theses, and Dissertations*, by Kate L. Turabian (see *ARBA* 88, entry 924), the MLA style has become popular with many teachers and students. This handbook should remain valuable and available.

Patricia M. Leach

833. Kline, Mary-Jo. **A Guide to Documentary Editing.** Baltimore, Md., Johns Hopkins University Press, 1987. 228p. illus. index. $29.50. LC 86-18507. ISBN 0-8018-3341-8.

As a guide to editing historical and literary material, this book succeeds in its intent to consider "alternative methods to deal with different—and sometimes widely different—bodies of documents." The author begins with an overview of documentary editing in this country, examining accomplishments of the congressional agency that serves historical editing projects and of organizations that create standards for literary texts. She also looks at the evolution in approaches to historical and literary editing.

Additional chapters discuss how to initiate an editorial project, organize documentary edition, and evaluate and transcribe source texts. With information on conventions of textual treatment, the application of editorial conventions, and some general rules, the guide presents important practical material for the documentary editor. Final advice on working with the publisher follows material on the mechanical aspects of establishing a text and preparing it for the printer. Suggested reading lists are provided for each topic, including works on computer usage in documentary editing.

Prepared for the Association for Documentary Editing, this guide offers practical information for all editors, students, and scholars who work with original documents. [R: C&RL, Jan 88, p. 67]   Renee B. Horowitz

834. Mandell, Judy, comp. and ed. **Fiction Writers Guidelines: Over 200 Periodical Editors' Instructions Reproduced.** Jefferson, N.C., McFarland, 1988. 316p. index. $20.95pa. LC 88-45206. ISBN 0-89950-249-0.

Ranging from *Aboriginal Science Fiction* to *Young Miss Magazine*, this book presents material from over 230 magazines about their publication guidelines. These guidelines include such information as format of submissions, type of manuscripts required, rate of payment, and availability of sample copies. Reader demographics also find their way into many of the descriptions. A number of magazines without specific guidelines do accept unsolicited manuscripts, and a short section at the end of the book addresses these publications.

Although the editor provides material about little-known literary magazines as well as familiar periodicals, all of the entries are interesting to browsers. For writers, students, or writing teachers, the information will be particularly useful. Entries are alphabetical, but a comprehensive index allows the researcher access to listings by subject.

Renee B. Horowitz

NEWSPAPERS AND MAGAZINES

Bibliographies

835. Hoerder, Dirk, and Christiane Harzig, eds. **The Immigrant Labor Press in North America, 1840s-1970s: An Annotated Bibliography. Volume 2: Migrants from Eastern and Southeastern Europe.** Westport, Conn., Greenwood Press, 1987. 725p. maps. index. (Bibliographies and Indexes in American History, No. 7). $65.00. LC 87-168. ISBN 0-313-26077-X.

836. Hoerder, Dirk, and Christiane Harzig, eds. **The Immigrant Labor Press in North America, 1840s-1970s: An Annotated Bibliography. Volume 3: Migrants from Southern and Western Europe.** Westport, Conn., Greenwood Press, 1987. 583p. maps. index. (Bibliographies and Indexes in American History, No. 8). $65.00. LC 87-168. ISBN 0-313-26078-8.

Both of these volumes continue the excellent standards set by the first title in this series, which covered migrants from northern Europe. The concept and scope are immense, and the three volumes together make an impressive contribution to the research literature of the labor movement. At the same time these books provide a foundation for research into cultural history of the North American working class: coverage here includes only non-English language labor and radical periodical publications of the United States and Canada written by and for immigrants.

The contents of each book includes a thoroughly developed user's guide to the format, along with extensively annotated introductory essays on the labor press in North America, linguistic fragmentation of multilingualism among labor migrants, the individual language sections (each compiled to a format by different scholars), and a combined title index at the back—which unfortunately has no listings for nonroman script. None of the indexes in this series has a nonroman index. Covered in volume 2 are Poles, Byelorussians, Russians, Lithuanians, Latvians, Estonians, Czechs, Slovaks, Hungarians, Ukrainians, Carpatho-Rusyns, Yugoslavians, Bulgarians, Albanians, Romanians, Greeks, Armenians, and Jews. Volume 3 covers Italians, Spaniards, British Isles natives, Dutch, French, and Germans.

Each language group has its own annotated section; this is the heart of each volume. These sections contain formatted data about the compilers, about the areas in which the language was spoken (normally, in 1910 for comparison's sake), an explanation of the library and depository symbols, and a section bibliography. Introductory essays survey each language labor group. The annotated bibliography contains virtually all periodicals that appeared more than once a year: titles are translated into English or rendered into roman script; the first editor, the first and last issues, and the frequency are noted; nonroman scripts are reproduced; depository collections are noted for physical copies of the periodicals. Normally, each entry would have a descriptive history or tracing of the periodical for name changes, changes of philosophy, impact, and so forth. Each section concludes with title, place, and chronological indexes to the periodicals.

One major highlight of the series is that it also includes Canada, which is as it should be since languages in the New World knew no political boundaries until recently. This is an excellent work, at a fairly reasonable price, and it should be mounted onto a computer database as soon as possible to allow for comprehensive searching. [R: Choice, June 88, p. 1536; C&RL, July 88, p. 342]   Dean Tudor

837. Widor, Claude, comp. **The Samizdat Press in China's Provinces, 1979-1981: An Annotated Guide.** Stanford, Calif., Hoover Institution Press, 1987. 157p. index. (Hoover Press Bibliographical Series, 70). $11.95pa. LC 87-13559. ISBN 0-8179-2702-6.

This annotated list of eighty-eight journals, mostly mimeographed, published in various parts of China outside Beijing during the brief period of the democracy movement, 1979-1981, is a useful supplement to an earlier work by the Hoover Institution on War, Revolution and Peace, *Unofficial Documents of the Democracy Movement in Communist China 1978-1981* (see *ARBA* 88, entry 695).

The journal titles in this guide are arranged by province and within each province by city. In addition to the pertinent bibliographic information for each journal (indicating the title, issues published, dates, and number of pages), background information on the movement in each city and descriptive notes about each journal are the most important and useful features of the guide—which reflects the personal knowledge and perhaps first-hand observation of events of the compiler. Even though the movement was

short-lived and many of the journal editors were arrested and jailed, researchers on the recent history and politics of China will find the publications very useful in understanding the mind and thoughts of Chinese people today. The significance of these publications now collected and preserved in the East Asian Collection of the Hoover Institution will be made better known through this guide.

Hwa-Wei Lee

Biographies

838. Edwards, Julia. **Women of the World: The Great Foreign Correspondents.** Boston, Houghton Mifflin, 1988. 275p. illus. index. $17.95. LC 87-37593. ISBN 0-395-44486-1.

This engaging book gives a highly readable overview of American women who have served as foreign correspondents, spotlighting the leading journalists. It serves not only as a reference tool, but also as a source of inspiration for anyone striving to follow in the footsteps of these intrepid women.

Edwards does not give in-depth biographies; they range from passing references to chapter-long sketches which cover the individual's life and work, and her influence and impact on journalism and public opinion. The work is well researched, with information coming from biographies, writings, personal correspondence, and interviews. The chapter references at the end of the book are excellent. The index is quite thorough, which is extremely important considering the ambiguous chapter headings.

Although the biographies of some of the women included in this book can be found in other sources, such as the Dictionary of Literary Biography series, no other source offers the coordinated, comprehensive, personal coverage provided here. The lively, conversational style, open admiration, and solid research combine to produce a work suitable for any library collection. [R: LJ, Aug 88, p. 155]

Susan Davis Herring

839. Riley, Sam G., ed. **American Magazine Journalists, 1741-1850.** Detroit, Gale, 1988. 430p. illus. bibliog. index. (Dictionary of Literary Biography, Vol. 73). $95.00. LC 88-17586. ISBN 0-8103-4551-X.

The first of a three-part set in the Dictionary of Literary Biography series, this work covers forty-six American magazine journalists whose lives and careers spanned the period from 1741 to 1850. Among the distinguished personalities included are Ralph Waldo Emerson, Benjamin Franklin, Thomas Paine, Edgar Allan Poe, and Noah Webster. Entries include major positions held, a four- to six-page essay high-lighting the journalist's life and career, a bibliography of secondary sources, and information on which libraries or historical societies have special collections about the journalists. A black-and-white photograph or painting of each journalist is provided, along with many other interesting photographs which enhance the text. In the back of the volume are a two-page check-list of further readings on early American periodical publication and a cumulative index of all the persons included in all volumes of DLB to date. The table of contents contains the names of all the journalists found in the work. The volume is well researched and the writing is clear and lively, making it an excellent addition to this distinguished series.

Marilyn Strong Noronha

Directories

840.   **Bacon's Publicity Checker 1988.** 36th ed. Chicago, Bacon Publishing, 1987. 2v. index. $145.00/set spiralbound. ISSN 0162-3125.

In two volumes, this is a handy guide to magazines and newspapers in the United States and Canada. The first volume lists over seventy-two hundred magazines and newsletters in 195 market classifications from "Advertising" to "Woodworking." In addition to title, address, telephone number, editor, circulation, frequency and publication date, fourteen types of publicity codes indicate if an entry includes such features as new product announcements, letters, and book reviews. Symbol codes to the right of each listing offer other specialized information. Access is facilitated by the numerical index of market classifications which show the number of publications within each group and the page number of the appropriate section. The related market classifications listed at the start of each section are useful for cross-reference. The first volume concludes with an index of all publications under the various classifications and an index of multiple publishers.

The second volume follows a similar format for U.S. and Canadian newspapers. Over 1,750 general interest daily newspapers are alphabetized by state, then city within the state, with a comprehensive editorial coding block at the bottom of each page indicating specific contents and features. The next section covers over seventy-seven hundred weekly and semiweekly U.S. newspapers. The volume concludes with a number of special listings, such as news syndicates, newspaper printed magazines, a black press newspaper index, and the top one hundred ADI markets.

Although some of this information is available in other sources (such as *Editor and Publisher International Year Book* [Editor & Publisher, 1924-]), these two volumes, with their yellow revision sheets for easy updating, are a valuable source of data on the contemporary press.

Michael Ann Moskowitz

841.   Thompson, Julius E. **The Black Press in Mississippi, 1865-1985: A Directory.** West Cornwall, Conn., Locust Hill Press, 1988. 144p. illus. maps. bibliog. index. $25.00. LC 88-561. ISBN 0-933951-16-7.

This directory is the first comprehensive publication that covers the black press of any single state. Because the basic history of blacks in Mississippi is not well represented in the literature, this source also helps to fill a void that currently exists. Thompson's directory provides us with references to the written and recorded words and activities of the black leadership in Mississippi.

The black press in this volume includes not only newspapers but also newsletters, college catalogs, pamphlets, fraternal organs, and religious publications. The four hundred papers that are known to have been published from 1865 to 1985 serve as concrete products that represent the history and culture of blacks both in times of extreme racism and improved relations.

The main body of the directory is an alphabetical listing county by county. Publications for each county appear in the following arrangement, as available: publication name, dates of publication, frequency, number of pages, size in inches, subscription rate, circulation, name of editor/publisher, short description of publication, and location of the publication's files (for some, there are no known copies).

There are five useful indexes: title, publisher/editor, organization/institution, city, and chronological. This source will be useful to scholars in communications, history, folklore, and library science. Even high school teachers, parents, and ordinary citizens seeking elusive artifacts to an important aspect of the black experience in the South will benefit from this publication.

Academic and public libraries will enhance their collections covering black history by acquiring this significant resource.

R. Errol Lam

Handbooks

842.   Schwarzlose, Richard A. **Newspapers: A Reference Guide.** Westport, Conn., Greenwood

Press, 1987. 417p. index. (American Popular Culture). $55.00. LC 87-246. ISBN 0-313-23613-5.

While this book is useful and informative for the communications scholar and library, its price and its depth may put it out of the reach of the regular library and student. It is a very comprehensive introduction to the literature about and by American newspapers. It is essentially a historical overview, with sourcebook data about the different American regions, chronologies, and biographies of great newspapers and journalists. There is some material here on newspapers and technology (the production side), but not much. This book appears to be one of a series of spinoffs from the *Handbook of American Popular Culture* (see *ARBA* 80, entry 1099; *ARBA* 81, entry 1140; and *ARBA* 83, entry 1063), a three-volume work from Greenwood Press. In volume 3, published in 1981, there is a thirty-four page section on "American Newspapers," authored by Schwarzlose, and it forms the basis for the current, much-expanded book. Both the 1981 guide and this current book detail major research collections and provide annotations for the major books and periodicals. Libraries on a tight budget might wish to peruse the *Handbook of American Popular Culture* first before deciding to purchase *Newspapers*. [R: RBB, 1 Feb 88, p. 918]

Dean Tudor

Indexes

843. Alternative Press Index: An Index to Alternative and Radical Publications. Baltimore, Md., Alternative Press Center, 1988. 127p. $25.00 (4 issues); $110.00 (4 issues) (institutions). LC 76-24027. ISSN 0002-662X.

The *Alternative Press Index* covers over two hundred established, nonmainstream journals and newspapers in the current events, social sciences, and humanities subject areas. The editorial style of the index is designed to make the information thoroughly accessible, from the extensive introductory section to the plain English, current usage subject headings.

The "How to Use the Index" section is a good explanation of the construction of the entries and the criteria for article selection. The list of periodicals indexed provides information on publisher, frequency, cost, subject coverage, ISSN, and, most helpfully for interlibrary loan use, the OCLC record number for each title. The editors include notes of title changes, cessations and suspensions, and a list of periodicals with special issues during the index coverage (it

appears quarterly) with the topic of each special issue.

The subject headings are very well chosen and more than adequately cross-referenced. The index provides subject access only: there is no access by author's name.

This index should be in all public and college/university libraries of medium size and larger. Although not all libraries will hold the periodicals indexed, these are classics of the radical press and library users should have access to their contents. [R: RBB, 1 June 88, p. 1647]   Linda A. Naru

844. Canadian News Index 1987. Volume 11. Julie de Martigny, ed. Toronto, Micromedia, 1988. 1063p. price not reported. ISSN 0225-7459.

This is the annual cumulation of a monthly index to seven daily Canadian newspapers. It began in 1977 as the *Canadian Newspaper Index* and changed in 1980 to the *Canadian News Index*. It is also available through Dialog online searching as Canadian Business and Current Affairs (which also includes the online versions of the Canadian Magazine Index and the Canadian Business Index, both Micromedia publications that index magazine and business publications' articles). Being available online means that the data are more quickly and easily retrieved. But all references are to microfilmed copies of the finished product, and while this poses no problem for the magazines which only come out in one edition, there are newspapers that change throughout the day and appear differently on a "national" basis, as well as appearing differently as an online searchable database. The *Globe and Mail*, from Toronto, thus has several different "editions," some for metro Toronto, the national edition, and the online edition. The one indexed here is for the microfilmed edition, which is the metro Toronto edition and not the national edition. Also covered are the papers from Calgary, Halifax, Montreal, Vancouver and Winnipeg. The *CNI* has a full explanation of usage that is clear and readable. Selection criteria include letters to the editors, reviews of books and the arts, and indication of photographs, but there is nothing on extremely local material nor continuing columnists. There is also a personal name index for information on individuals to accompany the main subject index. Some articles are available through the Canadian Press wire service; most others can be ordered from the National Library in Ottawa at $0.25 a page (good value here!).

Dean Tudor

RADIO

845. The Music Radio Directory, 1987/88. San Anselmo, Calif., Augie Blume/Music Industry Resources, 1987. 92p. $29.95pa. ISBN 0-932521-03-7.

Primarily of interest to those in the "music and recording fields" (p. v), this directory contains more than four thousand station listings, which are considered by the editor to be "musically significant in the promotion and marketing of music" (p. v).

Included in the listings of radio stations are "reference codes" that inform the reader about each station (CJ = Cajun music, BZ = Brazilian, etc.).

Also included are brief sections aimed at a variety of readers who might need practical advice: "Tips for the Musician in the World of Business," "More Basic Tips for Musicians," "Getting Radio Airplay," and other, similar advice.

While of use to those who create or promote music, because of the rapid changes in station formats, even these users should be aware that the information given may need updating. [R: RBB, 1 Jan 88, p. 768]

M. David Guttman

TELECOMMUNICATION

846. Hudson, Heather E. **A Bibliography of Telecommunications and Socio-Economic Development.** Norwood, Mass., Artech House, 1988. 241p. index. $40.00pa. LC 87-35089. ISBN 0-89006-288-9.

For $40.00 you get a computer search of about fifteen databases on the socioeconomic aspects of new technologies. Databases searched are ABI/Inform, Books in Print, Dissertation Abstracts, Economic Literature Index, ERIC, Foreign Trade and Economic Abstracts, GPO Monthly Catalog, InfoTrac, INSPEC, NTIS, PAIS, Social SciSearch, Sociological Abstracts, and Soviet Science and Technology. One also gets a short essay (eight pages) on recent developments (ends in 1985) in telecommunications.

The book is arranged alphabetically by main entry up to page 208, where one finds another ten-page computer search tacked on from who knows what database. A typical entry consists of a bibliographic citation sufficient enough to locate the item, but no indication of which data file it comes from. "The bibliography was initially compiled on a mainframe computer," which I might add has a very poor quality uppercase only line printer. The publisher has the text of the citations on a floppy at an unknown price. The volume is copyrighted by the author, as are presumably the database files by their owners. There is a "key word" index to the entry numbers. It is actually a topical/class index in which one has to guess the topics, since there is no index to the indexing scheme. If you want to buy a book that is a computerized literature search on this topic with keyword indexing under terms such as *research*, then this is the book for you.

A useful bibliography on the subject, but alas three years out-of-date and not very attractive to look at. Needs updating and better indexing.

Ralph Lee Scott

847. Passport to World Band Radio, 1989. Lawrence Magne, ed. Penn's Park, Pa., International Broadcasting Services; distr., Lake Bluff, Ill., Quality Books, 1988. 415p. illus. maps. $14.95pa. ISBN 0-914941-17-8; ISSN 0897-0157.

Passport to World Band Radio contains nineteen articles about radio programming around the world, a buyer's guide to world band radios, and an hour-by-hour guide to radio programs throughout the world. The glossaries and guides are printed in three languages. The book has a directory of advertisers which will interest the world band radio buff.

The popular magazine-type articles are informative, entertaining, and appropriate. Titles include "Escape from Iran: How World Band Radio Saved My Life," "World Band Radio, A Real Part of My Life: An Interview with James A. Michener," "What's on Radio France in English," "Canada Airs Popular Program for World Band Listeners," and "World Band Radio in the Twenty-first Century."

The buyer's guide presents comparative ratings and makes recommendations for the purchase of radios and related equipment. Under "Editor's Choice," recommendations are made by price range: under $100.00, $100.00 to $150.00, and so on up to world band radios selling for over $1,000.00. Pictures and specifications of the radios are shown, followed by a discussion of the advantages and disadvantages of each.

Anyone with a world band radio should own this work because of the wealth of information contained, including the guide for selecting and listening to world band radio programs. [R: RBB, 1 Sept 88, p. 52]

William E. Hug

TELEVISION, AUDIO, AND VIDEO

Bibliographies

848. Garay, Ronald. **Cable Television: A Reference Guide to Information.** Westport, Conn., Greenwood Press, 1988. 177p. index. $39.95. LC 87-24955. ISBN 0-313-24751-X.

In four brief decades, cable television has experienced explosive growth technologically, financially, and in its social impact. With all of its energies focused on growth and survival, however, the industry has done a notoriously terrible job of documenting itself; what information resources exist are scattered and of inconsistent quality. Garay's work will at least provide researchers with a map of those resources that are available.

Cable Television is an extended bibliographic essay on approximately four hundred print resources (books, government documents, and periodical articles) available to researchers on cable television topics. The five chapters cover general sources; business and industry/system economics; program services, program content, uses and effects, viewing habits, and criticism; cable law and regulations; and videotex. Sources cited have been published between 1980 and 1987.

With the exception of the general sources section, each chapter begins with an overview of its topic. These introductions are lengthy (ten to twenty-five pages), clearly written, and up-to-date, and will be extremely helpful to the researcher trying to understand the current or historical context of cable television issues.

After the introduction comes a source overview that identifies subject-related books and book chapters, government documents, and periodical articles. Next comes the chapter bibliography, which provides brief, unannotated bibliographic citations for each of the publications mentioned. (It is important to note that the citations list only publisher and publication date—neither pages, prices, nor ISBNs have been included, which lessens *Cable Television*'s usefulness as a collection tool.) An appendix lists fourteen cable-related agencies and associations, but does not indicate what their particular role within or relationship to the cable industry is, nor what information resources they might provide. A ten-page index concludes the work.

Garay's book is intended as neither a handbook for the industry nor a collection development tool for libraries, although as the only information resource guide on cable television, it might well end up functioning as both. Its organization, currency, and comprehensiveness, however, make it an incredibly useful tool for communications researchers and educators, students of the industry, and others exploring issues in this complex area. People in these groups owe Garay a real debt of gratitude; he has saved them months of work. [R: Choice, Sept 88, p. 103]   G. Kim Dority

849. **Words on Cassette 1987/88: A Comprehensive Bibliography of Spoken Word Audiocassettes.** New York, R. R. Bowker, 1987. 1486p. index. $85.00pa. ISBN 0-8352-2383-3.

First published in 1985 (see *ARBA* 86, entry 904) this third edition has expanded to include thirty thousand titles from over six hundred producers. The preceding editions were well received and quickly considered definitive—now even more so; *Library Journal* selected *On Cassette* as one of the top reference books of the year. The expansion of titles since 1985 has come about because of demand; spoken word audiocassettes are growing in popularity and have impelled major publishing houses to develop separate departments just for their production. Bowker editors, no less, have kept up with the proliferating titles and for this edition have made a special effort to cover in greater depth medical and professional audiocassettes. If unfamiliar with this work, *Words on Cassette* has six indexes: title, author, reader/performer, subject, producer-distributor/title, and producers and distributors. Throughout, unabridged titles are noted to indicate completeness of a work. Most of the titles are for sale, though some are marked rental before the price. Also noted in the listings is whether the work is a dramatization or from an old radio show, if applicable. There are a few foreign-language entries, but many more foreign-language instruction cassettes, which most libraries will readily look to for acquisition. The whole audiocassette industry is one to watch in the coming years; the producers and distributors index alone demonstrates the vitality and variety of its products. From the American Atheist Press offering cassettes of its radio series to Yale University offering cassettes exploring Chinese culture, there is something for everyone. Social historians will likewise find the listings of interest; many of the titles are self-help or religious appeals or even outright propaganda no different from the book world—but because they are spoken by professional speakers will the impact be more pronounced? Recommended for all libraries, here is another exemplary Bowker reference work. [R: RLR, Nov 88, pp. 340-41]

Bill Bailey

Biographies

850.   Adir, Karin. **The Great Clowns of American Television.** Jefferson, N.C., McFarland, 1988. 260p. illus. bibliog. index. $25.95. LC 88-42642. ISBN 0-89950-300-4.

Though quite a bit of material has been produced on the great clowns of the cinema, such as Charlie Chaplin, W. C. Fields, and Buster Keaton, very little can be found that documents the lives and work of the prominent comedians of television. Labeled "a labor of love" by the author, this is a collection of biographies of eighteen funny men and women of the small screen: Lucille Ball, Milton Berle, Carol Burnett, Sid Caesar, Imogene Coca, Tim Conway, Jackie Gleason, Danny Kaye, Ernie Kovacs, Olsen and Johnson, Martha Raye, Soupy Sales, Red Skelton, Dick Van Dyke, Flip Wilson, Jonathan Winters, and Ed Wynn.

The only criterion for the selection of these individuals is the fact that they have been prominent "clowns" of television during the past thirty-five years. For those individuals not included, such as Don Knotts, Johnny Carson, and Rowen and Martin, the author simply states that "perhaps he or she will turn up in the next volume." The coverage is rather uneven, ranging from three to twenty-seven pages in length per individual, but the sketches are well written and provide information on the early years of the comic figure, marriages and personal challenges, anecdotes, the characters they created, styles, and a representative dialog or sketch description. Black-and-white photographs are included. An index directs the reader to other comic figures mentioned within the sketches.

Despite its shortcomings, the book provides quite a bit of insight into the lives of these clowns of television and is easily read from cover to cover. It would be an interesting addition to many collections.

Susan R. Penney

Dictionaries and Encyclopedias

851.   Jones, Glenn R. **Jones Dictionary of Cable Television Terminology: Including Related Computer & Satellite Definitions.** 3d ed. Englewood, Colo., Jones 21st Century, 1988. 108p. $14.95. ISBN 0-9453-7300-7.

The ever-changing cable industry's terms and vocabulary are comprehensively covered in this up-to-date volume of Glenn R. Jones's dictionary. Even though some sources, such as *Delson's Dictionary of Cable, Video and Satellite Terms* (see *ARBA* 84, entry 1086) and *Les Brown's Encyclopedia of Television* (see *ARBA* 83, entry 1111) contain some of the commonly

used words of the cable and satellite industries, Jones's book of over sixteen hundred terms is a more complete, accurate, and current representation. The various areas covered include operations, marketing, management, programming, systems, and regulatory issues.

There are over 250 *see, see also*, and *compare to* references that are especially useful to nontechnical persons. Also included are over five hundred industry-related agencies, associations, and services both national and international. This dictionary will be useful to many kinds of users: lawyers, business professionals, technical writers, teachers, and students or any citizen interested in the cable industry. Even though the volume is a bit expensive, most libraries, especially academic, special, and large public libraries, will find that this dictionary is a valuable addition to their collections. [R: BR, Nov/Dec 88, p. 48; Choice, Nov 88, p. 462]

R. Errol Lam

852.   White, Glenn D. **The Audio Dictionary.** Seattle, Wash., University of Washington Press, 1987. 291p. illus. bibliog. $30.00; $14.95pa. LC 87-15939. ISBN 0-295-96527-4; 0-295-96528-2pa.

Although some of the definitions here may be too sophisticated for the average home audiophile or studio engineer, this dictionary is a good first attempt to bring together and clarify the terminology of audio electronics. Entries are cross-referenced and frequently include several paragraphs of information. Coverage is extensive – from "Absolute Pitch" to "Zero Reference," though some obvious terms, like mini plug connector and phono plus, are not included. Additional illustrations and diagrams would be helpful in demonstrating many of the explanations. The dictionary concludes with several appendices of interest to hi-fi enthusiasts and an annotated bibliography of books and periodicals. [R: RBB, 15 June 88, pp. 1715-16]

Michael Ann Moskowitz

Directories

853.   **AVMP 1988: Audio Video Market Place: The Complete A/V Business Directory.** New York, R. R. Bowker, 1988. 693p. $65.00pa. LC 69-18201. ISBN 0-8352-2270-5; ISSN 0067-0553.

AVMP is a one-stop information source for suppliers of audiovisual, video, and other high tech communicaiton products and services in the United States. The sixteenth edition covers twelve hundred products of five thousand companies classified by type of service and indexed in a variety of ways. Descriptions of companies are included with contact information provided.

In addition to commercial companies, there are directories for associations connected with the industry, film and television commissions listed by state, a list of awards and festivals, a calendar of professional association meetings for 1988-1989, a list of professional periodicals, and an annotated bibliography of professional reference books.

The book is directed toward those persons needing information about software producers and distributors, production companies, production facilities, video services, cable programming, sound recording, music scoring, music and sound effects libraries, equipment manufacturers, distributors and dealers, and unions and guilds. This means that dealers, audiovisual production companies, audiovisual libraries, and school district media centers will need access to this directory on an annual basis. The directory is current and under continuous revision. An indispensable guide for its intended audience.   David V. Loertscher

854. *Variety*'s **Complete Home Video Directory 1988.** New York, R. R. Bowker, 1988. 852p. index. $99.95pa. ISBN 0-8352-2500-3; ISSN 0000-1015.

This first edition promises to be a comprehensive guide to home video. The main volume provides descriptive and ordering information on more than twenty-five thousand available videos. Quarterly cumulative updates including all new releases announced and available are planned. There are seven clearly tabbed sections and indexes. The main section is an alphabetical title list which gives such standard information as release date, running time, credits, awards, ordering information, and a brief descriptive annotation. There are a directory of services and suppliers and indexes of producers and distributors, awards, and cast and directors. Two special indexes, one to genres and one to closed-captioned titles, are very helpful. There are ninety categories and subcategories in the genre index, which provides access by such special interest areas as foreign films, horror films, documentaries, how-to films, and silents. Adult video listings are not included in this basic volume but are available without annotations in a separately bound volume as part of the subscription. Since the price of this volume probably puts it beyond the reach of most individuals, it would be a welcome addition to any reference collection serving a clientele with an interest in home video. [R: LJ, 1 May 88, p. 72; RBB, 15 Oct 88, p. 391]   Barbara E. Kemp

Discographies

855. Debenham, Warren. **Laughter on Record: A Comedy Discography.** Metuchen, N.J., Scarecrow, 1988. 369p. index. $35.00. LC 87-35938. ISBN 0-8108-2094-3.

This volume treats the somewhat narrow subject of comedy long-playing recordings. The discography contains over forty-three hundred entries sequentially numbered and arranged by artist(s) or performance group. Each listing includes the title, record number, reissues and foreign issues, and incidental information. The date of each recording is important information that is not given. The incidental information is sparse and no attempt is made at even a brief annotation or listing of selections from a record composed of more than a single comedy routine. Also included is a directory of several companies that produce comedy records and retail outlets that deal in out-of-date records. There is an index of the dominant theme of each respective record (e.g., air travel, insurance, school, etc.). The gathering and compilation of the titles are important; however, a researcher desiring specific information on a particular record would use this volume sparingly. [R: RBB, 15 Nov 88, p. 550; WLB, Oct 88, p. 106]   Jackson Kesler

Handbooks

856. Gianakos, Larry James. **Television Drama Series Programming: A Comprehensive Chronicle, 1982-1984.** Metuchen, N.J., Scarecrow, 1987. 830p. index. $62.50. LC 85-30428. ISBN 0-8108-1876-0.

Volume 5 of this series covers dramatic television programming from fall 1982 to the end of summer 1984. After the "Overview" chapter, which is a critical review of the two television seasons, the author presents the detailed complete weekly prime-time television schedules with times, days, and dates of very program. Following this section, each drama series is enumerated program-by-program. "Specials" and television movies are also listed and described in the regular program lists or in the "Overview" chapter. The title of the individual episode, the director, the writer, featured players, and notable events such as the date of introduction of a new character are given for most of the entries. Series which began previous to fall 1982 are listed first, and those that began fall 1982 or later follow. While the title suggests that this material is the main thrust of this volume, the section takes up only about two-fifths of the book. The remainder is supplementary material, which updates, through 31 January 1985, any of the four previous volumes.

The treatment of entries is uneven. In some cases, a brief description of the episode's storyline is included, while in many cases it is not. The lack of even a few words of description in many entries limits the value of the lists and may prove frustrating for information seekers. On the other hand, instead of description, sometimes the author's opinionated and political comments are intrusive in a work which no doubt is intended to be a comprehensive record of the medium rather than a critical review of it. In some sections, only month and day of the air date are noted but not the year. It saves space, but it is confusing for the user.

The appendix lists should be of value to educators and entertainment programmers. But none of the specialized lists, overview section, program specials, or television movies are included in the index, only the series titles. The index covers all five volumes, which is an important consideration because the researcher may need to consult two volumes or more to find a particular answer. This work cannot be effectively used without the complete set. The complicated patchwork format makes browsing difficult.

Libraries will have to weigh the limitations of using these five volumes against the load of information they contain. Some of the information can be found in numerous other sources on historical television programming. Recommended only for more comprehensive collections unless a more extensive index to the set becomes available. [R: RBB, 15 May 88, p. 1588]

Gary R. Cocozzoli

857. Herx, Henry, and Tony Zaza, eds. **The Family Guide to Movies on Video: The Moral and Entertainment Values of 5,000 Movies on TV and Videocassette.** New York, Crossroad Publishing, 1988. 331p. $27.50; $12.95pa. LC 88-1398. ISBN 0-8245-0816-5; 0-8245-0817-3pa.

Any parent or fan of television movies and videocassettes will benefit from this guide. It contains descriptions and evaluations of approximately five thousand motion pictures released in the United States from 1966 to 1987. Each listing contains a summary of the plot, the film's value (entertainment, information, etc.), and its appropriateness for different age groups. Two ratings are included: the United States Catholic Conference Department of Communication (USCC) and the Motion Picture Association of America (MPAA).

For the many people who like "good" movies, the guide is an invaluable tool. It is also an easy way to identify "morally offensive" films

if this fare is preferred. The films are arranged alphabetically by title and followed by the date the film was released. Annotations are well written but with the obvious bias of the editors about what is moral, obscene, violent, and so on.

The work contains an appendix that lists recommended motion pictures for family viewing. Films are grouped by subjects such as adventure, fantasy, drama, comedy, and the like. Separate lists divide films into categories, such as teens and adults, the Walt Disney productions, and documentaries. [R: WLB, Nov 88, p. 125]   William E. Hug

858. Marill, Alvin H. **Movies Made for Television: The Telefeature and the Mini-Series 1964-1986.** New York, New York Zoetrope, 1987. 576p. illus. index. $39.95; $19.95pa. LC 87-043022; 87-042898pa. ISBN 0-918432-80-4; 0-918432-85-5pa.

Updating an earlier edition to include programs through 1986, this volume lists more than twenty-one hundred television movies and miniseries. This is an increase of more than three hundred titles over the original edition. Films and miniseries made for PBS are not included, but those made for Home Box Office, Showtime, The Disney Channel, and some independent stations are. To be included, a television movie must be a separate, self-contained entity, not an episode or episodes of a continuing series or part of an anthology series. The author also states that he has added credit information to some original entries. The main section now is an alphabetical listing of titles in which each entry gives extensive cast and credit information, premiere date, a brief plot summary, background notes when appropriate, and pertinent awards information. There is a chronological index, as well as indexes of producers, directors, writers, and actors. Anyone needing information on this sometimes elusive video genre should find this comprehensive encyclopedia very useful. [R: Choice, Mar 88, pp. 1104, 1106]

Barbara E. Kemp

859. **The Producer's Masterguide 1988: The International Production Manual for Motion Pictures, Broadcast Television, Commercials, Cable and Videotape Industries.** 8th ed. Shmuel Bension, comp. and ed. New York, New York Production Manual, 1988. 488p. illus. index. $79.95pa. LC 83-641703. ISBN 0-935744-07-X; ISSN 0732-6653.

It is amazing that this work does not appear in the latest edition of Sheehy. It was reviewed in *ARBA 86* (entry 920) and yet does not appear in other standard compilations on resources for business information. This is too bad, since it has a wealth of information that very likely is not available elsewhere in the detail and care shown here for one of the larger and more complicated business operations in the world today. Clearly explained are the completion bond, types of insurance needed, copyright procedures including a reproducible form; and how to obtain a MPAA rating and how much it will cost. U.S. production information tells what to expect if you want to film on federal property and the problems you will face trying to import performing talent (as the editors note, it is difficult to get the U.S. Department of Labor to evaluate performers: "a prima ballerina and a chorus girl are in the same category: they both 'kick'").

Thirty-four states are covered for their specific requirements on production within their borders. Los Angeles, New York City, and the District of Columbia receive additional listings. Canada, the Caribbean, New Zealand, and the United Kingdom are similarly treated, with the new additions of Australia and Israel. A huge section with the latest contract information is devoted to the unions and guilds. After all of this comes 141 pages of directory information on such unusual information as trained animals, aerial photography, catering services, costumes, sources for stock footage, special effects producers, and stunt performers. The largest category goes to the producers and what their specialties may be. The categories cover almost any angle being sought by anyone approaching the motion picture/video field. Any agency claiming to be a resource on business information would have this at least on a periodic basis, while those with extensive production activity in their area would need the annual updating.

Gerald R. Shields

860.   Schwartz, David, Steve Ryan, and Fred Wostbrock. **The Encyclopedia of TV Game Shows.** New York, New York Zoetrope, 1987. 587p. illus. index. $39.95. LC 87-42900. ISBN 0-918432-87-1.

It is hard to believe that since 1946 over five hundred game shows have aired on television. Of that number many did not enjoy a long run due either to a shaky premise, the wrong host, or a too complicated structure. Unless the reader has been a television addict for all those years, most of these game shows are unfamiliar. "It's in the Bag," "Camouflage," "Funny You Should Ask," and "Split Personality" are a few examples. But the twenty longest running game shows are well known and still talked about. "What's My Line?" "I've Got a Secret," "You Bet Your Life," and "To Tell the Truth" hold the top four positions. This encyclopedia is greatly nostalgic, full of photographs and anecdotes about each show. Entire careers unfold here. Tom Kennedy has hosted no less than fourteen game shows; Johnny Jacobs has announced for seventeen of them; and to set the record straight "Who Do You Trust?" was not Johnny Carson's first television work – it was on another game show three years before, "Earn Your Vacation." For anyone interested in analyzing why some game shows make it while others fall flat, this is the source. The authors do not provide much assistance except to outline the premise of the show and to give the running dates. A behind-the-scenes look at what caused the demise of certain shows would have been just the right touch. Otherwise, everything else is pleasing: design, layout, and typography. The indexes and appendices are excellent and every photograph is crystal-clear. Because no other reference book like this one exists, public libraries will want to showcase it in a popular culture exhibit. [R: RBB, 1 May 88, pp. 1484-85]

Bill Bailey

861.   Wiener, Tom. **The Book of Video Lists.** Lanham, Md., Madison Books/University Press of America, 1988. 417p. index. $8.95pa. LC 88-19853. ISBN 0-8191-7011-9.

Reported to be the first guide designed for the customer as a movie selection guide in video rental shops, this volume contains over four thousand movie titles. The first part of the book divides the film titles into twelve categories: adventure/action, classics, comedy, cult films, drama, foreign films, horror, kid/family movies, musicals, suspense, science fiction/fantasy, and westerns. Within these categories are found numerous checklists of leading stars and directors and various subcategories such as gangster pictures or political thrillers. The second part is a title index of films arranged alphabetically. Information found here includes year of release, color, running time, a brief statement about the subject matter, notes of rating, and a symbol indicating in which of the twelve categories the film is listed. A checklist at the end of the volume lists by name the best known stars and directors and the symbol for the category where that person's films are found.

The major drawback to the volume is that one cannot easily locate information due to the lack of an index and table of contents. The title index would be more useful placed first in the volume. The user must read the introduction and the "how-to" sections to make any sense of the contents. The book provides very good film information in a concise format but the reader will need a great deal of patience to seek it out.

Marilyn Strong Noronha

21 Decorative Arts

GENERAL WORKS

862. de Winter, Patrick M. **European Decorative Arts 1400-1600: An Annotated Bibliography.** Boston, G. K. Hall, 1988. 543p. index. (Reference Publications in Art History). $75.00. LC 87-31071. ISBN 0-8161-8612-X.

The brilliant period of late Gothic and Renaissance decorative arts in Europe is celebrated in this bibliography of over twenty-two hundred entries covering the secular as well as the ecclesiastical world of these highly productive eras on the Continent and Great Britain. The book will be used primarily by those engaged in academic research in art history and by collectors for reading in their own particular field of interest.

The author is curator of the medieval and Renaissance collections at the Cleveland Museum of Art. He has included periodical articles plus exhibition and auction catalogs as part of his overall policy in the listings of the thirty-seven categories of materials under which he has organized a multitude of individual entries. The entries are annotated, which adds immensely to the permanent value of any bibliographic summary. Lengthy listings appear under "Secular Plate and Devotional Objects" (sixty-six pages), "Ceramics" (fifty pages), "Furniture" (thirty-five pages), "Arms and Armor" (thirty-three pages), and "Tapestries" (twenty-seven pages). Many researchers will be grateful for coverage of more specific topics such as seals, plaquettes, church bells, lecturns, scales, tools, silks, musical instruments, or rock crystal. In his introduction, the author points out that it was during the 1830s that the upper middle class began seriously to collect in the areas of his expertise. Therefore, the citations reflect writings from the past century or so with a stated emphasis on published research during the past quarter of a century and addressed to the English-speaking reader. Although many of the entries are fairly esoteric, users can expect to locate the material with a minimum of inconvenience in this time of library networking and photocopy.

Securely bound and concluding with three indexes for author, title, and the location of notable private and permanent collections, this erudite and thorough listing is a paradigm of serious bibliography for reference use by the art history community specializing in particular materials from a specific and prolific era. [R: RQ, Winter 88, pp. 266-67]

William J. Dane

863. Dizik, A. Allen. **Concise Encyclopedia of Interior Design.** 2d ed. New York, Van Nostrand Reinhold, 1988. 220p. illus. bibliog. $36.95. LC 88-5560. ISBN 0-442-22109-6.

A practical short-entry reference book, this encyclopedia is in some ways closer to a dictionary, due to the brevity of many of its entries. Aimed at serving the homemaker, the design student, and the semiprofessional decorator, it is also a handy ready-reference volume for the professional designer.

The scope is broad with the expected articles on furniture periods, furniture and room arrangements, fabrics, wall and floor coverings, and lighting, among others. Much valuable material also relates to the allied disciplines of fine arts, architecture, antiques, and construction.

The alphabetically arranged articles and definitions are well cross-referenced. For example, in the four-paragraph entry for "American Colonial" there are referrals to thirteen related entries. While many subjects are covered by a one-sentence definition, many others such as color, draperies, lighting, paint, and Spanish furniture, to list a few, may cover two to four pages. A number of charts and tables are included for such subjects as estimating tile coverage, types of carpet fibers, wallpaper coverage calculations, periods and styles of furniture, and fabric-to-leather conversion tables, all of which are useful to amateur and professional alike. The four pages of line drawings which are included illustrate principles of furniture arrangement and the various standard architectural symbols employed in drawing plans and elevations. Although the book could benefit perhaps from more illustrations, it is a highly competent, comprehensive, up-to-date reference tool. [R: Choice, Nov 88, p. 458; RBB, 15 Dec 88, pp. 688-89]   G. Joan Burns

864. Duncan, Alastair, ed. **The Encyclopedia of Art Deco.** New York, E. P. Dutton, 1988. 192p. illus. (part col.). bibliog. index. $29.95. ISBN 0-525-24613-4.

Art deco is a genuine visual style which flourished during the turbulent years from 1920 to 1940. Decorative art objects and architectural details from the period continue to fascinate and attract collectors, curators, and a multitude of informed enthusiasts. Much has been written about the style and its principal creators, especially over the past decade, both in books and periodical literature. This new one-volume summary is extremely well done and is a most welcome addition to the literature of the period. Edited by Christie's specialist, Alastair Duncan, who wrote the introduction and the sections on architecture and paintings, graphics, and bookbinding, the text includes the research of five other specialists who have written on sculpture, lighting, ceramics, metalwork, jewelry, and textiles plus furniture and interior decoration, thus covering the major classifications of art deco material. This text also provides a summary selection of the major artisans and objects, thus justifying an encyclopedic approach. Running along the lower section of each page of text are succinct biographies of the major contributors of the era, and these several hundred entries add greatly to the reference value of the book. The bibliographical data have been edited to the bone to provide only the pertinent facts pointing out the importance of the individual to the entire art deco period. Several hundred artists are listed, from Aalto to Zorach, as well as stellar figures such as Puiforcat, Ruhlmann, Marinot, Daum, Chareau, Brandt, and Cassandre. The biographies are set apart on a blue wash background, which is only one of the delights in the design and layout of this international effort. Some of the 350 illustrations are in color and all are clear in their details. The placement of the illustrations, captions, and chapter and section headings is so beautiful that each page seems colorful and a visual delight. The overall design is highly successful and entirely compatible with the art deco look. Modestly priced, this summary of the art

deco style has considerable reference value both to novices and seasoned experts. [R: LJ, Aug 88, p. 150]   William J. Dane

865. Newman, Harold. **An Illustrated Dictionary of Silverware: 2,373 Entries, Relating to British and North American Wares....** New York, Thames and Hudson; distr., New York, W. W. Norton, 1987. 366p. illus. (part col.). $39.95. LC 86-51576. ISBN 0-500-23456-6.

Much like Clayton's *The Collector's Dictionary of the Silver and Gold of Great Britain and North America* (see *ARBA* 86, entry 968), this dictionary is an excellent alphabetical listing of the decorative techniques, designers and makers, styles, and wares of the field. It covers Great Britain from 1500 to the present (including Ireland up to 1921) and North America (Canada, Mexico, and the United States) from the colonial period to the present.

The volume contains 2,373 brief entries, each a short paragraph, that provide comprehensive coverage for those various categories and countries along with a wide assortment of clear black-and-white photographs to accompany many entries. There are, in addition, a few color photographs designed to illustrate the sumptuous nature of some large silver pieces. The entries are clear and concise and offer useful specific information. One especially useful feature is the inclusion of appropriate bibliographic citations at the end of many of the entries. The work concentrates on topics such as makers, styles, and terms rather than on a miscellaneous assortment of pieces, as do other works such as *Sotheby's Directory of Silver 1600-1940* (see *ARBA* 87, entry 948). Thus, with Clayton's dictionary, it is a more useful reference tool to libraries because it is likely to provide answers to the specific kinds of questions about pieces and designers/makers that even sophisticated users may ask. [R: Choice, Mar 88, p. 1068; LJ, 15 Feb 88, pp. 160-61]   Norman D. Stevens

COLLECTING

Antiques

866. Andacht, Sandra. **Oriental Antiques & Art: An Identification and Value Guide.** Greensboro, N.C., Wallace-Homestead, 1987. 428p. illus. (part col.). index. $15.95pa. LC 87-50296. ISBN 0-87069-485-5.

Since there is no preface explaining the scope and purpose of the guide, confusion begins with the title and the question becomes: Which countries in the orient are included? Examination reveals that Chinese and Japanese antiques are emphasized. Included are genuine antiques (items over one hundred years old) and collectibles (nonantique items). The largest section concerns Chinese porcelain. Within this section are color photographs of the more popular Chinese export items. Color and black-and-white photographs will help beginning collectors to identify correctly certain inexpensive late nineteenth- and twentieth-century export items. The introductions to the various sections seem to be abridged versions of articles originally printed in antique trade magazines. These brief discussions do not help users understand market values nor do they serve to help beginners distinguish antiques from reproductions, a major problem in the world of oriental art.

There is no satisfactory explanation for most of the prices given, an important consideration given the cost of genuine Chinese and Japanese antiques. Some references are made to auction prices realized at Christie's, New York City, but it is not always clear which of the two Christie auction houses is concerned; Christie's East is a smaller house dealing in run-of-the-mill items. The author's experience as an appraiser seems to account for all but a few of the prices given. An experienced appraiser who contributes articles to trade magazines, Andacht is editor and publisher of *Orientalia Journal*.

This price guide may be of interest to the nonspecialist antique dealer. Beginning collectors having little knowledge of oriental antiques should avoid the guide as it might inadvertently serve to encourage them to pay too much for antiques that are simply nineteenth- and twentieth-century reproductions. Librarians are advised to select and purchase special museum publications devoted to Chinese and Japanese art.

Milton H. Crouch

867. Kelman, Keith, and Renee Kelman, comps. **The National Antique Show Directory: A Listing of Antique Shows for 1988 Arranged Geographically and Chronologically.** 2d ed. La Jolla, Calif., National Antique Show Directory, 1987. 234p. maps. $24.95pa.

This directory fills the need for a complete listing of antique shows presented throughout the calendar year across the United States. It will be of most interest and value to avid collectors and active dealers. The compilers have divided the fifty states into eight geographic regions with the principal list arranged chronologically by the opening dates of the many shows in 1988. Naturally, Hawaii and Alaska and the District of Columbia are included. A system for the listing of shows starting on the same day in the same region has been carefully worked out following a common-sense formula

that is easy to comprehend at a glance. The precise location for each show is listed along with the hours of opening, the number of dealers expected to exhibit, the admission charge, and the name of the promoter or manager. If some of the specifics are not known, the notation *N/A* is indicated. The greatest number of entries appear under the Northeast Region, which includes New England plus New York state, and the fewest entries are for the Northwest Region, which has only sixteen preposted shows for 1988.

A caveat recommends that readers confirm all details before they actually set out to attend shows far from their home base. The text is printed in capitals from typescript copy with entries nicely spaced to maximize legibility and to make the detailed information more readily available at a glance. This is only the second edition of the directory, which quickly becomes outdated as the months move along during the year for which the data were posted. However, there is no similar publication with all antique show information in one place. Therefore, it is a useful reference for the growing public and professional community vitally interested in antiques and ancillary collectibles. [R: RBB, 15 May 88, p. 1585]   William J. Dane

Baseball Cards

868. **The Complete Book of Collectible Baseball Cards.** By the Editors of *Consumer Guide.* Lincolnwood, Ill., Publications International, 1987. 424p. illus. (part col.). index. $14.95. ISBN 0-88176-414-0.

This is indeed a "complete book" only if one accepts the editors' definition of "collectible." Neither older card sets that are too obscure, rare, or expensive nor newer minor league or reprint sets meet their definition. One may question those limitations although the editors are right when they suggest that a book without limitations would be impossible to publish. There are other negatives: the book is dated (the last year included is 1986), and many of the prices listed are obsolete (the price for some sets has more than doubled).

What it does cover, it covers very well. In reverse chronological order, card sets (both national and regional) are described and evaluated under the following headings: specifications, history, features "for" and "against" the set, value (included are long-term investment possibilities), and most interestingly, "noteworthy cards." Here the peculiarities of each set are outlined, including major rookie cards, particularly scarce cards, errors and other idiosyncrasies that may make the set valuable. Here is information both the novice and experienced collector will appreciate. Illustrations for most sets are included. Altogether over 400 sets are described, from the 1886 Old Judge to the 1986 Topps.

The book includes a glossary and an index. The forty pages of attractive color reproductions of cards add to the book's appeal.

John R. Muether

869. Wright, Jim, and Jean-Paul Emard. **Baseball Card & Collectibles Dealer Directory, 1988.** Westport, Conn., Meckler, 1988. 210p. index. $10.95pa. ISBN 0-88736-269-9; ISSN 0896-8519.

It is no secret that baseball memorabilia has become big business. The *Wall Street Journal* recently labeled card collecting as one of the best investments today. *Sports Illustrated* described it as a $200 million per year business. Hundreds are returning to a hobby after over twenty-year layoffs, and many of them are rummaging their attics in search of their long-lost treasures. With the growth of the hobby has come the rapid proliferation of baseball card shows and dealers.

This guide attempts to perform an important function for collectors. By listing eleven hundred dealers of baseball memorabilia, it purports to provide "a one-stop source for dealers and collectors alike" (p. xiii). The directory is divided into four sections: an alphabetical listing (with the full listing of the dealers' addresses), indexes by kinds of collectibles, geographical index (which is helpful to the collector who is traveling), and a dealer name and number index.

The directory is heavy on advertisements. While these are often enjoyable to study and compare (there is an index to advertisers), they can be intrusive in finding information, and the prices listed in the ads are sure to be dated soon.

But the ultimate frustration in using this guide is that many dealers are not listed. (I have found none of the dozen or so dealers that I have consulted included.) This is less than the comprehensive resource that the introduction claims that it is, an inevitable problem in documenting a field that is growing so rapidly. Our hope is that future editions (it is intended as an annual) will be more complete.

John R. Muether

Books

870. LeFontaine, Joseph Raymond. **A Handbook for Booklovers: A Survey of Collectible Authors, Books, and Values.** Buffalo, N.Y.,

Prometheus Books, 1988. 612p. bibliog. $39.95. LC 88-15128. ISBN 0-87975-491-5.

This handbook supplies three main kinds of information: (1) the current market value of some thirty-seven hundred collectible (primarily American and British) books in various fiction and nonfiction genres; (2) the pseudonyms of various authors; and (3) the name, date, publisher, and place of publication of the first books of some eighteen hundred collectible authors. The remaining chapters comprise a brief overview of book collecting and its terminology and a list of collectible book illustrators. There are five appendices: a list of North American book dealers who do book searches, a list of North American book dealers who issue catalogs, a selected list of books about books, a five-page dictionary of foreign words and phrases, and a two-page table of how to price books of less than mint condition. Unfortunately, there is neither an author nor a title index. Although there is a lot of useful information in this handbook, the heart of the book—the price guide chapters—suffers from the omission of many major collectible authors and the inclusion of too few titles when an author is included. In the price guide chapter on science fiction, fantasy, and horror books, for example, the following major collectible authors are omitted: Ramsey Campbell, Philip K. Dick, Philip Jose Farmer, Stephen King, Larry Niven, Olaf Stapledon, and Roger Zelazny. Similarly, in the chapter on crime and mystery, such major collectible authors as Earl Stanley Garner, John D. MacDonald, Ngaio Marsh, Robert Parker, and Rex Stout are omitted and only two titles are listed for Dorothy Sayers, whereas seventy-two titles are listed for the less well known Edward Aarons. This handbook is thus a disappointingly uncomprehensive price guide and cannot adequately serve as a substitute for either the catalogs of major specialty dealers or *Bookman's Price Index* (see *ARBA 86*, entry 649).

Joseph Cataio

Coins

871. Breen, Walter. **Walter Breen's Complete Encyclopedia of U.S. and Colonial Coins.** New York, Doubleday, 1988. 754p. illus. index. $75.00. LC 79-6855. ISBN 0-385-14207-2.

This smashing book is it! It is without any question *the* definitive book on colonial and U.S. coins of all kinds, a landmark publication in the field of numismatics and a reference work of truly lasting value. Breen carefully defines and describes in detail 8,035 coins, and also provides over 4,000 black-and-white illustrations that depict not only the obverse and reverse of significant coins but also in many cases important details, representing almost every major and minor American coin from the first brass Bermuda shillings of 1616 to contemporary sandwich coins. Only a few minor categories (e.g., Philippine, Cuban, and Puerto Rican issues) are deliberately omitted. In addition to the detailed descriptions of the coins, there are precise and well-written introductory pieces to each of the forty-nine chapters, which are grouped into seven major parts, that provide a fascinating background and history for the particular type of coin. Arranged topically in chronological order, each of the chapters deals with a discrete set of coins (e.g., coinage of the Kingdom of Hawaii). Each individual coin is carefully numbered in a rough chronological sequence that is easy to follow, especially if one reads carefully the page of simple instructions on how to use the book. Wisely omitting price information, which is clearly out of place in an encyclopedia of permanent value, Breen provides for almost every item, except in cases where the data have not survived, information about the historical circumstances of issue, physical characteristics, designer, engraver, mint of issue, quantity issued, and level of rarity. This fascinating guide is not only an indispensable resource for information about U.S. coins but also an important adjunct to the study of coinage as a minor aspect of American history. [R: Choice, Nov 88, p. 455; LJ, 1 Sept 88, p. 162; RBB, 15 Dec 88, p. 695]

Norman D. Stevens

872. Rulau, Russell. **U.S. Trade Tokens 1866-1889: A Catalog of the Private Coinage and Advertising Tokens of an Industrializing America....** 2d ed. Iola, Wis., Krause Publications, 1988. 334p. illus. index. $17.95pa. LC 85-050403. ISBN 0-87341-026-2.

After completing his valuable five-volume series (*Early American Tokens, 1700-1832* [Krause, 1983]; *Hard Times Tokens, 1832-1844* [Krause, 1987]; *United States Merchant Tokens, 1845-1860* [see *ARBA* 87, entry 1914]; *United States Trade Tokens, 1866-1889* (see *ARBA* 84, entry 850]; and *Tokens of the Gay Nineties* [Krause, 1987]), which provides a comprehensive view of the various tokens used for trade purposes in lieu of money, Rulau has started over. The second edition of the 1866-1889 volume is a completely revised, updated, and greatly expanded text made possible, in part, by the wealth of additional information generated by the pioneering work of the first edition. There are probably twice as many tokens listed, many previously unidentified

"mavericks" have now been tracked down, and many others have had at least their possible dates of issuance narrowed down. The introductory material could still benefit from additional detail but is considerably better than that in the first edition. Here, once again, is a straightforward alphabetical listing by state, and within state by issuer, of an amazing variety of the different kinds of tokens issued in the period, such as store cards; advertising checks; work, job, picker, and railroad checks and talleys; saloon and billiard tokens; checks for value; exposition and festival medalets; and counterstamped coins. Some categories of tokens, such as transportation and military tokens, are reasonably excluded because of the existence of other comprehensive catalogs that cover them. Once again, for what Rulau still justifies as convenience, a number of British, Canadian, and other foreign tokens are included. That may be convenient but, given the title, few people are likely to look for information on foreign tokens here. For collectors of these unusual items, which should include many local historians, this revised edition is a must. Libraries with the first edition will probably want to update it. Libraries with a clientele interested in the social, commercial, and advertising history of the United States should also consider this since it is a useful volume that sheds a great deal of interesting light on several odd aspects of that history.

Norman D. Stevens

Glass

873. Edwards, Bill. **The Standard Encyclopedia of Carnival Glass.** 2d ed. Paducah, Ky., Collector Books, 1988. 223p. illus. (col.). $24.95. ISBN 0-89145-372-5.

Since publication of the first edition in 1982, the market for carnival glass, that colorful pressed and iridized glass produced between 1905 and 1930, has continued to grow. The new edition of this work covers hundreds of patterns, alphabetically listed from "Absentee Dragon" (a name hated by author Edwards) to "Zipper Variant." Identifications are brief but informative and are accompanied by bright, clear photographs, all of which are in color. The layout of the work is excellent, with the illustrations on the righthand page and the descriptive text on the lefthand page opposite. It appears that all known household patterns of this sometimes elusive glass have been covered, including certain utilitarian commercial products like the Golden Wedding Whiskey bottle and the Jackman Whiskey bottle as well as a few advertising pieces and souvenir items. The work begins with a very brief introduction preceded by an author's note, then furnishes an informative history of the five major companies in terms of production: Dugan, Fenton, Imperial, Millersburg, and Northwood. Lesser companies follow, including non-American manufacturers. Most important is the provision of a separate price guide, now in its seventh edition, which provides values for every item covered in the encyclopedia. (This is free with purchase of the encyclopedia, but sells for $7.95 as a separate item.) The pair together should be a useful purchase for the hobbyists and collectors who seek such information.   Ron Blazek

Toys

874. Boileau, Claude, Huynh-Dinh Khuong, and Thomas A. Young. **Encyclopaedia of Military Models 1/72.** Blue Ridge Summit, Pa., TAB Books, 1988. 204p. illus. (part col.). $28.95; $19.60pa. LC 88-6298. ISBN 0-8306-8283-X; 0-8306-8383-6pa.

This book is a reference guide to nearly fifty-five hundred models—primarily model airplane kits—that have been manufactured in 1:72 scale during the last fifty years. This scale was popularized during World War II, when 1/6-inch-to-the-foot aircraft "recognition models" were used in training observers to distinguish enemy from friendly aircraft. Today 1:72 scale is by far the most popular scale for static models of aircraft, and literally billions of kits have been produced in this size.

The core of this encyclopedia is a ninety-page list of fifty-five hundred models. The entries are arranged by prototype (manufacturer and model), subdivided by kit manufacturer. Each entry includes information on the type of model (hobby kit, recognition model, toy, or desk ornament) and the materials used (plastics of various types, wood, etc.), but not on kit production dates or quantities produced. Nearly 85 percent of the models listed are of aircraft, but lists are also provided of 1:72 scale missiles, spacecraft, science fiction equipment, vehicles, warships, etc. Names and current (or last-known) addresses are included for about 250 kit manufacturers.

The balance of the book consists of about 120 color photographs illustrating the box covers of about 470 kits, as well as about 75 completed models. Captions describing the completed models and about 90 of the kits provide a variety of information on the prototypes and the kit manufacturers.

This book is aimed primarily at people attempting to build models of specific prototypes or with a collector's interest in old kits. It provides a vast amount of well-organized infor-

mation on an elusive subject and appears to be the most complete work in the area.
Frederick A. Schlipf

875. Osterhoff, Robert J., ed. **Greenberg's Guide to Lionel Prewar Parts & Instruction Sheets.** Sykesville, Md., Greenberg Publishing, 1987. 398p. illus. index. $35.00pa. LC 87-8567. ISBN 0-89778-059-0.

This guide provides a wide variety of useful reference information for people who want to repair or operate Lionel trains made before World War II. It consists of three types of documents. Half the book is devoted to reproductions of parts lists that Lionel distributed to its authorized service stations. Although the oldest of these dates from 1922, most are from the 1930s, when Lionel began to provide its dealers with more detailed and accurate repair information. The sheets identify and provide catalog numbers for the parts used in various pieces of Lionel equipment.

The second section of the book consists of about 175 pages reproduced from the instruction sheets and manuals that accompanied Lionel equipment. Although these sheets were widely distributed at the time the trains were made, many copies have been lost in the intervening half century.

The third section is an eighteen-page list of sources of modern replacement parts. It has been decades since Lionel stocked replacement parts for prewar trains, and people who want to repair them depend on a number of small firms that make duplicates of the most frequently needed parts. This section lists—for each Lionel part number—which of twenty-one firms make replacements for that part. There is also a brief index by part number.

Greenberg's Guide should prove to be an extremely useful reference tool and an important companion volume to Greenberg's impressive, four-volume reproduction of post-World War II Lionel service manuals, *Greenberg's Lionel Service Manual* (Greenberg Publishing, 1985), edited by Isaac D. Smith.
Frederick A. Schlipf

Other Collectibles

876. Danforth, Ellen Zak. **Nesting Weights, Einsatzgewichte and Piles à Godets: A Catalog of Nested Cup Weights in the Edward Clark Streeter Collection of Weights and Measures.** Hamden, Conn., for Connecticut Academy of Arts and Sciences by Archon Books/Shoe String Press, 1988. 115p. illus. bibliog. index. (Connecticut Academy of Arts and Sciences

Transactions, Vol. 50). $18.50pa. LC 87-33492. ISBN 0-208-02220-1.

Nested cup weights, also known as *Einsatzsgewichte* or *piles à godet*, are not the kind of everyday collectible found at the local flea market or even the kind of antique found at the fanciest antique show. They are a highly specialized set of cup-shaped weights that fit into one another with a lid to cover the whole set. These weights were used from the sixteenth through the nineteenth centuries to weigh household commodities, precious metals, and coins in commercial settings. They were carefully calibrated scientific measuring devices and, as such, are of special interest to those interested in the history of commerce and science. This brief catalog of a collection of eighty such items in the Edward Clark Streeter collection of weights and measures at Yale University provides a detailed description of those nested cup weights. Each item is precisely cataloged to provide essential information about the type, date, place of manufacture, place of use, mass quantity, theoretical mass, numerical system, numerical breakdown, actual mass, maker's marks, verification stamps, adjustments, form, decoration, dimensions, condition, and provenance. Each entry is also accompanied by a clear black-and-white photograph. An excellent introduction describes in some detail the history and use of these devices, while a brief but comprehensive two-page bibliography provides ample information for those who wish to pursue further study of these weights. This is an outstanding catalog of an unusual and historically valuable kind of item, but the subject and the content are so highly specialized as to appeal only to a few historians and collectors. This is clearly not a book likely to be in high demand.

Norman D. Stevens

CRAFTS

877. *American Craft* **1988-89 Guide to Craft Galleries & Shops USA.** Lois Moran, Frank Wright, and Joyce Tognini, eds. Washington, D.C., American Craft Council, 1988. 56p. $5.00pa.

Issued as a supplement to the April/May 1988 issue of *American Craft* magazine (though it is also available separately), this little directory lists 614 galleries and shops selling crafts in the United States. The arrangement is geographical, first by state and then city. Information provided includes address, telephone number, owner and director names, year founded, type of crafts offered, and artists regularly represented. As stated on the title page, the purpose is "to provide a central source of information for both readers of *American Craft* magazine and the interested public." In order to be included, a gallery must have hosted at least one solo exhibition or group show of crafts during 1987 and/or have had at least 50 percent of its merchandise in one-of-a-kind items. In addition, the gallery had to complete a questionnaire. Display advertising was also accepted. Unfortunately, these criteria for inclusion are not explained in the directory itself.

Overall, this is a valuable publication. Virtually nothing else is available that covers this field so widely. The layout is attractive and the cost very reasonable. Because the editors relied on returned questionnaires for their information, it is not as comprehensive as one might wish. However, there is a clearly stated hope that future editions will be more inclusive. A problem for libraries is the flimsy construction, which will require rebinding in order to tolerate even moderate use.

Diane Richards

878. Ellis, Charles Grant. **Oriental Carpets in the Philadelphia Museum of Art.** Philadelphia, Philadelphia Museum of Art; distr., Philadelphia, University of Pennsylvania Press, 1988. 304p. illus. (part col.). $59.95; $28.00pa. LC 87-32713. ISBN 0-8122-7959-X; 0-87633-070-7pa.

Charles Ellis, various curators of the Philadelphia Museum of Art, and members of the University of Pennsylvania Press have created the best book now available on classic rugs and carpets. This beautifully produced work sets a standard by which other works devoted to oriental rugs produced during the classic period (sixteenth through the eighteenth centuries) will be compared. The only other reference work in English that is nearly as good is M. S. Dimand's *Oriental Rugs in the Metropolitan Museum of Art* (New York Graphic Society, 1973). Important works that complement this new work are Joseph V. McMullan's *Islamic Carpets* (Near Eastern Art Research Center, 1965), Kurt Erdmann's *Oriental Carpets* (Crosby Press, 1976), *Islamic Carpets and Textiles in the Keir Collection* (Faber and Faber, 1978), by Friedrich Spuhler, and *Antique Rugs from the Near East* (Cornell University Press, 1984), by Wilhelm von Bode and Ernst Kuhnel. Two of these titles, those by von Bode and Kuhnel and Erdmann, were translated from the German by Charles Ellis.

Essay-length discussions focus on structure, design elements, date of manufacture, dyes, place, and importance of each carpet in textile history. Technical analysis for each carpet includes information on size, warp, weft, ply of wool, and condition. One element included in the technical information that might confuse users is the description of "quality." Terms such as *ordinary, fair,* and *fairly good* are not defined in the introductory chapters.

Illustrations of paintings including rugs like those found within this collection are used to aid the reader's understanding of the iconography of carpets, the evolution of design elements, and methods for dating. Another feature that helps place this work in a separate category from other books on antique carpets is including in each discussion pictures of similar rugs housed in other museum collections. All textiles located within the Philadelphia Museum of Art are illustrated in color; pictures of paintings and similar rugs in other museums are in black-and-white. All illustrations are excellent.

Perhaps the highlight of the work is its discussion of Turkish rugs, an important feature of the museum's collection. Because of the many examples in the collection, coverage of Turkish rugs is better than that provided by a recent book describing carpets in the Topkapi Museum, *The Topkapi Saray Museum Carpets* (New York Graphic Society, 1987), by Hulye Tezcan. However, the strength of the Topkapi's collection is Turkish prayer rugs, making the Tezcan book another work complementing the Ellis catalog.

Citations to references are in the form of footnotes (a time saver for scholars). There is an outstanding, and necessary, glossary.

Milton H. Crouch

879. The Guild: A Sourcebook of American Craft Artists. New York, Kraus Sikes, 1988. 462p. illus. (col.). index. $60.00pa. ISBN 0-9616012-3-X; ISSN 0885-3975.

This attractive directory serves to describe the work of 370 craftspeople. The stated purpose of the directory is to help introduce craft artists to designers and architects, the primary clientele for some of the expensive larger items. There is a variety of work included, from small items for the dining room table to large architectural works made of metal, wood, and glass. All entries combine photographs, a brief written description and, for many, cost information. The color photographs are excellent. Placed throughout the book are brief commentaries written by people involved in the arts and crafts business. Some of these offer practical advice to the potential user; others are superficial.

The directory includes a listing of craft centers arranged by state and a listing, again by state, of the craftspeople discussed. This is a commercial product and a guide to the works of a few selected crafts artists. The photographs

tell the story and, unlike works of art, the crafts illustrated contain no mysteries.

Milton H. Crouch

880. McKendry, Blake. A Dictionary of Folk Artists in Canada: From the 17th Century to the Present.... Elginburg, Ont., Blake McKendry, 1988. 287p. $35.00 spiralbound. ISBN 0-9693298-0-6.

Folk art embraces a wide field in Canada since it must include the multicultural expression, the indigenous work of native peoples, and those born in Canada from the "second generation" onwards. Accordingly, McKendry explains his definitions for folk art, primitive art, naive art, provincial art, and amateur art. He also includes in his masterful work on identification the popular portrait, topographical, genre, religious, and decorative artists of the seventeenth, eighteenth, and nineteenth centuries. There are three thousand entries here arranged alphabetically by the artist's last, or known, name. Each entry includes the name, the life dates, the part of Canada where best known, the folk art forms and materials used, and references to one or more of the 276 biographical tools cited for further details. A typical entry would read "Allard, Emile (b.1873), Saint Mathieu, Quebec. Yard art, models of houses, and a church. de Grosbois, 1978" (which refers to the latter's *Les Patenteux du Quebec,* Les Editions Parti, Montreal).

This is a "processed" book of 8½-by-11-inch pages, spiralbound to open flat, and easy enough to add to or update. McKendry used WordPerfect software for the database disks, and he notes that these are available from him for searching (but no price is reported).

Dean Tudor

881. McRae, Bobbi A. The Fiberworks Directory of Self-Published Books on the Fiber Arts. Austin, Tex., Fiberworks, 1988. 58p. illus. index. $11.95pa. LC 87-30587. ISBN 0-944577-00-8.

Fiber arts include basketry, embroidery, felt making, knitting, quilting, weaving, etc. McRae has collected information on over 150 books in the field published as "labors of love" by the crafts people themselves. Arranged alphabetically by title, each entry describes the book's contents and gives complete ordering information. Sometimes, a bit about the author is included. A subject index makes for easy access to the material. The directory is illustrated with black-and-white photographs and drawings, making it a delight to peruse. Suitable for libraries that serve experienced crafters who are on the lookout for instruction and inspiration.   Deborah Hammer

882. Oppelt, Norman T. **Southwestern Pottery: An Annotated Bibliography and List of Types and Wares.** 2d ed. Metuchen, N.J., Scarecrow, 1988. 325p. illus. index. $35.00. LC 88-6424. ISBN 0-8108-2119-2.

Achieving the status of "standard reference work" usually takes several editions; Oppelt did it with the first edition of this work. The new edition contains 300 more annotations, bringing the total to 965. There are 180 new pottery types or variety names, which bring that total to 1,240 type, ware, or variety names. A few of the additions are pre-1975, the cut-off date for the first edition, but the vast majority are recent publications. The cut-off date for this edition was 1986. One new feature is the inclusion of dates for any dated pottery type. The annotations are a little longer now, running seventy-five to one hundred words for many entries rather than the thirty to forty words in the first edition. Oppelt also includes synonyms for all types known to have two or more names. What is most apparent from this edition is that there is still little uniformity in the Southwestern pottery taxonomic system. Researchers can use the work in three ways: specific pottery types or wares can be studied using the "List of Southwestern Pottery Types and Wares"; a topical/geographical approach is feasible using the index; and the publications of a particular researcher are brought together in the annotation section. The list of types is most useful as it provides date, synonym, and references to annotations that describe the pottery as well as publications with illustrations. A check of twenty-five books and articles on Southwestern pottery showed the thoroughness of the compiler; the only flaw was that he did not include a "slightly revised" (1978) version of a 1969 cited work by Robert Lister and Florence Lister, *Anasazi Pottery* (rev. ed., University of New Mexico Press, 1978). Without a copy of the earlier work it is impossible to tell how great a difference exists between the two versions and how serious the omission really is. No matter, this is an important work for any collection serving the needs of Southwestern archaeologists.   G. Edward Evans

883. Oshins, Lisa Turner, comp. **Quilt Collections: A Directory for the United States and Canada.** Washington, D.C., Acropolis Books, 1987. 255p. illus. (part col.). bibliog. $24.95; $18.95pa. LC 87-17455. ISBN 0-87491-845-6; 0-87491-844-8pa. (May be obtained from American Folklife Center, Library of Congress, Washington, D.C.).

Almost every community includes quilt makers, quilt researchers, and quilt aficionados. This listing of collections has been compiled for the American Folklife Center at the Library of Congress. It is probably not comprehensive, and definitely should be updated periodically.

Each entry is for a collection of at least five quilts or large documentary holdings. In each case, the most significant holding or the highlight of the quilt collection is mentioned. Also noted are study services; public services; any publications; and of course, the location with address, telephone number, mailing address, and times open to the public.

While at first glance this book may not appear to be of great interest to the reading public, quilters are a breed apart. A quilter would be overjoyed to be able to plan vacations based on the information in this book: being able to visit collections in each and every state and province, being able to compare historical and regional variations, and being able to write ahead for permission to do research. Listings are by state/province and are very convenient.

It is hoped that this book will be made available in every public library, especially in areas where much quilting is done.
        Judith E. H. Odiorne

884. Porter, Frank W., III, comp. **Native American Basketry: An Annotated Bibliography.** Westport, Conn., Greenwood Press, 1988. 249p. index. (Art Reference Collection, No. 10). $39.95. LC 87-37570. ISBN 0-313-25363-3.

With 1,128 entries this comprehensive bibliography, which covers every aspect of information about native American basket making in North America published in the past one hundred years, is by far the best source of single information currently available on the subject. Arranged by the broadly defined geographic and cultural areas (e.g., Great Basin) of North America that correspond to the distribution of native Americans and their basket styles and techniques, this bibliography lists almost every article, book, dissertation, and/or thesis that makes even passing reference to the subject. In each of the eleven sections the entries are arranged alphabetically by author and each entry provides standard bibliographic information along with a brief annotation that characterizes the nature of the item. Separate author and subject indexes, both keyed directly to the bibliographic entry, provide additional access to the wealth of information found here. Greater selectivity, since some of the items clearly have very little to do with the subject, and an indication of the location of the more obscure items might have improved what is otherwise an impressive and useful contribution for those interested in native Americans and/or baskets and basket making. [R: Choice, Oct 88, p. 295; RBB, 1 Nov 88, p. 464]   Norman D. Stevens

885.   Ramsay, Caroline C. **The International Directory of Resources for Artisans.** Washington, D.C., Crafts Center, 1988. 116p. $59.95pa.

The continued growth of the craft movement throughout the world has created increasing demand by artisans for information to help them in creating, developing, producing, and marketing their work. This directory, which is the first attempt to provide a comprehensive source of such information, is a bold and valuable endeavor especially since it has an international focus. However, the information for Africa, Asia, Europe, Latin America, and the Middle East, which is arranged under those headings and then alphabetically by country, is limited and by no means complete, concerned primarily with a few arts organizations, marketing groups, and government agencies in each country. The entries under Canada in the North American section are equally brief.

The United States entries are far more comprehensive and up-to-date. This section represents, for most purposes, the true immediate value of this directory. It contains fairly lengthy listings for arts organizations, experts, financial organizations, foundations, government agencies, law, marketing organizations, multilateral organizations, private voluntary organizations, refugee groups, schools, and suppliers. The entries under each of these headings are arranged alphabetically by state and then alphabetically by the name of the organization.

Throughout the directory the only information provided is the complete address and telephone number for each organization and, in some cases, the name of a contact person. Despite its limitations this directory should prove to be of real benefit as a starting point for artisans as they pursue their work, as well as to collectors of contemporary arts and crafts as they look for shops and galleries in which to purchase such work.   Norman D. Stevens

886.   Rogers, Barbara Radcliffe. **The Encyclopaedia of Everlastings: The Complete Guide to Growing, Preserving, and Arranging Dried Flowers.** New York, Weidenfeld & Nicolson, 1988. 191p. illus. (part col.). maps. bibliog. index. $19.95. LC 87-22514. ISBN 1-555-84133-3.

Organized alphabetically, by Latin name with an index of common names, this encyclopedia covers over two hundred plants and flowers suitable for growing, collecting, preserving, and arranging. The introductory matter

of the book contains a description of the various methods of plant preservation, methods and tools for arranging, a garden zone map, and a diagram of a flower. A list of sources for seeds and supplies and a list of recommended field guides conclude the work. The body of the book is devoted to the description and illustration of the plants themselves. Provided with each entry is information on the region where the flower or plant is found, how to gather or grow it, its height, effective preservation techniques, and how to use it to best advantage. Each entry is accompanied by a watercolor illustration.

The author states that the purpose of the book is "to broaden the horizons and enrich the resources of anyone who enjoys flowers" and to "[encourage] readers to see the potential for beautiful everlastings everywhere" (introduction). This is a tall order to fill; however, with its beautiful illustrations and brief but informative descriptions, the book does serve to assist the more experienced and to inspire the novice. It is recommended primarily to public libraries. [R: BL, 1 Apr 88, p. 1302]   Susan R. Penney

887.   Von Rosenstiel, Helene, and Gail Caskey Winkler. **Floor Coverings for Historic Buildings: A Guide to Selecting Reproductions.** Washington, D.C., Preservation Press, 1988. 283p. illus. bibliog. $12.95pa. LC 87-22310. ISBN 0-89133-130-1.

With the high level of current interest in the careful restoration of historic houses and the use of period furnishings by many who live in older houses, information about contemporary sources of supply for appropriate materials is in demand. The book under review is an excellent source of such information for a complete range of materials used to finish floors, including wood, brick, stone, tile, linoleum, vinyl, matting, and carpeting. A concise introduction provides a variety of useful background information on such matters as levels of authenticity, the technologies of floor coverings, documentation, and installation. It is followed by a comprehensive directory of current sources for appropriate coverings arranged by period (1750-1800, 1800-1840, 1840-1875, 1875-1900, and 1900-1930), and within each period by the type of covering (e.g., wood flooring). A description of specific coverings, and how they were produced and used, is followed by entries that describe in some detail available products by manufacturer. A brief appendix alphabetically lists the suppliers of floor coverings, providing address and telephone number(s) and indicating the kinds of coverings they manufacture or supply. An excellent glossary defines all of the various terms. Finally, a brief bibliography provides a list of sources for additional old and new information about historic floor coverings. Throughout, a series of black-and-white photographs provide a good representative picture of a variety of types and styles of floor coverings that make the text more meaningful. As a careful guide to a specific line of products for use in historic and older houses, this is a useful addition to interior design collections.

Norman D. Stevens

FASHION AND COSTUME

888. Calasibetta, Charlotte Mankey. **Fairchild's Dictionary of Fashion.** 2d ed. New York, Fairchild, 1988. 749p. illus. (part col.). $50.00. LC 88-80198. ISBN 0-87005-635-2.

Following the first edition by six years, this new volume contains over 15,000 definitions of terms from the world of fashion. The broad scope of the material covers all centuries from classical to modern and goes beyond historical costume terminology to include cultural, nationalist, stylistic, and artistic terms as well. The entries are arranged alphabetically, and in certain cases over ninety broad categories are established under which are grouped related terms, which in turn are alphabetized under the respective section (e.g., aprons, dresses, and shoes). A separate index for these categories is provided. The book contains over 500 black-and-white drawings and sixteen pages of full-color illustrations that are cross-referenced to the text. The definitions are quite succinct and are more useful for identification than descriptive purposes. Additional cross-referencing citations for related entries are given. There is an index of biographical entries of famous fashion designers with personal photographs as well as examples of each designer's work. A notable weakness of the volume is the omission of a bibliography for further reference to compensate for the brevity of the entry information. Nevertheless, the scope and currency of the entries make the volume a valuable addition to a reference library. [R: Choice, Oct 88, p. 284; RBB, 15 Dec 88, p. 690]

Jackson Kesler

889. Racinet, Albert. **The Historical Encyclopedia of Costumes.** New York, Facts on File, 1988. 320p. illus. (part col.). index. $40.00. LC 88-11186. ISBN 0-8160-1976-2.

This volume is a modern edition in English of the original six-volume *History of World Costume* first issued between 1876 and 1888 by Auguste Racinet, a French expert on costume. This edition has been redesigned, translated, and organized into four principal sections: the ancient world; nineteenth-century antique civilizations; Europe from Byzantium to the 1880s; and traditional costumes of the 1880s. Each section is then subdivided by regions, countries, and empires. The distinguishing feature is the more than two thousand reproductions, the majority in color, of Racinet's original lithographs. These are presented on every other page with facing pages of text providing descriptions of the costumes and general background information. Attention is given also to accessories, with the areas of ornamentation and architectural settings occasionally included. Unfortunately Racinet did not include the sources for the illustrations. A brief introductory background is provided for each section, and the descriptive notes are explanatory but very brief with no bibliographic suggestions for further investigation. There is a limited index, but it does not include the geographical headings. The book's attempted scope is broad and all-encompassing; perhaps it is so broad to the detriment that no area is adequately covered. The book will be best used for only a superficial introduction, and serious costumers and researchers will have to go elsewhere. [R: LJ, Dec 88, p. 96]

Jackson Kesler

PHOTOGRAPHY

890. Edwards, Gary. **International Guide to Nineteenth-Century Photographers and Their Works.** Boston, G. K. Hall, 1987. 591p. $50.00. LC 87-25120. ISBN 0-8161-8938-2.

A comprehensive guide to nineteenth-century photographers and their works, this directory, the only one of its kind, includes four thousand photographers both famous and obscure. Information was compiled from over three hundred catalogers from major U.S. and British dealers and auction houses dealing in specialized photographic sales.

This important reference tool for collectors, dealers, auction houses, specialized research libraries, rare book dealers, and local historical societies is arranged alphabetically by author's last name. For each photographer the guide provides nationality, dates of birth and death, principal subject matter, inclusive dates for earliest and latest known photographs, processes and formats used, studio location, geographic range for topographic or documentary photographers, and locations of photographs in sales catalogs. [R: Choice, July/Aug 88, p. 1687; RBB, 15 June 88, pp. 1721-22; RQ, Summer 88, p. 575; WLB, Apr 88, pp. 102-3]

Thomas L. Hart

891.   Naylor, Colin, ed. **Contemporary Photographers.** 2d ed. Chicago, St. James Press, 1988. 1145p. illus. (Contemporary Arts Series, Vol. 3). $120.00. ISBN 0-912289-79-1.

This huge compilation of fact and opinion covers the lives and accomplishments of 750 photographers who have been judged as important contributors to the technical and esthetic status of the art today. The editor and his team of advisors have produced an essential reference work for all those involved with photography in the final decades of the twentieth century.

Worldwide in coverage, the entry for each photographer includes a biography, listings of individual and group shows as well as public gallery and museum holdings, and a bibliography. Living photographers were invited to prepare a statement and to select a single representative photograph of their work for reproduction. Entries conclude with a signed critical essay prepared by one of the 175 contributors selected from the international community of experts. Many major photographers who are now deceased are included as a tribute to their lasting contribution to the current state of the art. Examples include Lewis Hine, Atget, Stieglitz, Cecil Beaton, Robert Capa, and Carl Van Vechten. A few painters such as David Hockney, Robert Rauschenberg, and Andy Warhol are included because of their long preoccupation with photography.

However, this outstanding publication is not to be regarded primarily as a historical survey, as the emphasis is squarely on the contemporary. An earlier edition appeared in 1982 and covered 650 photographers in 837 pages, so the second edition is considerably enlarged. The hundreds of black-and-white photographs are totally absorbing. The weight of this large book requires an especially strong binding, which it has, along with other solidly presented production features found in other titles in the Contemporary Arts Series. In summary, this is an outstanding reference work due to a carefully considered format, extensive scope, and massive documentation by authorities. [R: Choice, July/Aug 88, p. 1672; RBB, 1 Sept 88, p. 46]

William J. Dane

22 Fine Arts

GENERAL WORKS

Bibliographies

892. Burt, Eugene C. **Ethnoart: Africa, Oceania, and the Americas: A Bibliography of Theses and Dissertations.** New York, Garland, 1988. 191p. index. (Garland Reference Library of the Humanities, Vol. 840). $29.00. LC 88-7207. ISBN 0-8240-7545-5.

Ethnoart is defined as the visual arts of the traditional peoples of Africa, Oceania, and the Americas. It is a term that has gained prominence in the last twenty years, although interest in the subject dates to the nineteenth century, when it was referred to as primitive or tribal art. University departments in anthropology, art, sociology, and folklore have been active in the subject especially since the 1960s, and have produced valuable dissertations and theses. In this bibliography, Eugene Burt arranges these sources by area. Chapters cover Africa, Latin America, North America, and Oceania, and subdivisions cover specific tribes and areas. Indexes at the back of the book allow cross-referencing by author, date, institution, and subject. The indexing is thorough and useful in the bibliography, but the main entries could have also used some of this thorough treatment. The information in the entries is minimal: author, title, degree, institution, date, and length. Other references such as *Ethnic Folklife Dissertations from the United States and Canada*, by Catherine Hiebert Kerst (Library of Congress, 1986) show the benefits of a more complete listing. It includes the university department where the work was completed, the University Microfilms order number, a citation for publication of the abstract in *Dissertation Abstracts, American Doctoral Dissertations,* or *Dissertation Abstracts International*, and citation of publication information including the Library of Congress number, if the work was revised for a book or monograph. In addition, the bibliographer annotated the dissertation's contents. Such added information in *Ethnoart* would have greatly enhanced the appeal of the book for library, museum, scholar, and student use.   Simon J. Bronner

893. Chapman, Gretel. **Mosan Art: An Annotated Bibliography.** Boston, G. K. Hall, 1988. 363p. index. (Reference Publications in Art History). $55.00. LC 87-26611. ISBN 0-8161-8329-5.

One of the toughest aspects of doing research on medieval art is finding the source material. The diligent investigator must use a variety of European languages, locate obscure society publications, and generally operate without much help from indexes. Happily, *Mosan Art* offers some hope for researchers in one of the most fascinating and important periods of the Middle Ages.

The Mosan area of the Meuse Valley (Belgium/Netherlands) was a vital center between the ninth and midthirteenth centuries. Notable for the Reims and Court School manuscripts of the ninth century, Mosan artists were later known for enamel work, goldsmithing, and sculpture of a "classicizing" bent in the later Romanesque period. Chapman's useful introduction points out some of the knotty problems of Mosan scholarship and pinpoints a few of the landmark opinions.

The body of the volume is composed of bibliographic entries with short annotations. The general organization distinguishes between reference works, works on historical and ancillary sciences like numismatics, important collections, major exhibitions, and general surveys before concluding with chapters on artistic media, period studies, and individual artists. College students will probably get the most use out of the three later chapters, especially the sections on famous twelfth-century metalworkers Renier of Huy and Nicholas of Verdun. Author and subject indexes help direct wider-ranging and advanced queries.

The audience for *Mosan Art* will be found in academic institutions with medieval art and history curricula. That audience is not large, but this excellent bibliography will make an important reduction in the amount of midnight oil burnt in its quest for knowledge. [R: Choice, Sept 88, p. 76]   Stephanie C. Sigala

894. Coulson, William D. E., and Patricia N. Freiert. **Greek and Roman Art, Architecture, and Archaeology: An Annotated Bibliography.** 2d ed. New York, Garland, 1987. 204p. index. (Garland Reference Library of the Humanities, Vol. 580). $38.00. LC 84-48860. ISBN 0-8240-8756-9.

The beginning student of ancient culture may welcome this readable volume, the second edition of Coulson's 1975 bibliography. Its contents include over 350 annotated entries, subdivided into eight chapters by topic and culture. The title of the volume describes its major focus, but there are also appendices noting special bibliographical sources, important series, museum publications, biographies, books on the classical tradition, and some novels. It is very exemplary for what it does, except that it excludes many of the most important sources of information about the Greeks, Romans, and Etruscans.

The problems of this volume lie in the nature of classical studies, which are notoriously conservative and pedantic. Many of the most useful books are out-of-print, expensive, and/or in German and thus excluded. Coulson's guidelines explicitly include only current in-print materials under $30.00; most are in English. Also attempting to appeal to the broadest possible audience, both novels appealing to a fifth-grade audience and scholarly excavation reports are included. A narrower focus would have made this bibliography more valuable, despite the problems in scope. As it is, the primary audience for this work will be public and secondary school libraries. Most academic libraries may not want to consider it. For them, the perennial index *L'annee Philologique* and the venerable *Pauly-Wissowa* remain the best resources for students at sophomore level and above.   Stephanie C. Sigala

895. Kaufman, Edward, and Sharon Irish. **Medievalism: An Annotated Bibliography of Recent Research in the Architecture and Art of Britain and North America.** New York, Garland, 1988. 279p. index. (Garland Reference Library of the Humanities, Vol. 791). $46.00. LC 88-11072. ISBN 0-8240-7896-9.

Renewed interest in the study of the Gothic and its influence has created a wealth of recent scholarly publications. This work catalogs the most significant articles and books published between 1960 and 1984, with generous references to major or important works occurring outside these dates. A useful preface instructs the user on the parameters and arrangement of the volume. The authors, both architectural historians, have provided a complete and very well-written introduction which supplies a solid groundwork for tracing historical development of the study of medievalism. The ease with which the user will locate intended subjects is to be commended. The volume is divided into five general parts: architecture and architectural crafts in Great Britain and Ireland; John Ruskin and William Morris; painting and sculpture in Great Britain; architecture in North America; and painting and sculpture in North America. These are further broken down by general works, monographs of architects (or artists), places and buildings, and more. The section on architecture in North America is sensibly presented alphabetically by province and state. The index is unusually complete. Finally, the annotations are often so interesting and informative that browsing through the bibliography becomes a profitable pastime.

Octavia Porter Randolph

896. Kaufmann, Thomas DaCosta. **Art and Architecture in Central Europe, 1550-1620: An Annotated Bibliography.** Boston, G. K. Hall, 1988. 316p. index. (Reference Publications in Art History). $45.00. LC 88-1816. ISBN 0-8161-8594-8.

Kaufmann, an associate professor in the Department of Art and Archaeology at Princeton University, brings sound credentials to the task of compiling this bibliography. He is the author of major books as well as numerous reviews and articles on the subject of Central European art and architecture and has been the recipient of a number of related fellowships and prizes.

The substantial introduction suggests that the past neglect by art historians of the time period and geographic region, in large part the Holy Roman Empire without the Low Countries and Lorraine, is unmerited given the quality and quantity of the work to be found there. An added purpose of the bibliography is to open up the present available scholarship on this "Mannerism" period to English-speaking scholars and thus encourage further study of the art and architecture of Central Europe.

The text following the introduction is divided into twenty-three major categories, the first being "Sources" and the second "General Works." The latter includes subdivisions on patronage, architecture, sculpture, painting, drawings, and applied arts. The following twenty sections focus on regional or artistic centers including Austria, Augsburg, Bavaria, Bohemia, Cologne, Hesse, Lower Saxony, Nuremberg, Switzerland, Westphalia, and Württemberg, among others. Each of these sections covers general studies, architecture, sculpture, painting, and related fine arts. The final section considers traveling artists.

The more than fourteen hundred entries are restricted to published sources, primary or secondary, dissertations in print or on film and available in the United States, nineteenth-century books, periodicals, and exhibition and collection catalogs. They are arranged by author within each category and medium, with full bibliographic citations and concise, informative annotations. Although the time period and geographic location seem somewhat limited, the wealth of material available in this selective bibliography indicates the importance of the subject to art historians. This is a distinguished reference tool and is a worthy addition to the G. K. Hall list. [R: Choice, Oct 88, p. 292]

G. Joan Burns

Biographies

897.   Seymour, Nancy N. **An Index-Dictionary of Chinese Artists, Collectors, and Connoisseurs with Character Identification by Modified Stroke Count: Including over 5,000 Chinese Names and Biographies....** Metuchen, N.J., Scarecrow, 1988. 987p. bibliog. $82.50. LC 87-28704. ISBN 0-8108-2091-9.

The long title serves to introduce users to this ingenious new reference work designed to help identify Chinese artists, collectors, and connoisseurs. An examination of the bibliography indicates that most of the artists included here are painters or calligraphers. The keystone of the work is an alphabetized listing of artists arranged by surname. In addition to an artist's complete name (Wade-Giles romanization is used), entries include the Pinyin form of the name, dynasty or period during which the artist lived, alternate names, a brief biographical statement for purposes of quick identification, number of strokes in the character of the surname, full script characters for each name, and reference(s) to at least one of twenty-six important collected biographical sources.

The second part of the work is devoted to explaining the nature of Chinese signatures. The purpose of this section is to help those unable to read Chinese to identify those Chinese signatures they encounter during their research. There is a useful index to modified stroke

counts that helps those properly prepared to isolate possible signatures. The strokes are broken down one to five up to twenty-eight to thirty-seven. Just browsing this section might enable the lucky user to identify signatures.

This is a complicated work to use and most people will need to spend several hours studying the section explaining the nature of Chinese signatures. However, scholars able to read the language will find the biographical references useful; those unable to read Chinese or identify a signature will appreciate the author's efforts to help them identify major artists.

Artists whose signatures are often forged are not identified. However, that major problem is beyond the scope of this work. [R: LJ, 1 May 88, pp. 71-72]   Milton H. Crouch

Dictionaries and Encyclopedias

898.   Cummings, Paul. **Dictionary of Contemporary American Artists.** 5th ed. New York, St. Martin's Press, 1988. 738p. illus. bibliog. $65.00. LC 82-7337. ISBN 0-312-00232-7.

The fifth edition of Cummings's reference standard continues both the strengths and weaknesses of older editions (see *ARBA* 83, entry 851 and *ARBA* 78, entry 823). Each new edition shows a conscientious attention to the details of documenting an ever-increasing number of American artists active in the last fifty years. From this book we learn important dates; education; teaching background; commissions; awards; address; dealer address; one-man, retrospective, and group exhibitions; some collection names; and some bibliography for each of the 900 artists selected. As in the past, there are an index and a name pronunciation guide, a key to museums and institutions cited (which unfortunately contains some errors), a gallery list, and fifty pages of bibliography. The updated information makes each edition worth purchasing.

The major weakness of the volume continues to be its misleading title. One would normally expect the "contemporary" artists covered to be living, but this work seems always to have had a strong retrospective cast. Nearly a quarter of the artists included are deceased (many for decades) and few are younger than forty. In fact, no one born after 1949 has been included. A close reading of the introduction makes the selection policy clear, but then one does not always read introductions closely. An alternative international source is *Contemporary Artists* (see *ARBA* 84, entry 833), which is useful for its critical essay and long bibliography about each artist. *Who's Who in American Art* (17th ed., see *ARBA* 88, entry 1011) is yet another choice for biographical information on currently active artists. [R: RBB, 15 Sept 88, pp. 132, 134]   Stephanie C. Sigala

899. Earls, Irene. **Renaissance Art: A Topical Dictionary.** Westport, Conn., Greenwood Press, 1987. 345p. bibliog. index. $55.00. LC 87-250. ISBN 0-313-24658-0.

Over eight hundred definitions and descriptions of key words and phrases relating to the art of the Renaissance in Italy and northern Europe make up this new art dictionary. The iconography of Renaissance painting, sculpture, and many of the decorative arts was drawn chiefly from the mythology of classical antiquity and the books of the Old and New Testaments. These timeless subjects are described in carefully edited entries for ready-reference. Art techniques and materials are also discussed, including woodcut and priming, gesso and terracotta. Major rulers such as Francis I, Henry VIII, the Medici, Pope Paul III, and Sultan Mohammed II are properly placed in the history of the visual arts of the period.

The many complicated legends, classical myths, and stories based on the literature of religion illustrated in Renaissance art are confusing to the contemporary viewer. Some examples of these subjects are Calumny or Tityus from mythology and Abner or Drusiana from the Bible. Collectors and art historians will find the Seven Acts of Mercy, the Seven Deadly Sins, and Seven Liberal Arts, and the Seven Sorrows of the Virgin neatly listed and described for quick information.

The compiler, Irene Earls, is an experienced teacher, well qualified to relate the most succinct details in her text. This topical dictionary covering one of the most productive periods in art history should prove to be beneficial to the informed layperson in viewing Renaissance collections as well as to seasoned curators, librarians, dealers, and collectors who need the essential facts and authoritative definitions. [R: Choice, Apr 88, p. 1220; RBB, 15 Feb 88, p. 986]   William J. Dane

900. **Encyclopedia of World Art. Volume XVII. Supplement II.** David Eggenberger, ed.-in-chief. Palatine, Ill., Fondazione Giorgio Cini with Jack Heraty, 1987. 1v. (various paging). illus. (part col.). index. $99.50. LC 87-080314. ISBN 0-910081-01-8.

Although this volume needs to be acquired in order to preserve the integrity of the original multivolume set, it is also worth considering as an entirely separate work of recent art scholarship. This volume revises and restates some earlier premises and bases this new historical account on recent scholarship, field studies, and archaeological discoveries. It reflects the changes brought to light during the twenty years since the foundation work was published. This work of Italian scholarship is arranged according to four main topics: the origins of art and the ancient world, the Orient and other non-European civilizations, the Middle Ages and the Modern Era, and the twentieth century and problems of contemporary criticism. Each of the broad topical divisions is further broken down into subtopics. All of the articles are signed. Preliminary pages list the contributing scholars, their positions, and institutional affiliations. Erudite essays explore the history and philosophical bases of various areas of art. Kitsch, which was not considered at all in the original set, or in the volume 16 supplement, herein gets scholarly attention in a five-page article. Semiotics is surveyed, and brought up-to-date. The article on photography by Daniela Palazzoli is a first-rate survey.

One never catches up with the avant garde, and this is a historical work. Although the publication date is 1987, the logistics involved in negotiating with scholars, gathering the articles, coordinating, and editing, plus having it printed and bound means that much of the writing was done a year or more prior to publication. Bibliographies follow each article, and in some cases are as extensive as five or more pages of citations. Both journal articles and monographs are cited, which date from around 1960 through the mid-1970s. The polyglot listings have the Russian-, Arabic-, and Asian-language titles transliterated into the Western alphabet. The articles refer to illustrative matter at the back of the book in an appendix containing 176 plates. This volume is not as well indexed as the volume 16 supplement.   Frank J. Anderson

901. **The Oxford Dictionary of Art.** Ian Chilvers and Harold Osborne, eds. New York, Oxford University Press, 1988. 548p. $39.95. ISBN 0-19-866133-9.

Every academic and public library will want a copy of the *Oxford Dictionary of Art*, but some libraries may want to order an extra for the ready-reference librarian. A successor to the *Oxford Companion* titles on art (1970), decorative arts (1975), and twentieth-century art (1981), the three thousand new volume entries have been rewritten extensively, shortened, and updated for quick consultations. Like other one-volume comprehensive guides to art, the majority of the entries in the new work describe the significance of individual artists. Most of the entries are two or three paragraphs, however, so the sort of factual detail one might find in a biographical dictionary has been eliminated in favor of well-considered, but succinct, historical assessment. New in this work are hard-to-find descriptions of contemporary art historical terms ("luminism," or "School of Paris") that have come into general use only in the last decade. There is also a recognition of the business of art history by a greater number of entries on significant art historians (Alois Riegl, for example) and important institutions (the Prado Museum or the auction firm of Christie's).

Some things are missing from the dictionary. Long articles on national art histories familiar from the *Oxford Companion*s are now banished, as are pictures and bibliography. Architects and architecture are only discussed in relation to other media, and non-Western art forms are ignored unless they have affected European art traditions. Because of these subject limitations, one might wish for another less inclusive title, but what this dictionary sets out to do it does well; it will become a reference standard. [R: Choice, Dec 88, p. 631; LJ, 15 Oct 88, p. 84]   Stephanie C. Sigala

Directories

902. **ArtsAmerica Fine Art Film & Video Source Book 1987.** Greenwich, Conn., Arts-America, 1987. 79p. index. $12.95pa.

A marvelous resource for educators, librarians, and program planners, this volume—along with an eight-page 1988 supplement ($3.00)—includes approximately 750 documentary films and videos available for rental or purchase. The major section of this catalog is subdivided first by time period, then by discipline and country. In all instances, artists are designated by country of birth, rather than residence. Each entry contains basic production information, ordering and rental information, and a one hundred to two hundred-word annotation of the item in question.

In addition to the major sections are listings of films with particular audiences or subjects which fall outside of the main categories. These include films and videos treating specific museum collections, museum professionals, techniques of art production, items which span more than two centuries in their time coverage, and items which are part of a series. Also included are separate indexes by artist or architect, by title, and by distributor. A final section contains ordering information as well as listing information.

Highly recommended as a ready-reference, selection, and acquisition tool for academic, public, high school, and pertinent special library and museum collections. This title is likely to

remain a key reference work for years to come.
                    Edmund F. SantaVicca

903. Davidson, Martha, Carlota Duarte, and Raúl Solano Núñez, eds. **Picture Collections: Mexico: A Guide to Picture Sources in the United Mexican States.** Metuchen, N.J., Scarecrow, 1988. 292p. illus. bibliog. index. $49.50. LC 87-28475. ISBN 0-8108-2074-9.

For the research worker wishing to tap the extensive heritage of pictorial materials now scattered in the archives, museums, libraries, and private collections of Mexico, this is a highly useful reference work. As a guide to sources of photographs, drawings, paintings, prints, maps, diagrams, and other two-dimensional images concerning Mexico, it will be of most interest to the worker in the socio-humanistic fields. The guide lists over five hundred sources, each with the name of the institution or individual, address, telephone number, type of material, subjects covered, availability, and comments. There is a useful glossary of pictorial terms in common usage in Mexico. Particularly helpful are the six indexes listing entries alphabetically by source, location of materials, artist, geography, personal name of individual pictured, and topic. Attractively bound in gold on red, the volume has 292 numbered pages in addition to thirty-two glossy pages of black-and-white illustrations. [R: Choice, Nov 88, pp. 456, 458]

                    Adam E. Cappello

904. Green, Laura R., ed. **Money for Artists: A Guide to Grants and Awards for Individual Artists.** New York, ACA Books/American Council for the Arts, 1987. 241p. index. $16.95; $9.95pa. LC 87-18711. ISBN 0-915400-58-8; 0-915400-59-6pa.

Relatively unique among guides to funding, this directory distinguishes itself by identifying monies available directly to individual artists, whether those monies be through grants or awards. The work is arranged in five major sections—literary arts, media arts, multidisciplinary arts, performing arts, and visual arts. Each section opens with a brief introductory essay, followed by an alphabetical listing of sources. Information for each entry includes name, address, telephone number, type of award or grant available, eligibility and special requirements, pertinent art forms, number of awards, deadline for applications, and instructions on how to apply.

Four indexes supplement the text: awards, organizations (by name), organizations (by state), and organizations (by discipline). Following these are brief profiles of the Center for

Arts Information and the American Council for the Arts.

As many artists experience frustration by having to apply for monies through institutional, rather than individual, identity, this volume should find an eager audience. Recommended for academic and public libraries, for museums and arts centers, and for other pertinent special libraries.   Edmund F. SantaVicca

905. Katlan, Alexander W. **American Artists' Materials Suppliers Directory: Nineteenth Century: New York 1810-1899; Boston 1823-1887.** Park Ridge, N.J., Noyes Publications, 1987. 460p. illus. bibliog. $64.00. LC 87-12283. ISBN 0-8155-5064-2.

Unsigned nineteenth-century American paintings can be dated by the unique stencil mark or label left behind by the art supply firm that initially prepared the canvas. To aid art owners, art galleries, museums, conservation laboratories, and auction houses in the process of researching a painting's origin, painting conservator Alexander Katlan has compiled this very specialized directory to nineteenth-century art supply firms. Approximately thirty-seven hundred firms from the New York and Boston areas were identified and listed in alphabetical order in part 2 of the directory. Included are addresses and dates for when these firms were in existence.

Part 1 gives historical information on the beginnings of the *artist colorman*, that is, one who prepared the canvasses and mixed the paints for the artists. Brief histories on eight of the major art supply firms are presented. Black-and-white photographs and illustrations of the various stencil marks and labels are shown in part 6.

A concise introduction giving the purpose and scope of this work would have been beneficial. Coverage is limited to New York and Boston. Katlan says stencil marks have been found from many other U.S. cities and suggests that more research should be done in this area.

This work will be most appreciated by the select group of individuals who have hands-on access to American nineteenth-century paintings, a limited audience indeed.

Mary Frances White

906. McLaughlin, John, ed. **A Guide to National and State Arts Education Services.** New York, ACA Books/American Council for the Arts, 1987. 84p. index. $14.95pa. LC 87-18712. ISBN 0-915400-60-X.

The American Council for the Arts has compiled a handy guide to 191 organizations that provide arts education services. This guide

is intended to help individuals and institutions locate art-related resources on the state and national level.

The guide is divided into six sections: "State Arts Agencies" (including "Regional"), "State Departments of Education," "State Arts Education Alliances," "National Arts Educational Associations," "National Arts Service Organizations," and "National Education Associations." Organizations in the three state sections are arranged in alphabetical order by state postal abbreviations, for example, Alaska, AK, precedes Alabama, AL. In the three national sections, the entries are arranged in alphabetical order by organization name.

Each entry includes the organization's address, telephone number, name of contact person, goal statement, publications, art education services, and list of art forms served such as dance, folk art, visual art, media, creative writing, crafts, theater, and music. Also provided is the annual budget and the percentage allotted to arts education. The list of arts education services will probably be of most interest to the guide user. The services include the following: advocacy, artist residencies, consulting services, curriculum development, designing projects, funding, library collection, setting up exhibits, speakers' bureau, student workshops, and teacher workshops. Two helpful indexes complete the guide: "Index to Organizations" and "Index of Personnel."

This guide should be of special value to individuals and institutions involved in arts education. Librarians will appreciate the ease with which they can access this difficult-to-find information.   Mary Frances White

907. Porter, Robert A., ed. **Guide to Corporate Giving in the Arts 4.** New York, ACA Books/American Council for the Arts, 1987. 481p. index. $60.00. LC 87-18738. ISBN 0-915400-56-1.

This book is a standard reference for thousands of arts organizations in the United States. It identifies 505 corporations who have supported museums, orchestras, public communications media, theater, opera, and other arts activities, as well as providing comparative statistical data about them.

The bulk of the newest edition's almost five hundred pages is composed of the guide, which profiles in alphabetical order the leading corporations that supported the arts in 1986. We learn, for example, Anheuser-Busch's corporate contact name, the company's preferred charitable causes, requirements for funding applications, its preferred arts organizations or activities, and grant evaluation criteria. The alphabetical guide is supported by an all-important geographical index, an index of types of art activities favored, an index of types of support, and an index of "in-kind" services offered.

For some art organizations, the information in the guide will be well known. After all, charitable giving to the arts is less than 10 percent of all giving and the number of companies in any geographical area is small. What may be of greater general interest is the introduction to the fourth edition, which discusses current trends and preferences in corporate support for the arts. Several charts with long-term giving trends are included in this introduction and a three-page list gives a company-by-company giving profile from 1979 to 1986. This comparative information expands the audience for the volume from the individual development department to the large public or academic library. This volume should sit side by side with the more general *Foundation Directory* (see *ARBA* 86, entry 41) and the *Taft Corporate Giving Directory* (see *ARBA* 86, entry 809) in any arts administration resource center. [R: Choice, Apr 88, p. 1222; WLB, Feb 88, p. 100]

Stephanie C. Sigala

908. Werenko, John D., ed. and comp. **Guide to American Art Schools.** Boston, G. K. Hall, 1987. 281p. maps. index. $45.00. LC 87-20296. ISBN 0-8161-8792-4.

Touted as the "first in-depth guide to academic and non-academic professional education and training in visual art and design," this guide profiles 384 of the 1,653 art programs in the United States. Its compiler is an assistant dean and director of admissions at the Herron School of Art and has put his experience to good effect. He has created a handy compendium of accredited schools, many offering the MFA or BFA degrees, in an easy-to-use format for the high school or undergraduate student. In it one can find relevant names and addresses as well as enrollment statistics, degrees offered, history of program, admissions policy, and myriad other practical facts.

Most academic institutions and high school counselors should own a copy of this book. The introduction highlighting application procedures makes the book worth purchase. Despite this recommendation, there are a few idiosyncrasies users should note. Information was compiled between 1985 and 1987 through questionnaires and from school catalogs with the result that the text is dry. It would have been useful to have a list of tenured faculty and a sample of student/faculty ratios in order to make a judgment on, say, the best glass pro-

gram. Another complicating factor is that large universities with multiple programs covering the visual arts have been limited to one entry for the "Art Department" thus omitting some separate programs in architecture, art history, and art education. While it is unlikely that final enrollment decisions will be made solely on the information in this book, it should be easier to evaluate programs than it is. For these reasons, this guide rates a B+, not an A. [R: BR, May/June 88, p. 37; Choice, May 88, pp. 1386, 1388; LJ, 15 Feb 88, p. 162; RQ, Summer 88, pp. 574-75; VOYA, June 88, p. 107; WLB, Apr 88, pp. 99-100]

Stephanie C. Sigala

Indexes

909. Falk, Peter Hastings, ed. **The Annual Exhibition Record of the Pennsylvania Academy of the Fine Arts 1807-1870....** rev. ed. Madison, Conn., Sound View Press, 1988. 472p. $89.00. LC 88-90530. ISBN 0-932087-03-5.

This is the first volume of a three-volume series indexing the annual exhibition catalogs of the Pennsylvania Academy of the Fine Arts. The academy is the nation's oldest art museum and thus played an integral part in the promotion and collection of art in nineteenth-century America. Volume 1 is a revised and enlarged edition of Anna Wells Rutledge's original *Cumulative Record of Exhibition Catalogues, 1807-1870* (American Philosophical Society, 1955). Volume 2 will index records from 1876 to 1913 and volume 3 from 1914 to 1969.

More than twenty-five thousand works of art are indexed, including paintings, drawings, and sculpture. The works are indexed by artist, owner, and subject. In the index by artist, the artists' names are arranged in alphabetical order with their vital dates. Entries are listed chronologically by year of exhibition. The title of the artwork is followed by the owner's name in italics. Abbreviations are used to distinguish special exhibits, stationary paintings, and exhibits sponsored by the Artists' Fund Society of Philadelphia. This portion of the three-part index gives the most complete citations to the exhibition catalogs.

A brief but informative history of the academy is provided in the foreword. There is also an addendum which covers material from five catalogs not found in the first edition. This is a fine edition with sturdy binding, heavy acid-free paper, and clear print.

Original copies of the annual exhibition catalogs are available at several locations as well as on microfilm from the Archives of American Art, Smithsonian Institution. This is an important reference work for art historians, collectors, dealers, and librarians.

Mary Frances White

ARCHITECTURE

Bibliographies

910. Atkinson, Steven D. **Solar Home Planning: A Bibliography and a Guide.** Metuchen, N.J., Scarecrow, 1988. 343p. index. $29.50. LC 87-32341. ISBN 0-8108-2098-6.

Although the energy crunch has temporarily abated, interest in solar energy continues. As the price tag on fossil fuels grows higher, both in dollars and environmental damage, the need to continue development of solar power will grow.

This bibliography provides a good place to begin an in-depth search for information. The author has included over two thousand citations dating from 1975 to 1986 and includes references to directories, monographs, articles, bibliographies, computer software, and other sources. Most are from North American publications and thus should be readily available in the United States.

The work is organized first by type of materials: bibliographies, directories, indexes and abstracts, databases, articles, monographs, associations, research centers, libraries, periodicals, software, and films and videos. Within each type of material the citations are further subdivided by topics in the field. Examples of topics are solar architecture, solar design, solar research, solar economics, photovoltaic solar retrofits, and superinsulation. The citations are numbered and the references in the indexes are to the citation number rather than the page number. Each citation contains the appropriate bibliographic information.

The author has aimed his work at lay people interested in solar power as well as architects, contractors, city planners, educators, engineers, lawyers, and librarians. There are both an author and a title index but no subject index. There is a detailed table of contents. The sections on computer software, databases, and videos are especially useful. [R: Choice, Oct 88, p. 283; RBB, Aug 88, p. 1907]

Susan Ebershoff-Coles

911. Belcher, Margaret. **A. W. N. Pugin: An Annotated Critical Bibliography.** London, Mansell; distr., Rutherford, N.J., Publishers Distribution Center, 1987. 495p. illus. index. $117.00. LC 86-18265. ISBN 0-7201-1774-7.

This is a work of immense scholarship. For the adherents and critics alike of Augustus Welby Northmore Pugin, Belcher has provided the definitive annotated reference to his published works. In his tragically brief life (1812-1852), Pugin designed and wrote on nearly every aspect of what came to be called the Gothic Revival: chapels and cathedrals, vestments and stained glass, jewelry, tilework, and bookbinding. The book is divided into the following main sections: publications by Pugin, including books, books of etchings, pamphlets, and published letters; illustrations by Pugin for the work of others; works sometimes attributed to Pugin; and publications about him. Entries typically contain full title; half title; description of text, including listing of illustrations or chapters; locations in which the work can currently be found; notations on additional editions of the same work; and a brief descriptive essay on the work which places it in context with Pugin's life and other works. A fifth section is an extremely useful biographical glossary of Pugin's contemporaries. A thorough index and a number of illustrations of Pugin's etchings complete the work. As befits a lifetime investment, the volume is beautifully printed on crisp white paper and is a pleasure to use. [R: Choice, June 88, p. 1529]   Octavia Porter Randolph

912. Doumato, Lamia. **Architecture and Women: A Bibliography Documenting Women Architects, Landscape Architects, Designers, Architectural Critics and Writers and Women in Related Fields Working in the United States.** New York, Garland, 1988. 269p. illus. index. (Garland Reference Library of the Humanities, Vol. 886). $40.00. LC 88-17698. ISBN 0-8240-4105-4.

Architects are so little known among the general American populace that few citizens can name one beyond Frank Lloyd Wright. Given this lack of public profile, how much greater is the shadow of obscurity in which women architects languish. The compiler of this bibliography states as her goal the encouragement of research on the history of American women in architecture and its related fields. This volume brings to light the names of 128 American women, past and present, who are notable as architects, landscape architects, critics, garden writers, reformers, and planners. The volume begins with a list of extant published bibliographies, and continues through listings of monographs, dissertations and theses, exhibition catalogs, and periodical articles. This last category is drawn from publications as refreshingly diverse as *The Ladies Home Journal* and *Architectural Record*. The main body of the book comprises an alphabetical listing of the women themselves, including birth and death dates (if known), a simple title such as "Architect" or "Planner," a list of primary and secondary works, and exhibitions, if any. Twenty crisp black-and-white photographs illustrate the work of women designers of this century and the last. The alphabetical table of contents makes locating citations on a given woman quick and simple.

Octavia Porter Randolph

Chronologies

913. Yarwood, Doreen. **A Chronology of Western Architecture.** New York, Facts on File, 1987. 353p. illus. bibliog. index. $29.95. LC 87-13652. ISBN 0-8160-1861-8.

Doreen Yarwood has written a fine history of western architecture in this chronological presentation that begins with the Greek mainland and islands in 2000 B.C. and finishes with the United States, Australia, and Europe in 1970-1986. The text, which covers a time span of almost four thousand years, is divided into more than eighty sections, varying in length from a single double-page spread to as many as six double pages. The early civilizations are treated in long periods of time, generally several hundred years. However, from A.D. 1100 the material is covered in fifty-year periods with from three to five double pages devoted to each century.

In addition to such expected topics as Greek temples, Hellenistic orders and decoration, Byzantine, Gothic, and Renaissance architecture, there are other sections including "Castle Building and Town Defences," "Towards Palladianism," "Town Planning in the 18th and 19th Centuries," "Ferrovitreous Construction in the 19th Century," "In Search of New Architectural Forms 1870-1900," and several sections on modern architecture broken into fifteen- to twenty-year time periods. The highly readable text, free from professional jargon, provides essential support for the more than one thousand illustrations.

The physical format of the book is an important part of the presentation. Each double page has a general heading indicating the dates and style. The left-hand margin indicates the countries and areas considered, while the excellent illustrations, usually line drawings, extend over the double-page spread. There are two columns of text explaining social, political, or technological trends that relate closely to the illustrations. In the right-hand margin there is a column of information about contemporary world events or personalities to assist in placing the architectural developments of the period in broader perspective.

There are a brief introduction, a basic bibliography, a selective glossary, and a comprehensive index. Intended for the general reader and the beginning student, this is a useful, excellent approach to the subject. [R: Choice, July/Aug 88, p. 1686; SLJ, May 88, p. 35]

G. Joan Burns

Dictionaries and Encyclopedias

914. **Encyclopedia of Architecture Design, Engineering & Construction. Volume 1: Aalto, Alvar to Concrete—General Principles.** Joseph A. Wilkes, ed.-in-chief. New York, John Wiley, 1988. 749p. illus. (part col.). maps. $200.00. LC 87-25222. ISBN 0-471-80747-8.

This new series of encyclopedias is intended to be a comprehensive reference for educators, architects, engineers, students, consultants in acoustics, lighting, interior design, landscaping, and the construction industry. Technical articles are instructive, with good to excellent coverage of theory and general principles and concise discussions of technique. Essays on materials such as acrylics, adhesives, and concrete provide a useful primer for the student and additional background and history on use for design professionals. Distinct building types such as airports, amusement parks, and bridges, often not treated at all, are here presented with thorough historic background, examples, and engineering tenets. Inclusion of terms such as "Adaptive Use" (the reuse of existing structures for new purposes; e.g., an elementary school converted to housing for the elderly) brings the general reader into thought-provoking contact with some of the late twentieth century's most perplexing and satisfying design challenges. This compensates for the colorless biographies of architecture's greatest figures, which are almost uniformly dry and lacking in elegance and substance—a surprising deficiency in a work from the American Institute of Architects.

This volume's large format and clear print on crisp white paper make reading a pleasure. Black-and-white photographs and many drawings and graphs enrich the text. The lengthy section, "Color in Architecture," is illustrated by four pages of small, beautifully chosen and reproduced color photographs. [R: Choice, Nov 88, pp. 458, 460; RBB, 1 Oct 88, pp. 222-23]

Octavia Porter Randolph

Handbooks

915. Gans, Deborah. **The Le Corbusier Guide.** Princeton, N.J., Princeton Architectural Press, 1987. 192p. illus. maps. index. $17.00pa. LC 87-22301. ISBN 0-910413-23-1.

This work can be used as a travel guide for a tour of Le Corbusier architecture and has value as a reference book of the sixty-nine extant Le Corbusier buildings.

The travel guide features of the work include arrangement by geographical location of the buildings (the majority are in Paris and other sites in France and the others are located throughout the world). The author devotes two to three pages to each building: standard information includes the name of the building, date, street address, policies for public visiting, suggestions for touring the surrounding areas, and directions via public transportation systems and automobiles. The entry provides a description of each building and its meaning in the Le Corbusier *oeuvre*, small but adequate black-and-white photographs, and floor plans and other drawings of each building.

The reference features also will enhance the traveler's use of this work. There is an excellent essay on the philosophy and impact of Le Corbusier's art, a biographical note, and a glossary of general architectural terms and terms formulated by Le Corbusier. There is an index that includes place names, personal names, and building names, and bibliographical notes arranged by building.

Linda A. Naru

916.   Woodbridge, Sally B. **California Architecture: Historic American Buildings Survey.** San Francisco, Calif., Chronicle Books, 1988. 274p. illus. bibliog. index. $35.00; $19.95pa. LC 88-23688. ISBN 0-87701-553-8; 0-87701-538-4pa.

Sponsored by the Historic American Buildings Survey (HABS) and the California Historical Society, this work consists of two main parts, the first of which is a brief history of architecture in California from early missions to colorful movie theaters. Buildings are described against a background of local history and anecdote, with rather little reference to architecture in other areas. The account is engrossing; familiar structures such as the Carson house (Eureka), the Gamble house (Pasadena), and the since-destroyed Richfield Building (Los Angeles) mingle with other, equally interesting works.

The second part, the HABS catalog, is arranged alphabetically by town, giving for each building such information as materials, size, shape, roof type, chimneys, date of construction, and reference to documents and photographs available in the Library of Congress.

Photographs (black-and-white) are clear, as are most drawings. Both are provided generously. A brief glossary for nonarchitects and a few maps for non-Californians would have been helpful features.

Competently researched and well written, this work is recommended for college and medium-sized public libraries everywhere.

Robert N. Broadus

GRAPHIC ARTS

917.   Axsom, Richard H., with Phylis Floyd. **The Prints of Ellsworth Kelly: A Catalogue Raisonné 1949-1985.** New York, published with American Federation of Arts by Hudson Hills Press; distr., New York, Rizzoli, 1987. 200p. illus. (part col.). bibliog. index. $50.00. LC 87-3079. ISBN 0-933920-84-9.

Richard Axsom and collaborator Phylis Floyd have written the first scholarly catalogue raisonné on the prints of contemporary artist Ellsworth Kelly. Kelly, a painter, sculptor, and printmaker, is known for his nonobjective art. His images are mostly flat, hard-edged color fields with roots in abstract, minimalist art. Kelly's participation in the creation of this work confirms its accuracy of information and gives the reader many of the artist's personal insights.

An informative introductory essay begins the work. The catalogue raisonné consists of a chronological display of Kelly's prints from 1949 to 1985. The reproduced prints are either in color or duotone. Each print is documented with title, date, measurements, media, printing sequence, proof information, and comments. The work concludes with a chronology of important dates beginning with Kelly's birth in 1923, a glossary of terms relating to printing processes and materials, a bibliography that emphasizes his printmaking activities, and an index.

The book is well bound; the paper and color quality are excellent. Unfortunately, the text is in a soft gray tone that may be difficult for some to read.

This catalog will be of special interest to print collectors, scholars, and connoisseurs.

Mary Frances White

918.   Karpinski, Caroline. **Italian Printmaking, Fifteenth and Sixteenth Centuries: An Annotated Bibliography.** Boston, G. K. Hall, 1987. 305p. index. (Reference Publications in Art History). $45.00. LC 86-19509. ISBN 0-8161-8556-5.

This new volume in G. K. Hall's series of bibliographies on the Italian Renaissance focuses on prints, printmakers, and printmaking. It is divided into sixteen sections and includes references to encyclopedic-type works; histories (general as well as specific); iconographic studies; works illustrating the uses of the print; descriptions of collections (arranged geographically); and information on printmakers, designers, publishers, and so forth. Three indexes provide access to names of authors, printmakers and publishers, and subjects.

The author, a former curator of prints at the Metropolitan Museum, New York, has excellent credentials for this undertaking. So many entries relating to the subject have been pulled together in this single volume that it will ease the work of identifying the literature for students researching in the field. However, the book is marred by too many instances of awkward style, overly abbreviated annotations, and incorrect syntax (e.g., p. 94: "No artists cited respecting some scintillating plates."), which fail to convey the author's point.　　　Carole Franklin Vidali

919.　Lumsdaine, Joycelyn Pang, and Thomas O'Sullivan, comps. **The Prints of Adolf Dehn: A Catalogue Raisonné.** St. Paul, Minn., Minnesota Historical Society, 1987. 268p. illus. (part col.). bibliog. index. $75.00. LC 87-7776. ISBN 0-87351-203-0.

This catalogue raisonné is based on Lumsdaine's thesis, completed in 1974, at the University of California at Los Angeles. After his death in 1968, Dehn's widow, Virginia, preserved intact his master set of prints while seeking a permanent repository for the set and a publisher for the catalog. When she donated the set to the Minnesota Historical Society in 1985, her goals were fulfilled.

This catalog contains descriptions of 665 of Dehn's black-and-white and color prints of both nature and human nature, from biting satires to sensitive landscape studies inspired by his wide travels. His prints show style, inventiveness, and exuberance.

Today his lithographs are in the major museums in America, and he was twice awarded a Guggenheim fellowship for his contributions to lithography.

Two essays on Dehn's life and career by Richard W. Cox and Clinton Adams precede this catalog. An index of titles, a select bibliography, a chronology, and a list of major exhibitions conclude the volume.

An excellent addition to an art department of a public library, or an art museum library. [R: Choice, July/Aug 88, p. 1684]
　　　Kathleen J. Voigt

920.　Wilson, Raymond L. **Index of American Print Exhibitions, 1882-1940.** Metuchen, N.J., Scarecrow, 1988. 906p. $82.50. LC 88-15640. ISBN 0-8108-2139-7.

American printmaking flourished from the 1880s to the early twentieth century, when photomechanical and screen processes were developed. This index presents a chronological listing of exhibition catalogs from American print societies and international expositions. The first two-thirds of this work covers exhibition information. After the name of the catalog and exhibition date, the artists' names are presented alphabetically and are followed by their print titles. If the medium (e.g., lithograph) was given in the catalog it is indicated by the title. An index of artists concludes the work.

The stated aim of the author "is to make available a reference to individual prints and printmakers represented at the annual salons of the leading societies" (p. v). This information is clearly presented and helpful to researchers. But for those trying to identify a print that may not be signed or titled, this work is lacking in coverage. Important distinguishing features, such as measurements and date of creation, are excluded. A title index was not included, which makes it almost impossible to locate the artist. The inclusion of this valuable information would expand this work to a two-volume set.

This specialized index will be of use to collectors, dealers, museum professionals, and other print enthusiasts.
　　　Mary Frances White

PAINTING AND DRAWING

921.　**The Index of Paintings Sold in the British Isles during the Nineteenth Century. Volume I: 1801-1805.** Burton B. Fredericksen with Julia I. Armstrong and Doris A. Mendenhall, eds. Santa Barbara, Calif., ABC-Clio, 1988. 1047p. $90.00. LC 88-3369. ISBN 0-87436-526-0.

An ambitious and intricately detailed record of paintings sold in Britain during the past century is launched with this massive volume, which lists thousands of entries for works sold during the first five years of the nineteenth century. Nineteen additional volumes are in process as part of the Getty History Information Program and each will include the auction records of a five-year span. A fascinating essay on the development of the London art market during the late eighteenth and early nineteenth centuries serves as an introduction to the listings and it is essential to read the concise description of the indexes and their arrangement to effectively use the myriad details. As many as eighteen items of data may be supplied for each work with annotations, inscriptions, and notes included. The most useful index is the major listing by artist's name but there are also indexes for the catalogs which were consulted as well as one for the owners of the works. The index has major importance as London established itself as the center for the international art trade of the era. The catalogs from which the listings were culled were generally printed in small editions, perhaps one to two hundred copies at the most. They are therefore difficult to locate. London was the home market for the majority of the sales and the files of the Christie firm were of substantial value, as were other catalogs held by the Courtould Institute, the Victoria and Albert Museum, the National Gallery in London, the British Library, and the British Museum. The appearance of long lists of sales of works by Reni, Rubens, Rembrandt, Poussin, the Carracci, Angelica Kauffman, and Van Dyck clearly defines art interests of the time along with the record of who was buying and selling. The scale of the completed twenty-volume set is immense and the editors as well as the Getty Program are to be commended by the art research community for undertaking such a gigantic reference project.

William J. Dane

922. Shaw, James Byam, and George Knox. **The Robert Lehman Collection. VI: Italian Eighteenth-Century Drawings.** New York, Metropolitan Museum of Art, with Princeton, N.J., Princeton University Press, 1987. 261p. illus. bibliog. index. $65.00. LC 86-12519. ISBN 0-691-04046-X.

The Metropolitan's impressive series on the Robert Lehman Collection continues with a second exemplary volume. The new volume, like its predecessor, is admirable in every way; a meticulous attention to scholarly detail is complemented by attractive design and a multiplicity of illustrations.

The eighteenth-century Italian art world was dominated by the Venetians, so it is appropriate that two experts in Venetian art, Shaw and Knox, have been responsible for the catalog. Documented are a wide range of drawing styles from the careful views of Canaletto to the flashy chiaroscuro studies of Giovanni Battista Tiepolo. Among other artists included are Domenico Tiepolo, Giovanni Panini, Pietro Longhi, and Francesco Guardi.

Arranged in alphabetical order by artist name, each section includes a brief biographical and stylistic summary about the artist as well as a catalog entry and a black-and-white illustration for each drawing. In addition, two or three paragraphs comment on each work and note bibliographical, provenance, and exhibition history. Completing the volume are an extensive general bibliography, an exhibition list, an index of artist names, and an index of previous owners. Every information need has been anticipated by the authors.

In sum, the publications of the Lehman Collection seem destined to be landmarks in art history. They should be in every art research library.   Stephanie C. Sigala

923. Scott, Randall W. **Comic Books and Strips: An Information Sourcebook.** Phoenix, Ariz., Oryx Press, 1988. 152p. index. $30.00pa. LC 88-22377. ISBN 0-89774-389-X.

This is an annotated bibliography of 989 mostly post-1970 English-language books and periodicals about or containing comic books and comic strips (books on animation and cartoons are excluded as are individual journal articles). Section 1 is a core library collection of eighty-eight books and twelve periodicals deemed by the author the most important titles published to date (through 1987). Section 2 lists 310 books about comics; section 3, 525 books that reprint comics; section 4, 54 periodicals about comic books; and section 5, 43 libraries with large comic book collections and/or comic book-related materials. Items in each section are descriptively annotated (usually in less than forty words) and are arranged either alphabetically by author or alphabetically by title. There are three indexes: author, title, and subject. This is a useful and carefully done work which nevertheless would have been even better had it included doctoral dissertations, collections of political and social commentary cartoons (such as those by Jules Feiffer, Pat Oliphant, and various *The New Yorker* cartoonists), and the small mass market paperbacks reprinting selections from *Mad, Peanuts,* and *Pogo.* In addition, some titles listed in sections 2 and 3 seem worthy of being included in the core collection, particularly the Russ Cochran reprints of the E.C. comics and the three reference works by Michael Fleisher.

Joseph Cataio

924. Weinberg, Robert. **A Biographical Dictionary of Science Fiction and Fantasy Artists.** Westport, Conn., Greenwood Press, 1988. 346p. bibliog. index. $49.95. LC 87-17651. ISBN 0-313-24349-2.

Nearly 280 artists and illustrators whose creations grace the covers and interiors of science fiction/fantasy books and magazines are described in this volume. The entries (with a few exceptions) are more detailed and the coverage is more comprehensive than that offered by *The Encyclopedia of Science Fiction and Fantasy* (see *ARBA* 75, entry 1330 and *ARBA* 79, entry 1204), *The Visual Encyclopedia of Science Fiction* (see *ARBA* 79, entry 1202), or *The Science Fiction Encyclopedia* (see *ARBA* 80, entry 1212). The author's background combines extensive research in the science fiction/fantasy field with experience as an art dealer.

Prefatory material includes an introduction, an explanation of how to use the book, and a list of abbreviations. A brief history of science fiction art is followed by the artist biographies (arranged alphabetically with cross-references and *see* references), an overview of still-existing art materials, and a list of the art awards in science fiction. A select bibliography is provided, along with an index of the biographical entries and a general index.

While some of the entries provide only a brief description of the artist, most provide a biographical sketch, an estimate of the artist's influence, notes on techniques used, and quotations from the artists concerning their work. The writing is crisp and clear, with emphatic critical evaluations. Particularly valuable is the appended indicative listing of published work for most artists (divided into hardback and paperbound covers, and magazine illustrations). A representative test sample of the data proved accurate.

The dictionary is admittedly incomplete. Major missing artists include P. Bruillet, H. R. Giger, J. Giraud, Jack Kirby, and K. Thole. As another measure of comprehensiveness, about 40 percent of the artists whose illustrations appear in *The Science Fiction Encyclopedia* are not given entries. The coverage is occasionally uneven (despite the fact that John Berkey is described as "the American master of science fiction hardware art," his entry occupies less than one-quarter of a page), and the occasional misspelling or missed cross-reference was noted. Overall, however, these flaws do not detract from the substance of this work, although its value could be enhanced considerably if a representative illustration of each artist's work had been included.

In summary, clearly printed on good-quality paper in a sturdy binding, this volume fills a major gap in science fiction studies, and can serve effectively both as a ready-reference source and as a scholarly index to materials which otherwise would be difficult (if not impossible) to find. [R: LJ, 15 June 88, p. 53; RBB, Aug 88, pp. 1896, 1898]

John Howard Oxley

SCULPTURE

925. Lyman, Thomas W., with Daniel Smartt. **French Romanesque Sculpture: An Annotated Bibliography.** Boston, G. K. Hall, 1987. 450p. index. (Reference Publications in Art History). $49.00. LC 86-29390. ISBN 0-8161-8330-9.

It is the opinion of the scholarly compilers of this extensive bibliography that Romanesque sculpture in France had as decisive an impact on European culture as did the architectural style of the earlier Roman Empire. Both then and now, the audience for this sculptured work consisted of clericals and laypersons, as the majority of the pieces were created as public art. The bibliography covers sculpture from the eleventh and twelfth centuries in lands claimed by the French monarchy during that time plus Corsica and Alsace, in addition to adjoining centers in Italy and Germany. The listings are separated into three major time segments and include 2,173 annotated entries. The period divisions are for the times when the texts appeared: 1700-1900, 1900-1944, and 1945 to the present. The majority of entries, over twelve hundred, were published after 1944, and this fact provides ample evidence as to the reason the editors selected this subject as part of their series of reference publications in art history. Each of the three categories includes a historical introduction, followed by separate listings for articles, books, and catalogs, with the entries arranged chronologically as they appeared in print. Names of celebrated authorities in the field appear again and again, as would be anticipated. These include Viollet-Le-Duc, Arthur Kingsley Porter, Puig i Cadafalch, Marcel Aubert, Kenneth Conant, Marcel Durliat, and Henri Focillon. The international art history community has been deeply absorbed in French Romanesque sculpture since the end of World War II, and this meticulously organized bibliographic survey is an essential reference service for contemporary researchers. An index of seventy-one pages is absolutely essential for maximum use of this specialized listing, which strives to be inclusive and which will be of great value to enthusiasts of medieval art.

William J. Dane

23 Language and Linguistics

GENERAL WORKS

Bibliographies

926. Beard, Robert, and Bogdan Szymanek, comps. **Bibliography of Morphology 1960-1985.** Philadelphia, John Benjamins, 1988. 193p. index. (Amsterdam Studies in the Theory and History of Linguistic Science. Series V: Library & Information Sources in Linguistics, Vol. 18). $29.00. LC 87-30008. ISBN 90-272-3742-5.

In its broadest sense, morphology is an essential part of the grammar of a language; it is also a branch of linguistics that focuses on the study of structures or forms of words and on types of word formation. The new bibliography represents a selective collection of major and some minor works of hundreds of morphologists throughout the world.

The primary focus of the two compilers has been on contemporary theoretical morphology and its development in the past twenty-five years. This restriction automatically eliminates even the most influential works published before 1960. The decision to list only published works further excludes a vast body of dissertations on morphology.

The main part (pp. 1-162) consists of detailed entries arranged alphabetically by authors. No categorization or classification by areas of research has been attempted here. An essential and very thorough subject index makes it possible to search for studies on the basis of various subject areas, as well as branches or schools of morphology (such as autonomous, autosegmental, categorial, lexical, natural, transformational). Another important reference tool is the language index, which alphabetically lists over 250 languages with names of authors who analyzed or discussed a particular language in their morphological works included in the main part of the book.

The interrelationships between morphology and phonology, semantics, syntax, and other branches of linguistics, and the bearing of morphological studies on interdisciplinary research in psycholinguistics, neurolinguistics, or sociolinguistics, will make this bibliography attractive to students and professionals in several fields of language-related research. [R: Choice, Sept 88, pp. 73-74]   Lev I. Soudek

927. **Dictionaries, Encyclopedias, and Other Word-Related Books: A Classed Guide....** 4th ed. Annie M. Brewer, ed. Detroit, Gale, 1988. 2v. index. $495.00/set. LC 87-83314. ISBN 0-8103-0440-6.

This sizable work of over thirteen hundred pages in two volumes is a bibliography of some thirty-five thousand dictionaries, glossaries, lexicons, encyclopedias, thesauri, topical indexes, and other collections of words from many fields of research and areas of interest. Entries are arranged according to the Library of Congress Subject Classification system, with broad headings listing general works on a given area first, followed by more specific entries. One of the welcome improvements of this revised and updated fourth edition is a detailed subject/title index which facilitates searching for wider related areas, as well as for highly specialized topics.

A few examples will show the range and depth of this remarkable collection: works pertaining to the general subject of the English language take up almost one hundred pages, with three columns per page. They include standard monolingual, bilingual, and polyglot dictionaries, as well as specialized dictionaries of synonyms, antonyms, neologisms, abbreviations, idioms, phrasal verbs, slang, and many others.

For more esoteric areas, persons interested in, for instance, terms pertaining to wine will find as many as seventeen dictionaries dealing with wines and wine making. Similarly, in a few minutes, one can locate five dictionaries of pathology or six glossaries of linguistic terminology.   Lev I. Soudek

928.   Fisiak, Jacek, comp. and ed. **A Bibliography of Writings for the History of the English Language.** 2d ed. New York, Walter de Gruyter, 1987. 216p. index. $66.00. LC 87-24015. ISBN 0-89925-057-2.

This second edition of Jacek Fisiak's *Bibliography of Writings for the History of the English Language* is a useful and workmanlike tool for specialists. The 1983 edition, out of print since 1985, was "conceived in the process of writing a history of English for Polish students" (*Journal of English Linguistics* 17 [1984]: 116). The new edition, which is half again as long as the first, not only repeats older pertinent material but also adds items appearing since 1983 (p. vii).

Professor Fisiak considers the works of approximately fifteen hundred authors, classing them under topics ranging from bibliographies, memorial volumes, general lexicography, histories of English and historical grammars to grammar, word-formation, vocabulary and semantics, foreign elements, varieties and dialects, and sociolinguistics. Articles appearing in the "Memorial Volumes" are accessible through the author index at the back of the volume. The index is accurate as far as it goes; but it would be better if expanded by titles and subject terms. In general, a lexical and grammatical orientation seems to drive selection. Theoretical and large-unit constructs like syntax are relatively underrepresented.

One probably cannot find better coverage of the history of Old and Middle English in any other single volume. Except for dialectology, earlier modern English is the practical outer limit for historical studies of the language; and this state of affairs is reflected in the present work. The entries are all clear and uniformly styled, although they lack annotations. This is not a perfect tool; but users will, nonetheless, award it very high marks.

Judith M. Brugger

929.   Gazdar, Gerald, and others. **Natural Language Processing in the 1980s: A Bibliography.** Stanford, Calif., Center for the Study of Language and Information, 1987. 240p. index. (CSLI Lecture Notes, No. 12). $24.95; $9.95pa. LC 87-27644. ISBN 0-937073-26-1; 0-937073-28-8pa.

This bibliography of 1,764 items reporting on work in natural language processing (NLP) as it has been conducted in the 1980s is a valuable collection for the increasing numbers of scholars and researchers concerned with the field. Produced by the Center for the Study of Language and Information, the contents are drawn from journals, conference and workshop proceedings, and edited collections on NLP per se, or application of logic programming to NLP tasks. The entries are arranged alphabetically by first author, with alternate access via subsequent authors or keyword-in-context (KWIC), based on terms from titles of the papers. Although the KWIC index provides some subject access, it does not provide sufficient entries to this wealth of information. Indexing devoid of intellectual analysis of the indexed pieces is always somewhat dissatisfactory, even in situations like this where the majority of titles are quite reflective of the subjects covered. An admirable aspect of this effort is the availability of the bibliography for online searching by anyone with access to the same academic computer network. Alternatively, a disk containing a machine-readable copy of the file can be purchased. Since the bibliography is going to be updated continually, it will be of great value to those active in the field. However, its lack of well-designed subject access will make it less so to those new to the field of natural language processing.

Elizabeth D. Liddy

930.   Gordon, W. Terrence. **Semantics: A Bibliography, 1979-1985.** Metuchen, N.J., Scarecrow, 1987. 292p. index. $27.50. LC 87-16344. ISBN 0-8108-2055-2.

As a companion to the same author's 1980 work (see *ARBA* 81, entry 1143) that supplied an interdisciplinary bibliography for 1965-1978, this useful volume begins where the earlier work ended. The four disciplines included are anthropology, linguistics, philosophy, and psychology. In a short introduction, the author explains that considerable scholarship exists in anthropology in the areas of color terms and kinship terminology. Linguistic semantics has produced increasing amounts of research and controversy, while semantics continues to be an area of interest for philosophers. A new branch of study for psychologists is "the semantics of child language ... which was all but ignored a few short years ago."

To provide a comprehensive bibliography for scholars in the above disciplines, Gordon begins with a listing of books, then organizes article and paper entries by topic. The longest sections are on definitions and models of meaning, the semantics of parts of speech, semantics and syntax, and the semantics of child language. Other topics include associative series in the lexicon, kinship terminology, color terms, negation, idioms, comparative semantics, and semantic universals.

With over one thousand annotated listings in English, French, German, Italian, Portuguese, and Spanish, this volume is an excellent resource for the researcher in semantics. Its interdisciplinary focus is another valuable aspect.

Renee B. Horowitz

931.   Markus, Manfred, and Josef Wallmannsberger. **English-German Contrastive Linguistics: A Bibliography.** New York, Peter Lang, 1987. 108p. index. (European University Studies. Series 14: Anglo-Saxon Language and Literature, Vol. 174). $14.60pa. ISBN 3-8204-0146-6.

This specialized reference work focuses on the interdisciplinary area of contrastive linguistics, also known as contrastive analysis or contrastive grammar. For decades, researchers in this field have attempted to compare and contrast the systems and subsystems of two or more languages either for purposes of linguistic theory or, more frequently, for the practical needs of language pedagogy.

Having survived periods of euphoria as well as of skepticism, contrastive linguistics has made a remarkable comeback, especially in recent studies of European linguists and language-teaching specialists.

Although the new bibliography focuses on English-German contrastive studies, it does include scores of books, dissertations, articles, and papers dealing with more general aspects of linguistic contrasts. The work is divided into eleven sections corresponding to the subsystems of language (such as phonetics and phonology, lexicology and morphology, syntax, semantics, pragmatics, etc.) or to activities such as translation or pedagogical applications.

An author index facilitates searching. In the absence of cross-referencing, some entries reappear in several sections. The bibliography should be useful not only for theoretical linguists but also for researchers in applied linguistics and for teachers of German and English.

Lev I. Soudek

932.   Tajima, Matsuji, comp. **Old and Middle English Language Studies: A Classified Bibliography 1923-1985.** Philadelphia, John Benjamins, 1988. 391p. index. (Amsterdam Studies in the Theory and History of Linguistic Science. Series V: Library & Information Sources in Linguistics, Vol. 13). $46.00. LC 88-10429. ISBN 90-272-3732-8.

Matsuji Tajima established his bibliographic credentials two years ago as the coauthor of a first-rate bibliography on Noam Chomsky (see *ARBA* 88, entry 1051). According to the author, his new bibliography is the result of over ten years of research. It covers a period from the final entries of 1922, listed in A. G. Kennedy's *Bibliography of Writings on the English Language* (Yale University Press, 1927), and provides a very systematic, comprehensive, and detailed coverage through 1985, including a few selected titles published as late as 1987.

Unlike Kennedy's all-inclusive bibliography, however, Tajima's work has an exclusive focus on Old English and Middle English language studies. It lists monographs, books, dissertations, articles, and reviews, divided into fourteen broad thematic areas, such as grammars, orthography and punctuation, phonology and phonetics, morphology, syntax, lexicology and word formation, dialectology, and others.

Some entries display cross-references to related works. Reviews are conveniently grouped under the entry for the book reviewed. Throughout the bibliography, great care has been taken to respect the various orthographies of authors' names and entry titles. A reliable index of names (pp. 357-91) lists all authors, editors, collaborators, translators, reviewers, and other contributors mentioned, with numerical references to the main part of the bibliography.

The 3,913 entries document a vast body of truly international scholarship that has traditionally focused on the Old English and Middle English areas of historical linguistics. Thanks to a patient, systematic, and meticulous bibliographer, the results of that scholarship are now more accessible to others.   Lev I. Soudek

Dictionaries and Encyclopedias

933.   **The Cambridge Encyclopedia of Language.** By David Crystal. New York, Cambridge University Press, 1987. 472p. illus. index. $39.50. LC 86-32637. ISBN 0-521-26438-3.

David Crystal's fine reference work is the first encyclopedic survey of knowledge about language and of the many kinds, schools, and branches of linguistic science. As an outstanding British linguist, founder and editor of *Linguistic Abstracts*, Crystal comes well prepared for such a task. His recent *Dictionary of Linguistics and Phonetics* (see *ARBA* 86, entry 1040), has become a superior reference tool used by linguists throughout the world.

His encyclopedia superby documents the immense expansion of research and knowledge about language and languages in the second half of our century, the branching out of linguistics into several specialized sciences and various interdisciplinary study areas, and the current proliferation of linguistic terminology.

The encyclopedia consists of eleven parts subdivided into sixty-five self-contained thematic sections. Each section focuses on a major area of language study: detailed information is presented in the form of lucid and succinct essays that include frequent and very useful cross-references to other sections where related topics are discussed. Hundreds of tables, maps, data charts, photographs, drawings, newspaper clippings, and cartoons illustrate the text and provide further synoptic information or exemplification.

The appendices include a glossary of over a thousand terms (with brief definitions) that occur in the text, a table of hundreds of the world's living languages, useful notes directing the user to further sources of information on respective topics, and an extensive list of references. Three meticulously organized indexes (of languages, authors, and topics) make searching quite a joyful activity.

The quantity and quality of included information is amazing. Composed by an individual, this is a truly unique and monumental reference work. [R: Choice, June 88, p. 1532; LJ, 1 May 88, p. 71; RBB, 15 June 88, p. 1716; WLB, May 88, p. 106]   Lev I. Soudek

Handbooks

934. Paulston, Christina Bratt, ed. **International Handbook of Bilingualism and Bilingual Education.** Westport, Conn., Greenwood Press, 1988. 603p. bibliog. index. $85.00. LC 87-263. ISBN 0-313-24484-7.

There are very few monolingual nations in the world; in most countries bilingualism (or even multilingualism) is the norm. It has been estimated that over two-thirds of the world's population is bilingual or multilingual.

The various aspects, types, degrees, and social manifestations of bilingualism/multilingualism can be and have been approached from the points of view of several disciplines. This new handbook, edited by a prominent scholar in applied linguistics, presents a detailed, informative, and scholarly survey of a wide range of multilingual situations in many parts of the world.

An introductory essay by the editor provides the necessary theoretical background for understanding basic concepts of linguistic, psychological, sociological, and political approaches to some manifestations of bilingualism and multilingualism. A well-written general chapter by Sarah Thomason surveys current

linguistic thinking concerning the origins of language, language families, and diversification.

The main part of this fine sourcebook consists of twenty-five case studies by contributors from various countries, describing specific bilingual/multilingual situations in many parts of the globe. Together with well-known and frequently quoted language situations, such as those in Belgium, Canada, or Switzerland, the studies include detailed descriptions of bilingualism in mainland China, the Soviet Union, several South American countries, various parts of Africa, and many other nations. A thought-provoking study on language behavior and attitudes towards bilingualism in the United States contains many interesting details and observations on minority languages and their relations to English. Most case studies include valuable bibliographies for further study.

Despite the general unifying theme, these studies show an amazing diversity of approaches and implications. In varying proportions, they bring up problems of language planning, spread, maintenance, shift, split, revival, and even language death. Other studies focus on diglossia, assimilation, political dominance, ethnicity, and nationalism.

An author index and a language index enhance the usefulness and accessibility of this important contribution to the study and understanding of global multilingualism.

Lev I. Soudek

ENGLISH-LANGUAGE DICTIONARIES

General Works

935. Barnhart, David K. **The Barnhart Dictionary Companion Index (1982-1985).** Cold Spring, N.Y., Lexik House, 1987. 102p. $45.00. LC 86-81562. ISBN 0-936368-05-5.

This Barnhart dictionary is an index to the words and phrases defined in the first four volumes of the quarterly journal, *The Barnhart Dictionary Companion*. The *Companion* defines new words, new meanings for existing words, and changed usages, giving one or more citations showing how each entry is used and indicating frequency of use.

This index does indeed provide an alphabetical index of terms (with variations) giving volume, number, and page on which the definitions are found for some three thousand words. In addition, alphabetical word lists are provided for broad subjects such as social studies and common vocabulary.

Etymological lists include entries under such headings as "Borrowings," "Loan Translations," "Folk Etymology," "Compounds," and "Usage." This set of lists is generally in alphabetical order with no additional explanation, but the "Borrowings" list is broken down by the country of origin and "Loan Translations" are followed by the language from which they were translated. The part of speech is indicated for "Compounds."

The third supplemental section is "Formative Elements of Words and Phrases." In this section, "all of the prefixes, suffixes, words or combining forms which appear within words and phrases" (introduction), are given in boldface type in alphabetical order, surrounded by the rest of the word or phrase.

While each issue of the *Companion* has an index which cumulates for the volume year, this index provides users with one alphabetical finding list for the first four volumes of the *Companion*.

The subject lists allow the user to examine a limited field of new words. The etymological lists give the scholar or the dilettante a quick look at the impact of new words on the language. The "Formative Elements" section would probably be of most interest to scholars or linguists.

At the present time the index covers four of the six volumes published, each of which has its own volume index. Many users may, therefore, choose to forego acquisition of the index until such time as it covers a larger number of volumes or there is more demand for the supplements. Others, especially linguists, and editors doing much writing demanding both currency and accuracy, may find the index a useful shortcut.   Betty Jo Buckingham

936. O'Neill, Robert Keating, comp. **English-Language Dictionaries, 1604-1900: The Catalog of the Warren N. and Suzanne B. Cordell Collection.** Westport, Conn., Greenwood Press, 1988. 480p. index. (Bibliographies and Indexes in Library and Information Science, No. 1). $85.00. LC 87-35947. ISBN 0-313-25522-9.

In 1969 and again in 1974, Warren Cordell made a gift of the dictionaries he had collected to Indiana State University. By 1975 the collection totaled some five thousand titles and has continued to grow through additional gifts and university acquisitions. This catalog lists the 2,328 English-language dictionary titles in the collection known to have been published prior to 1900. Entries are arranged alphabetically by author including compiler or editor. Following the author entry title, publication statement, collation, and notes are given. Notes are brief

and include prices found in the book as well as information about the condition of the title. Provenance is given after notes, and in general includes book labels or plates, early ownership, inscriptions, and significant notes. The final entry is for references used in research of the Cordell entries. There is a subject index.

While not a catalog of the entire collection, *English-Language Dictionaries* is a significant work, and one that language scholars and bibliographers will find useful. It is far more comprehensive than M. M. Mathew's *Survey of English Dictionaries* (repr., Russell & Russell, 1966), and large academic libraries will want to purchase it. It is hoped that another catalog of this collection will be published to fill in the gaps, since the Cordell Collection is now one of the chief repositories of dictionaries in the United States.

    Helen M. Gothberg

Abridged

937. **The American Heritage Illustrated Encyclopedic Dictionary.** Boston, Houghton Mifflin, 1987. 1920p. illus. (part col.). maps. $55.00. LC 87-4039. ISBN 0-395-44295-8.

The *American Heritage Illustrated Encyclopedic Dictionary* (*AHD*) offers a combination of encyclopedia and dictionary functions. As a dictionary, it provides guidance to the pronunciation, spelling, syllabification, and meaning of approximately 180,000 entry terms incorporating some 200,000 meanings. Quotations, synonyms, etymologies, usage notes, and cross-references illustrate variations of meaning within entries.

As an encyclopedia, the work offers 295 longer (though still brief) "feature" articles, on the informational level of a good youth encyclopedia, that cover selected subjects under headings such as time zone, river, postimpressionism, map projection, Leonardo da Vinci, dinosaur, Bronze Age, American Revolution, etc. It also provides some twenty-three hundred small maps and other color illustrations followed by glosses. Both kinds of material supplement rather than take the place of entries occurring alphabetically in the text, and both are set apart from the main text. The pictures and glosses appear vertically in left and right margins. Larger maps and "feature" articles are defined in blocks within the text. There are no cross-references between main text and supplementary material, which may occur on a following page. Illustrations were chosen for their informative and visual attributes, but no discernible policy governs selection of topics for feature articles, though coverage seems best in biography, geography, the general sciences, and fine arts.

This edition of the *AHD* should not be compared with unabridged dictionaries (which approach 340,000 items) or other scholarly reference works, though it does have approximately the same number range of entries/meanings as its own 1969 and 1982 versions. Its lexicon, updated until "the last days before the book went to press," emphasizes North American vocabulary and usage, omitting certain raunchily explicit terms that appeared in earlier editions and most of the scholarly apparatus, like the appendix of Indo-European root words, that distinguished the others.

Despite any shortcomings, the combination of encyclopedic and dictionary functions is intriguing and attractively presented. The print is easy to read, colors are clear, and the large, sturdily bound volume, printed on nonreflecting paper, lies flat when opened. It should make a popular addition to any library. Before purchasing, however, buyers should see entry 938 for a comparison with the *Reader's Digest Illustrated Encyclopedic Dictionary*. [R: Choice, May 88, p. 1377; RBB, 15 Apr 88, p. 1400; WLB, Feb 88, p. 96]

Mary Jo Walker

938. Reader's Digest Illustrated Encyclopedic Dictionary. Pleasantville, N.Y., Reader's Digest Association, 1987. 2v. illus. (part col.). maps. $49.95/set. LC 87-9650. ISBN 0-89577-269-8.

This Reader's Digest dictionary (*RDD*) shares the same database, including lexicon, illustrations, and other features, as the *American Heritage Illustrated Encyclopedic Dictionary* (see entry 937). In fact, the two works evidently are fraternal twins, with two obvious differences: the first two words of their titles and the fact that the *RDD* has divided its text into two volumes that display the same quality of binding, paper, printing, etc., as the *AHD*'s single volume.

Otherwise, whether compared page by page (each has 1,920), entry by entry (each claims 180,000), illustration by illustration (each claims 2,300), or feature article by feature article, the two works seem identical. The two also share the same preliminary use instructions (the *RDD* uses highlighting here, which makes scanning easier); the same concluding list of acknowledgments; the same editorial boards (though listed in different order in each); and the same truncated, curiously uninformative preface signed simply "The Editor." Interestingly, this preface claims that each work is "a new type of dictionary," and carefully makes no mention of previous publication history.

There is one more difference between the two works: price. The *RDD* costs $5.05 less than the *AHD*. All things considered, buyers will have to decide whether they prefer a one- or two-volume format, and whether they want to pay a little more (or less) for what they may consider a more (or slightly less) prestigious name.

Mary Jo Walker

939. Webster's New World Dictionary of American English. 3d ed. Victoria Neufeldt, ed. New York, Webster's New World; distr., New York, Prentice Hall Press, 1988. 1574p. illus. $16.95; $17.95 (thumb-indexed). LC 88-1712. ISBN 0-13-949280-1; 0-13-947169-3 (thumb-indexed).

In the past what has separated the *New World* from competing desk dictionaries is its emphasis on current American English; the lucid "plain English" style of its definitions; and its outstanding coverage of the idiomatic, colloquial, and slang vocabulary of American English. The third edition carries on this tradition admirably.

Containing 170,000 entries and four million words of text, the *New World* emphasizes words of American origin such as *downsize*, *hickory*, *psychobabble*, *green light*, and eleven thousand others marked with an asterisk. It also includes illustrations, the largest type size of any American desk dictionary, and, of particular interest to professional writers, it distinguishes between preferred and less preferred breaks for line-end hyphenation.

Like *Webster's Ninth New Collegiate Dictionary* (see *ARBA* 84, entry 1026) definitions are given in historical order. The *New World* is much stronger in etymologies than the *American Heritage Dictionary* (2d college ed., Houghton-Mifflin, 1982) and is comparable to *Webster's Ninth*. The *New World* has more extensive usage explanations and examples than *Webster's Ninth*, and in general it is also better on usage than the *American Heritage*, though the *American Heritage* is also very good and in most cases the difference is slight, with the edge going to the *New World*.

Among American desk dictionaries, the *New World* basically occupies the middle ground between the stodgier *Webster's Ninth* and the glitzier *American Heritage*. The definitions of the *New World* stand out as being more concise and readable than either of its principal competitors. The *New World* is also stronger than its competitors in the area of new words, colloquialisms, and idiomatic phrases. The *New World* is an essential American reference for every library regardless of budget or clientele.

No other dictionary or combination of dictionaries can be used to duplicate its contents.

Dennis Dillon

Eponyms

940. Tuleja, Tad. **Namesakes: An Entertaining Guide to the Origins of More Than 300 Words Named for People.** New York, McGraw-Hill, 1987. 226p. bibliog. index. $7.95pa. LC 86-15216. ISBN 0-07-065436-0.

The 1980s have been a good decade for eponyms. Tad Tuleja's *Namesakes* is the fifth monographic work to appear on this topic since Allan Wolk's unspectacular *Everyday Words from Names of People and Places* (see *ARBA* 81, entry 1161). The book to beat in this field, though, is Robert Hendrickson's *Dictionary of Eponyms* (see *ARBA* 86, entry 1051), formerly published as *Human Words* (Chilton, 1972). For one thing, Hendrickson's work is much bigger. Its thirty-five hundred words simply overpower Tuleja's three hundred.

Tuleja has published satirical and/or humorous origins for the more curious English locutions in his *The Cat's Pajamas* (Fawcett, 1987). In *Namesakes* his engaging prose style pays off. His entry for "Pap smear" (pp. 145-46) for example, provides the reader with a few details from the private life of Dr. Papanicolaou that Hendrickson's article does not. On the other hand, Hendrickson's work is often more apropos. His entry for *ampere* (pp. 11-12) for example, focuses on the historical situation of that word's adaptation into English, rather than on the life of the scientist André Marie Ampère.

There are also organizational differences. In Tuleja's volume, the first entry under *guns* is *shrapnel* (p. 82). Obviously, the index at the back is a necessary textual component. Whereas Tuleja alphabetizes "according to Hoyle" in the "H's" (p. 91), Hendrickson puts it in the "A's." Tuleja's "A's" read like entries from a juvenile dictionary of Greek mythology: Achilles heel, Adonis, aphrodisiac, Atlas (pp. 3-8). To his credit, none of these entries appears in Hendrickson. A large percentage of his material is, however, redundant. *Namesakes* is not a "mesmerizing" (p. 122) work, but it is not a "gargantuan" (p. 73) flop, either.

Judith M. Brugger

Etymology

941. Barnhart, Robert K., ed. **The Barnhart Dictionary of Etymology.** Bronx, N.Y., H. W. Wilson, 1988. 1284p. bibliog. $59.00. LC 87-27994. ISBN 0-8242-0745-9.

This dictionary "traces the origins of the basic vocabulary of modern English." It contains "over 30,000 entries," and emphasizes language "development, especially from the point of view of American English" (p. xiii). It includes glossaries of language and linguistic terms, works cited in entries, a bibliography, historical information, and "Explanatory Notes."

Entries give pronunciation "for hard or unusual words"; part of speech; definition (for most words); date; language(s) borrowed from and likely forms in those languages; other forms of the word including other parts of speech, with separate history if needed; and cross-references. The book may contain over thirty thousand entries if main entries *and* subdivisions are counted. Random sample counts of main entries result in estimates closer to twenty thousand.

Except for the prefatory material on "Proto-Germanic and Indo-European" which presents a challenge to the layperson, the dictionary is easy to use. It includes terms that have become popular within the last generation or two, such as yuppie (1984) and WASP (1960), and older terms, some still commonly used and some uncommon today, such as warlock (before 950), and yclept (before 1350).

As with any dictionary, there are words or meanings one looks for and does not find. *Trews* is afforded neither an entry nor a reference under "trousers." "Card" does not include the sense in the statement, "You are a card."

The *Oxford Dictionary of English Etymology* (Oxford, 1966) included more discrete words, usually literary terms or words more likely to be found in English works, where the discrete words offered by *Barnhart* tend to be newer or American English terms. The *Barnhart* entries are longer and include dates (generally omitted in the *Oxford Dictionary*) and many more citations. While no etymological dictionary examined by the reviewer can compete in thoroughness with the different editions of the *Oxford English Dictionary*, the *Barnhart Dictionary* gives more detail for more English language words than the *Oxford Dictionary of Etymology*, or the *Concise Oxford Dictionary of Etymology* (see *ARBA* 87, entry 1020). Schools and libraries wishing to emphasize American English or to have more detail in a single volume dictionary will prefer *Barnhart*. Those concerned with older terms may wish to provide the 1966 *Oxford Dictionary* as well. [R: RBB, 15 Dec 88, pp. 687-88]

Betty Jo Buckingham

942. Black, Donald Chain. **Spoonerisms, Sycophants, and Sops.** New York, Harper & Row, 1988. 134p. index. $15.95. LC 87-45832. ISBN 0-06-015886-7.

The word *spoonerism* is derived from the humorous inversions of the Reverend Spooner who is reported once to have referred to the British Queen as "that queer old dean." If you do not know what *sycophants* and *sops* are, you will find them defined in this enjoyable word-book. Questions such as "Which would you rather *not* be?" and "What do these words have in common?" pull the reader into the discourse that follows. The reader may discover words such as *booboisie* (coined by H. L. Mencken from *boob* + *bourgeoisie*), *hoi polloi*, and *canaille*, all used contemptuously.

Spoonerisms, Sycophants and Sops is a clever volume which is indexed for usefulness. However, the lack of a pronunciation guide for words such as *colporteur, egregiously, billet-doux* and *trompe l'oeil* will undoubtedly be a disadvantage for many; nor is there any attempt to show the use of words in a sentence. This little book is not geared to reference work, but will be enjoyed by word buffs of moderate sophistication as part of the library's circulating collection from senior high school through college. However, most of these words can be found in slang and/or historical dictionaries.

Helen M. Gothberg

943. Ciardi, John. **Good Words to You: An All-New Dictionary and Native's Guide to the Unknown American Language.** New York, Harper & Row, 1987. 343p. $19.95. LC 86-45647. ISBN 0-06-015691-0.

This is the third of Ciardi's etymological dictionaries. In the foreword to the first, *A Browser's Dictionary* (see *ARBA* 81, entry 1159) Ciardi says that he will make several of them "before collating the whole into some future obsessive tome." Since this great etymologist, translator, poet, critic, and teacher died just weeks before the appearance of *Good Words to You*, it is uncertain whether any such compilation will be done. We can only hope it will.

There are those who think Ciardi's etymological work is not, well, serious enough: Paul Stuewe called *A Second Browser's Dictionary* (Harper, 1983) "banal" and "silly" (*Quill & Quire* 49 [August 1983]: 41). Actually Ciardi conveys a feeling of deep involvement in all three of his dictionaries. The foreword of *Good Words to You* represents in verse part of the prose message of the foreword in *A Second Browser's Dictionary*. Ciardi hones his definition of *alibi* for all three volumes. But after all, right there on pages 124 and 125 of *Good Words*

to You, Ciardi does illustrate the meaning of *fungible* by presenting a little drama involving Michelangelo's *David*, three plastic Madonnas, and his Social Security check. Blatantly discursive and truly subjective, it is not a highbrow style. *Good Words to You* frivolously includes, moreover, such queer and/or rare words as *tec* (p. 278), *tic dollaroo* (p. 279), and *Brooklyn* (p. 51ff).

Granted, *Good Words to You* is not serious in the way that the *Oxford English Dictionary* is. Considered either alone or together with the first two browser's dictionaries, however, it does have personality, wit, common sense, and a Johnsonesque *je ne sais quoi*.

Judith M. Brugger

944. Morris, William, and Mary Morris. **Morris Dictionary of Word and Phrase Origins.** 2d ed. New York, Harper & Row, 1988. 669p. index. $25.00. LC 87-45651. ISBN 0-06-015862-X.

This is the second edition of a three-volume work published between 1962 and 1971 and then updated and compiled into one volume in 1977 (see *ARBA* 78, entry 1032). Random comparisons between these editions lead me to conclude that apparently all of the entries in the first edition are included verbatim in the second. So, while there are numerous new entries in the second edition, this is not a revision of the first edition.

As the authors freely admit, this is a reference book that is meant to amuse as well as to inform: "The purpose of this volume – if it may be said to have a purpose other than to entertain and enlighten – is to lay before you some of the results of many years of exploration of the more casual byways of the fascinating science, etymology" (introduction). Readers who believe that a book's entertainment value may detract from its ability to inform will be skeptical of this book. The book is addressed to a general, not a scholarly audience, and is meant to be browsed as much as consulted. It is similar to numerous other popular etymological dictionaries, such as *The Facts on File Encyclopedia of Word and Phrase Origins* (see *ARBA* 88, entry 1066), to cite just one recent example.

As is true with many other types of reference questions, reference librarians seem to be duty-bound to check more than one source when in doubt about an etymology. If, on the other hand, a reader is just browsing dictionaries like these for diversion, the Morrises have written a very friendly companion. For example, in addition to reminding us of the origin of the word *browsing* as a type of animal feeding, the authors suggest that browsing a book or a library may therefore be considered "nibbling, so to speak, at learning." Unfortunately, some of the entries I nibbled at in this dictionary, while they satisfied me as to what a particular word or term meant, did not tell me how its meaning was derived. For instance, it is not sufficient to be told that "a Monday morning quarterback" is equivalent to saying "anyone can be an expert on strategy after the game is over." The editors forget that a non-American reader may not know that *quarterback* is a football term or that Monday is significant because most football games are played on weekends. If a library can afford it, this is another useful and amusing, though not indispensable, etymological dictionary. [R: RBB, 1 Oct 88, p. 243]

David Isaacson

945.   Rees, Nigel. **Why Do We Say...? Words and Sayings and Where They Come From.** London, Blandford Press; distr., New York, Sterling Publishing, 1987. 224p. $17.95. ISBN 0-7137-1944-3.

Why do we say such things as "talking nineteen to the dozen," "sowing his wild oats," or "one's name is Mudd?" The answers to these and approximately five hundred other such words and phrases are to be found in *Why Do We Say...?* by Nigel Rees.

After locating the word or phrase (which this reviewer found by looking for the keyword), there are interesting definitions and explanations following. For example, "guillotine for executive equipment" gets the name "guillotine" from the French physician Dr. Joseph-Ignace Guillotine, who did *not* invent the guillotine. This "humane and painless" device, used for severing a person's head, was used in Italy and other places and was adapted by Dr. Antoine Louise, who lived from 1723 to 1792. This device, known in France as "La Veuve" or "The Widow," was pensioned off in 1981 when the French National Assembly eliminated the death penalty.

For many of these entries sources are cited, a list of which is given on pages 7-8 of this volume.

Why Do We Say...? is similar to such books as *A Hog on Ice and Other Curious Expressions* (Harper & Row, 1985), *Heavens to Betsy* (Harper & Row, 1980), and *Thereby Hangs a Tale* (Harper & Row, 1985). However, this reviewer has found using *Why Do We Say...?* somewhat tedious, as there is no index and determining the keyword or phrase is not always easy. Even so, the book deserves a place in reference collections, especially those in high school and university libraries.

Nigel Rees has also written *Nudge, Nudge, Wink, Wink* (Sterling, 1987), another collection of humorous words and phrases. Other credentials of this person were not obtainable.

Jefferson D. Caskey

Foreign Terms

946.   **Loanwords Dictionary: A Lexicon of More Than 6,500 Words and Phrases Encountered in English Contexts That Are Not Fully Assimilated into English....** Laurence Urdang and Frank R. Abate, eds. Detroit, Gale, 1988. 324p. $80.00. LC 87-25089. ISBN 0-8103-1543-2.

While the *cognoscenti* may find this book less than authoritative, it is nevertheless too specialized for the *hoi polloi*. The italicized terms in the previous sentence are not simply foreign words that have been incorporated into English. More specifically, they meet the three selection criteria established by the editors for what they call a *loanword*: namely, that the term (1) "maintains some measure of its foreign orthography, pronunciation, or flavor"; (2) "is freely and commonly used in English contexts"; and (3) if originally specialized or technical, has become generalized in application or is from a field that attracts broad general interest" (preface).

A user will consult a dictionary like this one (1) to ascertain the present meaning of a loanword; (2) to discover its original, or literal meaning in the foreign language; (3) to find out how the word is pronounced in English; and (4) to get some guidance as to appropriate usage. *Loanwords* is rather useful in fulfilling the first two purposes, but, unfortunately, gives no pronunciation symbols, and usually does not offer prescriptive advice. Thus, for example, referring back to the first sentence of this review, *Loanwords* informs us that the word *cognoscenti* is the plural in Italian of *cognoscente* and that it means either "a connoisseur" or "an elite group that is thought to possess superior knowledge." Helpful as this entry is, it does not inform us whether we should pronounce this word as the Italians do or whether we should Anglicize it. One might also argue that while related, the words *cognoscenti* and *connoisseur* are not synonyms.

Somewhat more helpfully, the entry for *hoi polloi* in *Loanwords* informs us: "(Greek) (lit., 'the many') the common people; the masses (often said with an attitude of superiority)." Although we still need to consult another source for pronunciation, we do get some usage advice in this entry. But what we do not learn is that in the course of English usage, or rather misusage, this term has sometimes come to mean the opposite of the masses. Webster's third unabridged dictionary notes that *hoi polloi* may, in fact, mean "people of distinction or wealth or elevated social status." In other words, *hoi polloi* can mean *cognoscenti*. *Loanwords* not only does not tell us that this term is frequently used in this way, but that, strictly speaking, English users should never say *the hoi polloi* since *hoi* means *the* in Greek.

Many of these loanwords are included in general dictionaries, especially unabridged ones, and some of these words are used so commonly in English by so many people as hardly to seem foreign (e.g., *kosher, tango,* and *papier mâché*). It should be noted that although this source contains more than sixty-five hundred words and phrases, many more entries than this can be found in more specialized lexicons. Potential users of this dictionary should also know that numerous similar dictionaries already exist, including, to cite just two of the more recent titles, Kevin Guinagh's *Dictionary of Foreign Phrases and Abbreviations*, third edition (see *ARBA 84*, entry 1027), and B. A. Phythian's *A Concise Dictionary of Foreign Expressions* (see *ARBA 84*, entry 1028).

Since most unabridged dictionaries include many of these words and may in fact also include aids to pronunciation and usage, this book is not an essential purchase. [R: Choice, Apr 88, p. 1223; RBB, 15 May 88, p. 1584; WLB, Feb 88, p. 101]   David Isaacson

Idioms, Colloquialisms, and Special Usage

947.   Bryson, Bill. **The Facts on File Dictionary of Troublesome Words.** rev. ed. New York, Facts on File, 1987. 192p. bibliog. $17.95. LC 87-33046. ISBN 0-8160-1933-9.

Those who have ever tried to figure out when to use *amid, between,* and *among* or when to use *can* and when to use *may* or whether a married person can be *celibate* will appreciate books like Bryson's, now out in a revised edition. Presumably, a revision either changes earlier statements or errors or it enlarges the work by adding new entries. Which of these (both?) is achieved here is unclear, because nowhere in his witty introduction does Bryson allude to any earlier edition. The existence of the 1984 original, in fact, is inferred only from promotion which the publishers sent along with the review copy.

That aside, Bryson provides a wonderful little dictionary of clever and accurate distinctions between (and among) like-seeming words

and phrases. English being perhaps the most idiosyncratic of languages, with few rules and many exceptions, books of this sort are always welcome, in the ongoing attempt of careful speakers and writers to bring order to the chaos that is our living, growing, changing mother tongue. No biographical information about Bryson is found within the covers of the book, but clues in entries, spelling, and liberal quotation from the *Times* without a city preceding it would suggest that he is British, which puts a particular spin on his definitions and distinctions that does not always apply on this side of the pond.

It is not abundantly clear how this book is best employed. It is not the sort of thing you would carry around, nor is it intended to be a comprehensive dictionary. Rather, it is the kind of work you might intend to consult for one nugget of clarification or information. But the eye is drawn upward, downward, and across the page to other points of distinction, and on to other pages. The overall effect is too much for one's mind to absorb, but there is much to be gained in effective communication skills from reading, say, two pages a day, and trying to retain the distinctions Bryson makes so well the next time one is writing or speaking. This title is recommended, but libraries owning the first edition probably can get along without this one. Browse through it; then, perhaps, you will know the correct spelling of *guttural*, you can tell others correctly whether the weekend experience you had was sensuous or sensual, and whether you had been served or serviced by the Internal Revenue Service. [R: RBB, 15 Nov 88, pp. 552-53]   Bruce A. Shuman

948.   Chapman, Robert L., ed. **American Slang.** New York, Perennial Library/Harper & Row, 1987. 499p. $8.95pa. LC 87-45028. ISBN 0-06-096160-0.

From the very first page this fascinating book is worth getting to know. Those who are interested in the English language and the way it can be used—and misused—will find the following covered in the preface: "History of Slang Lexicography," the worthwhile section entitled "How This Book Was Made," and finally, another rather lengthy section entitled "What Is Slang?"

Following the preface is a useful guide to the dictionary, which explains the main entries, the impact symbols which identify the words as *taboo* or *vulgar*, the pronunciations, part-of-speech labels, variant forms, dating labels, provenance labels, derivations, and cross-references. The body of the book is replete with words and "terms not to be lightly used in polite society" (p. vii). The intent is to provide a lexicographical history of the times.

Each entry is given in alphabetical order. The part of speech of each of these entries follows, with definitions and *see* references. In many instances a sentence follows to illustrate its use, and when known, its origin.

American Slang is an abridgment of the *New Dictionary of American Slang* (see *ARBA* 88, entry 1076). It should be in all university and public libraries, along with Eric Partridge's *A Dictionary of Slang and Unconventional English* (Macmillan, 1985) and Harold Wentworth and Stuart Berg Flexner's *Dictionary of American Slang* (Crowell, 1975).

Jefferson D. Caskey

949. **A Dictionary of American Idioms.** 2d ed. Revised and updated by Adam Makkai. Hauppauge, N.Y., Barron's Educational Series, 1987. 398p. $11.95pa. LC 84-9247. ISBN 0-8120-3899-1.

For almost twenty years *A Dictionary of American Idioms* has been considered the pre-eminent dictionary of idioms. The first edition, by Maxine Tull Boatner, John Edward Gates, and Adam Makkai, was published in 1977 by Rowman & Littlefield. It was revised by Adam Makkai for this second edition. This volume updates considerably the ever-growing English language. Numerous changes and additions are found in this new work. Included are new slang and informal regional expressions.

Every person who is actively involved in the English language will find this dictionary valuable. For example, the person whose native language is other than English will find the meaning of "kick the bucket" along with a sentence to illustrate the meaning in standard English, and the native speaker of American English will find new slang, clichés, and proverbial expressions that are not in the 1977 edition.

A Dictionary of American Idioms is useful and most usable. The introduction has detailed explanations on what an idiom is, how to use the dictionary, types of entry, parts of speech labels, and restrictive use labels.

In addition to the sentences given to illustrate usage, each entry is classified according to part of speech and whether it would be considered slang, vulgar, or cliché. The numerous cross-references greatly enhance locating variant ways in which the idiom may be found.

In this second edition, this dictionary should be in every American library. Students, teachers, writers, readers, and those who speak or write English as a second language will need access to it. [R: BR, Sept/Oct 88, p. 51; Choice,

July/Aug 88, p. 1672; RBB, 15 Nov 88, pp. 550, 552; SLJ, May 88, pp. 29-30]

Jefferson D. Caskey

950. Green, Jonathon. **Dictionary of Jargon.** New York, Routledge, Chapman & Hall, 1987. 616p. bibliog. $49.95. LC 87-4960. ISBN 0-7100-9919-3.

As with even the best general dictionaries of living languages, dictionaries of jargon can never be called complete. Containing approximately twenty-one thousand words, phrases, acronyms, abbreviations, professional slang, and verbal shorthand, this current volume is an updating of Jonathon Green's earlier work on jargon, *Newspeak* (Methuen, 1983).

Green explains in the introduction that jargon falls into different groups: the masking of facts, professional shorthand, regional dialects, technological developments, humor taken from the job, and the way workers play with the language.

The entries give the part of speech of each word or phrase, the profession or trade group to which it belongs, and a clear, adequate definition. In many instances there are cross-references to appropriate synonyms.

As a lexicographer, the author has published *The Cynic's Lexicon* (St. Martin, 1984) and *The Dictionary of Contemporary Slang* (Stein and Day, 1985). The *Dictionary of Jargon* would be essential to all libraries needing up-to-date dictionaries in this aspect of the vibrant English language. [R: Choice, Mar 88, p. 1064]

Jefferson D. Caskey

951. Henke, James T. **Gutter Life and Language in the Early "Street" Literature of England: A Glossary of Terms and Topics Chiefly of the Sixteenth and Seventeenth Centuries.** West Cornwall, Conn., Locust Hill Press, 1988. 339p. bibliog. index. $30.00. LC 88-8827. ISBN 0-933951-17-5.

This book contains 805 glossary entries on "obscene" terms and topics found in such "literary ephemerata" of sixteenth- and seventeenth-century England as "ballads, printed song lyrics, broad-side sheets, jestbooks, pamphlets" and other such items.

The entries range alphabetically from *Adamites* (a religious sect that may have practiced religious nudity), through *mustard pot* (the vagina), to *yellow hose* (a sign of jealousy). Each entry contains a definition, a source and context, and often an editorial comment and cross-referencing. The book is a bawdy browser's delight. Who can pass over such eye-catchers as *female fire-ships* (syphilitic prostitutes), *ennulus anti-cornutus* (a charm to prevent cuckolding), *pyeman* (a lascivious male), and *Pickadilly cramp* (a venereal disease)?

But a topic index makes the book also a handy reference tool. And in finding that whores were called *unsavory lamps*, and their customers *cully-rompers*, and that anal intercourse was a *cathedral exercise*, and a diseased penis a *running nagg*, one hears the truth in John Updike's observation that the writer faced with the choice between medical and obscene terms must "choose the words given the force and life of colloquial usage." [R: Choice, Dec 88, p. 628]   Edward J. Gallagher

952. Lewin, Esther, and Albert E. Lewin. **The Thesaurus of Slang: 150,000 Uncensored Contemporary Slang Terms, Common Idioms, and Colloquialisms....** New York, Facts on File, 1988. 435p. bibliog. $40.00. LC 88-6985. ISBN 0-8160-1742-5.

If you are looking for a slang word in this thesaurus, chances are you will find it from its "150,000 uncensored contemporary slang terms, common idioms, and colloquialisms" (title page). But there is a difference that may slow up the searchers if they do not know the English word to begin with. Instead of translating slang into standard English, the opposite is followed. Under each entry the slang terms are listed. For example, the entry *teacher* is entered as a noun followed by "prof, teach, babysitter, grind, guru, slave driver, snap. (See also SCHOLAR.)" (p. 378). In addition to slang, the nicknames of the United States and many cities are included.

The Thesaurus of Slang is unique. It is about as comprehensive as a dictionary of slang can be. Researchers, writers, and word buffs will find it most helpful. [R: Choice, Nov 88, p. 462; LJ, 1 June 88, p. 104; RBB, 1 Sept 88, p. 57; WLB, Oct 88, pp. 111-12]

Jefferson D. Caskey

953. Lewis, Norman. **The New American Dictionary of Good English: An A-Z Guide to Grammar and Correct Usage.** New York, New American Library, 1987. 294p. $4.95pa. LC 87-62469. ISBN 0-451-15023-6.

This paperback volume contains over twenty-five hundred entries which attempt to provide the answers to questions readers may have about grammar or correct usage. The grammatical terminology in the dictionary is based on structural and transformational grammar. A brief explanation is given in the front of the book regarding related terminology. The part of speech is indicated for headwords, but few are pronounced. When pronunciation is indicated, it is for words such as *abaci* or *sarcophagi*, and the phonic alphabet is used.

Headwords appear in boldface print slightly to the left of the text, with guide words appearing at the top of each column on a double-column page, making entries easy to locate.

Troublesome words such as *farther, further* and *lie, lay* are given very full treatment, with the latter receiving about four pages. An interesting feature of this book is that within long, complicated entry explanations, there are occasionally self-tests for the reader to check his or her understanding of the information presented. The dictionary has a friendly tone which young people would like. For example, under *lie, lay* we find the following statement: "But wait! The thorniest problem occurs in the *past tense:*." Recommendations for "correct" usage reflect current American English, and in this sense can be contrasted with E. S. C. Weiner's *The Oxford Guide to English Usage* (Oxford University Press, 1983). The latter is more formal, British with American usage indicated, more comprehensive, and hardbound.

In addition to troublesome words, there are entries for parts of speech. *Noun* is given seventeen pages of text, making this dictionary a grammar book as well as a usage book. Another useful feature is that words which are sometimes confused with one another in meaning are included. An example is *feebleminded, cretinous, moronic, imbecilic, idiotic*; or *chairman, chairwoman, chairperson* where uncertainty of use is involved. This dictionary would be a good book to circulate in collections aimed at junior high or high school students and adult readers in either college or public libraries. It has limited use as a reference source due to its size and binding.

Helen M. Gothberg

954. **Linguistic Atlas of the Gulf States. Volume Two: General Index for the Linguistic Atlas of the Gulf States.** Lee Pederson, Susan Leas McDaniel, and Carol M. Adams, eds. Athens, Ga., University of Georgia Press, 1988. 440p. $60.00. LC 83-24139. ISBN 0-8203-0972-9.

This *General Index* is a summary of the *Linguistic Atlas of the Gulf States* (*LAGS*), first published in 1986. Included are index entries in a headword, with the total number of times the word appears in the *LAGS* concordance given in parentheses. Generally the part of speech is given for the word used in the concordance. Following is the protocol page, which provides the line number of the first or principal instance of the word.

Personal names published in the concordance are omitted in the index unless they refer to historical or popular figures. Also omitted are contractions with nouns. Phrases are given only when they are proper nouns, worksheet items, noun plus noun structures, and verbs plus postpositionals. For the most part, lengthy phrases and other structures are excluded.

It must be emphasized that this index can never be complete in itself but must be used along with the concordance to *LAGS*. All scholarly libraries will need both the *Linguistic Atlas of the Gulf States* and this *General Index* for their linguistic collections.

Jefferson D. Caskey

955.   Malotte, Stan, ed. **The Painless Path to Proper English Usage.** New York, St. Martin's Press, c1986, 1987. 127p. illus. bibliog. index. $6.95pa. LC 87-4469. ISBN 0-312-00714-0.

This work presents a selection of 126 of "the most frequently confused pairs of words in our language" and briefly explains the correct usage of each in a short paragraph sprinkled with clever mnemonic devices, followed by a cartoon illustrating and summarizing the lesson. Examples of the confusable pairs range alphabetically from *accept/except* to *your/you're*, including other such aggravating annoyers as *fewer/less*, *everyday/every day*, *farther/further*, and *that/which*.

All of these can of course be found in standard usage books and dictionaries, though certainly not so charmingly presented. *The Painless Path* should make a good supplementary teaching tool in English classes and deserves a place in junior high through junior college libraries.

Mary Jo Walker

956.   Randall, Bernice. **Webster's New World Guide to Current American Usage.** New York, Webster's New World/Simon & Schuster, 1988. 420p. $16.95. ISBN 0-13-947821-3.

Fowler (*A Dictionary of Modern English Usage*, Oxford University Press, 1965) and Partridge (*Usage and Abusage*, Penguin, 1963) are the masters of British-English usage; Americans have traditionally relied on Follett (*Modern American Usage*, Hill & Wang, 1966). William Morris and Mary Morris's *Harper's Dictionary of Contemporary Usage* (see *ARBA* 86, entry 1047) and Copperud's much under-reviewed *American Usage and Style, the Consensus* (Van Nostrand Reinhold, 1980) are just two of Follett's serious challengers. Bernice Randall's *Guide to Current American Usage* is another.

Randall advocates a commonsense approach to usage in a comfortably readable style. Unlike the Morrises, she does not consult expert panels. She does, however, occasionally refer to the Morrises' work; see, for example, the entry for *hopefully* (pp. 146-48). Sometimes Randall

enters the problem word or phrase directly ("hung or hanged?" p. 156). Other times the troublesome locution generates an illustrative phrase, to which the writer is referred by *see* reference, for example, "should or would?" (p. 292) *see* "Shall you return? We should like that" (p. 285). Knotty grammatical concepts are also accessible by *see* reference. For example, dangling elliptical clauses (p. 76) are discussed under the heading "Covered with onions, relish, and ketchup, I ate a hot dog at the ball park" (p. 71). There is an excellent article on *can* (p. 49), but no entry for *kind of*, or any pronouncement on the current lust for *speak* at the expense of *talk*. (I long for an authoritative description of this phenomenon.) Adequate bibliographical references are given in the back, grouped under the entry to which they refer. One more picayunish complaint: the page numbers are on the spine side of the page rather than near the edges. [R: RBB, 15 Nov 88, pp. 556-57; RQ, Winter 88, pp. 272-74; WLB, Oct 88, pp. 111-12]

Judith M. Brugger

957.   Roberts, Philip Davies. **Plain English: A User's Guide.** New York, Viking Penguin, 1987. 191p. bibliog. index. $5.95pa. ISBN 0-14-008407-X.

There are many small handbooks that deal separately with style, usage, and grammar. *Plain English* covers all these aspects of English and more. The various sections of the book include: "Grammar," "Vocabulary," "Typography," "Dialects," and "Style." In addition information about how to write letters, a short bibliography, an explanation of irregular verbs, and definitions of grammatical terms are included. There is an index to the book. The main section of *Plain English* is on usage.

The preface states that a prescriptive rather than descriptive approach is taken. The "Vocabulary" section reflects this emphasis, and many of the common errors in writing and speech are covered here. For example, *irregardless* (p. 72) is defined as a word that "is not part of standard English." In the explanation of the differences between *flaunt* and *flout* (p. 58), we find some variances in the definition supplied for *flout* not found in other style manuals and dictionaries. Fowler's *Dictionary of Modern English Usage* (Clarendon Press, 1965), Evans's *Dictionary of Contemporary Usage* (Random House, 1957), and the *Random House Dictionary* (see *ARBA* 88, entry 1095) are in agreement in defining *flout* as having to do with "disdain" or "scorn." This work, which has a British slant, defines it as to "disobey openly."

Plain English notes some deviations between American and British English that are interesting and useful; and in the section on typography, the word *point* is used to avoid either the American *period* or the British *full stop*. Although the British slant of *Plain English* may bother some readers, it is a useful quick reference for those commonly occurring questions regarding the English language. It would be especially useful to foreign-language students, not only for "correct" use of English words, but for the basic grammar which is included. It is suitable for high school and college libraries as a circulating volume and as a quick reference tool for libraries that need something inexpensive. *The New American Dictionary of Good English* (see entry 953) is a similar book on American grammar and correct usage and should be considered for purchase along with *Plain English*.

Helen M. Gothberg

958. Urdang, Laurence. **The Dictionary of Confusable Words.** New York, Facts on File, 1988. 391p. index. $29.95. LC 88-045090. ISBN 0-8160-1650-X.

Laurence Urdang, the former editor-in-chief of the *Random House Dictionary* and author of several books on the lexicon of English, has compiled a useful, interesting, and quite unique reference tool. His focus is on confusable lexical units.

Conventional dictionaries concentrate on defining individual word denotations (and some connotations) and only occasionally offer sporadic information on similar or contrastive meanings of other words; it is not their main purpose to compare and contrast sets of words or to signal areas of potential confusion. In this respect, Urdang's dictionary, with its focus on confusable word sets, provides vital supplementary information.

As lexical and semantic confusability has many causes and many faces, it is no surprise to find a great variety of word sets in Urdang's eclectic collection. The dictionary lists and explains hundreds of pairs or groups of words, such as *adapt/adopt*, *affect/effect*, *appraise/apprise*, *complement/compliment*, *principal/principle*, etc., where graphic similarities often cause semantic mix-ups. Urdang also discusses useful differences in meaning in pairs such as *amoral/immoral* and *disinterested/uninterested*, exemplifies semantic shades of *classic/classical* and *economic/economical*, and provides useful explanations of sets like *balcony/terrace/deck/porch/veranda/patio* or *oculist/optometrist/optician/ophthalmologist*. The dictionary even tells us that we should not *assume/presume* that *brandy* is always *cognac*. Scores of antonyms (such as *emigrant/immigrant*, *ener-*

vate/innervate) and many other easily confusable word sets enhance the value of this useful reference work.

An alphabetical index (pp. 329-91) lists over five thousand entries and terms discussed for comparison or contrast. [R: Choice, Nov 88, p. 470; RBB, 15 Nov 88, p. 553; WLB, June 88, p. 138]   Lev I. Soudek

959. Urdang, Laurence. **The Whole Ball of Wax and Other Colloquial Phrases: What They Mean & How They Started.** New York, Perigee Books/Putnam, 1988. 157p. illus. index. $8.95 pa. LC 87-26132. ISBN 0-399-51436-8.

Urdang makes no pretense to comprehensiveness, which is available in the three-volume *Idioms & Phrases Index* (Gale, 1983). He selected his words, phrases, and expressions mainly for their curiosity value, "either because they have odd or interesting etymologies or because the expressions themselves reveal something useful about the way the language is used." The *Morris Dictionary of Word and Phrase Origins* (Harper & Row, 1977) and John Ciardi's *A Browser's Dictionary* (see *ARBA* 81, entry 1159) and *A Second Browser's Dictionary* (Harper & Row, 1983) are the most familiar references. Urdang cannot compete with them for sheer volume of inclusions. But he can add to what they have already collected; for example, "piss on ice" and "play footsie" are not in Morris or Ciardi. Urdang's title expression, "whole ball of wax," can be found in Morris but not in Ciardi, and with it controversy arises. Urdang states "there is no evidence found for its use outside of American English," while Morris convincingly demonstrates that it was born from British law (parceling of property). Of course differences of opinion occur in the unsure art of etymology. "Drugstore cowboy," "raring to go," and "stir-crazy" are other unique entries in Urdang. Word books are such a delight to have around. This one is no less entertaining than the others. Recommended.   Bill Bailey

960. **Webster's New World Dictionary of Quotable Definitions.** 2d ed. Eugene E. Brussell, ed. New York, Simon & Schuster, 1988. 674p. index. $14.95pa. LC 88-15087. ISBN 0-13-948159-1.

Words, those symbols of communication, have always fascinated man. For us librarians, they have been our life's blood, our soul's moly. But shelves lined with mere dictionaries are not much help to the librarian or the wordsmith. With the emergence of the *Webster's New World Dictionary of Quotable Definitions* in 1970, editor Eugene Brussell changed all that. Now writers, editors, researchers, speakers, and other word-workers can find new meaning in meaning.

No one will ever forget Dorothy Parker's word play on horticulture. Now, in this fully revised and expanded version of the *Dictionary*, no one will ever forget William James's definition of success as the "bitch-goddess," or John Barrymore's comparison of a footnote to "running downstairs to answer the doorbell on the first night of marriage." Though a bona fide reference tool, catalogers may find it hard to get this book out of the processing unit and onto the shelves. Once there, it is certain not to stay long.

The arrangement is alphabetical, with subjects and individual names listed together. An index of the authors of the definitions follows. Cross-references are also included. The book is as easy and as simple to use as a dictionary, but delightfully more fun.

The dictionary is tied to no one century, pilfering, as it does, from Aristotle to Frank Zappa. The inclusion of scholarly definitions, popular, literary, folk, and philosophical word-plays make this tool a book for all seasons.

Mark Y. Herring

Juvenile

961. The Lincoln Writing Dictionary for Children. San Diego, Calif., Harcourt Brace Jovanovich, 1988. 901p. illus. (part col.). $17.95. ISBN 0-15-152394-0.

The compilers of this new dictionary for children explain their choice of title by stating: "In Abraham Lincoln's time, people ... *read* dictionaries." In order to make their dictionary readable they have included several features which they claim have disappeared from most dictionaries: quotations from noted authors, essays on the origin and uses of language, and guidance on correct usage. The thirty-five thousand entry words in the dictionary were drawn from a computerized survey of over ten million words of running text, although the sources of the texts are not given. Many recent words are defined: *AIDS*, *VCR* and *microwave oven*; but *crack* as a drug is not included nor is *interactive* or *gay* in the sense of homosexual (also excluded) or *street people*. Because the vocabulary comes from printed sources, most slang and vulgar words are omitted, as are all the terms which refer to sexuality, even the most basic ones such as *genital* and *penis*. The book is well designed with comfortably large, clear print and many useful and attractive drawings and color photographs to illustrate definitions. Authors whose works are quoted include writers as diverse as Matthew Arnold, Raymond Chandler,

Dorothy Parker, and Toni Morrison. Many quotations are lively and interesting and blocked sections of text give sensible tips on writing. The compilers have succeeded in producing a dictionary which is fun to read and which should help children in their written work. Although it is not an all-purpose dictionary, it deserves a place in school and public libraries. [R: WLB, Dec 88, p. 118]

Adele M. Fasick

Other English-Speaking Countries

962. The Australian Concise Oxford Dictionary of Current English. George W. Turner, ed. New York, Oxford University Press, 1987. 1340p. $29.95. ISBN 0-19-554619-9.

Australian English, one of several varieties of global English, began its distinct development in 1788 with the establishment of a British penal colony in a location that is now a tiny spot in the sprawling city of Sydney.

This first edition of the *Australian Concise Oxford Dictionary* has been published in time for Australia's bicentennial celebration. The new Australian version is based on the seventh edition of the highly successful *Concise Oxford Dictionary of Current English* (see *ARBA* 83, entry 1074). That model has now been thoroughly and meticulously revised and supplemented by G. W. Turner. A leading lexicographer and author of *The English Language in Australia and New Zealand* (1966), Turner has done a superb job in preparing this new Australian version. He has added thousands of lexical units current in Australian English, such as technical terminology, words of aboriginal origin, slang terms, Australian colloquialisms, and many others.

The new dictionary contains over forty-five thousand main entries and close to eighty-thousand secondary lexical items, with concise information on etymology, general or regional usage, and pronunciation. Many entries are characterized by illustrative phrases showing prevalent usage. The introduction includes a succinct description of major features of Australian English pronunciation.

Turner's new Australian version is a fine piece of lexicography, a contribution to the study and use of Australian English, and a useful tool for those who work with or are interested in that quite specific variety of the English language. [R: Choice, Sept 88, p. 73]

Lev I. Soudek

963. Branford, Jean. A Dictionary of South African English. 3d ed. New York, Oxford

University Press, 1987. 444p. $27.00. ISBN 0-19-570427-4.

Jean Branford, a prominent South African lexicographer, and a group of her collaborators published the first edition of this unconventional dictionary in 1978. She then updated it moderately in her second edition in 1980. The new third edition of 1987 includes substantial revisions and a considerable number of additions.

This is a "regional" dictionary of one of the several global varieties of English. The focus is on nonstandard South Africanisms; that is, terms used by English-speaking South Africans of any race. Vocabulary items that can be found in general dictionaries of standard English (British or American) have been included only if they have acquired significantly different denotative meanings in South African English.

Many of the lexical units included reflect the influence of diverse languages and races that have left their mark on the history, culture, struggles, aspirations, and the current volatile situation of a sharply divided society. A significant number of terms come from Dutch or from its Afrikaans variety, others are loanwords from the Bantu language group, from several languages of India, Malaysia, and from some European languages other than Dutch or English.

Several South Africanisms, such as *apartheid*, *commandeer*, *commando,* and *trek*, have found their way into the standard lexicon of "world" English. A few more will follow, but the majority of the approximately five thousand entries comprising this new dictionary will apparently remain on the level of unconventional regionalisms characterizing the use and users of English in South Africa. In this respect, the new dictionary is an authoritative reference work that records the ingredients and, through its authentic and fascinating quotations, chronicles the history and growth of a distinct variety of English.   Lev I. Soudek

964.   Lougheed, W. C. **Writings on Canadian English 1976-1987: A Selective, Annotated Bibliography.** Kingston, Ont., Queen's University, 1988. 66p. index. (Strathy Language Unit Occasional Papers, No. 2). $5.00pa. ISBN 0-88911-510-9.

This source updates a bibliography compiled by W. S. Avis and A. M. Kinloch, *Writings on Canadian English, 1792-1975* (Toronto, Fitzhenry and Whiteside, 1978). The term *Canadian English* is defined to include what various linguists describe as general Canadian English (central/prairie English), or the English of the Canadian regions, or Canadian English, central

prairie or regional. The three hundred items in this bibliography include books, parts of books, journal articles, theses, conference papers, and other kinds of publications. Each item is annotated, with the more important publications receiving longer descriptions.

In addition to this bibliography, researchers in Canadian English will benefit from other activities of the Strathy Language Unit of Queen's University. As described at length in the introduction to this work, the Strathy Language Unit maintains an extensive computerized file of scholarship on the uses of Canadian English. This file will facilitate further updates of this bibliography as well as more specialized inquiries into particular aspects of Canadian English.   David Isaacson

965.   Thain, Chris. **Cold as a Bay Street Banker's Heart: The Ultimate Prairie Phrase Book.** Saskatoon, Sask., Western Producer Prairie Books, 1987. 165p. illus. $9.95pa. ISBN 0-88833-216-5.

This is a nice easy book on phrases and idioms of the Canadian prairie provinces, gleaned from 199 weekly and 6 daily newspapers in Western Canada. The material is listed alphabetically in true dictionary fashion, but unfortunately nothing appears to be sourced. Thus, words and phrases are defined, but they are not derived. The six hundred terms, with relevant cross-references to related entries, are a curious mixture of strictly local phrases, well-known phrases with peculiar local usages, and phrases that developed on a national basis across Canada rather than just on the prairies. Some regional ones include "arrogant as an elevator" (referring to the massive height of the grain elevators) and "Codland" (referring to Newfoundland); some universal ones are "back 40" and "claim jumper." "Gumbo" here means sticky, heavy clay soil. Some others are the "Anderson cart" (referring to a cut-down, rear wheels only, automobile pulled by a horse, named after Alberta's Premier Anderson) and the "Bennett buggy" (referring to a four-wheel engineless car pulled by a horse, named after Canada's federal Prime Minister R. B. Bennett) – both terms coming from the Depression, naturally. Good fun, useful, and affordable for most Canadian studies programs.

Dean Tudor

966.   Upton, Clive, Stewart Sanderson, and John Widdowson. **Word Maps: A Dialect Atlas of England.** New York, Croom Helm/Routledge, Chapman & Hall, 1987. 228p. maps. bibliog. index. $57.50. LC 87-675293. ISBN 0-7099-4410-1.

This atlas consists of 200 dialect maps of England, 61 devoted to representing pronunciation and 139 to vocabulary. These maps were produced as a result of The Survey of English Dialects, a study undertaken by the University of Leeds between 1948 and 1961, in which field workers collected information in 313 mainly rural localities. The speakers surveyed were usually elderly, local-born, and with little formal education, so that the speech recorded would not be overly influenced by television, radio, or other social factors tending to diminish regional linguistic variations. Most of the books resulting from this survey have been scholarly, such as *The Linguistic Atlas of England* (see *ARBA* 80, entry 1106) and *A Word Geography of England* (Academic Press, 1975). Unlike these books, *Word Maps* does not require the user to follow detailed instructions or to have prior linguistic expertise.

The maps are arranged alphabetically by title: titles are words or groups of words readily understood by speakers of standard English. Different dialect areas on the maps are delineated by easy to read boldface lines indicating where a word or pronunciation is dominant. Some words have only one variation, such as *child* and *bairn*, while others have numerous dialectical equivalents, such as *silly*, *soft*, *barmy*, *fond*, *daft*, *gormless*, *cakey*, and *addle-headed*. Pronunciation maps use a respelling system rather than phonetic script, making it easier for the general reader to distinguish sounds. A very well-written introduction not only explains how to read the maps but also provides an excellent concise history of dialects in England.

While there may be some use for this atlas by itself, most users will probably also want to consult various general dictionaries, such as *The Oxford English Dictionary*, as well as more specialized ones, such as *The English Dialect Dictionary* (London: Henry Froude, 1898), in order to put words into a fuller context. Specialists needing more detailed maps will need to consult the aforementioned more academic publications resulting from The Survey of English Dialects.   David Isaacson

---

Spelling Guides

967. Cummings, D. W. **American English Spelling: An Informal Description.** Baltimore, Md., Johns Hopkins University Press, 1988. 555p. bibliog. index. $49.50. LC 86-30537. ISBN 0-8018-3443-0.

This reference work might be subtitled "and more than you ever wanted to know about spelling in the English language." It is one of the most comprehensive volumes on the subject that you will find. The preface notes that "much important work has been done on the study of English orthography ... [so] that we now understand the English spelling system." Cummings certainly makes a monumental effort to see that we do. The book is divided into four sections. The first section presents the approach to orthographic analysis upon which the book is based. The second section covers tactical rules. Here we find many of the rules remembered from school days but considerably expanded. For example, there is the third syllable rule, the voiced "th," the stress front shift rule, and others. The third section describes three major procedural rules, and the fourth section — the largest — deals in some detail with the major and minor correspondences between the sounds of American English and their spellings.

This is not a reference resource for the casual albeit educated reader to explore as a means of improving his or her spelling. It is a work intended for the serious student/scholar of American English, its spelling, and its formation. To this end it is a worthwhile addition to the library.

Helen M. Gothberg

968. **Webster's Spell It Right Dictionary.** Paul Heacock, ed. New York, Perigee Books/Putnam, 1987. 298p. $9.95pa. LC 86-18722. ISBN 0-399-51294-2.

The idea behind this guide is to provide a time-saving device for the poor speller. When puzzled about spelling a word correctly, the user can sound it out as near as possible, then look up the near-miss. Across from it will be the correct spelling. In this manner a guess can be turned into positive identification. The one catch is that the user may not be able to come up with the same wrong spelling as the editor (e.g., *natierel* for *natural*, *pyarrea* for *pyorrhea*, and *sleier* for *slayer* might not be the usual mental confusion). Some of the mistaken spelling is downright wild: *joojetsoo*, *hiccuff*, and *consimmet*. These could just as easily have been *jewjitsue*, *hickup*, and *consuemate*.

Included are the twenty-five thousand most commonly misspelled words, listed in columns. For a meaning of any one of them, a regular dictionary must be consulted. The editor contends that the misspellings are prevalent ones, but most users would do better compiling their own list side-by-side with correct spellings.

In short, misspelling is idiosyncratic. To make full use of this guide the user has to study the flubs first and learn them before trying to zero in on the misspelling to find the correct spelling. There is little profit in that. Libraries do not need such a backward tool. Recommended only for individuals who feel comfortable with it.   Bill Bailey

Thesauri

969. Roget's Thesaurus of English Words and Phrases. London, Longman, Brown, Green, and Longmans, 1852; repr., London, Bloomsbury; distr., Detroit, Gale, 1987. 418p. index. $49.95. ISBN 0-7475-0105-X.

Why a facsimile first edition? As a useful desk tool, the first edition has been superseded. The thesaurus itself is some eleven thousand words poorer than the third "international" edition, which in turn lacks the vocabulary of automation and the sexual revolution included in the fourth (see *ARBA* 78, entry 1041). The front material to the facsimile is shockingly modest: the third "international" edition has a better biography of Roget. As an archival preservation, the facsimile first edition may be useful for someone compiling a history of the genre, although the raw data for such a comparison are still to be collected. Laurence Urdang's introduction dismisses the question by saying that there is "no telling" how many editions of the *Thesaurus* have been published to date. Roget's own reprinted introduction is an essay on the linguistic reasoning that informs his classification scheme, which is, as Urdang says, both "curious" and "nineteenth-century".

One could, however, spend hours making astonishing comparisons between the first edition and any newer one. In the index of the facsimile first edition, *sex* subsumes two ideas: "kind, 75" and "women, 374." In the third edition, *sex* encompasses two nouns: "gender, 418" and "womankind, 420.3." The third edition adds the verbal and the adjectival ideas of *sex* to its index, while the facsimile first edition does not admit the transposition. Because the facsimile first edition prints the hierarchical arrangement of ideas in parallel columns of antonyms, endless insights into the English manner can be very quickly gleaned. Whereas, for example, *love* (897) in the sense of *lover* generates twenty-four synonyms; *hate* (898) in the sense of *object of hatred*, generates only three.   Judith M. Brugger

NON-ENGLISH-LANGUAGE DICTIONARIES

Arabic

970. Stevens, Virginia, and Maurice Salib, comps. **A Pocket Dictionary of the Spoken**

Arabic of Cairo: English-Arabic. Cairo, American University in Cairo Press; distr., New York, Columbia University Press, 1987. 211p. $12.95 pa. ISBN 977-424-167-3.

This dictionary is an extended version of a previous edition of the same title by Maurice Salib. It gives the phonetic transcription of colloquial Arabic words used in the streets of Cairo for some four thousand alphabetically listed English words. It is aimed at English-speaking visitors and residents of Egypt who are studying or have studied classical Arabic, to serve them in communicating with natives outside the classroom. In fact, some knowledge of Arabic is necessary to derive the full benefit of this dictionary. The book is a bit awkwardly sized (4¼ by 8 inches) and is printed with relatively large letters on heavy duty paper, which makes it rather bulky to fit comfortably into a normal pocket. Although it may be useful to tourists, the principal beneficiaries of this dictionary will be individuals who are in Cairo for an extended stay and are making an exerted effort to become conversant in the colloquial Arabic of the city. Given the regional differences of dialect, users will have some difficulty in communicating with the rural natives of the South, hence the title of the dictionary, which specifies it as for the "Arabic of Cairo."

Garabed Eknoyan

Chinese

971. Defu, Wang, Qiang Zhenxin, and Zhou Zongxin, comps. **A Chinese-English Handbook of Idioms.** New York, Hippocrene Books, c1981, 1987. 603p. index. $8.95. ISBN 0-87052-454-2.

This is a handy guide to over 4,000 Chinese idioms with 150,000 English translations. The Chinese entries are transcribed in Hanyu pinyin. The translations are mostly precise, giving consideration to the characteristics of the Chinese origin and the English language. Literal translations, along with free translations as well as English idioms and phrases, are provided for each entry. These Chinese idioms provide users some of the vivid images that have been inspiring Chinese conversation for thousands of years. They also offer interesting insights into the habits of the Chinese language and thought of the Chinese culture. This handbook should be useful to translators, English teachers, and students as well as foreign scholars who are learning Chinese.

All idioms are transcribed with Chinese phonetic alphabets and arranged alphabetically. Idioms with their first characters sharing the same transcription are arranged according to the tone levels of their first characters in the following order: level, rising, falling-rising, and falling. Every idiom is supplied with one or more English translations arranged in the order of: literal translation, free translation, English idiom or proverb synonymous with or corresponding to the Chinese idiom, and English word equivalent to the Chinese idiom. This handbook also contains an "Index to Syllables of Hanyu Pinyin" and a "Stroke Index" in which the idioms are arranged according to the number of strokes of their characters. [R: Choice, May 88, p. 1380]

Betty L. Tsai

972. **A New English-Chinese Dictionary.** rev. ed. Compiled by The Editing Group of *A New English-Chinese Dictionary*. Seattle, Wash., University of Washington Press, 1988. 1769p. $19.95. ISBN 0-295-96609-2.

This comprehensive English-Chinese dictionary was compiled by a group of over seventy scholars from the Fudan University, the Shanghai Teachers' University, the Shanghai Institute of Foreign Languages, and a number of other institutions in China. All of them are well-known institutions.

The dictionary defines a total of more than eighty thousand English words, including derivations and compound words. Entries include pronunciation, part of speech, derivation, usage, knowledge, definition (in Chinese simplified characters), compounds and phrases including the word, and illustrative sentences. Its first edition, under the same title, was published in 1975. Over six hundred changes have been made. Also included in this revised and enlarged edition is a supplement of over four thousand new words and words that have changed in meaning or morphology. New entries include such words as *AIDS* and *video cassette*.

Nine appendices include a list of irregular English verbs; lists of ranks in the U.S. and British armed forces, with Chinese equivalents; tables of weights and measures (metric and U.S./British), with Chinese equivalents; lists of common marks and symbols, with Chinese names; and conversion tables of complex-to-simplified-to-complex Chinese characters.

The dictionary is an essential and useful tool especially for its supplement. However, it would be even better if the supplement had been merged into its main section.

Betty L. Tsai

973. Schuessler, Axel. **A Dictionary of Early Zhou Chinese.** Honolulu, University of Hawaii Press, 1987. 876p. $45.00. LC 87-13863. ISBN 0-8248-1111-9.

Chinese is one of the longest living languages today. It has developed over three thousand years with traceable changes. This dictionary records the language of the Western Zhou bronze inscriptions (ca. 1050 B.C.-770 B.C.). A lexical inventory of ancient Chinese language is by no means a simple task especially as it is done in English by a western scholar. Because much of the writing from this period is obscure, study is considered very difficult even for Chinese linguists. Despite its unique nature and specialty, this dictionary may only be of interest to a very small group of readers and find its place in highly specialized East Asian collections.

Hwa-Wei Lee

French

974. **Harrap's French Vocabulary.** Compiled by LEXUS with others. Lincolnwood, Ill., National Textbook, 1987. 1v. (various paging). index. $4.95pa. ISBN 0-8442-1822-7.

This compact, pocket-sized book is intended for those who are learning French. It is not a dictionary but a guide to build a modern French vocabulary. Approximately six thousand words and phrases are listed in sixty-four broad subject areas, such as "Describing People" and "Adventures and Dreams." Each section is further divided into thematic groupings. For instance, the section on emotions includes groupings for anger, sadness, fear and worry, and joy and happiness. There is an alphabetical index which refers the user from an English term to the appropriate section, and many sections have *see also* references to other sections with related vocabulary. As is the case with many French-English reference works, the English base for the vocabulary is British rather than American English. In fact, it has been designed for those taking the British General Certificate of Secondary Education (GCSE) exam. This can present a problem for the American user who is not familiar with the British form of such common terms as *truck*, *elevator*, or *automobile trunk*. Another problem is that it is not always easy to determine the section in which a term might appear, and the index of terms does not list all terms included in the sections. It also does not always reference all sections in which a term does appear. Overall, the size and arrangement of the book make it more valuable for an individual user rather than use in a library reference collection.

Barbara E. Kemp

975. **Harrap's Pocket French-English Dictionary. Dictionnaire Anglais-Français.** By

Michael Janes. London, Harrap and Lincolnwood, Ill., National Textbook, 1988. 679p. $9.95pa. ISBN 0-245-54508-5.

This is a completely revised edition which strives to give "translations of the most useful French and English vocabulary." It succeeds admirably at this goal, considering its small size, and holds the further attributes of currency, superior clarity, and ample guidance in grammar, pronunciation, and translation. Sentences illustrating idioms and common usages are abundant. In addition, one of the best features of this dictionary is the inclusion of careful translations for subtle differences in meaning: for example, French translations for both *imbued* (with ideas) and *imbued* (with feeling) are provided. Derivative forms are consistently included, as are masculine and feminine endings. The dictionary identifies colloquial usages as well as British and American terms, which are fairly equally represented. A "field" indicator, such as history or cookery, is also included where appropriate.

A special section lists French regular and irregular verb conjugations; spelling anomalies of -er verbs; English irregular verb conjugations; and numbers, days, and months with examples of their usage ("a week from Monday = lundi en huit," "three times out of ten = trois fois sur dix"). In addition, two pages of general grammar notes—one for each language—guide the user in making conventional plurals, participles, and so on.

This dictionary will be of equal value to speakers of either language, an effort at which pocket dictionaries often fail. It is bound in a durable, flexible plastic cover and its pages are printed clearly. While it is too large (about 4½ by 7 inches) to actually fit into most pockets, this is altogether a superior small bilingual dictionary.   Emily L. Werrell

976. **Petit Lexique de la France Contemporaine: Français-Anglais. A Pocket Dictionary of Contemporary France.** By Claudie Cox. New York, Berg; distr., New York, St. Martin's Press, 1988. 117p. $9.95pa. LC 87-18226. ISBN 0-85496-534-3.

This dictionary is "intended to serve as a useful companion to courses on 'Contemporary France'" (preface). It does focus specifically on the vocabulary one would encounter in French newspapers and magazines having to do with politics, current affairs, and everyday life. Synonyms are plentiful. The chapters cover broad areas such as political institutions and education, with each chapter further subdivided into appropriate subject areas. The entries are not, however, organized any further within each

subdivision, alphabetically or otherwise. This arrangement will make the dictionary time-consuming to use, as the subdivisions each contain at least fifty words or phrases, all of which must be read through in order to find a particular one. There is no index. The pages are arranged in columns, with the French word on the left side and the English translation on the right.

Another drawback for American students is the dictionary's British slant. *Petrol* is used instead of *gasoline*, *holiday* instead of *vacation*, and *to read law* instead of *to study law*. The translation for *un parlementaire* is given simply as *MP*. This abbreviation would have to be spelled out *Member of Parliament* to be of use to most American students.

Although there are a couple of new words and phrases in this dictionary which might be difficult to find elsewhere (such as translations for SDI), students looking up current French words would do better with an up-to-date edition of a standard high-quality dictionary such as the *French-English, English-French Dictionary* (Larousse, n.d.), or one of several more thorough and better-organized pocket dictionaries currently on the market.

Emily L. Werrell

Greek Romany

977. Messing, Gordon M. **A Glossary of Greek Romany As Spoken in Agia Varvara (Athens).** Columbus, Ohio, Slavica, 1987. 175p. $14.95pa. ISBN 0-89357-187-3.

A Glossary of Greek Romany is a highly specialized work which will be of interest to a very limited audience, primarily linguists. Gordon Messing deliberately restricted his focus to a specific community of Greek gypsies, "several hundred families with a great many children" (p. 7) who live in Agia Varvara, a suburb of northwest Athens. The glossary lists Romany words and phrases commonly used by members of this particular gypsy group, but "it is far from being a complete lexicon of the dialect" (p. 9).

An introduction briefly covers grammatical structure and other topics of linguistic interest, such as gender, plurals, declension of nouns, adjectives, pronouns, and conjugation of verbs. This section also includes some sample Greek Romany texts with analysis and translations. A select bibliography lists six references frequently cited in the glossary and the abbreviations for them.

The Romany-English glossary itself is the most substantial section of the work (pp. 39-140); but for many users, a brief index, the English-Romany word list (pp. 141-75), will be equally important. The index pairs English words and the Greek Romany equivalents which appear in the glossary.

Since Greek Romany is exclusively a spoken language with no written tradition, glossary entries are the author's "representation of the actually occurring Romany sounds" (p. 36). The entries are listed in English-language alphabetical order and include numerous examples of typical usage. Although there are some cross-references, use of them is not consistent, as the author himself admits. Etymological notes are not usually given for native Romany words, but are provided for words of Greek, Turkish, or Slavic origin.

Lydia W. Wasylenko

Russian

978. Leed, Richard L., and Slava Paperno, comps. **5000 Russian Words: With All Their Inflected Forms and Other Grammatical Information. A Russian-English Dictionary with an English-Russian Word Index and an Appendix on Russian Endings.** Columbus, Ohio, Slavica, c1986, 1987. 322p. $17.95pa. ISBN 0-89357-170-9.

This dictionary presents complete inflectional information for the five thousand words selected. Drawing on the basic vocabulary lists used in seven introductory textbooks, the compilers have also added words based on several well-defined criteria. They have used authoritative dictionaries as sources for inflectional and aspect information, most notably the works of A. A. Zalizniak. Fifteen specific features of the dictionary, such as aspect partners and homonym inclusion, are well defined in the preface.

Entries, or headwords, are followed by the morphological information necessary for construction of the inflected forms. Below this line is a display of inflected forms.

Addressed to both students and teachers, this dictionary should prove a valuable addition to tools supporting Russian-language study. It can be used either as a quick check of spelling for a particular form, or as a guide to constructing that form. Similar works in English have been devoted to Russian verbs: D. B. Powers, *A Dictionary of Irregular Russian Verb Forms* (Wiley, 1968) and E. Daum and W. Schenk, *A Dictionary of Russian Verbs*, third edition (Hippocrene, 1986).

An English-Russian word index is included to facilitate use of the dictionary. The appendix provides grammatical rules and paradigms.

Cyrillic entries are in large, clear print, with morphological information and displays in smaller, but legible, print. The dictionary is also available in electronic format from the compilers.

Cheryl Kern-Simirenko

Spanish

979. Butt, John, and Carmen Benjamin. **A New Reference Grammar of Modern Spanish.** London, Edward Arnold; distr., New York, Routledge, Chapman & Hall, 1988. 431p. index. $69.50. ISBN 0-7131-6502-2.

Two British scholars (King's College, London) have produced an excellent reference grammar of the Spanish language of the twentieth century. Comments are made when Spanish American Spanish may differ from peninsular Spanish. Examples of usage are shown with quotations from both Spanish and Spanish American authors and publications.

This grammar is divided into thirty-three chapters with an appendix on pronunciation. There is also an index. The authors note that "the approach and terminology of the grammar are conservative and points are often clarified by example rather than by theoretical argument, which is kept to a minimum" (p. ix). This means that the grammatical terms, while those of a pre-World War II era, are those more widely known and used by more people. The terminology of descriptive or transformational linguistics would only render the volume less useful and available only to those who specialize or have specialized in the grammar of these linguistic schools.

The student in the United States will find English words not generally in his or her vocabulary. Terms such as *detached house, cinema* (movie theater), and *to drink down in one go* will only continue to show the differences in vocabulary between the two major divisions of the English-speaking world and should not interfere with the user's comprehension of the text.

The grammatical rules are clearly stated, with illustrative examples. It admirably fulfills its purpose of offering the "intermediate and advanced English-speaking students, e.g., pre-university and university students, teachers, translators and self-taught students, a reasonably detailed account of the morphology and syntax of the Spanish of educated conversation and plain prose in Spain and Latin America in the late twentieth century" (p. vi). Those who teach advanced grammar courses will find many of their questions answered and libraries should add to their collections this outstanding reference grammar of one of the world's major languages.

Hensley C. Woodbridge

Yiddish

980. Bratkowsky, Joan G. **Yiddish Linguistics: A Multilingual Bibliography.** New York, Garland, 1988. 407p. index. (Garland Reference Library of the Humanities, Vol. 140). $58.00. LC 87-34196. ISBN 0-8240-9804-8.

This scholarly bibliography was prepared as a supplement to *Yiddish Language and Folklore: A Selective Bibliography for Research*, by Uriel Weinreich and Beatrice Weinreich (The Hague, Mouton, 1959). It is a comprehensive listing of publications dealing with all aspects of Yiddish linguistics which post-date the Weinreich bibliography. The material is arranged in broad subject categories reflecting the major academic divisions of the field of linguistics. Within each category citations, numbered consecutively, are grouped according to language: works in English, then works in Yiddish, followed by works in other languages. Items within each language category are further arranged alphabetically by author, then chronologically by date of publication. Cross-references are included. Reviews of items follow the work under review. Items not examined personally by the compiler are indicated. Citations are given in the original script. There are occasional short, descriptive annotations. An introduction clearly discusses the scope and limitations of the work. A detailed table of contents presents the basic thematic organization of the bibliography. The work concludes with a name index. The paper (acid free) and binding are of high quality, although the type is of manuscript or "typewriter style." The work represents an important, scholarly contribution to this field, and would be a valuable addition to academic and research library collections, as well as being appropriate for religious and theological libraries in institutions where Yiddish is being taught or where there is an interest in this language.

Susan J. Freiband

981. Coldoff, Harry. **A Yiddish Dictionary in Transliteration.** Toronto, Proclaim Publications, 1988. 223p. illus. $39.95pa.; $29.95pa. (U.S.). ISBN 0-919415-03-2.

This dictionary of the Yiddish language includes an English-Yiddish section aimed at English speakers wanting to enlarge their knowledge of Yiddish vocabulary and idiom without having to read Hebrew characters. It contains Yiddish equivalents of common English words in everyday use. There is also a Yiddish-English section containing a more elaborate definition and example of usage for each word. Americanized words appearing regularly in Yiddish-English dictionaries are excluded. The two main sections include idioms and idiomatic phrases. In addition, there are several separate short sections containing specialized vocabulary of the plant world, the animal world, weather, family relations, time, numbers, proper names, anecdotes, curses, death/cemeteries/God, and the zodiac. The transliteration follows the accepted YIVO standard. The author, a lover of Yiddish, has romanized according to the northeastern (or Lithuanian) Yiddish pronunciation. In addition to a short definition, the derivation of each word is given. Works by eminent Yiddish authorities have been followed for pronunciation, translation, and derivation. The dictionary includes a short "Notes for the User" section, as well as a brief introduction and foreword. This is not a scholarly, detailed, or exhaustive compilation, but rather a selective, popular presentation, according to the author, "a modest compilation." The format uses double columns and boldface type to enhance readability. Although the margins are narrow, the type is large and clear and the paper of good quality. The dictionary is a valuable addition to Judaic studies materials in academic libraries, and to reference collections in public, temple, synagogue, and community center libraries.

Susan J. Freiband

LANGUAGE BOOKS FOR TRAVELERS

982. Holt, Daniel D., and Grace Massey Holt. **Korean at a Glance: Phrase Book and Dictionary for Travelers.** Hauppauge, N.Y., Barron's Educational Series, 1988. 385p. illus. $5.95pa. LC 88-3355. ISBN 0-8120-3998-X.

This is a collection of useful phrases and sentences distributed by topic, as we would expect in a book of this type. The present collection can be considered better than the average manual of this type for several reasons. First, the cultural embedding of each topical section is highly informative: the reader learns what to see in Seoul, how to use trains, how to behave in various situations, etc. Second, many sentences are constructed in such a way that they can be modified, and possible modifications are indicated in a clear, simple way. With the use of the dictionary, many sentences can be produced by lexical insertion into the variable slots. Third, the book takes into consideration the "ethnography of talking" and makes the user thoroughly aware of, for example, the various levels of politeness which must be observed in felicitous Korean discourse. There are blemishes in the book: for example, on page 266 there is a table of the complete Han-gul alphabet, but the transcription of none of the 164 signs is given (the survey of pronunciation on page 2 and following does not suffice for the purpose). But on the whole, this book is a good specimen of the genre of manuals.   L. Zgusta

983. Talking Business in Japanese: Dictionary and Reference for International Business. By Nobuo Akiyama and Carol Akiyama. Hauppauge, N.Y., Barron's Educational Series, 1988. 425p. illus. maps. $6.95pa. LC 87-19601. ISBN 0-8120-3848-7.

Nobuo Akiyama and Carol Akiyama are the authors of *Japanese at a Glance* (see *ARBA* 87, entry 1058), portions of which are reprinted in this title. A basic words and phrases section provides frequently used short sentences illustrating how to ask questions, talk to taxi drivers, and alert others of health problems. The major section is a three-part business dictionary which lists business terms in English/Japanese and Japanese/English. Part 3 lists keywords associated with specific industries, such as chinaware and tableware, electricity and electronics, or motor vehicles. For each Japanese phrase or vocabulary item used, both the Japanese writing and the Hepburn spelling (most common system of Romanization) are given. Included is a brief section on pronunciation. There is no discussion of grammar, so most users will not understand how to construct a sentence even if they use the dictionary to locate necessary words. If memorized, the phrases could be helpful under certain circumstances, but most users will not be able to make changes in set phrases to express a new idea.

Sections within the dictionary are not marked to facilitate use. The next edition would benefit by using color codes or thumb indexing to identify the dictionary's sections. Too much of the dictionary—over forty pages—is taken up with information easily located in travel guides: customs, passports and visas, temperature and climate, travel tips, major hotels.

Libraries are better served by standard dictionaries such as *Kenkyusha's New English-Japanese Dictionary on Bilingual Principles* (Kenkyusha, 1960) or *The Oxford-Duden Pictorial English Japanese Dictionary* (see *ARBA* 84, entry 1063). Individuals are better served by the authors's *Japanese at a Glance*.

Milton H. Crouch

24 Literature

GENERAL WORKS

Bibliographies

984. Sargent, Lyman Tower. **British and American Utopian Literature, 1516-1985: An Annotated, Chronological Bibliography.** New York, Garland, 1988. 559p. index. (Garland Reference Library of the Humanities, Vol. 831). $75.00. LC 88-2546. ISBN 0-8240-0694-1.

A chronological list of utopian fiction first published in English (with a few Latin titles, such as More's *Utopia*), this is a major revision of a work under the same title published by G. K. Hall in 1979. In addition to works clearly meeting the definition of "utopian" and "fiction" (defined in a brief introduction), Sargent provides some that are probably "nonfiction," although holding these to a "higher" (undefined) standard of utopianism. Contrary to the earlier work, he does include a large number of short stories that discuss only some aspects of a society.

The work is arranged by year of first appearance in English, subarranged by author. Each entry includes standard bibliographic information (but *not* the usual analytical bibliographic apparatus), location symbols of libraries where the author examined a copy, and, as appropriate, references to Lyle Wright's *American Fiction* (Huntington Library, 1969). All listed titles were personally examined, and a brief annotation justifies each title's inclusion. Access is provided by a complete author index (both real name and pseudonym) and separate title index.

The 1979 edition was almost wholly ignored by reviewers in favor of Glenn Negley's *Utopian Literature: A Bibliography* (see *ARBA* 79, entry 1181), which is much less complete, although covering more ground (all nations, and with some secondary works). Within its limits, Sargent's work is definitive, although it would have been better to include the 1979 version of the introduction and to retain the list of secondary works. Any library with a research interest in utopias, political fiction, or science fiction should get this book. Unfortunately, given the price, less comprehensive collections that already have the earlier edition should carefully consider demand before purchasing this.

One last thought: How much longer will it be before this sort of growing bibliographical work becomes available in updatable machine-readable form (e.g., Cauzin SOFTSTRIP or floppy disks)? [R: Choice, Oct 88, p. 296]

James H. Sweetland

985. Schatzberg, Walter, Ronald A. Waite, and Jonathan K. Johnson, eds. **The Relations of Literature and Science: An Annotated Bibliography of Scholarship, 1880-1980.** New York, Modern Language Association of America, 1987. 458p. index. $40.00; $19.75pa. LC 87-26241. ISBN 0-87352-172-2; 0-87352-173-0pa.

This work consolidates the Modern Language Association's bibliographies of scholarship on the relations of literature and science, which have been compiled annually since 1939 and published in various sources. The editors have made some "significant additions and deletions," namely, the addition of references from 1880 to 1939, and the deletion of general studies which do not deal specifically with literature and science. Excepting the first chapter, which includes general studies on the interaction of the two fields, the bibliography is organized in broad chronological categories (Middle Ages, Renaissance), with each chapter further subdivided into studies and surveys and individual authors. Scholarship relating to the literary qualities of a scientist's work, works which compare literature and science, and works which treat science in literature are all included. Biological and physical sciences, natural history, and pseudosciences such as phrenology are represented. The twenty-five hundred items are limited to the literature of the West, primarily American, English, French, and German.

The subject index is clear and thorough. Entries are included for individual authors as well as for specific areas of science (animal magnetism, thermodynamics). Where appropriate, subject entries are further broken down by author; for example, under embryology one finds references to entries for Beckett, Blake, Darwin, Erasmus, Huxley, Sterne, Svevo, and Tennyson. For access to scholarship by a particular critic, there is a separate author index. The editors have created a valuable interdisciplinary research tool for scholars and students of literature and the history of science. Its usefulness will be enhanced by the planned supplement covering scholarship of the 1980s. [R: Choice, July/Aug 88, pp. 1676-77]

Emily L. Werrell

Biographies

986. **Contemporary Authors: Autobiography Series. Volume 6.** Adele Sarkissian, ed. Detroit, Gale, 1988. 453p. illus. index. $88.00. LC 84-647879. ISBN 0-8103-4505-6; ISSN 0748-0636.

987. **Contemporary Authors: Autobiography Series. Volume 7.** Mark Zadrozny, ed. Detroit, Gale, 1988. 429p. illus. index. $92.00. LC 84-647879. ISBN 0-8103-4456-4; ISSN 0748-0636.

This unique series was created to fill a gap in literary reference works: there have been no brief autobiographies of current writers collected in one source. For most of these writers, many of whom have only recently been recognized, autobiographical information is unavailable elsewhere. As stated in the preface, this work provides "an opportunity for writers ... to let their readers know how they see themselves and their work, what carefully laid plans or turns of luck brought them to this time and place, what objects of their passion and pity arouse them enough to tell us." Volume 6 concentrates on novelists and poets, including Nikki Giovanni, D. Keith Mano, and Dee Brown. Volume 7 covers, among others, Andrew Greeley, Jamake Highwater, and David Ray. As in the main *Contemporary Authors* set, the writers represented here fall into a broad range of categories, including literary criticism, nonfiction, drama, film, and television.

Each volume contains sixteen essays, the scope and style of which were left entirely to the authors. As a result, some are chatty and entertaining, others are introspective, matter-of-fact, or poetic. Some are chock full of facts, names, and dates; others leave the reader with a "feeling" for the author's thoughts about life and literature. Karl Shapiro's is written in the third person, and Arnold Wesker's is a "miniauto-biography in three acts and a prologue." All of them make fascinating reading.

Each essay is accompanied by photographs supplied by the writer. The only feature added by the editorial staff is a bibliography of book-length works for each writer. The index provides adequate access to names or titles mentioned in this or previous volumes. Some of the other Gale literary series index one another. While *Contemporary Authors: Autobiography Series* is indexed in several other Gale sets, its own index is limited to volumes within the series.

An autobiography series is a great idea, and this particular one is an interesting and unusual companion to existing sources for literary biography and criticism.

Emily L. Werrell

988. Magill, Frank N., ed. **The Nobel Prize Winners: Literature.** Englewood Cliffs, N.J., Salem Press, 1987. 3v. illus. index. $210.00/set. LC 88-6469. ISBN 0-89356-541-5.

This set is the first in a projected series about Nobel laureates in all areas, so subsequent volumes will cover peace, physics, chemistry, physiology or medicine, and economics. Volume 1 of this set begins with an interpretive essay tracing the sometimes quite controversial history of the Nobel Prize for Literature, first awarded in 1901. A table is also provided listing the winners' names, dates of birth, death, and award years, as well as the nationalities and literary genres for which the laureates are best known. Most of the rest of the set is then devoted to separate essays in chronological order on each laureate through Joseph Brodsky, the winner in 1987. Preceding each article is a photograph of the laureate. The articles, each about thirty-five hundred words long, are arranged in a standard format. To facilitate ready-reference, at the head of each article are the winner's name, place and date of birth and death, language(s) in which he or she wrote, and major genres. A brief one- or two-sentence summary of why the laureate won the prize is given in italics (in words taken from the official citation). The text of each article then covers (1) a synopsis of the points made by the presenter of the award and a summary of the laureate's Nobel lecture or acceptance speech (including Jean Paul Sartre's letter explaining his refusal of the award); (2) a survey of international reactions to the choice; (3) a brief biography; (4) a review of the laureate's major works; and (5) a list, by genre, of principal works by the laureate, as well as some significant critical works about him or her. A separate author/title index allows readers to locate laureates by country and genre, and each volume begins with a complete alphabetical list of the laureates.

This set will be very useful to students tracing patterns among various laureates. It will also be valuable for information about now obscure laureates. Readers just seeking information about well-known winners, such as Kipling or Faulkner, do not, of course, need this set, since so many other sources provide that information in greater depth. But readers wanting to know why these writers won the Nobel Prize, or who need information about less well-known writers—such as Sully Prudhomme and Verner von Heidenstam—will welcome this set.

Readers interested in sources devoted to *all* of the Nobel winners may want to consult two recent works: *Nobel Prize Winners: An H. W. Wilson Biographical Dictionary* (see *ARBA* 88, entry 32) and *The Who's Who of Nobel Prize Winners* (see *ARBA* 88, entry 33). [R: RBB, 15 Nov 88, p. 555]   David Isaacson

Dictionaries and Encyclopedias

989. Legat, Michael. **The Illustrated Dictionary of Western Literature.** New York, Continuum, 1987. 352p. illus. (part col.). $29.50. LC 87-19991. ISBN 0-8264-0393-X.

For the purposes of this nicely illustrated literary dictionary, "Western" includes writers from every continent and almost every country with the exception of the Middle East and Far East. Thus Russian writers are included, as are African, Latin American, American, and European writers. As would be expected, the two thousand entries in the dictionary are arranged alphabetically. Length of the articles varies from one sentence to up to one page. Most entries cover authors and specific works; movements and literary terms are covered only minimally. There are two appendices: the first provides examples of various kinds of verse, such as heroic verse, sonnets, lyrics; the second is a list of authors included in the dictionary, arranged chronologically by birth date. While some biographical entries are quite lengthy, most are short, listing major works and dates, and neglecting any comment on literary style, importance, or themes. There are almost no additional references or cross-references to other entries. In addition to the lack of cross-references, terms appear in some definitions which should be defined elsewhere but are not. For example, Kingsley Amis is defined as one of the "angry young men" and Roland Barthes is described as a "leading member of the Structuralist movement." Neither *angry young men* nor *Structuralist* is defined in the dictionary, and an interested reader would be forced to find the definition in a more comprehensive work. Although the book is nicely illustrated, on at least one

occasion (a painting of D. H. Lawrence) the author has failed to credit the artist (whose name does, however, appear in the painting itself). This dictionary will be of greatest interest to general readers and beginning students of literature, but will not replace standard literary dictionaries or encyclopedias. [R: RBB, 1 Apr 88, p. 1322]   Jean M. Parker

990. Prince, Gerald. **A Dictionary of Narratology.** Lincoln, Neb., University of Nebraska Press, 1987. 118p. bibliog. $17.95. LC 87-4998. ISBN 0-8032-3678-6.

This dictionary is not simply another dictionary of literary terms. Although one will find literary terms defined in the dictionary, the terms included are chosen based on their importance specifically to the study of narratology. As defined by the dictionary, narratology "studies the nature, form, and functioning of narrative," and is not restricted to the study of literature; thus, narratology covers many disciplines, including history, religion, mythology, and conversation. Prince, professor of French at the University of Pennsylvania, states that he covers all important traditions of narratology, from Aristotle to the present, but that he concentrates on recent works of the French narratologists. This technical dictionary attempts to establish common definitions for the terminology of narratology. As such, while some terms appear in other dictionaries (to literature or rhetoric, for example) the definitions for the terms relate specifically to the study of narrative. Therefore, the dictionary attempts to distinguish meanings that in narratology vary from their meanings in other fields (e.g., "voice"). Arrangement is alphabetical, with references, cross-references, and related terms clearly indicated in the text. Definitions conclude with references to seminal works discussing the specific subject or term. The dictionary concludes with a thorough and useful bibliography of sources. The *Dictionary of Narratology* is an important contribution to a growing field. [R: Choice, Sept 88, p. 88; RQ, Summer 88, pp. 570, 572]   Jean M. Parker

Handbooks

991. **The Cambridge Guide to Literature in English.** Ian Ousby, ed. New York, Cambridge University Press, 1988. 1109p. illus. $37.50. LC 87-33129. ISBN 0-521-26751-X.

Although technically this book is not related to *The Cambridge Guide to English Literature* (see *ARBA* 85, entry 1004), and although it does not acknowledge any relationship, the later volume appears to be a revision of the earlier one. *The Cambridge Guide to English Literature* was criticized by *ARBA*'s reviewer because it tried to cover literature written in English all over the world, not just in Britain. *Literature in English* avoids that problem with its title change, but it might create the impression that it deals with literature *translated* into English as well as originally written in English (it does not cover translations).

The major use of this volume will be for ready-reference: it is a handy source to check biographical data about authors, significant literary works, definitions of literary terms, information about schools of literary criticism, identification of literary allusions, descriptions of genres, etc. Appropriately, major works and major authors receive more space than minor ones.

Although many of the three hundred illustrations and some of the text of *The Cambridge Guide to English Literature* remain the same, many new entries are included and old ones are revised. Each volume has much in common: the same number of pages; primary descriptions and identifications of entries, rather than extensive interpretations; and numerous cross-references to other entries. In addition, both consider non-English writers only in relation to English writers; both have separate entries on authors and on their major works; and both include numerous entries on subjects related to literature.

However, the differences between these volumes are also significant. *Cambridge* has a considerably broader geographical scope that includes writers in English from countries outside the United Kingdom. *Cambridge* provides entries for the Indian novelist Mulk Anand, the American children's writer Frank Baum, and the Canadian poet Leonard Cohen. While none of these are in the Oxford volume, it does include the sculptor John Flaxman, the biographer Michael Holroyd, and the composer Gustav Holst—all British nationals the Cambridge volume did not have room to include.

Since each volume contains much not included in the other, libraries with sufficient budgets may want to purchase both.

David Isaacson

992. **Contemporary Literary Criticism: Excerpts from Criticism of the Works of Today's Novelists, Poets, Playwrights, Short Story Writ-**

ers, Scriptwriters, and Other Creative Writers. Volume 45. Daniel G. Marowski, Roger Matuz, and Robyn V. Young, eds. Detroit, Gale, 1987. 784p. illus. index. $92.00. LC 76-38938. ISBN 0-8103-4419-X; ISSN 0091-3421.

Now at volume 45 of the series, *Contemporary Literary Criticism* continues to present excerpts from criticism on a wide range of contemporary authors, including novelists, short story writers, poets, playwrights, mystery writers, science fiction writers, nonfiction writers, screenwriters, and others.

Volume 45 includes recent criticisms on approximately fifteen authors appearing in previous volumes (including Edward M. Forster, William Stanley Merwin, Howard Moss, John James Osborne, Delmore Schwartz, John Steinbeck, and Tennessee Williams), plus criticism on authors not covered in earlier editions (such as Kathy Acker, Tom Clancy, Rex Warner, and Yuri Trifonov). Selection criteria appear to be rather broad, and authors may be chosen for inclusion for a number of reasons. The "publication of a critically acclaimed new work, the reception of a major literary award, or the dramatization of a literary work as a film or television screenplay" constitute rather obvious grounds for inclusion, while standards less easily defined include "authors of considerable public interest" and "literary and social critics whose insights are considered valuable and informative."

Beginning with volume 40, a title index has been provided which lists all titles reviewed in *CLC* in alphabetical order. Access is also facilitated through the cumulative indexes to authors, nationalities, and titles. Beginning with volume 27, the cumulative index to authors includes cross-references to such Gale offerings as *Contemporary Authors, Children's Literature Review, Dictionary of Literary Biography, Nineteenth-Century Literature Criticism, Twentieth-Century Literary Criticism,* and *Something about the Author.*

As indicated in past reviews, this well-indexed and handy reference tool becomes more valuable with the publication of each new volume. Most libraries should begin or continue to have standing orders for it.

Susan R. Penney

993. **Critical Survey of Literary Theory.** Frank N. Magill, ed. Englewood Cliffs, N.J., Salem

Press, 1987. 4v. index. $300.00/set. LC 88-
11424. ISBN 0-89356-390-0.

In the tradition of Magill's surveys in other
literary topics, this set provides information
necessary to initiate research on literary theory.
The four volumes give basic biographical information and summaries of the influence, opinions, and work of 257 major writers and
critics. The last volume also includes a series of
essays on the history of literary theory and
discussions of major movements. These solid
survey articles trace the development of various
theories through the work of influential
authors, with plentiful quotes and paraphrasing, and should prove especially helpful to students seeking an overview of the topic. A
glossary provides short definitions, which often
suffer from the typical fault of defining specialized terms with jargon. A highly useful index
lists authors, works, and theories; the entries for
theories refer the user not only to the essays but
also to leading writers and their works.

This set is a good selection for any public,
college, or university library trying to serve
students embarking on research in literary
theory or criticism. It is not a final solution;
students will inevitably have to delve deeper into
the topic to understand it, but brief bibliographies following each article assist in that.
Despite gallant efforts by the writers, the subject
matter is often obscure and the requirements for
brevity necessarily limit the extent of clarification possible, but that comes with the territory.
Overall, this set provides a thoughtful overview
and analysis of major theories and theorists.
Two caveats must be noted: the set deals with
theories on prose and poetry only, and the
emphasis is almost exclusively on European and
American theory, with essays on Chinese and
Japanese theory providing token recognition of
the rest of the world. [R: WLB, Dec 88, p. 117]
— Susan Davis Herring

994. **Twentieth-Century Literary Criticism:
Excerpts from Criticism of the Works of
Novelists, Poets, Playwrights, Short Story
Writers, and Other Creative Writers.... Volume
24.** Dennis Poupard, Marie Lazzari, and
Thomas Ligotti, eds. Detroit, Gale, 1987. 686p.
illus. index. $92.00. LC 76-46132. ISBN 0-8103-
2406-7; ISSN 0276-8178.

995. **Twentieth-Century Literary Criticism:
Excerpts from Criticism of the Works of
Novelists, Poets, Playwrights, Short Story
Writers, and Other Creative Writers.... Volume
25.** Dennis Poupard, Marie Lazzari, and
Thomas Ligotti, eds. Detroit, Gale, 1988. 672p.

illus. index. $92.00. LC 76-46132. ISBN 0-8103-
2407-5; ISSN 0276-8178.

Designed to serve as an "introduction for
the student of twentieth-century literature to the
authors of the period 1900 to 1960 and to the
most significant commentators on these
authors" (preface), this ongoing series now
numbers twenty-five volumes. The first volume,
which appeared in 1978, covered thirty-eight
writers. Volume 24 discusses eighteen authors,
providing more in-depth coverage for each one.
Volume 25 discusses nineteen authors.

Some of the authors covered in volume 24
are Max Beerbohm, Frank Harris, Frank Norris, and Mary Webb; critics include Edmund
Wilson, Katherine Anne Porter, Virginia
Woolf, and H. L. Mencken. In addition, two
author entries are devoted to criticism on a
single, major work—Sherwood Anderson's
Winesburg, Ohio and Henry James's *The Turn
of the Screw.* Volume 25 covers Bret Harte,
Edgar Lee Masters, and Oswald Spengler,
among others. Joseph Conrad's *Nostromo* is the
major work it considers.

Author entries covering an entire career
begin with early criticism to reflect initial reactions, followed by later criticism to indicate
changing perspectives on a writer's work. Current retrospective analyses provide the student
with modern critical thinking to complete the
chronological presentation of criticism on the
author's work.

Arranged alphabetically, each entry includes a portrait of the author, biographical information, a list of the author's principal works,
the critical excerpts, and a brief bibliography of
additional works about the author. The critical
essays include explanatory notes about the
critic, the type of criticism, and the bibliographical citations. The explanatory notes provide
valuable background material concerning the
criticism, which, for a student, is helpful indeed.
As noted in an earlier *ARBA* review, "the
editors ... have done an admirable job in selecting pertinent critical writing" (see *ARBA* 84, entries 1110-13).

An important feature appearing for the
first time, with volume 24, is a cumulative index
to titles of works discussed in the series since its
inception. Cumulative indexes to authors and
nationalities and an appendix identifying the
sources of the excerpts are also included in each
volume. Literature students are well served by
this comprehensive, balanced series.
— Carmel A. Huestis

Indexes

996. Index Guide to Modern American Literature and Modern British Literature. (An Index Guide to Volumes 1-5 of *Modern American Literature*, Compiled and Edited by Dorothy Nyren Curley et al., and Volumes 1-5 of *Modern British Literature*, Compiled and Edited by Ruth Z. Temple et al.). New York, Ungar Publishing, 1988. 114p. (Library of Literary Criticism). $29.95. LC 87-23734. ISBN 0-8044-3055-1.

This slim volume provides easy access to two valuable publications, *Modern American Literature* and *Modern British Literature*. Providing a comprehensive index to the first five volumes of both publications, it covers more than 830 authors and some 3,500 critics' studies of those authors.

The index is divided into two sections. The first lists authors covered by both publications; the second provides an index to the critics' writings. Although some indexing is provided by both publications themselves, students and scholars alike will find this combined index a much handier tool to use. [R: RBB, 1 Mar 88, p. 1101]   Elizabeth Patterson

CHILDREN'S LITERATURE

Bibliographies

997. Books for the Gifted Child. Volume 2. By Paula Hauser and Gail A. Nelson. New York, R. R. Bowker, 1988. 244p. index. (Serving Special Needs). $32.95. LC 79-27431. ISBN 0-8352-2467-8.

Building on the model of a previous volume, Hauser and Nelson have assembled a list of 195 beginning, intermediate, and advanced titles published in the 1980s for the gifted reader. Titles have been selected based on their potential to challenge readers with abstractions, ambiguities, and other reasoning tasks. In addition, books eliciting an emotional or an imaginative response were included. The books are arranged alphabetically by author and contain lengthy descriptive annotations. There is a title, level, and subject index. Chapter 1 of the book provides an essay on the gifted student and describes various types of literature of interest to this group.

While the titles seem to have been selected carefully, the book suffers from a flawed structure. If the book had been arranged by theme, or if there had been an extensive theme index (the subject index is too brief), and if the annotations would have suggested uses of the book with the gifted reader (only a few comments of this nature are given occasionally), the book would have been a better prescriptive source. As structured, the annotations are too long, and the user has to spend an inordinate amount of time reading before the volume can serve the needs of a teacher of the gifted or a librarian short on time.

Recommended as a checklist against the current collection if the library can afford it.
          David V. Loertscher

998. Booth, David, Larry Swartz, and Meguido Zola. Choosing Children's Books. Markham, Ont., Pembroke, 1987. 176p. index. $9.95pa. ISBN 0-921217-12-9.

This new annotated bibliography of books for children up to age 14 is an endeavor of three devotees of children's literature who have selected these titles on the basis of their experience with children. The list is divided into four age groups (birth-5, 5-8, 8-11, and 11-14). The authors have attempted to group the books within the age divisions by genre or theme, as well as give a section of read-aloud books. Books typically read by adults to children are arranged alphabetically, while those read by children on their own are given in order of difficulty. The variety of organizational aspects proves both useful and confusing. With only an author index, a user could search several sections before locating a title whose author is not remembered.

Some choices of groupings are obviously arbitrary. Why should *Tex* by S. E. Hinton be included in the section for young adolescent "Reluctant and Remedial Readers" instead of "Fiction for Developing Readers" or the theme section "Relationships"?

Annotations are concise and helpful, and each is followed by titles of other books by the same author, sequels to the listed book, and other books in the series. The strongest feature of this bibliography is the quality of the literature recommended. As a source for choosing good books to share with children, this book is useful. For ease of use, this source has limitations.   Patricia Tipton Sharp

999. Children's Books of the Year. 1988 ed. New York, Child Study Children's Book Committee, Bank Street College, 1988. 55p. illus. index. $4.00pa.

Any number of organizations publish brief lists of books of the year for various age groups. These include state library associations that involve students in making their choices, and national associations that issue brief lists of best books selected by librarians and teachers. There are fewer organizations which offer frequently published, inexpensive lists of children's books. Among those that are still available are the Association for Childhood Education International's list (now quadrennial) and the annual list from the Library of Congress.

This offering has been an annual publication for fifty years, making it one of the most reliable lists. It includes some six hundred books published in 1987 or late 1986, whittled down from three thousand reviewed. They are grouped for ages five and under, ages five through eight, ages eight and up, and special interests. These categories are further divided by type of book for the age level categories, and by broad subject areas for special interests.

Entries are in alphabetical order by title, with author, illustrator, publisher, price, and a brief annotation given. There are indexes of titles, authors, and illustrators, and a list of publishers. The publishers list seemed short, but all the publishers whose entries were checked were on the list. The committee is "a voluntary group of about thirty parents, teachers, librarians, writers, illustrators, and psychologists" who review books using criteria based on "suitability of text and illustrations for the age for which the book is intended; the author's sincerity and respect for the young reader; the credibility of characterization and plot; the authenticity of background of time and place; the treatment of ethnic and religious differences; the absence of race, sex, and age stereotypes; and the quality of writing" ("About This List"). This year the committee is offering a separate *Paperback Books for Children through Age 14*.

The *Children's Books of the Year* list has the advantage of being an annual upon which one can depend. The criteria are appropriate. Many of the authors and illustrators are standard entries on children's book lists. It would be nice to have a clear designation of the affiliation of the group of reviewers, but fifty years have brought them wide acceptance and have given this document a solid position among annual reviews of children's literature.

Betty Jo Buckingham

1000. Gagnon, André, and Ann Gagnon, eds. **Canadian Books for Young People. Livres Canadiens pour la Jeunesse.** 4th ed. Cheektowaga, N.Y. and Toronto, University of Toronto Press, 1988. 186p. illus. index. $14.95pa. ISBN 0-8020-6662-3.

With the increasing number of Canadian children's books published in recent years, André Gagnon and Ann Gagnon faced a formidable task in updating the 1980 edition of this work, but they have succeeded in producing a valuable selection aid. In this edition they have

compiled a selective list of more than twenty-five hundred titles, both English and French, with brief annotations in the language of publication. The annotations are concise and most are entirely descriptive, although occasionally an evaluative comment slips in. Within each language section, the arrangement is by subject: picture books, science, arts, fiction, and so forth. The age range covered is from preschool to eighteen, and each title is assigned an approximate age level. There are separate sections for professional media in each language as well as useful listings of award books, periodicals, and publishers' series. The three indexes—author, title, and illustrators—integrate the two languages. Information given for each item includes ISBN and price, thus making the book useful as a buying guide, although the short in-print life of Canadian children's books will make disappointments inevitable. The double-column pages and small but legible type, as well as the line drawings used to separate sections, make for an attractive, compact compilation of information which will be helpful for children's librarians and others who wish to build a collection of Canadian children's books.

Adele M. Fasick

1001. **High Interest Easy Reading for Junior and Senior High School Students.** 5th ed. By Dorothy Matthews and the Committee to Revise *High Interest-Easy Reading* of the National Council of Teachers of English. Urbana, Ill., National Council of Teachers of English, 1988. 115p. index. $6.25pa. LC 88-1430. ISBN 0-8141-2096-2.

The fifth edition of this booklist for adolescents who are not eager readers describes 367 fiction and nonfiction titles published between 1984 and 1986. Some classic favorites published earlier are also included.

The National Council of Teachers of English has established a committee, chaired by Matthews, to revise and update *High Interest Easy Reading*. Teachers, school media specialists, parents, public librarians, and students themselves can rely on this popular selection tool for identifying books that have particular appeal to students and are useful in completing assignments in various areas of the curriculum. According to the introduction (p. vii), books included here are either exciting stories, contain "suspenseful action, likeable characters," or are concerned with topics that are part of the young adult's everyday life and culture.

Entries are arranged alphabetically by author under twenty-three subject headings, some of which are fantasy and science fiction, love and friendship, real people, sports, technology, ghosts and the supernatural, mystery, how-to books, and humor. Each entry includes complete bibliographic description (including total page numbers) and International Standard Book Number for ease in ordering. Annotations always indicate the age of the leading character(s) and provide a brief summary of the story or subject content. [R: BR, Sept/Oct 88, p. 50; RBB, 1 Sept 88, pp. 48, 50; VOYA, Aug 88, pp. 153-54]   Lois Buttlar

1002. Horner, Catherine Townsend. **The Single-Parent Family in Children's Books: An Annotated Bibliography.** 2d ed. Metuchen, N.J., Scarecrow, 1988. 339p. index. $29.50. LC 87-26403. ISBN 0-8108-2065-X.

The single-parent family has always been represented in children's literature. Prior to the 1960s, the cause of single parenthood in books was invariably widowhood or orphanhood with a single guardian (e.g., Sydney's *Five Little Peppers* and Hergan's *Mrs. Wiggs of the Cabbage Patch*). With the sexual revolution of the 1960s and 1970s, a leap in the divorce rate, and the emergence of the popular psychology movement eventually came the publication of books that deal realistically with death, divorce, separation, desertion, remarriage, binuclear families, and never-married mothers. Today there are a wealth of books that deal with these topics multidimensionally and provide literary expression in the popular children's genres of mystery, adventure, fantasy, contemporary realism, humor, topical books, science fiction, and historical fiction.

Horner's comprehensive bibliography annotates and rates 596 fiction and 26 nonfiction titles published between 1965 and 1986 that pertain to families fractured by divorce, desertion, separation, or the death of a parent; unmarried mothers or other single adults as heads of households; and the protracted absence of one parent from a traditional two-parent home. Some modern classics and old favorites published prior to 1965 are also reviewed.

The bibliography is intended for professionals and lay persons interested in identifying a variety of reading materials for children from nontraditional homes. Clearly annotated and arranged, the bibliography provides valuable access to titles that speak to the need of millions of children and their families now living in single-parent households in the United States. [R: BR, Nov/Dec 88, p. 47; RBB, Aug 88, p. 1907; VOYA, Dec 88, p. 257]

Debbie Burnham-Kidwell

1003. Howard, Elizabeth F. **America as Story: Historical Fiction for Secondary Schools.**
Chicago, American Library Association, 1988. 137p. index. $15.00pa. LC 88-3453. ISBN 0-8389-0492-0.

Designed to assist teachers and librarians in selecting novels which will stimulate students' interest in history, this guide identifies over 150 novels, most published in the last twenty years, which portray the experiences and feelings of ordinary people living through key periods in American history. An emphasis is placed on themes involving the experiences of fictional young people, such as "building a sod house on the Nebraska prairie, following the North Star with a bold band of escaping slaves, or parachuting into enemy territory after a B-17 is shot down" (p. xii).

The book is arranged in seven broad chronological/topical categories: colonial America; the American Revolution and the new nation; the Civil War and Reconstruction; westward expansion and the native American response; immigration, industrialization, and urbanization; the jazz age and the Depression; and America in the modern world. Entries consist of the title of the book and its imprint, indication of the reading level, a short annotation introducing the plot, a comment on historicity, and suggestions for reports or activities. As the author indicates, the suggested activities are just that— suggestions. Teachers, librarians, and students are expected to devise additional follow-up activities.

Some of the standard bibliographies consulted by the author were H. W. Wilson's *Senior High School Catalog* (see *ARBA* 88, entry 640) and *Junior High School Catalog* (see *ARBA* 86, entry 596), *The American History Book List for High Schools* (National Council for the Social Studies, 1971), the National Council of Teachers of English lists for junior and senior high schools, and *Books for the Teen Age* (see *ARBA* 87, entry 618). Additional titles were suggested by quite a few "knowledgeable" individuals named in the acknowledgments section. Because the guide focuses on more recent books, generally 1940 to 1986, some of the older classics such as *Uncle Tom's Cabin* have been omitted. However, a sampling of the material includes such works as *Johnny Tremain, Across Five Aprils, My Antonia, The Jungle, The Grapes of Wrath,* and *The Bridges at Toko-ri,* as well as the even more recent *1787, Roots: The Saga of an American Family, Bold Journey: West with Lewis and Clark, The Tempering,* and *A Woman of Independent Means.* This would be a useful tool for teachers and librarians who want to bring the social studies curriculum to life by showing students through contemporary literature that history is the story of real people's lives. [R: BL, 1 Oct 88, pp. 259-60; RBB, 15 Nov 88, p. 550]

Susan R. Penney

1004. Lipson, Eden Ross. **The New York Times Parent's Guide to the Best Books for Children.** New York, Times Books/Random House, 1988. 421p. illus. bibliog. index. $22.95; $12.95pa. LC 87-40587. ISBN 0-8129-1649-2; 0-8129-1688-3pa.

A selective guide to nearly one thousand of the best books for children published in the United States, the volume includes "a mixture of classic, standard and distinguished new titles.... Some are noble classics, some are just fun; others may be helpful directly or indirectly as they address real issues children face" (p. xii).

The main titles are numbered consecutively and grouped according to text level from wordless through books for middle and advanced readers. Books are listed alphabetically by title within each section. For each title, the following bibliographic information is provided: author, illustrator, publisher in hardcover and paperback, date of original publication, and a notation of awards, if any. As the author is Children's Book Editor of *The New York Times*, she has included mention of *The Times* Best Illustrated winners. The annotations, highly colored by Lipson's "own tastes and enthusiasms" (p. xiv), are very brief, usually only a sentence or two. A unique feature of the book is the variety of indexes; there are title, author, and illustrator indexes; "Age-Appropriate Indexes"; "Read-Aloud Index"; and "Special Subject Indexes," with categories such as "Adoption," "Biography/Autobiography," and "Growing Up."

The author's admittedly subjective selection criteria have produced a collection in which the balance is slightly skewed. Most recognized titles are included, but a few are not. As for authors included, Lipson makes some interesting choices. William Steig has ten titles; Dr. Seuss only seven. Beverly Cleary has only four titles; Lorna Balian none at all. Jane Yolen rates seven. Barbara Cooney has only one, and that not one of her best. In view of the fact that more objective selection criteria were not applied, buyers should be aware that this is really *"Eden Ross Lipson's Parent's Guide to the Best Books for Children."*

Carmel A. Huestis

1005. Lukenbill, W. Bernard, and Sharon Lee Stewart, comps. and eds. **Youth Literature: An Interdisciplinary, Annotated Guide to North American Dissertation Research, 1930-1985.** New York, Garland, 1988. 466p. index. (Gar-

land Reference Library of Social Science, Vol. 400). $65.00. LC 87-38077. ISBN 0-8240-8498-5.

Youth Literature is a selective interdisciplinary guide to youth literature from 1930 to 1985. It is intended as an update and expansion of the 1972 work *A Working Bibliography of American Doctoral Dissertations in Children's and Adolescents' Literature, 1930-1971* (see *ARBA* 74, entry 1292) by Lukenbill. This present volume gives titles and annotations for over fifteen hundred doctoral studies conducted at major North American universities on the subject of youth literature.

The editors broadly define "youth" as the period of life from preschool to about age eighteen. The wide range of topics covered (e.g., social attitudes and values, minority cultures, and political environment) illustrates the interrelatedness of youth literature to such disciplines as sociology, psychology, anthropology, and history. Generic studies about reading and reading environments, types of literature, and literary criticisms are also included.

Dissertation Abstracts International (*DAI*) is the primary source for titles selected. The arrangement is simple with just two major divisions—part 1 lists the titles and annotations arranged alphabetically by author, and part 2 is a subject index to the dissertations listed. Cross-references are provided.

The bibliographic citations for each title include author, title of dissertation, university accepting the dissertation, date of degree, and *DAI* reference number. The annotations, based on *DAI* abstracts, are clear and concise, range in length from about twenty to one hundred words, and are descriptive rather than critical. A few titles (less than 10 percent) have no annotations because they were not given in *DAI*.

This work is useful to anyone interested in youth literature. Those planning a study dealing with this literature have in one source a variety of research designs from which to choose.

Dianne Brinkley Catlett

1006. Marantz, Sylvia S., and Kenneth A. Marantz. **The Art of Children's Picture Books: A Selective Reference Guide.** New York, Garland, 1988. 165p. index. (Garland Reference Library of the Humanities, Vol. 825). $27.00. LC 88-1704. ISBN 0-8240-2745-0.

This annotated 451-item bibliography provides selected primary and secondary sources on the art and illustration of children's literature. Most of the sources have been published within the past twenty-five years, with emphasis on the more recent sources located in the United States. The sources listed include books, periodicals, articles, videotapes, films, filmstrips, and dissertations and theses. The subjects presented in the bibliography are the history of children's picture books, how a picture book is made, criticism of children's picture books, including their use with children, anthologies of artists, information on individual artists, guides and aids to further research, and locations of some collections and archival materials on picture books and their creators. Artist, author, and title indexes provide easy access to the information. This will prove to be an excellent resource for those with special interests in the art of children's literature.

Marilyn Strong Noronha

1007. Nakamura, Joyce, ed. **High-interest Books for Teens: A Guide to Book Reviews and Biographical Sources.** 2d ed. Detroit, Gale, 1988. 539p. index. $95.00. LC 81-6889. ISBN 0-8103-1830-X.

Over thirty-five hundred fiction and nonfiction titles by two thousand authors, of special interest to junior and senior high school students, with sources of critical reviews about them are listed in this reference tool aimed at librarians, classroom teachers, and reading tutors. This second edition updates and expands the first edition published by Gale in 1981.

Titles included have been recommended in reading lists by educators, librarians, and publishers as especially appropriate for enticing students with learning disabilities, or those who need to improve their reading skills, to read. They have been identified as "high interest/low-readability level" materials and include both contemporary works and favorite classics by familiar authors.

In the main body of the work, "Guide to Book Reviews and Biographical Sources," entries are arranged by author (or pseudonym), with dates of birth and death (if applicable) indicated. At least one citation to a source of further biographical information follows. For individual books by each author, a list of citations to evaluations of the title in reviewing periodicals is provided. Subject headings and cross-references to name variants/pseudonyms, co-authors/adapters or authors of adapted works under which other books have been written and reviewed are also indicated. Two brief sections, "Book Review Sources Cited" and "Biographical Sources Cited," give complete names of biography and review sources indicated by abbreviations or codes in the entry. In addition to a title index, the second edition has included a very useful subject index with over 500 categories popular with young adults, such as adventure stories, mystery and detective stories, sports, occult sciences, motorcycles and motorcycle

racing, rock music and musicians, and family life and family problems. Subject headings are those used by the Library of Congress and also from the *Sears List of Subject Headings.*

While recommended lists for students whose chronological age exceeds their reading ability are not hard to find, a tool that identifies in one place all sources of reviews for each title is a definite asset. [R: RBB, Aug 88, p. 1903; VOYA, Aug 88, p. 153]

Lois Buttlar

1008. **The Newbery & Caldecott Awards 1988: A Complete Listing of Medal and Honor Books.** Chicago, Association for Library Service to Children, American Library Association, 1988. 40p. index. $5.00pa. ISBN 0-8389-7209-8.

This work is a useful compilation of the Newbery and Caldecott award winners and runners-up from the inception of each award through 1988. Listings for each award are in reverse chronological order and include title, author, illustrator (for Caldecott books), and publisher. A brief history of the award precedes the chronological list.

Although this information is available in many children's literature textbooks, purchasing guides, and professional journals, this is still a useful booklet. Unlike *Hornbook Magazine's* Newbery and Caldecott Medal series, which includes acceptance speeches, book notes, excerpts, illustrations, and other useful information, *The Newbery & Caldecott Awards* is just a list. This is the information most requested by students, parents, and other laypersons. It is exactly the type of material classroom teachers, children's literature professors, and librarians working with children use most often. Recommended.

Carol J. Veitch

1009. Roberts, Patricia L. **Alphabet Books as a Key to Language Patterns: An Annotated Action Bibliography.** Hamden, Conn., Library Professional Publications/Shoe String Press, 1987. 263p. index. $27.50. LC 87-3216. ISBN 0-208-02151-5.

This reference source focuses on language patterns in alphabet books. After a comprehensive introduction to language patterns and their efficacy for children's language, literacy, and learning skills, Roberts analyzes nearly five hundred alphabet books for language patterns. The introduction addresses research findings about language patterning, then discusses numerous types of language patterns and patterns as a means of playing with language, making oral responses, writing, etc. This introduction is both useful and well organized.

The bibliography is organized into categories by the language patterns used in the book. Each entry is by author's last name, has an annotation, and gives the suggested age level. Annotations typically describe the book's approach, provide response activities, and specify the language pattern used. Some titles are designated "Recommended." An index of authors and titles is also included.

Having the source be inclusive means that some entries are not outstanding literary or artistic examples, and books which use the alphabet merely as a vehicle for organization are also included (*Ancient Egypt from A to Z, The Smurf ABC Book*, etc.).

This resource is an excellent source for the wide variety of alphabet books available, and it is an interesting application of language patterns. [R: BL, 1 Oct 87, p. 327]

Patricia Tipton Sharp

1010.   Schon, Isabel. **A Hispanic Heritage, Series III: A Guide to Juvenile Books about Hispanic People and Cultures.** Metuchen, N.J., Scarecrow, 1988. 150p. index. $17.50. LC 88-18094. ISBN 0-8108-2133-8.

Once again Isabel Schon has produced a quality guide to assist librarians and teachers in developing and broadening the reading interests of children and young adults, particularly in the selection of literature about the Hispanic culture. This work contains evaluative, not merely descriptive, annotations of hundreds of fiction and nonfiction (including biographies) books arranged by specific country or geographic region. Users can quickly locate books about Argentina, Nicaragua, Spain, or the United States through the table of contents. Separate author, title, and subject indexes round out the work.

Entries include "most in-print books in English published since 1984 in the United States," and noteworthy titles are designated with an asterisk. Citations include standard bibliographic information, as well as price and grade/audience level designations. Schon includes refreshingly candid, clearly written, personal comments to describe the books, and does not hesitate to state strengths and weaknesses. Her insights range from "this is an excellent tribute" to "this is definitely the wrong book to introduce children to Mexico."

Although entries are not numbered, the arrangement of the book is logical and easy to use. Excellent as a collection development tool, this is an affordable book which will be useful to academic, school, and public libraries.

Ilene F. Rockman

1011.   Wear, Terri A. **Horse Stories: An Annotated Bibliography of Books for All Ages.** Metuchen, N.J., Scarecrow, 1987. 277p. index. $27.50. LC 87-13050. ISBN 0-8108-1998-8.

Over fifteen hundred titles dealing with equine fiction are arranged here according to age group. The compiler has interpreted "horse stories" quite broadly, and thus includes fiction on donkeys, mules, merry-go-round horses, rocking horses, and toy horses. She excludes unicorns and most Westerns, arguing that the latter "usually are not horse stories" (p. vi). On the other hand, books such as *The Mammoth Hunters, The Good Master,* and *Madeleine in London* are included, while McKinley's *The Blue Sword* and *The Hero and the Crown* are excluded, thus proving that one person's horse story may be ignored by another horse lover. The one-sentence summaries for each entry are concise but thorough. Some especially helpful features include information on series and sequels and a mention if the book was still in print as of November 1986. There are no notations of Newbery or other award winners, and an author index would have been a useful addition to the title and subject indexes since the entries are by age group, but these are minor quibbles. Public librarians will find this a useful and reasonably priced tool for helping patrons of any age who are looking for another good horse book. [R: BR, May/June 88, pp. 48-49; RBB, 1 May 88, pp. 1486-87; RLR, Nov 88, pp. 333-34; VOYA, Oct 88, p. 210]

Marilyn R. Pukkila

1012.   Williams, Jane A. **Who Reads What When: Literature Selections for Children Ages Three through Thirteen.** Placerville, Calif., Bluestocking Press, 1988. 60p. index. $3.95pa. LC 87-27854. ISBN 0-942617-01-0.

This bibliography of children's books was compiled using literature recommendations from the Textbook Evaluation Reports, private school recommended reading lists, and the author's own favorites for parents to use in helping their children choose books. There are three lists of indexes: age, title, and author. Unless parents have read the introductory section, they will be rather confused by the format of the indexes. The age index lists selections at suggested age levels for reading. Several of these indicated reading levels seem inappropriate (e.g., *Freckles* and *Island of the Blue Dolphins* for a nine-year-old). The number following the titles in the other indexes refers to the age level rather than a page number. As the author indicates, many of the titles are out-of-print and may not be accessible. There are many important authors and titles missing from this compilation, especially at the lower level (Carle, Keats, Zion). Nancy Larrick's *A Parent's Guide to Children's Reading* (see *ARBA* 84, entry 608) contains many of the same selections and is much easier to use. Many of the titles included in *Who Reads What When* are not found in either *Children's Catalog* or *The Elementary School Library Collection*, which are basic standards for book selection. No list is all-inclusive, and this should be used only as a supplement if additional reading lists are desired. Not recommended as an important tool. [R: JAL, Mar 88, p. 45; LJ, 1 Apr 88, p. 83]　　Mary J. Stanley

1013. Wilson, George, and Joyce Moss. **Books for Children to Read Alone: A Guide for Parents and Librarians.** New York, R. R. Bowker, 1988. 184p. index. $32.95. LC 88-10430. ISBN 0-8352-2346-9.

Over four hundred books have been listed and annotated for the child in grades 1 through 3 to use for independent reading as opposed to a list of books to be read to a child. The list is arranged by reading level in seven chapters, starting with wordless books and continuing by half grade levels through grade 3. Each chapter is further arranged by easy, average, and challenging for that level (for example, books for the first half of grade 1, readability: 1.0-1.4). Titles are listed first for easy reference and then each title is listed with a descriptive paragraph, followed by its genre and subject headings.

The authors note that while the list is arranged by reading level (Spache and Fry), they did consult with children about the titles and tried to take their suggestions. However, this is the point at which the list fails. If librarians and children waited to enjoy the books listed until they had gained the recommended reading level, they would miss many good titles, and many more would no longer be of interest. For example, the list recommends waiting until the second half of grade 3 before reading *Where the Wild Things Are, The Biggest Bear,* and *Jumanji.* Waiting until the first half of grade 3 is recommended before reading *Stone Soup, Strega Nona,* and *Lyle, Lyle, Crocodile.* While the advocates of teaching reading through literature could use this list because of the good titles it contains, the grade level structure would have to be ignored. As librarians know, children will rise to meet more difficult vocabulary when the interest level in a book is high.

Other features of the book are flawed. The subject headings suggested for the items are too much like *Sears* and too little like Bowker's excellent *A to Zoo* list, which bring out story themes. Likewise, the alphabetical listing of authors puts Dr. Seuss in the "Ds."

The list has some good titles and one could argue about many which were excluded, such as *Green Eggs and Ham.* Overall, the list is useful for its inclusions, but should not be used as the authors have structured the list. [R: LJ, Dec 88, p. 96]　　David V. Loertscher

1014. **Your Reading: A Booklist for Junior High and Middle School Students.** 7th ed. James E. Davis and Hazel K. Davis, eds., and the Committee on the Junior High and Middle School Booklist, NCTE. Urbana, Ill., National Council of Teachers of English, 1988. 494p. index. $12.95pa. LC 88-25148. ISBN 0-8141-5939-7.

In the seventh edition of *Your Reading*, the National Council of Teachers of English continues its practice of evaluating, recommending, and annotating books of interest to students in the fifth through ninth grades. Although aimed primarily at students, this now-standard reference source is valuable as a selection aid for teachers, librarians, and parents who need help in sifting through the myriad of new titles for this age group that appear each year.

After considering approximately six thousand books published between 1983 and 1987, NCTE's Committee on the Junior High and Middle School Booklist chose almost two thousand titles for inclusion. Selection was made on the basis of both audience appeal and literary merit, with books of exceptional literary merit receiving a special annotation. The titles are grouped by subject and literary type or both into sixty-one highly diverse categories (e.g., "Abuse," "Picture Books for Older Readers," "Historical Novels," "Computers," "Death and Dying," "Dating and Love," "Fantasy," and "Trivia"). Within each category the books are arranged alphabetically by author. Each entry provides author, title, publication, collation, and ISBN information, and is briefly, yet effectively, annotated. In keeping with the focus of the book, these annotations are written to appeal directly to the student reader, not the adult; and in most cases they succeed remarkably well. The book is concluded by an author index, a title index, and a directory of publishers.

Concise, accessible, and well arranged, this latest edition of a standard juvenile reference work should be welcomed both by students and interested adults and deserves a place on the reference shelves of most junior high and middle school libraries.

Kristin Ramsdell

Biographies

1015. Bingham, Jane M., ed. **Writers for Children: Critical Studies of Major Authors since the Seventeenth Century.** New York, Scribner's, 1988. 661p. index. $90.00. LC 87-16011. ISBN 0-684-18165-7.

"A critical guide to selected classics in children's literature ... important writers from the seventeenth century to the first part of the twentieth century. It includes eighty-four original critical essays, alphabetically arranged with selected bibliographies" (introduction). Beginning with Louisa May Alcott and ending with Charlotte Mary Yonge, each essay is by a named, often noted, contributor, and while entries vary in length, most cover the subject quite fully.

There are a listing of contributors with their backgrounds and credentials and a full index of important persons, titles, and events mentioned.

This extremely interesting and well-written reference work is aimed at scholars and critics in the field of children's literature, and is obviously of great interest and value to children's librarians, students, and researchers in the field as well as those who are concerned with this delightful and important area of literature. Useful (maybe even essential) for academic libraries as well as public and school libraries of any size. [R: Choice, Feb 88, p. 890; WLB, Jan 88, pp. 98-99]   Eleanor Elving Schwartz

1016. Rollock, Barbara. **Black Authors and Illustrators of Children's Books: A Biographical Dictionary.** New York, Garland, 1988. 130p. illus. bibliog. (Garland Reference Library of the Humanities, Vol. 660). $25.00. LC 87-25748. ISBN 0-8240-8580-9.

Black authors and illustrators (115) from the United States, Africa, Canada, and Great Britain whose works have been published in the United States are profiled in this biographical dictionary. Intended to "represent those black authors who have made or are making literary history in the world of children's books" (p. xi), the collection includes subjects whose works were published as early as the 1930s, although most are from the 1970s and 1980s.

Each profile includes a biographical sketch plus a bibliography of the subject's work for children. The sketches range in length from about 30 to 350 words; most are very brief. "Bibliographical Sources and References" (p. xiii) lists seventeen sources for more information. Also included in the collection are fifty-one black-and-white photographs of people and book covers.   Nancy Courtney

1017. **Something about the Author: Facts and Pictures about Authors and Illustrators of Books for Young People. Volume 49.** Anne Commire, ed. Detroit, Gale, 1987. 310p. illus. index. $68.00. LC 72-27107. ISBN 0-8103-2259-5; ISSN 0276-816X.

Following the tradition of earlier volumes, *Something about the Author* (*SATA*) contains both personal and professional material about authors of children's literature. Generously illustrated articles enable children and young adults to learn more about their favorite authors. Continuing the format of long biographical features, brief entries, and obituary notices, Commire has added to this edition full biographies of Frank Bonham, Chester Gould, and Leon Uris, among others. Among those included with brief entries are Jan Andrews, Tamore Pierce, and Agnes S. P. Szudek. Obituaries include Elizabeth Coatsworth, Paul Galdone, and Jane Quigg. With effort made for complete coverage, each biographical entry contains correct name, personal information, career facts, writings and information concerning them, any adaptations, sidelights, and references to other sources. Few changes have occurred since *SATA* was last reviewed (see *ARBA 85*, entries 1026-1029) and it continues to be recommended as an excellent source for children and young adults seeking biographical information on authors.   Anna Grace Patterson

Handbooks

1018. Adamson, Lynda G. **A Reference Guide to Historical Fiction for Children and Young Adults.** Westport, Conn., Greenwood Press, 1987. 401p. bibliog. index. $49.95. LC 87-7533. ISBN 0-313-25002-2.

This comprehensive, historical fiction guide describes the works written since 1940 of eighty award-winning authors. Main entries are accessible alphabetically by the author's last name. Specific titles, main characters, historical personages, places, and important historical aspects of several novels can be found via a similar alphabetical progression. Within each author's entry are a bibliography of the author's works, a description of his or her honors, a lengthy annotation of each cited title, and a summary of the author's general themes and style. Two useful appendices provide access by classifying titles according to historical periods and by Fry Readability levels. In addition, there are two appendices: a bibliography on writing historical novels by writers cited in the guide, and a secondary bibliography about the authors and historical novels cited in the guide.

The integration of author, people, place, historical event, and main character entries is disconcerting. The guide would be improved by listing, for example, characters in a separate part of the book. Coverage of these entries is also somewhat uneven. For example, a paragraph is devoted to Lindisfarne, while there are no entries for Confucius, Buddha, or Adolph Hitler. These flaws are minor, however, when considering the potential use for this book. The titles cited are covered more thoroughly than in Nilsen and Donelson's *Literature for Today's Young Adults* (2d ed., Scott Foresman, 1985), Irwin's *Guide to Historical Fiction* (see *ARBA* 73, entry 1252), the *Children's Catalog* (see *ARBA* 86, entry 821), and *Senior High School Library Catalog* (see *ARBA* 88, entry 640). The book is a valuable resource for teachers, parents, and school and public librarians who wish to compile bibliographies and reading lists or simply acquire more knowledge about historically based fictional works. [R: RBB, 15 Feb 88, pp. 984, 986; RQ, Spring 88, pp. 433-34]

Kathleen W. Craver

1019.   Gillespie, John T., with Corinne J. Naden. **Juniorplots 3: A Book Talk Guide for Use with Readers Ages 12-16.** New York, R. R. Bowker, 1987. 352p. index. $24.95. LC 87-27305. ISBN 0-8352-2367-1.

Juniorplots 3 is similar in format to *Juniorplots* (Bowker, 1967) and *More Juniorplots* (Bowker, 1977) although this work does not include any introductory material on booktalking techniques. Instead, it refers the reader to several resources on the topic.

Juniorplots 3 gives detailed plot summaries of eighty books which have proven popular with adolescent readers (grade 6 through high school). The selected titles have been recommended in at least two standard reviewing sources and meet the interests and needs of young adults of different reading levels and developmental stages. Titles were grouped into eight subjects/genre: teenage life and concerns, adventure and mystery stories, science fiction and fantasy, historical fiction, sports fiction, biography and true adventure, guidance and health, and the world around us. The first category contains the largest number of titles.

As with the previous *Juniorplots*, a detailed plot summary is followed by an enumeration of primary and secondary themes. Suggestions are given for booktalks, including paginations for selections to read aloud. Six to eight related titles are briefly described, with bibliographic data also provided. When biographical data were found on the author of the featured book,

appropriate citations are provided for follow-up research.

A welcome addition to the professional collections of public and school librarians working with young adults. Highly recommended. [R: RBB, 1 June 88, p. 1659; SLJ, Sept 88, p. 126]

Carol J. Veitch

1020.   Hendrickson, Linnea. **Children's Literature: A Guide to the Criticism.** Boston, G. K. Hall, 1987. 664p. index. (Reference Publication in Literature). $35.00. LC 86-19455. ISBN 0-8161-8670-7.

This guide to criticism in the field of children's literature demonstrates the extent to which the field has gained stature as an academic discipline during the past fifteen years. No specific dates of coverage are given, but the number of articles from the 1970s and 1980s indicates the growth in the field. Few of the books analyzed were published earlier than 1960, although a few classics such as those by Paul Hazard (1944) and Lillian H. Smith (1953) are included. The compiler states that "the starting point ... was the critical sources." Journals and books were examined to find books and articles that "provide insight into the work or topic discussed" and "say something significant or enlightening." In addition to books and journal articles, a number of unpublished dissertations and ERIC documents are listed. The bibliography is divided into two sections: "Authors and Their Works," and "Subjects, Themes and Genres." Indexes to authors, titles, subjects, and critics are also included, thus providing easy access for almost any purpose. Annotations are brief and descriptive, indicating the scope of the item but not evaluating its contribution. A six-page appendix lists reference works and journals in children's literature. Students of children's literature, teachers, and librarians will find this a compact, useful guide to a variety of critical articles. [R: Choice, May 87, p. 1380; RBB, 15 June 87, p. 1576]   Adele M. Fasick

1021.   Kobrin, Beverly. **Eyeopeners! How to Choose and Use Children's Books about Real People, Places, and Things.** New York, Viking Penguin, 1988. 317p. illus. bibliog. index. $16.95; $7.95pa. LC 88-40115. ISBN 0-670-82073-3; 0-14-046830-7pa.

"Are you a parent, a grandparent, a teacher, a librarian, a friend of one, about to become one, or any combination thereof? If so, this book is a bundle of ideas just for you—a passel of persuasive prose about the pros of children's nonfiction books" (p. 1). Thus the author gives her own best summary of what the book is about and whom it is for. Over five hundred trade books (i.e., not textbooks and not fiction) are organized by subject, with a more detailed subject index and an index of authors, titles, and illustrators to provide still more thorough access. Every entry is vividly discussed, and frequently accompanied by tips for projects to link the books to children's everyday experiences. Kobrin's material is gender inclusive and sensitive to the issues of race, disabilities, and nontraditional families. She includes books for "difficult" topics such as death, alcoholism, sex, and divorce, as well as the more standard fare of dinosaurs, lasers, cars, grandparents, music, zoos, outerspace, etc. All materials mentioned were in-print and available as of the beginning of 1988.

The first portion of the work is a handbook addressed to the various types of adults who bring children and books together. In this section, Kobrin's energetic creativity shines forth with suggestions that are stimulating and relevant. She reminds adults to teach children to read critically, to be aware of points of view, dates of publication, and potential biases. She reminds teachers to consult with librarians before giving out assignments, and offers librarians suggestions on how to encourage reading.

Kobrin is dedicated to the notion that both nonfiction and fiction together comprise literature, and her enthusiasm is infectious. This book is more than just a bibliography or a handbook; it is a celebration of the very best that can happen when children and books are brought together. [R: BL, 1 Oct 88, p. 331]

Marilyn R. Pukkila

1022.   Jones, Dolores Blythe. **Children's Literature Awards and Winners: A Directory of Prizes, Authors, and Illustrators.** 2d ed. Detroit, Neal-Schuman with Gale, 1988. 671p. index. $92.00. LC 84-643512. ISBN 0-8103-2741-4; ISSN 0749-3096.

The second edition of this work is divided into four parts: directory of awards, authors and illustrators, selected bibliography, and indexes. Four types of indexes are offered: award, subject index of awards, author/illustrator, and title.

The directory of awards includes the name and address of the sponsoring organization, purpose and history of the award, frequency, selection criteria, award categories, rules and regulations, and form of award. Award recipients are listed from the award's inception to 1987, and entries include author, title, illustrator, translator, publisher, and date of publication. Awards that have been discontinued are included in the list.

The most important tools for the reader are the indexes. The newly added author/illustrator and title indexes are straightforward and easy to use, yet the reader may encounter difficulties using the award index and subject index of awards, the latter also being new to this edition. These two would benefit from more extensive cross-referencing to bridge the disparity between official title and commonly used titles, such as the Sequoyah Children's Book Award versus the Oklahoma Sequoyah Children's Book Award.

Further, the subject index of awards should be more comprehensive. There is no access by state to all the awards originating in that state. For example, the Charlie May Simon Award, if placed under the heading of Arkansas, would be easier for the reader to locate than under the Children's Choice subject heading. Perhaps a fifth index of awards by state could be created for successive editions.

Children's Literature Awards & Winners is more extensive than its counterpart, *Children's Books: Awards & Prizes*, compiled by The Children's Book Council, though it is also more expensive. Each is published periodically. For the library who can afford the price, its collection will benefit from having this reference source. [R: RBB, 15 Dec 88, p. 688]

Susan M. Sigman

1023.   Reed, Arthea J. S. **Comics to Classics: A Parent's Guide to Books for Teens and Preteens.** Newark, Del., International Reading Association, 1988. 121p. illus. $8.95pa. LC 88-10171. ISBN 0-87207-798-5.

This is a practical, commonsense guide to young adult literature. Like Jim Trelease's *Read Aloud Handbook*, it provides a basic introduction for parents who are interested in their children's reading. The first chapters of Reed's book discuss the physical and emotional development of preteens and teenagers. Chapters 6 and 7 are annotated bibliographies of books which should appeal to most adolescents. They are arranged by topic and coded for reading interest levels. Chapters 8 and 9 discuss ways to share books with young people and include a discussion of the positive and negative effects of television on the reading of adolescents. The last section of the book includes book selection tips, sources for buying and borrowing books, and a bibliography of books and magazines about adolescents.

This book is a good introduction to the topic of books and the adolescent reader. Parents will find it both interesting and useful. It could also be used as a supplementary textbook in young adult literature courses. Both public and school libraries will find it a valuable addition to their collections. [R: BL, 15 Nov 88, p. 516]   Carol J. Veitch

1024. Spirt, Diana L. **Introducing Bookplots 3: A Book Talk Guide for Use with Readers Ages 8-12.** New York, R. R. Bowker, 1988. 352p. index. $39.95. LC 87-37513. ISBN 0-8352-2345-0.

Librarians, teachers, and other adults looking for books suitable for children in grades 3 to 6 (ages eight to twelve) will find many excellent suggestions in this collection by Diana Spirt. Like her previous books, *Introducing Books* (see *ARBA* 71, entry 136) and *Introducing More Books* (see *ARBA* 79, entry 235), this volume concentrates on quality books and groups them thematically under headings such as "Making Friends," "Developing Values," "Forming a View of the World," and "Understanding Social Problems." Books are arranged alphabetically by author within each section, but additional guidance is given by a "Reading Ladder" section in which titles are arranged by age level and difficulty. There are also author/title/illustrator and subject indexes. For each of the eighty-one featured books the author provides a lengthy plot summary. The pattern is to start with a paragraph about the author's previous works, describe the book cover and illustrations, and then move to a summary of the plot. Occasionally these summaries are confusing (see "The Boy and the Devil," p. 82), but most of them give a clear account of the book. A thematic analysis of each book and suggestions about how to discuss it as well as a listing of related materials are included. Since the books were published between 1979 and 1986, many of the titles will be new to librarians, especially those working in small libraries. This book could be used as a selection aid as well as a booktalk guide in many libraries. [R: RBB, 1 Sept 88, pp. 50, 52; SLJ, Sept 88, p. 126]   Adele M. Fasick

1025. Walker, Elinor, comp. **Book Bait: Detailed Notes on Adult Books Popular with Young People.** 4th ed. Chicago, American Library Association, 1988. 166p. index. $10.95pa. LC 88-987. ISBN 0-8389-0491-2.

The fourth edition of this excellent young adult readers' guide is based upon ninety-six selections made by a group of fifteen teenagers in grades 7 through 9. Books include works of fiction, biography, autobiography, and nonfiction. Each "main entry" contains a three-quarter page summary of the book, a paragraph highlighting its notable qualities, passages recommended for booktalking, and brief annotations of additional genre titles. The selections retain

some entries from the third edition, such as *Ann Frank: The Diary of a Young Girl*, but most titles, such as *Into the Mouth of the Cat: The Story of Lance Sijan, Hero of Vietnam*, are new recommendations. Spanning a spectrum of fifty subjects from adventure, civil rights, courage, danger, and fantasy to the generation gap, minorities, sex, suspense, and women's rights, *Book Bait* provides school and public librarians with a wealth of popular, appealing young adult books to booktalk and recommend to adolescents. The annotations are carefully written and related titles are well chosen. Objectionable language and sex scenes are also appropriately noted for specific titles. Also included are a subject index of main entries and a title index. This new edition should be considered an essential purchase for all public and secondary school libraries. [R: BL, 1 Oct 88, p. 259]   Kathleen W. Craver

Indexes

1026. Shields, Nancy E. **Index to Literary Criticism for Young Adults.** Metuchen, N.J., Scarecrow, 1988. 410p. $32.50. LC 87-37. ISBN 0-8108-2112-5.

Geared toward the novice researcher, this index lists four thousand plus authors who are covered in a small selection of standard library reference books. *British Writers* (see *ARBA* 88, entry 1199) and *Nineteenth-Century Literature Criticism* (see *ARBA* 86, entry 1086) are examples of the reference books chosen for availability and wealth of information.

Contemporary authors as well as those of the past are indexed alphabetically, with book, volume, and publisher information following in an abridged form, discarding awkward abbreviations and keys. Cross-references aid the researcher with pseudonyms and variant name spellings, but authors with multiple pen names have all books listed for each. In special cases subject headings and page numbers are provided.

It should be kept in mind that this book provides a starting place for research. The researcher's success will result from following the bibliographical map provided in the reference books indexed. [R: RBB, 15 Sept 88, pp. 138, 140; VOYA, Dec 88, p. 259; WLB, Sept 88, pp. 95-96]   Patricia M. Leach

1027. **Young Adult Book Review Index 1987.** Barbara Beach and Beverly Anne Baer, eds. Detroit, Gale, 1988. 451p. $85.00. ISBN 0-8103-4373-8; ISSN 0897-7402.

This new annual incorporates all the review citations for books and periodicals from *Book*

Review Index that at least one reviewer recommended for persons ages eleven through seventeen (16,800 review citations from about sixty-three hundred books and periodicals). It also contains citations for books if the targeted audiences overlap each end of the range, and books originally written for adults, but evaluated for young adults by one or more reviewers. *Book Review Index* now indexes more than 465 periodicals.

Each entry includes the author's or editor's name in boldface type; the title; the illustrator in parentheses; an abbreviation of the reviewing source with the date, volume number, and page on which the review appears; and a letter code identifying the type of book being reviewed, if appropriate (c = book for children ten and younger, a = adult, y = young adults eleven and older, r = reference work, and p = periodical).

Endsheets give a listing of the periodical abbreviations. A name and address list of publications indexed as well as illustrator and title indexes are included.

This is a good, single, concise source for needed information on young adult literature. Libraries already owning *Book Review Index* may not want to purchase this specialized title unless they have a separate department for young adults.   Kathleen J. Voigt

CLASSICAL LITERATURE

1028. Classical and Medieval Literature Criticism: Excerpts from Criticism of the Works of World Authors from Classical Antiquity through the Fourteenth Century.... Volume 1. Dennis Poupard, Jelena O. Krstovic, and Thomas Ligotti, eds. Detroit, Gale, 1988. 607p. illus. index. $80.00. ISBN 0-8103-2350-8; ISSN 0896-0011.

The Gale preface to this series admits that the ancient and medieval periods "provide the foundation of all subsequent literatures." C. S. Lewis, the great medieval critic, once remarked that the medieval period made the Renaissance look like a ripple in the ocean of literature, so vast was that former period's influence. Gale's *Classical and Medieval Literature Criticism* (*CMLC*) proves both these contentions.

The series will provide commentary and introduction to literature from antiquity to the fourteenth century. *CMLC* does not deviate from the standards set by very similar Gale works such as *Twentieth-Century Literature Criticism* (see entries 994-995), *Nineteenth-Century Literature Criticism* (see *ARBA* 86, entry 1086), and *Shakespearean Criticism* (see *ARBA* 85, entry 1119). Each volume will treat several major figures of the period, providing

pertinent biographical materials about the authors, when known, bibliographic and critical materials following, along with philological, linguistic, and historical facts. This first volume covers Homer, who is eponymous for the classical period, Apuleius for the age of Rome, *Beowulf* and *The Song of Roland* for medieval Europe, and Lady Murasaki for ancient Japan. With this volume, Gale will now be able to claim literary coverage from ancient times to the current Nobel Prize winner.

Since each volume will present an overview of major criticism on the authors, only four to six authors will be included in each five hundred-page tome of the series. While this promises more generous coverage, it also promises Gale another long-running series. It promises librarians a rich treasure-trove of satisfying answers, but it also promises to take up considerable shelfspace. In light of what the series will bring, however, shelfspace, while important, should not be considered an issue.

The index of *CMLC* will cumulate in the same manner as other Gale volumes. Each volume will also include the names of authors who appear in other Gale volumes of similar type, such as those mentioned above.

With such great authors as Abelard, the *Batrachomyomachia*, Norse Sagas, and Virgil scheduled, *CMLC* promises to be another Gale jewel in its already fabulous mine of works. [R: BR, Sept/Oct 88, p. 51; Choice, July/Aug 88, p. 1672; RBB, 15 May 88, pp. 1580-81; WLB, May 88, p. 108]   Mark Y. Herring

1029. Classical and Medieval Literature Criticism: Excerpts from Criticism of the Works of World Authors from Classical Antiquity through the Fourteenth Century.... Volume 2. Jelena O. Krstovic, ed. Detroit, Gale, 1988. 508p. illus. index. $85.00. ISBN 0-8103-2350-8; ISSN 0896-0011.

This second volume of *CMLC* adds to our understanding of that rich legacy left by the ancient period and the Middle Ages. Included in this volume are *Alf Layla wa-Layla*, better known as the *Arabian Nights; Hrafnkels saga Freysgoda* (*Hrafnkel's Saga*), and Li Po, also known as Li Bai or Li T'ai-po, the Chinese poet whom Ezra Pound made known to readers with his translation of *Cathay*. Li Po is a Romantic poet, often celebrating the love of love and wine, with the latter usually outdistancing the former. Li Po and his contemporary, Tu Fu, are generally considered the two greatest Chinese poets.

Rounding out this volume is the magnificent *Sir Gawain and the Green Knight*, and the works of Sophocles. *Sir Gawain* is that delightful tale about chivalry, courage, and the proclivity of the human psyche to fall victim to hypocrisy. The piece on Sophocles focuses on his major works and provides the reader with critics such as Aristotle, Adam Smith, Hegel, and Edmund Wilson.

The *CMLC* again regales the reader with excellent writing, even that not penned by the various "greats" that pepper the Gale volumes. Librarians who have begun this series will want to be sure to keep it up; librarians who have missed it should be chagrined, and begin collecting the series immediately.   Mark Y. Herring

DRAMA

1030. **Ottemiller's Index to Plays in Collections: An Author and Title Index to Plays Appearing in Collections Published between 1900 and 1985.** 7th ed. By Billie M. Connor and Helene G. Mochedlover. Metuchen, N.J., Scarecrow, 1988. 564p. index. (Index to Plays in Collections). $42.50. LC 87-34160. ISBN 0-8108-2081-1.

Why quibble with a standard reference work? Full-length plays published in collections get loving treatment and an ever expanding scope in this collection which updates the sixth edition by ten years (see *ARBA* 77, entry 996). Many series and multiple sets have been added as well as 250 new collection sources, including many Canadian, South African, Australian, and oriental works as well as emerging ethnic, feminist, and gay genres. The text retains its three main services: an author index, a title index, and a list of collections analyzed and the codes used in the other parts of the index. Great effort is made to account for any variances in title, author spellings, or names, plus those who may be listed as part of the creative process such as joint author, translator, adapter, or musical composer. Larger collections have been adding this compilation, and it is listed in the tenth edition of Eugene Sheehy's *Guide to Reference Books* (see *ARBA* 87, entry 17). Cooperative networks that may have overlooked this work may wish to reconsider because of the ability of this tool to point out sources for multiple copies, thus helping play reading groups and some classroom situations meet their needs. Even such rare attributions as *Arden of Feversham* appear under the Shakespeare entry as well as the more prolific and believable Anonymous. [R: RBB, 1 Sept 88, p. 52]
                                           Gerald R. Shields

1031. **Play Index 1983-1987: An Index to 3,964 Plays.** Juliette Yaakov and John Greenfieldt, eds. Bronx, N.Y., H. W. Wilson, 1988.

522p. $55.00. LC 64-1054. ISSN 0554-3037.

Indexing nearly four thousand plays published during the five-year period 1983-1987, this newest volume of the *Play Index* (like its predecessors) contains plays and plays in collections that have been written in or translated into English. Some plays published before 1983 but omitted from the previous volume of *Play Index* are now included. Listing every kind of dramatic script, from puppet performances to radio and television plays to classical drama, this series is broad in its appeal and usefulness.

All four sections provide valuable information. In part 1 entries give detailed facts about individual plays with alphabetical listings under author, title, and subject. Author entries give the name of the author, the title of the play, a brief descriptive note, the number of acts and scenes, the size of the cast, and the number of characters. In the case of single plays, the publisher, date, and pagination are given as well as the ISBN designation and the Library of Congress card number when available. Title and subject entries refer the user to the appropriate author entry. Symbols indicate plays for children at the elementary school level and the young adult level (grades seven through ten).

For those interested in producing, directing, or acting in a particular play, part 2 helps locate plays by number of players or readers. It is divided into six sections: all male cast, all female cast, mixed cast, puppet plays, unidentified cast, and variable cast. Part 3 ("List of Collections Indexed") and part 4 ("Directory of Publishers and Distributors") assist users in locating texts for specific dramas indexed.

For all those interested in contemporary drama—casual reader and serious scholar, audience member and performer, producer and director—all seven volumes of the *Play Index* series provide invaluable information.
                                           Colby H. Kullman

FICTION

General Works

1032. Beacham, Walton, and Suzanne Niemeyer, eds. **Popular World Fiction: 1900-Present.** Washington, D.C., Beacham Publishing, 1987. 4v. index. $249.00/set. LC 87-19545. ISBN 0-933833-08-3.

This four-volume work, originally issued in 1986, attempts to provide an alternate summary overview to English and American fiction that students have had available to them in a variety of other forms, such as *Contemporary Novelists* (see *ARBA* 83, entry 1141), *Twentieth Century Literary Criticism* (see *ARBA* 84, entries 1110-

1113), and Frank Magill's series of valuable publications. Beacham and Niemeyer have a very tough act to follow, and they do not succeed.

Over 170 authors, primarily American and British, are included in this collection. The only criterion for inclusion is that the author is "best-selling," a guideline very erratically observed. Saul Bellow is included, but John Updike and Kurt Vonnegut are not. Louis L'Amour is covered, but Danielle Steele is not. Victoria Holt is here, but not Georgette Heyer.

Each entry contains a brief publishing history, a summary of the author's "critical reception," and a brief analysis of each title listed (covering major themes, techniques, and adaptations of the work). Rounding out the entry are a list of related titles by the author and a summary of critical reviews. Each volume contains two identical appendices. The first lists all titles covered in a broad subject arrangement, described as "social issues and themes." The second appendix reverses this approach, listing titles and the "social issues" they cover. Volume 4 contains an additional index of titles by genre, and a cumulative author/title index.

The coverage of this work is so erratic, the quality of the essays so uneven, and the concept so much better addressed in many other works, that it is hard to find any justification for purchasing this publication. It is strongly *not* recommended. [R: RBB, 15 May 88, pp. 1586-87; WLB, Apr 88, p. 103]

                         Elizabeth Patterson

1033.   Drew, Bernard A. **Action Series and Sequels: A Bibliography of Espionage, Vigilante, and Soldier-of-Fortune Novels.** New York, Garland, 1988. 328p. illus. index. (Garland Bibliographies on Series and Sequels; Garland Reference Library of the Humanities, Vol. 842). $49.00. LC 88-11007. ISBN 0-8240-8396-2.

Preceded in the series by science fiction, mystery, and western genres, *Action Series and Sequels* deals with series featuring spies, rogues, criminals, cops, private eyes, villains, vigilantes, and other adventurers that had their beginnings primarily in the pulp and paperback thrillers. As author Drew points out, the action genre was generally regarded as having little literary merit; yet there have been thousands of readers who have enjoyed the likes of Nick Carter, Fu Manchu, Tugboat Annie, G-8 and his Battle Aces, the Shadow, and Doc Savage.

The 750 series entries are alphabetically arranged by the first major word in the series name or by the last name of the leading character. Each entry lists the series type, major characters, chronologically arranged books in

the series, movie or television appearances, and reissues in paperback. Appendix A consists of eighteen categories of action novels, including those mentioned above. Appendix B lists boys' and girls' books, movie and television tie-ins, heroines, and ethnic heroes. Included also are an alphabetical author index referring to the number(s) of the series; a title index, similarly referenced; and a bibliography that will clearly interest "action" fans. Public and academic libraries should find this attractively formatted – but fairly expensive – volume a useful addition.   Charles R. Andrews

1034.   Menendez, Albert J. **The Catholic Novel: An Annotated Bibliography.** New York, Garland, 1988. 323p. index. (Garland Reference Library of the Humanities, Vol. 690). $40.00. LC 88-1718. ISBN 0-8240-8534-5.

There seems to be no satisfactory definition of the term *Catholic novel* or agreement about when such a genre began. To establish some parameters and to differentiate the Catholic novel from other kinds of religious fiction, the compiler of this valuable reference tool has formulated his own working definition: "A Catholic novel is one which reflects the values, cultures and conflicts of the Roman Catholic faith and its community." Accordingly, he cites such classics as Manzoni's *The Betrothed,* Huysmans's *En Route,* Bloy's *The Woman Who Was Poor,* Greene's *The Power and the Glory*, and Waugh's *Brideshead Revisited*; but excludes the works of such authors as Flannery O'Connor. In O'Connor's case, she wrote mainly short stories and her novels draw essentially upon the fundamentalistic Protestant heritage of her native Georgia. Omitted also are so-called anti-Catholic novels (most of which are puerile, subliterary, and based on misrepresentation, ignorance, and bigotry). So-called anticlerical novels, which have had a long and honorable heritage in European literature, however, are included, as well as long works of fiction, however captious or hypercritical, written by lapsed Catholics, Protestants, and non-Christians, that reflect aspects of Catholicism. In all, 1,703 major works of fiction are cited, as well as 489 books and essays illustrative of the genre. The earliest titles date from the 1820s, when the Catholic novel first emerged. All nations and periods of time are included, as examination of the detailed subject index indicates. A title index allows for quick reference to the novels themselves, which are succinctly annotated in the body of this bibliography and listed under the names of their authors. An added *lagniape* is offered the reader: the author has appended his own nominations for the "100 Greatest Catholic

Novels." [R: Choice, Nov 88, p. 464; WLB, Sept 88, p. 92]   G. A. Cevasco

1035. Olderr, Steven. **Olderr's Fiction Index 1987.** Chicago, St. James Press, 1988. 331p. $50.00. ISBN 0-912289-85-6.

The first of a proposed annual publication, this printed computer database indexes 1,739 adult fiction titles (hardbound or paperback) published in 1987. Olderr obtained data from reviews printed in *Booklist, Library Journal,* and *Publishers Weekly.* A few titles reviewed in *School Library Journal* are indexed also. Each work has a main entry by author. Similar to a main entry catalog, this listing includes author, U.S. and U.K. title, imprint (both U.K. and U.S. if different), up to nine topical headings, and review sources. Brief entries (author and title only) are included for second authors, series titles, and U.S. and/or U.K. titles.

Integrated into the author/title arrangement are the topical headings given to each title. A title may appear in up to nine different subject categories assigned by the *Index*'s author as the reviews of the book were read. Topical headings are much more extensive than Library of Congress or Sears subjects that might be assigned to the work. Such topics as the timespan of the novel, geographical place, name of principal character, and theme of the book are included. The index thus becomes a thorough topical guide to the year's output. In addition, the tone of the review has been judged by the author and converted to a starred rating system similar to a restaurant guide.

The in-depth indexing of fiction reviews is the major strength of the work, and as such, it is an excellent tool for selection and analysis of the year's output in fiction. However, the index is extremely difficult to read. Output on a laser printer in a three-column format, the author, title, and topical entries are very difficult to differentiate. Had the authors spent more time manipulating the data into a more traditional bibliographic format, the work would have been much easier to use. Hopefully, later editions will take care of this problem.

For those libraries who want an in-depth fiction index to adult fiction, this work is a satisfactory, if difficult-to-use source.

David V. Loertscher

Crime and Mystery

1036. Barnes, Melvyn. **Murder in Print: A Guide to Two Centuries of Crime Fiction.** London, Barn Owl Books; distr., Peoria, Ill., Spoon River Press, c1986, 1987. 244p. index. $22.00. ISBN 0-9509057-4-7.

Barnes's earlier work in this field was *Best Detective Fiction* (see *ARBA* 76, entry 1202), but *Murder in Print* is more extensive than its predecessor and is not just a revised edition. In prose chapters ordered roughly chronologically, Barnes examines nearly five hundred books by 260 writers, ranging from William Godwin's *Things As They Are, or, The Adventures of Caleb Williams* to Martin Cruz Smith's *Gorky Park.*

As is often the case with such lists, it is made up of two types of books: the "milestones," important works in the development of mystery fiction, which have held their historical worth over the years; and those books which the author feels are, for one reason or another, interesting. Those in the latter category have usually been exceptionally well written, or have introduced some new technique or style, or have better-than-usual plots or characterization; for the mystery fan, this is the heart of the book because here are found the gems and curiosities that may have been overlooked. "Thrillers" and gothics have generally not been included.

For each book is given the first date(s) of British and American publication, alternate titles, and author's real name and pseudonym. Full bibliographical details are not given, nor is any attempt made at full coverage of all titles in the genre. This is appropriate for this "guide" because it really is a history of the genre more than anything else.

Both beginning and experienced readers of mystery fiction will find much to delight and inform them in *Murder in Print.* Barnes's style is casual, his information accurate, and his judgments sound.   Philip R. Rider

1037. Cook, Michael L., and Stephen T. Miller. **Mystery, Detective, and Espionage Fiction: A Checklist of Fiction in U.S. Pulp Magazines, 1915-1974.** New York, Garland, 1988. 2v. index. (Fiction in the Pulp Magazines, Vol. 1; Garland Reference Library of the Humanities, Vol. 838). $100.00/set. LC 88-7190. ISBN 0-8240-7539-0.

Few types of literary works are as difficult to identify bibliographically as the old-time pulp magazines. Published on wood pulp paper, issues have now become brittle and fragile with age, and the relatively few copies in existence are in private collections and libraries.

The authors of *Mystery, Detective, and Espionage Fiction* have fulfilled the monumental task of identifying by title, date, volume, and issue the contents of pulp magazines published in these three categories. In the first section of their two-volume bibliography, magazines are listed alphabetically by title, with each known issue identified by volume and issue number. Authors and titles of individual stories in each issue are also listed. An appendix in volume 1 alphabetically lists periodical titles and includes a summary of publication data, while titles are organized chronologically in the section "Magazine Chronological Commencement Dates." Volume 2 is a comprehensive author index.

Cook and Miller are longtime devotees of pulp magazines and crime fiction; indeed, Cook has published a half-dozen books in this field, including *Monthly Murders* (see *ARBA 83*, entry 1158) and *Mystery, Detective, and Espionage Magazines* (see *ARBA 85*, entry 1038).

Although *Mystery, Detective, and Espionage Fiction* is not an essential purchase for most libraries, it belongs in institutions that actively collect pulp magazines. One caveat, however: the bibliography is reproduced directly from original computer-typed pages, with each page reduced to fit Garland's format. The resulting minuscule type size makes for difficult reading, particularly since pages are single spaced. [R: WLB, Dec 88, p. 120]   Jack Bales

1038. Hubin, Allen J. **1981-1985 Supplement to Crime Fiction 1749-1980.** New York, Garland, 1988. 260p. (Garland Reference Library of the Humanities, Vol. 766). $32.00. LC 87-23637. ISBN 0-8240-7596-X.

This is a supplement to Hubin's original comprehensive bibliography of mystery and detective fiction (see *ARBA 85*, entry 1040). The supplement has the same design, layout, and selection criteria as the original; but in addition, it now includes citations to films based on crime fiction, cited in the original bibliography or in the supplement.

The supplement adds 6,900 new book titles, gives additional information on 4,300 previously cited titles, identifies 440 new series, and includes 3,200 films. Arranged by author, the supplement includes indexes to titles, settings, series, movie titles, screenwriters, and directors. A well-organized and useful bibliography for both the academic scholar and the mystery fan, it allows users to quickly search for another book by the same author, or for another mystery set in a particular place such as the art world, or for another book about the same series character, or even for all the movies based on a particular book.

Like the original, the supplement is printed on acid free paper and sturdily bound in the same color cover and with the same size paper. There is no comparable work nor any other source that begins to approach the comprehensive scope and scholarly attention to detail of Hubin's bibliography. Its only drawback is its

small type size, but this is made up for, in part, by large, clear headings on every page. Highly recommended.   Dennis Dillon

1039. Keating, H. R. F. **Crime & Mystery: The 100 Best Books.** New York, Carroll & Graf, 1987. 219p. index. $15.95. LC 87-17377. ISBN 0-88184-345-8.

In the introduction to this delightful book, the author writes that its title should more properly be: "One Hundred Very Good Crime and Mystery Books, Taking into Account That No Author Should Be Represented by More Than Three Titles (So As to Be Fair to Others) and Allowing for a Little Personal Idiosyncracy in Naming One or Two Whom the Majority of Other Commentators Might Not Have Chosen Very Readily." Though less catchy, that title is more apt and says much about both the style and content of the book.

Keating, himself a fine mystery writer, writes two-page critiques of the one hundred best ("simply the books I have most enjoyed") mysteries ranging from Poe to P. D. James. The arrangement is chronological, and the book functions in part as a history of the genre. Readers will find many favorites here: Doyle, Christie, Sayers, Stout, Chandler, Queen, Rendell, Wambaugh, etc. But the "Little Personal Idiosyncracy" also admits some that are less familiar: Ethel Lina White, John Franklin Bardin, Guy Cullingford, and others. Part of the attraction of the book lies in the discovery of these relatively obscure authors.

But it is not the list itself that gives this book its appeal (there have been other such lists). The charm of the book is in Keating's graceful and frequently humorous style. Each essay is self-contained, and Keating makes no attempt to approach each novel in the same way. But whether his subject is publishing history, biography, historical setting, or literary criticism, Keating is a joy to read. Who else would compare John D. MacDonald to Charles Dickens? This is not a book in which to look up information; it is a book to *read*.

Philip R. Rider

Gothic

1040. Fisher, Benjamin Franklin, IV. **The Gothic's Gothic: Study Aids to the Tradition of the Tale of Terror.** New York, Garland, 1988. 485p. index. (Garland Reference Library of the Humanities, Vol. 567). $67.00. LC 88-18059. ISBN 0-8240-8784-4.

More than twenty-six hundred entries appear in this annotated bibliography of materials related to Gothicism in British and American literature. Although citations usually are to secondary materials, primary sources which allude to Gothicism also have been listed. Coverage is intended to fill the gaps in standard sources and extends from the end of the eighteenth century to 1979, the publication date of the first annual bibliography of Gothic materials in the journal, *Gothic*. The author has included many formats, such as books, dissertations, articles, and even the graphic arts. Therefore, the coverage is quite broad and in general is quite helpful. Some entries, however, such as citations to *Playboy* cartoons, are both unexpected and of questionable research value. There are two sections to the bibliography. The first, and largest part, is devoted to listings of the authors treated, while the shorter section treats broad topics related to Gothicism. The arrangement of the author section is a general chronological order according to the time when an author's work first began attracting attention, rather than by birth date of the author. There is no apparent order to the sequence of part 2, so the table of contents must be consulted. Three indexes (author/artist/subject, title, critic) provide access to the citations, but coverage does not seem to be consistent. Not all personal names mentioned in the annotations can be found in the index, but there is no clear reason given as to why some were indexed and others were excluded. The chronological listing of the authors does give the user some idea of the development of Gothicism, but it makes the work more difficult to use. Overall, this bibliography will be helpful to students and researchers, but its effectiveness is diminished by the problems of arrangement and indexing.

Barbara E. Kemp

1041. Frank, Frederick S. **Gothic Fiction: A Master List of Twentieth Century Criticism and Research.** Westport, Conn., Meckler, 1988. 193p. index. (Meckler's Bibliographies on Science Fiction, Fantasy, and Horror, 3). $34.95. LC 87-24705. ISBN 0-88736-218-4.

This bibliography of serious works on Gothic fiction attempts to be more comprehensive and international in scope than any bibliography on this topic to date. The work is divided into clearly defined chapters, beginning with English Gothic fiction. Arrangement is by author within each segment and all citations are numbered consecutively. Works include doctoral dissertations and are not limited to the English language. The first chapter covers primary and secondary bibliographic and other reference works. The second deals with literary histories, theories, and genre studies. Then follow the individual author studies and listings

of works in special subject areas. Works dealing with American Gothic fiction follow the same pattern. There are also chapters on the French and German Gothic novels and one dealing with other countries. Fourteen British and ten American Gothic writers receive special segments of the bibliography.

The chapter on individual American authors also contains a segment on later American Gothic writers (1850-1985). This segment includes Faulkner, Flannery O'Connor, and Stephen King. Yet another chapter lists works on special Gothic themes such as the evil eye, science fiction Gothic, and writing the Gothic novel. Three additional chapters include listings of studies on the Wandering Jew and the "double figure," werewolfery and vampirism, and the Gothic film. Two indexes are provided: critics and authors/artists. Each index cites the number of the citation rather than a page number.

This is a thorough treatment of the subject and does fill a need in the in-depth study of the role and influence of the Gothic novel. [R: Choice, July/Aug 88, pp. 1674-75]

Susan Ebershoff-Coles

Science Fiction, Fantasy, and Horror

1042. Barron, Neil, ed. **Anatomy of Wonder: A Critical Guide to Science Fiction.** 3d ed. New York, R. R. Bowker, 1987. 874p. index. $39.95. LC 87-9305. ISBN 0-8352-2312-4.

Aptly titled, this book provides an anatomy of its subject, establishing the framework that interconnects the myriad aspects of science fiction from early to modern times. The third edition, again edited by Neil Barron, expands coverage though its scope remains essentially the same as the first and second editions (see *ARBA* 77, entry 1173 and *ARBA* 82, entry 1300), which had in turn expanded articles that Barron first published in *Choice* in January 1970 and September 1973.

Statistically, the third edition annotates and evaluates twenty-six hundred titles organized in sixteen bibliographic essays under three main sections: English-language science fiction, foreign-language science fiction, and research aids. Articles in the first two sections, written by established names such as Thomas Clareson, Joe De Bolt, and Brian Stableford, trace the emergence of science fiction, examine its development from 1918 to 1986, and discuss science fiction for children and young adults and in thirteen countries besides the United States and Great Britain. With the exception of an essay on teaching materials by Muriel Becker, the ten chapters in the research aids section are by Barron and Hal Hall and cover general reference works; history and criticism; biographical studies; television, film, and illustration; magazines; and notable library and private collections, and suggest a core collection checklist. Most of the essays are followed by annotated bibliographies, with item numbers that serve as cross-references to themes and items discussed elsewhere. There are also author, subject, and title indexes.

This reviewer has often used the various editions of *Anatomy of Wonder*, but in examining it for review discovered new information and fresh insights into interrelationships. If forced to select a reference work in science fiction/fantasy to take to the proverbial desert island, *Anatomy of Wonder* would be first choice. Barron received the Pilgrim Award in 1982 for his overall contributions to scholarship in the field. No *Wonder*. [R: JOYS, Spring 88, p. 368; RBB, 1 May 88, p. 1482; VOYA, June 88, p. 105]   Mary Jo Walker

1043. Jaffery, Sheldon. **Future and Fantastic Worlds: A Bibliographical Retrospective of DAW Books (1972-1987).** Mercer Island, Wash., Starmont House, 1987. 297p. index. (Starmont Reference Guide, No. 4). $29.95; $19.95pa. LC 87-9901. ISBN 1-55742-003-3; 1-55742-002-5pa.

This is a "bibliographical retrospective" of DAW books published between 1972 and 1987. If you do not know what a DAW book is, this retrospective will probably be of minimal interest and utility. According to Jaffery, a DAW book is "4¼" wide and 7" long, and somewhere around ½" to ¾" thick, depending on the book, and, for a number of years, it was mostly yellow (especially on the spine), which makes it pretty distinctive when you're searching the stacks of used paperback stores to complete your collection" (p. x). More specifically, DAW books are paperback science fiction/fantasy novels or collections of short stories published by the firm founded by Donald A. Wollheim.

The author's short introduction includes information regarding the edition/printing and numbering of DAW books buried in a morass of informal comments about the genre in general and Wollheim in particular. The main section of the work is a numerical listing (by collector's number) of DAW books. Each entry includes author, title, publishing history (when appropriate), cover artist, number of pages, original price, and a short summary of the novel's plot (which, in most cases, is taken from back cover blurbs). In some instances, a brief

bibliographer's note is added providing additional information about a particular title. There are author/title, artist/title, and title indexes, which makes this retrospective easy to use.

The author's presentation is informal to the point of distraction. While the "irreverent and amusing" observations are somewhat appropriate to a research work on genre literature, when carried to an extreme they become the unwarranted focus of attention. This reference work will be of limited interest to fans of the genre and of special interest to collectors of DAW books.

       Larry G. Chrisman

1044. **Science Fiction and Fantasy Research Index. Volume 7.** Hal W. Hall and Jan Swanbeck, comps. San Bernardino, Calif., Borgo Press, 1987. 197p. $24.95. ISBN 0-8095-6103-3.

Users familiar with Hall's *Science Fiction and Fantasy Reference Index, 1878-1985* (see *ARBA* 88, entry 1152) and his earlier *Science Fiction Book Review Indexes* (1923-1973; 1974-1979; 1980-1984 – for the first and third, respectively, see *ARBA* 76, entry 1206 and *ARBA* 87, entry 1121) will welcome this volume as the first supplement to the *SFFRI, 1878-1985*.

As stated in the introduction, the *SFFRI*, with its wide coverage of books, chapters from books, and articles from periodicals and newspapers, may be viewed as a combination of the *Readers' Guide* and the *Essay and General Literature Index*. According to Hall, material included here has not appeared in his earlier publications. The bulk of the entries appear to be from 1986. The small type is computer-generated; characters are not fully formed, but the book is easily readable. Right margins are not justified.

The volume is divided into two sections. The first is an alphabetically arranged list of author entries, followed by a subject index which Hall refers to as the "heart" of the volume. Among its hundreds of subject headings one will find authors (Bradbury, Sturgeon, Vonnegut), films (*Back to the Future, Legend, Mad Max*), and various subjects (space travel, special effects, teaching science fiction). Citations are printed in full each time they appear.

Libraries with strong science fiction holdings and serious researchers will doubtless want this reasonably priced index, even with the knowledge that another high-priced, five-year cumulation will be forthcoming.

       Charles R. Andrews

Short Stories

1045. Hooper, Brad. Short Story Writers and Their Works: A Guide to the Best. Chicago, American Library Association, 1988. 60p. index. $14.95pa. LC 88-10393. ISBN 0-8389-0485-8.

This "readers' advisory tool" for short story lovers is a disappointment. A fifty-seven-page booklet, this "guide to the best" is highly personal in its selections, does not cite enough examples of each author's works, and is altogether incomplete. The first chapter, "Masters of the Past," includes sixty-one authors, lumping all deceased writers together, so that Malamud, who died in 1986, is with Hawthorne, who died in 1864. "Contemporary Masters" covers only twenty-six authors. Although these are all well selected, the gaps are enormous. For example, of the forty writers selected for the prestigious 1987 O. Henry Prize short story collection or the 1987 Best American Short Stories anthology, only five were listed in the Hooper guide. Even thinner are the "Genre Stories" chapter, which includes ten authors, and the "Anthologies" chapter, which suggests only two of the many fine collections available annually.

Because the public—and the publishers—have "rediscovered" the short story, a guide to short story writers would be extremely useful to libraries. This book, however, is not the one we have been waiting for.   Rhea Joyce Rubin

1046. Short Story Criticism: Excerpts from Criticism of the Works of Short Fiction Writers. [Volume 1]. Laurie Lanzen Harris and Sheila Fitzgerald, eds. Detroit, Gale, 1988. 575p. illus. index. $70.00. ISBN 0-8103-2550-0; ISSN 0895-9439.

Limited to literary criticism of short fiction, this is the first volume of a projected series dedicated to surveying such critical response to major authors. The fourteen writers in this volume include Edgar Allan Poe and Guy de Maupassant, creators of the modern short story. Other entries survey criticism of the short stories of Sherwood Anderson, J. G. Ballard, John Cheever, G. K. Chesterton, William Faulkner, Mary Wilkins Freeman, Ernest Hemingway, Herman Melville, Flannery O'Connor, James Thurber, Jean Toomer, and Eudora Welty.

Each entry provides biographical information and a critical introduction followed by a list of that author's principal works. Criticism is presented chronologically to give the researcher a historical overview. An appendix lists all sources used in the volume, followed by cumulative author and title indexes for the complete Gale Literary Criticism series (GLC).

Although, as the editors point out, some essays have appeared in previous volumes of the GLC, most of the material is new to this series, which presents a more comprehensive treatment of each author than GLC format permits. If the projected volumes do appear, this series will be an excellent resource for students, researchers, and anyone else interested in the shorter works of major writers. [R: BR, Sept/Oct 88, p. 52; Choice, July/Aug 88, p. 1678; RBB, 15 May 88, pp. 1587-88; WLB, May 88, p. 108]
                              Renee B. Horowitz

POETRY

1047. Poetry Index Annual 1987: A Title, Author, First Line and Subject Index to Poetry in Anthologies. By the Editorial Board, Roth Publishing, Inc. Great Neck, N.Y., Roth Publishing, 1988. 328p. $54.00. ISBN 0-89609-269-0; ISSN 0736-3966.

With a nod of recognition to such standard works as *Granger's Index to Poetry*, the editorial board of *Poetry Index Annual* claims its work to be "the first and only work to systematically index *all* poetry anthologies as they are published." The editors add: "Being cumulative, each annual edition is a permanent volume which complements and supplements preceding issues; no superseding issues will be published. Taken together, the annual editions will form an ongoing and comprehensive title, author, and subject index to anthologized verse."

A noble aim, to be sure, but one that raises a number of questions, viz: *All* poetry anthologies? In all languages? In all countries? Hardly. While international in scope (the present volume includes Bulgarian, Indian, Sicilian, and Welsh poetry, among others), fifty-five anthologies, the number covered in this volume, would not appear to be exhaustive. This index does appear to make a good stab at *English-language* poetry anthologies, wherever they may be published.

Another question derives from the meaning of the word *cumulative*. While each volume complements and supplements previous ones, they are cumulative only in the sense that taken in the aggregate, they present a "cumulative" index. However, each volume is discrete and is not cumulative in the usual sense of that word. A final question has to do with the subject headings, which appear in italics throughout each index. Librarians who use catalogs and indexes like to know the authority list from which such a list is constructed, and no such indication is given here.

With these caveats and concerns, one must admit that this volume will complement, not only previous volumes in the series, but the "standard" poetry indexes as well. It is more international in scope and, though not mentioned in the title, it even indexes foreign-language poems by translator. First-line entries, which did not appear in some early volumes, have been restored. For those libraries needing increased access to poetry published in anthologies, this series, even with its imperfections, is certainly worthy of serious consideration.

Edwin S. Gleaves

NATIONAL LITERATURE

American Literature

GENERAL WORKS

Bibliographies

1048. Bain, Robert, and Joseph M. Flora, eds. **Fifty Southern Writers before 1900: A Bio-Bibliographical Sourcebook.** Westport, Conn., Greenwood Press, 1987. 601p. index. $75.00. LC 86-31832. ISBN 0-313-24518-5.

A companion volume to *Fifty Southern Writers after 1900* (see entry 1049), *Fifty Southern Writers before 1900* takes as its province "the work of half a hundred Southerners whose careers ended before 1900 or thereabouts, whose works often appear in anthologies of Southern and American writing, and whose books figure prominently in the history of Southern letters." Beginning with Captain John Smith and ending with Grace King and Charles W. Chestnut (who both died in 1932), this volume confronts historical events from 1607 to 1900, including the first settlements, the introduction of slavery, the revolutionary war, the adoption of the Constitution, the Southern expansion across the mountains and into the Old Southwest, the growing controversy over slavery and secession, the devastating War between the States and equally devastating Reconstruction, and the rocky road to reunion. The range of writers covered includes major authors (William Byrd, Thomas Jefferson, Edgar Allan Poe, Mark Twain, and Kate Chopin, to mention a few) as well as lesser-known Southern authors (such as Robert Beverley, William Alexander Caruthers, and Augusta Jane Evans Wilson).

Focusing mostly on those nineteenth-century authors whose works give a sense of the long background behind the Southern renascence, this volume offers students and teachers an overview of the writers' lives and works. Each essay is divided into five sections: a biographical sketch, a discussion of the author's major themes, an assessment of the scholarship

on each writer, a chronological list of the author's works, and a bibliography of selected criticism. A comprehensive index provides easy access to authors and their works as well as to major themes, literary movements, and historical events.

Written by knowledgeable scholars, the essays and bibliographies in this volume (and its companion) are so carefully researched and aptly detailed that they are of value to the specialist in Southern studies as well as the student looking for useful introductory materials about a specific author or work.

Colby H. Kullman

1049. Flora, Joseph M., and Robert Bain, eds. **Fifty Southern Writers after 1900: A Bio-Bibliographical Sourcebook.** Westport, Conn., Greenwood Press, 1987. 628p. index. $75.00. LC 86-19460. ISBN 0-313-24519-3.

The editors have provided an outstanding biographical, bibliographical, and critical sourcebook for information about the Southern renascence writers who published between 1919 and mid-century (including such diverse writers as Thomas Wolfe, Richard Wright, Ellen Glasgow, Alan Tate, and Eudora Welty) as well as for the new generation of Southern writers who have published within the last three decades (Harry Crews, Doris Betts, Ernest Gaines, Reynolds Price, and Ann Tyler).

Written by a knowledgeable scholar, each article contains five parts: a biographical sketch, a discussion of the author's major themes, an assessment of the scholarship, a chronological list of the author's works, and a bibliography of selected criticism. The editors wisely recommend that readers working with this bio-bibliography (and its companion volume *Fifty Southern Writers before 1900*, see entry 1048) complement their study by also reading *The History of Southern Literature*, edited by Louis D. Rubin, Jr. (Louisiana State University Press, 1985).

The eight-page introductory essay provides an excellent condensed overview of Southern literature of the twentieth century by discussing Southern writing before and after the turn of the century; by presenting those authors who first questioned the "moonlight and magnolias" genteel tradition; and by explaining the significance of the Fugitive Era, the Agrarians, and black Southern writers as well as the importance of individual authors (James Weldon Johnson, Thomas Wolfe, Richard Wright, William Faulkner, and Ellen Glasgow).

Detailed information about these and many other twentieth-century Southern writers who have achieved regional and national reputations may be found in the first-rate essays that follow this introductory history. This reference book is highly recommended for community as well as university libraries.   Colby H. Kullman

1050. Foster, M. Marie Booth, comp. **Southern Black Creative Writers, 1829-1953: Biobibliographies.** Westport, Conn., Greenwood Press, 1988. 113p. (Bibliographies and Indexes in Afro-American and African Studies, No. 22). $29.95. LC 88-5595. ISBN 0-313-26207-1.

This publication contains bio-bibliographical information on nearly two hundred Southern black writers. While the names one expects to see—Arna Bontemps, Frank Yerby, Frances Harper, W. E. B. DuBois—are included, other writers who have not been so felicitously dealt with by time—Alice Dunbar-Nelson and Mary Weston Ford come to mind—also appear. The volume opens with an essay on the historical periods covered: 1829-1865, Reconstruction to 1912, 1913-1928, and "Oppressed, Depressed, Suppressed, but Determined 1829-1953" (this latter turns out to be a typographical error for 1929-1953, *cf.* pp. xiv and 81). Following this essay are the entries themselves. It is sometimes difficult to read this section because the authors' names appear in a typeface identical to that of the entry itself, set apart only by blank lines above and below. Moreover, the information contained in the entries seems sometimes to have been brought over wholesale from another source without much editorial adjustment. Compare, for example, Abram Hill's entry in *Southern Black Creative Writers* (*SBCW*) (p. 36) with the one in Edward Mapp's *Directory of Blacks in the Performing Arts* (see *ARBA* 79, entry 1016), a directory cited as a source for *SBCW* (p. 109). *SBCW* states that Hill earned his bachelor's degree in 1937 from Lincoln University. To my certain knowledge, there are Lincoln universities in Tennessee, Missouri, and Pennsylvania—but to my consternation, *SBCW* does not distinguish between them. The fact that Mapp does not include the state name is really no excuse for Foster. The criterion for inclusion in *SBCW* is birth date, birth place, and race. Thomas Ward, for example, who was born in 1908 in Louisiana, is included (p. 67), although he left the South at thirteen, and all of his creative life seems to have been spent in the North.

In the back of the volume are author listings sorted by date and state. Authors can be listed more than once here. W. E. B. DuBois, for example, appears under 1866-1912 (p. 79) as well as under 1913-1928 (p. 80).

This work's editorial control is truly insufficient. One can only hope that this material will be handled more seriously in the future.   Judith M. Brugger

Biographies

1051. Harris, Trudier, and Thadious M. Davis, eds. **Afro-American Writers, 1940-1955.** Detroit, Gale, 1988. 389p. illus. bibliog. index. (Dictionary of Literary Biography, Vol. 76). $95.00. LC 88-21423. ISBN 0-8103-4554-4.

This "sixth and final volume in [the DLB] series devoted exclusively to Afro-American writers" (p. xi) covers twenty-six novelists, poets, playwrights, biographers, screenwriters, and essayists who published significant works between 1940 and 1955. Other volumes in the subseries cover fiction writers after 1955 (see *ARBA* 85, entry 1056), dramatists and prose writers after 1955 (see *ARBA* 86, entry 1132), poets after 1955 (see *ARBA* 86, entry 1155), writers before the Harlem Renaissance (see *ARBA* 87, entry 1069), and writers from the Harlem Renaissance to 1940 (see *ARBA* 88, entry 1158). The essays in this volume begin with a list of works by each writer followed by discussions (punctuated with photographs) of each writer's life and works, and conclude with selected references to critical works (not linked to the text) and locations of papers. Essay length varies for each author based on his or her renown (e.g., three pages for William Blackwell Branch, twenty-three for Richard Wright). References are often insufficient (e.g., two references for J. Saunders Redding, three for Melvin Tolson, four for Margaret Walker), although the entry for Ralph Ellison has eighty-one references. The essays are well written, some critical, some simply descriptive, by little-known scholars (although Robert Farnsworth composed the Tolson entry), and all significant authors of the period are covered (e.g., Gwendolyn Brooks, Robert Hayden, Chester Himes, Ann Petry). Three additional essays describe the Hatch-Billops Collection, the Moorland-Spingarn Research Center, and the Schomburg Center. A superfluous reprint of the readily available December 1950 issue of *Phylon* expands the text by sixty-two pages, space that could have been better used for an analytical index. The work concludes with a forty-six-item general bibliography and the usual DLB cumulative index.   Robert Aken

Chronologies

1052. Rood, Karen L., ed. **American Literary Almanac: From 1608 to the Present: An Original Compendium of Facts and Anecdotes about Literary Life in the United States of**

America. New York, Facts on File, 1988. 427p. illus. bibliog. index. $29.95. LC 88-3689. ISBN 0-8160-1245-8.

In a style that evokes the miscellany offered by early American almanacs, the present work presents itself as a reference work in narrative form. Its nineteen chapters, written by several contributors, approach American literary history thematically, emphasizing biography and anecdote. An introductory history of American almanacs (by "Benjamin Franklin V") sets the tone. Succeeding chapters survey milestones in American literary culture; list literary pseudonyms; relate, in a gossipy manner, "politics, sex, and other vices in the lives of American writers"; and quote from tombstones and last words. The almanac's traditionally biographical emphasis ignores postmodern concerns (one will search in vain for any mention of, for instance, the Yale critics). Yet chapters such as "Schooldays," which lists colleges and discusses the authors who attended each, and "Writers Who Went to War and Wrote about It," which recounts the experiences of individual writers, offer valid and valuable approaches to the topics at hand. The almanac includes a basic bibliography, ample black-and-white photographs, and a detailed index that allows a reader to locate the facts buried within the anecdotes. [R: BR, Nov/Dec 88, p. 45; Choice, Nov 88, pp. 484-85]

William S. Brockman

Handbooks

1053. Colonization to the American Renaissance, 1640-1865. Detroit, Gale, 1988. 415p. illus. index. (Concise Dictionary of American Literary Biography). $60.00. LC 88-2328. ISBN 0-8103-1819-9.

This work is the second volume in the six-volume Concise Dictionary of American Literary Biography (CDALB) series aimed at high schools, junior colleges, and smaller libraries that do not need or cannot afford the forty-six volumes in American literature alone now in the valued Dictionary of Literary Biography (DLB).

This volume contains substantial biocritical essays with bibliographies on the twenty-three American authors from the colonial through the Romantic periods determined by a large survey to be most important to a precollege audience: Bradstreet, Brown, Bryant, Cooper, Douglas, Emerson, Franklin, Fuller, Garrison, Hawthorne, Holmes, Irving, Jefferson, Longfellow, Lowell, Mather, Melville, Paine, Poe, Thoreau, Wheatley, Whitman, Whittier. (Not much call for Taylor and Edwards in these circles?)

The entries are taken without abridgment from the parent DLB, but the bibliographies have been updated to include recent criticism and works especially useful to precollege students. The most important addition, however, is a "contextual diagram"—quite handy for reviewing, seeing connections, or for generating research projects—that lists key topics in six areas for each author: places, influences and relationships, literary movements and forms, major themes, cultural and artistic influences, social and economic influences.

Just as the parent DLB has, CDALB will quickly become a standard reference work for its audience.   Edward J. Gallagher

1054. Dictionary of Literary Biography Documentary Series: An Illustrated Chronicle. Volume Five: American Transcendentalists. Joel Myerson, ed. Detroit, Gale, 1988. 437p. illus. bibliog. index. $95.00. LC 82-1105. ISBN 0-8103-2639-6.

Ralph Waldo Emerson and Henry Thoreau are perhaps the only American transcendentalists whose names are recognized by most educated people today, but many other individual thinkers influenced and were influenced by these two luminaries. Volume 5 of the *DLB Documentary Series* reprints some of the less known writings of this group: literary criticism by Margaret Fuller and Orestes A. Brownson; philosophical essays by James Freeman Clarke and Theodore Parker; and personal reminiscences by Nathaniel Hawthorne, Louisa May Alcott, and Henry Thoreau. Two short sections of the book are devoted to the experimental communities associated with this movement, Brook Farm and Fruitlands. An essay on transcendentalism by Alexander Kern discusses the ideas and writings of more than thirty individuals who contributed to the introduction and development of the transcendentalist movement in America. A wide selection of illustrations of people, places, and texts break up the solid, double-column pages, while a list of further readings and a cumulative index to the series round out the volume. Although the format of the volume is rather forbidding for casual browsing, this book provides students with many important texts of the period and will be a useful addition to both public and university library collections.   Adele M. Fasick

1055. Fried, Lewis, ed. Handbook of American-Jewish Literature: An Analytical Guide to Topics, Themes, and Sources. Westport, Conn., Greenwood Press, 1988. 539p. bibliog. index. $65.00. LC 87-292. ISBN 0-313-24593-2.

One can agree with Lewis Fried, the editor of this collection of essays, that "American-Jewish literature has a commanding strength in expressing the interior, communitarian, and yet public nature of Jewish life" (p. 11). The emphasis of this publication is placed on the Jewish literary culture created by Eastern European Jewish immigrants and their descendants covering American Jewish letters including Jewish American fiction, drama, poetry, literary criticism, autobiography, and other topics. Most contributors to this handbook are affiliated with American and other universities or various Jewish organizations. It is interesting to note that one essay of this publication is devoted to German Jewish and American Jewish literature (Gershon Shaked, pp. 391-415), and another to "Eastern Europe in American-Jewish Writing," by Asher Z. Milbauer (pp. 357-90). However, the last topic covers mainly Russia, and the author did not provide a clear definition of "Eastern Europe," which in this case, would be necessary and appropriate. It would be interesting to find in this handbook separate essays on American Jewish writing pertaining to Poland, Ukraine, Hungary, Rumania, Lithuania, and other East European countries with large Jewish populations prior to World War II. Probably in the next revised edition Fried will consider these important topics in the context of the development of Jewish literature in the United States.

The handbook has strong bibliographical features. Each essay includes a bibliography and one section is devoted to selected reference materials and resources. From the reference point of view, this is an important feature of this collection of articles. In general, the eighteen essays presented in this volume provide an in-depth interpretation of the spirit and ideological basis of American Jewish literature and literary criticism. Probably an additional essay on reference sources pertaining to Jewish literary culture would enhance the scope of this noted publication. Lewis Fried should be congratulated for a well-executed project. [R: LJ, 15 Mar 88, p. 51]

Lubomyr R. Wynar

1056. Holte, James Craig. **The Ethnic I: A Sourcebook for Ethnic-American Autobiography.** Westport, Conn., Greenwood Press, 1988. 210p. index. $39.95. LC 87-23650. ISBN 0-313-24463-4.

Descriptive studies and criticisms of major autobiographical works by twenty-nine ethnic American writers comprise the contents of this sourcebook. The work begins with a brief essay, "Introduction: Personal Voices from the New World," in which Holte discusses the particular conventions of the autobiography as a literary genre, emphasizing its ability to combine both history and literature as well as the objectivity of

facts and the subjectivity of the perceptions of personal experience.

Holte also points out two major approaches taken to the ethnic autobiography: (1) as a chronicle of the transformation or conversion of the ethnic or immigrant from outside the dominant culture to an accepted, often successful, insider; and (2) as recorded observations of instances in which the majority culture has not included individuals who, because of race, sex, class, language, or their own volition, failed to be assimilated into the mainstream of society. He points out that, in either case, the writer may have experienced some kind of transformation, and says that "the very language used to describe ethnic and immigrant experience underscores the notion of change and conversion" (p. 6).

Autobiographies described that represent the first success story of conversion include those of writer Mary Antin, steelmaker Andrew Carnegie, and film director Frank Capra. Some that exemplify rejection of the individual of or by the American community include personal narratives of Emma Goldman, Black Elk, and Malcolm X.

The twenty-nine accounts included represent a wide range of personal experiences, from well-known and popular works (e.g., Nicky Cruz's *Run, Baby, Run; Iacocca;* and Booker T. Washington's *Up from Slavery*) to those that are less familiar, or even obscure, such as black writer Zora Neal Hurston's *Dust Tracks on a Road: The Autobiography of Mary Jane Hill Anderson.* The titles cover a period of over 150 years, from the personal recollections of Mary Jane Hill Anderson, who was born in 1827, to contemporary accounts of *The Woman Warrior* (1976) by Maxine Hong Kingston, and Lee Iacocca's *Iacocca* (1984).

Entries are arranged alphabetically by author and include a brief biographical sketch of the writer; descriptive comments about his or her autobiography, including selected excerpts; a critical analysis of the work; and a bibliography of further references. The work is not indexed, but is concluded with a "Bibliographical Essay" examining ethnic and immigrant writing in American literature as a growing field of intellectual investigation. While the amount of coverage given to literary criticism is rather limited in each of these narratives, the descriptions of the ethnic American's emotions and experiences are rich and vivid, making this a unique sourcebook for readers from a historical, sociological, and literary perspective.

Lois Buttlar

1057. Inge, M. Thomas, ed. **Handbook of American Popular Literature.** Westport, Conn.,

Greenwood Press, 1988. 408p. index. $55.00. LC 87-32294. ISBN 0-313-25405-2.

Inge's collection of essays covering popular literature should be required reading of all persons doing reader's advisory work with adults and young adults, in addition to scholars of literature and general patrons who have reading hobbies. An outgrowth of Inge's previous work, *Handbook of American Popular Culture* (see *ARBA* 83, entry 1063), the fifteen essays (five original to this work) have been updated and revised for this publication. Essays cover detective novels, fantasy, Gothic novels, romance, science fiction, and westerns, among others. Each essay covers the historical development of the literature, reference works, research centers, and useful publications. Each has been written by a specialist. Highly recommended. [R: LJ, 15 Oct 88, p. 83; RBB, 15 Nov 88, p. 554]

David V. Loertscher

1058. Jay, Gregory S., ed. **Modern American Critics, 1920-1955.** Detroit, Gale, 1988. 384p. illus. bibliog. index. (Dictionary of Literary Biography, Vol. 63). $92.00. LC 87-25138. ISBN 0-8103-1741-9.

This volume, like others in the series, may be used profitably by itself, although some of the essays are interconnected with other volumes in the series. Devoted to analyses of the major writings of modern American critics who flourished between 1920 and 1955, it includes essays ranging in length from ten to twenty pages on twenty-five literary and cultural critics. These include figures with a worldwide, secure reputation such as T. S. Eliot, Kenneth Burke, H. L. Mencken, Edmund Wilson, Lionel Trilling, Ezra Pound, Lewis Mumford, Allen Tate, John Crowe Ransom, and Cleanth Brooks, as well as less well-known critics such as R. S. Crane and Waldo Frank. Some of these men, such as Mencken, Mumford, and Wilson (no women are included—a judgment that, it can be argued, does not reflect sexism but rather the relative paucity of influential women critics in this period), are significant for their cultural, not simply their literary commentary. Others are, or were, well-known creative writers as well as critics, such as Eliot, Pound, Ransom, and Tate. Some of these figures were considerably more influential during their lifetimes or earlier in their careers than they are today, such as Irving Babbit, Randolph Bourne, Van Wyck Brooks, and Vernon Parrington. Some have been very prolific, such as Van Wyck Brooks, Burke, Mencken, Mumford, Trilling, and Wilson. Others, while less prolific, have made very important contributions with one or a few books, such as F. O. Matthiessen with his

American Renaissance and Parrington with the three volumes of *Main Currents in American Thought.*

Each of these essays provides an introductory discussion of the lives and ideas of these critics, with greater emphasis, appropriately, on the ideas. Most of the critics here are responsible for creating academic criticism, although a few, like Kenneth Burke, have made brilliant contributions without obtaining a college degree or holding a regular academic job. Each of the twenty-five writers of these essays presents balanced assessments, not hagiography. All of the essays sampled by this reviewer assume that the reader is at least somewhat familiar with literature, though the editor has been careful to see that a general, literate audience will find these critiques accessible. Each essay begins with a summary paragraph describing the most significant contributions of the critic, so one does not have to read the whole essay if one only needs a quick overview. A brief bibliography of the critic's most important works, a selected list of works about the critic, and the location of his papers are also provided. A well-chosen photograph or two also accompanies each entry. A special glossary of literary terms frequently used by these critics will be included at the end of the second volume devoted to these twentieth-century American critics.

While it is not difficult to obtain biographical and analytical information about the more famous of these men in other literary reference tools, this volume is handy because it brings these twenty-five together. Although there is no summary essay attempting the admittedly difficult task of categorizing these sometimes very diverse thinkers, many of these essays make comparisons to other critics covered in this volume. Recommended especially for academic audiences. [R: Choice, May 88, p. 1384]

David Isaacson

1059. Jay, Gregory S., ed. **Modern American Critics since 1955.** Detroit, Gale, 1988. 397p. illus. bibliog. index. (Dictionary of Literary Biography, Vol. 67). $92.00. LC 87-30283. ISBN 0-8103-1745-1.

Covering individuals who have played a prominent role in contemporary American literary criticism, this volume complements *Modern American Critics, 1920-1955* (see entry 1058), which is published as volume 63 of the Dictionary of Literary Biography series. Other volumes of the DLB treat American literary critics of the nineteenth century.

By focusing on the major proponents of contemporary literary theories, *Modern American Critics since 1955* reflects the various trends in interpreting literature that have developed during the past several decades, such as theoretical criticism, feminist criticism, Afro-American criticism, and deconstruction. Among the twenty-seven critics it treats are M. H. Abrams, Harold Bloom, Northrop Frye, Alfred Kazin, Adrienne Rich, and Susan Sontag.

Following the format established in previous volumes of the DLB, entries are arranged alphabetically by individual. The signed essays, which average about ten pages each, usually include some biographical information; however, the major emphasis is on the individual's career and the literary theories espoused in his or her writings. A bibliography of the critic's books, edited works, and periodical articles appears at the beginning of each entry, and a brief list of secondary references follows most of the essays. In addition, each article is accompanied by one or more photographs.

Supplementing the text is a useful glossary that provides explanations of the principal terms, schools, concepts, and movements (e.g., reader-response criticism, semiotics, deconstruction) associated with modern literary criticism. An additional appendix reprints three papers addressing "The Limits of Pluralism," written by Wayne C. Booth, M. H. Abrams, and J. Hillis Miller, who represent differing critical views.

A selective list of works recommended for additional reading precedes the cumulative index, which cites entries contained in all the DLB volumes published to date as well as the *DLB Yearbook* and the *DLB Documentary Series.* This index would be more useful if topical articles were indexed under their subjects rather than their titles. For example, "An Interview with Peter S. Prescott" is listed under "Interview" rather than "Prescott," while "A Field Guide to Recent Schools of American Poetry" is entered under "Field" rather than "American Poetry."

Although *Contemporary Literary Critics* (see *ARBA* 83, entry 1140) covers over four times as many individuals, it surprisingly does not include eleven of the critics treated in this volume, nor does it provide the detailed assessment offered by this work. This will be an important addition to academic and other libraries that support scholarly research in the field of literary criticism. [R: Choice, May 88, p. 1384]   Marie Ellis

1060.   **A Literary History of the American West.** J. Golden Taylor and others, eds. Fort Worth, Tex., Texas Christian University Press; distr., College Station, Tex., Texas A & M

University Press, 1987. 1353p. illus. bibliog. index. $79.50. LC 85-50538. ISBN 0-87565-021-X.

This massive volume provides not only a synthesis of the many movements, trends, and genres of western literature, but also gives good biographical and literary analysis of several hundred writers of narrative, fiction, poetry, drama, and film scripts, from early oral traditions and folklore to the work of the recently deceased Louis L'Amour. No aspect of literature is overlooked—travel, romance, heroic fiction, poetry, drama, film, and essays.

The major divisions of the work are: "Encountering the West," subdivided into such topics as "Across the Wide Missouri" and "Precursors of the Western Novel"; the next division, part 2, is subdivided geographically, with excellent biographies and criticism of over forty major writers—Mark Twain, Mary Austin, and others in the Far West, J. Frank Dobie and Paul Horgan as examples in the Southwest, Willa Cather, Mari Sandoz, and others for the Middle West, and Vardis Fisher and Bernard De Voto as typical of the Rocky Mountain region. The final major division is entitled "Rediscovering the West" and includes such essays as "Indian Poetry," "Contemporary Western Drama," and "Western Movies since 1960," with a final essay on modern trends in western radio, television, film, and print.

Each of the more than eighty essays is by a different author, usually an established authority in that field. Each is followed by an excellent bibliography of both primary and secondary sources. A list of contributors, giving affiliation and listing a few of the person's writings, a list of 126 "Major Reference Sources" for the book as a whole, and an excellent index of names and subjects are included. This is a monumental work which should be in every library with a collection dealing with the West. [R: LJ, 15 Apr 88, p. 33]

Raymund F. Wood

1061.   Rathbun, John W., and Monica M. Grecu, eds. **American Literary Critics and Scholars, 1850-1880.** Detroit, Gale, 1988. 352p. illus. bibliog. index. (Dictionary of Literary Biography, Vol. 64). $92.00. LC 87-25802. ISBN 0-8103-1742-7.

This volume, the second of three designed to comprehensively survey contributions of nineteenth-century critics and scholars to letters in the United States, covers the years 1850-1880, a thirty-year period which witnessed social and political strain, internecine warfare, and cultural transformations. The majority of writers and critics lived in New England and

New York, with the publishing industry a nexus between them.

Like previous volumes in the DLB, volume sixty-four provides an illustrated bio-critical essay for each of some thirty-five authors represented. Among those covered are the well-known Mark Twain, Bret Harte, and Walt Whitman; the less-known Francis James Child, Henry Joseph Ruggles, and Parke Godwin. Each essay typically contains a chronological discussion of their lives and works. Appended to each essay are a primary bibliography of books and major articles and a secondary bibliography of critical works, as well as information about published letters and the location of collected papers.

A fifty-five page cumulative index lists all authors represented in the DLB (volumes 1-64), the *DLB Yearbook* (1980-1986), and the *DLB Documentary Series* (1-4). What is missing is a subject index to material in this volume. Whitman, for example, did not aspire to be a literary critic, yet during his career he reviewed the works of a host of writers ranging from the ancient classics to his contemporaries. There is no way to compare and contrast his views with those of other critics of his time on such leading figures as Poe, Hawthorne, Thoreau, Longfellow, and so on without laboriously searching out their names in the other thirty-four essays making up this volume. Undoubtedly, the editors of the DLB will provide such a comprehensive index when the series is fully complete; but, regrettably, *American Literary Critics and Scholars, 1850-1880* is not a "self-contained" reference tool. [R: Choice, July/Aug 88, p. 1671]　　　　G. A. Cevasco

1062. Rathbun, John W., and Monica M. Grecu, eds. **American Literary Critics and Scholars, 1880-1900.** Detroit, Gale, 1988. 374p. illus. bibliog. index. (Dictionary of Literary Biography, Vol. 71). $95.00. LC 88-10879. ISBN 0-8103-1749-4.

This volume in the well-known Dictionary of Literary Biography series is the last in a three-volume study of American literary critics and scholars of the nineteenth century. Among the thirty-six authors covered in the book are Ambrose Bierce, Hamlin Garland, Henry James, Frank Norris, and George Santayana.

As with all the volumes in the DLB, the essay covering each person studied provides biographical and critical information, a list of major writings, and a secondary bibliography noting biographies, significant periodical articles, and the location of the writer's personal papers and manuscripts. Although advanced students will naturally have to supplement their research with more in-depth material, beginning researchers can find a great deal here that will be of interest—as can the reference librarian desiring to help these patrons.

All libraries carrying the DLB will probably add this volume, although the ever-rising cost of each book, along with Gale's proliferation of inevitable spinoffs (Documentary Series, Yearbooks, and now Concise Series), will eventually cause acquisition librarians to look hard at each purchase. Another problem is the rather sloppy indexing. Although each volume in the DLB contains a cumulative index, if the name of a person included in an essay is not in the article's title, then access to that name can be found only through a broad, hard to find generic heading. For example, researchers wanting information on mystery writers Dashiell Hammett or Raymond Chandler will look through the index in vain unless they are familiar with the entry "Tough-Guy Literature."　　　　Jack Bales

DRAMA

1063. Peterson, Bernard L., Jr. **Contemporary Black American Playwrights and Their Plays: A Biographical Directory and Dramatic Index.** Westport, Conn., Greenwood Press, 1988. 625p. bibliog. index. $75.00. LC 87-17814. ISBN 0-313-25190-8.

The main entries in this valuable reference work are by individuals active in writing for the stage (spoken and musical), television, radio, and film, since 1950, even if some works have remained unpublished and unperformed. The biographical sketches which follow are terse but informative, and include current addresses. The plays are described by genre (drama, tragicomedy, domestic comedy, etc., although it can be anticipated these terms do not come from a list of standardized terms), date of production, synopsis of plot, location of the scripts (including films and recordings), and other information of value. The foreword is by James V. Hatch, a highly respected archivist in the field. Appendices cover additional materials deposited in special collections and works by other writers about which insufficient information has been located. The bibliographic aids are excellent.

Although a new edition is already projected, this initial venture provides significant data not available elsewhere. As a stimulus for research, perhaps the next edition will add a topical index to the existing ones (titles and general) so that one might be led to consider the treatment of recurring themes, such as bicultural values, miscegenation, sexual orientation, and domestic issues. Because this publication appears not to have been produced by computer, the cut-off date seems to be 1984. Producers, theater devotees, cultural historians, and Americanists will welcome this acquisition.

                    Dominique-René de Lerma

FICTION

1064. Realism, Naturalism, and Local Color, 1865-1917. Detroit, Gale, 1988. 392p. illus. index. (Concise Dictionary of American Literary Biography, Vol. 2). $60.00. LC 88-6016. ISBN 0-8103-1821-0.

Projected as a six-volume set, the Concise Dictionary of American Literary Biography series is designed to bring together the most significant American authors covered in the Dictionary of Literary Biography series. It is intended for high school, junior college, and small and medium-sized public libraries that cannot afford or do not need the more comprehensive coverage of the DLB. Gale is publishing this set out of sequence; volume 5, *The New Consciousness, 1941-1968* (see *ARBA* 88, entry 1162), appeared in 1987, while volume 1, *Colonization to the American Renaissance, 1640-1865* (see entry 1053) was published in 1988.

This volume features twenty-two major writers who were active from the end of the Civil War to the beginning of U.S. involvement in World War I, a period characterized by the rising popularity of local color literature and by the development of realism and naturalism in American writing. Among those covered are Louisa May Alcott, Samuel Clemens, Emily Dickinson, Bret Harte, Carl Sandburg, and Edith Wharton. The alphabetically arranged entries include essentially the same lengthy biographical and critical articles that appeared in the DLB. However, the essays and bibliographies have been updated as necessary to reflect recent scholarship, and brief annotations have been added to most of the items in the secondary bibliographies. In addition, a full-page chart at the beginning of each article briefly outlines the individuals, literary movements, and events that influenced the writer and identifies the major themes of his or her works. While the essays have not been abridged, the number of illustrations and photographs accompanying each article has been reduced to about one-third of those appearing in the DLB.

A cumulative index covers the individuals treated in this volume and in the two previously published volumes of the CDALB. The index identifies each volume by dates of coverage rather than by volume number.

This work would have been greatly enhanced by an introductory essay providing an overview of the period and placing the authors covered within the political, historical, and social context in which they wrote. The absence of such an introduction seriously diminishes the value of arranging the set by literary period rather than alphabetically. In addition, the omission of such writers as Sidney Lanier, Upton Sinclair, and Hamlin Garland is questionable.

Although one wishes that the editors had chosen to cover more authors by reducing the length of the entries, the CDALB will be a welcome alternative to those libraries that have been unable to purchase the DLB. [R: Choice, Nov 88, p. 466; LJ, 15 June 88, pp. 66-67; RBB, 1 Sept 88, pp. 45-46]   Marie Ellis

1065. White, Ray Lewis. Index to *Best American Short Stories* and *O. Henry Prize Stories*. Boston, G. K. Hall, 1988. 183p. (Reference Publication in Literature). $35.00. LC 87-28112. ISBN 0-8161-8955-2.

Although both *Best American Short Stories* (*BASS*) and its supplements (see *ARBA* 86, entry 1101 for a review of the 1979-1983 supplement) and *O. Henry Prize Stories* (*OHPS*) are indexed in *Short Story Index*, this new volume is a useful tool. It will be most valuable either in libraries which purchase *BASS* and *OHPS* but do not buy heavily in short stories generally, or in those which do not subscribe to *Short Story Index*. *BASS* and *OHPS* are indexed separately by author and title, and jointly by title. In addition, there are introductory essays about each series and a chronological list of all short stories since 1927 that have won the O. Henry Prize.

                    Rhea Joyce Rubin

HUMOR

1066. Gale, Steven H., ed. Encyclopedia of American Humorists. New York, Garland, 1988. 557p. index. (Garland Reference Library of the Humanities, Vol. 633). $75.00. LC 87-8642. ISBN 0-8240-8644-9.

This book does not pretend to be an all-inclusive reference on every American humorist who ever penned a line. So one will find omissions, and perhaps a favorite funnyman is missing from these pages. For instance, there are no articles on Richard Bissell, George Shepard Chappell (Captain Traprock), Bill Cosby, or Lewis Grizzard. And the only one of the colonial "Connecticut Wits" included is John Trumbull. In his preface the editor reveals the processes, and problems, of selecting those writers who are included.

This will be a useful volume, with its information on 135 American and Canadian humorists from colonial times to the present. It includes newspaper columnists, stand-up comedians, and script writers as well as book-length authors. It is alphabetically arranged from Franklin P. Adams through Matthew Franklin Whittier. Vital statistics, a biographical sketch, a literary analysis, a bibliography, and a list of secondary sources are given for each humorist. Each article is signed by the contributor. Following the text there is an alphabetical list of contributors with curriculum vitae and area of expertise. The length of the articles varies, with a few receiving longer entries than might be warranted (e.g., Erma Bombeck with three pages and Woody Allen with six and a half pages, versus four columns for Garrison Keillor). The text is presented in a two-column format, with good typography and adequate leading contributing to legibility. It is well indexed, well bound, and lies flat when opened so that the researcher need not wrestle with the book while copying information. [R: Choice, June 88, p. 1532; LJ, 1 May 88, p. 71; RBB, Aug 88, pp. 1901-2; WLB, June 88, p. 140]

Frank J. Anderson

1067. Sloane, David E. E., ed. **American Humor Magazines and Comic Periodicals.** Westport, Conn., Greenwood Press, 1987. 648p. bibliog. index. (Historical Guides to the World's Periodicals and Newspapers). $75.00. LC 86-27155. ISBN 0-313-23956-8.

This most recent volume in Greenwood's Historical Guides series is a reference book arranged with the user's needs in mind. Layout, design, and typography contribute to accessing the information. The book is signature sewn and sturdily bound. It is useful for the general reader and the scholar. Preliminary matter includes a foreword by Stanley Trachtenberg, an authority on American humor; an editor's preface explaining the book's arrangement; and acknowledgments. A nineteen-page introduction surveys the history of American humor magazines, and a handy list of library codes as used in the *Union List of Serials* is included.

The text of the book is arranged in four parts. Part 1, "Magazine Profiles," is arranged alphabetically by magazine title and runs from *Abracadabra*, a short-lived magazine published in Maine in 1808, through *Ziff's*, a Chicago publication of the 1920s. Between these titles are more than one hundred other magazines from the almost forgotten to such well-known titles as *Judge, Life,* and *Mad.* For each title considered there are thoughtful, signed essays relating the type of humor to contemporary American culture. The essays cover publishing history, writers, artists, and publishers, and give an assessment of the impact of the magazine on

American politics and mores. "Information Sources," following the essays, provides a bibliography, index sources, reprint editions, and locations of libraries holding the title. The publication history gives title and title changes, volume and issue data, publisher and place of publication, editors, and circulation information. The length of the essays varies; *Captain Billy's Whiz-Bang* gets five pages, *Harvard Lampoon* ten, *Mad* seven, and *The New Yorker* twelve. Part 2, "Brief Listings," also arranged alphabetically by title, provides epitomes of a paragraph or two of less important, or short-lived magazines. Part 3, "Additional Magazines," is primarily a listing of unexamined titles derived from the *Catalogue of Copyright Entries: Periodicals.* Part 4, "Genre Essays," includes "College Humor Magazines" by George A. Test; "Scholarly Humor Magazines" by George A. Test and Don Nilsen; and "Humor in American Almanacs" by Robert Secor. "A Chronological List of Humor Magazines" lists more than one thousand titles dating from 1757 through 1985. This section concludes with a selected bibliography, a forty-seven-page index, and a credentialed list of contributors. Sloane is an English professor at the University of New Haven and is the author of several books and numerous articles on American humor and humorists. [R: Choice, Jan 88, p. 741; LJ, 15 Mar 88, p. 51]

Frank J. Anderson

INDIVIDUAL AUTHORS

Edward Albee

1068. Giantvalley, Scott. **Edward Albee: A Reference Guide.** Boston, G. K. Hall, 1987. 459p. index. (Reference Guide to Literature). $45.00. LC 87-25047. ISBN 0-8161-8783-5.

This comprehensive, annotated bibliography of material written by and about Edward Albee includes reviews and interviews from daily newspapers, popular magazines, and the entertainment press as well as the standard academic criticism and a large number of books and articles from other countries. The resulting volume does, indeed, live up to the author's intent: "to provide a richly detailed overview of the critical reputation of a major American writer as he approaches his fourth decade of public scrutiny."

Items are listed alphabetically within the year of publication. Although the annotations strictly summarize the originals (without evaluation), they manage to indicate the relative value of items as they chronicle Albee's development. Annotations also indicate the presence of illustrations, with "Portrait" indicating a photograph of Albee, and "Photograph" indicating a production photograph of the play discussed in the entry. A detailed index provides a means of locating items by author, publication, and subject.

Thanks to Giantvalley's scholarly achievement in this book, it is possible to trace through primary and secondary sources Albee's growth from the premiere of *Zoo Story* in Berlin on 28 September 1959 to his smash hit (despite mixed reviews) with *Who's Afraid of Virginia Woolf?*, to his stage adaptation of Carson McCuller's *Ballad of the Sad Cafe*, to his enigmatic *Tiny Alice* and his unmitigated disasters *Lolita* and *Man*. This easy-to-use bibliographical guide will soon be in need of updating as Albee is still writing and his major plays continue to be performed and reviewed around the world.

Colby H. Kullman

Edward Bellamy

1069.   Widdicombe, Richard Toby. **Edward Bellamy: An Annotated Bibliography of Secondary Criticism.** New York, Garland, 1988. 587p. index. (Garland Reference Library of the Humanities, Vol. 827). $77.00. LC 87-37686. ISBN 0-8240-8563-9.

In this exhaustive—and exhausting—bibliography of secondary, and in some cases tertiary, material on the life and works of Edward Bellamy (1850-1898), best known as the author of *Looking Backward* (1888), Widdicombe has produced a valuable guide for students of nineteenth-century American literature. There are 2,275 entries arranged alphabetically by author in separate sections for books, articles, theses and dissertations, chapters and subchapters of books, introductions and headnotes, reviews, "sequels" and ripostes, citations and references, and reprinted extracts from journals and newspapers. There is even a section containing twenty-five spurious and unlocated references. The main listing then concludes with yet another ten entries added after the completion of the work, bringing the total number of entries for material on Bellamy published from 1878 to October 1987 to 2,310 items. The main focus is on English-language material, for which a comprehensive search has been conducted; there is also a wide range of material in various foreign languages although Widdicombe has not conducted an exhaustive search for such materials. Each entry, with the exception of those for theses and dissertations, is briefly but carefully annotated to indicate the significance of the item. There are separate alphabetical indexes for authors, titles, journal titles, and subjects. This is, of course, *the* definitive bibliography on

Bellamy, a minor writer whose utopian *Looking Backward* brought him instant fame and generated most of the references in this bibliography.

Norman D. Stevens

James Fenimore Cooper

1070.   Summerlin, Mitchell Eugene. **A Dictionary to the Novels of James Fenimore Cooper.** Greenwood, Fla., Penkevill, 1987. 372p. index. $30.00. ISBN 0-913283-18-5.

James Fenimore Cooper wrote thirty-two novels from 1820 to 1851, establishing himself as the first major American novelist. He peopled these romances with rather predictable characters, who are the main subject of this dictionary. Summerlin here lists all the characters of Cooper's works in one alphabetical arrangement and identifies their roles, attributes, occasionally their specific actions, and the novel in which they appear.

Entries range from a sentence for some generic types (lawyer) to three pages for Natty Bumppo. *See* references are also used. There are separate lists of animals and inanimate objects, ships' names, and an index of proper names arranged by the novel in which they appear. For good measure the author adds a forty-page essay on character types found in Cooper's works. The dictionary portion may help to clear up readers' confusion on subjects such as the many nicknames used for Natty Bumppo through the five novels in which he appears. The essay is a fairly good depiction of the somewhat conventional characters found in Cooper's fiction and might serve as a guide to any one novel.

John P. Schmitt

Emily Dickinson

1071.   Dandurand, Karen. **Dickinson Scholarship: An Annotated Bibliography 1969-1985.** New York, Garland, 1988. 203p. index. (Garland Reference Library of the Humanities, Vol. 636). $25.00. LC 87-34558. ISBN 0-8240-8641-4.

Like others in the series, this bibliography consists, in large part, of typewritten (or computer-generated) copy submitted camera-ready by the author. This material, which is the heart of the book, is relatively error-free. More importantly, it fills a gap in Dickinson scholarship by providing an annotated bibliography of the books, articles, chapters, and dissertations published during the period indicated in the title. Nearly eight hundred items, most of them with annotations, appear in the work, followed by an index of poems discussed, a general subject index, and an author index, all of which would be useful to the student and the scholar seeking commentary on Dickinson's life and work. English-language materials, which compose the greater part of the citations, are usually annotated, while those in foreign languages are not annotated.

Like other Garland publications in the series, this work is printed on acid-free, 250-year-life paper. However, this work probably should not have been published in its present form. Apparently the preface and the introduction, which are typeset, were never proofread; they are rife with glaring errors in spelling ("Dicckinson" and "Throeau," "perticularly" and "particulary," "Erwein" instead of "Eberwein"), grammar ("The book ... are concerned with these issues"), punctuation, and typography. Thus, a potentially useful work is seriously marred by careless editing and an apparent rush to publish.

Edwin S. Gleaves

E. L. Doctorow

1072. Tokarczyk, Michelle M. **E. L. Doctorow: An Annotated Bibliography.** New York, Garland, 1988. 132p. index. (Garland Reference Library of the Humanities, Vol. 811). $22.00. LC 88-16106. ISBN 0-8240-7246-4.

The author has divided this annotated, comprehensive bibliography of materials by and about Doctorow into four parts. In part 1, "Primary Sources," books, short fiction, political and cultural criticism, literary essays, and Doctorow's produced play, *Drinks before Dinner*, are listed chronologically. Everything but the books is annotated. Part 2, "Secondary Sources," treats books, articles, film, dissertations, and interviews, followed by book, drama, and film reviews. Part 3, identified as "a somewhat unusual feature for a literary bibliography," consists of thirty-seven selected references to the 1953 case of Ethel and Julius Rosenberg. This section provides helpful background to *The Book of Daniel*, Doctorow's historical novel having a unique relationship to the Rosenbergs. Name and title indexes conclude the volume. Tokarczyk's reasonably priced study should have a fairly broad research appeal, as Doctorow is one of those contemporary novelists "whose work reaches both popular and academic readers." Charles R. Andrews

F. Scott Fitzgerald

1073. Bruccoli, Matthew J. **F. Scott Fitzgerald: A Descriptive Bibliography.** rev. ed. Pittsburgh, Pa., University of Pittsburgh Press; distr., New York, Harper & Row, 1988. 479p. illus. index. (Pittsburgh Series in Bibliography). $100.00. LC 87-40220. ISBN 0-8229-3560-0.

The amazingly prolific Bruccoli has revised his original descriptive survey of F. Scott Fitzgerald's writings (see *ARBA* 73, entry 1280), which was the second volume published in the Pittsburgh Series in Bibliography. Bruccoli had updated the bibliography with a supplement published in 1980; now he has completely revised the original work and has incorporated many previously elusive Fitzgerald pieces. This volume represents a true revision of the material rather than an expanded version of the earlier bibliography. Bruccoli has eliminated several sections that appeared in the first compilation (mimeographed film scripts, movies made from Fitzgerald's work, book contracts, braille editions, material from auction catalogs, and republications of short pieces), and has not included everything that appeared in the 1980 supplement (such as a complete listing of all foreign-language translations).

Other sections of the bibliography remain intact, from "Separate Publications" to "Movie Work," with additional entries found in most of the sections. Bruccoli has retained an appendix listing the writings of Zelda Fitzgerald, has added a page of "Compiler's Notes," and has expanded the list of "Principal Works about Fitzgerald" from forty to sixty-one titles. There is also a long and detailed index, which lists names as well as titles for every piece of writing cited in the bibliography.

As with the first edition, this bibliography is generously illustrated with photographs of dust jackets (including several British Penguin paperback editions) and title pages. This is a volume that is essential for all American literature collections and is a perfect complement to the critical bibliographic work done on Fitzgerald by Jackson R. Bryer (see *ARBA* 85, entry 1073). Thomas A. Karel

Robert Gover

1074. Hargraves, Michael. **Robert Gover: A Descriptive Bibliography.** Westport, Conn., Meckler, 1988. 95p. illus. index. $29.50. LC 87-16489. ISBN 0-88736-165-X.

Robert Gover is probably best known for his novel *One Hundred Dollar Misunderstanding*, published in 1961, which the compiler of this bibliography ranks with *Catcher in the Rye* and *The Adventures of Huckleberry Finn*. While there is reason to dispute this assessment, it is fair to say that Gover is a somewhat avant-garde writer who was quite popular for awhile in the 1960s, but who has, until recently, been virtually unknown (two of his novels are currently being considered as films). This bibliography should help to resurrect interest in Gover's work. It includes a foreword by Gover's novelist friend Herbert Gold and a frank, sometimes embarrassingly confessional, but also humorous "Mini-Autobiography" by Gover himself.

The bibliography is divided into six sections: (1) original books, including precise descriptions of first and subsequent editions and reviews; (2) contributions to other published books; (3) contributions to periodicals; (4) translations of original editions; (5) biographical and/or critical works on Gover; and (6) miscellaneous items, including, for example, screenplays, dust jacket blurbs, and mentions in other books. A number of illustrations are included of facsimiles of title pages, dust jacket front covers, etc. An index lists book and article titles, other authors, and cross-references.

David Isaacson

Henry James

1075. Bender, Claire E., and Todd K. Bender. **A Concordance to Henry James's** *The Turn of the Screw.* New York, Garland, 1988. 251p. (Garland Reference Library of the Humanities, Vol. 828). $48.00. LC 87-32834. ISBN 0-8240-4147-X.

This is the third volume in an ongoing research project to analyze Henry James's lexicon. The first concordance, published in 1985, was to the novel *The American* (see *ARBA* 87, entry 1147); the second concordance was devoted to a novella, *Daisy Miller* (see *ARBA* 88, entry 1178). This major project is sponsored by the University of Wisconsin and is being edited by Todd K. Bender. Librarians interested in the overall plan for the James Archive should consult Bender's article, "Literary Texts in Electronic Storage: The Editorial Potential (*Computers and the Humanities* 10 [July/August 1976]: 193-99). The overall plan is also discussed in the preface to the first concordance in the series, *The American.* Simply stated, plans are to produce concordances for one version of each of James's novels and stories. So far, the New York Edition has been used. The second stage of the project is to "add all significant variant states for each text so that collations may be made facilitating the creation of a sound scholarly edition of James's texts." The third stage will include the following information for each word used by James in his published works: part of speech, function in the sentence, phonetic value, name of speaker uttering the word, the audience hearing the word. A final volume will contain all James's vocabulary showing the date of each word's appearance and frequency of occurrence.

The final volume(s) will not obviate the need for the larger academic libraries to purchase these concordances to individual works now being produced. These concordances include sentence fragments in which the word appears along with page and line references to the New York Edition. There are listings of high- and low-frequency words. These listings enable users to identify words easily and make quick calculations. [R: Choice, July/Aug 88, p. 1671]   Milton H. Crouch

Anne Morrow Lindbergh

1076. Wurz, Trude. **Anne Morrow Lindbergh: The Literary Reputation: A Primary and Annotated Secondary Bibliography.** New York, Garland, 1988. 92p. index. (Garland Reference Library of the Humanities, Vol. 556). $22.00. LC 88-12064. ISBN 0-8240-7248-0.

This bibliography is a substantially good work that lacks in the presentation. The bibliography itself is divided into four major sections: (1) Lindbergh's books; (2) her articles, essays, and prefaces; (3) her poems; and (4) writings about her. The two middle sections constitute a careful, numbered, chronological listing of works by Lindbergh in the stated genre. The fourth section, also carefully numbered and chronologically arranged, lists and briefly annotates articles about her. Unfortunately, the index in the back of the volume lists authors and titles only, no subjects.

In the first section, Wurz's beautifully explicit descriptions of the first editions is marred by Garland's inability to provide her with a typeface that includes an exclamation point (p. 8) and square brackets (p. 5). The penned-in punctuation that this edition features sits weirdly among the minute precision of Wurz's bibliographic descriptions. There is also a problem with the miscellanea section (pp. xvii-xix). Here the citations to interviews, letters, etc., are simply double-spaced without indentations, in a uniform typeface that leaves the reader somewhat confused as to the limits of the entry. Wurz's editors should have followed the same procedure here that they did in the readable fourth section devoted to articles about Lindbergh's writing.

Lindbergh captured the public imagination as aviator, writer, and mother. We await bibliographies on the other persona.

Judith M. Brugger

William March

1077. Simmonds, Roy S. **William March: An Annotated Checklist.** University, Ala., University of Alabama Press, 1988. 191p. $16.95. LC 86-30786. ISBN 0-8173-0361-8.

Though he is the author of one of the best known fictional studies of World War I, *Company K,* little study has been done on the work of author William March Campbell. This checklist expands on the compiler's previous bibliographic studies, providing a fairly comprehensive publication record of works by and about March.

The checklist is divided into two sections, primary and secondary materials. Primary materials include a chronological list of all known editions of March's novels, short stories, fables, and miscellaneous writings. Brief annotations about each edition are included. The secondary materials section is subdivided into three units: known dramatic and film adaptations of March's work (most notably his novel, *The Bad Seed),* biographical and critical studies of March, and selected reviews of his writing. The two latter sections also include lengthy excerpts from the sources cited. A brief biography of March also is included.

Scholars of twentieth-century American literature will find this checklist a helpful tool, pulling together interesting information on this little-studied writer from a variety of sources. This work will be of particular value to libraries with very strong collections in the area. [R: Choice, Oct 88, p. 297]

Elizabeth Patterson

Herman Melville

1078.   Sealts, Merton M., Jr. **Melville's Reading.** rev. ed. Columbia, S.C., University of South Carolina Press, 1988. 296p. illus. index. $35.00. LC 87-16186. ISBN 0-87249-515-9.

It is not surprising that a prodigious writer like Melville was also a prodigious reader. Nor does it necessarily detract from his genius to know that Melville freely borrowed, often without attribution, from other writers for his own works. Sealts, with this major revision and enlargement of a book originally published in 1966, makes it easier for other scholars to ascertain which books Melville owned or borrowed and therefore to make some deductions about what he read. The first part of this book is a lengthy discussion of Melville's reading, with separate chapters devoted to suggesting influences and sources for each of Melville's major works. Part 2 consists of an alphabetical list by author of books both owned and borrowed by Melville and his immediate family. "Books" is defined broadly to include pamphlets and periodicals. Sealts's annotations indicate whether Melville marked or made comments in these books and where the books are located, if known. Appendices list twelve other books that

have been advertised as belonging to Melville but about which Sealts has doubts, a list of other books bought by Melville's relatives which might have been part of his reading, a list of the books in the library of one of the ships Melville sailed on as a young man, and fifty-one call slips for books charged to Melville from the New York Society Library during 1890 and 1891 (a patron's right to privacy apparently does not extend to the famous or the dead).

As Sealts is careful to stress, the mere fact that Melville owned or borrowed a book is, of course, no proof he read or used that book as a source in his own writing. But this very carefully documented study does allow scholars to make more probable attributions of sources, and should prevent some merely idle speculations. Users of this study are also advised to consult the complementary *Melville's Sources* by Mary Bercaw (see *ARBA* 88, entry 1183), which is a checklist of secondary works claiming that Melville used particular sources. Sealts's study does *not* cite works which Melville may have used as sources but for which no proof exists that he owned or borrowed them. Bercaw's work, on the other hand, is an annotated bibliography of thousands of source studies, which is especially valuable because she evaluates the reliability of these source attributions. Melville scholars engaged in this kind of detective work will need to consult both Bercaw and Sealts.

David Isaacson

H. L. Mencken

1079.   Bulsterbaum, Allison. **H. L. Mencken: A Research Guide.** New York, Garland, 1988. 267p. index. (Garland Reference Library of the Humanities, Vol. 776). $42.00. LC 87-36668. ISBN 0-8240-6634-0.

A challenge for any bibliographer is to track the writings by and about H. L. Mencken, the prolific and opinionated "Sage of Baltimore" who flourished in the first half of the twentieth century. Until now, the only comprehensive Mencken bibliography has been the monumental and ongoing work begun by Betty Adler in 1961 (*H. L. M.: The Mencken Bibliography,* Books on Demand) and updated by the "bibliographic checklist" published in the journal *Menckeniana* and two supplements published by the Enoch Pratt Free Library in 1971 (also edited by Adler) and 1986 (edited by Vincent Fitzpatrick). Bulsterbaum has compiled a highly selective bibliography, which is intended to be more accessible than the Adler/Fitzpatrick compilation. It is recommended more for the "general reader and newcomer to Mencken" than for the true Mencken scholars and aficionados (whose numbers are legion). Bulsterbaum provides a very useful and entertaining twelve-page introduction to Mencken's life and career, and carefully spells out the limitations of this bibliography.

The first half of the bibliography consists of Mencken's writings, organized by type of publication: full-length works and collaborations, pamphlets, essays, magazine articles, newspaper articles, and contributions to other books (introductions, prefaces, chapters, encyclopedia entries). There is a separate section listing anthologies, collections, and selections of Mencken's work; a final section lists collections of Mencken letters, as well as other collections that include letters written by Mencken (e.g., Faulkner, Fitzgerald, Dreiser).

The secondary bibliography is also divided by type of material: bibliographies (Mencken himself compiled the first significant bibliography of his writings, published in 1920 under a pseudonym), biographical works, books and pamphlets, chapters of books, articles, mentions, dissertations, and five forthcoming works (including an edition of Mencken's diaries and a major new biography).

Almost all of the items in this bibliography contain brief annotations; some offer just a few words of elaboration, others are paragraph-length. The bibliography is well organized, easy to use, and fun to browse through. Indexes to authors and subjects are keyed to item numbers (the bibliography contains 1,315 separate items). As with other Garland publications, this book is printed on acid-free paper and has tightly sewn signatures. This is highly recommended for most academic libraries—and any library in the greater Baltimore region.

Thomas A. Karel

Toni Morrison

1080. Middleton, David L. **Toni Morrison: An Annotated Bibliography.** New York, Garland, 1987. 186p. illus. index. (Garland Reference Library of the Humanities, Vol. 767). $36.00. LC 87-15031. ISBN 0-8240-7970-1.

Finally, a book-length bibliography of Toni Morrison! Standard bibliographies and lists lead the searcher to most of the information cited in this bibliography; although this efficient volume is in no way denigrated by that. While it may, at first, not seem customary for scholarly bibliographies to include references to publications such as *Newsweek* (item 78) and *Vogue* (item 46), the fact is that some of Morrison's most interesting interviews were published in such places. Conversely, without the microform

collection at the Schomburg Center, items 36 and 45 are hard to come by.

The carefully and unexpectedly thorough annotations immensely enhance the value of the work. Indeed, the annotations are informative and thought-provoking in a most illuminating way. They are little essays written in complete sentences, the only kind of annotation that this reviewer finds really palatable.

The material is clearly organized into sections comprising both Morrison's own work and works about her. First there is a listing of the novels (without annotations), then the poetry, essays, and interviews. Next are the critical works which deal with her larger opus, followed by critical articles on specific titles. Last are listings of her awards, honors, memberships, and a postscript on *Beloved*. The index is adequate without being spectacular. No entries for popular (versus scholarly) sources or biblical referents are given.

Morrison is a fairly new writer, but a stellar one. This bibliography is a timely compilation of the record of her impact. [R: Choice, July/Aug 88, p. 1676]   Judith M. Brugger

Frank Norris

1081. McElrath, Joseph R., Jr. **Frank Norris and *The Wave*: A Bibliography.** New York, Garland, 1988. 161p. index. (Garland Reference Library of the Humanities, Vol. 801). $28.00. LC 88-5863. ISBN 0-8240-6616-2.

At the turn of the century, especially in the 1890s, *The Wave* (a weekly magazine) addressed the ladies and gentlemen of upper middle class San Francisco. The purpose of this slim volume is to establish the record of what Frank Norris wrote for *The Wave* during the 1890s when he was its employee.

Identifying Norris's writings from *The Wave* is no small task. One mannerism of high-toned publications of the time was that of unsigned works; another was the use of pseudonyms. As a result, consistent identification of a single author was tricky indeed. Thus, there have been many answers to the question "What did Norris write?"

The author of this bibliography has divided this work into three sections: "*Wave* Writings by Frank Norris," "Explanatory Notes," and "*Wave* Writings Previously Attributed to Frank Norris." An extensive "Introduction" describes *The Wave*, its head (John O'Hara Cosgrave), the difficulties in determining authorship, and the reasons for attributing but 165 articles to Norris.

The first section merely indicates the year and volume of *The Wave*, the title of the article, the day it appeared and how it was or was not signed. The "Explanatory Notes" in the following section describe these writings. This arrangement is most inconvenient especially because the explanatory notes do not include the articles' titles. Thus, one is constantly flipping back and forth between the two sections. The arrangement of the third section, where citations and notes are kept together, is far preferable.

Although the arrangement described above is annoying, it should not deter libraries from purchasing this volume. If nothing else, it will undoubtedly add to the controversy of which articles are truly of Frank Norris's authorship. Recommended for research collections focusing on American literature.

Marjorie E. Bloss

Eugene O'Neill

1082. Smith, Madeline, and Richard Eaton. **Eugene O'Neill: An Annotated Bibliography.** New York, Garland, 1988. 320p. index. (Garland Reference Library of the Humanities, Vol. 860). $44.00. LC 88-11264. ISBN 0-8240-0691-7.

This bibliography was initially designed to update Jordan Y. Miller's *Eugene O'Neill and the American Critic*, second edition, revised (Archon, 1973), but it was expanded from Miller's American scope to international coverage. This volume covers 1973 to 1985, with a few 1971 and 1972 entries not included in Miller's earlier work on O'Neill. This work also drew heavily on G. Fridshtein's *Iudzhin O'Nil: bibliograficheskii ukazatel* (Moscow: Kniga, n.d.) for non-English-language material. The bibliography is divided into sections covering books and parts of books; dissertations; periodical publications in English; foreign-language publications; English-language productions and reviews; foreign-language productions and reviews; miscellaneous adaptations, television and radio productions, audio and film recordings, and fictional representations of O'Neill's life; editions of primary works; and translations. An index of plays and an index of authors refer to entry numbers in the bibliography. In each section entries are annotated and arranged alphabetically by year. This volume will prove useful in identifying the broad range of material written about American playwright Eugene O'Neill, but it is weak in annotations of foreign-language materials. An introduction to this work would have been of interest, but there is none. It does not include, in the index of plays, a play entitled *Gold* (1921) mentioned in the O'Neill entry in James D. Hart's *The Concise Oxford Companion to American Literature* (see *ARBA* 87, entry 1130). The computer type-

face used is small and boring; the paper used is flimsy.

Maureen Pastine

Sylvia Plath

1083. Tabor, Stephen. **Sylvia Plath: An Analytical Bibliography.** Westport, Conn., Meckler Publishing, 1987. 268p. index. $47.50. LC 86-8625. ISBN 0-88736-100-5.

With the publication of Sylvia Plath's *Johnny Panic and the Bible of Dreams* (1977) and her *Collected Poems* (1981) a task was completed, providing a relatively complete gathering of the writings of Plath, one of America's great modern poets. This effort was the labor of her husband, Ted Hughes, and her sister-in-law, Olwyn Hughes. From this work of seventeen years came over twenty posthumous books and pamphlets and over one hundred other writings that had been published in periodicals. From this prolific output numerous changes were made, reflecting, no doubt, the art of a poet who labored for perfection in her work.

Some earlier bibliographies were published, although they could not be complete until there was an ingathering of Plath's works. Among these earlier bibliographies are *A Chronological Checklist of the Periodical Publications of Sylvia Plath* (University of Exeter, American Documents Centre, 1970), *Sylvia Plath: A Bibliography* (Scarecrow Press, 1978), *Sylvia Plath and Anne Sexton: A Reference Guide* (G. K. Hall, 1974), and "Bibliography: Sylvia Plath" (*Hecate* 1 [July 1975]: 95-112).

Tabor's work includes physical descriptions of the books, the poems and prose are organized under uniform titles, and textual variants of the poems are clearly noted. Listed in this bibliography are separate works by the poet, works edited by her, her contributions to periodicals, and recordings and broadcasts. Also included are manuscripts, works about her, and translations. The index is thorough and most usable. Also of interest to scholars and researchers is that the introduction calls attention to the outstanding Sylvia Plath collections at Smith College and Indiana University. [R: Choice, Sept 87, p. 94]

Jefferson D. Caskey

Edwin Arlington Robinson

1084. Boswell, Jeanetta. **Edwin Arlington Robinson and the Critics: A Bibliography of Secondary Sources with Selective Annotations.** Metuchen, N.J., Scarecrow, 1988. 285p. index. (Scarecrow Author Bibliographies, No. 80). $30.00. LC 87-32324. ISBN 0-8108-2076-5.

Robinson was one of the most widely recognized U.S. poets at the time of his death in

1935, but today he is primarily known for the short, dramatic poems written early in his career. Boswell has documented his reception by critics and biographers from the 1890s to the 1980s in this, her eighth title for the Scarecrow Author Bibliographies series.

Boswell lists 1,383 items including monographs, parts of books, periodical and newspaper articles, reference books, book reviews, theses, pamphlets, and some anthologies containing Robinson's poetry. The entries are arranged by author and most citations are annotated, paraphrasing the words of the author. A few French, German, and Italian citations appear. Boswell concludes the bibliography with a subject index referring to individual poems and books, proper names, and a few broad themes (romanticism, philosophy, reputation, etc.).

There are a few oddities about this otherwise thorough work. Boswell incorrectly cites the 1948 edition of Robert E. Spiller's *Literary History of the United States* for the chapter that appears in the 1974 revised fourth edition (Macmillan). She cites the eleventh edition of *The Reader's Adviser* (1968) but not the more recent twelfth edition (R. R. Bowker, 1974). Missing is David Pownall's *Articles on Twentieth Century Literature* (Kraus-Thomson, 1978) while Jacob Blanck's *Bibliography of American Literature* is here, but with the annotation "E. A. Robinson not represented." Librarians may want to examine this work against Nancy C. Joyner's *Edwin Arlington Robinson* (G. K. Hall, 1978, o.p.). Both are nearly comprehensive efforts, but many libraries will need only one. [R: Choice, Oct 88, p. 284]

John P. Schmitt

Carl Sandburg

1085. Salwak, Dale. **Carl Sandburg: A Reference Guide.** Boston, G. K. Hall, 1988. 175p. index. (Reference Guide to Literature). $35.00. LC 88-12048. ISBN 0-8161-8821-1.

It should hardly come as a surprise that the bibliographies treating a man who was a poet, a biographer, a historian, a troubadour, a novelist, and an author of children's stories are scattered and fragmentary in scope. This latest effort lists those earlier efforts. Two among these merit mention. Members of the Library of Congress's General Reference and Bibliography, Manuscript, and Music Divisions, assisted by other divisions, compiled the bibliography included in Mark Van Doren's *Carl Sandburg* (Government Printing Office, 1969), an appreciation of the writer. That bibliography identifies and briefly describes primary works in LC's

collections. The other worthy of mention is the bibliography of criticism published between 1950 and 1975 that William White contributed to *The Vision of This Land: Studies of Vachel Lindsay, Edgar Lee Masters, and Carl Sandburg* (Western Illinois University Press, 1976).

Salwak's bibliography does not attempt to replicate nor compete with the LC bibliography. Indeed, he simply lists Sandburg's books by title chronologically in this book's prefatory section. His scope is much broader than White's, listing secondary works from both scholarly and popular sources published from 1904 through 1987. He has arranged these by year and alphabetically by author within year. In addition to the standard bibliographic information necessary for identification and retrieval of the books, articles, book chapters, and dissertations, Salwak's entries include brief descriptive annotations. The annotations bear out the analysis Salwak offers in his introduction of the Sandburgian critical heritage and its sharp divisions over seven decades. A consolidated author/title/subject index cites items by year and item number within that year.

Although Salwak makes no claims for comprehensiveness, this is the most extensive bibliography of secondary works on the writings of a distinctively American voice. As such, it is an essential tool to any student or scholar who wants to augment the body of Sandburg criticism.

James Rettig

Gertrude Stein

1086. Kellner, Bruce, ed. **A Gertrude Stein Companion: Content with the Example.** Westport, Conn., Greenwood Press, 1988. 352p. illus. bibliog. index. $49.95. LC 88-3126. ISBN 0-313-25078-2.

Years ago I was defeated by Robert Bartlett Haas's *A Primer for the Gradual Understanding of Gertrude Stein* (Black Sparrow Press, 1971). I am not proud of this fact: Haas's book, as I came to realize, was the queen of the Stein textbooks. Having reigned for its seventeen years, however, Haas's *Primer* has recently had to yield the palm to Kellner's *A Gertrude Stein Companion*. Try sitting down in your living room encircled by the eight volumes of the *Yale Gertrude Stein* (1980), your neglected Haas, and your new copy of Kellner's; Kellner's is the book that you will find most useful. It is a first-class reference book.

The book is divided into six major sections, supplemented by a useful introduction. First, Kellner treats Stein's works in a kind of *catalogue raisonné* (bibliography seems too pallid a word for these annotations). Then there are ten explanatory articles of varying pointedness, including my favorite one by Marjorie Perloff, and seven poems-as-criticism. In part 3, "Friends and Enemies," Kellner has alphabetically arranged entries on the people in and out of Stein's life. There is a typographical error in the Ezra Pound entry (p. 242), where the abbreviation *DLE* has displaced the correct acronym *DLB*. Part 4, "Gertrude Stein's ABC," is a delightful compendium of her random pronouncements on everything from "Accuracy" ("Accuracy is by and by to be slightly poisoned by inaccuracy") to "Zero" ("So Zero is a hero"). Taken together, the annotated bibliography and the (separate) list of works consulted will please even the most persnickety librarian/scholar/crazed poet.   Judith M. Brugger

Nathaniel Tarn

1087. Bartlett, Lee. **Nathaniel Tarn: A Descriptive Bibliography.** Jefferson, N.C., McFarland, 1987. 125p. illus. index. (American Poetry Contemporary Bibliography Series, No. 2). $25.00. LC 87-43064. ISBN 0-89950-296-2.

This descriptive bibliography in this young series of contemporary American poets covers the full range of Nathaniel Tarn's contributions as poet, anthropologist, editor, and translator through 1986. French-born (1928), British-and-American educated, Tarn continues to write poetry at his home in Santa Fe, having taken early retirement from Rutgers University in 1984.

Following Tarn's seventeen-page foreword, the book is divided into five chronologically arranged parts. Part A treats books, pamphlets, and broadsides; part B, items edited, translated, and introduced; part C, contributions to periodicals; part D, translations; and part E, contributions to anthologies. Three appendices complete the study: "Heteronyms," a listing of various works which Tarn published under two different names (Michael Tavriger and E. Michael Mendelson); "Cape Editions," a title listing of thirty-eight volumes published by Jonathan Cape under Tarn's editorship; and annotated checklists of Tarn's criticism and reviews.

Essentially only the largest university and research libraries supporting graduate or honors courses in modern poetry will need this bibliography. [R: Choice, May 88, p. 1378]
                Charles R. Andrews

Diane Wakoski

1088. Newton, Robert. **Diane Wakoski: A Descriptive Bibliography.** Jefferson, N.C.,

McFarland, 1987. 136p. illus. index. (American Poetry Contemporary Bibliography Series, No. 1). $25.00. LC 87-43065. ISBN 0-89950-297-0.

This descriptive bibliography on the twentieth-century poet Diane Wakoski is the first of a planned series on significant contemporary American poets. It is divided into six major sections: books, pamphlets, and broadsides; co-authored books; periodical contributions; contributions to anthologies; translations; and published interviews. A brief chronology in the first part of the volume covers the author's early history and publication record. The volume ends with a checklist of reviews and criticism. Entries provide information obtained from (and quasifacsimiles of) the title page, and include "information on the collation, pagination, binding, dust jacket, publication, and contents of the work." The author began his work with "bibliographies by G. P. Lepper, Walter Hamady, Bradford Morrow and Seamus Cooney." This descriptive bibliography is an important work for scholars completing research on an important contemporary poet, adding to the growing list of critical works relating to the long-neglected women writers and poets. [R: Choice, May 88, p. 1378]   Maureen Pastine

Alice Malsenior Walker

1089. Pratt, Louis H., and Darnell D. Pratt. **Alice Malsenior Walker: An Annotated Bibliography: 1968-1986.** Westport, Conn., Meckler, 1988. 162p. index. (Meckler's Studies and Bibliographies on Black Americans, 1). $42.50. LC 87-34816. ISBN 0-88736-156-0.

Alice Walker's novel *The Color Purple* was a major literary success in book form. It was the making of the novel into a movie, however, that made it accessible to an even wider audience. It is no surprise, then, that the vast majority of this annotated bibliography deals predominantly with *The Color Purple* even though Walker has written eleven other books.

This bibliography is divided into primary sources and secondary sources. The entry in each section contains a short analysis of its contents. An index of Walker's works, secondary authors and the titles of their works, and subjects concludes the bibliography.

With the exception of *The Color Purple* there is little substance to this bibliography. Although Walker is an American Book Award winner, she won this award for a single work rather than a cumulation of her writings. This is not meant to detract from *The Color Purple* but to indicate that not much has been written about many of her other works. It also indicates that readers will have some difficulty tracking down primary sources. A new book in which Walker gathers her speeches and some journal articles together in a single volume, *Living by the Word* (Harcourt Brace Jovanovich) should help alleviate this problem.

In and of itself, this bibliography is recommended. This is done with the caveat, however, that it is primarily a one-book bibliography. [R: Choice, Sept 88, pp. 86, 88]

Marjorie E. Bloss

Richard Wright

1090. Kinnamon, Keneth, with others, comps. **A Richard Wright Bibliography: Fifty Years of Criticism and Commentary, 1933-1982.** Westport, Conn., Greenwood Press, 1988. 983p. index. (Bibliographies and Indexes in Afro-American and African Studies, No. 19). $85.00. LC 87-27831. ISBN 0-313-25411-7.

This is not only the major bibliography of secondary materials dealing with Wright: its compiler's claim that these 13,117 items constitute "the most comprehensive such list ever compiled for any American writer" (preface) indicates accurately its breadth. The bibliography includes not only the usual reviews, dissertations, articles, and books, but extends to items generally ignored in author bibliographies, such as entries in *MLA Abstracts*, bestseller lists, publishers' blurbs, articles in standard reference books, entries in published library catalogs, and passing references in works dealing with other authors. Items from some fifty countries have been included.

Citations are arranged chronologically by year, and within each year, by author. Entry numbers give the year and a sequential number within the year. An annotation briefly describes each entry. The index lists all authors, titles of books cited, a selection of broad subject entries for places, organizations, literary or formal categories (such as characterization or bibliographies), and titles of Wright's works.

The arrangement and cogent annotations allow one to follow Wright's reception through the years and in various countries. But those searching for criticism of a particular work will encounter problems in using the index. What is a user seeking criticism of, for instance, *Native Son* to make of the roughly thirty-five hundred entry numbers given? Even though an asterisk identifies entry numbers of special importance, those so identified still number in the hundreds. The bibliography's scope will prove an obstacle to undergraduates and others whose needs would be met more efficiently by a more selective compilation. Yet the bibliography's absolutely thorough coverage, complemented by its

meticulously accurate presentation (this reviewer found no typographical errors), may indeed, as the compiler hopes, "expand current notions of what constitutes a total literary reputation" (preface). [R: Choice, Sept 88, p. 82]

William S. Brockman

POETRY

1091. Caskey, Jefferson D., comp. **Index to Poetry in Popular Periodicals, 1960-1964.** Westport, Conn., Greenwood Press, 1988. 232p. $49.95. LC 87-32277. ISBN 0-313-24810-9.

Index to Poetry in Popular Periodicals is a companion volume to an earlier work covering the period 1955-1959. It is a title, first line, author, and subject index to poetry published in general American periodicals indexed in H. W. Wilson's *Readers' Guide to Periodical Literature*. Poets represented range from the well known and established (such as Robert Fly, e. e. cummings, Robert Frost, Ogden Nash, Sylvia Plath, and Anne Sexton) to the less famous and light verse writers (such as Richard Armour, Jack Matthews, Jane Merchant, and Helen Singer). There is a good sampling, from the more scholarly poetry published in periodicals such as *American Scholar* and *Yale Review,* to the lighter verse published in *McCall's* and *Redbook.*

This volume is an excellent source for poems or light verse to fit special occasions. It includes many poems that will never be included in sources such as *Granger's Index to Poetry* (see *ARBA* 88, entry 1155), *Chicorel Index to Poetry in Anthologies and Collections in Print 1975-77* (see *ARBA* 80, entry 1188), and other indexes to more scholarly poetry. The entries are divided into four sections: title, first line, author, and subject. The title index and the list of abbreviations of periodicals in the front of the volume provide location information. The title entries provide the entry number (the number to which the user is referred from the author, first line, and subject indexes), full title of the poem, poet's surname and first and middle initials, periodical title abbreviation, volume number of periodical, date of issue, and pages where the poem is located.

Maureen Pastine

1092. Catalá, Rafael, and James D. Anderson, with others. **Index of American Periodical Verse: 1986.** Metuchen, N.J., Scarecrow, 1988. 526p. $37.50. LC 73-3060. ISBN 0-8108-2149-4.

This index is a familiar reference source. (For a review of the 1982 edition, see *ARBA* 86, entry 1156.) This sixteenth volume for 1986 consists of poems from 246 periodicals that were published in the United States, Canada, and

Puerto Rico. From the periodicals come approximately sixteen thousand poems written by nearly six thousand poets or translators.

The author index is the key to locating a particular poem. The names of the poets are in alphabetical order and are numbered. The entry for each poem includes an abbreviated title of the name of the periodical, its volume and issue number, followed by date of issue, and the number of the page on which the poem is printed. The title index, in two columns, lists alphabetically the title or first line of the poems that are completely indexed under the poet's or translator's name. Following these titles are the entry numbers that must be referred to under the author entries.

Other important sections for using this index are the introduction, which assists with names and cross-references, the format and arrangement of the entries, and abbreviations; and the lists of periodicals that were added, those that were deleted, and those that were indexed. For those that were deleted and those that were indexed the name of the editor, place, and address of publication are given. For those deleted, the reason for deletion is given; for those indexed the editor's name, address of publication, and cost of a subscription or single issue are given.

The compilers are Rafael Catalá, a poet, critic, and teacher of poetry and literary theory; James D. Anderson, who specializes in the design and evaluation of textual databases for information retrieval; and Sarah Park Anderson and Martha Salberger, now retired librarians, who indexed many of the general publications.

Such a work is always a major undertaking. *Index of American Periodical Verse* renders a major service to poets, to teachers of poetry, and to reference librarians especially for its indexing of "little" and regional periodicals. For future volumes, poetry editors are invited to submit sample issues of their publications in order that they might be considered for inclusion in subsequent volumes of the index.

Jefferson D. Caskey

1093. Moss, William. **Confederate Broadside Poems: An Annotated Descriptive Bibliography Based on the Collection of the Z. Smith Reynolds Library of Wake Forest University.** Westport, Conn., Meckler, 1988. 173p. illus. index. $44.50. LC 87-28156. ISBN 0-88736-163-3.

This book describes the holdings of "one of the largest gatherings of Confederate Broadside verse" in the country. Most of the collection was recently acquired (1967-1976), and it contains "hitherto unlisted items," suggesting that more material exists.

The book, which contains illustrations of fifteen items, describes 228 Confederate broadside poems and another twenty-two non-broadside and non-Confederate items in enough detail for scholars, librarians, and collectors: author and printing information, attributions, dimensions, the first two lines of the work, and cross-references to other major listings.

Moss provides an admirably concise yet comprehensive introduction which moves from "The Call to Pens," through the feeble response from the literary establishment, to a discussion of the numerous popular poets, the means through which their work circulated, and current resources for studying them.

Moss, citing the value new historical criticism places on minor writers, senses that the study of such popular poetry will reveal facts and truths about the Confederacy that may be in opposition to what we would like to believe about it or what the Southern establishment would have us believe.

Edward J. Gallagher

British Literature

GENERAL WORKS

1094. **Index of English Literary Manuscripts. Volume II: 1625-1700. Part I: Behn-King.** Peter Beal, comp. Bronx, N.Y., H. W. Wilson, 1987. 645p. illus. $280.00. LC 79-88658. ISBN 0-7201-1855-7.

1095. **Index of English Literary Manuscripts. Volume III: 1700-1800. Part I: Addison-Fielding.** Margaret M. Smith, comp. Bronx, N.Y., H. W. Wilson, 1986. 357p. illus. $250.00. LC 79-88658. ISBN 0-7201-1779-8.

The purpose of this large and impressive project is to make readily available a descriptive index of the manuscripts of a selected list of British and Irish writers of the period 1450 to 1900. Publication began in 1980 with the two parts of volume I (1450-1625) and has included, in addition to the volumes reviewed here, the first part of volume IV. Another five volumes are planned: volume II, part 2; volume III, part 2; volume IV, parts 2 and 3; and an index volume. Users should consult the general introduction in volume I, part 1, for a description of the scope and method of presentation of the project, but they should also read the preface to the individual volume they will be working with, for the project has evolved and some details of its arrangement of materials have changed.

For each author an attempt has been made to list all literary manuscripts (details on nonliterary works are often provided in the introduction). Each manuscript is described briefly, with its present location noted, and some information on provenance. Full details on the physical manuscript are usually not given. The introductory essay to each author is generally very full, discussing the manuscripts, manuscript annotations and signatures, questionable manuscripts, and printed editions. Scholarship on these matters is often mentioned, but a separate listing of such works would have been handy.

Among the twenty-six authors covered in volume II, part 1, are Sir Thomas Browne, Carew, Congreve, Cowley, Dryden, Herrick, and Hobbes. Among the twenty-one in volume III, part 1, are Addison, Boswell, Burns, Cowper, Defoe, and Fielding. The argument could be made that more minor authors and/or anonymous works should have been included because information on these figures is less accessible. The corollary to this can be seen in the editor's treatment of Blake: although he is included, he is accorded only introductory notes because his manuscripts have already been thoroughly described elsewhere. Similarly, Henry Carey is represented only by an introductory note mentioning a single manuscript letter and a few later transcripts. It would seem that this space might have been better used.

Overall, this is a very good series that gathers in one place much valuable, but often scattered, information. Despite the price, research libraries will need to acquire these volumes.　　Philip R. Rider

1096. Schlueter, Paul, and June Schlueter, eds. **An Encyclopedia of British Women Writers.** New York, Garland, 1988. 516p. index. (Garland Reference Library of the Humanities, Vol. 818). $75.00. LC 88-21393. ISBN 0-8240-8449-7.

This biographical dictionary covers approximately four hundred women writers who spent a major portion of their lives in the British Isles. Thus, it includes not only British-born authors such as Jane Austen and Virginia Woolf but also writers like Mary Lavin and Ngaio Marsh, who were born in other countries but produced a significant body of their work while living in England. Although medieval and Renaissance personalities are included, the majority of the writers treated are from the eighteenth through twentieth centuries. Coverage of contemporary British authors, such as Fay Weldon and Anita Brookner, is especially strong.

The alphabetically arranged entries combine biographical information with a critical overview of each writer's work. Contributed by subject specialists, the signed articles range in length from one-half to three and one-half pages. The scope encompasses not only creative writers such as novelists, poets, dramatists, and children's authors but also critics, biographers, diarists, translators, and other prose writers. Some of these women (e.g., Florence Nightingale and Ellen Terry) are better known for careers other than writing.

Bibliographies at the end of each entry provide a chronological list of the author's published works and a selective list of secondary sources. Among the latter are abbreviated citations to standard biographical and literary reference works that include entries on the individual. The secondary references do not provide the titles of articles, nor do they include pagination, a particularly serious omission when the citations are to newspaper or periodical articles. However, the bibliographies are commendably up-to-date, often including citations to 1987 publications.

The index includes all authors covered and provides cross-references from pseudonyms and other alternative forms of their names. It also selectively indexes topics discussed in the entries. A particularly useful feature is the detailed breakdown of genre headings. For example, the "fiction" entry is further subdivided into over thirty categories, ranging from "adventure" to "working class."

Similar in concept to *American Women Writers* (4v., Ungar, 1979-1983), this work complements that set and enlarges upon the coverage of *A Dictionary of British and American Women Writers, 1660-1800* (see *ARBA* 86, entry 1079). Most libraries that support in-depth research in British literature or history or in women's studies will want to add this volume to their collections.

　　Marie Ellis

FICTION

1097. Benstock, Bernard, and Thomas F. Staley, eds. **British Mystery Writers, 1860-1919.** Detroit, Gale, 1988. 389p. illus. bibliog. index. (Dictionary of Literary Biography, Vol. 70). $95.00. LC 88-11465. ISBN 0-8103-1748-6.

Ever since the discovery of crime, people have relished stories of suspense and intrigue. *British Mystery Writers, 1860-1919* is the seventieth volume in the biographical-bibliographical series known collectively as the Dictionary of Literary Biography. It is also the first volume of that series to be devoted to the roots of mystery fiction. Subsequent volumes will cover the "Golden Age of British Mysteries" and trace the development of the genre up to the present.

During the later half of the nineteenth century, Britain was the breeding ground for a new style of writing which grew out of the Gothic novel into a middle-culture literary style that forever blurred the line between serious literature and popular fiction. The writers of this period were the foundation builders for modern mystery fiction, which has, in its many manifestations, gone on to become both a popular form as well as a means of serious literary expression.

Familiar members of the genre such as Sir Arthur Conan Doyle, Sax Rohmer, and H. G. Wells are covered as well as some of the less well-known ground breakers: Angus Reach, Fergus Hume, and Charles Dickens. Well-written biographical and critical essays focus on thirty-five writers covered by this volume. As the foreword explains, "just as an author is influenced by his surroundings, so is the reader's understanding of the author enhanced by a knowledge of his environment." Each signed essay is accompanied by a bibliography of the authors major works and articles, a short list of critical works and the location of their collected papers.

Following the traditional DLB format, *British Mystery Writers, 1860-1919* is copiously illustrated with portraits, scenes from the author's life, illustrations, book jackets and stills from films based on their works. The volume contains a cumulative index for the entire series and a list of contributors. A "Books for Further Reading" section lists seventy-five titles on the art, history, style of crime and detection fiction.

An excellent addition for libraries with strong mystery collections or for reference collections supporting research in popular literature.   Steven J. Schmidt

1098. Oleksiw, Susan. **A Reader's Guide to the Classic British Mystery.** Boston, G. K. Hall, 1988. 585p. $29.95. LC 88-1735. ISBN 0-8161-8787-8.

Now there is an easy way to help lovers of the British mystery story to find another book "just like this one." *A Reader's Guide to the Classic British Mystery* bills itself as the first "complete" guide to the genre, covering 121 authors and 1,440 novels and novellas published between 1886 and 1985. The entries are listed alphabetically by author with the titles grouped chronologically by character. Hercule Poirot, Agatha Christie's earliest creation, is listed first, followed by Ariadne Oliver, Tommy Tuppence Beresford, and so on. The titles in each series are arranged according to the time of the story, either as stated by the author or as surmised by Oleksiw. This unique feature allows readers to

follow the career of their favorite sleuth in a logical order. A short annotation accompanies each entry, giving the flavor of the story without revealing any of the secrets of the plot.

Access is through any of seven indexes. Authors are linked to their creations; fictional sleuths with their creators. There are indexes based upon the setting of the story (courtroom, racecourse, etc.), time period (2,000 B.C. to 1959) and the occupation of the main character (housewife, amateur detective, etc.). Another section presents titles where the author's special knowledge brings the book to life. For example, Dick Francis and his inside knowledge of the horse racing world, or Jonathon Gash and the antiques trade. A brief discussion of the British Class System, a breakdown of metropolitan and county police ranks, and a pair of county maps are also included in the volume.

A Reader's Guide to the Classic British Mystery is entertaining and extremely useful, but I found the limits of its scope a bit annoying. The author's definition of the phrase "classic British mystery" is never really stated. American writers, such as Martha Grimes, are included, but Dr. Salt, the crusty physician created by the noted British author J. B. Priestly, is not. Another conspicuous omission is the progenitor of the classic British detective, Sherlock Holmes.

While books about mysteries may abound, *A Reader's Guide to the Classic British Mystery* fills an important gap in the literature by providing direct and easy access to companion works and introducing readers to similar titles in the genre. [R: RBB, 1 Sept 88, pp. 55-56]
Steven J. Schmidt

INDIVIDUAL AUTHORS

Algernon Blackwood

1099. Ashley, Mike. **Algernon Blackwood: A Bio-Bibliography.** Westport, Conn., Greenwood Press, 1987. 349p. index. (Bio-Bibliographies in World Literature, No. 1). $39.95. LC 87-17808. ISBN 0-313-25158-4.

Still some years away from completing the only full-scale biography of Algernon Blackwood (1896-1951), author Ashley has temporarily filled the gap with this biographical and bibliographical study of this master supernaturalist. A brief foreword by Ramsey Campbell, the author's introduction, a chronology of important dates, and an excellent thirty-three-page biographical essay—"The Man Who Was Uncle Paul"—precede the main part of the work.

Part 1 of the bibliography lists Blackwood's works: the books, short fiction, nonfiction, poetry and songs, plays and dramas, radio and television broadcasts, films, recorded works, unpublished or unbroadcast manuscripts, and untraced items. Complete descriptive annotations are included, as well as the names of the collections in which the short stories appear. Part 2 lists adaptations of Blackwood's works by others in various media. Part 3 includes works about Blackwood: a selected secondary bibliography, reviews, radio documentaries, and portraits and photographs. The twenty-seven-page part 4 consists of five useful "source indexes," including publisher, periodical, and anthologist. Concluding the volume are various appendices—translated books and foreign editions and significant library and archives holdings—and four indexes: locale and theme, chronological, alphabetical, and personal name.

All research libraries, as well as those with representative Blackwood and fantasy/science fiction holdings, will want this major, comprehensive study. [R: Choice, Apr 88, p. 1219]

Charles R. Andrews

William Blake

1100. Damon, S. Foster. **A Blake Dictionary: The Ideas and Symbols of William Blake.** rev. ed. Hanover, N.H., for Brown University Press by University Press of New England, 1988. 532p. illus. maps. bibliog. index. $18.00pa. LC 87-40509. ISBN 0-87451-436-3.

Since its publication in 1965, S. Foster Damon's *A Blake Dictionary* (Brown University Press, 1965) has remained an essential resource for both basic and advanced research on William Blake. This "Revised edition with a new foreword and annotated bibliography" by Morris Eaves was prompted by a sense that "people entering strange territory want up-to-date guidebooks" (p. ix) as well as a certainty that Damon's dictionary was "probably consulted more than any other by people reading Blake for the first time" (p. 463). The chief problem with Damon's original work was its lack of a cumulative index of any sort. Arrangement, although "impersonally" alphabetical, represents Damon's "very personal account of his understanding of Blake." On the one hand, Damon's dictionary is an index of specific words, phrases, allusions, themes, concepts, and other elements in Blake's writing while, on the other hand, it includes entries for a term such as *nudity* which Damon defines as "a word Blake never used and probably despised" (p. 303). Similarly, although Damon provides an entry for "BYRON and Napoleon," an entry for

Napoleon must be discovered under "BONAPARTE and Byron." Damon explains Blake's understanding of sex, hell, and women, but not love, heaven, and men. Eaves published a full list of the entries included and omitted in Damon's dictionary in *Blake Studies* (University of Tulsa, 1970-). The index compiled by Eaves cumulates the subjects of Damon's entries as well as references to other pervasive subjects. These include references to Blake's works, such as *The Songs of Innocence* and *Jerusalem*, as well as to topics like art, the American and the French revolutions, and Milton. For the first time explications and interpretations that were previously largely buried are now conveniently accessible. The "revision" consists mainly of adding the index. Side-by-side comparison of the texts of the two editions reveals a few textual differences. However, it seems that no new entries are added, no entries are revised, no new cross-references are provided, and no bibliographic references are updated. The state of Blake scholarship embodied by the revision, as a result, dates from the 1960s. Nonetheless, the increased access makes this paperback edition a worthwhile purchase even for libraries that own the original edition.

James K. Bracken

George Gordon Byron

1101. Page, Norman. **A Byron Chronology.** Boston, G. K. Hall, 1988. 117p. maps. bibliog. index. $35.00. LC 87-24776. ISBN 0-8161-8952-8.

The aim of the several volumes in this series of chronologies (other published or forthcoming volumes cover Dickens, Wordsworth, Virginia Woolf, and George Eliot) is to assemble from authoritative sources the "chronological facts of an author's life ... [so that they] can be seen at a glance" (p. vii). Page's *A Byron Chronology* at first glance seems to offer an attractive alternative to the "time-consuming and frustrating occupation" of digging through the varieties of biographical and autobiographical sources about the most romantic English poet, author of "She Walks in Beauty," *Childe Harold's Pilgrimage, Don Juan,* and *A Vision of Judgment,* among others. To provide a "record of Byron's life from year to year," Page has reduced to their component facts the primary materials of Byron's biography.

The chronology is most heavily indebted to Leslie A. Marchand's edition of *Byron's Letters and Journals* (Harvard University Press, 1973-1981) as well as Page's *Byron: Interviews and Recollections* (Humanities Press, 1985). Accounts of Byron by his contemporaries, including Leigh Hunt, Sir Walter Scott, Percy Bysshe

Shelley, and Mary Shelley, are also used. These are listed in an appended "Select Bibliography." Unfortunately, specific bibliographic citations to these sources are not generally or consistently provided in the chronology. As a result, scholars who want fuller treatments of the events still need to submit to "time-consuming and frustrating" digging in these sources. Page insists that what emerges in the chronology is a "clear if not complete picture" of Byron's career as well as "some striking juxtapositions—of Byron's public and private doings, for instance, and of the conduct of his various relationships and the connection between his social and personal life and the composition of his poems (p. ix). Despite this claim and the great value of convenient packaging of factual data, however, this chronology is not a place to look for biographical or critical insights about Byron. Users will have to identify similar "juxtapositions" and other themes in Byron's life for themselves. All in all, this makes using the chronology not all that satisfying, unless one needs to know something about a specific date in Byron's life.

In addition to the "Select Bibliography," the chronology includes brief biographical sketches of selected members of Byron's family and friends as well as associates and acquaintances. Separate indexes cite "Byron's Writings"; "People," chiefly valuable for identifying individuals who commented on Byron or on whom Byron commented; and "Topics." The latter index is rather disappointing in its slimness. Single references to "breakfast" and "burning alive" lead to events of little significance. At the same time, Page misses several opportunities to index similar events that moved Byron to comment, like witnessing executions on 18 May 1812 and 19 May 1817, among others. Only libraries intent on maintaining definitive collections on Byron need to consider this chronology. [R: Choice, Dec 88, p. 622; WLB, Sept 88, pp. 90, 92]

James K. Bracken

Lewis Carroll

1102. Fordyce, Rachel. **Lewis Carroll: A Reference Guide.** Boston, G. K. Hall, 1988. 160p. index. (Reference Publication in Literature). $40.00. LC 88-16527. ISBN 0-8161-8925-0.

An impressively wide range of subjects is represented in this annotated bibliography. Works treating Carroll not just as an author, but also "as photographer, logician, mathematician, and ... friend of children" (preface) are plentiful. Sources published during the last three decades are emphasized, and early works are also included, so it expands on Edward

Guiliano's *Lewis Carroll: An Annotated International Bibliography, 1960-1977* (University of Virginia Press, 1980). Despite its broad scope, however, Fordyce's book has a damaging flaw: its index is entirely inadequate for its straight alphabetical arrangement. Major recurring themes, such as "nonsense," are missing from the index. The introduction states that "the topic that dominates Carroll literary criticism and analysis is influence," and eighty-nine entries discuss the subject. However, these can be found only providing one knows the name of the person who influenced or was influenced by Carroll; otherwise, they are inaccessible, as "influence" is not an index term. Entries about several other topics, including women, juvenilia, and philosophy, were also found to be inaccessible through the index. While a number of biographies can be found under "Dodgson," at least six others are lost for want of indexing. Two other noticeable omissions from the index are entries that would provide access to the general critical works, such as collections of essays, and to the bibliographies of secondary materials like Guiliano's.

The introduction serves well as a review of research on Lewis Carroll, and because it is written in the style of a bibliographic essay, it alleviates to a small degree the shortcomings of the index. Still, those who use this bibliography would be wise to read it from cover to cover in order to be sure that nothing is missed.

Emily L. Werrell

Geoffrey Chaucer

1103. Baird-Lange, Lorrayne Y., and Hildegard Schnuttgen. **A Bibliography of Chaucer 1974-1985.** Hamden, Conn., Archon Books/ Shoe String Press, 1988. 344p. index. $39.50. LC 87-35157. ISBN 0-208-02134-5.

Scholars have long been mesmerized by that "Chaucerian" facility of the grand master to depict the natural object in its most precise form. In some ways, Chaucer would be flattered by all this attention, and even depict himself sardonically, while still remaining abashed. Yet the attention is overdue. Speakers of English must come to understand that Shakespeare, genius though he was, does not sit alone in his class, but with a host of others. Indeed, in some respects, Shakespeare's very talent emerges from the dust and rabble of characters that issued from the mind of the inimitable Chaucer.

The present text is a scholar's delight, a librarian's jewel, and an undergraduate's treasure trove. For in each case, the authors have managed to please all. For the scholar, there are inclusiveness and comprehensiveness; for the librarian, there are indexes (subject and author) and every imaginable category of Chaucerian works from print to nonprint; and for the student, there are articles and books in abundance to advance every essay, to enliven every term paper.

An entertaining introduction by Baird-Lange opens the text, providing the reader with an aerial view of the subject matter to come. Here texts are explained, and especially good works named, making this introduction the broth to this stew of a study. Following this comes the bibliography proper, which contains articles and books (for which reviews are cited) on Chaucer's life, his manuscripts, textual studies, general criticism, influence and illusions, writing style, language and word studies. Follow this by articles and books on the *Canterbury Tales*, sections on other longer works, lyrics and shorter poems, specious works and lost works, and backgrounds of every description (religious, historical, philosophic, scientific, and musical) and what emerges is truly a remarkable volume. The authors have added sections on facsimiles, medieval women's studies, and pedagogy from the previous twelve-year study, *Bibliography of Chaucer 1964-1974* (G. K. Hall, 1977).

Author and subject indexes (no title) round out this excellent addition to Chaucerian studies.   Mark Y. Herring

1104.   Peck, Russell A. **Chaucer's** *Romaunt of the Rose* **and** *Boece, Treatise on the Astrolabe, Equatorie of the Planetis,* **Lost Works, and Chaucerian Apocrypha: An Annotated Bibliography 1900 to 1985.** Toronto and Cheektowaga, N.Y., published with University of Rochester by University of Toronto Press, 1988. 402p. index. (Chaucer Bibliographies, 2). $60.00. ISBN 0-8020-2493-9.

This second volume in the Chaucer Bibliographies series provides a comprehensive annotated bibliography of twentieth-century scholarship of Chaucer's "longer, independent" (p. ix) translations, *The Romaunt of the Rose* and *Boece*; his scientific writings, *The Treatise on the Astrolabe* and *The Equatorie of the Planetis*; his "lost works," including *Origines upon the Maudeleyne*, *Wretched Engendring of Mankynde*, and *Book of the Leoun*; and over two dozen apocryphal works, such as the *Tale of Gamelyn, The Plowman's Tale,* and *Testament of Cresseid.* For more details about the series, users should consult the "General Editors' Preface" in volume 1 by the same author, *Chaucer's Lyrics and Anelida and Arcite: An Annotated Bibliography, 1900 to 1980* (Toronto, 1983).

These volumes of the Chaucer Bibliographies are the best now available for the particular works of Chaucer that are included. Volume 2, including entries for over 750 editions and studies, is especially noteworthy for the inclusion of background works. For example, besides editions and criticism of Chaucer's *Boece*, Peck also cites other Latin editions and modern translations of Boethius's work as well as critical interpretations and discussions of "Boethius: The Man and His Work." Similarly, for *The Treatise on the Astrolabe*, Peck includes a section of selected background studies of medieval astronomy. Studies of Chaucer's audiences of the fifteenth and sixteenth centuries are listed in the section for the apocrypha. As in volume 1, Peck's annotations are exceptionally thorough and detailed. The numerous non-English-language studies are fully described. Although Peck largely refrains from critical evaluation in the annotations, he frequently cites and describes reviews of significant studies. While many of the sorts of errors that plagued volume 1 (as noted by R. T. Lenaghan in *Speculum*, 60 (1985), 709-10) seem to have been avoided, volume 2 is not without flaws. For example, item 306 is nowhere to be found in the text, which skips from 305 to 307. It is cited in the index, however, and is presumably Olga Fischer's article on the Alfredian and Chaucerian Boethius. Despite similar deficiencies, when completed the Chaucer Bibliographies will be the best available for this century's Chaucer scholarship. Scholars, graduate students, and advanced undergraduates will certainly find Peck's work as useful as it is impressive. Students making their first acquaintance with research on Chaucer, on the other hand, will find it more convenient to consult Mark Allen and John H. Fisher's *The Essential Chaucer: An Annotated Bibliography of Major Modern Studies* (see *ARBA* 88, entry 1212) or, especially, John Leyerle and Anne Quick's *Chaucer: A Bibliographical Introduction* (see *ARBA* 87, entry 1174). [R: Choice, Oct 88, p. 294]   James K. Bracken

John Cleland

1105.   Coleman, Samuel S., and Michael J. Preston. **A KWIC Concordance to John Cleland's** *Memoirs of a Woman of Pleasure.* New York, Garland, 1988. 627p. (Garland Reference Library of the Humanities, Vol. 829). $100.00. LC 87-36615. ISBN 0-8240-8515-9.

John Cleland's *Memoirs of a Woman of Pleasure* is perhaps better known to Americans as *Fanny Hill*, the controversial eighteenth-century English novel that was banned from publication in the United States until 1963.

Generally recognized as the first pornographic novel in English, it has been variously described by critics as "humorless indecency unadorned" (Ralph Thompson) and as "a comic sexual romance" (Malcolm Bradbury).

This concordance to *Memoirs of a Woman of Pleasure* is based on the Oxford University Press edition of the novel, which was edited by Peter Sabor and published as part of the World's Classics series in 1985. The format is similar to that of other KWIC (Keyword-in-Context) concordances issued by Garland. Arrangement is alphabetical, with each word used by Cleland appearing in boldface type along the left side of the page, followed by the number of times it occurs. Each occurrence of the word is then displayed in approximately the center of a line of context. These listings are arranged alphabetically by the word immediately following the keyword. The appropriate volume, page, and line number in the Sabor edition are provided to the left of each citation. Although high-frequency words, such as articles, prepositions, conjunctions, and forms of the verb "to be" are listed in the concordance and the number of their occurrences is noted, their contexts are omitted.

Following the main body of the concordance is a "ranking frequency list," which groups words according to how often they appear in the novel. Concluding the volume is a brief supplementary concordance that notes the instances of "three consecutive substantive words in common" (p. xiv).

This work will be of value primarily to large university and research libraries that support scholars involved in textual criticism.

Marie Ellis

Charles Dickens

1106. Page, Norman. **A Dickens Chronology.** Boston, G. K. Hall, 1988. 156p. bibliog. index. $35.00. LC 87-25209. ISBN 0-8161-8949-8.

Expanding on a chronology the author included in his 1984 publication, *A Dickens Companion* (Schocken), Norman Page has produced a detailed "alternative biography" of Dickens's life and work. Based on Dickens's letters, speeches, numerous biographies of the writer and his contemporaries, and on selected newspapers and magazines such as *The Dickensian*, Page has amassed a comprehensive record of events, often providing a weekly, and sometimes daily record of Dickens's activities. Items are arranged by year, month, and specific day, if known. A modest subject index is provided, divided into three sections: references to Dickens's writings, personal names, and places.

This work will prove a particularly handy reference for scholars and advanced students. It provides an easy, at-a-glance resource to the events and activities Dickens was involved in throughout his career. The annotations are sometimes quite lengthy, and almost always make for fascinating reading. This work is an unexpected and pleasant addition to the wealth of materials on the work and life of Dickens. [R: Choice, Dec 88, p. 622; WLB, Sept 88, pp. 90, 92] Elizabeth Patterson

1107. Schlicke, Priscilla, and Paul Schlicke. *The Old Curiosity Shop*: **An Annotated Bibliography.** New York, Garland, 1988. 495p. index. (Garland Dickens Bibliographies, Vol. 9; Garland Reference Library of the Humanities, Vol. 708). $67.00. LC 88-4359. ISBN 0-8240-8512-4.

This annotated bibliography gives an account of Dickens's novel in its manuscript, proof, and printed versions, as well as an extensive survey of editions, adaptations, and responses to the novel from 1840 to 1985. As do previous volumes of the Garland Dickens Bibliographies series, this work contains entries dealing with the text of the novel, entries describing critical commentary on the novel, and entries indicating adaptations of it. Unlike other works, the volume includes a large number of nonscholarly, nonintellectual, and even unintelligent responses to Dickens's work. Annotations total 1,486.

The work is divided into three parts: text, studies, and adaptations. The text includes letters, manuscripts, editions, and bibliographical studies. The studies section consists of contemporary reviews and nineteenth- and twentieth-century criticisms. The final section contains film, stage, radio and television adaptations, parodies, and plagiarisms.

The volume concludes with a single index, which contains in one alphabetical listing characters, subject headings, names of authors, illustrators, adapters, and so on. Dickens's works are listed under their title, but works of other authors are only listed under the author's name. The index would have been better had all titles been listed; also, a divided index is generally easier to use and is certainly preferred by this reviewer.

Janet R. Ivey

Margaret Drabble

1108. Packer, Joan Garrett. **Margaret Drabble: An Annotated Bibliography.** New York, Garland, 1988. 189p. index. (Garland Reference Library of the Humanities, Vol. 913). $27.00. LC 88-23468. ISBN 0-8240-5937-9.

After a compact biographical introduction, this bibliography lists Margaret Drabble's novels, short stories, plays, and (here the annotations begin) nonfiction and edited texts (e.g., Wordsworth, Woolf, Hardy), reviews and essays (again, many are about Wordsworth, Woolf, and Hardy, but there are unexpected entries—Jane Fonda, Dirk Bogarde, Updike). The last part, two and a half times as long as the first, yet highly selective, consists of bibliographies (five of them), books and dissertations (twenty-three—all but one or two are by women), articles in books and journals, and reviews (some by big-name critics, such as Malcolm Muggeridge, Joyce Carol Oates, C. P. Snow, John Updike, Donald Davie, Angus Wilson, Frank Kermode, Roy Fuller, John Wain, V. S. Pritchett, Denis Donaghue, and Margaret Atwood). All bibliographical entries, it should be noted, are in the English language. From Parker's conscientious annotations alone one gets insights into Drabble's works (themes and influences, but not craft) and a clear view of critical reception. On almost every page, it is stated or implied that Drabble is "moral" or "over-moral" (what is "feminine morality"?); obviously the vast majority of commentators, as summarized, see her not as a novelist, but as an intensely, and vaguely, moral sociologist.

Paul H. Stacy

George Eliot

1109. Levine, George, with Patricia O'Hara. **An Annotated Critical Bibliography of George Eliot.** New York, St. Martin's Press, 1988. 128p. index. $35.00. LC 88-3044. ISBN 0-312-01959-9.

This bibliography provides a selective record of George Eliot scholarship covering approximately 1945-1985. Works are arranged under twelve broad subject categories, such as general essays and full-length critical studies. These broad subject categories are followed by separate groupings of materials focusing on individual books by Eliot, as well as her poetry and stories. Within each category items are listed chronologically, and within each year alphabetically. Brief annotations, some no more than a sentence in length, accompany each entry. A very brief subject index is provided, as well as an index to contributors.

This volume serves as a useful accompaniment to Constance Fulmer's *George Eliot: A Reference Guide* (see *ARBA* 79, entry 1239), updating and expanding on that helpful tool. This new bibliography also provides some interesting topical approaches to Eliot's works; particularly fascinating are the sections on feminism and feminist thought, and philosophy and religion. One would have wished for a fuller, more detailed subject index for this work, but even so researchers and students alike should find this new bibliography a useful one. [R: Choice, Nov 88, p. 462]

Elizabeth Patterson

George Herbert

1110. Roberts, John R. **George Herbert: An Annotated Bibliography of Modern Criticism, 1905-1984.** rev. ed. Columbia, Mo., University of Missouri Press, 1988. 433p. index. $39.00. LC 87-19095. ISBN 0-8262-0487-2.

This revised edition of Roberts's wide-ranging bibliography adds 653 new entries to the 800 from the first edition (see *ARBA* 80, entry 1275). Most of these items were written between 1974 and 1984, although earlier works have been added as well, particularly foreign-language works (most in Japanese). C. A. Patrides has collected and reprinted 64 works that predate Roberts's coverage in *George Herbert: The Critical Heritage* (Routledge & Kegan Paul, 1983).

The arrangement remains chronological, with detailed descriptive annotations, many containing revealing quotations from the cited work. Coverage includes all modern editions, translations, critical books, monographs, critical articles from 152 journals, biographical works, bibliographic essays, and pertinent but minor reviews and commentary. Dissertations are excluded.

The main shortcoming of this work remains the inadequate subject index. Specific items (e.g., pilgrimage, imagery, metrics, mimesis, ecstasy, pain) are the focus of several entries but are not listed in the subject index. Moreover, many entries are so broad that they cause frustration. For example, "Bible (Old Testament, New Testament, biblical figures)" has 153 references with no breakdown to specific books or persons, and no cross-references to separately listed books (e.g., Psalms). The author index and "Index of Herbert's Works Mentioned in Annotations" are complete and accurate.

Roberts's work remains an essential guide to twentieth-century Herbert criticism. Commentary on Herbert's work has greatly increased in this half of the twentieth century, and Roberts is planning a second revision. One hopes he will strengthen the subject index to provide better access to his excellent compilation.

Robert Aken

C. S. (Clive Staples) Lewis

1111. McLaughlin, Sara Park, and Mark O. Webb. **A Word Index to the Poetry of C. S. Lewis.** West Cornwall, Conn., Locust Hill Press, 1988. 232p. $30.00. LC 88-17562. ISBN 0-933951-21-3.

Commemorating the twenty-fifth anniversary of Lewis's death, the publication of *A Word Index* will be a welcomed addition to scholarship on C. S. Lewis. Carrying the claim as the first index to any of his writings makes the work of greater value. Three collections of poems are indexed: *Poems, Narrative Poems,* and *Spirits in Bondage.* These poems cover Lewis's poetry from his younger, atheistic days to his later life as a Christian.

With several editions of the collected poems available, the authors chose abbreviated titles of the books, codes for the poems, and line numbers over page numbers. A chart at the front of the index identifies each poem numerically. A list of words not indexed (prepositions and articles) follows. Foreign words were also omitted, which is a mistake since Lewis is famous for his fluency in several languages. The text, which was computer-generated, is clear and easy to use.   Patricia M. Leach

E. V. (Edward Verrall) Lucas

1112. Prance, Claude A. **E. V. Lucas and His Books.** West Cornwall, Conn., Locust Hill Press, 1988. 243p. $35.00. LC 88-15728. ISBN 0-933951-19-1.

Edward Verrall Lucas (1868-1938) was a prolific British writer, perhaps best known as an editor and biographer of Charles Lamb. Lucas was also a poet, novelist, writer of children's fiction, essayist, anthologist, diarist, and travel writer. He continues to be popular in the United States as well as England, but this annotated bibliography seeks to make Lucas better known. After a chronology of the life of Lucas, Prance provides a detailed account of the most important events in his life, with special attention to major writings.

The bibliography itself consists of four major sections: (1) a chronological list of Lucas's books and pamphlets (including those edited by and with introductions by Lucas), (2) contributions by Lucas to periodicals, (3) selected works about Lucas (including autobiographical writings), and (4) some books reprinting Lucas's works. Five separate alphabetical lists provide access to books and pamphlets; books edited, selected, or introduced by Lucas; essays, sketches, and short stories; verses; and selected subjects and genres of Lucas's books and essays.

Prance seems just as devoted an admirer of Lucas as Lucas was of Charles Lamb. This bibliography will be indispensable to readers interested in identifying the hundreds of publications of this very productive author.
     David Isaacson

George Moore

1113. Gilcher, Edwin, with Robert S. Becker and Clinton K. Krauss. **Supplement to** *A Bibliography of George Moore.* Westport, Conn., Meckler, 1988. 95p. index. $29.95. LC 87-18593. ISBN 0-88736-199-4.

Gilcher's *A Bibliography of George Moore* (see *ARBA* 71, entry 1488) is the definitive authority listing the many publications of this author. Although Moore died as long ago as 1933, he was so prolific and wrote for such a variety of hard-to-identify publications that this supplement correcting and adding entries to the original bibliography is quite useful to Moore scholars. Additions and corrections are limited to the sections devoted to listing Moore's books, pamphlets, and publications in periodicals. Additions and errata are presented in the same sequence and with the same typography as the original bibliography; this supplement, therefore, cannot be used apart from the parent bibliography. In his preface Gilcher says that he believes more publications by Moore will continue to be located, but since an entirely new edition of this bibliography will not be published "in the forseeable future" he issued this supplement.

Moore researchers may also be interested in Robert Langenfeld's recently published *George Moore: An Annotated Secondary Bibliography of Writings about Him* (see *ARBA* 88, entry 1221).   David Isaacson

Iris Murdoch

1114. Begnal, Kate. **Iris Murdoch: A Reference Guide.** Boston, G. K. Hall, 1987. 198p. index. (Reference Guide to Literature). $35.00. LC 87-25042. ISBN 0-8161-8646-4.

This reference guide demonstrates the increasing critical acclaim received by a modern British writer. The first major bibliography by Thomas T. Tominaga and Wilma Schneidermeyer, *Iris Murdoch and Muriel Sparks: A Bibliography* (Scarecrow, 1976) covered writings by and about Iris Murdoch up to 1975, including all secondary works found. This guide expands that work through 1983 but omits the "brief reviews, uninformative plot summaries, encyclopedias, literary histories, and foreign commentary difficult to obtain." The importance of this guide, in relation to the first bibliography by Tominaga and Schneidermeyer, is the inclusion of annotations in the section on secondary sources. The introduction and annotations clearly delineate the "critical reception of Murdoch's books" and illustrate her "popular as well as academic reputation." The chronological arrangement makes it more difficult to locate criticism of a particular work (even though the index is a key to this criticism), but it is most effective in developing the critical controversy surrounding Iris Murdoch and the growing interest in her work. Over the years, the annotations show, the initial disappointments have diminished and the critics have focused more on her strengths in "flexibility of style" and "intellect and sensitivity." As the author intimates, Iris Murdoch is moving from "the honorable second rank of artists" to "emerge as a writer of considerable stature," with comparisons to Virginia Woolf, E. M. Forster, Jane Austen, Doris Lessing, and Vladimir Nabokov, to name but a few. [R: Choice, May 88, p. 1378]

Maureen Pastine

Walter H. Pater

1115. Wright, Samuel. **An Informative Index to the Writings of Walter H. Pater.** West Cornwall, Conn., Locust Hill Press, 1987. 460p. $40.00. LC 87-22852. ISBN 0-933951-11-6.

This work is an index, not to one title, but to several: the life work, in fact, of Walter Pater, the critic/essayist/novelist whose works, like those of many other late Victorians, are coming back into fashion, and whose views of art are receiving new critical acclaim.

The idea of a multivolume subject index (not a concordance) is hardly common among reference publications, but not at all a bad idea when the subject permits such a work. An index to each book, the compiler maintains, "would fail to illuminate Pater's overall perspective on any particular subject. The breadth of Pater's interests is not always recognized" (preface). Fortunately for this indexer, the Pater canon is finite enough to be indexed in one volume, which, in this instance, covers the following works from the New Library Edition of the Works by Walter Pater (1910 and many reprints): *Appreciations with an Essay on "Style," Essays from "The Guardian," Gaston de Latour, Greek Studies, Imaginary Portraits, Marius the Epicurean, Miscellaneous Studies, Plato and Platonism,* and *The Renaissance.* Also included are Pater's *Uncollected Essays*

(1903), *Sketches and Reviews*, and six uncollected articles in magazines of his day. Had the compiler waited another year or so, he would have had access to a later and more reliable text of Pater's works: *Walter Pater: Three Major Texts*, edited by William E. Buckler (New York University Press, 1986).

Of particular interest in this index are the explanatory notes that accompany all but the most obvious entries, for example, "Diadumenos [statue by Polycleitus (q.v.) of an athletic youth 'binding the filet or crown of victory upon his head.' There are many copies]." Thus this "index" becomes a kind of dictionary to Pater's vast array of Greco-Roman references, though not, to be sure, an encyclopedia.

This reference work can be complemented (or preceded) by Wright's *Bibliography of the Writings of Walter H. Pater* (see *ARBA* 76, entry 1281) and Franklin E. Court's *Walter Pater: An Annotated Bibliography of Writings about Him* (see *ARBA* 81, entry 1323).

Edwin S. Gleaves

Alexander Pope

1116. Berry, Reginald. **A Pope Chronology.** Boston, G. K. Hall, 1988. 221p. bibliog. index. $35.00. LC 87-24772. ISBN 0-8161-8951-X.

This book is the first in a projected series of chronologies from the publisher. The intention is to provide a biographical digest, outlining by date the events of the author's life and career. It is not supposed that this approach will replace conventional biography which, with greater available space, can explore in depth such subjects as influence, cause and effect, and reception, and can carefully develop arguments in considerable detail. Instead, it presents the facts of its subject's life, in day-to-day diary form, drawn from reliable sources—that is, it is a reference book.

A Pope Chronology begins on Monday, 21 May 1688, with Pope's birth at 6:45 p.m., and ends on 14 June 1744 with the proving of Pope's will. In between, Pope's daily life is chronicled, much of it drawn from the five-volume *Correspondence* edited by George Sherburn (Clarendon Press, 1956). Information on other persons, such as John Gay and Jonathan Swift, is presented as it touches on Pope. Following the chronology is a list of principal persons and places mentioned and a very brief bibliography. The volume concludes with a full and competent index.

Although the book is certainly readable, its primary use will be as a quick and reliable source of biographical information. As such, it will no doubt be found very useful by Pope scholars. This reviewer's only suggestion is that sources be cited for more of the specific details so that the user might easily find more expanded information. [R: Choice, Dec 88, p. 622; WLB, Sept 88, pp. 90, 92]   Philip R. Rider

William Shakespeare

1117. DeLoach, Charles, comp. **The Quotable Shakespeare: A Topical Dictionary.** Jefferson, N.C., McFarland, 1988. 544p. index. $39.95. LC 87-35362. ISBN 0-89950-303-9.

As quotation books go, DeLoach's is a good one; 6,516 consecutively numbered quotations from the plays, poems, and sonnets of Shakespeare illustrate one thousand single-word topics arranged alphabetically. The book is prefaced by a (rather redundant, as the book is in dictionary format) table of contents, and includes topical and character indexes. The former helps access quotations of similar subjects under diverse headings.

For the most part, DeLoach does a good job of retaining the intrinsic sense of each quotation, as well as arranging them under the most appropriate subject heading. There are, however, a few failures. For example, most of Hamlet's address to the actors in Act 3 is rightly placed under the topic *acting*, yet his admonition in that address to "suit the action to the word [and] the word to the action," while clearly about acting, is inexplicably placed under the heading *tact*. In this case, the topical index fails to provide the appropriate cross-reference. DeLoach also provides variant textual readings of the quotations, if they are important to the sense of the quotation, and glosses obscure or archaic words.

Libraries that support a clientele with intensive Shakespeare-related research or interest may find this volume useful and fairly inexpensive. For others, *Bartlett's Quotations* will still provide the user with the most well-known and frequently used Shakespearean quotations. [R: BR, Nov/Dec 88, p. 48; Choice, Dec 88, pp. 624, 626; RBB, 1 Nov 88, pp. 464-65; WLB, Sept 88, p. 96]   James Edgar Stephenson

1118. Michael, Nancy C. **Pericles: An Annotated Bibliography.** New York, Garland, 1987. 289p. index. (Garland Shakespeare Bibliographies, No. 13; Garland Reference Library of the Humanities, Vol. 424). $43.00. LC 87-17295. ISBN 0-8240-9113-2.

This annotated bibliography continues the excellent tradition of Garland's Shakespeare Bibliographies series. As was the case with *Timon of Athens* (see *ARBA* 87, entry 1192), *Pericles* is one of the least known or performed

works of Shakespeare. Despite being a remote play, this volume consists of 816 annotations. Eight categories divide the work: "Criticism"; "Sources, Analogues, and Background"; "Dating"; "Authorship and Textual Studies"; "Bibliographies and Concordances"; "Editions"; "Stage History and Recorded Performances"; and "Adaptations, Influences, Synopses, and Excerpts." Works written between 1940 and 1985 are included and items within each category are arranged chronologically. The annotations are concise and to the point. The index is in a single dictionary format. Despite the obscurity of *Pericles*, this work would have been improved had there been divided indexes as in others of the Garland Shakespeare series. [R: Choice, Apr 88, p. 1223]

     Janet R. Ivey

1119. Micheli, Linda McJ., comp. **Henry VIII: An Annotated Bibliography.** New York, Garland, 1988. 444p. index. (Garland Shakespeare Bibliographies, No. 15; Garland Reference Library of the Humanities, Vol. 540). $62.00. LC 84-45381. ISBN 0-8240-8836-0.

This bibliography, part of the Garland Shakespeare Bibliographies series, follows the format of the previous volumes. As the editor points out, the bibliography covers "books, chapters, articles, editions, translations, dissertations, reviews, notices of production, analogues, and accounts of the influence of the play on other works and writers" (p. xxix). The period covered is from 1940 to 1984, but the reader will discover that coverage is also comprehensive for items before 1940. Though many items after 1984 are also included, the coverage of this period is spotty and unpredictable. The volume consists of an introduction; the bibliography, which is subdivided into ten sections; and a general index. The introduction, based on extensive research and written with much care, surveys the state of the scholarship on *Henry VIII*, covering such areas as authorship; overview of critical issues; sources and backgrounds; dating; textual studies; editions, adaptations, and translations; stage history; and analogues and influence. The bibliography proper covers nearly a thousand items divided into the following areas: criticism; authorship; sources and backgrounds; dating; textual studies; editions and adaptations; translations; stage history; influences, analogues, and miscellaneous; and bibliographies. Except for a number of typographical errors in the translation section, this bibliography is thoroughly satisfactory and very useful to scholars and students alike.

     Geraldo U. de Sousa

1120. Pearson, D'Orsay W., comp. **Two Gentlemen of Verona: An Annotated Bibliography.** New York, Garland, 1988. 251p. index. (Garland Shakespeare Bibliographies, No. 16; Garland Reference Library of the Humanities, Vol. 847). $37.00. LC 88-16544. ISBN 0-8240-5641-8.

Shakespeare's *Two Gentlemen of Verona* has long been unpopular with producers, readers, and literary critics, the latter having produced only a small body of critical writing about the play. D'Orsay W. Pearson, the compiler of this newest entry in the Garland Shakespeare Bibliographies series, reveals that "of all the plays in the canon, *Two Gentlemen* was considered the least likely candidate for producing a book-length bibliography." Nevertheless, Pearson has produced a fine annotated bibliography devoted to the play, with citations culled from books, periodicals, and doctoral dissertations, providing a comprehensive view of past and current commentary with little or no padding. Each consecutively numbered entry is given a full bibliographic citation and a nonjudgmental annotation which summarizes the article's major points. The combined author/subject index cross-references all of the citations. What is particularly welcome in this bibliography is a true "world view," with foreign-language publications frequently cited and annotated. In short, this is not a "makeshift" publication, but as essential a purchase as all of the Garland Shakespeare Bibliographies.

James Edgar Stephenson

1121. Roberts, Josephine A., comp. **Richard II: An Annotated Bibliography.** New York, Garland, 1988. 2v. index. (Garland Shakespeare Bibliographies, No. 14; Garland Reference Library of the Humanities, Vol. 833). $110.00/ set. LC 88-2697. ISBN 0-8240-8588-4.

This is volume 14 of the Garland Shakespeare Bibliographies series. Like the previous volumes, it provides comprehensive coverage for the years 1940-1982, but it also includes significant scholarship prior to 1940 and many items dated from 1983 to 1987. The scholarly introduction offers an overview of critical analyses of the play, sources, textual history and problems, genre studies, adaptations, and film versions. The first volume contains the introduction and criticism. The second volume includes separate sections on sources and historical background; dating; textual studies; individual editions; complete and collected editions; influence, adaptations, and altered versions; staging and stage history; criticism of films and other media; translations; and bibliographies. The entries, which are arranged by the year of original publication, provide complete biblio-

graphical information as well as lengthy, detailed annotations describing the item and summarizing its content. Many scholarly works published in foreign languages are also summarized, thus giving the reader access to a large body of material not available in English translation. The compiler also lists items, such as numerous dissertations, that she did not examine. This is probably one of the most complete, detailed bibliographies on any single Shakespeare play; it inspires awe and admiration for anyone who would undertake such a massive project. I find no faults, not even minor ones, with this monumental, definitive bibliography, which eventually will be updated but not superseded. [R: Choice, Nov 88, p. 468]

Geraldo U. de Sousa

1122. Woodbridge, Linda. **Shakespeare: A Selective Bibliography of Modern Criticism.** West Cornwall, Conn., Locust Hill Press, 1988. 266p. index. $20.00. LC 87-31134. ISBN 0-933951-14-0.

Linda Woodbridge's *Shakespeare: A Selective Bibliography of Modern Criticism* is a small book with modest aspirations. Unfortunately, its aspirations are *too* modest.

This is an enumerative bibliography of modern Shakespeare criticism (i.e., books or articles written between 1900 and 1985) grouped together under general subject headings. Under the "Individual Plays and Poems" section, the citations are further grouped by specific work. An author index accesses individual citations. Each citation is numbered consecutively for convenient referencing, and most abbreviations for journal titles are avoided. Woodbridge accurately describes these features of the bibliography as "user friendly."

This bibliography is not annotated, which was a deliberate decision by the compiler. Woodbridge confesses in her preface that she "[is] not a great admirer of annotation as many scholars are," and defends her decision to jettison annotations, as they "distort a critical argument in the same way that ... [a] plot summary distorts a work of fiction." Further, she says, annotations would increase the book size or decrease the number of citations. Consequently, the user must rely on the title of the work alone to determine its quality or critical thrust – and titles of articles of literary criticism are notoriously vague. If annotations are desired, Woodbridge perversely recommends that the reader turn to Larry Champion's annotated bibliography *The Essential Shakespeare* (see *ARBA* 87, entry 1189).

Woodbridge's main objective was to produce a "portable, inexpensive working bibliography which a Shakespeare student might carry about all year," yet even there this bibliography fails, as the hardbound format and twenty dollar price tag testifies. Libraries should bypass this volume in favor of the annual Shakespeare bibliographies published by the PMLA and *Shakespeare Quarterly*, the aforementioned Champion bibliography, or the excellent Garland Shakespeare Bibliographies series. [R: Choice, June 88, p. 1541]

James Edgar Stephenson

George Bernard Shaw

1123. Adams, Elsie B., with Donald C. Haberman, comps. and eds. **G. B. Shaw: An Annotated Bibliography of Writings about Him. Volume II: 1931-1956.** DeKalb, Ill., Northern Illinois University Press, 1987. 667p. index. (Annotated Secondary Bibliography Series on English Literature in Transition, 1880-1920). $45.00. LC 86-8649. ISBN 0-87580-121-8.

Volume 2 of this projected three-volume bibliography lists 2,394 citations to secondary works and follows the format and extensive coverage of volume 3 (see *ARBA* 88, entry 1225). During the years covered by the present volume, Shaw, who died in 1950, was "at the apogee of his fame" (introduction): writings about him react to his prodigious output as a writer, his socialist politics, and performances of new plays and revivals of his classics written earlier in the century. Works listed span some twenty-one languages and include literary, theatrical, and cinema reviews; critical works; biographies; dissertations; articles in encyclopedias; and works of a more general nature in which Shaw's own works are discussed. Citations are arranged by year of publication and by author within each year. An annotation succinctly paraphrases each entry. Indexes list authors, titles of secondary works, titles of periodicals and newspapers, foreign languages, and titles of primary works.

William S. Brockman

Percy Bysshe Shelley

1124. Engelberg, Karsten Klejs. **The Making of the Shelley Myth: An Annotated Bibliography of Criticism of Percy Bysshe Shelley 1822-1860.** London, Mansell and Westport, Conn., Meckler, 1988. 468p. index. $59.50. ISBN 0-88736-298-2.

Scholars of Shelley will welcome this annotated bibliography of one of the most interesting poets, in terms of both his work and his life. The bibliography is nonevaluative but gives the reader a clear idea of the content of the citation. The author has used the considerable resources of the Bodleian Library, The British Library, and the Manchester Public Library to pull together this impressive bibliography.

The work is more than a bibliography, however. The first eighty-two pages consist of four chapters in which a defense of Shelley and a rationale for the "Shelley Myth" is presented. The author clearly has prejudices and a thesis here. It would have been better, however, to have written a separate monograph on the topic and allow the bibliography to stand on its own clear merits. In essence, this is one and a fraction of a book. The four chapters need expansion and amplification.

The bibliography is excellent, but the four essays need work. This is highly recommended for research collections in British literature; other libraries are not likely to find it useful or used. [R: Choice, Oct 88, p. 290]

C. D. Hurt

Alan Sillitoe

1125. Gerard, David. **Alan Sillitoe: A Bibliography.** Westport, Conn., Meckler, 1988. 175p. index. $47.50. LC 87-34748. ISBN 0-88736-104-8.

Gerard's compilation is the first book-length bibliography to appear on contemporary novelist Sillitoe, who is best known for his powerful descriptions of British working class life in works such as *Saturday Night and Sunday Morning* (Knopf, 1959) and *The Loneliness of the Long Distance Runner* (New American Library, 1971). A forerunner is found in R. J. Stanton's *Bibliography of Modern British Novelists* (see *ARBA* 79, entry 1230), but the present work is much more comprehensive and up-to-date.

The beginning section is a descriptive bibliography of first editions of the author's books, with other editions and translations also noted for each work. This is followed by a chronological listing of his contributions to books and periodicals. Section C lists materials of critical and biographical interest in alphabetical order by author, and D is devoted to reviews of Sillitoe's works. The final two parts cover films and plays, including relevant reviews and critical articles, and radio and television programs and sound recordings. The time period covered is 1950 through 1987, although most of the critical studies are dated 1986 or earlier. An enthusiastic introduction discusses Sillitoe's background and main themes. An index to authors and titles is provided.

This is a useful effort, particularly as a primary bibliography; Sillitoe scholars and libraries collecting twentieth-century British literature will want to own it.

Willa Schmidt

John Skelton

1126. Fox, Alistair, and Gregory Waite, eds. **A Concordance to the Complete English Poems of John Skelton.** Ithaca, N.Y., Cornell University Press, 1987. 1001p. index. $49.50. LC 87-47552. ISBN 0-8014-1944-1.

This, the first published concordance to any of the works of John Skelton, is a much needed addition to existing scholarly resources not only for advanced research on Skelton but also on early sixteenth-century English literature and language in general. The concordance is based on *John Skelton: The Complete English Poems*, edited by John Scattergood (Yale, 1983), which supersedes Alexander Dyce's *The Poetical Works of John Skelton* (Thomas Rodd, 1843) as the standard edition. Additionally, significant variants from selected fifteenth- and sixteenth-century manuscript and printed texts are identified, permitting the reconstruction of those texts. As in other concordances in the series, frequency, modern spellings, and compound-word indexes are appended. Other appendices present a fresh transcription of the radically variant manuscript version of *Collyn Clout* and a word index to this text.

The concordance's most obvious shortcoming owes to the decision to index only Skelton's English-language vocabulary rather than the complete texts of the English poems as prepared by Scattergood. The omission of Skelton's foreign words and phrases is particularly unfortunate. Fox and Waite acknowledge that it is "the idiosyncratic stylistic and linguistic habits that make Skelton a unique genius" (p. viii). As J. A. Burrow points out in reviewing Scattergood's edition, a significant portion of Skelton's English poetry consists of "classical Greek and Latin tags, phrases of scholastic and liturgical Latin, and scraps of French, Spanish, Dutch and even Welsh ... jumbled together higgledy-piggledy" (*TLS* [15 April 1983]: 372). On the one hand, Fox and Waite index each "chuk" in Skelton's "Good yere and good luk,/ With chuk, chuk, chuk, chuk" ("Garlande," 11. 1003-1004), as well as words like "troly-loly-lo" ("Agaynste a Comely Coystrowne," 1. 15) and "te he," "ta ha," and "bo ho" ("Replycacion," 1. 75), while on the other hand exclude the more meaningful Latin of "And yet ye supposed/ *Respondere ad quantum,*/But ye were *confuse tantum,*/Surrendering your supposycions,/For

there ye myst your quosshons" ("Replycacion," 11. 109-113). Including Skelton's non-English vocabulary would have greatly increased the concordance's usefulness in linguistic research. Even appended indexes of Skelton's foreign vocabulary would have made the work more valuable to scholars.

Despite this limitation, the concordance will certainly provide more than "a modest impetus" (p. ix) toward the study of Skelton. With this work, Scattergood's edition, and Robert S. Kinsman's *John Skelton, Early Tudor Laureate: An Annotated Bibliography, c.1488-1977* (G. K. Hall, 1979), scholars are at last adequately equipped to intensify research. [R: Choice, June 88, p. 1534]   James K. Bracken

Montague Summers

1127. Frank, Frederick S. **Montague Summers: A Bibliographical Portrait.** Metuchen, N.J., Scarecrow, 1988. 277p. index. (Great Bibliographers Series, No. 7). $29.50. LC 88-10048. ISBN 0-8108-2136-2.

A useful research tool for those involved in the study of literature, drama, religion, and publishing itself, this volume presents a somewhat panoramic view of a somewhat unique writer and researcher. Frank has compiled a variety of perspectives on the Reverend Montague Summers. These perspectives include an opening section that presents three interpretative essays on Summers. The next major section includes selections from Summers's writings in three major areas: the Restoration theater, the Gothic novel, and demonology and witchcraft. A third and final section includes a biographical chronology and annotated bibliography of works by Montague Summers. Entries include full bibliographic information accompanied by evaluative or interpretative remarks, some of which are quite lengthy. Frank has also provided indexes by author, artist, actor, and title.

As Summers has always appeared to be somewhat of an enigma in terms of intellectual pursuits and literary research, this volume should find use among a variety of audiences. Recommended for most academic libraries, and public libraries whose community of users might reasonably be drawn to the volume.

Edmund F. SantaVicca

Anthony Trollope

1128. Gerould, Winifred Gregory, and James Thayer Gerould. **A Guide to Trollope.** Princeton, N.J., Princeton University Press, c1976, 1987. 256p. maps. $40.00; $12.95pa. LC 48-7405. ISBN 0-691-06053-3; 0-691-01441-8pa.

Republication of this guide after forty years proves that Trollope's star is still in the ascendant. There are those who would even claim that he has reached the zenith of a cult figure. Trollope's novels, especially *The Warden* and *Barchester Towers*, continue to be read with avid interest; for despite his many faults, no other writer has depicted so clearly and so completely the virtues and shortcomings of the clerical and the political society of his day. Additionally, no other Victorian knew the countryside as well as he, the postal inspector who penetrated into every corner of it. The breadth of his interest in the men and women he met is reflected in his characters, whom he always treated kindly. However weak or vicious he drew them, he always—unlike Dickens, with whom he is frequently compared—hinted at traits that relieved their baseness.

This reference tool is an alphabetical record of all such characters and locales found in his more than sixty novels and stories. In many cases the identifications are in Trollope's own words, taken from the works as they are. Included is a brief plot summary of each story. Trollope's own estimate of an individual work as found in his *Autobiography* (1883) is also given, plus occasional comments by critics. Of special help are nine maps based upon the author's own geographical indications of various narratives.

An inexpensive paper edition is available to all Trollopians for their personal libraries. Reference collections (whose 1948 edition of this work should be shelf-worn by now) will require the more substantial clothbound edition.

G. A. Cevasco

John Wain

1129. Gerard, David. **John Wain: A Bibliography.** Westport, Conn., Meckler, 1987. 235p. index. $47.50. LC 87-7959. ISBN 0-88736-103-X.

This bibliography of a well-established, prolific contemporary British writer covers John Wain's career from the late 1940s to 1986. It begins with a critical introduction to Wain's writings: the novels, the short stories, the poetry, and the criticism. The major body of the volume is divided into five sections: books by Wain; contributions to books and periodicals; materials of critical and biographical interest; reviews of works by Wain; and radio, television, and sound recordings. Entries are arranged chronologically, except for the section of reference sources (critical and biographical works about Wain) which are arranged alphabetically by author. In the first section, the first British

edition is described in full, including number of copies, binding, cover, illustrations, print style, and typeface. Other editions and translations follow the main entry. "First appearances of essays, poems and short stories are listed in the second section with a reference to the volume in which they were later collected." The work also includes an index referring to entry numbers for personal names and titles of works. The bibliography is comprehensive and easy to read and use even though the print is small. Varied typefaces and spacing help. I found the prefatory remarks on location of printed materials and manuscript holdings particularly useful. In addition the author includes a note on availability of scripts of radio, television, and sound recordings by Wain. This first book-length bibliography on Wain is an important contribution to the extensive critical and biographical material published on this major British short story writer, novelist, poet, essayist, and critic. [R: Choice, Nov 88, p. 460]

Maureen Pastine

Arthur Waley

1130. Johns, Francis A. **A Bibliography of Arthur Waley.** 2d ed. Atlantic Highlands, N.J., Athlone Press; distr., Atlantic Highlands, N.J., Humanities Press, 1988. 160p. index. $70.00. LC 87-18706. ISBN 0-485-11344-9.

The first edition of this descriptive bibliography was published by the Rutgers University Press (1968). This second edition is photoduplicated on thinner paper stock and is not as attractive as the printed older edition. The photograph of Arthur Waley found in the earlier edition has not been included here. However, the descriptive entries, the typography, the citations to journals and anthologies, and the indexing and cross-referencing are all excellently thought-out and executed. The bibliography is a model of its kind. The book's original organization remains the same. The sections that have been expanded are "Book Reviews," "Miscellaneous," "Some Appearances in Anthologies," and the final section, "Material on Arthur Waley."

The descriptive format for published books and their contents contains references to Waley translations published in periodicals prior to their inclusion in a published book. Subsequent reprintings in other published works are often noted. Johns's comments or footnotes are extremely important, serving to clarify problems and aid scholars. Citations to critical comment on Waley's contribution as a translator of oriental literature will save hours of hunting through other published bibliographies for this information. The bibliography includes all known material up to December 1985.

Milton H. Crouch

H. G. Wells

1131. Scheick, William J., and J. Randolph Cox. **H. G. Wells: A Reference Guide.** Boston, G. K. Hall, 1988. 430p. index. (Reference Guide to Literature). $45.00. LC 88-5220. ISBN 0-8161-8946-3.

This work provides the researcher with a bibliography of works by Wells as well as a listing of articles and books about the man and his writings published between 1895 and 1986. The author plans to update the work in a supplement, to be published in *English Literature in Transition* (Arizona State University, Department of English, 1963-). Other works of note are Geoffrey H. Wells's *A Bibliography of the Works of H. G. Wells, 1893-1925* (Routledge, 1925), *H. G. Wells, 1866-1946: A Centenary Booklist* by James Thirsk (Ealing Central Library, 1966), *A Bibliography of H. G. Wells* by Fred A. Chappell (Norwood, 1977, c1924), and the Bromley Public Libraries's *Catalogue of the H. G. Wells Collection* (Bromley Public Libraries, 1974). In addition, the H. G. Wells Society has recently published the fourth edition of its *Comprehensive Bibliography* (H. G. Wells Society, 1986).

The primary sources in this reference guide are arranged chronologically within categories such as fiction (with collected editions set apart), nonfiction, and letters. In books consisting of collections of short stories or essays, the individual works are enumerated, a useful feature. The main body of the book is an extensive annotated listing of secondary literature. Annotations range from a single sentence to a paragraph in length, and frequently characterize the author's reactions to Wells. An index by author, editor, and translator completes the work. Researchers may be frustrated by the lack of a subject index. Libraries will also need to purchase the H. G. Wells Society bibliography for more complete information on the primary sources. [R: Choice, Nov 88, p. 468]

Maureen B. Lambert

William Wordsworth

1132. Pinion, F. B. **A Wordsworth Chronology.** Boston, G. K. Hall, 1988. 255p. maps. bibliog. index. $35.00. LC 87-25208. ISBN 0-8161-8950-1.

Pinion covers selected facts of Wordsworth's life in this volume of G. K. Hall's Literary Chronology series. This work also includes four black-and-white maps of appropriate areas of England and Scotland, twenty-four biographical sketches of "Persons of Importance in Wordsworth's Life," a twenty-five-item bibliography of sources, and thorough indexes to subjects and Wordsworth's poetry and prose. Although Pinion finds Mark L. Reed's *Wordsworth: The Chronology of the Early Years, 1770-1799* (Harvard, 1967) and *Wordsworth: The Chronology of the Middle Years, 1800-1815* (Harvard, 1975) "probably too acronymic and conjectural for all but those who wish to specialize in Wordsworth biography" (p. 235), Reed's works remain definitive for the period covered. Over half of Pinion's work covers the period following 1815 (a projected third volume of Reed's will cover the later years), and he does add some facts drawn from recent publications (including Beth Darlington's *The Love Letters of William and Mary Wordsworth* [Cornell, 1981]). He does not, however, provide the discussion and documentation Reed does in extensive footnoting, source references, cross-references, and appendices. Reed also includes a chronological listing of Wordsworth's works with cross-references to the main chronology. The index in Reed's book fails to list every reference in the text; Pinion's is exhaustive.

Pinion's work will be useful to those seeking an outline of events in Wordsworth's life and for its coverage of the later years; Reed remains essential for the scholar. [R: Choice, Dec 88, p. 622; WLB, Sept 88, pp. 90, 92]

Robert Aken

POETRY

1133. Kallich, Martin. **British Poetry and the American Revolution: A Bibliographical Survey of Books and Pamphlets, Journals and Magazines, Newspapers, and Prints 1755-1800.** Troy, N.Y., Whitston Publishing, 1988. 2v. index. $150.00/set. LC 86-50943. ISBN 0-87875-318-4.

Kallich's book provides detailed entries for over fifty-six hundred poems about Britain's American colonies—more specifically, "about domestic and political affairs that affected the colonies" (p. xii)—published in books, pamphlets, magazines, newspapers, broadsides, and miscellaneous prints in Great Britain in the period 1763 to 1783, with selective coverage from 1755 through 1800. As such, Kallich's bibliography, first, affords comprehensive bibliographic coverage of contemporary verse accounts of revolutionary America from the British point of view and, second, potentially serves as an index or finding aid for these accounts in that many are now included in widely accessible microform collections.

Coverage of books and pamphlets expands on that previously offered by Joseph Sabin's *Bibliotheca Americana* (Repr., N. Israel, 1961-1962) and Thomas R. Adams's *The American Controversy: A Bibliographical Study of the British Pamphlets about the American Disputes, 1764-1783* (see *ARBA* 82, entry 397), as well as, for American reprints, Charles Evans's *American Bibliography* (Repr., Peter Smith, 1941). Heavily relying on notices in contemporary sources like the *Monthly Review* and the *Critical Review*, Kallich identifies about five hundred poems published as books and pamphlets. Significant attention is given to analysis of the period's poetical collections, or "miscellanies," that typically reprinted quantities of verse. Here Kallich's bibliography offers useful access to the microform collections that include materials in Sabin and Evans. The bibliography's value will doubtless increase as the *Eighteenth Century Short Title Catalogue* project continues and additional titles are microfilmed.

Arrangement in the catalog is chronological by years, with convenient subdivisions for books and pamphlets, serials, and prints. Entries are generally (as opposed to bibliographically) descriptive, including full bibliographic data; transcriptions of first lines, with line counts; Evans and Sabin numbers; references to contemporary notices (in the *Monthly Review*, for example); locations of copies in British and American libraries, brief descriptions of meter and stanzaic form; and very useful annotations that describe the subjects of the verses and attempt to give their historical contexts. A poem's publishing history is also noted when appropriate. Separate indexes of authors (with subdivisions for poems) and anonymous poems; topics, including persons, places, events, themes, and subjects; and verse forms conclude volume 2.

All in all, Kallich's *British Poetry and the American Revolution* offers a very useful complement to Gillian B. Anderson's *Freedom's Voice in Poetry and Song* (see *ARBA* 79, entry 958), which indexes poetry and lyrics in 126 colonial newspapers, as well as to the basic research bibliographies and collections mentioned previously. Both Anderson's and Kallich's bibliographies should be regarded as important purchases for libraries supporting research on the period of the American Revolution. Medium-sized and small academic libraries supporting courses in American studies and owning some of the major microform collections with materials on this period should consider Kallich's not inexpensive bibliography as a valuable investment.   James K. Bracken

Australian Literature

1134. Pierce, Peter, and others, eds. **The Oxford Literary Guide to Australia.** New York, Oxford University Press, 1987. 344p. illus. (part col.). maps. $59.00. ISBN 0-19-554592-3.

This lavishly photographed work will find more utility on the coffee table than on the reference shelves. Produced by the Association for the Study of Australian Literature, it indeed provides "a kaleidescope of glimpses into Australia's history" (foreword), but like a kaleidescope, it must be experienced in bits and pieces. One must be cautioned that any attempt to use it for quick reference will be frustrated.

The format is geographical, arranged by territory, and then alphabetically by specific place—these individual entries consist of towns, townships, rivers, suburbs, and mountains. There is an index by author name, which provides the specific geographic location for the works by that author; one must then turn to the territory section, and flip through the entries until the correct one is found. Page numbers would have been helpful. Maps at the back aid those not familiar with Australia's geography, but a strictly alphabetical place index would have been better. Main entries are a succinct sentence or two describing what the author accomplished in the place listed, and sometimes briefly excerpt a creative work if it captures the atmosphere of the area.

One could painlessly learn much about Australia's landscape and history by dipping into this book at leisure. The two hundred plus photographs, about twenty of which are plates, make it a real pleasure to read. It would be valuable in travel collections and in libraries with extensive holdings in literature. [R: RBB, 15 Nov 88, p. 555]   Maureen B. Lambert

Brazilian Literature

1135. Stern, Irwin, ed. **Dictionary of Brazilian Literature.** Westport, Conn., Greenwood Press, 1988. 402p. maps. index. $65.00. LC 87-17744. ISBN 0-313-24932-6.

Written and compiled by forty-six specialists on Brazilian studies, this dictionary contains approximately three hundred entries on Brazilian writers and literary and cultural movements ranging from the colonial to the contemporary periods. The length of the entries varies according to the relative importance of the figure or literary movement. In addition to a biographical list of the contributors, the dictionary also includes a comparative chronology (1500-1987) of Brazilian history, Brazilian literature, and non-Brazilian literature. There is a fourteen-page introduction to "Brazilian Literature in Cultural Perspective," which, as the editor points out, "presents a global perspective on the development of Brazilian literature within the culture" (p. xv) and a bibliography of Brazilian studies. The dictionary proper consists of two types of entries: authors (arranged in alphabetical order) and themes and movements. Some of these entries are very short; others are quite detailed. Some of the articles are particularly outstanding, for example: "Slavery and Literature" and "Contemporary Black Literature," both written by James H. Kennedy; "Theater History," by Leslie Damasceno; "Film and Literature," by Randal Johnson; and "Children's Literature," by Marisa Lajolo. These and other entries offer information not easily available from other sources in English. Each entry includes a bibliography on additional selected works, translations, and criticism. Scholars, students, and general readers will find this superb dictionary to be of enormous value. [R: Choice, Oct 88, p. 286]

Geraldo U. de Sousa

Canadian Literature

1136.   Deahl, James, and Bruce Meyer, eds. **Poetry Markets for Canadians.** 3d ed. Toronto, League of Canadian Poets, 1987. 58p. $10.00pa.

This directory updates information previously contained in *Poetry Markets in Canada*, the last edition of which was published in 1984. Most of the book lists Canadian book and periodical publishers which accept poetry. A few publishers in the United States, Great Britain, and Australia are also included. Excluded are French-language sources, since, as a rule, the Canadian French and English poetry markets function separately from one another.

Besides the lists of book and magazine poetry publishers, this directory includes a number of pages of practical advice for new poets about submitting their poems to magazines; a list of writers' workshops; advice about negotiating book contracts; a list of literary awards; markets for oral poetry (radio, television, and public readings); and a list of resources, including other directories of publishers, writers' organizations, and Canadian government resources.

Canadian poets interested in a wider American market need to consult standard directories

such as *Writer's Market* (see *ARBA* 88, entry 925), *The Poet's Marketplace* (see *ARBA* 85, entry 779), *The International Directory of Little Magazines and Small Presses* (see entry 583), and *Literary Marketplace.*

The League of Canadian Poets, which publishes this directory, also sponsors poetry readings; offers manuscript evaluation; administers literary prizes; hosts international festivals; and publishes a newsletter, a members' directory, and various books. Considering the modest price and the fact that many of these publishers will not be found in other directories, this is a recommended purchase for many Canadian (and some American) libraries.

David Isaacson

1137.   **An Index to the Contents of the Periodical Canadian Literature. Supplement 1: Nos. 103-107.** By Glenn Clever. Ottawa, Tecumseh Press, 1987. 34p. $6.95pa. ISBN 0-919662-18-8.

1138.   **An Index to the Contents of the Periodical Canadian Literature. Supplement 2: Nos. 108-111.** By Glenn Clever. Ottawa, Tecumseh Press, 1987. 26p. $5.95pa. ISBN 0-919662-19-6.

1139.   **An Index to the Contents of the Periodical Canadian Literature. Supplement 3: Nos. 112-115.** By Glenn Clever. Ottawa, Tecumseh Press, 1988. 38p. $6.35pa. ISBN 0-919662-20-X.

The latest publications in the series of indexes to the journal *Canadian Literature* cover volumes 103 through 115 and are designed to supplement the index to volumes 1 through 102 published in 1984.

Each of the three supplements begins with a list of subject headings used in the supplement. Many of these headings are very broad (e.g., "Canada, reference works") and may be of limited use. Articles are indexed by subject including personal names. Articles about individual works, including book reviews, are listed under the authors of those works. Book reviews are designated by asterisks. Poetry and other creative works appear in *Canadian Literature* listed also under their authors. The extensive index names many books passingly mentioned in text but neither discussed nor reviewed. No description of the scope of the index nor any instructions for its use are offered in the supplements.

These supplements will be of interest to those who found the previous index to *Canadian Literature* helpful and to those who require extensive access to the contents of *Canadian Literature*. Its French language articles in particular may not be indexed adequately elsewhere. Others finding the contents of *Canadian*

Literature covered in other sources (e.g., *Humanities Index*) should consider this a discretionary purchase.　　　Gari-Anne Patzwald

1140.　Lecker, Robert, and Jack David, eds. **The Annotated Bibliography of Canada's Major Authors. Volume Seven.** Toronto, ECW Press; distr., Boston, G. K. Hall, 1987. 477p. index. $48.00. ISBN 0-920763-11-1. (This may be obtained in Canada in paperback from ECW Press, $28.00pa., ISBN 0-920763-12-X.)

This annotated bibliography of nineteenth- and twentieth-century French- and English-Canadian major authors and poets is the seventh in a series of eight volumes, and it is available in a hardbound or paperback format. Coverage includes only four authors: Marian Engel, Anne Hébert, Robert Kroetsch, and Thomas H. Raddall. Each volume includes works by and about the writers covered. Each bibliography includes books, broadsides, audiovisual materials, manuscripts, contributions to books and periodicals, and miscellaneous works by the author. Works about the author include books, articles, theses and dissertations, interviews, audiovisual materials, awards and honors, and selected reviews of the author's works. There is an index to critics listed in the bibliography. The listings by the authors include all book editions reprints, revisions, translations, excerpted work, or retitled works. The sections are organized chronologically within genres to ensure a sense of "the relation between creative output and shifting critical response." The cut-off date for inclusion of materials was 1985. The manuscripts section identifies the comprehensiveness, contents, and location of manuscript collections, a valuable asset for the scholar/researcher. The annotations are particularly valuable, as they often include thought-provoking quotations from the author's works or controversial comments from the critics.

It would have been helpful to have, in each volume, a listing of the authors covered in other volumes. It would also have been useful to know the editors' criteria for those included in the series.　　　Maureen Pastine

1141.　**Literary Archives Guide. Guide des Archives Littéraires.** Ottawa, National Archives of Canada, 1988. 59p. free pa. ISBN 0-662-55424-8.

The National Archives of Canada has produced a bilingual (French and English) guide to post-Confederation literary collections acquired by its Manuscript Division before 30 September 1987. Included are papers of poets, writers of fiction and nonfiction prose, children's authors, critics, journalists, editors, publishers, and anthologists, as well as literary organizations. Entries are arranged alphabetically by subject. Each entry indicates call number, inclusive dates of the collection, size, and availability of microfilm and/or a finding aid. Brief essays give biographical information, describe highlights of the collections, and list other prominent people about whom the collection contains significant material. There are also cross-references to related collections. The guide also includes guidelines and instructions for use of the Manuscript Division's collections and invites researchers to contact the Division for more detailed information about specific collections. This brief guide provides a general overview and summary of literary collections of the Manuscript Division. It will complement other recent guides to Canadian archival and manuscript resources and will be a helpful starting point for those planning to use the National Archives's literary collections.

Gari-Anne Patzwald

1142.　Lochhead, Douglas G., comp. **A Checklist of Nineteenth Century Canadian Poetry in English: The Maritimes.** Sackville, N.B., Centre for Canadian Studies, Mount Allison University, 1987. 1v. (unpaged). $7.50pa.

This 8½-by-11-inch paperback checklist was printed in a 1987 preliminary edition of two hundred copies as part of "a larger work which will embrace all of Canada during the years 1800-1899." According to the preface, it was "originally based on R. E. Walters's *A Checklist of Canadian Literature* ... second edition, revised and enlarged (1972)." This edition includes more titles and editions along with a record of the holdings of many North American libraries. *A Preliminary Checklist of Nineteenth Century Canadian Poetry in English* (Sackville, New Brunswick, Centre for Canadian Studies, Mount Allison University, 1976) was the precursor of this 1987 checklist. This work should prove to be of greatest value to special collections librarians and scholars interested in nineteenth-century Canadian literature. It lists approximately 315 works by early Canadian poets. Entries are arranged alphabetically by poet (many are anonymous) and include title of the work, place of publication, publisher, date, and number of pages, along with abbreviations of Canadian and North American libraries holding the publications. This "attempt to compile a listing of all known titles of nineteenth century English Canadian poetry" will add to our knowledge of Canadian history and literature, and the works listed will provide a fascinating glimpse of the schoolroom and social circle, public worship, emigration, music, women's roles, politics, and legends and beliefs of the times.

Maureen Pastine

1143.　Moritz, Albert, and Theresa Moritz. **The Oxford Illustrated Literary Guide to Canada.** Don Mills, Ont., Oxford University Press, 1987. 246p. illus. index. $45.00. ISBN 0-19-540596-X.

This concise illustrated literary history of Canada surveys the literary past and present of the country from the standpoint of regions and places: Newfoundland and Labrador, Nova Scotia, Prince Edward Island, New Brunswick, Quebec, Ontario, Manitoba, Saskatchewan, Alberta, British Columbia, Northwest Territories, and Yukon Territory. This approach provides a fascinating historical sketch of over five hundred cities and environments, allowing the scholar to trace curiosities, connections, and coincidences and significance of relationships of literary output from different authors living and working in the same places, albeit during different time periods.

Under the name of the region, the entries are arranged alphabetically by place and provide brief accounts of the essayists, humorists, poets, novelists, preachers, folk song writers, dramatists, explorers, and adventurers whose names are in boldface type and who have brought unknown places to our attention, or who have transformed an insignificant event into major literary work. The entries are filled with anecdotes, biographies, brief synopses of literary works, sites of buildings and houses long gone, and locations and addresses of writers now deceased. This volume will be loved by trivia experts and travelers, recreational readers and serious scholars. Newspaper articles, tragic events, and everyday occurrences forming the basis of novels, poems, and songs are frequently mentioned, as are the famous and not-so-famous visitors who wrote major works around a region or place or who kept diaries of the life of the times. The black-and-white photographs scattered liberally throughout the volume add to the enjoyment of browsing through its pages. The index provides an alphabetical listing, by surname, of all literary and other historical figures named throughout this one-volume literary history. [R: Choice, Sept 88, p. 84; RBB, 1 Oct 88, p. 244; WLB, June 88, pp. 142-43]

Maureen Pastine

1144.　New, W. H., ed. **Canadian Writers, 1920-1959: First Series.** Detroit, Gale, 1988. 417p. illus. index. (Dictionary of Literary Biography, Vol. 68). $95.00. LC 88-724. ISBN 0-8103-1746-X.

The sixty-eighth volume in the Dictionary of Literary Biography is the first of two volumes on Canadian writers who established their reputations between 1920 and 1959. It begins with an excellent introductory essay by editor W. H. New. The following sections on individual authors begin with lists of works by the subjects. These cover all major works but are not exhaustive (e.g., books by Gabrielle Roy are included but not her contributions to periodicals). Essays, written by scholars, emphasize the subject's professional development and describe major works. These essays are professionally written and informative, if frequently subjective, and careful editing has made them remarkably similar in scope. Where available, selected interviews, biographies, critical works, and manuscripts are included. The black-and-white photographs of authors may be useful, but the numerous reproductions of dust jackets serve only to pad the volume. A supplementary reading list is appended.

To use this volume effectively, one will need access to its proposed companion volume and to the volumes covering the previous and subsequent periods of Canadian literature. Although valuable for its inclusion of literary figures not often bound elsewhere (e.g., editor Alan Crawley), due to its somewhat subjective nature, its limitations as a ready-reference source, and its high price, this volume's potential usefulness should be carefully assessed before purchase is considered by all but libraries serving specialists in Canadian studies. [R: Choice, Nov 88, p. 456]

Gari-Anne Patzwald

1145.　**Who's Who in the League of Canadian Poets.** 3d ed. Stephen Scobie, ed. Toronto, League of Canadian Poets, 1988. 227p. illus. bibliog. $19.95pa. ISBN 0-9690327-4-9.

Each entry submitted by more than two hundred professionally published and performing poets includes a photograph, a biographical sketch, awards, major publications, a selection of anthologies in which the poet's work is included, and excerpts from critical comments and reviews. Although a membership directory cannot be comprehensive, this one includes most of English Canada's major poets as well as new voices from across the country. A useful appendix identifies sixty-nine current poetry magazines and forty-nine publishers of poetry, all with addresses. Since the previous edition was published in 1980 book selectors will welcome the current title lists in this handy biographical directory.

Patricia Fleming

Chilean Literature

1146.　Woodbridge, Hensley C., and David S. Zubatsky. **Pablo Neruda: An Annotated Bibliography of Biographical and Critical Studies.** New York, Garland, 1988. 629p. index. (Garland Reference Library of the Humanities, Vol. 593). $80.00. LC 84-48872. ISBN 0-8240-8732-1.

Pablo Neruda, one of the best known and perhaps most controversial Spanish American writers and political activists, has invited much critical response to his works and life throughout the world. This bibliogrpahy, which briefly annotates and summarizes over two thousand items, is the most comprehensive bibliography yet published on Neruda, encompassing the following major sections: (1) list of previous bibliographies; (2) biographical studies, arranged chronologically, including material on Neruda's life as well as posthumous tributes, celebrations, movies and documentaries—material that would be useful to Neruda's biographers; (3) personal testimony and reminiscences about the author from Neruda's contemporaries; and (4) critical studies of Neruda's poetry, prose, contributions as a journalist, letters, translations, and drama (e.g., *Fulgor y muerte de Joaquin Murieta*). Other sections focus on Neruda's manuscripts, influence, and reputation, and there are extensive subject, title, and author indexes. This bibliography combines comprehensive coverage with brief descriptive, rather than critical, annotations of material published not only in the United States and Western Europe but also in Spanish America, Brazil, Japan, and the Soviet Union. The annotations excerpt opening and concluding comments that indicate the item's scope and coverage. Full bibliographical data are provided for most of the items, but, as the compilers indicate, this has not been possible for all because of the inaccessibility of some of the material. Both the scholar and the general reader will undoubtedly be very pleased with this excellent bibliography. [R: Choice, July/Aug 88, p. 1679]

Geraldo U. de Sousa

Chinese Literature

1147.　Berry, Margaret. **The Chinese Classic Novels: An Annotated Bibliography of Chiefly English-language Studies.** New York, Garland, 1988. 302p. illus. index. (Garland Reference Library of the Humanities, Vol. 775). $42.00. LC 88-4816. ISBN 0-8240-6633-2.

The author has carefully selected the most important published criticism on six novels: *The Romance of the Three Kingdoms*, *The Water Margin, Monkey, or Journey to the West, The Golden Lotus, The Scholars, The Dream of the Red Chamber*. For each novel, she includes an excellent essay discussing possible sources, interpretations, major schools of criticism, and problems associated with particular translations. These essays are followed by annotated citations to those books, journal articles, and dissertations providing the best discussions of the novels. The annotations are evaluative. A reading of these introductory essays and annotations provides an understanding of each novel's literary merits and an appreciation of its place in the development of the Chinese novel. There is no doubt about the best available translation of a novel, making this a good selection guide within this narrow subject. In addition to specific critical comment for each novel there is also a bibliography of general sources. Here, one finds articles on those people who have written about the Chinese novel (Pearl S. Buck) and articles written by the leading scholars. There is a complete author/title index.

This excellent subject bibliography complements two other important works, Jordan D. Paper's *Guide to Chinese Prose* (G. K. Hall, 1984) and Meishi Tsai's *Contemporary Chinese Novels and Short Stories, 1949-1974: An Annotated Bibliography* (see *ARBA* 80, entry 1291). [R: Choice, Dec 88, pp. 621-22]

Milton H. Crouch

Czechoslovakian Literature

1148.　Brand, Glen. **Milan Kundera: An Annotated Bibliography.** New York, Garland, 1988. 133p. index. (Garland Reference Library of the Humanities, Vol. 820). $23.00. LC 87-29201. ISBN 0-8240-7544-7.

Now in exile in France, the Czech novelist Milan Kundera, ironically, may be better known abroad than in his native land. Since shortly after the Soviet military invasion in 1968, Kundera's writings have been banned in Czechoslovakia. But Kundera's international reputation seems assured, and this annotated primary and secondary bibliography will help to increase scholarly attention to his work. The primary bibliography includes separate sections for poetry, dramatic works, short stories, novels, translations of other writers' works into Czech by Kundera, prefaces and afterwords to works by other writers, screenplays, artworks, full length critical work, critical essays, speeches, and interviews. The secondary bibliography has separate sections for full-length studies, general secondary works, criticism of Kundera's plays, and criticism of films based on his work, with separate sections listing criticism of each of

Kundera's books (novels and collections of short stories).

The primary bibliography includes translations of Kundera's works into other languages; the secondary bibliography includes criticism in French, Spanish, Italian, German, Czech (not much since 1968 has been published about Kundera in his native language), and English. (Since Kundera has lived in France since 1975 a special focus has been placed on French publications.) Brand's annotations are objective and descriptive, although he makes occasional brief evaluative comments and devotes longer annotations to the more significant works. A concise, critical introduction to Kundera's major works is also included. [R: Choice, Sept 88, p. 76]

David Isaacson

Filipino Literature

1149.   Valeros, Florentino B., and Estrellita Valeros-Gruenberg. **Filipino Writers in English (A Biographical and Bibliographical Directory).** Quezon City, Philippines, New Day; distr., Detroit, Cellar Book Shop, 1987. 236p. $11.75 pa. ISBN 971-10-0285-X.

This excellent reference source contains biographical and bibliographical information on Filipino writers in English, past and present, at home or abroad. It includes sketches of both purely literary as well as nonliterary writers (such as historians, sociologists, and journalists), and this feature enhances its value.

The entries are arranged in alphabetical order by author's last name and include a wide variety of data: "name, type of writer, year and place of birth, work experience starting from the latest and working back in time, education including schools, honors and awards, published works with place and date of publication, and prizes and awards won. In some cases excerpts from critics' comments have been included" (p. vii).

The style is informal, almost chatty, and is easily readable. The entries are enriched by frequent critical comments on various aspects of the writers' lives and works.

Filipino Writers in English is the only guide of its kind and is packed with interesting and valuable information. Interestingly enough, the two well-qualified authors are a father and daughter writing team.   Marshall E. Nunn

French Literature

1150.   Brosman, Catharine Savage, ed. **French Novelists, 1900-1930.** Detroit, Gale, 1988. 381p. illus. bibliog. index. (Dictionary of Literary

Biography, Vol. 65). $95.00. LC 87-25822. ISBN 0-8103-1743-5.

1151.   Brosman, Catharine Savage, ed. **French Novelists, 1930-1960.** Detroit, Gale, 1988. 478p. illus. bibliog. index. (Dictionary of Literary Biography, Vol. 72). $95.00. LC 88-16462. ISBN 0-8103-4550-1.

These two volumes of the popular, well-established reference series, DLB, include fifty biocritical essays that trace the novelists' lives, writings, influences, and reputations. (A third volume on the post-1960 period is planned.) The entries provide excellent summaries and starting points for studies by undergraduates, the general public, and scholars. The length of each entry is related to the quantity and critical reception of the author's writings, for example, twenty-five pages for Colette, fourteen for Yourcenar, thirty-six for Proust, and four for Maurice Genevoix. Each entry includes a list of the author's works and usually several photographs, a list of references, and the location of collections of manuscripts and letters.

In the foreword the editor discusses the scope of the volumes, the selection of authors, and the characteristics of twentieth-century French fiction. At the end of the book a short bibliography of books for further reading lists bibliographies, histories, and criticism of French literature. In volume 65, on the period 1900-1930, an appendix reprints the presentations and acceptance remarks of four Nobel laureates. Both volumes 65 and 72, like all DLB volumes, have a cumulative index to the main entries in the volumes published to date in the DLB, the DLB *Yearbook*, and the DLB *Documentary Series*. Whereas this index is handy at times, a serious inconvenience is the lack of an index of the many persons, titles, and concepts in each volume.   Joyce Duncan Falk

1152.   **French XX Bibliography: Critical and Biographical References for the Study of French Literature since 1885. Volume VIII, No. 4, Issue No. 39.** Douglas W. Alden, Peter C. Hoy, and Christine M. Zunz, eds. Selinsgrove, Pa., Susquehanna University Press; distr., Cranbury, N.J., Associated University Presses, 1988. 1v. (various paging). $78.00pa. LC 77-648803. ISBN 0-941664-86-4; ISSN 0085-0888.

The basic format of this annual bibliography has not changed since it was first reviewed in *ARBA* 79 (see entry 1266). Over nine thousand citations to biographical and critical material relating to French literature since 1885 are listed in one of three parts: general subjects, author subjects, and cinema. As can be seen, literature is broadly defined and entries are found for both theatrical and film directors and actors. Entries also identify the source of information or the library in which the item was examined. Items not verified are identified as an indirect reference. Although the bibliography offers impressive coverage of its field, there are a few drawbacks. A first-time user is likely to be confused by the lack of explanation of how the volume in hand is related to those of previous years. After some examination the user gets the idea that paging in the series is continuous and that references to certain citation prefix letters appear in earlier volumes, but this is not stated in the volume. In comparison to the revised format of the *MLA International Bibliography*, the *French XX Bibliography* lacks the enhanced access points which lets the *MLA International Bibliography* user more quickly and accurately identify relevant citations, but the extensive coverage provided by the *French XX Bibliography* still makes it a valuable resource for research libraries.

Barbara E. Kemp

German Literature

1153. Elfe, Wolfgang D., and James Hardin, eds. **Contemporary German Fiction Writers: First Series.** Detroit, Gale, 1988. 413p. illus. bibliog. index. (Dictionary of Literary Biography, Vol. 69). $95.00. LC 88-11164. ISBN 0-8103-1747-8.

This volume of the now familiar Dictionary of Literary Biography series covers West German, East German, and Swiss-German fiction writers who established their literary reputations in the decade following World War II. A companion volume (see entry 1154) surveys writers who achieved notoriety after the mid-1950s. Post-war Austrian authors will be covered in yet another volume of the series.

As with other German literature titles in the DLB series, the articles in this volume are solid, informative, and generally well written. Each provides an overview of the author's life and works which are described within the larger context of recent German literary history. The volume as a whole documents several important characteristics of post-war German literature, including its attempt to come to terms with the Nazi past and the war, the different directions taken by literature in East and West Germany, and the role of "Gruppe 47."

One problematic aspect is the volume's inclusion of a number of writers who now are virtually forgotten. Of the forty-three authors covered, seven have no entries in the *Oxford Companion to German Literature* (see *ARBA* 88, entry 1246), and as many as half are unlikely

to receive noticeable attention from American readers.

The scope of the volume is also problematic. Several of the authors are primarily known as poets, dramatists, or essayists, and, despite the editor's insistence that the focus is prose fiction, the articles which cover these writers include discussions of their nonfiction works. One wonders if much of this material will be duplicated in future series volumes on German poetry, drama, and prose.

The main value of *Contemporary German Fiction Writers* for American audiences will be the coverage it provides of the better-known literary figures. While information on these authors is easily available—for example, the *Encyclopedia of World Literature in the 20th Century* (for reviews of volumes 3 and 4, see *ARBA* 84, entry 1103 and *ARBA* 85, entry 992) includes eighteen of the writers—this volume provides excellent and substantive survey articles and bibliographies. Librarians will need to decide if these advantages justify the $95.00 price.

For additional comments on the DLB series see *German Fiction Writers 1885-1913* (entry 1155). [R: Choice, Dec 88, p. 624]

Ray English

1154. Elfe, Wolfgang D., and James Hardin, eds. **Contemporary German Fiction Writers: Second Series.** Detroit, Gale, 1988. 367p. illus. bibliog. index. (Dictionary of Literary Biography, Vol. 75). $95.00. LC 88-23267. ISBN 0-8103-4553-6.

This volume is the fourth in the Dictionary of Literary Biography series to deal with German fiction writers and the second to feature contemporary writers, i.e., those whose reputations were established after World War II. The subjects of *Contemporary German Fiction Writers: First Series* (see entry 1153) were adults during the Hitler period and World War II and for the most part achieved renown in the post-World War I decade. The *Second Series* provides a continuation, highlighting significant authors who were born between 1917 and 1946 and who gained recognition between the mid-1950s and the mid-1970s.

Thirty-nine writers are included. Of these, four are Swiss and fourteen are East German. (Austrian writers will be covered in a future volume.) Some, such as Günter Grass, Martin Walser and Christa Wolf are internationally famous; others, Ludwig Fels and E. Y. Meyer, for example, are little known outside their own countries. Feminist writers such as Gabriele Wohmann and Irmgard Morgner are represented somewhat sparsely: only seven of the names belong to women. Writers of varied genres appear such as Michael Ende (fantasy) and Willi Heinrich (popular literature). Prose fiction is emphasized though some writers, such as Johannes Bobrowski and Sarah Kirsch, are better known for other genres.

As usual, an excellent bio-bibliographical essay and lists of primary and secondary literature are provided for each author by an established scholar in the field. Photographs and other pertinent illustrations enhance the book. Two appendices contain reprinted articles on efforts of postwar German writers to deal with their recent pasts and immediate futures. Highly selective as it is, this compilation provides an attractive, useful tool for introducing English speakers to modern German literature. The cost may keep all but the largest libraries from purchasing the series, however.

Willa Schmidt

1155. Hardin, James, ed. **German Fiction Writers, 1885-1913.** Detroit, Gale, 1988. 2pts. illus. bibliog. index. (Dictionary of Literary Biography, Vol. 66). $190.00/set. LC 87-29300. ISBN 0-8103-1744-3.

This latest volume in the expansive Dictionary of Literary Biography covers thirty-eight German novelists and short fiction writers who were born during the second half of the nineteenth century and whose first significant literary works were published between 1885 and 1913. About a third of the entries are for noted literary figures; the remainder are either less known or obscure.

Following the standard format of the series, entries include full primary bibliographies, extensive biographical and critical articles, selective secondary bibliographies, and notes on the location of manuscripts and papers. Also included are an appendix of seven reprinted essays on German culture and history, a glossary of German historical terms, and a checklist of additional readings.

The essays for each author are substantive, generally well written, and contain much more than simple biography. Most succeed in conveying a sense of the author's *oeuvre* and its importance within the larger context of German literary history. They often also include surprisingly full discussions of individual works. For the less known figures, these articles will in many instances be the most extensive treatment available in English. Some of them may prompt critical revaluation.

Those libraries considering this set should weigh the excellent quality of its contents against several other factors. First, biographical and critical material on the prominent authors it

covers is readily available in English. Patrons of libraries other than those which serve active graduate programs in German literature are unlikely to be interested in the more obscure figures that are included. Finally, the set is very costly, due in part to a large amount of non-essential material. Approximately half of the set's space is taken up by illustrations, reprinted essays, and a cumulative index for the series.

The cost of existing DLB volumes now totals over $7,000.00, and no end to the series is in sight. Libraries should therefore evaluate carefully the need for this and each future volume in the series. The publisher should also consider whether or not libraries and their patrons would be better served by a series—at least for the foreign-language literatures—of leaner, more modestly illustrated volumes that cover only more significant authors and larger time spans. [R: Choice, July/Aug 88, p. 1675]

Ray English

Indic Literature

1156. **Encyclopaedia of Indian Literature. Volume I: A-Devo.** Amaresh Datta, ed. New Delhi, Sahitya Akademi; distr., Columbia, Mo., South Asia Books, 1987. 987p. $64.00.

The Indian civilization is one of the oldest in the world. It has a history of over five thousand years and has much to offer to scholars, researchers, and others. Indian literature has played a dominant part in the development of India and Indians. Volume 1 of the proposed five-volume set of the *Encyclopaedia of Indian Literature* is a welcome addition to all collections.

The encyclopedia is arranged alphabetically by authors and titles. It deals with the literature in twenty-two Indian languages, including Assames, Bengali, Dogri, English, Gujarati, Hindi, Kashmiri, Maithili, Marathi, Nepali, Punjabi, Sanskrit, Sindhi, Telugu, and Urdu. In addition, there are a few entries in Pali, Prakrit, and Apabhramsha languages. All entries are comprehensive in scope and the language of the literature of each entry is given in parentheses. All entries are authoritative and include a bibliography on each topic.

This work provides a true picture of Indian literature and is an excellent tool even for self-education. The encyclopedia deals with ancient, medieval, and modern Indian literature and includes all important aspects.

This important reference work is the result of elaborate planning and hard work of many well-known Indian writers. It is recommended for all types of libraries interested in developing collections on India and for those scholars, researchers, and others who are interested in learning about Indian literature and its development through the ages.

                              Ravindra Nath Sharma

1157. International Encyclopaedia of Indian Literature: Sanskrit, Pali, Prakrit & Apabhramsa. Volume 1. rev. ed. By Gaṅgā Rām Garg. Delhi, India, Mittal; distr., Columbia, Mo., South Asia Books, 1987. 2pts. index. $98.00/set. ISBN 0-8364-231-6X (pt.1); 0-8364-2161-2 (pt.2).

It has been difficult to find material on ancient Indian literature due to a lack of sources. Gaṅgā Rām Garg, a well-known Indian scholar, has filled a major gap by preparing this much-needed encyclopedia in two volumes. The purpose of this encyclopedia is to introduce researchers and other interested readers to scholars and their writings to 1981 on ancient Indian languages in Sanskrit, Pali, Prakrit, and Apabhramsa. There are over two thousand entries arranged in alphabetical order. They include well-known scholars from all over the world who have contributed to the development of ancient Indian languages; major classical epics and other works such as Vedas, Brahmanas, Upanishads, Puranas, Mahabharata, Ramayana, and Buddhist and Jaina texts; yoga, architecture, astronomy, and other important old works. In brief, the encyclopedia includes people, places, and great scholarly works not only from India but from Australia, Europe, Japan, Mongolia, Thailand, and the United States. Entries give complete information, and they vary in length from a few lines to a few pages depending on the importance of the entry. An additional attraction of this well-prepared, well-written encyclopedia is an excellent introduction written by the editor covering many subjects including drama, philosophy, Sanskrit, Pali, and Prakrit literature, astronomy, mathematics and music. The encyclopedia includes an author index for the benefit of researchers. It is certainly an invaluable and excellent reference source for the study of Indian literature and languages. It is highly recommended for all libraries interested in developing their collections on India.   Ravindra Nath Sharma

Irish Literature

1158. Barale, Michèle Aina, and Rubin Rabinovitz. **A KWIC Concordance to Samuel Beckett's Trilogy: *Molloy, Malone Dies*, and *The Unnamable*.** New York, Garland, 1988. 2v. (Garland Reference Library of the Humanities, Vol. 753). $175.00/set. LC 87-38471. ISBN 0-8240-8394-6.

Although Samuel Beckett is best known to the world for his 1952 play *Waiting for Godot*, he himself has insisted that his novels are of greater literary importance. Should history prove him right, we are fortunate that this first concordance of his works covers the trilogy at the heart of his fiction. All three novels were originally written in French. The compilers base their undertaking on the translated editions published by Grove Press in 1955, 1956, and 1958 respectively.

Volume 1 covers words beginning with letters A through L; volume 2 includes M through Z plus ranked lists of word frequencies for each novel. A preface by Barale gives detailed explanations of method and format. Of 185,180 total words, 67,291 have been concorded, that is, arranged not only alphabetically but also shown as they appear in each work within a line of text, or in context. Articles, pronouns, and other less significant words are included in the alphabetical sequence with only their overall frequency of occurrence. Painstaking scholarly intervention has tempered impressively the computer's lack of discrimination. Rabinovitz's introduction provides a convincing argument for the usefulness of a concordance in the study of Beckett's works in particular, namely, the latter's love of word and phrase repetition. Examples drawn from the texts support this contention.

Hardcore Beckett scholars will no doubt agree. The price, however, may make even large academic libraries balk at purchasing an item which will be used by only a very few.

                              Willa Schmidt

1159. Lane, Denis, and Carol McCrory Lane, comps. and eds. **Modern Irish Literature.** New York, Ungar Publishing, Crossroad/Ungar/Continuum, 1988. 736p. bibliog. index. (Library of Literary Criticism). $95.00. LC 87-5090. ISBN 0-8044-3144-2.

The expansion of Ungar's Library of Literary Criticism series continues with this volume, which features excerpts from critical commentary on eighty-seven twentieth-century Irish writers. In addition to well-known figures such as Samuel Beckett, James Joyce, and George Bernard Shaw, the compilation also includes less-renowned individuals, such as Padraic Fallon, Kate O'Brien, and James Plunkett.

Arrangement is alphabetical by author. Within each entry critical excerpts from periodicals, newspapers, and books are reprinted chronologically. Following each selection is a complete bibliographical citation to the original source. The number of excerpts provided for an author ranges from four to twenty-four, reflecting his or her literary prominence. Selections vary in length, but many cover at least one page. Primary bibliographies, which list each writer's principal works chronologically and identify the genre of each title, appear in a separate section near the end of the volume. Most of these also include a citation to either a separately published bibliography or a biographical or critical source that includes a bibliography. The useful index to critics includes many prominent writers, a number of whom are themselves the subjects of entries in this work (e.g., Benedict Kiely, Sean O'Faolain, and W. B. Yeats).

Fifty-six of the authors in this volume are also treated in at least one other compilation of criticism: forty-eight are covered by either Gale's *Contemporary Literary Criticism* (see entry 992) or *Twentieth-Century Literary Criticism* (see entries 994-995) series, while thirty-five are included in Chelsea House's six-volume *Twentieth-Century British Literature* (1987). In addition, Ungar's own *Modern British Literature* (for review of *Volume 5: Second Supplement*, see *ARBA* 87, entry 1163) features thirty-one of these Irish writers, five of whom also appear in *Major Modern Dramatists*, volume 1 (see *ARBA* 85, entry 1009).

Although the duplication of specific selections does not appear to be significant, most libraries probably do not need all of these sources. *Modern Irish Literature* offers the advantage of bringing together authors of a particular nationality in a convenient single volume. Moreover, it covers thirty-one authors not represented in the other critical compilations with which it was compared. [R: RBB, 15 Oct 88, pp. 388, 391]   Marie Ellis

Latin American Literature

1160.   Bhalla, Alok. Latin American Writers: A Bibliography with Critical and Biographical Introductions. New York, Envoy Press; distr., New York, Apt Books, 1987. 174p. index. $22.50. LC 87-80661. ISBN 0-938719-20-3.

This bibliography covers eighteen major Spanish-American literary figures. Brazilian writers are not included, although the title and the preface (by referring to original works in Portuguese [p. v]) imply that they are. The entry for each author includes a biographical and critical introduction, and bibliographies of the author's original works, his works in English translation, and criticism in English.

The introductions combine biographical data (sometimes scant, as in the case of Jose Lezama Lima) with rather subjective discussions of the philosophical or ideological viewpoints

which inform the writer's literary efforts, and summaries of or comments on major works. The cut-off date for the accompanying bibliographies is about 1985, although a very few 1986 imprints were noted.

This work suffers from careless editing; misspellings are common. Two glaring errors which were repeated were the spelling of Argentina as Argentinia (pp. 10 and 41 in the section headings), and that of the last name of the Nicaraguan dictator, Anastasio Somoza, as Samoza (p. 27, twice in the same paragraph). The quality of the printing is rather poor and diacritics in Spanish-language words are totally lacking.

Although this work does not provide any information which cannot be pieced together by consulting other sources, it does supply bibliographic data for English translations and criticism in English in one place for the limited number of Latin American authors that it covers. It is therefore a useful tool for libraries supporting teaching and research in Latin American literature.   Ann Hartness

1161.   Rela, Walter, comp. A Bibliographical Guide to Spanish American Literature: Twentieth-Century Sources. Westport, Conn., Greenwood Press, 1988. 381p. index. (Bibliographies and Indexes in World Literature, No. 13). $49.95. LC 88-15443. ISBN 0-313-25861-9.

Rela is an internationally known student and bibliographer of Spanish American literature. This volume, with an emphasis on material published in Spanish and English, is divided into four major parts: bibliographies, dictionaries, history and criticism, and anthologies. These are subdivided, sometimes by country and by genre within each country.

This volume of 1,884 entries, many of which are annotated, should be in any library with an interest in Spanish American literature. It includes items as recent as 1986. It contains an author index, which is an index both of the critics whose works are listed and of authors mentioned in the annotations.

Various other sections might have been added. I would liked to have seen a section on bibliographies of Latin American literature in translation or a listing, at least, of separately published indexes to Spanish American literary journals. However, the work stands well on its merits.

It is almost impossible to keep up-to-date in such a broad field. Rela lists only the first volume of the *Diccionario de la literatura cubana*. The second volume was published in 1984. He lists only the 1978 edition of Luis María Sánchez López's *Diccionario de escritores colombianos*. The third revised and enlarged edition appeared in 1985. It is a pity that there is no annotation to warn the user of the poor quality of Smulewicz's *Diccionario de la literatura chilena*. Proofreading of the French leaves much to be desired; other typographical errors do not impede the use of this outstanding new reference work.   Hensley C. Woodbridge

Nigerian Literature

1162. Coger, Greta M. K., comp. **Index of Subjects, Proverbs, and Themes in the Writings of Wole Soyinka.** Westport, Conn., Greenwood Press, 1988. 311p. bibliog. (Bibliographies and Indexes in Afro-American and African Studies, No. 21). $49.95. LC 88-160. ISBN 0-313-25712-4.

It is exceedingly difficult to escape hyperbole in reviewing this comprehensive index to the themes, proverbs, and subjects in the writings of the Nobel Laureate, Wole Soyinka. The author has done a remarkable and painstaking job of identifying by keywords the ideas, objects, and subjects in the works of the Nigerian writer. The scope of this work is unbelievable. In the "themes" section *alone*, twenty thousand items are listed. There is extensive cross-referencing from one section to another. It should be stressed as well that the utility of this work goes well beyond Soyinka studies. Researchers pursuing topics as diverse as the religious meaning of Yoruba traditional Ifa divination and political corruption will find this index helpful. While this work is admittedly one which will be used intensively and extensively by a select few, it is a work which should be on the shelves of all academic libraries.

Dorothy C. Woodson

Russian Literature

1163. Clowes, Edith W. **Maksim Gorky: A Reference Guide.** Boston, G. K. Hall, 1987. 226p. index. (Reference Guide to Literature). $35.00. LC 87-20. ISBN 0-8161-8722-3.

The compiler's goal in preparing this annotated bibliography/reference guide of Maksim Gorky's works was "to encourage recent efforts at a reassessment by presenting a large variety of approaches and evaluations and by raising as many questions about Gorky's life and art as possible." Clowes devotes particular attention "to periods, issues, and themes about which scholars disagree." This first English-language research bibliography is therefore not intended to duplicate the many existing Soviet bibliographies on Gorky. Clowes's book does include

Soviet memoir and archival materials as well as a good representation of the major Soviet critical approaches. In addition, she also incorporates Western and Russian émigré writing on Gorky.

The book is divided into four parts. The first is an excellent scholarly introduction to Gorky that focuses with clarity on "patterns in critical reading and biography writing." The second part is a primary bibliography (unannotated) that provides a chronological listing of Gorky's famous stories and critical essays, major novels, and plays mentioned in part 3. The third part, arranged chronologically, contains annotated listings of secondary works. The fourth and last part consists of author and subject indexes.

This well-planned and well-executed volume is everything a research guide is supposed to be: the introductory essay sketches the main patterns of critical reception, the bibliographies list the works needed for further research, and the indexes provide easy access to the contents of the guide. Gorky scholars will greatly appreciate Clowes's work.   Robert H. Burger

1164. Kasack, Wolfgang. **Dictionary of Russian Literature since 1917.** New York, Columbia University Press, 1988. 502p. index. $55.00. LC 87-20838. ISBN 0-231-05242-1.

This volume is a translation of Wolfgang Kasack's *Lexikon der russischen Literatur ab 1917* (1976) and its supplement (1986), which have been recognized as an excellent reference source for post-1917 Russian literature. They contain more authors for this period than either Victor Terras's *Handbook of Russian Literature* (see *ARBA* 86, entry 1221) or Harry B. Weber's *Modern Encyclopedia of Russian and Soviet Literatures* (Academic International Press, 1977-1984). Note that this is not a dictionary of Soviet literature, but Russian literature: Kasack has subordinated national boundaries to language. The dictionary contains only authors, not critics, literary scholars, or translators, unless they have produced belles lettres as well. The 619 author entries are divided into a biographical section and a section dealing with the author's work (primary and secondary sources). The biographical portion includes data expected in such entries, as well as father's occupation, course of study, beginning of literary activity, membership in the Communist Party, date of emigration when applicable, pseudonyms used, and position in writers' unions. The translated entries are well executed and read smoothly; the bibliographic apparatus is accurate and easily decipherable. The dictionary also has eighty-seven subject entries that include journals, literary circles, movements, etc. Access to the volume is enhanced by both name and subject indexes.

This volume is a major reference work for modern Russian literature and will serve as a reliable source for many years to come.

Robert H. Burger

1165. Stevanovic, Bosiljka, and Vladimir Wertsman. **Free Voices in Russian Literature, 1950s-1980s: A Bio-Bibliographical Guide.** New York, Russica, 1987. 510p. ("Russica" Bibliography Series, No. 4). $87.50. LC 84-61344. ISBN 0-89830-090-8.

The phenomenon known as *samizdat*— self-publishing—began to emerge with Khruschev's ascent to power and rising hopes for greater freedom of individual expression. When these hopes were dashed and censorship returned, writers were forced to circulate their works privately, and copies eventually found their way to the West, where they were published by the émigré press. This body of "unofficial" Russian writing has attained major importance in world literature. The emphasis in *Free Voices* is on the writers who have produced it. It includes biographical and bibliographical data on over nine hundred authors who live, or lived, in the Soviet Union. It is not intended as a comprehensive guide to Soviet political dissidents or to Russian *samizdat* literature, but is limited to those authors whose work, regardless of genre or literary or political affiliation, was rejected by the censor, smuggled out of the country, and published in the émigré press. It was compiled exclusively from Russian-language publications that appeared in the West between 1957 and 1985. The work is arranged alphabetically by author. Each entry includes birth and death dates when available and a brief description, which may include educational background and political and publication activities. This is followed by a list of published writings. An effort was made to obtain biographical information directly from the authors now living in the West; where this was not possible, information was drawn from any other available source. The identity of those authors using pen names was revealed only when this information was public knowledge, or with the author's consent. A similar bibliographical work is Josephine Woll's *Soviet Dissident Literature: A Critical Guide* (see *ARBA* 84, entry 1217). Her emphasis is on the writings, rather than the authors, so there is little biographical information; however, she also includes English-language publications, as well as works which may have been published officially but in censored form, or may have circulated underground before being published

officially. Scholars of modern Russian history and literature will find in these two works a very comprehensive guide to this important body of Russian literature. [R: Choice, Jan 88, p. 752]

Sara J. Richardson

Spanish and Portuguese Literatures

1166. Schneider, Marshall J., and Irwin Stern, comps. and eds. **Modern Spanish and Portuguese Literatures.** New York, Continuum, 1988. 615p. index. (Library of Literary Criticism). $85.00. LC 87-13754. ISBN 0-8044-3280-5.

This volume presents a selection of criticism of the works of some eighty major twentieth-century authors writing in Spanish, Catalon, Galician, and Portuguese. Nearly eight hundred citations are included in all. The volume is arranged in two sections: Spain and Portugal. The authors are listed alphabetically in each section with the critical excerpts arranged chronologically within each section on the author. The volume concludes with full citations for works mentioned and an index of the critics cited. One can assume that citations through the mid-1980s are included although this is only implied.

The review of this work is met with mixed emotions. On one hand, there have been few works published that concentrate on Spanish and Portuguese literatures. Consequently, almost anything published quickly fills a need and a definite void. On the other hand, it is precisely this eagerness to build a critical collection in this subject area that makes us willing to purchase whatever is available. This is not to say that *Modern Spanish and Portuguese Literatures* has not been carefully compiled; it is evident that it has been.

Some nagging questions remain unanswered, however. What were the bases for including some critiques while (most likely) omitting others? A bibliography listing works not actually quoted would have provided added depth. Obviously (from the volume's two major sections) only European Spanish and Portuguese writers have been included. Is the reason for omitting South and Central American authors purely a space consideration? Is another volume planned in which these authors will be included?

All of this is to say that this work is most definitely recommended and unquestionably will receive much use. One cannot help but feel, however, that there are some glaring omissions. [R: LJ, 15 Mar 88, p. 51]

Marjorie E. Bloss

25 Music

GENERAL WORKS

Bibliographies

1167. Brockman, William S. **Music: A Guide to the Reference Literature.** Littleton, Colo., Libraries Unlimited, 1987. 254p. index. (Reference Sources in the Humanities Series). $38.50. LC 87-26462. ISBN 0-87287-526-1.

Is yet another guide to music research materials really necessary? The answer is yes in the case of Brockman's excellent work. Vincent Duckles's *Music Reference and Research Materials,* third edition (see *ARBA* 75, entry 1123) is now seriously out-of-date, and Guy A. Marco's *Information on Music* (see *ARBA* 76, entry 989; *ARBA* 78, entry 894; and *ARBA* 85, entry 1159) can be somewhat forbidding because of its arrangement and completeness. Brockman has aimed at a selective guide to the most important and useful tools in the field, and concentrates on English-language materials. The book is arranged by sensible and useful broad categories. It is beautifully printed so that titles stand out prominently in boldface type. The annotations are first rate, and not only describe the books, but note weaknesses and problems, and refer to other titles of related interest. The listing of resource guides (such as the Garland Composer Resource Manuals) as a group is very useful. The sections devoted to current periodicals, and associations, research centers, and other organizations are excellent, and will lead researchers beyond the titles mentioned. The subject index is complete, and does lead the user to all the appropriate materials, so that one does not need to know the exact name of a society to find it.

The book's selectivity does mean that many important titles are not listed here, but I cannot fault the choices since it seems to me that the most important of several rival works has always been the one chosen for inclusion.

Having worked with these materials and those in need of them for many years I am very impressed by Brockman's choice of materials, his organization of them into useful groups, and by the informative but informal tone of the annotations. This superb book does just what the title promises. But speaking of titles, why, oh why was the spine title limited to the one word *music* when the subtitle is the thing that should catch the browser's eye on music shelves? [R: Choice, Oct 88, p. 284; RBB, 1 Oct 88, p. 243]

George Louis Mayer

1168. Brookhart, Edward. **Music in American Higher Education: An Annotated Bibliography.** Warren, Mich., published for College Music Society by Harmonie Park Press, 1988. 245p. index. (Bibliographies in American Music, No. 10). $35.00. LC 87-33238. ISBN 0-89990-042-9.

This work is based on an unpublished bibliography begun by Henry L. Cady. As completed by Brookhart it is limited to the *history* of music in American higher education between the years 1830 and 1985. Arrangement is by eight broad topics subdivided as necessary: general music sources, nonmusic sources, role of music in higher education, characteristics and qualifications of students, faculty, administration and accreditation, histories of individual institutions, and special topics. Almost all of the thirteen hundred citations are briefly annotated. A comparison with the bibliography accompanying the article "Education in music, higher" in the *New Grove Dictionary of American Music* (presumably not cited in Brookhart because of the 1986 publication date) reveals several omissions, perhaps justified by this tool's emphasis on history. (It also revealed two misspelled names—in the *New Grove*!) Brookhart's bibliography belongs in any academic library supporting music or education. [R: Choice, Dec 88, p. 622]

Robert Skinner

1169. Horn, David, with Richard Jackson. **The Literature of American Music in Books and Folk Music Collections: A Fully Annotated Bibliography. Supplement I.** Metuchen, N.J., Scarecrow, 1988. 570p. index. $49.50. LC 87-9630. ISBN 0-8108-1997-X.

A first supplement to its identically-named forebear (see *ARBA* 78, entry 893), this book covers American music from 1975 through 1980 with fully-annotated entries. In addition, appendices A and B contain books published from 1981 to 1985 and revised editions of important books listed in the earlier text. That book was included in *A Basic Music Library: Essential Scores and Books* (American Library Association, 1978). The present *Supplement* is of comparable quality and essentiality and should be included in future lists.

In one respect, the *Supplement* differs in emphasis from its brother: "In the base volume one musical area, jazz, was treated more selectively than others," lest it wind up dominating the others. Here, the section on "Rock, Pop, and Rock and Roll" was reduced because it is well covered by *The Literature of Rock, II: 1979-1983*, by Frank Hoffmann and B. Lee Cooper (see *ARBA* 87, entry 1269) and *Popular Music: A Reference Guide* by Roman Iwaschkin (see *ARBA* 87, entry 1262). Of course, the book as a whole exhibits much selectiveness. Its mission: "to include all English-language material known to the compilers and judged to be of interest." Minor books and items unseen by the compilers have been kept in, but without annotations. As in the original (for the obvious reason of manageability) certain formats were left out: periodical articles, dissertations, serials, fiction, popular songs collections, "art" music scores, and general reference works.

Substantial annotations add much to the value of this work. Descriptive and often critical, they indicate that the authors do indeed know their material. Opinions are expressed with confidence. When a book is bad, or could have profited from having a stronger editor, they tell us. Randall Rafferty

1170. Jackson, Roland. **Performance Practice, Medieval to Contemporary: A Bibliographic Guide.** New York, Garland, 1988. 518p. index. (Music Research and Information Guides, Vol. 9; Garland Reference Library of the Humanities, Vol. 790). $73.00. LC 87-25900. ISBN 0-8240-1512-6.

The attempt by modern performers to duplicate or approximate the way a composer wanted his music to sound by the interpretation of imprecise musical notation and the study of written commentaries contemporary with the composer is what gives the topic of performance practice its importance. The documentation is enormous, covers many centuries and a wide variety of topics such as tempi, pitch, rhythm and ornamentation. A bibliography is one thing, but a bibliographic guide, the subtitle chosen by the author, is something else—and something much superior, if well done. This guide has assembled, sorted, organized, and annotated the books, articles and dissertations of this complex subject matter which have appeared in English, French, German, and Italian. Jackson has gathered them into the kind of sensible arrangement a user would hope to find.

The introductory survey and each of the chronological sections which follow have been divided into the following categories: general studies, composers, forms and genres (opera, etc.), media (voice and instruments), tempo, added notes (ornamentation, etc.), altered notes (dynamic nuances, etc.), pitch and tuning. The ninth to thirteenth centuries are grouped by monody and polyphony, and each section thereafter is by century. There are additional sections, "Reflections on Performance Practice," and an index of theorists. The subject index is detailed and thorough, and there is also an author index.

This is a major guide to a very important subject. Any library serving a serious musical public must have this work. It is not too specialized. It is not too expensive. It must be purchased. [R: Choice, July/Aug 88, p. 1675]

George Louis Mayer

1171. Krummel, D. W. **Bibliographical Handbook of American Music.** Champaign, Ill., University of Illinois Press, 1987. 269p. index. (Music in American Life). $24.95. LC 87-20597. ISBN 0-252-01450-2.

D. W. Krummel is a writer and bibliographer of substantial note, one of the compilers of *Resources of American Music History* (see *ARBA* 82, entry 1027). His handbook follows a bibliographical path through books, articles, dissertations, and databases that offer the researcher assistance in locating music, writings, ephemera, and recordings pertaining to music in and of the United States. One of the strengths of the handbook is its coverage both of sources specific to music and of general sources.

Presented as an annotated bibliography of roughly seven hundred items, the handbook is organized into chapters within four overall sections. "Chronological Perspectives" surveys the major national retrospective and current bibliographies, as well as review sources. "Contextual Perspectives" examines bibliographies devoted to regions, ethnic or other groups, or persons. "Musical Mediums and Genres" surveys bibliographies devoted to the many "musics" subsumed under the "American" rubric: concert, vernacular (folk, jazz, rock), popular, and sacred. "Bibliographical Forms" covers guides to and bibliographies of collections and writings about music, discographies and bibliographies of discographies, guides to sheet music collecting, and surveys of music publishing. The index lists authors, editors, and other names connected with publications, titles, and selected subjects.

Interspersed among the citations are cogent bibliographical essays which draw out the features of important reference works and set in historical or cultural context the art of musical research. These include a history of the *Catalog of Copyright Entries* (Copyright Office, 1906-) which examines its changing contents and format in relation to the publication of music in the twentieth century, and a short history of music collecting in the United States and its influence on the growth of music library collections.

As is any good bibliography, the handbook is more than a listing of diverse elements: it is an intellectual entity which defines a literature. Its selection of appropriate citations, effective organization, evaluative annotations, and informed essays make it a marvelously useful and, considering the price, inexpensive resource. [R: Choice, Sept 88, pp. 82, 84; LJ, Jan 88, p. 77]

William S. Brockman

1172. Lister, Craig. **The Musical Microcomputer: A Resource Guide.** New York, Garland, 1988. 172p. index. (Garland Reference Library of the Humanities, Vol. 854). $26.00. LC 88-11723. ISBN 0-8240-8442-X.

Lister's work represents the first published bibliography devoted exclusively to microcomputers and music. He organizes the topic into six categories: bibliography, history, and criticism; composition and theory; education and musicianship (where the abbreviation CAD stands for computer-assisted-drill rather than the more commonly understood computer-aided-design); interfaces (e.g., MIDI); programming; and synthesis. Resources covered include anthologies, books, dissertations, journal articles, and—it is important to emphasize—software. Annotations are short but accurate, although one wonders why a few items were not available for inspection. Where possible, book and software reviews by others are cited. I did not note any major omissions in printed material except, obviously, for volumes not yet in publication. Coverage of software is selective, leaving more comprehensive listings and commentary to

books such as Barton Bartle's *Computer Software in Music and Music Education* (see *ARBA* 88, entry 1287). Lister's bibliography includes author, title, and software indexes, and two appendices present a list of relevant journals and a checklist of twenty books for the small music library. Highly recommended.

Robert Skinner

1173. Wenk, Arthur, comp. **Analyses of Nineteenth- and Twentieth-Century Music: 1940-1985.** Canton, Mass., Music Library Association, 1987. 370p. index. (MLA Index and Bibliography Series, No. 25). $29.00pa. LC 87-5675. ISBN 0-914954-36-9.

This is Wenk's fourth contribution to the MLA Index and Bibliography Series in what is a combining and updating of his earlier efforts. The index consists of 370 pages (5,664 entries) of both English- and foreign-language sources. In the introduction, Wenk states that "the purpose of this index is to provide rapid access to technical materials of an analytical nature contained in periodicals, monographs, festschriften, and dissertations." It is important to note that this work indexes only analyses and not research discussing a composer's "life and works." Examples of subjects discussed in an analysis include reductive techniques, syntax formulation, set-theoretic approaches, and a given work's relation to the norms of its genre.

Wenk pleads that by its nature a work of this kind is doomed to incompleteness, but a wide range of predominantly European composers, the well known and not so well known, are included, with Beethoven and Schoenberg in a virtual tie for the most entries, 287 and 289, respectively. Analyses of Americans such as Barber, Cage, Hovhaness, and Piston can also be found.

Entries are arranged by composer and, for those composers having ten or more entries by work, title, or genre. There is also an author index. Each entry includes the composer, the author, title, and source of the analysis, and the name of the work being analyzed if it is not clear from the article's title. Each entry includes the abbreviated title of the periodical, festschrift, or monograph in which it is found, and the use of the abbreviations list is essential.

Although very specialized material is covered in this work, it has a clear, understandable format. Appropriate for music libraries and large academic libraries. [R: RQ, Spring 88, pp. 420-21]

Phillip P. Powell

Biographies

1174. The Concise Baker's Biographical Dictionary of Musicians. By Nicolas Slonimsky. New York, Schirmer Books/Macmillan, 1988. 1407p. $35.00. LC 87-32328. ISBN 0-02-872411-9.

The seventh edition of *Baker's Biographical Dictionary* (see *ARBA* 86, entry 1232) included approximately thirteen thousand entries and was published in an unwieldy single volume of 2,577 pages, an increase of over 400 pages from the sixth edition. This concise version of *Baker's* seventh edition has been reduced by over 1,100 pages and the number of entries has been reduced to about half that of the parent volume. No changes in content have been made in the entries, although a necrology has been included to update death dates. Rather, entries for secondary figures, such as music critics, church organists, librarians, theorists, and commentators have been eliminated, as have those of minor composers and popular music idols not deemed to be of lasting value.

Baker's, of course, is a basic music reference tool. For those libraries which do not own the seventh edition and find it difficult to afford, for general reference collections, and for librarians needing a desk copy (such as catalogers), the *Concise Baker's* is a bargain at $35.00. For libraries already owning the seventh edition, and not needing an additional, smaller, less expensive resource, the purchase of this volume seems unnecessary.   Allie Wise Goudy

1175. LePage, Jane Weiner. **Women Composers, Conductors, and Musicians of the Twentieth Century: Selected Biographies. Volume III.** Metuchen, N.J., Scarecrow, 1988. 323p. illus. index. $32.50. LC 80-12162. ISBN 0-8108-2082-X.

This book follows two other volumes of the same title (see *ARBA* 81, entry 1038, and *ARBA* 84, entry 884). Like the previous volumes it offers biographies of women musicians, in this case Grazyna Bacewicz, Betty Beath, Anne Boyd, Sylvia Caduff, Ann Carr-Boyd, Gloria Coates, Selma Epstein, Nicola LeFanu, Priscilla McLean, Elizabeth Maconchy, Mary Mageau, Ursula Mamlok, Priaulx Rainier, Shulamit Ran, Ruth Schonthal, Margaret Sutherland, Joan Tower, and Gillian Whitehead. The articles are based on interviews with each musician (or a family member) as well as writings, often newspaper articles, about the women and reviews of their works. A list of compositions selected by the composer accompanies each appropriate article, as do a discography, a list of publishers, and a list of record companies. Although interesting and informative, the articles on these musicians are very informal and chatty in style, often colored by the author's views. A useful addition to this volume would have been a bibliography of other sources containing information on these musicians.

Allie Wise Goudy

Catalogs and Collections

1176. Krasker, Tommy, and Robert Kimball. **Catalog of the American Musical: Musicals of Irving Berlin, George & Ira Gershwin, Cole Porter, Richard Rodgers & Lorenz Hart.** Washington, D.C., National Institute for Music Theater, 1988. 442p. illus. index. $60.00pa. LC 87-061421. ISBN 0-9618575-0-1.

This volume is the first in a series of reference works that attempt to document the location of all original piano and vocal scores, lyrics, libretti, and orchestral scores of American musicals. The current volume treats the seventy-five musical productions of Irving Berlin, George and Ira Gershwin, Cole Porter, and Richard Rogers and Lorenz Hart.

Each of the sections starts with a short biographical and career sketch of the composer and lyricist. Information about each of the musicals includes a plot summary, production information, orchestration information, locations of original material, rental status, music publisher, and other information sources about the work. Location information is also given for each of the show's musical numbers (used and unused). Location abbreviation and rental agency appendices are provided as well as a song index.

This reference work will be a boon to the historian of the American musical in terms of locating original manuscripts and scores. It will also be an invaluable tool for those interested in reconstructing and producing musicals in their original form. [R: RBB, 15 Sept 88, p. 132]

Charles Neuringer

1177. Stiverson, Cynthia Zignego. **Colonial Williamsburg Music: A Descriptive Catalogue of the Printed Eighteenth- and Nineteenth-Century Music in the Collections of the Colonial Williamsburg Foundation.** West Cornwall, Conn., Locust Hill Press, 1988. 189p. index. $25.00. LC 88-15733. ISBN 0-933951-18-3.

This is an attractively printed catalog of 333 eighteenth-century and 185 nineteenth-century musical imprints, arranged by author (or by title if an author is lacking) in each of the two sections. Introductory essays by Arthur Rhea (music consultant to Colonial Williamsburg, 1950-1961), James S. Darling (organist and choirmaster, Bruton Parish Church of Williamsburg), and author Stiverson (former research librarian for the Colonial Williamsburg Foundation) describe the building of this collection and its purpose (to provide authentic sources in support of musical activities at Colonial Williamsburg, particularly at the Bruton Parish Church and the Royal Governor's Palace). Scholarly care has been taken to identify as many publication dates as possible. Notes concerning the provenance, Virginia association (e.g., listing in the 1783 inventory of Thomas Jefferson's library), and physical description (pagination, binding, etc.) of individual items are included. An index of names and titles provides additional points of access.   John E. Druesedow, Jr.

Dictionaries and Encyclopedias

1178. Del Mar, Norman. **The Anchor Companion to the Orchestra.** Garden City, N.Y., Anchor Press/Doubleday, 1987. 266p. illus. $19.95; $10.95pa. ISBN 0-385-24081-3; 0-385-24082-1pa.

There are 250 entries describing essential aspects of the orchestra in this compact companion book for concert goers and enthusiasts of serious music. Del Mar is widely admired in Great Britain as a teacher at the Royal College of Music, where instruction in conducting is his particular forte. He has also written four earlier music books which were well received by the international music community. This guide is presented in ready-reference format and in alphabetical order by major topics and subspecies for maximum practicality. Quite naturally many entries are for the myriad instruments which make up the huge orchestras which are necessary to perform compositions of many twentieth-century composers. One also finds ample descriptions of some of the more popular aspects of orchestral performance today such as chamber orchestra, flute, brass, and electrical amplification. Applause, audience, program books and notes, and platform arrangement are subjects of interest to both the musician and the concert goer. As the author is English, many of the examples cited for composition and experience are based on the works of British composers and musical history and anecdotes from the same geographic locale. This is well illustrated by the description under *national anthem*, which centers squarely on "God Save the Queen." In summary, this is a successful new music reference book of the handy variety. It is available in an inexpensive paperback edition for reliable reference to members of today's concert hall audience, for collectors of orchestral recordings, for music students, and for librarians, too.   William J. Dane

1179. Wadhams, Wayne. **Dictionary of Music Production and Engineering Terminology.** New York, Schirmer Books/Macmillan, 1988. 257p. illus. bibliog. $29.95. LC 87-30998. ISBN 0-02-872691-X.

Wayne Wadhams has had a varied career as a writer, performer, and producer in the entertainment industry. His practical experience was called on by the Berklee College of Music in planning and setting up its department of Music Production and Engineering, which has been in operation since 1983. This dictionary began as a glossary intended for use in the college. It seems to be the first book of its type. The book is needed and it was done by the right person.

In the past few years the once separate worlds of recording, television, and motion pictures have become more or less one as professionals move about in all media. This entertainment world is a mix of creative people, lawyers, promoters, and engineers, and all must speak the same language. This book is the key to this mix of technology and jargon.

The author has presented the material in the best possible way. Definitions are clear and concise. The illustrations by Robin Coxe-Yeldham are just as clear and unfussy and complement the text perfectly. The publisher has also cooperated by designing a book which makes the important things stand out on the pages in large type with sufficient space between entries for easy use. Few books this practical are so attractive and pleasurable to use.

Each definition has been keyed with one or more letters, such as *A* for advertising and *R* for record industry, to clarify its source. The key is repeated in small type at the bottom of every page in the dictionary part of the book, another nicety. A separate section of standard units and measures defines words such as *footcandle* and *hertz*, which most of us have heard of, as well as others such as *gauss*, *oersted*, and *weber*, which have not come our way before. The selected bibliography is especially useful in a field such as this. An admirable book. [R: RQ, Summer 88, p. 570]   George Louis Mayer

Directories

1180. **The Music Business Directory, 1987/88.** San Anselmo, Calif., Augie Blume/Music Industry Resources, 1987. 99p. $29.95pa. ISBN 0-932521-02-9.

The most important thing to point out about this book is that it is a directory to the record business, not the music business. It is one of a group of three directories. The other two (which I have not seen) are *The 1988 California Music Directory* (Augie Blume, 1987), which from the description does cover both the music and record businesses, and *The 1988 Music Radio Directory* (Augie Blume, 1987), which lists "4,200 musically significant and promotable radio stations." All three are available from the same publisher in both book and disc form.

From the business point of view, the importance of this directory is that it directs the user to individuals within companies by position and responsibility. Each entry is coded with basic information about the department's output (such as ethnic, folk, etc.) and the job of the person listed (such as regional promotion person, etc.). The large companies have multiple listings to cover the full range of the companies' activities and staff. Thus, Elektra Records has thirty-five entries covering both East and West coast activities.

The list is far from complete for the classical record business, since it has no entries for major specialized foreign labels which would direct the user to the importer/distributor listed. More cross-references would be useful. Introductory sections are devoted to basic tips for musicians approaching the music business. They are excerpted from a forthcoming musicians' handbook being prepared by Augie Blume. The information is basic but accurate and of use to the novice.

This is basically a promotional and marketing tool, and from this point of view it is excellent and valuable. It should be of value to business and performing arts libraries in large urban centers that provide this kind of detailed information. It goes beyond the kind of good, basic listings to be found in *The Album Network Yellow Pages of Rock '88* (Album Network, 1988) and *Billboard's 1988 International Buyer's Guide* (Billboard Publications, 1987). [R: RBB, 1 Jan 88, p. 768]

George Louis Mayer

1181. **Music Directory Canada '88.** Toronto, CM Books, 1988. 607p. bibliog. $24.95pa. ISSN 0820-0416.

Many of the major forms of music which are created and performed in the world of the 1980s are found in the Canada of today, and this six-hundred-page directory provides the facts for fifty categories of Canadian music activity. Over three thousand individuals and firms are listed under type of institution or enterprise such as lawyers, financial services, and management companies with the largest listing under artist contacts. For performers, the citations for concert promoters, music festivals, night clubs, opera companies, and symphony orchestras are most relevant. The recording and video industries in Canada are prosperous, as

evidenced by multiple listings for these services ranging from the availability of studio spaces through distribution facilities for completed productions. Of special interest are the listings of Canadian award winners and music libraries and a selected discography of Canadian performers which reveals that Gordon Lightfoot, Anne Murray, the very special Buffy Sainte-Marie, and Neil Young are hugely popular with Canadian audiences as well as with countless fans in the United States. Nine opera companies and fifty-six symphony orchestras are listed as currently performing in Canada.

The first edition of this directory was published in 1983. This updated listing has thousands of factual entries for 1988 telephone numbers and addresses plus annotations, and all are compactly arranged under the most logical groupings. Now that trade between the United States and Canada is relatively barrier free, all facets of Canadian business are of increasing interest. This handy directory has considerable reference value to musicians and also to the business community of the United States and Canada. [R: RBB, 15 Sept 88, p. 140]

William J. Dane

1182. **Musical America's Festivals '88.** Shirley Fleming, ed. New York, ABC Consumer Magazine, 1988. 63p. illus. index. $9.95pa.

Festivals '88 is a magazine-like publication composed primarily of the entries for American and foreign music festivals found in the 1988 edition of *Musical America International Directory of the Performing Arts*. Approximately one thousand festivals are listed, following exactly the same format as that of the directory, except that there is additional information on some seventy-five festivals (supplied by festival promoters) as well as some advertisements containing useful information. Supplementing the entries are short articles on Tanglewood, Aspen, Yale at Norfolk, and American festivals in general. Unfortunately, the entries are arranged geographically and there is no index. If you have the directory, it comes down to whether or not the additional information is worth $10.00. If you do not have the directory, *Festivals '88* will answer with current information some of the most common questions music librarians receive as people plan their vacations.

Robert Skinner

1183. Uscher, Nancy. **The Schirmer Guide to Schools of Music and Conservatories throughout the World.** New York, Schirmer Books/ Macmillan, 1988. 635p. index. $60.00. LC 88-1518. ISBN 0-02-873030-5.

This lengthy volume provides extensive information on more than 750 music departments, schools, and conservatories throughout the world. For a U.S. school to be included, the institution had to offer a master's degree or employ more than ten full-time faculty above the rank of instructor. For European countries, only those schools that prepare students to be professional musicians are included. In non-European countries, guidelines for inclusion vary according to what seemed appropriate for that country. Entries for each institution include a brief history and academic information such as enrollment, number of faculty (faculty names are not included), entrance requirements and admission procedures, degrees offered, and areas of study. Information is also provided on facilities, special programs, and financial aid. Occasionally the author comments on some aspect of the institution that is particularly noteworthy. Information on U.S. schools is much more detailed than that for foreign institutions. An especially useful feature of this guide is its three indexes: an index by institutions, an index to program areas, and an index to instruments taught.

By way of comparison, the *Music Industry Directory 1983* (see *ARBA* 85, entry 1166) offers much less information about the music departments it lists, but as it is not selective, many more departments are included. Which source one would consult would depend on the type and extent of information being sought. *The Schirmer Guide* is an excellent resource and will be a valuable addition to music reference collections. [R: Choice, Nov 88, p. 470; LJ, 15 Oct 88, p. 84; RBB, 15 Dec 88, p. 693; WLB, Sept 88, p. 97]   Allie Wise Goudy

Discographies

1184. *CD* **Review Digest: The Guide to English Language Reviews of All Music Recorded on Compact Discs. Volume 2: No. 1.** Janet Grimes, ed. Voorheesville, N.Y., Peri Press, 1988. 239p. index. $35.00 (4 issues). ISSN 0890-0213.

1185. *CD* **Review Digest Annual: The Guide to Reviews of All Music on Compact Disc. Volume 1: 1983-1987.** Janet Grimes, ed. Voorheesville, N.Y., Peri Press, 1988. 2 pts. index. $135.00/set. ISBN 0-9617844-0-7; ISSN 0893-5173.

The volumes under review constitute the first in a new series which aims to cite all compact disc and videodisc reviews appearing in some fifty English-language magazines. The

initial installment consists of two volumes devoted to discs released between 1983 and 1987 and a continuing series of quarterly supplements with annual cumulations covering new releases. Unlike Richard LeSueurs's more familiar "Index to CD and Record Reviews," which appears in the *Notes* of the Music Library Association, the *Digest* includes SPARS codes, total duration, reviewers' names, approximate word counts, and short review excerpts for many (but not all) discs, as well as coverage of over twice as many periodicals. Volume 1 is devoted to classical recordings, volume 2 to jazz, popular, soundtrack/cast recordings, and videodiscs, as well as indexes for both volumes. Arrangement is alphabetical by composer for recordings with single works by not more than three persons; otherwise, it is by performer (*Notes*, incidentally, uses record label). Each entry is numbered, facilitating internal references. Indexes are provided for show composers, labels, reviewers, titles, and performers.

There is no question that this could be a most useful work, both for record collectors and for those who select recordings for libraries. Librarians, at least, will find that the review quotations often provide sufficient information to obviate referring to the original. In spite of the amount of material, a spot check showed few mistakes (a couple of missing diacritical marks; at least one missing entry for Roy Hemming in the index of reviewers). There are, however, aspects which definitely need to be improved. To begin with, the type in general is too small and the names of compositions within a composer's entry (or album titles within a performer's entry) are not sufficiently distinguished typographically from the mass of information surrounding each entry. Several persons I showed the classical volume to found it sufficiently tedious to read and they eventually gave up. Particularly difficult to find, unless you are looking for them, are the references to couplings elsewhere in the volume (see the listing for Schubert's *Unfinished Symphony* for examples). More seriously, the *Digest* often omits some or all of the titles for pieces in anthologies. Sometimes this seems capricious, as in the case of an entry which lists seven Renaissance choral works on the album but leaves out the last two. In other cases, we get only the information typically found in *Schwann* — "French orchestral music" (works by Berlioz, Ravel, Dukas, Saint-Saens, Debussy, Chabrier) — with no indication of the actual pieces performed. Since this information is almost always available in the information accompanying reviews, it should not be too much trouble to include here. This, together with a second try at the graphic design level, would help this publicaiton fulfill its promise.

Robert Skinner

1186. Greenfield, Edward, Robert Layton, and Ivan March. **The New Penguin Guide to Compact Discs and Cassettes.** New York, Viking Penguin, 1988. 1366p. $14.95pa. ISBN 0-14-046829-3.

Just a short time ago no one was predicting that compact discs and cassettes would bring to an end the era of the long-playing vinyl disc as quickly as it has come. Guides to CDs which appeared even a short time ago were of little value since so few performances were available in this format. This massive tome, with its tiny print, shows just how quickly things have changed, and how short a time it has taken for the major companies to remaster major releases in their catalogs into the CD format. This guide, therefore, can compare performances of new digitally recorded versions with the digitally remastered versions from the LP era.

Readers familiar with the same authors' *Complete Penguin Stereo Record and Cassette Guide* (see *ARBA* 86, entry 1268) and their reviews in the British periodical *Gramophone* already know that these critics are trustworthy and usually quite eloquent in expressing their opinions. A certain favoritism toward British performers seems to an American reader to assert itself from time to time, but the evaluations seem unbiased and sound for the most part. Both long and short reviews concentrate on the essentials and give a good sense of the performances and sound quality of the releases. They are especially good in pointing out the quality of cassettes.

The only factual error I have discovered is in the review of performances of Verdi's *Macbeth.* It states that Leonard Warren died on the stage of the Metropolitan in this role but he had died in *La Forza del Destino.*

Arrangement is by composer. Those with many entries have been divided into categories: orchestral music, chamber music, vocal music, et cetera. A short section on recitals is added for those recordings which could not be included by composer. One longs for a performer index, but there is none. Every effort has been made to include American release information when necessary. This is an excellent guide.

George Louis Mayer

1187. Harris, Steve. **Film, Television and Stage Music on Phonograph Records: A Discography.** Jefferson, N.C., McFarland, 1988. 445p. bibliog. index. $49.95. LC 87-42509. ISBN 0-89950-251-2.

This reference contains just under twelve thousand titles of films, television productions, and stage works for which a discography exists, each medium having its own alphabet. Liberal use of abbreviations is essential if so much information is to be provided within one volume, but these will not have the user often flipping back to the introductory pages for explanations. Each entry is numbered consecutively, in boldface print, while the title is not, which tends to slow down rapid reference. The scope is not limited to U.S. productions, but the medium and recording must have had an American release. The cut-off date is the end of 1986. The names of the composers and conductors (or principal musical performers) are given, but not the cast, producer, or other contributors. There is only one index, that being reserved for composers, giving further focus to the goals and offering additional restrictions to the reference value of this undertaking. The frontmatter, somewhat self-laudatory, provides definitions and orientation. Those buffs of these media, concerned with the composers of the music employed and the issue of recordings, will find this an important resource, beautifully produced, with a few typographical errors and liberal capitalization of foreign titles. [R: Choice, Oct 88, p. 292; RBB, 1 Oct 88, p. 240; VOYA, Dec 88, p. 258]

Dominique-René de Lerma

Handbooks

1188. Craven, Robert R., ed. **Symphony Orchestras of the World: Selected Profiles.** Westport, Conn., Greenwood Press, 1987. 468p. bibliog. index. $75.00. LC 86-29452. ISBN 0-313-24073-6.

While *Symphony Orchestras of the United States* (see *ARBA* 87, entry 1238) offers coverage for its geographical area, this publication covers 118 foreign ensembles from forty-two countries, including the Americas, Asia, the South Pacific, Europe, Israel, and Egypt. This is then about two-thirds of the potential, the remainder not being qualified because of some practical (albeit it severe) criteria related to repertoire, recordings, and reviews. Basic data for those excluded are found in the annual listings of Musical America's *International Directory of the Performing Arts* (see *ARBA* 88, entry 1279). The entries (by country, then city) are cited in English (the native name is generally often provided), with a description of the ensemble's history, budget, repertoire, and hall. A chronology of music directors is provided, with literary sources for additional information, the address, and telephone number. The entries for various countries were written by a regional authority. Backmatter includes a chronological perspective of the scene, starting with 1530 when the Bavarian State Orchestra was established as a court ensemble. The selected bibliography includes previously cited material along with the new, and following the index are sketches on the contributors and translators. This work will be immediately practical for those needing information on the world's major orchestras and conductors. [R: Choice, Mar 88, p. 1110]

Dominique-René de Lerma

Indexes

1189. The Music Educators Journal: Cumulative Index 1914-1987: Including the Music Supervisors' Bulletin and the Music Supervisors' Journal. By Arne Jon Arneson. Stevens Point, Wis., Index House, 1987. 380p. $59.95pa. LC 87-28941. ISBN 0-936697-01-6.

MEJ is the official periodical of the Music Educators National Conference, which represents all aspects of music education in American schools, colleges, universities, and teacher preparation organizations. Individuals working in the field of music education are also encouraged to join this nonprofit organization, which has regional divisions across the United States. This index covers material published over a span of seventy-three years and therefore surveys the major trends in the teaching of music in America during most of the twentieth century. Three separate indexes have been compiled to cover the authors of articles, subjects, and books reviewed over the past seven decades. Review of scores, recordings, films, and computer software are not included. The most useful section of this index for subject specialists and education majors is that arranged by subject. This makes up more than 200 of the total of 380 pages. Articles appearing in *MEJ* are generally brief. Contemporary topics such as rock music, black music, and electronic music receive only minimal attention. However, music education, instruments, voice, war, and education are topics with ample coverage since 1914. Libraries and researchers directly involved with music education and its history will find this index of value chiefly for the survey factor of the articles in the long run of the periodical, which tracks the constantly changing philosophy and classroom approach to academic music education across the United States.

William J. Dane

1190. The Music Index: A Subject-Author Guide to Music Periodical Literature. Volume 33-34: 1981-1982. Warren, Mich., Harmonie Park Press, 1987. 1087p. $475.00. LC 50-13627. ISBN 0-89990-041-0.

1191. The Music Index: A Subject-Author Guide to Music Periodical Literature. Volume 39: 1987 Subject Heading List. Warren, Mich., Harmonie Park Press, 1987. 154p. $745.00/yr. LC 50-13627. ISBN 0-89990-029-1.

This monumental music reference work provides the key to unlocking countless articles, obituaries, book reviews, and myriad other music subjects covered in over 350 periodicals from twenty nations. First issued in 1949, this two-year cumulation is representative of the superb job of organization achieved by the editors of this notable bibliographic summary. With nearly eleven hundred pages covering a two-year span, this is without doubt the major single source to find periodical information devoted to music in Europe and America. The indexing covers all aspects of the volatile and mercurial world of popular music by covering material in such contemporary standard magazines as *Billboard*, *Rolling Stone*, *Spin*, and *Variety* while also including the world of opera, musical instruments, and essential regional and national publications in the discipline. New technical developments of our era are thoroughly treated and include video, compact discs, tape cassettes, electronic music, and computer sound synthesis. Music biography is brilliantly summarized. For example, the literature on major composers is rich and varied, as evidenced by five columns of entries for Richard Strauss, Stravinsky, and Beethoven; nineteen obituary notices to record the death of Samuel Barber in 1981; and a full column of entries for the Rolling Stones and another for the Beatles. Music therapy, copyright, drugs, page turners, auditions, and piano tuning are also covered, and these provide some indication of the diversity of material. A subject heading list with cross-references is published annually. This is highly useful in facilitating maximum use of the index and is also helpful to those compiling institutional or personal vertical files.

The index is currently published in twelve monthly numbers. Music librarians have long hoped that annual cumulations could be published immediately after each year has run its course and thus be current and more efficient to use. The editor plans to compile and publish the two-year cumulations on a more up-to-date basis, and this is good news indeed for musicologists, students, and the library world. This publication is truly a major reference work and is without question an essential bibliographic service for all institutions and individuals seriously concerned with the music world past, present and future.   William J. Dane

1192. **The Recording Locator 1988.** rev. ed. San Jose, Calif., Resource Publications, 1987. 1047p. $160.00pa. ISBN 0-89390-115-6.

The 1988 revised edition of *The Recording Locator* comprises indexes intended to offer accessibility to more than 100,000 recorded Christian song and album titles. It incorporates the information from the 1987 supplements as well as "a comprehensive list of releases accurate as of July 1987 with as many releases projected for August or later as possible" (p. 5). The three major indexes, each separate and each arranged alphabetically, list music by song title, artist, and album title. Titles of group names beginning with numbers precede the alphabetical listing in each index, a small but very helpful adjustment to the normal alphabetical arrangement. There are also accompaniment tape listings by song title and by artist, a music video listing, and the publisher list. The availability codes included in the artist, album, and accompaniment listings indicate each title's availability as LP record, single 45, compact disc, 8-track cartridge, and cassette tape. Out-of-print albums are so marked. This is the first edition of *The Recording Locator* to include compact disc availability, and the first to include a music video listing. *The Recording Locator* is to be updated by three supplements. The neatness and consistency of the page layout, the small but very clear print, and the good-quality paper all combine to make it easy to read, an important attribute for the busy user.

This is a good resource book for locating particular songs contained in albums (in song listing), or for finding a complete listing of all the titles contained in an album (in the artist listing rather than the album listing). *The Recording Locator* does index only one genre of recorded music, and is self-described as "a single source of information about recorded music for the religious music retailer" (p. 5). An earlier edition states that "contemporary and Gospel artists are particularly well represented; classical artists, less so" (preface to the 1982-1983 edition). This is still true. However, this index would be useful in many public libraries, college and university music libraries, and most retail record stores. It is particularly useful for the retail store which does not want to keep a large stock of recordings in a genre which, like much popular music, has a high production and a fast out-of-print rate. [R: RBB, 15 Nov 88, pp. 554-55]

Dorothy E. Jones

COMPOSERS

1193. Antokoletz, Elliott. **Béla Bartók: A Guide to Research.** New York, Garland, 1988. 356p. index. (Garland Reference Library of the Humanities, Vol. 691). $52.00. LC 87-36053. ISBN 0-8240-7747-4.

Antokoletz (University of Texas at Austin) must now know more about Bartók than anyone. The most satisfactory aspect of this excellent study guide is its selectivity. The author has not attempted to give us everything, but has sorted out the most important sources, and these are the ones he lists and annotates. This is a wise guide, and he is to be thanked for sorting these materials out for us.

The guide begins with a history of the composer's musical development, and goes on to a list of his works, a list of primary sources, biographical and historical studies, studies of the musical compositions, and discussions of institutional sources for Bartók research. The indexes cover author/title, Bartók's compositions, proper names, and subjects. The arrangement does necessitate the using of the index to compositions constantly, because the writings on any particular composition are not grouped together. I was frustrated at my first attempts to use this guide by checking what many of us would call "Bluebeard's Castle" and finding no entry until I looked under the more precise "Duke Bluebeard's Castle," which led me to the Hungarian title. My next attempt was under "Bagatelles." No entry. I had to remember their number to find them under "Fourteen Bagatelles." This bothers me a bit. Not everyone in need of this guide knows that some of his works contain five, four, seven, or eight songs, pieces, sketches, or improvisations.

The section of institutional sources contains a list of computerized databases. The subject index is excellent and picks up on such items as the Fibonacci Series, which is an important feature of the composer's work, and not so easy to locate in discussions of his methods.

I have nothing but admiration for this excellent work. I only wish that the computer typeface were more attractive and easier on the eye. This one is particularily nasty. [R: Choice, Sept 88, p. 73]   George Louis Mayer

1194. Appleby, David P. **Heitor Villa-Lobos: A Bio-Bibliography.** Westport, Conn., Greenwood Press, 1988. 358p. index. (Bio-Bibliographies in Music, No. 9). $45.00. LC 87-28042. ISBN 0-313-25346-3.

Published a year after the centenary of Villa-Lobos's birth, this ninth volume in Greenwood's series of bio-bibliographies provides a wealth of data on a composer about whom little information has been available, especially in a single English-language source.

A brief (five pages) yet informative biographical sketch introduces the volume. The greater part of the book is devoted to a chronological catalog of 567 works identified as complete and/or published. Works are cited alphabetically within each year or groups of years. Information about dates of composition, commissions, dedications, first performances, and publishers is provided. Following is a list of additional works (incomplete, fragmentary, or lacking reliable dates) and "Errata."

The second major section is a substantial, though selective, discography of representative recordings of the composer's music. It includes recordings "currently available, unavailable recordings of good quality, and ... recordings originally issued as LPs ... released for the Villa-Lobos Centennial year ... in CD (compact disc)." A twenty-five-page bibliography cites books and articles separately. Unfortunately, only the books are annotated and these very briefly; the articles are not. Even if space was a consideration, at least major articles should have been annotated.

Two appendices provide an alphabetical and a classified list of compositions, respectively, with references back to the catalog proper. A lengthy index includes names of performers, concert locations, and compositions (including short pieces arranged by Villa-Lobos and movements from larger works that have been performed separately).

Carole Franklin Vidali

1195. Block, Geoffrey. **Charles Ives: A Bio-Bibliography.** Westport, Conn., Greenwood Press, 1988. 422p. index. (Bio-Bibliographies in Music, No. 14). $49.95. LC 88-21316. ISBN 0-313-25404-4.

The treatment of individuals within this excellent series of reference books uses a standard format which is modified and expanded as the specific subject requires. In the case of Charles Ives (1874-1954), the format consists of a terse biographical sketch, a register of works, a discography, and a classified bibliography followed by appendices and indexes. The biography has parenthetical references to the bibliography, as does the works list (which carefully annotates duration, instrumentation, premiere, and publications). The discography is not comprehensive, but other sources for additional data are listed. The bibliographies, chronologically ordered, include useful annotations. The general index and index of authors provide alternate access to the information. Ives

is excellently treated, although one might wish for a single-source discography. His music merits this attention. This volume will receive heavy use in all academic music libraries.

Dominique-René de Lerma

1196. Boenke, Heidi M., comp. **Flute Music by Women Composers: An Annotated Catalog.** Westport, Conn., Greenwood Press, 1988. 201p. bibliog. index. (Music Reference Collection, No. 16). $37.95. LC 88-21317. ISBN 0-313-26019-2.

The publication of this catalog adds another volume to the growing list of books concentrating on women's role in music. This particular book presents flute compositions—solo, concertos, chamber works—written by women composers from all over the world. The vast majority of composers are from the twentieth century. The author has included any composition she could find, even if complete information was unavailable. Most of the entries, however, which are alphabetically arranged by composer, include brief biographical information about the composer, a list of flute compositions with instrumentation, publisher, and date of publication. Also included, when available, are a record number and date, an OCLC number, and an item number from the *National Union Catalog*. Indexes are provided which allow access by instrumentation and title. These are useful, although the instrumentation index would be improved if several of the categories, such as "Duets," "Flute and Strings," "Other Small Ensembles," and "Other Large Ensembles," were subarranged by specific instruments. Users will appreciate the thoroughness of the information within the entries. The book is recommended to conservatory libraries, large and medium-sized academic music collections, and larger public libraries needing specialized resources. Allie Wise Goudy

1197. Christensen, Jean, and Jesper Christensen. **From Arnold Schoenberg's Literary Legacy: A Catalog of Neglected Items.** Warren, Mich., Harmonie Park Press, 1988. 164p. illus. bibliog. index. (Detroit Studies in Music Bibliography, No. 59). $35.00. LC 87-29627. ISBN 0-89990-036-4.

This is a catalog of the portion of Schoenberg's literary works which has not hitherto been cataloged. Based on Schoenberg's own scheme for arranging his writings, it is arranged by category/subject, then chronologically. For each item the compilers have supplied a descriptive annotation and a physical description. (It would greatly facilitate the use of the book if the list of abbreviations used in the descriptions were printed on the inside front cover; although it is perfectly reasonable to list the abbreviations as the last piece of information before the actual catalog, it causes a good deal of searching to find the undistinguishable pages which are the key to the abbreviations when using the catalog.) The annotations contain a great deal of information; where appropriate they cite published and/or translated versions of the item. The volume includes a detailed index. Complementary to published Schoenberg catalogs, this volume will be an essential acquisition for historically oriented music libraries.

Carol June Bradley

1198.   Citron, Marcia J. **Cécile Chaminade: A Bio-Bibliography.** Westport, Conn., Greenwood Press, 1988. 243p. index. (Bio-Bibliographies in Music, No. 15). $39.95. LC 88-21315. ISBN 0-313-25319-6.

The popularity of Cécile Chaminade (1857-1944) in the United States was no doubt at its peak during the autumn of 1908, when the composer-pianist appeared on tour in such cities as New York, Philadelphia, Cincinnati, Minneapolis, Chicago, and St. Louis, where the tour was proclaimed in the *Daily Globe Democrat* as "the most important musical event since the last tour of Rubenstein [sic] in this country" (Citron, citation B354). The road to fame was well paved: nine years earlier, *The Etude* had unabashedly described Chaminade as "the greatest of female composers" (November 1899, p. 349). But since World War I, her star has been in decline both here and elsewhere. If there is to be a resurgence of interest in this Parisian-born student of Benjamin Godard (1849-1895) and others, the present work could well become the bibliographical cornerstone. Marcia J. Citron has scrutinized family memorabilia and other sources in putting together probably the most accurate biography of Chaminade available (pp. 3-32); in addition, the author has provided a well-nigh complete list of published and unpublished works (with annotations for selected performances), an impressive discography including piano-roll recordings, and a discriminatingly annotated bibliography of 479 (!) citations, plus three appendices and an index. The whole appears to be thoroughly cross-indexed.

John E. Druesedow, Jr.

1199.   Cohen, Aaron I. **International Encyclopedia of Women Composers.** 2d ed. New York, Books & Music (USA), 1987. 2v. illus. bibliog. $125.00/set. LC 86-72857. ISBN 0-9617485-2-4.

The first edition of this valuable reference work (see *ARBA* 83, entry 945) has been out of print for several years, and it is good to have an expanded, two-volume version available costing less than the original! The new edition contains over 1,230 pages (over 600 pages longer than the original) and covers 1,200 more composers. It includes 572 photographs. The original appendices listed lacuna; composers arranged by various criteria including country, century, instrument, occupation; an extensive bibliography; and other information. Cohen has added lists of operas by women, compositions influenced by Shakespeare, pseudonyms, and a discography of LPs. Although the first edition was generally well received, the compiler and his staff have taken a number of criticisms to heart. It is particularly gratifying to see female composers (most notably, Amy Marcy Beach) listed first under their own names rather than their husbands' names. Although this set will not replace other more specialized resources (especially those dealing with popular music), it belongs in every music collection. [R: Choice, Sept 88, p. 76]

Robert Skinner

1200.   Craggs, Stewart R. **Arthur Bliss: A Bio-Bibliography.** Westport, Conn., Greenwood Press, 1988. 183p. index. (Bio-Bibliographies in Music, No. 13). $37.95. LC 88-10975. ISBN 0-313-25739-6.

The "Bio" section of this study is a brief ten pages, but it does give the basic facts of the life and career of the composer. Bliss was thoroughly a British composer—even becoming in 1953 the Master of the Queen's Music—despite having an American father and an American wife, and being very much aware of the continental activities of his European contemporaries such as Stravinsky, Milhaud, and Poulenc.

The major parts of this book are works and performances, publishing directory, discography, bibliography, alphabetical list of main compositions, chronicle of main compositions, and the index. The important and necessary things are all here, but there are aspects of the organization and of the information given which I find disappointing and incomplete. Some researchers will be frustrated by these weaknesses.

I do not like the fact that the suites from Bliss's ballets do not get separate entries as separate works but that information about them gets buried within the body of the main ballet entries (and the index is no help). Also, works that were substantially reworked into new compositions do not get separate entries. The work which started out as a concerto for piano, tenor voice, strings and percussion was later transformed into a concerto for two pianos and orchestra (and still later a concerto for two pianos (three hands) and orchestra. There are no separate entries. All appear under the original. The index in this case does lead one to the entry, however. Even the lists of main compositions ignore these separate works. The publishing directory merely gives "no longer extant" status to several of Bliss's publishers. What serious researchers and performers need to know is information about who now controls the rights, who now has rental copies, etc., for firms no longer in business. The discography is limited to long-playing discs and is selective. It should have been a complete and detailed discography.

The bibliography entries are excellent and are well annotated. This will be the most useful section of the book. [R: Choice, Dec 88, p. 624]

George Louis Mayer

1201. DeBoer, Kee, and John B. Ahouse. **Daniel Pinkham: A Bio-Bibliography.** Westport, Conn., Greenwood Press, 1988. 238p. index. (Bio-Bibliographies in Music, No. 12). $39.95. LC 88-157. ISBN 0-313-25503-2.

Since his graduation from Harvard with a major in music, the prolific American composer Daniel Pinkham has written more than three hundred works. These compositions span his entire career from the mid-1940s to date as composer, performer, and teacher.

This volume begins with a ten-page biography, hence the claim in the subtitle "a bio-bibliography." While these ten pages are informative, they are but a chronological overview of Pinkham's musical life and style. I am not convinced it deserves such prominent mention.

The rest of the work pertains to Pinkham's compositions, first subdivided by medium (e.g., works for orchestra, solo organ, mixed chorus). Each of these is numbered sequentially as it appears in this volume. (A chronological listing comprises appendix 1.) They are cross-referenced where appropriate to the listings in the section on discography and bibliography. The entries found in the bibliography are short, annotated descriptions of reviews or program notes. Four appendices and an index conclude the work: a chronological listing of Pinkham's works, an alphabetical listing of works, any literary texts used in Pinkham's works, and biblical sources of texts.

All in all, this work breaks new ground by its very existence. The importance of chronicling the works of a composer during his lifetime and opinions about those works shortly after they were composed cannot be underestimated. This volume will provide valuable assistance to musicians, scholars, and students of twentieth-century music. [R: Choice, Nov 88, p. 458]

Marjorie E. Bloss

1202. **The Great Composers: Their Lives and Times.** David Buxton and Sue Lyon, eds. Freeport, N.Y., Marshall Cavendish, 1987. 11v. illus. (part col.). index. $299.95/set. LC 86-31294. ISBN 0-86307-776-5.

Aimed at the casual, but informed, listener of serious music, *The Great Composers* series provides biographical information, listening helps and advice, and cultural, social, and political background for composers from the Baroque through the late Romantic Periods. The eleven-volume set includes twenty-one major composers and is arranged as follows: Volume 1—Mozart; volume 2—Beethoven; volume 3—Tchaikovsky; volume 4—Albinoni, Corelli, Handel, Pachelbel, Purcell, Rameau, Telemann, and Vivaldi; volume 5—Bach and Haydn; volume 6—Chopin, Liszt, Schubert; volume 7—Brahms and Mahler; volume 8—Berlioz, Mendelssohn, and Schumann. Volumes 9 and 10 are guides to classical music and opera, respectively; and volume 11 contains a general index, a composer index, and a music form index. In addition to the "Composer's Life," "Listener's Guide," and "In the Background" sections, each composer volume contains a bibliography, a section on contemporary composers not included among those featured in the series, and an index. The two "guide" volumes also include bibliographies and indexes.

The real strength of this set is in neither the breadth nor the depth of its coverage (these are both better addressed by the standard surveys of music and numerous individual composer biographies already available), but rather in the fact that it integrates the composer's life, music, and environment and presents the information in a readable, easily understood fashion. The slim volumes are extensively illustrated, attractive, and exceptionally well bound (except for one volume of the review copy that was placed in its case upside down!) and should withstand fairly heavy use.

While obviously not intended as a definitive scholarly resource, this set will satisfy many beginning music appreciation needs and through the bibliographies will provide access to more in-depth information. Most appropriate for public, secondary school, and home library collections. [R: RBB, 1 Apr 88, p. 1321; WLB, Mar 88, p. 99]   Kristin Ramsdell

1203. Grim, William E. **Max Reger: A Bio-Bibliography.** Westport, Conn., Greenwood Press, 1988. 270p. index. (Bio-Bibliographies in Music, No. 7). $37.95. LC 87-25153. ISBN 0-313-25311-0.

Max Reger was an eminent composer in Germany during the late nineteenth and early twentieth centuries. Extensive research has been devoted to him in Germanic countries, and a critical edition of his works, published by Breitkopf & Härtel, is almost complete. In English-speaking countries, however, Reger is much less well known. The author has attempted to rectify this lack of recognition through the publication of this bibliography. The main portion of the bibliography includes 1,894 entries arranged by format: periodical articles, bibliographies, biographies, monographic studies, writings by Reger, etc. Many entries are annotated. This section is preceded by a brief biography; a list of works, publishers, and first performances; and a discography. It is followed by two appendices — a chronological list of Reger's works and a list of works by genre — and an index. Because the main section of the bibliography is not classified by topic, the entries can be somewhat difficult to access. The index includes only names, places, and compositions and thus offers no subject access. A feature of great value in locating information on a particular work is the second section noted above, "Works and Performances," which also includes references to entries in other sections of the book which pertain to specific compositions. The volume is recommended for music research collections. [R: Choice, June 88, p. 1534]

Allie Wise Goudy

1204. Hammond, Frederick. **Girolamo Frescobaldi: A Guide to Research.** New York, Garland, 1988. 412p. illus. bibliog. index. (Garland Composer Resource Manuals, Vol. 9; Garland Reference Library of the Humanities, Vol. 672). $52.00. LC 87-25914. ISBN 0-8240-8555-8.

A mother lode of information concerning Frescobaldi (1583-1643) and his milieu, this guide begins with "corrections and additions" to the author's *Girolamo Frescobaldi* (Harvard University, 1983), a major monograph of the life and works variety. Immediately following is a "documentary biography," a chronology of Frescobaldi's life interlaced with relevant artistic and political events. There are chapters on "places" (including Roman churches, palaces, institutions, and academies, all individually described), "persons" (brief biographies of about four hundred figures whose lives directly or indirectly touched the subject), "current and future research," and "performance" (translations of the prefaces of Frescobaldi's published works); especially to be noted is the chapter on "useful knowledge," a labor-saving compendium of practical data (e.g., on contemporary currency, bookkeeping, the postal system, weights and measures, archival sources). Two appendices ("Check-List of Documentary Mate-

rials Referring to Frescobaldi" and "Other Archival Materials"), a 123-page bibliography, a discography of 89 citations, and an index of names and subjects complete this exhaustive reference study, a worthy complement to the author's above-mentioned monograph. [R: Choice, Oct 88, p. 292]

John E. Druesedow, Jr.

1205. Howard, Patricia. **Christoph Willibald Gluck: A Guide to Research.** New York, Garland, 1987. 178p. illus. index. (Garland Composer Resource Manuals, Vol. 8; Garland Reference Library of the Humanities, Vol. 716). $32.00. LC 87-12027. ISBN 0-8240-8451-9.

Howard probably first encountered much of her source material in writing *Gluck and the Birth of Modern Opera* (London: Barrie & Rockliff, 1963), and has continued to explore it for the subsequent articles she has written about Gluck's works over the last quarter of a century. This research guide has the authority of a specialist sharing insights. Her level-headed approach appeals to me. She is very specific about where she has been selective (because of many good sources) and where she has less critically been more inclusive (because of the paucity of sources). She is honest and straightforward about omitted sources which might have been included had she had the opportunity to see them. She is also very direct and informative about the quality of the source materials, and gives warnings about some aspects of some otherwise reliable writings. Her annotations are compact but give very specific information about content, quality, and usefulness. In short, they are models of what annotations of this type should be. Users of this guide will have many reasons to be grateful to Howard for her skills, generosity, and practicality.

Gluck's compositions are listed with valuable information about the collected editions and the resources of major European libraries for manuscripts. She covers the sources and resources for Gluck's life and works in general and in connection with specific compositions. She adds a valuable section about Gluck's collaborators in the theater which covers choreographers, designers, librettists, singers, theater management, and archives. Indexes are by authors, proper names, and Gluck's works. This guide is valuable to students of this somewhat enigmatic composer, who was so aptly described after his death by Christian Shubart as one who "belonged to no school and who founded no tradition," but whose works continue to fascinate and please music lovers.

George Louis Mayer

1206. Kushner, David Z. **Ernest Bloch: A Guide to Research.** New York, Garland, 1988. 345p. illus. bibliog. index. (Garland Composer Resource Manuals, Vol. 14; Garland Reference Library of the Humanities, Vol. 796). $47.00. LC 88-11297. ISBN 0-8240-7789-X.

Like other volumes in Garland's Composer series, this is a bibliography of the subject's works and of secondary material devoted to him. A short opening biography of Bloch examines aspects of his compositions that have led to his popular identification as a "Jewish" composer. An annotated bibliography of literature by and about Bloch includes 579 entries arranged by author and occupies most of the volume. As the preface notes, "the literature about Bloch is largely fragmented"; consequently, the bibliography includes not only articles and book-length works but also entries in reference works, pages from standard histories, newspaper articles, program notes, and LP liner notes. Further chapters list Bloch's works, recordings of his works, the holdings in archives and repositories of manuscripts and other items relating to Bloch, festivals and retrospectives devoted to Bloch, Bloch's own program notes, honors and awards given to Bloch, winners of the Ernest Bloch Award Competition, and holders of the Ernest Bloch professorships at Berkeley. Indexes cover authors, proper names, Bloch's compositions, and subjects in the bibliography and throughout the volume. Since the bibliography is arranged by author, the author index is redundant; nevertheless, the guide as a whole is thorough and well organized.

William S. Brockman

1207. Ossenkop, David. **Hugo Wolf: A Guide to Research.** New York, Garland, 1988. 329p. index. (Garland Composer Resource Manuals, Vol. 15; Garland Reference Library of the Humanities, Vol. 747). $51.00. LC 88-16323. ISBN 0-8240-8474-8.

In producing this comprehensive bibliographic guide to the work and life of Hugo Wolf, David Ossenkop has provided the music scholar, student, and performing artist with access to much material that has previously been scattered, unlisted, or insufficiently documented. While earlier sources such as Margarete Saary's *Personalität und musikdramatische Kreativität Hugo Wolfs* (1984) and the major biographical work on Wolf, Frank Walker's *Hugo Wolf: A Biography* (1951; 2d ed., 1968), both include extensive bibliographies, Ossenkop's guide casts a broader net, greatly expanding and updating the coverage of both.

The guide is divided into three major parts: "The Works of Hugo Wolf," "Bibliography,"

and "Guide to Further Research." The section on works covers both Wolf's musical compositions, divided by type, and his critical writings; complete listings of each are provided. The musical entries include title, first lines of vocal compositions, authors of texts, key, date of composition, date of publication, location in the *Sämtliche Werke*, and other relevant information. A brief prefatory section on the publication history is especially helpful.

The heart of this guide is a selective bibliography of just under five hundred primary and secondary sources published between 1890 and 1986. Divided into the following sections—"General Background Studies," "Collections of Essays on Wolf," "Biographical Sources on Wolf," "Wolf as Critic," and "Wolf as Composer"—the bibliography covers material in all Western languages and includes books, essays, periodical articles, program notes, significant record linear notes, and important unpublished doctoral dissertations. Reviews and biographical articles considered to be ephemeral are generally excluded. In addition, the general sources bibliography is highly selective; only those materials containing significant information relative to Wolf are included. Complete bibliographic information for each entry is included and all entries are annotated.

The final section of the guide, aimed at future researchers, is divided into the following sections: "The Internationale Hugo Wolf-Gesellschaft," "Primary Source Materials in Libraries and Collections," "Directions for Future Research," and "Directory of Hugo Wolf Scholars." An introductory biographical sketch and two indexes, one to Wolf's works, the other to general topics, complete the guide.

Scholarly, well-organized, and comprehensive, this bibliographic guide will be of primary interest to Wolf scholars, but would be a useful addition to most academic music library collections, especially those with a strong emphasis in the Romantic period or vocal music.

Kristin Ramsdell

1208. Patterson, Donald L., and Janet L. Patterson. **Vincent Persichetti: A Bio-Bibliography.** Westport, Conn., Greenwood Press, 1988. 336p. index. (Bio-Bibliographies in Music, No. 16). $49.95. LC 88-25084. ISBN 0-313-25335-8.

Persichetti's importance as a composer began in the 1940s and continued until his death in 1987. He also had a long career as a teacher and his influence reached out in many directions in the American musical scene of his generation.

The Pattersons have done a superb job in preparing this bio-bibliography. I regret, as will other readers, that the biography section is only about twenty pages long, since it is so interesting, but the main feature of this work is to deliver information about the composer's works and what has been written about them, and this the authors do extremely well.

The main section of the book is the works and performances section, which is a classified list (piano music, orchestral music, etc.). Each entry gives full information about the work, publication data, premiere information and, for major works, information about other important performances. The largest and most useful part of the book is the "Bibliography about Persichetti." Entries in the works and performances section refer to entries in this bibliography section. This is a long list which is arranged alphabetically by author. Users must consult this section of the book with care and thoroughness in order not to overlook articles which are about their main concerns, since the cross-referencing can only tie together works and articles about these specific works and not, for example, more general articles about the composer's choral works or harpsichord works. Appendices provide lists of Persichetti's works by opus number, by alphabet, and by chronology. The discography is limited to commercially issued recordings but is extensive and contains recordings by small and specialized companies. The index is first-rate. A useful and attractive guide.

George Louis Mayer

1209. Pemberton, Carol A. **Lowell Mason: A Bio-Bibliography.** Westport, Conn., Greenwood Press, 1988. 206p. index. (Bio-Bibliographies in Music, No. 11). $37.95. LC 87-37569. ISBN 0-313-25881-3.

Lowell Mason (1792-1872) was a member of an earlier American musical dynasty, a seminal figure in music education, and is well known for his contributions to Protestant hymnology. The author provides a biography on Mason, an extensively annotated chronology of his publications, and a bibliography of his writings and those about him by others. The classified works list directs the reader to the chronology of publications, followed by an alphabetical register of the same titles. Prior to the general index is reprinted an excerpt from Mason's thoughts on pedagogy. The manual will prove helpful to Americanists interested in the period and subject, and will be particularly useful for studying the history of music education in this country. [R: Choice, Oct 88, p. 327]

Dominique-René de Lerma

1210. Picker, Martin. **Johannes Ockeghem and Jacob Obrecht: A Guide to Research.** New York, Garland, 1988. 203p. index. (Garland Composer Resource Manuals, Vol. 13). $29.00. LC 88-4175. ISBN 0-8240-8381-4.

Some of the most useful reference books to appear in recent years are the guides to the works of individual composers, such as the Garland Composer Resource Manuals and the Bio-Bibliographies in Music of Greenwood Press. Picker's new research guide on Ockeghem and Obrecht belongs to the Garland series and is exemplary. Individual chapters separately treat the lives and works of the two composers, but combine listings of sources, bibliography, and discography. How useful it is to be able to look up a composition, such as Ockeghem's famous *Missa Mi-Mi*, and find in one place a brief assessment of the mass's importance, a listing of movements with number of measures, contemporary sources, sigla for modern editions and to the relevant historical and analytical literature, and a list of domestic and foreign recordings. Information is often repeated or elaborated at relevant points; thus there are separate lists of prints and manuscript sources as well as an annotated bibliography of items cited throughout the book. Two minor quibbles: even though it is not difficult to locate individual works in the genre-arranged composition lists, an index of works as well as the one included for names would be a time saver; second, the sections on the compositions of Ockeghem and Obrecht would be easier to read if more use had been made of italics, underlining, and other alternatives. More to the point, one has to question why, with laser printers widely available, typescript or letter quality printing was used for the production of this book. [R: Choice, Nov 88, p. 466]

Robert Skinner

1211. Talbot, Michael. **Antonio Vivaldi: A Guide to Research.** New York, Garland, 1988. 197p. illus. index. (Garland Composer Resource Manuals, Vol. 12; Garland Reference Library of the Humanities, Vol. 757). $33.00. LC 88-2521.

This guide, by an acknowledged Vivaldi scholar, identifies both manuscripts—including letters and nonmusical documents—and printed sources relevant to the study of Vivaldi's life and music. The book begins with a short biography of its subject and proceeds into the four sections of the bibliography: sources concerning Vivaldi's life and works, sources of Vivaldi's music, iconography, and Vivaldi research today. The body of the book is segments 1 and 3-5, in which the entries are arranged chronologically, then alphabetically, rather than topically. In most cases, the cited writings of an individual scholar are grouped together. A subject and topical index is built on key words in titles and the compiler's annotations.

There is an addition to the compiler's discussion of addresses of libraries (p. 155): *Canada and the United States*, second revised edition, was published by Bärenreiter in 1983; volumes 4 and 5 (Australia, Israel, Japan, New Zealand; Czechoslovakia, Hungary, Poland, Yugoslavia) now complete the series published under the aegis of the International Inventory of Musical Sources (Répertoire International des Sources Musicales).

As with the others in this series, the volume will be an automatic purchase by historically oriented music libraries. [R: Choice, Sept 88, p. 90]   Carol June Bradley

1212. Thomerson, Kathleen. **Jean Langlais: A Bio-Bibliolgraphy.** Westport, Conn., Greenwood Press, 1988. 191p. index. (Bio-Bibliographies in Music, No. 10). $37.95. LC 87-37550. ISBN 0-313-25547-4.

Jean Langlais, the blind French organist, teacher, and composer, has had a great impact on the organ music and organ playing of this century. Kathleen Thomerson, herself an organist and teacher, has studied privately with Langlais in Paris and has performed many of his works. She has honored her mentor with this excellent bio-bibliography, which is the first study of the composer to be published in English.

The biography and two interviews with the composer and his wife cover only twenty pages, but they cover the important points and give us a good picture of the man and the musician. The bulk of the book is devoted to his works. A chronological listing of his works includes dates of composition, publisher information, and information about the work's premiere.

A discography includes commercial and private recordings of Langlais's works and also his recordings of the works of other composers. The bibliography comprises the largest section of the book. It lists general sources and articles and reviews of specific works—listed, as I like them to be, under the individual works. Most sources are in French and English, but there are a few listings in German and other languages. Each entry is annotated and gives an idea what the article covers, and sometimes has brief quotes from it. This will probably be the section of the book which will be most useful for organists and students. Those who make use of it will have reason to thank the author for her care and thoroughness. The appendix has a list of Langlais's works, with opus numbers newly assigned by his wife. This is published here for the first time. In addition to the general index, the book contains separate indexes for authors and translators and for Langlais's compositions.

An excellent and useful reference work.
                              George Louis Mayer

1213. Yeomans, David. **Bartók for Piano.** Bloomington, Ind., Indiana University Press, 1988. 163p. bibliog. index. $27.50. LC 87-45436. ISBN 0-253-31006-7.

This chronological listing of more than four hundred separate piano pieces and movements by Béla Bartók covers year of publication; editions; timing; difficulty; bibliographic references; and commentary on form, interpretation, and influence of folk music. Front matter includes a short survey of Bartók's career as teacher and pianist. Appendices contain listings of Bartók's solo piano works in order of technical and musical difficulty, publishers of his works, editions and transcriptions by Bartók of other composers' works, and teaching editions and collections of his piano compositions. The compositions are listed chronologically using "Sz. numbers" (András Szöllösy's cataloging system of Bartók's compositions). *Bartók for Piano* is a very useful and informative survey of Bartók's solo piano music. There is a need for works such as this, that is, an in-depth descriptive examination of a composer's compositions. Too often one finds only cursory examinations of a composer's works, usually relegated to a short chapter in a predominantly biographical volume. This is not the case for David Yeomans's *Bartók for Piano*; his coverage of the solo works is well done, with specific attention to historical background and to musical aspects of each piano composition. Yeomans's descriptive annotations of the *Mikrokosmos* pieces contain more detail than offered in Benjamin Suchoff's *Guide to Bartók's Mikrokosmos* (Da Capo Press, 1982). David Yeomans's *Bartók for Piano* is a must for pianists, pedagogues, and library reference divisions.   Robert Palmieri

INSTRUMENTS

Percussion

1214. Bajzek, Dieter. **Percussion: An Annotated Bibliography with Special Emphasis on Contemporary Notation and Performance.** Metuchen, N.J., Scarecrow, 1988. 185p. index. $18.50. LC 87-32389. ISBN 0-8108-2107-9.

Just under fifteen hundred annotated entries are provided in this reference, particularly designed to be helpful for composers, students, and performers interested in contemporary issues. The Austro-Australian compiler reveals his knowledge of the field in his terse annotations and has drawn on books, articles, and graduate papers for his material. Most of these are in English (which is both practical and restrictive), with a few in other languages. The absence of access to diacriticals is a small point, as are the typographical errors. Citations are provided alphabetically by author under the appropriate categories (handbooks, repair, notation, performance practice, and research, with special sections for non-Western topics). The appendices include recommended analyses and transcriptions, important bibliographies and reviews, and information on journals whose issues were consulted. An index of authors concludes this manual, which will be most useful to those from the concert, jazz, popular, and ethnic worlds of percussion. [R: Choice, Oct 88, p. 284]   Dominique-René de Lerma

Piano

1215.   Fine, Larry. **The Piano Book: A Guide to Buying a New or Used Piano.** Jamaica Plain, Mass., Brookside Press, 1987. 186p. illus. index. $24.95; $14.95pa. LC 87-70448. ISBN 0-9617512-1-5; 0-9617512-0-7pa.

The author, who writes a regular column in *Keyboard Magazine*, has compiled a handy, easy to understand volume covering the art of buying a used or new piano, reviews of various brand name pianos, sales gimmicks to be wary of, descriptions of integral parts of the instrument, special attention to Steinways, care and servicing, moving and storage, and much more. The book makes an excellent introduction to the piano for shoppers as well as dealers and pianists of all levels. It is written in nontechnical language by an experienced and candid technician who offers the reader straightforward information. Especially interesting is the appraisal (from terrible to excellent) of approximately two hundred pianos manufactured by leading firms. The astute foreword by Keith Jarrett presents the pianists' view of the piano technician. The only feature notably absent is a bibliography, which would be useful for added, in-depth study. Included are illustrations, an index to trade names, and a glossary/index. Highly recommended as the best "how-to" book on the subject of purchasing pianos available.
Robert Palmieri

1216.   Maxwell, Carolyn, and Geraldine Gant Luethi, eds. **Mozart: Solo Piano Literature.** Boulder, Colo., Maxwell Music Evaluation,

1987. 345p. illus. bibliog. index. $13.95pa. ISBN 0-912531-04-5.

This reference guide to the solo piano literature of W. A. Mozart has a format similar to the previous four volumes in the Maxwell Music Evolution series (on Haydn, Schumann, Scarlatti, and Shubert). A brief foreword describes the purpose and organizational scheme of the book. Each of Mozart's piano compositions is listed in chapters entitled "The Early Years (1761-1777)," "The London Notebook," "Works without K. Numbers," "Later Years (1778-1791)," "Six Viennese Sonatinas," and "Sonatas and Variations." The entry for each composition contains the title, followed by the original Köchel number, the revised Köchel number, a grade level, brief notes on the history of the piece, and some comments on the character and style. Published sources for the piece are given, with editor and publisher. The grade levels are "an admittedly subjective judgement that is defined on page 333" (p. i). A short (usually three to five measures) incipit, intended for identification purposes, is included for each work, and for each separate movement or section of a work. There are also notes on the number of measures in the piece and on the "technique," or technical attributes and demands, of the piece.

The guide is obviously directed toward teachers of piano or motivated students who want to expand their repertoire. It is useful for locating small or obscure compositions contained in collections. It is also a useful tool for identifying several pieces at similar levels of difficulty or several pieces which offer the student similar kinds of technical practice. An alphabetical listing of publishers, with the full name and address, would be a useful addition to the book.

Lack of editorial care mars the volume and diminishes its credibility as a scholarly work. A book title is placed within quotation marks in one place and is underlined in another. The umlauts in the name Köchel are sometimes included, sometimes omitted. This reviewer could not find any confirmation of the accuracy of the bibliographic data given for the primary reference source used for titles and K. numbers.

Recommended for piano teachers and students.   Dorothy E. Jones

MUSICAL FORMS

Band

1217.   Rasmussen, Richard Michael. **Recorded Concert Band Music, 1950-1987: A Selected,**

Annotated Listing. Jefferson, N.C., McFarland, 1988. 442p. index. $45.00. LC 88-42522. ISBN 0-89950-318-7.

Access to band music recordings, previously limited to Kenneth W. Berger's *Band Discography* (Berger Band, 1955) and *Band Encyclopedia* (Band Association, 1960), has been updated and expanded by Rasmussen (author of *The UFO Literature*, see *ARBA* 86, entry 747). The focus is on U.S. LP recordings, but some European (e.g., Molenaar's Band Series) and Japanese (e.g., Tokyo Kosei Series) works are included. Few marches are listed; emphasis is instead on an "active band repertoire" (p. 2) including new, traditional, and experimental works. "Major compositions" (p. 3) are included, with most grade 3 or above.

Over seventeen hundred composition entries (both in- and out-of-print) are arranged alphabetically by composer, arranger, or transcriber; and include album title, performing ensemble, conductor, date of recording or issuance, label, record number, and, usually, a descriptive annotation. The format of entries with multiple recordings makes it difficult to distinguish one recording citation from another, and Rasmussen rarely distinguishes among the recordings in terms of quality. He also fails to reveal the length of each piece and the other works on each record. The data, however, are rarely inaccurate (entry 1134 does have an incorrect record number), and the annotations provide some background and technical descriptions of the piece. Additional sections include an overview of the major band music series (with background on bands and conductors), an appendix listing record companies and distributors (with brief descriptions of their concentration), and a very detailed and accurate index to composers, transcribers, composition titles (but not albums), performers, conductors, and types of music (both thematic and instrumental).

Norman Lloyd Owen's foreword places woodwind and brass music in a cultural and historical context and designates Rasmussen's work as primarily a selection tool for band directors looking for music for performance. This work has a broader audience, however, including students, music collectors, and interested listeners.   Robert Aken

Choral

1218. DeVenney, David P. **Early American Choral Music: An Annotated Guide.** Berkeley, Calif., Fallen Leaf Press, 1988. 149p. bibliog. index. (Fallen Leaf Reference Books in Music, No. 10). $19.95pa. LC 88-3617. ISBN 0-914913-09-3.

Intended for use by choral performers in colleges, schools, and churches, this is a descriptive catalog of choral music composed in the United States between 1670 and 1825; it is a companion volume to DeVenney's *Nineteenth-Century American Choral Music: An Annotated Guide* (see *ARBA* 88, entry 1302). Only "serious, art music" written for full chorus (i.e., more than one voice to a part) is included; hymns and psalm tunes, arrangements of other composers' works, stage works, and separately published choruses from larger works are excluded. Not surprisingly, sacred music strongly predominates, and the secular music is largely patriotic in theme.

After a brief introduction, the catalog of 859 works, arranged alphabetically by composer and title, follows. Most listings include, at least, data on performing forces required, source of the text, location of the original manuscript, and publication; they may also indicate performing time (if over ten minutes) and include citations to the bibliography. Fullness of data varies considerably from entry to entry, however. The catalog is followed by a 127-item bibliography and multiple indexes: by type of chorus, sacred/secular, title, authors and sources of texts, and, finally, a separate index to the bibliography. Appended are a list of printed music collections utilized by the compiler, and a directory of publishers. This is a useful guide to a body of music that deserves to be better known.

Paul B. Cors

1219. **Secular Choral Music in Print.** 2d ed. F. Mark Daugherty and Susan H. Simon, eds. Philadelphia, Musicdata, 1987. 2v. index. (Music-in-Print Series, Vol. 2). $195.00/set. LC 87-24749. ISBN 0-88478-020-1.

1220. **Secular Choral Music in Print: Arranger Index.** 2d ed. Philadelphia, Musicdata, 1987. 128p. (Music-in-Print Series, Vol. 2c). $35.00. LC 87-24033. ISBN 0-88478-021-X.

Bibliographic control of music scores presents so many problems that all libraries collecting in that format will find this a helpful tool, though the price will be a stumbling block for some. Users will also have to recognize that works of this type inevitably begin to obsolesce even before publication as titles listed go out-of-print (although scores tend to have longer print lives than books) and new titles continue to be published.

The scope is nominally worldwide, but pragmatically is mostly limited to the United States, Canada, and Western Europe. Volume 2 contains a complete directory of all publishers covered, with full mailing addresses and, when applicable, a noting of U.S. distributors.

Composers and titles are interfiled in a single alphabetical list, with full data usually given under the composer entry and a cross-reference from the title (except, of course, when title main entry is appropriate, as for anonymous works and anthologies). A normal entry includes composer, title, vocal forces, accompaniment, format, publisher, catalog number, price in U.S. dollars, and an entry number. Arrangers are stated; lyricists are not. Not all entries are complete; prices are often not given for foreign publications. Composers' names may not always follow current cataloging rules and there are instances of multiple listings for what appears to be the same person, but these are only minor inconveniences. Once the basic format is learned, the work is easy to use.

The alphabetical *Arranger Index* may occasionally be useful, but it is not an essential purchase, as it contains no data not present in the main volumes.   Paul B. Cors

Church

1221. McKinnon, James, ed. **Music in Early Christian Literature.** New York, Cambridge University Press, 1987. 180p. index. (Cambridge Readings in the Literature of Music). $39.50. LC 86-21545. ISBN 0-521-30497-0.

This book provides a collection of some four hundred passages on music from early Christian literature – New Testament to ca. A.D. 450 – translated from the original Greek, Latin, and Syriac. The translations were all newly prepared for the volume. The ideal McKinnon followed in preparing the translations was that of literalness. He did not ignore the demands of idiomatic English, but in every case where there was a choice between a graceful English expression which almost fitted the meaning and a somewhat more awkward one which still more closely fitted it, the latter was chosen.

The subject of liturgical chant is the focus of this collection, but it also provides evidence of early Christian attitudes toward pagan musical culture and of Christian musical imagery. Each of the eleven chapters covers a specific chronological and regional span, with its authors appearing in chronological order. An introduction outlines the major subjects and themes of the original source material. There are a brief historical commentary at the beginning of each chapter and brief biographical notes on each author in turn. Each literary source is succinctly described and each literary passage is briefly summarized or placed in historical perspective.

Since there are no musical sources from this period, remarks about music in literary sources are a singular source of some knowledge of early Christian liturgical music. McKinnon has made a large and representative collection of this material conveniently available to scholars and students of early Christian music.

Avery T. Sharp

1222. **The Music Locator 1988.** 4th ed. San Jose, Calif., Resource Publications, 1988. 1193p. $110.00pa. ISBN 0-89390-111-3.

The Music Locator is organized in much the same way as its companion publication, *The Recording Locator.* The size of *The Music Locator* has more than doubled since the third edition in 1984. It now contains 114,328 titles of printed Christian music (preface), with information on how to find each through a publisher or in a songbook. There are a title index, a composer index, a "Categorized Index," a songbook list, and a publisher list. The "Categorized Index" is a theme or subject index deriving from parts of the liturgical service and year as well as using general subject categories. Each category is then subdivided by six music styles: children's music, folk, gospel, contemporary, rock, and traditional. The rock category is new to this edition.

There are both a "Quick Guide to the Music Locator" (p. 5) and a clearly written page on "How to Use the Music Locator" (p. 7). However, since there are many letter or number codes in each index (for copyright date, publisher, style, theme, songbook reference), "how-to-use" notes at the beginning of each index would have greatly enhanced ease of use. Copyright information on page 9 and in an essay in the appendix can save the user time and worry.

The Music Locator is designed as a resource for music dealers, publishers, researchers, musicians, and liturgists. Hard to find music in collections is made accessible. Useful for locating items to fill orders, it is also a most helpful planning and finding tool for choral directors or ministers of music who need to locate specific titles or who plan their music in advance to assure thematic cohesiveness. [R: RBB, 15 Nov 88, pp. 554-55]

Dorothy E. Jones

1223. **Sacred Choral Music in Print. 1988 Supplement.** Susan H. Simon, ed. Philadelphia, Musicdata, 1988. 277p. index. (Music-in-Print Series, Vol. 1s). $85.00. LC 88-25247. ISBN 0-88478-022-8.

This supplement to the second edition of *Sacred Choral Music in Print* (see *ARBA* 87, entry 1251) is a welcome update of a practical, well-organized bibliography which aims to "provide as complete a list as possible of sacred choral music in print throughout the world" (preface). It contains entries for sacred choral music which is included in the 1986 annual supplement, as well as new music published since 1985. The arrangement of the supplement follows that of its parent publication. The main body of the book is the "Composer/Title Index," a single alphabetical listing by composer, composition title and cross-references. The cross-referencing is abundant. Most compositions can be identified and located even if one starts searching with minimal bibliographic information. For example, a composition can usually be located by its original title, a translated title, a popular title or a subtitle.

The "Composer/Title Index" is followed by an "Arranger Index" and a "Publisher Directory." The "Publisher Directory" is the master list for the whole Music-in-Print series, so all publishers listed in the directory do not appear in this supplement. Publisher entries include the U.S. distributing agents.

Information in entries is from the publishers. The "Guide to Use" section at the front of the volume explains the codes and symbols in each entry specifying instrumentation, collections, etc.

Detailed descriptive and ordering information make this listing a quite complete access tool, useful for music stores, for church musicians and choral conductors in general.

Dorothy E. Jones

Classical

1224.   Gray, John, comp. **Blacks in Classical Music: A Bibliographical Guide to Composers, Performers, and Ensembles.** Westport, Conn., Greenwood Press, 1988. 280p. index. (Music Reference Collection, No. 15). $39.95. LC 87-37567. ISBN 0-313-26056-7.

In the past decade, there have been several significant reference books treating different aspects of Afro-American cultural history. The present volume readily merits such recognition, all the more because it addresses an area too often thought out of the mainstream. The composers, conductors, instrumentalists, singers, and opera companies are each provided with their own alphabets of unannotated entries, prefaced by general references. Included are not only the major figures, but several rather new on the scene. Reference materials (indexes, discographies, graduate papers, and encyclopedic

works) have their own section, followed by bibliographic guides to special collections. Authors and artists have separate indexes. This publication is worthy of highest consideration by all school and public libraries, and deserves extensive use for all academic applications, starting with the undergraduate student. [R: Choice, Dec 88, p. 628]

Dominique-René de Lerma

1225.   Rosenberg, Kenyon C. **A Basic Classical and Operatic Recordings Collection for Libraries.** Metuchen, N.J., Scarecrow, 1987. 255p. $27.50. LC 87-12747. ISBN 0-8108-2041-2.

It is important to note that this guide is to long-playing discs and cassettes only. The author, an experienced reviewer who will be remembered as the classical recordings editor for *Library Journal* and *Previews*, is at work on a guide to compact discs.

I doubt anyone could compile a basic list (of anything) which would please everyone and be beyond criticism. All such lists must contain a certain bias based on personal preference. Rosenberg seems to have made an effort to restrict his choices to time-honored "classic" performances and those of big-name superstar performers. Thus, recordings by Dame Joan Sutherland, Luciano Pavarotti, and Leontyne Price, etc., dominate the operatic choices. Recordings by pianists such as Artur Rubinstein and Vladimir Horowitz; violinists such as Isaac Stern and Jascha Heifetz; and conductors such as Bruno Walter, Herbert von Karajan, and Otto Klemperer are featured throughout these pages. These are safe choices in most cases, but these big names do not always represent, in my view, the best possible choices for some specific works. I would not myself recommend Sutherland's recordings of all Bellini operas over those of Maria Callas (whose name I have not been able to find here—not even for her *Tosca*, generally accepted to be more of a classic than the ones given here). But this is a good, sound basic list, with notations for price and other important considerations.

What bothers me more than the choices for recordings is the chosen repertory. Rosenberg features orchestral, chamber, and solo instrumental music over the song literature. There are no listings for the songs of Debussy, Ives, Fauré, Poulenc, Brahms, Sibelius, and other composers whose songs are among their major works. And I cannot understand the absence of Debussy's *Pelléas et Mélisande* in a list which includes the much less important *Lakmé* and *Mignon*.

The other thing about this list that I do not like is the choice of so many large, multidisc sets. These are difficult for libraries to catalog effectively, since they usually get a standard title such as "Orchestral Works. Selections" rather than individual title listings which the public needs, and libraries need for circulation. Many of these sets do not have side-breaks which permit breaking them up into smaller packages.

Users of this guide are encouraged to supplement its suggestions with information from other sources such as current record magazines. [R: RBB, 15 Dec 87, p. 684]

George Louis Mayer

Opera

1226. **The Definitive Kobbé's Opera Book.** rev. ed. Earl of Harewood, ed. New York, Putnam, 1987. 1404p. illus. index. $35.00. LC 86-18705. ISBN 0-399-13180-9.

Kobbé is the name most of us associate with the very best in opera plots. Gustave Kobbé's original work appeared in 1919 (after his death) as *The Complete Opera Book*. It has been revised and reprinted many times since with major revisions in 1954 and 1976 by Lord Harewood. This latest edition is no more "definitive" than Kobbé's was "complete," but each edition has been geared to its audience at the time of its appearance.

Over three hundred titles are represented. The criterion for inclusion was, and remains, basically those operas which a traveling opera goer (English or American) would be likely to meet at home and abroad. Some weightier factors such as historical importance also enter in, but the book's contents do reflect what works of the past are being revived and what new works are successful as well as the standard repertory. The contents also show changing tastes very vividly. The Handel section is new and contains eight operas. The Donizetti, Bellini, and Rossini additions reflect the legacy of the Callas/Sutherland/Horne/Sills careers. Other composers whose representation has been expanded considerably are Verdi, Janacek, and Prokofiev (with five more each); Britten (with nine); Smetana and Menotti (with three); and Tchaikovsky (with two). Composers represented for the first time are Chabrier, Moniuszko, Poulenc, Shostakovich, Walton, Tippett, Birtwistle, Martinu, Szymanowski, Penderecki, Blitzstein, Glass, Ginastera, Nielsen, Sallinen, Ullmann, Weill, von Einem, Zimmermann, Ligeti, Henze, Reimann, Knussen, and Fauré (some with multiple entries — six for Hanze!). Twenty titles have been dropped from the 1976 revision, and in some cases one opera by a composer has been substituted for another. Some users will want to

hold on to the older edition for these titles. The contents pages are much improved by now listing all titles. All other features are (thank God!) as they were.

For all his distinguished work as an administrator with several opera companies and festivals among others, Lord Harewood has probably done more for opera lovers with his excellent revisions of Kobbé than in any other way. He has revised some old entries and has written the new ones himself. We are in his debt. [R: RBB, 15 Jan 88, pp. 840, 842]

George Louis Mayer

1227. Jacobs, Arthur, and Stanley Sadie. **Great Opera Classics.** rev. ed. New York, Gramercy; distr., New York, Crown, 1987. 563p. music. bibliog. $12.95. LC 87-8547. ISBN 0-517-64108-9.

Let the book selector beware! Although it is not indicated anywhere in the book itself, this work has been issued earlier by two other publishers under two other titles: *The Pan Book of Opera* (Pan Books, 1984) and *The Limelight Book of Opera* (see *ARBA* 87, entry 1257). It is not, however, as the Library of Congress cataloging record erroneously states, a reprint of the 1964 edition of *The Pan Book of Opera*; the 1984 edition has been substantially expanded and revised.

By any name, it is a useful if selective guide to eighty-seven of the most frequently performed and recorded operas, written by two of Britain's leading musicologists. The entries include a short historical introduction, a detailed plot summary, and a brief analysis of selected musical excerpts. The arrangement is essentially chronological. The work cannot compare in breadth of coverage to the standard reference, *The Definitive Kobbé's Opera Book*, edited by the Earl of Harewood (see entry 1226), which covers some 340 operas, nor to *The Metropolitan Opera Stories of the Great Operas*, edited by John Freeman (see *ARBA* 86, entry 1274), which covers 150 operas and provides considerable information on American performances.

Paul B. Cors

POPULAR

General Works

1228. **The Billboard Book of Top 40 Albums.** By Joel Whitburn. New York, Billboard, 1987. 330p. illus. index. $16.95pa. LC 87-24982. ISBN 0-8230-7513-3.

When you realize that Joel Whitburn has a record collection of some thirty thousand albums, including a copy of every album to ever appear in the *Billboard* Top 200, the reason that he is uniquely qualified to compile this book becomes clear. To anyone who is serious about popular music and its vagaries, the *Billboard* magazine singles and album charts, and especially the higher positions on those charts, is an event not to be missed each week. The practice of album chart watching, which may begin innocently enough through happenstance, soon grows into a commitment. The budding chartophile is hooked, like the baseball fan who reads the averages. He also wants to look back, to check out which records were the most popular for the longest times. Hence the need for books such as this, the *Billboard Book of Top 40 Albums*, which offers, in alphabetical order by name of artist, the chart history of every album to make it into the first forty positions since the advent of *Billboard*'s charts in 1955, the dawn of rock and roll. Two companion books, *The Billboard Book of Top 40 Hits* (see *ARBA* 84, entry 905) and *The Billboard Book of Number One Hits* (see *ARBA* 86, entry 1275), have demonstrated the usefulness of this format for reference. Entries include date, position, and weeks in the top 40, artist biographies, singles from an album that made the top 10, and label. Separate sections include the top soundtracks, original casts, television shows, label compilations, concerts/festivals, Christmas, and others. It contains some forty-seven hundred titles, which comes to 25 percent of all the albums to have ever made the top 200.

This is another of those reference books in pop music that, once opened, is hard to close, for it is a source of pleasure and satisfaction. It is helped by crisp layout and use of a second color to highlight names. [R: LJ, 1 Feb 88, p. 60]   Randall Rafferty

1229. Cohen-Stratyner, Barbara, ed. **Popular Music, 1900-1919: An Annotated Guide to American Popular Songs....** Detroit, Gale, 1988. 656p. index. $70.00. LC 88-21191. ISBN 0-8103-2595-0.

As is true with the other volumes in this set, this guide documents the years within its range significantly. Entries are alphabetized and span a variety of media—recordings, television, films, musicals, and the like, having their own index (a chronological index is provided). Authors of texts and composers (also indexed) are cited with titles, along with original publishers. Annotations on performances and performers (also indexed) appear as the editor thought necessary. While the value to musicians might be evident, the value to Americanists might be overlooked. Here, in music, is a social history of the first two decades of this country,

with numerous references to major events such as the First World War and personalities, J. P. Morgan, for example. Compiling this volume is an experienced bibliographer who has followed the criteria established by the series' originator, Nat Shapiro. With its companions, this work documents its material splendidly and should be added to any major collection.

Dominique-René de Lerma

1230. Connor, D. Russell. **Benny Goodman: Listen to His Legacy.** Metuchen, N.J., Institute of Jazz Studies and Scarecrow, 1988. 357p. index. (Studies in Jazz, No. 6). $49.50. LC 87-32069. ISBN 0-8108-2095-1.

In an approach similar to other titles in the Studies in Jazz series, *Benny Goodman* presents a complete discography of the subject's recordings within a biographical framework. It derives from similar, but earlier works by the author, beginning with *BG—Off the Record* (Gaildonna Publishers, 1958), followed by *BG—On the Record* (Arlington House, 1969), then by *The Record of a Legend—Benny Goodman* (Greenwood press, 1985). The present work chronologically details recording sessions beginning with Goodman's first recording in 1926 at the age of 17 and ending with a concert recording days before his death in 1986. Each entry specifies the date and place of the recording session, the musicians, the works performed, and labels and numbers of recordings issued. A notable feature of the discography is its inclusion of "air checks"—noncommercial or unauthorized recordings made from broadcasts, films, or concerts. The author's ongoing narrative between the discographical entries provides concurrent biographical details and evaluates the recording quality or the recorded performances. This unusually fine production from Scarecrow uses a wide range of typefaces to differentiate between varieties of discographical data, and features a number of full-page black-and-white photographs.

William S. Brockman

1231. Hoffmann, Frank, and George Albert with Lee Ann Hoffmann, comps. **The Cash Box Album Charts, 1955-1974.** Metuchen, N.J., Scarecrow, 1988. 512p. index. $42.50. LC 87-12716. ISBN 0-8108-2005-6.

Cash Box is the title of a New York City-based weekly trade journal that tracks the coin machine, music, and record industries. Since the early 1950s it has provided charts of the best-selling record albums. The book under review is an integration of the chart positions of the top albums during the twenty-year period 1955-1974, an era dominated by rock and roll, with a heavy undercurrent of folk, blues, soul, and ballads. It was the heyday of rock and pop, when the music charts and cash registers were fueled by Elvis Presley, the Beatles, and the "British invasion."

This book can be useful. Short of sorting through old issues of *Cash Box*, no other source can so quickly answer the twin questions that intrigue many a babyboomer: "How high did that album go and how long did it stay on the charts?" At first, the *Cash Box* charts included just ten positions, but with the growth of the album format at the expense of the single, the number of positions was expanded until it reached 175 in 1973. A typical entry shows name of artist, date of release, album title, label and number, and the unique feature—a week-by-week listing of its chart positions. There is also an album title index after the artist index. Arrangement is alphabetical by last name of artist or, as is so frequently the case in the world of rock, by the first word when there is no last name—Herman's Hermits, for example. Collaborative efforts, with many artists on one record, are listed under their respective titles (e.g., "Hey, Let's Twist" [Original Film Soundtrack]).

A companion volume is *The Cash Box Album Charts, 1975-1985* (Scarecrow, 1987). [R: WLB, May 88, pp. 106, 108]

Randall Rafferty

Folk

1232. Elliker, Calvin. **Stephen Collins Foster: A Guide to Research.** New York, Garland, 1988. 197p. index. (Garland Composer Resource Manuals, Vol. 10; Garland Reference Library of the Humanities, Vol. 782). $30.00. LC 87-35853. ISBN 0-8240-6640-5.

This book was written "to serve the research needs of both the general public and the scholarly community" concerning written and other materials on the life and music of Stephen Collins Foster, the first American to support himself as a composer. A secondary aim might have been to correct some of the misconceptions and outright myths that have grown up around his name since his death in an almost penniless state in 1864. His nostalgic, sentimental songs were so popular during and after his life that Foster has become a cult figure to many people. The books, articles, and films about Foster have frequently taken liberties with the facts of his life. In Hollywood, especially, his story has been embroidered with fanciful detail. This first research guide attempts to point out errors and omissions in the record. It also documents the growing cadre of articles that dispute the notion of Foster as the "native genius,"

whose melodies sprang full-blown from his head, in favor of the revisionist view which holds that he was a "careful, well-trained composer." It consists of a list of Foster's works, a list of selected editions of his works, a bibliography of materials about Foster, an iconography, a list of realia or personal effects, his surviving letters, memorials listed state by state, dramatic and literary tributes, and musical tributes. Elliker has added informative comments to practically every entry. According to the publishers, his clearly organized book is the first bibiliographical work on Stephen Foster to appear in thirty years. [R: Choice, Sept 88, p. 78]

Randall Rafferty

1233. Graham, Ronnie. **The Da Capo Guide to Contemporary African Music.** New York, Da Capo Press, 1988. 315p. illus. maps. bibliog. index. $13.95pa. LC 87-31073. ISBN 0-306-80325-9.

The goal of this guide to contemporary African music "is to document the commercially available LP recordings of Africa's leading musicians in an effort to widen the scope of appreciation and deepen our historical understanding of the modern music of Africa. It is, therefore, basically a discography, to which have been added elements of biography, history and economic analysis" (p. 1). A quick perusal of the text leads one to conclude that the guide achieves its objective. Scholars and novices alike should find something of interest here. The beginner will find the historical and biographical information a useful introduction to contemporary African music, while more experienced readers should find it useful to consult the work as a discography.

Arrangement is by geographical areas of Africa, with chapters on individual countries and regions. Maps are provided which facilitate understanding of historical and economic information. There is a select bibliography of four and one-half pages and a relatively detailed index of eight pages. Fourteen pages of black-and-white portraits are inserted as a kind of "midsection."

There is a wealth of information included in this reference guide and everything about it (format, style, etc.) leads the reader to one conclusion: it is not only informative and easy to use, but fun to browse through. This title should become the basic reference source on its subject. [R: LJ, July 88, p. 82]

Larry G. Chrisman

Jazz

1234. Crowther, Bruce, and Mike Pinfold. **The Jazz Singers: From Ragtime to the New**

Wave. London, Blandford Press; distr., New York, Sterling Publishing, c1986, 1988. 224p. illus. bibliog. index. $12.95pa. ISBN 0-7137-2047-6.

This is an interesting and readable account of the jazz singer in music. Some two hundred vocalists who have performed on disc from the turn of the century up through the modern jazz age are described. Covered are such unique artists as Louis Armstrong, B. B. King, Ma Rainey, and Billie Holiday, in a narrative text, usually in chronological chapters. Unfortunately, this book is not a reference book in dictionary arrangement style. Access to the individuals is through the entries in the index, and many performers are scattered throughout the book. All of the page references must be tracked down.

On a larger level, there are more important things remiss in this book. One is that the definition of "jazz singer" is wide-ranging, for it embraces blues, soul, popular and stage singers, and big band vocalists. Only the latter can be regarded as anywhere near being "jazz." I am not being picky over the criteria for inclusion, but I do wish to draw librarians' attention to the fact that data about blues, soul, and popular and stage performers are available elsewhere and in better shape (i.e., dictionary arrangement). All Crowther and Pinfold have done is provide a context for the better-than-bland singers. There are some photographs, some recommended discs (with no reasons or choices made for specific titles), and some additional reading. Curiously, Henry Pleasants's major epic, *The Great American Popular Singers* (Simon & Schuster, 1974), is missing from this bibliography. *The Jazz Singers* is a useful and enjoyable book to read, but slight to consult.

Dean Tudor

1235. Cuscuna, Michael, and Michel Ruppli, comps. **The Blue Note Label: A Discography.** Westport, Conn., Greenwood Press, 1988. 510p. illus. index. (Discographies, No. 29). $75.00. LC 88-162. ISBN 0-313-22018-2.

Little can be said about discographies with which Michael Ruppli is associated except to point them out and make sure that appropriate audiences buy the book. It is a case of either you need it or you do not. Ruppli has been working on jazz discographies for over fifteen years; his previously published works for Greenwood Press have included the labels of Atlantic Records, Prestige, Savoy, Chess, Verve, Clef, and King Records. With Blue Note Cuscuna and Ruppli have defined the jazz releases from perhaps the most important of the early "independent" labels (it released starting in 1939).

They deliver almost all of what they promise. No discography is ever complete, but their diligence results in about 99.9 percent completeness and about the same level for accuracy. That is all anybody could ask for. In arrangement, the book follows a standard discographic pattern established by Brian Rust over twenty-five years ago. Sessions are listed in chronological order with all available information on personnel, recording locations and dates, and master and issue numbers. Reissues, of course, are covered, as well as reissues leased from other labels. Name changes of the company's owners over the years are also taken into account. All of this is followed by single numerical listings, album numerical listings, compact disc numerical listings, and cassette numerical listings. At the end there is an index of artists who played on the various session dates. A masterful work, of high exactitude in standards, and certainly recommended for those libraries that provide discographic jazz information.

Dean Tudor

1236. Harris, Steve. **Jazz on Compact Disc: A Critical Guide to the Best Recordings.** New York, Harmony Books/Crown, 1987. 176p. illus. (part col.). index. $13.95pa. LC 87-7383. ISBN 0-517-56688-5.

Both new recordings and reissues of older recordings are rapidly becoming available on compact disc. This buyer's guide, written by a seasoned British reviewer of recordings and audio equipment, presents an "essential" selection of discs by seventy-nine performers. A short biographical sketch introduces each performer. The author then details from one to several of the performer's discs, noting the title, duration, compositions, recording date, manufacturer and number, and method of recording and transfer to disc. A short narrative evaluation of each disc provides the basis for a summary award of from one to three stars for the performance and recording quality. Color photographs of performers and discs appear on nearly every page.

Though the selection is well balanced between new recordings and reissues, the author has made some choices that seem inappropriate to a selection dubbed "essential" (introduction), such as recordings by Stanley Jordan and Eberhard Weber. Readers should keep in mind that the author has included recordings issued in Britain, which will sometimes appear under a different number or even label from the American version. Yet, the author's informed comments along with an introductory list of one hundred "best" recordings selected from those detailed in the book should help those who, confronted with a bewildering profusion of newly released discs, wish to make reasoned purchases.   William S. Brockman

1237. Timner, W. E., comp. **Ellingtonia: The Recorded Music of Duke Ellington and His Sidemen.** 3d ed. Metuchen, N.J., Institute of Jazz Studies and Scarecrow, 1988. 534p. (Studies in Jazz, No. 7). $49.50. LC 86-21967. ISBN 0-8108-1934-1.

Timner chronicles Ellington's prolific recordings from a session in 1923 as a member of Snowden's Novelty Orchestra through his last concerts in 1974 — well over one thousand recordings from not only studio performances but also movies, concerts and dances, and television and radio broadcasts. The work's format follows that of other titles in the Studies in Jazz series. A chronological listing of sessions notes the date, personnel, location, and compositions performed. A significant limitation of *Ellingtonia* is its restriction of discographical data to the labels and numbers of only first issues of recordings, and consequent omission of reissues such as the many LP compilations of recent years. A bonus of Timner's compilation is a separate listing of recordings with groups other than Ellington's by sidemen such as Johnny Hodges and Cootie Williams who for years were closely associated with him. An alphabetical listing of Ellington's compositions notes the dates of all recorded performances of each. A chronological table traces the presence or absence of musicians from session to session, but does not allow alphabetical access to individual names. This third edition follows two privately published earlier editions. Its limitations as a discography are minor compared to its value as a finely detailed chronology.

William S. Brockman

Rock

1238. Banney, Howard F. **Return to Sender: The First Complete Discography of Elvis Tribute & Novelty Records, 1956-1986.** Ann Arbor, Mich., Pierian Press, 1987. 318p. illus. index. (Rock & Roll Reference Series, No. 29). $29.50; $39.50 (institutions). LC 87-61977. ISBN 0-87650-238-9.

Ten years after his death, the legend of Elvis is as strong as ever. Over seven hundred Elvis impersonators currently fuel the fires of fans' adoration, while a staggering number of "tribute" records have been released to honor the performer whose disciples call him "The King." The present work lists more than one thousand recordings by other artists, from the early days to the present, which in some way praise, parody, or refer to Elvis. The compiler, himself an avid fan who has been a serious collector in this particular genre since 1972, lists both singles and albums, together with comments about whether the performer sounds like Elvis and the song's specific tie-in, such as "mentions Elvis' name."

Recordings listed range from the extensive treatment of *Pat Boone Sings Guess Who?* (an entire album of songs originally recorded by Elvis) to singles which include mere mention of the name Elvis. Some are comic, like Weird Al Yankovich's, while others ("Jesus, Here Comes Elvis") attempt a religious perspective. About every half-dozen pages there is a full page of black-and-white photographs of album covers, which lends a nice sense of atmosphere.

Three good indexes are provided, by performer, song and album title, and record number, and the entry number system is conveniently arranged, making for easy use. The introduction includes some interesting charts and graphs, showing Elvis tribute/novelty records by year and country of origin. While many of these recordings come from Canada, England, and Germany, the vast majority (ca. 78 percent) originate in the United States. [R: WLB, May 88, p. 112]

Richard W. Grefrath

1239. Bianco, David. **Heat Wave: The Motown Fact Book.** Ann Arbor, Mich., Pierian Press, 1988. 524p. illus. index. (Rock & Roll Reference Series, No. 25). $39.50; $49.50 (institutions). LC 86-60558. ISBN 0-87650-204-4.

This work is the first publication in the Rock & Roll Reference series to be devoted to the output of a label rather than a performer. The decision to focus on Motown Records could not be more justified, however, the "Motown sound" was probably the most important American contribution to popular music during the 1960s and early 1970s. The label is not as vital today as it was, yet it remains overwhelmingly popular by recycling old hits in various collections and formats for nostalgic "baby boomers" (the "Big Chill" generation). While the Pierian Press may be exploiting this same demograpahic group with *Heat Wave*, the publication is an excellent production nevertheless. Part 1 is a collective biography of Motown artists and executives, with separate entries for each figure or group. Entries for important figures are illustrated with publicity photographs and accompanied by brief discographies. Part 2 is a chronology which details artist and label developments by year and month. Part 3 is a very useful "biography" of Motown-related labels. Parts 4-7, which comprise the largest portion of the book, are comprehensive discographies and indexes of U.S. and UK releases. This information will be of little interest to the general reader, but will be of particular interest to record collectors and fans. The book is physically larger than previous titles in the series, and the binding is durable and attractive. In short, this is a typically excellent entry in the series and is highly recommended. [R: WLB, Oct 88, pp. 108-9]

James Edgar Stephenson

1240.   Kocandrle, Mirek. **The History of Rock and Roll: A Selective Discography.** Boston, G. K. Hall, 1988. 297p. index. $35.00. LC 88-21200. ISBN 0-8161-8956-0.

Mirek Kocandrle's work is a good idea; a book-length discography of seminal or representative recordings tracing rock and roll's history and current stylists would be a useful tool. The resulting production, however, fails to bring the good idea to a satisfactory fruition. In this discography, artists are classified by musical style. Each artist entry is accompanied by a list of song and album titles. Many of the artist entries have dates added, and some who recorded under pseudonyms or nicknames have their true names listed (although Kocandrle is not consistent in this practice). The recordings selected for inclusion have been graded by Kocandrle and judged to be "worthy of grades of B and better." The discographic information included consists only of year of release and label name, although either or both of these are omitted at times. No release numbers are included, and the provided information is sometimes misleading (as when Kocandrle provides the original year of release, yet credits a label which re-released the recording years later). U.S. and U.K. releases are not differentiated. Song titles and album titles are distinguished by typography (album titles are in italics), but these are sometimes confused. Where the book fails most dismally, however, is in the classification of performers. Here Kocandrle reveals his lack of familiarity with individual performers and misunderstanding of styles, with laughable mistakes in judgment. (One typical example: Kocandrle classifies the Ink Spots and the Mills Brothers under the heading "White Harmony Groups," along with the Four Freshmen, the Crew Cuts, and the Andrews Sisters.) In short, *The History of Rock and Roll: A Selective Discography* is a disaster—a poorly executed production of inadequate research and misinformation.   James Edgar Stephenson

1241.   Prakel, David. **Rock 'n' Roll on Compact Disc: A Critical Guide to the Best Recordings.** New York, Harmony Books/Crown, 1987. 176p. illus. (part col.). index. $13.95pa. LC 87-7382. ISBN 0-517-56687-7.

David Prakel's buying guide is superior to its competitor, Bill Shapiro's *The CD Rock & Roll Library* (see entry 1242), in virtually all respects. Prakel arranges his CD reviews alphabetically by artist rather than the cumbersome chronological/alphabetical approach of Shapiro. Each of Prakel's reviews lists album contents, American and English release numbers and labels, and total playing time. Prakel uses a quantitative system (from one "star" to three) for grading a CD's "desirability" and "recording"—that is, for quality of performance and quality of reproduction on CD. This double grade provides the reader with a clearer picture of a CD's relative merits or faults compared with the analog disc release. Each performer or group is introduced by biographical information, and all entries are graced by at least one color illustration of an album cover. As part of the book's general introductory material, Prakel includes a well-illustrated article, "Introducing Compact Disc." This article provides an accessible introduction to CD technology, including the processes of recording and manufacturing compact discs.

As with all critical guides produced by a single author, one must make allowances for the author's tastes and prejudices in this guide. For the most part, Prakel's critical opinions are mainstream, and unlikely to elicit outrage or controversy. All considered, this is a good rock music CD buying guide that will not disappoint. [R: VOYA, Apr 88, p. 52]

James Edgar Stephenson

1242.   Shapiro, Bill. **The CD Rock & Roll Library: 30 Years of Rock & Roll on Compact Disc.** Kansas City, Mo., Andrews and McMeel, 1988. 188p. bibliog. index. $8.95pa. LC 88-6261. ISBN 0-8362-7947-6.

Unlike classical music buffs, fans of rock music have never needed "buying guides" to assist with their purchases. The emergence and widespread acceptance of the compact disc, however, has apparently created a need for such a guide. Now there are two buying guides for "rock music on CD": David Prakel's *Rock 'n' Roll on Compact Disc* (see entry 1241) and this title. Shapiro's guide, although less expensive, is a considerably lesser effort.

Shapiro's reviews are arranged by decade—the fifties to the eighties. Each decade occupies a chapter, and each era/chapter is introduced with a "history" of the time and its music. Within each decade, reviews are arranged alphabetically by artist, and Shapiro includes some brief biographical information for these artists. As the reviews of individual works are arranged by the original release (or recording) date, artists whose works have spanned multiple decades are represented in the appropriate chapters. Consequently, a user desiring to read a review of a specific Rolling Stones album, for instance, must either remember the decade of the album's release, or locate the album in the index. Along with the index, Shapiro appends a listing of the "top 100 rock compact discs" and a bibliography. The book's introductory material consists of chapters titled "The Music" (which attempts [without success] to summarize the history of rock music in three and a half pages), "The Technology" (a brief introduction to the CD) and "The Ratings."

The individual reviews list American album title, label, and release number, as well as total time, and a letter "grade" (from *A* to *F*) by which Shapiro rates each CD. There is only one grade for each CD, so it is often difficult to determine what Shapiro finds worthy of praise or damnation—performance or sound quality. Further, the reviews do not include track listings, a feature especially missed in the reviews of compilation CDs. Finally, in regard to Shapiro's critical opinion: apart from a few aberrations, they are solidly mainstream and uncontroversial.

In summary, Shapiro's book is mostly impractical, and spoiled by less than useful filler. Libraries or individuals in need of a buying guide of rock CDs are advised to skip this book in favor of Prakel's. [R: Choice, Nov 88, p. 468]

James Edgar Stephenson

26 Mythology, Folklore, and Popular Customs

FOLKLORE

1243. Ashliman, D. L. **A Guide to Folktales in the English Language: Based on the Aarne-Thompson Classification System.** Westport, Conn., Greenwood Press, 1987. 368p. bibliog. index. (Bibliographies and Indexes in World Literature, No. 11). $45.00. LC 87-15017. ISBN 0-313-25961-5.

In order to describe this guide, it is necessary first to explain the Aarne-Thompson system for classifying folktales, on which it is based. This system, which is widely used among folklorists, assigns a number to each of about twenty-five hundred basic plots, or "tale types." Variations of tales can then be placed in appropriate categories; as a result, folktale themes are easily identified and studied regardless of slight variations in plot or their original language or country. The Aarne-Thompson tales are generally limited to those of European or Near Eastern origin, and this guide is designed to help locate texts of these tales published in English-language collections.

Ashliman has arranged the tale types by Aarne-Thompson number. For each, a brief plot synopsis is provided, followed by citations to published variants. The author has rewritten the Aarne-Thompson summaries in order to accurately describe the English-language versions. Because there are so many variants of each folktale, the lists of sources are not comprehensive, concentrating instead on "a few reliable editions."

A separate list of the Grimms's tales is included, with the type number for each story. Also included are a bibliography of secondary literature and a bibliography of the folktale collections cited in the body of the book. The index provides access to the tale types by title and by keyword.

While many tale-type indexes exist for specific countries, regions, or subjects, this guide is unique in that it indexes English-language versions of most of the tales included in the Aarne-Thompson catalog, and is not limited to a particular type, format, or nationality. As such, it fills a gap in folklore reference sources and will be of great use to folklorists, students, storytellers, and librarians. [R: C&RL, July 88, p. 345]

Emily L. Werrell

1244. Glazer, Mark, comp. **A Dictionary of Mexican American Proverbs.** Westport, Conn., Greenwood Press, 1987. 347p. index. $39.95. LC 87-23721. ISBN 0-313-25385-4.

Few book-length collections exist of Mexican-American proverbs. This dictionary should interest the folklorist and students of proverbs and of the Spanish language in the United States. It is based on a collection of proverbs from the Lower Rio Grande Valley of Texas which has been deposited in the Rio Grande Folklore Archive at the Pan American University (Edinburg, Texas).

"The dictionary is based on a collection of 3,485 items, 986 of which are proverbs and the remaining 2,499 being duplicates and/or variants of these proverbs.... The form of entry includes the following information: the proverb in its original Spanish form(s), an English translation or interpretation, contextual information, and demographic data on the informant of the proverb. The entries in the dictionary include the proverbs collated from the collection form plus annotations from published sources, which complete each entry" (p. xii).

There are two appendices: tabular summary data and proverb collection form as well as two indexes, one arranged by the Spanish keyword and one by the English word.

The bibliography is extremely useful, but poorly proofread. Accent marks are missing from Spanish titles; publishers are omitted without an indication that they do not appear in the cited volume. There is no suggestion as to how the dictionaries of Americanisms in the bibliography were chosen.

Much effort has gone into the collection of these proverbs and their scholarly annotation. It will be an invaluable source for those who wish to study Mexican-American proverbs in the future. [R: Choice, Mar 88, p. 1064]

Hensley C. Woodbridge

1245. **The Macmillan Book of Proverbs, Maxims, and Famous Phrases.** By Burton Stevenson. New York, Macmillan, c1976, 1987. 2957p. index. $75.00. LC 86-16275. ISBN 0-02-614500-6.

Every library needs as many quotation books as it can possibly afford if reference queries are to be satisfied at any acceptable rate. Macmillan has reprinted an original volume issued in 1948 under the title *Home Book of Proverbs, Maxims, and Familiar Phrases.* One cannot help wondering why the change in title. To bring a standard reference tool back into print is welcomed, but duplicate copies are likely to be purchased by the unsuspecting—an unhappy thought in tight economic times.

As for the volume itself, the quotations are topically arranged with an important word index at the end. Each quotation has its source and often contains useful reference information such as the original quote in its original language. The print is small, but the almost three thousand pages are sure to provide a treasury needed in most libraries.

David V. Loertscher

1246. Owomoyela, Oyekan. **A Kì í: Yorùbá Proscriptive and Prescriptive Proverbs.** Lanham, Md., University Press of America, 1988. 388p. bibliog. index. $30.25. LC 87-23021. ISBN 0-8191-6502-6.

Yoruba is one of the most widely spoken languages in Nigeria. It is a major language in Nigeria and is also spoken in some other West African countries such as Ghana and Sierra Leone. What Oyekan Owomoyela has done is simplify most of those idiomatic expressions and proverbs in Yoruba so as to make the language easily understood by those who speak it and may wish to study it.

This work is the first of its kind and will be very useful to the general public and scholarly community. It contains a vital and informative historical chronology in the introduction as well as 875 idiomatic and proverbial entries in

Yoruba with succinct explanations that correspond to the Yoruba cultural and historical context.

This work is recommended to most libraries and to scholars and students of African languages and linguistics.

Felix Eme Unaeze

1247. Walls, Robert E., comp. and ed. **Bibliography of Washington State Folklore and Folklife: Selected and Partially Annotated.** Seattle, Wash., for Washington State Folklife Council by University of Washington Press, 1987. 301p. index. $35.00. LC 87-21940. ISBN 0-295-96514-2.

This selective bibliography of over twenty-one hundred citations on Washington State folklore and folklife was developed as a popular planning guide for more scholarly research. It is the most comprehensive guide available to the rich cultural and physical diversity of the state, with some focus on Oregon, Idaho, and British Columbia. In addition to coverage of many different native American cultures in the state, other cultures such as Afro-Americans, Scandinavians, Asian-Americans, Russians, Germans, and Finnish-Americans are included. Citations on regional and oral histories, pioneer life, fishing, logging, farming, and mining abound. Other citations cover special groups such as the Shakers, the Hutterites, Doukobors, and Sephardim. Information can be found on tall tales and legends, pioneer recipes, folk art and architecture, women's roles in early pioneer days, Western farming customs, petroglyph and pictograph sites, early native traditions, place names, branding irons, and fruit box labeling. Citations published through 1984 are annotated and arranged by author. An extensive subject and name index is useful in identifying citations on broad and narrow subject interests. A select list of sound recordings, compiled by Jens Lund, Washington State folklorist, is included. It is unfortunate that a similar listing of special library collections and film/video collections held in the state are not included in similar special sections. Even so, the bibliography is fascinating and does provide items of interest to folklorists, historians, anthropologists, librarians, and anyone interested in American studies, native American studies, other ethnic and minority studies, and regional and local history of the Pacific Northwest. There are a few errors, mostly typographical, and I would thus caution the researcher to check entries carefully before citing sources exactly as listed. The second entry, for example, lists G. K. Hall (publisher) as "B.K. Hall." [R: Choice, Sept 88, p. 92]

Maureen Pastine

1248. Yetiv, Isaac. **1,001 Proverbs from Tunisia.** Washington, D.C., Three Continents Press, 1987. 152p. index. $22.00; $10.00pa. LC 87-10230. ISBN 0-89410-615-5; 0-89410-616-3pa.

Churchill once remarked that reading quote books improved the mind; being in the neighborhood, so to speak, of so many great minds must surely prove contagious. That, of course, was before Kahil Gibran gave us quotes to drive the mind to mediocrity or worse. It is not so much that these proverbs from Tunisia are monolithically bathetic, as that they are earnestly too hard to follow in our language. That is a polite way of saying that everything may have been lost in translation.

The proverbs are arranged in alphabetical order, according to the Arabic. Under each is a transliteration, followed by an explanation. The effect is like a joke book with the "ha-has" added after each punch line. But this may be owing to the translation: one must simply be there, and know the right language to boot.

Having damned with such slight praise, one must be quick to add that Isaac Yetiv has done a masterful job of putting a pleasant face on a rather transmogrified visage. Tunisia (its traditional name Ifriqiyah, an Arabic form of the Roman name for Africa) is an independent country in North Africa, and rich in culture, tradition, and history. The Jewish connection is no accident. The original Jewish population, who obtained French citizenship under the protectorate, has continued to decline ever since Tunisia's independence.

The problem with the book, however, is not its rich history, or even its obvious play upon our age's Third World mania. Rather the problem is with the proverbs themselves: "Offer her to a pig, he will say, 'I am in a hurry' " or "Hit him with a bean, he will break." What about, "A slug, and they poured salt on it"; or perhaps this one: "Urinate in the wrecked slums before they become mosques." Finally, my favorite simile, "Like the lung, soft but without fat." These proverbs are understandable in an ambiguous way. Use them as quotes, however, and one is likely to end up like dirt—on the ground.   Mark Y. Herring

MYTHOLOGY

1249. Lindow, John. **Scandinavian Mythology: An Annotated Bibliography.** New York, Garland, 1988. 593p. index. (Garland Folklore Bibliographies, Vol. 13). $43.00. LC 87-29280. ISBN 0-8240-9173-6.

The more than three thousand annotated entries in this comprehensive bibliography treat a body of mythology recorded mostly in thirteenth-century Iceland and dealing with Scandinavian pagan gods. The entries are alphabetically arranged by author, and the annotations are primarily descriptive; their lengths "offer a clue" to the compiler's view of the relative importance of the works cited. The articles indexed are mostly in languages other than English (Swedish, Norwegian, Danish, German), but all annotations are in English.

Lindow's choice of a large (89 pages), alphabetical single index rather than several indexes, each covering a specific category (e.g., place names or texts), grew out of a belief that users would find it easier and faster to use. Index entries are appropriately subdivided. For example, there are 113 subdivisions under Thor, dealing with such topics as his search for the Midgard serpent, his relationship to Odin and Loki, and his association with the oak tree.

Large academic, public, and research libraries will seriously want to consider the purchase of this outstanding scholarly achievement. [R: Choice, July/Aug 88, p. 1675]

Charles R. Andrews

1250. Mercatante, Anthony S. **The Facts on File Encyclopedia of World Mythology and Legend.** New York, Facts on File, 1988. 807p. illus. bibliog. index. $95.00. LC 84-21218. ISBN 0-8160-1049-8.

Myth, legend, folktale, fable—all of these appeal to the mysterious and supernatural interests of people. Many may wonder about their origins, others may be concerned with how they have influenced literature and art. As a work to be both browsed and searched with a purpose, Mercatante's encyclopedia will satisfy the curious and the studious.

Over four hundred interesting black-and-white illustrations enhance the more than three thousand entries. Succinct and clearly written, the short articles describe the subject, give dates and historical facts (if applicable), and list works in which the subject appears (in most cases). Some have cross-references to other topics in the text. Brief plot summaries accompany title entries (e.g., *The Odyssey*) and as often as not the meaning of a name or term is included (e.g., Morgan le Fay means bright, great fairy). Subjects vary from historical characters to the fictional, saints to rulers, fantastic creatures and animals to sacred relics. Yet in the reviewer's mind some common entries have been excluded. For example, while "Troll" has its own article, both "Fairy" and "Dwarf" can only be located by using the general index or by stumbling onto a cross-reference. There is a chance that such omissions may discourage a younger reader.

Several research aids are included. A bibliography of primary and secondary sources with short annotations is divided by culture and nation, subject, and type of collection (e.g., fable collections). The text states that all major works are listed, but the reviewer is puzzled by the omission of Edith Hamilton's *Mythology* (New American Library, 1971) which is still in print. Yet the bibliography is extensive in scope and would lead the reader to many valuable sources. Another help is the key to variant spellings which provides reference from the less familiar to the most common spelling. (All of the encyclopedia entries are spelled in the most common spelling.) The list is incomplete, however, for some variant spellings, such as leprecaun and luchorpain for "leprechaun," are missing. The book concludes with a large general index as well as a cultural and ethnic index. Both are excellent.

There is so much information in this encyclopedia, both obscure and well known, that any library or collection would benefit by its inclusion.   Patricia M. Leach

POPULAR CUSTOMS

1251. Dunkling, Leslie. **A Dictionary of Days.** New York, Facts on File, 1988. 156p. illus. $18.95. LC 88-3825. ISBN 0-8160-1416-9.

This cleverly conceived, well-executed, fun reference work, is an alphabetical listing of over 850 "named" days, both fact and fiction. Provided are concise explanations for each day listed as well as a calendar for those who need a special event for a particular day. Just prior to the calendar is an explanation that many of the days listed cannot be linked to a specific *date*. Some are "moveable," such as Easter, while others fall at a distinct time each year but have no fixed date (the example given is Thanksgiving, which always falls on the third Thursday in November, but, of course, the date of that third Thursday varies from year to year).

The days listed range from solemn and serious to light and whimsical. Major Christian and Jewish holidays are listed but Islam appears to be represented solely by Ramadan. Important U.S. and British public holidays and celebration days are noted, but the dictionary is at its best when listing less well-known or downright fanciful days. Among days worthy of note (and worthy of celebration, now that we know of their existence) are "insipid day" (a day when nothing happens), "loaf day" (a nineteenth-century U.S. creation indicating a day when workers have nothing to do but "loaf"), and the should-be all-time favorite, the "unbirthday."

In spite of the light tone of some of the descriptions (befitting the seriousness of the occasion), the historical explanations for those events that *have* histories (both real and fanciful) are concise and informative. When dealing with a day of importance to many or to just a few, Dunkling writes in a sober and respectful manner. *A Dictionary of Days* should find a home in public, academic, and school libraries. [R: BR, Nov/Dec 88, p. 48; LJ, 15 Apr 88, p. 74; RBB, Aug 88, p. 1900; WLB, May 88, p. 109]

Ellen Broidy

1252. **Etiquette: Charlotte Ford's Guide to Modern Manners.** By Charlotte Ford. New York, Clarkson N. Potter; distr., New York, Crown, 1988. 524p. index. $19.95. LC 87-32893. ISBN 0-517-56823-3.

This revised edition of Charlotte Ford's book of etiquette continues to place emphasis on graciousness and consideration for others rather than rigid adherence to strict rules of proper behavior. Her advice helps people to deal gracefully with the many perplexing situations frequently faced in a world where social norms are constantly changing. Several recent concerns of the 1980s are reflected in her suggestions for "visiting a friend with AIDS" and "safer sex." A new section on teenage etiquette addresses topics of special concern for this age group and provides information on matters such as the rites and rituals of dating, conduct at a friend's house, proms, and preparing for the first job interview. Modern lifestyles are addressed with topics on how to handle guests who abuse drugs or alcohol, life after divorce, birth announcements for unmarried parents, and dealing with sexual harassment in the workplace.

Keeping in mind the renewed formality of the past decade, etiquette for the time-honored traditions of weddings, parties, correspondence, business, travel, sports and games, etc., is adequately covered also. The table of contents in this edition has been made more concise and the index redone, which facilitates locating the necessary information for any social situation. The book is comprehensive and the writing clear and interesting. It should have a wide audience among all age groups from every walk of life. [R: LJ, 15 Oct 88, p. 90]

Marilyn Strong Noronha

1253. **The Official Directory of Festivals, Sports & Special Events: Directory.** 2d ed. Lesa Ukman, ed. Chicago, International Events Group, 1987. 350p. index. $119.00 spiralbound. ISBN 0-944807-00-3; ISSN 0894-0649.

This expensive, commercial directory is explicitly a "reference guide to the most important sponsorship opportunities" for festivals, sports, and special events, with emphasis on attendance, budget, and media coverage, as well as "vision, authenticity, and imagery." Events with and without sponsors are included. All of the one thousand plus events, however, which have been selected "hold promise for sponsors."

Primary arrangement is alphabetical by location: states (and cities therein), Canadian provinces, and a few foreign countries. Each entry includes the official name of the event; the contact person, with address and telephone number; date(s); site; event characteristics (television coverage, food/beverage availability, stages, fireworks, program book, entertainment, free or ticketed admission, attendance, budget); sponsors; and a more detailed event description. There are also event indexes by category (bowling, golf, sailing, etc.), month, and title, all of which refer the user to the location index. Concluding the directory, which, incidentally, carries a modest amount of advertising, is an "Industry Yellow Pages," a subject-arranged list of advertisers with complete contact information. Principal purchasers will probably be chambers of commerce, special libraries, and large business reference collections.   Charles R. Andrews

27 Performing Arts

GENERAL WORKS

1254. Franck, Irene M., and David M. Brownstone. **Performers and Players.** New York, Facts on File, 1988. 196p. illus. bibliog. index. (Work throughout History). $16.95. LC 87-30340. ISBN 0-8160-1443-4.

This volume presents a comprehensive survey of persons who participate or perform in fields usually referred to as entertainment, such as actors, athletes, dancers, directors, musicians, puppeteers, racers, and variety entertainers. Included for each occupation are the history of the vocation, its socioeconomic status, the specific tasks performed, and the changes technology and society have wrought.

In addition to the easy to read text, illustrations, a comprehensive index, and suggestions for further reading enhance this volume as a reference work.

Part of the series entitled Work throughout History, this is for young readers 10 and up. The entire set explores occupations as they have evolved and are executed throughout the world. It will be a valuable addition to middle and high school libraries.

Sara R. Mack

1255. Kirkpatrick, D. L., ed. **Contemporary Dramatists.** 4th ed. Chicago, St. James Press, 1988. 785p. index. $85.00. ISBN 0-912289-62-7.

The biographies of over three hundred living contemporary dramatists writing in English comprise this directory. There are also supplements on writers for screen, radio, and television; musical librettists, theater groups; and seven recently deceased dramatists who are regarded as essentially contemporary. Selected by a panel of advisers and arranged alphabetically, each entry consists of a biography, a complete survey of produced and/or published plays arranged chronologically, a listing of all other published books by type, and a signed essay.

Some entrants provided a personal comment on their work. Valuable specific information is also included when available, such as location of manuscript collections, critical studies and bibliography, agents, addresses, and related theatrical activities. The entries for the writers included in the supplements deal only with directly related professional writing. There is a title index. This volume, although limited in selection, provides a great amount of information for every major contemporary dramatist presented in a logical and readily accessible form. Such data are not readily available anywhere else. This volume qualifies as a major biographical research source. [R: Choice, Oct 88, p. 286; RBB, 1 Dec 88, p. 630]

Jackson Kesler

1256. Lyman, Darryl. **Great Jews on Stage and Screen.** Middle Village, N.Y., Jonathan David, 1987. 279p. illus. index. $19.95. LC 87-4214. ISBN 0-8246-0328-1.

Defining a Jew as "anyone who was born of a Jewish mother or who converted to Judaism," Lyman presents one hundred biographies of Jewish performers from the theater, film, and television. Each one-to-three-page biography includes a biographical sketch; a large black-and-white photograph; and a list of the biographee's "selected performances" on stage, film, radio, and television. These major biographies are followed by twenty-five pages of thumbnail sketches of Jewish performers, including many—such as Isaac Stern, Paul Simon, Bob Dylan, and Roberta Peters—that one would expect to find in Lyman's companion volume, *Great Jews in Music* (1986).

Although most of the information presented in this volume will be readily found in *Current Biography* and/or standard entertainment biographies, these sketches are very easy to read and provide an ethnic overview that is not available in other sources. On the other hand, how many readers looking for information on Erich von Stroheim, Dinah Shore, or Marilyn

Monroe would know to consult this book? Lyman does not explain why some entertainers are given major biographies and others only a one- or two-sentence sketch. For instance, Stella Adler, Anouk Aimée, Sara Bernhardt, and Alvin Epstein are all reduced to thumbnail sketches, while Henry Houdini, who is certainly not remembered for his six film roles, is presented in a three-page major biography. [R: RBB, Aug 88, p. 1903]

Michael Ann Moskowitz

1257.   Slide, Anthony, Patricia King Hanson, and Stephen L. Hanson, comps. **Sourcebook for the Performing Arts: A Directory of Collections, Resources, Scholars, and Critics in Theatre, Film, and Television.** Westport, Conn., Greenwood Press, 1988. 227p. index. $45.00. LC 87-23630. ISBN 0-313-24872-9.

Comprehensive in its directory approach to resources in television, radio, theater, and film, this work attempts to bring together a miscellany of information previously available only through searching many varied reference tools. The first section, arranged alphabetically by state, profiles institutions with major collections pertinent to the disciplines involved. Each entry presents name, address, telephone number, and a brief description of holdings. This section is followed by another that presents brief biographical information on leading critics, academics, historians, librarians, archivists, and scholars in the areas of the performing arts. Together, these two sections comprise the bulk of the directory.

A third and final section, "Useful Addresses," gives basic directory information in the following categories: bookshops, journals and magazines, specialist publishers, organizations, major motion picture and television studios and production companies in the U.S., U.S. film commissions, international film commissions, and television networks.

The index covers only entries in the first two sections, thereby limiting access to the entire volume. Recommended for academic and public library ready-reference collections. [R: Choice, Sept 88, p. 90; LJ, 1 Apr 88, p. 80]

Edmund F. SantaVicca

1258.   Smith, Ronald L. **Comedy on Record: The Complete Critical Discography.** New York, Garland, 1988. 728p. (Garland Reference Library of the Humanities, Vol. 724). $55.00. LC 87-35969. ISBN 0-8240-8461-6.

This amusing, frustrating work opens with a subtitle that belies its limited scope. *The Complete Critical Discography* is, in reality, a listing of comedy records published in America between 1957 and 1987; more specifically, the author concentrates his efforts on those records which a collector might hope to find in the bins of a local used record shop. For most entries, the author lists the name of the comedian, the record label and number, a brief biographical sketch summarizing the comedian's career, and samples of dialog from the recording. The book is arranged by name only; there is no index.

This work is itself a form of entertainment, since the author has included extensive examples of comedy routines transcribed from the recordings he reviews. In addition, the author gives freely of his own opinions regarding the relative merits of each work.

Libraries and serious collectors of comedy on record may wish for more bibliographic information and fewer transcribed comedy routines, particularly since most recorded comedy seems to lose its humor in print. Dates of recordings are rarely given, and an index would have been a useful addition for locating comedians who appeared often in minor roles on one another's albums. [R: LJ, Aug 88, p. 151; RBB, 15 Nov 88, p. 550; WLB, Oct 88, p. 106]

Daniel Uchitelle

DANCE

1259.   Studwell, William E., and David A. Hamilton. **Ballet Plot Index: A Guide to Locating Plots and Descriptions of Ballets and Associated Material.** New York, Garland, 1987. 249p. (Garland Reference Library of the Humanities, Vol. 756). $40.00. LC 87-19758. ISBN 0-8240-8385-7.

The literature of ballet abounds with information concerning individual ballets; the problem lies in identifying and locating it. This reference book attempts to do just that for sixteen hundred ballets of all types and periods and from all Western nations. Toward that end, fifty-four books in several languages published between 1926 and 1982, are indexed. While serving mainly as a guide to plots and descriptions, this volume also indicates the location of associated material. Such information may consist of historical references, bibliographical notes, musical themes, and criticism and analysis.

Codes, both for sources indexed and for type of peripheral material, as used in the main section, are listed in the beginning of the book. The ballet index, alphabetically arranged by original title, with cross-references from variant titles, is preceded by a helpful guide illustrating its use. A composer index lists composers mentioned in the main section, including names of ballets with which they are associated.

Entries contain the ballet's title, the composer, date of first performance, any variant titles, and codes for sources of information. Each code is followed by a symbol in parentheses identifying the type of associated material present.

Although other guides to individual ballets exist, this one is unique in the number of titles included. Besides the sheer volume of entries, related data covered provide valuable supplementary information. This comprehensive index should prove to be a useful addition to research collections on dance. [R: Choice, Apr 88, p. 1226; WLB, Mar 88, p. 96]

Anita Zutis

FILM

Bibliographies

1260. Eberly, Stephen L. **Patty Duke: A Bio-Bibliography**. Westport, Conn., Greenwood Press, 1988. 88p. illus. index. (Bio-Bibliographies in the Performing Arts, No. 3). $29.95. LC 87-37565. ISBN 0-313-25675-6.

The versatile Patty Duke is among the few actors who have successfully made the transition from child stardom to a distinguished acting career as an adult. Best remembered for her portrayal of Helen Keller in *The Miracle Worker* on film and on Broadway, Patty Duke has played wide-ranging roles, including the President of the United States. The present work provides a list of these many triumphs, with distinct chapters for awards, discography, filmography, plays, and television appearances. An episode-by-episode guide to Duke's three television series, *The Patty Duke Show, It Takes Two,* and *Hail to the Chief*, variously furnishes cast, credits, synopsis, and excerpts from *Variety* reviews.

Coverage is somewhat skimpy here and there. The filmography and television appearance entries lack plot synopses, the television series episode entries lack casts, and the 45 rpm/ LP recording entries lack dates. The entries in the bibliography, most of which seem to be lurid magazine articles like "My Husband Is Not the Father of My Baby," are mostly unannotated. The index utilizes a confusing alphanumeric entry-number system which is not entirely sequential.

In a dozen full-page, black-and-white photographs, nearly all show Patty performing in some of her many roles, including the famous dual role of Patty and Cathy Lane, look-alike cousins. As the few pages of prefatory biography explain, the "Patty and Cathy" image

was tough to shake and badly affected her subsequent career.   Richard W. Grefrath

1261. Matzen, Robert D. **Carole Lombard: A Bio-Bibliography**. Westport, Conn., Greenwood Press, 1988. 167p. illus. index. (Bio-Bibliographies in the Performing Arts, No. 4). $35.95. LC 88-15429. ISBN 0-313-26286-1.

Lombard is a Hollywood legend as much for her offscreen wit, salty vocabulary, famous husbands and lovers, and airplane crash death at age 33 as for her screen performances. This bio-bibliography (fourth in a series that includes volumes devoted to Milos Forman, Kate Smith, and Patty Duke) starts with a thirty-nine-page biography which offers an overview of Lombard's career and lovelife, and concludes with a 154-item annotated bibliography. In between there are a filmography, a short piece the actress wrote about studio publicity in 1938, two fan magazine articles about Lombard from the same year, some samples of the Lombard wit, a report on the "strange death" in a 1934 shooting accident of Lombard's "great love" crooner Russ Columbo, fifteen photographs, and the Civil Aeronautics Board report of the 1942 plane crash that claimed Lombard's life. The emphasis throughout is on Lombard's personality and romances, with little in-depth analysis of her as either a person or a screen performer. The extensive bibliography includes a number of substantive works, but a majority of the 45 books (many of them Hollywood memoirs) and 109 articles (most from popular magazines of the 1930s) seem likely to be more gossipy than scholarly. For large cinema collections.

Joseph W. Palmer

1262. Nachbar, Jack, Jackie R. Donath, and Chris Foran. **Western Films 2: An Annotated Critical Bibliography from 1974 to 1987**. New York, Garland, 1988. 308p. index. (Garland Reference Library of the Humanities, Vol. 638). $40.00. LC 87-38487. ISBN 0-8240-8640-6.

This sequel to *Western Films: An Annotated Bibliography* (Garland, 1975), has the same problem that it had before. According to the review (see *ARBA* 76, entry 1050), the assigned numbering system complicates rather than simplifies finding articles. Still, the annotations are excellent: they are critical as well as descriptive. The bibliography covers English-language, mainly American, publications from 1974 to the early part of 1987. As before, it is divided into ten categories, including selected reference sources, criticism, performers, history, theory, etc. One section brings the first edition up-to-date by gathering articles missed in the 1975 compilation. An interesting introduction addresses the "death of the Western film as a significant factor in American cultural life." Perhaps this is a premature death knell. This volume, while three times the size of the first one (308 pages versus 98 pages), is more than three times as expensive ($40.00 versus $12.00). Appendices add additional material of interest and a list of "fan" and "collector" Western periodical names and addresses. The volume ends with an author/subject index. [R: Choice, Oct 88, p. 294]

Elizabeth Futas

1263. Steene, Birgitta. **Ingmar Bergman: A Guide to References and Resources.** Boston, G. K. Hall, 1987. 342p. bibliog. index. (Reference Publication in Film). $50.00. LC 86-25839. ISBN 0-8161-7961-1.

A film director of Bergman's stature deserves a richly detailed bibliographic study, and Steene has the credentials the task calls for. A Swedish-American film scholar, Steene has written or edited several books on Bergman and compiled a staggering amount of critical material along the way. For this "resource guide"—an annotated bibliography accompanying review essays—she limits herself to "important critical and biographical information available" with some partiality for U.S. and West European articles, reviews, essays, books, and dissertations. The Swedish press is particularly well covered, but the majority of the cited works are in English. The result is impressive both for the quantity of material uncovered and for the value-added annotations.

She divides her work into eight sections, beginning with two brief, narrative chapters on Bergman's life and films. Section 3 is a 155-page study of each film, including synopses, credits, notes, critical commentary, and accounts of the contemporary reception. A film like *Cries and Whispers* alone generates seventy-four citations in this section. Writings about the director, interviews, and general studies of his work occupy the next seventy-five pages. Here Steene has compiled mini-bibliographic essays on topics such as Bergman's views on women and psychological approaches to Bergman's films. A section of primary works lists Bergman's screenplays, unpublished scripts, and lectures. Finally, shorter chapters cover his career in theater, television, and film production, and list relevant archives and distributors.

Minor difficulties include a name index which is not perfectly alphabetical and a few verbal miscues (*exappropriation* for expropriation, *bending arms* for arm wrestling). Nonetheless, Steene's resource guide is a fitting summary of the immense interest spawned by Europe's

dominant film director over the last four decades.

John P. Schmitt

1264. Wolfe, Charles. **Frank Capra: A Guide to References and Resources.** Boston, G. K. Hall, 1987. 464p. bibliog. index. (Reference Publication in Film). $50.00. LC 86-27095. ISBN 0-8161-8507-7.

Anyone seriously interested in film is presumably interested in the movies of Frank Capra and, therefore, in this remarkably useful and thorough reference work. Not everyone will need the last two units of this book—archival sources (listing forty-six collections of Capra material) and film distributors—nor will many find the twenty-page biography indispensable, although it is indeed more objective and wieldy than Capra's own 513-page *The Name above the Title: An Autobiography* (1971). Wolfe's filmography of Capra lists each of the fifty-seven films, with credits, detailed synopses, and notes. It is hard to find a book with notes more intriguing than these (about production, sources, casting, censorship, remakes). For most film students, the heart of the book will be the 220-page annotated bibliography (this must have taken years of work) listing (1) writings about Frank Capra, (2) writings by and interviews with Frank Capra (in his own confessions, some on film and videotape, Capra explains his own morality, politics, aesthetics, religion, pacifism, and Hollywood problems, always managing to be personal without being gossipy), and (3) other film-related activity (including unfinished projects). The first part, the bibliography, is enormous, covering 1922 to 1981. (What a pity to end there; so many fine books and articles have appeared since then.) Many of these eleven hundred bibliography entries are routine reviews, of course, but some are articles, essays, letters, or chapters of extremely thoughtful observations (Lewis Jacobs, Graham Greene, Mark Van Doren, James Agee, Peter Bogdanovich, François Truffaut, Pudovkin, Pauline Kael, Malcolm Lowry, Pare Lorentz, Mack Sennett, Georges Sadoul). A reference book like this is like InfoTrac: it pays for itself many times in saved energy and time.

Paul H. Stacy

Biographies

1265. Holston, Kim. **Starlet: Biographies, Filmographies, TV Credits and Photos of 54 Famous and Not So Famous Leading Ladies in the Sixties.** Jefferson, N.C., McFarland, 1988. 299p. illus. bibliog. index. $39.95. LC 87-43209. ISBN 0-89950-307-1.

Promoted as future stars, the fifty-four women profiled here all gained popularity in the 1960s. All were leading ladies at one time, but only a few, like Natalie Wood or Jane Fonda, went on to attain superstardom. Each entry contains black-and-white illustrations consisting of publicity shots and stills from the individual's movies, and details the starlet's career development. Among the sources used are coworkers, critics, and the women themselves. A filmography and a list of television credits complete the portrait.

A general bibliography and individual ones, including reviews, letters, interviews, articles, and monographs follow. Additional access points are provided by the index. Insight into the last decade of Hollywood's "star system" is obtained through fifty-four accounts of women who have experienced it. This compendium sheds new light on a period of radical change in American cinema.

Anita Zutis

1266.   Miller, Lynn Fieldman. **The Hand That Holds the Camera: Interviews with Women Film and Video Directors.** New York, Garland, 1988. 271p. illus. (Garland Reference Library of the Humanities, Vol. 688). $27.00. LC 87-32871. ISBN 0-8240-8530-2.

The premises that "the hand that holds the camera" determines the images of women in films and that there is a "women's culture expressed through the minds and experiences of women" are the subject of the book's short introduction. It details the characteristics of the work of the women interviewed, selected as examples of how a woman's direction makes a difference. The directors, some quite young and some more experienced, are Doris Chase, Michelle Citron, Kavery Dutta, Tami Gold, Amalie Rothschild, Meg Switzgable, and Linda Yellen. Of the seven interviews, one was done in 1987 and six from 1982 to 1985. Each one is accompanied by a photograph of the artist, a brief biographical-professional sketch, and a list of her films and videos. There are an additional nineteen photographs.

Besides providing insights into issues about women in films and filmmaking, the interviews are sources for historical and critical studies and offer opinions and practical information for young artists on the direction, production, business, and technical aspects of making films and videos. Perhaps interviews were the only way to capture these insights and information, but they also try the reader's patience and waste space on inane remarks such as: "everyone suggests that women be teachers" (p. 20); "You should send her a letter.... Oh, I did. You did?"

(p. 142); and "I don't want to take up too much of your time" (p. 270).

Woefully lacking is any index, which is needed to locate the many references to persons, titles, institutions, and issues in the interviews.

Joyce Duncan Falk

1267.   Monaco, James. **Who's Who in American Film Now.** 2d ed. New York, New York Zoetrope, 1987. 388p. $39.95. LC 87-43024. ISBN 0-918432-63-4.

This book covers six thousand films, made between 1975 and 1986, and over eleven thousand people who worked on those films. It is arranged in thirteen chapters by the craft of the individuals who worked on the films. The chapters are arranged in the sequence usually followed in the stages of movie production. Thus, the first chapter is given to the writers; then are listed producers of all sorts; directors; actors and actresses; production designers; art directors, etc.; costume designers; cinematographers; sound on the set and off, recording and editing; choreographers; music; special effects; and finally, the editors. The entries within each chapter are alphabetically arranged by surname with the titles of the films and the date made listed in chronological order. Unfortunately, there is not a master index for all thirteen chapters, and so, for individuals who do a great variety of things with a movie, such as Woody Allen, Mel Brooks, or Harold Ramis, one will have to go through all the chapters to gather complete information. An introductory chapter is included that deals with the salaries paid to film people. The information in this publication is taken from BASELINE, a comprehensive database for the film and television industry, which was started by the author. Even though there is no biographical information about the people included, this should prove to be a useful source for relatively current information on the activities of individuals in the American film industry. [R: RBB, 1 Jan 88, p. 770]

Robert L. Turner, Jr.

1268.   Palmer, Scott. **A Who's Who of Australian and New Zealand Film Actors: The Sound Era.** Metuchen, N.J., Scarecrow, 1988. 171p. bibliog. $20.00. LC 87-32215. ISBN 0-8108-2090-0.

"Who's who" leads you to expect more than you get from this little book. "Who Was in What" would be a more accurate title, since the work merely consists of names of film actors of Australian/New Zealand origin or citizenship and lists of films in which they appeared. Some of the actors are unexpected (and well covered in other reference books): Errol Flynn, Judith

Anderson, silent comedians Snub Pollard and Billy Bevan, 1930s comedian Leon Errol. Others are obscure: Frederick Esmelton, Marshal Crosby, Anouska Hempel. Information given is minimal: name, sometimes year of birth and death, a brief blurb ("Australian leading lady of films and television of the eighties"), and a chronological list giving titles and years of films in which they appeared (*High Rolling* 1977, *My Brilliant Career* 1979). Hollywood, British, and television films are included. Indeed, they seem to far outnumber Australian films although there is no way to know since there is no indication of which films are which. The value of the book is enhanced by a twenty-eight-page introductory essay which chronicles the development of the Australian film industry between 1896 and 1983 (with a couple of paragraphs on the 1986 film *Crocodile Dundee* tossed in at the end) and by a bibliography of twenty-five relevant monographs published between 1964 and 1984. I am not sure there is much need for this little volume, but cinema collections should find it of some value.   Joseph W. Palmer

1269. Wakeman, John, ed. **World Film Directors. Volume I: 1890-1945.** Bronx, N.Y., H. W. Wilson, 1987. 1247p. illus. $90.00. LC 87-29569. ISBN 0-8242-0757-2.

1270. Wakeman, John, ed. **World Film Directors. Volume II: 1945-1985.** Bronx, N.Y., H. W. Wilson, 1988. 1205p. illus. $90.00. LC 87-29560. ISBN 0-8242-0763-7.

By providing introductions to the work and lives of about four hundred of the world's best-known film directors from the beginning of cinema to the present, *World Film Directors: 1890-1945* and *1945-1985* succeed in doing for filmmakers what *Twentieth Century Authors* (H. W. Wilson, 1955), *World Authors* (see *ARBA* 86, entry 1080), and other works in the Wilson Company's authors series do for writers. Making no claims to original research, this two-volume work brings together in one place information previously scattered throughout many reference books, monographs, histories, critical essays, reviews, and interviews.

Whether the user seeks a definition of George Cukor's style, information about Sergio Leone's best and worst "spaghetti Westerns," commentary on Vittorio de Sica's view of each script as a highly structured artifact, an analysis of the use of color in Jean Renoir's 1951 film adaptation of Rumer Godden's *The River*, an explanation for the tremendous success of Ken Russell's 1969 adaptation of D. H. Lawrence's *Women in Love*, or a reason for the celebration of Stanley Kubrick's *Lolita* as an "epic comedy

of frustration rather than lust," the answers to tens of thousands of such queries may be easily found in this monumental pair of reference books.

Arranged alphabetically, the entries in *World Film Directors* provide a fifteen hundred to eight thousand word essay on each director and offer a summary of the director's films, an analysis of the filmmaker's early development, a commentary on significant influences on the artist, a discussion of the major films directed, information on casting and production, a complete filmography of the director, and a selected bibliography of relevant books and articles. Each article is often highlighted with first-person statements by the directors themselves, the deliberations of academic critics, and the spontaneous responses of good reviewers.

Well aware of the difficulty of providing "a fair summation of representative critical response," the authors of the articles have skillfully charted the "dazzling flux" of reputations that "have soared or plummeted with sobering abruptness," trying to be as comprehensive and objective as "time, space, and patience" allow. In order to keep the project to a manageable size, editor John Wakeman interprets "directors" rather strictly and excludes figures who are best known as animators or producers. He also admits that in selecting directors he has favored those who have films that can be seen in the United States, Great Britain, and other English-speaking countries. Consequently, the "emerging or flourishing cinemas of the Third World have perhaps received less attention than they deserve."

Although intended primarily for students and movie goers, these volumes will also be an invaluable aid to scholars, for nowhere else is so much information about filmmakers available in a reference guide. Individuals and libraries interested in any aspect of film will find *World Film Directors* a much-used companion. [R: BR, May/June 88, p. 49; Choice, Apr 88, p. 1226; LJ, 15 Apr 88, p. 75; RBB, 15 Nov 88, p. 548; WLB, Mar 88, p. 104]   Colby H. Kullman

Dictionaries and Encyclopedias

1271. Buscombe, Edward, ed. **The BFI Companion to the Western.** New York, Atheneum, 1988. 432p. illus. (part col.). maps. bibliog. $60.00. LC 88-10402. ISBN 0-689-11962-3.

While several Western film "guides," notably *Shoot-em-ups* (see *ARBA* 87, entry 1294), *Western Films* (see *ARBA* 83, entry 1000), and *Western Movies* (see *ARBA* 88, entry 1356) have been published in the U.S. in the last decades, this is a British "companion" to the genre. Though the spelling ("armoury" and "labour") is British, the monetary units are in dollars, and the *Companion* will be welcomed by aficionados of the film. Instead of merely listing or briefly commenting, or both, on hundreds of Westerns, the editors try to explore the source for the Western's continued popularity in both theater and television presentations. They try to provide an interpretive history of the making of Westerns as well.

This is done mostly in the "Culture & History" section (pp. 55-246), arranged alphabetically by specific name ("Abilene, Kansas" to "Emiliano Zapata") and by broad topic ("Costume," "Cowboy," "Horses," "Indians," "Photography," etc.). These entries range from a short paragraph to three or four pages and are well-written analyses or explanations of their subjects. There are illustrations, many in color, in a separate section.

A listing of about 300 "key Westerns" includes fairly long story analyses for each, a brief technical notation, and a partial listing of players.

This is followed by a listing of "film makers," mostly actors, with some producers and directors. The emphasis is on criticism, often a full page. Following each analysis is a complete listing, by year, of all films in which the person appeared (or directed or produced, etc.).

Finally there is a listing of about 260 films made for television, including "Little House on the Prairie" and the Reagan-hosted "Death Valley Days." The appendix contains an extensive bibliography; a list of alternative titles (usually the French, German, Italian, or Spanish titles of U.S. films); some statistical tables; and a kind of finding tool called "Cross-References." There is no single index since most portions of the book are already alphabetical.

Raymund F. Wood

1272. Fernett, Gene. **American Film Studios: An Historical Encyclopedia.** Jefferson, N.C., McFarland, 1988. 295p. illus. bibliog. index. $35.00. LC 88-42514. ISBN 0-89950-250-4.

The author, who has spent many years in the film industry as a director and scriptwriter as well as being a college professor and big-band leader, has written a fascinating history of the American film studio. He covers in detail over sixty studios, with entries ranging in length from one to nine pages and referring to many more within each entry. This is not an exhaustive treatment, since according to the Los Angeles Chamber of Commerce there were forty-nine film studios in that city alone in 1921. Each entry gives a brief history of the studio from the beginning to its demise, naming the major people involved with the studio, including owners, producers, directors, and actors. Often included are historical pictures of the studio, as well as pictures of promotional materials for some of the films shot there. There is a very detailed index that includes people, places, studios, and films. This work presents a lively glimpse not only of the American studios, but also of the film industry. It is informative and enjoyable to read.   Robert L. Turner, Jr.

1273. Grant, John. **Encyclopedia of Walt Disney's Animated Characters.** New York, Harper & Row, 1987. 320p. illus. (part col.). bibliog. index. $35.00. LC 87-45052. ISBN 0-06-015777-1.

Character is the operative word here. It is the concept by which Walt Disney Studios was able to create the hundreds of unique, true-to-life animated personalities that are depicted in this two-part encyclopedia. The parts are chronologically arranged. The first treats characters from Disney shorts, in order of their first appearance. Each entry traces the development of the character through various shorts and ends with a filmography. The second chronicles animated feature films, including those with only animated sequences. The film's credits, history, and a synopsis of the plot are included, and its characters (major and minor) are described and analyzed. Both sections are well illustrated with stills from the films, and contain numerous cross-references to additional information.

An extensive bibliography is included, and by using the comprehensive indexes, one may locate a character through a variety of access points.

The arrangement of the encyclopedia allows for a historic perspective on the art of animation. That, and the thorough research conducted in the Walt Disney Archives, contribute to making this an authoritative and comprehensive work, as well as a highly readable and entertaining one. As is pointed out, this compilation makes a unique contribution to the study of Disney's animated characters.

Anita Zutis

1274. **The International Dictionary of Films and Filmmakers: Volume V: Title Index.** James Vinson and Greg S. Faller, eds. Chicago, St. James Press, 1987. 494p. $60.00. ISBN 0-912289-86-4.

With the publication of this fifth and final index volume, the user is able to locate biographical and career information on seven hundred actors and actresses, five hundred directors, five hundred writers and production artists, and the five hundred films with which they were related. The work is arranged alphabetically by film title. Surnames of the artists associated with each particular film follow the title, with a number after the name indicating the volume in which complete information about that person can be located.

The coverage is not the same for each film. For some only one name is given, while others have many, since inclusion is based entirely upon the individuals covered in the series. It would not be possible to find information on all important persons associated with most of the films. There is no name index, but since each of the four volumes has an alphabetical listing of the persons included in the front, this does not seem to present a problem.

The volume has little use on its own but it is a very necessary part of the series, since it provides the only access by film title and is a necessity for libraries who have the series. [R: Choice, June 88, p. 1536; RBB, Aug 88, pp. 1904-5]   Marilyn Strong Noronha

1275. Konigsberg, Ira. **The Complete Film Dictionary.** New York, New American Library, 1987. 420p. illus. $24.95. LC 87-5747. ISBN 0-453-00564-0.

"Complete" refers to the author's attempt to include terms related to all aspects of motion pictures—technique, production, history, criticism, and theory—in one reference book. Coverage, while extensive, is not really "complete," and the book in no way replaces standard reference tools such as the 1969 *Focal Encyclopedia of Film and Television Techniques* (see *ARBA* 70, v. 2, p. 33). The thirty-five hundred entries vary from single-sentence definitions, to paragraph and page-long explanations, to encyclopedia-like articles several pages in length on topics such as film, film theory, lighting, sound, and special effects. Explanations are clear and avoid jargon; nonspecialists should find them easy to understand. Dozens of excellent line drawings illustrate types of equipment and technical terms, while numerous stills from classic motion pictures draw attention to explanations of film genres and aesthetic techniques. If I were to make a single improvement to this book, I would add bibliographic references to each of the longer articles. While most provide good introductions to their topics, suggestions for further reading would be a great help to readers who want more information. This dictionary is a good value which will be a particularly useful addition to the reference shelves of smaller libraries. Larger libraries will find that it nicely updates and complements

other reference books in their collections. [R: LJ, 15 Apr 88, p. 33; RBB, 15 Jan 88, p. 840; SLJ, May 88, p. 35]   Joseph W. Palmer

1276. Langman, Larry. **Encyclopedia of American Film Comedy. Moving-pictures.** New York, Garland, 1987. 639p. illus. (Garland Reference Library of the Humanities, Vol. 744). $60.00. LC 87-11837. ISBN 0-8240-8496-9.

This is an attempt to bring together in one volume "all the major American screen comedians, comediennes, comedy teams, light actors and actresses, and directors and screenwriters who have contributed substantially to silent and sound comedy films" (p. vii). Arrangement is alphabetical by name of performer, director, screenwriter, comedy team, etc. There are ample cross-references throughout the dictionary arrangement.

Two special features of this work are the inclusion of selected "landmark" films as separate entries and samples of routines and humor in the entries on comics and selected films. The latter feature is entertaining but adds little to the value of this title as a reference work. What is the basis for including some "routines" while excluding others, and why are play-on-word routines (e.g., the surely/Shirley routine from *Airplane* and the sanity clause/Santy Claus routine from *Night at the Opera*) included when printing such dialog destroys the "joke"?

Reading a random selection of entries disclosed some errors/omissions, generally minor in nature. For example, in the *Airplane* entry, Lloyd Bridges is incorrectly identified as Robert Hays's former commander when the role was portrayed by Robert Stack, and *Lost in America* is excluded from the "filmography" on Albert Brooks even though these selected lists are stated to include the first and last credit of each individual entered.

In spite of its shortcomings, this work provides informative and entertaining reading for anyone interested in film comedy. It should be a useful supplement to the major reference works on film in general and on American film in particular. [R: Choice, July/Aug 88, p. 1675; LJ, 15 Apr 88, p. 74; RBB, Aug 88, p. 1901; WLB, Apr 88, pp. 100-1]   Larry G. Chrisman

Directories

1277. Thorpe, Frances, ed. **International Directory of Film and TV Documentation Centres.** Chicago, St. James Press, 1988. 140p. $45.00. ISBN 0-912289-29-5.

The previously titled *FIAF (International Federation of Film Archives) Directory of Film and TV Documentation Sources* now appears under this title. The number of entries has grown since the 1976 original edition to a total of 104, including 40 new entries. Forty-seven countries are represented, with updated information on the library and documentation services offered by these film schools, state institutions, and specialty agencies. The archival bent of these collections becomes clear upon reading the description of the holdings, which can hold in addition to books and periodicals, scripts, clippings, stills, posters, festival programs, press books, scrapbooks, production files and diaries, sound recordings, slides, videos, and special publications produced by the center. There are an index to special collections and a list of FIAF members, associates, and observers. Previous editions have not been reviewed in *ARBA* nor does the title appear in Sheehy's *Guide to Reference Books* (see *ARBA* 87, entry 17). Two similar publications have a heavy U.S. emphasis: *Motion Pictures, Television, and Radio: A Union Catalogue of Manuscript and Special Collections* (see *ARBA* 79, entry 1165) by Linda Harris Mehr, and *Film Study Collections: A Guide to Their Development and Use* (see *ARBA* 80, entry 1023) by Nancy Allen. Institutions with a clientele greatly given to research will need this important tool.

Gerald R. Shields

Filmographies

1278. Banerjee, Shampa, and Anil Srivastava. **One Hundred Indian Feature Films: An Annotated Filmography.** New York, Garland, 1988. 205p. illus. index. (Garland Reference Library of the Humanities, Vol. 915). $36.00. LC 88-22716. ISBN 0-8240-3647-6.

The authors began work on this filmography intending to include a representative selection, recommended by an advisory panel, of Indian feature films from the start of the sound era to the present. Inclusion of films ultimately was determined by accessibility to information on the films. The authors acknowledge certain missing elements in this filmography, but have had to struggle with a lack of documentation on the cinema in India.

The work originated as a project under the National Film Heritage program at the Centre for Development of Instructional Technology in Delhi and with some cooperation with the Library of Congress (LC) in its attempts to build a collection of India cinema. Several of the films included are in LC's collection, along with many of the film scripts.

The dates of the films included in this work are 1932 through 1986. The films are arranged in alphabetical order by their original-language titles. Each entry includes the title in English translation, running time, date, credits, and a thorough plot summary. Following the data about each film are a brief essay on its artistic merits and a discussion that sets the film in its political and sociological contexts.

The book has twelve pages of black-and-white stills, a general index, an index of English titles, and a chronological index. It is printed on acid-free paper. Linda A. Naru

1279. Bogle, Donald. **Blacks in American Films and Television: An Encyclopedia.** New York, Garland, 1988. 510p. illus. index. (Garland Reference Library of the Humanities, Vol. 604). $60.00. LC 87-29241. ISBN 0-8240-8715-1.

Bogle is the leading historian of black portrayals and performances in the entertainment industry. His reputation was established by *Toms, Coons, Mulattos, Mammies & Bucks: An Interpretive History of Blacks in American Films* (Viking, 1973) and *Brown Sugar: Eighty Years of America's Black Female Superstars* (Harmony Books, 1982). Here he offers facts about and highly charged critical evaluations of over 260 Hollywood and independent films and more than 100 television series, specials, and movies. All have featured black performers and, in Bogle's opinion, reflected racial attitudes. A "Profiles" section looks at and critiques the careers of about one hundred black performers and a handful of directors. Good illustrations abound. There are an up-to-date bibliography and a substantial index. My only real criticism concerns the decision to organize the volume as an alphabetical encyclopedia with a skimpy nine-line table of contents. Given the importance of an historical perspective, it would have been more useful to arrange the films and programs chronologically and to include a detailed listing of titles and "Profiles" in the table of contents. This is a meaty volume crammed with facts and strong opinions. It is sure to be a valued reference book in public and academic libraries. [R: Choice, Sept 88, p. 74; LJ, 1 Sept 88, p. 161; RBB, 1 Oct 88, p. 223]

Joseph W. Palmer

1280. Dye, David. **Child and Youth Actors: Filmographies of Their Entire Careers, 1914-1985.** Jefferson, N.C., McFarland, 1988. 310p. illus. bibliog. index. $24.95. LC 87-46441. ISBN 0-89950-247-4.

To be included in this book, an actor or actress had to have at least two performing credits. The entry for each person contains the person's name (both assumed and real), the date and place of birth, death date, series information, chronological listing of roles, and trivia notes. Included in the chronological listing are movies (general releases), including year released, title of the movie, production, company, and the character portrayed; movies (made for television), including year released, title of the movie, station (followed by TVM, made for television), segment title, if needed, and character portrayed; series, including the year released, title of the series, station, date (month and day) that the episode was aired, and the character portrayed; and any work on the stage, including year, title of the production, name of the theater, city in which it was performed, and the character portrayed. An asterisk precedes the title of a movie or series in which the person was scheduled to appear but did not. There is a bibliography, as well as a title index of movies, plays, television series, and made for television movies.

There are errors in this book. For example, for the movie *Andy Hardy's Private Secretary*, the date of release is given as 1940 for one of the actors and 1941 for all the others, and one of the characters in the movie, Polly Benedict, is misnamed Polly Hardy. In the entry for Kurt Russell many of his movies for the Disney studios were not listed. However, this is an interesting and worthwhile addition to the reference collection, since much of this information would be fairly difficult to find. [R: Choice, Nov 88, p. 458; LJ, 1 Sept 88, p. 162; VOYA, Dec 88, p. 258]

Robert L. Turner, Jr.

1281. Carr, Robert E., and R. M. Hayes. **Wide Screen Movies: A History and Filmography of Wide Gauge Filmmaking.** Jefferson, N.C., McFarland, 1988. 502p. illus. index. $39.95. LC 86-43093. ISBN 0-89950-242-3.

This work will be most appreciated by motion picture buffs who understand anamorphic film processes, aspect ratios, pulldown, compression, angular visual field, and other esoterica related to the mechanics of film production and projection. The authors assume a high level of subject expertise from their readers, and reward them with a comprehensive directory of wide screen motion picture formats. These include not only such common processes as CinemaScope and Techniscope, but also such obscure technologies as Daieiscope, Samcinescope, Tohoscope, and Sovscope.

Though not mentioned in this work's title, a large section of the book is devoted to theatrical presentation techniques that do not involve wide screens at all, such as Sensurround and Smell-O-Vision. The book concludes with a two hundred-page filmography of wide gauge and large format films, giving complete credits and

casts. [R: RBB, 15 Sept 88, pp. 141-42; RQ, Winter 88, p. 274]   Daniel Uchitelle

1282. **Film/Video Canadiana 1985-1986: A Guide to Canadian Films and Videos Produced in 1985 and 1986. Film/Video Canadiana 1985-1986.** Montreal, published for National Library of Canada and National Archives of Canada by National Film Board of Canada, 1988. 618p. index. $35.00pa.; $40.00pa. (U.S.). ISSN 0836-1001.

Film Canadiana (see *ARBA* 87, entry 1299), the exhaustive annual compendium of Canadian motion picture production, has now become *Film/Video Canadiana*. It encompasses both videotape and film produced in the calendar years 1985 and 1986 by Canadian production companies or independent producers, including short films, experimental videos, commercials, cartoons, educational films, and medical training videos; in short, virtually the entire output of the Canadian film and video industry.

Each entry lists complete production and format data, as well as providing a synopsis of the work. There are no less than eight separate indexes, including PRECIS subject and broad category subject indexes, plus a directory of Canadian film/video producers and distributors, including addresses and telephone numbers.

The bibliographic data contained in this volume may also be obtained online through UTLAS or through FORMAT, the online retrieval system of the National Film Board of Canada.   Daniel Uchitelle

1283. **500 Best British and Foreign Films to Buy, Rent or Videotape.** By The National Board of Review of Motion Pictures and the editors of *Films in Review*. Jerry Vermilye, ed. New York, William Morrow, 1988. 526p. $25.00; $12.95pa. LC 87-28260. ISBN 0-688-07798-6; 0-688-06897-9pa.

The five hundred films in this book were selected by The National Board of Review of Motion Pictures and the editors of *Films in Review*, the Board's main publication. As explained in the preface, The National Board was founded in 1909 to serve as protector of sorts for the fledgling motion picture business. Many of those who wrote the reviews in this book are also writers for *Films in Review*. The contributors are briefly identified; however, the reviews themselves are unsigned.

Reviews are of uniformly high quality, very readable, and packed with knowledge, insight, and opinion that could only be the result of a deep involvement in the history and technique of filmmaking. Though they are relatively brief, running less than a page in length, the reviews are very good at providing the details a consumer in a videotape store must have in order to make an informed judgment. They cite story, direction, and performances, and place the film in the voting and in awards.

The films are arranged alphabetically, with title in the language of origin. Entries include running time, nationality, year of release, cast, director, whether black-and-white or color, and availability—name of distributor when known, or "TV only" if known to be unavailable either for rental or purchase. A note as to whether a film is subtitled or dubbed into English is added for many foreign-language films.

This is a useful book, and would be an excellent choice for video stores and public libraries that serve a sophisticated clientele. The succinct, nearly page-long reviews are more satisfying than the terse comments in *Halliwell's Film Guide* (see *ARBA* 87, entry 1300). A companion volume—*500 Best American Films to Buy, Rent or Videotape* (Pocket Books, 1985)—completes the series. [R: LJ, 15 Feb 88, p. 160]

Randall Rafferty

1284. Palmer, Scott. **British Film Actors' Credits, 1895-1987.** Jefferson, N.C., McFarland, 1988. 917p. $55.00. LC 87-31098. ISBN 0-89950-316-0.

The author's objective in writing this book was to list every British actor who appeared in films from the beginning of the silent era through 1987 and to compile a complete filmography for each actor.

The general rules for selection were that the actor was a British or British Commonwealth performer and worked on at least three films. The films listed include television and non-British productions.

The work is divided into two sections. The second part covers films made from 1895 to 1928 and includes actors with no screen credits after 1928. The first section covers 1929 through 1987, and includes all actors who worked in both silents and talkies.

Within each section, actors are listed in alphabetical order. Entries in part 1 have birth and death dates, a pithy description of the actor's career (for example, for Karel Stepanek: "Czechoslovakian-born character actor in Britain from the early 40s, often cast as Nazi officer or other sinister characters"), and a chronological list of films. Entries in part 2 include name and film credits only.

Special sections list actors with honorary titles, those who have won film awards, and those who have appeared in one hundred or more films.

The information packed into the career summaries is often quite helpful, especially references to an "actor's" primary vocation and citations to autobiographies.

Commendably, this book is published on acid-free paper. The work contains no indexes. It is an appropriate acquisition for the comprehensive film collection.

Linda A. Naru

1285. **Rating the Movies: For Home Video, TV, and Cable.** rev. ed. By the editors of *Consumer Guide* and Jay A. Brown. Skokie, Ill., Consumer Guide Books, 1987. 512p. illus. $13.95pa. LC 87-62000. ISBN 0-88176-450-7.

This guide lists in alphabetical order more than thirty-three hundred films released between 1930 and the late 1980s. Each entry gives the release date; indicates availability on videocassette, and in closed captions for the hearing impaired; gives a rating from no stars to four stars; and provides a brief review. The review lists the principal actors and director, some critical commentary, the Motion Picture Association of America (MPAA) rating if available, any Academy Awards or nominations in major categories, and the running time for the theatrical release. Color is assumed, so only black-and-white films are specifically identified. Scattered throughout the book are brief profiles of thirty-five major stars. This guide will be especially helpful to those who want to decide on whether to watch a film on regular or cable television or to rent a videocassette. Although the videocassette availability information will change rather quickly, the rest of the information should be interesting to the home viewer.

Barbara E. Kemp

Handbooks

1286. Kinnard, Roy. **Beasts and Behemoths: Prehistoric Creatures in the Movies.** Metuchen, N.J., Scarecrow, 1988. 179p. illus. index. $22.50. LC 87-23424. ISBN 0-8108-2062-5.

Covering thirty-six live-action films released from 1925 to 1985, this book is devoted to prehistoric monsters, a subgenre of the monster film. In general the author has chosen the best or most noteworthy feature-length films, but has included examples of some of the worst. It should be noted that artificially created monsters, such as the giant ants in *Them*, are not included. Listed in chronological order, each entry gives cast and production credits, a critical commentary, and often comments and information from interviews with those involved with the productions. The latter, along with many of the photographs, give some valuable insight into the various techniques used to bring the prehistoric monsters to life. Additional information is provided in a brief introduction and the introductory chapter, "Silent Prehistory." Two appendices list live-action, feature-length prehistoric monster films (implying U.S. films), and live-action Japanese feature films in the same subgenre. There are also personal name and title indexes. Although many of these films are covered in other volumes, such as Alan Frank's *The Horror Film Handbook* and *The Science Fiction and Fantasy Film Handbook* (see *ARBA* 84, entries 965-66), this slim volume will appeal to many monster film fans and those who are interested in special effects.

Barbara E. Kemp

1287. Parish, James Robert, and Michael R. Pitts. **The Great Western Pictures II.** Metuchen, N.J., Scarecrow, 1988. 428p. illus. $45.00. LC 88-6528. ISBN 0-8108-2106-0.

One of a series of *The Great ... Pictures*, this one is a follow-up to the 1976 volume, *The Great Western Pictures*, and frequent references to this volume, called B/V (Basic Volume) are to be found. The editors state that their purpose was to include in this second volume some Westerns that have appeared since 1976, but their main focus is on titles omitted from the B/V for various reasons. They also wished to give a more rounded look at the Western film field. This is done in part by including films which, in their own words, "range from classics to the bottom-of-the-barrel." There are also a few foreign-language films, mostly made in Germany.

Each entry gives name of producing company and date; running time; names of responsible people (producer, director, music, camera, etc.); actors' names, each followed by name of character played, in parentheses; a brief account of how the film came to be made, and whether it has any "son of ...," or television descendants, or other matters of interest; a plot summary, in which the actor-character roles are reversed, the name of the character being followed by the name of the actor/actress in parentheses; and a brief criticism of the film, sometimes quoting *Variety* or some other film reviewing medium.

The reviews and summaries are written in a sprightly tone, Western films being often referred to as "oaters" or "sagebrushers," and the text is full of colorful expressions: a companion is a "side-kick," villains are "dastardly," and in one place a fight between a hero and villain is termed "a corker."

About every fifth film has a black-and-white illustration, usually a still from the movie, but occasionally a reproduction of the placard used in advertising the film. Unfortunately there is no index of any kind. [R: Choice, Dec 88, p. 632]

Raymund F. Wood

THEATER

Bibliographies

1288. Forys, Marsha. **Antonio Buero Vallejo and Alfonso Sastre: An Annotated Bibliography.** Metuchen, N.J., Scarecrow, 1988. 209p. index. (Scarecrow Author Bibliographies, No. 81). $22.50. LC 87-32385. ISBN 0-8108-2100-1.

These men were two very important contemporary Spanish playwrights who managed to make a significant mark during the Franco regime as social commentators. Buero Vallejo was known as a transcendental realist and Sastre was primarily a social theorist operating in a sort-of "underground" obscurity. Thus, one has more citations and publications than the other, but their influence on modern Spanish theater is of equal importance. This selective bibliographic record ends at the beginning of 1987. Books, dissertations, theses, journals, magazines, and newspapers are the source materials. There is also a small section of unverified citations for each author. The introduction to this compilation is in English and Spanish. The titles are almost exclusively in Spanish and the annotations are in English. There is an index of critics. This is a useful addition to this successful bibliographic series. [R: Choice, Sept 88, p. 80]

Gerald R. Shields

1289. Heck, Thomas F. **Commedia dell'arte: A Guide to the Primary and Secondary Literature.** New York, Garland, 1988. 450p. index. (Garland Reference Library of the Humanities, Vol. 786). $62.00. LC 87-29210. ISBN 0-8240-6644-8.

The main key to tapping the vast amount of material contained in this scholarly volume is an understanding of the initially confusing and arbitrary use of abbreviations, terminology, and usage. However, investigation justifies the adopted system in view of the scope of materials. The book organizes, annotates, and indexes the field of the subject and its literature, regardless of language, into 808 entries. Books, articles, dissertations, source manuscripts, exhibition catalogs, and iconographic material of all kinds are cited. Following an introductory chapter, the study covers the scenarios, historical studies, diffusion, actors, stock characters, improvisation, dance and music, revivals, iconography, and literature of the topic. An appendix of scenarios by title is provided as well as a bibliography and general index. This would be a valuable source for scholars and students of this important era of world theater. [R: Choice, Dec 88, p. 628]   Jackson Kesler

1290. King, Christine E., and Brenda Coven. **Joseph Papp and the New York Shakespeare Festival: An Annotated Bibliography.** New York, Garland, 1988. 369p. index. (Garland Reference Library of the Humanities, Vol. 793). $54.00. LC 87-25921. ISBN 0-8240-6609-X.

The name of Joseph Papp is almost synonymous with that of his organization, the New York Shakespeare Festival. Both have contributed significantly to the history of American theater since the 1950s, and are chronicled in this selective bibliography. Over 900 references were derived from periodical and newspaper indexes, subject bibliographies, government documents, works on the American theater, databases, and clipping files.

An introduction detailing Papp's life and career and the development of the Festival precedes a section, chronologically arranged, of material by Papp. This includes articles, letters, columns, interviews, and testimony at congressional hearings. Writings about him consist first of books and articles, arranged by author, and then of daily newspaper articles, chronologically listed. The latter provide the most abundant and detailed information. A chronology of major productions from 1951 to 1986 contains citations to the *New York Times* opening night reviews, and includes plays directed by Papp, as well as those produced by him and the Festival. A list of major productions by title, and indexes by author and subject enhance the work's usefulness.

This bibliography provides a single source of information about an influential force in New York cultural life for the past thirty years. As such, it would be a welcome addition to collections of American theater history.

Anita Zutis

1291. Kolin, Philip C. **David Rabe: A Stage History and a Primary and Secondary Bibliography.** New York, Garland, 1988. 273p. index. (Garland Reference Library of the Humanities, Vol. 795). $35.00. LC 87-21155. ISBN 0-8240-6611-1.

Philip Kolin has gathered together a vast amount of bibliographical material on playwright David Rabe. The author presents a lengthy biographical-chronological essay dealing with Rabe's writings (newspaper stories, movie and theatrical reviews, as well as a stage history of the playwright's dramas). This reference work presents a primary bibliography of Rabe's plays, screenplays, novels, short stories, poems, journalistic efforts, books, plays and movie reviews, as well as interviews and translations. A secondary bibliography lists all known writings about Rabe's work and influence in the theater. Several of the items in this latter bibliography are annotated. A combined name and subject index, giving both page number references and bibliography item number references, is also supplied.

This reference work is the product of exhaustive and scholarly research and is an invaluable tool for those interested in this playwright, as well as those readers concerned with the history of current drama.

Charles Neuringer

1292. Langhans, Edward A. **Eighteenth Century British and Irish Promptbooks: A Descriptive Bibliography.** Westport, Conn., Greenwood Press, 1987. 268p. illus. index. (Bibliographies and Indexes in the Performing Arts, No. 6). $49.95. LC 87-23638. ISBN 0-313-24029-9.

Truly a work of scholarship, lovingly put together with the kind of professionalism that restores faith in the learning possibilities of the descriptive bibliography. Langhans has already established his reputation for his knowledge of the Restoration period in theatrical history, especially in his commentary and reproduction of several promptbooks published in 1981 by Southern Illinois Press. In this work he describes over 380 promptbooks and related documents, including citations from other sources that turned out to be either nonexistent or missing. Entries include the location, shelfmark, production for which the promptbook was prepared, type of marginal notes contained therein, and citations to books or articles that have dealt with the described copy. The introductory material is a short course in the art of prompting, a glossary of abbreviations, and commentary on play production during the period. This is an obvious choice for all research collections and any director's library that may someday face a production of an eighteenth-century play.   Gerald R. Shields

Chronologies

1293. Sampson, Henry T. **The Ghost Walks: A Chronological History of Blacks in Show Business, 1865-1910.** Metuchen, N.J., Scarecrow, 1988. 570p. illus. index. $47.50. LC 87-27973. ISBN 0-8108-2070-6.

The history of black American entertainment, from its origins at the end of the Civil War to the first decade of the twentieth century, is traced in this illustrated chronology. Original source material, obtained mostly from libraries, includes newspaper reviews, playbills, theater programs, letters, biographical sketches, and critical commentary. Rare photographs, from abroad as well as from the United States, enhance the narrative.

Entries document the development of black entertainment from minstrel shows to involvement with all facets of popular entertainment, such as burlesque, circus, vaudeville, and musical comedy. The business of show business is included as well; it led to the formation of a black film industry years later. An index is provided.

This work serves as a prolog to the author's previous books, *Blacks in Blackface* (see *ARBA* 81, entry 1059) and *Blacks in Black and White* (see *ARBA* 78, entry 950). The chronology links the first fledgling efforts of blacks to the achievements of the emerging stars of the 1920s.

While entries are detailed, bibliographical annotations are often lacking, and no bibliography exists for those wishing to do further research. Such information would add to the usefulness of this historical account.

Anita Zutis

Dictionaries and Encyclopedias

1294. Courtney, Richard. **Dictionary of Developmental Drama: The Use of Terminology in Educational Drama, Theatre Education, Creative Dramatics, Children's Theatre, Drama Therapy, and Related Areas.** Springfield, Ill., Charles C. Thomas, 1987. 153p. bibliog. $28.50. LC 86-30193. ISBN 0-398-05313-8.

This dictionary contains (by the publisher's count) 956 terms selected for use in the area of educational drama and related areas plus significant terms from related disciplines such as anthropology, psychology, sociology, and foreign languages. The compiler does not seem to have clear criteria for the choice of entries, as many of them seem to have only a vague relationship or bearing to the title and/or subject. The vast majority of definitions are generally so abbreviated as to be of uncertain and questionable value. At best only the most elementary beginner in the field would find any value in the definitions, much less a graduate student, researcher, or practitioner. In many cases the inclusion of illustrative material would have been helpful. There is a brief concluding list of references and journals.   Jackson Kesler

Directories

1295. Frick, John W., and Carlton Ward, eds. **Directory of Historic American Theatres.** Westport, Conn., Greenwood Press, 1987. 347p. illus. bibliog. index. $45.00. LC 87-10709. ISBN 0-313-24868-0.

Detailed comparative studies of our nineteenth- and early twentieth-century theaters are now possible thanks to this directory, which provides scholars with information about nearly nine hundred surviving buildings that can be visited, studied, and surveyed. The theaters included were built before 1915, were designed for the presentation of live entertainment and movies (with live performances the principal attraction), and are extant even though they may not be used for their original purpose. Theaters used primarily for vaudeville have been included while those that were essentially motion picture houses have been excluded.

Divided into two sections, each arranged alphabetically by state and then by city, with theaters recorded alphabetically within each city, this informative guide first presents data about those theaters that have been documented, giving seating capacity, stage dimensions, famous performers who have appeared there, and type of productions staged as well as factual information about the building itself. The second section lists those buildings known to exist but for which no information could be found.

Here one may discover many interesting details of theatrical and architectural interest. Ford's Theatre in the District of Columbia was originally built as a Baptist church in 1833. It was not until 1861 that the conversion of the structure into a theater was begun. When Lotta Crabtree owned Boston's State Theatre, she lived next door in the Hotel Brewster, which was connected to the theater by a tunnel. Persons who appeared at the Springer Opera House in Columbus, Georgia, included Franklin D. Roosevelt, John L. Sullivan, and William Jennings Bryan.

Although much work remains to be done in gathering information about historic American theaters, editors Frick and Ward have put together an invaluable reference guide that will be of great assistance to theater scholars, architectural historians, and historic preservationists. [R: Choice, Apr 88, p. 1256; C&RL, July 88, pp. 346-47; RBB, 15 June 88, pp. 1718-19; WLB, May 88, p. 110]

Colby H. Kullman

1296. Lynch, Richard Chigley, comp. **Broadway on Record: A Directory of New York Cast Recordings of Musical Shows, 1931-1986.** Westport, Conn., Greenwood Press, 1987. 347p. index. (Discographies, No. 28). $37.95. LC 87-11822. ISBN 0-313-25523-7.

The comprehensive coverage of this volume makes it an invaluable research source for collectors, performers, scholars, and general devotees of the modern American Broadway musical. In covering the period from *The Band Wagon* in 1931 to *Me and My Girl* in 1986 the compiler provides full information on 459 show albums with some four thousand song titles. Entries are arranged alphabetically by musical title and each includes vital production information: opening date and name of theater; revivals; composer, lyricist, and conductor credits; cast members who sing on the recording; and each song and who performs it. Complete discographic data include record label and number of the original and any reissues or multiple recordings; type of recording; and mode (disc, tape, or compact disc). An index of performers identifies the albums on which each person appears. There is a separate index for composers, lyricists, and musical directors. This would be an appropriate choice for music and theater collections as well as large public libraries. [R: Choice, Mar 88, p. 1108; RBB, 1 Feb 88, pp. 913-14; RQ, Spring 88, p. 422; WLB, Mar 88, p. 96]

Jackson Kesler

1297. Richel, Veronica C., comp. **The German Stage, 1767-1890: A Directory of Playwrights and Plays.** Westport, Conn., Greenwood Press, 1988. 230p. index. (Bibliographies and Indexes in the Performing Arts, No. 7). $39.95. LC 87-25155. ISBN 0-313-24990-3.

This reference work is an invaluable tool for specialists interested in the German stage between the years 1767 and 1890. That interval covers from the first attempt to establish a German national theater to the demise of the German neo-romantic movement and the beginnings of modern realism in Germany. The author hopes to facilitate further investigations of the German repertory of that period by recording the production of over four thousand plays in ten selected German cities.

The citations in this reference work are presented alphabetically by playwright. Each citation supplies the place and date of the birth and death of the playwright, biographical source, title of play, genre, date of publication of the play (if any), and date and city of performance. The citations are brief and composed mostly of abbreviations. Various abbreviation tables are supplied. This format makes this reference work somewhat awkward to use, since the reader must constantly refer to the various abbreviation tables to decipher the citations. A play title index is also supplied. [R: Choice, June 88, p. 1540; C&RL, July 88, p. 347]

Charles Neuringer

Handbooks

1298. Bergan, Ronald. **The Great Theatres of London: An Illustrated Companion.** San Francisco, Calif., Chronicle Books, 1987. 200p. illus. (part col.). index. $14.95pa. LC 88-15337. ISBN 0-87701-571-6.

While not a scholarly work, this volume will delight London theater lovers. It contains short descriptions of forty-four London theaters. Each of the alphabetized entries gives something of the theater's history, architecture, plays performed there, and a listing of the great actors appearing on their boards. A sampling of stories both true and mythical linked to each theater enlivens the book's appeal.

The volume is heavily illustrated. Its two-page introduction scans the history of London theaters. Twenty other theaters are described in single-paragraph treatment. An index is also supplied.

Charles Neuringer

1299. Bordman, Gerald. **The Concise Oxford Companion to American Theatre.** New York, Oxford University Press, 1987. 451p. $24.95. LC 86-33294. ISBN 0-19-505121-1.

When Gerald Bordman's *Oxford Companion to the American Theatre* (Oxford University Press) appeared in 1984, it quickly established itself as the standard one-volume reference on the American stage. This 1987 abridgment of the massive original volume eliminates many entries on minor plays and figures, while it preserves those articles that are of the widest general interest.

Hundreds of biographical sketches and summaries of individual plays illuminate the major achievements of playwrights such as William Dunlap, Eugene O'Neill, Elmer Rice, Lillian Hellman, Arthur Miller, William Inge, David Mamet, David Rabe, and Sam Shepard. Also included are essays on significant performers, directors, and producers (ranging from Edwin Booth to Joseph Jefferson, Colleen Dewhurst to James Earl Jones, Sidney Kingsley to Joseph Papp). While extensive coverage is given to the great tradition of the American musical, the often neglected achievements of the nineteenth century are also represented. Here one may find information on American theater companies (such as Houston's Alley Theatre, the Dallas Theatre Center, and the Oregon Shakespeare Festival Association), theater structures (Charleston's Dock Street Theatre, New York's Lyceum Theatre, and Philadelphia's Arch Street Theatre, for example), and types of theater (mime, theater-in-the-round, off-Broadway theater).

Updated information on contemporary topics as well as many new articles make this "concise" edition of more than two thousand entries an excellent companion to the 1984 volume. An outstanding resource for theater scholars, it is also an enjoyable text for anyone interested in the world of theater, as the articles are clearly written and well informed.

Colby H. Kullman

1300.   Simas, Rick. **The Musicals No One Came to See: A Guidebook to Four Decades of Musical-Comedy Casualties on Broadway, Off-Broadway and in Out-of-Town Try-out, 1943-1983.** New York, Garland, 1987. 639p. illus. index. $50.00. LC 87-25095. ISBN 0-8240-8804-2.

While regional, summer stock, educational, and community theaters are often hard put to find unique, interesting musical shows to perform, each season a number of productions close after short runs, and are, therefore, never promoted and made available by licensing agencies. The shows remain virtually unknown. This volume aims to interest theater groups in producing these musicals, commercially unsuccessful in New York, perhaps through no fault of the playwright or composer.

Five sources were used to locate, verify, and document the 577 shows indexed here, premiering in New York between 1948 and 1981. Opening chapters assist in locating cast albums, tapes, sheet music, and librettos; offer advice on making the necessary contacts; and explain the arrangement and content of entries. The four categories of musicals are Broadway shows, off-Broadway shows, shows that closed in try-outs or preview, and shows that ran longer than three hundred performances but are currently unavailable for production. Under these categories, entries provide a general profile of the musical. Each contains the title, facts about the production, location of additional information, the availability of associated material, and critical citations. Indexes provide more access by show title; opening date; sources of adaptations; and names of source authors, librettists, composers, and lyricists.

Future, updated editions are promised, and will ensure the continued usefulness to the theater-producing community of this thoroughly researched guidebook. [R: RBB, 15 June 88, p. 1722]

Anita Zutis

1301.   Slide, Anthony, ed. **Selected Vaudeville Criticism.** Metuchen, N.J., Scarecrow, 1988. 308p. index. $29.50. LC 87-28553. ISBN 0-8108-2052-8.

The editor of this volume has gathered together a mixture of reviews of over 130 well-known performers from the "Golden Era" of vaudeville (i.e., that part of the twentieth century before the cinema displaced it as *the* popular entertainment). Thirteen essays about vaudeville are also reprinted.

The reviews and essays are reprinted in full. The length and number of reviews of particular performers vary a great deal. All the material reprinted in this volume comes from professional and popular periodicals of the time. A list of critics and the performers they reviewed is also supplied at the end of the volume. (No page references are given.)

The editor has not supplied a rationale for the selection of particular entries. Even though they are fascinating to read, they do not by themselves shed much light on the status and history of this now extinct entertainment form. The theater historian may be able to reconstruct the history of vaudeville from a close reading of the essays, but such a task is beyond the general reader. It is suggested that the general reader use this volume as a supplement to one of the many histories of vaudeville available to the public. On the other hand, the selections reprinted are a joy to read. While this volume falls short of scholarly orientation, it is a source from which to get a dim glimmer of what vaudeville was like.

Charles Neuringer

1302.   Willis, John. **Theatre World: 1986-1987 Season. Volume 43.** New York, Crown, 1988. 251p. illus. index. $35.00. LC 73-82953. ISBN 0-517-56828-4.

The forty-third annual edition of *Theatre World* continues to provide a complete list of Broadway productions and personnel, including actors, replacements, producers, directors, authors, composers, costume designers, lighting technicians, press agents, and opening and closing dates for plays presented between 1 June 1986 and 31 May 1987. Also included are numerous photographs of the plays and their players, and hundreds of short biographies. Off-Broadway, touring companies, and regional theater productions are included as well. The entire work is tied together with a thorough index.

Virtually any question involving who did what in the theater world in 1987 can be answered with this volume. A standard reference work, recommended for performing arts reference collections.

Daniel Uchitelle

28 Philosophy

BIBLIOGRAPHIES

1303. Navia, Luis E., and Ellen L. Katz. **Socrates: An Annotated Bibliography.** New York, Garland, 1988. 536p. index. (Garland Reference Library of the Humanities, Vol. 844). $67.00. LC 88-10264. ISBN 0-8240-5740-6.

This important annotated bibliography of over nineteen hundred representative entries covers a wide spectrum of scholarship on Socrates and his influence. Included works encompass all historical periods through 1987, concentrating on materials written in or translated into English, French, German, Ancient Greek, Italian, Latin, Portuguese, and Spanish. A variety of works is represented: books, chapters, dissertations, journal and newspaper articles, and conference proceedings. The section on Socrates's influence contains references to literature, opera, television, and film.

Socrates is organized into twenty-three sections, including primary and secondary sources, the Socratic problem, biographical literature, special studies, and other reference works. Works that pertain to more than one section are cross-listed. The bibliography also provides a list of journal and periodical titles with place of publication and an index of authors.

Navia and Katz introduce each of the twenty-three bibliographic sections with at least a brief description of what is included. Introductions to the earliest sections, which provide editions and translations of primary sources, give an overview of the scholarly discussions concerning these sources.

The authors' characterization of their annotations as merely descriptive does not do justice to their work. Navia and Katz succinctly identify major issues, arguments, and conclusions of each of the works listed. Not only do they lead the reader to the major works, but through the annotations and organization, they sketch the dimensions of Socratic scholarship.

The one disappointment of this work is the uneven quality of the print, although it is not so poor that it detracts from the worth of the work itself.

This bibliography is highly recommended for all academic libraries because of its potential use for specialists and for those who need an introductory overview of Socratic scholarship.

Joan B. Fiscella

1304. Potter, Karl H., with Austin B. Creel and Edwin Gerow. **Guide to Indian Philosophy.** Boston, G. K. Hall, 1988. 159p. index. (Asian Philosophies and Religions Resource Guides). $37.50. LC 88-7031. ISBN 0-8161-7904-2.

This is a selective bibliography of English-language *secondary* studies on Indian philosophy. It lists and annotates 884 books and articles published up to 1985 (later in a few instances), with some emphasis on works published since 1975. Articles must be at least ten pages in length. A fair proportion are in a few key journals, notably *Philosophy East and West* and the *Journal of Indian Philosophy*. All items are arranged in a single alphabetical sequence by author. This arrangement places the burden for subject access on the two indexes: one for names, including not only personal names but also the names of works treated as subjects, and one for other subject terms, including Sanskrit as well as English-language terms. The subject index is reasonably well done but not faultless. For example, an article comparing Buddhism with Western existential philosophies could not be located under either existentialism or Buddhism. Another, on free will, was not listed under freedom of the will.

Chief editor Karl Potter brings solid credentials to his work on this publication. Himself the author of eight items listed in this guide, he is also the general editor of the *Encyclopedia of Indian Philosophies* (see *ARBA* 83, entry 1055) and of its bibliography volume (see

517

ARBA 85, entry 1279). The latter, a massive and comprehensive bibliography, is to be distinguished from the work under review, which is far more modest by virtue of its selectivity and the restriction to English-language secondary literature, but within its scope more helpful to the nonspecialist by virtue of its descriptive annotations. The annotations, incidentally, are at times refreshingly informal.

The meaning of "Indian philosophy" for the purpose of this guide is left somewhat indefinite. The preface indicates, rather vaguely, that the compilers intend by it mainly "the subject of bondage and liberation and the methods of gaining the latter." This characterization, whatever one might read into it, is applied loosely enough that the bibliography encompasses all the usual subdivisions of philosophy, from epistemology, metaphysics, and logic to ethics and social, political, and legal philosophy. At the same time, the compilers have attempted, they say, to include only works having philosophical as opposed to "religious" or "literary" relevance. These distinctions are not defined, despite their notoriously problematic character in relation to Indian thought. [R: Choice, Dec 88, p. 632]   Hans E. Bynagle

1305.   Taylor, Donald S. **R. G. Collingwood: A Bibliogrpahy: The Complete Manuscripts and Publications, Selected Secondary Writings, with Selective Annotation.** New York, Garland, 1988. 279p. index. (Garland Bibliographies of Modern Critics and Critical Schools, Vol. 11; Garland Reference Library of the Humanities, Vol. 810). $40.00. LC 88-4041. ISBN 0-8240-7797-0.

Collingwood was a major figure in twentieth-century philosophy of history and art, as well as in the archaeology of Roman Britain. Taylor, who has written several pieces on this thinker, here compiles both a primary and a secondary bibliography. The primary bibliography attempts to be comprehensive of all materials written by Collingwood, including the large number of manuscripts and letters held in the Bodleian; this section is largely reprinted from volume 24 of *History and Theory* (1960-). The secondary bibliography contains a selected list of almost two hundred books, articles, and essays concerning the philosopher's thought on two topics: history and art. Though selective, it appears to include most major books and a wide range of shorter pieces.

Just as the sources in the secondary portion are chosen with a focus, Taylor follows this focus in annotating the primary bibliography. Only those works which cover history or aesthetics are annotated (sometimes to several pages in length); all others are unannotated. The annotations themselves are quite useful, especially in placing any of Collingwood's works in the context of his other publications. The detail of some of these summaries, combined with the forty-page introduction, can serve as a brief introduction to this philosopher for the unfamiliar. But in spite of the quality of annotating present, one wishes that more of the original materials had been annotated; the topical filter used to select what to abstract (and what to include as secondary literature) is limiting. However, what *is* here will be very useful in most academic libraries. [R: Choice, Nov 88, p. 470]   Christopher W. Nolan

BIOGRAPHIES

1306.   Bales, Eugene F. **A Ready Reference to Philosophy East and West.** Lanham, Md., University Press of America, 1988. 289p. index. $24.50. ISBN 0-8191-6640-4.

"Ready-reference" can mean a multitude of things, but here it refers to an outline history of philosophy that mainly strings together brief summaries of individual philosophers and, to some extent, schools of philosophy. These summaries are comparable in length and content to the alphabetically arranged entries typically found in single-volume philosophical dictionaries, notably Antony Flew's *Dictionary of Philosophy* (see *ARBA* 80, entry 1086), although Bales includes more individuals than Flew or any other current dictionary. To this extent, then, Bale's "ready-reference" might function somewhat similarly to a dictionary, with the advantage of placing each summary within its appropriate historical context. This function, moreover, is facilitated by two "quick alphabetical indexes" placed in the front, one to philosophers and another to philosophical theories and movements. On the other hand, it is possible to describe this as simply an exceptionally compressed history, and not necessarily to be treated as a reference work. Aimed at undergraduate philosophy students and the general reader, it is competently done, though it lacks the authoritative touch of most compact histories turned out by more "mainstream" publishers. The inclusion of Eastern philosophy (here confined to Indian and Chinese) along with Western philosophy in a single volume is a fairly unusual benefit, as is the attention to Russian philosophy under twentieth-century Western philosophy. This is the sort of work that comes in handy now and then, even if it cannot be recommended as a priority acquisition for most libraries. [R: Choice, May 88, p. 1378]   Hans E. Bynagle

1307. Kennedy, Leonard A. **A Catalogue of Thomists, 1270-1900.** Houston, Tex., Center for Thomistic Studies, University of St. Thomas; distr., Notre Dame, Ind., University of Notre Dame Press, 1987. 240p. index. $29.95. LC 86-72913. ISBN 0-268-00763-2.

Kennedy provides a sort of biographical checklist of Thomists, that is, theologians and philosophers who follow the thought of St. Thomas Aquinas. He has included those thinkers who claimed to be (or are described as) Thomists, as well as those whose book titles seemed to indicate Thomistic work. The entry for each of the approximately two thousand people listed includes birth and death dates, if known, up to three titles of works written by that person, and an indication of what sources provide fuller biographic or bibliographic information. The thinkers are arranged chronologically by century, then by religious order, and finally by country of origin. The table of contents contains a tabulation of the number of entries in each category, allowing one to get an overview of the interest in Thomas's thought during different eras and among different religious groups. A name index concludes the volume.

This work may be useful to those doing historical research on less-known figures in the Thomistic school, principally for identification. But it will probably be peripheral for those researching the major figures of the tradition, on whom much more comprehensive reference materials are available. The amount of information provided on any figure here is quite minimal. Also, the author notes that difficult to pursue items were often omitted, so the potential use of this as a comprehensive catalog of a major intellectual school is diminished.

Christopher W. Nolan

29 Religion

GENERAL WORKS

Bibliographies

1308. Hunt, Thomas C., and James C. Carper. **Religious Colleges and Universities in America: A Selected Bibliography.** New York, Garland, 1988. 374p. index. (Garland Reference Library of Social Science, Vol. 422). $54.00. LC 88-14737. ISBN 0-8240-6648-0.

Thirty-five contributors have combined efforts in this sequel to *Religious Schools*, published in 1986 (see *ARBA* 87, entry 326). Here the subject is "private colleges and universities that are, or have been, religiously affiliated" (introduction). After one chapter on general works and two chapters on the relationship of government to religious higher education, the bulk of this work is spread among twenty-five chapters organized by denominational traditions. Although the diversity of schools represented does require, as the introduction suggests, some variety of arrangement, this work would have been helped by greater standardization of design. For example, the chapter on Presbyterian colleges is arranged alphabetically by school, but the chapter on Reformed colleges lists entries by author.

There are other organizational problems. Gordon College is listed under Bible Schools, although for a long time it has been a liberal arts school. Wheaton College (Illinois) is found both under independent colleges and United Church of Christ colleges. Many double entries result. Schools that are no longer religious in character, like Harvard University, are included, but the explanation is unclear. William Ringstenberg's *The Christian College* can be found in four different places. Some chapters have helpful introductory essays and annotated entries, but others have neither.

These problems will no doubt frustrate the user. However, for the extent of coverage (there are about twenty-three hundred entries), one must speak appreciatively of the achievement of the compilers. Together with its predecessor and the forthcoming *Religious Seminaries* (scheduled for 1989), *Religious Colleges and Universities* will be part of a significant bibliographic trilogy on American religious education. Author and subject indexes complete the work.

John R. Muether

1309. Pearl, Patricia. **Children's Religious Books: An Annotated Bibliography.** New York, Garland, 1988. 316p. index. (Garland Reference Library of the Humanities, Vol. 689). $45.00. LC 87-14374. ISBN 0-8240-8531-0.

This comprehensive, annotated bibliography of religious books for children is a welcome addition to the field. Patricia Pearl has assembled a list of 1,123 entries which gives an overview of children's literature that has some overt religious theme. The age range is preschool to grade 6.

The bibliography is arranged by subject and then by author. Eight of the ten major subject categories are Christian. Sections 9 and 10 cover Judaism and non-Judeo-Christian religions. Pearl comments in the preface that the list appears weighted toward Protestant Christianity, but she correctly explains that Protestant Christian publishers have a large output of children's religious books. Books from Roman Catholic, Jewish, Hindu, and Baha'i publishing houses are included.

Annotations for each entry are appropriately descriptive of religious aspects and more critical in literary and illustrative concepts. Annotations are well written and helpful. Each annotation is numbered to correspond to the ones found in the author and title indexes. A directory of religious publishers is also included.

This new bibliographic source is a major development in the neglected field of children's religious literature. Highly recommended. [R: RBB, Aug 88, p. 1899]

Patricia Tipton Sharp

1310. Pearl, Patricia. **Religious Books for Children: An Annotated Bibliography.** rev. ed. Portland, Oreg., Church and Synagogue Library Association, 1988. 36p. index. $6.95pa. LC 83-7339. ISBN 0-915324-21-0.

The Church and Synagogue Library Association has published a revised edition of its 1983 annotated bibliography by Patricia Pearl, librarian for the First Presbyterian Church in Martinsdale, Virginia. "Religion" is interpreted to mean mostly the Judeo-Christian faith, although three of the thirty-six pages are devoted to "Conflict and Ecumenism," Buddhism, Hinduism, Islam, native American faith, and Sikhism. Every entry is annotated, and includes prices (as of June 1988) and ages appropriate for the material. The author has aimed for currency, so only imprints from 1980 on are included. Entries are by a detailed subject arrangement, with additional access through separate author and title indexes.

The annotations show some sensitivity to race and gender, and comment critically on style and content when appropriate. Despite inclusion of other faiths, the emphasis is largely mainstream Christian, and because of this and the dates of publication, this bibliography would be most helpful for Christian church librarians seeking to update an already existing collection of materials for children ages preschool through sixth grade. [R: BL, 1 Oct 88, p. 331]

Marilyn R. Pukkila

Dictionaries and Encyclopedias

1311. Bishop, Peter, and Michael Darton, eds. **The Encyclopedia of World Faiths: An Illustrated Survey of the World's Living Religions.** New York, Facts on File, 1987. 352p. illus. (part col.). maps. bibliog. index. $40.00. ISBN 0-8160-1860-X.

For students and general readers, this encyclopedia provides an excellent introduction to the great variety of religious beliefs and practices found in the world today. An authoritative list of contributors, comprehensive content presentation, and extensive, detailed illustrations will make this encyclopedia a popular addition to general library collections.

Defining religion according to Ninian Smart's model, which suggests that the six dimensions of religion are ritual, myth, doctrine, ethics, social, and experiential, the

editors have compiled articles on twelve major religions: Judaism, Zoroastrianism, Christianity, Islam, Babism and the Baha'i Faith, Hinduism, Jainism, Buddhism, Sikhism, Confucianism, Taoism, and Shinto. Each article deals in particulars, outlining the main features of the religion according to Smart's model.

Chapters are also included on the general nature of religion, the relevance of religion in the modern world, and on new religious movements in modern Western society and among primal peoples. New religious movements in modern Western society refer primarily to religions that were founded in the 1950s or earlier and attracted widespread attention during the 1960s and 1970s. There are no references to "new age spiritualism."

To aid readers in visually comparing and contrasting the practices and beliefs of different faiths, eight color sections are presented under the themes of faith and life, gods and gurus, religious leaders, prophets and teachers, death and afterlife, festivals, myths and legends, and life cycles. These special sections are interspersed within the chapters without clear indications of where chapter text ends or is picked up again. Because these sections are of interest for their photography and the opportunity to make comparisons, they should have been listed in the table of contents and otherwise noted and highlighted.

Finally, this reviewer would have preferred to see a more comprehensive index. For example, some entries I would have liked to have found were *women*, *icons*, and a cross-reference from the Protestant Episcopal Church to Anglican Communion (this last omission is no doubt due to the fact that the encyclopedia was first published in the United Kingdom). [R: BR, Sept/Oct 88, p. 51; Choice, May 88, p. 1420; LJ, 15 Mar 88, p. 51; RBB, Aug 88, pp. 1902-3]

Debbie Burnham-Kidwell

1312. **The Encyclopedia of American Religions: Religious Creeds: A Compilation of More Than 450 Creeds, Confessions, Statements of Faith, and Summaries of Doctrine....** J. Gordon Melton, ed. Detroit, Gale, 1988. 838p. index. $125.00. LC 87-30384. ISBN 0-8103-2132-7.

J. Gordon Melton of the Institute for the Study of American Religion in Santa Barbara, California, has produced another monumental reference work under the Gale imprint. This title follows the same organizational scheme Melton used in his *Encyclopedia of American Religions* (see *ARBA* 88, entry 1390), with religious families arranged into twenty-three chapters and further subdivided according to denominations and sects.

This work presents the text of more than 450 creeds, confessions, and statements of belief from denominations in the United States and Canada representing Christian, Jewish, Islamic, Buddhist, and Hindu traditions as well as various minor groups (an area of special expertise for the compiler).

A major consideration here is the reliability of the texts produced. The compiler has made no attempt to provide "detailed textual analysis, or variant readings of a text, except in those few cases in which contemporary Christian churches disagree over the exact wording of the older creeds" (p. xxi). Melton has corrected typographical errors and altered formats for stylistic consistency and clarity but has retained authentic wording, grammar, and punctuation. He appends a brief note to each creed placing it in an appropriate historical context. He concludes with a creed/organization name and keyword index.

In attempts to present creeds currently acknowledged by religious groups operating in the United States and Canada, Melton's work does not replace collections that illustrate changes in creedal statements over time. Thus, Philip Schaff's *The Creeds of Christendom* (Harper, 1919), John Leath's *Creeds of the Churches* (John Knox, 1982), and Arthur C. Cochrane's *Reformed Confessions of the 16th Century* (Westminster, 1966) remain as useful as before in tracing the historical development of ideas. What Melton offers is an up-to-date collection unmatched by any other recent source. [R: Choice, July/Aug 88, p. 1674; LJ, 15 May 88, p. 77; RBB, Aug 88, p. 1902; WLB, May 88, p. 110]   John Mark Tucker

1313.   **The Encyclopedia of Religion. Volume 16: Index.** Mircea Eliade, ed.-in-chief. New York, Macmillan, 1987. 482p. index. $1,200.00/set (Volume 16 included in price of set). LC 86-5432. ISBN 0-02-909890-4.

Following by almost a year the fifteen base volumes of the *Encyclopedia of Religion* (see *ARBA* 88, entry 1392), the index volume, number 16, brings to a welcome conclusion this stupendous scholarly project. As promised, it includes not only a "thorough topical index," which lives fully up to expectations, but also a thirty-page synoptic outline of contents. The latter can expedite use by offering at a glance the principal articles on a given religion or group of religions (say, African traditional religions), or on a major theme (e.g., science and religion), followed by lists of (typically) "supporting articles" and "related articles," and sometimes other

subdivisions appropriate to the topic. Also in this volume is the directory of contributors, which identifies institutional affiliations as well as specific articles contributed.

Hans E. Bynagle

Handbooks

1314.   Ward, Hiley H. **My Friends' Beliefs: A Young Reader's Guide to World Religions.** New York, Walker, 1988. 183p. illus. maps. index. $18.95. LC 87-29953. ISBN 0-8027-6792-3.

Hiley H. Ward's interests in ecumenicity and in young people, both apparent in his previous publications, are brought together in this book. It contains profiles of the major groupings of the world's religious bodies. Each profile begins with a brief history of the religion, incorporating stories which illustrate the roots of some of the major emphases or themes of the faith. The history is followed by a discussion of its requirements and the practices of its members. Next is a discussion of branches of the religion, plus a list of interesting bits of information called "Things to Know," and an explanation of the holy days and the major symbols of the faith. The contemporary customs and practices of each group are presented through the eyes of one young member, whose picture introduces the profile and the section in which the young member discusses his beliefs and what he does as a member of that faith.

The first part of the book consists of chapters entitled "The Jewish Path," "The Hindu Path," "The Buddhist Path," "The Islamic Path," and "The Christian Path." Pages 67-168 treat various Christian groups: Roman Catholics, Greek Orthodox, Episcopalians, Lutherans, Presbyterians, Methodists, Baptists, Pentecostals, and then, in one final chapter, "Other Groups."

The book is attractively laid out and is short enough to invite rather than intimidate young readers. The inherent difficulties of "explaining" theological terms concisely, with the added challenge of making the explanation clear to young minds, are apparent in such sentences as: "Grace means the life of God in us or God dwelling in us, and with it one enters heaven" (p. 74). A little more precision in editing would have given the book more clarity and polish. For example, in the description of the Five Pillars of Islam (pp. 47-51), the names of two of the pillars are italicized but the other three are not. This is an attractive, interesting book for public and school libraries and the libraries of religious institutions. [R: VOYA, Aug 88, pp. 151-52]   Dorothy E. Jones

Periodicals and Serials

1315. Fieg, Eugene C., Jr., comp. **Religion Journals and Serials: An Analytical Guide.** Westport, Conn., Greenwood Press, 1988. 218p. index. (Annotated Bibliographies of Serials: A Subject Approach, No. 13). $45.00. LC 87-32276. ISBN 0-313-24513-4.

This bibliography of 328 titles in English was selected from approximately nineteen hundred religious journals and serials. Primary emphasis is placed on the major Eastern and Western traditions, although selected others appear in the categories primal religions, spiritualism, and modern faiths. The last category has five entries: one each for Mormonism, religious humanism, and Baha'i, and two for secular humanism. The six entries in spiritualism cover psychical research, healing, and "formative spirituality."

Bibliographic information for many though not all entries is fairly extensive. Names of editors, as well as information on whether a journal is illustrated and/or accepts advertising might have been omitted since updated information could be verified easily in other sources. Fully one-fifth of the volume is devoted to indexes: geographic, title, subject, audience, and publisher, the last perhaps less useful than the others. Of the twenty chapters, the one on Eastern religions has only nine entries. More extensive coverage is allotted to Christianity, which is subdivided into some nine sections, among them Bible studies, history of Christianity, practical theology, and ecumenism. In this context, the subject index provides some additional access which can also appear arbitrary. For example, there are subject entries for the Lutheran Church and the Church of England, but none for Presbyterians. While audience is an obvious consideration for collection development, a separate index is unnecessary since the target audience is listed in each entry.

The annotations themselves lack stylistic grace. Ponderous declarative sentences, coupled with monotonous phraseology, confuse rather than clarify. Verbosity and editorializing appear.

The volume purports to address the needs of both scholars and collection development librarians. However, the results are less impressive than they might have been. [R: Choice, Oct 88, p. 290]   Bernice Bergup

BIBLE STUDIES

1316. The Eerdmans Analytical Concordance to the Revised Standard Version of the Bible. Richard E. Whitaker with James E. Goehring and Research Personnel of the Institute for Antiquity and Christianity, comps. Grand Rapids, Mich., William B. Eerdmans, 1988. 1548p. index. $49.95. ISBN 0-8028-2403-X.

The Revised Standard Version (RSV) of the Bible is a widely used and well-respected English translation of the Old Testament, New Testament, and Apocrypha. It is read by students, laypersons, ministers, and scholars. This concordance can easily and profitably be used by each group.

The basis of this computer-generated concordance is an alphabetical listing in English of almost every word found in the RSV. (Proper names and most numerals are listed separately.) Each English word (or sometimes phrase) is followed by the Hebrew, Greek, Aramaic, or Latin expressions that correspond to it. It is seen that the same English word frequently represents a number of different words in the original languages.

After this material, there is the citation (by chapter and verse) of each occurrence of the word in the RSV, the context of this usage (by quoting surrounding material), and a reference to indicate which particular word in Hebrew, Greek, or other original language is being translated. Those who have no familiarity with the ancient languages will pass over the non-English data; however, individuals with only a little bit of such knowledge will be able to use the data surprisingly well. Of course, full usage of the analytical features (including separate indexes of Hebrew, Greek, Aramaic, and Latin words) is reserved for those with competence in the biblical languages.

Since this is a concordance only to the RSV, it cannot be used equally well with any other English version. However, the RSV is a mainline translation, and much of its vocabulary will be found in other texts, especially those in the King James tradition. In sum, this well-conceived and sturdily bound volume should find a place in the reference section of most libraries. [R: WLB, Nov 88, p. 124]

Leonard J. Greenspoon

1317. The Eerdmans Bible Dictionary. By W. H. Gispen and others. Allen C. Myers, rev. ed. Grand Rapids, Mich., William B. Eerdmans, 1987. 1094p. illus. maps. (col.). $29.95. LC 87-13239. ISBN 0-8028-2402-1.

This new one-volume comprehensive dictionary (nearly five thousand entries within 1,094 pages) is an expanded and updated translation of the 1975 edition of the Dutch *Bijbelse Encyclopedie*. First published in 1950 under the editorship of distinguished New Testament scholar F. W. Grosheide, the work was thoroughly revised and published in two volumes in 1975. The revision incorporated articles from yet another work edited by Grosheide, the *Christelijke Encyclopedie*. This first English edition, expanded still further by the inclusion of entries on topics not previously treated, reflects recent archaeological discoveries and includes insights from literary, historical, and sociological studies. Most major items from the earlier work have also been revised and expanded. Forty-eight persons—not readily recognized—from a variety of denominational stances have contributed unsigned articles to this "primarily evangelical" work which identifies every person and place named in the Bible, explains important biblical theology concepts, examines the contents and background of each book of the Bible, and describes physical and cultural aspects of the world of the Bible. The writers have addressed a broad spectrum of divergent points of interpretation.

This edition is based on the Revised Standard Version, but attention is given to alternate readings in other modern translations, frequently via *see* references. The work, in compact format (6 by 9¼ inches) includes a list of abbreviations, a transliteration scheme, and pronunciation guide; a limited number of illustrations, tables, charts, and line drawings; and a twelve-page collection of Hammond colored maps (located in the middle). Bibliographies have been added, but only to a small number of entries.

The work surpasses in quality *The New Westminster Dictionary of the Bible*, edited by Henry Snyder Gehman (see *ARBA* 71, entry 1322) and *Dictionary of the Bible*, by John L. McKenzie (Bruce, 1965). It is more current than *The New Bible Dictionary*, edited by J. D. Douglas (Tyndale, 1982), and *Zondervan Pictorial Biblical Dictionary*, edited by M. C. Tenney (Zondervau, 1969). It is equal to the newer *Harper's Bible Dictionary*, edited by Paul A. Achtemeier (see *ARBA* 86, entry 1382), even though the perspectives taken by these two are obviously different. It merits, and has already received, high praise from a variety of scholars, as evidenced by the quotes on the book jacket. [R: RBB, 15 Jan 88, pp. 842, 844]

Glenn R. Wittig

1318.   Fausset, A. R. **Home Bible Study Dictionary.** Grand Rapids, Mich., Kregel Publications, 1987. 753p. illus. index. $18.95pa. LC 87-16883. ISBN 0-8254-2625-1.

This Bible dictionary is a reprint of an edition originally printed in the late 1800s. It has the substance of other dictionaries plus extensive articles on such subjects as Antichrist,

inspiration, millennium, prayer, etc. There are also six hundred line drawings which help one visualize obscure Bible places and objects. It is alphabetically arranged, with a scripture index which will assist in finding answers to questions on specific Bible verses.

This is a classic work, worthy of reprint. It would be helpful had the publisher provided more background information about the author. The print is extremely small, but readable.

Thomas L. Hart

1319.   Gonen, Rivka. **Biblical Holy Places: An Illustrated Guide.** New York, Macmillan, 1987. 288p. illus. (part col.). maps. index. $17.95pa. ISBN 0-02-085140-5.

This is a descriptive guide to selected lands and landmarks mentioned in the Bible—both the Old and New Testament. Each of the 210 entries offers: (1) a glimpse of the past, including the biblical significance of each place featured, (2) a contemporary viewpoint, and (3) relevant biblical references. There is also information about archaeological developments. Impressive color photographs accompany most of the sites described here. In addition, there are maps, which further enhance the usefulness of this volume to travelers, biblical scholars, and students of the Middle East.

Entries are arranged alphabetically, first by country, then by place name. As might be expected, the primary emphasis is on Jerusalem, Bethlehem, Nazareth, and Rome. However, the guide gives coverage to many other sites mentioned in the Bible, particularly those in and around the Mediterranean, including the lands inhabited by or visited by biblical prophets and apostles.

There is a "Historical Outline" naming major events and developments dating from Paleolithic times to the mid-nineteenth century, which the reader may refer to for historical perspective. An index with cross-references completes the volume.   Dianne Brinkley Catlett

1320.   Green, Jay P., and others, eds. **A Concise Lexicon to the Biblical Languages.** Peabody, Mass., Hendrickson, 1987. 1v. (various paging). $14.95pa. ISBN 0-913573-85-X.

This book consists of a short dictionary of biblical Hebrew (253 pages) and a New Testament Greek dictionary (143 pages). In both parts, the user is given the grammatical description of the entry word, its most important occurrences, and its basic English equivalents; if possible, the basis of the word's derivation is also given. In the Hebrew part, the meanings of the derivative conjugations (*Piel, Hitpael,* etc.)

are given under the root but as a separate sense of the verb.

The original feature of this lexicon consists in the fact that cross-references within each entry direct the user to further information to be found in several basic books of reference. Each Hebrew and Greek entry is numbered by the number under which the entry word appears in *Strong's Exhaustive Concordance* (Broadman, 1978). In addition, the Hebrew entry words are cross-referenced to the respective entries in Brown, Driver, and Briggs's *Gesenius Hebrew and English Lexicon* (Clarendon Press, 1952); the Greek entries are cross-referenced to Bauer, Arndt, and Gingrich's *A Greek-English Lexicon,* to Thayer's *Greek-English Lexicon,* and to Kittel's *Theologisches Wörterbuch zum Neuen Testament* (Stuggart, 1932-1972). It is this cross-referencing that makes this book a very practical tool that will save much time for the user whose desire to learn more is stronger than his knowledge of the biblical languages.

L. Zgusta

1321. **Harper's Bible Commentary.** James L. Mays and others, eds. San Francisco, Calif., Harper & Row, 1988. 1326p. illus. (part col.). maps. index. $32.50; $34.95 (thumb-indexed). LC 88-45148. ISBN 0-06-065541-0; 0-06-065542-9 (thumb-indexed).

Harper's Bible Commentary (*HBC*) is the first completely new one-volume biblical commentary to appear in a decade. Produced under the auspices of the Society of Biblical Literature, it serves as a companion to the recently released *Harper's Bible Dictionary* (*HBD*). In fact, throughout, *HBC* uses a reference system to direct the reader to further information in *HBD*. Both volumes are intended to present the results of mainstream biblical scholarship. Thus, this work can be seen as the successor to *Peake's Commentary on the Bible.* It is divided into eight parts: "Introduction," consisting of general essays, "The Biblical Story: Genesis to Esther," "Psalms and Wisdom," "The Prophetic Books," "The Apocrypha," "The Gospels and Acts," "The Pauline Letters," and "The General Letters to the Churches." In addition to the general essays there are other appropriately placed short essays which develop special topics (e.g., "Women in Genesis," "Jeremiah's Symbolic Actions," and "The Miracles of Jesus in Mark"). The list of contributors is an impressive who's who of contemporary biblical scholarship. Many of the authors have produced (or are producing) major works on the writings/subjects they have been assigned in *HBC.*

The appearance of another commentary should be justified, and in this case it is.

Biblical studies and related disciplines have not stood still in the past decade. This is especially true in the application of sociological and literary theory to the biblical world and literature. Some of the contributors to *HBC* are leaders in these areas and all are well versed in them. The awareness of the value of sociological and literary studies in understanding the Bible text is reflected in the introductions to and the section-by-section commentaries on the individual books and in several of the general introductory essays. Scholarly expertise is everywhere apparent but not usually obtrusive. The text will be easily understood by all users above the young adult level. Therefore, this volume is recommended for all public and academic collections.

Craig W. Beard

1322. Hupper, William G., comp. and ed. **An Index to English Periodical Literature on the Old Testament and Ancient Near Eastern Studies. Volume II.** Metuchen, N.J., American Theological Library Association and Scarecrow, 1988. 502p. (ATLA Bibliography Series, No. 21). $45.00. LC 86-31448. ISBN 0-8108-2126-5.

This is the second source in a series which is an analytical index to periodical literature from 1769 to 1969. Volume 2 includes over seven thousand references from more than six hundred journals to articles on ancient Near Eastern history; ancient Near Eastern personalities; nations and peoples; chronology of the ancient Near East, including biblical (Hebrew), Assyrian, Babylonian, Egyptian, Greek, and Ptolemaic chronology; scientific thought in the ancient Near East; astronomy/astrology; ecological and meteorological studies; demography; place names; geological studies; geographical studies; levitical cities of refuge; and an alphabetical listing of articles on cities and places within Israel/Palestine, with nearly three hundred entries for Jerusalem. The author estimates that there will be over 100,000 entries when all of the volumes are completed. This source uses a classification scheme similar to one in an earlier work by Bruce Metzger, *Index to Periodical Literature on Christ and the Gospels* (Leider, Netherlands: E. J. Brill, 1966).

Research scholars might prefer descriptive and critical annotations, but this source does include a detailed classification of the entries which will make it very useful. The author states that 90 percent of volume 3 was complete at the printing of this source, volume 4 is in the computer, and work had begun on volume 5. The editor feels that volumes 4 and 5 will be highlights of the series, consisting of the articles dealing directly with the Hebrew scriptures, both critically and exegetically. A subject/author index is planned when all of the volumes are complete.   Thomas L. Hart

1323. The International Standard Bible Encyclopedia. Volume Four: Q-Z. rev. ed. Geoffrey W. Bromiley and others, eds. Grand Rapids, Mich., William B. Eerdmans, 1988. 1211p. illus. (part col.). maps. $39.95. LC 79-12280. ISBN 0-8028-8164-5.

In 1929 the Howard-Severance Company copyrighted the completed edition of the *International Standard Bible Encyclopedia* (*ISBE*), an important multivolume work that had been in continual production since its debut in 1915. The *ISBE* quickly won acclaim for solid biblical scholarship, its popularity being signified by its continual availability. Throughout most of its recent history, it has been sold in five-volume reprints by one of the leading evangelical publishing houses, William B. Eerdmans of Grand Rapids, Michigan.

After more than fifteen years of extensive rewriting and careful editorial work, Eerdmans completes, with this volume, a fully revised *ISBE* under the capable editorship of Geoffrey W. Bromiley. (For reviews of the first three volumes, see *ARBA* 80, entry 1056; *ARBA* 83, entry 1037; and *ARBA* 87, entry 1358). Associate editors Everett F. Harrison (New Testament), Roland K. Harrison (Old Testament), and William Sanford Lasor (biblical geography and archaeology) assisted Bromiley, Emeritus Professor of Church History and Historical Theology at Fuller Theological Seminary. These men, along with Gerald H. Wilson and Edgar W. Smith, Jr., constitute a solid corps of premier biblical scholars. With volume 4 the *ISBE* maintains the standards of scholarship, practicality, and thoroughness of coverage that characterize the first three and, taken together, the four revised volumes substantially enhance the traditions established in an earlier generation.

Typical entries identify the Greek or Hebrew origins of terms, references to biblical passages, historically based definitions, and brief bibliographical sources. Volume 4 alone reproduces more than five hundred photographs, including thirty-three color plates and eighty-six maps. The revised *ISBE* includes articles on every name of a person or place mentioned in the Bible as well as other terms that have ethical or theological meaning. It is based on the Revised Standard Version and contains references to the King James Version and the *New English Bible*. Students, pastors, and researchers engaged in serious study will want to begin with the new *ISBE*; devoted students of the Bible selecting only one research aid of any kind, whether it be dictionary, concordance, encyclopedia, or commentary, should choose the new *ISBE*. [R: RBB, 15 Dec 88, pp. 691-92]

John Mark Tucker

1324. Pritchard, James B., ed. The Harper Atlas of the Bible. San Francisco, Calif., Harper & Row, 1987. 254p. illus. (part col.). maps. index. $49.95. LC 86-675550. ISBN 0-06-181883-6.

This Harper atlas is a refreshing new look at combining scripture with photographs, drawings, and maps from a new perspective. This source conveys an almost tangible sense of the land, events, and people as portrayed in the Bible. It presents the historical eras – from the Old Testament, intertestamental, and the New Testament periods through Byzantine Palestine – but it also covers the important background to the times, including color spreads on customs, beliefs, and practices of the times as well as a glimpse into everyday life. Reading the text is a fascinating experience. It details ancient scripts, crafts, industries, the equipment of war, and considerably more.

The atlas includes an extensive chronology, a glossary summarizing biographical details of most of the biblical personalities involved, and an exhaustive place-name index that gives biblical and extra-biblical names with their exact location on the Palestine grid. This source provides a new perspective because of its inclusion of recent archaeological excavations. This information was never available in previous biblical atlases.

The book jacket provides a unique view of the Middle East. It is an airplane view from Egypt, looking toward Babylonia. This is the only time this perspective is provided. It illustrates the strategic location of Israel. Throughout the source there are new, refreshing illustrations with the maps. However, the drawing of Solomon's Jerusalem is disappointing; it looks like a series of mud huts. It may be accurate in scale, but not in architectural detail as described in the accompanying text. The view of Jerusalem at the time of Jesus portrays a feeling of grandeur, because the architectural detail is more distinct. A wonderful addition to the area of Bible atlases, setting a new standard of quality. [R: Choice, Feb 88, p. 886; LJ, Jan 88, pp. 76-77; LJ, 15 Apr 88, p. 33; RBB, 15 Feb 88, pp. 982, 984]

Thomas L. Hart

1325. Unger, Merrill F. The New Unger's Bible Dictionary. rev. ed. Chicago, Moody Press, 1988. 1400p. illus. (part col.). maps. index. $29.95. LC 88-9189. ISBN 0-8024-9037-9.

A number of one-volume Bible dictionaries currently on the market are characterized by practical arrangement and scholarly yet clear definitions. Moody Press, a "ministry" of the Moody Bible Institute, stakes its claim to a rightful share of this market with *The New Unger's Bible Dictionary*. The seriousness with which Moody approached this project is indicated in its selection of R. K. Harrison (Emeritus Professor of Old Testament at Wycliffe College, Toronto) as editor, accompanied by Howard F. Vos and Cyril J. Barber.

Unger's was originally written by Merrill F. Unger, a graduate of the doctoral program in semitics at Johns Hopkins University and former professor of Old Testament studies at Dallas Theological Seminary. Unger wrote numerous religious works, including the popular *Unger's Bible Handbook*, and he traced the origins of the present volume to the *Bible Encyclopedia*, edited by Charles Randall Barnes (Eaton and Mains, 1903). The Barnes source, issued variously in two-volume and three-volume sets, was compressed into one volume in 1913 as *The People's Bible Encyclopedia*, which emerged as an early twentieth-century model of the one-volume Bible dictionary. As Unger himself noted in introducing his first edition, he was indebted to William Smith's *Dictionary of the Bible* (Fleming H. Revell, 192?) and other various religious encyclopedias.

The present volume claims four special emphases: (1) archaeological information based on the latest contributions to scientific biblical archaeology, (2) historical-geographical characteristics of Near Eastern lands as they affected the Bible, (3) biographical entries about figures connected to biblical places and events, and (4) doctrinal beliefs widely held throughout Christendom. *The New Unger's* is based on the *New American Standard Bible*, with additional quotations from the King James Version and the *New International Version*. Three hundred photographs, two hundred illustrations, and fifty maps accompany the text. Students, pastors, and researchers will be pleased with this solid and reliable source, with its fine physical appearance and accurate definitions.

John Mark Tucker

1326. Watson, Francis. **A Guide to the New Testament**. Totowa, N.J., Barnes & Noble Books, 1987. 198p. maps. $24.95. LC 87-14531. ISBN 0-389-20767-5.

Francis Watson has, by his own admission, not prepared a Bible dictionary, although it is in alphabetical order. Nor does his guide appear to resemble a handbook discussing each book of the Bible in order of its appearance. Instead he has prepared a "guide book" in which he has limited the entries "to make space for adequate discussion" (p. vii) with the purpose of discussing "various features of the New Testament as objectively as possible ..." (p. x) to help people study the Bible.

This guide presents "points which seem to [Watson] to be most interesting or relevant" (p. viii) from Abba to Zechariah. Watson avoids scholarly terms such as *parousia*, including them, however, in the cross-references index. He applies the historical-critical method to the guide, recognizing that there is some legitimate opposition to rigid application of the method.

The author provides a cross-reference index including the approximately 200 topics addressed in the book and around 150 cross-references. The user is guided to other topics by superscript numbers in the body of the text which refer to topics or subtopics in the cross-references index. This seems clumsy and unlikely to encourage users to pursue the additional information.

Watson appears to have reached his goals of readability and objectivity. His discussion of the virgin birth, for example, carefully outlines the reasons for the major opposing views without losing reader interest. He gives a careful explanation of the controversy between Paul and the Jewish Christians in Jerusalem, pointing out the difference in presentation in Acts and in Paul's writing. His explanations accurately reflect the understanding of scholars of the New Testament.

Watson points out the doubtful authorship of some of "Paul's" letters, but does not always present the authors who have been proposed. Blair's *Illustrated Bible Handbook* (see *ARBA* 88, entry 1401), for instance, gives Apollos, Luke, Barnabas, Clement, Silvanus, Philip, Priscilla, and Origen as suggested authors of Hebrews. Watson notes merely that there is no agreement.

Seminarians and pastors will probably find little use for Watson's guide, since they would have available multiple-volume dictionaries and handbooks. But serious laypersons, such as Sunday school teachers, and, therefore, church libraries, would find *A Guide to the New Testament* a useful supplement to a one-volume Bible dictionary which would cover many more topics but with much less detail. It could also be used by laypersons to support Bible handbooks because of its alphabetical order and concentration on selected topics.

Betty Jo Buckingham

BUDDHISM

1327. Soothill, William Edward, and Lewis Hodous, comps. **A Dictionary of Chinese Buddhist Terms: With Sanskrit and English Equivalents and a Sanskrit-Pali Index.** Delhi, India, Motilal Banarsidass; distr., Columbia, Mo., South Asia Books, c1937, 1987. 510p. index. $44.00. ISBN 81-208-0319-1.

When originally published in 1937, this resource was the first dictionary of Chinese Mahayana Buddhist terms in English. Identical reprints in 1975 and now 1987 still have no other competition. The compilers have put together a "working dictionary" for those dealing with the Chinese texts of canonical Buddhist documents. The necessity of such a reference source is dictated by the difficulty of working with a variety of Chinese translations of Sanskrit and Pali originals. Users will find this dictionary suitable only when working from the Chinese texts; there is no index from English terms or concepts to the Chinese, and no transliterations of the Chinese characters are given.

Entries are arranged by the number of strokes in the initial Chinese character. Following the main entry is the definition in English and, frequently, a discussion of related concepts. The definitions are generally clear, though some knowledge of Buddhist ideas is occasionally necessary in order to interpret the meanings. The introduction includes a list of Chinese characters that are particularly troublesome to identify, and an index to Sanskrit and Pali words used in the definitions completes the work.

Users needing help with the Chinese texts will find this tool important. Those more common readers who need definitions of English, Pali, or Sanskrit terms may wish to use T. O. Ling's *A Dictionary of Buddhism* (see *ARBA* 73, entry 1109) or C. Humphreys's *A Popular Dictionary of Buddhism* (see *ARBA* 77, entry 1038).   Christopher W. Nolan

CHRISTIANITY

Almanacs

1328. Blake, William D. **An Almanac of the Christian Church.** Minneapolis, Minn., Bethany House, 1987. 400p. index. $8.95pa. LC 87-32643. ISBN 0-87123-897-7.

Blake's compilation inherits the tradition popularized in the late nineteenth century by Robert Chambers, whose *Book of Days* underwent several editions over a period of nearly forty years. More recent sources in the same vein include Jane Hatch's *The American Book of Days*, third edition (see *ARBA* 80, entry 1098), Ruth Gregory's *Anniversaries and Holidays*, fourth edition (see *ARBA* 85, entry 1230), and Howard V. Harper's *Days and Customs of All Faiths* (Fleet, 1957). By choosing the almanac format, Blake aims for the general reader, claiming that "undiluted history can become oppressively time-consuming and, to some, quite boring" (p. 10). These brief entries accordingly ask little of the reader but offer much in return.

The scope of this work is primarily Protestant, but includes Catholic references as well. References are drawn from events, movements, official documents, publications, and correspondence from the lives of "hundreds of the church's earliest theologians and pastors, missionaries and hymnwriters, evangelists and Bible scholars, denominational and religious leaders" (p. 10). Generally, some six to eight entries are given for each date in the year; the compiler quotes heavily from hymn writers and from authors of religious and theological works. A sample from August 26th notes Michelangelo's commission to carve the *Pieta* (1498); the death of Adam Clarke, English Methodist clergyman and commentator (1832); the publication of the American Standard Version of the *New Testament* (1901); and a quotation from Christian statesman Dag Hammarskjöld (1956): "Bless your uneasiness as a sign that there is still life in you" (pp. 236-37). This almanac may be used for study, devotional, or entertainment purposes. It is an honorable contribution to an honorable tradition.

John Mark Tucker

Archives

1329. Heuser, Frederick J., Jr. **A Guide to Foreign Missionary Manuscripts in the Presbyterian Historical Society.** Westport, Conn., Greenwood Press, 1988. 108p. illus. maps. index. (Publication of The Presbyterian Historical Society; Bibliographies and Indexes in World History, No. 11). $39.95. LC 87-34088. ISBN 0-313-26249-7.

The Presbyterian Historical Society contains the national archives for the Presbyterian Church (U.S.A.). Since its founding it has gathered materials related to American Presbyterianism. This guide is limited to the society's manuscript and archival materials that document missionary work outside of the continental United States. It does not include PHS's extensive published holdings, photographs, and oral history collections.

Even with these limitations of scope, this little book remains valuable, and not only for documenting the work of American Presbyterians abroad. It is important also for the study of developing Third World countries and especially for the Western influences on those countries.

The guide is arranged geographically (Africa, Asia, and the Middle East) and sub-arranged by country. For each country, an overview of missionary activity is given. Each country's archival collections begin with files of the secretaries of the foreign mission board; the other collections are generally the papers of the missionaries who labored in those fields. The size of each collection is described, followed by two- or three-paragraph summaries of the contents (including biographical sketches of the missionaries). Altogether the work lists 109 collections.

There is an extensive index that includes names, places, and subjects. Also included is a brief history of Presbyterian missions. Some maps and photographs round out the work.

John R. Muether

1330. **Resources for Canadian Mennonite Studies: An Inventory and Guide to Archival Holdings at the Mennonite Heritage Centre.** Winnipeg, Man., Mennonite Heritage Centre, 1988. 135p. illus. bibliog. index. $7.50pa. ISBN 0-921258-00-3.

The Mennonite Heritage Centre has produced an excellent guide to its archival holdings. The guide briefly describes the center, its various collections (e.g., archives, audiovisuals, maps), and services and accommodations available to researchers.

The focus of the guide is on the archives and its three major categories of records: Mennonite church organizations, Mennonite congregations, and individuals. Descriptions of collections are divided into two sections: detailed descriptions of twenty-four major collections and brief descriptions of seventy-nine others. The former include a chronology of major events in the life of the person or organization; a list of relevant books, articles, theses, and dissertations; a summary of the composition of the collection which also indicates the availability of a finding aid; a provenance statement describing the collection's origins; and a scope and content note describing the contents of the collection in considerable detail. The brief descriptions omit the chronology and combine and summarize other parts of the description. The guide concludes with a select bibliography and an index.

An attractive format and concise, readable writing make the guide very easy to use. Its low price is refreshing. This is an outstanding example of a guide of its kind. It will go far toward making researchers aware of the center's resources and encouraging their use. It will also save distant researchers wasted trips and large telephone bills. Highly recommended wherever subject interest warrants.

Gari-Anne Patzwald

Bibliographies

1331.   Crumb, Lawrence N. **The Oxford Movement and Its Leaders: A Bibliography of Secondary and Lesser Primary Sources.** Metuchen, N.J., American Theological Library Association and Scarecrow, 1988. 706p. index. (ATLA Bibliography Series, No. 24). $62.50. LC 88-10217. ISBN 0-8108-2141-9.

The Reform Act of 1832 wrought all kinds of political, social, and religious changes throughout England. On 14 July 1833, to defend the established church against devastating encroachments of Parliament, John Keble preached on "national apostasy" at Oxford University. His sermon struck a responsive chord in those loyal to High Church ideals who refused to accept Parliament's implication that the church was the state's creature. Little did Keble realize that his sermon would initiate what was soon dubbed the "Oxford Movement." Today the term implies to some the entire Catholic movement in the Church of England; others define the movement more narrowly.

This bibliography limits the Oxford Movement to the first generation of Catholic versus Protestant activity, beginning with Keble's sermon of 1833 and ending in 1850 when the Gorham Judgment confirmed Keble's worst fears. Even within such a restriction, this volume lists some 5,688 citations to books, pamphlets, articles, theses, manuscripts, microforms, and tapes on the subject. Since this bibliography is primarily one of secondary sources, it excludes the works of Keble, John Henry Newman, and Edward Bouverie Pusey (the three most important figures in the movement), but it does list the works of many lesser associated figures. Arrangement is chronological, with detailed author, periodical, and subject indexes. The length of this bibliography prohibited annotations, as a preface explains while stating purpose and format. An introduction provides an excellent summary of the movement and a four-page chronology supplies important dates. An added feature is an appendix of 197 items listing editions, translations, and commentaries on Newman's *Apologia pro Vita Sua.* [R: Choice, Dec 88, p. 624]

G. A. Cevasco

1332. Elliott, Mark R., ed. **Christianity and Marxism Worldwide: An Annotated Bibliography.** Wheaton, Ill., Institute for the Study of Christianity and Marxism, Wheaton College, 1988. 136p. index. $12.00pa.

The comparison of Christianity with other world ideologies benefits the growth of important subdisciplines as well as the intellectual development of the students and faculty involved. Especially commendable is the concern of a reputable academic institution to advance cross-disciplinary dialog by establishing an institute for such a purpose. Wheaton College, long recognized for its special commitments to the Christian faith, hosts the Institute for the Study of Christianity and Marxism. Mark R. Elliott, the Institute's director, edited this work, the production of which was underwritten by a grant from the Fieldstead Institute.

The resulting work is an inexpensively produced paperback identifying about 350 items and arranged into the following chapters: "Theory," "The Soviet Union," "Eastern Europe," "China," "Asia outside China," "Latin American Liberation Theology," and "Africa." Each chapter features a brief essay on definitional and bibliographic issues written by scholars with substantial international experience and with backgrounds from the fields of political science, history, or religious studies.

Elliott describes this bibliography as his response to the questions he is asked most frequently: "What should I read on Christianity and Marxism?" Or, more specifically, "Where should I *begin reading* on the church in the Soviet Union, or in China, or wherever?" The published result is a handy guide to the ethos of Christian churches in Marxist/socialistic societies, largely but not exclusively in Third World settings. Elliott cautions that the "interface of Christianity and Marxism is sharp, jagged, and blood-stained" and, thus, that readers of the literature (he has identified) should anticipate a style of language that "stirs mighty and conflicting passions all across ... political and theological spectrums."   John Mark Tucker

1333. Jarboe, Betty M. **John and Charles Wesley: A Bibliography.** Metuchen, N.J., American Theological Library Association and Scarecrow, 1987. 404p. index. (ATLA Bibliography Series, No. 22). $39.50. LC 87-13005. ISBN 0-8108-2039-0.

John Wesley, the founder of Methodism, also influenced many educational, medical, political, and social aspects of English life. In addition, he had a strong impact on the American religious revival known as the "Second Great Awakening." This comprehensive bibliography includes writings about the Wesleys from 1791 to the 1980s. References to their parents, Samuel and Susanna, are also included. The compiler, a librarian at Indiana University, searched thirty indexes and abstracting services manually, plus seven computer databases. She also visited a number of libraries in England and the United States having collections of Wesleyana.

The bibliography is organized by format: bibliographies, books, articles, dissertations, poetry, drama, fiction, juvenile works, and miscellanea. Over 150 non-English-language publications are listed in part 2, arranged alphabetically by author. Library locations are indicated for hard-to-find items; repositories include those in the United States, Australia, England, Scotland, and Wales. The topical index, keyed to item numbers, uses LC subject headings, keyword indexing, and two specialized authorities.

This thorough compilation should stand as the definitive source on the Wesleys for years to come. [R: Choice, May 88, p. 1382]

Gary D. Barber

1334. Rowe, Kenneth E., comp. and ed. **United Methodist Studies: Basic Bibliographies.** rev. ed. Nashville, Tenn., Abingdon, 1987. 80p. $3.50pa. LC 87-11495. ISBN 0-687-43110-7.

The purpose of this compact (5¼ by 8 inches), handy compendium, as clearly stated at the beginning, "is to provide a selected list of the basic resources for students and instructors of seminary-level courses in United Methodist history, doctrine, and polity." This work also establishes "minimum standards for libraries to support such courses." Numbered items (903) have been organized topically in eight parts: general resources, history, doctrine, polity, audiovisual resources, for children and youth, for new and continuing adult members, and basic library for students. Most parts contain a variety of subdivisions. "In addition to listing standard texts, past and present, emphasis has been placed on selecting the best modern critical interpretations in book form still in print." Occasionally key journal articles are also included. Annotations, when offered, are minimal.

I have three criticisms to make. First, part 6, "For Children and Youth," and part 7, "For New and Continuing Adult Members," while extremely short (two pages and only twenty-one items), run counter to the stated purpose of the work as a whole. Second, the section in part 1 on periodicals, certainly valuable in and of itself, seems to be comprehensive in coverage rather than selective (i.e., it goes beyond "minimum standard" requirements). Finally, the work also lacks an author/title, or at least an author, index.   Glenn R. Wittig

1335. Snyderwine, L. Thomas, ed. **Research-ing the Development of Lay Leadership in the Catholic Church since Vatican II: Bibliographi-cal Abstracts.** Lewiston, N.Y., Edwin Mellen Press, 1987. 192p. index. (Roman Catholic Studies, Vol. 1). $49.95. LC 87-12224. ISBN 0-88946-241-0.

Among some of the more important changes wrought by the Second Vatican Council are those dealing with the collegial paradigm for teaching and governance, and the emergence of the laity as an active force in ecclesial ministry. Input from lay and religious sessions ensured a fruitful dialog at the Fall 1987 Episcopal Synod on the Laity. Problems and needs surfaced, issues such as lay formation, lay spirituality, tensions in religious-lay ministry, and the role of women in the church. Any scholar or well-informed reader who wants to research and reflect upon such issues will find this volume of considerable help, for it contains abstracts of the most important books and articles on lay leadership written between 1957 and 1986.

Three separate indexes – author, title, and subject – allow quick access to material in the three hundred or so abstracts, which are, for the most part, objectively written. Any conclusions reached after reading these abstracts will prob-ably be a consequence of perspectives and values already held. There are undoubtedly some who will conclude that the laity has over-stepped the parameters endorsed by Vatican II. Others may contend that lay leadership is main-ly a matter of tokenism. Most readers should make the inference that lay leadership in the church today, though perhaps still in its adoles-cence, is evolving into a mature expression of its proper capabilities.

                                        G. A. Cevasco

1336. Swartley, Willard M., and Cornelius J. Dyck, eds. **Annotated Bibliography of Menno-nite Writings on War and Peace: 1930-1980.** Scottdale, Pa., Herald Press, 1987. 740p. index. $59.95. LC 87-14932. ISBN 0-8361-1292-X.

The Institute for Mennonite Studies has prepared a bibliography of approximately ten thousand English-language items related to peace and war issues written, printed, or pub-lished in North America by Mennonites. The period covered is approximately 1930 through 1980, a time of significant intellectual ferment in Mennonite circles. Publications selected include books, articles, news reports, editorials, letters to editors, poetry, theses, and dissertations. The majority appeared in Mennonite magazines.

The items are arranged under seventeen major subject headings (e.g., "The Bible, Peace, and War"; "Church and State"; "Conscientious Objection"; "Justice"), with appropriate sub-headings. Items relating significantly to more than one heading are repeated as necessary. The editors have defined their topic broadly to in-clude justice and civil rights issues that many may consider only peripherally, if at all, related to war and peace. Annotations, which are one or two sentences in length, vary in usefulness. Many fail to indicate the item's relevance to its subject heading or to describe the contents meaningfully. An author index is included.

As members of an historic peace church, Mennonites have been at the forefront in the articulation of nonresistance, peace, and justice positions, and this bibliography should interest students of twentieth-century religious, politi-cal, and social thought. It is a valuable addition to the growing body of scholarly publications from Herald Press because it provides access to materials not indexed elsewhere. It is recom-mended wherever interest warrants and finances permit its purchase. [R: Choice, Sept 88, p. 73]

                                        Gari-Anne Patzwald

Biographies

1337. Kleinz, John P. **The Who's Who of Heaven: Saints for All Seasons.** Westminster, Md., Christian Classics, 1987. 334p. bibliog. $12.95pa. LC 87-071420. ISBN 0-87061-136-4.

Before Vatican Council II, collections of lives of saints and biographies of individual saints were prominent on Catholic publishers' lists. Today there are not so many of these items, but books about saints written in recent years are invariably of better quality from the historian's and theologian's perspective. *The Who's Who of Heaven* is a good example of this "new hagiography." Painstaking research (sup-ported by over a dozen pages of notes) here records the lives of those saints considered to have the most modern appeal, those saints whose lives demonstrate that sanctity is remark-ably varied and readily capable of imitation – even in today's world.

An introduction delves into the question "What is a saint?" and explains why such indi-viduals are worthy of veneration. The first and longest chapter concentrates on Mary, the Queen of Saints, treats the myriad of ways Catholics honor her, explains the origin of various Marian hymns, and concludes with a history of popular Marian shrines. Among the seven chapters that follow are those devoted to remarkable men and women who should serve as role models for priests, nuns, and all

Christians; to missionaries who were martyred in the Americas, Africa, China, Japan, and New Guinea; to foundresses of viable religious congregations; to certain medieval saints; and to several contemporaries who someday may be beatified and canonized.

Although this volume lacks an index, it does have a detailed table of contents and a six-page bibliography. *Who's Who of Heaven* actually is more of a spiritual reader than a ready-reference tool, but still of value to large theology collections. [R: BL, 1 Jan 88, p. 732]
G. A. Cevasco

1338. Woodbridge, John D., ed. **Great Leaders of the Christian Church.** Chicago, Moody Press, 1988. 384p. illus. (part col.). maps. bibliog. index. $22.95. LC 87-34974. ISBN 0-8024-9051-4.

Presented here are brief biographies of sixty-four persons considered to be "some of the most important leaders of the Christian church" (p. 9). They span the history of Christianity from the first to the twentieth century and include biblical figures (Peter, Paul, and John), popes (Leo the Great, Gregory the Great, and Innocent III), reformers (Luther, Zwingli, and Calvin), and evangelists (C. H. Spurgeon, D. L. Moody, and Billy Graham). Each chapter consists of a one-page sketch (most with a chronology) and the biography proper. Timecharts and topical essays interspersed throughout the text supplement the biographies. A select bibliography suggests sources of material by and about the biographees for further study.

A work of this sort must necessarily be selective, and this one is. However, the selection criteria are not spelled out and the reader is left wondering why certain individuals are included and others are not (e.g., why William Wilberforce and not Martin Luther King?). In spite of this, there can be little disagreement over those chosen for inclusion.

The quality of the work varies, as it will with multi-author products, but overall both text and illustrations are very good. The biographies are marked by fairness and well-rounded presentation (with the exception of the treatment of Calvin, which borders on eulogy). They also have generally overcome a major problem of condensed treatments, that of clarity. There are occasions, though, when laypersons will need to go elsewhere for clarification of unfamiliar terminology and concepts.

Biographical information on most of the biographees can be found, often in concise form, in other sources. So, where is this volume's niche? It will serve the smaller libraries which are unable to afford the several larger works through which the material is scattered. For them it will provide a high-quality alternative.
Craig W. Beard

Dictionaries and Encyclopedias

1339. Broderick, Robert C., ed. **The Catholic Encyclopedia.** rev. ed. Nashville, Tenn., Thomas Nelson, 1987. 613p. illus. $19.95. LC 87-1529. ISBN 0-8407-5544-9.

Changes in this revised edition are more in format and typography than in substance. The volume is smaller, as is the print, and the photographs and pictures are not included, though the pen and ink illustrations remain. Most of the substantive changes are those related to changes in the Code of Canon Law, promulgated in 1983. The editor points out that the purpose of the revised edition is to bring these changes to the reader together with clarifications that may add to the understanding of the present-day church. In spite of this stated purpose, however, the emphasis seems to be more on historical entries than those relating to the present-day church. One wonders why some items such as "The Battle of Lepanto," "Montessori Method," and "Logic" should be included at all when they are readily available in other reference books. Most of the articles are the same as in the earlier volume although thirty-five new articles have been added. There are now the articles "Liberation Theology" and "Women, Ordination of," though surprisingly the article "Women" remains the same. Paragraphs have been added to a few articles, such as "Annulment," "Process, Due," and "Canon Law," but the work as a whole does not seem to reflect the profound discussions going on in the church today. This is particularly true of areas relating to the role of women in the church and peace and justice issues. On the positive side, the articles are generally clear, well written, and well documented. For those who want definitions of traditional "Catholic" terms, such as *papacy, indulgences,* or *canonization,* or a Catholic interpretation of such terms as *Marxism, evolution,* or *euthansia,* the volume is very useful. It would have been helpful, however, if a list of contributors could have been included and if there were additional cross-references.

Lucille Whalen

1340. **The New Dictionary of Theology.** Joseph A. Komonchak, Mary Collins, and Dermot A. Lane, eds. Wilmington, Del., Michael Glazier, 1987. 1112p. $59.95. LC 87-82327. ISBN 0-89453-609-5.

This dictionary provides a discussion of the major areas in theology based on their historical as well as contemporary significance for Catholic faith. The articles represent both traditional and contemporary theological positions currently held since Vatican II. Since all the contributors are from the English-speaking world, the insights from biblical, liturgical, traditional, and magisterial theology are more precise for the American audience than those found in collections that are translations from other languages.

College or seminary teachers and those responsible for religious education in parishes will find this reference work an uneven source. The reader needs to be aware of each author's theological bias when assessing the merits of an article. This is especially true if the reader is investigating issues such as sin, justice, or sexuality.

Topics such as feminist theology, cults, and economics are welcome additions. Major topics such as church, grace, and creation receive full treatment. Words no longer of general use, such as *Monarchianism* or *co-redemption*, receive minimal attention. *The New Dictionary of Theology* strives to use inclusive language, yet the major article on the church uses the model of "communion and brotherhood." The bibliographical additions after each article are helpful; a general index would have improved this collection.

This book is a real asset for those wishing to gain a sense of where Catholic theology is situated today. [R: Choice, Apr 88, pp. 1223-24; LJ, 1 Mar 88, pp. 61-62; WLB, May 88, p. 111]　Marie Alexis Navarro

Handbooks

1341. Brackney, William Henry. **The Baptists.** Westport, Conn., Greenwood Press, 1988. 327p. index. (Denominations in America, No. 2). $49.95. LC 87-15047. ISBN 0-313-23822-7.

This work consists of two major parts. The first is a thematic approach which gives rather lengthy essays on various phases of Baptist history: "An Overview of Baptist History," "The Bible: Authority or Battleground?" "A New Vision for the Church," "Sacraments/Ordinances: Signs of Faith," "A New Way: Voluntary Religion," and "The Struggle for Religious Liberty"; and the second covers biographies of Baptist leaders, both those of earliest times and some of the outstanding ones who are still active.

There are copious footnotes at the conclusion of part 1, and at the end of each biography are bibliographies that will be appropriate for those seeking more detailed information about these personalities. Following part 2 are two appendices, one a chronology of dates beginning

with John Smyth in 1609 and ending with Jerry Falwell in 1979. The second of the appendices is "The International Baptist Family," which lists in tabular form the number of churches and their membership in the United States, Canada, Europe, Africa, Asia, and Latin America. Also of value is the bibliographic essay on pages 296-315. Finally, there is a detailed index.

William Brackney is vice-president, dean, and professor of the history of Christianity at the Eastern Baptist Theological Seminary. He is also an editor of the *American Baptist Quarterly*, has written three other books on Baptists and American religious history, and has contributed numerous articles to professional journals. He has also served as executive director of the American Baptist Historical Society.

The Baptists will find a welcome place in all seminary, church, and church-related libraries. Its excellent bibliographies will lead the scholar of religion and religious history to more exhaustive materials. [R: Choice, Sept 88, p. 146; RQ, Winter 88, pp. 264-65]

Jefferson D. Caskey

JUDAISM

1342. Brisman, Shimeon. **A History and Guide to Judaic Encyclopedias and Lexicons.** Cincinnati, Ohio, Hebrew Union College Press; distr., Hoboken, N.J., KTAV, 1987. 502p. index. (Jewish Research Literature, Vol. 2; Bibliographica Judaica, Vol. 11). $49.50. LC 87-25969. ISBN 0-87820-909-3.

This bibliographic guide aims to identify, document, and evaluate the hundreds of different types of Judaic encyclopedias and lexicons published worldwide during the nineteenth and twentieth centuries. It was undertaken starting in 1978 with support from the University of California at Los Angeles and the National Endowment for the Humanities. The author, a noted scholar in the field of Jewish bibliography, has been Jewish Studies bibliographer and lecturer at the University of California at Los Angeles since 1962. The book includes more than 360 Judaic encyclopedias and lexicons written in more than a dozen languages. Only those works devoted entirely to Judaic topics are included.

After an introductory chapter dealing with various attempts to publish Judaic encyclopedias during the nineteenth and twentieth centuries, the book is divided into nine chapters. Each focuses on a specific type of Judaic encyclopedia and lexicon, including, for example, general, talmudic-rabbinic, Bible, Judaism, biographical, works on the Holy Land, the state of Israel, and Zionism. The chapters consist of a historical description of the types of encyclopedias/lexicons and a chronological listing of specific works. The complete bibliographic information is included, as well as a brief descriptive annotation, a statement on the purpose and organization of the work, the added title, the editor, and brief citations to reviews of the work. There is a listing of abbreviations used in these citations, as well as a complete listing of sources, magazines, and collective works and monographs. The book is extensively footnoted. Two detailed indexes, one to the narrative and footnotes and another to the chronological lists, conclude the work. This guide is an extremely valuable scholarly resource for Judaic study collections in academic, theological, temple, or synagogue libraries. In addition to providing important information for students, scholars, and researchers, it is an excellent collection development tool for librarians building reference collections in this area. [R: Choice, Apr 88, p. 1220]   Susan J. Freiband

1343. Nadell, Pamela S. **Conservative Judaism in America: A Biographical Dictionary and Sourcebook.** Westport, Conn., Greenwood Press, 1988. 409p. bibliog. index. (Jewish Denominations in America). $55.00. LC 87-31782. ISBN 0-313-24205-4.

This book documents the lives and careers of the most important leaders in the Conservative Jewish movement in the United States. It also provides a brief history of the movement and its central institutions. The majority of the work consists of biographical sketches of some 130 key conservative leaders, mostly rabbis. Each entry includes, in addition to the essential biographical data, an evaluation of the figure's contributions to the development of American conservatism, a bibliography of the individual's major writings, and selected references about him or her. The preface discusses the approach toward the selection of leaders who are included in the dictionary. In addition to the biographical dictionary, three essays (based on printed sources) present the history, ideology, and organization of Conservative Judaism. The Jewish Theological Seminary of America, the Rabbinical Assembly, and the United Synagogue of America are discussed in these essays. Each includes extensive bibliographical notes. The book concludes with a series of appendices listing the names and dates of the leaders of the most important Conservative and Reconstructionist associations. There are also a glossary of Hebrew terms, and a sixteen-page bibliography of resources for further study. The bibliography, arranged by types of materials, includes both primary and secondary sources. There is an extensive subject index, including cross-references. The author is Associate Professor of Jewish Studies and History at American University, and a specialist in modern American Jewish history. The book is an important contribution to American Jewish scholarship. It serves as a valuable resource for students and scholars in understanding the Conservative movement, and would be an excellent addition to reference collections in the area of Jewish studies in academic, public, and special libraries. It is also especially important for Judaica collections in temple, synagogue, community center, and day school libraries.

Susan J. Freiband

Part IV

SCIENCE
AND
TECHNOLOGY

30 Science and Technology in General

BIBLIOGRAPHIES

1344. Hurt, C. D. **Information Sources in Science and Technology.** Englewood, Colo., Libraries Unlimited, 1988. 362p. index. (Library Science Text Series). $29.50; $21.50pa. LC 88-22977. ISBN 0-87287-581-4; 0-87287-582-2pa.

The Library Science Text series has been and continues to be a useful set of resources for the professional librarian. This publication is the latest work in the series that identifies major titles in the pure and applied sciences. The structure is similar to earlier science guides, that is, there are sections — seventeen in this title — organized first by subject (e.g., history of science, physics, biomedical sciences) and then by type of publication (e.g., guides to the literature, encyclopedias, directories). Hurt is Director of the Graduate Library School at the University of Arizona, and his brief introduction on the characteristics of scientific and technical literature credits three graduate students for their assistance in identifying and verifying the citations. Hurt also acknowledges the value of another recent guide: Ching-chih Chen's source book, *Scientific and Technical Information Sources*, 2d ed. (see *ARBA* 88, entry 1433).

Each topical section is briefly introduced by a description of the field. For example, chapter 10, "Zoology," begins with three paragraphs that define the discipline, summarize its historical foundation, note the foci of the literature, and zoology's relationship to other scientific or technical disciplines. The author/title index and the subject index refer to the entries by number; there are 2,027 titles included in the work. Each entry, as in the past, averages three or four sentences of annotation and is generally descriptive. Some annotations note the sophistication of a title, its value or importance, or its use.

This title compares with other guides to scientific literature listing some of the same sources as well as some selected uniquely by Hurt. As he notes (p. xiv), "By no means are the sources listed here a complete listing of sources available. An effort was made to include the most important and useful items. This is a subjective judgment, likely to meet with some disapproval in certain cases." Regardless, this addition to the Library Science Text series will be an automatic acquisition for both library science collections and science reference.

Laurel Grotzinger

1345. O'Connell, Susan M., Valerie J. Montenegro, and Kathryn Wolff, comps. and eds. **The Best Science Books & A-V Materials for Children: An Annotated List of Science and Mathematics Books, Films, Filmstrips, and Videocassettes....** Washington, D.C., American Association for the Advancement of Science, 1988. 335p. index. $20.00. LC 88-10575. ISBN 0-87168-316-4.

This must-purchase bibliography covers twelve hundred books and audiovisual materials which have received either "recommended" or "highly recommended" review ratings in the review journal *Science Books & Films* from 1982 through 1987. The bibliography is arranged in classified order by science topic and contains complete bibliographic information and the original review. Indexes to authors, title, subjects, and series are provided, plus a distributors' index. For libraries that already subscribe to *Science Books & Film*, the bibliography provides a convenient, one-stop list. For those that cannot afford that periodical, this bibliography is a must. Its reasonable price tag makes it the best tool for building science collections for children available on the market.

David V. Loertscher

1346. Richter, Bernice, and Duane Wenzel, comps. **The Museum of Science and Industry Basic List of Children's Science Books 1988.** Chicago, American Library Association, 1988. 72p. index. $11.95pa. LC 87-641170. ISBN 0-8389-0499-8.

This title is the third annual update of *Museum of Science and Industry Basic List of Children's Science Books, 1973-1984* (see *ARBA* 86, entry 1415). It is the product of an annual book fair held by the museum where publishers of books for grades K-12 are invited to send copies of their best books for exhibit. Each title received is examined by the museum staff, reviews in current periodicals are checked, and the in-print status is researched. The book is then annotated and rated for quality by one or several museum staff and then printed in subject arrangement.

Each entry contains bibliographic information, grade level, a quality rating, a brief descriptive annotation, and a listing of reviews from current review media. A directory of publishers, a listing of sourcebooks for adults, and a list of science magazines and review journals are appended. Both title and author indexes are also included.

As a source for determining the quality of the publications, the list is flawed. The museum staffer may have rated the book as "not recommended," but the annotation gives no clue to the reason. The user will have to trace the reviews listed at the end of the annotation to discover the problems encountered by the reviewer. Of what use, then, is this publication? For libraries who already subscribe to *Appraisal* (Children's Science Book Review Commission, 1967-), *Bulletin of the Center for Children's Books* (University of Chicago Press, 1958-), *Booklist* (American Library Association, 1901-), and *Science Books & Films* (American Association for the Advancement of Science, 1975-), there will be little need for this publication since the books are reviewed much more thoroughly in those sources. However, for the small library that cannot afford to subscribe to those publications, this list can be considered a substitution, although for an extra $12.00, the library can get a subscription to *Appraisal* which is the best review journal in the field of science.

David V. Loertscher

CHRONOLOGIES

1347. Turner, Anthony. **Early Scientific Instruments: Europe 1400-1800.** London, Sotheby's; distr., New York, Harper & Row, 1987. 320p. illus. (part col.). bibliog. index. $115.00. LC 87-060453. ISBN 0-85667-319-6.

Anthony Turner, author of several monographs, catalogs, and numerous articles on scientific instruments, has produced a handsome, beautifully illustrated volume on a variety of devices used by scientists in Europe during the fifteenth through the nineteenth century. The work is not a true reference volume since Turner has chosen to limit his coverage to Europe and to exclude "all kinds of medical instruments and ... chemical apparatus and the prehistory of the instruments of specialised [sic] subjects such as oceanography" (p. 9). Moreover, he readily admits that the structure is "avowedly a work of synthesis and *haute vulgarisation*; ... [it is] narrative and chronological" (p. 9).

The six chapters of the work are indicative of Turner's approach: (1) "The Instruments of Later Medieval Europe," (2) "The Development of an Instrument-making Trade," (3) "The Instruments of Renaissance Europe," (4) "New Instruments and 'New Philosophy': Instrument-making in the 'Scientific Revolution,'" (5) "Scientist, Craftsman, Patron: The Heyday of the Mathematical Practitioner," and (6) "Contrasting Collections: The Instruments of Charles Boyle, 4th Earl of Orrery and of Horace-Bénédict de Saussure." There are copious footnotes, an extensive bibliography, and a detailed index to add to the quality of the volume. Heavy emphasis is given to astronomical or mathematical items such as the astrolabe, sundial, microscope, telescope, and a variety of "measuring" instruments. As noted, the volume is well-illustrated with superb color plates as well as dozens of black-and-white photographs. Each illustration has a caption, explanation and source, that is, the international public or private collection where located.

Turner's preface establishes the limitations of the work when he states that "the text of this work is by necessity broad, generalised and impressionistic in approach" (p. 9). On the other hand, his scholarship is such that the narrative themes (e.g., "the mathematisation of a subject provoked the development of new instruments to enable men to avoid calculating." [p. 8]) provide a valuable interpretation of how instruments relate to the scientific revolution. Most librarians would turn first to Turner's 1975 text, coauthored with Harriet Wynter, that is entitled *Scientific Instruments* (see *ARBA* 77, entry 1279) for basic questions about early scientific devices. However, this volume is one that any library serving the general college-level public would wish to acquire.

Laurel Grotzinger

DICTIONARIES AND ENCYCLOPEDIAS

1348.   Chambers Science and Technology Dictionary. new ed. Peter M. B. Walker, ed. New York, Cambridge University Press, 1988. 1008p. $39.50. ISBN 1-85296-150-3.

This revision of the well-known reference book continues to uphold the dictionary's reputation for comprehensiveness and quality. The forty-five thousand entries represent over one hundred areas in science and technology including chemistry, engineering, botany, zoology, medical science, physics, architecture, behavioral science, computing, building, mathematics, biology, paper, electronics, telecommunications, textiles, and printing. These entries were selected by the editor and forty-two collaborators who are competent specialists in their fields of interest.

The layout of the dictionary makes it easy to use. The alphabetically arranged terms are in boldface type followed by the scientific discipline in italics (in parentheses), then the definition. Cross-references are in boldface; italics are also used for alternate forms or names and emphasis.

The appendices include chemical formulas, a table of chemical elements, a periodic table classification of the animal and plant kingdoms, a geological table, physical concepts in SI units, and SI conversion factors.

This new edition fulfills its purpose of being useful both to the layperson and the professional, but will not replace the expert's own specialist dictionaries. Such a revision represents a great deal of effort. It is extremely difficult to keep up with the many new developments in science and technology and to be aware of all the evolving terms. It is good for readers to have a selection of technological dictionaries available to them since no one dictionary can contain every conceivable term. This excellent dictionary provides comprehensive coverage of science and technology with concise, accurate, and descriptive definitions of terms. [R: LJ, 1 Nov 88, pp. 90-91]   Anne C. Roess

1349.   Durbin, Paul T. A Dictionary of Concepts in the Philosophy of Science. Westport, Conn., Greenwood Press, 1988. 362p. bibliog. index. (Reference Sources for the Social Sciences and Humanities, No. 6). $59.96. LC 87-32293. ISBN 0-313-22979-1.

This dictionary defines and provides the historical context of about one hundred concepts important in the philosophy of science. The topics range from major schools of thought and theories (such as laws and science, sociobiology, and evolution) to particular methods used in science (such as induction and confirmation). The text averages about two to three pages per concept and follows a consistent pattern: basic definition(s), historical development of the idea, and position of the concept in contemporary debates. A list of references cited in the text provides a core bibliography after each discussion, and the author frequently gives suggestions for additional sources of information. Cross-references are sprinkled generously through the text, and a detailed subject index is provided.

Durbin usually does a fine job of converting sophisticated topics into summaries that are not laden with jargon. However, users with no background in philosophy may find that some entries remain somewhat complex. Durbin presents various perspectives on the many topics which engender substantial scholarly debate, only occasionally coming down on one side of an issue (e.g., indeterminism). Although the lists of references give access to many key historical works, it is unfortunate that more citations to materials published after 1980 were not included. This work covers more specific topics than does the classic *Encyclopedia of Philosophy* (Macmillan, 1973) and contains frequently longer (but fewer) articles than W. F. Bynum, *Dictionary of the History of Science* (see *ARBA* 83, entry 1266), with which it has considerable overlap.   Christopher W. Nolan

1350.   The Encyclopedic Dictionary of Science. Candida Hunt and Monica Byles, eds. New York, Facts on File, 1988. 256p. illus. (part col.). maps. $29.95. LC 88-16396. ISBN 0-8160-2021-3.

Large, clear, colorful illustrations are the high point of this new scientific dictionary. The illustrations and format make this appear to be a popular work, but the type size and language are of academic style. Although intended for students and the general public, it is not suitable for the nonscientifically oriented. Many of the definitions require familiarity with technical language. Cross-references to terms and illustrations are plentiful. The list of Nobel Prize winners is a plus, but a list of abbreviations might have been more useful.

The dictionary covers physics, chemistry, environmental sciences, biology, and medicine, and gives brief biographies of important persons. It does not cover mathematics or engineering, notably civil engineering although internal combustion engines and space exploration are included. Overall, it is less comprehensive than the standards like *Van Nostrand's Scientific*

Encyclopedia (see *ARBA* 84, entry 1229) and its definitions are shorter than *Van Nostrand* essays but longer than those in the *McGraw-Hill Dictionary of Scientific and Technical Terms* (see *ARBA* 84, entry 1234). Although insufficient as the only scientific dictionary in a collection, it would supplement the others quite well. With its illustrations and low price, this is a worthwhile addition to any public, high school or college library.   Susan Davis Herring

1351. Junge, Hans-Dieter. **Pocket Dictionary of Laboratory Equipment: English/German. Taschenwörterbuch Laborausrüstung.** New York, VCH, 1987. 201p. $28.00pa. ISBN 0-89573-596-2.

In handy, small-sized paperback format, this pocket dictionary contains over twenty-five hundred terms, mostly nouns, comprising a comprehensive vocabulary of laboratory equipment in chemistry, medicine, metallurgy, biochemistry, food, pulp and paper industries, and other fields. In the two parts, English-German and German-English, the source language is in boldface type. The preface and instructions are in both English and German.

Compound words are cross-listed for convenient use (e.g., *capsule sorting device* can be found under *capsule, sorting,* and *device*). Instead of cross-references, the translations are given for each entry for easy use. As is common in scientific literature, the American spelling is given preference, but in many instances, the British spelling is included in parentheses in both parts of the dictionary. Gender is indicated for all German nouns.

Andreas E. Mueller

1352. **The New Illustrated Science and Invention Encyclopedia.** Westport, Conn., H. S. Stuttman and Freeport, N.Y., Marshall Cavendish, 1988. 27v. illus. (part col.). maps. index. $399.95/set. LC 85-30973. ISBN 0-86307-491-X.

Edited by Donald Clarke, this set of twenty-six volumes provides well-balanced, but brief, information on hundreds of topics in the area of science and technology. The text is accompanied by many illustrations, mostly in color, plus some diagrams. The keystones of this encyclopedia, as stated in the introduction, are as follows: "it has an easily understandable, yet detailed and authoritative, text written by experts who understand well the importance of communicating detailed technical information in a lucid, well-organized style that makes it easily assimilated by a broad spectrum of readers ... [and] the encyclopedia features extensive use of detailed informative color photographs

and drawings that complement the text and make the entire work a valuable learning aid." A list of staff credits and contributors is found in volume 26.

Indeed, the text is readable and the illustrations are quite good. As with most Cavendish publications, it should be kept in mind that *The New Illustrated Science and Invention Encyclopedia* is a British product. Nevertheless, the information is well balanced, and an article on algae in volume 1 will serve to illustrate this point. In the article, algae is defined as a varied group of primitive plants ranging in size from microscopic single cells to giant kelp. A brief description and historical information follow, plus a "fact sheet" and several cross-references (e.g., cell, drug, protein, etc.), forming a well-rounded, informative article.

The previous edition of this encyclopedia was reviewed under the title of *Growing Up with Science: The Illustrated Encyclopedia of Invention* in *ARBA* 85 (see entry 1330). At that time we indicated that this is "an excellent work for children who want an introduction to science or who desire a reference book on their own level to learn about new topics." Unfortunately, no bibliography of other sources is provided for the young reader. However, despite this one deficiency, our previous recommendation and criticism are also valid for the *New Illustrated Science and Invention Encyclopedia.* [R: RBB, 15 Sept 88, p. 141]   Bohdan S. Wynar

1353. **New Polytechnic Dictionary of Spanish and English Language. Nuevo Diccionario Politechnico de las Lenguas Española e Inglesa.** By Federico Beigbeder Atienza. Madrid, Diaz de Santos; distr., Philadelphia, Taylor & Francis, 1988. 2v. $300.00/set. ISBN 84-86251-71-0.

The language of technology increases constantly, and the usual bilingual dictionary can only deal with a fraction of the new vocabulary. This volume provides data on terms in biogenetics, environment, genetic engineering, air space technology, computer science and many other phases of present-day technology. Despite the introductory material, the emphasis is on the Spanish of Spain and the English of England.

This dictionary is up-to-date and accurate and is of the greatest value to translators of technical material and to those who desire to read the scientific and technical literature published in the other language.

These volumes should be a first choice for purchase by libraries with collections of recent Spanish technological literature or for libraries in the Spanish-speaking world with scientific and technical periodicals. Libraries in universities that provide graduate degrees in the fields covered by this dictionary will find them an indispensable addition to their collections.

While more than 99.9 percent of the vocabulary is technical in nature, one cannot help but be surprised to find such words as baby, perambulator (but not baby carriage), and pancake (as something to eat). Little attempt is made to differentiate meanings. Thus the word *about* has fourteen Spanish meanings, all of which are not used interchangeably. Each volume has an appendix or group of appendices. The English-Spanish volume has a section that lists abbreviations, acronyms and chemical symbols. The Spanish-English volume has six appendices – conversion tables for weights and measures, and so forth.

Beigbeder Atienza and his Spanish publisher are to be congratulated on the publication of this extremely valuable and useful dictionary. This is the fullest and most up-to-date bilingual dictionary of its kind, and one can only hope that from time to time new editions will keep it current.   Hensley C. Woodbridge

DIRECTORIES

1354. **Directory of Testing Laboratories.** 1988 ed. Compiled by ASTM. Philadelphia, ASTM, 1987. 252p. index. $50.00pa. ISBN 0-8031-0973-3; ISSN 0895-7886.

This directory "lists the locations and capabilities of testing laboratories that perform services for a fee" (p. vi). There are over nine hundred entries in this edition. The editors state that a laboratory's inclusion in this directory does not constitute an endorsement or certification by ASTM.

In the main section of the directory, the laboratories are listed geographically by state, city, and then foreign country. Each entry includes the following information: lab name, address, areas of specialization, fields of testing/services, materials and products tested, lab equipment, testing capabilities and applications, type and number of professional staff, and locations of branch sites. While the information for each laboratory is fairly detailed, there are two sections, fields of testing/services and materials and products, that are coded. The user must continually refer to two different lists of codes to decipher a laboratory's services and testing abilities. This makes the directory somewhat cumbersome to use. There are two indexes: alphabetical by laboratory name and a subject index which incorporates the terms used in the fields of testing and laboratory services.

The directory may provide a useful starting point for those seeking laboratory testing services; however, it is by no means complete. The

reviewer is aware of several reputable laboratories in one state alone that are not included here. Other sources, such as the directory published by the American Council of Independent Laboratories, contacts with local libraries and technical organizations, and telephone directories should also be consulted.

Last published in 1982, the directory will be updated and published annually beginning with the 1988 edition. Perhaps the editors will take a more aggressive role in soliciting additional laboratories for inclusion in future editions.

Diane Montag

HANDBOOKS AND YEARBOOKS

1355. **The Facts on File Scientific Yearbook 1988.** Margaret DiCanio, ed. New York, Facts on File, 1988. 216p. illus. (part col.). index. $27.50. LC 85-642413. ISBN 0-8160-1889-8; ISSN 0883-0800.

This is the latest volume in an annual series of scientific yearbooks for high school students, published under its current title since 1985. In common with other scientific yearbooks, this one is devoted to a review of the previous year in science, along with articles of interest to its target audience. Its thirty articles are grouped under the three broad categories of life sciences, earth and space science, and physical science and mathematics. Some are expected, such as those dealing with AIDS and superconductors, while some are not so common, such as a useful explanation of the differences between conservationists, preservationists, environmentalists, and ecologists, terms too often used interchangeably.

The readable articles are unsigned and well indexed. There are many good illustrations, some produced especially for this volume. An appendix provides a listing of the winners of major scientific awards and prizes for the year under review.   Donald J. Marion

1356.   Franck, Irene M., and David M. Brownstone. **Scientists and Technologists.** New York, Facts on File, 1988. 212p. illus. bibliog. index. (Work throughout History). $14.95. LC 87-19959. ISBN 0-8160-1450-7.

One of a fifteen-volume set, this book describes developments in science and technology from ancient times to the present day. Most notably, physicists, astronomers, mathematicians, engineers, chemists, alchemists, and biologists are included here, as are a few others.

Each occupation is introduced with a brief definition and a broad statement about its very early beginnings. Developments, famous scientists, and the accomplishments through the ages and in many lands are described in language that is far too sophisticated for the intended juvenile audience. The authors talk about the "vulnerability of the Ptolemaic model" in geography, and the "existence of ... a symmetrical inverse of the Compton effect (wave-particle dualism), when [Louis de Broglie] showed that there was also a particle-wave dualism." This is difficult material to understand, but is especially so in the case of this book because few terms are defined in the text, and no glossary is provided. The chapters vary widely in length, from the mere four paragraphs that describe the work of cartographers to the twenty-four-page chapter on astronomers.

There are other shortcomings. While it is only to be expected for authors to have cross-references to related occupations in the other volumes of the series, to cite these referenced volumes as "forthcoming" will only confuse the reader, especially once they are available. The skimpy annotated bibliography has limited use. The annotation for another Facts on File publication reads: "A valuable new survey"—a less than valuable annotation. In addition, smaller public and school libraries are not likely to have the works cited here by scholarly publishers such as Oxford University Press. The illustrations are adequate, consisting mostly of woodcuts and black-and-white photographs. The index, which is printed in a small and difficult to read typeface, has few cross-references. Leonardo da Vinci is listed uner "Vinci, Leonardo da," with no cross-reference under "da Vinci."

Already published titles in the Work throughout History series are *Artists and Artisans*, *Builders*, *Clothiers*, *Financiers and Traders*, *Harvesters*, *Healers*, *Helpers and Aides*, *Leaders and Lawyers*, *Manufacturers and Miners*, *Performers and Players*, *Restaurateurs and Innkeepers*, *Scholars and Priests*, and *Warriors and Adventurers*. For high school and public libraries. [R: BR, May/June 88, p. 42; VOYA, Aug 88, p. 145]   Kerry L. Kresse

1357.   Mount, Ellis, and Barbara A. List. **Milestones in Science and Technology: The Ready Reference Guide to Discoveries, Inventions, and Facts.** Phoenix, Ariz., Oryx Press, 1987. 141p. bibliog. index. $29.50. LC 87-12352. ISBN 0-89774-260-5.

This is an eclectic and meandering mixture of one thousand inventions and discoveries that the authors feel to be milestones in the categories of science and technology. As is the case in these types of reference works, the selection is highly subjective. Limited to the natural

sciences, emphasis is on medicine and related disciplines, astronomy, engineering, and the physical sciences. The biological sciences outside medicine are given cursory attention. Many of the included entries would appear on most lists of important discoveries, but some are questionable. A few entries, such as the Herzprung-Russell diagram of stellar evolution and the Ekman layer (a term in oceanography), seem too advanced in theory and application for inclusion in a book that is based on bibliographical sources "apt to be found in most medium-sized public libraries." Others come right out of the blue (e.g., the glass eye and the videocassette recorder). Every school child studies the six simple machines that are the basis for all other machines: wedge, wheel and axle, pulley, inclined plane, lever, and screw. Without these, other inventions would not be possible, yet only three have their own entries in this book.

The entries are arranged in alphabetical order by the name of the invention or discovery. Averaging one hundred words in length, they provide a very brief description of the item, the inventor or discoverer, and the date. Also included is one reference for additional reading. The authors admit that there are often opposing viewpoints regarding the exact dates and names connected with inventions, and used their "best judgment" in selecting the published reference. In such cases, at least two references should have been provided, or a mention made in the text.

Indexes for personal names, dates, nation of discovery, and broad subject categories allow further access to the topics. The annotated bibliography provides sixty-one references, and they are the sources used in the text. An adequate tool for public libraries only. [R: Choice, Apr 88, p. 1223; RBB, 1 Apr 88, p. 1324; SLJ, May 88, p. 33; VOYA, Apr 88, p. 52; WLB, Jan 88, p. 102]   Kerry L. Kresse

INDEXES

1358.   **Applied Science & Technology Index 1987.** Joyce M. Howard and Mila Braigen, eds. Bronx, N.Y., H. W. Wilson, 1988. 2388p. sold on service basis. LC 14-5408. ISSN 0003-6986.

Now in its thirtieth year, this familiar Wilson publication indexes 350 English-language periodicals, 44 more titles than it did ten years ago. The subjects covered remain essentially the same compared to 1978, with the exception of two new fields: atmospheric sciences and mineralogy. The major difference, however, between ten years ago and now, is that the index is now also available in machine-readable form, both online and on compact disk, along with the other indexes in the Wilson family. Access via computer is faster, easier, and more expensive than using this paper version.

In addition to indexing technical publications in fields such as chemistry, engineering, physics, computer science, geology, and so on, *Applied Science and Technology Index* also selectively covers general science publications such as *Science*, *Scientific American*, and *American Scientist*, as well as some semipopular serials such as *Byte*, *Datamation*, *QST*, and *Sea Technology*. There is, therefore, some overlap with Wilson's *General Science Index* (see *ARBA 88*, entry 1453).

Access to information is by subject only. Entries include article title, author, journal title, and citation data (volume, pagination, date), as well as an indication of references, charts, diagrams, and other illustrations. Access is facilitated by *see* and *see also* references. The 2,388-page 1987 volume includes a 30-page index of book reviews which appeared in the indexed serials. Appropriate for academic and large public libraries.   Robert A. Seal

1359.   Finnegan, Robert. **Product and Process: An Index to the Way Things Work.** Metuchen, N.J., Scarecrow, 1988. 238p. $25.00. LC 88-6691. ISBN 0-8108-2113-3.

"How does it work?" is one of the perennial questions, and numerous volumes have appeared providing answers. Now this index provides a guide to twenty of these reference works.

The author has done his job well. The products and processes mentioned in the title include such broad-ranging topics as forest ecology, wounds and injuries, pregnancy, and lunar engineering as well as the expected hot air balloons, simple machines and nuclear power plants. The headings reflect the terms used in the books indexed, with cross-references provided. This limited vocabulary presents occasional difficulties, as the terms used in the index are not necessarily those a patron would request; some imagination is beneficial.

The twenty books indexed are standard, commonly available, single-volume references. A workable selection of them should be found in even the smallest public or school library. With its moderate price and wide-ranging approach, this will be a useful tool for any public, school, or college library.
Susan Davis Herring

1360.   Pilger, Mary Anne. **Science Experiments Index for Young People.** Englewood, Colo., Libraries Unlimited, 1988. 239p. $35.00. LC 88-13870. ISBN 0-87287-671-3.

This unique guide, one in a series of data books, indexes science experiments and demonstrations found in 694 elementary and intermediate science books dating from 1941 through 1988. In addition to books specific to the physical sciences, books dealing with models, math concepts that can be related to the science fields, social science experiments, and food and nutrition experiments are included.

The volume is organized in a manner easy to use by adults and children. The first section is an alphabetical list of subject headings, including a three- to eight-word description, a book number, and the book pages where the experiments can be found. The second section of the volume contains book references arranged by book number.

The subjects cover a vast range of experiments, beginning with an entry for "ABACUS how to count" through "ZOO ANIMALS behavior." Children will have little difficulty selecting simple and complex science projects and teachers have ready access to information on exhibits and demonstrations. Unfortunately, subject headings lack cross-references and inversion of headings leads to different references, for example: "BALLOONS—HOT AIR ... how to make" (178) and "HOT AIR BALLOONS ... make a hot air balloon" (564). The user, finding information under one heading, may not think to look under another.

The volume is also available in disk format for Apple II, Macintosh, and IBM microcomputers from the publisher for $30.00. The disk contains the same information but allows a library to tailor the index to its collection, and perhaps locate subjects more readily. At the price, both print and disk versions are welcome additions to library collections.
Andrew G. Torok

PERIODICALS AND SERIALS

1361.   **Encyclopedia of Associations Association Periodicals: A Directory of Publications.... Volume 2: Science, Medicine, and Technology.** Dennis M. Allard and Robert C. Thomas, eds. Detroit, Gale, 1987. 1v. (various paging). index. $60.00. ISBN 0-8103-2062-2; ISSN 0894-3869.

In their introduction the editors state that the periodicals covered in this "encyclopedia" are basically those published by the nonprofit organizations covered in Gales's *Encyclopedia of Associations, Volume 2: National Organizations of the U.S.*

Many of the organizations whose publications are included in *Science, Medicine and*

Technology are quite specialized and the periodicals they publish follow suit: *Private Doctor Newsletter*, *Wilderness Medicine*, *Bovine Practitioner*, *Jewish Braille Review*, and *Vintage Airplane*, for example.

The organization of this encyclopedia is straightforward. The main body is arranged alphabetically by title within assigned subject headings. There are both a title/keyword index and an association index which provides a listing of publications under each sponsoring organization. Entries include organization name, address, and telephone number; subject description; features; editor(s); frequency; price, circulation; and whether advertising is accepted. Volume 1 covers business, finance, industry, and trade, while volume 3 covers the social sciences, education, and humanities.

Association periodicals often provide a unique source of information, particularly for statistics, people, reading lists, and regional activities. Volume 2 of *Encyclopedia of Associations Association Periodicals* is recommended to those active in the fields covered as well as for academic and public libraries with strong science/technology collections.

Diane Montag

THESAURI

1362. **SPINES Thesaurus: A Controlled and Structured Vocabulary for Information Processing in the Field of Science and Technology for Development.** Compiled by Division of Science and Technology Policies, UNESCO. Paris, UNESCO; distr., Lanham, Md., UNI-PUB, 1988. 2v. (Science Policy Studies and Documents, No. 50). $57.00pa./set. ISBN 92-3-102257-1.

The *SPINES* (Science and Technology Policy Information Exchange System) *Thesaurus* was produced under a UNESCO program to promote the management and international exchange of information. The *Thesaurus* is a controlled and structured vocabulary of 11,464 terms and 78,153 semantic relations which are used in connection with the scientific, technological, and socioeconomic aspects of development at local, national, regional, and international levels. The present volumes are an English 1987 edition of the revised 1984 version, originally published in 1976. It also provides for the translation of French, Spanish, and Portuguese descriptors into English equivalents.

The first volume provides a detailed introduction, directions for use, an alphabetical list of English descriptors with relations, a brief bibliography, previous titles from the series, and names and addresses for national distributors of UNESCO publications. Volume 2 contains a list of international organizations and projects, a thematic list of descriptors, a permuted list of descriptors, and the multilingual relations.

The *Thesaurus* has been used by governments and institutions to process science and technology policy documents, for ongoing research projects, with documents dealing with economic and social development, to facilitate searching computerized databases, and for preparing bibliographic newsletters. While of limited value to most collections, university libraries and information centers may wish to consider the *Thesaurus* for specialized needs.

Andrew G. Torok

1363. **Thesaurus of Scientific, Technical, and Engineering Terms.** New York, Hemisphere Publishing, 1988. 1v. (various paging). $125.00. LC 87-21113. ISBN 0-89116-794-3.

This thesaurus is a reproduction of the well-known *NASA Thesaurus*, 1985 edition plus supplement. This single hardbound volume cumulates, in one physical volume, volume 1 (hierarchical listing), volume 2 (access vocabulary), and the supplement of May 1986. The generic structure is presented in volume 1, showing broader terms and narrower terms in indented fashion under the GS reference. The cross-reference structure also includes the standard, related term (RT), use (USE), and used for (UF) references. The thesaurus includes array terms ( ), defined as terms with meaning either too broad or too ambiguous for effective indexing or retrieval. An array term refers to a generous list of more specific terms. The second volume is an alphabetical listing of the thesaurus terms and cross-reference terms, including permuted terms and embedded terms to give increased access to the hierarchies in volume 1. The 1986 supplement is bound in this single volume between volumes 1 and 2. This reproduction would be more valuable if this supplement had been incorporated within the text itself.

This is an exact reproduction of the original. The only difference this reviewer could find is in the examples used in the introductory explanations found at the front of the text. The *NASA Thesaurus* is a well-known language tool in the field of science and technology which may be used for searching, but is primarily of use in indexing. Libraries considering purchase should investigate the price difference between this copy and the original NTIS publication. [R: SBF, Sept/Oct 88, p. 3]

Lorna K. Rees-Potter

31 Agricultural and Resource Sciences

AGRICULTURAL SCIENCES

General Works

ACRONYMS AND ABBREVIATIONS

1364. Abbreviations Used by FAO for International Organizations, Congresses, Commissions, Committees, Etc. 4th ed. Rome, Food and Agriculture Organization of the United Nations; distr., Lanham, Md., UNIPUB, 1988. 205p. bibliog. (FAO Terminology Bulletin, No. 27). $20.25pa. ISBN 92-5-002659-5.

In an attempt to keep up with the growing number of abbreviations in its field, the Food and Agriculture Organization of the United Nations (FAO) has once again revised *Abbreviations Used by FAO*. This fourth edition, number 27 in the FAO Terminology Bulletin series, contains nine hundred entries primarily gleaned from FAO's Terminology and Reference Section. Entries are arranged alphabetically by the English abbreviation, with French and Spanish equivalents following. For those abbreviations and names which do not have an official English, French, or Spanish equivalent, the most commonly used translations and abbreviations, if any, are listed. A composite listing of all the abbreviations allows one to look up the French or Spanish abbreviation and find out which entry to go to for counterpart terms. Also included is a bibliography of the sources used, along with a listing of the FAO Terminology Bulletins and Terminology Notes issued to date.   Angela Marie Thor

BIBLIOGRAPHIES

1365. Guither, Harold D., and Harold G. Halcrow. **The American Farm Crisis: An Annotated Bibliography with Analytical Introductions.** Ann Arbor, Mich., Pierian Press, 1988.

164p. index. (Resources in Contemporary Issues). $40.00pa. LC 87-32846. ISBN 0-87650-240-0.

This book is a historical perspective on agriculture, and concentrates on the authors' opinion of the best techniques to manage the current farm situation. The authors are optimistic and state that solving the "farm problem" will center around the status of farm people, the scientific and technological revolution in agriculture, farm economy, farm production potential, domestic and world markets, and the necessity of American farms to grow and prosper. The book also outlines adjustments that must be made to the farm economy, steps at which these adjustments can be made, and the broader effects of farm people on the rural, national, and world economy.

The book is divided into chapters that discuss the American farm and tradition, the scientific and technological revolution in farming, the evolution of farm business management, the evolution in market and marketing of agricultural products, the farm and its setting in the rural community, government farm commodity programs, transforming traditional goals for times ahead, and educational programs for implementing change. Each chapter also contains an antedated bibliography which is quite helpful. The chapters are followed by a chronology of contemporary farm policies and the American farm and a glossary of agriculture and food policy terms. The book is well indexed, with author and title indexes. It is well printed on average paper with adequate binding and is a paperback. It would be quite useful to anyone interested in the future of American agriculture. [R: RBB, Aug 88, pp. 1895-96]
                    Herbert W. Ockerman

DIRECTORIES

1366. Sanzone, Susan J., Jenny Burman, and Mary Agnes Hage, eds. **Healthy Harvest II: A**

Directory of Sustainable Agriculture & Horticulture Organizations 1987-1988. Washington, D.C., Potomac Valley Press, 1987. 119p. illus. index. $10.95pa. ISBN 0-938443-01-1.

This biannual publication lists alphabetically approximately six hundred organizations, seed sources, and publications interested in sustainable agriculture, which is a system of agriculture in which yields are maintained over time. Each group was invited in previous editions to submit their own information and discuss in their own words their structure and the mission they are trying to accomplish, which are as varied as the organizations themselves. Many of the entries are from the United States, but organizations from other countries are also included. This directory also has a subject and geographical index. The publication is 8½ by 11 inches; the paper, printing, and binding are of average quality. The book would be useful for people wanting information on organizations that are interested in sustainable agriculture. [R: RBB, 1 May 88, p. 1486]

Herbert W. Ockerman

HANDBOOKS

1367. **Pesticide Fact Handbook.** By U.S. Environmental Protection Agency. Park Ridge, N.J., Noyes Publications, 1988. 827p. index. $96.00. LC 87-31528. ISBN 0-8155-1145-0.

The Environmental Protection Agency (EPA) participates in regulatory activities involving all manner of chemicals, and one aspect of this work results in issuing pesticide fact sheets on individual chemicals (or less commonly, chemical groups) that provide a description of (1) the chemical, (2) use patterns, (3) science findings regarding toxicity, (4) EPA's regulatory position and rationale, (5) major data gaps, and (6) the EPA contact person. The EPA uses these fact sheets as a communication tool to update interested parties on EPA's views on chemicals under scrutiny. EPA's regulatory position and rationale and their view of major data gaps represent information unique to these fact sheets. The handbook is a compilation of 130 fact sheets and of interest to parties wishing to follow the work of the EPA at a leisurely and inexpensive pace (each fact sheet is available when printed at about ten times the cost of the compilation). There are some typographical errors and the ubiquitous use of arcane acronyms detracts somewhat, but a glossary helps and the common name, generic name, and trade name indexes are useful. The information represented is not, however, adequately documented save for listing the contact person. Esoteric notations like (40 CFR 180.259) on P687 no doubt

direct the reader to another reference, but this is not explained. The book would be strengthened by adding a brief user's guide to EPA fact sheets introduction to the handbook.

Marvin K. Harris

Food Science and Technology

BIBLIOGRAPHIES

1368. Harrison, Gail G., Osman M. Galal, and Mary E. Mohs, comps. **Food and Nutrition in the Middle East, 1970-1986: An Annotated Bibliography.** Westport, Conn., Greenwood Press, 1988. 258p. index. (Bibliographies and Indexes in Science and Technology, No. 4). $39.95. LC 87-34023. ISBN 0-313-26188-1.

Greenwood Press is an eminent source of scholarly bibliographies today. The intent of this work is to continue the work of *A Decade of Nutrition Research in the Arab World* (Beirut: American University) and it focuses on the world's population that consumes "primarily the Middle Eastern diet." The work does not define that diet, and this may blur the intent since diet varies widely, even within the Arab world or Islamic populations.

The bibliography is organized first by Middle Eastern country, then in reverse chronological order, not by author or title. The eight principal countries included are Egypt, Iran, Iraq, Israel, Lebanon, Saudi Arabia, Sudan, and Turkey; there are then sections on the Middle East as a whole, other countries, and non-country specific. Its index is arranged first by country, then by broad subject. A user looking for one of the "other" countries by name will be out of luck, since the index does not facilitate this type of search.

The work does not include a list of the journal title abbreviations used or a bibliographic listing; this is a major omission, since many of the titles are so generically shortened that it is almost impossible to ascertain a title, let alone any other bibliographic data. For example, what title is "*J. Med.*" in an international bibliography? The book's typeface is clear, but lacks any boldface or other font differences to accentuate material, producing a rather dull format; some titles have not been underlined.

The work is esoteric and would not find much use except for a highly specialized nutrition or perhaps Middle Eastern studies-related library.

Robert D. Adamshick

1369. Orta, John. **Computer Applications in Nutrition and Dietetics: An Annotated Bibliography.** New York, Garland, 1988. 242p. index. (Garland Reference Library of Social Science,

Vol. 428). $32.00. LC 87-30450. ISBN 0-8240-6621-9.

This bibliography is a collection of 201 annotated citations. The majority of the entries are drawn from twenty-five academic and professional journals. Inclusion dates are from 1958 to 1987.

Special features include an author, title, and subject index with a glossary. A detailed outline of the areas covered by the American Dietetic Association's "Registration Examination for Dietitians" serves as a topical framework for the annotations. Major subject areas are normal nutrition, community nutrition, management, food service, operations, and food science. Not all of the sections listed in the outline have representative citations. Annotations are for the most part noncritical and lean heavily towards the descriptive.

The selection of sources for this text was a by-product of the author's dissertation on the same subject. This work is aimed toward the undergraduate to graduate student who needs to place current developments in a historical context. Recommended for libraries serving this clientele. [R: Choice, Sept 88, p. 86]

Peter B. Kaatrude

1370. Wheaton, Barbara Ketcham, and Patricia Kelly. **Bibliography of Culinary History: Food Resources in Eastern Massachusetts.** Boston, G. K. Hall, [1988]. 379p. index. $75.00. ISBN 0-8161-0455-7.

"Since Eve ate apples, much depends on dinner," wrote Byron. Barbara Wheaton and Patricia Kelly have compiled a feast of works on which centuries of dinners have depended, in this bibliography of culinary history resources. They have included primary resources published before 1920, or more recent works dealing with these subjects, from the collections of the American Antiquarian Society; the Boston Athenaeum; the Boston Public Library; the Essex Institute in Salem, Massachusetts; all the departmental libraries of Harvard University; the Massachusetts Historical Society; and the libraries of the Minuteman Network, a regional consortium of public and college libraries. They have also included works microfilmed in the Goldsmiths'-Kress Library of Economic History series, the History of Women series, and the Schlesinger Library Cookery microfilms. Their definition of culinary history is relatively broad, since besides cookbooks, they have included treatises on nutrition, household planning and management, and table etiquette, to name just a few. Books about alcoholic beverages are excluded, because of the great number of them. The authors provide complete bibliographic

information for each work, but no annotations. There are indexes by title, topic, and country of origin. The country index is further subdivided by date of publication. The location of works in the libraries included is indicated. While this could be considered something of a novelty work, it would be particularly useful for collections that support strong programs in women's studies or nineteenth-century social history.

Sallie H. Barringer

DICTIONARIES AND ENCYCLOPEDIAS

1371. Adrian, J., G. Legrand, and R. Frangne. **Dictionary of Food and Nutrition.** Chichester, England, Ellis Horwood and New York, VCH, 1988. 233p. illus. (Ellis Horwood Series in Food Science and Technology). $47.00. LC 87-2999. ISBN 0-89573-404-4.

This is a translation of a 1981 French book. Aimed at scientists and technicians in the field of food sciences, this dictionary contains data relating to the chemistry, physiology, biochemistry, nutrition, and processing of food. The entries are brief but contain structural diagrams, charts, and tables when necessary. *See* references abound and are indicated by boldface type. Appendices contain food composition tables and formula structures. The text is enlivened by woodcuts throughout. Quite specialized, the dictionary needs to be purchased only by institutions that support advanced studies in food sciences.

Deborah Hammer

1372. Hughes, Christopher C. **The Additives Guide.** New York, John Wiley, 1987. 146p. bibliog. index. $46.95. LC 87-2122. ISBN 0-471-91496-7.

This slim volume provides a fascinating introduction to the common additives found in food. The first few chapters define additives, and describe their history, functions, and health risks. The main portion of the book is a glossary of individual additives and classes of additives used in the United States, Canada, Australia, and the EEC countries. (There is a slight British emphasis.) For each additive or class, the common name, E-number, chemical formula, and synonyms are listed. Also provided are a description of the additive, its function, and any known beneficial or adverse effects on humans.

Following the glossary is a brief bibliography, somewhat annotated, of books and articles relating to additives. In addition, there is an index of synonyms and minor additives.

Although there are more detailed guides to additives, such as the *CRC Handbook of Food Additives* (see *ARBA* 74, entry 1714), this work is strong on readability. While it is not an exhaustive reference guide, it is an interesting preface to the subject. Whether for the avid label reader who wants to know what ditolyethylenediamine on the margarine box is, or for the nutritionist, this book can be a helpful resource. Unfortunately, its high price will be a deterrent to many.

Deborah Pearson Reeber

1373. **Larousse Gastronomique.** Jenifer Harvey Lang, ed. New York, Crown, 1988. 1193p. illus. (part col.). index. $50.00. LC 88-1178. ISBN 0-517-57032-7.

This enormous work is a delight to the mind as well as the eye (and a delight to the palate if you use the recipes). It is unquestionably the "world's greatest culinary encyclopedia," synthesizing the science of nutrition and the art of cooking and providing a monumental historical overview of classical cuisine.

First published in 1938 and revised in 1971, *Larousse Gastronomique* has long been considered a basic textbook for the student of classic French cuisine. This edition was completely rewritten, in French, by Robert J. Courtine, the gastronomy editor of *Le Monde*, who updated, expanded, and modernized it to include a wide variety of the world's cuisines. These changes have expanded the scope of the work but do not alter its traditional orientation. Lang has Americanized the English translation, adding American measurements and clarifying British terms ("double cream" is translated to "heavy cream"). American regional cuisines are covered, and entries on wines have been greatly amplified, so that every wine-producing region in the world is covered.

Approximately one thousand photographs and drawings, the majority in color, adorn the pages of this beautiful book. Articles on specific dishes, famous chefs, sauces, cooking terms and techniques, utensils, geographic regions and their cuisines, wines and liqueurs, customs, and four thousand marvelous recipes (mostly French) combine to make this volume one of extraordinary interest to anyone who appreciates the art of gastronomy. An essential purchase for all public libraries.

Shirley Lambert

1374. Lichine, Alexis, and others. **Alexis Lichine's New Encyclopedia of Wines & Spirits.** 5th ed. New York, Alfred A. Knopf/Random House, 1987. 771p. maps. bibliog. index. $45.00. LC 85-2590. ISBN 0-394-56262-3.

In the world of wines and wine books, the name of Alexis Lichine stands tall, along with such luminaries as Hugh Johnson, Frank Schoonmaker, and André Simon. The current title, first published in 1967 and reprinted and updated often, has become a tradition among wine encyclopedias. There is little wonder when one considers the information it offers between its covers. Ten essay chapters covering fifty-six pages deal with the history of wine and how it is made, wine and food, value and wines, and additional information on spirits. The heart of the book consists of alphabetically arranged articles (varying greatly in length) on wines, wine terms, wine-growing regions, and wine-producing nations. Six appendices provide detailed listings of French and German wines, conversion tables, vintage charts, and other quick-reference information. The fifth edition incorporates ten thousand changes in a completely reset text.

Its scope notwithstanding, Lichine's "general survey of the wines and spirits of the world" has some major limitations as a reference book. First, although the maps are useful, they are the only illustrations in the book. More important is the question of balance. Although this encyclopedia features excellent entries on the wines of many nations (seventy-five-pages on the United States) among its alphabetical entries, it is primarily a book on European—and especially French—wines. A high percentage of the short entries in the book relate to French wines and wine-growing areas, and the extensive appendices include only French and German wines, excluding the largest wine-producing nation in the world, Italy. The great American achievements with the Cabernet Sauvignon and the Chardonnay grapes are scarcely mentioned in the entries under those grape names. In truth, hardly any name associated with American viticulture is found outside the article on the United States, whereas geographical regions from France and European nations appear frequently. French chateaux abound throughout the text. The result is an unbalanced book that is better for browsing than for finding reference information on many of the wines of the world.

This is not to deny the French their place of importance in the world of wines, but simply to point out that this encyclopedia bears a striking resemblance to *Alexis Lichine's Guide to the Wines and Vineyards of France* (Alfred A. Knopf, 1982).

Edwin S. Gleaves

1375. **The New Frank Schoonmaker Encyclopedia of Wine.** Revised by Alexis Bespaloff. New York, William Morrow, 1988. 624p. maps. $22.95. LC 88-5270. ISBN 0-688-05749-7.

Originally published in 1964 (and last revised in 1978 by Julius Wile), this book is certainly welcomed back as a basic starting point for knowledge about wine producing regions of the world. It serves as a quick reference, made even better through the updated and (in many cases) entirely new charts of figures for the American wine industry. While there are four hundred new entries, the editor has eliminated some older ones. For example, in the "A" section, there is no longer an entry for "Alambrado," a Spanish term for a bottle enclosed in an open wine netting (yet many Spanish wines still appear on the American market with this netting in place). There are no entries for "Altar wines," "Albanello" from Sicily, "Ammerschwihr" from Alsace, "Ampuis" from the Rhone, the Spanish "Añada," and others. While there are more than twenty new maps specially drawn for this edition, there are no longer any reproductions of wine labels. Every article has changed, even "Fino" and "Labrusca," which never in themselves have changed over the centuries. With renewed interest in Italy, new interest in Australia and California and other U.S. areas, there is something for everybody in this book. The fifty pages of appendices include charts and lists of appropriately good wines. Another useful feature is the pronunciation guide after each entry so that the reader will not feel like a klutz when asking for a particular wine in a store or at a restaurant.

If there can be any faults it is that there is no index for the fine tuning of subject topics; to make matters worse, there are no internal cross-references, and thus the materials are just not linked together as they should be. Another bad point is that the entry headings are in green ink – they simply do not stand out the way the former edition's plain capital letters did. Still, the price is exceptional, and the book remains a good value (at least until the next general encyclopedia of wine is published). [R: LJ, 1 Nov 88, p. 91]   Dean Tudor

1376. Sotheby's World Wine Encyclopedia: A Comprehensive Reference Guide to the Wines of the World. By Tom Stevenson. Boston, Little, Brown, 1988. 480p. illus. (part col.). maps. index. $40.00. LC 88-61237. ISBN 0-8212-1690-2.

If a good reference book can be recognized by its comprehensiveness, accuracy, ease of use, and copiousness of illustrations, then this guide to wines qualifies as a good – no, an excellent – reference work. Unlike some wine guides that are limited to text and maps, this work abounds with illustrative material: maps, charts, tables, symbols, color paintings and color photographs, and full-color reproductions of wine labels from all over the world. Indeed, the purview of the book is global; while devoting two

hundred pages to the wines of France, it does not neglect the other wine-producing countries of Europe (including the USSR), North and South Africa, North and South America, Australia and New Zealand, and even the Far East.

This coverage is framed by an excellent introduction and appendices that include a helpful glossary and a vintage guide through 1987 that itself is worldwide, including France, Germany, Italy, Spain, Portugal, the United States, and Australia. Of course, such coverage is gained at the loss of some detail, but as compressed as it is, this guide is highly readable and informative – and not without the personal opinions of the author on even the most insignificant wines of the lesser known wine-producing countries. Eye-catching vignettes, such as "What Makes Pétrus the World's Most Expensive Wine?" add special zest to an already lively book.

This encyclopedia belongs on the reference shelf along with such names as Hugh Johnson, Alexis Lichine, André Simon, and Frank Schoonmaker. As a reasonably priced gift book, it should also find its way to the coffee tables of lucky oenophiles everywhere.

Edwin S. Gleaves

1377. Traditional Food Plants: A Resource Book.... Rome, Food and Agriculture Organization of the United Nations; distr., Lanham, Md., UNIPUB, 1988. 593p. illus. bibliog. (FAO Food and Nutrition Paper, 42). $30.00pa. ISBN 92-5-102557-6.

A team of FAO researchers has selected for inclusion and detailed discussion 110 plant species indigenous to eastern and southern Africa. Their objective is to help reintroduce traditional food plants as a "key element in household food security," food plants that will help sustain the population when it is difficult to obtain the major cereals: wheat, rice, and maize. The first part (forty-one pages) of the handbook describes the basic scientific principles of nutrition in relation to the nutritional problems in eastern Africa. The second part (490 pages) lists and describes the value of individual plants. Plant descriptions include scientific names and synonyms, vernacular names, general description and distribution, food value and preparation, storage, ecology, cultivation, and references. The main emphasis is on food value and food uses. Recipes are not included, but suggestions for mixing foods together are made frequently. Each description is accompanied by good line drawings showing the entire plant, fruit, flower, and leaves. The work contains a good bibliography and many helpful tables and appendices, including a table illustrating language groups, a glossary of botanical terms, a table showing eco-climatic zones, and a list of the names and addresses of specific research organizations within Africa.

The handbook is not typeset, but the photographic reproduction of typescript is well done. Unfortunately, there is no comprehensive index listing all common plant names given within the work (English, French, Sudan, Kenya, Tanzania, Malawi, Zimbabwe, Zambia, Uganda, Ethiopia) and scientific names. However, there is an alphabetical listing by scientific name of all plants and their common English name. The absence of an index is a minor omission in this important work, perhaps supremely important to millions of people. Many of the plants discussed would also flourish in the southeastern United States.

Milton H. Crouch

DIRECTORIES

1378. Kocs, N. J., ed. **Arrow's Complete Guide to Mail Order Foods.** Ardmore, Pa., Arrow Clearinghouse, 1987. 157p. illus. index. $19.95pa. LC 87-71024. ISBN 0-944894-07-0.

This bare bones guide to mail order foods is arranged alphabetically by company under twelve broad chapter headings (e.g., cheese, ethnic foods, coffee). Each entry gives the company's name, address, telephone number, and a listing of the foods offered. There are both a product index and an index to company names. Kocs did her research by collecting over six hundred catalogs and brochures from companies throughout North America. These catalogs are almost a must for potential purchasers to help them flesh out the brief descriptions offered here. As a guide to these companies and their catalogs, this is a fine volume that can easily be used for reference work. [R: RBB, 15 Sept 88, pp. 130, 132]   Deborah Hammer

HANDBOOKS

1379. Campbell-Platt, Geoffrey. **Fermented Foods of the World: A Dictionary and Guide.** Stoneham, Mass., Butterworths, 1987. 291p. $44.95. LC 86-33392. ISBN 0-407-00313-4.

An alphabetical listing of fermented foods consisting of beverages, cereals, dairy, fish, fruit and vegetables, legumes, meat, and starch products from all over the world. For each specific food Campbell-Platt gives its origin, microbiology and biochemistry, composition and nutritive value, methods of production, types available, and method of consumption. References to the literature are given for most entries and there are many *see* references from

local terms to more general foodstuffs. Though fermented foods include many that are widely enjoyed, this scholarly dictionary is not for everyone. Intended for "researchers, food scientists, technologists, nutritionists, biotechnologists, microbiologists, information scientists, product developers [and] people involved in food inspection and control," this volume is recommended only for the largest research collections.   Deborah Hammer

1380. **Commodity Review and Outlook 1986-87.** By Food and Agriculture Organization of the United Nations. Rome, Food and Agriculture Organization of the United Nations; distr., Lanham, Md., UNIPUB, 1987. 125p. (FAO Economic and Social Development Series, No. 43). $30.00pa. ISBN 92-5-102524-X.

Information about the international commodity trade is sometimes difficult for librarians to locate. This volume will be of use in business and agricultural collections because it begins with a general review of the international commodity market for the past year. This includes a global review of agricultural trade, macroeconomic factors affecting commodity prospects, and international policy responses to the trade problems of developing countries. Most of the book consists of reviews and outlooks about specific commodities such as sugar, coffee, cocoa, tea, bananas, peppers, oilseeds, rice, wheat, meat, milk, cotton, jute, rubber, hides and skins, citrus fruits, wine, tobacco, fishing products, and forest products. A final special feature is an essay on the "world pulse economy."   Beth M. Paskoff

1381. **FAO Production Yearbook, 1987. Vol. 41.** Rome, Food and Agriculture Organization of the United Nations; distr., Lanham, Md., UNIPUB, 1988. 351p. (FAO Statistics Series, No. 82). $30.00. ISBN 92-5-002671-4.

This yearbook, written in English, French, and Spanish, is principally a list of agricultural production tables. It contains an introduction, explanatory notes, notes on tables, country notes, and a list of countries. Tables include land usage, irrigation, population, agricultural population, and economically active population. FAO index numbers of agricultural production are also included. Production information on approximately seventy crops, information on livestock number and animal products, including slaughter numbers, average dressed carcass weight, and production of meat from slaughtered animals are tabulated. Milk, cheese, and other livestock products are covered. Food supply in relation to basic nutritional components is also listed. Means of production, including farm machinery, pesticides, and prices (including index numbers of prices) are also given.

Most information is for a number of years, frequently going back through 1975 and concluding with 1987. The book would be extremely useful for anyone needing production figures of an international scope for agricultural products produced in specific countries. It would also be useful for those looking for international trends in production. The book is well printed, well bound on good quality paper, and even though much of it is computer printed, it is easy to read and the type is of sufficient size to make it useful.   Herbert W. Ockerman

1382. Kraus, Barbara. **Calorie Guide to Brand Names and Basic Foods, 1988.** rev. ed. New York, New American Library, 1988. 147p. $2.75pa. ISBN 0-451-15149-6.

1383. Kraus, Barbara. **Carbohydrate Guide to Brand Names and Basic Foods, 1988.** rev. ed. New York, New American Library, 1988. 145p. $2.75pa. ISBN 0-451-15151-8.

These "portable guides" are based on Kraus's *Calories and Carbohydrates* (New American Library, 1987), which lists over eight thousand brand name and basic foods. The arrangement is alphabetical, though inconsistent in the sense that there is a generic entry for cheese which includes all cheeses, but no entry for cereal; in that case, each individual cereal has its own entry under its brand name. Fast food restaurants' menus are listed, as are a plethora of new and popular frozen foods. The entries are brief, giving only name, portion size, and number of calories/carbohydrates. The virtue of these paperbacks is that they are updated yearly and reflect the latest nutritional information and newly available products. The drawback is that they are clearly intended to be an item for people to have with them at all times and as such should be a personal purchase. If a library has a current edition of Kraus's guide these books are unnecessary. If not, buy the paperbacks as a reference to update but do not try to supply the entire dieting community with personal copies.   Deborah Hammer

1384. Mott, Lawrie, and Karen Snyder. **Pesticide Alert: A Guide to Pesticides in Fruits and Vegetables.** San Francisco, Calif., Sierra Club Books; distr., New York, Random House, 1987. 179p. illus. bibliog. index. $15.95; $6.95 pa. LC 87-42965. ISBN 0-87156-728-8; 0-87156-726-1pa.

The accuracy of this book, the resources to which it points the reader (organizations for further information and involvement), and the clarity of organization (e.g., tabular presentations of the five pesticides most frequently found in twenty-six fruits and vegetables) more than justify its modest price. On the surface, the book seems a bit tedious because of the repetition, but embedded in the individual accounts of fruits and vegetables are as many fascinating bits of information (e.g., each person in the United States eats eight pounds of carrots a year) as grim ones (e.g., 68 percent of fruits and vegetables are coated with or contain residues of pesticides, or their breakdown products or carriers, that are known carcinogens); the good news reciprocal of the carcinogen prevalence is that 68 percent of the surface residues can be reduced by washing. In fact, it is the consumer intervention that the authors hope to stimulate: consumers can ask their stores to stock organically grown produce (and then buy it), and they can resist the enculturation of cosmetic enhancements like wax (that trap surface residues). This book is made all the more useful by an intelligible glossary, indexes by pesticide and produce type, and suggestions for further reading (including the must read, for the "next" generation, *Silent Spring* by Rachel Carson). The illustrations are marvelous.

Diane M. Calabrese

1385. Vine, Richard P. **Wine Appreciation: A Comprehensive User's Guide to the World's Wines and Vineyards.** New York, Facts on File, 1988. 679p. illus. maps. bibliog. index. $60.00. LC 87-12831. ISBN 0-8160-1148-6.

Vine is coordinator of enology and viticulture at Mississippi State University; he is also a wine consultant to American Airlines. This explains, in part, why his book *Wine Appreciation* is pedantic in the extreme. Unfortunately, it does not look like a textbook, nor does it sell for one. The price and cover mislead the consumer into believing that it is a "compendium" wine book that could prove of value. Such is not the case, for the text and the tone clearly suggest that the book is meant for students: it reads like a textbook. The book was originally announced as selling for $35.00, but it came in at $60.00. What happened? There is no value for the dollar here as there is for Hugh Johnson's wine reference books. The excessively large typeface, the panorama of white space, the lack of color, the uselessly magnified black-and-white reproductions of meaningless wine labels suggest a certain padding. The book could have been issued in paperback at $9.95. The topics include the usual: origin of wine; production and distribution system; tasting of wine; a country-by-country assessment (120 pages for the United

States; six pages for Canada – and there is out-of-date information about Ontario wines with only a brief survey of ownership without any tasting notes); an all-too-brief bibliography that omits some of the leading wine books; and only an eleven-page index (in large type) that omits small, but not necessarily minute, topics. In sum, there are too many lists of data without any cohesion; much better material can be found elsewhere, such as in the Johnson books. Not recommended.   Dean Tudor

Forestry

1386. Kricher, John C. **A Field Guide to Eastern Forests: North America.** Boston, Houghton Mifflin, 1988. 368p. illus. (part col.). index. (Peterson Field Guide Series). $22.95; $14.95 pa. LC 87-35247. ISBN 0-395-35346-7; 0-395-47953-3pa.

For most people interested in nature, a Peterson Field Guide was a first purchase. Unfortunately, you needed to "specialize," one guide for birds, another for trees, still another for flowers, and the list goes on. Those with large backpacks (and strong backs) could identify any species they wanted. But what these guides could not do was to explain the "whys" of how nature worked. Back in 1985, the Audubon Society came out with "second generation" field guides that looked at all the species in a particular habitat. Kricher has created much the same type of guide in *Eastern Forests*.

As with the Audubon Society's *Eastern Forests* (Knopf, 1985), Kricher's guide deals with interpretation rather than identification. All species in a particular habitat are considered, from the insects to trees, and their interaction is discussed. The differences between the Peterson version and the Audubon version are mainly cosmetic; drawings in Peterson versus photographs in Audubon, and the smaller, more easily handled size of the Peterson.

Chapters are arranged by observable patterns, for example, "Disturbance and Pioneer Plants" or "Patterns of Spring." Each chapter describes the particular pattern and tells you how to find the details for this pattern in the field. The chapter ends with a brief questionnaire to "help you learn how to see ecologically" (p. 3), a great tool for those involved in interpretive programs.

As with the other guides in the series, *Eastern Forests* employs the Peterson system of using field marks for identification. Cross-references are made between the text and the illustrations and vice versa, along with referencing other chapters when appropriate. The overall intent is interpretation of nature rather than

species identification, so do not expect a comprehensive field guide. Species are chosen because they characterize an area or interact in a meaningful way. For those looking for a greater understanding of their natural environment, this book provides a great compendium of information scattered about in books and journal articles. But do not expect to be able to throw out all your other field guides. [R: WLB, Dec 88, pp. 117-18]   Angela Marie Thor

1387. Patterson, Douglas. **Commercial Timbers of the World.** 5th ed. Brookfield, Vt., Gower Publishing, 1988. 339p. illus. bibliog. index. $74.95. ISBN 0-291-39718-2.

The first edition of this work appeared in 1948 under the title *Concise Encyclopedia of World Timbers* (Philosophical Library), by F. H. Titmuss. Other editions were published in 1949, 1959, and 1971. These earlier editions emphasized the architectural and engineering requirements of timber; the new edition continues to cover these requirements but also includes a good discussion of the properties of timber and timber processing. One section provides a discussion of materials such as plywoods and fiberboards, developed for manufactured items and in some ways superior to solid wood. Information on individual timbers includes scientific and common names, range, wood characteristics (graining, texture), storage considerations, use (including some possible uses of bark), and conservation.

As an identification aid, small drawings depicting end-grain structure are provided. These are well done but are probably not as helpful to most users as the author would hope. The handbook does not include detailed identification keys. A superior identification guide is H. A. Core's *Wood Structure and Identification* (Syracuse University Press, 1979). Core's work has a good key to identification and truly magnificent halftone illustrations showing end-grain structure. The illustrations are photomirographs that represent the structure one sees with a light microscope. The information given in the Patterson book focusing on wood properties makes it a good companion to the Core work. Two other important works are William G. Keating's *Properties and Uses of Timbers* (Texas A & M University Press, 1982) and the Timber Research and Development Association's *Timbers of the World* (2v., Construction Press, 1979-1980).

Douglas Patterson's handbook faces stiff competition, but its coverage of timber properties meets a practical need and it should be included in those libraries supporting a forestry program.   Milton H. Crouch

1388. Taylor's Guide to Trees. Boston, Houghton Mifflin, 1988. 479p. illus. (part col.). maps. index. (Taylor's Guides to Gardening). $14.95pa. LC 87-26247. ISBN 0-395-46783-7.

Covering nearly two hundred popular trees, this guide shows the homeowner how to select, plant, and care for trees. Introductory chapters explain how to select trees based on temperature zones in North America, landscaping with trees, planting methods, and problem trees to avoid.

The color plates are organized in sections: deciduous ornamentals, deciduous shade trees, broadleaf evergreens, and needleleaf evergreens. These sections contain photographs of each tree with flower or fruit, and information on height, blooming season, and hardiness zones. Species descriptions are arranged under each genus. For each genus there is a brief "How to Grow" paragraph. Species descriptions contain morphological details and advice on soil and climate conditions favored. Appendices cover tree maintenance, disease and pest control, record keeping, and a chart for tree selection based on several factors such as drought tolerance, city conditions, fall color, and suitable soil type.

The species descriptions are clear and complete. The photographs are excellent. The guide is very well organized and easy to use, and allows the user to take into account the many factors involved in tree selection. By comparison Richard Gorer's *Trees and Shrubs* (see *ARBA* 78, entry 1492) has similar species descriptions, but none of the chapters and appendices found in *Taylor's Guide to Trees* that are so useful for the homeowner ready to purchase a tree. The latter is highly recommended.   John Laurence Kelland

Horticulture

1389. Beckett, Kenneth A., with the Royal Horticultural Society. **The RHS Encyclopedia of House Plants Including Greenhouse Plants.** Topsfield, Mass., Salem House, 1987. 491p. illus. (part col.). index. $34.95. LC 87-4546. ISBN 0-88162-285-0.

Culminating forty years of experience as a professional horticulturalist, the author introduces this book as a truly comprehensive work intended for serious collectors of plants. Following the introduction, the author provides a readable, highly illustrated discussion of background and general care under the following topics: history of house plants, plant origin, selection and cultivating, special groups, maintenance and propagation, pests and diseases, and sources for unusual species.

The bulk of the book is devoted to listing over four thousand plant species with nearly one thousand color photographs of excellent specimens. As the name "encyclopedia" suggests, the book covers many not-so-common plants ranging from cacti to aquatic plants. For North American readers, the title "house plants" is confusing, since many shrubs and some trees usually grown out of doors are included. On the other hand, highly cultivated flowering plants such as roses, irises, and tulips are not elaborated upon. Equally surprising is the inclusion of tomatoes and sweet potatoes. Numerous entries of orchids and other tropical plants grown only by professionals are extremely valuable for ambitious ornamental plant enthusiasts.

The entries are arranged alphabetically by genus names. For each genus, the origin of the plant(s), the general description and care, and word/name origin are provided, followed by the pictoral key for environment, light, temperature, water requirements, as well as mature plant shape. Three variable types are considered for each set of requirements, while the shapes are chosen from ten different forms. After the general genus discussion, commonly cultivated species are listed with further information on the origin and specific characteristics, including possible height in both centimeters and inches. Common names are given for some of the species. The 273-word morphological glossary, which follows the genera description, is particularly helpful because the terms used may be too technical for the layman. The index of common names appears after the glossary.

The comprehensiveness of this book, with its focus on a wide variety of indoor and outdoor plants, makes it quite valuable for horticulturalists and botanists. Its lack of basic growing information such as soil type, fertilizer, or force-flowering, makes this book impractical for average house-plant lovers unless it is used in conjunction with other popular house plant books.

Mitsuko Williams

1390. Brookes, John, Kenneth A. Beckett, and Thomas H. Everett. **The Gardener's Index of Plants & Flowers.** New York, Macmillan, 1987. 272p. illus. (part col.). maps. $14.95pa. LC 86-20708. ISBN 0-02-049100-X.

This book is meant to provide an overview of outdoor gardening, with the accent on planning a decorative/landscaped garden. It can be used to pinpoint specific plants to be used in specific locations (both geographic and a specific corner with a specific problem in a specific garden), and also for designing a landscaped setting for a home.

The information presented is accurate and attractively laid out. The only difficulty is that it presupposes a reader to be very highly organized: decide exactly what is to be put where, and then go out and buy the exact plant(s) needed. Much of the information is given in chart formation, listing size, type, shape, needs, and uses, along with other pertinent data for similar varieties of plants (trees, shrubs, climbing plants, perennials, etc.).

Much, if not all, of this data will be included in other books, such as the multi-volume set of the *Time-Life Encyclopedia of Gardening* (Time-Life Books, 1971-) already found in most public libraries. However, this book could be a useful addition to a personal library, or as a reference tool in a small public library that does not already have a gardening reference section.

Judith E. H. Odiorne

1391. Clevely, A. M. **The Total Garden: A Complete Guide to Integrating Flowers, Herbs, Fruits and Vegetables.** New York, Harmony Books/Crown, 1988. 192p. illus. (part col.). bibliog. index. $25.00. LC 88-81387. ISBN 0-517-57054-8.

As the introduction states, this book "is an attempt to marry gardening tradition that is centuries old with modern techniques and varieties, to produce an alternative and decorative way of raising fruit, vegetables and herbs." The emphasis here is on decorative, as the text is filled with pages of colored illustrations of lush gardens and foliage.

In three major sections, fruits, herbs, and vegetables, the reader will find clear and detailed information for sowing, raising, and harvesting. Growing seasons, fruit yield, ornamental value, varieties, pruning, soil preparation, and seed germination are examples of the many areas covered with both the novice and experienced gardener in mind. A chart delineating the various climate zones offers further aid as well as a glossary of unfamiliar terms. General discussions on such topics as tools, soils, sowing and planting, feeding and watering, weeds, and first aid make the book complete.

Because the text refrains from technical jargon, this information will be useful to anyone interested in gardening.   Patricia M. Leach

1392. **Knott's Handbook for Vegetable Growers.** 3d ed. By Oscar A. Lorenz and Donald N. Maynard. New York, John Wiley, 1988. 456p. illus. index. $24.95 spiralbound. LC 87-25224. ISBN 0-471-85240-6.

Knott's handbook is a one-stop compendium on vegetable production. An excellent, up-to-date book on commercial vegetable (and strawberry) production, the volume also contains a wealth of information for the home gardener. Topics include planting, soils, fertilizer, water, pests, weed control, harvesting, storage, seed production, and greenhouse vegetable production. This third edition, which was first published in 1956, contains updated information on high technology growing of vegetables, such as gel seeding, seed priming, polyethylene mulches, and precision seeding. Numerous tables, charts, and diagrams of interest to vegetable growers pepper the work. An insect identification section contains most of the line illustrations in the volume. The volume comes in a handy spiral binding that facilitates use in the field. Libraries with clients interested in commercial or home vegetable growing will find this a heavily used reference work.

Ralph Lee Scott

1393. Logan, William Bryant. **The Gardener's Book of Sources.** New York, Viking Penguin, 1988. 271p. illus. index. $12.95pa. LC 87-40306. ISBN 0-14-046761-0.

This book is not comprehensive; however, the author/compiler claims to have listed the best and most unusual resources in the gardening world. The stated purposes of the book are to put a reader in contact with companies, books, magazines, and individuals who can give them what they need for virtually any sort of gardening and to focus on gardening as a human pursuit, classifying nurseries, clubs, books, magazines, designers, and suppliers by their attitudes towards gardening.

The annotated contents run for twelve pages, listing contents without pages: the index functions as a better guide to finding specific information. Each entry lists an address, cost (if any), what is available, and something about either the place or the item. The scope covers books and catalogs, plants (indoor plants, outdoor plants, all kinds), tools, furniture, landscape architecture and design, and regional sources and sources of sources.

The design and layout are interesting: interspersed among the entries are small line drawings and sidebars of quotations from various books (listed by page, not by author in alphabetical sequence as in a regular bibliography) which are of interest.

Possibly useful in a public library as a reference tool, but sure to become dated quickly (addresses and costs will change), and too expensive to be very useful to individual home libraries.

Judith E. H. Odiorne

1394. McCann, Joy L. **Gardener's Index for 1987.** Kansas City, Mo., CompuDex Press, 1988. 155p. $12.00pa. ISBN 0-945621-01-9; ISSN 0897-5175.

Originally begun for personal convenience in locating articles in periodicals dealing exclusively with gardening, this is the second year *Gardener's Index* has been published.

The best reason for its inclusion on library shelves is that it indexes six periodicals, four of which are not included in the *Readers' Guide to Periodical Literature.* In this source, articles in those magazines are now accessible. The magazines included in this index are *American Horticulturist, Flower and Garden, Garden, Horticulture, National Gardening,* and *Rodale's Organic Gardening.* General magazines that deal in part with gardening, such as *Better Homes and Gardens* or *House and Garden,* are not included (though they are listed in *Readers' Guide*).

Articles are indexed by subject, with a subject guide included, as well as by title and author. Information is also given about each of the magazines in question, with the correct assumption that a reader of one may well enjoy reading others. Since this index was begun to help individual gardeners, it was assumed that many of them subscribed to several of these periodicals already. If not, addresses and rates are given so a reader can write to the magazine in question to begin a subscription.

Since many readers are also gardeners, and since most public libraries already subscribe to one or more of the magazines not indexed in *Readers' Guide,* this would be a very welcome purchase. [R: RBB, 15 Sept 88, p. 136]

Judith E. H. Odiorne

1395. Smith, Miranda, and Anna Carr. **Rodale's Garden Insect, Disease & Weed Identification Guide.** Emmaus, Pa., Rodale Press, 1988. 328p. illus. (part col.). bibliog. index. $21.95; $15.95pa. LC 88-4969. ISBN 0-87857-578-0; 0-87857-759-9pa.

For those who enjoy gardening, there seems to be a constant battle against "invaders." Rodale Press has added a weapon to your arsenal, an identification guide to those pests. The guide covers over two hundred common insects, diseases, and weeds listed in their own sections.

The first portion of the book deals with insects. Two keys, one for larval stages and one for adult and nymph stages, lead to the correct insect group. From there, the insects are arranged alphabetically by common name. Each entry has a black-and-white illustration of the insect, and where needed, illustrations of the larval stage and/or the damage inflicted. For the fifty worst pests, a color photograph depicting the insect and the damages is provided in the back of the book. Each entry gives information on the range, description, life cycle, feeding habits, and host plants. For those which are truly problems, there is information on prevention and control. Beneficial insects, and those which cause minimal damage, have no such listing.

Diseases are categorized by the organism causing the problem (e.g., fungus or virus), and are then alphabetized by common name. Color photographs for all of the diseases are located in the back of the book, with cross-references. The narrative covers the range, description, life cycle, host plants, transmission, and prevention and control. For other items of special interest, a notes section is included. A chart listing each vegetable and its diseases aids the reader in finding a particular problem. The weeds are grouped by annual, biennial, perennial, and woody perennial, then arranged alphabetically by common name. A few of the most common weeds have color photographs, but one must mainly rely on the black-and-white illustrations which accompany each entry. The mature plant is depicted, and when useful, illustrations of the seed, seedling, and/or flower are included. Entry information includes range, description, life cycle, and prevention and control, along with the occasional footnote.

Each section has a short glossary. The index includes the common and scientific names of all entries, as well as the common names of the host plants. In keeping with Rodale's philosophy, the prevention and control methods are all organic. An overview begins each section and supplies general information about the pests covered in that section. A brief list of mail-order sources of natural controls is also included.

Angela Marie Thor

RESOURCE SCIENCES

Energy Resources

GENERAL WORKS

1396. **Alternative Sources of Energy: ASE: The Magazine of the Independent Power Production Industry, December, 1987. 1988 Directory.** Milaca, Minn., Alternative Sources of Energy, 1987. 96p. index. (ASE, No. 96). $4.95 pa. ISBN 0-91732886-8; ISSN 0146-1001.

This is the second annual directory of the Independent Power Production Industry. It is divided into two parts. The first lists companies alphabetically by name regardless of the technology used. The second part lists the companies by the technology used to produce energy. The technologies covered include cogeneration, in which one system produces both electricity and thermal power, usually in the form of steam; district heating, which provides heating and cooling to a number of buildings from one central boiler; geothermal, which is generating electricity from geothermal hot spots in the earth; hydroelectric, which is producing electricity by water power and which is the most widely used renewable energy source around the world; photovoltaics, in which semiconductor materials convert sunlight directly into electricity; solar thermal electric, in which the sun's energy is used to drive a generating turbine; solid fuels – biomass, in which agricultural wastes are used for producing electricity; waste-to-energy systems, in which wastes are burned to produce electricity; electrical equipment; and windpower, in which electricity is produced using the wind. The entries in the first part consist of the company name, address, telephone number, and contact person. The entries in the second section are a listing of company names under the categories developers/owners/operators, manufacturers, services, and "other." After part 2 are a listing of trade groups, a listing of federal and state agencies, and a professional directory. This is a very good, inexpensive, source.   Robert L. Turner, Jr.

1397. Anthony, L. J., ed. **Information Sources in Energy Technology.** Stoneham, Mass., Butterworths, 1988. 324p. maps. index. (Butterworths Guides to Information Sources). $105.00. LC 87-33749. ISBN 0-408-03050-X.

This work is arranged in three parts with sixteen chapters, written by nine contributors, all of whom have had much experience in their respective fields of energy. The first part is on energy in general and consists of five chapters dealing with international energy agencies, national energy agencies, and primary and secondary sources of information. The second part is composed of five chapters on fuel technology, including combustion, steam and boiler plants, electrical energy, energy conservation, and energy and the environment. Part 3 deals with specific energy sources. A chapter is given to solid fuels; liquid fuels; gaseous fuels; nuclear energy; solar and geothermal energy; and alternate energy sources such as ocean energy, wind energy, biomass, and flywheels. Most of the chapters have bibliographies. The chapters are well written and cover vast amounts of current materials. However, the emphasis is primarily on British sources. There is also an index to

subjects, information services, and organizations. This will be a useful, though expensive, guide. [R: LAR, 14 Oct 88, p. 597]
Robert L. Turner, Jr.

1398. Pross, Catherine, and Mary Dwyer-Rigby, comps. **Sustaining Earth: A Bibliography of the Holdings of the Ecology Action Resource Centre, Halifax, Canada.** Halifax, N.S., School of Library and Information Studies, Dalhousie University, 1988. 302p. (Occasional Paper, No. 44). $18.00 spiral-bound. ISBN 0-7703-9718-2.

This bibliography encompasses an eclectic collection of articles, clippings, and volumes held by the Ecology Action Resource Centre in Halifax, Canada. Although the center began to accumulate holdings in 1970, most of the entries in the volume cluster between 1977 and 1983; no materials dated later than 1987 are included. The table of contents reflects a great deal of thought about the subcategories into which the materials fit, and would facilitate a search for resources by a user interested in specific topics (e.g., tidal energy). The compilers refer to "grey" entries for which some bibliographic data are missing or hypothesized (bracketed); it is difficult to imagine how such entries are useful (i.e., [land use – clippings]), particularly when the bibliography does not reveal how to obtain copies of the materials in the collection. There are over six thousand entries; some seem out of place (i.e., an entry on women and law under environmental law) and there are some errors (e.g., the running head on tidal energy continues over wind energy), but on the whole the modest price would probably return the investment to those environmentalists who search the literature in part by browsing. A particularly useful feature of the bibliography is the list of serials held by the center. The emphasis of the collection – not surprisingly – is regional: there are few holdings on tropical forests, but many on wood energy.   Diane M. Calabrese

OIL AND GAS

1399. **Financial Times Who's Who in World Oil & Gas.** 8th ed. Chicago, St. James Press, 1988. 308p. index. $105.00. ISBN 0-912289-84-8.

This book contains biographical information on 1,029 corporate personnel, 181 consultants, 195 academics and research staff members, and 133 politicians (ministers of energy, etc.) involved with the oil and gas industry. Information supplied for each person varies, but typically includes such information as current appointment, previous appointments, business address, telephone number, directorships, publications, and degrees earned. Listings are arranged alphabetically within sections for each of the four categories of personnel. Indexes listing all personnel alphabetically and by company are included at the end of the book.

Representatives of many, but not nearly all, the companies listed in the *Financial Times Oil and Gas International Year Book 1988* (see *ARBA* 87, entry 1441, for a review of the 1986 edition) are included in this book. Only one or two officers of some important companies (for instance, Amerada Hess and BP America) are included, and only a small proportion of the many consultants and academics involved with the industry are listed. While the detailed personal information in this book will certainly be useful, the book's use is limited by the inclusion of only a small proportion of the personnel involved with the oil and gas industry.

Joseph Hannibal

1400. **Worldwide Refining and Gas Processing Directory, 1989.** 46th ed. Donna Barnett, ed. Tulsa, Okla., PennWell Books, 1988. 488p. index. $110.00pa. ISSN 0277-0962.

Produced by the publisher of the *Oil & Gas Journal*, this well-known directory provides statistical and directory-type information on companies involved in crude oil and natural gas processing. Refining companies are listed alphabetically, country-by-country, in sections for the United States, Canada, Africa, Europe, Latin America, and the Middle East. Gas processing companies are similarly listed for the United States and Canada. Each entry contains company address; telephone, telex, and fax numbers; company description; names of personnel; and plant locations. The engineering and/or construction section lists worldwide companies offering a wide range of services including plant and equipment design construction, economic studies, and instrumentation. Company and office addresses, telephone numbers, company description, and personnel are listed. This is a good source for locating a contractor or consulting firm. Company and geographical indexes are also available to the user.

The directory also contains worldwide statistical surveys which were prepared by the *Oil & Gas Journal*. The refining surveys cover refinery locations, capacities, types of processing, products, construction, and catalysts, while the gas processing survey covers plants, capacities, process, and product volumes produced.

The publisher is well known for its comprehensive oil and gas directories. This one, which has long provided refining and gas processing

information for the oil and gas industries, continues to be a very valuable and useful reference tool.

Anne C. Roess

Environmental Science

1401. **California Environmental Directory: A Guide to Organizations and Resources.** 4th ed. Thaddeus C. (Ted) Trzyna and Ilze Gotelli, eds. Claremont, Calif., California Institute of Public Affairs, 1988. 100p. maps. bibliog. index. $40.00pa. LC 77-642158. ISBN 0-912102-85-3.

The fourth edition of the *California Environmental Directory* is divided into six parts. The guide provides addresses and telephone numbers and an overview of the activities of the various governmental, public, and private environmental interest groups with regard to California. Part 1 is the user's guide to who does what in the state of California. Part 2 lists the various federal government departments and agencies. Part 3 lists the state of California governmental activities. Part 4 lists international, interstate, regional, and local agencies. Part 5 includes various associations and independent environmental centers. Part 6 outlines public and private college and university environmental programs. The book is rounded out with an appendix of useful reference books, a description of the California Institute of Public Affairs, and an index of organizations. This is a very useful reference guide for California libraries and for companies, institutions, or organizations with activities in California. It is the most comprehensive listing and useful environmental directory for California.

David R. Fuller

1402. Farmer, Penny, comp. **Lead Pollution from Motor Vehicles 1974-86: A Select Bibliography.** New York, with Technical Communications by Elsevier Science Publishing, 1987. 95p. index. $45.00. LC 86-24013. ISBN 1-85166-066-6.

The absence of an explanation about how the references included in this bibliography were selected represents the only deficiency in the work. Penny Farmer's careful attention to detail (including the mention of whether articles contain illustrations, graphs, and tables, and whether the publication is a supplement or regular issue) suggests the reader should trust her judgment and assume that the four hundred references selected for the bibliography are representative of the literature. Most of the references are annotated lucidly by the compiler. The remainder include either the abstract of the original article or no annotation; the inclusion of references without annotations is not explained but it may be because the title (e.g., "The Beetle and Spider Fauna of Meadows Affected by Traffic Pollution") reveals the content. References on all aspects of lead pollution from ecological effects to regional surveys of effects to legislation are included.

Anyone concerned with policy issues relating to the management of lead pollution from motor vehicles will find the volume useful. The organizations index and personal author index to references facilitate the search for references to the involvement of particular groups in lead pollution management and policy. Moreover, the annotations supplied by the compiler are so good one can learn from reading them. [R: Choice, May 88, p. 1380]

Diane M. Calabrese

1403.   Frankena, Frederick, and Joann Koelln Frankena. **Citizen Participation in Environmental Affairs, 1970-1986: A Bibliography.** New York, AMS Press, 1988. 154p. (AMS Studies in Social History, No. 8). $45.00. LC 87-45800. ISBN 0-404-61608-9.

This bibliography is divided into five subject areas. The environmental decision making chapter covers air pollution, education, environmental action, environmental management, environmentalism, government, impact assessment, information/communication, litigation, planning, pollution, toxic and hazardous substances/wastes, and water pollution. The energy-related decision making chapter covers references on alternative energy development, community energy development, conventional energy development, electric power/utilities, energy action, government, nuclear power, radioactive waste, and transportation.

The chapter on natural resources decision making discusses coastal zone management, forest resources, land use, natural resources action, natural resources management, natural resources planning, parks, recreation and wildlife, resource development, resource recycling, water resources, and weather modification.

The environmental mediation chapter is a special category with references on public concern and resolving environmental problems. Likewise, the chapter on science and technology decision making provides appropriate references on the subject of public involvement in general.

This reference should be of interest to a large audience, from governmental planners and environmental advocacy groups to the general public. It is recommended as a useful reference source for most public libraries and a definite necessity for academic and governmental libraries, particularly any libraries supporting environmental studies or practices. [R: Choice, Dec 88, p. 626]   David R. Fuller

1404.   Goldsmith, Edward, and Nicholas Hildyard, eds. **The Earth Report: The Essential Guide to Global Ecological Issues.** Los Angeles, Calif., Price Stern Sloan, 1988. 240p. illus. maps. index. $19.95; $12.95pa. LC 87-21451. ISBN 0-89586-673-0; 0-89596-678-1pa.

This is an excellent small resource for anyone concerned with the state of our world and its environment. It will be found useful by professors, reporters, journalists, students, political leaders, and concerned citizens.

The report is divided into two parts. Part 1 comprises a series of essays dealing with some of the major environmental issues of our time by some of the most authoritative voices on these issues. Included are "Man and the Natural Order," by Donald Worster; "The Politics of Food Aid," by Lloyd Timberlake; "Nuclear Energy after Chernobyl," by Peter Bunyard; "Man and Gaia," by James Lovelock; "Acid Rain and Forest Decline," by Don Hinrichsen; and "Water Fit to Drink?" by Armin Maywald, Uwe Lahl, and Barbara Zeschmar-Lahl. These essays are all timely and well done and are especially valuable as up-to-date information on these issues. Part 2 consists of an encyclopedic listing of major environmental concerns. Included here are four hundred shorter articles arranged alphabetically. The entries are strictly alphabetical; thus 2, 4, 5-T follows tropical forests and precedes 2, 4-D. These entries carry both internal cross-references to each other, and additional cross-references set at the end of each entry. A series of codes enables the reader to use these cross-references with considerable ease. The amount of information that has been condensed into this small volume of only 240 pages (including acknowledgments) is staggering. One can find information on almost every environmental issue that might be of interest. It is truly a job well done. This book deserves a place on the bookshelf of every environmentalist, educator, political leader, and concerned citizen. It is hoped it will be read, especially by those in leadership positions, because the information presented is of survival significance. Highly recommended.   John C. Jahoda

1405.   Grayson, Lesley, comp. and ed. **Acid Rain & the Environment 1984-1988: A Select Bibliography.** London, British Library Science Reference and Information Service and Letchworth, England, Technical Communications; distr., Corning, N.Y., Air Science, 1988. 240p. index. $55.00pa. ISBN 0-7123-0757-5(British

Library Science Reference and Information Service); 0-946655-25-1(Technical Communications).

"I'm doing a paper on acid rain." Reference librarians probably hear this remark a number of times a semester, and *Acid Rain and the Environment* can offer an up-to-date bibliography to get students started. Technical Communications, along with the British Library Science and Information Service, produced their first acid rain bibliography in 1984, covering the literature from 1980 to 1984. This edition picks up where the last left off, and deals with 1984 to March 1988. The bibliography "reviews a substantial selection of the published literature" (p. ii), including journal articles, books, proceedings, and government reports. Coverage is international, and all references are available at either the British Library Science Reference and Information Service or through the Library's Document Supply Centre.

Entries include a full bibliographic citation, along with a brief abstract. The bibliography is divided into five subject areas: the issue, the scientific controversy, research, the effects, and the litigation strategies. There are further subdivisions within each area, and the entries are then arranged alphabetically by title. Access by author, organization, or project is provided by alphabetical indexes. An additional ten pages of unindexed references which arrived after the deadline bring the bibliography up-to-date with the March 1988 cutoff. A large number of the materials appear in standard journals and U.S. government documents, making them accessible to American users. Though selective in nature, the coverage seems more than adequate to serve most needs.

Angela Marie Thor

1406. Jessup, Deborah Hitchcock, ed. **Guide to State Environmental Programs.** Washington, D.C., BNA Books, 1988. 578p. maps. $40.00pa. LC 88-6373. ISBN 0-87179-583-3.

This book is an incredible and extremely useful reference tool. The foreword clearly and concisely explains the intent and organization of the contents. The intent is to assist the wide variety of prospective users through the morass of both the federal and individual state environmental laws and programs. The first portion of the book outlines the federal laws and programs related to environmental protection and cleanup, including the Clean Air Act, the Clean Water Act, groundwater protection, Corps of Engineers water protection programs, the Resource Conservation and Recovery Act, SARA Title III Spill Reporting, and coastal zone protection.

This book summarizes each of the environmental programs of every state in the nation, in alphabetical order. In addition to the summaries, the chapters include "first contacts" for more specific information on programs, telephone numbers of the individual state agencies outlined in the book, permit information and fees, spill reporting addresses and telephone numbers, and the individual approach to environmental protection.

Appendix A includes telephone directories of the Environmental Protection Agency and the Army Corps of Engineers. Appendix B provides state and local directories for the state economic development agencies, and many of the individual state agencies. This book is highly recommended as a reference tool. It is about as close to a "one-stop-shopping-guide" on environmental programs as one is likely to find. [R: Choice, Dec 88, p. 630; RBB, 15 Dec 88, p. 691]

David R. Fuller

1407. Nordquist, Joan, comp. **Toxic Waste: Regulatory, Health, International Concerns.** Santa Cruz, Calif., Reference and Research Services, 1988. 64p. (Contemporary Social Issues: A Bibliographic Series, No. 11). $15.00pa. ISBN 0-937855-21-9.

The compiler of this volume has given a great deal of thought to topical subdivisions, which include chemical waste, nuclear waste, transportation of toxic waste, federal policy, and state policy. The bibliography succeeds in providing the user with references to literature representing many viewpoints (the stated goal). However, the bibliography is deficient in several ways: there is no clear statement about how the references for inclusion were selected, how comprehensive a literature review was culled to produce it, and how it happened that the dates for references cluster in the years 1985-1987. On the other hand, a strong feature of the bibliography is the list of organizations from which pamphlets can be obtained. This bibliographic series would probably be most useful to public libraries because it meets the needs of reference users seeking a quick immersion in a topic, and not a comprehensive one.

Diane M. Calabrese

1408. Seidel, Egon, comp. **Dictionary of Environmental Protection Technology: In Four Languages: English, German, French, Russian.** New York, Elsevier Science Publishing, 1988. 527p. index. $144.75. LC 86-32746. ISBN 0-444-98971-4.

This dictionary will certainly facilitate discussion and research into issues of environmental protection across major language barriers. It records English, German, French, and

Russian equivalents for a *comprehensive* list of technical terms used in the contemporary environmental literature. Alphabetized according to the English usage, the dictionary acknowledges that most important papers and international conferences are written and conducted in English. The other three languages which are included do, however, rank next in importance. Active international scholars will, therefore, find the volume extremely useful.

Gary W. Yohe

1409.   Vozzo, Steven F., comp. **International Directory of Acid Deposition Researchers.** 1985-86 ed. St. Paul, Minn., Acid Rain Foundation, [1987?]. 177p. index. $10.00pa. ISBN 0-935577-08-4.

The authors of this directory note that their "chain-letter" approach to assembly may have missed some very important and interested researchers. This is true. For example, Paul Godfrey, head of the University of Massachusetts Acid Rain Monitoring Project, is not included. However, once this imperfection is noted, it should be stated that overall this is a very useful directory, and perhaps the only one of its kind. The purpose of the book is to facilitate the exchange of information among scientists interested in acidic deposition and effects. The directory is intended to serve as a starting point facilitating communication and interaction among scientists. Each individual is listed by name, address, telephone number, and discipline. The listings are arranged geographically (country, state, province). The appendix includes a subject index and an alphabetical index. This field is an active, dynamic, and vitally important area of research and this guide should fill a real need.   John C. Jahoda

Natural Resources

1410.   James, William, and David Short, eds. **Natural Resources and Development: An Annotated Bibliography.** Buffalo, N.Y., William S. Hein, 1987. 297p. $38.50. LC 87-81840. ISBN 0-89941-577-6.

The title of this book is misleading, as only articles, most published in legal periodicals during the past fifteen years, are included. Most articles address issues related to federal and state law. Articles are arranged by subject and alphabetically by title under subject. Subjects include mines and minerals, oil and gas, taxation, synthetic fuels, and environmental law. Annotations are short and descriptive. There is no index, but the table of contents is very detailed and abundant *see* references are supplied.

This work is intended to be a quick reference to the legal literature on natural resources and to make researchers in other fields more aware of this literature. However, citations of articles, while in proper legal style, will be disconcerting to those accustomed to more complete citations (authors' names are not always supplied, etc.). Also, titles of publications are abbreviated, and no list of abbreviations is provided, and, because of a large amount of wasted space (the annotations are double spaced!), this book is much longer than it need have been.

Still, this bibliography can serve as a useful entry into the legal literature on natural resources for researchers in the United States. Larger law libraries will have most of the publications cited.

Joseph Hannibal

32 Biological Sciences

BIOLOGY

1411. Brigitte T. Darnay and Margaret Labash Young, eds. **Life Sciences Organizations and Agencies Directory: A Guide to Approximately 8,000 Organizations and Agencies....** Detroit, Gale, 1988. 864p. index. $155.00. LC 87-29090. ISBN 0-8103-1826-1.

Directories are central to the reference services that librarians are able to provide. Gale Research Company is well known for the directories it has published in the past, and the editors have an understanding of the market for new publications. This directory of life sciences organizations and agencies is based in part on material from eight other Gale directories, and provides a specialized focus that life sciences librarians will appreciate. It can serve as a companion volume to the *Scientific and Technical Organizations and Agencies Directory* (see *ARBA* 86, entry 1436) and the *Medical and Health Information Directory* (see *ARBA* 86, entries 1608-1609).

The life sciences, as defined for this volume, include all of the agricultural sciences, environmental sciences, food sciences, veterinary sciences, and biotechnology, as well as botany, zoology, and microbiology. Each chapter is devoted to a single type of organization, with entries within the chapter arranged either alphabetically or geographically. There are chapters on U.S. and international associations, as well as botanic gardens, state and federal agencies, educational institutions, research centers, consulting firms, standards organizations, and libraries. Because several chapters have an international coverage, there is a list of the names of countries as they are used in the directory. A single index to master names and keywords is quite complete. Although there is no geographic index, most states and countries can be located in this index, especially if the location is in the name of the organization.

An advisory board of leading life sciences librarians contributed to the planning of this directory. The editors note that there will be future editions, and that they plan to expand the coverage to meet the needs of users. *Life Sciences Organizations and Agencies Directory* will be a frequently used addition to any life sciences or agriculture library, and is recommended to them for purchase. [R: Choice, Sept 88, p. 84; LJ, July 88, p. 72; RBB, 15 May 88, p. 1584]

Beth M. Paskoff

1412. Coffin, Barbara, and Lee Pfannmuller, eds. **Minnesota's Endangered Flora and Fauna.** Minneapolis, Minn., for Natural Heritage and Nongame Wildlife Programs by University of Minnesota Press, 1988. 473p. illus. (part col.). maps. index. $49.50; $16.95pa. LC 87-30141. ISBN 0-8166-1688-4; 0-8166-1689-2pa.

There has been a great deal of interest generated recently in the recording of endangered species; this book is an excellent example of such a publication that exemplifies good planning, sound organization, knowledgeable authority, and attractive execution. The result of a state legislative mandate, *Minnesota's Endangered Flora and Fauna* covers three hundred native Minnesota species in a total of eleven chapters, written by thirty authors chosen for their recognized expertise in the fields of botany, ornithology, mammalogy, herpetology, ichthyology, and invertebrate zoology. The introduction to the volume provides historical context, and a thorough discussion of the Minnesota Endangered Species Program, the Minnesota landscape, and a list of selected references. Instructions for using the volume are carefully described and defined; there are appendices for species distribution by county for plants and animals, and for presenting the Minnesota statute requiring the production of this document.

Chapters are arranged by broad category of floral and faunal groups, including lists classifying species by "endangered," "threatened," and "special concern." A brief introduction to each chapter sets the stage for individual species accounts, supplying scientific and common name, synonyms, official status, basis for the species's status, preferred habitat, aid to identification, references, distribution map, and illustrations. The book does not provide comprehensive treatment of the biology of each species, nor is there any attempt to supplant taxonomic keys, which the editors warn will surely be necessary to identify some of the more difficult or rare species. There is a complete index for all names.

This reference work was designed to provide information and assistance to a wide range of individuals including biologists, students, planners, developers, and interested citizens who seek understanding of Minnesota's unique natural environment, and show concern for preserving its natural heritage. The book succeeds admirably.   Elisabeth B. Davis

1413. Maclean, Norman. **Dictionary of Genetics & Cell Biology.** New York, New York University Press; distr., New York, Columbia University Press, 1987. 422p. illus. $60.00. LC 87-28153. ISBN 0-8147-5438-4.

The fields of genetics and cell biology have changed radically in the last decades, growing and merging, and incorporating aspects of molecular biology, developmental biology, and microbiology, among other fields. Interest in these subjects transcends traditional academic circles, as well, since they are at the center of research in biotechnology, cancer, and AIDS. This dictionary brings together terms from genetics, cell biology, and many closely related fields, in a format which is accessible to both professionals and intelligent laypersons.

Terms are listed in alphabetical order, with numerous cross-references from synonyms, related terms, and abbreviations. A wide subject area is covered, from classical and population genetics to molecular biology. While the definitions (of lengths ranging from a single sentence to several pages) are complete enough to satisfy workers in the field, the writing is lucid enough to be readable by just about anyone. Several appendices add to the usefulness of this book: a list of common and Latin names of key organisms used in genetics and cell biology, lists of numbers of chromosomes and amounts of DNA in key species, and a taxonomic classification of living organisms. [R: Choice, Sept 88, p. 84; RBB, 15 Sept 88, p. 134; SBF, Nov/Dec 88, p. 75]   Carol L. Noll

1414. Margulis, Lynn, and Karlene V. Schwartz. **Five Kingdoms: An Illustrated Guide to the Phyla of Life on Earth.** 2d ed. New York, W. H. Freeman, 1988. 376p. illus. bibliog. index. $35.95; $24.95pa. LC 87-210. ISBN 0-7167-1885-5; 0-7167-1912-6pa.

The typical course in biology progresses from cells to whole organisms including their functions. Rarely can biologists, who study one or two organisms intensively assist beginning biology students in understanding the broad spectrum of life on earth, or encouraging students' interests in evolutionary history. The authors deserve major applause for succeeding at both goals. The book's understandable organization and description of life forms will appeal to the book's target audience of science students and laypersons.

The book consists of five chapters: "Prokaryotae," "Protoctista," "Fungi," "Animalia," and "Plantae." Each chapter begins with a general discussion of the evolutionary relationships among the phyla discussed and is followed by two-page descriptions of each phylum. The description format for ninety-two phyla (seventeen prokaryotic, twenty-seven protoctist, five fungi, thirty-three animal, and ten plant) includes three elements: a brief text, a typical habitat based on one of the five different scenes, and illustrations of one or two species. The illustrations consist of a photograph and a labeled anatomical drawing of the organism(s). Each photograph is accompanied by a key showing how that organism can be visualized: by naked eye, hand lens and light, scanning electron or transmission electron microscope. The appendix consists of an extensive index, a glossary of 734 terms, and a list of about 1,000 genera with respective phylum and common names.

This book makes taxonomic studies fun and relates it well to all aspects of biological studies whether microbiology, botany, or ecology. This edition incorporates many discoveries and developments occurring since the publication of the first edition in 1982. As a guiding light in the maze of ten million species over three billion years of evolution, this book is highly recommended for a wide variety of readers, from high school students to the specialists.   Mitsuko Williams

1415. McIver, Tom. **Anti-Evolution: An Annotated Bibliography.** Jefferson, N.C., McFarland, 1988. 385p. index. $39.95. LC 88-42683. ISBN 0-89950-313-5.

This volume contains annotated bibliographic entries on 1,852 publications which the author considers to be anti-evolutionary in theme or in interpretation. McIver's definition of anti-evolution is unusually broad, but revolves around opposition of Protestant fundamentalist creationism to Darwinian evolution. Most included titles relate to this narrow focus, but his broad definition produces unexpected bedfellows. Pro-evolution works critical of Darwinian evolution are included if they seem "motivated by extra-scientific concerns" or if they were quoted "by creationists as if they were hostile to evolution itself" (p. xi). Works advocating psychic and occult evolution and evolution guided by extraterrestrial beings are also listed.

Most cited publications are books and pamphlets. Journal and periodical articles, unless issued as separates, are excluded, as are most, but not all, films, videos, and other visual media. McIver makes no claim of complete coverage of "anti-evolution" literature and a casual perusal of books in this reviewer's library indicated omitted titles.

All entries are listed alphabetically by author and numbered sequentially. Typical entries include author(s), title, edition or volume number, date, publisher, and descriptive comments, although inconsistencies in both format and content of the citations are numerous. Most listings include brief comments on illustrations, tables, and indexes, but do not refer to the pagination or length of publications being described.

The author attempts to describe most cited publications concisely and objectively and to avoid interpretations which might be considered polemic by objective readers. Citation annotation lengths vary considerably and many titles lack content descriptions entirely. Some descriptions are written with complete sentences, while others are composed partially or entirely of brief phrases. Numerous abbreviated words and initials are undefined and left to the reader to interpret (e.g., on p. 185: "Morris points out it has been a decade since he left VPI to found CHC and ICR, and notes that ICR has been the dominant force in creation-science").

The preface and introduction focus on the author's intentions and methods. Indexes for author names, titles, and subjects terminate the book. This book has value primarily as a single-source reference for persons needing capsulized descriptions of many anti-evolution and/or creationism-oriented books and pamphlets.

                         Edmund D. Keiser, Jr.

1416. Singleton, Paul, and Diana Sainsbury. **Dictionary of Microbiology and Molecular Biology.** 2d ed. New York, John Wiley, 1987. 1019p. illus. $150.00. LC 87-19047. ISBN 0-471-91114-3.

As scientific progress forces researchers further into specialization, communication among them becomes more and more difficult because the terms used in a given field take on new meanings and are rarely clearly defined outside each specific, narrow subject area. This dictionary provides a linguistic bridge for one of the fastest growing branches of science, microbial and molecular biology. Just how much this bridge was needed is evident in its size, which has more than doubled since the publication of the first edition, *Dictionary of Microbiology* (see *ARBA* 80, entry 1359).

The uniqueness of this dictionary is in its concise and clear description of terms, followed by some up-to-date references where those terms are discussed extensively. The references are not necessarily the source where the terms were originally used, but rather the most recent, review-type sources for location of related papers. The references are both books and journals seldom dating before 1980. The book references are numbered; the journal references are listed in full with journal titles abbreviated to the extreme. Illustrations, though small in number, include formulas, tables, processes, instruments, and chemical structures. Appendices include a series of specific pathways, biosyntheses, and fermentation processes. The usefulness of this dictionary extends to specialists and beginning science students. It provides answers to many basic questions sometimes only found by painful paging of textbooks. For example, under "air," microbes contained in air as well as sampling methods are discussed.

Despite the slight inconvenience caused by the use of the British spelling, this dictionary is extremely comprehensive and easy to use. It will be a worthwhile addition to all laboratories and life science libraries.   Mitsuko Williams

1417. Tootill, Elizabeth, ed. **The Facts on File Dictionary of Biology.** rev. ed. New York, Facts on File, 1988. 326p. illus. $19.95. LC 88-045476. ISBN 0-8160-1865-0.

When it comes to reference books in the biological sciences, newer is better, since anything more than a few years old is out-of-date. This is a revision and enlargement of a 1981 work, with added material from the fast-moving fields of molecular biology, genetics, and immunology. Like the previous version, the coverage is broad, from traditional fields such as botany and anatomy, to the newer, more technical fields. Definitions are written in clear, nontechnical English, with numerous cross-references to related terms. There are very few illustrations, most of them of chemical pathways or cellular anatomy. This is a good basic dictionary for students and laypersons whose work involves biological concepts or terminology.

Carol L. Noll

BOTANY

General Works

1418. Boudreault-Lapointe, Lise. **Vocabulaire de Biotechnologie Végétale. Plant Biotechnology Vocabulary.** Ottawa, Canadian Government Publishing Centre, 1988. 77p. bibliog. (Terminology Bulletin, 180). price not reported. pa. ISBN 0-660-53993-4.

Biotechnology is a rapidly developing field and as with any such field its terminology develops and changes quickly. This brief dictionary is aimed at helping writers to use standarized vocabulary, particularly those who in Canada write in both French and English. The terms and definitions are presented in parallel columns alphabetized by the English term. Although covering only the plant aspects of the subject, when compared with J. Coombs's much more extensive treatment, *Dictionary of Biotechnology* (see *ARBA* 88, entry 1610), this compilation comes out very well in having the most important terms and even having thirty-seven terms not in Coombs. The definitions are clear and concise, with the French definitions sometimes more extensive than the English ones. Also useful is the seven-and-one-half-page bibliography of monographs and periodical articles used in preparing this dictionary.

Emanuel D. Rudolph

1419. **The Marshall Cavendish Illustrated Encyclopedia of Plants and Earth Sciences.** David M. Moore, ed.-in-chief. Freeport, N.Y., Marshall Cavendish, 1988. 10v. illus. (part col.). maps. index. $299.95/set. LC 87-23927. ISBN 0-86307-901-6.

It is a measure of the relative importance we accord the plant and animal kingdoms that while there are several multivolume encyclopedias of the animal world (including the massive *Grzimek's Animal Life Encyclopedia* (see *ARBA* 73, entry 1459), until now there have been no comparable reference works for plants. Yet it is on the photosynthesis of plants that all but a handful of the world's ecosystems depend. Furthermore, plants are disappearing from nature due to the effects of humans more rapidly even than are animals. This encyclopedia, the work of more than 120 botanists and geologists, will go a long way toward restoring a balance in natural history reference collections and increasing popular appreciation of the plant world and the geological basis of plant communities.

The ten-volume encyclopedia is divided into four main parts. Volumes 1, 2, and part of 3 are an alphabetical dictionary of the most important groups of plants, listed under scientific generic names and common names. The emphasis in the descriptions of over two thousand plants is on those which are either used in some way by people, or are of particular scientific interest. Many important groups of plants have more than one entry. For example, the peppers can be found under *capsicum* (the genus) and under the common names "chile peppers," "cayenne" and "green peppers." Asterisks beside key words in each article link related terms. Most entries are one paragraph long, but there are a few dozen multipage articles on major crop groups (e.g., "rootcrops") and important botanical groups (e.g., "fungi"). Many articles are accompanied by clear and informative color photographs.

The second section of the encyclopedia (the remainder of volume 3, and volumes 4 and 5) is a comprehensive survey of the families of flowering plants. The majority of the more than three hundred plant families are described in articles which average one page long. The essays, by specialists, are arranged in traditional taxonomic order, and give the number of genera and species, distribution, descriptions, and discussion of the economic and scientific importance of each family. Articles on each family are accompanied by maps of geographic distribution and beautiful paintings of representative flowers, fruit, and foliage.

Part 3 of this encyclopedia (volumes 6 and 7) is a survey of the entire subject of plant ecology. There is a history of humankind's exploration of the plant world and the development of methodologies to study plant ecology, and chapters describing both methods and results in the fields of plant geography, ecology, paleobotany, and evolution. Then there are detailed descriptions of the world's vegetation types and zones, and last a thorough treatment of humankind's past and present effects on it all. While the fields of plant physiology and molecular biology are only briefly discussed, the coverage of ecological and evolutionary botany is first rate, comprehensible, and accompanied by numerous helpful photographs, charts, and diagrams.

Volumes 8 and 9 are really a basic textbook on geology, from the special viewpoint of trying to understand the evolution and distribution of plants. There are discussions of all the geological forces which determine the environment, and detailed dictionaries of fossils and minerals.

Volume 10 links this complex and diversified reference source together with alphabetical and thematic indexes, a glossary, and an extensive bibliography. This is an outstanding work, with fascinating snippets of information and beautiful illustrations on every page. Despite the multipart arrangement, the central goal of explaining the diversity of plants and their importance to our world is met throughout. [R: WLB, Dec 88, pp. 117-18]   Carol L. Noll

1420. Young, Michael. **Collins Guide to the Botanical Gardens in Britain.** London, Collins; distr., Topsfield, Mass., Salem House, 1987. 160p. illus. (part col.). maps. bibliog. index. $24.95. ISBN 0-00-218213-0.

While this book fills an empty niche, it is a curious and not entirely successful hybrid between a proper guidebook and a coffee table decoration. As a guide, it lists twenty-eight British botanical gardens, providing details as to location, hours, fees, contents, and history of each. Discussions range from two to ten pages in length and are chatty, with mention of some plants of horticultural interest. The coffee table aspect is provided by the 8-by-11-inch format, the chatty text, and the color pictures.

As a guide, the book is not entirely successful, as its size precludes easy transport, and its coverage is not complete, hitting only the larger and more conspicuous gardens. As a coffee table book, it seems short, and the photographs are not especially numerous; further, they are cursed by poor registration and color separation.

However, I am not aware of any other nontechnical guide to the botanical gardens of this area, and it is pleasant reading. Those seeking detailed listing of botanical gardens should consult D. M. Henderson and H. T. Prentice's *International Directory of Botanical Gardens*, third edition (Utrecht, Bohn, Scheltema & Holkema, 1977).   Bruce H. Tiffney

Aquatic Plants

1421. Kraus, E. Jean Wilson. **A Guide to Ocean Dune Plants Common to North Carolina.** Chapel Hill, N.C., published for University of North Carolina Sea Grant College Program by University of North Carolina Press, 1988. 72p. illus. maps. index. $4.50pa. LC 87-40515. ISBN 0-8078-4212-5.

This thin volume is a very basic guide to the coastal flora and vegetation of North Carolina, suitable for use by the casual, nonscientific visitor to these shores. It commences with a concise summary of the factors that influence the distribution of vegetation in the coastal environment. A visual glossary of botanical terms leads to simple keys arranged by plant habit (e.g.,

shrub, herb, etc.). Some fifty plants are described, each accompanied by a simple line drawing illustrating key characters and a brief text. Short descriptions of plants not illustrated, references, and indexes complete the book. I would hesitate to call this a "reference" book, as it serves more the purpose of public education, and does it well. Those requiring a reference to the coastal flora of North Carolina might consider, in order of increasing complexity, G. M. Silberhorn's *Common Plants of the Mid-Atlantic Coast: A Field Guide* (see *ARBA* 83, entry 1324) or A. E. Radford, H. E. Ahles, and C. R. Bell's *A Manual of the Vascular Flora of the Carolinas* (University of North Carolina Press, 1968).

Bruce H. Tiffney

Flowering Plants

1422. Cox, Peter A., and Kenneth N. E. Cox. **Encyclopedia of Rhododendron Hybrids.** Portland, Oreg., Timber Press; distr., Portland, Oreg., ISBS, 1988. 318p. illus. (col.). bibliog. index. $59.95. LC 88-2203. ISBN 0-88192-108-4.

Rhododendrons have been hybridized since the early 1800s. A hybrid is not necessarily better just because it is new, but it can be better suited for the climate or have other advantages. Many hybrids, however, are sold without adequate information, and can be "bud-tender, disease prone, straggly, ugly, shy-flowering, or they may have been grafted on an unsuitable rootstock."

This book was designed to help avoid such pitfalls, and to help people locate the kinds of rhododendron that they will enjoy. The approximately two thousand plants described in this book are available through major nurseries in Britain, Europe, Canada, Australia, New Zealand, and the United States. Most Japanese hybrids were not included.

Each entry is evaluated, with additional information as to when and by whom it was hybridized. A glossary provides more information. Names and addresses of rhododendron societies are given for people who want to obtain further inforamtion. The bibliography lists periodicals and yearbooks in addition to books. Nonprint media may or may not be available through the societies.

Unfortunately, the cost will prevent this book finding its way into the public libraries where it would get the most use.

Judith E. H. Odiorne

1423. Hayward, John. **A New Key to Wild Flowers.** New York, Cambridge University

Press, 1988. 278p. illus. index. $49.50. LC 86-4249. ISBN 0-521-24268-1.

Inexcusably missing from the title is "of the British Isles." That aside, this is a superb basic key enabling the nonspecialist to identify all but the most unusual of ferns, conifers, or flowering plants found in the British Isles. It is, however, only a key. No descriptions of species morphology, ecology, or distribution are given beyond those used in the identification. For these data, the user is expected to refer to a technical flora.

The key is not based upon the usual dichotomous approach, but rather upon an ingenious nested series of descriptive comments which lead the user to a species identification. The descriptive phrases are often accompanied by small, clear drawings which highlight specific characteristics. An excellent and illustrated glossary provides definitions of terms used in the key proper. More advanced users familiar with angiosperm systematics will welcome the fact that the latter portion of the key is broken down by families, permitting one to refer to the family keys without having to deal with the more general portions of the key first.

Without beating such a work to death in the field, it is inappropriate to praise it unreservedly. However, on a reading examination, this seems an excellent contribution, and well worthy of imitation in other areas of the world.

Bruce H. Tiffney

1424. Mohlenbrock, Robert H. **Wildflowers: A Quick Identification Guide to the Wildflowers of North America.** New York, Macmillan, 1987. 203p. illus. (part col.). maps. bibliog. index. (Macmillan Field Guides). $24.95. LC 86-21614. ISBN 0-02-585440-2.

This Macmillan Field Guide is a handsome and handy tool for those with a casual interest in wildflower identification. It treats relatively few species – a mere 304 of the estimated 20,600 flowering plants found in North America. But the entries are selected carefully to include many of the most common wildflowers likely to be encountered by hikers and suburbanites in all parts of America north of Mexico.

Species are arranged by color and flower shape, in a convenient format of four entries per page, with text and color photographs on facing pages. Photographs are clear and beautiful, and descriptions are brief, giving flowering season, habitat, range, and some background comments. There is minimal use of specialized terminology, backed up by good introductory material and pictorial and textual glossaries. There are also appendices describing the families of flowering plants, and listing names and addresses of wildflower societies.

There are more complete guides to North American wildflowers – the *Audubon Society Field Guides to North American Wildflowers* (see *ARBA* 80, entries 1381 and 1383) and *Guide to Field Identification: Wildflowers of North America* (see *ARBA* 86, entry 1502), to name two. But for the limited purpose of a simple, efficient guide to the most common wildflowers, this new book is an attractive option.

Carol L. Noll

1425. Polunin, Oleg, and Adam Stainton. **Concise Flowers of the Himalaya.** New York, Oxford University Press, 1987. 283p. illus. (part col.). index. $39.95. ISBN 0-19-561832-7.

The Himalayan region, here defined as Kashmir to Nepal, contains a diverse flora that has attracted the attention of increasing numbers of tourists. The authors published *Flowers of the Himalaya* (Oxford University Press) in 1984 as a guide to the more common and colorful members of this flora. The original volume assumed the user was able to identify plant families, and presented keys only at the generic level for the larger families. Individual species descriptions were concise, and included information about the habitat, site ecology, and morphology of the plant. Additional sections included an excellent introduction, a well-illustrated glossary, and an index. The chief joy of the work was the seventy plus pages of beautiful line drawings and nearly seven hundred botanically excellent color photographs. The work lacked the breadth of coverage and depth of treatment to be a true "flora," but remains a superlative guidebook to the more common and obvious elements of the Himalayan flora.

In an attempt to lower the price and bulk of the book, and to increase its audience, the authors have issued this abbreviated version, retaining the drawings, color photographs, glossary, and index, but cutting some 500 of the original 1,495 species descriptions and the introductory material. In addition, the generic keys to the larger families were eliminated, and many generic descriptions were rewritten, sometimes with loss of information, sometimes with a gain in clarity. I personally feel that the reduction in coverage, particularly the loss of generic keys, makes this a less useful version, and would urge libraries to acquire the original, rather than the pruned version. [R: Choice, Oct 88, p. 343]

Bruce H. Tiffney

1426. Polunin, Oleg, and B. E. Smythies. **Flowers of South-West Europe: A Field Guide.** New York, Oxford University Press, c1973, 1988. 480p. illus. (part col.). maps. bibliog.

index. $22.50pa. LC 87-28242. ISBN 0-19-288178-7.

This book is a botanical tour guide to Spain, Portugal, and southwestern France. After introductory material and a summary of the biogeographic and ecological features of the area, twenty-three "plant hunting regions" are briefly described. Note is taken of particular locales of interest, often with driving or hiking instructions. The characteristic plants of the area are summed up in one to four pages of excellent line drawings, and the plant communities illustrated in one to several fine color photographs.

The bulk of the book contains over twenty-four hundred species descriptions organized by family. Keys are provided only to species; the user is expected to know families and to use the illustrations to sort out genera. Some species descriptions are accompanied by line drawings illustrating plant habit, and comparative drawings are provided for large or difficult genera. Excellent color photographs of representative members of each genus are at the back of the book, linked to the descriptions by a numbering scheme. A brief bibliography and indexes of plants, place names, and common names (in four languages) complete the volumes. Brevity begets exclusion. The keys and pictures restrict identfication to flowering material, and coverage is only of the most common two-thirds of the regional flora. The authors suggest that these problems be overcome by using this volume in conjunction with Polunin's larger *Flowers of Europe: A Field Guide* (see *ARBA* 70, vol. 2, p. 121-22).   Bruce H. Tiffney

1427. Polunin, Oleg, with Robin S. Wright. **A Concise Guide to the Flowers of Britain and Europe.** New York, Oxford University Press, c1972, 1987. 107p. illus. (part col.). index. (Oxford Paperback Reference). $13.95pa. LC 86-28497. ISBN 0-19-217630-7.

This is intended as a "quick and dirty," one-stop guide to over one thousand flowering plants in Eastern and Western Europe and the British Isles. Identification is accomplished either by matching the unknown to the color photographs at the rear, or by using the pictorial key. The former approach presupposes knowledge of the family to which the unknown belongs. The latter approach leads one through a nested set of groups based on plant habit, flower color, flower size, plant size, flower shape, flower arrangement, and geographical distribution. This process suggests one or more taxa with which the unknown may be compared, again using the pictures at the rear. The beginner will be helped by an excellent illus-

trated glossary, but the species descriptions in the body of the work focus on distinguishing characteristics, and are painfully brief.

The book is an abbreviated version of Polunin's *Flowers of Europe: A Field Guide* (see *ARBA* 70, vol. 2, pp. 121-22) which uses the same color photographs, but additionally provides extensive keys to families, genera, and species; excellent drawings; and extensive species descriptions. I would use the original, which is not even that much larger than the "concise" version.   Bruce H. Tiffney

1428. Wampler, Fred. **Wildflowers of Indiana.** Bloomington, Ind., Indiana University Press, 1988. 177p. illus. (col.). bibliog. index. $45.00. LC 88-45102. ISBN 0-253-36573-2.

The first thing to note about this magnificent book is that it is *not* a field guide. Besides the large size (approximately 10 by 13 inches), the quality and beauty of the illustrations make this a book to be savored at home or in the library, not to be lugged around outdoors. Although Fred Wampler has provided a readable and informative text, his wife Maryrose Wampler's artwork is the reason for this publication. The book includes eighty full-page, full-color plates of unique watercolors of plants grouped in their natural surroundings, often including insects, mushrooms, lichens, and other details of the habitat. Wampler's style, with luminous colors and interesting use of the white spaces on the page, is artistically pleasing and realistic at the same time.

While this is primarily a book of wildflower art, the introduction, filled with information on the Indiana climate, hardiness zones, and methods of studying wildflowers, and the glossary, bibliography, and index make it a useful reference book as well. The plates are arranged by blooming season, and the text includes information on the natural history of the plants pictured, where particular specimens were found, and charming anecdotes of the author's painting trips. It should be noted that Indiana's flora is fairly typical of the Midwest, and overlaps quite a bit with the Northeastern states' also, so this book should have wide appeal.

Carol L. Noll

Fungi

1429. Bessette, Alan, and Walter J. Sundberg. **Mushrooms: A Quick Reference Guide to Mushrooms of North America.** New York, Macmillan, 1987. 173p. illus. (col.). bibliog. index. (Macmillan Field Guides). $24.95. LC 87-14034. ISBN 0-02-615260-6.

In the past few years, books on mushroom identification have been springing up like, well, mushrooms. This new offering is a paradoxical one, in that it is obviously for beginners, picturing and describing only two hundred of the most common species, and lacking a dichotomous key, but having some features such as chapters on chemical testing and microscopic features of interest only to the most advanced mushroom fanciers.

Like the other Macmillan field guides, the strong points of this book are the simple format and exceptional pictures. There are three superb color pictures on each page, with clear, concise descriptions on facing pages. Arrangement is in groups based on obvious similarities of shape and form. An identification outline at the end of the book sends the reader to the appropriate mushroom group in the guide. A checklist of field characteristics in the introductory material and the illustrated glossary on the front papers give the beginner valuable information for use in the field.

Despite the quality presentation of this book, as a beginner's guide it deserves a word of warning. The authors list as edible with caution several members of the genus *Amanita*, close relatives of the deadliest mushrooms in North America. While an expert can probably always tell members of this genus apart, beginners are prone to making mistakes. A safer approach is taken by most other authors of field guides for amateurs, including Smith and Weber's *The Mushroom Hunter's Field Guide* (see *ARBA* 82, entry 1466) and Miller and Miller's *Mushrooms in Color* (see *ARBA* 82, entry 1465), who recommend enjoying *Amanita*s for their graceful beauty, but leaving the tasting to the experts. [R: SBF, Sept/Oct 88, pp. 25-26]

Carol L. Noll

1430. Rossman, Amy Y., Mary E. Palm, and Linda J. Spielman. **A Literature Guide for the Identification of Plant Pathogenic Fungi.** St. Paul, Minn., APS Press, 1987. 252p. index. $24.00pa. LC 87-070764. ISBN 0-89054-080-2.

This is not a mycology text but a guide intended for pathologists and mycologists needing to review the literature for a specific genus. Successful use depends on the user's ability to identify a genus without the help of identification keys. No easy task, even for advanced students. Citations to the literature are listed under each of the 607 genera included. The organization of the work is alphabetically by genus. An outstanding feature of the guide is a selected bibliography of reference sources. The authors have identified those essential sources needed to help specialists place a fungus within its proper

class, order, family, and genus. These essential sources contain the keys to identification and must be within a library's collection or in a laboratory if this guide is to be of use.

Citations to books and journal articles are complete. Periodical titles are abbreviated, but this will cause few problems for specialists and they can be readily identified by reference librarians. There is an index to all authors cited in the work. The index to genera included in the work is complete.

This printed guide saves time for those wishing to review the printed literature. A spot check would indicate citations are current through 1986. Two bibliography databases, AGRICOLA and BIOSIS, can be used to update the bibliography. These online searches are made easy since search terms (genus and order) are supplied by the bibliography.

Milton H. Crouch

Grasses and Weeds

1431. Williams, Gareth, and Károly Hunyadi, comps. **Dictionary of Weeds of Eastern Europe: Their Common Names and Importance in Latin, Albanian, Bulgarian, Czech, German, English, Greek, Hungarian, Polish, Romanian, Russian, Serbo-Croat and Slovak.** New York, Elsevier Science Publishing, 1987. 479p. index. $144.00. LC 87-575. ISBN 0-444-98969-2.

This is the companion volume to *Elsevier's Dictionary of Weeds of Western Europe*, published in 1982 (see *ARBA* 83, entry 1327). Like its companion, this dictionary groups common weed names under the scientific name (1,868 names) and lists common names by language. Within the scientific or Latin grouping of names, symbols are used to indicate the importance of the species as a weed in the geographical area in which the language is spoken. The listing of English common names makes this a useful work for Americans. Weeds of East Germany are included in this volume. It is amazing how few of the weeds found in the eastern areas of Germany are located in the western geographical area (included in the first volume). A review of some twenty common German names would indicate that weeds have the same common name throughout the country. Users may use the dictionary to identify those weeds indigenous to all areas of Europe or identified in only one or two geographical areas.

The two volumes making up this dictionary are not identical. The titles differ and this volume is not thumb indexed. The publisher indicates that supplements will be needed since weed populations are not static. In the meantime, this is a useful listing by common names of weeds

found in Europe and should promote cooperative efforts to control them.

Milton H. Crouch

Medicinal and Edible Plants

1432.   MacLeod, Heather, and Barbara Mac-
Donald. **Edible Wild Plants of Nova Scotia.**
Halifax, N.S., Nimbus Publishing, 1988. 135p.
illus. index. $9.95pa. ISBN 0-920852-98-X.

Listed in this work are more than fifty
edible wild plants that grow in Nova Scotia. The
authors say there are many more wild edibles of
the area, but that they have experimented only
with the ones mentioned. The plants are
grouped under these headings: woodland
edibles, foods from fields and waste places,
plants from ponds and streams, delicacies from
the seashore, and fruits of bogs and barrens.
Also included are brief sections on other useful
plants and plants to avoid.

Little information is included in the two
latter sections. However, in the main sections
each plant is illustrated with a line drawing and
text material is provided on the facing page.
Information provided includes scientific and
common names, family, other names, description, season, habitat, and edibility. Instructions
are provided on how to prepare the plant for
eating, and occasionally supposed medicinal
properties of the plant are mentioned.

Theodora Andrews

Trees and Shrubs

1433.   Courtright, Gordon. **Trees and Shrubs
for Temperate Climates.** 3d ed. Portland,
Oreg., Timber Press; distr., Portland, Oreg,
ISBS, 1988. 239p. illus. (col.). index. $45.00.
LC 87-36433. ISBN 0-88192-097-5.

This is the third edition of a work formerly
entitled *Trees and Shrubs for Western Gardens*
(see *ARBA* 81, entry 1642). It is written as a
practical guide for the home gardener. The text
is brief and all plants are illustrated with color
photographs. Its coverage is restricted to plants
readily available in retail nurseries and suited to
the temperate climate. Plants are arranged by
height and type. Two indexes permit cross-
referencing between botanic and common
names. Minimum temperatures are indicated for
each plant. A five-number code is used to indicate planting conditions for each species. After
the main entry section, several lists cover flower
colors, trees for dry and damp conditions, trees
resistant to oak root fungus, and those resistant
to deer.

The color photographs are excellent, showing trees in home settings. There is much useful
information on planting conditions and locations in the yard. Plate numbers are indicated in
the botanic name index but not in the common
name index, an inconvenience. The temperature
zone guide lacks the usual map. The homeowner
will find this a very useful guide in tree or shrub
selection.   John Laurence Kelland

1434.   Duncan, Wilbur H., and Marion B.
Duncan. **Trees of the Southeastern United
States.** Athens, Ga., University of Georgia
Press, 1988. 322p. illus. (part col.). maps. index.
(Wormsloe Foundation Publication, No. 18).
$19.95. LC 87-5837. ISBN 0-8203-0954-0.

This important new regional field guide accomplishes the impossible: it is suitable for use
by both professional botanists and enthusiastic
amateurs. To accomplish this, the authors
group trees into eleven major categories based
on distinctive features and within these categories by family or genus. The line drawings of
distinctive features (leaves, flowers, fruit) are
some of the best to be found in any guide. Leaf
illustrations, showing edges and blade bases, are
particularly helpful. Good color illustrations
show distinctive identifying features. Dichotomous keys (arranged in couplets that offer a
choice between two opposing characteristics or
sets of characteristics) are well thought out.
These keys will prove helpful to self-taught
botanists wishing to make more effective use of
the guide over a period of years. The glossary
contains 149 terms; the index is complete. This
close-to-ideal guide lacks two features: for the
beginner, there are no silhouettes showing the
form of mature trees, and for the botanist, there
are no winter keys.

With the exception of Texas, the Southeast
includes all the former Confederate states
(Florida north of Levy County on the Gulf
Coast and Flagler County on the Atlantic Coast)
plus Kentucky, West Virginia, Maryland, and
Delaware. These borders are somewhat artificial
since distribution maps and descriptions indicate that most of the 306 species included are
also found in adjacent states. Including the
complete range for each species is another outstanding feature of the work, making it a useful
purchase for libraries located in the mid-
Atlantic and midwestern states.

Descriptions include particulars of a tree's
abundance or rarity, its habitats, and its flowering or pollen-shedding period. Information on
susceptibility to disease, insects, or fire is
included. Poisonous features are identified.
Utilization by wildlife and humans are provided
for many species.   Milton H. Crouch

1435. Hightshoe, Gary L. **Native Trees, Shrubs, and Vines for Urban and Rural America: A Planting Design Manual for Environmental Designers.** New York, Van Nostrand Reinhold, 1988. 819p. illus. maps. bibliog. index. $79.95. LC 87-18911. ISBN 0-442-23274-8.

This comprehensive work responds to the information environmental designer's need to choose native trees, shrubs, and vines suitable for the American environment. The intent of the book is to provide the layperson, student, and professional with material that will clarify plant interrelationships so that plants will be selected that will survive and be healthy as well as attractive.

The work is divided into two main sections: native trees and native shrubs and vines. Each of these is further subdivided into two sections. The first, "Elimination Key," describes different factors usually considered in selecting plantings. More than 250 plants are classified by such characteristics as form; branching; foliage; flower and fruit; suitable ecological habitats; and cultural requirements such as soil, hardiness, and similar species. The second part, "Master Plates," presents drawings or photographs of the plants with separate illustrations of twigs, leaves, flowers, and fruits. There is a map of the United States showing native regions. The plants' characteristics are listed and described on pages facing the illustrations. Also included in the book are tables showing in squares of color the foliage coloration of the plants during the four seasons of the year. All illustrations are in black-and-white.

The author of the book is a professor of landscape architecture.

Theodora Andrews

1436. Mohlenbrock, Robert H., and John W. Thieret. **Trees: A Quick Reference Guide to Trees of North America.** New York, Macmillan, 1987. 155p. illus. (part col.). maps. bibliog. index. (Macmillan Field Guide). $24.95. LC 87-14033. ISBN 0-02-585460-7.

This handbook is a part of the Macmillan Field Guide series and is "designed with the novice in mind." Included are 232 of the most common trees located north of Mexico; trees located in south Florida are excluded. The guide is divided into two sections: "Conifers" and "Hardwoods." The index lists popular and scientific names; popular names are included under the type of tree, for example, the Pacific yew is indexed, "Yew, Pacific." There are a brief glossary and a bibliography listing some of the more important monographs, including several excellent U.S. government publications.

The illustrations are good, but, with the exception of the conifers, which are arranged according to leaf structure, there are no helpful keys to aid identification. There are no color keys to flowers and fruits; the section on conifers does not include a key to cones. The guide does not include a winter key to help identify nonevergreens. There are maps showing ranges, but useful tree silhouettes are not included for most of the trees discussed. Bark is not pictured or often discussed as a key to identification. Poisonous leaves or fruits are not always readily identified, nor is there an index entry serving to gather the names of those trees having poisonous leaves, seeds, or fruits.

The Audubon Society Field Guides to North American Trees (see *ARBA* 81, entries 1453 and 1454) is a better purchase for libraries and individuals.   Milton H. Crouch

1437. Petrides, George A. **A Field Guide to Eastern Trees: Eastern United States and Canada.** Boston, Houghton Mifflin, 1988. 272p. illus. (part col.). maps. bibliog. index. (Peterson Field Guide Series, 11). $19.95; $13.95pa. LC 87-22591. ISBN 0-395-46730-6; 0-395-46732-2pa.

This is a much revised version of Petrides's *Field Guide to Trees and Shrubs* (see *ARBA* 73, entry 1428). The previous guide covered eastern Canada and northeastern United States. The area treated in the new edition includes all of eastern Canada and the United States east of the Great Plains. The new guide includes 455 species of trees, but shrubs are no longer covered.

Descriptions are organized into six groups according to leaf morphology. Color plates include leaf, twig, and flower or fruit. A new feature is the identification chart next to each plate. This allows the user to distinguish similar species by cross-checking field marks. Range maps represent a welcome new feature. Appendices include a key to trees found only in Florida, a key to trees in winter, and a plant classification chart.

The species descriptions are detailed. The illustrations are entirely new, and far more detailed and true to life than the clear but stylized ones of the previous edition. The illustrations are arranged to allow immediate identification of like species. This is an excellent guide and should be in every collection containing field guides.   John Laurence Kelland

NATURAL HISTORY

1438. Johnson, Carolyn M., comp. **Discovering Nature with Young People: An Annotated Bibliography and Selection Guide.** Westport,

Conn., Greenwood Press, 1987. 495p. index. $49.95. LC 87-8694. ISBN 0-313-23823-5.

This is a listing of several thousand items, of just about every conceivable media type (books, slide sets, computer programs, posters), all dealing with some aspect of nature or humans' relationship to the natural world. Relatively few are concerned with the scientific study of nature. The focus here is on a more general "nature appreciation." A large section deals with literary, artistic, and musical interpretations of nature. The result is that there is a lot of chaff in with the wheat. Do the sound track albums from the *Wizard of Oz* and *Annie* really have much to do with nature study?

The bibliography is divided into sections of materials for young people (mostly ages 8-16), and materials for the educators, librarians, and youth group users who are the intended audience for the book. Most items have brief annotations; many have addresses of supplying organizations. In addition, there are lists of such things as publishers and distributors, contests and awards, and nature associations. There are indexes by authors, titles, media types, and fairly broad subject areas.

Since there exist other, more specific sourcebooks for science teachers, this book will be of most use to teachers of art and literature, and elementary teachers who want to give a natural history slant to their curriculum. [R: BR, Sept/Oct 88, p. 50; RQ, Summer 88, pp. 572-73]   Carol L. Noll

ZOOLOGY

Birds

1439. Ali, Salim, and S. Dillon Ripley. **Compact Handbook of the Birds of India and Pakistan: Together with Those of Bangladesh, Nepal, Bhutan and Sri Lanka.** 2d ed. New York, Oxford University Press, 1987. 737p. illus. (part col.). maps. bibliog. index. $98.00. ISBN 0-19-562063-1.

Here reproduced in smaller format, four pages on one page, is the complete text of the authors' magisterial *Handbook of the Birds of India and Pakistan* (10v. Oxford University Press, 1968-1974) including the revised text of volumes 1-4. Ripley and the late Ali have a tradition of prodigious production of books on birds of the subcontinent, the later ones somewhat derivative, beginning with their authoritative *Synopsis of the Birds of India and Pakistan* (Bombay Natural History Society, 1961), a detailed listing, the numbering system of which forms the basis for the organization of the

earlier *Handbook*. The 104 plates of the *Compact Handbook*, some in color for the first time, have only minor changes from those in *A Pictorial Guide to the Birds of the Indian Subcontinent* (Oxford University Press, 1983) by Ali and Ripley and are by the respected American artist John Henry Dick. The plates and line drawings in the *Handbook* were interspersed throughout the text. Most were in turn derived from older area monographs and have the charm and beauty (as well as the incompleteness) of another time. Most plates in the first edition of the *Compact Handbook* consist of these older ones. Dick's attractive paintings in the *Pictorial Guide* and this *Compact Handbook* depict for the first time all twelve hundred species and are conveniently grouped in one section. For those who have not purchased the ten-volume *Handbook*, volumes 6-10 of which are out-of-print although undergoing revision, this compact edition is a superb alternative. However, at $98.00 and 12½ by 8¼ inches it has considerable heft in its own right. For each species the text has sections on local names, size, field characters, status, distribution and habitat, habits, breeding, museum diagnosis, measurements, food, color of bare parts, voices and calls, and migration as appropriate, plus a distribution map and often a text figure. An excellent production which belongs in every major library concerned with ornithology. Highly recommended.   Henry T. Armistead

1440. Andrle, Robert F., and Janet R. Carroll. **The Atlas of Breeding Birds in New York State.** Ithaca, N.Y., Cornell University Press, 1988. 551p. illus. maps. bibliog. index. $29.95. LC 87-47867. ISBN 0-8014-1691-4.

Atlases of wild bird populations originated in Europe and are now in progress in much of North America, especially the eastern United States. This excellent New York volume documents the presence, or lack of it, of 242 species in 5,323 sectors ("atlas blocks") of the state during the period 1980-1984 as determined by over forty-three hundred volunteer field observers. For each species there is a high-quality, full-page map indicating its breeding status in the blocks where it is recorded. On the opposite page are signed summaries of this information as well as authoritative accounts of the species' historical status, distribution, and abundance in New York. These text writeups provide a fine historical overview and make full use of existing literature. This New York atlas is an extremely fine production of the highest quality. The line drawings for each species, done by several artists, are also very pleasing and accurate.

Appendices describe the state's ecozones, natural and manmade environments (e.g., rock quarry, urban vacant lot, etc.), and breeding season tables with egg dates, nestling and incubation periods, etc. The extensive introductory material and plastic, transparent overlays ($12.95 extra) featuring forest types, altitude, precipitation, etc., are also very well done.

With atlases either completed or underway for neighboring Ontario, Vermont, and Pennsylvania plus other nearby states and provinces, the published results of these massive, cooperative field studies should prove invaluable to ecologists, wildlife biologists, state and county officials, federal agencies, and others for environmental planning, environmental impact statements, and resource management. They provide baseline data which should be useful for decades. Highly recommended.

Henry T. Armistead

1441.	Clark, William S. **A Field Guide to Hawks of North America.** Boston, Houghton Mifflin, 1987. 198p. illus. (part col.). maps. bibliog. index. (Peterson Field Guide Series, 35). $19.95; $13.95pa. LC 87-4528. ISBN 0-395-36001-3; 0-395-44112-9pa.

This addition to the Peterson Field Guide Series serves the growing hawk-watching community among bird enthusiasts. It is unusual in covering only one order of birds, the diurnal raptors, or hawks and their relatives. While most guides cover several hundred species, here the thirty-nine native and accidental North American species are treated. The species accounts are much longer than those in previous field guides, including description, similar species, flight patterns, status and distribution, behavior, unusual plumages, and more. Species accounts are arranged in phylogenetic sequence, and a range map accompanies each. The birds are illustrated with color plates and black-and-white photographs. Introductory material provides guidance on recognizing the general types (accipiters, kites, falcons, etc.) and includes silhouettes of each.

The color plates are very detailed, in fact more so than those in Peterson's *A Field Guide to the Birds* (see *ARBA* 82, entry 1483). This is important because each species is illustrated in male, female, immature, regional variant, and subtle transitional plumages, very helpful to the observer in the field. The photographs are not uniformly clear, but they supplement the plates and provide an overall impression of the birds as one would observe them under less than ideal conditions. This is a nicely executed, well-organized field guide, and will greatly facilitate hawk identification. [R: LJ, 15 Apr 88, p. 31]

John Laurence Kelland

1442.	Farrand, John, Jr. **Eastern Birds.** New York, McGraw-Hill, 1988. 484p. illus. (part col.). index. (Audubon Handbook). $13.50pa. LC 87-3430. ISBN 0-07-019976-0.

The publishing of this book will surely be hailed in the bird-watching world as a major event. John Farrand, Jr., was coauthor of the 1977 *Audubon Society Field Guide to North American Birds: Eastern Region* (see *ARBA* 78, entry 1315), but this new work is a vast improvement over that somewhat flawed offering. Instead of arrangement by appearance, color, and habitat, which was the revolutionary experiment of the 1977 field guide, the author has returned to a more usable, modified phylogenetic arrangement. The main improvement, however, is in placing the pictures and text on the same page, rather than having color plates and species descriptions in separate halves of the guidebook.

Birders argue endlessly over which is better in a bird guide, photographs or idealized paintings such as those in the Peterson guides (see *ARBA* 82, entry 1483). Suffice it to say, if photographs are your personal preference, this is the book for you. The photographs are clear and beautiful, and most birds are shown in several poses and stages of maturity. Close-ups of facial and other features are also included. Although the format of one species per page sacrifices the at-a-glance comparisons possible with other field guides, there are several pages of photographs in the introductory section comparing different swans, geese, raptors, ducks, and gulls in flight. The text, both in the introductory chapters on bird-watching and in the individual species entries, is uniformly readable and informative. Particularly useful is a section under each bird on similar species and how to differentiate between them. There are textual descriptions of the range of each species, but no range maps. The author has included handy graphs showing the relative size of each bird. This is an outstanding new bird guide, and although it probably would not supplant previous guides, it will be a welcome addition to the field. [R: Choice, Mar 88, p. 1064]

Carol L. Noll

1443.	Harrison, Peter. **A Field Guide to Seabirds of the World.** New York, Stephen Greene Press/Viking Penguin, 1987. 317p. illus. (part col.). maps. bibliog. index. $24.95pa. ISBN 0-8289-0610-6.

This guide is splendidly illustrated with 741 seabird color photographs which were selected from over sixty thousand slides. Included are photographs of some of the rarest and most enigmatic birds in the world, the Amsterdam albatross, the Chinese black-headed gull, the relict gull, and the near-extinct short-tailed albatross. As such it represents the largest and most complete collection of seabird photographs ever published. In a few cases very rare species have been illustrated with paintings instead of photographs because no photographs were available. In addition to the photographic plates the book includes features commonly found in the better field guides: descriptive text, including English and scientific name; size information, etc.; distribution maps; identification information; habitat information; distribution information; and information on similar species. A unique feature of this guide is an illustrated key to the Procellariiformes (Tubenoses), which includes ninety-two species in twenty-three genera and covers twenty-four pages. A short bibliography and a cross-referenced index to scientific and common names are also included. The index is designed to be used as a seabird checklist or life list. Finally, this beautiful photographic collection, valuable information, and identification aid are nicely packaged in a handy, pocket-sized guide that can go along into the field. Highly recommended for both the professional naturalist and amateur seabird enthusiast.

John C. Jahoda

1444. Isler, Morton L., and Phyllis R. Isler. **The Tanagers: Natural History, Distribution, and Identification.** Washington, D.C., Smithsonian Institution Press, 1987. 404p. illus. (part col.). maps. bibliog. index. $70.00; $49.95pa. LC 85-11747. ISBN 0-87474-552-7; 0-87474-553-5pa.

Do not be fooled by the shape and format of this book, which are that of a field guide (and indeed it will undoubtedly serve as such). In reality, it is a full-fledged monograph, covering all the known 242 species of tanagers (a few only recently discovered), one of the most attractive subfamilies of birds in the New World.

A short general introduction is followed by a list of abbreviations, a fine glossary, and the bulk of the book, a detailed account of each species. The species accounts include verbal descriptions (cross-referenced to the plates), geographic and elevational ranges (including maps), habitat and behavior, vocalizations, breeding behavior, and sources.

The authors have combed ornithological resources – museums, the literature, unpublished material – added to their own observations in the field, to present the most current information. In a discipline where individual findings are often jealously guarded, an unusual number of well-known field ornithologists have contributed extensive unpublished notes of their observations. All such contributions are meticulously acknowledged throughout the text.

There is an innovative feature for the Summer, Scarlet, and Western Tanagers – separate accounts for summer and winter habitats. Hepatic Tanager is treated as three subspecies.

There are thirty-two color plates illustrating every species, many not only male and female but subadult and subspecies as well, with brief descriptions on facing pages cross-referenced to the text. A complete list of references and an alphabetical index round out the volume. This volume is an extraordinary achievement and deserves the widespread recognition it will undoubtedly receive.   Syd Schoenwetter

1445. Lever, Christopher. **Naturalized Birds of the World.** Harlow, England, Longman Scientific & Technical and New York, John Wiley, 1987. 615p. illus. maps. bibliog. index. $130.00. LC 86-28727. ISBN 0-470-20789-2.

Naturalized exotic species are animals (or plants) introduced outside their native range, which have gone on to form reproducing populations in their new habitats. The examples are many and varied, as are the reasons for introduction. Ring-necked pheasants, native to Asia, were released in the United States in a variety of locations as game birds. In many areas they thrived and became a favorite game species. The ubiquitous house sparrow was introduced in the midnineteenth century from Europe as a form of insect control. It soon became a pest. And the starling, the most serious pest bird in North America, was first introduced into Central Park by an eccentric millionaire who wanted to establish in the United States populations of all birds mentioned in Shakespeare.

The object of this guidebook is to detail "when, where, how, and by whom various birds now living in the wild state were introduced, and what effects – for good or ill, they have had on the native biota." The author is an acknowledged expert on the subject who has also written *Naturalized Animals of the British Isles* (Hutchinson, 1977) and *Naturalized Mammals of the World* (John Wiley, n.d.). He has provided a thorough and fascinating guide to the subject. Birds are arranged in taxonomical order, with chapters for each species. Entries include maps of natural and naturalized distributions, sketches of the birds, and detailed histories of naturalization in each location in which new populations of the bird have become established. In particular, the author concentrates on important ecological consequences of each example. Every article includes numerous references, and there is a fifty-two-page bibliography at the end of the book. Complete geographical and species indexes make this an outstanding reference source.   Carol L. Noll

1446.   Madge, Steve, and Hilary Burn. **Waterfowl: An Identification Guide to the Ducks, Geese and Swans of the World.** Boston, Houghton Mifflin, 1988. 298p. illus. (part col.). maps. bibliog. index. $35.00. LC 87-26186. ISBN 0-395-46727-6.

Waterfowl doubtless appeal to more people – birders, hunters, aviarists, even casual zoo visitors – than any other order of birds, and were probably the first birds to be domesticated by humans as a source of food and feathers, so it is not surprising that there is a large body of literature, scholarly and popular, dealing with the anatidae. This is, however, the first field guide to cover all the world's wild waterfowl, in virtually every important plumage variant; as an identification manual, it has no equal.

The first section consists of 47 colored plates accompanied by range maps and brief descriptions emphasizing field marks. This is followed by 155 species accounts, which include English and Latin names, further field identification data, voice, description, subspecies (if any), habits, habitat, distribution, population statistics (conservation concerns are noted when relevant), and citations to the bibliography. Line drawings accompany some accounts. A few readily identifiable subspecies (especially those that have sometimes been regarded as full species) are treated separately, and there are brief accounts of those species known or believed to have become extinct in the past century. Both sections are taxonomically arranged according to B. C. Livezey's 1986 classification scheme. There is an index of common and scientific names. The treatment is rigorous but not excessively technical, suitable for public, academic, and many secondary school libraries. [R: Choice, Oct 88, pp. 292, 294; LJ, July 88, p. 72]   Paul B. Cors

1447.   Martin, Brian P. **World Birds.** Enfield, England, Guinness Books; distr., New York, Sterling Publishing, 1987. 192p. illus. (part col.). maps. index. $19.95. ISBN 0-85112-891-2.

As might be assumed from the publisher, this is primarily a collection of avian superlatives: largest, smallest, most abundant, rarest, etc. It is more than just a random collection of facts for trivia fans, however; the author is obviously well grounded in ornithology and is careful in assessing data, so the book can give the reader some understanding of the basics of bird biology. The consistent emphasis on conservation is also a virtue. One can, by consulting the index, find specific bits of information, but one can also read the book through as a monograph; libraries may well find it as useful in the circulating collection as on the reference shelves.

The writing is straightforward without being simplistic, and can be understood by persons with only a minimal background in ornithology. No serious factual or typographical errors are apparent; there are a few repetitious passages. Many American readers may have difficulties with the book's strong British emphasis, however. The use of unfamiliar terminology (how many readers will recognize *ringing* as the British equivalent of *banding*?), the use of birds common in Britain but unknown in North America as examples of phenomena being discussed, and the inclusion of numerous "the – est bird in Britain" entries with no comparable entries for North American species are likely to be problems. All measurements are given in both metric and "traditional" terms, however.   Paul B. Cors

1448.   Palmer, Ralph S., ed. **Handbook of North American Birds. [Diurnal Raptors]. Volume 4: Family Cathartidae ... [and] Family Accipitridae (first part).... Volume 5: Family Accipitridae (concluded) ... [and] Family Falconidae....** New Haven, Conn., Yale University Press, 1988. 2pts. illus. (part col.). maps. index. $80.00/set. LC 62-8259. ISBN 0-300-04062-8 (v.4 and v.5).

The earlier volumes of this set have already established its importance as a major reference work; these volumes continue to maintain their predecessors' standard, so all libraries owning the earlier volumes will want to acquire these also. The only disappointment is the extremely slow publication rate; volume 1 appeared in 1962 and volumes 2-3 in 1976 (see *ARBA* 77, entry 1384).

This continues to be a work of multiple authorship; the individual contributions are signed, but no complete list of the authors and their credentials is provided. Articles are based both on a comprehensive review of the literature and primary research by their authors; the bibliography is very extensive, but continues to use the awkward run-on format of the earlier volumes and is somewhat hard to use.

North America is defined as the United States and Canada, Baja California, Bermuda, Greenland, and Hawaii (the only endemic Hawaiian raptor, the Hawaiian hawk, is excluded, however). Arrangement is in taxonomic sequence, essentially following current A.O.U. practice; the Cathartidae are retained in the traditional location, though most current thought puts them in the Ciconiiformes. There are three levels of accounts: full coverage is given to species regularly occurring in the region; less detailed coverage is given to species of verified but only occasional occurrence; and two species for which unverified sight records exist are briefly footnoted. The full accounts provide data on description, subspecies, field identification, voice, habitat, distribution, migration, banding status, reproduction, survival, habits, and food.

Though written primarily for a scholarly audience, the book is within the comprehension of serious amateurs; it should also interest most falconers. [R: LJ, 1 Sept 88, p. 163]

Paul B. Cors

1449.　Pulich, Warren M. **The Birds of North Central Texas.** College Station, Tex., Texas A & M University Press, 1988. 439p. illus. maps. index. (W. L. Moody, Jr., Natural History Series, No. 9). $45.00; $16.95pa. LC 87-9143. ISBN 0-89096-319-3; 0-89096-322-3pa.

Regional avifaunal studies usually cover entire states or larger geographic areas, but Texas is so large and ecologically diverse that monographs covering only part of the state are reasonable. This work covers a thirty-two-county region approximately centered on Fort Worth. Originally mostly grassland except for riparian hardwood forest along the major rivers, the region has now been much altered by agriculture, urbanization, and the damming of the rivers to create many large reservoirs in an area devoid of natural lakes.

Following an introductory section discussing the ecology of the region and the methodology of the study are the taxonomically arranged accounts of the 385 species of verified occurrence in the region. Appropriately, since information on the identification and biology of these species is readily available elsewhere, these accounts deal with the birds' geographic and seasonal occurrence in the region, including nesting records. Coverage is comprehensive and authoritative, based largely on the author's own studies augmented by examination of other ornithologists' records. Most accounts include a range map. Appended are brief accounts of thirty-three species "of uncertain occurrence" and a checklist by county. Also included are a comprehensive bibliography and an index of common and scientific names. This is an excellent addition to the growing list of regional bird books.　　　　　Paul B. Cors

1450.　Robinson, Jane Washburn. **A Birder's Guide to Japan.** Santa Monica, Calif., Ibis Publishing; distr., Ithaca, N.Y., Cornell University Press, 1987. 358p. maps. index. $14.95pa. ISBN 0-934797-02-1.

Japan's birds have been the subject of comprehensive, modern English-language books only since 1982, when *A Field Guide to the Birds of Japan* (Kodansha, 1985) appeared. Jane Robinson was the editor of this excellent reference book, the first complete guide in English to Japanese birds. Her latest book deserves to be equally well received. In it she describes forty-nine areas of major importance to birders. Fifty-seven detailed maps enhance her site descriptions. For each site there are sections on best seasons for visits; bird specialties; a general, introductory paragraph; transportation; directions; the site and its birds; time required; food and rest accommodations; sources for maps; useful Kanji (mostly town names); and a general end "note." There are also three useful appendices: references and resources, essential Kanji, and a list of target birds of special interest. The lengthy introductory section should be invaluable to anyone visiting Japan, covering such topics as food, good manners and meeting the Japanese, safety and the police, and making arrangements and getting help. The cover photograph of Japanese cranes in a gentle snow fall is both appropriate and exquisite.

The index is for bird names only. The indexing of place names would have added to the book's value. Although all other major islands (including remote Okinawa and the other Ryukyus) have site guides, there do not seem to be any for Shikoku. Otherwise this is an excellent, exemplary guide which deserves the widest possible dissemination. It is a pleasure to recommend.　　　　　Henry T. Armistead

1451.　Toups, Judith A., and Jerome A. Jackson. **Birds and Birding on the Mississippi Coast.** Jackson, Miss., University Press of Mississippi, 1987. 303p. illus. maps. index. $17.95. LC 87-2216. ISBN 0-87805-31606.

Like the pieces in a jig-saw puzzle, bird-finding guides for the entire United States are gradually being filled in. About half are entire state guides, but many concentrate on a particular area or region. This volume covers Hancock, Harrison, and Jackson counties on the gulf coast of Mississippi. (It is hard to understand why an overall map of the entire area is not included.)

More than half the book consists of a listing for each species in the area. Each listing (357 species) compresses into one paragraph a load

of information about how many birds have occurred, where, and when. This is supplemented
by bar graphs at the end of the book giving a
bird's eye view of much the same information.

The rest of the volume is a site guide. Each
location is described in precise detail with
specific information on habitat, location, and
birding spots. Each is accompanied by a map
and an account of which birds may be found
and how to get there. There are a separate
chapter on birding around the calendar and a
whimsical chapter on an imaginary big birding
day.

This is a workmanlike job. While there are
no significant hot spots to inspire avid birders to
come running to the Mississippi shore from the
ends of the earth, for the resident and migrant
birders the book is an essential tool and will be
much appreciated.

Syd Schoenwetter

1452. Zimmerman, John L., and Sebastian T.
Patti. **A Guide to Bird Finding in Kansas and
Western Missouri.** Lawrence, Kans., University
Press of Kansas, 1988. 244p. illus. maps.
bibliog. index. $22.50; $9.95pa. LC 87-34655.
ISBN 0-7006-0365-4; 0-7006-0366-2pa.

Kansas's location in the geographic center
of the United States has given the state an
unusually large and diverse avifauna, in which
both Eastern and Western species can be found.
If the state is, correctly, thought of as mainly
prairie, it nevertheless does contain several types
of forest habitat, and the prairie itself is not
homogeneous. The authors recognize six different prairie types, each with its own distinctive
bird life. Within the area covered by this handbook, which includes the western edge of
Missouri, some 345 species of birds regularly
abide.

A brief introduction summarizes the biogeography of the region; following this is the
description of individual areas and their birds,
arranged by major habitats from southeast to
northwest, subarranged alphabetically by place.
Regional maps locate the areas covered, and
there are more detailed maps of some sites of
special interest. The emphasis is on places open
to the public, focusing especially on parks and
wildlife refuges. The descriptions are clearly
written and very precise in giving directions for
reaching the areas described. Appendices include a complete checklist of the birds of the
region, suggestions on where to look for a number of less common species, and a brief bibliography. There are indexes of bird names and
place names.

Paul B. Cors

Butterflies

1453. Mitchell, Robert T., and Herbert S.
Zim. **Butterflies and Moths: A Guide to the
More Common American Species.** rev. ed. New
York, Golden Press/Western Publishing, 1987.
160p. illus. (part col.). maps. index. $3.95pa.
LC 64-24907. ISBN 0-307-24052-5.

This compact and economical guide introduces the butterflies and moths of North
America via a selected group (about 4 percent of
known species) of the most "common, widespread, important and unusual." The vivid illustrations and brief descriptions make it possible
for novices to use the guide in their gardens to
identify diurnal swallowtails, sulfurs, and
whites, or to put names with the forms of noc-
turnal species of satyrs and fritillaries. Even
species that sometimes stray into the United
States from the tropics (e.g., the Heliconians,
such as the zebra butterfly) are included in the
guide. An index to scientific names makes it
possible to move on to more complete sources
of information about particular species. The
distribution maps provided for about 10 percent
of the species in the book would have better
been offered for all of them. The eighteen introductory pages survey the life history of the order
of butterflies and moths, and balance comments
on collecting and rearing techniques with advice
on conservation, the importance of butterfly
gardening, and the reasons for collecting sparingly. Names and addresses of organizations
that promote conservation and knowledge of
butterflies are cited. A mention of the butterfly
production centers (e.g., Callaway Gardens)
that are developing in the United States (to
introduce a wide segment of the population to
the diversity and complexity of the group)
would improve a future edition.

Diane M. Calabrese

Domestic Animals

1454. Anderson, Janice. **The Cat-a-logue.** Enfield, England, Guinness Books; distr., New
York, Sterling Publishing, 1987. 128p. illus.
$7.95. ISBN 0-85112-484-4.

Devoted entirely to cats, this slim volume
treats us to facts and feats about the "biggest,
smallest, earliest, rarest, most expensive, and
most famous" of all cats, in a format that is vintage Guinness. Designed as a pocket book, it is
crammed full of line drawings, photographs,
cartoons, stories, anecdotes, and breed lists,
among many, many other items. The contents
are divided into six chapters: "Cats and Us"
(genealogy, caring societies), "The Inimitable

Cat" (physical aspects, maternal instinct, endurance records, famous cats), "The Pedigree Cat" (recognized British breeds, some North American cats, cat shows), "The Cat in the Language" (in literature, nursery rhymes), "Cats in the Arts" (performing cats, in the movies), and "Cult of the Cat" (witchcraft, superstitions).

All illustrations are in black-and-white and some are not reproduced well (see, for example, pages 15 and 111). However, the wide variety of photographs and drawings offers a charming and playful view of the cat world. The major missing feature is an index, sure to be a terrible nuisance for anyone hoping to find (refind) information. In order to locate information on specific British breeds one must turn to page 52 and scan the entire chapter to be sure nothing was missed.

The entire book is set in a very narrow two-column format. No column width exceeds 1½ to 1¾ inches, and the text is not justified. Light typeface is used for the body of the text and boldface text is used for emphasis (names of famous people, places). Reading the book is a real chore because so much boldface appears, often three entire lines in a row, that it is difficult to catch the meaning of the very brief entries, since the eye cannot make the transition from light typeface to dark typeface quickly enough. Names of famous people and places are on every page, but no sources are given for quotations or the myriad "facts" regarding what someone said, did, and thought about his or her relationship with their cat(s).

The book is fun and informative for a cursory overview of all things *cat* and can be recommended for public or school libraries. In no way will this book help you select a cat for a pet or help you determine your suitability to own one. For assistance in that area, see *Harper's Illustrated Handbook of Cats* (see *ARBA* 86, entry 1526), a guide to the breeds of cats recognized in North America, with cat registries, advice on showing cats, and detailed information on their care.   Judy Gay Matthews

1455.   Kwalwasser, Amy, and Carolyn Banks. **The Horse Lover's Guide to Texas.** Austin, Tex., Texas Monthly Press, 1988. 683p. $14.95 pa. LC 88-2245. ISBN 0-87719-104-2.

Do you need to find a top cutting trainer for your quarter horse? Need a place to stable your friends on the long drive across Texas? Looking for a rodeo? Perhaps a horse auction? This guide presents a unique compilation of information for the horse lover – too bad it is limited to Texas.

There are three main sections: activities, breeds, and services. Each contains alphabetical

directory listings by county under specific subjects. For example, under activities, main subjects include cutting, distance riding, dressage, foxhunting, polo, rodeo, therapeutic riding, and racing, among others. Ranches, trainers, drivers, rodeo riders, and racetracks are listed under their respective counties. Brief descriptions are given for each activity, and, in some cases, for ranches and individuals.

The second section, on breeds, is divided by breed or type of horse, including mustangs, mules, miniature horses, and warmbloods, along with the "standard" breeds. Unfortunately, the information here is far from complete. Directories from the various breed associations are much more accurate. The final section, on services, covers camps, colleges, creative services such as artists and photographers, facilities, insurance companies, veterinarians, saddlemakers, and a tremendous variety of other equine-related specialties.

A useful publication for public libraries in and around Texas, as well as for individual horsemen, this book is the first of its kind other than a few state directories sponsored by local periodicals, which tend to be very superficial. A really useful reference would be a national directory with this same type of information, updated every few years.

Shirley Lambert

Fishes

1456.   Axelrod, Herbert R., and others. **Dr. Axelrod's Mini-Atlas of Freshwater Aquarium Fishes.** mini-ed. Neptune, N.J., T.F.H. Publications, 1987. 992p. illus. (part col.). index. $19.95. ISBN 0-86622-385-1.

This book is an aquarium lover's dream. Covered in the front matter are an extensive list of symbols to identify the sex of the fishes, their feeding habits, reproduction, aquarium lighting, temperament, swimming habits, pH of the water, and how large they grow. The preface expounds on the various items of the symbols list, including charts of metric and liquid measures, useful discussions of how to photograph fish in a set-up aquarium, in a film frame, and how to handle live fish out of water in preparation for photography. There is a six-page discussion of the family *Cichlidae*, specifically those cichlids found in Central and South America and one species from Texas. These fish are very popular with aquarists because they are hardy, easy to sex and breed, very colorful, friendly, and many become tame enough to take food from their owner's hands.

The truly outstanding aspect of this work is the over eighteen hundred full-color photographs (640 pages). These approximately 4-by-2½-inch photographs faithfully reproduce the wonderful colors of the fish as well as show form and texture, and represent 99 percent of the fish that hobbyists would encounter. Beneath each photograph are the scientific name of the fish and a string of symbols that relate back to the symbols list. This portion of the guide should serve as a quick means of identification for specialists and nonspecialists, and represents a major contribution to the identification of the many varieties of aquaria fish available.

Almost a "book within a book" is the "Aquarium Maintenance, Plants, and Fish Breeding" section (250 pages), preceded by its own separate table of contents. Included in this section is information on the tank and other equipment, how to set up an aquarium, fish anatomy and physiology, tank water and the intricacies of maintaining it properly, food and feeding, various families of fish, health problems and cures, live plants, and breeding characteristics. Virtually every page of this section has wonderful color photographs of disease conditions, anomalies of certain species, water plants, and breeding and birthing phases.

There are two indexes: one covers the section on aquarium maintenance, plants, and breeding, and the other is a separate scientific names index, which includes codes indicating geographic distribution of the fish (AF = Africa, NA = North America, TA = Tropical America, etc.).

Considering the high cost of many reference books today, the price of this volume is truly astounding given the excellent production aspects that are evident: heavy coated paper stock for clear reproduction of the photographs, sewn signatures to ensure that the work will hold together under heavy use, heavy-duty dust jacket, and strong cover boards. This book is an absolutely essential reference work for anyone interested in the identification and care of freshwater aquarium fishes.

Judy Gay Matthews

1457.   Dore, Ian, and Claus Frimodt. **An Illustrated Guide to Shrimp of the World.** Hedehusene, Denmark, Scandinavian Fishing Year Book and Huntington, N.Y., Osprey Books, 1987. 229p. illus. (part col.). maps. bibliog. index. $85.00. LC 87-13994. ISBN 0-943738-20-2.

An excellent introduction to the biology and economics of shrimp, the book is divided into four major sections (chapters). Chapter 1 is a brief (two pages) statement of the purpose and structure of the book. The book really starts with chapter 2, which is a layperson's guide to the identification of shrimp. Terms are described and problems of identification are discussed. Chapter 3 is called the "shrimp encyclopedia" and gives in alphabetical order information of value to shrimp producers and users. Definitions, descriptions, and comments are provided. Chapter 4 is the most striking section, consisting of an illustrated guide to shrimp identification. Color pictures, drawings, and maps are provided for seventy species of shrimp and one species of krill (*Euphausia superba*). The authors note that although the color pictures represent the appearance of live shrimp, the enormous individual variation means that there is no such thing as a correct color. Shrimp are usually translucent when alive, which makes colors difficult to define.

This book is directed toward industry use, and is not intended for scientific use. The authors note that proper scientific identification requires much more detailed descriptions than those given and the use of systematic taxonomy. In light of this the primary interest and use for this volume will be for those involved in the shrimp industry. However, it will serve as a useful "field guide" for others, including amateur and professional scientists interested in marine biology. Recommended for the purpose for which it is obviously intended.

John C. Jahoda

Insects

1458.   Johnson, Warren T., and Howard H. Lyon. **Insects That Feed on Trees and Shrubs.** 2d ed. Ithaca, N.Y., Comstock Publishing/ Cornell University Press, 1988. 556p. illus. (part col.). bibliog. index. $49.95. LC 87-25074. ISBN 0-8014-2108-X.

This second edition has increased the color plates by approximately 10 percent, reorganized old plates, and greatly expanded black-and-white illustrations; these revisions have made a very good book better, and together with *Diseases of Trees and Shrubs* (see *ARBA 88*, entry 1543), provides broad coverage for pest identification by tree and shrub specialists. The identification and diagnosis of insect and mite problems on woody ornamental plants must precede actions to solve problems. This well-illustrated and tightly written text provides the biology, life history, illustrations, references, and other information on about nine hundred arthropod species associated with common trees and shrubs. These constitute the primary problems that ornamentalists, homeowners, pest control operators, city foresters, etc., are likely to encounter, even though only about one-third of the arthropod species that could be encountered are represented. The format includes a one-page readers' guide that categorizes pests by general host type and subdivides each type by plant part fed upon or feeding mode. (For example: conifer pests; leaf feeders; bagworms, results in referring the reader to plates 80-81, containing nine color photographs and a page of text describing bagworms.) The insect index and host plant index also access this information. This work is relatively user-friendly, allowing a good chance for diagnosis from several directions using the host plant, the insect, or symptoms as starting points. Browsing is also pleasurable because of the succinct text and attractive photographs that give the book coffee table as well as desk reference status. The glossary and sources of information on pests and pest control sections provide additional information. The omission of the ubiquitous and regularly encountered honeydew aphids of pecan (*Monellia caryella* and *Monelliopsis pecanis*), while discussing numerous other minor species, is an example of the difficulties encountered by the authors in selecting material and interpreting references. Specialists on arthropods of other plants may have similar criticisms. Nevertheless, the authors have successfully compiled the most comprehensive and best-illustrated text on this subject to date. This is an excellent reference for the interested layperson and others seeking an overview of this area.   Marvin K. Harris

Mammals

1459. Burton, John A., with Vivien G. Burton. **The Collins Guide to the Rare Mammals of the World.** Lexington, Mass., Stephen Greene Press; distr., New York, Viking Penguin, 1988. 240p. illus. (part col.). maps. bibliog. index. $30.00. ISBN 0-8289-0658-0.

As the world slides ever closer to an ecological Armageddon, interest in endangered species is growing. Unfortunately the number of extinctions in the twentieth century is unprecedented and catastrophic, and the will to stop this escalating problem seems sadly lacking. Yet some continue to try. This work attempts to identify and describe all the mammal species which might be considered threatened. There is no reliable single source of information on threatened mammals. The 1986 *IUCN Red List of Threatened Animals* depends on data received from other sources and so is incomplete. *Walker's Mammals of the World* and *Red Data Books* and regional sources were used in this compilation as well as the IUCN list.

The authors provide a useful chapter on how to use the guide and explain abbreviations, acronyms, the categories, and the checklist given at the end of the book. The text gives a brief description of the mammal along with notes on its biology and ecology and a summary of its status in the wild and in captivity and notes on the protection given it. There are ninety-eight color plates, with each animal drawn from life whenever possible. Each is drawn approximately to scale within each plate. Each mammal also has a black-and-white distribution map. The entry for each species is numbered and the index refers to this number rather than a page number. Appendix 1 is a checklist of species and lists both the common and scientific names, the species number in the book, its rating, IUCN category, and the CITES appendix number if applicable. A supplemental list and a bibliography are also provided.   Susan Ebershoff-Coles

1460. Jones, J. Knox, Jr., and Elmer C. Birney. **Handbook of Mammals of the North-Central States.** Minneapolis, Minn., University of Minnesota Press, 1988. 346p. illus. maps. $29.50; $15.95pa. LC 86-4302. ISBN 0-8166-1419-9; 0-8166-1420-2pa.

The work begins with a brief discussion of the environmental characteristics of the north central states. For the purposes of this book the north central states are defined as Minnesota, Iowa, Wisconsin, Illinois, Michigan, Indiana, and Ohio. The initial discussion includes the geological past, the physiography and drainage patterns, soils, climate, vegetation and, of course, human influences. The second section provides an account of zoogeographic patterns. The bulk of the work is then devoted to the various species one may expect to encounter in one or more of these seven states.

There are ninety-nine native and five introduced species identified. Each has a photograph, a distribution map of its range within the seven-state area, and an insert showing distribution nationally. The written discussion of each animal is kept to about one page and includes data on distribution, a description, natural history, and selected references. The listing of mammals is arranged in phylogenetic sequence by order, family, and genus. Species are then listed alphabetically within genus. The introduced or possibly occurring species are treated separately. Information in this section is much more limited.

The work includes a glossary of terms used in mammalogy, a list of the references given in the text, and an index to the vernacular and scientific names of each animal. The book is a solid, basic introduction to mammals occurring in these states and provides a guide to identification, making it useful in the field.

Susan Ebersoff-Coles

1461. Wolfe, Linda D. **Field Primatology: A Guide to Research.** New York, Garland, 1987. 288p. index. (Garland Reference Library of Social Science, Vol. 356). $43.00. LC 87-23811. ISBN 0-8240-8552-3.

This new bibliography complements *Behavioral Development of Nonhuman Primates* (Plenum, 1980) by F. R. Akins; an excellent reference source by J. H. Wolfheim, *Primates of the World* (see *ARBA* 84, entry 1354); and a specialized bibliography, *The Baboon* (Southwest Foundation for Research and Education, 1964-), the last supplement of which is dated 1971. Wolfe's bibliography includes 1,072 annotated entries and concentrates "on the writings of researchers who went into the field, conducted a behavioral study of freeranging alloprimates, and published a report." Annotations serve to describe the book or article selected for inclusion and concentrate on major findings. Information on the research site and years of study is included if known. Perusal of these annotations will enable users to know what to expect before locating sources in a library or requesting them through interlibrary loan. Bibliographic citations are complete for both books and journal articles.

A good subject index increases the reference value of this bibliography. The author has gathered scholarly writings on primates or alloprimates (the author's preferred term) by using common names (baboon, chimpanzee) and geographical names. Entries are gathered by broad subject category (conservation, ecology) and specific categories: fruit eating, crop raiding, drills, baby parking, urine marking. College students will be able to comb these subject entries to identify ideas for research papers. Specialists using the "Primate Genus Index" will locate entries if the genus is mentioned in the title of a cited source or the author has been able to identify genus by a careful reading of the text. A special taxonomic listing of primates serves to help nonspecialists make use of the "Primate Genus Index." [R: Choice, Apr 88, p. 1226]

Milton H. Crouch

1462. Zeveloff, Samuel I. **Mammals of the Intermountain West.** Salt Lake City, Utah, University of Utah Press, 1988. 365p. illus. (part col.). maps. bibliog. index. $40.00; $19.95pa. LC 88-20462. ISBN 0-87480-296-2; 0-87480-327-6pa.

The intermountain West of North America includes the states of Utah and Nevada but is an area that is not easily defined. It generally refers to the space between the Sierra Nevada and the Rocky Mountains. The author has chosen as his boundaries a map developed during a symposium on intermountain biogeography and published in the Great Basin Naturalist Memoirs series. The region includes all of Utah, almost all of Nevada, a small slice of eastern California, the southeastern quarter of Oregon, the southern two-fifths of Idaho, the southwestern quarter of Wyoming, western Colorado, a corner of northwestern New Mexico, and a section of northern Arizona. It encompasses the eastern flank of the Sierra Nevada, the Great Basin, the Snake River Plains, the northern two-thirds of the Colorado Plateau, and several major Rocky Mountain ranges.

The species accounts are concise and easily understood. Measurements are only given in inches. Metric equivalents should have been included, even though the intended audience appears to be primarily nonscientists. Farrell R. Collett's paintings and drawings render a certain charm to the guide. In treatment this guide is very much like many other mammalian field guides and follows the standard format of introduction, mammalian characteristics, and species accounts. The introduction does include some information about the region and its ecology and the interpretation of regional mammalian faunal relationships. Recommended to those specifically interested in the mammals of the area.

John C. Jahoda

1463. Zim, Herbert S., and Donald F. Hoffmeister. **Mammals: A Guide to Familiar American Species.** rev. ed. New York, Golden Press/ Western Publishing, 1987. 160p. illus. (part col.). maps. bibliog. index. $3.95pa. LC 61-8320. ISBN 0-307-24058-4.

This is one in a standard series of Golden guides. The guides have been around for many years and have proved their usefulness many times over. This one is small, easily portable, and really far more valuable in a home reference collection than behind a library reference desk.

The introductory section gives a few tips on seeing, observing, and photographing mammals as well as general information on ranges, species, numbers, and the uses of ecological niches of mammals. The descriptions of mammals are accompanied by a color drawing and a small range map. Size, color, and a general description of the animal and its habits are provided in the written section. Most mammals have a page each although a few animals have a slightly longer description. A list of scientific names and an index are provided. Carry this in your pocket on your daily walks. There are many other guides more useful for daily reference work in most libraries.

Susan Ebershoff-Coles

Marine Animals

1464. Halstead, Bruce W. **Poisonous and Venomous Marine Animals of the World.** 2d ed. Princeton, N.J., Darwin Press, 1988. 1v. (various paging). illus. (part col.). index. $250.00. LC 84-70414. ISBN 0-87850-050-2.

This major work is the leading reference in marine biotoxicology and medicine. It has been rigorously revised and presents in one volume an encyclopedic work on toxic marine organisms. Major topics in marine zootoxicology are covered, including scientific and common names, basic biology, geographical distribution, mechanisms of intoxication, clinical characteristics, pathology, treatment, prevention, public health aspects, pharmacology, and chemistry. The text is clear, authoritative, and well documented. Almost all the organisms covered are also illustrated. The coverage includes all marine invertebrate and vertebrate phyla (protists, sponges, hydroids, jellyfishes, mollusks, worms, arthropods, starfish, sharks, fishes, sea snakes, marine turtles, and marine mammals). Five hundred and fifty different species receive coverage. Some of these are well known for their venomous or toxic effects, others are less well known, especially those causing occasional poisoning due to toxic flesh or organs. Organisms of this kind include such species as the polar bear (toxic liver and kidneys), the sperm whale, and the green turtle. The text includes in excess of three hundred photographs, drawings, and graphs; twenty-three tables; and thirteen maps. In addition there are 288 pages of plates which include more than seven hundred photographs and illustrations. Three hundred and ninety of these are in full color. The artwork includes anatomical drawings and photomicrographs of venom organs. Also provided is an extensive bibliography (following each chapter) which includes thousands of references, and a comprehensive glossary of new and little-known terms.

This is the authoritative text on this subject and will be of indispensable value to anyone involved with poisonous or venomous marine animals including biologists, oceanographers, physicians, first aid workers, scuba divers and skin divers, biochemists, physiologists, toxicologists, medical schools and hospitals, and

libraries. It is also an excellent resource for those interested in the basic biology of the species covered. Highly recommended. A must inclusion in any medical library located in a region where marine toxicology problems might occur. [R: LJ, 15 Oct 88, p. 83]

John C. Jahoda

1465. Ruppert, Edward, and Richard Fox. **Seashore Animals of the Southeast: A Guide to Common Shallow-Water Invertebrates of the Southeastern Atlantic Coast.** Columbia, S.C., University of South Carolina Press, 1988. 429p. illus. (part col.). maps. bibliog. index. $34.95; $24.95pa. LC 87-27349. ISBN 0-87249-534-5; 0-87249-535-3pa.

This nice little field guide fills the need for a layperson's guide to this region. Excellent field guides are available for the Northeast, the Florida Keys, and the Pacific Coast, but until now a good shallow water invertebrate guide for the Southeast has been missing. The style is clear and easily understood. Of the approximately one thousand species of coastal marine invertebrates to be found in the Southeast, 740 of the most common forms are discussed and 360 are illustrated, identified, and described in adequate detail. The illustrations are excellent and include one hundred color photographs, seventy-five black-and-white photographs, and two hundred line drawings. All the photographs and line drawings are new. The photographic technique employed is simple but the results are excellent. Descriptions include information on identification, biology, and ecology. An illustrated key helps with the identification of unknown animals to major phyla. The bulk of the guide is devoted to a taxonomically arranged description of the organisms. This is followed by an excellent section on the major groups of marine animals, a section on abiotic factors and marine ecology. Also included are a glossary, a list of selected references, a section on animal taxonomy, and an index to scientific and common names. This field guide should be a welcome addition to the library of anyone interested in the invertebrate life of the Southeastern United States, including beachcombers, fishermen, natural history lovers, marine biologists, and students.

John C. Jahoda

Reptiles and Amphibians

1466. Garrett, Judith M., and David G. Barker. **A Field Guide to Reptiles and Amphibians of Texas.** Austin, Tex., Texas Monthly Press, 1987. 225p. illus. (part col.). maps. index. (Texas Monthly Field Guide Series). $21.95;

$14.95pa. LC 87-17971. ISBN 0-87719-068-2; 0-87719-091-7pa.

Taxonomists traditionally have been divided into two camps: lumpers who like to group species together, and splitters who like to separate them out. So too we find field guides, some lumping all the species of a particular region together, and others separating out a state here, a county there. *A Field Guide to Reptiles and Amphibians of Texas* joins the growing ranks of state guides "split off" from the regionals. This guide, number 4 in the Texas Monthly Press Field Guide Series, covers all amphibians and reptiles (excluding snakes, which have their own volume) found in Texas. A total of 167 species and subspecies are included.

Entries are arranged alphabetically by class, then within the class by order, family, genus, species, and subspecies. The index, composed of family, common, and scientific names, indicates the page numbers for the descriptive entry and the photograph. A small glossary is included as well as a bibliography of sources consulted. Appendix 1 provides a list of threatened and endangered species, while appendix 2 offers locality information for the photographs.

Each entry contains a graphic description of the species, along with the range, habitat, behavior, and reproductive cycle. For the toads and frogs, a description of their call is included to aid in identification. The photographs are arranged in the same order as the species descriptions and occupy the center of the book. Since there are no cross-references between the written entry and the photograph, the index must be used to go back and forth between the two. The photographs, however, are some of the finest I have seen: clear, sharp, and seemingly ready to leap off the page. Range maps, which consist of a simple outline of Texas, illustrate the approximate location of the species. Though a written description of the range is also included, the visual interpretation would have been enhanced by including the county borders.

Angela Marie Thor

1467. Welch, K. R. G. **Snakes of the Orient: A Checklist.** Malabar, Fla., Krieger, 1988. 183p. bibliog. index. $22.50. LC 86-27298. ISBN 0-89464-203-0.

The Orient as defined here includes Pakistan east to China and south through Asia, including Japan, the Philippines, Indonesia, and Papua New Guinea. This is an area that has been greatly neglected by herpetologists in comparison to the rest of the world. This listing should focus attention on this region of rich fauna and help to encourage its study. Entries are listed by present-day name, original name and reference, type locality, distribution, and recent taxonomic references (if any). The appendix includes a list of region references, a bibliography, an index to the genera, and an index to species and subspecies. This volume is solely a taxonomic listing; it provides no identification aids such as keys or illustrations, which somewhat limits its usefulness. It will most likely need to be used in conjunction with some other source of reference such as the regional references that are listed. Overall this checklist should prove to be a valuable quick reference to the species of snakes from this part of the world and should be of use to both professional herpetologists and snake fanciers.

John C. Jahoda

33 Engineering

GENERAL WORKS

1468. Engineering Research Centres: A World Directory of Organizations and Programmes. 2d ed. Harlow, England, Longman; distr., Detroit, Gale, 1988. 599p. index. $400.00. ISBN 0-582-01778-5.

This second edition contains descriptions of about eight thousand engineering research centers in eighty-seven countries. These centers are defined as industrial centers, official laboratories, and major university or technical college laboratories which carry out, promote, or fund research in aerodynamics, structural aeronautics, industrial and mechanical engineering, transportation (road, rail, and ship technology), civil engineering, and fluid mechanics.

Names of the centers are listed alphabetically in boldface type within each country. For centers such as universities which have different laboratories or departments administered by them, the headings are weighted; that is, each successive heading which is in smaller boldface type shows this relationship.

Each entry gives the center's name in the original language and in English, the address, telephone number, telex and facsimile numbers, status (type of center), product range, affiliation or parent organization, names of directors, departments or divisions, annual expenditures, activities, publications, and liaison (names of firms or organizations for which a center has performed substantial research). Asterisks next to a center's name indicate that the center did not respond. Unfortunately, there are quite a few of these. The entry data range from very little to very detailed, again depending on the response. The year a center was founded is not included.

Each center is assigned a number within each country. The subject and titles of establishment indexes refer to the centers by a country chapter code, such as "bul 5" for the fifth entry in the Bulgaria chapter. *See also* references are used, though in the subject index there is no *see also* for *civil* or *chemical engineering* under *engineering*. Some of the subjects have many country number codes which will require a great deal of page flipping by the user. For example, the term *mechanical engineering* contains fifty lines of codes. The country codes are useful for narrowing a search to a specific country.

This directory is part of the Longman Reference on Research series, which includes volumes on other types of laboratories or research centers. It is a valuable reference tool for hard to find data on research organizations—a useful addition in this area.

Anne C. Roess

ACOUSTICAL ENGINEERING

1469. Parker, Sybil P., ed. **Acoustics Source Book.** New York, McGraw-Hill, 1988. 333p. illus. index. (McGraw-Hill Science Reference Series). $35.00. LC 88-8884. ISBN 0-07-045508-2.

This book consists of selected entries from the sixth edition of the *McGraw-Hill Encyclopedia of Science and Technology* (see *ARBA* 88, entry 1448) on acoustics and sound. The selected articles have been collected and rearranged so that the entries are no longer in alphabetical order but are grouped into chapters covering basic concepts, physics of sound, sound transducers, etc. In fact, even the introduction is from the encyclopedia: it is the article which defines acoustics.

As befits a book formed from encyclopedia entries, each article includes *see* references. These references have been edited to exclude references to material not included in this book. For example, the article in the encyclopedia on acoustical imaging references architectural acoustics and optical image. The reference to optical image has been dropped since this topic is not included in the *Acoustics Source Book*.

The bibliographies at the end of the articles have also been slightly edited. For example, the acoustic emission bibliography in the encyclopedia has four entries, while that in the *Acoustics Source Book* has two and one of these is not cited in the encyclopedia. This is interesting since the articles appear to be the same in both books.

This is repackaging at its best, since it does offer an overview which can be either checked out or purchased.   Susan B. Ardis

ASTRONAUTICAL ENGINEERING

1470. Bond, Peter. **Heroes in Space: From Gagarin to Challenger.** New York, Basil Blackwell, 1987. 467p. illus. index. $24.95. LC 86-31004. ISBN 0-631-15349-7.

From the flight of *Vostok 1* in April 1961 to the *Challenger* disaster in January 1986, there have been 116 manned space flights involving nearly two hundred astronauts or cosmonauts. Over the past twenty-five years many words have been written about these flights, and today much of our outlook on technology, economy, and social values has been affected by them. Except for a few books and movies such as *The Right Stuff* and a few personal accounts by astronauts, there has not been a comprehensive portrait of the astronauts and cosmonauts dealing with their personalities, experiences, and feelings in relationship to their specific missions. This book, written by a freelance but knowledgeable writer, accomplishes this in a straightforward, comprehensive way that will attract all readers from young adults to seasoned space buffs. The comparison of the American and Soviet space missions and the feeling of tension between them is maintained throughout the book. The accounts are believable, well documented, and well illustrated. It is a pity the book ends with the *Challenger* disaster, but it is hoped that the future story will be one of increasing cooperation in man's space endeavors.
      Robert J. Havlik

1471. King-Hele, D. G., and others, comps. **The RAE Table of Earth Satellites 1957-1986.** 3d ed. New York, Stockton Press/Grove's Dictionaries of Music, 1987. 936p. illus. index. $130.00. LC 87-10204. ISBN 0-935859-05-5; ISSN 0265-3931.

This handbook of tables covers 2,869 launches that sent seventeen thousand satellites into Earth orbit. The senior author, D. G. King-Hele of the Royal Aircraft Establishment, Farnborough, Hants., England, is a world authority on the orbits of Earth satellites, both inside of and outside of its atmosphere, and of their use

in research. He has gained recognition as a Fellow of the Royal Society, London, partly from this work.

The introduction covers how the table began and grew (including a facsimile of the original one-page table conceived of and issued by Doreen Walker in 1958), the number of launches, name and designation, satellite orbits, guide to the table (twelve columns of data), methods used to compile the table, and launch sites. There is a steady refrain throughout of the difficulty of extrapolating all physical details and orbits of USSR satellites (by far the most numerous ones), while the United States and international ones have such information available publicly.

The main body of the text is the reproduction of 892 typed masters held at RAE. The "flavor" of the group pride that has kept this project going for nearly thirty years is illustrated by this quotation from the acknowledgments: "We particularly thank those who have for many years accurately filed the data on the 17000 satellites, and the many typists who have not only typed the Table skilfully and accurately but have also cheerfully tackled the far worse problem of making thousands of amendments to the masters" (p. xvii). (One is reminded of projects in humanities reference works undertaken by religious orders!)

Anyone fortunate enough to have visited RAE Farnborough more than once has been impressed by the extreme breadth of their researchers, and of the excellent analyses of research results using the proverbial "one sharp pencil" instead of elaborate hardware. This table is quite within this tradition and merits a place on the astronautical sciences reference shelf alongside such other classics as Jane's *All the World's Aircraft* (see *ARBA* 87, entry 1728). The latest edition should always be purchased, as the changes are numerous. [R: Choice, May 88, p. 1384]   E. B. Jackson

1472. Pisano, Dominick A., and Cathleen S. Lewis, eds. **Air and Space History: An Annotated Bibliography.** New York, Garland, 1988. 571p. illus. index. (Garland Reference Library of the Humanities, Vol. 834). $75.00. LC 88-342. ISBN 0-8240-8543-4.

Although aeronautics and space science are relatively new disciplines, the scope of concerns is so broad that it has been difficult to draw together all the bits and pieces to get an idea of the historical aspects of their development. With the aid of the staff of the National Air and Space Museum, Garland has issued as cohesive a bibliography of air and space history as is possible. Wisely, they have divided the materials into three major groups: general sources on both air and space, including bibliographies, general sources, research sources, biography, institutional, political, social, and cultural issues; air, including aerospace engineering, aircraft, helicopters and autogiros, balloons and airships, propulsion, communication, navigation, meteorology, equipment, military aviation, air transport, general aviation, events, and safety; and space, including early rockets through World War II, launch vehicles, propulsion and ballistics, missiles, launch sites, satellites, space sciences, applications, military uses of space, manned programs, and speculation on space flight. Some readers may miss their favorite book but discretion had to be used to whittle the volume down to over two thousand references. The annotations are excellent and the organization allows one to find related materials easily despite the fact that there is only an author index.

Robert J. Havlik

1473. Sheridan, Anneli, and Judy Mills, comps. **Directory of Aerospace Educational Programs in Canada, the United States and Abroad.** Downsview, Ont., Institute for Aerospace Studies, University of Toronto, 1988. 76p. bibliog. index. $15.00 spiralbound.

The Institute for Aerospace Studies at the University of Toronto offers the most well-known academic program in aerospace in Canada. Graduates frequently migrate to the United States or other parts of the world for more specialized study. To meet the students' need for information about other aerospace education programs in the world, the institute decided to compile a directory for their own use, but they soon realized the value of such a work to other institutions. Compiled from available sources, the work lists academic programs, technical/commission programs, and international programs arranged by continent and then by country. Data include the name of the institution, degrees and awards, a short statement of programs offered, number of faculty members, cost of study, whom to contact, and a list of the latest calendars or catalogs available at UTIAS. A unique feature of the U.S. academic program listing is a rating of the institution's graduate and undergraduate programs taken from the 1985 *Gourman Reports*. There is also an institution index.   Robert J. Havlik

1474. Waldman, Harry. **The Dictionary of SDI.** Wilmington, Del., Scholarly Resources, 1988. 182p. illus. maps. $35.00; $19.95pa. LC 87-12477. ISBN 0-8420-2281-3; 0-8420-2295-3pa.

While almost everyone is conscious of the existence of the strategic defense initiative (SDI), few are knowledgeable about its technology or the international, political, or economic effects that such a massive research and defense project as this involves. The term *Star Wars* can in no way define its complexity or the passions it has generated at both international and scientific levels. Harry Waldman, who has already published several engineering dictionaries, now returns to his earlier experience in the field of missile technology to try to clarify and simplify some of the major engineering problems involved in SDI deployment. The dictionary is in straight alphabetical form and defines over eight hundred terms and acronyms currently in use in the fields of ballistic missile defense, arms control, research and development, countermoves to defense, and Soviet capabilities. It also discusses the role of various U.S. allies, and some of the personalities involved in research and management of SDI-related projects. There are many illustrations of systems and concepts. Also included are copies of the 1972 ABM treaty and names and affiliations of the Defensive Technologies Study Team. The book is fascinating and frightening but necessary for librarians or media people who may be asked or need a starting point for further information and understanding of this new technology that could affect the peace of the world. [R: Choice, Sept 88, p. 90; WLB, June 88, pp. 140-41]

Robert J. Havlik

CHEMICAL ENGINEERING

1475. Becher, Paul, ed. **Encyclopedia of Emulsion Technology. Volume 3: Basic Theory Measurement Applications.** New York, Marcel Dekker, 1987. 437p. illus. index. $115.00. LC 82-18257. ISBN 0-8247-1878-X.

This third volume in the series serves as a supplement to the first two volumes: *Basic Theory* (see *ARBA* 84, entry 1282) and *Applications*. It also introduces a new topic, measurements.

The "chapters" are, in reality, small monographs on the various topics by experts in the field. Illustrations are provided where appropriate, and more than 550 bibliographic references are furnished. The appendix consists of a thorough bibliography on HLB (hydrophile-lipophile balance).

This volume will be a required purchase for those libraries holding the first two volumes in the series. The entire series should be seriously considered by libraries serving chemical engineers and chemists working in the field.

Edwin D. Posey

1476. Chemical Engineering Faculties 1988-1989. Volume 37. Keith P. Johnston, ed. New York, American Institute of Chemical Engineers, [1988]. 242p. index. $40.00pa. ISBN 0-8169-0447-2.

Academic directories get much use in college and university libraries. Whether it is addresses of academic institutions, their programs, or names of their faculty, a bank of reference books is available to supply the need. The broader the coverage of the work, however, the less up-to-date it is, due mainly to the mobility of the academic community. Directories put out by societies or subject-oriented associations have an advantage, however, since they are limited in their scope and have a built-in membership or chapter list upon which to base their data gathering. *Chemical Engineering Faculties* is one of the most useful of the latter type. The directory lists chemical engineering departments throughout the world. It gives a summary of their accreditation status and graduate admissions office for the interested student. It gives the departmental faculty by rank and telephone number, when available, for faculty contacts. It gives the name and title of the chief administrating officer and placement supervisor for other users. The alphabetical index of the faculty is especially valuable for tracking down theses advisors, book authors, and colleagues in chemical engineering. This annual publication is not only a good reference, it is a good communications tool.

Robert J. Havlik

1477. Dorman, Phae H. **Chemical Industries: An Information Sourcebook.** Phoenix, Ariz., Oryx Press, 1988. 95p. index. (Oryx Sourcebook Series in Business and Management, No. 9). $29.50. LC 87-23180. ISBN 0-89774-257-5.

The major objective of Dorman's bibliography is to provide sources of business-related information needed to conduct comprehensive chemical market analyses for industries manufacturing chemicals and allied products. Emphasis is on current English-language or national sources, and over 90 percent of the 557 entries are U.S. publications. There is a core library collection of 158 entries to the most essential sources followed by a categorical arrangement of 399 citations to specialized information sources for eleven industry groups: agricultural chemicals and food; cleaning preparations and cosmetics; drugs and pharmaceuticals; electronics; minerals and metals; paints, coatings, and adhesives; paper and allied products; petrochemicals and energy; plastics and packaging; rubber; and textiles. These two sections comprise the bulk of the text and are subdivid-

ed by type of source as follows: biographical directories; electronics retrieval systems; encyclopedias, dictionaries, and handbooks; indexes, abstracts, and continuing services; newspapers, journals, and newsletters; and U.S. government publications. The core library collection also contains a list of recent books on chemical information sources. The majority of entries are annotated. Generally annotations are concise, factual statements; special features in particular issues of journals are indicated. Descriptive information for computer databases is more extensive. Explanatory paragraphs precede literature subdivisions in the core library collection and industry groupings in the categorical arrangement. There are two annotated lists of associations and of consultant sources, arranged by the same industry groups and giving complete addresses. These are largely located in the United States. The list of consultant sources is preceded by an annotated list of directories for locating experts and consultants in the chemical industry. There are three indexes: author, title, and subject. Of these, only the title index is accurate. The author index contains many incorrect citation references (e.g., Dickson, Cheryl L., 458-60 should refer to citations 445-447, and Nass, L. J., 503 should refer to citation 490). The subject index also contains many incorrect citation references, usually off by only one digit (e.g., "Food, frozen" refers to citations 200, 208 when actual citations are 199 and 207; "Biotechnology" refers to citations 165-88, 241, 252, and 244-245 when only citations 164, 187, 240, 251, 243-244 are biotechnology titles). Adding to the confusion is the fact that though each index is preceded by a statement pointing out that numbers in italics refer to page numbers and all others refer to citation numbers, it is difficult to distinguish numbers in italics from other numbering. Better editorial supervision could easily have prevented this unfortunate drawback to an otherwise good and useful compilation of chemical industry business sources. [R: Choice, July/Aug 88, p. 1674]

Virginia E. Yagello

1478. Encyclopedia of Chemical Processing and Design. 28: Lactic Acid to Magnesium Supply-Demand Relationships. John J. McKetta and William A. Cunningham, eds. New York, Marcel Dekker, 1988. 498p. illus. $135.00. LC 75-40646. ISBN 0-8247-2478-X.

This venerable set, begun in 1976, is projected to be finished in some forty-five volumes. The aim of the editors, as set forth in volume 1, is to cover all aspects of chemical processes, especially those of economic significance. To this end, an impressive editorial board has been assembled from both industry and academia.

The articles tend to be rather long: the volume at hand, for example, uses nearly five hundred pages to cover forty articles. The articles are well illustrated where required with line drawings, flow charts, and graphs and charts. Appended bibliographies tend to be rather short. Where the material has been published elsewhere, this fact is generally noted. The work suffers from the lack of a comprehensive index, but obviously this is impractical until the set has been completed.

The work must inevitably be compared to the standard of the industry, that is, the *Kirk-Othmer Concise Encyclopedia of Chemical Technology* (see *ARBA* 86, entry 1561). While an article-by-article comparison is not within the scope of this review, some impressions might be helpful to potential purchasers. For similar articles, *Kirk-Othmer* tends to have longer and more useful bibliographic references. The arrangement of the two works differs in that *Kirk-Othmer* tends to get more specific: it has sections on wool and waterproofing, for example, while McKetta and Cunningham have articles such as "Liquids, Thermal Conductivity Estimation" and "Lubricating Oils I: Manufacturing Processes."

We would assume that academic libraries supporting strong chemical engineering programs will want to acquire both works simply because different treatments of the same material will be of value. Due to the cost per volume ($115.00 per volume by subscription), most other libraries will probably opt for one or the other.   Edwin D. Posey

1479. **Encyclopedia of Fluid Mechanics. Volume 7: Rheology and Non-Newtonian Flows.** N. P. Cheremisinoff, ed. Houston, Tex., Gulf Publishing, 1988. 1185p. illus. index. $195.00. LC 85-9742. ISBN 0-87201-540-8.

Last year Gulf Publishing began to issue the extensive and comprehensive, *Encyclopedia of Fluid Mechanics* (see *ARBA* 88, entry 1592). The series is now projected to cover twelve volumes over the next few years supplemented by the *Annual Reviews in Fluid Mechanics* (Gulf Publishing, 1988-) and the *International Journal of Engineering Fluid Mechanics* (Gulf Publishing, 1988-). Volume 7 of the encyclopedia includes thirty-five authoritative chapters on rheology and non-Newtonian flows grouped in three major sections: "Flow Dynamics and Transport Phenomena," "Slippage and Drag Phenomena," and "Polymer Rheology and Processing." Rheology, the science of deformation and flow of materials in response to stress, is especially important in today's chemical and food industries. Oils, foodstuffs, whole blood and polymers, for example, do not follow the simple Newtonian equations for mixing and fluid flow and need special considerations for processing and transport. This volume sums up the current knowledge in solving these problems with extensive tables, charts, equations and bibliographic references. Future volumes will cover aerodynamics and compressible flows; polymer flow engineering; subsurface and groundwater flow phenomena; gas dynamics and plasma flows; and advanced numerical flow modeling.
                                        Robert J. Havlik

1480. Meyer, Rudolf. **Explosives.** 3d rev. ed. New York, VCH, 1987. 452p. illus. bibliog. index. $75.00pa. LC 87-6191. ISBN 0-89573-600-4.

This handbook has a long history, starting in 1932 with the publication of a booklet titled *Explosivstoffe*. In 1961 it was substantially revised and updated under the title *Handbook of Industrial and Military Explosives*.

As the author clearly states, "this book is not intended as a systematic presentation of the science of explosives." For this the user should consult "Encyclopedia of Explosives and Related Items" edited by Seymour M. Kaye, a report released by the U.S. Armament Research and Development Large Caliber Weapons Systems Laboratory in 1960. Rather the objective is to provide fundamental information on the subject of explosives and individual explosives. Approximately five hundred entries are arranged in alphabetical order and include brief descriptions of properties, manufacturing methods, and application of 120 explosives; descriptions of 60 additives, fuels, and oxidizing agents; and test methods and information on caps and casings. Basic thermodynamic data for many explosives are given in extensive tables.

The large bibliography is arranged by subject or type of material and includes such categories as applications, manuals, pyrotechnics, theories of detonation, and governmental regulations. The index serves two purposes, as an entry point for the alphabetical listings and as a technical dictionary defining words without reference to the text.

The audience for this book would be anyone needing fundamental information on individual explosives. The descriptions and illustrations are quite clear and in many cases were checked for accuracy by the manufacturer.
                                        Susan B. Ardis

CIVIL ENGINEERING

1481.   Brinker, Russell C., and Roy Minnick, eds. **The Surveying Handbook.** New York, Van Nostrand Reinhold, 1987. 1270p. illus. index. $82.95. LC 87-8217. ISBN 0-442-21423-5.

This most timely work follows the classic formula for handbooks: each major subdivision of the subject is assigned to specialists, who then compile concise treatments for inclusion.

In this case, the specialists are well chosen from industry, government, and academia, and list impressive credentials for their respective tasks.

Some twenty-six chapters and 1,270 pages treat all major aspects of the field of surveying. The latest instruments and methods are discussed in detail, with illustrations where appropriate. There are even two chapters on land litigation and courtroom techniques, surely important parts of the surveyor's practice. Bibliographic references are appended to most chapters for further reading. The work is well illustrated with maps, charts, drawings, and photographs.

This important handbook has no serious competitor, and is strongly recommended for all engineering collections, law libraries, most public libraries, and, of course, for individual purchase by practitioners. [R: Choice, Mar 88, p. 1072]   Edwin D. Posey

1482.   Gaylord, Edwin H., Jr., and Charles N. Gaylord, eds. **Concrete Structures Reference Guide.** New York, McGraw-Hill, 1988. 1v. (various paging). illus. index. (McGraw-Hill Engineering Reference Guide Series). $34.50. LC 88-12708. ISBN 0-07-023067-6.

This guide on concrete structures is an abridged version of the second edition of the co-editors' previous work, *Structural Engineering Handbook* (see *ARBA* 80, entry 1603). The six sections of the guide, all written by recognized specialists, are "Design of Reinforced Concrete Structural Members," "Design of Prestressed Concrete Structural Members," "Concrete Construction Methods," "Masonry Construction," "Thin-Shell Concrete Structures," and "Reinforced-Concrete Bunkers and Silos." Additional references are given at the end of some sections. The book ends with an index. Intended as a quick reference tool, this work provides concise, basic, and handy information on the design of concrete structures for practicing engineers, architects, and designers.

Hwa-Wei Lee

1483.   Grandchamp-Tupula, Mariette. **Lexique des Barrages. Glossary on Dams.** Ottawa, Canadian Government Publishing Centre, 1987. 83p. bibliog. (Terminology Bulletin, 178). $8.00pa.; $9.60pa.(U.S.). ISBN 0-660-53886-5.

This handy volume covers the major terms relating to dams in both English to French and vice versa. It compares favorably with its predecessor, *Glossary of Words and Phrases Related to Dams* (Paris: International Commission on Large Dams, 1978), in that more terms are covered. Since English and French are the "official languages" of the International Commission, this Canadian work will be of value to the larger community of scientists and engineers concerned with the topic. Recommended for all libraries concerned with the international literature on dam construction and maintenance.   Edwin D. Posey

1484.   Jackson, Donald C. **Great American Bridges and Dams.** Washington, D.C., Preservation Press, 1988. 357p. illus. bibliog. index. (Great American Places Series). $16.95pa. LC 87-22309. ISBN 0-89133-129-8.

This attractive guidebook, filled with photographs, contains useful descriptions of some 330 selected American bridges and dams and well-written historical notes on these examples of American engineering and technology. Written by a historian of technology and published by the National Trust for Historical Preservation, the guide emphasizes older bridges and dams of technological or historical significance. It covers a full range of types and sizes of bridges and dams that have contributed to America's development. Prefacing the guide is a chapter on the history of bridges, "Bridges: Spanning the Nation," and one on the history of dams, "Dams: Controlling a Precious Resource." Two other chapters are "Saving Bridges and Dams" and "Epilogue: The Ones That Got Away." The main body, comprising three-fourths of the guide, groups the bridges and dams into six geographical regions which are divided by state and then by city or site, arranged alphabetically. Each entry is highlighted by key details in the outside margin showing the name, location, engineer, construction company, and year of completion. The entries generally provide one or two paragraphs of narration about the structure. The guide also has sections of further readings, information sources, and photographic sources, and an index at the end.

Because the wealth and breadth of information it contains is likely to appeal to the general reader as well as the specialist, the guide should be a part of any historical, engineering, or travel collection in large and medium-sized libraries. [R: LJ, 1 June 88, pp. 102, 104]

Hwa-Wei Lee

1485. McMullan, Randall. **Dictionary of Building.** New York, Nichols/GP Publishing, 1988. 262p. illus. $44.50. LC 88-12598. ISBN 0-89397-319-X.

This reference offers brief definitions of modern terms used in building construction. The terms are ones in general use in the British Isles and North America. Entries are cross-referenced, and a brief section containing diagrams supplements the entries. The book will be useful to students of building trades and construction engineering, but somewhat less so to students of architecture. The emphasis is clearly on technical and institutional terms, and matters of style, region, history, bibliography, and scholarship are left to another work. Even granted its focus on construction, the work could have benefited from more diagrams and photographs integrated into the text, and more discussion of variance among terms. Although the language used in the definitions is simple and direct, the definitions themselves often appear cursory or incomplete. More indication of the context in which the words are used and elaboration on technical matters would have also helped the library user.

Simon J. Bronner

ELECTRICAL ENGINEERING AND ELECTRONICS

1486. Chalmers, B. J., ed. **Electric Motor Handbook.** Stoneham, Mass., Butterworths, 1988. 546p. illus. (part col.). index. $120.00. LC 87-20887. ISBN 0-408-00707-9.

A large amount of power in the world is supplied through electric motors. Because of the glamour of electronics fewer and fewer students are studying this field of electrical engineering. Most texts on electric motors are devoted to methods of performance analysis and even less on design. This new handbook has tried to draw together expert advice and knowledge on plant design, equipment specifications, commissioning, operation, and maintenance. Because of the vast number and types of electric motors available, this handbook has limited itself to rotating motors above ten kilowatts. This eliminates the more common machines used in small industry. Topics covered include characteristics, environment, selection, variable-speed drives and motor control, materials and motor components, insulation, ancillary equipment, works and acceptance testing, installation, site testing and commissioning, maintenance, and failures. There is also a chapter on units, dimensions, and conversion factors. The handbook is sanctioned by the Manchester (England) Machines Research

Group, and is designed to supplement the J & P Transformer and Switchgear books.

Robert J. Havlik

1487. Douglas-Young, John. **Illustrated Encyclopedic Dictionary of Electronics.** 2d ed. Englewood Cliffs, N.J., Prentice-Hall, 1987. 692p. illus. $42.95; $16.95pa. LC 86-21272. ISBN 0-13-450701-0; 0-13-451006-2pa.

The second edition has been enlarged and revised since this book was first published in 1984. Like the previous edition, this one is arranged in alphabetical order and has extensive cross-references. The entries consist of thousands of electronic terms, with illustrations and brief definitions. However, if an individual entry is part of a larger concept or subject covered by a more extensive writeup, the title of the latter is given. All entries are interfiled in one sequence. A good example of the power and usefulness of these cross-references is found in the "Charge carrier" entry, which references the larger topic "Semiconductors." The semiconductor entry consists of seven and a half pages of text and includes references to "Optoelectronics" and "Transistors and Transistor Circuits."

The text is clearly written and heavily illustrated with functional drawings, schematics, diagrams, and tables. The author has several electronic reference books, including *Microelectronics: Standard Manual and Guide* (Prentice-Hall, 1983) to his credit. [R: BR, Nov/Dec 88, p. 49; RBB, 15 Dec 88, p. 691]

Susan B. Ardis

1488. Ishibashi, Seiichi. **Dictionary of Electronics and Electrical Engineering: English-Japanese-German-Russian.** 3d ed. New York, Plenum, 1987. 1v. (various paging). index. $195.00pa. ISBN 0-306-42749-4.

This dictionary is an outstanding compilation of technical vocabulary entries in electronics, communications, and electrical engineering. The present publication provides the translation of over forty-two thousand technical terms from English into Japanese, German, and Russian. Cross-references arranged logically in the respective native language are also given so that translation from any language to the other three is possible. As a third edition, the present publication has been extensively enlarged to contain terminology from recent technical developments including automation, data processing, and instrumentation. Entries from other engineering areas including nucleonics, mechanical engineering, civil engineering, architecture, and economics, and from the basic sciences such as mathematics, physics, and chemistry are also included. In addition, many verbs, adjectives, and adverbs are also included to facilitate usage. A supplementary section at the end lists translations of commonly used abbreviations and units in the four languages.

This publication can be used in a number of ways. For established scientists and researchers, the dictionary can be used to translate papers published in the other three languages. It also provides the common usage of technical terms to facilitate international communications. For foreign students, it provides a valuable cross-reference from one language to the others. This publication is highly recommended for any technical or college libraries.

John Y. Cheung

1489. Kaufman, Milton, Arthur H. Seidman, and Perry J. Sheneman, eds. **Electronics Sourcebook for Technicians and Engineers.** New York, McGraw-Hill, 1988. 1v. (various paging). illus. index. $22.95pa. LC 87-33626. ISBN 0-07-033559-1.

In the process of reviewing electronics reference books for academic libraries, it is easy to forget that professors still send their broken television sets or electronic instruments out to be fixed by a technician. These persons need basic information on the latest electronic components to properly perform their job. This book, which is a paperback condensation of the authors' *Handbook for Electronics Engineering Technicians*, second edition (see *ARBA* 85, entry 1507) has this audience in mind. There are twenty-four sections, starting with characteristics of resistors, capacitors, coils, and magnetic circuits and ending with digital multimeters and oscilloscope measurements. For each section are given a definition of terms and parameters; a breakdown of the various types of characteristics of components; an analysis of the basic and special functions; detailed practical problems and clearly worked-out solutions; and clarifying charts, tables, nomographs, and illustrations. The book's basic and direct approach will make it valuable for anyone interested in learning more about electronic components and how they work.

Robert J. Havlik

1490. Turner, Rufus P., and Stan Gibilisco. **The Illustrated Dictionary of Electronics.** 4th ed. Blue Ridge Summit, Pa., TAB Books, 1988. 648p. illus. $36.95; $23.95pa. LC 88-2252. ISBN 0-8306-0900-8; 0-8306-2900-9pa.

This is an updated, revised, and expanded edition of a well-received dictionary (see *ARBA* 86, entry 1574). Several hundred new additions have been made to this edition.

The overall editorial focus has not changed. This is an excellent tool for electronics in the broadest sense. It contains a great deal of jargon and trade terms not found in more technical or narrow dictionaries and encyclopedias. As the title indicates, it is illustrated and illustrated well. The illustrations are all line drawings but in the world of electronics line drawings often convey much more than a photograph.

The definitions are concise and to the point. Where appropriate, the reader is directed to other terms. The majority of the definitions are very brief, but given the breadth of the definition of electronics, they accurately reflect the subject.

This work is highly recommended for virtually any collection which deals with electronics in any form. A good technical dictionary is needed to balance out the collection, but this dictionary goes a long way toward satisfying the majority of informational questions dealing with electronics.

C. D. Hurt

GENETIC ENGINEERING

1491. Coombs, J., and Y. R. Alston. **The Biotechnology Directory 1988: Products, Companies, Research and Organizations.** New York, Stockton Press/Grove's Dictionaries of Music, 1987. 500p. index. $150.00pa. LC 83-12138. ISBN 0-935859-13-6.

This large, expensive reference work lists the products, companies, and organizations active in the important field of biotechnology. Biotechnology, as defined by the authors, includes industrial microbiology, pharmaceuticals, fermentation, biomass, genetic engineering, and many related areas.

A brief overview of the field is followed by a list of international organizations classified by their interests. A useful section on information services points the reader to relevant databases, abstracting services, periodicals, and newsletters in the field. Next, a listing of governmental departments and private associations involved in biotechnology is provided for the major countries of the world.

The bulk of the work is contained in the section "Companies and Organizations: Products, Research and Services Buyers Guide." The products and services offered by these companies are accessed by a separate "Products, Research and Services Buyers Guide" at the end of the volume. The new user would be well advised to study the various indexes and their relationships; having done this, the work should be accessible to knowledgeable practitioners in the field.

Due to the highly volatile nature of this field, well-produced guides such as the volume at hand are very useful. This directory will be of value to private companies active in biotechnology, as well as to academic and special libraries serving clienteles involved in related research.

Edwin D. Posey

1492. Federal Biotechnology Information Resources Directory. Washington, D.C., OMEC International, 1987. 151p. index. (Biotechnology Information Series). $95.00pa. ISBN 0-931283-03-5.

1493. Federal Biotechnology Programs Directory. Washington, D.C., OMEC International, 1987. 162p. index. (Biotechnology Information Series). $95.00pa. ISBN 0-931283-02-7.

These two directories provide broad coverage of federal programs and information resources in biotechnology and related life and chemical sciences research and development, commercialization, regulation, and policy. Biotechnology is defined as the controlled use of biological agents such as microbes or cellular components for beneficial purposes. This includes all forms of life when such forms are manipulated at a molecular level to produce a predicted result. These publications are based upon work supported by the U.S. Department of Agriculture, Agricultural Research Service, and the National Agricultural Library.

Both are arranged by federal agency and department under which the different programs and information resources are listed. Contact persons are listed for the reader to obtain additional information. Users' guides clearly explain the formats. There are contact individual indexes as well as an organization/program index and an organization/information resource index. The separate information resource index in the information resources directory should have been eliminated, as it is confusing to the reader because it has duplicate entries, such as those for the National Agricultural Library. The reader would assume that the organization/information resource index would cover everything.

The programs directory describes basic research programs by giving general information about each organization's mission, followed by abstract summaries on current biotechnology programs. Cross-references to related entries are used in both directories. The information resources directory emphasizes those resources relevant to assessments of the public and environmental safety of biotechnology and novel organisms, products, and processes. This means that information resources

on chemical-biological effects, toxicology, organism and chemical identity and properties, and hazards are well represented. Information resources include both internal ones (i.e., those generated and operated by agency personnel) and external ones (those produced by external contractors and grantees but funded by federal programs). All types of information resources are covered, including major organism, culture, germplasm and specimen collections, chemical repositories, and relevant artificial intelligence resources.

These two directories should prove to be useful reference tools. The reader will obtain a good introduction to this field which can be pursued more in depth by means of the contact persons listed. If the reader is looking for a specific organism, culture, etc., he or she will not find it here. The publisher has published other reference materials in biotechnology, and is well versed in this field.

Anne C. Roess

1494. Genetic Engineering and Biotechnology Related Firms Worldwide Directory 1988/89: Technical Highlights & Funding Sources. 7th ed. Kingston, N.J., Sittig & Noyes, 1988. 489p. bibliog. index. $240.00pa. ISSN 0890-0906.

This compendium lists nearly two thousand U.S. firms specializing in the fields mentioned in the title, plus those from fifty-seven different foreign countries. Intermingled with the laboratories and factories is an extensive listing of sources of venture capital.

United States firms comprise the first listing, in alphabetical order by the name of the firm. A breakdown by state follows, with the city of location indicated. The companies are characterized by some twenty-six activity codes, and the companies are indexed by these codes —for instance, this index makes it simple to identify companies by major interest—reagents, fermentation, etc. These indexes apply only to U.S. firms; the foreign companies are merely listed by country. Most of the entries for U.S. firms also provide brief sketches of the company's interests.

This work should be compared to Mark Dibner's *Biotechnology Guide U.S.A.: Companies, Data and Analysis* (see entry 212). Dibner only lists some 360 companies in this field and omits coverage of venture capital sources. The entries in Dibner give considerably more information than does the volume under review; for example, details of personnel, major product lines, standard classification codes for the products, etc.

The work at hand will probably be of primary interest to investors, and is recommended for large urban public libraries, special libraries serving financial institutions, and academic libraries supporting programs in business and industrial administration.

　　　　　　　　　　　　　　　　Edwin D. Posey

1495. Nordquist, Joan, comp. **Biotechnology and Society.** Santa Cruz, Calif., Reference and Research Services, 1987. 64p. (Contemporary Social Issues: A Bibliographic Series, No. 8). $15.00pa. ISBN 0-937855-15-4.

The entries in this bibliography are arranged under seven broad headings: "Biotechnology and Society – General"; "Biotechnology: Legal and Regulatory Aspects"; "Biotechnology and Agriculture"; "Medical and Reproductive Technologies"; "Biotechnology and Biological Weapons and Warfare"; "The University/Corporate Research Relationship"; and "Resources." Each of the first six headings is divided into books, documents, pamphlets, and articles.

Scanning the entries reveals a strong concentration on genetic engineering and recombinant DNA. Inasmuch as these topics have attracted a great deal of public concern, this might be an appropriate weighting. More seriously, this reviewer notes that most articles seem to be from relatively obscure magazines. *Science* and *Nature*, in particular, have provided extensive coverage on these topics, but most of the articles are not reported in this bibliography.

This publication seems to be a marginal addition to collections with extensive holdings in the represented areas; however, it might be of value to medium-sized public libraries.

　　　　　　　　　　　　　　　　Edwin D. Posey

MATERIALS SCIENCE

1496. **Engineered Materials Handbook. Volume 1: Composites.** Cyril A. Dostal and others, eds. Metals Park, Ohio, ASM International, 1987. 983p. illus. index. $104.00. LC 87-19265. ISBN 0-87170-279-7.

This state-of-the-art handbook on composites is volume 1 of *Engineered Materials Handbook*, issued by the American Society for Metals. This new series treats the new materials in the same manner as the seventeen-volume *Metals Handbook*, ninth edition, covers metals and metalworking. Coverage is extensive and varied, reflecting current interest and developments in composites.

The composites volume includes properties and forms of components of composites, analysis and design, testing, and applications. Composites, by handbook definition, include thermoset polymer matrix materials, reinforced with continuous fibers, used mostly for primary structural applications in the aerospace industries. Some metal, carbon/graphite, and ceramic matrix composites are also included. Reinforced plastics will be covered in volume 2 of the series.

The industry, academic, and government contributors to this encyclopedic treatment of composites vary in length of articles and inclusion of references, and all sections are current and pertinent. Each section opens with an introductory overview on the general subject, followed by subsections on specific aspects such as static strength and adhesives specifications. Authors are very straightforward in stating where technology is under development and more research is needed, and the evaluative comments are useful.

Graphics are excellent; a good glossary, an extensive index, and an abbreviations section round out the volume. The handbook is large but relatively easy to handle, and given the amount of material included, the price is reasonable.

This series is off to a good start, and the set will be the standard reference on composites. Industrial, chemical, and mechanical engineering, as well as materials science collections should include this series. The American Society for Metals has produced an essential reference book.

　　　　　　　　　　　　　　　　Marilyn Stark

1497. **High-Temperature Property Data: Ferrous Alloys.** M. F. Rothman, ed. Metals Park, Ohio, ASM International, 1988. 1v. (various paging). bibliog. $128.00. ISBN 0-87170-243-6.

While the purpose of this book is to gather high-temperature data on ferrous alloys in a convenient, accessible form, it is worth mentioning that this was accomplished by the utilization of personal computers and existing software. The new technique has allowed editing, table preparation, graph presentation, and page copy to be set up at great cost savings and allows the option of saving the data for future electronically searchable databases. The data were collected from thirty of the most important metallurgical reference books, most of which were published by the American Society for Metals. The ferrous alloys are grouped into eleven categories: irons, carbon steels, alloy steels, ASTM steels, elevated-temperature service steels, ultrahigh strength steels, tool steels, maraging steels, wrought stainless steels, ACI casting alloys, and wrought iron-nickel alloys and iron-nickel super alloys. After a general description and summary of the main characteristics and uses of the alloy, tables and graphs of composition, physical properties, and mechanical properties at high temperatures are given. There is no index, so the user must know the type of alloy being considered beforehand. A second volume on high-temperature properties of nonferrous alloys will appear soon.

Robert J. Havlik

1498. Metals Handbook. Volume 14: Forming and Forging. 9th ed. Joseph R. Davis and others, eds. Metals Park, Ohio, ASM International, 1988. 978p. illus. index. $88.00. LC 78-14934. ISBN 0-87170-020-4.

This prestigous handbook has long been recognized as a primary source for metals information. With the publication of this volume, plus the preceding volume on powder metallurgy and the volume to follow on casting, the handbook will contain comprehensive information on metal forming processes.

The format of this volume provides detailed coverage of many topics related to forming and forging. The articles are very well written and illustrated, with photographs, line drawings, and charts where applicable.

Literally hundreds of writers and reviewers have contributed to this volume. When purchased as a component of the complete set, it will be highly useful to engineers working in these areas. It will also be useful for manufacturing establishments employing these techniques.

Recommended for all engineering libraries, special libraries of manufacturing establishments, and larger public libraries.

Edwin D. Posey

1499. Metals Handbook. Volume 15: Casting. 9th ed. Joseph R. Davis and others, eds. Metals Park, Ohio, ASM International, 1988. 937p. illus. maps. index. $104.00. LC 78-14934. ISBN 0-87170-021-2.

Casting is the making of a metal shape by pouring or injecting liquid metal into a mold, in contrast to shaping by mechanical means. The earliest known castings are more than ten thousand years old and the process has evolved from magic to an art to the complex, interdisciplinary science it is today. Volume 5 of the eighth edition of the *Metals Handbook* covered both casting and forging, but since the body of knowledge has doubled over the past ten years, volume 15 of the ninth edition stands alone, covering 937 pages. There are over seventy articles by nearly two hundred authors. All aspects of metal casting, including historical developments, liquid metal processing, solidification, patterns, molding and casting processes, foundry equipment and processing, design considerations, ferrous and nonferrous casting

alloys, and computer applications are covered. As in the other volumes of the *Metals Handbook* there is a glossary of terms used, as well as a metric conversion guide, abbreviations and symbols, and extensive index. The quality of the articles as well as the illustrations and references are the same high quality of the other volumes in the set.

Robert J. Havlik

1500. Worldwide Guide to Equivalent Irons and Steels. 2d ed. Harold M. Cobb, ed. Metals Park, Ohio, ASM International, 1987. 1v. (various paging). index. $120.00. LC 87-072577. ISBN 0-87170-305-X.

1501. Worldwide Guide to Equivalent Nonferrous Metals and Alloys. 2d ed. Harold M. Cobb, ed. Metals Park, Ohio, ASM International, 1987. 1v. (various paging). index. $120.00. LC 87-072576. ISBN 0-87170-306-8.

Just as surely as "All Gaul is divided into three parts," all engineering materials are so divided: ferrous (irons and steels), nonferrous metals, and nonmetallic materials (plastics, ceramics, glasses, etc.). Governmental agencies and professional societies exist whose prime or sole purpose is to describe precisely what the physical and chemical properties must be for the materials to be labeled as "Meets _____ Specification no. _____" or "Meets _____ Standard no. _____." As these phrases exist in binding legal documents as contracts or "RFPs," the urgency of the patron's need for accurate and up-to-date answers is clear. This, coupled with the rather small *number* of inquiries, means justification of typically high-unit-cost reference materials needs special emphasis.

The volumes cited in the headings (totalling over one thousand pages by count) are really twins and need to be reviewed together. They are comprehensive in that they each include data from twenty-three different international and national bodies and which in some three thousand cases at least are linked by the Uniform Numbering System (UNS) of ASTM/ASM—a high recommendation. (In answer to the implied question of "Who needs such detail," the reviewer's desk is two miles from a widely acclaimed bridge whose completion date was delayed one year, as the Korean steel supplied did not meet the specifications and had to be replaced from that country.)

Based on the space occupied, the following is the importance of subjects: volume 1— wrought carbon steels, wrought stainless ... steels, wrought alloy steels, tool steels, cast steels, and cast iron; volume 2—wrought aluminum, wrought copper, cast aluminum, cast copper, magnesium, nickel, titanium, lead, zinc, and tin. Adequate introductions explaining the tables and significance of each of the nine column headings into which the pages are formed are provided, as well as indexes to UNS Number, Specification Number, and Designations. Current updates to the data cited are available in ASM's "MetSel/2" disk-based database.

There is a need to supplement the above by graphs and diagrams of the several alloys and metals, if one is to surely select an item for a specific application. A first possibility is *Metals Handbook Desk Edition* (see *ARBA* 86, entry 1577) or ASM's earlier *Engineering Properties of Steel* by Phillip Harvey (ASM, 1982). Elegant but looseleaf handbooks of newer materials are those of the Battell Columbus Laboratories Metals and Ceramics Information Center, prepared under Department of Defense auspices. (Examples include ones on structural alloys and on aerospace structural metals.) A rather more pedestrian looseleaf service with more data than diagrams is *Alloy Digest: Data on World-Wide Metals and Alloys* (Alloys Digest, 1952-).

Unless the absolute currency of filing of updates is assured, the use of looseleaf services in the crucial area of specifications and standards of engineering materials is a disservice to the pressured users.

E. B. Jackson

MECHANICAL ENGINEERING

1502. Fluid Mechanics Source Book. Sybil P. Parker, ed. New York, McGraw-Hill, 1988. 274p. illus. index. (McGraw-Hill Science Reference Series). $45.00. LC 87-36638. ISBN 0-07-045502-3.

Fluid mechanics is an important topic in most areas of engineering, and as such has a large spectrum of users and applications. Some users require in-depth treatment on specific problems, and others need a quick review to get an idea of what they are dealing with. This book is for the latter category. In essence it assembles 105 separate topics, including fluid statics, fluid flow, and fluid dynamics and both nonviscous and viscous flow, from the sixth edition of the *McGraw-Hill Encyclopedia of Science and Technology* (see *ARBA* 88, entry 1448) and arranges them by topic to save extensive cross-references within the original volumes. The editors have published similar collections in optics, physical chemistry, solid-state physics, and spectroscopy. A disappointment is that no special introduction was written for this volume. (It is also a reprint of an article in the encyclopedia, minus the references.) For an academic

library a copy of the encyclopedia would cover all topics; this would be better than acquiring the specific volumes. For a research library the recent *Encyclopedia of Fluid Mechanics* (see *ARBA* 88, entry 1592) would be best.

Robert J. Havlik

1503. Machinery's Handbook: A Reference Book for the Mechanical Engineer, Designer, Manufacturing Engineer, Draftsman, Toolmaker, and Machinist. 23d ed. By Erik Oberg, Franklin D. Jones, and Holbrook L. Horton. New York, Industrial Press, 1988. 2511p. illus. index. $55.00; $65.00 (thumb-indexed). LC 87-31093. ISBN 0-8311-1200-X; 0-8311-0900-9 (thumb-indexed).

This engineering handbook covers machine shop practice and other aspects of practical mechanical engineering in an exemplary manner, and has done so for seventy-five years. It is another example of a "mature" reference tool that remains dependable and predictable.

All engineering libraries serving undergraduates, vocational/community trade schools, and job retraining centers would buy not only this volume, but also the practical companion, *Machinery's Handbook Guide to the Use of Tables and Formulas* (Industrial Press, 1988). The latter includes worked examples and problems for class and home study. Engineering libraries dedicated to engineering science could get by with alternate editions, unless they were intrigued by the new section on numerical control and machinery noise (pp. 1117-69). As would be expected, updating has concentrated on new specifications and standards numbers and an ever deeper intrusion of metrics into the veteran text. A successful effort has been made to rearrange topics in a more meaningful manner. This is a useful tool.

E. B. Jackson

MINING ENGINEERING

1504. Stark, Marilyn McAnally. **Mining and Mineral Industries: An Information Sourcebook.** Phoenix, Ariz., Oryx Press, 1988. 124p. index. (Oryx Sourcebook Series in Business and Management, No. 10). $33.00. LC 87-23189. ISBN 0-89774-295-8.

This annotated bibliography, compiled by the head of reference at the Colorado School of Mines, is arranged according to type of reference, such as dictionaries, indexes, and databases. Items covered include recent reference volumes, periodicals, journals, and selected nonprint materials. Since government documents are an integral part of mining and mineral industries, they are not treated as a separate category but are integrated with the other types of literature. Most of the citations are from the 1970s and 1980s and vary from introductory to extremely technical and scholarly.

To be included materials must specifically deal with mineral industries, which are defined as exploration for ore, mineral processing, and marketing. General business sources and metallurgical materials are not included unless a significant portion relates directly to the mineral industries. However, because mining is an international activity which has political and economic ramifications, both types of information are covered as they relate to this industry.

The materials are well indexed, with separate author, title, and subject indexes keyed to citation number. Of special interest is the section "Core Library Collection," which contains an overview and quick access sources relevant to the entire industry. For those collections with a strong interest in mining or those business collections with an interest in this industry. [R: Choice, July/Aug 88, p. 1718]

Susan B. Ardis

NUCLEAR ENGINEERING

1505.   Bierlein, Lawrence W. **Red Book on Transportation of Hazardous Materials.** 2d ed. New York, Van Nostrand Reinhold, 1988. 1203p. index. $96.95. LC 86-32558. ISBN 0-442-21044-2.

Appendices comprise two-thirds of this tome; they provide vapor pressure curves for inflammable liquids (many running inexplicably beyond the grids), the United Nations recommendations on transport of dangerous goods, the preambles to Department of Transportation notices and amendments (dockets HM-1 to HM-198), and what the author labels "pertinent" materials statutes. Anyone who will be engaged in the transportation of hazardous materials, however, will find it necessary to secure separate copies of the government regulations which are cited and broadly outlined in the chapters (thirty-two). The volume itself touches upon all components of hazardous transportation from the types of authorized vehicles and containers to issues of liability and the right of a community "to know," and cites relevant regulations. An index provides a quick reference to most topical issues, but to only a few encoded forms of regulations (dockets, OMR, etc.).

The volume provides an excellent resource for those who seek a clarification of the difference among such regulations as those developed by the Occupational Safety and Health Administration, those encompassed by the Environmental Protection Agency Super

fund, and those included in the UN "Orange Book." The dichotomous keys for the determination of proper DOT shipping names are a particularly useful feature of the volume, as is the list of addresses (with some telex and telephone numbers) of organizing groups in countries which participate in the regulation of dangerous international maritime goods.

Diane M. Calabrese

1506.   Hassler, Peggy M. **Three Mile Island: A Reader's Guide to Selected Government Publications and Government-Sponsored Research Publications.** Metuchen, N.J., Scarecrow, 1988. 214p. index. $25.00. LC 88-10086. ISBN 0-8108-2118-4.

The 1979 Three Mile Island nuclear power plant incident has spawned a veritable flood of books, journal articles, technical reports, conference papers, newspaper accounts, and other analyses. This modest bibliography takes as its province "selected government publications and government-sponsored research publications." Pennsylvania government and county publications are included, along with those of the federal government. More than half of the 668 items are government-sponsored technical reports, in addition to which there are some one hundred journal articles and over two hundred reports of hearings by various governmental bodies.

A clear and well-written introduction is followed by a glossary of terms, and both author and subject indexes are appended. Each bibliographical entry is followed by a succinct description of its contents.

In view of the widespread interest in the possible effects of nuclear accidents, it is felt that this bibliography will be useful to a variety of libraries and their patrons. Clear ordering information, including NTIS order numbers and even OCLC numbers when available, increases the potential utility of this bibliography.

Recommended for academic libraries, public libraries, and those special libraries with an interest in the subject.

Edwin D. Posey

1507.   Lau, Foo-Sun. **A Dictionary of Nuclear Power and Waste Management with Abbreviations and Acronyms.** Letchworth, England, Research Studies Press and New York, John Wiley, 1987. 396p. bibliog. (Research Studies in Nuclear Technology, 1). $170.00. LC 87-4288. ISBNM 0-471-91517-3.

This is an eclectic, interesting dictionary. It includes terms from high technology as well as popular jargon such as *NIMBY* (Not in My Backyard). Much of the material comes from nuclear engineering, as might be guessed. There are additional terms from geology and medicine listed, "which have a specific application" (introduction). It is unclear what criteria were used to determine inclusion of geologic and medical terms.

The majority of the definitions are brief, approximately thirty to forty words long. Care with terminology and circular references is evident. The major impact of this work will be the beginnings of standardization into the field of nuclear power and waste management. SI units are used throughout and standardized values for specific measurements are used wherever possible.

The major drawback to the work is not the content, but the price. It appears to be produced from author-supplied copy with only minor typographical work. Libraries and information centers with tight budgets are urged to wait for a comparable dictionary at a more reasonable price. I recommend the content but fault the publishers for what is, in my opinion, price gouging.   C. D. Hurt

1508. Wood, M. Sandra, and Suzanne M. Shultz, comps. **Three Mile Island: A Selectively Annotated Bibliography.** Westport, Conn., Greenwood Press, 1988. 309p. index. (Bibliographies and Indexes in Science and Technology, No. 3). $47.95. LC 87-37547. ISBN 0-313-25573-3.

This bibliography is both ambitious and successful in its coverage of the literature generated by the 1979 accident at Three Mile Island (TMI). The bibliography sparkles with clarity: a subject index guides the user to the literature via a comprehensive list of topics (including humor) and a cross-referenced author index. Broad headings (e.g., health effects, industry issues) for nonfederal publications make it possible to browse by topic. And, the compilation of the titles in the section on popular literature provides in itself a quick immersion in the patterns of thoughts and sentiments since 1979. The volume is exemplary as one that has been proofread meticulously. The scope and integrity of the bibliography merit it a place in any reference library. The only peculiar (self-effacing, perhaps?) aspect of the book is the absence of the names and titles of the compilers at the conclusion of their preface. [R: Choice, Dec 88, p. 634]

Diane M. Calabrese

PETROLEUM ENGINEERING

1509. Myers, Arnold, Diana Edmonds, and Karen Donegani. **Offshore Information Guide.**
Berkhamsted, England, ASR Books; distr., Tulsa, Okla., PennWell Books, 1988. 1v. (various paging). bibliog. index. $140.00 spiral-bound. ISBN 0-906528-03-8.

This work is an unusual and interesting combination of bibliography and directory, covering various facets of information on offshore operations, especially petroleum and marine engineering. This British publication merges *Current Bibliography of Offshore Technology, Offshore Literature Classification,* and *Guide to Information Sources in Marine Technology.*

The classed ninety-eight-page bibliography covers reports, symposia, books, and pamphlets, sometimes in categories, such as OCS maps, rather than individual items. Core information, most published within the last five years, comes mostly from North Sea operations. Author, sponsoring organization, and general subject indexes follow the bibliography. Using the bibliography, a librarian can collect a comprehensive core collection of offshore technology information, from platforms to waste disposal. The classed arrangement is unfamiliar, so the bibliography requires some time and effort to use effectively.

Information services and databases are separate sections of the guide, color-coded for quick access. The detailed description of information services includes specialties and contact persons at places like Aberdeen City Libraries and Society for Underwater Technology. Name indexes follow each section. Stockbroker research reports are also covered.

The directory combines agencies, publishers, government bureaus, and companies – from OPEC to Oildom Publishing to Paint Research Association. The wide-ranging, inclusive directory ties together many different types of sources on offshore engineering. All publishers and information sources from the bibliography are included, with address and telephone, telex, and fax numbers.

The guide will be useful in developing and broadening offshore technology collections and then as a ready-reference directory. The spiral-bound format is convenient. Recommended for petroleum and marine engineering collections, especially those with a North Sea focus.

Marilyn Stark

SAFETY ENGINEERING

1510. **Dictionary of Terms Used in the Safety Profession.** 3d ed. Stanley A. Abercrombie, comp. and ed. Des Plaines, Ill., American Society of Safety Engineers, 1988. 72p. $25.00pa. ISBN 0-939874-79-2.

ASSE is the oldest and largest national safety organization in the United States. Major interests include safety management, consulting, engineering, risk management/insurance, public sector, healthcare, and construction. With such broad interests the terminology of health and safety matters in these areas can get quite complicated. In 1971 the first comprehensive *Dictionary of Terms ... * appeared. This third edition contains approximately fifteen hundred terms, definitions, and cross-references, found in more than three hundred disciplines and subject areas. The terms reflect many of the current concerns and recent advances of interest to safety professionals, such as *AIDS, biohazards, prospective nuclear waste,* and *the Zephinie escape chute*, as well as everyday terms from *Abbreviated Injury Scale (AIS)* to *X-rays*. Appendix A lists the abbreviations, names, and addresses of over two hundred professional organizations concerned with safety and occupational health, and appendix B annotates more than a dozen printed or online sources of information. This is an interesting dictionary with wide applicability.

Robert J. Havlik

1511. Directory of Safety Related Computer Resources. 1987 ed. By Engineering Division, American Society of Safety Engineers. Des Plaines, Ill., American Society of Safety Engineers, 1987. 3v. bibliog. index. $15.00pa./vol. ISBN 0-939874-75-X (v.1); 0-939874-76-8 (v.2); 0-939874-77-6 (v.3).

Volume 1 consists of a directory of software, volume 2 a directory of databases, and volume 3 a listing of systems and hardware. It was interesting to note that there is a computer game in this area called "Three Mile Island." Each volume is a stand-alone product arranged in alphabetical order by the name of the product. Volumes 1 and 3 are then further subdivided into large subjects, such as chemical safety, fire protection, and weather.

The individual volumes are not indexed and there is no overall index to the set. This is a very specialized reference tool for safety consultants.

Susan B. Ardis

SANITARY ENGINEERING

1512. Biron, Paul J. **Terminology of Water Supply and Environmental Sanitation: English-French. Terminologie de L'approvisionnement en Eau et de L'assainissement de Milieu.** Washington, D.C., World Bank, 1987. 171p. (World Bank-UNICEF Glossary). $23.00pa. LC 85-16863. ISBN 0-8213-0585-9.

The author states that he "attempts to provide the user with a handy French/English glossary of the terms more frequently used in connection with water supply and environmental sanitation" (p. 1), especially terms and descriptions used by equipment manufacturers and suppliers. This glossary is arranged in a straightforward manner with sections for English-French and French-English. Multiple or equivalent translations are listed when they exist. Translations having different meanings are also listed, as are cross-references to related terms. There are two appendices: a list of diseases related to the lack of water supply and/or sanitation and a compilation of conversion factors and equivalents commonly used by those involved in these fields.

This volume assumes a basic knowledge of English and/or French. The intent here is to offer an easy-to-use guide to the jargon or technical language of a specific subject area. This glossary would be useful to those involved in the fields of water supply, sanitation, and environmental engineering on an international level, or for assistance in translating or understanding foreign publications covering these subjects.

Diane Montag

STEAM ENGINEERING

1513. Boiler Operator's Dictionary: A Quick Reference of Boiler Operation Terminology. Lionel Edward LaRocque, comp. Phil Roman, ed. Troy, Mich., Business News Publishing, 1988. 151p. $7.95pa. LC 87-18417. ISBN 0-912524-41-3.

This is a pocket-sized, quick reference dictionary dealing with boilers and the technology associated with them. Terms listed are those encountered in normal boiler operation. The information supplied is not in-depth; definitions are clear, concise, and range in length from twelve to twenty words. Lacking a preface or introduction, the intent of the work appears to be a quick source for those who are literally on-site; this is where the book will find its greatest audience. The definitions are too simplistic for academic or special collections, and the scope precludes recommending it for public or school library collections.

Although the book may have a limited market, it fills that niche nicely. Those seeking more expansive definitions should consult *Van Nostrand's Scientific Encyclopedia* (6th ed. Van Nostrand Reinhold, 1983) or the *ASME Boiler and Pressure Vessel Code* (American Society of Mechanical Engineers, 1986). Recommended for a boiler operator's collection only.

C. D. Hurt

34   Health Sciences

GENERAL WORKS

Bibliographies

1514. Chitty, Mary Glen, with Natalie Schatz, comps. **Federal Information Sources in Health and Medicine: A Selected Annotated Bibliography.** Westport, Conn., Greenwood Press, 1988. 306p. index. (Bibliographies and Indexes in Medical Studies, No. 1). $49.95. LC 88-226. ISBN 0-313-25530-X.

Even those librarians with less than a passing interest in the health sciences should take note of this new reference work. Here in one place are annotations for twelve hundred government publications and a hundred federal databases. The authors use a liberal definition of what constitutes a government publication but essentially the book has references to GPO depository publications, NTIS titles, and selected documents only available directly from federal agencies. Using 1980 as a cut-off date for most nonserial publications, Chitty and Schatz have compiled this bibliography using serials, indexes, federal laws and regulations, handbooks, reports, and directories. Material from some ninety federal agencies is represented in this volume.

Entries include author, title, document availability, publication date, pagination, and SUDOC and NTIS numbers. What the entries do not include are the GPO stock numbers or the format. The authors feel that because so many publications are found in both print and microfiche it is best to consult the *Monthly Catalog* for format identification. This is really the only regrettable omission. The entries are grouped into over forty general chapters. An appendix for discontinued publications and another for addresses of major federal agencies also are included. A twenty-eight-page index assists the user in finding material about specific subjects.

This is an important new reference book. No one has to be reminded how difficult it is to gain access to relevant government documents in any field let alone one so specialized. This book helps fill this access gap. It is strongly recommended for government depository libraries, health sciences libraries, and general academic libraries. [R: Choice, Dec 88, p. 622]

Tom Smith

1515. Haselbauer, Kathleen J. **A Research Guide to the Health Sciences: Medical, Nutritional, and Environmental.** Westport, Conn., Greenwood Press, 1987. 655p. index. (Reference Sources for the Social Sciences and Humanities, No. 4). $49.95. LC 87-17592. ISBN 0-313-25530-9.

The primary purpose of this reference tool is to assist researchers at all levels, students from undergraduate through graduate programs, clinicians, and scientists in finding the answers to their reference questions when an experienced medical librarian is not available.

Over two thousand sources (the cut-off date for inclusion of items is 1986) are cited and arranged by broad category, including general works (e.g., research guides, bibliographies, indexes and abstracts, etc.), basic sciences supporting clinical medicine (e.g., anatomy and physiology, biochemistry, biophysics, etc.), social aspects of the health sciences (e.g., bioethics, medical economics, and legal and forensic medicine), and medical specialties (e.g., diagnosis, psychiatry, public health). The subtitle may be somewhat misleading, in that it suggests a special emphasis on the nutritional and environmental when, in fact, those aspects are simply included along with many other topics.

Each section usually begins with a useful definition or description of the area which sets the stage for the annotations which follow. Unlike many comprehensive bibliographies which are composed simply of descriptions of content, the strength of this reference work is the inclusion of critical evaluations and comparisons with other like works. Liberal use of cross-referencing provides guidance to related areas and relevant works.

A short glossary defines generic terms used throughout the work, such as *Atlas*, *Handbook*, etc. A comprehensive index of titles, authors, and subjects concludes the volume. In addition to the primary audience, students and practitioners in the health sciences, librarians who provide reference services in these areas would find this a very useful volume. [R: RBB, 15 June 88, p. 1724]

Sherrilynne Fuller

1516. Leppa, Carol J., and Connie Miller, eds. **Women's Health Perspectives: An Annual Review. Volume 1.** Phoenix, Ariz., Oryx Press, 1988. 238p. index. $45.00. LC 88-19676. ISBN 0-89774-452-7.

Women's health is an emerging field of study rapidly gaining the attention of researchers and health care providers. While this literature is proliferating, it has not necessarily been organized in a meaningful and useful way. Traditionally resources have focused on particular topics, such as psychological and medical aspects of induced abortion, reproductive rights, childbirth, and the baby boom, thus seemingly limiting the scope of women's health. This present work begins a new annual series which will critically examine timely topics of concern in women's health.

Reflecting the broad scope and interdisciplinary nature of women's health issues, this first volume focuses on areas such as women's access to health information, mental health, alcohol and drugs, sexuality, older women, and women as health care providers. Each chapter, written by an expert(s) in that area, begins with a well-documented overview, and is followed by evaluative annotations of selected journal articles, dissertations, and monographs on that subject. The editors, noting that this is not a comprehensive bibliography, do claim that the items selected "focus on women, women as active and knowledgeable participants, and the connection of health care information to quality of life." The citations represent material published mainly within the last five years, although there are also some significant earlier works. Contributors' credentials, backgrounds, professional interests, and addresses are identified, thus enabling users to communicate with the authors. In addition, three unannotated bibliographies on abuse, cancer, and osteoporosis as well as a subject and author index are included.

Judith Ann Erlen

1517. **Medical and Health Care Books and Serials in Print 1988: An Index to Literature in the Health Sciences.** 17th ed. New York, R. R. Bowker, 1988. 2v. $139.95/set. LC 77-94389. ISBN 0-8352-2470-8; ISSN 0000-085X.

The information in this index, the seventeenth annual cumulation, is excerpted from the databases of the Bowker Company's Database Publishing Group, the same databases from which *Books in Print* and the other indexes in the "In Print" line are produced. The serials have been selected from the database used to produce *Ulrich's International Periodicals Directory* (see *ARBA* 88, entry 93).

There are 62,466 entries for books and 12,103 entries for serials, arranged under Library of Congress subject headings. The first volume contains both the subject index and the author index for books, and volume 2 contains the title index for books and the subject and title indexes for serials. A publisher list concludes volume 2.

The Bowker indexes are such a basic and standard part of the library's acquisitions and bibliographic apparatus that those libraries interested in the medical and health care areas will welcome the new annual edition. A previous edition, the fourteenth, was reviewed in *ARBA* 86, entry 1596.   Necia A. Musser

1518. Smallwood, Carol, comp. **Health Resource Builder: Free and Inexpensive Materials for Librarians and Teachers.** Jefferson, N.C., McFarland, 1988. 251p. index. $15.95pa. LC 88-42639. ISBN 0-89950-359-4.

This is a bibliography of associations, government departments, foundations, institutes, etc., in the health care area, arranged by medical topic, for example, aging, blindness, cholesterol, food additives, and so on. Over four hundred medical conditions are listed. Many of the associations appear under more than one medical condition. For instance, the Cancer Information Service; Merck Sharp & Dohme Health Information Services; and Public Affairs Pamphlets are cited frequently.

The information for each association includes full address, telephone number, and types of publications issued. The associations are then repeated in an alphabetical listing under the types of materials they publish: audiovisual material, bibliographies, health care databases, indexes, and so forth. There are also three useful appendices: "State and Regional Offices of Public Agencies," "National Health Observances Calendar," and "Hotlines and Other Special Telephone Numbers." A good, comprehensive subject and name index concludes the work.

Despite the repetitive agency information, this is a well-made bibliography which should be helpful to many kinds of health professionals, as well as to school, public, and academic librarians. The book is softcover, but with a sewn binding, and should hold up well for reference use.   Necia A. Musser

Dictionaries and Encyclopedias

1519. **The Columbia Encyclopedia of Nutrition.** Myron Winick and others, comps. and eds. New York, Putnam, 1988. 349p. index. $19.95. LC 87-10782. ISBN 0-399-13298-8.

This reference work is intended to provide the lay reader with current and authoritative information about nutrition. The editors do not claim that this volume is comprehensive, but rather that "it has focused on those issues in nutrition and diet which most concern us in our desire to lower our risk for certain diseases and to promote good health and well being" (p. 8). These objectives are accomplished in this work. The editorial board is composed of nutrition experts who are or were recently on the faculty of the Institute of Human Nutrition, Columbia University College of Physicians and Surgeons. The book presents summaries of data on human nutrition. Some one hundred entries are organized alphabetically. Among the topics included are vitamins, caffeine, salt, reducing plans, and cancer prevention. In addition to presenting basic information and recommendations on each topic, the editors supply evidence to support their advice. *See* references to related topics are provided. The volume is written in a clear, simple to understand manner. A variety of tables and a few sample menus are included. An index is provided at the end of the volume. No references or bibliographies are included, so the reader has no easy way to follow up on or learn more about the information provided. [R: LJ, 1 June 88, p. 102; RBB, 15 Sept 88, p. 132]
                    Jacqueline Wilson

1520. Last, John M., ed. **A Dictionary of Epidemiology.** 2d ed. New York, Oxford University Press, 1988. 141p. bibliog. $24.95; $12.95pa. LC 87-31409. ISBN 0-19-505480-6; 0-19-505481-4pa.

Epidemiology is defined in this dictionary as the study of the distribution and determinants of health-related states of events in specified populations and the application of this study to the control of health problems. Since the field is growing rapidly, this little book defines perhaps one thousand terms and is twenty-seven pages larger than the previous edition published five years ago. It uses thoughtful

definitions and good typography to clarify terms for those whose first language is not English and for individuals working in peripheral fields. The boundaries are broad: terms derive from fields of sociology, biostatistics, probability theory, and biology as well as medicine. Typically, the entries explain the underlying concepts. When synonyms exist, definitions are usually entered under the most commonly used term and are cross-referenced from alternates. Although the editor tried to avoid jargon and initialisms, the dictionary does contain some widely used slang as well as a few eponyms and acronyms, and contains some brief, interesting biographical entries for important figures in epidemiology.
                    Marda Woodbury

1521. Rhea, Joseph C., J. Steven Ott, and Jay M. Shafritz. **The Facts on File Dictionary of Health Care Management.** New York, Facts on File, 1988. 692p. bibliog. $35.00. LC 87-6831. ISBN 0-8160-1637-2.

In the world of health administrators the NRA (National Rehabilitation Association) represents the interests of rehabilitation specialists, and fixed charges relate to hospital accounting practices. This new Facts on File volume does an excellent job of capturing the specialized language, jargon, and acronyms used by managers in all types of health care organizations. It also contains a significant number of entries from other fields, such as accounting and labor relations, that health care managers will find helpful. There are gaps, particularly in the financial and legal aspects of health administration, but these will not detract from the value of this reference work to most users. The one serious fault lies in inconsistent cross-referencing of acronyms. Rounding out the volume are a useful chronology of important historical events in health delivery and financing, and a brief, but well-selected, bibliography of additional source materials. [R: Choice, Dec 88, p. 632]
                    Bruce Stuart

Directories

1522. **Directory of Biomedical and Health Care Grants 1988.** Phoenix, Ariz., Oryx Press, 1988. 402p. index. $74.50pa. LC 85-15562. ISBN 0-89774-383-0; ISSN 0883-5330.

This book, containing descriptions of over twenty-three hundred health-related funding programs, is produced from the GRANTS database — the source for the larger *Directory of Research Grants* (*DRG*).

The directory consists of a main section and three indexes. The main section is arranged alphabetically by program title and includes grants from the AAAS Prize for Behavioral Science Research to the Mary C. Zahasky Memorial Awards. Following each program title is an annotation describing the program's goals. Subsequent to the annotation is information on eligibility requirements, application/renewal, funding amount, sponsor, and contact address. The quality and length of these descriptions vary, but there is generally enough information to point potential applicants in the right direction.

Following the main section are a subject index, a sponsoring organization index, and a sponsoring-organizations-by-type index. The subject index is helpful, but falls short of the claim that it is very detailed. There are, for example, no sections on dietetics or blindness, nor are there cross-references to them. The same weakness is true for the sponsoring organization index. Subject access would be greatly enhanced by an upgrading of the cross-references (i.e., broader terms, narrower terms, related terms) in all the indexes.

Despite the limitations of the subject access, this directory is a worthwhile purchase for the small hospital library. Larger public and academic libraries should continue to purchase the *DRG*, as all the information included in this book is encompassed in the larger *DRG*. Purchase of both the *Directory of Biomedical and Health Care Grants* and the *DRG* is not necessary, except by larger academic health sciences centers. Although more recent information is available in the GRANTS database, browsing a print version is frequently desirable. Subsequent editions should provide better cross-references and subject access to the printed directory.

Patrice O'Donovan

1523. **Directory of Nursing Homes.** 3d ed. Phoenix, Ariz., Oryx Press, 1988. 1262p. index. $175.00pa. LC 84-18994. ISBN 0-89774-414-4; ISSN 0888-7624.

Because of an increasing aging population, society continues to need current information about long-term care facilities. The third edition of this directory follows the same format of the previous edition as it lists agencies according to city and state and uses data from self-report questionnaires on administration, licensure, number of beds, certification, ownership, admissions requirements, staff, language spoken, available facilities, and activities provided. The compilers note that if agencies failed to return questionnaires, the data available on those facilities were checked for accuracy against state licensing directories. An affiliation index and a list of all facilities is again included.

This latest edition contains several new and useful features. Chain-owned facilities are identified, and a list of corporate nursing home headquarters with addresses and telephone numbers is appended. There are two short, informative articles about financing long-term care written by experts in this area. Additionally, the introduction cites important aspects of new federal legislation which will have an impact on the services provided by nursing homes and the rights of those residents.

While the directory provides an overview of more than sixteen thousand long-term care facilities, the compilers continue to advise that persons visit and compare agencies before making decisions about placement, since inclusion does not mean endorsement. [R: RBB, 1 Dec 88, p. 621]   Judith Ann Erlen

1524. **Health Devices Sourcebook 1988: A Directory of Medical Devices Trade Names, and Manufacturers....** Plymouth Meeting, Pa., ECRI, 1987. 1v. (various paging). $165.00. ISBN 0-941417-02-6; ISSN 0278-3452.

1525. **Medical Device Register 1988. Volume 1: U.S. & Canada.** Stamford, Conn., Medical Device Register, 1987. 1v. (various paging). index. $170.00. LC 81-645923. ISBN 0-942036-18-2.

The 1988 edition of *Health Devices Sourcebook* for operators of health care facilities is divided into eight sections: product categories, product listing (main section), manufacturers' product lines, trade names, manufacturers' directory, equipment services, service companies, and numerical listings; users may thus approach the needed information from various starting points. The two new sections, equipment services and service companies, deal with access to used and leased equipment. Every legitimate product descriptor has a unique five-digit International Medical Device Code number, which may be used for filing systems, computerized inventory, purchasing orders, etc. Each American and Canadian service company or manufacturer has its own numerical designation; over sixty-four hundred furnished information. Entries under products include a list of manufacturers with their numbers, addresses, and telephone numbers, and may include the typical price range and references to ECRI's evaluations in their journal *Health Devices*, or technical descriptions in their *Product Comparison System* publications. The 1988 edition of the *Medical Device Register* (*MDR*) covers over ten thousand manufacturers and suppliers. It uses the FDA product code. Considerable detail is provided in the supplier profiles. The introductory material announces a new volume 2, *International Edition*, and *MedSpec*, consisting of pictures and other descriptive material provided by manufacturers, fully cross-referenced to *MDR*. The publisher's claim to being "the first and only specifying and buying guide on medical equipment and supplies available" is obviously refuted by *Health Devices*. Larger medical and research institutions may prefer *MDR* for its greater coverage and somewhat more detailed information.

Harriette M. Cluxton

1526. Medical Technology Assessment Directory: A Pilot Reference to Organizations, Assessments, and Information Resources. Clifford Goodman, ed. Washington, D.C., National Academy Press, 1988. 662p. index. $250.00. LC 88-5358. ISBN 0-309-03829-4.

This directory is a product of the Council on Health Care Technology, which was mandated by the U.S. Congress "to oversee the development and operation of an information clearinghouse for ... health care technology assessments" (p. xvii). The subtitle refers to the directory as a "pilot reference" and, consequently, while it is quite inclusive (featuring government agencies, corporations, associations, and research and educational institutions, mostly in the United States), it is not exhaustive. Plans call for the directory to be expanded and to serve as the basis for creation of a computerized database.

The directory is divided into five parts. Part 1 comprises profiles of sixty-eight assessment programs with citations to completed, ongoing, and planned assessments. Part 2 is a thesaurus and a listing of report citations according to the thesaurus terminology. Part 3 describes seventy-three information sources on technology assessment, including computerized databases. Part 4 describes seventy-two organizations which do not normally produce assessments but which are active in the technology field. Part 5 is a listing of all organizations included in the directory. Particularly noteworthy is the inclusion of materials often outside the information mainstream, such as industry publications, marketing reports, regulatory reports, and proceedings.

While one might fault the organization of the directory, which results in some repetition of information, it is an impressive initial effort to bring together information in an area in which rapid change, proliferation of products, high costs, and the potential impact on life and death medical decisions make the availability of information critical. This is an essential resource for all involved in the development, assessment, purchase, and use of health care technology. [R: Choice, Oct 88, p. 294]

Gari-Anne Patzwald

1527. Sunshine, Linda, and John W. Wright. **The Best Hospitals in America.** New York, Henry Holt, 1987. 371p. index. $22.95. LC 87-7535. ISBN 0-8050-0583-8.

The authors of this book purport to have selected the best hospitals in the United States. Sunshine and Wright, writers by profession, made their selection after considering recommendations of physicians, using data from government sources, reviewing professional and popular publications, and interviewing staffs from 150 hospitals. The end result is a profile of sixty-four hospitals and medical centers. Children's hospitals were excluded from the study. The criteria for final selection were based on the needs and concerns of the patients. These "best" hospitals are arranged by state (only twenty-seven states are represented), with indexes to names of medical specialists and a general subject index. The authors, to their credit, showed familiarity with the Joint Commission on Accreditation of Hospitals (JCAH), the Commission on Professional and Hospital Activities (CPHA), and the Health Care Financing Administration (HCFA).

The profiles of these hospitals are characterized by cogent narrative, covering from four to six pages per entry. Also covered are the hospital's reputation, an outline of services, patient profile, number of operations and type, specialties, a statistical profile (beds, occupancy rate, average patient stay, annual admissions, births, staffing, well-known specialists, research funding and projects, room charges, address and telephone numbers, and admissions policies).

There are some built-in defects in this book. First, it's far too selective. The District of Columbia, which has several medical centers, is not even represented. Second, with the rapid pace of technology and changing staffs and specialists, these data—indeed the whole book—may well be outdated in several years. In spite of these problems the authors have provided useful comparative data in their consumer-oriented guide for the hospitals they selected. Recommended for large public libraries. [R: RBB, 1 Dec 88, p. 624]   Tom Smith

Handbooks

1528. The Columbia University School of Public Health Complete Guide to Health and Well-Being after 50. Robert J. Weiss and Genell

J. Subak-Sharpe, eds. New York, Times Books/ Random House, 1988. 335p. illus. index. $24.95. LC 87-10005. ISBN 0-8129-1325-6.

This work is said to be a reflection of the Columbia University School of Public Health's optimism and concern for the physical and emotional health of those over age fifty. It provides information about specific diseases and practical aspects of a healthful lifestyle.

The presentation is in five parts: health and fitness, emotional well-being and relationships, a preventive approach to diseases of aging, health resources for older people, and death. In addition to text material the book contains much information in useful tables, including guidelines for a healthy diet, exercise, dealing with stress, and drugs to treat various conditions. The section on health resources provides information on use of the health care system, including Medicare, Medicaid, private insurance, and health maintenance organizations. [R: LJ, 15 Apr 88, p. 74]   Theodora Andrews

1529. The New Child Health Encyclopedia: The Complete Guide for Parents. By Boston Children's Hospital. Frederick H. Lovejoy, ed. New York, Delacorte Press/Dell Publishing, 1987. 740p. illus. index. $39.95; $19.95pa. LC 87-6809. ISBN 0-385-29541-3; 0-385-29597-9pa.

Since children are the future adults of society, protecting the health of and providing quality health care for children are topics with far-reaching implications for parents, health care professionals, and society. This book shares the combined experience and knowledge of many Boston Children's Hospital health professionals and has as its target audience parents and child care workers. The major goal of this volume is to enable parents to promote children's health and well being; however, it is not intended to substitute for a health maintenance program for children.

This book is divided into four sections. Section 1, "Keeping Children Healthy," provides an overview of growth and development with a chart outlining age and developmental level in relation to specific areas such as communication and mastery, as well as a discussion of practical suggestions for promoting a child's physical and mental well being. Part 2, "Finding Health Care for Children," helps prepare the user for a child's hospitalization or visit to the doctor's office. There is a useful discussion on informed consent and rights of patients and parents. The third section, "Emergencies," explains ways that parents can prepare for possible emergencies and can intervene when such situations arise. The last section, "Diseases and Symptoms," contains current information on signs and symptoms, diagnosis, cause, treatment, and prevention of almost three hundred health concerns. The editors note that the contents of the first three sections should be read by all persons caring for children and that the last section is designed as a reference tool and is to be read only as necessary. The clearly presented content is thorough without being too technical, and is enhanced by the illustrations. [R: LJ, 15 Nov 87, p. 72]   Judith Ann Erlen

1530. Pearman, William A., and Philip Starr. Medicare: A Handbook on the History and Issues of Health Care Services for the Elderly. New York, Garland, 1988. 158p. bibliog. index. (Garland Reference Library of Social Science, Vol. 406). $22.00. LC 88-2423. ISBN 0-8240-8391-1.

This slim volume purports to be a basic sourcebook for references to the Medicare program from 1965 to the mid-1980s. It begins with a review essay that outlines, in the barest of detail, the characteristics of Medicare coverage, program history, and current issues. The essay is marred by factual inaccuracies, misinterpretations of program benefits, and unsubstantiated opinion. It contains no references. The bibliography that follows represents a highly idiosyncratic collection of 288 references including many unpublished papers from professional association meetings. The material is organized alphabetically by first author. There are neither subject headings nor cross-references. A sentence or two of annotation is provided for about a third of the bibliographic entries. The authors provide no indication of why the selected entries were chosen nor what criteria led to the exclusion of literally thousands of other works on Medicare. Given the sparse coverage of the topic, a surprisingly large number of entries have no direct bearing on the Medicare program at all! The last half of the book is a chronological listing of *New York Times* references to Medicare, Medicaid, national health insurance, and sundry other issues. A five-page subject index rounds out the volume. The subject references are keyed to page number rather than bibliographic entry, further reducing the value of the work.   Bruce Stuart

1531. Saltman, Richard B., ed. The International Handbook of Health-Care Systems. Westport, Conn., Greenwood Press, 1988. 403p. index. $65.00. LC 87-17797. ISBN 0-313-24111-2.

This is more a compendium than a reference book, with not-quite-parallel accounts of the basic features of twenty-one national health care systems, mostly in developed countries. While these range from Australia to the United States, eight of the twenty-one are in European countries, only three (Argentina, Brazil, and Columbia) are Latin American nations, and only three (Egypt, Mozambique, and Nigeria) are African.

Typically, these accounts, by various authors, provide a historical overview, some basic information on geography and population, statistics on health services (these differ widely — for example, Australian health indicators demonstrate that the health status of Australia is comparable with most developed countries — *if* the aboriginal population is excluded), information on the structure and financing of the national health care system, current issues, future trends, and information sources.

The work is valuable in providing background for health statistics from different sources. As it shows common problems and widely varying approaches to solutions, it is a useful research tool for comparative studies.

Marda Woodbury

Indexes

1532. **Health Media Review Index 1984-86: A Guide to Reviews and Descriptions of Commercially Available Nonprint Material....** Deborah J. McCalpin, ed. Metuchen, N.J., Scarecrow, 1988. 751p. $52.50. LC 88-18452. ISBN 0-8108-2172-9.

This index updates the original volume, published in 1985 (see *ARBA* 86, entry 1618). It indexes reviews and descriptions of nonprint media from over one hundred health-related journals. Since the distributor of each piece of media is cited, the index becomes a means of selecting and ordering as well. A possible drawback is that media not reviewed in the journals examined do not appear in the index. Reviews of works intended for both laypersons and practitioners are mentioned. Major sections of the index include a list of journals examined with their descriptions, media arranged by subject (using MeSH), media arranged by title, and a list of distributors. If the user understands that this is not a listing of *all* media on health-related subjects, one will find it a highly useful guide to works of this nature, and an invaluable aid to collection-building.

Philip A. Metzger

MEDICINE

General Works

ACRONYMS AND ABBREVIATIONS

1533. Davis, Neil M. **Medical Abbreviations: 5500 Conveniences at the Expense of Communications and Safety.** 4th ed. Huntingdon Valley, Pa., Neil M. Davis, 1988. 139p. $7.95pa. LC 88-70072. ISBN 0-931431-04-2.

The author makes known his bias against the indiscriminate use of medical abbreviations in his subtitle. He makes his point again in the preface, calling his list "a testimonial to the problems and dangers associated with most undefined abbreviations." He shows that many medical abbreviations can refer to a number of conditions. For instance, PA can mean pulmonary artery, pernicious anemia, physician's assistant, or even pineapple. He especially discourages the use of abbreviations in medical prescriptions, citing some instances of unfortunate results from the misinterpretation of abbreviations and symbols.

This small 4-by-6-inch paperback book packs in fifty-five hundred current abbreviations, acronyms, and symbols. While the book is apt to get lost on the shelf among larger reference works because of its diminutive size, it does fill a need for anyone having to cope with medical records. It will be of primary interest to medical and health libraries, and to hospital personnel generally.

Necia A. Musser

1534. Hamilton, Betty, and Barbara Guidos. **MASA: Medical Acronyms, Symbols, & Abbreviations.** 2d ed. New York, Neal-Schuman, 1988. 277p. $45.00. LC 87-31455. ISBN 1-55570-012-8.

The second edition of *MASA* contains over thirty thousand entries, an increase of over ten thousand from the first edition (see *ARBA* 85, entry 1540). The work consists of abbreviations and acronyms listed alphabetically. These are accompanied by "explanations" which consist of word(s) or phrase(s) for which the acronym or abbreviation may stand. Many of the acronyms or abbreviations have several entries; *A*, for example, has over sixty-five entries, ranging from *Absidia* to *water (aqua)*. Many of the explanations are followed by cross-references to other abbreviations or explanations. The user should have a general idea of what to look for to avoid having to find potential "explanations" here and then having to go to a regular medical dictionary or text for further information. A complete set of "explanations," followed by dictionary definition, would be ideal, although the size would prove unwieldy.

Although "symbols" appears in the title, less than two of the 277 pages contain symbols. These appear following the main acronyms/ abbreviations section.

As a quick reference guide, this title is recommended for use by libraries, researchers, physicians, and medical records departments of hospitals. It is one of the most thorough guides of its type available and the authors have done a good job of gathering the information into one place. [R: RBB, 1 May 88, pp. 1487-88]

Patrice O'Donovan

BIOGRAPHIES

1535. O'Connor, W. J. **Founders of British Physiology: A Biographical Dictionary, 1820-1885.** Manchester, England, Manchester University Press; distr., New York, St. Martin's Press, 1988. 278p. index. $49.95. ISBN 0-7190-2537-0.

The core of this book consists of the biographical sketches of the over one hundred most important British physiologists in Victorian England. The principal source of these sketches is the obituaries of the individuals covered that appeared in the scientific periodicals of the time. To be sure, these are not critical or interpretative sketches, but they do reveal the prevailing opinion of the listed individuals' scientific contributions and the relevant basic facts about the sequence of their progression through their professional careers. The individual entries are not arranged alphabetically, and as such this is not strictly a dictionary as the book's subtitle implies; rather, they are grouped into the period in which the listed physiologists worked and into the institutions to which they were attached. Part 1 of the book covers the period 1820-1835, when physiology was still part of anatomical and clinical medicine. Part 2 covers the period 1835-1870, when physiology became a discipline taught in medical schools and hospitals. Part 3 covers the period 1870-1885, when experimental physiology emerged and flourished as a new discipline of scientific information. A short explanatory essay introduces each period covered and each of the institutions covered. These interpretative essays are easily discerned by their larger typeset, are scholarly, and taken together form a concise history of the development of physiology in Britain during that critical period when physiology established itself as an independent discipline within the medical sciences. This book is well worth reading, not only by those interested in British physiology but also by anyone concerned with the history of medicine and the development of physiology. [R: Choice, Oct 88, p. 294]

Garabed Eknoyan

DICTIONARIES AND ENCYCLOPEDIAS

1536. Anderson, Kenneth. **Symptoms after 40.** New York, Arbor House, 1987. 324p. $19.95. LC 86-32242. ISBN 0-87795-879-3.

Today the public wants information about how to be healthy, how to stay healthy, and how to interpret what health professionals have said. Self-help books related to various aspects of health care and written for the lay public are readily available in public libraries and bookstores. *Symptoms after 40* is another of these books. While it is frequently beneficial for laypersons to be informed, self-help books can also have a negative effect in that individuals may delay seeking necessary professional advice.

The title of this volume is misleading as it suggests that the age of forty is a demarcation point related to health. Not all the content is relevant only for persons over forty years of age. Some of the content applicable to persons under forty includes amenorrhea, hernia, and progeria. In addition this book contains material other than symptoms. For example, there are descriptions of conditions such as laryngeal cancer and abdominal hernia, medical and surgical treatments such as laminectomy, physiological functions of various hormones, and drug groups such as laxative and antitussive.

This volume is a dictionary of health-related terms. Cross-references to related terms are noted where appropriate. The content reflects current medical trends (e.g., suggesting lumpectomy as a treatment for breast cancer and providing research findings related to osteoporosis. The user, however, would need to be familiar with human anatomy or else would need another resource in order to understand terms such as the hypothalamus and pituitary gland. In addition, the user would find it helpful to have diagrams of anatomical parts such as the kidney and the brain stem. While the author has written and edited other health-related books, one wonders if he is qualified to write this particular volume, as nowhere is his educational background stated.

Judith Ann Erlen

1537. **Black's Medical Dictionary.** 35th ed. C. W. H. Havard, ed. Totowa, N.J., Barnes &

Noble Books, 1987. 750p. illus. $36.95. ISBN 0-389-20745-4.

Although this thirty-fifth edition of a classic text has been thoroughly rewritten and many new subjects have been added, the intention is unchanged: to describe medical practice as clearly and concisely as possible. The book itself is concise (with only forty-five hundred terms or phrases); the perspective and spelling are British. Although the cover notes that it "has proved itself invaluable to nurses and physiotherapists, to radiographers and medical secretaries, to medical students and practitioners," its greatest value – and its most appropriate niche – seems to be as a medical dictionary for the intelligent layperson. Its entries are exceptionally well written and informative, often explaining disease from a patient's perspective rather than a practitioner's. The book is quite current and includes definitions of many terms in fields related to medicine (e.g., the genetic code, nutrition, ultrasound, speech therapy, etc.). Characteristically, without wasting words, the book provides more background and context than are available in dictionaries for physicians, such as *Stedman's Medical Dictionary, Illustrated* (see *ARBA* 83, entry 1445), or nurses such as *Taber's Cyclopedic Medical Dictionary* edited by Clayton L. Thomas (see *ARBA* 86, entry 1627). For several terms I checked in all three; *Black's* was superior in providing what an intelligent layperson would like to know. *Black's* would seem most valuable in public libraries or libraries oriented towards patient education.

Marda Woodbury

1538. Dorland's Illustrated Medical Dictionary. 27th ed. Philadelphia, W. B. Saunders, 1988. 1888p. illus. $38.95 (thumb-indexed). LC 78-50050. ISBN 0-7216-3154-1.

This is an updating of the last (1981) edition of the classic, standard medical dictionary. Changes include a reduction in page size, making the volume a bit less unwieldy, redrawing of some illustrations, and of course many additions and revisions of terms, particularly in the fields of immunology, bacteriology, infectious diseases, and enzymology.

Make no mistake, this is a traditional, very technical medical dictionary, not particularly accessible to the layperson. In particular, the grouping of all terms consisting of two or more words as subentries under the noun can be confusing to anyone unfamiliar with medical dictionaries. For example, the term *acquired immune deficiency syndrome* will be found under the entry *syndrome*, along with several hundred other named syndromes. A medical dictionary which has adopted a strictly alpha-betical listing, such as the excellent *Webster's Medical Desk Dictionary* (see *ARBA* 87, entry 1604), is more accessible to the general user. However, *Dorland's* remains the choice for professional use, since it provides a higher level of technical information than any other single-volume source. [R: RBB, 1 Dec 88, pp. 620-21]

Carol L. Noll

1539. Encyclopaedia of Indian Medicine. S. K. Ramachandra Rao, ed. Bombay, India, Popular Prakashan; distr., Columbia, Mo., South Asia Books, 1985-1987. 3v. illus. bibliog. $121.00/set.

The Indian medicine covered in this encyclopedia is the indigenous medicine of India, which beginning in antiquity gradually evolved into a disciplined body of health-related concepts, methods, and practices. Through the ages and in the course of its cultural encounters it has been influenced by, and in turn affected, Arabic, Greek, Persian, Chinese, and other oriental schools of medicine. The knowledge thus accrued, known as Ayurveda or the Science of Life, is integrated into the Vedic Corpus. It is the purpose of the present text to present to the Western reader an overview of this discipline of health care which is still very much in vogue in India.

The first volume covers the history, personalities, and events that influenced the evolution of Indian medicine. The second volume exposes the basic concepts, including philosophical and metaphysical principles, engendered in Indian medicine. The third volume presents the conceptual framework of diagnosis and rationale of treatment in the practice of Indian medicine. Each volume is prefaced by an introductory précis which gives an overview of the topics covered. This is followed by a series of alphabetical entries describing the components of the topic considered in that volume. An appendix to each volume gives appropriate source materials, illustrations, and selected translations from original Sanskrit texts.

This is an inclusive and informative text that belongs on the shelf of every institution or individual with any interest in the history of medicine. It is well written, easy to use, and goes a long way in exposing concepts not readily accessible in commonly available texts on the subject. It represents the first half of the project undertaken by the author. A planned additional three-volume set dealing with diseases, drugs, materia medica, and folk medicine is scheduled for the future and should be eagerly awaited.

Garabed Eknoyan

1540. Encyclopedia of Medical Devices and Instrumentation. John G. Webster, ed. New York, John Wiley, 1988. 4v. illus. index. $450.00/set. LC 87-29608. ISBN 0-471-82936-6.

The relationship of medicine and instrumentation is a rapidly expanding, complex subject. This large, four-volume encyclopedia contains over 250 articles by specialists on the impact of physics, computers, and engineering on many of the specialty and subspecialty fields of medicine.

Each article provides the background to and the current status of specific aspects of medical devices and instrumentation. Articles present condensed information, varying in length from several pages to over ten, though each topic is worthy of book-length treatment. Subject coverage ranges in scope from specific instruments (endoscopes, pacemakers) to broad topics (biomedical engineering education, human factors in medical devices). Major strengths of these articles include up-to-date bibliographies, useful illustrations, brief historical overviews for most topics, and thorough cross-indexing in the text. A comprehensive index is also provided. No effort is made to cover broad public health concerns or medical specialties which do not make use of devices.

This compilation is extremely useful for health care professionals trying to keep up with the expanding field of medical devices and instrumentation; however, the highly scientific language makes these volumes of little use to the general public, despite the claims to this effect by the editor. It is also unlikely that the editor's claims for total comprehensive coverage and to "describe every aspect of medical devices and instrumentation" (volume 1, p. 1) are realistic. [R: Choice, Oct 88, p. 290]

Jonathon Erlen

1541. Firkin, B. G., and J. A. Whitworth. **Dictionary of Medical Eponyms.** Park Ridge, N.J., Parthenon, 1987. 591p. illus. $48.00. ISBN 0-940813-15-7.

Medical terminology is replete with diagnostic entities identified by the name of the individuals who first identified them. The traditional use of eponyms over the years has resulted in their adoption as the accepted diagnostic term with little, if any, knowledge by their users of anything about the origin of the eponym, the background of the individual after whom the disease or syndrome is named, or the history of the disease. The authors of this text have undertaken the laudable task of compiling a practical reference book that would provide this information. Entries made are listed alphabetically, and give a brief, at times superficial, description of the entity; a short background history of the recognition of the entity; a brief biography of the individual after whom it is named; and occasionally a picture of the person.

The entries are selective to the extent that the absolute majority are those used in internal medicine, with only a few from other specialties. There is also considerable variability in the detail provided for each entry. The two authors' subspecialties of nephrology and hematology are clearly reflected in the detail the eponyms in these two fields receive, as compared to the paucity of information given for some of the other subspecialties. The authors acknowledge this deficiency in their introductory remarks and express the intent to remedy it in future editions.

The input of collaborators from other disciplines of medicine and more hard work by the authors is bound to make future editions of this dictionary more inclusive and as such more useful. Still, this is a jewel of a book that provides under one cover information that is otherwise difficult to obtain. It certainly belongs on the shelf of every medical library as well as that of anyone with the slightest interest in the history of medicine.

Garabed Eknoyan

1542. Rothenberg, Robert E. **The New American Medical Dictionary and Health Manual.** 5th ed. New York, New American Library, 1988. 555p. illus. $4.95pa. ISBN 0-451-15152-6.

"To translate medical terms into language that can be easily understood," and to "supply medical information in simple form so that it can be interpreted readily by those who are unfamiliar with medical matters" is a valid purpose and was probably even more laudable when the first edition of this work appeared in 1962. In light of the growth of health consumerism and its burgeoning literature, plus almost daily television coverage of "medical matters," the fifth edition of the *Medical Dictionary* seems oversimplified. It briefly explains in easy, nontechnical language over nine thousand medical terms and diseases, often with accompanying diagrams.

The *Health Manual* (150 pages) consists largely of charts and tables on anatomy, first aid, laboratory tests, diets, life expectancy, child development, etc., for quick reference in the home. Nearly one-third of it merely reprints *Your Medicare Handbook* (Social Security Administration, 1986). Most libraries will prefer the more sophisticated *Signet/Mosby Medical Encyclopedia* (see entry 1543).

Harriette M. Cluxton

1543. **The Signet/Mosby Medical Encyclopedia.** Kenneth N. Anderson, ed. New York, New American Library, c1985, 1987. 685p. $5.95pa. ISBN 0-451-15059-7.

Based on the well-known Mosby *Medical and Nursing Dictionary*, this "newest and largest health reference ... in pocketbook size" (eighteen thousand entries) contains a tremendous amount of useful information on health care as well as quite thorough definitions of medical terms in understandable language. Related terms are grouped under the primary entry: this book is both dictionary and encyclopedia. Cross-referencing is extensive; pronunciation is often indicated. Particularly useful is the inclusion of many commonly prescribed drugs by brand names (e.g., Lanoxin), with indication of generic name and use. A cross-reference guide on such information and one on common drug interactions are among fourteen appendices, mostly charts and tables on contagious and sexually transmitted diseases, dietary requirements, etc.

Material has been checked for accuracy and currency by health professionals, and is surprisingly comprehensive although concisely presented. Libraries will find this useful for quick reference when conventional medical dictionaries and texts might be superfluous. Although some material is unique to this title, and some differently presented than in *The New American Medical Dictionary and Health Manual* (see entry 1542), the generally more in-depth coverage will be well worth the extra dollar to most health-conscious purchasers.

Harriette M. Cluxton

DIRECTORIES

1544. **ABMS Compendium of Certified Medical Specialists.** 2d ed. Evanston, Ill., American Board of Medical Specialties, 1988. 7v. index. $240.00/set. ISBN 0-934277-12-5; ISSN 0884-1543.

This is the second edition of a compendium listing professional information on members of all currently board-approved medical specialties. It is the updated version of the first edition that was released two years ago. The diplomates who have met the certification requirements of their respective boards are listed alphabetically under separate sections devoted to each specialty board. The certification of the diplomates listed has been verified with the individual boards, but the biographical information provided has been furnished by the diplomates themselves. Each biographical sketch provides the name, date and place of birth, education,

training, certification date, professional membership, address, and often telephone number. Each specialty section is preceded by the requirements and governing rules of that board, and followed by a geographic index listing the specialists by state and city of location. The seventh volume of the compendium is a master alphabetical index of all the specialists listed in the first six volumes. The compendium is scheduled to be updated every two years. A 1989 supplement to this edition is included with each order and will be shipped to purchasers in June 1989. [R: RBB, 1 Dec 88, p. 621]

Garabed Eknoyan

1545. Kurian, George Thomas. **Global Guide to Medical Information.** New York, Elsevier Science Publishing, 1988. 808p. index. $85.00. LC 88-3915. ISBN 0-444-01300-8.

Recent studies have shown that medical practices vary widely throughout the world. The aim of this book is to facilitate the flow of medical information across national and linguistic borders. The book has ninety-eight sections, the largest of which is a list of periodicals arranged by subject. There are also sections dealing with international and regional organizations; research institutes; national associations; publishers; online databases; symposia; and indexes, bibliographies, and statistics.

If all of the above listings were annotated and well researched, this would be a tremendously useful volume. However, most have only the name of the publication or organization, address, and sometimes a telephone number. Many of the associations have only a name and a city. The one exception is the section on online databases, which gives complete information on the scope, coverage, and producers.

Although the three-volume *Medical and Health Information Directory* (see *ARBA* 86, entries 1608 and 1609 and *ARBA* 87, entry 1589) has less of an international focus, it includes much more detail for most English-language publications and associations, and is a better choice for all except those libraries with a clear need for truly international coverage. [R: LJ, 15 Sept 88, p. 75]   Carol L. Noll

HANDBOOKS

1546. Covington, Timothy R., and J. Frank McClendon. **Sex Care: The Complete Guide to Safe and Healthy Sex.** New York, Pocket Books/Simon & Schuster, 1987. 402p. illus. index. $8.95pa. ISBN 0-671-52398-8.

Optimal sexual health is not guaranteed; it requires fundamental knowledge and consistent application. The authors, a pharmacist and a public service advertiser, present an excellent work designed for the layperson to help understand, improve, and maintain a healthful, fulfilling sex life. After a short but thorough discussion of male and female anatomy, the proper use, safety, effectiveness, adverse effects, and special considerations of contraceptives and contraceptive methods are presented. Included is information on IUDs, condoms, creams, gels and foams, sterilization, abstinence, and the rhythm method. The next lengthy section provides information on sexually transmitted diseases. This well-written section includes much of the most current information on the symptoms, treatments, and prevention methods of gonorrhea, herpes, syphilis, PID, and AIDS. A final section discusses special considerations in sexual health. Problems such as premenstrual syndrome (PMS), toxic shock syndrome, abortion, hygiene, and sexual myths are discussed in a frank and objective manner. This work is strongly written; the information is nonjudgmental and useful. Highly recommended for all libraries. Charts, tables, and an index are provided.   Julie M. Mueller

1547. **General Surgery.** By the Diagram Group. New York, Facts on File, 1988. 1v. (various paging). illus. index. (Surgery on File). $75.00 looseleaf with binder. LC 88-11256. ISBN 0-8160-1774-3.

1548. **Obstetrics and Gynecology.** By the Diagram Group. New York, Facts on File, 1988. 1v. (various paging). illus. index. (Surgery on File). $75.00 looseleaf with binder. LC 88-3690. ISBN 0-8160-1768-9.

These are the first two volumes, by health professionals, of a planned series of five designed to serve as resource material for patient information. Future volumes will cover surgical procedures in pediatrics; orthopedics and trauma; and diseases of the eye, ear, nose, and throat. Each volume of the series covers selections of the most commonly practiced diagnostic, operative, and therapeutic procedures within the specialty covered in that volume. Some fifty procedures are covered in each volume. Each entry is illustrated by one or more simple anatomical diagrams demonstrating the steps involved in performing the procedure. The accompanying text explains in easy to understand lay terms what the procedure is, its indications and why it is performed, what its benefits and risks are, how it is done and any preparation that may be necessary for it, what to expect afterwards in terms of complications, and what

to do in terms of after-care during the convalescence period. Each procedure is covered on the two sides of one of the looseleaf, heavy duty pages and is printed in a large typeface with black-and-white diagrams. All the material is free of copyright restrictions and grants the purchaser permission to duplicate the material for patient education and for nonprofit use.

The need for providing patients undergoing any procedure with a general idea of what to expect has long been recognized by the medical profession, with most physicians going to great lengths to brief patients. This perceived necessity to inform patients in order to reassure them has been reinforced by the judicial system in malpractice cases. In response to this need a host of patient information material has become available over the past decades. Most of this has been generated for individual specialties and is varied in scope and content. The present volumes provide a uniform approach, are easy to use and understand, and make it possible to give the patient a copy to take home for reading in a more leisurely setting. As such, they should be a welcome addition to institutions, generalists, and specialists involved in the delivery of health care. [R: RBB, 1 Dec 88, p. 623]

Garabed Eknoyan

1549. **Listen to Your Body: A Head-to-Toe Guide to More Than 400 Common Symptoms, Their Causes and Best Treatments.** By Ellen Michaud, Lila L. Anastas, and the Editors of *Prevention Magazine.* Emmaus, Pa., Rodale Press, 1988. 525p. index. $27.95. LC 87-26402. ISBN 0-87857-728-9.

This easy to use source of medical information was compiled by a team that included a public health nurse and a professional writer, with the assistance of the editors of *Prevention Magazine* and a professional review board of twenty-eight distinguished medical doctors and dentists. It arranges more than four hundred common symptoms alphabetically in some nineteen chapters that proceed (alphabetically) from abdomen and digestive system to whole body symptoms. All major areas are covered, cross-referenced, and indexed thoroughly.

Chapter introductions generally start out with a list of significant symptoms ("See your doctor immediately if ..."). Symptom presentations are clear, concise, current, and interesting to read; they are followed by common causes and recommended procedures. A reviewer who evaluated the chapter on digestive diseases felt that the discussions were excellent and suited to students and faculty in the health sciences as well as to laypersons. "Many texts focus on deadly disorders and neglect the ordinary but important complaints of otherwise healthy people. All of us working in the health professions need to be reminded regularly of the most common complaints that affect our health care consumers." For these consumers, this guide is clear, convenient, and well arranged. [R: LJ, Jan 88, p. 77]   Marda Woodbury

Psychiatry

1550. Diagnostic and Statistical Manual of Mental Disorders: DSM-III-R. 3d ed. Washington, D.C., American Psychiatric Association, 1987. 567p. index. $39.95; $29.95pa. LC 87-1458. ISBN 0-89042-018-1; 0-89042-019-Xpa.

This volume is the revision of the third edition of the American Psychiatric Association's *Diagnostic and Statistical Manual of Mental Disorders*, also known as *DSM-III*. Soon after its publication, *DSM-III* became widely accepted in the United States as the language of the mental health field. Recent major book and journal articles in psychiatry and related fields have made extensive reference to *DSM-III* or adopted its terminology and concepts.

The American Psychiatric Association assembled twenty-six committees of experts to review the previous edition and to make suggestions for updating it. The stated purpose of *DSM-III-R* is "to provide clear descriptions of diagnostic categories in order to enable clinicians and investigators to diagnose, communicate about, study, and treat the various mental disorders." This book shows evidence of the time and care which went into its preparation. The goals appear to have been accomplished.

The basic features of *DSM-III-R* include the *DSM-III-R* classification including axes I and II categories and codes; a section on using the book; diagnostic categories with text and criteria; eight appendices including proposed diagnostic categories needing further study, decision trees for differential diagnosis, glossary of technical terms, annotated comparative listing of *DSM-III* and *DSM-III-R*, a historical review on ICD-9 glossary and classification, ICD-9-CM classification, and more. There are also symptom and diagnostic indexes. Future editions are planned. [R: RBB, 1 Dec 88, p. 623]   Jacqueline Wilson

1551. Evans, Glen, and Norman L. Farberow. **The Encyclopedia of Suicide.** New York, Facts on File, 1988. 434p. maps. bibliog. index. $40.00. LC 88-11173. ISBN 0-8160-1397-7.

This reference work brings together information about psychological, political, legal, socioeconomic, and sociological aspects of suicide. There are over five hundred entries of varying length and detail. Many of the entries are cross-referenced. While no reference can be truly exhaustive or free from editorial orientations and interests, the encyclopedia makes a good start towards intergrating facts, data, and theories about self-destructive behavior. This reference work will be of interest to both students and the casual reader. It may be of limited utility for those researchers and scholars already well acquainted with the field of suicidology.

Of special interest is the excellent introductory essay on the history of suicide by Norman L. Farberow. Two appendices dealing with suicide statistics are very informative. A useful listing of a wide variety of agencies dealing with suicide and other self-destructive behavior comprises a third appendix. A source bibliography for this reference work and an index are supplied. [R: LJ, Aug 88, p. 151; RBB, 15 Nov 88, p. 552]   Charles Neuringer

1552. Skodol, Andrew E., and Robert L. Spitzer, eds. **An Annotated Bibliography of DSM-III.** Washington, D.C., American Psychiatric Press, 1987. 649p. index. $38.50. ISBN 0-88048-257-5.

The *Diagnostic and Statistical Manual of Mental Disorders* (see entry 1550), published by the American Psychiatric Association in 1987, has become the official nomenclature and classification system of mental disorders in the United States. In order to assist in an empirical and theoretical evaluation of *DSM-III* from the perspectives of academic and clinical psychiatry and psychology, this current annotated bibliography was prepared. It was also the intent of the editors to include all of the data available to the American Psychiatric Association's Work Group to Revise DSM-III, which was completed and published *DSM-III-Revised* (*DSM-III-R*) concurrently with the preparation of this volume. This bibliography focuses on issues in the classification of mental disorders generated by the introduction of *DSM-III*. The work is divided into five major sections: general overview, review of diagnostic areas, annotations of 300 selected articles, complete bibliographic listing of all (2,010) relevant articles, and subject index. Internationally known experts in psychiatric diagnosis were invited to prepare the overviews. The bibliography mainly contains references to English-language journal articles published between 1980 and July 1986. Some books and book chapters are included. The editors state that the bibliography is for use by researchers, teachers, clinicians, and professional students of psychopathology. The work is written at an advanced level and assumes knowledge of the fundamentals of psycho-pathology, the basic principles of *DSM-III*, and experience using the literature of psychiatry and psychology.   Jacqueline Wilson

1553.   Stone, Evelyn M., comp. and ed. **American Psychiatric Glossary.** 6th ed. Washington, D.C., American Psychiatric Press, 1988. 143p. bibliog. $19.95. LC 87-26972. ISBN 0-88048-275-3.

This brief guide to the terminology used in the field of psychiatry is now in its sixth edition. It gives easy, short definitions of terms related to diseases, drugs, and treatments, and brief references to prominent individuals in the field. It incorporates the revised nomenclature of the American Psychiatric Association's new *Diagnostic and Statistical Manual of Mental Disorders: DSM-III-R* (see entry 1550). Diagnostic terms are cross-referenced to allow use by those familiar with older nomenclature. Experts in the field of psychiatry are credited for their contribution of definitions or advice. In addition to the glossary, there is a short list of commonly used abbreviations and also concise tables of commonly abused drugs, legal terms, neurologic deficits, psychological tests, research terms, and schools of psychiatry.

The preface states that the purpose of the work is to keep users aware of current terminology in the field of psychiatry. This glossary achieves this purpose. The intended audience is not clearly identified. Early editions were for use by psychiatrists and other mental health professionals; however, the 1984 trade edition – which has essentially the same format as the current edition – was written for the layperson. Earlier editions indicated that this was the glossary of the American Psychiatric Association, but this edition makes no claim to be an official publication of that organization.

Jacqueline Wilson

1554.   Thomas, Claudewell S., and Jacob Jay Lindenthal, eds. **Psychiatry and Mental Health Science Handbook.** St. Louis, Mo., Warren H. Green, 1988. 267p. index. $39.95pa. ISBN 0-87527-473-0.

This handbook aims to present information about a variety of mental health issues. The thirteen chapters, dealing with such topics as brain disorders, schizophrenia, substance abuse, etc., were written by separate contributors. The writers use different formats for each review. A bibliography is attached to each contribution. The scope of the reviews is limited by space. Only superficial information on these important topics can be presented in 264 pages. A short index is supplied. The reader may find this book

useful as a starting point for gathering knowledge about these topics, but should also consult one of the more detailed handbooks such as Silvano Arieti's multivolume *American Handbook of Psychiatry* (Basic Books, 1974).

Charles Neuringer

Specific Conditions and Diseases

GENERAL WORKS

1555.   Mulvihill, Mary Lou. **Human Diseases: A Systematic Approach.** 2d ed. East Norwalk, Conn., Appleton & Lange, 1987. 411p. illus. bibliog. index. $22.95pa. LC 86-14649. ISBN 0-8385-3895-9.

This fine work is designed for students of the allied health fields or for anyone interested in the body's functions. It is divided into two parts. Part 1 discusses the general mechanisms of disease and introduces fundamental terminology including etiology, immunity, prognosis, symptoms, neoplasia, and inflammation. Terms are clearly explained and enhanced by numerous large, high-quality diagrams and black-and-white photographs. Part 2 discusses the most commonly occurring diseases of the various systems such as cardiovascular, excretory, digestive, and respiratory. The emphasis of the work is on the malfunction of an organ in contrast to the normal organ. This innovative approach helps the reader to obtain a better sense of the disease. This fine work would be an excellent addition to public libraries or to health information libraries. References, a glossary, and an index are included.   Julie M. Mueller

1556.   Smith, Wrynn. **Diabetes, Liver, and Digestive Disease.** New York, Facts on File, 1988. 164p. illus. bibliog. index. (Profile of Health and Disease in America). $35.00. LC 87-24532. ISBN 0-8160-1459-0.

This publication is part of a series in which each book is devoted to a different medical specialty. Gathered together is diverse statistical evidence relating to health issues, such as the demographics of the disease; disease patterns of different groups of people based on age, sex, and cultural group; and causes of the disease. In addition, historical and current statistics on the incidence, prevalence, and mortality are covered. Data for different geographical areas of the United States as well as international data are presented. The use of various medicines and surgical procedures is discussed, and the length of hospital stay, treatment costs, and major controversies are dealt with. Much of the information is given in charts and graphs. Sections cover the problem of digestive diseases, major digestive diseases, diseases of the liver, diabetes, and renal disease. A short glossary is included.

The book would be a good first place to consult when factual statistical information on the aforementioned diseases is needed.

Theodora Andrews

AIDS

1557. Collected Papers on AIDS Research, 1976-1986. Philadelphia, BIOSIS, 1987. 1v. (various paging). index. (BIOSIS Perspectives Series). $95.00pa. ISBN 0-916246-15-9.

This retrospective bibliography includes 4,643 citations to papers and other published research on AIDS. Although the first description of AIDS was published in 1981, references to earlier articles are included if those articles described neoplasms and opportunistic infections associated with AIDS in at-risk populations. The major part of the bibliography comprises references, arranged alphabetically by author or title and keyed with sequential reference numbers. Information included (though not consistently) is author(s); author address; source publication and bibliographic information; author title, in English; words added to clarify title; abstract or synopsis; subject descriptors; and taxonomic categories describing organisms mentioned in the source document. The two remaining sections are an author index and a subject index, both keyed to the sequential reference number used in the main section. This work can be supplemented by *AIDS Research Today*, a monthly update with an annual cumulative index ($120.00/yr.).

The primary audience for this tool will be medical researchers, physicians, and students in various health care curricula. Recommended for strong health sciences and medical libraries, and larger academic or research libraries.

Edmund F. SantaVicca

1558. Halleron, Trish A., and Janet I. Pisaneschi, eds. **AIDS Information Resources Directory.** New York, AmFAR, 1988. 192p. index. $10.00pa. ISBN 0-9620363-0-7; ISSN 0897-9693.

A well-conceived, well-executed and well-organized work, this volume results from the painstaking work of a multitude of individuals and organizations throughout the country as well as the review of all materials by thirty-four AIDS specialists. The volume is arranged in four major sections. The first of these, "A

Guide to Selected AIDS Educational Materials," includes a listing of resources (brochures, posters, audiovisual materials) arranged by primary target audience (e.g., Black community, college and university students, health care community, parents, etc.). Each entry contains descriptive and ordering information, as well as reviewer's comments. The remaining three sections, "Producer & Distributor Information," "Late Entries & Materials under Development," and "A Collection of References, Resources & Service Information (Not Reviewed)," each provide similar information. In addition, four indexes are provided as a guide to materials and resources. These include alphabetical listings of: (1) titles, with a product type designation; (2) organizations and agencies; (3) titles, sorted by type of material; and (4) titles available in languages other than English.

This is a major resource that should be in every school, public and academic library, as well as health care collections. It will prove to be a key tool for AIDS educators, librarians and students. Parent groups involved in community education will also benefit.

Edmund F. SantaVicca

1559. Lingle, Virginia A., and M. Sandra Wood. **How to Find Information about AIDS.** New York, Harrington Park Press, 1988. 130p. bibliog. index. $6.95pa. LC 88-6192. ISBN 0-918393-52-3.

Although the authors indicate that the purpose of this work is "to assist the health professional and the general public alike" (p. vii), the emphasis seems to be to serve some of the information needs of the health care professions regarding AIDS. By no means exhaustive, the volume functions best as an inexpensive directory to selected organizations, health departments, hotlines, online sources of information, and audiovisual producers, and to federal agencies, research institutions, and grant funding sources. In most instances, entries are brief and accompanied by one or two lines of annotation. The authors include a section on print sources of information, which includes full bibliographic citations and brief annotations. Most of the items included, however, are primarily geared toward the health care professions.

The strength of this work is to be found in its use as a directory; even then, it should be supplemented by other works. Recommended for medical libraries and smaller collections in health care facilities. Some public libraries might also take advantage of the low price to acquire such a handy directory. [R: Choice, Dec 88, p. 630; RBB, 1 Oct 88, p. 241]

Edmund F. SantaVicca

1560. Malinowsky, H. Robert, and Gerald J. Perry. **AIDS Information Sourcebook.** Phoenix, Ariz., Oryx Press, 1988. 85p. bibliog. index. $24.50pa. LC 87-31337. ISBN 0-89774-419-5.

For libraries with limited funds, this work should be useful as a single-volume handbook on AIDS. Other libraries will want to consider it for purchase as a supplement to monographs and articles. The work has three major divisions. The first is a useful chronology of AIDS from June 1981 to November 1987. The second is a directory of organizations concerned with AIDS. This is arranged alphabetically by state, then by name of organization. Directory information is provided, followed by an organizational profile indicating staffing, budget, funding source, library, outreach, network affiliation, additional information, available literature, and languages spoken. An alphabetical index to organizations is provided. The final section of this work is an enumerative and partially annotated bibliography of articles, bibliographies, books, films, periodicals, and plays on the subject of AIDS. A separate subject index is provided.

Highly recommended for all public, academic, and medical libraries, and for collections emphasizing AIDS education. A very useful handbook. [R: Choice, July/Aug 88, p. 1671; RBB, 1 June 88, p. 1648; RBB 15 June 88, p. 1715; WLB, May 88, pp. 103-4]

Edmund F. SantaVicca

1561. Nordquist, Joan, comp. **AIDS: Political, Social, International Aspects.** Santa Cruz, Calif., Reference and Research Services, 1988. 72p. (Contemporary Social Issues: A Bibliographic Series, No. 10). $15.00pa. ISBN 0-937855-19-7.

A bibliography of books, pamphlets, documents, and articles on the subject of AIDS, this work will prove useful in many library reference settings – from secondary through university, as well as public and special. Arranged in eighteen thematic sections, with each section subdivided by format, this work covers social and political issues, public policy, state and local policy, legal aspects, blood testing, the insurance industry, the safety of the blood supply, workplace issues, drug research, minorities, women, children, drug users, prisons, and international aspects (with a subsection on Africa). Standard bibliographic information is presented, with entries being selected for inclusion on the basis of varied perspectives on the topic. Most articles cited have been published within the past three years.

Also included are sections on bibliographies, resources, organizations, and periodicals focused on AIDS. Selective as it is, this bibliography should allow most researchers to begin work in the field. Quite affordable, this work is recommended highly for all libraries. Academic and other large research collections will need to supplement this with other bibliographies and online searching.   Edmund F. SantaVicca

1562. Tyckoson, David A. **AIDS 1987 (Acquired Immune Deficiency Syndrome).** Phoenix, Ariz., Oryx Press, 1988. 153p. index. (Oryx Science Bibliographies, Vol. 11). $29.50pa. LC 87-28217. ISBN 0-89774-434-9.

An update of two previous volumes in this series, by the same author, and with the same generic title, the current volume includes annotations of 637 books, articles, and other publications released from mid-1986 to mid-1987. Prefaced by a research review, the bibliography is arranged under thirty-one classed headings, each treating a narrow aspect of the larger subject. Tyckoson provides a complete bibliographic citation, accompanied by a fifty to one-hundred-word annotation, for each entry. The author index is coded to entry number. Among the many subtopics included are AIDS in minorities; AIDS in correctional facilities; patent disputes over the AIDS virus; international aspects of AIDS; testing and the blood supply; heterosexual transmission; moral and religious aspects; legal, political, and social aspects; victims, caregivers and friends; and employment and workplace issues.

As a reference tool, this work should be in most libraries. It is invaluable for its selection of key articles on the subject of AIDS, and will provide the user with a handy guide to the literature. Given the lack of similar bibliographies on this topic, this work is well worth the investment. Highly recommended. [R: VOYA, Apr 88, p. 52; WLB, May 88, pp. 103-4]

Edmund F. SantaVicca

1563. Tyckoson, David A. **AIDS 1988. Part 1.** Phoenix, Ariz., Oryx Press, 1988. 139p. index. (AIDS Bibliography Series). $19.50pa. ISBN 0-89774-504-3.

The fourth in a series of AIDS bibliographies compiled by Tyckoson, this volume breaks from tradition by covering only a six-month period rather than a complete year. Articles (550) published between January and June 1988 are included, with full bibliographic description accompanied by a fifty to one-hundred-word annotation. One of the key advantages of the work is the arrangement of entries into approximately thirty categories, each focused on a facet of AIDS, from general to specific. Examples include "AIDS and Children," "Business Response to AIDS," "Discrimination against AIDS Victims," and "Patient Zero: Gaetan Dugas." Other facets treated include AIDS education, cures and vaccines, heterosexual transmission, psychological aspects, research funding, and media treatment.

Tyckoson should be celebrated for creating and maintaining a key bibliographic access series that will prove useful in virtually any information delivery environment—health care facilities, libraries, service organizations, and governmental and policy making offices. A key and very highly recommended reference tool.

Edmund F. SantaVicca

ALLERGIES

1564. **Allergy Products Directory.** 2d ed. By Staff of the American Allergy Association. Menlo Park, Calif., Allergy Publications, 1987. 122p. $9.95pa. LC 87-070885. ISBN 0-9616708-2-7.

One of the most frustrating aspects of living with allergies is the necessity of tracking down specialized products and services. This booklet is meant as a source for names, addresses, and telephone numbers of companies of interest to allergy sufferers. There are listings for suppliers of air cleaning equipment, specialized cookbooks, cosmetics, all-cotton clothes, foods free of particular allergens, and lists of organizations which can provide information or assistance. Besides addresses and telephone numbers, brief descriptions of the services or products available from each source are given.

This guide has no index, and the chapter headings are somewhat confusing. Sometimnes companies are listed under the type of sales (mail order or toll-free telephone orders), not under the type of products offered, so finding all sources of interest can take some digging. There are no ratings or information on reliability, so the buyer should beware. Still, this is a unique directory which will benefit anyone with allergy problems.

Carol L. Noll

BIRTH RELATED CONDITIONS

1565. **International Bibliography of Fertility Technology 1983-1987.** Philadelphia, BIOSIS, 1988. 1v. (various paging). index. (International Bibliography Series). $90.00pa. ISBN 0-916246-18-3.

The Bio Sciences Information Services, which produces *Biological Abstracts*, has compiled this annotated bibliography covering the available literature published from 1983 through 1987 on the various aspects of fertility technology. This reference tool includes coverage of journal articles, patents, monographs, and meeting papers.

This bibliography is divided into three sections. The reference segment provides 4,049 annotated listings of material on fertility technology research. The annotations vary in length from a few words to an extensive paragraph. Each citation presents complete bibliographic information, including the address of the first author of the item. An author index covers up to ten authors for each cited listing. The subject index is organized by key words or phrases found in the titles of cited items or added to the reference citations by this bibliography's indexers.

As useful as this reference work appears to be, there is one glaring weakness, namely the total absence of an explanatory introductory statement. The reader is left to guess at the scope of topics included in this bibliography, any limitations used for selecting cited items, and the overall purpose for the creation of such a reference tool. Despite this major failing this volume is the only large-scale bibliography currently available in the field of fertility technology.

Jonathon Erlen and
Judith Ann Erlen

1566. Kelley-Buchanan, Christine, with Ellen Thro. **Peace of Mind during Pregnancy: An A-Z Guide to the Substances That Could Affect Your Unborn Baby.** New York, Facts on File, 1988. 367p. index. $24.95. LC 88-045295. ISBN 0-8160-1907-X.

In the early 1960s the level of awareness of the medical community and society in general was raised about the teratogenic effects of drugs in pregnancy when infants whose mothers had taken thalidomide were born with various limb malformations. Research has demonstrated that there are many substances and diseases that can have adverse affects on the fetus depending on when the pregnant woman ingests the substance, is exposed to the hazardous material, or contacts the disease. The result is that doctors are advising women in the childbearing years to be cautious in their use of or exposure to possible teratogens.

The author has based this clearly written and very timely book on her experience as one of the three founders of the California Teratogen Registry. This volume, written for expectant parents, is a guide for evaluating the safety of substances in order to avoid potentially harmful ones, not a substitute for physician consultation. The introductory chapters describe how to use the book, risks in pregnancy, and the effects of substances on the fetus. Each entry contains information about the substance, time of exposure, risk, pregnancy outcome, and documentation of risk. Because of the limited research on many of these substances, the author states no known adverse effects and suggests caution when using them. References are cited for each entry. For some items such as emetrol and antihistamines, natural remedies to use instead are identified. The author notes that although they are helpful, they have not been scientifically tested.

There are a few tables which would have been better placed with the substance category instead of the next entry. Cyclosporine was not included, yet women following transplant surgery are becoming pregnant. The publisher is correcting the omission of brand names of substances in the index by developing an addendum for existing books and revising the index for future printings. [R: RBB, 1 Sept 88, p. 52]

Judith Ann Erlen

1567. Nordquist, Joan, comp. **Reproductive Rights.** Santa Cruz, Calif., Reference and Research Services, 1988. 68p. (Contemporary Social Issues: A Bibliographic Series, No. 9). $15.00pa. ISBN 0-937855-17-0.

Focused bibliographies provide a quick ready-reference tool for the clinician and/or researcher. *Reproductive Rights,* number 9 in the series Contemporary Social Issues, is such a timely and timesaving work centering on a crucial societal concern. The books and articles included were predominantly published within the last five years and describe legal, ethical, religious, and feminist perspectives, among others, on the topic, thus demonstrating the wide range of resources used to compile this unannotated bibliography. No specific criteria for inclusion of items are identified.

This reference work is topically organized (e.g., abortion, fetal rights, paternal rights, and reproductive technologies). Citations for each topic are alphabetized by author, identified in boldface type, and separated into books and articles. There is a list of names and addresses of organizations concerned with reproductive rights; however, no telephone numbers are included.

Inaccuracies in citing authors' names in several citations suggest that the user needs to be aware that other such errors may exist. Even though this work is not exhaustive (it does not claim to be) and the items are not annotated,

this reference tool will be useful for someone wanting quick access to current material on this subject without doing a computer search.

Judith Ann Erlen

1568. Sachdev, Paul, ed. **International Handbook on Abortion.** Westport, Conn., Greenwood Press, 1988. 520p. index. $75.00. LC 87-11994. ISBN 0-313-23463-9.

Abortion remains a legally and morally controversial means of terminating a pregnancy despite the liberalization of laws in many countries. Not infrequently researchers desire information on various aspects of abortion in their own country, as well as in other countries. This volume, compiled by an editor who has produced other studies on this topic, will enable investigators to gain access to current data on abortion practices in thirty countries. While this book is international in scope, it is limited in that the USSR, many of the African nations, and the countries in the United Arab Republic, for example, are not included. Yet individuals will be able to compare policies of the thirty included countries without having to search through the literature to identify trends related to abortion, birth control, and fertility. For example, the liberal policies of Singapore and China can be contrasted with the restrictive policies of Indonesia and South Africa, where abortion is illegal. The index enables the user to easily compare various countries and abortion policies and practices.

The introductory chapter provides an overview of the book's contents. The other chapters are arranged according to country. Each chapter has been written by persons from that country who have appropriate qualifications. The authors discuss how the various governments developed abortion legislation; what influenced these decisions such as the historical perspective, the demographic picture, and the impact on fertility; and what changes in the policy on or attitudes toward abortion have occurred. Each chapter is well documented and contains appropriate tables displaying statistics on abortion and fertility through the mid-1980s. The countries of Latin America are discussed together; however, tables enable the user to make comparisons on abortion, fertility, and contraception between and among the countries. [R: WLB, Oct 88, p. 110]

Judith Ann Erlen and
Jonathon Erlen

1569. Winter, Eugenia B., comp. **Psychological and Medical Aspects of Induced Abortion: A Selective, Annotated Bibliography, 1970-1986.** Westport, Conn., Greenwood Press,

1988. 162p. index. (Bibliographies and Indexes in Women's Studies, No. 7). $37.95. LC 88-194. ISBN 0-313-26100-8.

Well-organized, focused annotated bibliographies provide researchers with easy accessibility to sometimes difficult to locate material. This work by Eugenia B. Winter accomplishes this goal in relation to induced abortion, which she defines as "elective (voluntary) abortion."

The compiler has alphabetically arranged five hundred selected items into ten broad areas which are described in the introduction, including general works on induced abortion, abortion techniques, counseling, morbidity, and mortality. Additionally, there is an author/subject/title index to further facilitate the retrieval of information. Cross-references are used where appropriate. The entries meet specified criteria identified in the preface and include standard as well as representative books, articles from journals that are easily accessible, dissertations, and audiovisual resources. The writer indicates if a citation is an editorial and notes a specific chapter in a book when a book also focuses on other topics. The annotations provide enough information for the user to grasp the main ideas of any study. Only occasionally does the compiler make a value judgment about a particular work. Because of the emotional nature of induced abortion, the author has tried to present material in a nonbiased manner. [R: Choice, Dec 88, p. 633; RBB, 15 Dec 88, p. 693]
Judith Ann Erlen

CANCER

1570. Vaillancourt, Pauline M., comp. **Cancer Journals and Serials: An Analytical Guide.** Westport, Conn., Greenwood Press, 1988. 259p. index. (Annotated Bibliographies of Serials: A Subject Approach, No. 11). $45.00. LC 87-29580. ISBN 0-313-24055-8.

This is the eleventh volume in the Greenwood Press series of annotated bibliographies of serials. Other titles in the series have covered library science, philosophy, dentistry, economics, agriculture, finance, marine science, history, aging, and anthropology. The intent of the series is to make the task of serial selection more systematic by identifying and annotating currently published English-language serials. The author of the present volume is Professor Emerita at SUNY-Albany and a medical library consultant.

The bibliography lists 423 journals pertinent to cancer research. The basic medical journals, such as *JAMA* and *New England Journal of Medicine*, are included, as well as the broad coverage science journals such as *Science* and *Nature*. Since cancer research is a part of many medical specialties, most specialized medical journals are also included. In fact, the bibliography is so all-encompassing it might well have been titled *Medical Journals and Serials*.

For each title extensive information collected by questionnaire is given: date founded, sponsor, title changes, mergers, frequency, price, circulation, policy on manuscript selection, and indexes and databases in which the title is included. The annotations, while often lengthy, are descriptive rather than evaluative. There are four indexes: by publisher, by geographic area, by subject, and by sponsor. An appendix contains those titles which have ceased publication or for which data could not be verified. A useful feature is the ICRBD (International Cancer Research Data Bank) rankings in the annotations. In summary, a wealth of information has been gathered here, useful to any library beginning or expanding a medical collection.
Necia A. Musser

HEART DISEASES

1571. Ervin, Gary W. **Memory Bank for Critical Care: EKGs and Cardiac Drugs.** 3d ed. Baltimore, Md., Williams & Wilkins, 1988. 277p. illus. bibliog. $16.95 spiralbound. LC 88-5453. ISBN 0-683-02820-0.

This spiralbound, pocket-sized reference manual is intended for the use of nursing and related health professionals working in a hospital-based coronary critical care facility. The first two-thirds of the text is devoted to electrocardiographic tracings of the principal abnormalities encountered clinically in a critical care unit. The format followed is to illustrate a segment of the typical abnormal tracing followed by two or three brief explanatory sentences. The explanatory comments are written in simple, easy to understand language aimed mainly at the novice. The last third of the manual covers the major cardiovascular drugs used in the critical care setting. The generic and trade name of each drug, its uses, dosages, route of administration, and adverse effects are highlighted in brief sentences. The bibliography consists of seven general texts on cardiology, electrocardiography, and drugs. Overall, this manual should benefit its intended audience.
Garabed Eknoyan

MEDICAL GENETICS

1572. McKusick, Victor A. **Mendelian Inheritance in Man: Catalogs of Autosomal Dominant, Autosomal Recessive, and X-Linked**

Phenotypes. 8th ed. Baltimore, Md., Johns Hopkins University Press, 1988. 1626p. index. $85.00. LC 88-9328. ISBN 0-8108-3691-3.

One of the major recent breakthroughs in medicine has been the revolution in genetics. The deciphering of the genetic code, coupled with the technological advances that allowed the fragmentation, cloning, sequencing, and mapping of the human gene, has resulted in a quantitative and qualitative leap of knowledge in a field that only two decades ago was relegated to a few scanty pages in standard textbooks of medicine. The present volume is the eighth edition of a catalog of this ever-expanding information on the genetics of autosomal and sex-linked diseases. Each of the 4,344 entries consists of five parts: (1) a title, including synonyms; (2) a brief description of the clinical features or phenotype; (3) the nature of the basic defect; (4) a summary of the genetic information; and (5) key and up-to-date references through August 1987. Two indexes are provided, for authors and titles. The latter includes alternative designations, distinctive symptoms and signs, gene symbols, and acronyms. Three appendices provide a listing of the molecular defects in Mendelian disorders, a presentation of the human gene map, and a list of mutations for which cell lines are available from the Mutant Cell Repository. An online version of the book is also available.

The cost of this catalog of the nosology and genetics of hereditary diseases is a bargain for the amount of information provided. It belongs on the shelves of every medical library and anyone remotely interested in inherited diseases. Written by a founding father of modern genetics, this book is the perfect example of how a caring and fecund mind utilizing available computer methodology can produce a polished and integrated product that is essential not only to all geneticists, but also to anyone in practice seeking the latest genetic advice to give patients and their families.   Garabed Eknoyan

RHEUMATIC AND SKIN DISEASES

1573. Smith, Wrynn. **Rheumatic and Skin Disease.** New York, Facts on File, 1988. 113p. bibliog. index. (Profile of Health and Disease in America). $35.00. LC 87-33090. ISBN 0-8160-1456-6.

This is one of a planned series of volumes on the demographic profile of the principal diseases that afflict Americans. Prior volumes have covered such topics as cardiovascular, gastrointestinal, and mental diseases. The present volume, in the same general format as its predecessors, provides a short definition of the specific diseases covered, written simply enough to be understood by the lay reader, then presents the demographics of each disease in charts, tables, and graphs with a brief explanatory commentary on each. As with the other volumes in the series, the breadth of statistical data presented on incidence, prevalence, morbidity, and mortality is quite impressive. Only one ten-page chapter of the present volume covers diseases of the skin, while the other five chapters, of about the same length each, are devoted to rheumatic diseases. The rheumatic diseases covered are musculoskeletal diseases, arthritis (osteoarthritis, rheumatoid arthritis, gout), systemic diseases associated with musculoskeletal symptoms, osteomyelitis, and other bone diseases. A note on methodology, a short glossary, and a limited bibliography take up the final twenty pages of this short monograph. Only one of the cited references was published in 1983, while most of the others are from the 1960s and 1970s. By the same token the bulk of the statistical data included is from the 1970s, with only a few tables providing data from 1981. This temporal limitation notwithstanding, this is a useful reference volume for anyone seeking information on the general demographics of the diseases covered. Financial planners and legislators would probably be the principal audience who would find this text specially valuable.

Garabed Eknoyan

SPORTS INJURIES

1574. Williams, J. P. R., ed. **Barron's Sports Injuries Handbook.** Hauppauge, N.Y., Barron's Educational Series, 1988. 160p. illus. (part col.). index. $12.95. LC 87-37426. ISBN 0-8120-5915-8.

A trio of orthopedic surgeons collaborated on this sports medicine handbook. The need for proper conditioning is the main issue that resonates throughout this text, the primary focus of which is the prevention, diagnosis, and treatment of sports injuries. The audience the authors seem to have targeted are the millions who participate regularly in some sports activity.

Preventive medicine when it comes to sports and the weekend sportsman is a vastly over-simplified notion. Hence this book is for the layperson. The authors have divided their book into four sections. The first deals with general fitness, protective equipment, and getting fit. This section has an excellent chapter on stretching exercises. Section 2 has an injuries guide along with anatomical charts and narrative by body area of general injuries. A brief third chapter covers first aid, and the last chapter looks at injuries specific to particular sports.

This is a very elementary text focusing on only a few aspects of sports medicine. For a more thorough treatment of the subject there is Greg R. McLatchie's *Essentials of Sports Medicine* (Churchill-Livingstone, 1986); *Sports Medicine*, by Steven Roy (Prentice Hall, 1983) or even *The ABC's of Sports Medicine*, by James H. McMaster (Krieger, 1982). This book is excellent for coaches and public libraries. It does have its place, but that place may not necessarily be in a reference collection.

Tom Smith

NURSING

1575. Bullough, Vern L., Olga Maranjian Church, and Alice P. Stein. **American Nursing: A Biographical Dictionary.** New York, Garland, 1988. 358p. illus. (Garland Reference Library of Social Science, Vol. 368). $60.00. LC 87-29076. ISBN 0-8240-8540-X.

This dictionary lists 175 women and two men, all but one deceased, who made significant contributions to nursing, not always as "trained" professionals. While the *American Journal of Nursing* and the early *Trained Nurse and Hospital Review* often carried obituaries of these nurses, personal data were usually lacking; few were included in the who's who or *Current Biography* types of reference books; and nursing history texts were rarely known outside the schools. The feminist movement has focused attention on nursing as a research area. As the editors point out, further research could well be done on almost all of the figures included here, as well as on the large number who it is hoped will appear in a projected second volume. They also acknowledge that the group is "heavily weighted toward the East and Midwest."

The articles follow a pattern in which each author (there are seventy contributors) tries to state in the first paragraph exactly who the biographee was and what she accomplished for the nursing profession or American society in general. This is followed by what personal information is known, career activities and honors, the books and articles written by the person, a bibliography, and the contributor's name. Indexes list persons under decades of birth, beginning with "before 1840"; first nursing school attended; areas of special interest or accomplishment (e.g., Sanger is under "public activity"); and states or countries of birth.

A great deal about the development of nursing in America—its history, education, military and public health service, organizations, etc.—can be learned from this dictionary of its leaders. It should prove a worthy addition to the sociological reference series of which it is a part; its appeal is far wider than merely to the health sciences. [R: Choice, Oct 88, p. 283]

Harriette M. Cluxton

1576. **Educational Outcomes: Assessment of Quality—An Annotated Bibliography.** New York, National League for Nursing, 1987. 62p. price not reported. pa. ISBN 0-88737-372-0.

1577. **Educational Outcomes: Assessment of Quality—A Directory of Student Outcome Measurements Utilized by Nursing Programs in the United States.** New York, National League for Nursing, 1987. 51p. index. price not reported. pa. ISBN 0-88737-392-5.

These two volumes represent the findings from two aspects of the Accreditation Outcomes Project of the National League for Nursing. This investigation was undertaken to delineate and assess student outcome data as a measure of quality of a nursing education program.

The annotated bibliography is the first published resource of this project. This reference tool does not claim to be comprehensive; however, it does cover over two hundred articles, dissertations, unpublished papers, and books that focus on current research related to student outcomes and program outcomes at all levels of nursing education. While there are a few works dating back to the mid-1960s, most have been published since 1980. The contents are organized alphabetically according to topics that reflect various skills, competencies, or attitudes of nursing students. Non-nursing works that discuss the same concept with students in other health professions are included but are placed in separate categories.

The second volume is a directory of measurements of student outcomes. The first section lists nursing student behaviors, attitudes, and competencies and the schools of nursing that measure these particular variables. This is not a complete listing of all programs measuring a particular variable as it includes only those programs who voluntarily submitted data on their current efforts at measuring outcomes. The second section of the book includes a directory of the nursing schools alphabetically arranged by state.

Both of these volumes should serve as useful resources for nurse educators as they develop evaluative instruments to measure student outcomes and to monitor the quality of educational programs. In addition, the directory should facilitate networking among educators about the use of various measurement tools.

Judith Ann Erlen

1578. Kaufman, Martin, ed. **Dictionary of American Nursing Biography.** Westport, Conn., Greenwood Press, 1988. 462p. index. $49.95. LC 87-25454. ISBN 0-313-24520-7.

With the recent emergence of the scholarly discipline of the history of nursing, there is a need for quality reference tools in this field. Martin Kaufman's new nursing biographical dictionary, an outgrowth of his 1984 publication covering American physicians, is a useful reference work for anyone interested in the history of nursing.

This volume contains one- to five-page biographical sketches of 196 nineteenth- and twentieth-century pioneers who contributed to American nursing. Selection criteria included the significance of the individual's contributions to nursing and the ability of the research team to find fairly complete biographical material about the person. Only individuals who died prior to 31 January 1987 and who met the selection criteria are included. The biographical sketches cover nursing leaders in a variety of nursing fields, such as education, public health, administration, and the military. For those persons selected the following information is provided: education, family background, career highlights, contributions to the evolution of nursing, and a list of their main publications and locations of additional bibliographic material. Unfortunately, this last segment does not include recent journal articles about these noteworthy pioneers in nursing. Appendices which list these nursing leaders by place of birth, state where they worked during most of their careers, and their nursing specialty, along with a comprehensive index, provide easy access to the useful information in this book. [R: Choice, Oct 88, p. 283]

Judith A. Erlen and
Jonathon Erlen

PHARMACY AND PHARMACEUTICAL SCIENCES

Bibliographies

1579. Huls, Mary Ellen, comp. **Food Additives and Their Impact on Health.** Phoenix, Ariz., Oryx Press, 1988. 69p. index. (Oryx Science Bibliographies, Vol. 12). $16.00pa. LC 87-34885. ISBN 0-89774-433-0.

This is the twelfth volume in the Oryx Science Bibliographies series. Other topics covered include AIDS, Alzheimer's, animal experimentation, mass extinctions (dinosaurs, etc.), and earthquake predictions. These off-the-shelf bibliographies are a godsend for librarians, who can use them not just as a subject listing but for bibliographic instruction as well. All of the offerings in the series offer fully annotated English-language sources with emphasis on current materials that are readily available in most undergraduate, public, or medical libraries.

This latest edition on food additives is especially good. There are 251 citations culled from a wide spectrum of journal literature. Included are technical articles from *Food Technology* and *Food Engineering* and medical opinions found in *JAMA, Lancet,* and *The Annals of Allergy* as well as the more mundane and popular offerings from *Time, Scientific American,* and *Vogue.* This variety of sources makes for a flexible tool to use even in the most anemic of journal collections. A seven-page introduction reviews the research in the following areas: adverse effects of food additives, regulating food safety, nitrites and nitrates, antioxidants, sulfites, monosodium glutamate, artificial sweeteners (cyclamate, saccharin, aspartame), diet and behavioral disorders, and artificial colors. In all cases the choice of inclusion was sound, and the annotations are comprehensible to even the most inexperienced layperson.

This book costs $16.00. I doubt that anyone could produce an in-house publication of equal quality for less. Highly recommended for undergraduate libraries. [R: VOYA, Aug 88, p. 154]

Tom Smith

Dictionaries and Encyclopedias

1580. Bycroft, B. W., ed. **Dictionary of Antibiotics and Related Substances.** New York, Routledge, Chapman & Hall, 1988. 944p. illus. index. $620.00. LC 87-24902. ISBN 0-412-25450-6.

The intent of this impressive work is to list every known well-defined microbial compound showing antibiotic activity. Also, interpreting the term *antibiotic* broadly, the compilers have listed other substances such as biologically active substances from sources other than microorganisms and some semisynthetics. The well-known and respected *Dictionary of Organic Compounds* (originally edited by I. M. Heilbron) has served as a model for this specialized dictionary. However, the new work is not a spinoff; it contains approximately 75 percent new material. More than eight thousand compounds are included within four thousand entries.

The entries of the dictionary are arranged alphabetically by chemical name. There are indexes by name (synonymous terms), molecular formula, Chemical Abstracts Service registry number, and type of compound. Each entry usually includes the following: name and synonyms, structure diagram, Chemical Abstracts Service registry number, molecular formula, molecular weight, microbiological source, type, physical description, physical data, *Registry of Toxic Effects of Chemical Substances* number, toxicity data, use, and several literature references. Included is an introductory chapter which provides descriptions of main antibiotic types.

Supplemental volumes are planned for the future in order to keep the work up-to-date. Also, the material, along with that from the publisher's other chemical dictionaries, is available from a database known as HEILBRON. It is accessible online via Dialog.

Although the price of this dictionary is extremely high, it is highly regarded and very valuable for anyone who works with antibiotics. [R: Choice, July/Aug 88, p. 1672]

Theodora Andrews

1581. Hodgson, Ernest, Richard B. Mailman, and Janice E. Chambers. **Dictionary of Toxicology.** New York, Van Nostrand Reinhold, 1988. 395p. illus. bibliog. $67.95. ISBN 0-442-31842-1.

No other work comparable to this one exists, and it promised to be quite useful. It defines significant terms and concepts encountered in the field of toxicology, providing both a broad and a specialized view.

More than sixty experts contributed to the dictionary, which includes entries for toxic chemicals, measurement of toxicity, diagnosis and treatment of poisonings, environmental pollutants, regulations, organizations, and government bodies in North America and Western Europe. Also included are terms that have a relationship to toxicology, such as anatomical, biochemical, pathological, and physiological terms. Diagrams and structures of compounds are often provided. The entries are usually about a paragraph in length, but some are a column long.

The authors of the dictionary believe that it will be of most value to graduate and undergraduate students and to scientists in fields other than toxicology. Although toxicologists will use it also, experts in the field need less assistance with terminology.   Theodora Andrews

1582. Jefferson, James W., and others. **Lithium Encyclopedia for Clinical Practice.** 2d ed. Washington, D.C., American Psychiatric Press, 1987. 744p. index. $21.50 spiralbound. LC 86-28685. ISBN 0-88048-230-3.

The first edition of this work was published in 1983 and reflected a review of more than ninety-five hundred citations. Only three-and-one-half years later the literature regarding the clinical uses of lithium has grown to more than fifteen thousand citations, hence this new edition. An online database of references facilitated the preparation of this work.

Lithium, according to the authors, "produces the most dramatic therapeutic improvement of any drug used in psychiatry." This comprehensive work is divided into over 120 sections ranging from lithium in combination with other drugs (e.g., antihypertensive drugs) to hematological and neurological effects of lithium. The synopses are based on the pertinent lithium literature, modified, as necessary, to remain consistent with the clinical experience of the authors. Each section concludes with a list of pertinent references. A detailed index completes the volume.

The authors' stated aim is to "provide clinicians, researchers, and interested laypersons with up-to-date topical information about lithium and its clinical use." They have succeeded.

Sherrilynne Fuller

1583. Swarbrick, James, and James C. Boylan, eds. **Encyclopedia of Pharmaceutical Technology. Volume 1: Absorption of Drugs to Bioavailability of Drugs and Bioequivalence.** New York, Marcel Dekker, 1988. 494p. illus. $150.00. LC 88-25664. ISBN 0-8247-2800-9.

This is the first volume of a comprehensive work that will probably comprise ten to twelve volumes when it is completed. The plan is to complete approximately two volumes per year over the next few years. The editors, who are well-known individuals from academia and industry, felt that the need for such a work was obvious and that it would become a valuable resource for colleagues in pharmaceutical industry, education, and government. Significant advances in recent years in the understanding of disease processes, therapeutics, and the need to optimize drug delivery in the body have brought about an increased awareness of the role of the dosage form. *Pharmaceutical technology* embraces a level of expertise in the design, development, manufacture, testing, and regulation of drugs and dosage forms.

The editors have defined the scope of the encyclopedia to include broadly the discovery, development, regulation, manufacturing, and commercialization of drugs and dosage forms. It is to include such disciplines as pharmaceutics, pharmacokinetics, analytical chemistry, quality assurance, toxicology, and manufacturing processes. The articles are long, averaging more than twenty pages in length.

The noted contributors to this volume are all from the United States or Europe, but future volumes are to include articles contributed by experts from other countries.

Theodora Andrews

Directories

1584. Sittig, Marshall, and Janne S. Kowalski. **Drug Companies & Products World Guide.** Kingston, N.J., Sittig & Noyes, 1988. 596p. $120.00pa.

This is a companion volume to Marshall Sittig's *Pharmaceutical Manufacturing Encyclopedia*, second edition (Noyes Publications, 1988). The latter describes in two volumes the manufacturing processes for about thirteen hundred pharmaceuticals marketed around the world. The material in the encyclopedia has been rearranged, modified, and updated to provide the basic information given in the guide under review. It will serve as a point of access to the information in the larger encyclopedia as well as a source in itself.

The guide is an international list of pharmaceutical companies, arranged alphabetically, with a representative list of their products. Both generic and trade names are provided. Additional information given is the company address, telephone number, function of each product, and the year it was introduced. Once a reader has identified a product of interest, he can then look it up by generic name in the two-volume encyclopedia and learn about how it is manufactured, including raw materials consumed, reaction conditions, and product separation techniques. The material has been obtained from patent literature, and, in addition, other literature references are supplied.

To be of most value the two works should be used together. The guide contains no index of product names. The only feature it contains that is not found in the encyclopedia is the listing of products under the company names. A somewhat similar publication is *World Pharmaceuticals Directory* (Unlisted Drugs, 1988).

Theodora Andrews

Handbooks

1585. **AARP Pharmacy Service Prescription Drug Handbook.** Washington, D.C., American Association of Retired Persons and Glenview, Ill., Scott, Foresman, 1988. 940p. illus. (col.). index. $25.00. LC 87-16661. ISBN 0-673-24887-9.

This reference work for older persons was produced by the American Association of Retired Persons Pharmacy Service, which is the largest private, nonprofit mail service pharmacy in the world. The service, which addresses specifically the needs of those fifty years of age and older, felt obliged to make the information they present available to a wide audience, including those who monitor drug use in the older persons they care for. The elderly consume more than 30 percent of the prescription drugs sold in the United States.

The book is made up of thirteen chapters, each covering medically related disorders, such as disorders of the heart and blood vessels. Preceding the listing of drugs for each condition is a brief medical guide which provides an overview of the problem. Following are "drug charts" that summarize, in tabular form, information about the medicines that may be prescribed for the condition or disease. A limited number of drugs are included, only those most commonly described and used by older persons. Also, many over the counter drugs are not included.

The "drug charts" cover the condition involved, drug category, names (brand and generic), dosage forms and strengths, a drug profile or description, instructions to follow before using the drug, specific restrictions while taking the drug, side effects, storage instructions, information on stopping or interrupting therapy, and special considerations for those over sixty-five.

The book also includes some brief introductory material on saving money on drugs, a guide to over-the-counter medicines, and traveling. There is also a color section identifying tablets and capsules. Indexes of drug names and medical conditions are provided.

The work is authentic; the advisory board is made up of specialists in medicine and pharmacology. The biggest drawback of the book is that not very many drugs are listed.

Theodora Andrews

1586. Anderson, Kenneth, and Lois Anderson. **Orphan Drugs.** rev. ed. Los Angeles, Calif., Body Press/Price Stern Sloan, 1987. 253p. bibliog. index. $14.95pa. LC 87-35933. ISBN 0-89586-643-9.

Orphan drugs, so called because no U.S. pharmaceutical company has "adopted" them, are available in foreign countries but are not manufactured or sold in the United States. They lack Food and Drug Administration approval.

Obtaining approval requires lengthy expensive testing, and because orphan drugs usually are of value only for obscure diseases, they are not profitable to test and sell. In addition, they may be difficult to patent. The author's view is that these products should be readily available in the United States. He thinks U.S. government regulations are too restrictive, although Congress has taken some action recently to encourage development of these drugs.

The book provides the reader with information on about 192 generic (1,535 brand-name) valuable drugs that are available overseas. The book is divided into six sections: "Introduction," which provides background on the problem, "Symptoms Directory," "Orphan Drug Directory," "Sources Directory," "Bibliography," and "Index of Names." The orphan drug directory section, which makes up most of the book, lists the drugs alphabetically by generic name. Monographs about a page in length give this information: brand name(s), actions and uses, precautions, dosage and administration, and source (names of manufacturers or laboratories that can provide the drug).

Health professionals and researchers may find the book useful in locating drugs for investigatory use or to identify products patients may have obtained in foreign countries. Practicing physicians may obtain authorization from the Food and Drug Administration to treat patients with orphan drugs on an investigational basis.

Theodora Andrews

1587.   **Complete Book of Vitamins & Minerals.** By the Editors of *Consumer Guide.* Lincolnwood, Ill., Publications International, 1988. 320p. index. $3.95pa. ISBN 0-451-15747-8.

Written for the consumer, this work provides medically sound, up-to-date information on the function of nutrients, their value, and dangers of deficiency and overdose. The authors suggest that vitamins and mineral supplements be used only if a physician so prescribes.

First the reader is advised to eat a proper balanced diet. Next, the vitamins and minerals are discussed separately at some length with history, function, food sources, dietary requirements, deficiency, and use and misuse considered. The last section, about one-third of the book, "Supplement Product Profiles," provides monographs on popularly prescribed products. Information given includes name (including trade names), manufacturer, dosage form, nutrients included (many are combination multivitamin and mineral products), and comments such as a safety evaluation and precautions.

Other guides similar to this one are available, such as *Complete Guide to Vitamins, Minerals & Supplements,* by G. H. Winter (see entry 1590).   Theodora Andrews

1588.   **Drug Facts and Comparisons.** 1988 ed. Philadelphia, J. B. Lippincott, 1987. 2283p. illus. index. $69.50; $129.00 looseleaf. ISBN 0-932686-88-5; ISSN 0277-9714.

This publication has gone through considerable evolution since its inception in 1945. Published monthly in looseleaf format under the title *Facts and Comparisons,* it was barely half the size of the current compendium. Since 1982 when its title was changed, a bound annual edition has been made available in addition to the looseleaf edition. The latter is kept up-to-date with monthly replacement or supplementary pages. The bound edition is not supplemented between editions. In 1977 a microfiche edition was made available, which also provides the monthly updating.

The work is quite comprehensive, containing information on over ten thousand drug products available in the United States, including some over-the-counter products.

Drug Facts and Comparisons has long been one of the standard sources of drug information for health professionals. It is somewhat unique in at least two respects — first, its format provides for easy comparison of the therapeutic aspects of similar products, and second, through a cost index figure, it provides an indication of the relative prices of similar or identical products.

The organization of the work is by therapeutic class of drugs. In addition to the tables that provide for the comparison of products, monographs are included on each drug. In general, the following information is provided: actions, indications, contraindications, warnings and precautions, drug interactions, adverse reactions, overdosage information, patient information, and administration and dosage.

Theodora Andrews

1589.   **The Family Physician's Compendium of Drug Therapy.** Edwin S. Geffner, ed. New York, McGraw-Hill, 1987. 1899p. illus. (col.). index. $29.95. ISBN 0-07-023237-7.

Although little indication is given of it, this compendium seems to be the first volume of what may become an annual series. It describes nearly all medications routinely prescribed or recommended by family physicians. The information provided is based on that supplied by the manufacturers of the drugs.

Introductory chapters include a drug identification guide (in color); a directory of manufacturer product imprint codes; a list of information resources with addresses (drug information centers, poison control centers, pain clinics, etc.); essential pharmacokinetic data; and a section listing new products, revised drug information, and some miscellaneous agents. The bulk of the book is made up of about forty chapters which list drugs divided into therapeutic categories such as antianxiety agents, antidepressants, diuretics, etc. About each drug the following information is usually given: brand name, composition, manufacturer, dosage forms, strengths available, dosages, contraindications, adverse reactions, drug interactions, and altered laboratory values. A glossary of terms is appended.

The information offered in the compendium seems useful and reliable, but it does not add a great deal to what is found in many other of the available drug compendia. [R: RBB, 15 May 88, p. 1582]

Theodora Andrews

1590.   Griffith, H. Winter. **Complete Guide to Vitamins, Minerals & Supplements.** Tucson, Ariz., Fisher Books, 1988. 510p. index. $9.95 pa. LC 87-25156. ISBN 1-55561-006-4.

The author of this work is a physician who has written several other reference books for consumers. He has presented most of the material in the work in chart form as he did in earlier publications, such as *Complete Guide to Prescription and Non-Prescription Drugs*, fifth edition (Body Press, 1988).

The introductory section of the book (about twenty pages) presents a discussion of vitamins, minerals, supplements, and herbs. The bulk of the book is made up of sections of charts covering vitamins, minerals, amino acids and nucleic acids, other supplements, and medicinal herbs. In each section the entries are alphabetical by the best known name of the substance. Each entry in most sections provides information on dosage, benefits (proven and unproven), deficiency symptoms, natural food sources, recommended dosage, possible adverse reactions, side effects, overdose, medical test effects, interactions with medication, and reports about proven and unproven claims. A glossary and a section on brand names are provided.

The charts in the section on medicinal herbs are a bit different. They give basic information, known effects, unproven speculated benefits, warnings and precautions, toxicity, and adverse reactions or overdose symptoms. About two hundred herbs are listed. Also included is a section rating the toxicity of herbs.

Although no literature references are provided, the material presented seems authentic.

[R: LJ, 15 Feb 88, p. 160; RBB, 15 June 88, pp. 1716, 1718]   Theodora Andrews

1591.   **Handbook on Injectable Drugs.** 5th ed. By Lawrence A. Trissel. Bethesda, Md., American Society of Hospital Pharmacists, 1988. 757p. bibliog. index. $60.00. ISBN 0-930530-85-3.

This is the fifth edition of a work first published in 1977. It has somewhat more pages than the fourth edition, but it covers about the same number of drugs. It provides information on some 240 injectable drug products commercially available in the United States, as well as information on about 60 investigational drugs. Also included, in tabular format, is a section on the composition and characteristics of the commercially available intravenous infusion solutions, and there is also an appendix which provides parenteral nutrition solution formulas. Previously existing information has been updated, and new literature references have been added throughout.

The monographs on the commercial drugs are arranged alphabetically by nonproprietary name. Trade names are listed in the index. Each monograph includes trade name(s), manufacturer, description, dosage, stability compatibility information, and miscellaneous other information.

The primary intent of the work is to organize and summarize in a concise, standardized format the results of research on parenteral drug stability and compatibility. It is a valuable work for pharmacists and other practitioners who prepare and use intravenous drugs. The publisher also has made available an abbreviated version of the handbook called *Pocket Guide to Injectable Drugs* (see entry 1597).

Theodora Andrews

1592.   Katcher, Brian S. **Prescription Drugs: An Indispensable Guide for People over Fifty.** New York, Atheneum, 1988. 357p. bibliog. index. $22.50. LC 87-19587. ISBN 0-689-11915-1.

This book was written because the author perceived a need for specific information for individuals over fifty, who are more likely than others to require medication, take drugs in combination, and suffer unpleasant side effects. Only ninety-two generic drugs are listed, those most commonly taken by the older patient. Each drug, however, is described in more detail than most books for the patient provide. Emphasized are drugs for arthritis, high blood pressure, heart problems, and diabetes.

The presentation is in two sections. The first, "The Pharmacology of Aging," describes how aging affects the patient's response to drugs and explains how the risk of adverse drug reactions can be minimized. The second section, which makes up most of the book, lists the drugs with several pages of helpful information about each. Included is such information as other names, action, side effects, interactions, use with food or alcoholic beverages, and how age affects the response to the drug. The index lists popular brand names as well as generic names.

The author of this book is a pharmacist and teacher who has also coauthored a widely used textbook on the clinical use of drugs. [R: BL, 15 Jan 88, pp. 816-17; LJ, Jan 88, p. 76]

Theodora Andrews

1593. Liska, Ken. **The Pharmacist's Guide to the Most Misused and Abused Drugs in America.** New York, Macmillan, 1988. 278p. $9.95 pa. LC 87-36847. ISBN 0-02-059340-6.

The viewpoint of the author of this work, who is a pharmacist and a professor, is that Americans are overdosing themselves with both prescription and nonprescription drugs. His book may help clear up misconceptions about the use of drugs. The intended audience is the consumer.

The book is in dictionary format. Most of the entries are drug names (including street drugs), but categories of drugs, medical terminology, and miscellaneous information are also included. There is no index, but cross-references are provided. There are a few pages on testing for drugs of abuse. The entries for the drugs usually include: other names, source, pharmacological classification, dose, drug and food interactions, adverse effects, and abuse potential. Most of the monographs are about a half-page in length, but a few are several pages long. A short glossary is provided.

Theodora Andrews

1594. **Medication Teaching Manual: A Guide for Patient Counseling.** 4th ed. Bethesda, Md., American Society of Hospital Pharmacists, 1987. 428p. index. $30.00pa. ISBN 0-930530-78-0.

Patients frequently are advised by their physicians to take various medications. While the doctors may explain briefly the purposes of the drug, how and when to take it, and a few common side effects, patients often are unable to remember everything they have been told. This volume, prepared by the American Society of Hospital Pharmacists, provides patient teaching guides for approximately four hundred commonly prescribed medications.

The medications are arranged alphabetically by generic name and are on separate pages so that they can easily be duplicated and given to patients by their physicians or pharmacists. The information is presented in readily understandable terminology for the public. The content includes trade names, why prescribed, when to be used, how to be used, special instructions, side effects, other precautions, and storage conditions. There is a separate section on chemotherapeutic agents that includes valuable explanations about treatment information, side effects and precautions, and nutrition.

The appendices specify helpful interventions for nausea and mouth discomfort, and for increasing calories, protein, and appetite. There is also a useful bilingual directory of prescription orders (English-Spanish). The index lists the drugs by generic and trade names, thus allowing for easy access to the contents.

Judith Ann Erlen and
Jonathon Erlen

1595. **Prescription Drugs.** new and updated ed. By the Editors of *Consumer Guide* and Nicola Giacona. Lincolnwood, Ill., Publications International, 1987. 991p. illus. (part col.). $6.95pa. ISBN 0-451-15169-0.

There are a number of guides to prescription and nonprescription drugs intended for the consumer. In general they provide information on using drugs safely, and they fill a need.

Introductory chapters of this book cover filling the prescription, administering medication correctly, coping with side effects, and how drugs work. The bulk of the work consists of a list of drug profiles for the most commonly prescribed drugs, arranged alphabetically by generic name. Each profile includes brand names, manufacturers, pharmacologic or chemical class of drug, ingredients, dosage forms, storage instructions, uses, how to take the medication, side effects, interactions, and warnings. More than twelve hundred brand names are included. A special section, "Tablet/Capsule Identificaiton Guide," provides color photographs of more than three hundred commonly prescribed drugs. It can be used to help identify medicines. A separate list of Canadian brand names has been supplied.

The material presented in the book seems to be authentic, and it should prove useful since it provides information that the physician or pharmacist may have failed to make clear.

Theodora Andrews

1596. **Statistics on Narcotic Drugs for 1986: Furnished by Governments in Accordance with**

the International Treaties. By International Narcotics Control Board, Vienna. New York, United Nations, 1987. 106p. $17.00pa. ISBN 92-1-048040-6; ISSN 0566-7658. S/N E/F/S.87. XI.1.

The title of this publication says it all. It is a tabulation of the licit production and consumption of narcotic and psychotropic agents reported by the governments of 123 sovereign countries, in accordance with internationally agreed protocols, to the International Narcotics Control Board of the United Nations in Vienna. The board publishes an annual report and four technical reports. The present volume is its 1986 report. The text and tables are trilingual (English, French, and Spanish). Its contents should be useful to all those concerned with issues pertinent to the international cultivation, production, manufacture, and utilization of narcotic and psychotropic substances either to ensure the legitimate availability of these agents or to prevent their illicit production and trafficking.   Garabed Eknoyan

1597. Trissel, Lawrence A. **Pocket Guide to Injectable Drugs.** 1987 ed. Bethesda, Md., American Society of Hospital Pharmacists, 1987. 209p. index. $15.00pa. ISBN 0-930530-72-1.

This is an abbreviated version of Trissel's *Handbook on Injectable Drugs*, fourth edition (American Society of Hospital Pharmacists, 1986). Since some data are not included in the brief edition, it is suggested that the *Pocket Guide* be used in conjunction with the larger work.

The brief guide contains monographs on one hundred drug products which are frequently used injectables. Each monograph provides the following information: (1) a reference to the longer handbook, (2) a description, (3) products (including some trade names and perhaps sizes, strengths, and volumes in which the drug is supplied), (4) preparation (instructions for administration), (5) dosage and routes of administration, (6) stability, and (7) compatibility table. The tables are composed of lists of common intravenous infusion solutions and drugs. The entries are designated as compatible, incompatible, or conditional/equivocal.

The guide should prove valuable to nurses, pharmacists, and physicians in hospital settings.
Theodora Andrews

Indexes

1598. **American Drug Index 1988.** 32d ed. Norman F. Billups and Shirley M. Billups, eds. Philadelphia, J. B. Lippincott, 1988. 726p. $25.50. LC 55-6286. ISBN 0-932686-25-7.

This index, a compact annual publication, lists, identifies, gives brief information about, and correlates pharmaceuticals. It is especially valuable because drugs and drug products are steadily multiplying, and many similar products are available. The main section presents brief monographs with the drugs arranged alphabetically. They are listed by generic and chemical name. In addition, synonyms that are in general use are included, many of which are trade names. Many cross-references are provided. The inclusion of the variety of names is an outstanding feature of the work. It is also possible to find information on drug combinations when only one major ingredient is known.

The information given in each entry includes manufacturer, generic and/or chemical name, composition, strength, pharmaceutical forms available, package size, dosage, and use. In addition to the monographs section, which makes up most of the book, there are ten other sections including common abbreviations used in medical orders, approximate practical equivalents, common systems of weights and measures, a glossary, new USP and NF (United States Pharmacopeia and National Formulary) monographs, container and storage requirements for sterile USP drugs, oral dosage forms that should not be crushed, pharmaceutical company labeler code index, and a list of pharmaceutical manufacturers and/or drug distributors.

This publication is highly recommended for all who deal with pharmaceuticals. There are many publications that give information about drug products, and although this one is more compact than most, it still provides essential material.
Theodora Andrews

35 High Technology

CD-ROM

1599. CD-ROMs in Print 1988-1989: An International Guide. Jean-Paul Emard, comp. Westport, Conn., Meckler, 1988. 164p. index. $37.50 pa. ISBN 0-88736-274-5; ISSN 0891-8198.

Given the rate at which CD-ROM products are appearing, any directory would be out-of-date before it was ever published, and Meckler's *CD-ROMs in Print* is no exception. As long as the reader harbors no unrealistic expectations of current awareness, Emard's thorough and painstaking volume will yield quantities of useful data that are not available elsewhere in so convenient a form. This new edition of *CD-ROMs in Print* includes 239 entries arranged alphabetically by CD-ROM title. Each entry lists the data provider; the producer and/or distributor; the type(s) of drive(s) needed; the search software; computer requirements; price; and descriptive information about subject, content, and use. Numerous indexes provide a variety of additional access points. A "ROM Drive Index" lists all the products that can be used with each of the seven different drives, and a software index does the same for software. A subject index groups the products under broad subject headings. A type index divides products into five primary categories: catalog processing, database, public access catalog, reference, and demonstration disks; some of the primary categories have subdivisions. Acronyms associated with products are listed with cross-references to the titles under which the entries appear. Three other listings, wrongly called indexes since no references appear to the relevant products, provide the addresses, telephone numbers, and contact persons for data providers and CD-ROM and software producers. This book cannot pretend to be comprehensive but it is one of the best sources of the most information about compact disk products available on the market. Most libraries and many individuals will want a copy in their reference collections.

Connie Miller

1600. Elshami, Ahmed M. CD-ROM: An Annotated Bibliography. Englewood, Colo., Libraries Unlimited, 1988. 138p. index. $24.50pa. LC 88-13908. ISBN 0-87287-702-7.

This annotated bibliography, available also, ironically, on CD-ROM, is intended for a broad audience of librarians, computer systems professionals, and subject specialists. The 725 entries, which include articles, books, documents, theses, and dissertations, are arranged in twelve broad subject categories. Example categories are general references, technology, optical and magnetic media, production, applications, and marketing. Within each of these categories the items are further subdivided by more refined subject rubrics and arranged alphabetically by author. *See also* cross-references have been used to relate the categories to one another. Each item, which is numbered sequentially, is annotated with brief, cogent descriptions of contents. When appropriate, entries also contain ISBN, LCCN, and LC call numbers.

In addition to the detailed table of contents, access to the items listed is enhanced by an author index, title index, and a subject index.

This work will prove to be extremely useful to anyone needing information on CD-ROM and related technologies because it pulls together a literature now scattered over a wide variety of journals and other sources. As the author readily admits, selectivity was sacrificed for comprehensiveness. This bibliography is also available on diskettes for IBM, Macintosh, and Apple II computers.

Robert H. Burger

COMPUTING

General Works

BIBLIOGRAPHIES

1601. Bibliographic Guide to Computer Science 1987. Boston, G. K. Hall, 1988. 252p.

$150.00. ISBN 0-8161-7070-3; ISSN 0896-8098.

This guide lists approximately two thousand monographs, serials, technical reports and theses in the field of computer science that were cataloged at the libraries of Stanford University and the Massachusetts Institute of Technology between 1 September 1986 and 31 August 1987. Most of the items, therefore, are 1985 and 1986 imprints but works published as early as 1963 are also included.

The bibliography is arranged like a dictionary catalog with author entries and subject entries interfiled. Each main entry consists of AACR2 descriptive cataloging and Library of Congress subject headings, as well as ISBN and Dewey and LC numbers. Entries under boldface LC subject headings are condensed or abbreviated forms of the main entry. Call numbers for both Stanford and MIT copies of the described items are given. Finally, cross-references for subject headings are provided.

This work would be especially useful for those libraries that do not have bibliographic access to RLIN (Research Libraries Information Network) and, therefore, cannot search that bibliographic data, or for any library that is still forced to rely on printed bibliographies. For libraries not falling into these two categories, the work would be handy, at best.

Robert H. Burger

1602. Cox, John, Peter Hartley, and Doug Walton. **Keyguide to Information Sources in CAD/CAM.** Lawrence, Kans., Ergosyst, 1988. 257p. bibliog. index. $65.00. LC 88-9185. ISBN 0-916313-15-8.

Although there have been at least two other bibliographies written about portions of CAD/CAM (computer-aided design/computer-aided manufacture) literature, this work appears to be the first to provide background and directory information plus listings of print and electronic sources discussing CAD/CAM.

The guide is divided into three parts: survey of CAD/CAM and its information sources, bibliography, and directory of organizations. At the beginning of the book, the authors have included a glossary of terms and initialisms, appropriate for the novice and experienced user alike. Part 1 is a series of lengthy historical and bibliographic essays covering such topics as the history of CAD/CAM, CAD/CAM's scope, libraries and information services, online information sources, and audiovisual material, just to name a few. The extensive critically annotated bibliography in part 2 lists indexes and abstracting services, books, journals, information services, handbooks, conference proceedings, newsletters, reports, year-

books, and directories that range from general to specific. Like everything else in the guide, the sources reported are international in scope, both English and non-English. Part 3, the annotated directory of organizations, is a list reporting the scope and interests of international, national, and regional organizations from the likes of the United States, United Kingdom, and the Soviet Union, to Paraguay, Sri Lanka, and New Zealand—any country which has an interest in CAD/CAM issues.

The authors have compiled an impressive list of sources for the researcher. The annotations, which describe virtually every entry, are clearly written. The index gives easy access by author, title, and subject. This work would be an appropriate addition to any collection of high-tech resources.   Phillip P. Powell

1603. Nissley, Meta, comp. **Health Hazards of Video Display Terminals: A Comprehensive, Annotated Bibliography on a Critical Issue of Workplace Health and Safety.** 3d ed. Chico, Calif., Ryan Research International, 1987. 63p. index. (Information Alert Series, No. 4). $9.95 pa. LC 87-90423. ISBN 0-942158-04-0.

There is a debate going on between those who feel video display terminals are dangerous to health and those who believe that the displays are perfectly safe. This is a list of books, papers, and reports that have some relevance to this discussion. Also included is a list of manufacturers of video display terminals.

The book does not evaluate these materials; nor does it summarize the issue or summarize any of the items cited. The list of manufacturers is of questionable utility: many of the companies are small computer firms who do not manufacture displays but assemble them, together with computer chips and keyboards. This bibliography will soon be out of date. If it contained summaries of issues and of cited literature, it might be worth buying and cataloging.

Steven L. Tanimoto

1604. Zureik, Elia, and Dianne Hartling. **The Social Context of the New Information and Communication Technologies: A Bibliography.** New York, Peter Lang, 1987. 310p. (American University Studies. Series XV: Communications, Vol. 2). $35.00. LC 87-3450. ISBN 0-8204-0413-6.

In this bibliography the editors have attempted to provide a major tool for bibliographic control of the rapidly expanding literature on the social context of information and communications technology. No one can fault them for lack of ambition nor the importance of their topic. Indeed, the social consequences of the new information and communications technologies may well turn out to be of far greater significance than any of the technologies themselves. The editors devised eighty codes to classify the more than six thousand entries in this book, which are from an electronic database at Queen's University.

Entries are arranged alphabetically by author, with these one- to two-letter codes preceding them. Codes cover such topics as artificial intelligence; computer-assisted design and manufacturing; copyright and patenting; computer crime; office, home, and factory work; robotics; unions; transborder data flow and funds transfer; women; and national distinctions (e.g., Canada, Western Europe, Third World). Entries may be assigned more than one code although the majority have only one or two.

Criticisms of this bibliography relate to organization, entry contents, and the coding system. Organization by author, while a common arrangement, does not seem practical given the lack of subject or category index. If one wanted all citations on artificial intelligence, one would have to manually search every single page of the book. A second criticism relates to the lack of annotations for entries. While other bibliographic data are complete, the lack of content summary for citations seems a fairly serious omission. This would, in fact, seem to be what could have distinguished this work from any other mere listing of bibliographic citations.

Finally, the subject access which the editors attempt is disappointing on several counts. First, the categories are often too broad to be helpful in locating specific information. For example, banking, insurance, financial institutions, and commerce are all lumped together. Privacy (freedom, data protection, surveillance, etc.) comes before patents in the code list, which is confusing, and while one assumes this includes privacy of information, this is not indicated. Some codes, such as that for science fiction, seem out of place in the list, and a final criticism relates to the fact that science fiction (its code is HO, which is used for two entirely different subjects) is entirely out of order alphabetically and the code S which is used in the bibliography appears nowhere in the coding list. One could assume, since three citations by noted science fiction writer Arthur C. Clarke on page 61 have this S designation, that it is perhaps an error and should be something else, but one is not sure. Perhaps the category was an afterthought.

In summary, if one can overlook the overly broad categories, the inefficient organization, and the fact that most citations fall within a narrow range of years (mid- to late 1970s up to the early 1980s), one could find this bibliography useful. However, online searching by keywords or descriptors would probably be much quicker and more expedient and result in a more current bibliography for those who need references on the social implications of the new technologies. One must still applaud the efforts of these editors, because any large-scale bibliography is a tremendous amount of work and adds to bibliographic control of important topics such as this.   Carol Truett

BIOGRAPHIES

1605. Slater, Robert. **Portraits in Silicon.** Cambridge, Mass., MIT Press, 1987. 374p. illus. bibliog. index. $24.95. LC 87-2868. ISBN 0-262-19262-4.

This book is a stimulating and exciting collection of portraits about historical and present day individuals who have made significant contributions to the computer industry. These individuals are pioneers through their efforts and talents in different facets of the computer revolution. The book begins with the conceptualizers who laid the foundation of computing, the early inventors who built the first machines, and the early entrepreneurs who commercialized the computing industry. The book continues with those who made the computer smaller and more powerful, the hardware designers, and the software specialists. The book ends with those who brought the computer to the masses and a pioneer in computer science. There is a total of thirty-one portraits. The author discusses early figures such as Watson and Perot and their efforts in founding commercial computer companies. There are also biographies of Gates and Jobs, whose endeavors have made computers available to the general public. Each portrait is about eleven pages long and covers the challenges and crucial events leading to the particular contribution of the pioneer, in an unbiased, journalistic manner. Many of the portraits are written from direct interviews with the persons themselves and hence carry the flavor of the inventor's point of view. This book is nontechnical in nature and is written for the general public. It is highly recommended for all libraries. [R: SBF, Jan/Feb 88, p. 137]   John Y. Cheung

DICTIONARIES AND ENCYCLOPEDIAS

1606. Christian, Kaare. **The C and UNIX Dictionary: From Absolute Pathname to Zombie.** New York, John Wiley, 1988. 216p. $29.95;

$16.95pa. LC 88-14208. ISBN 0-471-60929-3; 0-471-60931-5pa.

This book is a useful collection of terms that are unique to the C and UNIX environment. The author has done a good job of selecting the terms to include in the text and has provided useful definitions and explanations of these terms. The examples of codes included are concise and effective. Few terms of general use to other areas of computer science have been included. I would prefer to have more items included that are UNIX and C jargon, such as *bang* (the exclamation mark), *white book* (the K&R text), *Dennis* (Dennis Ritchie), and *deathstar* (an AT&T logo).

A few definitions exhibit small problems: the *MERT* definition is not complete; there was a backslash missed in the *backslash* definition; describing *lex* as a lexical analyzer is not very helpful; and the *lint* definition has a wording problem. Some alternative definitions should be included, such as *strip* (to turn the eight bit off), *port* (an input/output hardware connection, often a RS232 coupler), and *code generator* (also an application generator).

Some UNIX gurus may consider things like *backspace, bell, form feed,* and *carriage return* to be escape sequences. However, they are treated as ASCII characters on many systems. I think that the escape sequence definition should be restricted to sequences like those that control printers and screens and actually contain an escape that the programmer must enter.

This is a very useful book for beginners in UNIX and C and useful as an occasional reference for experienced UNIX users.

John A. Jackman

1607.   **A Glossary of Computing Terms: An Introduction.** 5th ed. Edited by Glossary Working Party, British Computer Society. New York, Cambridge University Press, 1987. 73p. index. $3.95pa. LC 86-20738. ISBN 0-521-33261-3.

This volume's main distinction is that it presents entries not in alphabetical sequence, but rather within fifteen categories: applications, communications, data representation and structure, documentation, input and output, computer personnel, computers, programming languages, storage, operational processes, programming, machine architecture, systems software, truth tables and logic gates, and units (e.g., *giga*). An index in the front takes one to the relevant section, in some cases from like terms which are not actually included but whose definition is related to the term defined. Unfortunately, the index is not complete. For example, ASCII is mentioned in the entry for character codes but not directly in the index.

Definitions are terse, sometimes, as the book itself admits, making them of "limited use." (For example, the programming language LISP is defined as "used for list processing," with no indication of its wide employment in artificial intelligence.) In spite of this, the low cost of the book together with the topical arrangement makes it a satisfactory introduction or review for the major areas of computer science.

Robert Skinner

1608.   **McGraw-Hill Encyclopedia of Electronics and Computers.** 2d ed. Sybil P. Parker, ed. New York, McGraw-Hill, 1988. 1047p. illus. index. $75.00. LC 87-37592. ISBN 0-07-045499-X.

A one-volume encyclopedia composed of 520 articles, selected from the sixth edition of the *McGraw-Hill Encyclopedia of Science and Technology* (see *ARBA* 88, entry 1448), concentrating on electronics and computers. The subject matter ranges over diverse topics in these fields such as fabrication methods for integrated circuits, the flow of electricity through semiconducting materials, electromagnetic pulse, and the use of computers in areas such as robotics, data management systems, communications, and consumer products. This second edition contains 45 new and 120 revised articles (about a quarter of the articles appearing in the first edition). The articles are organized in alphabetical order with many keyword subheadings and numerous illustrations, photographs, tables, line drawings, and diagrams. The articles are clearly although technically written and most contain references to other articles in the volume and selected bibliographies. There is a useful index to the detailed contents of the articles at the back of the volume. The articles are written by noted authorities in these fields.

This encyclopedia is intended for the technically oriented lay or professional reader and will serve as a useful first reference source for technical terms and concepts. [R: RBB, 1 Oct 88, pp. 242-43]   Lorna K. Rees-Potter

1609.   Stark, Robin. **Encyclopedia of Lotus 1 2 3.** Blue Ridge Summit, Pa., TAB Books, 1987. 484p. index. $29.95; $19.95pa. LC 87-19839. ISBN 0-8306-7891-3; 0-8306-2891-6pa.

In spite of strong competition from other spreadsheets, Lotus 1-2-3 is probably the program most associated with the IBM personal computer. Such popularity has spawned numerous cottage industries ranging from templates, software enhancements, and, of course, books explaining how to get the most out of the program. Stark's work is "A complete cross-reference to all macros, commands, functions, applications, and troubleshooting." The book begins with a short introduction to Lotus, followed by 200 pages on commands, 150 on functions, 50 on macros, and a short section on companion programs that accompany Lotus, as well as the widely used HAL. Following this is a useful "Troubleshooting Guide" covering some of the frequently encountered error messages or questions. Explanations are clear and there are numerous examples. The author has gone out of his way to provide cross-references and there is a good index (in a spot check of the index, the only omission I discovered was the function @LOG(x), but there was an entry to the proper page under the term *logarithms*). Lotus users, and they are legion, will find this book a helpful tool.

Robert Skinner

DIRECTORIES

1610. Computing Information Directory: A Comprehensive Guide to the Computing Literature. 5th ed. Darlene Myers Hildebrandt, comp. and ed. Federal Way, Wash., Pedaro, 1988. 893p. index. $139.95pa. ISBN 0-933113-03-X; ISSN 0887-1175.

The main impetus of this reference guide is to list bibliographical data on over fifteen hundred computer publications. The computer industry has blossomed in the last two decades, as has the amount of literature published in the field. This book provides the tools to survey the extent of literature available. The bulk of this guide is an exhaustive listing of computer journals. The vast number of computer titles is cross-referenced to guide users to titles in similar and related areas. An exhaustive collection of computer-related items is also provided, including university computer center newsletters, computer books, dictionaries and glossaries, indexing and abstracting services, software sources, review sources, hardware sources, directories, encyclopedias and handbooks, and computer languages. Also included are six appendices dealing with Association for Computing Machinery (ACM) Special Interest Group (SIG) Proceedings from 1969 to 1985; historical guides to the computing literature; a bibliography of career and salary trends in the United States 1970-1986; expansion to the Library of Congress classification schedules QA 75 and QA 76, 1986 draft; and subject, publishers', and master indexes. This is a comprehensive guide to where computer information can be found. This book can be considered as a resource tool and is highly recommended as reference material for college and professional libraries.

John Y. Cheung

1611. The Optical Publishing Directory 1987. By Richard A. Bowers. Medford, N.J., Learned Information, 1987. 199p. bibliog. index. $45.00 looseleaf with binder. ISSN 0893-0317.

The optical publishing industry is making rapid advances in libraries and information-dependent enterprises. The industry, however, is not without its casualties. The first edition of this directory contained listings of forty-two products. Eighteen of those did not make it into this updated edition, which contains eighty-four titles currently available.

The directory has several sections. A "State of the Art" essay provides the reader with background information on CD-ROM and the impact of optical publishing on information markets. Extensive definitions of key terms and concepts associated with optical publishing are provided in a glossary. The "Product Profiles" section comprises nearly half the volume. Each profile includes information about the manufacturer, print equivalent, bibliographic type, optical format (CD-ROM, WORM, videodisc), product description, hardware specifications, software, and price. This section is arranged by name of the product.

An applications index groups entries by general subject, for example, business, medicine, etc. A product type index lists titles according to their format such as bibliographic, reference, statistical, etc. Additional information is provided on hardware vendors, CD-ROM manufacturers, videodisc players, and Write-Once vendors. A general index appears at the end of the book.

This directory contains a variety of valuable and difficult-to-find information about optical publishing. It is a welcome addition to the literature. [R: RBB, 1 Mar 88, pp. 1114-15]

Dennis J. Phillips

1612. Rogers, Helen, comp. Canadian Machine-Readable Databases: A Directory and Guide. Bases de Données Canadiennes Lisibles par Machine. Ottawa, National Library of Canada, 1987. 134p. index. $12.50pa.; $15.00 pa. (U.S.). ISBN 0-660-53734-6.

This publication is a bilingual (English and French) directory of approximately 450 databases in machine-readable form created and produced in Canada. The databases listed cover all disciplines from the humanities to the sciences. They may be textual, statistical, or videotex in nature and may be publicly accessible or not. The restriction is that they must be produced by a Canadian organization, firm, or individual. The preface indicates that the directory information is current as of June 1987 and will be updated with future editions. The directory is intended as a reference tool for the Canadian information industry, information scientists, and librarians in particular.

It is organized primarily in alphabetical order by the database name, with subject, database producers, online and offline service vendors, and database name reference lists. Each entry gives full information on the content and scope, coverage, language, updating, access conditions, and notes any print equivalent. The coverage appears excellent to this reviewer, listing a number of databases not publicly accessible that are often not found in such directories. It might be more useful in future editions to include some indication of the size and growth of the databases covered. There are some typographical errors in the text such as a duplication of index information in the subject index under "Leisure," and a transposition of some index entries under "Law" to "Library Catalogues." Hopefully the next edition will eliminate these errors through better editorial review. Recommended for libraries that provide online search services, especially if Canadian information is required.

Lorna K. Rees-Potter

HANDBOOKS AND YEARBOOKS

1613. Aleksander, Igor, and Ian Benson, eds. **The World Yearbook of New Generation Computing Research and Development.** Lawrence, Kans., Ergosyst, 1988. 821p. index. $150.00. ISBN 0-916313-14-X; ISSN 0953-7813.

The yearbook is the first of its kind to list those parties who are significantly involved in the research and development of new generation computing, that is, artificial intelligence systems, throughout the world. Most of the participants are researchers who actively participated in the International Joint Conference on Artificial Intelligence. Entries in the directory include the institution names, names of contact personnel, addresses, brief descriptions of current and future research projects, funding records, and literature references. All entries are categorized by country and alphabetically within each country. The bulk of the entries comes from groups within the United Kingdom and the United States. The second half of the yearbook contains a list of communication networks; major national and international funding agencies; and indexes of research institutions, personnel, keywords, and projects. This yearbook is a useful and handy reference guide for identifying some active researchers and their respective areas of interest in the field of

artificial intelligence. It is recommended for college and professional libraries.

John Y. Cheung

1614. **Computer Discount Shopping Guide.** Lincolnwood, Ill., Publications International, 1988. 160p. index. $6.95pa. ISBN 0-451-82195-5.

As the title implies, this publication is designed for the microcomputer home shopping market. After a lengthy and informative introduction on the pros and cons of home shopping, the main portion of the book presents 103 one-page profiles of companies selling a wide range of hardware, software, and computer peripherals. The companies appear to be drawn from a wide U.S. geographic region and include many of the better known mail order companies.

Information on each company includes a brief résumé, showroom locations, pricing and shipping policies (no actual dollar amounts), products sold, services, and ordering information. The remainder of the volume is divided into a series of indexes accessing the information presented in the company profiles. These consist of brands of desktop computers, portable computers, peripherals, software, used equipment, renting/leasing, supplies, onsite repair, and showroom locations.

While by no means comprehensive, this volume presents a great deal of useful information at a reasonable price. While obviously biased toward home shopping, the introduction also includes a section on how to handle problems with an order or with a merchant. The information will become quickly dated but the volume is still quite useful. Advertisements in trade journals should also be consulted for updates and additional companies.

Andrew G. Torok

1615. **Computer Industry Forecasts: The Source for Business Information on Computers, Related Equipment and Software.** Georgetown, Calif., Data Analysis Group, 1988. 373p. index. $250.00/yr. looseleaf with binder. ISSN 0883-931X.

This abstract service was formerly called *Computer Industry Abstracts* (see *ARBA* 88, entry 1717). Like its predecessor, this service presents statistics pulled from major computer and business journals. Each entry generally contains bibliographic information; a brief statement of what the statistics represent, such as "shipments of PC monochrome monitors," and then the statistics themselves in tabular form. Annual growth rates are computed when relevant. Statistics are easy to locate, because they are indexed by both company name and keyword. The comments on market trends have been dropped, although the Data Analysis Group presents their own four-year forecasts for major products. They also offer interpretive graphs and charts. The statistics emphasize market share, sales, and consumer usage.

By dropping the "Intelligence Report," this service has become more like *Predicasts Forecasts* (Predicasts, 1960-) than ever. It is, however, easier to read and interpret than *Predicasts*, and is, of course, limited only to computers, which it covers in more depth, especially specific brand names.

I received the fourth quarter 1988 issue in early November, long before the end of the quarter. It primarily covers material from June through September. In the volatile computer market recent information can be critical, and this source does as good a job at that as anything except an online database could. This type of specialized information is always expensive, and the price is what one might expect for this kind of specialized market information. In all, an important and useful source for those researching the computer market.

Susan V. McKimm

1616. **Handbook of Computer-Communications Standards.** By William Stallings and others. Indianapolis, Ind., Howard W. Sams, 1987. 3v. illus. index. $34.95/vol. LC 87-14062. ISBN 0-672-22664-2 (v.1); 0-672-22665-0 (v.2); 0-672-22666-9 (v.3).

This three-volume set covers computer communications standards of the Open Systems Interconnection Model (vol. 1), Local Area Networks (vol. 2), and the Department of Defense (vol. 3). These three areas are becoming especially important for computer communications. The information on these topics can be difficult to locate since much of it resides in technical documents and committee reports. Moreover, the technical aspects of communications can make this subject particularly difficult to grasp. This set will make the tasks of finding and assimilating the information easy and even pleasant.

It is well written, nicely laid out, and carefully edited. The treatment of difficult topics is remarkably easy to follow. Technical terms are defined carefully in the text and can be located using the index. Technical source documents are well referenced but these will seldom be needed by most readers since the treatment is so thorough.

Two features set these books apart from others on the topics—the figures and abstracts at the start of each chapter. While some of the figures are rather familiar, many are unique. These figures are definitely above average and more easily understood than many on these topics. The abstracts help the reader identify the contents rapidly and lead into the subject matter.

As the preface states, this set of books is ideal for the student, professional in data processing, information systems customer and designer, or implementer of computer communications. I recommend it highly.

John A. Jackman

1617. LaGasse, Charles E. **The Computer Resource Guide.** 1988 ed. Concord, Mass., Computer Insights, 1987. 84p. index. $24.00pa. LC 87-70697. ISBN 0-942199-00-6.

The guide serves as a first reference point for computer-related information, listing 240 primary computer resources under eighty-five subjects. Criteria for inclusion are as follows: subject areas must relate to computer systems, hardware, software, or services; resources chosen are unique, comprehensive, or well known. The list is intended to either locate the appropriate resource or assist the reader in finding it.

Resources are grouped by type (e.g., books, magazines, newsletters, catalogs, conference/exhibits, sourcebooks) under alphabetically arranged subject headings. These resources may be from public or private organizations, which can be for profit or nonprofit. Entries are briefly annotated.

Three alternative indexes list computer resources by type, vendor, and computer resource (to answer the question "Is a certain resource included?"). A special features section offers guidelines and advice as to recommended acquisitions, resources, and associations to join. A preview of the planned 1989 edition is provided, promising expanded subject areas and resource types, as well as the addition of more product-specific resources and U.S. government publications.

Cross-referencing among the subject areas would also be a valuable feature to consider, as more and more terms are used in computer jargon, and more assistance is needed to locate the desired item. [R: RBB, 1 June 88, p. 1654]

Anita Zutis

INDEXES

1618. **Master Index to SAS System Documentation for Personal Computers.** Cary, N.C., SAS Institute, 1987. 130p. $6.95pa. ISBN 1-55544-075-4.

1619. Master Index to SAS System Documentation, Version 5 Edition. Cary, N.C., SAS Institute, 1987. 224p. $7.95pa. ISBN 1-55544-047-9.

1620. Master Index to SUGI Proceedings. 1988 ed. Cary, N.C., SAS Institute, 1988. 144p. $8.00pa. ISBN 1-55544-306-0.

The first two indexes listed provide extremely detailed access to manuals and technical reports that document the SAS System for Personal Computers, Release 6.03 and for Version 5 of the SAS System on mainframes and minicomputers. These are comprehensive indexes that cover all users' guides, SAS Views, and titles in the SAS Series in Statistical Applications. These volumes are arranged alphabetically by subject. Subheading use is extensive.

The third index listed provides complete coverage to the SAS Users' Group International conference proceedings from SUGI 6 through SUGI 13 (1981-1988). This index is in two parts. Part 1 is a subject index, similar to the other two works. Part 2 is an author list of those who have written papers that appear in the different proceedings.

All three of these volumes would be extremely beneficial to anyone trying to find out as much as possible about specific aspects of SAS. The indexes are well crafted and cross-references are provided when needed.

Robert H. Burger

Microcomputing

1621. Dewey, Patrick R. Interactive Fiction and Adventure Games for Microcomputers 1988: An Annotated Directory. Westport, Conn., Meckler, 1988. 189p. illus. index. $39.50 pa. LC 87-16473. ISBN 0-88736-170-6.

The microcomputer revolution occurred at the time when the video game phenomenon was hitting the United States. It was only natural that programmers would create for the home computer market what was available in the video arcade. To some extent, the adventure game is a direct competitor with the video game. However, a new genre appeared for microcomputers which no video game could duplicate. This new genre was interactive fiction. The best known program of this type is "Zork," which can take an individual weeks or months to solve.

Dewey's purpose seems to be twofold. He attempts to list most of the adventure and interactive fiction for microcomputers. Those games he is personally familiar with, he describes in detail, and reviews their strengths and weaknesses. He does this with skill and

provides perceptive analyses. For the games he is not familiar with, he quotes or paraphrases the information given on the game box. Thus, the user can expect two completely different types of coverage.

General information given for each game includes name, producer, cost, hardware, grade or difficulty level, type, and a description. Coverage is excellent up to the end of 1987 and even includes publishers' descriptions of some games coming out in 1988.

Dewey's book is for game enthusiasts who want to build their repertoire, libraries which try to serve parents of game enthusiasts, educators who need to choose the best of interactive fiction, and computer stores who want a quick lookup reference for their computer customers. [R: JOYS, Spring 88, p. 365; RBB, 15 Sept 88, p. 140] David V. Loertscher

1622. Encyclopedia of Microcomputers. Volume 1: Access Methods to Assembly Language and Assemblers. Allen Kent and James G. Williams, eds. New York, Marcel Dekker, 1988. 434p. illus. $160.00. LC 87-15428. ISBN 0-8247-2700-2.

Designed as a companion to *Encyclopedia of Computer Science and Technology* (Marcel Dekker, 1975-), the intention of this encyclopedia is to produce a comprehensive work covering at least five hundred articles in ten volumes. The definition of *microcomputer* was a problem for the editor, since the distinction between microcomputers and mainframe computers has almost been erased.

The coverage is to include "the broad spectrum of microcomputer knowledge ... and is aimed at the needs of microcomputer hardware specialists, programmers, systems analysts, engineers, operations researchers, and mathematicians." Some of the articles are to be readable to the novice, others to the specialist.

An examination of the entries shows many entries on computer companies (most of which have been in business less than ten years) and technical articles such as "Aerospace Digital Crewstations," "ALGOL," and "Analytic Hierarchy Process." Very few of the entries would be of interest to the typical user of microcomputers who uses application programs or tries to keep up with trends in the field.

Recommended as a source for more technical articles.

David V. Loertscher

1623. Encyclopedia of Microcomputers. Volume 2: Authoring Systems for Interactive Video to Compiler Design. Allen Kent and James G. Williams, eds. New York, Marcel Dekker, 1988.

452p. illus. $160.00. LC 87-15428. ISBN 0-8247-2701-0.

Volume 2 of the multivolume *Encyclopedia of Microcomputers* covers twenty-five topics. Five profile computer companies or computer-related organizations: Burroughs, C. Itoh, CCITT, Century Analysis, and Commodore. Nine relate to programming, from the system level to authoring systems, including videodisc authoring systems, automated program generators, BASIC, benchmarking programming languages, BIOS, COBOL, command languages, Common LISP, and compiler design. Eight concern themselves with applications: automated forecasting, automated material handling, automated office information systems design, bilingual language processors, CAD/CAM from a management viewpoint, chemical engineering, civil engineering, and client-centered information processing. The three remaining entries cover microprocessor circuits, image data compression, and bibliographic control of microcomputer software.

Entries are signed and range from two pages to almost sixty. On the whole, they do an adequate job of covering their subjects for persons with only a moderate amount of computer literacy. Most authors have provided bibliographies, some with over one hundred items; however, citations are almost entirely before 1986 and this also reflects the currency of the entries themselves. There are a number of charts and a few photographs. The volume shows some problems in proofreading. Librarians familiar with the Dekker sets *Encyclopedia of Computer Science and Technology* (for reviews of vols. 2-6, see *ARBA* 78, entry 1523) and the *Encyclopedia of Library and Information Science* (for reviews of vols. 39-41, see *ARBA* 87, entries 578-580) will have a good idea as to what to expect from *Encyclopedia of Microcomputers*.   Robert Skinner

1624. Naiman, Arthur, ed. **The Macintosh Bible: Thousands of Basic and Advanced Tips, Tricks and Shortcuts Logically Organized and Fully Indexed.** 2d ed. Berkeley, Calif., Goldstein & Blair; distr., Emeryville, Calif., Publishers Group West, 1988. 759p. illus. index. $28.00pa. ISBN 0-940235-01-3.

Having had the opportunity to use the first edition of this work extensively, I was not surprised to find that the second edition is even better. It is a testament to the thoroughness of the original authors (Dale Coleman and Arthur Naiman) that the first edition remains useful today, almost two years after publication—not a short time in the volatile areas of microcomputer hardware and software. It is also helpful that

readers receive two free updates as part of the purchase price. In addition to the usual tips for users of specific programs and peripherals, new Macintosh users will find a good deal of useful information in the first hundred pages or so. If you purchase machine-specific books for your library, this should be one of them. (Incidentally, the book is also available for $79.95 accompanied by three disks which constitute *The Macintosh Bible: STAX! Edition.* The HyperCard version, which was not available for review, excerpts information from the printed volume.)   Robert Skinner

Software

1625. Eckhardt, Robert C. **Free (and Almost Free) Software for the Macintosh: An Illustrated and Rated Guide to over 1,000 of the Best Programs.** Portland, Oreg., dilithium Press; distr., New York, Crown, 1987. 413p. illus. $19.95pa. LC 86-29293. ISBN 0-517-56585-4.

Perhaps one of the better recommendations for a book is to start out by noting that the reviewer had thought highly enough of it to buy his own copy. Such is the case with Eckhardt's survey of over one thousand public domain and shareware programs for the Apple Macintosh, many of which are still of use. Although there have been other similar books, such as Bertram Gader and Manuel Nodar's *Mac Software for Pennies* (Warner Software/Warner Books, 1986), Eckhardt's is by far the most comprehensive. His descriptions are lengthy, illustrations well chosen, and evaluations fair. There are two problems with the volume: one avoidable, one not. The latter is that in spite of being quite current at the time of publication, there are several important new classes of materials not included, most notably those relating to HyperCard and the Macintosh II. More unfortunate is the lack of an index. One presumably was planned, as it is mentioned in the otherwise good section on bit-mapped ImageWriter fonts. As it is, for access points one is left with only the table of contents and wondering just what is in the section labeled "Whatnot" of chapter 9, "Everything Else."   Robert Skinner

ROBOTICS

1626. **International Encyclopedia of Robotics: Applications and Automation.** Richard C. Dorf, ed. New York, John Wiley, 1988. 3v. illus. index. $295.00/set. LC 87-37264. ISBN 0-471-87868-5.

Robotics is a relatively new field. In fact, Isaac Asimov is credited with coining the word in 1942. At that time he assumed it was the "proper scientific term for the systematic study of robots, their construction, maintenance and behavior." It is the goal of this encyclopedia to define the discipline and practice of robotics by bringing together the core knowledge and practice in the field with that from closely related fields. Included are numerous articles associated with theoretical aspects of robotics as well as articles dealing with both present and future applications of robotics in the factory, office, and home.

The encyclopedia is made up of signed articles by respected researchers in the field from both industry and academic, including many from European and Japanese companies or universities. Each article includes a bibliography as well as extensive cross-references to other articles. As behooves any major technical encyclopedia, this one has numerous tables and figures (over two thousand).

The articles are arranged in alphabetical order. For example, an article entitled "End-of-Arm-Tooling" follows an article titled "Employment, Impact." This would cause a problem were it not for an extensive index found at the end of volume 3. The index makes it possible to find all of the articles related to robotic arms, such as geometric design, arm-joints, or manipulators.

This is an attractive encyclopedia on a topic of great interest to many, not all of whom are engineers and computer scientists. The variety and shear number of topics covered is impressive. The articles "Art, Robotics In," "Kinematics," and "Robots in Japan" are good examples of the variety and depth of the articles found. They also demonstrate the variety of audience that should be attracted to this set. Not only should it be extremely popular, but it also is a good value for the money.

Susan B. Ardis

SECURITY

1627. Kidd, Stewart. **Dictionary of Industrial Security.** New York, Routledge & Kegan Paul/Methuen, 1987. 141p. illus. bibliog. $42.50. LC 87-4672. ISBN 0-7102-0794-8.

This dictionary provides an immediate reference to the complex methods and technology used in the protection of people, property, and information. The first of its kind, it provides an invaluable glossary of both British and U.S. terms in industrial security and crime prevention. In some one thousand entries, the dictionary gives comprehensive coverage of all areas central to security, such as alarm systems, access control systems, locks, lighting, organizations, and institutions. Diagrams are used to supple-

ment the text and an extensive network of cross-references guides the reader to useful related entries. Also, two appendices and a security bibliography are included. Appendix 1 contains a brief summary of British standards relating to industrial and domestic security, while appendix 2 contains a listing of some of the standards relevant to the U.S. security practice. The bibliography contains a list of books on security topics for mastering the security examinations administered by the American Society for Industrial Security (ASIS) and the International Professional Security Association (IPSA).

As the only dictionary on industrial security in existence, the book's purpose is to be of use not only to the security profession, but also to the nonspecialist. The book is, therefore, recommended to managers who have a supplementary responsibility for security or loss prevention, to police and military personnel with crime prevention and physical security duties, and to those studying for professional security qualification. [R: Choice, Mar 88, p. 1066; RBB, Aug 88, p. 1900]   Assad A. Tavakoli

1628. Longley, Dennis, and Michael Shain. **Data & Computer Security: Dictionary of Standards, Concepts and Terms.** New York, Stockton Press/Grove's Dictionaries of Music, 1987. 428p. illus. index. $100.00. LC 87-18024. ISBN 0-935859-17-9.

I found myself very interested in browsing through the maze of terminology on data and computer security that is covered in this volume. This was totally unexpected from a book with a rather unassuming title and covering an apparently dry topic. The authors meet the objective very well and even exceed the goal of providing a dictionary on the subject. Some terms have a few pages of explanation which help make the book more like a primer than a dictionary. I found the editing of this book to be excellent and the topics interesting, but the layout a bit peculiar. It is remarkably free of typographical errors, with clear descriptions and examples. The definitions are concise, with only a few slanted opinions, which one expects since many of the definitions rely on military and government documents with emphasis on the United States and United Kingdom.

A wide range of topics is included and context-specific definitions are provided. The topic selection mechanism is somewhat arbitrary but is appropriate for the target audience. A few statements are debatable. The statement that assembly language "greatly improves the comprehension of the program and enables modifications to be incorporated more readily" would be challenged by most readers. Names of many of the computer languages are retained today in all capitals (e.g., COBOL and FORTRAN) rather than lowercase. One of the most popular development languages today, C, was omitted.

The list of references is given in the introduction rather than at the end of the book. Similarly, the bibliography is placed at the beginning, which is highly unusual. Cross-references to topics are exhaustive and placed both in the subject index at the end of the book and in the text proper. The type style is poor around a few of the figures, but fine around most others. The alphabetical order is somewhat peculiar (e.g., approved, a priori control; rather than a priori control, approved).

This book is a valuable source of information for many individuals, both computer professionals and managers of companies that use computers heavily. It is recommended for a wide variety of professionals, but would be especially useful to those interested in government contracts with security requirements, or computer banking managers. [R: Choice, June 88, p. 1538; RBB, 15 June 88, p. 1718]

John A. Jackman

VIDEO DISCS

1629. Schwartz, Ed. **The Educators' Handbook to Interactive Videodisc.** 2d ed. Washington, D.C., Association for Educational Communications and Technology, 1987. 151p. bibliog. $22.95pa. LC 85-71983. ISBN 0-89240-049-8.

Although I did not have access to the first edition of the handbook, the foreword states that the book has gone through "extensive changes, clarifications, and corrections." The majority of this book is devoted to descriptions of laser videodisc players (home and industrial), video monitors and projectors, interfaces to connect a player to a computer, authoring software for developing instructional units using videodiscs, and, most extensively, a listing of available videodiscs of interest to educators. This latter section is divided into approximately sixty sections ranging from aeronautics to vocational education-telemarketing. In addition to a brief description of the videodisc's program, system requirements, publisher, and price are also indicated. For the earlier equipment sections, technical specifications are provided but no comparisons.

General information in a variety of areas relating to videodiscs and their control and playback is provided in the first seventeen pages. Persons unfamiliar with the technology will find these discussions useful, but will have to look elsewhere for in-depth treatments. The information on specific players and discs is helpful to have in one place, although I found several available pieces of equipment unmentioned (most notably the Macintosh and its videodisc controller software). Robert Skinner

36 Physical Sciences and Mathematics

ASTRONOMY

1630. Arp, Halton C., and Barry F. Madore. **A Catalogue of Southern Peculiar Galaxies and Associations. Volume II: Selected Photographs.** New York, Cambridge University Press, 1987. 1v. (various paging). illus. bibliog. $75.00. LC 86-11700. ISBN 0-521-33087-4.

Volume 1 of this useful set was an extensive compendium of numerical data on 6,445 unusual galaxies and groups of galaxies. This companion volume's purpose is to provide examples of the various galaxy types, arranged according to the classification used in the first tome. In most cases, the authors selected the "largest and most spectacular examples" to illustrate the form and evolution of each type of galaxy or association. Each section of the book is prefaced by a brief description of the characteristics of the category and subcategories in question.

The photographs are divided into twenty-five categories, including single, double, and triple galaxies, as well as larger groups. One can find examples of interacting galaxies, galaxies with jets, spiral galaxies, compact galaxies, ring galaxies, etc. Each photograph has an identifying number which indicates right ascension and declination of the photograph, as well as a "white bar, two arc minutes long, in the southeast corner" to provide a sense of scale. Like the first volume, this work is most appropriate for university and observatory libraries.

Robert A. Seal

1631. Henry, Richard C., and others. **Atlas of the Ultraviolet Sky.** Baltimore, Md., Johns Hopkins University Press, 1988. 457p. maps. index. $65.00. LC 88-45403. ISBN 0-8018-3738-3.

Based on data collected by TD-1, a European Space Research Organization satellite launched in 1972, this reference work consists of 212 pairs of celestial maps portraying the entire sky at both visible and ultraviolet wavelengths. In each pair, the lefthand diagram shows an $18° \times 18°$ portion of the sky with all naked-eye stars and a few fainter objects shown according to brightness. This map is for orientation purposes only. The righthand map presents the identical portion of the sky with the stars' brightness shown in the ultraviolet portion of the spectrum at a wavelength of 1,565 Angstroms.

Aimed at the professional astronomer, this atlas of 25,314 stars is the first comprehensive survey of the ultraviolet sky. It contains a well-written introduction which explains stellar ultraviolet radiation, describes study of stars at ultraviolet wavelengths, reviews the data used, and compares the distribution and location of stellar objects at both visible and ultraviolet wavelengths. There are two indexes (tables) which help a user with either celestial or galactic coordinates of a given object to quickly find the needed plate (map) in the atlas. Recommended for the observatory, special, or university library.

Robert A. Seal

1632. Kronk, Gary W. **Meteor Showers: A Descriptive Catalog.** Hillside, N.J., Enslow, 1988. 291p. index. (Enslow Astronomy Series). $24.50pa. LC 87-22159. ISBN 0-89490-072-2.

Meteoroids are generally believed to be non-icy solids that have been ejected from comets. A meteoroid that strikes the earth's atmosphere is a meteor and a group of meteors is a meteor shower. Because meteors orbit, their regular reappearance can be predicted.

To aid amateur observers and researchers, Kronk has compiled information on more than eighty meteor showers grouping them according to their month of appearance and their maximum duration. Each chapter represents a different month, and within the chapters showers are listed alphabetically by constellation of radiation or origin. A name index allows the reader easy access.

Each entry includes an observer's synopsis (times, duration and location of the shower), a historical overview (first sightings, important developments and interesting facts) and current orbital information. Data about brightness and color are also included when available. Appended are sections on definitions, shower associations, source abbreviations and the "D-criterion." The latter, used to analyze orbits, played an important role in deciding which meteor showers to include in this volume.

This descriptive catalog is an impressive compilation, containing a wealth of data and detailed information on meteor showers. It is an excellent sourcebook for both professional and amateur observers.   Karen S. Croneis

1633.   Moore, Patrick. **Patrick Moore's A-Z of Astronomy.** New York, W. W. Norton, c1986, 1987. 240p. illus. (part col.). index. $13.50pa. LC 87-11017. ISBN 0-393-30505-8.

With the rapid changes which take place in science, any specialized subject dictionary must be considered seriously for library purchase. This is especially the case when there have been relatively few such publications in a particular field over the years. In astronomy, the last such work to appear was Jeanne Hopkins's *Glossary of Astronomy and Astrophysics* (see *ARBA* 82, entry 1422). This new dictionary by Patrick Moore is a revised and updated version of an earlier work, and is aimed primarily at amateur and armchair astronomers, as are virtually all of Moore's prolific writings. The information is current as of mid-1985. There are numerous photographs, charts, graphs, and drawings (at least one to a page) to illustrate the definitions. One noteworthy and useful feature of this work not found in other astronomy dictionaries, at least none in recent years, is its inclusion of historical personages, events, and landmark publications in astronomy.

Donald J. Marion

1634.   Tirion, Wil, Barry Rappaport, and George Lovi. **Uranometria 2000.0. Volume I: The Northern Hemisphere to −6°.** Richmond, Va., Willmann-Bell, 1987. 259p. illus. maps. bibliog. $39.95. LC 87-14769. ISBN 0-943396-14-X.

The first of a two-volume set covering the entire sky, this superb celestial atlas includes more than 332,000 stars to 9.5 magnitude and more than 10,300 deep sky objects (galaxies, clusters, nebulae, quasars, etc.). Inspired by *Webb's Atlas of the Stars* (H. B. Webb, 1944), which included ninth magnitude objects but only covered the sky to −23° declination, and *Sky Atlas 2000.0* (Cambridge University Press, 1981), this work is a combination of computer plotting and inking, labeling, and illustration by hand.

The most comprehensive general purpose sky atlas ever published, *Uranometria 2000.0* is based on stellar data contained in the standard *Bonner Durchmusterung* (*BD*), its southern extension (*SBD*), and the *Cordova Durchmusterung* (*CoD*), and nonstellar data from the *Revised New General Catalogue* (*RNGC*) and the *Index Catalogue* (*IC*).

Certain to become *the* star atlas of the late twentieth and early to mid-twenty-first centuries, this fine work is not only very complete and easy to use, it is physically a very manageable size (9 by 12 inches), making it very handy for amateur field work. In addition to the 259 sky charts, volume 1 contains an introduction on how to use the atlas, and a lengthy history of uranography, the making of sky maps and atlases.

Aimed at the serious amateur and certain professional astronomers, *Uranometria 2000.0* would be an appropriate addition to both public and academic library reference shelves. Volume 2, planned for fall 1988, covers the Southern sky. [R: LJ, 15 Feb 88, pp. 161-62]

Robert A. Seal

1635.   Tully, R. Brent. **Nearby Galaxies Catalog.** New York, Cambridge University Press, 1988. 214p. bibliog. $49.50. LC 87-21044. ISBN 0-521-35299-1.

This companion volume to the *Nearby Galaxies Atlas* (Cambridge University Press, 1987) presents a variety of numerical data on 2,367 galaxies "with systematic velocities less than 3000 kilometers a second." The work is divided into three tables: a catalog of galaxies within forty megaparsecs, a reordering of the catalog by group affiliations, and the affiliation of rich clusters in supercluster complexes.

Table 1, the largest portion of the volume, has a detailed, six-page introduction describing each of the catalog's data elements: galaxy name, various coordinates, morphological type, local density, group affiliation, diameter, magnitudes, velocities, distance, luminosity, and others. Entries are presented, like many similar works, in order of ascending right ascension. Useful to both professional astronomers and serious amateurs, the book is appropriate for university, observatory, and certain other special libraries.   Robert A. Seal

CHEMISTRY

Bibliographies

1636. Ball, David W., and others. **A Bibliography of Matrix Isolation Spectroscopy: 1954-1985.** Houston, Tex., Rice University Press; distr., College Station, Tex., Texas A & M University Press, 1988. 643p. index. $90.00. LC 87-60695. ISBN 0-89263-266-6.

This book is a bibliography, purportedly comprehensive, of published references dealing with matrix isolation spectroscopy from its beginnings (1950s) to 1985. It first lists the "references," and then provides author, keyword, and formula indexes to these references. This otherwise useful work is marred by some rather serious errors.

The keyword index jumps from *munonium* to *nearest neighbors*, then resumes with *methylsubstuted* (sic) through *molecular*, hence to *nonradiative*, and in the process thoroughly confuses the user. There are other serious problems with the keyword index. It is unclear, for instance, why several pages are devoted to the index term *spectroscopy, infrared* when most of the references involve this term and it is scarcely a limiting factor.

When trying to use the formula index, one notes that the typefaces were not well chosen: the lowercase "l" as in "Cl" looks the same as the capital "I," the symbol for iodine. This is a potential source of confusion, especially since the authors have followed the widely used Hill system of ordering formulas, which results in arrangements which are perhaps less familiar to the librarian.

In checking for completeness, it was noted that the authors omitted at least one of their own papers. Citations generally seem to be a problem, especially when to other than standard journals; a NATO conference, for instance, is cited thus: NATO ADV.STUDY INST.SER. SER.C C76, 551 (1981) – no indication of publisher, name of conference, where held, etc. Timeliness is also a problem: one can but wonder why a bibliography with a 1988 imprint date covers only through 1985, especially since it is computer produced.

In short, the volume could have greatly benefited from some casual proofreading, as well as adherence to recognized standards for bibliographical citations.

Despite these deficiencies, in view of the prominence in the field of several of the editors

as well as the convenience of having these references neatly packaged, this volume will probably be a required purchase for libraries supporting strong chemistry programs, especially when those programs have substantial research components. The user will be well advised, however, to supplement this coverage with thorough online database searches.

Edwin D. Posey

Dictionaries and Encyclopedias

1637. Ash, Michael, and Irene Ash, comps. **Encyclopedia of Plastics, Polymers, and Resins. Volume IV.** New York, Chemical Publishing, 1988. 410p. $85.00. ISBN 0-8206-0325-2.

This hardbound, comprehensive compilation of over seven hundred plastics, polymers, and resins developed in the past five years is the updating supplement of the 1983 three-volume encyclopedia. Chemicals are listed in alphabetical order, followed by the company that developed them. Entries for each product contain a wealth of information. First a chemical description of the product is given, then its substance category and applications. Its form (e.g., pellet or powder) and molecular size and color are listed. When possible, general properties such as density, mechanical properties such as hardness and mold shrinking, thermal properties such as distortion temperature and flammability, and electrical properties such as dissipation and the chemical's dielectric constant are discussed. Other valuable information such as toxicity and storage handling are included.

Each product is referenced as to the source of the information. Running heads are provided for easy use. Included are a list of contributors and an index of abbreviations.

Andreas E. Mueller

1638. **Compendium of Chemical Terminology: IUPAC Recommendations.** Victor Gold and others, comps. Palo Alto, Calif., Blackwell Scientific Publications, 1987. 456p. illus. $69.60; $48.45pa. LC 86-32047. ISBN 0-632-01765-1; 0-632-01767-8pa.

There is no shortage of good chemical dictionaries. Most of these dictionaries are published by the standard scientific publishers. The *Compendium of Chemical Terminology* differs from the rest in that it is a publication of the International Union of Pure and Applied Chemistry. With this in mind, the editors set out to produce what is intended to be the authoritative dictionary of chemistry, based on strict IUPAC terminology.

The *Compendium* contains roughly thirty-one hundred entries. Compare this to the eleventh edition of *Hawley's Condensed Chemical Dictionary* (see *ARBA* 88, entry 1739). This popular chemical dictionary contains approximately sixteen thousand entries, more than four times the number of entries in the *Compendium*. The entries in the *Compendium* are taken from the five main areas of chemistry—analytical, inorganic, macromolecular, organic and physical chemistry. Not included are terms used specifically in applied or clinical chemistry. It is hoped that these and other areas will be included in future editions.

All definitions cite recommendations made by IUPAC commissions that have been published in various IUPAC publications dating from 1972 to 1985. Specifically, these include the IUPAC journal, *Pure and Applied Chemistry*, and the IUPAC rule books. The citation style used throughout the text is vague. The rule books are cited by their color (e.g., B.B., for Blue Book, the *IUPAC Nomenclature of Organic Chemistry*; or O.B., for Orange Book, the *IUPAC Compendium of Analytical Nomenclature*). The references to *Pure and Applied Chemistry* provide the user with year, volume and page. A bibliography with complete citations is provided. There are a few additional references to the chemical literature ranging from 1851 to 1980.

The definitions are brief, up to 150 words in length. Where appropriate, the entries are illustrated with graphs or equations. The quality of the definitions varies. For example, the definition for *radiation*, "A term embracing electromagnetic waves as well as fast moving particles," (p. 327) is poor. On the other hand, the definition for *isomorphous structures* is extensive, providing the user with seven illustrations and cross-references to three other entries. Even though dictionaries do not generally have indexes, one would be helpful with this work. Definitions for multi-word phrases are provided here, a big plus, but the cross-referencing is not always adequate.

The *Compendium* will not replace any of the current chemical dictionaries on reference shelves, but it is a necessary addition to any chemistry library. Future editions should provide expanded coverage of other areas of chemistry.

Kerry L. Kresse

1639. **Comprehensive Coordination Chemistry: The Synthesis, Reactions, Properties & Applications of Coordination Compounds.** Geoffrey Wilkinson, ed.-in-chief. Elmsford, N.Y., Pergamon Press, 1987. 7v. illus. index. $2,450.00/set. LC 86-12319. ISBN 0-08-026232-5.

A companion set to the highly regarded *Comprehensive Organometallic Chemistry* by the same publisher, this comprehensive, authoritative, state-of-the-art overview of coordination chemistry differentiates its coverage from the latter work by making an arbitrary distinction between those compounds with metal-carbon bonds that are considered organometallic and those considered coordination compounds. Deemed outside the scope of this volume are those compounds in which the number of metal-carbon bonds is at least half the coordination number of the metal and are thus classified as organometallic.

This seven-volume set consists of six text volumes comprising over sixty-five hundred pages and a cumulative subject and formula index volume. Each text volume has its own subject and formula index for rapid, easy access to subject matter. Though each volume carries separate paging, the 105 signed articles are grouped into sixty-seven chapters and subchapters numbered sequentially throughout the set, are written by 144 distinguished chemists actively engaged in research in eighteen countries. Clear, readable, critical presentation of information on the properties, uses, reactions, and methods of synthesis of coordination compounds as well as various spectroscopic techniques is enhanced by the extensive use of structural formulas, reaction schemes, figures, and tables. Numerous literature references accompany chapters, making them not only overviews of the subject but comprehensive literature reviews as well.

Volume 1 is divided into three sections. The first section covers history and nomenclature, coordination numbers and geometries, cages and clusters, isomerism, and ligand field theory. Section 2 reviews various reaction mechanisms, and section 3 covers complexes in aqueous and nonaqueous media. Volume 2 covers ligands, the chemical groups attached to metals. The arrangement of chapters is based on the nature of the binding atom.

Volumes 3, 4, and 5 parallel the arrangement of volume 2, classifying coordination compounds according to the Periodic Table. Complexes of specific ligands for each metal are discussed in the same sequence as is the discussion of parent ligands. Volume 3 describes main group and early transition elements, volume 4 middle transition elements, and volume 5 late transition elements. The greatest concentration of information is on chromium, molybdenum, ruthenium, cobalt, nickel, and copper. Unfortunately the publisher felt constrained to proceed with publication of these volumes despite the late receipt of manuscripts for three chapters, resulting in their inclusion at the end of the respective volumes rather than in their numbered sequence. In addition, two chapters were omitted entirely, with a note from the publisher to the effect that they would appear at some future time in the journal *Polyhedron*. Subsequently, purchasers of the set were notified that these missing chapters will be included in a supplement to be supplied free of charge. In these days of limited library budgets and inflated prices for library materials it is to be hoped that this cavalier attitude toward the publication of a major reference tool will not be emulated either by this or other publishers. As it is, because the original binding of these volumes is not sturdy enough to withstand the heavy reference use to which they will be subjected, libraries must expect to use part of already over-burdened bindery budgets for this purpose.

Types of applications in volume 6 range from electrochemical, photographic, and those pertaining to dyes and pigments, to extractive metallurgy. A section of chapters on uses of coordination compounds in synthesis and catalysis covers stoichiometric reactions, catalytic activation of small molecules, oxidation, Lewis acid catalysis, and the decomposition of water. Biological and medical aspects of applications include chapters on coordination compounds in biology, on applications in the nuclear fuel cycle, and on radiopharmacy. Of note here is the characteristic of all chapters for inclusion of critical evaluation of the topic under discussion together with indications of gaps in current knowledge.

Volume 7 contains three indexes: review articles and specialist texts, cumulative subject, and cumulative formula. The first of these is a novel index based on an unclassified, numbered title list of 1,707 reviews taken from thirty-seven primary and review serials. Classified subject indexing is provided by twenty-two access tables, each subdivided into specific topics and roughly aligned with the text of the preceding volumes of the set. The index is intended to be a comprehensive guide to the review literature of coordination chemistry for the years 1945 to early 1986. The cumulative subject index contains over twenty-five thousand entries to information found in the preceding text volumes on coordination complexes by type and specific complex, on general and specific organic compounds, on types of reactions, spectroscopic techniques, and various kinds of applications of coordination compounds. Common names as well as systematic names are used. Over twenty-eight thousand compounds found in the text, equations, reaction schemes, figures, and tables of the preceding six volumes are indexed in the

cumulative formula index. General classes of compounds are not indexed here, only specific compounds when they are of significance to the subject context. Arrangement of formulas is alphabetical according to a modified Hill System in which element symbols for metals appear first, followed by the symbols for carbon and hydrogen, and then any remaining element symbols in alphabetical order. Compounds with two or more metals are listed alphabetically under each metal symbol. Common ligand abbreviations used in the text are also used in the formula index. Under each entry are the structural formula for the compound and the volume and page references. In general there are very few typographical errors in this massive compilation of data on coordination chemistry, and though coverage of various areas varies by cut-off date, the overview is both comprehensive and quite up-to-date. [R: Choice, June 88, pp. 1530, 1532]   Virginia E. Yagello

1640. Daintith, John, ed. **The Facts on File Dictionary of Chemistry.** rev. ed. New York, Facts on File, 1988. 249p. illus. $19.95. LC 88-045477. ISBN 0-8160-1866-9.

The new edition of this dictionary adds approximately three hundred terms to the twenty-two hundred found in the first edition of the same name (see *ARBA* 82, entry 1436). The book is aimed at the high school and college student as well as laypersons with a need to identify basic chemical terms and reactions, new techniques and applications, and environmental issues such as acid rain and heavy metal pollution.

The number of entries does not come close to those found in comparable volumes, of which there are several, but the choice of terms and level of definitions come closer to the needs and understanding of the target market. Definitions are nontechnical and of sufficient length to provide a clear understanding of the material. Some forty-five line drawings illustrating chemical reactions and extensive cross-references add to the volume's utility. Tables at the back of the book include chemical elements with their symbols, proton numbers, and atomic weights; a brief list of physical constants; a list of elementary particles and related information; the Greek alphabet; and the periodic table. Not found in the dictionary are biographical data, information on major associations, Chemical Abstracts Service registry numbers, and systematic nomenclature.

While somewhat limited in scope, public and school libraries will welcome this volume for their collections.

Andrew G. Torok

1641. Edmundson, R. S., ed. and comp. **Dictionary of Organophosphorus Compounds.** New York, Routledge, Chapman & Hall, 1988. 1347p. illus. index. $725.00. LC 87-23936. ISBN 0-412-25790-4.

This is one of the latest entries in the distinguished series of organic chemistry reference works published by Chapman and Hall. Organophosphorus compounds are found in many places. They are used as crop protection agents and growth regulators, flame retardants, corrosion inhibitors, emulsifiers, and even as antistatic agents. They have myriad applications in pharmacology, chemotherapy, biochemistry, and industry. Many organophosphorus compounds are also highly toxic. The editors point out (in an all-but-impossible to miss fuchsia colored insert) that although toxic and hazardous properties are included in the text, the lack of a listing there does not mean that the compound is not dangerous. As society becomes more aware of the dangerous properties of many chemical compounds, this type of information cannot be repeated too often.

The introduction to the text provides the reader with a brief overview of the nomenclature of organophosphorus compounds. It is the nature of the structure of these compounds that makes them so useful. The nomenclature used within this work is IUPAC-based, and is also favored by Chemical Abstracts. The consistent use of this nomenclature throughout the chemical literature cannot be overlooked. In addition, a four-hundred-entry bibliography provides a comprehensive, but not exhaustive, list of additional books and reviews published from 1960 to 1987.

In much the same format as the other works in the series, five thousand organophosphorus compounds are listed alphabetically by name. According to the editors, only 10 percent of these entries appeared in the fifth edition of the *Dictionary of Organic Compounds* (Chapman & Hall, 1982). Derivatives, including esters, oxides, salts, etc., are added for many compounds, bringing the total number of compounds listed here to twenty thousand. Provided for the main entries, and many of the accompanying listings, are the Chemical Abstracts name, any alternative names, CAS registry number, molecular formula, structure, and some physical properties. A small number of references, including articles published through 1987 and those appearing in Soviet periodicals, are provided for most compounds. For all the Soviet references the editors have provided page numbers for the original Russian and the corresponding English translations, a true favor to researchers and librarians alike.

The work is well indexed, providing access by name, molecular formula, CAS registry number, type of compound (e.g., phosphenes), and a structural (ring) index.

The quality found in other Chapman and Hall reference works is evident here. Although the price is high, the information contained will be used by many researchers in many fields. It is highly recommended for academic and special libraries. For those who find the price of the *Dictionary of Organophosphorus Compounds* too high, the information is available on the HEILBRON database on DIALOG.

Kerry L. Kresse

1642. **Ullmann's Encyclopedia of Industrial Chemistry.** 5th ed. Wolfgang Gerhartz and others, eds. New York, VCH, 1987. 3v. illus. $180.00/vol. LC 84-25-829. ISBN 0-89573-158-4 (v.A8); 0-89573-159-2 (v.A9); 0-89573-160-6 (v.A10).

The three latest volumes of *Ullmann's* bring this new English-language version to about one-quarter of the way to completion (see *ARBA* 87, entries 1740 and 1741). With the publication of volume 1A in 1985, the publisher announced a production rate of three to four volumes each year until all thirty-eight are completed. Thus far, the timetable appears to be on schedule.

The subject of each volume illustrates well the coverage one will find in the individual volumes. Volume A8, *Coronary Therapeutics to Display Technology*, also includes substantial treatment of such topics as dental materials, detergents, etc. Volume 9A, *Dithiocarbamic Acid to Ethanol*, also includes extensive treatments of dyes, electrochemistry, and enzymes. Volume 10A, *Ethanolamines to Fibers*, includes substantial information on fertilizers and fats.

As with the other volumes of the set, each contains a list of contents, a list of cross-references, a table of symbols and units, conversion factors, prefixes, abbreviations, and the periodic table of the elements. The articles are lavishly illustrated with charts, diagrams, and tables and are thoroughly referenced.

It is anticipated that subsequent volumes of this set will be of the same high level of quality and authority. Clearly, it stands as one of the preeminent encyclopedias in the field of science and technology and should be acquired by any library that claims to offer comprehensive reference collections in chemistry and technology. The English-language version enhances its desirability. [R: Choice, Dec 88, pp. 632-33]

Cynthia A. Steinke

Handbooks

1643. Ash, Michael, and Irene Ash, comp. **What Every Chemical Technologist Wants to Know about.... Volume I: Emulsifiers and Wetting Agents.** New York, Chemical Publishing, 1988. 400p. $60.00. ISBN 0-8206-0326-0.

This is the first of six volumes in a new series intended to provide users with the information needed to determine which trademarked product is most appropriate for a particular application. The other volumes in the series are to cover dispersants, solvents, and solubilizers; plasticizers, stabilizers, and thickeners; conditioners, emollients, and lubricants; resins; and polymers and plastics. Volume 1 on emulsifiers and wetting agents contains 346 pages on 150 chemical products alphabetized by their most common generic chemical names, and some 50 pages of indexing. Entry information, organized under boldface subheadings, includes synonyms, structural and/or empirical formulas and Chemical Abstracts Service registry numbers when available, tradename equivalents followed by manufacturer's name in brackets, category of product, applications, properties, toxicity/handling, storage/handling, and standard packaging. Detail is specific to tradename products. The amount of information in entries varies according to the substance and the amount of information supplied by manufacturers. Applications range from farm products and cosmetics and toiletries to food, industrial, and pharmaceutical applications. Properties range from form, color, odor, and taste to solubility, flash point, acid number, etc., varying by product. There are three indexes: tradename products and generic equivalents, generic chemical synonyms and cross-references, and tradename product manufacturers. The first provides a quick cross-reference from tradename to generic main entries. The second index refers the user from synonym to the generic main entries in this and future volumes in the series. The third is an alphabetical listing of 154 chemical manufacturers from twenty countries worldwide, giving full address. Emphasis is on U.S. manufacturers (ninety-nine). A useful two-page list of abbreviations precedes the text. The binding is adequate and the format affords rapid access to the contents.

Virginia E. Yagello

1644. **Canadian Chemical Register 1986/1987.** Ottawa, Regional Industrial Expansion/Canadian Government Publishing Centre, 1987. 2v. price not reported/set. ISBN 0-662-15381-2.

The *Canadian Chemical Register* presents a definitive source for chemicals manufactured in Canada. The Canadian government published the *Register* in cooperation with the Canadian Chemical Producer's Association. The first volume includes an alphabetical listing of manufacturers, chemicals manufactured plus its status, and plant site. The second volume has chemicals listed alphabetically along with manufacturer and location. To be included in the work, a product must have one or more reaction steps, or a chemical separation process or both.

The *Register* is similar to the annual *Chemical Week Buyers' Guide* (McGraw-Hill) and the annual *OPD Chemical Buyers Directory* (Schnell) for the United States, but additional information appears in the *Canadian Chemical Register*. For instance, the data revision date—a reassuring gauge of currency—was published along with information that each company was contacted. Data should therefore be more current and complete than in some directories.

All chemicals listed are for sale unless status is given as captive or intermediate. Plant site of actual manufacture is included for each chemical. Address, telephone and telex are for company headquarters.

The review copy was received in late 1988 as a reprint, so obviously the *Register* found an appreciative audience. This valuable source for chemicals and the Canadian companies that manufacture them should be promptly updated, and the computer-produced format should help.

The *Register* serves as a source for chemicals in Canada and will be an excellent source within that country. Since free trade has opened between Canada and the United States, the *Register* should also be useful in the United States. The up-to-date survey, with dates noted, builds confidence in the information. This is a very good reference addition, published in English and also in French. [R: CLJ, Oct 88, p. 338]

Marilyn Stark

1645. Collins, P. M., ed. **Carbohydrates.** New York, Routledge, Chapman & Hall, 1987. 719p. illus. index. $195.00. LC 86-30995. ISBN 0-412-26960-0.

Carbohydrates is the latest volume in the Chapman and Hall Chemistry Sourcebook series. It is the second volume taken from the highly respected *Dictionary of Organic Compounds* (*DOC*), fifth edition (Chapman & Hall, 1982) and annual supplements. There are ten other volumes in the series based on the equally authoritative *Dictionary of Organometallic Compounds* (Chapman & Hall, 1984). Collection librarians, faced with straitened budgets, need to be cognizant of this new generation of publisher spinoffs made possible by electronic publishing, especially when the publisher omits mention of the derivative nature of the publication in the title page information and often from book ads, and library catalogers routinely omit the optional MARC 520 field, which conveys this information, from their cataloging.

This volume, obviously, has the same format and arrangement as its parent *DOC* volumes. Intended mainly for the synthetic carbohydrate chemist, it covers extensively monosaccharides and disaccharides and their derivatives, important oligo- and polysaccharides, and the most frequently occurring plant glycosides or those with unusual structures. It contains 2,242 alphabetically arranged main entries, which also include compound derivatives, and the usual name, molecular formula, and Chemical Abstracts Service registry number indexes. However, for introductory information regarding abbreviations, kinds of data in entries, and techniques used to depict compounds, the reader is referred to the introduction to the fifth edition of the *DOC*. There is also a computer-generated type of compound index which provides immediate access by structure to all entry compounds according to 102 structure types. Thus, at a glance, the chemist can locate, for example, all ribo-pentoses, 3-deoxy sugars, etc., covered in the text.

The chief value of this compilation lies in its convenience of access to a specific subset of compounds contained in the fifth edition *DOC* and annual supplements, plus some new compounds, additional synonyms, and derivative formulas which presumably will be incorporated in future supplements and/or a new edition of the *DOC*. A spot check comparison of a number of main entries did reveal some corrections and refinement of data as well as the addition of more recent literature references.

Virginia E. Yagello

1646. Hunting, Anthony L. L. **Encyclopedia of Conditioning Rinse Ingredients.** Cranford, N.J., Micelle Press, 1987. 492p. illus. bibliog. $89.00pa. LC 87-61071. ISBN 0-9608752-1-2.

Ever wonder what glyceryl stearate is, and exactly what it is doing in your creme rinse? This encyclopedia, a companion volume to the author's *Encyclopedia of Shampoo Ingredients* (see *ARBA* 85, entry 1486), provides a thorough treatment of more than 450 ingredients found in 250 commercially available conditioning rinses. The author begins with brief introductory remarks regarding the preparation and marketing of conditioning rinses. Following this are the detailed entries for the various ingredients. Included in the descriptions are the names associated with each ingredient, a Chemical Abstracts Service (CAS) registry number (if appropri-

ate), the chemical formula, physical data, safety information, the reason for use, cross-references to related compounds, suppliers, and a section of general comments that varies in length. These general comments are one of the most helpful parts of the book, describing everything from the chemistry of a compound to patent information, health aspects to FTC regulations.

Most of the information published here has been supplied by the manufacturers and suppliers. However, footnotes from the text (numbering more than five hundred) are compiled at the end of the book, proof that Hunting has done his homework. Appendices provide a list of suppliers and their addresses, marketing information, a handy chart tabulating ingredients and their properties and applications, and a ninety-four-item bibliography for additional reading.

This excellent guide is best suited for collections not only in cosmetic chemistry and cosmetology, but also dermatology. Large public libraries and academic libraries with good budgets may wish to consider this, too, because it can answer many of those questions regarding ingredients that the chemical dictionaries cannot. [R: Choice, June 88, p. 1536]

Kerry L. Kresse

1647. Maizell, Robert E. **How to Find Chemical Information: A Guide for Practicing Chemists, Educators, and Students.** 2d ed. New York, John Wiley, 1987. 402p. illus. index. $44.95. LC 86-15687. ISBN 0-471-86767-5.

This excellent second edition of a standard work has expanded and updated coverage since the 1979 edition. New chapters cover Chemical Abstracts use, other abstracts and indexes, U.S. government document information centers and sources, analytical chemistry sources, and trends. Reference materials are interpreted with tips on how to use them and what each covers. Cautions in using data, such as handbook data may not have been critically reviewed, are also included, a real benefit to the user. Data sources are evaluated and evaluation methods explained. The author says the guide is based on firsthand experience, and it shows extensive experience.

Classical tools and noteworthy new major sources are the focus, with strategies to enable constant updating. Chemistry is emphasized and chemical engineering is only lightly covered. A detailed table of contents provides easy access, in addition to extensive subject and name indexes. Unfortunately the review copy was missing pages 173-204, so chemical structure searching, full-text online searching, and reviews could not be checked.

The in-depth analysis of reference sources is thoughtful and useful. Even for those who constantly work with chemical information, nuggets of previously unknown data abound. Useful for practicing chemists, general libraries, and those with chemistry specialties.

Marilyn Stark

1648. Norback, Craig T., and Judith C. Norback, eds. **Hazardous Chemicals on File.** New York, Facts on File, 1988. 3v. index. $250.00/set looseleaf with binder. LC 86-32798. ISBN 0-8160-1353-5.

This is a guide for the general public seeking up-to-date, authoritative information on the characteristics of, and on how to protect oneself against, hazardous chemicals in the workplace. There are 327 main entries for the most common toxic chemical substances or groups of related substances, printed on sturdy sheets of 8½-by-11-inch buff-colored cover stock paper in three 3-ring binders. Entry names are commonly used chemical names, systematic names, and trade names; entries are arranged in alphabetical order, omitting prefixes and modifiers except for Greek letters, which are spelled out. Typical entries, in addition to molecular formulas, synonyms, appearance and odor, contain the following types of hazard information: permissible exposure limit, monitoring and measurement procedures, health hazards resulting from various kinds of exposure, recommended medical and emergency first-aid procedures to meet such exposure, methods for personal protection, leak and spill procedures, and waste disposal methods. The double-column outline format and use of varisized boldface headings facilitate ready access to specific hazard information. Technical terminology is avoided and abbreviations are explained at point of use.

Main entry information, which makes up the major portion of the set, is preceded and followed by two pamphlets on regular text paper. The first contains an alphabetical table of contents of main entry names plus an introduction giving background information on the services and regulations of the Occupational Safety and Health Administration (OSHA), its research arm, the National Institute for Occupational Safety and Health (NIOSH), and the Environmental Protection Agency (EPA) and associated government information centers and laboratories. There is a list of ten regional, seventy area, and eleven district offices of OSHA with addresses and telephone numbers, and a similar one of the ten EPA regional,

four field component, and three operations offices. The second pamphlet is an alphabetical substance index which includes synonyms; no use is made of cross-references to main entry names. The handbook format enables quick extraction of various portions of text on an "as needed" basis. Unlike far more comprehensive and technical compilations such as the sixth edition of N. Irving Sax's *Dangerous Properties of Industrial Materials* (1984) and even of its abbreviated version, *Hazardous Chemicals Desk Reference* (Van Nostrand Reinhold, 1987) which covers five thousand materials, this typical Facts on File publication, designed for ready-reference use by the general reader, is far more limited in coverage. [R: BR, Sept/Oct 88, pp. 51-52; Choice, Sept 88, p. 86]

Virginia E. Yagello

1649. **Physical Chemistry Source Book.** Sybil P. Parker, ed. New York, McGraw-Hill, 1988. 406p. illus. index. (McGraw-Hill Science Reference Series). $45.00. LC 87-36629. ISBN 0-07-045504-X.

Under the direction of Sybil Parker, editor-in-chief of the excellent reference work *McGraw-Hill Encyclopedia of Science and Technology* (see *ARBA* 88, entry 1448), the publishers are reassembling once again the sixth edition of the encyclopedia, this time into single-subject "source books." The so-called Science Reference Series culls articles and their accompanying illustrations directly from the sixth edition (and, in some cases, the fifth edition) into these source books. The *Physical Chemistry Source Book* contains 130 articles arranged in ten broad chapters covering most topics within physical chemistry.

The editors use the term "article" rather loosely here. While most seem to average three to four pages, the articles range in length from about eleven pages ("Molecular structure and spectra") to forty-one words ("Relative molecular mass"). The writing is clear and concise, one of the most valuable characteristics of McGraw-Hill's many scientific works. The articles are accompanied by a liberal number of good black-and-white illustrations, and for most, a brief bibliography.

The articles themselves are arranged in chapters by broad subject category: chemical thermodynamics, chemical reactions, surface chemistry, transport processes, matter (structure and properties), electrochemistry, electroanalytical chemistry, cells and batteries, optical phenomena, and specialized fields of study. An index provides adequate access to the material.

This volume and the rest of the new series are recommended especially for academic libraries that do not have the main set. The repackaging of material of this sort is also helpful if the new item is allowed to circulate. However, as there is no new material here, the main set will probably do for the libraries that have it. [R: Choice, Dec 88, p. 631]

Kerry L. Kresse

1650. **Spectroscopy Source Book.** Sybil P. Parker, ed. New York, McGraw-Hill, 1988. 288p. illus. index. (McGraw-Hill Science Reference Series). $40.00. LC 87-35254. ISBN 0-07-045505-8.

Most reference librarians are familiar with the *McGraw-Hill Encyclopedia of Science and Technology* (see ARBA 88, entry 1448) as well as the individual, subject-specific encyclopedias (e.g., *McGraw-Hill Encyclopedia of Astronomy*) that are derived from it. In a new effort to repackage this monumental work one more time, the publishers have begun a new series. The *Spectroscopy Source Book* is one of the first volumes in this series.

Taken directly (word for word, illustration for illustration) from the sixth edition of the *Encyclopedia of Science and Technology*, this reference book contains seventy articles that describe various aspects of spectroscopy. The articles are arranged by broad subject category in seven chapters: origin of spectra, instrumentation and techniques, analytical techniques, and the different types of spectroscopy—atomic and molecular, nuclear, microwave, microwave and radio frequency, and mass spectroscopy. The articles are written by experts, and vary in length from one to six pages. The black-and-white illustrations are plentiful, and the text is clear and concise. The index is adequate, with cross-referencing. The table of contents shows only the main headings, and would be more helpful if it listed the articles contained within each chapter. The material is written at an upper undergraduate level.

While repackaging of material published elsewhere can often be helpful to the user, especially if the new version is allowed to circulate, this reference volume is recommended only for those academic libraries that do not own the complete *Encyclopedia of Science and Technology*. However, if you do own the original set but wish to purchase this volume anyway, be aware that there is no new material here. [R: Choice, Dec 88, p. 631]

Kerry L. Kresse

Indexes

1651. **Index of Polymer Trade Names.** Compiled by Fachinformationszentrum Chemie GmbH. New York, VCH, 1987. 456p. $155.00. ISBN 0-89573-659-4.

Trade names of approximately twenty-four thousand polymers, monomers, and substances used in producing or processing polymers are listed alphabetically in this reference work. The publication is oriented toward the printed and online versions of *Chemical Abstracts*, with CAS registry numbers included where available and molecular formulas given as listed in the *Chemical Abstracts Formula Index*. Common names are also included for some polymers. Substances are coded according to type. Coverage is international, and the name of the producer is included if mentioned in the literature. Very few producers are listed, however, and those listed do not have address, or even country, added. When the trade name is found, the only information in most entries is the common name or chemical substance name and the type code. Contact points for more information would be useful.

The thirty-nine entries for various types of Teflon compare favorably with thirty-two in the *Chemical Abstracts Index Guide* (American Chemical Society, 1987). *Trade Names Dictionary* (see ARBA 80, entry 787) lists only three types of Teflon.

The CAS registry numbers are especially useful for online searching in CA File and other online databases keyed to registry numbers. This volume, along with *Merck Index* (Merck, 1983) will provide registry numbers for many chemical substances.

Because of its relatively narrow focus, this index is unlikely to be used by the general public or university undergraduates. Researchers and graduate students, as well as librarians in related scientific disciplines, may find it useful. Trade name information is needed, but this source provides limited added information. A list of company addresses is an extra feature which should be added. In addition, foreign publishing and the weak U.S. dollar result in the $155.00 purchase price, a deterrent to purchase for such a specialized book. Libraries with strong collections in polymers, chemical engineering, and materials science will probably be the major audience for this item.   Marilyn Stark

EARTH AND PLANETARY SCIENCE

General Works

1652. **Earth Science on File.** By David Lambert. New York, Facts on File, 1988. 1v.

(various paging). illus. maps. index. $145.00 looseleaf with binder. LC 88-21322. ISBN 0-8160-1625-9.

This book is intended "as a guide to the Earth and the Universe," as a source of "images" for photocopying, and as a basis for examination-paper illustrations. The book's narrative is limited to a single page foreword. The major content consists of three hundred black-and-white plates printed on heavy stock and an index to the plate locations of over fifteen hundred terms. The plates are organized into seven sections titled, respectively: "Earth and Space," "The Restless Rocks," "Air and Oceans," "Shaping the Surface," "Earth History," "Resources," and "Maps, Tables and Scales." The first six sections cover such topics as astronomy, geological evolution, fossil history, meteorology, oceanography, energy, and the environment. References to many of these topics are made in some form in every section. Outline maps of the continents and various comparison charts (e.g., metric-English measurement units, river lengths, waterfall heights) dominate the final section. Plate legends are minimal and explanations are absent for every plate.

The pages are looseleaf in a buckram ring binder. The inside front cover bears a reproduction certificate authorizing copying of the plates for nonprofit educational or private use. Virtually all plates have line drawings which will reproduce clearly by photocopying. The scientific correctness and completeness of many of the drawings leaves much to be desired. In the plates of section 5.000 ("Earth History"), most of the animals are unskillfully drawn. Many of the earth cross-sections portrayed in section 4.000 ("Shaping the Surface") are lacking in detail and will be useful only for the most elementary explanations.

The claim of being a guide to the Earth and the universe is pretentious. The absence of supporting narrative and details and a phenomenal boldness in artistic interpretations of scientific and physical realities do little to enhance such a bold statement. Many of the plates may have instructional value as teaching and testing aids at college and high school levels, but even these are unlikely to be competitive with the superior photocopy materials being produced by most textbook publishers today. This book is not satisfactory for general library purchase and will probably find its primary users to be junior high school and high school educators who wish simplified illustrative materials for teaching earth science courses.

Edmund D. Keiser, Jr.

1653. Emiliani, Cesare. **The Scientific Companion: Exploring the Physical World with Facts, Figures, and Formulas.** New York, John Wiley, 1988. 287p. illus. maps. bibliog. index. (Wiley Science Editions). $24.95; $14.95pa. LC 87-3010. ISBN 0-471-62483-7; 0-471-62484-5pa.

This unusual book is a cross between a textbook and a reference guide to the physical sciences. Eleven chapters of text outline basic concepts in physics, astronomy, geology, and even a little evolutionary biology. Emiliani introduces these concepts in a generally lucid, if dry, narrative that should be comprehensible to the interested general reader. Many photographs, charts, graphs, formulas, and drawings illustrate the discussion and lend it clarity. The appendices provide tables of physical constants, conversion factors, and the elements, as well as a reasonably detailed subject index.

This guide tackles its hugh scope credibly and will be interesting to browsers, but it does not succeed well as a reference book. First, the narrative style can make quick referral somewhat difficult. Second, the brevity of some explanatory material is confusing; for example, abbreviations heading some columns in the table of constants are not defined. Further, the conversion factor of Celsius to Fahrenheit temperatures is misleadingly incomplete, but labeled as "exact." Third, the list of references for further reading is quite minimal and contains only a few well-known textbooks and popular science materials. Fourth, the author does not always give sufficient weight to alternative scientific theories, such as those on the extinction of the dinosaurs. Finally, Emiliani expresses a positivistic perspective, including both a negative view of religions (pp. xi-xii) and an overly optimistic opinion of our current scientific knowledge ("only the ultimate question ... is still up in the air" [p. xi]), which may seem simplistic or offensive to some readers.

Christopher W. Nolan

Geology

1654. Chronic, Halka. **Roadside Geology of New Mexico.** Missoula, Mont., Mountain Press, 1987. 255p. illus. maps. bibliog. index. $9.95pa. LC 86-21748. ISBN 0-87842-209-9.

1655. Connor, Cathy, and Daniel O'Haire. **Roadside Geology of Alaska.** Missoula, Mont., Mountain Press, 1988. 250p. illus. maps. bibliog. index. (Roadside Geology Series). $12.95pa. LC 88-1651. ISBN 0-87842-213-7.

1656.   Lageson, David, and Darwin Spearing. **Roadside Geology of Wyoming.** Missoula, Mont., Mountain Press, 1988. 271p. illus. maps. bibliog. index. (Roadside Geology Series). $9.95pa. LC 88-1650. ISBN 0-87842-216-1.

It would surprise me if more than one driver in ten thousand ever considers the "scenery" being motored through. For that one driver, though, the *Roadside Geology* books are a boon. There is a fairly standard format: introductory material, sometimes a glossary, maps of several kinds, and, of course, a résumé of the "geology" along the major highways in each state. So far, the volumes comprise the *Roadside Geology of ...* (Alaska, Arizona, Colorado, Montana, Northern California, New York, New Mexico, Oregon, Vermont and New Hampshire, Virginia, Washington, Wyoming, and the Yellowstone country). Volumes for Idaho and Pennsylvania are in the works. All states will eventually be covered. Not every road trip can be described in this kind of book, so those of us who cut between the major highways will have to interpolate. I gave a copy of the Montana volume to a new-to-Montana physician who has taken one course in geology, many years before; he thought it the greatest thing since sliced bread! I suspect that anyone with even a mild interest in "rocks" will welcome each volume in the series. Good stuff for laypersons and itinerant geologists alike. The prices, incidentally, differ from volume to volume.

R. G. Schipf

1657.   **Directory of Geoscience Departments: United States & Canada.** 26th ed. Nicholas H. Claudy, ed. Alexandria, Va., American Geological Institute, 1987. 237p. index. $18.95pa. ISBN 0-913312-90-8; ISSN 0364-7811.

This is the most recent edition of the standard guide to departments of geological science and their faculties in North America. It is of value to students interested in possible institutions for undergraduate or graduate studies in earth sciences, to students seeking a geology field camp, and to laypeople and scientists seeking to locate specialists in the geosciences by geographic area.

The heart of this work is an alphabetical listing of geoscience departments by institutions within states and provinces. Each entry indicates the address and telephone number of the department, the present department head, and a list of faculty, with information on their degrees and area of specialty.

This material is supported by several separate indexes, including alphabetical listings of all institutions and faculty covered and an index grouping faculty by their research/teaching specialties. Short lists catalog institutions offering training in the teaching of earth sciences and institutions possessing library copies of the important reference tool *Bibliography and Index of Geology* (American Geological Institute). Finally, an alphabetical (by state and institution) index to field geology courses is provided, listing the starting date, place, credits offered, and whether outside students are accepted and at what level.

Bruce H. Tiffney

1658.   **The Field Guide to Geology.** By David Lambert and the Diagram Group. New York, Facts on File, 1988. 256p. illus. maps. bibliog. index. $22.95. LC 88-3751. ISBN 0-8160-1697-6.

This is an innovative, clearly descriptive, and enjoyable introductory earth science book. The book consists of hundreds of diagrams and photographs on practically all aspects of geology. The diagrams are exceptionally well executed with just the right blend of composition and text to clearly illustrate each of the subject areas. The formal text portion of each of the chapters is clearly and simply written to provide an easy understanding of the subject matter. An additional highlight of the book is a list of museums and geologic features around the world, to encourage further interest on the reader's part.

This book is highly recommended for any library from about the junior high school level to college. Public libraries should not pass up the opportunity to add this book to their collections.   David R. Fuller

1659.   Finkl, Charles W., Jr., ed. **The Encyclopedia of Field and General Geology.** New York, Van Nostrand Reinhold, 1988. 911p. illus. index. (Encyclopedia of Earth Sciences, Vol. 14). $89.95. LC 87-21618. ISBN 0-442-22499-0.

This is the companion to *The Encyclopedia of Applied Geology*, volume 13, in this series. The preface clearly describes the coverage and scope of the volume as being particularly "geared to the practical geologist." The preface also provides a list of specialized literature on the numerous aspects of field geology; a how-to-use-this-encyclopedia section; and five tables of standard units of measurement, symbols, conversion factors, and definitions. The preface is followed by an alphabetical listing of the main entries and a list of the contributors. The entries in the volume are nicely written and include tables, photographs, charts, and/or diagrams to supplement the text. Each entry ends with a list of cited references and cross-references to other entries in this volume and volume 13. The volume is completed by an author citation index and a very useful subject index.

This is truly a handy and useful book for the field geologist or any professional dealing with field-related earth science activities. As a reference tool for libraries, it is very useful. Its useful features include addresses and listings of the federal and state geological surveys, a table of selected map and chart reference collections around the world, a list of professional geological associations around the world, and geologic correlation charts. The book provides a nice overview of the subject matter and even includes such esoteric items as geomythology (myths, legends, and folklore about geology or geologic features) and geophilately (collecting postage stamps related to or depicting geologic features). The only detraction noted is that some of the type in the reproduced tables is too small or has lost some of its clarity; however, occurrences of this problem are few. The strengths of this book make it a very worthwhile and desirable reference. [R: Choice, Oct 88, p. 288]

David R. Fuller

1660.   **Glossary of Geology.** 3d ed. Robert L. Bates and Julia A. Jackson, eds. Alexandria, Va., American Geological Institute, 1987. 788p. $69.95. LC 87-3579. ISBN 0-913312-89-4.

This third edition of the *Glossary of Geology* contains well over thirty thousand terms (the publisher estimates that there are thirty-seven thousand). There are over one thousand more terms than in the second edition, which was published in 1980. Many definitions, which reflect North American usage, have been updated and over one hundred new references to the geological literature have been added. New in this edition is the division of terms into syllables, and the provision of accent marks for pronunciation when terms first appear. (Pronunciation was indicated for only a very few terms in the second edition.)

As in the second edition, an extensive list of specialists who have reviewed definitions, recommended corrections, etc., is provided, and an introduction explains features such as the type of alphabetization and use of brackets. The book is printed on acid-free paper.

This is the most comprehensive and authoritative dictionary of geology in English. It can serve as a model for dictionaries in other disciplines.

Joseph Hannibal

1661.   Lapidus, Dorothy Farris. **The Facts on File Dictionary of Geology and Geophysics.** New York, Facts on File, 1987. 347p. illus. $24.95. LC 82-7389. ISBN 0-87196-703-0.

This dictionary has more than three thousand entries, ranging in length from one word to more than a page. Coverage includes many terms commonly used in the major subfields of geology, including geophysics. Most terms are at least adequately defined and the accompanying illustrations are often helpful.

However, this book contains a number of errors and misleading statements. For instance, septa of nautiloids are incorrectly claimed to produce very wavy suture lines where they meet the outer shell, and the Cambrian *System* is erroneously defined as the oldest *period* of the Paleozoic. Also, some names of genera are italicized while others are not, and the book is in need of an introduction.

Some entries are very similar to those in Robert L. Bates and Julia A. Jackson's comprehensive and authoritative *Glossary of Geology* (see entry 1660) and Bates and Jackson's *Dictionary of Geological Terms* (see *ARBA 85*, entry 1686). Where there are minor differences in similar entries, the definitions in Bates and Jackson's works are often more precise. Despite the inclusion of illustrations and some more detailed entries, this book does not compare favorably to the *Dictionary of Geological Terms*, which has more entries and is similar in scope and intended audience. [R: Choice, June 88, p. 1538; LAR, 14 Oct 88, p. 609; RQ, Spring 88, p. 426; SBF, Sept/Oct 88, pp. 23-24]

Joseph Hannibal

1662.   Matthews, Rupert O. **The Atlas of Natural Wonders.** New York, Facts on File, 1988. 240p. illus. (part col.). maps. bibliog. index. $35.00. LC 88-16387. ISBN 0-8160-1993-2.

Fifty-two spectacular natural localities around the world, such as the Grand Canyon, the Congo Basin, the Dead Sea, New Zealand's Milford Sound, and England's Cheddar Gorge, are described in the main portion of this book. For each location there are a large page-and-a-half color photograph, a map showing the location of the site, and several additional illustrations. The accompanying text describes each locality in nontechnical terms, often elaborating on some aspect of the site or also discussing nearby features. The localities are arranged by longitude. The book also contains a short glossary, sections briefly describing forty-four additional localities and sixty-three national parks, a bibliography, and an index. The book is generally accurate, although a few geological terms could have been used with more care (tuff at one locality, for instance, is erroneously referred to as tufa).

This interesting and attractive book belongs to the coffee table genre. It also has some, albeit limited, value as a reference work. However, *Reader's Digest Natural Wonders of the World* (see *ARBA* 82, entry 1524) covers most of the main sites in this book as well as many additional localities, although with less detail on each locality; has a handier alphabetical arrangement; and has greater overall value as a reference work. [R: WLB, Nov 88, p. 121]

Joseph Hannibal

1663. **McGraw-Hill Encyclopedia of the Geological Sciences.** 2d ed. Sybil P. Parker, ed. New York, McGraw-Hill, 1988. 722p. illus. maps. index. $85.00. LC 87-35357. ISBN 0-07-045500-7.

A large number of the approximately five hundred articles in this second edition (see *ARBA* 79, entry 1418 for a review of the first edition) are revised or rewritten. The articles, covering topics in most major areas of geology, were selected from the well-received sixth edition of the *McGraw-Hill Encyclopedia of Science and Technology* (see *ARBA* 88, entry 1448). They are written and signed by specialists, and are intended for both professionals and nonspecialists. Overall, the text and accompanying illustrations (many new) are very good.

The extensive table of mineral species and a number of articles on paleontological topics included in the previous edition are not included in this edition. The omission of the paleontological articles is distressing, as there is much interest in this area. Also, there are some other, minor problems with the book, including scattered errors and inconsistencies (for instance, the Mississippian Period is once stated to be included within the Pennsylvanian Period; geologic time scales on pages 230 and 235 do not agree on many dates). Still, this is a very useful work, although not needed by those who already own the sixth edition of the *McGraw-Hill Encyclopedia of Science and Technology.* [R: RBB, 1 Oct 88, pp. 242-43]   Joseph Hannibal

1664. Rassam, G. N., J. Gravesteijn, and R. Potenza, eds. **Multilingual Thesaurus of Geosciences.** Elmsford, N.Y., Pergamon Press, 1988. 516p. bibliog. index. $120.00. LC 86-25353. ISBN 0-08-036431-4.

This thesaurus is a truly remarkable and useful tool, the result of fourteen years of international effort and cooperation. The primary goal of the publication is to better enable geoscience researchers to access international databases by providing geologic equivalents to approximately five thousand terms in six languages. The goal of the book has been achieved, and it is a credit to all of the participants involved.

The thesaurus is divided into four major parts. The first is the introduction, which clearly explains the history and rationale of the book, the methodology used, and its organization. The introduction is reproduced in each of the six languages (English, French, German, Russian, Spanish, and Italian).

The second section is the main list. This section is arranged in a spreadsheet format with each term listed in English at the left. The terms are arranged alphabetically and sequentially numbered. The number assigned is unique to each term and is used throughout the book and the indexes. The term is also assigned one of thirty-six "field of study codes" to assist in the description of the term's usage. Each term is then followed by six columns containing the equivalent term or phrase in each of the six languages and is printed in combinations of upper- and/or lowercase letters to indicate if the equivalent is a descriptor, nondescriptor, or "use for" expression of the term.

The third section of the book is the linguistic indexes. These indexes, like the introduction, are printed in each of the six languages. The indexes are alphabetically arranged and the words in the indexes are followed by the unique reference number of the term being described in the main list.

The final section is the field index. This section is only printed in English and is an alphabetically arranged listing of the field of study codes and the individual terms assigned to them in the book. Each of the terms is followed by its unique reference number.

This work is undoubtedly the first edition of a continuing effort. This is a necessary reference book for anyone or any institution involved in online searching in the geosciences and related fields. It is also a useful tool for geoscience research, regardless of the scientist's national language. [R: Choice, Sept 88, pp. 84, 86]   David R. Fuller

1665. Sarjeant, William A. S. **Geologists and the History of Geology: An International Bibliography from the Origins to 1978. Supplement 1979-1984 and Additions.** Melbourne, Fla., Krieger, 1987. 2v. index. $162.50/set. LC 87-3999. ISBN 0-89874-939-5.

This is the first five-year supplement to the previous bibliographic work. The two volumes also provide information on people and events previously unavailable to the author. Volume 1 is the bibliography, divided into general introduction; general works; historical accounts of societies, museums, and other institutions concerned with geology; histories of the petroleum industry; accounts of events significant in the history of geology; the individual geologists; and prospectors, diviners, and mining engineers. Volume 2 is composed of a number of indexes, including geologists by nationality and country; geologists by specialty; authors, editors, and translators; and women geologists.

The author very clearly describes the nature and selection criteria for the material in each of the sections in this set. This supplement has addressed and corrected some of the indexing shortfalls of the original volumes and has made the total work more functional. The overall intent of this reference as described in the introduction has been accomplished. The entire project is a remarkable undertaking and provides a very useful tool, not only to history of science students, but to anyone interested in the development of the field of geology. This is a necessary purchase for any person or institution possessing the original work and should be a motivating factor for considering the acquisition of both the original volume and this supplement.   David R. Fuller

1666.   Seyfert, Carl K., ed. **The Encyclopedia of Structural Geology and Plate Tectonics.** New York, Van Nostrand Reinhold, 1987. 876p. illus. maps. index. (Encyclopedia of Earth Sciences, Vol. 10). $89.95. LC 87-18879. ISBN 0-442-28125-0.

This encyclopedia contains more than one hundred alphabetically arranged entries, written by specialists, dealing with classical concepts of structural geology, such as strain, cleavage, and folding, as well as topics related to the more recent concept of plate tectonics, such as seafloor spreading and paleoclimatological evidence for continental drift. It is similar in format to other volumes in the same series, including *The Encyclopedia of Paleontology* (see *ARBA* 81, entry 1409) and *The Encyclopedia of Applied Geology* (see *ARBA* 85, entry 1687). Articles are signed and are usually followed by references and cross-references. Cross-references are also listed alphabetically in the body of the book. In addition there are subject and author citation indexes. The text is augmented by numerous figures, including diagrams, maps, and photographs.

The book does have some minor drawbacks. There is substantial overlap between some entries, the subject index could have been more comprehensive, some illustrations are poorly reproduced, and some newer references are not included.

Nonetheless, this is a solid, authoritative reference for use by geologists and college-level students of geology. [R: Choice, Mar 88, p. 1062]   Joseph Hannibal

1667.   Thompson, Susan J. **A Chronology of Geological Thinking from Antiquity to 1899.** Metuchen, N.J., Scarecrow, 1988. 320p. index. $29.50. LC 88-1493. ISBN 0-8108-2121-4.

This fascinating book is basically an annotated bibliography of geologic thought. The entries are arranged in chronological order, as documented by the date of first publication. The author and title of the first publication of the thought or concept precede the annotation. A source code follows each annotation. The source code refers to a list of sources and their abbreviations found at the back of this book. In addition to the list of sources, there are a bibliography of sources cited and an author index for easy reference. The chronological approach of this book provides a different outlook on the development of geologic thought. This reference is recommended particularly for geologic and history of science collections and academic courses. [R: WLB, Dec 88, p. 115]
David R. Fuller

Mineralogy

1668.   Read, P. G. **Dictionary of Gemmology.** 2d ed. Stoneham, Mass., Butterworths, 1988. 266p. illus. $49.95. ISBN 0-408-02925-0.

The stated intent of this dictionary was to produce concise and comprehensive descriptions of gems, scientific terms, and techniques as they apply to gemology in a single volume. The author has succeeded in his efforts. The dictionary entries are concisely and yet clearly written. Photographs and diagrams are nicely composed and reproduced to more fully illustrate instruments, characteristics, and techniques described in the text. The appendices at the end of the dictionary include balance systems, color and clarity grading standards for polished diamonds, sorting standards for rough gem diamonds, dispersion, units of measurement, tables of elements, table of fluorescence of principal gemstones, and constant characteristics of principal gemstones. Recommended as a good single-volume reference on gemstones, both at student and professional levels.
David R. Fuller

Paleontology

1669.   Dixon, Dougal, and others. **The Macmillan Illustrated Encyclopedia of Dinosaurs and Prehistoric Animals: A Visual Who's Who of Prehistoric Life.** New York, Macmillan, 1988. 312p. illus. (part col.). bibliog. index. $39.95. LC 88-1800. ISBN 0-02-580191-0.

This well-illustrated compendium is a major reference source of the who's who type on prehistoric life, describing some six hundred species of dinosaurs and other prehistoric animals. The material is presented in several chapters covering fishes, amphibians, reptiles, ruling reptiles, birds, mammal-like reptiles, and mammals. It concludes with a glossary, classification of vertebrates, bibliography, and an adequate index.

The text of this compendium is well written, and the illustrations are excellent. Dixon, author of the monograph *After Man: A Zoology of the Future* (St. Martin's Press, 1983), was assisted in the preparation of this encyclopedia by several other scholars, mostly British. The book was first published in London and was designed by Marshall Editions.

All in all, *The Macmillan Illustrated Encyclopedia of Dinosaurs and Prehistoric Animals* is a well executed compendium that will be of interest to school and public libraries.

Bohdan S. Wynar

MARINE SCIENCE

1670. Charton, Barbara. **The Facts on File Dictionary of Marine Science.** New York, Facts on File, 1988. 325p. illus. $22.95. LC 82-15715. ISBN 0-8160-1031-5.

Facts on File has again produced a basic dictionary volume for the general reader and student. The volume covers marine ecosystems, oceans, reefs, coastlines, waves, tides, marine plants and animals, and water chemistry. There is no table of contents, so it is not all that easy to find the helpful appendices covering the geologic time periods, a chronology of significant marine history from 609 B.C. to 1977, a taxonomic chart, and a rather strange list of "marine science research projects (such as "WMO World Meteorological Organization")."

The acknowledgments state that "no long project goes forward without aid, encouragement, etc.," which probably says more than this reviewer can about why the chronology and most of the entries in the book appear to end in the late 1970s. Recent material is sparse. (I did find a paragraph on Mel Fisher and the *Neustra Senora de Atocha* dated 1985.) Underwater archaeology is under *marine archaeology* with no cross-reference, despite a publisher's blurb that says "abundant cross references help make this volume a superb sourcebook." The entry under *ship* is very general and ends with the development of the *Great Eastern* (no date given, but it is 1858, and alas the end of marine technology!). The "abundant cross reference" says "see individual ships by type" but I was unable to find any. (I looked under *research vessel*, *canoe*, and *icebreaker* with no luck.) The line illustrations are the rather plain types one encounters in textbooks and are not credited as to origin. (Are they from the public domain? I rather like the chart Charton did of the Periodic Table of the Elements!)

The volume does have merit for high school and introductory university science students. For general basic reference collections. [R: Choice, Nov 88, p. 460; LJ, 15 June 88, p. 53; RBB, 1 Oct 88, pp. 238, 240]

Ralph Lee Scott

1671. Fielding, Ann, and Ed Robinson. **An Underwater Guide to Hawai'i.** Honolulu, University of Hawaii Press, 1987. 156p. illus. (col.). maps. bibliog. index. $14.95. LC 86-30841. ISBN 0-8248-1104-6.

With its clear, warm water, and unique lava and coral environment, the sea around the Hawaiian Islands is a scuba diver and snorkeler's paradise. This book gives a colorful, simple overview of the geology, ecology, and wildlife likely to be encountered by the underwater tourist.

Introductory chapters on formation of the Hawaiian Islands, their geographical isolation, the types of marine habitats found there, and the taxonomy of sea organisms are written in clear, nontechnical prose. The bulk of the book is a directory of species, from algae to marine mammals, consisting of 204 color photographs with very brief entries on each species. There is no key or other aid to identification, but the pictures are very good, and the types of organisms discussed are so different from each other that none seems necessary. This otherwise valuable work has one major flaw in that the index lists only Latin names of included species, excluding common names and concepts, making the index useless to most of the intended audience. Still, for the visitor to Hawaii and even those of us who can only dream, this is a colorful and informative guidebook.

Carol L. Noll

MATHEMATICS

1672. Campbell, Paul J., and Louise S. Grinstein. **Mathematics Education in Secondary Schools and Two-Year Colleges: A Sourcebook.** New York, Garland, 1988. 439p. bibliog. index. (Source Books on Education, Vol. 15; Garland Reference Library of Social Science, Vol. 377). $60.00. LC 88-2322. ISBN 0-8240-8522-1.

Aimed at helping teachers improve mathematics education at the secondary and junior college levels, this reference work intends to be a comprehensive sourcebook of information on the topic. Consisting of twenty chapters, each with a topical essay and an annotated bibliography, the book addresses "the questions of curricular goals, instruction in the core areas of the mathematics curriculum, and concern for special populations in the mathematics classroom."

Each chapter is written by an expert in the field of mathematics education. The essays present brief overviews of a variety of topics including theories of mathematical learning, problem solving, teaching the gifted, trends, and more. Chapter 20, "Resources," provides a listing of additional information sources such as organizations, newsletters, periodicals, films and videotapes, distributors and publishers, etc. Bibliographic citations are generally limited to the last fifteen to twenty years of the literature, so the material is up-to-date.

While the book's purpose is to serve as a sourcebook for mathematics educators, it will also be useful to the college student doing research on mathematics education. Unfortunately, its steep price will make many individuals, and libraries, think twice about buying a copy.   Robert A. Seal

1673. Encyclopedic Dictionary of Mathematics. 2d ed. By the Mathematical Society of Japan. Kiyosi Itô, ed. Cambridge, Mass., MIT Press, 1987. 4v. illus. index. $350.00/set. LC 86-21092. ISBN 0-262-09026-0.

The second edition of the *Encyclopedic Dictionary of Mathematics* will no doubt receive the same well-deserved praise as the 1977 edition (see *ARBA* 78, entry 1227). This outstanding four-volume set, a translation of the third edition of *Iwanami Sūgaku Ziten*, is the result of the work of almost two hundred distinguished Japanese mathematicians.

Nine years in the making, the new edition is greatly expanded. The number of pages has increased from 1,750 to 2,148, the number of volumes has doubled, the number of articles has gone from 436 to 450. The net increase of fourteen articles masquerades that over sixty-five new articles were added. About fifteen sections were changed, and nearly fifty others deleted or combined.

The dictionary is arranged alphabetically by article. Each section is subdivided and a list of references follows each article. There are informational articles on all topics in mathematics as well as biographical articles on nearly three dozen great mathematicians. Many references to Japanese textbooks in the first edition have replaced by comparable English language publications in this edition. Cross-references abound; key terms are boldfaced. Very detailed

subject and name indexes provide access to the wealth of information contained in *Encyclopedic Dictionary*. Every concept consisting of two or more words can be traced in the subject index using each of the component words. The name index now includes years of birth and death.

One welcome feature is that the indexes, appendices and backmatter are now in one volume, making them very easy to locate. The appendices consist of thirty numerical tables and tables of formulas. Included also are numerical and statistical table references, journals, publishers, special notations and both systematic and alphabetic lists of articles in the dictionary. Note that section 436 in the alphabetic list on page 1866 should be "Uniform Spaces," not "S-Matrices."

According to the foreword, the intent of this work is to "easily provide readers with every significant result of today's mathematics." This monumental work, unequalled by any, should be on the reference shelf of every academic library.   Karen S. Croneis

1674. Gibson, Carol, ed. The Facts on File Dictionary of Mathematics. rev. ed. New York, Facts on File, 1988. 235p. illus. $19.95. LC 88-045704. ISBN 0-8160-1867-7.

The publisher is known for clear, concise, and nontechnical dictionaries; this title does not deviate. The line drawings and the definitions are simplistic but informative. A broad view of mathematics is taken which results in inclusion of terms from tangential fields such as cartography and economics. This is a major weakness of the work. No consistency was noticed as to when the editor included some terms from ancillary fields and when other terms were not included. Mathematics alone deserves the full 235 pages in this slim volume.

The target audience is identified as "anyone who uses mathematics in everyday life" (dust jacket). A better audience might be students through junior college and the general public needing quick, nontechnical definitions.

This book will find good use in public and some academic collections for users who are unfamiliar with or have lost their familiarity with basic mathematics. The level and overly broad scope severely limit the utility of this dictionary.   C. D. Hurt

1675. Selected Tables in Mathematical Statistics. Volume 11. Edited by the Institute of Mathematical Statistics, R. E. Odeh and J. M. Davenport, eds. Providence, R.I., American Mathematical Society, 1988. 371p. $46.00. LC 74-6283. ISBN 0-8218-1911-9; ISSN 0094-8837.

In this era of precision, this selection of four statistical tables with all data presented at an accuracy of five decimals is a necessity for libraries. Modern methods of approximation have been used to correct inaccuracies in similar earlier tables.

Partially supported by the U.S. Army Research Office and by the Natural Sciences and Engineering Research Council of Canada, this volume contains tables of the one-sided and two-sided upper equi-coordinate percentage points of the central multivariate student t-distribution for equal and block correlations.

The authors reveal in detail their approach and formulas used to obtain the data and their advanced and extremely accurate methods of interpolation. One chapter is devoted to a comprehensive description of the different types of experiments for which the tables are intended. Concrete examples illustrating applications of the tables are given.

The tables are easy to read, with running heads throughout. All mathematical equations and formulas are numbered sequentially for easy reference. Included is a comparative chart of over twenty books containing multivariate student t-distributions.

Andreas E. Mueller

METEOROLOGY

1676.   Parker, Sybil P., ed. **Meteorology Source Book**. New York, McGraw-Hill, 1988. 304p. illus. maps. index. (McGraw-Hill Science Reference Series). $40.00. LC 88-15076. ISBN 0-07-045511-2.

The devastating fires which ravaged large areas of the West in 1988, especially those in Yellowstone National Park, may have some good effect if they have demonstrated the importance of meteorology to all of us. Meteorologists were "on duty" with fire crews, trying to predict fire paths and the like, and their work is well recognized. With all this, a readily available summary of a wide range of meteorological information may be just the ticket for the layperson as well as professionals. Actually, this volume, one in a series noted above, is taken from the several volumes of the *McGraw-Hill Encyclopedia of Science and Technology* (see *ARBA* 88, entry 1448) but it is arranged for ready-reference as well as study. The "chapter" headings outline the content: "The Atmosphere"; "Atmospheric Optical and Electrical Phenomena"; "Climate"; "Micrometeorology"; "Hydrometeorology"; "Weather"; "Instrumentation, Observation, and Forecasts"; and "Weather Modification." The illustrations (photographs, maps, and drawings) are well

done and sufficient. This volume will be a handy companion to those primarily concerned with the subject (e.g., physical geographers, foresters, meteorologists) but should also be presented to interested laypersons. This is an excellent compilation, modestly priced. Unfortunately, we still do not know if next Saturday will be a good day for the staff picnic.

R. G. Schipf

PHYSICS

1677.   Daintith, John, ed. **The Facts on File Dictionary of Physics**. rev. ed. New York, Facts on File, 1988. 235p. illus. $19.95. LC 88-045703. ISBN 0-8160-1868-5.

This book has good points and bad points. The good points follow. This is a very readable dictionary. The entries are short, but informative for a novice to physics. There is a good mixture of standard material with new discoveries and theory. An example of this latter point is the inclusion of new material in the entry on superconductivity. As a first stop in a nonscientific or technical collection, this is an excellent choice.

Now for the bad points. The book suffers from some flaws. Their severity depends on the use made of the dictionary. There is no entry, for example, under *superstrings*. Popular magazines contain the term, so why does not this dictionary? It does contain at least one curious entry: *overhead projector*. The definition is quite correct, but why is it included in *this* dictionary? Finally, there seems to be some confusion as to British versus U.S. spellings. For certain audiences, *colour* and *centre* may be confusing.

This is a good dictionary for small public and perhaps some community college collections.   C. D. Hurt

1678.   Parker, Sybil P., ed. **Nuclear and Particle Physics Source Book**. New York, McGraw-Hill, 1988. 529p. illus. index. (McGraw-Hill Science Reference Series). $45.00. LC 88-13483. ISBN 0-07-045509-0.

1679.   Parker, Sybil P., ed. **Optics Source Book**. New York, McGraw-Hill, 1988. 399p. illus. index. (McGraw-Hill Science Reference Series). $45.00. LC 87-36630. ISBN 0-07-045506-6.

1680.   Parker, Sybil P., ed. **Solid-State Physics Source Book**. New York, McGraw-Hill, 1988. 381p. illus. index. (McGraw-Hill Science Reference Series). $45.00. LC 87-35253. ISBN 0-07-045503-1.

These are all part of a new series derived from the sixth (1987) edition of the publisher's standard reference work, *McGraw-Hill Encyclopedia of Science and Technology* (see *ARBA* 88, entry 1448). There was an earlier effort by McGraw-Hill at bringing out a series of subject-specific, single-volume encyclopedias. In that attempt, spun off from the fifth edition, each volume focused on a broad subject category (e.g., chemistry or physics). The project was not a success, largely because of the interdependence of scientific disciplines which are that general. To take just one example, the volume on chemistry omitted any reference to quantum mechanics, since that subject was of course covered in the physics volume; yet a knowledge of quantum mechanics is essential to an understanding of modern chemistry.

However, this new series, with its narrower focus, seems to have succeeded where that earlier effort failed. The volumes under review here follow a similar pattern: articles from the more comprehensive work are selected for relevance to the subject of the individual volume, then abridged and categorized with related subtopics, providing a brief overview. Selected illustrations are also reprinted. Each article is signed, and includes a very selective bibliography, again culled from the unabridged article. The indexing appears to be comprehensive and accurate, increasing each volume's utility as a reference. Other volumes in the series are, or will be, devoted to acoustics, communications, computer science, fluid mechanics, meteorology, physical chemistry, and spectroscopy.

McGraw-Hill advertises that the series is intended for professionals, educators, and students, and this would seem the proper audience for it. Whereas each volume does offer a state-of-the-art overview that would be appropriate for science collections, meaningful reference work would demand the more comprehensive overview and cross-referencing found in the larger, multivolume encyclopedia. [R: Choice, Dec 88, p. 631]

Donald J. Marion

1681. Schubert, Joachim. **Dictionary of Effects and Phenomena in Physics: Descriptions, Applications, Tables.** New York, VCH, 1987. 140p. bibliog. $24.95. ISBN 0-89573-487-7.

This is a good, basic dictionary of effects and phenomena in physics. Although the audience is not made clear in the introduction or the notes to the reader, it appears to be directed to the undergraduate. The definitions are straightforward, with "standard" literature references.

These standard literature references lead the reader to the classic literature in the field.

The emphasis on standard works and standard definitions is very evident in some places. The superconductivity definition is very traditional, with the latest literature cited from 1965. Overall, the effect is to produce a work that is technically correct but not state-of-the-art.

This work is highly recommended for an undergraduate collection or a good public library collection. Its traditional approach and definitions preclude its utility in a research collection. [R: Choice, Oct 88, p. 296]

C. D. Hurt

1682. Sube, Ralf, comp. **Dictionary of High-Energy Physics in Four Languages: English, German, French, Russian.** New York, Elsevier Science Publishing, 1987. 163p. index. $95.25. LC 86-19782. ISBN 0-444-98983-8.

This is the latest in a sizable and growing number of specialized polyglot dictionaries from Elsevier, and it follows the format usually found in these. The arrangement is alphabetical by the English term, with parallel columns giving the equivalent expression in the other three languages. An alphanumeric term is provided for each of the approximately forty-five hundred terms listed, providing a key for cross-referencing the other three lists. Each entry also carries a two-letter code for classification into one of seven subject categories, such as particle accelerators, quantification, particle detection, etc. In common with most multilingual dictionaries, there are no definitions furnished, only equivalencies.

The literature searched for termionology included institutional research reports and conference proceedings, and seems to be about as current as one could reasonably expect in so fast-moving a field of pure science as high-energy physics (also called elementary particle physics).

As the compiler notes in his preface, the vast majority of the high-energy literature is written and published in either English or Russian, but access to the other two languages' literature can also be useful to the researcher. The volume is designed to stand alone, but complete coverage of nuclear physics and its applications would require acquisition of two previous dictionaries by the compiler. This dictionary is recommended as an up-to-date source, but its cost and narrow specialization will probably limit its appeal to physics and general physical science collections supporting research in this area.

Donald J. Marion

37 Transportation

GENERAL WORKS

1683. The Sophisticated Traveler's Pocket Guide to Airport Facilities and Ground Services 1988-89. Wilton, Conn., Market Dynamics Consultants, 1987. 211p. maps. index. $14.95 pa. LC 86-63679. ISBN 0-941521-01-X.

Designed for the frequent traveler, this breast pocket-sized manual provides information on both travel and the largest airports in the United States. The first third of the book presents travel information, including a discussion of the air travel industry, how to plan a trip, how to deal with airlines and airport services, health and safety tips, and issues confronting the traveler. Most of the information in this section is elementary and known to persons who travel frequently. For the beginning traveler, the section is useful.

The last two-thirds of the book presents detailed information on thirty-seven major airports in the United States. Most airport information is presented on two to four pages and includes an airport map, how to get around the airport, airport services, how to get into the city with approximate costs, how much time it takes to get downtown, and sites to see while in town.

As a frequent traveler, this reviewer scanned the guide for information that is always needed, particularly when going to cities for the first time. The biggest problem with this guide is its narrow coverage. Thirty-seven airports do not begin to cover the common destinations of business travelers. While information seems to be accurate for the airports covered, there are no "confidential tips" like many guides offer to help the traveler save money. For example, for Chicago O'Hare, the guide says that the CTA is $1.00 and convenient. That information would be more helpful if the guide said "safe, fastest way downtown, for travelers who have carry-on luggage; look for signs leading to the basement."

Who should buy this guide? Probably the beginner in business air travel would benefit the most. For the experienced traveler, a more comprehensive and "insider tip" guide would be much more useful. [R: RBB, 1 Oct 88, p. 222]

David V. Loertscher

AIR

1684. Smith, Myron J., Jr. **The Airline Bibliography: The Salem College Guide to Sources on Commercial Aviation. Volume II: Airliners and Foreign Air Transport.** West Cornwall, Conn., Locust Hill Press, 1988. 464p. illus. index. $75.00. LC 86-7149. ISBN 0-933951-12-4.

In addition to his role as librarian and professor at Salem College in West Virginia, Myron Smith is noted for his many extensive bibliographies covering topics from naval history to baseball. In 1986, he issued volume 1 of the *Airline Bibliography* (see *ARBA* 87, entry 1732), which was an extensive work dealing with U.S. airlines. Volume 2 deals with the historic, economic, and operational facets of foreign air transport; international associations and organizations; airliners; and airlines of the world outside of the United States. Over 689 journals were consulted and over thirteen thousand citations are given, more than twice the number in volume 1. An introductory reference section alone lists and reviews 392 reference books, abstracts, and directories that contain some degree of information on airlines. The airliners section gives a short description and historical review of all types of American and foreign airplanes used as airliners, followed by articles on their use. The same format applies for the airlines section, covering a worldwide range of carriers from the Instone Air Line (1919-1924) in England to Dragonair (1985-) in Hong Kong. There are extensive author and subject indexes.

Robert J. Havlik

GROUND

1685. Baldwin, Nick, and others. **The World Guide to Automobile Manufacturers.** New York, Facts on File, 1987. 544p. illus. (part col.). index. $50.00. LC 87-81834. ISBN 0-8160-1844-8.

One of the "other" authors is G. N. Georgano, author of a standard identification work, *The New Encyclopedia of Motorcars, 1885 to the Present,* now in its third edition (see *ARBA* 84, entry 1513). The other three authors are all well known for their work in automotive history. The guide is far more selective than the intentionally comprehensive encyclopedia: some one thousand marque entries rather than over forty-three hundred, many of the latter being obscure or even merely projected but never produced. Yet it will prove even more useful to persons interested in automotive history because of the fullness of the entries. According to Georgano (introduction), "every make of car with a life of ten years or more is listed, and many with less" (e.g., DeLorean). The emphasis is on corporate histories and the key people involved in them—bankers, engineers, designers, etc. Some 350 of the illustrations are in color (the encyclopedia has sixty-one in color out of some twenty-four hundred). Useful features are cross-references in the text (e.g., "Hartford—see Pope") and a detailed index of marques and individuals. There is also a six-page chronology of major events in automotive history; this seems to be of marginal usefulness. While not explicitly intended to be such, the guide will serve as an admirable supplement to the encyclopedia. [R: LJ, 15 Apr 88, p. 75; RBB, 15 May 88, p. 1588; WLB, Apr 88, p. 104]   Walter C. Allen

1686. Barger, Ralph L. **A Century of Pullman Cars. Volume One: Alphabetical List.** Sykesville, Md., Greenberg Publishing, 1988. 319p. illus. $49.95. LC 87-23611. ISBN 0-89778-061-2.

For generations, the name "Pullman" was synonymous with American train travel by sleeping car. During the century of its sleeping car operations, George M. Pullman's company operated a nearly monopolistic traveling hotel service that—at its peak—provided 175,000 accommodations nightly. On passenger trains the Pullman-operated cars were a separate world. No matter what the railroad, the staff on the Pullman cars were Pullman employees, and the service was nationally consistent in a way that coach travel could never be.

The habit of naming rather than numbering Pullman cars developed as a means of distinguishing Pullman equipment from that owned by the individual railroads, which almost always identified cars by number. By using names, Pullman avoided confusion in record keeping and kept travelers aware of the distinction between the coaches operated by individual railroads and Pullman equipment.

Volume 1 of *A Century of Pullman Cars* is an alphabetical list of nearly twenty thousand named cars owned by the Pullman company between the 1860s and 1968. The list is divided into three sections, based on type of equipment, including wooden cars (built 1859-1910), heavyweight steel cars (1910-1931), and lightweight (streamlined) steel cars (1934-1956). Information provided on each car includes type and number of accommodations, car builder, date built, the plan number, lot (order) number, etc. All the data are well organized and clearly presented, although the vocabulary may initially confuse those who know nothing about trains.

This is an impressive reference work and the most complete book on its subject. It should be extremely useful to both rail historians and model builders. Five additional volumes are planned in the set.

Frederick A. Schlipf

1687. *Consumer Guide* **Automobile Book: The Complete New Car Buying Guide.** 1988 ed. Skokie, Ill., Consumer Guide Books, 1988. 240p. illus. $7.95pa. ISBN 0-451-82168-8.

1688. *Consumer Guide* **Used Car Book.** 1988 ed. Skokie, Ill., Consumer Guide Books, 1988. 192p. illus. $6.95pa. ISBN 0-451-82175-0.

The 1988 edition of the continuing series of the *Automobile Book* features extensive sections on shopping, safety, insurance, consumer complaints, warranties and service contracts, and a glossary. Then there is a five-page "Best Buys" section, followed by 204 pages of "Buying Guide," compiled by make and model. Each entry includes a black-and-white picture, "What's New for '88," the characteristic for and against lines peculiar to this publisher's works on automobiles, a critical summary, basic specifications, prices, and notes on standard and optional equipment. The fors and againsts are much too simple, but the summaries are really critical and range from good to excellent. These are terser than the comments that may be found in *Consumer Reports, Road & Track, Car and Driver,* etc., which give far more detailed information on all aspects of evaluation. All in all, the *Automobile Book* has improved noticeably in recent years and, because of its compact format, it has become a reasonable (and reasonably priced) place to begin one's search for a new car. In addition to the *New Car Buying Guide,* there is a *Used Car Book* covering 1978-1988 models of most makes. It also has introductory sections, on shopping, how to read ads, prices, warranties, how to check out a used car, deal negotiation, contracts, consumer protection, etc., followed by some 150 pages on specific models. Entries include pictures, general remarks, price ranges (for good, average, and poor condition), brief specifications, and, very important, "Recall History." This feature alone makes the volume worth its modest price, even if some makes and models are excluded (e.g., Isuzu, Suzuki, Samurai).

Walter C. Allen

1689. Drury, george H., comp. **Guide to Tourist Railroads and Railroad Museums.** Milwaukee, Wis., Kalmbach Publishing, 1988. 248p. illus. maps. index. $9.95pa. LC 88-080173. ISBN 0-89024-090-6.

This is the second edition of an annual publication that is virtually identical in scope and format to the *Steam Passenger Service Directory* (see *ARBA* 87, entry 1744): a geographically arranged directory of tourist railroads and railroad museums in North America. Both list chiefly organizations operating scheduled trains with historical locomotives and cars, but both include some museums with only static displays and some miniature and model railroads of special interest. The guide is somewhat more liberal than the directory in admitting museums and miniature railroads, and therefore has about 20 percent more entries. Both cover only operations regularly open to the general public, and both are based upon data provided by the organizations themselves.

Entries cover name, operating equipment, displays, dates and hours of operation, schedules, admission fees and fares, availability of memberships, special events, a short list of nearby tourist attractions, mailing address, telephone number, special facilities (handicapped access is noted), and a brief narrative description. Most include a photograph, and a few include a map. Like the directory, the guide has several pages of discount coupons, which libraries may wish to remove. There is an alphabetical index of names.

To choose between the guide and directory is difficult; the guide is somewhat more comprehensive but also a bit more expensive ($9.95 versus $6.00). Many popular travel collections will want to acquire both.   Paul B. Cors

1690. **New Complete Book of Collectible Cars 1930-80.** rev. ed. By Richard M. Langworth, Graham Robson, and the auto editors of *Consumer Guide.* Skokie, Ill., Consumer Guide Books, 1987. 416p. illus. (part col.). $14.98. ISBN 0-88176-464-7.

The first edition of this work, covering the years 1940-1980, was published some ten years ago. The introduction to this second edition discusses selection criteria, prices and projections, and other features. The work itself is divided into two parts, American (228 pages) and foreign (174 pages). There are an eight-page detailed contents list and a one-and-one-half-page roster of "Milestone Cars" as recognized by the Milestone Cars Society. Most entries include a black-and-white photograph of a typical representative of the model and period; all include production numbers (totals only); a brief history; brief summaries of fors and againsts; summaries of specifications; and price estimates, current and projected. The principal weaknesses are the too-brief notes on specifications and the sometimes silly for/against notes (e.g., for, Ford V8 Super Deluxe Sportsman 1946-48, "It's a convertible"; against, Rolls-Royce Silver Dawn 1949-1955, "Too much like a Bentley?"). For detailed information the prospective purchaser will need to consult works on specific marques. Still, this is useful as an introduction to the major collectibles of the period, especially the "milestones."

Walter C. Allen

1691. Radlauer, Ed, and Ruth Radlauer. **Auto Tech Talk.** Chicago, Children's Press, 1987. 64p. illus. (part col.). (Tech Talk Books). $13.25; $3.95pa. LC 87-5195. ISBN 0-516-08258-2; 0-516-48258-0pa.

This small dictionary of automotive terms is intended for children. Definitions are brief (largely four to fifteen lines in a double-column, large-print format); simply but not insultingly written. Some of the definitions seem a little odd (e.g., *goodie, famous names*) or slightly preachy (*radio*) but most are to the point. Illustrations range from cartoons to excellent diagrams, although a few captions are questionable (e.g., *oil pump* is really a well-labeled diagram of an engine; *engine* is simply an unlabeled cutaway drawing of an engine). The clarity of the text and illustrations will make this useful for children and for adults who do not know a *jump start* from a *jack stand.*

Walter C. Allen

WATER

1692. Greenman, David, and E. C. Talbot-Booth, comps. **Jane's Warsaw Pact Merchant Ships Recognition Handbook.** New York, Jane's Publishing, 1987. 273p. illus. maps. index. $11.95pa. ISBN 0-7106-0455-6.

This 7½-by-5-inch landscape format pocketbook is intended to allow quick identification of Warsaw Pact merchant ships. Forty-five pages of introductory material are followed by 8 pages explaining the Talbot-Booth recognition system, 4 pages of glossary, 162 pages of ship drawings, and 64 pages of indexes. Some 840 drawings (most to 1:2400 scale) depict the complete range of Pact nonmilitary ships; each is followed by ship name and brief statistics; some ships have additional notes.

While handy and authoritative, as a recognition implement this volume suffers from several drawbacks. Four different drawing systems are used; one standard system would make recognition easier. Since small variations among sister ships create coding "homonyms," entries for several ships are repeated. As a result, some repeated ships have drawings which look *very* different, whereas others have drawings which appear identical. Some drawings are reproduced so faintly as to be nearly illegible (pp. 64, 70, 103, 114, 203); others are so dark that important detail is obscured (pp. 133, 138, 172, 175-76, 182, 195, and 197). Two indexes (one by drawing number, the other alphabetical) both refer to drawing number rather than page, impeding rapid content access.

This perfectbound paperback is printed on good quality paper. It is a highly specialized ready-reference tool, and cannot be used to supplant more extensive works on this topic.

John Howard Oxley

1693. Tver, David F. **The Norton Encyclopedic Dictionary of Navigation.** New York, W. W. Norton, 1987. 283p. illus. $19.95. LC 87-5659. ISBN 0-393-02406-7.

Modern navigators might employ an electronic computer to plot position and course, and derive data for inputting from signals sent by radio from an orbiting satellite or other sophisticated devices. This present work updates some of the terminology that a navigator needs to know. It is a combination dictionary of terms and an instruction manual in navigation. Written in a sort of techno-jargon, it is not for the uninitiated, because it requires some prior knowledge to be understandable. For instance, it goes on at some length about the information tabulated in *The Nautical Almanac*, but it never actually describes what the publication is, or who publishes it. It is also skimpy with cross-references. The book is divided into four parts: navigation, weather, navigational stars, and navigational alphabet. The navigational alphabet includes a black-and-white chart display of signal flags and pennants, but one has to refer to the alphabet in order to determine the flag colors. A chart in color would have been more useful. Many terms are referred to by initials or acronyms within the entries. An appendix of initialisms would have been useful; as would one of names and addresses of the various agencies that a mariner should know about.

Frank J. Anderson

Author/Title Index

Reference is to entry number.

A kì í: Yorùbá proscriptive & prescriptive proverbs, 1246

A to Z of Wall Street, 189

A. W. N. Pugin: an annotated critical bibliog, 911

AA touring England, 414

AARP pharmacy service prescription drug hndbk, 1585

Abate, Frank R., 946

Abbreviations used by FAO for int'l organizations ... , 4th ed, 1364

ABCs of Armageddon, 611

Abercrombie, Stanley A., 1510

ABMS compendium of certified medical specialists, 2d ed, 1544

Abrams, Irwin, 680

Abridged biography & genealogy master index, 65

Abuse of the elderly, 754

Access America, 406

ACCESS resource gd, 1988 ed, 681

Accounting to zoology: graduate fields defined, 308

Achtert, Walter S., 832

Acid rain & the environment 1984-88, 1405

Ackermann, Karen T., 378

Acoustics source bk, 1469

Action series & sequels, 1033

Adams, Carol M., 954

Adams, Elsie B., 1123

Adams, Michael, 139

Adamson, Lynda G., 1018

Additives gd, 1372

Adir, Karin, 850

Adrian, J., 1371

Adult literacy/illiteracy in the U.S., 324

Adventuring in Alaska, rev ed, 413

Adventuring in the Pacific, 417

Advertising & publicity resources for scholarly bks, 578

Africa: a directory of resources, 89

Africa bibliog 1986, 88

Afro-American writers, 1940-55, 1051

Agent Orange & Vietnam, 586

Agrawal, Surendra P., 177

Ahouse, John B., 1201

AIDS 1987 (Acquired Immune Deficiency Syndrome), 1562

AIDS 1988, pt.1, 1563

AIDS info resources directory, 1558

AIDS info sourcebk, 1560

AIDS: political, social, int'l aspects, 1561

Air & space hist, 1472

Airline bibliog, v.II, 1684

Akiyama, Carol, 983

Akiyama, Nobuo, 983

ALA hndbk of organization 1987/88 & membership directory, 539

ALA yrbk of lib & info services, v.13, 540

Alan Sillitoe: a bibliog, 1125

Alarid, William M., 201

Albanese, Sandy, 313

Albert, George, 1231

Alberta business who's who & directory, 3d ed, 159

Alden, Douglas W., 1152

Aleksander, Igor, 1613

Alexander, Robert J., 618

Alexis Lichine's new ency of wines & spirits, 5th ed, 1374

Algernon Blackwood: a bio-bibliog, 1099

Ali, Sheikh R., 638

Alice Malsenior Walker: an annotated bibliog, 1089

Allard, Denise M., 662

Allard, Dennis M., 1361

Allen, David Rayvern, 729

Allen, James Paul, 337

Allen, Martha Leslie, 821

Allergy products directory, 2d ed, 1564

Almanac of ...

    American women in the 20th century, 806

    British politics, 3d ed, 626

    the American people, 789

    the Christian church, 1328

    the federal judiciary, 510

    the unelected 1988, 642

Alphabet bks as a key to lang patterns, 1009

Alston, Y. R., 1491

Alternative press index, 843

Alternative sources of energy, 1988 directory, 1396

Ambert, Alba N., 262
America as story, 1003
America at the polls 2, 655
American advertising, 249
American Allergy Assn, staff of, 1564
American Antiquarian Society, staff of, 447
American artists' materials suppliers directory: 19th century, 905
American Banker 1988 yr bk, 202
American bk trade directory 1988-89, 579
American college regalia, 309
American Craft 1988-89 gd to craft galleries & shops USA, 877
American drug index 1988, 1598
American English spelling, 967
American farm crisis, 1365
American film studios, 1272
American Foundation for the Blind directory of services for blind & visually impaired persons in the U.S., 23d ed, 759
American governors & gubernatorial elections 1979-87, 653
American heritage illus encyclopedic dict, 937
American hist: a bibliographic review, v.III, 432
American Hist'l Assn, 450
American humor magazines & comic periodicals, 1067
American lib directory 1988-89, 535
American lib hist, 3d ed, 560
American literary almanac, 1052
American literary critics & scholars, 1850-80, 1061
American literary critics & scholars, 1880-1900, 1062
American magazine journalists, 1741-1850, 839
American nursing, 1575
American orators before 1900, 441
American psychiatric glossary, 6th ed, 1553
American Psychological Assn's gd to research support, 3d ed, 699
American slang, 948
American Society of Safety Engineers, Engineering Division, 1511
American univs & colleges, 13th ed, 280
America's first ladies, 443
Analyses of 19th-& 20th-century music: 1940-85, 1173
Anastas, Lila L., 1549
Anatomy of wonder, 3d ed, 1042
Anchor companion to the orchestra, 1178
Andacht, Sandra, 866
Anderson, James D., 1092
Anderson, Janice, 1454
Anderson, Kenneth, 1536, 1586
Anderson, Kenneth N., 1543
Anderson, Lois, 1586
Andrle, Robert F., 1440
Angelucci, Enzo, 597, 598, 599, 600, 601
Anglo-American relationship, 631

Animal magnetism, early hypnotism, & psychical research, 1766-1925, 702
Anne Morrow Lindbergh: the literary reputation, 1076
Annotated bibliog of ...
　Canada's major authors, v.7, 1140
　DSM-III, 1552
　Mennonite writings on war & peace: 1930-80, 1336
　Timothy Leary, 690
Annotated critical bibliog of George Eliot, 1109
Annual exhibition record of the Pa. Academy of the Fine Arts 1807-70 ..., rev ed, 909
Annual summary of investigations relating to reading July 1, 1986 to June 30, 1987, 269
Annuals & surveys appearing in legal periodicals, 520
Anthony, L. J., 1397
Anthropological fieldwork, 334
Anti-evolution: an annotated bibliog, 1415
Anti-intervention: a bibliographical introduction ..., 437
Antokoletz, Elliott, 1193
Antonio Buero Vallejo & Alfonso Sastre: an annotated bibliog, 1288
Antonio Vivaldi: a gd to research, 1211
Appleby, David P., 1194
Applied science & technology index 1987, 1358
Apterbach, Evelyn, 561
Arapaho Indians, 361
Architecture & women, 912
Archival & manuscript repositories in N.C., 423
Archives: a gd to the Nat'l Archives field branches, 428
Arden, Lynie, 223
Arizona place names, 397
Arlington Mgmt Pubs Ltd., 243
Armitage, Christopher M., 459
Arms & armour of the Crusading era 1050-1350, 614
Armstrong, Julia I., 921
Arneson, Arne Jon, 1189
Arp, Halton C., 1630
Arrow's complete gd to mail order foods, 1378
Art & architecture in central Europe, 1550-1620, 896
Art of children's picture bks, 1006
Arthur Bliss: a bio-bibliog, 1200
ArtsAmerica fine art film & video source bk 1987, 902
A's & B's of academic scholarship, 11th ed, 299
Ash, Irene, 1637, 1643
Ash, Michael, 1637, 1643
Ashley, Mike, 1099
Ashliman, D. L., 1243
Assassinations & executions, 620
ASSIA, v.1, no.3, 82
Association meeting directory, 2d ed, 48

ASTM, 1354
Atienza, Federico Beigbeder, 1353
Atkinson, Steven D., 910
Atlas of ...
   American hist, 429
   breeding birds in N.Y. state, 1440
   natural wonders, 1662
   Nazi Germany, 473
   the ultraviolet sky, 1631
   world affairs, 8th ed, 478
Audio dict, 852
Audiovisual material glossary, 552
Austin, Mary C., 105
Australian concise Oxford dict of current
   English, 962
Australians: a hist'l lib, 458
Author Aid/Research Associates Int'l, 829
Auto tech talk, 1691
Avatag Cultural Institute, 399
Aversa, Elizabeth, 817
AVMP 1988, 853
Avneyon, Eitan A., 203
Award voting, 716
Axe, Ruth Frey, 576
Axelrod, Herbert R., 1456
Axsom, Richard H., 917

Bacon's publicity checker 1988, 840
Baer, Beverly Anne, 1027
Bailey, Alvin R., Jr., 436
Bain, Robert, 1048, 1049
Bair, Frank E., 239
Baird-Lange, Lorrayne Y., 1103
Bajzek, Dieter, 1214
Balachandran, M., 204
Baldwin, Nick, 1685
Baldwin, Robert, 730
Bales, Eugene F., 1306
Ball, David W., 1636
Ballet plot index, 1259
Balzer, Howard, 731
Bancroft, Eleanor, 576
Banerjee, Shampa, 1278
Banks, Carolyn, 1455
Banney, Howard F., 1238
Baptists, 1341
Barale, Michèle Aina, 1158
Baratta, Joseph Preston, 672
Bard, Ray, 152
Barger, Ralph L., 1686
Barker, David G., 1466
Barnes, Melvyn, 1036
Barnes, Will C., 397
Barnett, Donna, 1400
Barnhart, David K., 935
Barnhart dict companion index (1982-85), 935
Barnhart dict of etymology, 941
Barnhart, Robert K., 941

Barron, Neil, 1042
Barron's Educ'l Series, Inc., editors of, 36
Barron's real estate hndbk, 2d ed, 252
Barron's sports injuries hndbk, 1574
Barron's student's concise ency, 36
Bartlett, Lee, 1087
Bartók for piano, 1213
Baseball card & collectibles dealer directory,
   1988, 869
Baseball research hndbk, 724
Baseball's best, 721
Basic classical & operatic recordings collections
   for libs, 1225
Basic Tex. bks, rev ed, 438
Basu, Asok, 102
Batchelor, Stephen, 418
Bateman New Zealand ency, 2d ed, 475
Bates, Robert L., 1660
Beach, Barbara, 1027
Beacham, Walton, 1032
Beal, Peter, 1094
Beard, Robert, 926
Beasts & behemoths, 1286
Beat the MBAs to the top!, 292
Beaumont, Roger, 603
Becher, Paul, 1475
Becker, Robert S., 1113
Beckett, Kenneth A., 1389, 1390
Begnal, Kate, 1114
Béla Bartók: a gd to research, 1193
Belcher, Margaret, 911
Belford, Gail T., 48
Bell, Carol Willsey, 369
Bellack, Alan S., 695
Bellamy, Patricia, 288
Bender, Claire E., 1075
Bender, Todd K., 1075
Benet's reader's ency, 3d ed, 816
Benjamin, Carmen, 979
Benjamin Franklin: a reference gd 1907-83, 434
Benny Goodman: listen to his legacy, 1230
Bension, Shmuel, 859
Benson, Hazel B., 688
Benson, Ian, 1613
Benstock, Bernard, 1097
Bercuson, David J., 468
Bergan, Ronald, 1298
Bergerson, Peter J., 686
Bergstone, David, 756
Berko, Robert L., 591
Bernard, Yolande, 256
Berry, Liba, 50
Berry, Margaret, 1147
Berry, Reginald, 1116
Bespaloff, Alexis, 1375
Bessette, Alan, 1429
Best hospitals in America, 1527
Best science bks & A-V materials for children,
   1345

BFI companion to the Western, 1271
Bhalla, Alok, 1160
Bianco, David, 1239
Biblical holy places, 1319
Bibliographic gd to anthropology & archaeology 1987, 331
Bibliographic gd to computer science 1987, 1601
Bibliographical gd to Spanish American lit, 1161
Bibliographical hndbk of American music, 1171
Bibliography of ...
    Arthur Waley, 2d ed, 1130
    Asian studies 1983, 103
    Canadian & comparative federalism, 1980-85, 617
    Chaucer 1974-85, 1103
    compensation planning & administration pubs 1975-85, 3d ed, 232
    culinary hist, 1370
    matrix isolation spectroscopy: 1954-85, 1636
    morphology 1960-85, 926
    published research of the World Employment Programme, 7th ed, 224
    telecommunications & socio-economic development, 846
    the Catawba, 352
    the works of Jean Piaget in the social sciences, 79
    Wash. state folklore & folklife, 1247
    writings for the hist of the English lang, 2d ed, 928
Bick, Patricia Ann, 147
Bierlein, Lawrence W., 1505
Bilingual educ & English as a 2d lang, 262
Billboard bk of top 40 albums, 1228
Billups, Norman F., 1598
Billups, Shirley M., 1598
Binding terms, 548
Bingham, Jane M., 1015
Biographical dict of ...
    American sports: football, 735
    Latin American & Caribbean political leaders, 618
    modern European radicals & socialists, v.1, 668
    science fiction & fantasy artists, 924
Biographical directory of anthropologists born before 1920, 332
Biographical directory of the Council of Economic Advisers, 150
Biotechnology & society, 1495
Biotechnology directory 1988, 1491
Biotechnology gd USA, 212
Biracree, Nancy, 789
Biracree, Tom, 789
Birder's gd to Japan, 1450
Birds & birding on the Miss. coast, 1451
Birds of N. central Tex., 1449
Birnbaum, Max, 282

Birney, Elmer C., 1460
Biron, Paul J., 1512
Bishop, Peter, 1311
Bizzarro, Salvatore, 131
Black authors & illustrators of children's bks, 1016
Black, Donald Chain, 942
Black leaders of the 19th century, 339
Black press in Miss., 1865-1985, 841
Blackfeet: an annotated bibliog, 359
Blackhurst, Hector, 88
Blacks in American films & television, 1279
Blacks in classical music, 1224
Black's medical dict, 35th ed, 1537
Blackwell ency of political institutions, 621
Blackwell ency of the Russian Revolution, 476
Blake dict, rev ed, 1100
Blake, Gerald, 140
Blake, William D., 1328
Blasio, Mary-Ann, 440
Blazek, Ron, 817
Block, Geoffrey, 1195
Bloomfield, Brynna C., 407
Blue bk of Canadian business 1987, 209
Blue Note label, 1235
Blum, Laurie, 180, 281
Blumer, Thomas J., 352
BNA Lib Staff, 511
BNA's directory of state courts judges & clerks, 2d ed, 511
Bochin, Hal, 635
Boehm, David A., 713
Boenke, Heidi M., 1196
Bogdanor, Vernon, 621
Boger, Karl, 210
Boggs, Michael D., 300
Bogle, Donald, 1279
Bohlander, Richard E., 295
Boileau, Claude, 874
Boiler operator's dict, 1513
Bolivia, 130
Bologna, Gregory L., 156
Bond, Peter, 1470
Bond, Robert E., 181
Book bait, 4th ed, 1025
Book of ...
    business anecdotes, 174
    days 1988, 60
    video lists, 861
Bookguide 1988-89, 580
Bookman's price index: subject series, v.1, 573
Books for ...
    children to read alone, 1013
    college libs, 3d ed, 6
    the gifted child, v.2, 997
Boone, Lalia, 398
Boorstein, Lucille, 519
Booth, David, 998
Borck, Jim Springer, 819

Bordman, Gerald, 1299
Bosnich, Victor W., 650
Boston Children's Hospital, 1529
Boswell, Jeanetta, 1084
Boucher, Lise, 625
Boudreault-Lapointe, Lise, 1418
Bourne, C. B., 515
Bowers, Richard A., 1611
Bowhunter's ency, 742
Bowker annual of lib & bk trade info 1988, 541
Bowker's forthcoming children's bks, v.1, no.4, 14
Bowker's law bks & serials in print 1988, 489
Bowman, James S., 628
Boyd, Andrew, 478
Boylan, James C., 1583
Brackney, William Henry, 1341
Brady, Anna, 807
Braigen, Mila, 1358
Brand, Glen, 1148
Branford, Jean, 963
Bratkowsky, Joan G., 980
Brautigam, Patsy, 558
Breen, Karen, 66
Breen, Walter, 871
Brereton, Mary M., 546
Brewer, Annie M., 927
Brinker, Russell C., 1481
Brisman, Shimeon, 1342
Britannica bk of the yr, 1988, 45
British bks in print 1987, 19
British Empire in the Victorian press, 1832-67, 461
British film actors' credits, 1895-1987, 1284
British hist'l statistics, 466
British military hist, 593
British mystery writers, 1860-1919, 1097
British newspapers & periodicals 1641-1700, 31
British Overseas Trade Board, 243
British poetry & the American Revolution, 1133
British sources of info, 119
Broadbent, Brenda, 263
Broadway on record: a directory ..., 1296
Brockman, William S., 1167
Broderick, Robert C., 1339
Bromiley, Geoffrey W., 1323
Brookes, John, 1390
Brookhart, Edward, 1168
Brooklyn Public Lib, Business Lib, 171
Brosman, Catharine Savage, 1150, 1151
Brown, Archibald, 499
Brown, Jay A., 1285
Brownstone, David M., 264, 345, 592, 1254, 1356
Broxis, P. F., 82
Bruccoli, Matthew J., 1073
Bruguier, Leonard R., 358
Bruhn, John G., 689

Brussell, Eugene E., 960
Bryant, Keith L., Jr., 213
Bryson, Bill, 947
Bubis, Gerald B., 350
Budgeting, pricing & cost controls, 178
Bullock, Alan, 37
Bullough, Vern L., 1575
Bully pulpit, 663
Bulsterbaum, Allison, 1079
Burke, John Gordon, 74
Burman, Jenny, 1366
Burn, Hilary, 1446
Burnham, Alan, 433
Burrill, Alexander M., 500
Burroughs, Lea, 818
Burt, Eugene C., 892
Burton, John A., 1459
Burton, Vivien G., 1459
Buscombe, Edward, 1271
Business acronyms, 145
Business & technical communication: a bibliog, 1975-85, 822
Business ethics & responsibility, 147
Business periodicals index: Aug 1986-July 1987, 170
Business rankings & salaries index, 171
Business serials of the U.S. govt, 2d ed, 173
Bustros, Charles G., 29
Butt, John, 979
Butterflies & moths, rev ed, 1453
Buttress, F. A., 1
Buxbaum, Melvin H., 434
Buxton, David, 1202
Buy bks where—sell bks where 1988-89, 585
Buy me! buy me!, 198
Bycroft, B. W., 1580
Byles, Monica, 1350
Byron chronology, 1101

C & UNIX dict, 1606
Cable television, 848
Calasibetta, Charlotte Mankey, 888
Calhoun, Milburn, 86
California architecture, 916
California environmental directory, 4th ed, 1401
Calorie gd to brand names & basic foods, 1988, 1382
Cambridge atlas of the Middle East & N. Africa, 140
Cambridge ency of lang, 933
Cambridge ency of the Middle East & N. Africa, 141
Cambridge gd to lit in English, 991
Camp, Roderic Ai, 135
Campbell, Paul J., 1672
Campbell-Platt, Geoffrey, 1379
Canada yr bk 1988, 110

Canadian almanac & directory 1988, 111
Canadian bks for young people, 4th ed, 1000
Canadian chemical register 1986/87, 1644
Canadian criminal justice hist, 526
Canadian ency, 2d ed, 112
Canadian machine-readable databases, 1612
Canadian magazine index 1987, 67
Canadian news index 1987, 844
Canadian Newspaper Services Int'l, 209
Canadian periodical index 1920-37, 68
Canadian statistics index 1988, 113
Canadian statistics index 1988 (suppl), 114
Canadian thesaurus 1988, 550
Canadian writers, 1920-59: 1st series, 1144
Canadian yrbk of int'l law, v.XXV, 515
Cancer journals & serials, 1570
Cannon, Donald M., 13
Capital punishment in America, 525
Carbohydrate gd to brand names & basic foods,
    1988, 1383
Carbohydrates, 1645
Carl Sandburg: a reference gd, 1085
Carlson, Raymond, 710
Carnes, Mark C., 25
Carole Lombard: a bio-bibliog, 1261
Carpatho-Rusyn studies, v.1, 470
Carper, James C., 1308
Carr, Anna, 1395
Carr, Robert E., 1281
Carroll, Janet R., 1440
Carruth, Gorton, 709
Carter, George, 467
Cartography of N. America 1500-1800, 385
Carvalho, Joseph, III, 439
Cash Box album charts, 1955-74, 1231
Caskey, Jefferson D., 1091
Casper, Dale E., 629
Cass, James, 282
Cassell & The Publishers Assn directory of
    publishing 1988, 581
Cassidy, Daniel J., 283, 316
Catalá, Rafael, 1092
Catalog of the American musical, 1176
Cataloging Service Bulletin index, nos.1-40,
    summer 1978-spring 1988, 553
Cataloging with copy, 2d ed, 554
Cat-a-logue, 1454
Catalogue of ...
    census returns on microfilm 1666-1891,
        790
    medieval & Renaissance manuscripts in
        the Beinecke Rare Bk & Manuscript
        Lib, Yale Univ, v.II, 483
    southern peculiar galaxies & assns, v.II, 1630
    Thomists, 1270-1900, 1307
Catholic ency, rev ed, 1339
Catholic novel, 1034
CBA plays America, 1988/89, 726
CCH Tax Law Editors, 257b

CD review digest annual, v.1, 1185
CD review digest, v.2, no.1, 1184
CD rock & roll lib, 1242
CD-ROM: an annotated bibliog, 1600
CD-ROMs in print 1988-89, 1599
Cécile Chaminade: a bio-bibliog, 1198
Center for Research Libs hndbk 1987, 30
Center for the Study of Women & Society,
    CUNY, 815
Cento città: a gd to the "100 cities & towns" of
    Italy, 416
Central America in the 19th & 20th centuries,
    125
Centre of Economic Forecasting, People's
    Republic of China, 165
Century of Pullman cars, v.1, 1686
Cerny, Johni, 370
Chalmers, B. J., 1486
Chambers bk of business quotations, 175
Chambers, Janice E., 1581
Chambers science & technology dict, new ed,
    1348
Chambers world gazetteer, 5th ed, 382
Champagne, Anthony, 636
Chandler, David, 588
Chandler, Lana J., 300
Chandler, Ralph C., 687
Chandler, Tertius, 800
Chant, Christopher, 604, 610
Chapman, Gretel, 893
Chapman, Karen J., 182
Chapman, Robert L., 948
Charles Ives: a bio-bibliog, 1195
Charness, Jeanie, 783
Charny, Israel W., 528
Charton, Barbara, 1670
Charts on file, 61
Chaucer's *Romaunt of the Rose* and *Boece,
    Treatise on the Astrolabe, Equatorie of
    the Planetis*, lost works, & Chaucerian
    apocrypha, 1104
Checklist of ...
    American imprints for 1838, 17
    American imprints for 1839, 18
    19th century Canadian poetry in English,
        1142
Check-list of pubs of H. H. Bancroft & Co 1857
    to 1870, 576
Chemical engineering faculties 1988-89, 1476
Chemical industries: an info sourcebk, 1477
Cheremisinoff, N. P., 1479
Chiang, Nancy S., 365
Chicano public catalog, 562
Child & youth actors, 1280
Children's bks of the yr, 1988 ed, 999
Children's britannica, 4th ed, 38
Children's ency & atlas, 39
Children's lit: a gd to the criticism, 1020
Children's lit awards & winners, 2d ed, 1022

Children's religious bks, 1309
Chilvers, Ian, 901
Chinese classic novels, 1147
Chinese-American heritage, 345
Chinese-English hndbk of idioms, 971
Chitty, Mary Glen, 1514
Chmielewski, Wendy E., 682
Choosing children's bks, 998
Christensen, Jean, 1197
Christensen, Jesper, 1197
Christian College Coalition, 285
Christian, Kaare, 1606
Christianity & Marxism worldwide, 1332
Christoph Willibald Gluck: a gd to research,
    1205
Chronic, Halka, 1654
Chronicle career index, 1988-89, 322
Chronicle student aid annual, 1988-89, 301
Chronicle vocational school manual, 1988-89,
    323
Chronology of geological thinking from
    antiquity to 1899, 1667
Chronology of Western architecture, 913
Church, Olga Maranjian, 1575
Ciardi, John, 943
Cities of the U.S., v.1, 801
Citizen participation in environmental affairs,
    1970-86, 1403
Citron, Marcia J., 1198
Civil War eyewitnesses, 435
Civilization of the ancient Mediterranean:
    Greece & Rome, 488
Clark, Judith Freeman, 806
Clark, Thomas L., 736
Clark, Virginia, 6
Clark, William S., 1441
Classical & medieval lit criticism, v.1, 1028
Classical & medieval lit criticism, v.2, 1029
Classification of institutions of higher educ,
    1987 ed, 302
Claudy, Nicholas H., 1657
Clay, Katherine, 270
Clegg, Melissa, 335
Clements, Frank A., 144
Clevely, A. M., 1391
Clever, Glenn, 1137, 1138, 1139
Clifton, James A., 357
Close, Arthur C., 156
Clowes, Edith W., 1163
Cobb, Harold M., 1500, 1501
Cockton, Peter, 464
Cocozzoli, Gary R., 109
Code of federal regulations index 1988, 519
Coffin, Barbara, 1412
Cogeneration & small power production
    manual, 2d ed, 220
Coger, Greta M. K., 1162
Cohen, Aaron I., 1199
Cohen, Daniel, 522

Cohen, Marjorie Adoff, 404
Cohen-Stratyner, Barbara, 1229
Colby, Robert W., 183
Cold as a Bay Street banker's heart, 965
Coldoff, Harry, 981
Cole, Garold L., 435
Cole, John Y., 49
Cole, Wayne, 625
Coleman, Samuel S., 1105
Colen, Donald J., 611
Collcutt, Martin, 108
Collected papers on AIDS research, 1976-86,
    1557
Collections & programs of the American
    Antiquarian Society, 447
Colledge, J. J., 607
College football records: Division I-A & the Ivy
    League, 1869-1984, 730
College hndbk foreign student suppl 1988-89,
    284
College hndbk 1988-89, 303
Collier's ency, 40
Collins dict of Canadian hist: 1867 to the
    present, 468
Collins gd to the botanical gardens of Britain,
    1420
Collins gd to the rare mammals of the world,
    1459
Collins, Mary, 1340
Collins, Mary Ellen, 268
Collins, P. M., 1645
Colonial Williamsburg music, 1177
Colonization to the American renaissance,
    1640-1865, 1053
Columbia ency of nutrition, 1519
Columbia Univ School of Public Health
    complete gd to health & well-being after
    50, 1528
Combat aircraft of ...
    WW II 1940-41, v.IV, 597
    WW II 1941-42, v.V, 598
    WW II 1942-43, v.VI, 599
    WW II 1943-44, v.VII, 600
    WW II 1944-45, v.VIII, 601
Combat fleets of the world 1988/89, 608
Comedy on record, 1258
Comic bks & strips, 923
Comics to classics, 1023
Commedia dell'arte: a gd to the primary &
    secondary lit, 1289
Commercial timbers of the world, 5th ed, 1387
Commire, Anne, 1017
Committee on the Junior High & Middle School
    Bklist, NCTE, 1014
Committee to Revise *High Interest-Easy
    Reading*, NCTE, 1001
Commodity review & outlook 1986-87, 1380
Common knowledge: a reader's gd to literary
    allusions, 820

Commonwealth yrbk 1988, 116
Community of the bk, 49
Compact hndbk of the birds of India &
    Pakistan, 2d ed, 1439
Companion to Calif., rev ed, 84
Companion to the French Revolution, 471
Company of Military Historians, 595
Comparative gd to American colleges, 13th ed,
    282
Comparative reading: an int'l bibliog, 272
Comparative statutory sources, 3d ed, 496
Compendium of ...
    American public opinion, 83
    armaments & military hardware, 610
    chemical terminology, 1638
Complete bk of ...
    collectible baseball cards, 868
    the Olympics, rev ed, 712
    vitamins & minerals, 1587
Complete car cost gd, 1988 ed, 194
Complete directory of large print bks & serials
    1988, 15
Complete film dict, 1275
Complete gd to federal & state benefits for
    veterans, their families & survivors, 10th
    ed, 591
Complete gd to vitamins, minerals &
    supplements, 1590
Comprehensive coordination chemistry, 1639
Computer applications in nutrition & dietetics,
    1369
Computer discount shopping gd, 1614
Computer industry forecasts, 1615
Computer resource gd, 1988 ed, 1617
Computer use in psychology, 694
Computers in educ, 312
Computing info directory, 5th ed, 1610
Concise Baker's biographical dict of musicians,
    1174
Concise dict of acronyms & initialisms, 2
Concise ency of interior design, 2d ed, 863
Concise flowers of the Himalaya, 1425
Concise gd to the flowers of Britain & Europe,
    1427
Concise law dict of words, phrases, & maxims
    ..., 507
Concise lexicon to the biblical langs, 1320
Concise Oxford companion to American
    theatre, 1299
Concise psychological dict, 696
Concordance to Henry James's *The Turn of the
    Screw*, 1075
Concordance to the complete English poems of
    John Skelton, 1126
Concrete structures reference gd, 1482
Condom bk: the essential gd ..., 775
Conetta, Carl, 683
Confederate broadside poems, 1093
Congress A to Z, 651

Congressional voting gd, 99th Congress, 650
Connor, Billie M., 1030
Connor, Cathy, 1655
Connor, D. Russell, 1230
Connors, Martin, 247
Conoley, Jane Close, 700
Conservative Judaism in America, 1343
Consider a Christian college, 285
Constitutions of the states, 517
Consultant's U.S. statistical gd & sourcefinder,
    rev ed, 162
Consumer Gd, auto editors of, 1690
Consumer Gd automobile bk, 1988 ed, 1687
Consumer Gd best-rated investments for 1988,
    184
Consumer Gd best-rated retirement cities &
    towns, 802
Consumer Gd consumer buying gd, 1988 ed, 195
Consumer Gd, editors of, 185, 868, 1285, 1587,
    1595
Consumer Gd 100 best-rated stocks, 185
Consumer Gd used car bk, 1988 ed, 1688
Consumer sourcebk, 5th ed, 196
Contemporary atlas of China, 387
Contemporary authors: autobiography series,
    v.6, 986
Contemporary authors: autobiography series,
    v.7, 987
Contemporary black American playwrights &
    their plays, 1063
Contemporary dramatists, 4th ed, 1255
Contemporary German fiction writers: 1st
    series, 1153
Contemporary German fiction writers: 2d
    series, 1154
Contemporary literary criticism, v.45, 992
Contemporary photographers, 2d ed, 891
Cook, Chris, 469
Cook, Michael L., 1037
Coombs, J., 1491
Corporate address bk, 155
Corporate foundation profiles, 5th ed, 767
Corporate technology directory, 1988 U.S. ed,
    211
Costa, Marie, 324
Couch, James V., 694
Couhat, Jean Labayle, 608
Coulson, William D. E., 894
County executive directory, 643
Courtney, Richard, 1294
Courtright, Gordon, 1433
Coven, Brenda, 1290
Covington, Timothy R., 1546
Cox, Claudie, 976
Cox, J. Randolph, 1131
Cox, John, 1602
Cox, Kenneth N. E., 1422
Cox, Peter A., 1422
Crabtree, Adam, 702

Craggs, Stewart R., 1200
Craven, Robert R., 1188
Creel, Austin B., 1304
Crime & mystery: the 100 best bks, 1039
Crime dict, rev ed, 523
Critical survey of literary theory, 993
Crowther, Bruce, 1234
Crumb, Lawrence N., 1331
Crystal, David, 933
Cuba: an annotated bibliog, 132
Culbertson, Judi, 24
Cultural atlas of Japan, 108
Cummings, D. W., 967
Cummings, Paul, 898
Cummins, Light Townsend, 436
Cumulative bk index 1986, 13
Cumulative index of sociology journals 1971-85,
    751
Cunningham, Scott, 703
Cunningham, William A., 1478
Cunningham's ency of crystal, gem & metal
    magic, 703
Curley, Dorothy Nyren, 996
Current biography yrbk 1987, 20
Current Christian bks, 1988-89, 16
Cuscuna, Michael, 1235
Cyclopedic dict of law, 506

Da Capo gd to contemporary African music,
    1233
Daintith, John, 1640, 1677
Damon, S. Foster, 1100
Dandurand, Karen, 1071
Danforth, Ellen Zak, 876
Daniel Pinkham: a bio-bibliog, 1201
Darch, Colin, 100
Darnay, Brigitte T., 1411
Darton, Michael, 1311
Data & computer security, 1628
Datta, Amaresh, 1156
Daugherty, F. Mark, 1219
Daume, Daphne, 45
Davenport, J. M., 1675
David, Jack, 1140
David Rabe: a stage hist ..., 1291
Davidson, Martha, 903
Davies, Maureen, 665
Davis, Hazel K., 1014
Davis, James E., 163, 1014
Davis, Joseph R., 1498, 1499
Davis, Neil M., 1533
Davis, Thadious M., 1051
Davis, Walter Goodwin, 375
Day, Alan J., 623
Day, Glenn, 637
De Lorme, Roland L., 431
de Martigny, Julie, 844
De Sola, Ralph, 523

de Winter, Patrick M., 862
Deahl, James, 1136
Deane, Bill, 716
Debenham, Warren, 855
DeBoer, Kee, 1201
Decalo, Samuel, 91, 93, 101
Definitive Kobbé's opera bk, rev ed, 1226
Defu, Wang, 971
Degenhardt, Henry W., 664
Del Mar, Norman, 1178
DeLashmitt, Eleanor, 520
DeLoach, Charles, 1117
Delson, Eric, 336
Denmark, 117
Desktop ency of banking, 206
Desktop ency of corporate finance &
    accounting, 179
Desktop reference to the Int'l Reading Assn
    1988-89, 273
Destroyers of WW II, 609
Development directory, 154
Developmental psychology in India 1975-86,
    693
DeVenney, David P., 1218
Dewdney, John, 140
Dewey, Patrick R., 1621
Diabetes, liver, & digestive disease, 1556
Diagnostic & statistical manual of mental
    disorders, 3d ed, 1550
Diagram Group, 61, 1547, 1548, 1658
Diamond greats, 725
Diane Wakoski: a descriptive bibliog, 1088
Dibner, Mark D., 212
DiCanio, Margaret, 1355
Dickens chronology, 1106
Dickinson scholarship: an annotated bibliog
    1969-85, 1071
Dickstein, Ruth, 551
Dictionaries, encys, & other word-related bks,
    4th ed, 927
Dictionary of ...
    accounting terms, 176
    American biography, suppl 8, 25
    American idioms, 2d ed, 949
    American nursing biography, 1578
    antibiotics & related substances, 1580
    battles, 588
    behavioral assessment techniques, 695
    Brazilian lit, 1135
    bldg, 1485
    Chinese Buddhist terms, 1327
    concepts in general psychology, 697
    concepts in physical geography, 383
    concepts in the philosophy of science,
        1349
    confusable words, 958
    contemporary American artists, 5th ed,
        898
    contemporary quotations, rev ed, 74

Dictionary of ... *(continued)*
  days, 1251
  demons, 704
  developmental drama, 1294
  early Zhou Chinese, 973
  effects & phenomena in physics, 1681
  electronics & electrical engineering, 3d
    ed, 1488
  environmental protection technology,
    1408
  epidemiology, 2d ed, 1520
  finance, 203
  folk artists in Canada, 880
  food & nutrition, 1371
  gambling & gaming, 736
  gemmology, 2d ed, 1668
  genetics & cell biology, 1413
  gerontology, 755
  high-energy physics in 4 langs, 1682
  industrial security, 1627
  jargon, 950
  legal quotations, 521
  literary biography documentary series,
    v.5, 1054
  marketing, 245
  mathematical games, puzzles, & amuse-
    ments, 737
  medical eponyms, 1541
  Mexican American proverbs, 1244
  microbiology & molecular biology, 2d
    ed, 1416
  modern Indian hist 1707-1947, 456
  music production & engineering terminol-
    ogy, 1179
  narratology, 990
  nuclear power & waste mgmt ..., 1507
  organophosphorus compounds, 1641
  outrageous quotations, 75
  Russian lit since 1917, 1164
  SDI, 1474
  S. African English, 3d ed, 963
  terms used in the safety profession, 3d
    ed, 1510
  the Middle Ages, v.10, 484
  the Middle Ages, v.11, 485
  the Middle Ages, v.12, 486
  the Vietnam War, 457
  toxicology, 1581
  weeds of eastern Europe, 1431
  words & phrases used in ancient & modern
    law, 501
Dictionary to the novels of James Fenimore
    Cooper, 1070
Die wunderbare neue welt, 448
Diem, Richard A., 312
DiPrima-LeConche, Patricia, 236
Directory for successful publishing in legal
    periodicals, 513

Directory of ...
  addiction professionals, 1988-89, 783
  aerospace educ'l programs in Canada, the
    U.S. & abroad, 1473
  agencies & organizations serving deaf-blind
    individuals, rev ed, 760
  American libs with genealogy or local hist
    collections, 569
  American research & technology 1988, 153
  American youth organizations, 1988-89, 785
  archives & manuscript repositories in the
    U.S., 2d ed, 424
  assns in Canada, 9th ed, 50
  biomedical & health care grants 1988, 1522
  bk, catalog, & magazine printers, 4th ed, 582
  congressional voting scores & interest group
    ratings, 656
  Europeanist anthropologists in N. America,
    335
  facilities & services for the learning disabled,
    1987-88, 320
  federal hist'l programs & activities, 450
  franchising organizations, 1988, 186
  geoscience depts: U.S. & Canada, 26th ed,
    1657
  historic American theatres, 1295
  intellectual property lawyers & patent agents,
    1988-89 ed, 512
  Islamic financial institutions, 207
  lib & info professionals, 536
  lib & info retrieval software for micro-
    computers, 3d ed, 559
  nat'l institutions of educ'l planning &
    administration in Asia & the Pacific,
    318
  New Brunswick museums & related institu-
    tions, 51
  nursing homes, 3d ed, 1523
  oral hist collections, 427
  overseas educ'l advising centers, 317
  residential facilities for emotionally handi-
    capped children & youth, 2d ed, 763
  safety related computer resources, 1987 ed,
    1511
  social science info courses, 1988, 81
  software in higher educ, 313
  software sources for higher educ, 314
  special libs & info centers 1987: Colo., S.D.,
    Utah, Wyo., 568
  telefacsimile sites in libs in the U.S. &
    Canada, 3d ed, 557
  testing laboratories, 1988 ed, 1354
  theme & amusement parks, 710
  travel agencies for the disabled, 403
  treasure hunting, prospecting, & related
    organizations, 745
  U.S. labor organizations, 1988-89 ed, 225
  U.S. mail drops, 197
  women's media, 1988, 821

Directory on European training institutions ... in ... diplomacy ... public administration & mgmt, economic & social development, 673

Discovering nature with young people, 1438

Dissertations & theses on Venezuelan topics, 1900-1985, 138

Division of Human Rights & Peace, 531, 685

Division of Science & Technology Policies, UNESCO, 1362

Dixon, Dougal, 1669

Dizik, A. Allen, 863

Doctoral dissertations on Asia, v.10, 106

Dodgers bibliog, 723

Doenecke, Justus D., 437

Dolnick, Sandy F., 769

Dominica, 134

Donath, Jackie R., 1262

Donegani, Karen, 1509

Dore, Ian, 1457

Dore, Susan Cole, 86

Dorf, Richard C., 1626

Dorgan, Charity Anne, 247

Dorland's illus medical dict, 27th ed, 1538

Dorman, Phae H., 1477

Dorsey dict of American govt & politics, 640

Dostal, Cyril A., 1496

Douglas-Young, John, 1487

Doumato, Lamia, 912

Dow Jones-Irwin investor's gd to online databases, 192

Dr. Axelrod's mini-atlas of freshwater aquarium fishes, mini-ed, 1456

Drew, Bernard A., 1033

Drug cos & products world gd, 1584

Drug facts & comparisons, 1988 ed, 1588

Drury, George H., 1689

Dryden, Laurel, 226

Duarte, Carlota, 903

Duffy, Bernard K., 441

Duffy, Susan, 808

Duncan, Alastair, 864

Duncan, Marion B., 1434

Duncan, Wilbur H., 1434

Dunkling, Leslie, 1251

Dunlap, Leslie W., 442

Dupuis, Diane L., 801

Durbin, Paul T., 8, 1349

Dutta, Ranjana, 693

Dwyer-Rigby, Mary, 1398

Dyck, Cornelius J., 1336

Dye, David, 1280

Dyer, Hilary, 559

Dying child: an annotated bibliog, 688

Dying, death, & grief, 758

E. L. Doctorow: an annotated bibliog, 1072

E. V. Lucas & his bks, 1112

Eadie, Bruce, 37

Earls, Irene, 899

Early American choral music, 1218

Early bks on cricket, 729

Early scientific instruments, 1347

Earth report, 1404

Earth science on file, 1652

Eastern birds, 1442

Eaton, Richard, 1082

Eberly, Stephen L., 1260

Echard, William E., 674

Eckhardt, Robert C., 1625

Economic Commission for Latin America & the Caribbean, 128

Economics: a resource bk for secondary schools, 163

Economist, The, 799

Edelheit, Abraham J., 351

Edelheit, Hershel, 351

Edible wild plants of Nova Scotia, 1432

Edmonds, Diana, 1509

Edmunds, R. David, 353

Edmundson, R. S., 1641

Education journals & serials, 268

Educational media & technology yrbk 1988, 263

Educational outcomes: ... a directory of student outcome measurements ..., 1577

Educational outcomes: ... an annotated bibliog, 1576

Educational Software Lib of Carnegie Mellon Univ, 314

Educators' hndbk to interactive videodisc, 2d ed, 1629

Edward Albee: a reference gd, 1068

Edward Bellamy: an annotated bibliog ..., 1069

Edwards, Bill, 873

Edwards, Charles J., 290

Edwards, Gary, 890

Edwards, Julia, 838

Edwin Arlington Robinson & the critics, 1084

Eerdmans analytical concordance to the Revised Standard Version of the Bible, 1316

Eerdmans Bible dict, 1317

Eggenberger, David, 21, 22, 900

Ehrlich, Eugene, 709

Eighteenth century: a current bibliog, n.s.9, 819

Eighteenth century British & Irish promptbks, 1292

Eiss, Harry Edwin, 737

Ekstrom, Brenda L., 803

Elections glossary, 625

Electric motor hndbk, 1486

Electronics sourcebk for technicians & engineers, 1489

Elementary school lib collection, 16th ed, 565

Eleuterio-Comer, Susan K., 349

Elfe, Wolfgang D., 1153, 1154

Eliade, Mircea, 1313

Elias, Stephen R., 504

Ellefson, Connie Lockhart, 380
Eller, William, 272
Elliker, Calvin, 1232
Ellingtonia, 3d ed, 1237
Elliot, Jeffrey M., 638
Elliot, Wendy, 370
Elliott, David L., 260
Elliott, Mark R., 1332
Elliott, Susan K., 152
Ellis, Charles Grant, 878
Elshami, Ahmed M., 1600
Elting, John R., 595
Ely, Donald P., 263
Emard, Jean-Paul, 869, 1599
Embree, Ainslie T., 455
Emerging stock markets factbk 1988, 187
Emerton, Bruce, 309
Emiliani, Cesare, 1653
Emmott, Bill, 151
Employment creation policies & strategies, 226
Employment of the learning disabled, 761
Encyclopaedia of ...
   everlastings, 886
   Indian lit, v.I, 1156
   Indian medicine, 1539
   military models 1/72, 874
Encyclopedia of ...
   American business hist & biography: rail-
      roads in the age of regulation, 1900-
      1980, 213
   American business hist & biography: rail-
      roads in the 19th century, 214
   American film comedy, 1276
   American humorists, 1066
   American intelligence & espionage, 639
   American religions: religious creeds, 1312
   architecture design, engineering & construc-
      tion, v.1, 914
   art deco, 864
   Asian hist, 455
   assns assn periodicals, v.2, 1361
   assns 1988, v.4, 52
   British women writers, 1096
   chemical processing & design, [v.]28, 1478
   conditioning rinse ingredients, 1646
   emulsion technology, v.3, 1475
   field & general geology, 1659
   fluid mechanics, v.7, 1479
   frontier biography, 446
   historic forts, 452
   human evolution & prehistory, 336
   legal info sources, 490
   lib & info science, v.42, 533
   lib & info science, v.43, 534
   Lotus 1 2 3, 1609
   magic & magicians, 738
   medical devices & instrumentation, 1540
   microcomputers, v.1, 1622
   microcomputers, v.2, 1623

   Native American tribes, 364
   pharmaceutical technology, v.1, 1583
   plastics, polymers, & resins, v.IV, 1637
   public affairs info sources, 78
   religion, v.16, 1313
   rhododendron hybrids, 1422
   school administration & supervision, 276
   statistical sciences, v.8, 793
   statistical sciences, v.9, 794
   structural geology & plate tectonics, 1666
   suicide, 1551
   technical market indicators, 183
   the world's air forces, 602
   TV game shows, 860
   Ukraine, v.II, 123
   unsolved crimes, 522
   Walt Disney's animated characters, 1273
   world art, v.XVII, suppl II, 900
   world biography, 20th century suppl, v.14, 21
   world biography, 20th century suppl, v.15, 22
   world faiths, 1311
Encyclopedic dict of mathematics, 2d ed, 1673
Encyclopedic dict of science, 1350
Engelberg, Karsten Klejs, 1124
Engineered materials hndbk, v.1, 1496
Engineering research centres, 2d ed, 1468
English, Arthur, 501
English-German contrastive linguistics, 931
English-lang dicts, 1604-1900, 936
Eponyms in psychology, 698
Ercolano, Patrick, 717
Erickson, Judith B., 785
Erlick, Louise S., 648
Ernest Bloch: a gd to research, 1206
Ervin, Gary W., 1571
Esanu, Warren H., 257a
Essential gd to wills, estates, trusts, & death
     taxes, updated & expanded ed, 518
Ethics & public policy, 686
Ethics & the professor, 278
Ethnic I: a sourcebk for ethnic-American
     autobiography, 1056
Ethnoart: Africa, Oceania, & the Americas, 892
Etiquette: Charlotte Ford's gd to modern
     manners, 1252
ETS test collection catalog, v.2, 325
Eugene O'Neill: an annotated bibliog, 1082
Eurofi (UK) Ltd., 205
European American elderly, 752
European Centre for Higher Educ, 319
European decorative arts 1400-1600, 862
European directory of non-official statistical
     sources 1988, 795
Evans, Glen, 1551
Everett, Jane, 775
Everett, Thomas H., 1390
Evidence continues to grow, 271
Evinger, William R., 796
Exploring common ground, 286

Explosives, 3d ed, 1480
Export sales & marketing manual, 240
Eyeopeners!, 1021

F. Scott Fitzgerald: a descriptive bibliog, rev ed, 1073
Facciola, Peter C., 824
Faces of America, 26
Fachinformationszentrum Chemie GmbH, 1651
Factor, Regis A., 164
Facts & dates of American sports, 709
Facts & figures on govt finance, 1988-89 ed, 257
Facts on File dict of ...
   archaeology, rev ed, 422
   biology, rev ed, 1417
   chemistry, rev ed, 1640
   geology & geophysics, 1661
   health care mgmt, 1521
   marine science, 1670
   mathematics, rev ed, 1674
   physics, rev ed, 1677
   troublesome words, rev ed, 947
Facts on File ency of world mythology & legend, 1250
Facts on File scientific yrbk 1988, 1355
Fairchild's dict of fashion, 2d ed, 888
Falk, Peter Hastings, 909
Faller, Greg S., 1274
Families in transition, 765
Family gd to movies on video, 857
Family law dict, 504
Family physician's compendium of drug therapy, 1589
Family therapy, 691
Famous judges & famous trials, 498
FAO production yrbk, 1987, 1381
Far East & Australasia 1988, 104
Farberow, Norman L., 1551
Farmer, Penny, 1402
Farrand, John, Jr., 1442
Farudi, Daryush, 585
Fausset, A. R., 1318
Federal biotechnology info resources directory, 1492
Federal biotechnology programs directory, 1493
Federal documents librarianship, 1879-1987, 56
Federal executive directory, 644
Federal info sources in health & medicine, 1514
Federal public policy on aging since 1960, 753
Federal regional executive directory, 645
Federal statistical data bases, 796
Federal Writers' Project of the Work Projects Administration, 409
Felknor, Bruce L., 542
Feminist literary criticism, 1975-81, 809
Fenton, Thomas P., 89, 624
Fermented foods of the world, 1379
Fernett, Gene, 1272

Ferrell, Robert H., 429
Fiberworks directory of self-published bks on the fiber arts, 881
Fiction writers gdlines, 834
Fieg, Eugene C., Jr., 1315
Field gd to ...
   eastern forests: N. America, 1386
   eastern trees: eastern U.S. & Canada, 1437
   geology, 1658
   hawks of N. America, 1441
   reptiles & amphibians of Tex., 1466
   seabirds of the world, 1443
Field primatology: a gd to research, 1461
Fielding, Ann, 1671
Fifty southern writers after 1900, 1049
Fifty southern writers before 1900, 1048
Filby, P. William, 367, 569
Filipino writers in English, 1149
Film, television & stage music on phonograph records, 1187
Film/video Canadiana 1985-86, 1282
Films in Review, editors of, 1283
Financial aid for the disabled & their families 1988-89, 762
Financial aid for veterans, military personnel & their dependents 1988-89, 297
Financial Post Moneywise Magazine dict of personal finance, 208
Financial Times industrial cos, 215
Financial Times who's who in world oil & gas, 8th ed, 1399
Findex 1988, 237
Fine, Larry, 1215
Finkl, Charles W., Jr., 1659
Finnegan, Robert, 1359
Firkin, B. G., 1541
Fisher, Benjamin Franklin, IV, 1040
Fisher, James C., 276
Fisiak, Jacek, 928
Fiske, Edward B., 305
Fitzgerald, Carol Bondhus, 432
Fitzgerald, Daniel, 408
Fitzgerald, Sheila, 1046
Five kingdoms, 2d ed, 1414
500 best British & foreign films to buy, rent or videotape, 1283
5000 Russian words, 978
Fleisher, Paul, 612
Fleming, Shirley, 1182
Flemming, Peter A., 677
Fletcher, Marvin, 605
Floor coverings for historic bldgs, 887
Flora, Joseph M., 1048, 1049
Florida almanac 1988-89, 85
Flowers of south-west Europe, 1426
Floyd, Phylis, 917
Fluid mechanics source bk, 1502
Flute music by women composers, 1196
FOCUS, 4th ed, 537

Food additives & their impact on health, 1579
Food & Agriculture Organization of the UN, 1380
Food & nutrition in the Middle East, 1970-86, 1368
Football register, 1988 ed, 731
Foran, Chris, 1262
Ford, Charlotte, 1252
Fordyce, Rachel, 1102
Foreign & Commonwealth Office, 116
Foreign policy of the French Second Empire, 674
Forrest, Joshua, 98
Forys, Marsha, 1288
Foster, Dennis L., 188
Foster, M. Marie Booth, 1050
Foundation Center source bk profiles Jan-Mar 1988, 768
Founders of British physiology, 1535
Four thousand yrs of urban growth, 800
Fowlie-Flores, Fay, 137
Fox, Alistair, 1126
Fox, Elyse H., 502
Fox, Richard, 1465
Fradin, Dennis Brindell, 23
Francis, Charles C., 642
Franck, Irene M., 264, 592, 1254, 1356
Frangne, R., 1371
Frank Capra: a gd to references & resources, 1264
Frank, Frederick S., 1041, 1127
Frank Norris & The Wave, 1081
Frankena, Frederick, 1403
Frankena, Joann Koelln, 1403
Fraser, P. M., 381
Fredericksen, Burton B., 921
Free (& almost free) software for the Macintosh, 1625
Free help from Uncle Sam to start your own business, 201
Free money for humanities & social sciences, 2d ed, 281
Free money for small businesses & entrepreneurs, 180
Free things for teachers, rev ed, 275
Free voices in Russian lit, 1950s-80s, 1165
Freedom in the world, 1987-88, 529
Freeman, Michael, 473
Freiert, Patricia N., 894
French novelists, 1900-1930, 1150
French novelists, 1930-60, 1151
French Romanesque sculpture, 925
French XX bibliog, v.VIII, no.4, issue no.39, 1152
French-English dict of legal & commercial terms, 505
French-English dict of legal words & phrases ..., 509
Frey, Robert L., 214

Frick, John W., 1295
Fried, Lewis, 1055
Friedman, Jack P., 252
Frimodt, Claus, 1457
From Abenaki to Zuni, 366
From Arnold Schoenberg's literary legacy, 1197
Frost, Elizabeth, 663
Frost, Wendy, 809
Fry, Ronald W., 306, 307
Fulton, Len, 583
Fundraising for nonprofit institutions, 769
Fungoes, floaters & fork balls, 717
Future & fantastic worlds, 1043

G. B. Shaw: an annotated bibliog ... , v.II, 1123
Gacs, Ute, 333
Gagnon, André, 1000
Gagnon, Ann, 1000
Gailey, Harry A., 94
Galal, Osman M., 1368
Gale, Steven H., 1066
Gambia, 95
Gamble, David P., 95
Gans, Deborah, 915
Garay, Ronald, 848
Gardener's bk of sources, 1393
Gardener's index for 1987, 1394
Gardener's index of plants & flowers, 1390
Garg, Gaṅgā Rām, 1157
Garland, Anne Witte, 813
Garraty, John A., 25
Garrett, Judith M., 1466
Gastil, Raymond D., 529
Gay/lesbian events of 1988, 776
Gaylord, Charles N., 1482
Gaylord, Edwin H., Jr., 1482
Gazdar, Gerald, 929
Gazetteer of Inuit place names in Nunavik (Quebec, Canada), 399
Geahigan, Priscilla C., 173
Geffner, Edwin S., 1589
Gélinas-Surprenant, Hélène, 746
Gender, unpaid labor, & the promotion of literacy, 326
Genealogical dict of Maine & N.H., 375
Genealogical periodical annual index, v.26, 378
Genealogical research & resources, 371
Genealogical research directory 1988, 368
General reference bks for adults, 32
General surgery, 1547
Genetic engineering & biotechnology related firms worldwide directory 1988/89, 1494
Genocide: a critical bibliographic review, 528
Geologists & the hist of geology, suppl 1979-84, 1665
Georg Lukacs, 669
George Herbert: an annotated bibliog ... , rev ed, 1110

Gerard, David, 1125, 1129
Gerbner, George, 825
Gerhartz, Wolfgang, 1642
German fiction writers, 1885-1913, 1155
German stage, 1767-1890, 1297
Gerould, James Thayer, 1128
Gerould, Winifred Gregory, 1128
Gerow, Edwin, 1304
Gertrude Stein companion, 1086
Gettings, Fred, 704
Ghost towns of Kans., 408
Ghost walks, 1293
Giacona, Nicola, 1595
Gianakos, Larry James, 856
Giantvalley, Scott, 1068
Gibaldi, Joseph, 832
Gibilisco, Stan, 1490
Gibraltar, 118
Gibson, Carol, 1674
Gibson, Ellen M., 516
Gifford, Courtney D., 225
Gilbert, Alan D., 458
Gilbert, Dennis A., 83
Gilbert, Sara, 770
Gilcher, Edwin, 1113
Gill, Kay, 196
Gillespie, John T., 1019
Gilmer, Lois C., 371
Gilmore, David D., 335
Girolamo Frescobaldi: a gd to research, 1204
GIS gd to 4-yr colleges, 1989, 287
Gispen, W. H., 1317
Glanze, Walter D., 775
Glazer, Mark, 1244
Glenn, Judith A., 810
Global gd to medical info, 1545
Global marketplace, 217
Glossary of ...
    computing terms, 5th ed, 1607
    dams, 1483
    geology, 3d ed, 1660
    Greek Romany as spoken in Agia Varvara
       (Athens), 977
Glossary Working Party, British Computer
    Society, 1607
Goehring, James E., 1316
Goeller, Priscilla S., 299
Goetz, Philip W., 44
Gold, Victor, 1638
Goldsmith, Edward, 1404
Goldstein, Amy J., 308
Gondolf, Edward W., 764
Gonen, Rivka, 1319
Good words to you, 943
Goodman, Clifford, 1526
Gordon, W. Terrence, 930
Gorman, G. E., 477
Gorton, Richard A., 276
Gotelli, Ilze, 1401

Gothic fiction: a master list ..., 1041
Gothic's gothic: study aids ..., 1040
Gotthold, Donald W., 124
Gotthold, Julia J., 124
Gould, Lewis L., 630
Government reference bks 86/87, 10th biennial
    v., 57
Government reference serials, 58
Graduate scholarship bk, 283
Graduate schools & financial aid, 3d ed, 288
Graham, Ronnie, 1233
Granatstein, J. L., 468
Grandchamp-Tupula, Mariette, 1483
Grant, John, 1273
Grant, Michael, 488
Grants & awards available to American writers,
    15th ed, 827
Grants for museums, 771
Grants register 1989-91, 289
Gravel, Pierre Bettez, 334
Gravesteijn, J., 1664
Gray, John, 1224
Grayson, Lesley, 1405
Great American bridges & dams, 1484
Great clowns of American television, 850
Great composers, 1202
Great Jews on stage & screen, 1256
Great leaders of the Christian church, 1338
Great lives from hist: ancient & medieval series,
    482
Great lives from hist: British & Commonwealth
    series, 463
Great opera classics, rev ed, 1227
Great theatres of London, 1298
Great vacations with your kids, 404
Great Western pictures II, 1287
Greatest 1st basemen of all time, 719
Greatest pitchers of all time, 720
Grecu, Monica M., 1061, 1062
Greek & Roman art, architecture, &
    archaeology, 2d ed, 894
Green, Jay P., 1320
Green, Jonathon, 950
Green, Laura R., 904
Greenberg, Stan, 711
Greenberg's gd to Lionel prewar parts & instruc-
    tion sheets, 875
Greenfield, Edward, 1186
Greenfield, Gerald Michael, 227
Greenfieldt, John, 1031
Greenman, David, 1692
Grenville, J. A. S., 675, 676
Grieb, Kenneth J., 125
Griffith, H. Winter, 1590
Grigory, Margit N., 671
Grim, William E., 1203
Grimes, Janet, 1184, 1185
Grinstein, Louise S., 1672
Gross, Jerome S., 255

Gross, Steve, 194
Grote, David, 820
Grover Cleveland: a bibliog, 633
Grover, David H., 606
Gubernatorial & presidential transitions, 628
Guidance Info System, editors of, 287
Guide to ...
  American art schools, 908
  bird finding in Kans. & western Mo., 1452
  corporate giving in the arts 4, 907
  current nat'l bibliogs in the Third World, 2d
    ed, 477
  documentary editing, 833
  federal funding for educ, 1988, 290
  folktales in the English lang, 1243
  foreign missionary manuscripts in the
    Presbyterian Hist'l Society, 1329
  income tax preparation, 1989 ed, 257a
  Indian philosophy, 1304
  local & family hist at the Newberry Lib, 377
  modern defense & strategy, 590
  nat'l & state arts educ services, 906
  nuclear weapons, 615
  ocean dune plants common to N.C., 1421
  sources on women in the Swarthmore College
    Peace Collection, 682
  state environmental programs, 1406
  statistical sources in money, banking, &
    finance, 204
  the *Archiv für Sozialwissenschaft und
    Sozialpolitik* Group, 1904-33, 164
  the hist of Mass., 439
  the hist of Tex., 436
  the Nat'l Archives of the U.S., 425
  the New Testament, 1326
  the presidential advisory commissions
    1973-84, 659
  tourist railroads & railroad museums, 1689
  Trollope, 1128
  writers conferences, 1989, 828
Guidos, Barbara, 1534
Guild: a sourcebk of American craft artists, 879
Guinness sports record bk, 1988-89, 713
Guither, Harold D., 1365
Gunson, Alison, 559
Gunston, Bill, 613
Gutierrez, David, 562
Gutter life & lang in the early "street" lit of
    England, 951
Guttmann, David, 752

H. G. Wells: a reference gd, 1131
H. L. Mencken: a research gd, 1079
Haberman, Donald C., 1123
Hage, Mary Agnes, 1366
Halcrow, Harold G., 1365
Halicki-Conrad, Adam, 561
Hall, Hal W., 1044

Halleron, Trish A., 1558
Halstead, Bruce W., 1464
Halter, Marilyn, 92
Hamilton, Betty, 1534
Hamilton, David A., 1259
Hamilton, Malcolm, 402
Hammond, Frederick, 1204
Hand that holds the camera, 1266
Handbook for bklovers, 870
Handbook for research in American hist, 451
Handbook of ...
  American popular lit, 1057
  American-Jewish lit, 1055
  British regiments, 604
  business info, 148
  computer-communications standards, 1616
  int'l business, 2d ed, 169
  int'l mgmt, 234
  Latin American studies, no.48, 126
  mammals of the north-central states, 1460
  N. American birds, vols.4-5, 1448
  state legislative leaders 1988, 652
  state police, highway patrols, & investigative
    agencies, 527
  the American frontier, v.I, 354
Handbook on injectable drugs, 5th ed, 1591
Hannings, Bud, 587
Hanson, Patricia King, 1257
Hanson, Stephen L., 1257
Hardin, James, 1153, 1154, 1155
Harewood, Earl of, 1226
Hargraves, Michael, 1074
Harnly, Caroline D., 586
Harper atlas of the Bible, 1324
Harper atlas of world hist, 479
Harper dict of modern thought, rev ed, 37
Harper's Bible commentary, 1321
Harrap's French vocabulary, 974
Harrap's pocket French-English dict, 975
Harris, Diana K., 755
Harris, Duncan, 267
Harris, Jack C., 252
Harris, Laurie Lanzen, 1046
Harris, Lorna B., 265
Harris, Sherwood, 265
Harris, Steve, 1187, 1236
Harris, Trudier, 1051
Harrison, Charles, 277
Harrison, Gail G., 1368
Harrison, Peter, 1443
Hart, James D., 84
Hartley, Peter, 1602
Hartling, Dianne, 1604
Harzig, Christiane, 835, 836
Haselbauer, Kathleen J., 1515
Hassler, Peggy M., 1506
Hauser, Paula, 997
Havard, C. W. H., 1537
Havighurst, Alfred F., 465

Hay, Peter, 174
Hayes, R. M., 1281
Hayward, John, 1423
Hazardous chemicals on file, 1648
Heacock, Paul, 968
Health devices sourcebk 1988, 1524
Health hazards of video display terminals, 3d
    ed, 1603
Health media review index 1984-86, 1532
Health resource builder, 1518
Healthy harvest II, 1366
Healy, Diana Dixon, 443
Heaney, H. J., 1
Heard, J. Norman, 354
Heat wave: the Motown fact bk, 1239
Heck, Thomas F., 1289
Hecker, Helen, 403
Hedges, Donna M., 761
Heffron, Mary J., 89, 624
Heggie, Grace, 68
Heitor Villa-Lobos: a bio-bibliog, 1194
Helen Keller Nat'l Center for Blind-Deaf Youths
    & Adults, 760
Help for children, 3d ed, 788
Henderson, Anne T., 271
Henderson, Bill, 62
Hendon, Donald W., 249
Hendrickson, Linnea, 1020
Henke, James T., 951
Henne, Robert E., 295
Henry, Richard C., 1631
Henry VIII: an annotated bibliog,
    1119
Herbert Marcuse, 80
Heroes in space, 1470
Herold, Jean, 238
Herring, Kenneth Lee, 699
Herring, Mark Youngblood, 278
Hersen, Michel, 695
Herx, Henry, 857
Heuser, Frederick J., Jr., 1329
High interest easy reading for junior & senior
    high school students, 5th ed, 1001
Higher educ in American life, 1636-1986,
    279
High-interest bks for teens, 2d ed, 1007
High-temperature property data: ferrous alloys,
    1497
Hightshoe, Gary L., 1435
Hildebrandt, Darlene Myers, 1610
Hildreth, Sandra S., 189
Hildyard, Nicholas, 1404
Hillman, Thomas A., 790
Himalayas: a classified social scientific bibliog,
    102
Hiram Johnson: a bio-bibliog, 635
Hispanic heritage, series III, 1010
Hispanic resource directory, 348
Historical atlas of Wash., 431

Historical dict of ...
    American industrial lang, 218
    Benin, 2d ed, 91
    Chad, 2d ed, 93
    Chile, 2d ed, 131
    Cuba, 133
    Guinea (Republic of Guinea/Conakry), 2d
       ed, 97
    N. American archaeology, 419
    the Gambia, 2d ed, 94
    the 1920s, 449
    the Republic of Cape Verde, 2d ed, 92
    the Republic of Guinea-Bissau, 2d ed, 98
    Togo, 2d ed, 101
Historical ency of costumes, 889
History & gd to Judaic encys & lexicons, 1342
History of rock & roll, 1240
Hladczuk, John, 272
Hockey gd, 1988-89 ed, 739
Hockey register, 1988-89 ed, 740
Hodgson, Ernest, 1581
Hodous, Lewis, 1327
Hoerder, Dirk, 835, 836
Hoffmann, Frank, 1231
Hoffmann, Lee Ann, 1231
Hoffmeister, Donald F., 1463
Hofmann, Paul, 416
Holocaust studies, 472
Holston, Kim, 1265
Holt, Daniel D., 982
Holt, Grace Massey, 982
Holte, James Craig, 1056
Home Bible study dict, 1318
Honig, Donald, 719, 720
Hooper, Brad, 1045
Hoover, Herbert T., 358
Hoppel, Joe, 718, 733
Horn, David, 1169
Horner, Catherine Townsend, 1002
Horowitz, Michael, 690
Horse lover's gd to Tex., 1455
Horse stories: an annotated bibliog ..., 1011
Horton, Holbrook L., 1503
Horvath, Laszlo, 129
Hourani, Albert, 141
How to ...
    find chemical info, 2d ed, 1647
    find info about AIDS, 1559
    look things up & find things out, 542
Howard, Edrice Marguerite, 310
Howard, Elizabeth F., 1003
Howard, Joyce M., 1358
Howard, Patricia, 1205
Hoy, Michael, 197
Hoy, Peter C., 1152
Hubbard, Linda S., 444
Huber, Thomas P., 383
Hubin, Allen J., 1038
Hudson, Heather E., 846

Hughes, Christopher C., 1372
Hugo Wolf: a gd to research, 1207
Hull, Debra L., 822
Huls, Mary Ellen, 1579
Human diseases, 2d ed, 1555
Human rights terminology in int'l law, 530
Humanities: a selective gd to info sources, 3d ed, 817
Hunt, Candida, 1350
Hunt, Thomas C., 1308
Hunting, Anthony L. L., 1646
Hunyadi, Karoly, 1431
Hupper, William G., 1322
Hurt, C. D., 1344
Hutchinson ency, 8th ed, 41
Hutchinson pocket ency, 42

IBI Int'l Business Intelligence development aid, 205
Idaho place names, 398
Ifkovic, John W., 439
Illustrated dict of ...
   electronics, 4th ed, 1490
   silverware, 865
   Western lit, 989
Illustrated ency of aircraft armament, 613
Illustrated encyclopedic dict of electronics, 2d ed, 1487
Illustrated gd to shrimp of the world, 1457
Illustrated world atlas, 388
Images of blacks in American culture, 341
Immigrant labor press in N. America, 1840s-1970s, v.2, 835
Immigrant labor press in N. America, 1840s-1970s, v.3, 836
Index gd to Modern American Lit & Modern British Lit, 996
Index of ...
   American periodical verse: 1986, 1092
   American print exhibitions, 1882-1940, 920
   English literary manuscripts, v.II, pt.I, 1094
   English literary manuscripts, v.III, pt.I, 1095
   majors 1988-89, 304
   paintings sold in the British Isles during the 19th century, v.I, 921
   polymer trade names, 1651
   subjects, proverbs, & themes in the writings of Wole Soyinka, 1162
Index to ...
   Afro-American reference resources, 342
   Best American Short Stories & O. Henry Prize Stories, 1065
   collective biographies for young readers, 4th ed, 66
   English periodical lit on the Old Testament & ancient Near Eastern studies, v.II, 1322
   federal programs & services 1987, 627

historic preservation periodicals, 453
journals in communication studies through 1985, 824
literary criticism for young adults, 1026
poetry in popular periodicals, 1960-64, 1091
Puerto Rican collective biography, 137
The Advocate, 1967-82, 777
the contents of the periodical Canadian Lit, suppl 1, 1137
the contents of the periodical Canadian Lit, suppl 2, 1138
the contents of the periodical Canadian Lit, suppl 3, 1139
the Iran-Contra Hearings summary report, 660
the Tower Commission report, 661
Index-dict of Chinese artists, collectors, & connoisseurs with character identification by modified stroke count, 897
Indian Ocean, 124
Indians of ...
   N. America: the Nanticoke, 355
   N. America: the Osage, 356
   N. America: the Potawatomi, 357
   N. America: the Yankton Sioux, 358
   N. & S. America, suppl, 365
INFO LINE taxonomy of human services, 780
Information & the future, 545
Information sources in energy technology, 1397
Information sources in science & technology, 1344
Informative index to the writings of Walter H. Pater, 1115
Inge, M. Thomas, 1057
Ingmar Bergman: a gd to references & resources, 1263
Input-output tables of China, 1981, 165
Insects that feed on trees & shrubs, 2d ed, 1458
Insider's gd to colleges, 1987-88, 291
Institut de Recherche et d'Histoire des Textes, 487
Institute for Antiquity & Christianity, Research Personnel, 1316
Institute of Geography of the Chinese Academy of Sciences, 791
Institute of Mathematical Statistics, 1675
Insurance industry, 222
Interactive fiction & adventure games for microcomputers 1988, 1621
Interlibrary loan policies directory, 3d ed, 558
International bibliog of fertility technology 1983-87, 1565
International bibliog of political science, v.XXXIV, 616
International Committee for Social Science Info & Doc, 616
International Congress calendar, v.3, 27th ed, 3
International dict of films & filmmakers: v.V, 1274

International directory of ...
  acid deposition researchers, 1985-86 ed, 1409
  film & TV documentation centres, 1277
  little magazines & small presses, 24th ed, 583
  medievalists, 6th ed, 487
  research institutions on higher educ, 2d ed, 319
  resources for artisans, 885
International ency of ...
  Indian lit, v.1, rev ed, 1157
  robotics, 1626
  women composers, 2d ed, 1199
International gd to ...
  accounting journals, 177
  19th-century photographers & their works, 890
  tipping, 199
International hndbk of bilingualism & bilingual educ, 934
International hndbk of health-care systems, 1531
International hndbk on abortion, 1568
International hndbk on race & race relations, 338
International marketing hndbk, 3d ed, 239
International Narcotics Control Board, Vienna, 1596
International relations dict, 4th ed, 679
International research centers directory 1988-89, 53
International scholarship bk, 316
International standard Bible ency, v.4, rev ed, 1323
International students & the lib, 561
International trade names dict 1988-89, 239a
International trade names dict 1988-89: company index, 239b
Internships, v.1, 306
Internships, v.2, 307
Introducing bkplots 3, 1024
Introducing children to the arts, 818
Inuit Elders of Nunavik, 399
Investment statistics locator, 182
Investor's info sourcebk, 190
Iran, 142
Iris Murdoch: a reference gd, 1114
Irish American material culture, 349
Irish records, 376
Irish research, 373
Irish, Sharon, 895
Ishibashi, Seiichi, 1488
Isler, Morton L., 1444
Isler, Phyllis R., 1444
Italian printmaking, 15th & 16th centuries, 918
Ito, Kiyosi, 1673

Jackson, Donald C., 1484
Jackson, Jerome A., 1451

Jackson, Julia A., 1660
Jackson, Paul, 119
Jackson, Richard, 1169
Jackson, Roland, 1170
Jacobs, Arthur, 1227
Jacobs, Sonia L., 346
Jaffery, Sheldon, 1043
Jagoe, John R., 240
James, Simon, 521
James, William, 1410
Janes, Michael, 975
Jane's Warsaw Pact merchant ships recognition hndbk, 1692
Jansen, Marius, 108
Japan marketing hndbk, 241
Japan trade directory 1988-89, 242
Japan's economic challenge, 109
Jarboe, Betty M., 1333
Jay, Gregory S., 1058, 1059
Jazz on compact disc, 1236
Jazz singers, 1234
Jean Langlais: a bio-bibliog, 1212
Jefferson, James W., 1582
Jelks, Edward B., 419
Jelks, Juliet C., 419
Jenkins, Esther C., 105
Jenkins, John H., 438
Jerusalem, the holy city, 143
Jessup, Deborah Hitchcock, 1406
Jewish world in modern times, 351
Job title index to SIC (Standard Industrial Classification) codes, 172
Johannes Ockeghem & Jacob Obrecht: a gd to research, 1210
John & Charles Wesley: a bibliog, 1333
John Wain: a bibliog, 1129
Johns, Francis A., 1130
Johnson, Barnabas D., 510
Johnson, Bryan R., 359
Johnson, Carolyn M., 1438
Johnson, Jonathan K., 985
Johnson, Keith A., 368
Johnson, Norman L., 793, 794
Johnson, Warren T., 1458
Johnston, Bernard, 40, 43
Johnston, Keith P., 1476
Joint Chiefs of Staff, 589
Jones, C. Lee, 557
Jones, Constance, 292
Jones dict of cable television terminology, 3d ed, 851
Jones, Dolores Blythe, 1022
Jones, Francine, 768
Jones, Franklin D., 1503
Jones, Glenn R., 851
Jones, J. Knox, Jr., 1460
Jordan, Gerald, 593
Jordon, Dorothy Ann, 404

Joseph Papp & the N.Y. Shakespeare festival, 1290
Joyner, Al, 513
Jud, G. Donald, 206
Junge, Hans-Dieter, 1351
Jungian literary criticism, 1920-80, 692
Juniorplots 3, 1019
Justice Louis D. Brandeis: a bibliog ..., 497
Justice, Noel D., 360

Kallich, Martin, 1133
Kanka, August Gerald, 121
Kanter, Hilary, 571
Kapp, Marshall B., 491
Karpinski, Caroline, 918
Kasack, Wolfgang, 1164
Kaston, Carren O., 49
Katcher, Brian S., 1592
Katlan, Alexander W., 905
Katz, Bernard S., 150
Katz, Ellen L., 1303
Kaufman, Edward, 895
Kaufman, Martin, 439, 1578
Kaufman, Milton, 1489
Kaufmann, Thomas DaCosta, 896
Kavass, Igor I., 492
Kaye, Kim R., 295
Keating, H. R. F., 1039
Kehde, Ned, 74
Kelley-Buchanan, Christine, 1566
Kellner, Bruce, 1086
Kelly, James R., 78
Kelly, Kevin, 823
Kelly, Matthew A., 228
Kelly, Patricia, 1370
Kelly, Robert E., 721
Kelman, Keith, 867
Kelman, Renee, 867
Kemp, Thomas J., 372
Kennedy, Leonard A., 1307
Kent, Allen, 533, 534, 1622, 1623
Keresztesi, Michael, 109
Key indicators of county growth 1970-2010, 166
Keyguide to info sources in business ethics, 167
Keyguide to info sources in CAD/CAM, 1602
Khuong, Huynh-Dinh, 874
Kidd, John, 692
Kidd, Stewart, 1627
Kimball, Robert, 1176
Kincade, William H., 681
King, Christine E., 1290
King, Kamla J., 511
King, Peter, 120
King-Hele, D. G., 1471
Kingston, Charles, 498
Kinnamon, Keneth, 1090
Kinnard, Roy, 1286
Kinnell, Susan K., 454

Kinney, J., Kendrick, 503
Kinsmen through time, 353
Kirchherr, Eugene C., 90
Kirkpatrick, D. L., 1255
Kirsh, Harvey J., 493
Kirsh: selected bibliog of construction law writings in Canada, 493
Kister, Kenneth F., 33
Kister's concise gd to best encys, 33
Kitzinger, Rachel, 488
Kleinz, John P., 1337
Kline, Mary-Jo, 833
Knight, David B., 665
Knirsch, Franco, 385
Knotsville, Betty Lou, 320
Knott's hndbk for vegetable growers, 3d ed, 1392
Knowledge Industry pubs 200, 1987 ed, 216
Knox, George, 922
Kobrin, Beverly, 1021
Kocandrle, Mirek, 1240
Kocs, N. J., 1378
Koek, Karin E., 52
Kolin, Philip C., 1291
Komonchak, Joseph A., 1340
Konigsberg, Ira, 1275
Korean at a glance, 982
Korsmeyer, Pamela, 154
Kotz, Samuel, 793, 794
Kowalski, Janne S., 1584
Kozokoff, Phyllis, 327
Kramer, Ilse E., 448
Kramer, Jack J., 700
Krasker, Tommy, 1176
Kraus, Barbara, 1382, 1383
Kraus, E. Jean Wilson, 1421
Krauss, Clinton K., 1113
Kremer, John, 582
Kricher, John C., 1386
Kronk, Gary W., 1632
Krstović, Jelena O., 1028, 1029
Krummel, D. W., 1171
Kubijovyč, Volodymyr, 123
Kumakura, Isao, 108
Kurian, George Thomas, 261, 311, 1545
Kushner, David Z., 1206
Kwalwasser, Amy, 1455
KWIC concordance to John Cleland's *Memoirs of a Woman of Pleasure*, 1105
KWIC concordance to Samuel Beckett's trilogy, 1158
Kyvig, David E., 440

Labor & industrial relations, 228
LaGasse, Charles E., 1617
Lageson, David, 1656
Lambert, David, 1652, 1658
Land, Brian, 50

Landis, Kenneth M., 192
Lane, Carol McCrory, 1159
Lane, Denis, 1159
Lane, Dermot A., 1340
Lang, Jenifer Harvey, 1373
Lang, Robert, 550
Langhans, Edward A., 1292
Langman, Larry, 1276
Language of sexuality, 779
Langworth, Richard M., 1690
Lantz, Judith C., 751
Lapidus, Dorothy Farris, 1661
Larkin, Robert P., 383
LaRocque, Lionel Edward, 1513
Larousse gastronomique, 1373
Larsen, John C., 426
Last, John M., 1520
Latham, Caroline, 27
Latin American labor organizations, 227
Latin American writers: a bibliog ..., 1160
Lau, Foo-Sun, 1507
Laughter on record, 855
Law bks in print, 5th ed, 494
Law dict & glossary: containing full defini-
    tions ... , 2d ed, 500
Law dict & glossary: primarily for the use of
    students ..., 503
Law lexicon, or dict of jurisprudence, 508
Law librarian's new product directory, 514
Lawless, Richard I., 99
Layton, Daphne Niobe, 772
Layton, Robert, 1186
Lazzari, Marie, 994, 995
Le Corbusier gd, 915
Lea, Richard S., 172
Lead pollution from motor vehicles 1974-86,
    1402
Learning resources programs that make a
    difference, 266
Leavitt, Judith A., 811
Lecker, Robert, 1140
Leed, Richard L., 978
LeFontaine, Joseph Raymond, 870
Legal aspects of health care for the elderly, 491
Legal research dict, 502
Legat, Michael, 989
Legrand, G., 1371
Lehman, Andrea E., 293
Leistritz, F. Larry, 803
Lemieux, Luci, 67
Lend a hand, 770
Lentz, Harris M., III, 620
Leonard, Robin D., 504
LePage, Jane Weiner, 1175
Leppa, Carol J., 1516
Lerner, Craig Alan, 289
Lesbianism: an annotated bibliog ... 1976-86,
    778
Lesko, Matthew, 190

Lester, DeeGee, 373
Lester, Paula E., 258
Lever, Christopher, 1445
Levine, George, 1109
Levine, Michael, 155
Lewin, Albert E., 952
Lewin, Esther, 952
Lewis Carroll: a reference gd, 1102
Lewis, Cathleen S., 1472
Lewis, Norman, 953
Lexicon of Greek personal names, v.I, 381
Lexique de la fiscalité, 256
Lexique de sports d'hiver, 746
Lexique des barrages, 1483
Lexique des élections, 625
LEXUS, 974
Libby, Charles Thornton, 375
Librarian career resource network directory,
    547
Libraries & special collections on Latin America
    & the Caribbean, 2d ed, 127
Library: a gd to the LDS Family Hist Lib, 370
Library & info science annual 1988, 543
Library & info science in China, 555
Library & info sources on women, 815
Library Assn yrbk 1988, 544
Library lit 1987, 546
Library-Anthropology Resource Group, 332
Libya, 99
Lichine, Alexis, 1374
Life sciences organizations & agencies directory,
    1411
Ligotti, Thomas, 994, 995, 1028
Lincoln writing dict for children, 961
Lincove, David A., 631
Lindenthal, Jacob Jay, 1554
Lindow, John, 1249
Lindquist, Carolyn Lloyd, 330
Lingle, Virginia A., 1559
Linguistic atlas of the Gulf states, v.2, 954
Lipson, Eden Ross, 1004
Liska, Ken, 1593
List, Barbara A., 1357
Listen to your body, 1549
Lister, Craig, 1172
Literary agents of N. America, 3d ed, 829
Literary archives gd, 1141
Literary hist of the American West, 1060
Literary presses in Canada, 1975-85, 574
Literature for children about Asians & Asian
    Americans, 105
Literature gd for the identification of plant
    pathogenic fungi, 1430
Literature of American music, suppl I, 1169
Lithium ency for clinical practice, 2d ed, 1582
Litwack, Leon, 339
LMP 1988, 584
Loanwords dict, 946
Lobban, Richard, 92, 98

Lobenstine, Joy C., 756
Lochhead, Douglas G., 1142
Logan, William Bryant, 1393
Longley, Dennis, 1628
Longman hndbk of modern European hist 1763-1985, 469
Longsdorf, George Foster, 506
Looney, Jim, 537
Lopez, Manuel D., 87
Lopos, George J., 294
LoPucki, Lynn M., 512
Lorenz, Oscar A., 1392
Lougheed, W. C., 964
Louis Wirth: a bio-bibliog, 749
Louisiana almanac 1988-89, 86
Lovejoy, Frederick H., 1529
Lovi, George, 1634
Lowell Mason: a bio-bibliog, 1209
Lubin, Bernard, 691
Lubitz, Wolfgang, 666
Luebking, Sandra Hargreaves, 428
Luethi, Geraldine Gant, 1216
Lukenbill, W. Bernard, 1005
Lumsdaine, Joycelyn Pang, 919
Lyman, Darryl, 1256
Lyman, Thomas W., 925
Lynch, Richard Chigley, 1296
Lyndon B. Johnson: a bibliog, v.2, 632
Lyon, Howard H., 1458
Lyon, Sue, 1202

MacDonald, Barbara, 1432
Macdonald, R. Bruce, 761
Macdonald, Roger, 127
Machinery's hndbk, 23d ed, 1503
Macintosh bible, 2d ed, 1624
Mackenzie, Kenneth R. H., 750
Mackesy, Eileen M., 69, 70
Maclean, Norman, 1413
MacLeod, Heather, 1432
Macmillan bk of proverbs, maxims, & famous phrases, 1245
Macmillan illus ency of dinosaurs & prehistoric animals, 1669
Madge, Steve, 1446
Madore, Barry F., 1630
Maggiore, Dolores J., 778
Magill, Frank N., 463, 482, 988, 993
Magne, Lawrence, 847
Magocsi, Paul Robert, 470
Mailman, Richard B., 1581
Maizell, Robert E., 1647
Major int'l treaties 1914-45, 675
Major int'l treaties since 1945, 676
Making of the Shelley myth, 1124
Makkai, Adam, 949
Maksim Gorky: a reference gd, 1163
Malbin, Michael J., 654

Malinowsky, H. Robert, 1560
Mallon, Bill, 714
Malone, Cheryl Knott, 326
Malotte, Stan, 955
Mammals: a gd to familiar American species, rev ed, 1463
Mammals of the intermountain west, 1462
Mandell, Judy, 834
Mann, Thomas E., 654
Mann, Thomas L., 332
Manser, Martin H., 175
Maoláin, Ciarán Ó., 667
Maram, Sheldon L., 227
Marantz, Kenneth A., 1006
Marantz, Sylvia S., 1006
March, Ivan, 1186
Marcus, Sharon J., 237
Margaret Drabble: an annotated bibliog, 1108
Margolis, Susanna, 417
Margulis, Lynn, 1414
Marill, Alvin H., 858
Marketing & sales mgmt, 238
Marketsearch int'l directory of published market research, 12th ed, 243
Markley, O. W., 545
Markus, Manfred, 931
Marowski, Daniel G., 992
Marsden, C. R. S., 75
Marsh, James H., 112
Marsh, Peter, 668
Marshall Cavendish illus ency of plants & earth sciences, 1419
Marszalek, John F., 633
Marth, Del, 85
Marth, Martha J., 85
Martial arts: an annotated bibliog, 743
Martin, Brian P., 1447
Martin, Dolores Moyano, 126
Marx, Robert F., 420
MASA: medical acronyms, symbols, & abbreviations, 2d ed, 1534
Mass murder: an annotated bibliog, 524
Master index to SAS system documentation for personal computers, 1618
Master index to SAS system documentation, version 5 ed, 1619
Master index to SUGI proceedings, 1988 ed, 1620
Mathematical Society of Japan, 1673
Mathematics educ in secondary schools & 2-yr colleges, 1672
Matlon, Ronald J., 824
Matney, William C., 344
Matricardi, Paolo, 597, 598, 599, 600, 601
Matthews, Dorothy, 1001
Matthews, E., 381
Matthews, Rupert O., 1662
Matuz, Roger, 992
Matzen, Robert D., 1261

Max Reger: a bio-bibliog, 1203
Maxwell, Carolyn, 1216
Maya ethnohistory, 474
Mayer, Ira, 216
Maynard, Donald N., 1392
Mays, James L., 1321
McAfee, Michael, 595
McCabe, Carol A., 320
McCalpin, Deborah J., 1532
McCann, Gary, 490
McCann, Joy L., 1394
McCauley, Rosemarie, 250
McClelland, Rosemary, 55, 113, 114
McClendon, J. Frank, 1546
McCormick, Regina, 163
McCullough, Prudence, 200
McDaniel, Susan Leas, 954
McElrath, Joseph R., Jr., 1081
McEvedy, Colin, 430
McGillivray, Alice V., 655
McGinnis, Carol, 374
McGrath, Daniel F., 573
McGraw-Hill ency of electronics & computers, 2d ed, 1608
McGraw-Hill ency of the geological sciences, 2d ed, 1663
McHugh, Francis P., 167
McIver, Tom, 1415
McKendry, Blake, 880
McKetta, John J., 1478
McKinnon, James, 1221
McKusick, Victor A., 1572
McLauchlan, Gordon, 475
McLaughlin, John, 906
McLaughlin, Judith A., 79
McLaughlin, Sara Park, 1111
McLean, Janice, 230
McMullan, Randall, 1485
McNeil, Barbara, 65
McPherson, Marion White, 697
McRae, Bobbi A., 881
Medical abbreviations, 4th ed, 1533
Medical & health care bks & serials in print 1988, 1517
Medical device register 1988, v.1, 1525
Medical technology assessment directory, 1526
Medicare: a hndbk ..., 1530
Medication teaching manual, 4th ed, 1594
Medievalism: an annotated bibliog ..., 895
Mehra, Parshotam, 456
Meier, August, 339
Melanson, Holly, 574
Melting pot bk of baby names, 380
Melton, J. Gordon, 1312
Melville's reading, rev ed, 1078
Memory bank for critical care: EKGs & cardiac drugs, 3d ed, 1571
Mendelian inheritance in man, 8th ed, 1572
Mendenhall, Doris A., 921

Menendez, Albert J., 1034
Mercatante, Anthony S., 1250
Merit students ency, 43
Messing, Gordon M., 977
Metals hndbk, v.14, 9th ed, 1498
Metals hndbk, v.15, 9th ed, 1499
Meteor showers: a descriptive catalog, 1632
Meteorology source bk, 1676
Metro insights, 1989 ed, 804
Meurs, Jos van, 692
Mexican autobiography/la autobiografía Mexicana, 28
Meyer, Bruce, 1136
Meyer, Robert S., 684
Meyer, Rudolf, 1480
Meyers, Thomas A., 183
Michael, Colette V., 340
Michael, Nancy C., 1118
Michaud, Ellen, 1549
Micheli, Linda McJ., 1119
Mickolus, Edward F., 677
MICROLOG 1987, 55
Middle East, 139
Middle East: a directory of resources, 624
Middleton, David L., 1080
Milan Kundera: an annotated bibliog, 1148
Miles, William, 634
Milestones in science & technology, 1357
Miletich, John J., 784
Military balance 1987-88, 594
Military uniforms in America, v.IV, 595
Miller, Connie, 1516
Miller, Herbert A., Jr., 191
Miller, Kenneth E., 117
Miller, Lynn Fieldman, 1266
Miller, Michael M., 347
Miller, Oscar J., 495
Miller, Stephen T., 1037
Miller, Stuart W., 2
Mills, J. J., 477
Mills, Judy, 1473
Mills, Victoria A., 551
Mining & mineral industries, 1504
Minnesota's endangered flora & fauna, 1412
Minnick, Roy, 1481
Minor presidential candidates & parties of 1988, 637
Mintz, Jerry, 274
Mitchell, B. R., 466
Mitchell, James V., Jr., 700
Mitchell, Jonathan, 140
Mitchell, Robert T., 1453
MLA directory of periodicals, 1988-89 ed, 69
MLA directory of periodicals, U.S. & Canada, 1988-89 ed, 70
MLA hndbk for writers of research papers, 3d ed, 832
Mochedlover, Helene G., 1030
Modern American critics, 1920-55, 1058

Modern American critics since 1955, 1059
Modern England 1901-84, 2d ed, 465
Modern Irish lit, 1159
Modern Spanish & Portuguese lits, 1166
Mohlenbrock, Robert H., 1424, 1436
Mohs, Mary E., 1368
Monaco, James, 1267
Monet, Ronald L., 628
Money for artists, 904
Monk, J. Thomas, 192
Monk, Susan S., 192
Montague Summers: a bibliographical portrait, 1127
Montenegro, Valerie J., 1345
Moore, David M., 1419
Moore, Patrick, 1633
Moorer, Dawson, 74
Moran, Lois, 877
Moritz, Albert, 1143
Moritz, Charles, 20
Moritz, Theresa, 1143
Morris dict of word & phrase origins, 2d ed, 944
Morris, Leslie R., 558
Morris, Mary, 944
Morris, William, 944
Morrison, Ian, 715
Morton, Herbert C., 575
Mosan art: an annotated bibliog, 893
Moskowitz, Jane M., 407
Moskowitz, Milton, 217
Moss, Joyce, 1013
Moss, William, 1093
Mostyn, Trevor, 141
Motor racing: the records, 715
Mott, Lawrie, 1384
Mount, Ellis, 1357
Movies made for television, 1964-86, 858
Moving to Ariz., 412
Mozambique, 100
Mozart: solo piano lit, 1216
Mullaney, Marie Marmo, 653
Müller-Wille, Ludger, 399
Mulligan, William H., Jr., 218
Multilingual thesaurus of geosciences, 1664
Mulvihill, Mary Lou, 1555
Municipal executive directory, 646
Munro, David, 382
Murder in print, 1036
Murray, Tracy, 169, 234
Museum of Science & Industry basic list of children's science bks 1988, 1346
Mushrooms: a quick reference gd to mushrooms of N. America, 1429
Music: a gd to the reference lit, 1167
Music business directory, 1987/88, 1180
Music directory Canada '88, 1181
Music educators journal: cumulative index 1914-87, 1189
Music in American higher educ, 1168

Music in early Christian lit, 1221
Music index, vols.33-34, 1190
Music index, v.39, 1191
Music locator 1988, 1222
Music radio directory, 1987/88, 845
Musical America's festivals '88, 1182
Musical microcomputer, 1172
Musicals no one came to see, 1300
My friends' beliefs, 1314
Myers, Allen C., 1317
Myers, Arnold, 1509
Myers, Robert A., 134
Myerson, Joel, 1054
Mystery, detective, and espionage fiction, 1037

Nā mea 'imi i ka wā kahiko: an annotated bibliog of Hawaiian archaeology, 421
Nachbar, Jack, 1262
Nadell, Pamela S., 1343
Naden, Corinne J., 1019
Nagar, Murari Lal, 71
Nagar, Sarla Devi, 71
Nagel, Kathleen Carter, 260
Nahrstedt, Mike, 733
Naiman, Arthur, 1624
Nakamura, Joyce, 1007
Names & nicknames of places & things, 401
Namesakes: ... gd to the origins of more than 300 words ..., 940
NASW register of clinical social workers: fall addendum to the 1987 5th ed, 781
Nathaniel Tarn: a descriptive bibliog, 1087
National antique show directory, 2d ed, 867
National Board of Review of Motion Pictures, 1283
National data bk: index, 12th ed, 774
National data bk, 12th ed, 773
National directory of ...
   alternative schools, 274
   corporate public affairs 1988, 156
   corporate training programs, 2d ed, 152
   educ'l programs in gerontology, 4th ed, 756
   product publicity sources, 1987/88 ed, 236
   retirement facilities, 2d ed, 757
   safety consultants, 13th ed, 229
National Hist'l Pubs & Records Commission, 424
National Hockey League sourcebk 1987-88, 741
National Trust, 415
National trust atlas, 3d ed, 415
National Trust for Historic Preservation Lib, Univ of Md., 453
National Trust for Scotland, 415
Nations within a nation, 362
Native American basketry, 884
Native trees, shrubs, & vines for urban & rural America, 1435
Natkiel, Richard, 429

Natural lang processing in the 1980s, 929
Natural resources & development, 1410
Naturalized birds of the world, 1445
Navabpour, Reza, 142
Navia, Luis E., 1303
Naylor, Colin, 891
NBA register, 1988-89 ed, 727
Nearby galaxies catalog, 1635
Negritude: an annotated bibliog, 340
Nelson, Carolyn, 31
Nelson, Gail A., 997
Nelson, Randy F., 743
Neri, Rita E., 244
Nesting weights, einsatzgewichte & piles à
    godets, 876
Netherlands, 120
Neufeldt, Victoria, 939
New American dict of good English, 953
New American medical dict & health manual,
    5th ed, 1542
New child health ency, 1529
New complete bk of collectible cars 1930-80, rev
    ed, 1690
New day/New Deal, 440
New dict of theology [Komonchak, Collins, &
    Lane, eds], 1340
New ency britannica, 15th ed, 44
New English-Chinese dict, rev ed, 972
New English-Chinese Dict, The Editing Group
    of, 972
New Frank Schoonmaker ency of wine, 1375
New illus science & invention ency, 1352
New int'l dict of acronyms in lib & info science
    & related fields, 532
New key to wild flowers, 1423
New law dict & institute of the whole law, 499
New Penguin gd to compact discs & cassettes,
    1186
New polytechnic dict of Spanish & English lang,
    1353
New reference grammar of modern Spanish, 979
New Unger's Bible dict, rev ed, 1325
New, W. H., 1144
New York: a gd to info & reference sources,
    1979-86, 87
New York City, the development of the
    metropolis, 433
New York legal research gd, 516
New York state directory 1988, 648
New York Times parent's gd to the best bks for
    children, 1004
Newbery & Caldecott awards 1988, 1008
Newman, Harold, 865
Newspapers: a reference gd, 842
Newton, Judy Ann, 678
Newton, Michael, 524, 678
Newton, Robert, 1088
Nicholls, David, 668
Nickson, R. Andrew, 136

Nicolle, David C., 614
Niemeyer, Suzanne, 1032
Niemi, Richard G., 657
1981-85 suppl to crime fiction 1749-1980, 1038
Nissley, Meta, 1603
Nobel Peace Prize & the laureates, 680
Nobel prize winners: lit, 988
Norback, Craig T., 329, 1648
Norback, Judith C., 1648
Nordquist, Joan, 80, 669, 747, 748, 1407, 1495,
    1561, 1567
North Carolina: the WPA gd ..., 409
Norton encyclopedic dict of navigation, 1693
Notable Americans, 4th ed, 444
Noyes, Sybil, 375
Nuclear & particle physics source bk, 1678
Number 1 in the USA, 63
Núñez, Raúl Solano, 903

Oberg, Erik, 1503
O'Brien, Nancy Patricia, 259
O'Brien, Philip M., 460
Obstetrics & gynecology, 1548
O'Connell, Susan M., 1345
O'Connor, W. J., 1535
Odeh, R. E., 1675
Official dict of military terms, 589
Official directory of festivals, sports & special
    events, 2d ed, 1253
Official NBA gd, 1988-89 ed, 728
Official 1988 Nat'l Football League record &
    fact bk, 734
Offshore info gd, 1509
O'Gara, Elaine, 830
O'Haire, Daniel, 1655
O'Hara, Patricia, 1109
O'Hara, Summer A., 53
Ohio gd to genealogical sources, 369
Old & Middle English lang studies, 932
Old Curiosity Shop: an annotated bibliog, 1107
Olderr, Steven, 1035
Olderr's fiction index 1987, 1035
Oleksiw, Susan, 1098
Olson, James S., 449, 457
Olson, Nancy B., 552, 553
Olton, Roy, 679
Olver, Graham, 505
Olympic games: the records, 711
Olympic record bk, 714
On being psychic, 705
One hundred Indian feature films, 1278
O'Neil, Rosanna M., 554
O'Neill, Robert Keating, 936
1,001 proverbs from Tunisia, 1248
Oppelt, Norman T., 882
Oppenheim, Joanne F., 198
Optical publishing directory 1987, 1611
Optics source bk, 1679

Oriental antiques & art, 866
Oriental carpets in the Philadelphia Museum of Art, 878
Original Cleartype business control atlas 1988, 146
Original Cleartype U.S. zip code atlas, 5
Oriol, William E., 753
Ornstein, Norman J., 654
Orphan drugs, rev ed, 1586
Orta, John, 1369
Osborn, Susan, 275
Osborne, Harold, 901
Oshins, Lisa Turner, 883
Ossenkop, David, 1207
Osterhoff, Robert J., 875
Ostrow, Rona, 245
O'Sullivan, Thomas, 919
Otaguro, Deborah, 328
O'Toole, G. J. A., 639
O'Toole, Thomas E., 97
Ott, J. Steven, 1521
Ottemiller's index to plays in collections, 7th ed, 1030
Our vice-presidents & second ladies, 442
Ousby, Ian, 991
Outlines of English hist, rev ed, 467
Owomoyela, Oyekan, 1246
Oxford dict of art, 901
Oxford illus literary gd to Canada, 1143
Oxford literary gd to Australia, 1134
Oxford movement & its leaders, 1331
Oyemade, Ura Jean, 787

Pablo Neruda: an annotated bibliog ..., 1146
Pacheleke, Calisto, 100
Packer, Joan Garrett, 1108
Page, Norman, 1101, 1106
Painless path to proper English usage, 955
Palliser, D. M., 462
Palm, Mary E., 1430
Palmegiano, E. M., 461
Palmer, R. E., 544
Palmer, Ralph S., 1448
Palmer, Scott, 1268, 1284
Paperno, Slava, 978
Paradis, Adrian A., 168
Paraguay, 136
Parapsychology: a reading & buying gd to the best bks in print, 706
Pardoe, Geoffrey K. C., 219
Parent, Roger H., 540
Parent-child attachment, 766
Parish, James Robert, 1287
Parker, Sybil P., 1469, 1502, 1608, 1649, 1650, 1663, 1676, 1678, 1679, 1680
Parry, R. B., 384
Passenger & immigration lists bibliog 1538-1900, 2d ed, 367

Passport to world band radio, 1989, 847
Paton, John, 46
Patrick Moore's A-Z of astronomy, 1633
Patten, Thomas H., Jr., 232
Patterson, Anna Grace, 543
Patterson, Donald L., 1208
Patterson, Douglas, 1387
Patterson, Janet L., 1208
Patti, Sebastian T., 1452
Patty Duke: a bio-bibliog, 1260
Paulston, Christina Bratt, 934
Paxton, John, 64, 471
Peace of mind during pregnancy, 1566
Peace organizations past & present, 684
Peace resource bk 1988-89, 683
Peacetime army 1900-1941, 605
Pearl, Patricia, 1309, 1310
Pearman, William A., 1530
Pearson, D'Orsay W., 1120
Peck, Russell A., 1104
Pederson, Lee, 954
Pemberton, Carol A., 1209
Penchansky, Mimi B., 561
Penguin atlas of N. American hist, 430
Pennant-Rea, Rupert, 151
People in hist, 454
People's voice: an annotated bibliog ..., 634
Percussion: an annotated bibliog ..., 1214
Pérez, Louis A., Jr., 132
Performance practice, medieval to contemporary, 1170
Performers & players, 1254
Pericles: an annotated bibliog, 1118
Perkins, C. R., 384
Permanent New Yorkers, 24
Peronism & the 3 Perons, 129
Perry, Gerald J., 1560
Perry, Jane Greverus, 410
Perry, John, 410
Personnel mgmt abstracts: accumulating index, 1987, v.33, no.4, 233
Pesticide alert, 1384
Pesticide fact hndbk, 1367
Peters, Gary L., 383
Peterson, Bernard L., Jr., 1063
Peterson, David A., 756
Peterson's college money hndbk 1989, 293
Peterson's gd to certificate programs at American colleges & univs, 294
Peterson's higher educ directory 1988, 295
Petit lexique de la France contemporaine, 976
Petrides, George A., 1437
Petriwsky, Eugene E., 346
Petrovsky, A. V., 696
Pfannmuller, Lee, 1412
Pharmacist's gd to the most misused & abused drugs in America, 1593
Philanthropy & voluntarism, 772
Philip's atlas of Canada & the world, 389

Physical chemistry source bk, 1649

Piano bk: a gd to buying a new or used piano, 1215

Pickard, Brent K., 744

Picker, Martin, 1210

Picture collections: Mexico, 903

Picture ency for children, 46

Pidgeon, Alice, 494

Pierce, Peter, 1134

Pilger, Mary Anne, 1360

Pinfold, Mike, 1234

Pinion, F. B., 1132

Pisaneschi, Janet I., 1558

Pisano, Dominick A., 1472

Pitts, Michael R., 1287

Place names of Africa, 1935-86, 90

Place-names of the world, rev ed, 400

Plain English, 957

Plano, Jack C., 679, 687

Plant closings, 231

Play index 1983-87, 1031

Pocket dict of ...
   contemporary France, 976
   laboratory equipment, 1351
   the spoken Arabic of Cairo, 970

Pocket economist, 2d ed, 151

Pocket gd to injectible drugs, 1987 ed, 1597

Poetry bkshop 1912-35, 577

Poetry index annual 1987, 1047

Poetry markets for Canadians, 3d ed, 1136

Poisonous & venomous marine animals of the world, 2d ed, 1464

Poland: an annotated bibliog of bks in English, 121

Poland, Ursula H., 570

Political dict of the Arab world, 622

Political parties of the world, 3d ed, 623

Polnaszek, Frank, 739, 740

Polunin, Oleg, 1425, 1426, 1427

Pope chronology, 1116

Popelka, Eleanor, 710

Popplestone, John A., 697

Popular music, 1900-1919, 1229

Popular world fiction: 1900-present, 1032

Population atlas of China, 791

Population Census Office, People's Republic of China, 791

Population info in 20th century census vols.: 1950-80, 792

Population, urbanization, & rural settlement in Ghana, 96

Porter, David L., 735

Porter, Frank W., III, 355, 884

Porter, Robert A., 907

Portinaro, Pierluigi, 385

Portrait of the stars & stripes, 587

Portraits in silicon, 1605

Postwar industrial policy in Japan, 210

Potenza, R., 1664

Potter, Karl H., 1304

Poupard, Dennis, 994, 995, 1028

Prakel, David, 1241

Prance, Claude A., 1112

Pratt, Darnell D., 1089

Pratt, Louis H., 1089

Prentice, Ann E., 543

Prescription drugs: an indispensable gd for people over 50, 1592

Prescription drugs, new & updated ed, 1595

Preservation educ directory, 5th ed, 556

Presley, John R., 207

Preston, Michael J., 1105

Prevention Magazine, editors of, 1549

Prézelin, Bernard, 608

Prince, Gerald, 990

Print Project, 200

Prints of Adolf Dehn, 919

Prints of Ellsworth Kelly, 917

Pritchard, James B., 1324

Pro football gd, 1988 ed, 732

Producer's mastergd 1988, 859

Product & process: an index to the way things work, 1359

Production & factory mgmt, 235

Professional reference for the office, 250

Professional resources catalogue 87, 321

Professional's gd to public relations services, 6th ed, 161

Project Head Start: past, present, & future trends ..., 787

Pross, Catherine, 1398

Provenance evidence, 549

Prucha, Francis Paul, 451

Prune bk, 658

Psychiatry & mental health science hndbk, 1554

Psychological & medical aspects of induced abortion, 1569

Public administration dict, 2d ed, 687

Public schools USA, 277

Public welfare directory, 1988/89, 782

Pulich, Warren M., 1449

Purchasing an en-cy-clo-pe-dia, 2d ed, 34

Purvis, James D., 143

Quick Canadian facts, 39th ed, 115

Quilt collections, 883

Quotable Shakespeare, 1117

R. G. Collingwood: a bibliog, 1305

Rabinovitz, Rubin, 1158

Racinet, Albert, 889

Radelet, Michael L., 525

Radical Right: a world directory, 667

Radlauer, Ed, 1691

Radlauer, Ruth, 1691

RAE table of earth satellites 1957-86, 3d ed, 1471
Raintree children's ency, 47
Ramsay, Caroline C., 885
Rand McNally atlas of world hist, rev ed, 480
Rand McNally cosmopolitan world atlas, 390
Rand McNally desk reference world atlas, 391
Rand McNally student's world atlas, 392
Rand McNally world atlas, 393
Rand McNally world atlas of nations, 394
Randall, Bernice, 956
Randall, Tom, 24
Rao, S. K. Ramachandra, 1539
Rappaport, Barry, 1634
Rare bks Slavica in the Univ of Colo. libs, Boulder, Colo., 346
Rasmussen, Richard Michael, 1217
Rassam, G. N., 1664
Rathbun, John W., 1061, 1062
Rating gd to franchises, 188
Rating the movies, rev ed, 1285
Read, P. G., 1668
Reader's adviser, v.4, 13th ed, 7
Reader's adviser, v.5, 13th ed, 8
Reader's adviser, v.6, 13th ed, 9
Reader's Digest America's historic places, 411
Reader's Digest illus encyclopedic dict, 938
Reader's gd to the classic British mystery, 1098
Ready reference to philosophy East & West, 1306
Real estate dict, 254
Real estate index: Jan 1975-June 1985, 253
Realism, naturalism, & local color, 1865-1917, 1064
Reams, Bernard D., Jr., 517
Recommended pubs for legal research 1978, 495
Recommended reference bks for small & medium-sized libs & media centers 1988, 10
Recorded concert band music, 1950-87, 1217
Recording locator 1988, 1192
Red bk on transportation of hazardous materials, 2d ed, 1505
Redekop, Paul, 707
Reed, Arthea J. S., 1023
Reed, John H., 745
Rees, Nigel, 945
Reese, William L., 7
Reference Bks Bulletin, Editorial Board of, 34
Reference bks bulletin 1986-87, 11
Reference bks for young readers, 35
Reference gd to hist'l fiction for children & young adults, 1018
Reference sources, 9th ed, 12
Reid, Darrel R., 617
Reidenbaugh, Lowell, 722
Reilly, Ann T., 512
Rela, Walter, 1161
Relations of lit & science, 985

Religion journals & serials, 1315
Religious bks for children, rev ed, 1310
Religious colleges & univs in America, 1308
Remarkable children: 20 who made hist, 23
Renaissance art: a topical dict, 899
Rentschler, Cathy, 546
Reo, Gloria J., 233
Reproductive rights, 1567
Research gd to the health sciences, 1515
Research in black hist, rev ed, 343
Research on men who batter, 764
Researcher's gd to archives & regional hist sources, 426
Researching the development of lay leadership in the Catholic church since Vatican II, 1335
Researching the Germans from Russia, 347
Resource/reading list 1987, 363
Resources for Canadian Mennonite studies, 1330
Resources for middle childhood, 786
Retirement benefit plans, 191
Return to sender, 1238
Revolutionary & dissident movements, 664
Rhea, Joseph C., 1521
Rheumatic & skin disease, 1573
RHS ency of house plants including greenhouse plants, 1389
Rich, Abby D., 290
Richard II: an annotated bibliog, 1121
Richard M. Nixon: a bibliographic exploration, 629
Richard Wright bibliog, 1090
Richardson, R. C., 481
Richel, Veronica C., 1297
Richter, Alan, 779
Richter, Bernice, 1346
Ridinger, Robert B. Marks, 334, 777
Right minds, 670
Riley, Sam G., 839
Rinderknecht, Carol, 17, 18
Ripley, S. Dillon, 1439
Roadside geology of ...
   Alaska, 1655
   N.Mex., 1654
   Wyo., 1656
Robert Gover: a descriptive bibliog, 1074
Robert Lehman collection, VI, 922
Roberts, John R., 1110
Roberts, Josephine A., 1121
Roberts, Patricia L., 1009
Roberts, Philip Davies, 957
Roberts, Robert B., 452
Robertson, David, 590
Robinson, Ed, 1671
Robinson, Jane Washburn, 1450
Robinson, Ruth E., 585
Robson, Graham, 1690
Rock 'n' roll on compact disc, 1241

Rodale's garden insect, disease & weed iden-
tification gd, 1395
Roell, Craig H., 630, 632
Rogers, Barbara Radcliffe, 886
Rogers, Helen, 1612
Rogers, Paul, 615
Rogers, Susan Carol, 335
Roget's thesaurus of English words & phrases,
969
Rollock, Barbara, 1016
Roman, Phil, 1513
Rood, Karen L., 1052
Room, Adrian, 400
Rose, Robert F., 173
Rosenbaum, Virginia K., 157
Rosenberg, Kenyon C., 1225
Rossman, Amy Y., 1430
Roth Publishing, Inc., Editorial Board, 1047
Rothenberg, Robert E., 1542
Rothman, M. F., 1497
Rotten reviews, 62
Rowe, Kenneth E., 1334
Royal Hist'l Society annual bibliog of British &
Irish hist: pubs of 1986, 462
Royal Horticultural Society, 1389
Royal Masonic cyclopaedia, 750
Royals, 27
Rugg, Frederick E., 296
Rugg's recommendations on the colleges
1988-89, 296
Rulau, Russell, 872
Ruppert, Edward, 1465
Ruppli, Michel, 1235
Rural community decline & revitalization, 803
Ruud, Inger Marie, 812
Ryan, Halford R., 441
Ryan, James G., 376
Ryan, Steve, 860

Sable, Martin H., 472
Sachare, Alex, 727, 728
Sachdev, Paul, 1568
Sacred choral music in print, 1988 suppl, 1223
Sader, Marion, 32, 35
Sadler, Judith DeBoard, 765
Sainsbury, Diana, 1416
Sainty, Malcolm R., 368
Sakol, Jeannie, 27
Salerno, Roger A., 749
Sales, Georgia, 780
Salib, Maurice, 970
Salim, Ali, 1439
Saltman, Richard B., 1531
Salwak, Dale, 1085
Salzmann, Zdeněk, 361
Sam Rayburn: a bio-bibliog, 636
Samizdat press in China's provinces, 1979-81,
837

Sampson, Henry T., 1293
Sanchez, James Joseph, 660, 661
Sanderson, Stewart, 966
Sanzone, Susan J., 1366
Saraswathi, T. S., 693
Sarfoh, Joseph A., 96
Sargent, Lyman Tower, 984
Sarjeant, William A. S., 1665
Sarkissian, Adele, 986
Sather, Leland B., 122
Saudi Arabia, rev ed, 144
Saving the Jewish family, 350
Sawoniak, Henryk, 532
Scammon, Richard M., 655
Scandinavian mythology, 1249
Schatz, Natalie, 1514
Schatzberg, Walter, 985
Scheick, William J., 1131
Schirmer gd to schools of music & conser-
vatories throughout the world, 1183
Schlachter, Gail Ann, 297, 762
Schlesinger, Benjamin, 754
Schlesinger, Rachel, 754
Schlicke, Paul, 1107
Schlicke, Priscilla, 1107
Schlueter, June, 1096
Schlueter, Paul, 1096
Schmidt, William D., 266
Schneider, Gail T., 276
Schneider, Marshall J., 1166
Schnuttgen, Hildegard, 1103
Scholars & priests, 264
Schon, Isabel, 1010
School administrator's resource gd, 270
School lib media annual 1988, 566
Schorr, Alan Edward, 56, 348
Schubert, Joachim, 1681
Schuessler, Axel, 973
Schuh, Dwight, 742
Schultz, Jon S., 496
Schulze, Suzanne, 792
Schwartz, David, 860
Schwartz, Ed, 1629
Schwartz, Karlene V., 1414
Schwartz, Mortimer D., 495
Schwarzkopf, LeRoy C., 57, 58
Schwarzlose, Richard A., 842
Science experiments index for young people,
1360
Science fiction & fantasy research index, v.7,
1044
Scientific companion, 1653
Scientists & technologists, 1356
Scobie, Stephen, 1145
Scott, David L., 193
Scott, James W., 431
Scott, Randall W., 923
Sealts, Merton M., Jr., 1078
Seashore animals of the Southeast, 1465

Seccombe, Matthew, 31
Secular choral music in print: arranger index, 2d ed, 1220
Secular choral music in print, 2d ed, 1219
Seidel, Egon, 1408
Seiden, Peggy, 314
Seidman, Arthur H., 1489
Select bibliog of women's studies, 1987, 810
Selected tables in mathematical statistics, v.11, 1675
Selected vaudeville criticism, 1301
Selective gd to colleges, 4th ed, 305
Self-determination: an interdisciplinary annotated bibliog, 665
Semantics: a bibliog, 1979-85, 930
Seminars directory, 1989, 158
Senior citizen educ programs, 327
Serials directory, 3d ed, 72
Series, 718
Sex care: the complete gd ..., 1546
Seyfert, Carl K., 1666
Seymour, Nancy N., 897
Shafritz, Jay M., 640, 1521
Shailor, Barbara A., 483
Shain, Michael, 1628
Shakespeare: a selective bibliog of modern criticism, 1122
Shapiro, Bill, 1242
Sharp, J. Michael, 656
Shavit, David, 641
Shaw, James Byam, 922
Shearer, Barbara S., 379
Shearer, Benjamin F., 379
Sheiman, Deborah Lovitky, 786
Sheneman, Perry J., 1489
Sheppard's int'l directory of print & map sellers, 386
Sheridan, Anneli, 1473
Sherman, Barbara Smiley, 763
Shields, Graham J., 118
Shields, Nancy E., 1026
Shim, Jae K., 176
Shimoni, Yaacov, 622
Ships of the Royal Navy, rev ed, 607
Shipwrecks in the Americas, rev ed, 420
Shirley Chisholm: a bibliog ..., 808
Shoebridge, Michele, 708
Short, David, 1410
Short story criticism, [v.1], 1046
Short story writers & their works, 1045
Shukman, Harold, 476
Shulman, Frank Joseph, 106
Shultz, Suzanne M., 1508
Shumaker, Walter A., 506
Siegel, Barry, 731
Siegel, Joel G., 176
Sierra Club gd to the natural areas of Idaho, Mont., & Wyo., 410
Sifakis, Stewart, 445

Sigler, Jay A., 338
SIGNAL: communication tools for the info age, 823
Signet/Mosby medical ency, 1543
Signorielli, Nancy, 825
Sikka, Anjoo, 693
Silverstein, Lorne, 159
Simas, Rick, 1300
Simmonds, Roy S., 1077
Simon, Ann, 783
Simon, Susan H., 1219, 1223
Simora, Filomena, 541
Simpson, James B., 76
Simpson, Michael A., 758
Simpson's contemporary quotations, 76
Single-parent family in children's bks, 2d ed, 1002
Singleton, Paul, 1416
Sinko, Peggy Tuck, 377
Sir Walter Ralegh: an annotated bibliog, 459
Sittig, Marshall, 1584
Sivin, Nathan, 387
Skier's gd to N. America, 744
Skodol, Andrew E., 1552
Slater, Robert, 1605
Slavens, Thomas P., 63
Slide, Anthony, 1257, 1301
Sloan, Dave, 727, 728, 732
Sloane, David E. E., 1067
Slonim, Maureen, 786
Slonimsky, Nicolas, 1174
Small business info source bk, 168
Smallwood, Carol, 1518
Smandych, Russell C., 526
Smartt, Daniel, 925
Smith, Allen, 427
Smith, Billy, 690
Smith, Carter, 26
Smith, Colleen, 537
Smith, Darren L., 53
Smith, Jane Bandy, 566
Smith, Jessie Carney, 341
Smith, Madeline, 1082
Smith, Margaret M., 1095
Smith, Miranda, 1395
Smith, Myron J., Jr., 723, 1684
Smith, Ronald L., 1258
Smith, Sweetman R., 245
Smith, Wrynn, 1556, 1573
Smythies, B. E., 1426
Snakes of the Orient, 1467
Snyder, Karen, 1384
Snyderwine, L. Thomas, 1335
Sobel, Robert, 150
Social & economic atlas of India, 107
Social & Human Sciences Documentation Centre, 81, 531, 685
Social context of the new info & communication technologies, 1604

Social Science Info & Documentation Committee, IFD, 81

Social support & health, 689

Society for Hist in the Federal Govt, 450

Sociology of sport, 707

Socrates: an annotated bibliog, 1303

Software for schools 1987-88, 315

Solar home planning, 910

Soled, Alex J., 518

Solid-state physics source bk, 1680

Somerville, James, 38

Something about the author, v.49, 1017

Soothill, William Edward, 1327

Sophisticated traveler's pocket gd to airport facilities & ground services 1988-89, 1683

Sotheby's world wine ency, 1376

Source bk of franchise opportunities, 1988 ed, 181

Sourcebook for the performing arts, 1257

Southern black creative writers, 1829-1953, 1050

Southwestern pottery, 2d ed, 882

Soviet law in English, 492

Soviet nomenklatura, 619

Space industry int'l, 219

Sparks, Linda, 309

Speaker's sourcebk, 77

Spearing, Darwin, 1656

Spears, Dee Ella, 69, 70

Special operations & elite units, 1939-88, 603

Spectroscopy source bk, 1650

Spiceland, J. David, 177

Spielman, Linda J., 1430

Spiewak, Scott A., 220

SPINES thesaurus, 1362

Spirt, Diana L., 1024

Spitzer, Robert L., 1552

Spokes, Penny, 11

Spoonerisms, sycophants, & sops, 942

Sporting News college football's 25 greatest teams, 733

Sporting News selects baseball's 25 greatest teams, 722

Spriggs, Matthew J. T., 421

Springberg, Judith, 511

Srivastava, Anil, 1278

Staar, Richard F., 671

Stainton, Adam, 1425

Staley, Thomas F., 1097

Stallings, William, 1616

Standard ency of carnival glass, 2d ed, 873

Standards Committee of the Rare Bks & Manuscripts Section, 548, 549

Stanley, Harold W., 657

Stanley, Sadie, 1227

Star, Nancy, 199

Stark, Marilyn McAnally, 1504

Stark, Robin, 1609

Starlet: biographies ..., 1265

Starr, Philip, 1530

State & local govt political dict, 638

State executive directory, 647

State legislative leadership, committees & staff 1987-88, 649

State names, seals, flags, & symbols, 379

State Statistical Bureau, People's Republic of China, 165, 805

Statesman's yr-bk, 125th ed, 64

Statistical yrbk for Latin America & the Caribbean, 1986 ed, 128

Statistical yrbk 1987, 797

Statistics on narcotic drugs for 1986, 1596

Stebbings, Chantal, 521

Steene, Birgitta, 1263

Stein, Alice P., 1575

Stephen Collins Foster: a gd to research, 1232

Stern, Irwin, 1135, 1166

Stevanovic, Bosiljka, 1165

Stevens, Virginia, 970

Stevenson, Burton, 1245

Stevenson, John, 469

Stevenson, Rosemary M., 342

Stevenson, Tom, 1376

Stewart, Sharon Lee, 1005

Stimson, Frederic Jesup, 507

Stiverson, Cynthia Zignego, 1177

Stoloff, Michael L., 694

Stone age spear & arrow points of the midcontinental & eastern U.S., 360

Stone, Evelyn M., 1553

Stormorken, Bjørn, 530

Strait, Jerry L., 596

Strait, Sandra S., 596

Straub, Deborah A., 801

Strauss, Diane Wheeler, 148

Strayer, Joseph R., 484, 485, 486

Strengthening the UN, 672

Stuart, Paul, 362

Student loan hndbk, 300

Studwell, William E., 1259

Study of hist, 481

Subak-Sharpe, Genell J., 1528

Sube, Ralf, 1682

Subject catalogue of the House of Commons parliamentary papers 1801-1900, 464

Suchlicki, Jaime, 133

Sudak, Diane, 327

Sulima, John P., 783

Sullivan, William M., 138

Summerlin, Mitchell Eugene, 1070

Sundberg, Walter J., 1429

Sunshine, Linda, 1527

Supplement to *A Bibliog of George Moore*, 1113

Supplement to the 9th Mental Measurements Yrbk, 700

Surdam, Wayne, 103

Survey of income & expenditure of urban
    households in China 1985, 805
Surveying hndbk, 1481
Sustaining Earth, 1398
Sutton, Margaret, 38
Swanbeck, Jan, 1044
Swanson, Alan, 122
Swarbrick, James, 1583
Swartley, Willard M., 1336
Swartz, Larry, 998
Swartzburg, Susan G., 556
Sweden, 122
Swidan, Eleanor A., 12
Sylvia Plath: an analytical bibliog, 1083
Symphony orchestras of the world, 1188
Symptoms after 40, 1536
Szucs, Loretto Dennis, 428
Szymanek, Bogdan, 926

T. E. Lawrence: a bibliog, 460
Tabor, Stephen, 1083
Tajima, Matsuji, 932
Takeover defenses: profiles of the Fortune 500,
    157
Talbot, Michael, 1211
Talbot-Booth, E. C., 1692
Talcott Parsons, 747
Talking business in Japanese, 983
Tanagers: natural hist, distribution, & iden-
    tification, 1444
Tanaka, Patricia Lehua, 421
Tattersall, Ian, 336
Tax Foundation, 257
Taxation glossary, 256
Taylor, Arlene G., 554
Taylor, Donald S., 1305
Taylor, J. Golden, 1060
Taylor, Michael J. H., 602
Taylor's gd to trees, 1388
Teacher job satisfaction, 258
Teacher's almanac 1988-89, 265
Technical, trade, & business school data hndbk
    1988-90: northeast/southeast regions,
    328
Tegeler, Dorothy, 412
Teitelbaum, Gene, 497
Television drama series programming, 1982-84,
    856
Temple, Ruth Z., 996
Terminology of water supply & environmental
    sanitation, 1512
Terrorism in the U.S. & Europe, 1800-1959, 678
Terrorism, 1980-87, 677
Test Collection, Educ'l Testing Service, 325
Test construction, 259
Textbooks in school & society, 260
Thain, Chris, 965
Theatre world: 1986-87 season, 1302

Theodor Adorno, 748
Thesaurus of ...
    psychological index terms, 5th ed, 701
    scientific, technical, & engineering terms,
        1363
    slang, 952
Thieret, John W., 1436
Thomas, Claudewell S., 1554
Thomas, Robert C., 1361
Thomerson, Kathleen, 1212
Thompson, Julius E., 841
Thompson, Susan J., 1667
Thomsett, Michael C., 254
Thorpe, Frances, 1277
Thrapp, Dan L., 446
Three Mile Island: a reader's gd ..., 1506
Three Mile Island: a selectively annotated
    bibliog, 1508
Thro, Ellen, 1566
Tibet gd, 418
Times family atlas of the world, 395
Timner, W. E., 1237
Tirion, Wil, 1634
Tobin, Patricia, 490
Tognini, Joyce, 877
Tokarczyk, Michelle M., 1072
Tomlinson, Gerald, 724
Toni Morrison: an annotated bibliog, 1080
Tools of the profession, 571
Tootill, Elizabeth, 1417
Torres, Donald A., 527
Total garden, 1391
Toups, Judith A., 1451
Towell, Julie E., 145
Towle, Laird C., 378
Toxic waste, 1407
Trade contacts in China, 246
Trade shows & professional exhibits directory,
    3d ed, 247
Tradeshow week data bk, 1988, 248
Traditional food plants, 1377
Training & development organizations direc-
    tory, 4th ed, 230
Trammell, Jeffrey B., 642
Trattner, John H., 658
Travel index: a gd to bks & articles, 1985-86, 402
Travel writer's markets, 1987-88 ed, 830
Traveling Jewish in America, rev ed, 407
Travis, Carole, 127
Treadway, Gary R., 631
Trees: a quick reference gd to trees of N.
    America, 1436
Trees & shrubs for temperate climates, 3d ed,
    1433
Trees of the southeastern U.S., 1434
Triffin, Nicholas, 494
Trissel, Lawrence A., 1591, 1597
Trombley, Stephen, 37
Trotsky bibliog, 2d ed, 666

Trujillo, Roberto G., 562
Trzyna, Thaddeus C. (Ted), 1401
Tuleja, Tad, 940
TULIP: the universal list of Indian periodicals,
    vols.1-4, 71
Tully, R. Brent, 1635
Turner, Anthony, 1347
Turner, Eugene James, 337
Turner, George W., 962
Turner, Rufus P., 1490
Tver, David F., 1693
Twentieth-century literary criticism, v.24, 994
Twentieth-century literary criticism, v.25, 995
Two Gentlemen of Verona: an annotated
    bibliog, 1120
Tyckoson, David A., 1562, 1563
Tyler, Elizabeth Ann, 343

Ukman, Lesa, 1253
Ullmann's ency of industrial chemistry,
    vols.A8-A10, 5th ed, 1642
Ulrich's int'l periodicals directory 1988-89, 73
UNCTC bibliog 1974-87, 149
Understanding the vocabulary of the nuclear
    arms race, 612
Underwater gd to Hawai'i, 1671
UNESCO Regional Office of Educ in Asia & the
    Pacific, 318
Unger, Merrill F., 1325
Uniglobe Travel, 405
Union of Int'l Assns, 3
United Methodist studies, rev ed, 1334
United Nations Institute for Training &
    Research (UNITAR), 673
University press bks for public libs, 10th ed, 563
University press bks for secondary school libs,
    20th ed, 567
Unterburger, Amy L., 65
Upshall, Michael, 41
Upton, Clive, 966
Uranometria 2000.0, v.I, 1634
Urdang, Laurence, 401, 946, 958, 959
U.S. Army ships & watercraft of WW II, 606
U.S. Environmental Protection Agency, 1367
U.S. govt pubs catalogs, 2d ed, 59
U.S. govt'l advisory organizations pubs on
    micrcofiche 1987, pt.2, 662
U.S. in the Middle East, 641
U.S. manufacturers directory, 1988-89 ed, 221
U.S. master tax gd, 1989, 257b
U.S. trade tokens 1866-89, 2d ed, 872
U.S./Japan foreign trade, 244
USA by numbers, 798
Uscher, Nancy, 1183

Vacation study abroad, 38th ed, 310
Vaillancourt, Pauline M., 1570

Valeros, Florentino B., 1149
Valeros-Gruenberg, Estrellita, 1149
Valiquette, Michele, 809
Van Couvering, John, 336
Van Ekeren, Glenn, 77
Vandiver, Margaret, 525
Variety's complete home video directory 1988,
    854
Veasey, Don M., 343
Vermilye, Jerry, 1283
Verrall, Catherine, 363
VGM's careers ency, 2d ed, 329
Vidal-Naquet, Pierre, 479
Vietnam War memorials, 596
Vikor, Desider L., 78
Vincent Persichetti: a bio-bibliog, 1208
Vine, Richard P., 1385
Vinson, James, 1274
Violence & terror in the mass media, 825
V.I.P. address bk, 1988-89, 54
Vital records hndbk, 372
Vital statistics on American politics, 657
Vital statistics on Congress, 1987-88, 654
Vocabulaire de biotechnologie vegetale,
    1418
Von Rosenstiel, Helene, 887
Vozzo, Steven F., 1409

Wadhams, Wayne, 1179
Wagner, Henry R., 576
Waite, Ellen J., 551
Waite, Gregory, 1126
Waite, Ronald A., 985
Wakeman, John, 1269, 1270
Waldman, Carl, 364
Waldman, Harry, 1474
Walker, Barbara G., 814
Walker, Elinor, 1025
Walker, Peter M. B., 1348
Wall Street words, 193
Wallechinsky, David, 712
Waller, Robert, 626
Wallmannsberger, Josef, 931
Walls, Karen, 690
Walls, Robert E., 1247
Walter Breen's complete ency of U.S. & colonial
    coins, 871
Walter, Ingo, 169, 234
Walton, Doug, 1602
Wampler, Fred, 1428
Ward, Carlton, 1295
Ward, Hiley H., 1314
Ward's business directory of U.S. private cos,
    160
Warriors & adventurers, 592
Washington, Valora, 787
Wasserman, Paul, 78, 490
Wasserstein, Bernard, 676

Waterfowl: an identification gd to the ducks, geese & swans of the world, 1446
Waters, T. A., 738
Watkins, Kathleen Pullan, 766
Watson, Francis, 1326
Watson, Louise, 45
Way, Harold E., 231
Wayburn, Peggy, 413
We the people: an atlas of America's ethnic diversity, 337
Wear, Terri A., 1011
Weatherson, Michael A., 635
Webb, Mark O., 1111
Webb, Walter, 170
Weber, R. David, 297, 762
Weber, Susan, 798
Webster, John G., 1540
Webster, Valerie J., 247
Webster's gd to business correspondence, 251
Webster's new world atlas, 396
Webster's new world dict of American English, 3d ed, 939
Webster's new world dict of quotable definitions, 2d ed, 960
Webster's new world gd to current American usage, 956
Webster's new world illus encyclopedic dict of real estate, 3d ed, 255
Webster's spell it right dict, 968
Weeks, Albert L., 619
Weeks, John M., 474
Wei, Karen T., 555
Weinberg, Robert, 924
Weiner, Alan R., 222
Weiner, Andrew, 208
Weiner, Richard, 161
Weinstein, Amy, 782
Weintraub, Sam, 269
Weiss, Carla M., 231
Weiss, Robert J., 1528
Welch, K. R. G., 1467
Wenk, Arthur, 1173
Wenzel, Duane, 1346
Werenko, John D., 908
Wertsman, Vladimir, 1165
West Virginia genealogy, 374
Westcott, Rich, 725
Western films 2, 1262
Wharton, J. J. S., 508
What every chemical technologist wants to know about, v.I, 1643
Wheatley, Janis, 55
Wheaton, Barbara Ketcham, 1370
Where to start career planning, 6th ed, 330
Whitaker, Katherine C., 743
Whitaker, Richard E., 1316
Whitaker's almanack 1988, 4
Whitburn, Joel, 1228
White, Glenn D., 852

White, Ray Lewis, 1065
White, Rhea A., 705, 706
Whitehouse, Ruth D., 422
Whiteley, Sandy, 11
Whitley, M. J., 609
Whitworth, J. A., 1541
Who reads what when, 1012
Who was who in the Civil War, 445
Whole ball of wax & other colloquial phrases, 959
Wholesale-by-mail catalog 1988, 200
Who's who among black Americans 1988, 344
Who's who in ...
    American film now, 2d ed, 1267
    Mexico today, 135
    special libs 1988-89, 572
    the Arab world 1988-89, 29
    the League of Canadian Poets, 3d ed, 1145
    the Writers' Union of Canada, 3d ed, 826
Who's who of Australian & New Zealand film actors, 1268
Who's who of heaven, 1337
Why do we say...?, 945
Widdicombe, Richard Toby, 1069
Widdowson, John, 966
Wide screen movies, 1281
Widor, Claude, 837
Wiener, Tom, 861
Wigge, Larry, 739, 740
Wiggins, James M., 54
Wildflowers: a quick identification gd to the wildflowers of N. America, 1424
Wildflowers of Ind., 1428
Wilkes, Joseph A., 914
Wilkinson, Geoffrey, 1639
William March: an annotated checklist, 1077
William McKinley: a bibliog, 630
Williams, Emelda L., 249
Williams, Gareth, 1431
Williams, J. P. R., 1574
Williams, James G., 1622, 1623
Williams, Jane A., 1012
Williamson, A., 509
Willis, John, 1302
Wilson, George, 1013
Wilson, Miriam J. Williams, 788
Wilson, Raymond L., 920
Wilson, Robert, 196
Wilson, Terry P., 356
Wiltshire, Carol, 67
Wine appreciation, 1385
Winick, Myron, 1519
Winkel, Lois, 565
Winkler, Gail Caskey, 887
Winter, Eugenia B., 1569
Winter sports glossary, 746
Wintle, Michael, 120
Witt, Maria, 532
Woelfel, Charles J., 178, 179, 206

Wolf, Carolyn E., 365
Wolfe, Charles, 1264
Wolfe, Gregory, 670
Wolfe, Linda D., 1461
Wolff, Kathryn, 1345
Wolfson, Evelyn, 366
Woman's dict of symbols & sacred objects, 814
Women activists, 813
Women & Judaism, 812
Women anthropologists, 333
Women composers, conductors, & musicians of
    the 20th century, v.III, 1175
Women in ...
    administration & mgmt, 811
    Ireland, 807
    LC's terms, 551
    sport, 708
Women of the world: the great foreign
    correspondents, 838
Women's health perspectives, v.1, 1516
Women's Resources Group, ACRL, 815
Wong, Betty, 761
Wong, Nancy C., 13
Wood, Donna, 239a, 239b
Wood, M. Sandra, 1508, 1559
Wood, R. Kent, 263
Woodbridge, Hensley C., 1146
Woodbridge, John D., 1338
Woodbridge, Linda, 1122
Woodbridge, Sally B., 916
Woods, Richard Donovon, 28
Woodward, Arthur, 260
Woolmer, J. Howard, 577
Word index to the poetry of C. S. Lewis,
    1111
Word maps: a dialect atlas of England, 966
Words on cassette 1987/88, 849
Wordsworth chronology, 1132
Work & alcohol abuse, 784
Work-at-home sourcebk, 2d ed, 223
World birds, 1447
World business travel gd, 405
World directory of ...
    biological & medical sciences libs, 570
    human rights teaching & research institutions,
        1988, 531
    peace research & training institutions 1988,
        685
World educ ency, 261
World film directors, v.I, 1269
World film directors, v.II, 1270
World gd to ...
    abbreviations of organizations, 8th ed, 1
    automobile manufacturers, 1685
    libs, 8th ed, 538
World in figures, 799
World list of univs, 17th ed, 298
World mapping today, 384
World yrbk of educ 1988, 267

World yrbk of new generation computing
    research & development, 1613
Worldwide gd to equivalent irons & steels, 2d
    ed, 1500
Worldwide gd to equivalent nonferrous metals
    & alloys, 2d ed, 1501
Worldwide refining & gas processing directory,
    1989, 1400
Wostbrock, Fred, 860
Wright, Frank, 877
Wright, Helen K., 540
Wright, Jim, 869
Wright, John W., 1527
Wright, Robin S., 1427
Wright, Samuel, 1115
Writers directory 1988-90, 831
Writers for children, 1015
Writings on Canadian English 1976-87, 964
Writings on scholarly communication, 575
Wurz, Trude, 1076
Wygant, Alice Chambers, 545
Wynar, Bohdan S., 10, 543

Yaakov, Juliette, 1031
Yale Daily News, staff of, 291
Yang, Hiyol, 170
Yaroshevsky, M. G., 696
Yarwood, Doreen, 913
Yeager, Gertrude M., 130
Yearbook of American univs & colleges,
    academic yr, 1986-87, 311
Yearbook on int'l communist affairs 1988, 671
Yeomans, David, 1213
Yetiv, Isaac, 1248
Yiddish dict in transliteration, 981
Yiddish linguistics, 980
Yoak, Stuart D., 517
Young adult bk review index 1987, 1027
Young adult 1987 annual bklist, 564
Young, Arthur P., 279, 560
Young, Margaret Labash, 1411
Young, Michael, 1420
Young, Robyn V., 992
Young, Thomas A., 874
Your reading, 7th ed, 1014
Youth lit: an interdisciplinary, annotated gd ...
    1930-85, 1005

Zacks Investment Research, 185
Zadrozny, Mark, 987
Zaza, Tony, 857
Zembicki, Christine, 235
Zesch, Steve, 733
Zeveloff, Samuel I., 1462
Zhenxin, Qiang, 971
Zim, Herbert S., 1453, 1463
Zimmerman, John L., 1452

Zimmerman, William E., 202
Zink, Steven D., 59, 659
Zola, Meguido, 998
Zonca, Darlene, 248
Zongxin, Zhou, 971

Zubatsky, David S., 1146
Zunz, Christine M., 1152
Zureik, Elia, 1604
Zusne, Leonard, 698
Zwaak, Leo, 530

Subject Index

Reference is to entry number.

Abbreviations, 1, 1364, 1507, 1533, 1534. *See also* Acronyms

Abortion, 1567, 1568, 1569

Abused women. *See* Spouse abuse

Accounting, 176, 177, 178, 179

Acid rain, 1405, 1409

Acoustical engineering, 1469

Acronyms, 2, 145, 532, 1507, 1534. *See also* Abbreviations

Actors, 1267, 1280
  Great Britain, 1284

Actresses, 1260, 1261, 1265, 1267, 1280
  Great Britain, 1284

Adorno, Theodor, 748

Adult education, 324, 327

Adventure stories, 1033. *See also* Detective and mystery stories

Advertising, 198, 249

Advocate, The, 777

Aeronautics, 1472, 1473

Aerospace. *See* Astronautics; Space flight

Africa, 88, 89, 90, 1233. *See also names of countries*

Afro-Americans. *See* Blacks

Agent Orange, 586

Aging, 491, 752, 753, 1528. *See also* Elderly abuse; Gerontology; Retirement

Agriculture, 1364

AIDS, 1557, 1558, 1559, 1560, 1561, 1562, 1563

Air forces, 597, 598, 599, 600, 601, 602

Airline industry, 1684

Airplanes, 874

Airports, 1683

Alaska, 413, 1655

Albee, Edward, 1068

Alcohol. *See* Wine and wine making

Alcoholism, 784

Allergy, 1564

Allusions, 820

Almanacs, 4, 265

Alternative education. *See* Education, alternative

American Antiquarian Society, 447

American drama, 1063, 1068, 1082

American Library Association, 539, 540

American literature, 984, 991, 996, 1048, 1049, 1050, 1051, 1052, 1053, 1054, 1055, 1056, 1057, 1058, 1059, 1061, 1062, 1066. *See also names of individual authors*

American poetry, 1071, 1083, 1084, 1085, 1087, 1088, 1091, 1092, 1093

Amphibians, 1466

Amusement parks, 710

Animal magnetism, 702

Anthropologists, 333, 335

Anthropology, 331, 332, 334

Antibiotics, 1580

Antiques, 866, 867, 876

Aquariums, 1456

Arabic language, 970

Arapaho Indians, 361

Archaeology, 331, 419, 421, 422

Architecture, 895, 896, 911, 912, 913, 914, 915, 916. *See also* Historic preservation

Archiv für Sozialwissenschaft und Sozialpolitik, 164

Archives, 423, 424, 426, 428, 448
  Canada, 1141

Area studies, 64, 116. *See also specific countries*

Argentina, 129

Arizona, 397, 412

Armaments, 610, 613, 614. *See also* Air forces; Armed forces

Armed forces, 609

Arrow-heads, 360

Art, 895, 900, 901, 904, 908, 922. *See also* Arts

Art galleries and museums, 909

Art, Chinese, 897

Art, Greco-Roman, 894

Art, Mosan, 893

Art, primitive, 892

Art, Renaissance, 899

Arthritis, 1573

Artificial intelligence, 1613

Artisans, 879, 885

Artists' materials, 905

Artists, American, 898

Arts, 341, 816, 896, 902, 906, 907. *See also* Art

Arts and children, 818

Asia, 103, 105, 106, 318, 455

Asian Americans, 105

Assassination, 620

Associations, institutions, etc., 48, 50, 52

Astronautics, 1472

Astronauts, 1470
Astronomy, 1630, 1631, 1632, 1633, 1634
Atlases, 39, 388, 389, 390, 391, 392, 393, 394,
     395, 396, 429, 473. *See also* individual
     countries and regions
Atomic energy. *See* Nuclear energy
Attack and defense, 1474
Audio-visual equipment, 852, 853
Audio-visual materials, 321
Australia, 458, 1268
Australian literature, 1134
Authority files, 550
Authors, 986, 987. *See also* Children's
     literature; *names of individual authors*
Authors, American, 1048, 1049
Authors, Black, 1016, 1050, 1051, 1080, 1089,
     1090
Authors, Canadian, 826, 1140, 1144
Authors, English, 1096, 1097
Authors, French, 1150, 1151
Authors, German, 1153, 1154, 1155
Authorship, 827, 828, 830, 831, 834, 1015. *See*
     also Publishers and publishing
Automobile industry and trade, 1685
Automobile racing, 715
Automobiles, 194, 1687, 1688, 1690, 1691
Aviation. *See* Aeronautics
Awards. *See* Rewards (prizes, etc.)

Ballet, 1259
Band music, 1217
Banks and banking, 202, 204, 205, 206, 207. *See*
     also Finance
Baptists, 1341
Bartók, Béla, 1193, 1213
Baseball, 716, 717, 718, 719, 720, 721, 722, 723,
     724, 725
Baseball cards, 868, 869
Basketball, 726, 727, 728
Battles, 588
Beckett, Samuel, 1158
Behavior, 695
Bellamy, Edward, 1069
Benin, 91
Bergman, Ingmar, 1263
Best American Short Stories, 1065
Bible, 1316, 1321
     dictionaries, 1317, 1318, 1320, 1323, 1325
Bible lands, 1319, 1324
Bible. N.T., 1326
Bible. O.T., 1322
Bibliographic societies, 49
Bibliography, 6, 571, 819, 1036
Bibliography, international, 13
Bibliography, national
     Great Britain, 19
     Third World, 477
     United States, 14, 15, 16, 17, 18

Bilingualism, 262, 934
Biochemical engineering, 1491
Biography, 20, 21, 22, 23, 28, 65, 66, 137,
     444
Biological libraries, 570
Biology, 1413, 1416, 1417
Biomedical engineering, 1540
Biotechnology, 212, 1491, 1492, 1493, 1494,
     1495
Birds, 1439, 1440, 1442, 1445, 1447, 1448, 1449,
     1450, 1451, 1452. *See also names*
     of birds
Blacks, 339, 340, 341, 342, 343, 344, 841, 1050,
     1279, 1293
Blackwood, Algernon, 1099
Blake, William, 1100
Blind, 759, 760
Bliss, Arthur, 1200
Bloch, Ernest, 1206
Boilers, 1513
Bolivia, 130
Book collecting, 573, 585, 870
Book reviews. *See* Books: reviews
Book selection, 6, 998, 1000, 1012
Book selection aids. *See* selection aids *under*
     types of libraries; subjects
Books and reading, 49, 998, 1004, 1014, 1019,
     1021, 1024. *See also* Book selection;
     Children's literature
Books
     conservation & restoration, 548, 549, 556
     reviews, 62, 1027
Bookselling, 579, 580, 585
Botanical gardens, 1420
Brandeis, Louis Dembitz, 497
Brazilian literature, 1135
Bridges, 1484
British literature. *See* English literature
British poetry. *See* English poetry
Buddhism, 1327
Buero Vallejo, Antonio, 1288
Building, 1485
Building laws, 493
Business, 145, 146, 148, 149, 159, 169, 170, 171,
     173, 213, 214
     quotations, maxims, etc., 174, 175
Business consultants, 162
Business education, 292
Business ethics, 147, 167
Butterflies, 1453
Byron, George Gordon, 1101

C (computer program language), 1606
Cable television, 848, 851
CAD/CAM systems, 1602
Caldecott award, 1008
Calendars, 3, 60
California, 84, 916, 1401

Canada, 110, 209, 515, 526, 964, 1282, 1612, 1644
  atlases, 389
  census, 790
  dictionaries, 112, 880
  directories, 50, 111, 159, 557, 1181, 1473, 1657
  government publications, 55
  handbooks, manuals, etc., 115, 1437
  history, 454, 468
  indexes, 844
  periodicals, 68, 70
  politics & government, 617, 625, 627
  statistics, 113, 114
Canadian literature, 1000, 1137, 1138, 1139, 1140, 1141, 1143, 1144
Canadian poetry, 1136, 1142, 1145
Cancer, 1570
Cape Verde, 92
Capital punishment, 525
Capra, Frank, 1264
Carbohydrates, 1645
Caribbean, 127, 128, 618
Carroll, Lewis, 1102
Cartography, 384, 385
Cartoon characters, 1273
Cataloging, 548, 549, 550, 551, 553, 554
  nonbook materials, 552
Cataloging Service Bulletin, 553
Catawba Indians, 352
Catholic Church, 1335, 1339
Cats, 1454
CD-ROM, 1599, 1600
Celebrities, 54
Cemeteries, 24
Central America, 125. *See also* Latin America
Chad, 93
Chaminade, Cécile, 1198
Charts, diagrams, etc., 61
Chaucer, Geoffrey, 1103, 1104
Chemical engineering, 1476, 1478
Chemical industries, 1477
Chemical processes, 1643
Chemistry, 1638, 1639, 1640, 1641, 1642, 1644, 1647, 1649, 1651
Child development, 786
Child welfare, 788
Children, 688, 788
  health care, 1529
Children's encyclopedias and dictionaries, 36, 38, 39, 46, 47, 961
Children's literature, 1002, 1006, 1009, 1012, 1014, 1015, 1016, 1017, 1020, 1021, 1023. *See also* Young adult literature
  awards, 1022
  bibliography, 14, 999, 1005, 1011, 1013, 1309
  selection aids, 565, 997, 1000, 1001, 1004, 1008, 1010, 1018, 1019, 1024, 1345, 1346, 1438

Children's reference books, 35
Chile, 131
Chilean literature, 1146
China, 165, 246, 387, 555, 791, 805, 837
Chinese Americans, 345
Chinese language, 971, 972, 973
Chinese literature, 1147
Chisholm, Shirley, 808
Choral music, 1218, 1219, 1220
Christian literature, 16, 1034
Christian literature for children, 1310
Christianity, 1328, 1332, 1338
Chronology, historical, 444, 587
Church music, 1192, 1209, 1221, 1222, 1223
Church of England, 1331
Church schools, 285, 1308
Cities and towns, 800, 801, 802
Civil engineering, 1482
Civil rights, 529. *See also* Human rights
Classical literature, 1028, 1029
Cleland, John, 1105
Cleveland, Grover, 633
Code of Federal Regulations, 519
Cogeneration of electric power and heat, 220
Coins, 871, 872
Collingwood, R. G., 1305
Comedians, 850, 855, 1258
Comic books, strips, etc., 923
Commerce, 239, 239a, 239b, 242, 246
Commercial correspondence, 251
Commodity exchanges, 1380
Commonwealth of Nations, 116
Communication, 822, 823, 824
Communism, 669, 671, 1332
Compact discs, 1186, 1241
Composers, 1193, 1194, 1195, 1197, 1198, 1199, 1200, 1201, 1202, 1203, 1204, 1205, 1206, 1207, 1208, 1210, 1211, 1212
Computer games, 1621
Computer industry, 1615
Computer music, 1172
Computer programs, 1609
Computer science, 1601
Computer-assisted instruction, 312, 314
Computers, 1604, 1605, 1607, 1608, 1610, 1613, 1616, 1617, 1628. *See also* Information storage and retrieval systems; Microcomputers
Condoms, 775
Confederate States of America, 1093
Conservation of books. *See* Books: conservation & restoration
Conservatism, 667, 670
Consolidation and merger of corporations, 157
Construction, 914
Construction industry, 493. *See also* Building
Consumer education, 194, 195, 196, 198, 199, 200, 1687, 1688
Cookery, 1373

Cooper, James Fenimore, 1070
Copy cataloging, 554
Corporations, 149, 152, 155, 156, 160, 211, 216, 217
Cosmology, 1653
Costume, 889
Cottage industries, 223
Council of Economic Advisers, 150
Cricket, 729
Crime and criminals, 522, 523, 524, 526
Crime in literature. *See* Detective and mystery stories
Criticism, 692, 809, 992, 994, 995, 1020, 1026, 1028, 1029, 1032, 1046, 1056
Critics, 1058, 1059, 1061, 1062, 1079
Cuba, 132, 133
Current events, 478
Czechoslovakian literature, 1148

Dams, 1483, 1484
Data base management, 1612
Deaf, 760
Death, 688, 758
Decorative art, 862, 864
Dehn, Adolf, 919
Demography, 166, 789, 790, 798
Demonology, 704
Denmark, 117
Depressions
   United States, 440
Detective and mystery stories, 1036, 1037, 1038, 1039, 1097, 1098
Dickens, Charles, 1106, 1107
Dickinson, Emily, 1071
Dinosaurs, 1669
Diseases, 1555, 1556
Dissenters, 664
Divorce
   law & legislation, 504
Doctorow, E. L., 1072
Dominica, 134
Drabble, Margaret, 1108
Drama, 1030, 1031, 1063, 1294
Dramatists, 1255
Dried flower arrangement, 886
Drug abuse, 1593. *See also* Substance abuse
Drugs, 1582, 1585, 1586, 1588, 1589, 1591, 1592, 1593, 1595, 1596, 1597, 1598.
   See also Pharmacology
Ducks, 1446
Duke, Patty, 1260

Earth sciences, 1419, 1652
Eastern Europe, 1431
Ecology, 1398. *See also* Environmental policy
Economic assistance, 154, 205
Economic forecasting, 165, 166

Economics, 109, 151, 163, 164
Economists, 150
Education, 260, 261, 268, 312. *See also*
   Universities and colleges; *specific kinds of education*
Education, alternative, 274
Education, bilingual, 262, 934
Education, elementary, 271, 315
Education, higher, 279, 288, 294, 295, 302, 310, 311, 313, 314, 319, 1657. *See also*
   Universities and colleges
Education, preschool, 787
Education, secondary, 277, 315
Educational innovations, 267
Educational software, 315
Educational technology, 263, 267
Elderly abuse, 754
Elections, 625, 634, 637, 655
Electric motors, 1486
Electrical engineering, 1488
Electronic data processing, 1604, 1628
Electronics, 1487, 1488, 1489, 1490, 1608
Eliot, George, 1109
Ellington, Duke, 1237
Emigration and immigration, 367
Employee fringe benefits, 191, 232
Employees, training of, 152, 230
Employment (economic theory), 224
Emulsions, 1475, 1643
Encyclopedias and dictionaries, 33, 34, 37, 40, 41, 42, 43, 44, 45
Endangered species, 1412
Energy, 1396
Engineering, 1468
English drama, 1117, 1118, 1119, 1120, 1121, 1122, 1123. *See also*
   Criticism
English language, 928, 932, 936
   dictionaries, 937, 938, 939
   juvenile, 961
   eponyms, 940
   etymology, 941, 942, 943, 944, 945
   foreign words & phrases, 946
   idioms & colloquialisms, 949, 950, 954, 959
   slang, 948, 952
   spelling, 967, 968
   terms & phrases, 935
   usage, 947, 953, 955, 956, 957, 958, 960, 969
English language in Australia, 962
English language in Canada, 964, 965
English language in Great Britain, 966
English language in South Africa, 963
English literature, 984, 991, 996, 1094, 1095, 1098. *See also names of individual authors*
English poetry, 1100, 1101, 1103, 1104, 1110, 1116, 1124, 1126, 1132, 1133

Entrepreneurs, 180, 201
Environmental policy, 1401, 1403, 1406
Environmental protection, 1404, 1408
Epidemiology, 1520
Espionage, 639
Estate planning, 518
Ethnic groups, 337, 1056
Ethnic press, 835, 836
Etiquette, 1252
Europe, 469, 678, 795, 1426, 1427
Evolution, 1415
Examinations, 259, 325
Executive advisory boards, 659
Exhibitions, 247, 248
Explosives, 1480
Export marketing, 240, 246

Facsimile transmission, 557
Family in literature, 1002
Family life, 765, 766
Family recreation, 404
Fanny Hill, 1105
Fantastic fiction, 924, 1044
Farm income, 1365
Fashion, 888
Federal aid, 290
Feminist literary criticism, 809
Fertility, 1565
Festivals, 1253
Fiction, 1032, 1035, 1064
Filipino literature, 1149
Films. *See* Moving-pictures
Finance, 179, 203, 204, 208
Fishes, 1456
Fitzgerald, F. Scott, 1073
Flags, 379
Floor coverings, 887
Florida, 85
Flowers, 1423, 1425, 1426
Fluid mechanics, 1479, 1502
Flute music, 1196
Folk artists, 880
Folk music, 1233
Folk songs, 1232
Folklore, 1243, 1247
Food, 1368, 1370, 1371, 1373, 1377, 1378, 1379,
    1381, 1382, 1383, 1579
Food additives, 1372
Football, 730, 731, 732, 733, 734, 735
Forecasting, 545, 799
Forestry, 1386
Foster, Stephen Collins, 1232
Foundations (philanthropic), 767, 768, 771,
    772, 773, 774
France, 674
    revolution, 1789-1799, 471
Franchises, 181, 186, 188
Franklin, Benjamin, 434

Free computer software, 1625
Free material, 275, 1518
Freemasonry, 750
French language, 505, 509, 974, 975, 976
French literature, 1148, 1152
Frescobaldi, Girolamo, 1204
Fund raising, 769
Fungi, 1430

Galaxies, 1635
Gambia, 94, 95
Gambling, 736
Game shows, 860
Games, 737
Garden pests, 1395
Gardening, 1391, 1393, 1394
Gazetteers, 382
Gay men. *See* Homosexuality
Geese, 1446
Gemmology, 1668
Genealogy, 65, 368, 369, 370, 371, 373, 374,
    375, 376, 377, 378, 569. *See also*
        Ships: passenger lists; *under place names*
Genetic engineering, 1494
Genetics, 1413
Genocide, 528
Geology, 1654, 1655, 1656, 1657, 1658, 1659,
    1660, 1661, 1663, 1664, 1665, 1666,
    1667
German drama, 1297
German literature, 1155
Germany, 473
Gerontology, 755, 756. *See also* Aging
Ghana, 96
Gibraltar, 118
Gifted children, 997
Gipsies
    language, 977
Glass, 873
Gluck, Christoph Willibald, Ritter von, 1205
Goodman, Benny, 1230
Gorky, Maksim, 1163
Gothic literature, 1040, 1041
Gover, Robert, 1074
Government publications. *See under names of*
    countries
Governors, 628, 653
Grants-in-aid, 771, 907. *See also* Scholarships
Great Britain, 119, 459, 461, 921, 1420
    armed forces, 604, 607
    biography, 27, 463, 1535
    foreign relations, 631
    history, 462, 465, 466, 467, 593
    politics & government, 626
Great Britain Parliament, 464
Greece, 381
Guinea, 97
Guinea-Bissau, 98
Gums and resins, 1637

Hair conditioners, 1646
Handicapped, 403, 406, 759, 760, 762
  care & treatment, 763
  employment, 761
Handicrafts, 877, 879, 881, 884
Hawaii, 421, 1671
Hawks, 1441
Hazardous substances, 1648
Hazardous wastes, 1407, 1505
Head Start, 787
Health, 1529
Health education, 1515, 1518, 1520
Health services administration, 1521
Heart disease, 1571
Henry VIII, 1119
Herbert, George, 1110
Himalayas, 102, 1425
Hispanic Americans, 348
Historic buildings, 415, 916
Historic preservation, 453
Historic sites, 411
Historical fiction, 1003, 1018
Historiography, 481
History, 819. *See also* Chronology, historical;
    World history; *individual
    countries*
History, ancient, 482, 488
Hockey, 739, 740, 741
Holidays, 1251
Holocaust, 472
Homosexuality, 776, 777, 778
Horses, 1011, 1455
Hospitals, 1527
House plants, 1389
Human evolution, 336
Human rights, 528, 530, 531. *See also* Civil
    rights
Humanities, 817, 819
Humorists, 1066
Hunting, 742

Idaho, 398
Illustrators, 924
India, 107, 456, 693, 1278, 1304, 1439, 1539
Indian Ocean, 124
Indiana, 1428
Indians, 892
Indians of North America, 352, 353, 354, 355,
    356, 357, 358, 359, 360, 361, 362, 364,
    365, 366, 419, 884. *See also names of
    tribes*
  Canada, 363
Indians of South America, 365
Indic language, 977
Indic literature, 71, 1156, 1157
Industry, 209, 210, 215, 218
  security measures, 1627
Industry and education, 286, 306, 307

Information science, 532, 533, 534, 536, 540,
    543, 545, 546, 555. *See also*
    Library science
Information services, 815
Information storage and retrieval systems, 1362,
    1602, 1618, 1619, 1620. *See also*
    Computers; Libraries: automation
Insects, 1458
Instructional materials centers, 266. *See also*
    School libraries
Insurance, 222
Intellectual property, 216, 512
Interior decoration, 863
International agencies, 52
International business enterprises, 154, 217
International economic relations, 169
International education, 310, 317, 318
International law, 496, 515
International relations, 673, 675, 676, 679
Interns, 286, 306, 307
Intervention (international law), 437
Inventions, 1357
Investments, 182, 183, 184, 185, 189, 190, 192,
    193
Iran, 142
Iran-Contra Hearings, 660
Ireland, 373, 376, 462, 807
Irish Americans, 349
Irish literature, 1158, 1159
Italy, 416
Ives, Charles, 1195

James, Henry, 1075
Japan, 108, 109, 210, 241, 242, 244, 1450
Japanese language, 983
Jazz music, 1234, 1235, 1236, 1237
Jerusalem, 143
Jewish families, 350
Jewish literature, 1055
Jews, 351, 1256
Job descriptions, 264, 592, 1254, 1356
Job evaluation, 172
Job satisfaction, 258
Johnson, Hiram, 635
Johnson, Lyndon B., 632
Journalists, 839
Judaism, 812, 1342, 1343
Judges, 497, 498, 510, 511

Kansas, 408, 1452
Kelly, Ellsworth, 917
Korean language, 982
Kundera, Milan, 1148

Labor and laboring classes, 223, 225, 226. *See
    also* Cottage industries

Labor laws and legislation, 228
Langlais, Jean, 1212
Language books for travelers, 982, 983
Languages, 926, 927, 933
Latin America, 126, 127, 128, 474, 618, 1010
Latin American literature, 1160, 1161
Law, 492, 515, 517, 519, 520
   bibliography, 489, 494, 495
   Canada, 493, 496
   dictionaries, 490, 499, 500, 501, 502, 503,
      504, 505, 506, 507, 508, 509
   directories, 511, 512, 513, 514
   quotations, maxims, etc., 521
   United States, 496
Lawrence, T. E., 460
Le Corbusier, 915
Lead-poisoning, 1402
League of Canadian Poets, 1145
Learning disabilities, 761
Learning disabled children, 320
Leary, Timothy Francis, 690
Legal research, 516, 517
Legislators, 635, 636
Lesbians. *See* Homosexuality
Lewis, C. S., 1111
Librarians, 536, 547
Libraries, 535, 538, 560. *See also specific types,*
   e.g., Public libraries
   automation, 559
   British Columbia, 537
Library Association, 544
Library cooperation, 558
Library orientation, 542, 561
Library science, 536, 540, 555. *See also*
   Information science
   dictionaries, 532, 533, 534
   handbooks, manuals, etc., 541, 543, 544
   indexes, 546
Library science as a profession, 547
Libya, 99
Life sciences, 1411, 1414
Lindbergh, Anne Morrow, 1076
Linguistics, 929, 931
Literacy, 324, 326
Literary agents, 829
Literature, 993
   dictionaries, 816, 986, 987, 989
Literature and science, 985
Literature, medieval, 1028, 1029
Lithium, 1582
Local government, 646
Lombard, Carole, 1261
Lotus 1-2-3 (computer program), 1609
Louisiana, 86
Lucas, E. V., 1112
Lukacs, Gyorgy, 669

Magic, 738
Mail-order catalogs, 200, 1378

Maine, 375
Malone Dies, 1158
Mammals, 1459, 1460, 1462, 1463
Management, 234, 811
Manufacturers, 221
Manuscripts, 424, 483, 833, 1094, 1095
Maps, 384, 386
March, William, 1077
Marcuse, Herbert, 80
Marine fauna, 1464, 1671
Marine invertebrates, 1465
Marine resources, 1670
Marketing, 236, 237, 238, 239, 239a, 239b, 241,
   243, 245, 247, 248, 840
Martial arts, 743
Mason, Lowell, 1209
Mass media, 825
Massachusetts, 439
Materials, 1496
Mathematics, 737, 1672, 1673, 1674, 1675
Matrix isolation spectroscopy, 1636
Mayas, 474
McKinley, William, 630
Mechanical engineering, 1503
Medical care, 1516, 1528, 1531, 1532, 1536,
   1542, 1544, 1549
Medical genetics, 1572
Medical instruments and apparatus, 1524, 1540
Medical laws and legislation, 491
Medical libraries, 570
Medical literature, 1514, 1517, 1532
Medical supplies, 1525
Medical technology, 1526
Medicare, 1530
Medicine, 1522, 1533, 1534, 1537, 1538, 1539,
   1541, 1542, 1543, 1545
Melville, Herman, 1078
Memoirs of a Woman of Pleasure, 1105
Men, 764
Mencken, H. L., 1079
Mennonites, 1330, 1336
Merchant ships, 1692
Metals, 1497, 1498, 1499, 1500, 1501
Meteorology, 1676
Meteors, 1632
Methodism, 1333
Methodist Church, 1334
Mexican American literature (Spanish), 562
Mexico, 28, 135, 903
Microcomputer software, 559
Microcomputers, 1614, 1622, 1623, 1624.
   See also Computers
Middle Ages, 482, 483, 484, 485, 486, 487, 614,
   895
Middle East, 29, 139, 140, 141, 622, 624, 641,
   1368. *See also names of individual*
   countries
Military art and science, 589
Military dependents, 297

Military history, 588, 593
Military policy, 590, 594
Military posts, 452
Minerals in nutrition, 1587, 1590
Mines and mineral resources, 1504
Minnesota, 1412
Minorities
   education (preschool), 787
Mississippi, 841, 1451
Missouri, 1452
Model trains, 875
Modern American Literature, 996
Modern British Literature, 996
Molloy, 1158
Moore, George, 1113
Morrison, Toni, 1080
Moths, 1453
Moving-picture actors and actresses, 1267, 1268
Moving-picture film collections, 1277
Moving-picture industry, 1272, 1274, 1275, 1276
Moving-picture producers and directors, 1263,
   1266, 1269, 1270
Moving-pictures, 857, 858, 861, 902, 1262, 1271,
   1278, 1279, 1281, 1282, 1283, 1285, 1286,
   1287
   production & direction, 859
Mozambique, 100
Mozart, Wolfgang Amadeus, 1216
Murder, 524
Murdoch, Iris, 1114
Museums, 51, 1689
Mushrooms, 1429
Music, 1173, 1177, 1225
   bibliography, 1167, 1168, 1169, 1170
   biography, 1174
   directories, 1181
   discography, 1186, 1187, 1217
   economic aspects, 1180
   handbooks, manuals, etc., 1183, 1184, 1185
   indexes, 1189, 1190, 1191
Music, American, 1171
Music festivals, 1182
Music in education, 1168, 1209
Music, popular (songs, etc.), 1228, 1229, 1230,
   1231
Music trade, 845, 1179
Musical revues, comedies, etc., 1176, 1296, 1300
Musicians, Black, 1224
Mythology, 1249, 1250

Names, geographical, 90, 397, 398, 399, 400,
   401
Names, personal, 380, 381
Nanticoke Indians, 355
Narration (rhetoric), 990
National Archives, 425
Natural history, 410, 417, 1438
Natural monuments, 1662

Natural resources, 1410
Naturalism in literature, 1113
Navies, 607, 608
Navigation, 1693
Near East
   antiquities, 1322
Neruda, Pablo, 1146
Netherlands, 120
New Hampshire, 375
New Mexico, 1654
New Quebec (Quebec), 399
New York (city), 24, 87, 433
New York (state), 87, 648, 1440
New York Shakespeare Festival, 1290
New Zealand, 475, 1268
Newberry Library, 377
Newbery award, 1008
Newspapers, 31, 835, 836, 837, 840, 841, 842,
   844
Nigeria, 1246
Nigerian literature, 1162
Nixon, Richard M., 629
Nobel prizes, 680, 988
Norris, Frank, 1081
North Africa, 140, 141
North America, 744
North Carolina, 409, 423, 1421
Nova Scotia, 1432
Nuclear energy, 1507
Nuclear physics, 1678
Nuclear power plants, 1506, 1508
Nuclear warfare, 611
Nuclear weapons, 612, 615
Nursing, 1575, 1576, 1577, 1578
Nursing homes, 1523
Nutrition, 1368, 1369, 1371, 1519

O'Neill, Eugene, 1082
O. Henry Prize Stories, 1065
Obrecht, Jacob, 1210
Obscene words, 951
Occult, 703
Oceania, 104, 417
Ockeghem, Johannes, 1210
Office practice, 250, 251
Old Curiosity Shop, 1107
Olympic games, 711, 712, 714
Opera, 1226, 1227
Optical storage devices, 1611
Oral history, 427
Orators, 441
Orchestra, 1178, 1188
Organic farming, 1366
Oriental literature, 1130
Osage Indians, 356
Oxford movement, 1331

Paintings, 921
Pakistan, 1439
Paleontology, 1286
Papp, Joseph, 1290
Paraguay, 136
Parapsychology, 705, 706
Parent and child, 766
Parsons, Talcott, 747
Patents, 512
Pater, Walter H., 1115
Peace, 680, 681, 682, 683, 684, 685, 1336
Pennsylvania Academy of the Fine Arts, 909
Pension trusts, 191
Percussion instruments, 1214
Performing arts, 1256, 1257. *See also* Ballet;
    Moving-pictures; Theater
Pericles, 1118
Periodicals, 71, 837, 840, 1067
    directories, 69, 70, 73, 583
    indexes, 67, 68, 453, 751, 824, 843
Peron, Eva, 129
Peron, Isabel, 129
Peron, Juan Domingo, 129
Persichetti, Vincent, 1208
Personnel management, 233
Pesticides, 1367, 1384
Petroleum industry, 1399, 1400, 1509
Pharmacology, 1583, 1584, 1589, 1591, 1592,
    1594, 1595. *See also* Drugs
Philosophers, 1303
Philosophy, 1305, 1306, 1307
Philosophy, Indic, 1304
Phonorecords, 855, 1225, 1296
Phonotapes, 849, 1186
Photography, 890, 891
Physical geography, 383
Physics, 1650, 1677, 1679, 1680, 1681, 1682
Physiology, 1535
Piaget, Jean, 79
Piano, 1213, 1216
Piano makers, 1215
Picture-books for children, 1006, 1009
Pictures, 903
Pinkham, Daniel, 1201
Plant diseases, 1395
Plant shutdowns, 231
Plants, 1389, 1390, 1419. *See also* Wild flowers
Plants, aquatic, 1421
Plants, edible, 1377, 1418, 1432
Plastics, 1637
Plath, Sylvia, 1083
Poetry Bookshop, 577
Poetry
    indexes, 1047
Poland, 121
Police, 527
Policy sciences, 156
Political ethics, 686
Political parties, 623

Political science, 616, 621
Pollution, 1402
Polymers, 1637
Polymers and polymerizations, 1651
Pope, Alexander, 1116
Population, 791, 792
Portuguese literature, 1166
Postal service, 197
Potawatomi Indians, 353, 357
Pottery, 882
Power resources, 1397
Pregnancy, 1566
Presbyterian Church, 1329
Presidents
    United States, 628, 629, 630, 632, 633, 637,
        655, 659, 663
    wives, 443
Presley, Elvis, 1238
Primates, 1461
Printers, 582
Prints, 920
Prints, American, 917, 919
Prints, Italian, 918
Production management, 235
Proverbs, 1244, 1245, 1246, 1248
Psychiatry, 1550, 1552, 1553, 1554
Psychological tests, 700
Psychology, 692, 693, 694, 696, 697, 698, 699,
    701
Psychotherapy, 691
Public administration, 687
Public libraries
    book lists, 563, 564
Public opinion polls, 83
Public relations, 161, 236
Public welfare, 782
Publishers and publishing, 541, 574, 575, 576,
    577, 578, 579, 581, 583, 584
Puerto Rico, 137
Pugin, Augustus Welby Northmore, 911

Quilts, 883
Quotations, 74, 75, 76, 77, 174, 663, 960.
    See also Quotations, maxims, etc.
    under certain subjects

Rabe, David, 1291
Race relations, 338
Radicals, 80, 667, 668, 690
Radio, 847
Radio stations, 845
Railroads, 213, 214, 1686, 1689
Raleigh, Walter, 459
Rare books, 549
Rayburn, Sam, 636
Reading, 269, 272, 273, 1023
Real estate, 252, 253, 254, 255

Realism in literature, 1064
Reference books, 7, 8, 9, 10, 11, 12, 32, 148,
    163, 438, 542, 927
Reger, Max, 1203
Registers of births, etc., 372
Religion, 1309, 1311, 1312, 1313, 1314, 1315
Renaissance, 483
Report writing, 832
Reproduction, 1567
Reptiles, 1466
Research, 575
Research, industrial, 153
Research institutes, 53, 319
Research libraries, 30
Retirement communities, 802
Retirement, places of, 757
Rewards (prizes, etc.), 680, 827, 988, 1022
Rheumatism, 1573
Rhododendron, 1422
Richard II, 1121
Robinson, Edwin Arlington, 1084
Robotics, 1626
Rock music, 1238, 1239, 1240, 1241, 1242
Royal families, 27
Rugs, Oriental, 878
Rural development, 803
Russia
    revolution, 1917-1921, 476
Russian Germans, 347
Russian language, 978
Russian literature, 666, 1163, 1164, 1165
Ruthenians, 470

Safety consultants, 229
Safety engineering, 229, 1510, 1511
Saints, 1337
Sandburg, Carl, 1085
Sanitary engineering, 1512
Sastre, Alfonso, 1288
Satellites, 1471
Saudi Arabia, 144
Scandinavia, 1249
Schoenberg, Arnold, 1197
Scholarships, 283, 289, 293, 316, 762, 904.
    See also Student aid
School administration and management, 318
School administrators, 270, 276
School libraries, 565, 566, 567
Science
    bibliography, 1344, 1345, 1346
    dictionaries, 1348, 1349, 1350, 1352,
        1361, 1362, 1363
    handbooks, manuals, etc., 1355
    indexes, 1358, 1360
Science fiction, 924, 1042, 1043, 1044
Scientific apparatus and instruments, 1347,
    1351
Sculpture, 925

Sea birds, 1443
Self-determination, 665
Semantics, 930
Seminars, 158
Sex, 779
Sex instruction, 1546
Shakespeare, William, 1118, 1119, 1120, 1121,
    1122
    quotations, maxims, etc., 1117
Shaw, George Bernard, 1123
Shelley, Percy Bysshe, 1124
Ships, 606, 609
    passenger lists, 367
Shipwrecks, 420
Short stories, 1045, 1046, 1065
Shrimps, 1457
Shrubs, 1433, 1435, 1436. *See also* Trees
Siksika Indians, 359
Sillitoe, Alan, 1125
Silverware, 865
Skelton, John, 1126
Skiing, 744
Skin
    diseases, 1573
Slavic literature, 346
Small business, 168, 180, 201
Snakes, 1467
Social psychology, 689
Social sciences, 78, 79, 81, 82
Social service, 780, 781, 782
Socialism, 1332
Socialists, 668
Sociologists, 748
Sociology, 707, 747, 749, 751
Socrates, 1303
Solar energy, 910
Solar houses, 910
Sound
    apparatus, 852
Soviet Union, 476, 492, 619
Soyinka, Wole, 1162
Space flight, 1470
Space industrialization, 219
Space sciences, 219
Spanish language, 979, 1353
Spanish literature, 1166
Spears, 360
Special librarians, 572
Special libraries, 127, 568, 569, 570, 571, 572
Spectrum analysis, 1650
Sports, 707, 708, 709, 713, 1253
Sports medicine, 1574
Spouse abuse, 764
Spy stories, 1033
Standard Industrial Classification Codes, 172
State birds, 379
State governments, 638, 647, 649, 652
Statistics, 64, 113, 114, 466, 657, 793, 794, 795,
    796, 797, 799, 1596, 1675

Stein, Gertrude, 1086
Stocks, 183, 184, 185, 187, 189, 193. *See also* Investments
Student aid, 281, 288, 290, 293, 297, 299, 300, 301. *See also* Scholarships
Students, foreign, 284, 561
Subject headings
  women, 551
Substance abuse, 783, 784
Suicide, 1551
Summers, Montague, 1127
Surgery, 1547, 1548
Surveying, 1481
Swans, 1446
Sweden, 122
Symbolism, 814
Synagogues, 407

Tanagers, 1444
Tarn, Nathaniel, 1087
Taxation, 256, 257, 257a, 257b
Teachers, 258, 278
Teaching, 265, 275
Technology, 211, 1344, 1348, 1353, 1358, 1359, 1361, 1362, 1363
Telecommunications, 846
Television programs, 856, 858, 860
Terrorism, 677, 678, 825
Testing laboratories, 1354
Texas, 436, 438, 1449, 1455, 1466
Textbooks, 260
Theater, 1288, 1289, 1290, 1291, 1293, 1294, 1295, 1296, 1297, 1298, 1299, 1302. *See also* Drama
  Great Britain, 1292
Theology, 1340. *See also* Religion
Thesauri, 969
Thomists, 1307
Three Mile Island Nuclear Power Plant, 1506, 1508
Tibet, 418
Timber, 1387
Tipping, 199
Togo, 101
Tower Commission Report, 661
Toxicology, 1581
Trade names, 239a, 239b, 1651
Trade-unions, 225, 227
Transcendentalism (New England), 1054
Translators, 1130
Travel, 403
  guide-books, 402, 405, 406, 407, 409, 410, 413, 414, 417, 744, 830
Treasure hunting, 745
Trees, 1388, 1433, 1434, 1435, 1436, 1437
Trials, 498
Trollope, Anthony, 1128
Trotsky, Leon, 666

Tunisia, 1248
Turn of the Screw, 1075
Two Gentlemen of Verona, 1120

Ukraine, 123, 470
Uniforms, military, 595
United Nations, 672
United States
  armed forces, 587, 603, 605
  biography, 24, 25, 26
  census, 792
  economic conditions, 789
  foreign relations, 244, 631, 641
  geography, 385
  government publications, 56, 57, 58, 59, 173, 662
  history, 343, 411, 426, 429, 430, 432, 435, 445, 446, 449, 450, 451, 454, 1133
  politics & government, 628, 638, 640, 642, 643, 644, 645, 647, 654, 657, 658, 678
  population, 798
  statistics, 796
United States Congress, 650, 651, 654, 656
Universities and colleges, 282, 285, 309. *See also* Education, higher
  bibliography, 1308
  curricula, 294, 296, 302, 304, 308
  directories, 280, 287, 291, 295, 298, 303, 305
UNIX (computer operating system), 1606
Unnamable, The, 1158
Urban policy, 800, 804, 805
Utopias, 984

Vaudeville, 1301
Vegetable gardening, 1392
Venezuela, 138
Veterans, 297, 591
Vice-Presidents, 442
Video discs, 1629
Video display terminals, 1603
Video tapes, 854, 857, 861, 902, 1282
Vietnamese Conflict, 1961-1975, 457, 586, 596
Villa-Lobos, Heitor, 1194
Violence, 825
Vitamins, 1587, 1590
Vivaldi, Antonio, 1211
Vocational education, 322, 323, 328, 330
Vocational guidance, 306, 307, 329
Volunteers, 326, 770, 772
Voting research, 650, 656

Wain, John, 1129
Wakoski, Diane, 1088
Waley, Arthur, 1130
Walker, Alice Malsenior, 1089

War, 1336
War stories, 1033
Washington (state), 431, 1247
Wave (San Francisco, Calif.), 1081
Weeds, 1431
Weights and measures, 876
Wells, H. G., 1131
Wesley, Charles, 1333
Wesley, John, 1333
West Virginia, 374
West, The, 1060
Western films, 1262, 1271, 1287
Wild flowers, 1424, 1427, 1428
Wine and wine making, 1374, 1375, 1376, 1385
Winter sports, 746
Wirth, Louis, 749
Wit and humor, 855, 1067
Wolf, Hugo, 1207
Women, 333, 682, 708, 806, 807, 810, 811, 812, 814, 815, 821, 912, 1266, 1516
Women authors, 1096
Women composers, 1196, 1199
Women in public life, 813
Women journalists, 838

Women musicians, 1175
Woodland Indians, 354
Wordsworth, William, 1132
Work environment, 218
World history, 479, 480
World politics, 478
World records, 63
World Series, 718
World War, 1939-1945, 606
Wright, Richard, 1090
Writers' Union of Canada, 826
Wyoming, 1656

Yankton Indians, 358
Yiddish language, 980, 981
Young adult literature, 564, 1003, 1005, 1007, 1018, 1023, 1025, 1026, 1027. *See also* Children's literature
Youth, 785

Zip code, 5